# J. S. BACH

OXFORD COMPOSER COMPANIONS

# *J. S. Bach*

EDITED BY MALCOLM BOYD

CONSULTANT EDITOR JOHN BUTT

**OXFORD**
UNIVERSITY PRESS

# OXFORD

UNIVERSITY PRESS

Great Clarendon Street, Oxford OX2 6DP

Oxford University Press is a department of the University of Oxford.
It furthers the University's objective of excellence in research, scholarship,
and education by publishing worldwide in

Oxford  New York

Auckland  Bangkok  Buenos Aires  Cape Town  Chennai
Dar es Salaam  Delhi  Hong Kong  Istanbul  Karachi  Kolkata
Kuala Lumpur  Madrid  Melbourne  Mexico City  Mumbai  Nairobi
São Paulo  Shanghai  Taipei  Tokyo  Toronto

Oxford is a registered trade mark of Oxford University Press
in the UK and in certain other countries

Published in the United States
by Oxford University Press Inc., New York

© Oxford University Press 1999

Database right Oxford University Press (maker)

First published 1999
First issued as an Oxford University Press Paperback 2003

British Library Cataloguing in Publication Data
Data available

Library of Congress Cataloging in Publication Data
Data available

ISBN 0-19-860620-6

3  5  7  9  10  8  6  4  2

Typeset by Alliance Photosettings, Pondicherry
Printed in Great Britain
on acid-free paper by
TJ International, Ltd, Padstow, Cornwall

# PREFACE

THIS volume, and the series of Composer Companions that it inaugurates, owes its inception to Michael Cox, who saw the need for a book to which one might turn for ready and reliable information about anything to do with Bach and his music. Although not the first of its kind (it is preceded by at least one German and two Japanese Bach lexicons laid out on similar lines), it is perhaps the first English-language attempt to deal comprehensively with the subject in an A–Z guide. I am grateful to Michael Cox not only for the initial idea and for inviting me to take it up, but also for his continued interest and support. Thanks are due also to his colleagues at Oxford University Press, particularly Pam Coote, Alison Jones, Wendy Tuckey, and Mary Worthington.

For agreeing to proof-read the whole volume I am indebted once more, as so often in the past, to David Wyn Jones, and the project has benefited in various ways from the help I have received from Beryl Boyd, Konrad Küster, Paula Lawrence, Mary Oleskiewicz, and Eva Zöllner. To these names should be added those of the 40 or so distinguished scholars who have contributed articles to the volume, and whose involvement with it has in many cases gone far beyond that. The assistance I received from Gill Jones and her library staff in the Music Department of the University of Wales, Cardiff, did much to ease the editorial process.

Above all my thanks go to John Butt, who interpreted his role as consultant editor in the most generous way possible, brought his energy and expertise to bear on practically all aspects of the volume, and proved in every respect to be the ideal Bach companion.

MALCOLM BOYD

*Cardiff, October 1998*

# CONTENTS

# LIST OF ILLUSTRATIONS

# List of Illustrations

# CONTRIBUTORS

*unsigned articles are the responsibility of the editor*

NA    **Nicholas Anderson** studied at New College, Oxford, and Durham University. For 20 years he worked for the BBC as a music producer, specializing in the Baroque repertory. Since 1991 he has acted as a consultant for the Erato and Teldec record companies, and has continued broadcasting, teaching, and writing. He is the author of *Baroque Music from Monteverdi to Handel* (1994) and has contributed to *The New Grove Dictionary of Music and Musicians* as well as to various symposiums and journals.

AB    **Alberto Basso** worked at the Turin Conservatory from 1961 to 1993, first as teacher and then as librarian. He is president of the Società Italiana di Musicologia and of the Istituto per i Beni Musicali in Piemonte, and vice-president of the Accademia Nazionale di Santa Cecilia. His numerous publications include *L'età di Bach e di Haendel* (1976), *Frau Musika: la vita e le opere di J. S. Bach* (1979–83), and *L'invenzione della gioia: musica e massoneria nell'età dei Lumi* (1994), and he has edited several important reference works, including the *Dizionario enciclopedico universale della musica e dei musicisti* (1983–90).

JB    **John Bergsagel** is professor of musicology at the University of Copenhagen. He studied at Cornell University with Donald Grout, and at Oxford with Jack Westrup, Egon Wellesz, and Frank Harrison. He taught at Oxford and at the University of Manchester, and moved to Denmark in 1970. He has published musicological studies on subjects ranging from the early Middle Ages to the 20th century.

GB    **Gregory Butler** is a noted Bach scholar, best known for his work on the original editions of the composer's works. He is also active in the areas of source studies, rhetorical-musical applications, Bach's compositional procedures, and, most recently, the Bach concertos. He is working on a collection of essays on Bach's late works and a monograph on Mozart's early concertos.

JAB    **John Butt** studied at Cambridge University and has held posts at the University of Aberdeen, Magdalene College Cambridge, and the University of California at Berkeley. In 1997 he returned to Cambridge as a university lecturer and fellow of King's College. His writings include the books *Bach Interpretation* (1990), *Bach: Mass in B Minor* (1991), and *Music Education and the Art of Performance in the German Baroque* (1994), and he has edited the *Cambridge Companion to Bach* (1997). He is currently working on a study of the philosophy and criticism of historical performance practice, and is also active as a performer (on organ and harpsichord) and conductor.

JJC    **Juan José Carreras** is professor of music at the University of Zaragoza and a member of the Neue Bach-Gesellschaft. He is well known and admired as a lecturer and organizer on the international conference circuit, and has published studies of seminal importance on Spanish music of the 17th and 18th centuries. He is co-editor of *Music in Eighteenth-Century Spain* (Cambridge, 1998).

TC    **Teresa Cascudo** studied Romance philology at the University of Zaragoza, and is researching for the Ph.D. on tradition and nationalism in Portuguese music of the 20th century. She works as a consultant for the Museu da Música Portuguesa, Lisbon, and her forthcoming publications include *Fernando Lopes-Graça: catálogo do espólio musical* and essays on Iberian symphonism (1779–1809) and on music and musicians at the Madrid court of Carlos IV.

LC    **Leon Coates** studied at St John's College, Cambridge, and since 1965 has been lecturer in music at Edinburgh University, where he teaches harmony, counterpoint, composition, and keyboard skills. He is active also as a composer, writer, and professional performer on harpsichord and piano, and is organist and choirmaster at the Church of St Andrew and St George, Edinburgh.

WC    **Walter Corten** teaches at the Conservatoire Royal de Musique and the Université Libre, Brussels. He has carried out research on the rediscovery of early music during the Romantic period and has also worked on numerical proportions in Baroque music, particularly that of Bach.

TTC    **Tim Crawford** studied the lute with Diana Poulton, and later with Michael Schaeffer in Cologne. He was a founder member of the Parley of Instruments, with whom he made several recordings. He has studied sources of music by Handel, Haydn, and Telemann and is currently editing the lute works of S. L. Weiß for *Das Erbe deutscher Musik*. At King's

# Contributors

College, London, he works on the application of information technology to musicological research.

SAC **Stephen A. Crist** is associate professor of music at Emory University. His articles have appeared in *Early Music, Bach Studies, Bach Perspectives, The Cambridge Companion to Bach*, and elsewhere. He has also published a facsimile edition of a Low German hymnal dating from Luther's time and is working on a book on the Bach arias. He is secretary and treasurer of the American Bach Society.

SFD **Stephen Daw** taught at the Birmingham Conservatoire until his retirement in 1997 and has been active in Bach research for nearly 30 years. His publications include *The Music of Johann Sebastian Bach: The Choral Works* (1981), articles on the Walther–Krebs organ manuscripts and Bach reception in England, and the introduction to a facsimile edition of *The Well-tempered Clavier* Book 2.

QF **Quentin Faulkner** is Steinhart distinguished professor of organ and music history at the University of Nebraska-Lincoln. He has written on the Bach organ and on aspects of performance practice in the *Westfield Center Newsletter, Bach*, and the *Bach-Jahrbuch*, and is the author of *J. S. Bach's Keyboard Technique: A Historical Introduction* (St Louis, Miss., 1984). He has also made an annotated English translation of Adlung's *Musica mechanica organædi*.

BH **Bruce Haynes** is internationally known as an innovative performer on the hautboy (early oboe). He taught at the Royal Conservatory in The Hague, 1972–83, and has published articles on the history of his instrument as well as the definitive book on its repertory. He is now working on a book on the origins, history, and performance of the hautboy.

SH **Simon Heighes** studied at Lancaster and Oxford Universities, and taught for a time at The Queen's and Oriel Colleges, Oxford. He is an active writer and broadcaster, and has worked with the European Union Baroque Orchestra. His publications include a study of the 18th-century musicians William and Philip Hayes and a performing version of Bach's *St Mark Passion*.

RH **Ryuichi Higuchi** studied musicology at Keio University, Tokyo, and in Tübingen, taking his Ph.D. with an edition of Bach cantatas for the *NBA* (I/34). He is now professor at the Meiji Gakuin University in Tokyo, and works also as a critic and conductor.

DLH **David Humphreys** is a lecturer in music at the University of Wales, Cardiff. He graduated at Cambridge University and went on to take the Ph.D. with a dissertation on the Elizabethan and Jacobean motet. He has since taken an interest in symbolism and attribution

problems in the music of Bach, on which he has published a book and several articles, and he has also undertaken research on the lutenist and composer Philip van Wilder.

NJ **Natalie Jenne** is a performer, lecturer, and author, and professor of music at Concordia University. She took the DMA degree at Stanford University, where she taught harpsichord. She has undertaken extensive research into Baroque dance and the music of J. S. Bach, is co-author with Meredith Little of *Dance and the Music of J. S. Bach* (1991), and has published articles in *Bach* and other journals.

RDPJ **Richard D. P. Jones** studied at Oxford under Jack Westrup and Joseph Kerman, and began his Bach studies under the informal supervision of Walter Emery. His numerous Bach editions include *Clavier-Übung I* (*NBA* V/1), the Violin Sonatas (OUP), and *The Well-tempered Clavier* (Associated Board), and he is working on a major study of Bach's keyboard music.

BK **Boris Katz** is head of the History and Analysis Department at the Musorgsky College, St Petersburg. He has published eight books and over 90 papers on various musical and literary topics, concentrating on Classical and modern Russian music, Bach, Mozart, and the interaction between literature and music. He has participated in numerous international symposiums and lectured at several American universities.

JK **John Koster,** for many years a professional harpsichord maker, is now conservator and associate professor of museum science at the University of South Dakota's Shrine to Music Museum. He is the author of numerous articles and the book *Keyboard Musical Instruments in the Museum of Fine Arts, Boston.*

KK **Konrad Küster** studied musicology and history at Tübingen University, where his *magister* thesis was on Johann Ludwig Bach. Since 1995 he has been professor of musicology at Freiburg University. He has published books on Mozart, the concert and concerto, and Beethoven. His Bach research has concentrated on the Thuringian environment, and his *Der junge Bach* appeared in 1996.

DL **David Lasocki** is head of reference services in the Music Library at Indiana University. He holds the Ph.D. in musicology from The University of Iowa. As a researcher he has concentrated on woodwind instruments, their social history, music, and performance practices.

RAL **Robin A. Leaver** is professor of sacred music at Westminster Choir College, Rider University, and visiting professor of liturgy at

# Contributors

Drew University. His books include *Bachs theologische Bibliothek* (1983) and *J. S. Bach and Scripture: Glosses from the Calov Bible Commentary* (1985), and he has published numerous essays in journals and symposiums, including the *Cambridge Companion to Bach* (1997).

ML  **Mark Lindley** served on the executive committee of *The New Grove Dictionary of Music and Musicians*, editing the articles on musical instruments, and on the editorial boards of *Performance Practice Review* and the *Journal of Music Theory*. His writings include *Mathematical Models of Musical Scales* (with Ronald Turner-Smith); *Lutes, Viols and Temperaments*; *Ars Ludendi*; *Early German Keyboard Fingerings*; and *Gandhi and Humanism*.

MEL  **Meredith Little** took the Ph.D. at Stanford University in 1967. She has taught at several universities in the USA, and has been a faculty member at the Aston Magna Academy. She is co-author with Natalie Jenne of *Dance and the Music of J. S. Bach* (1991), co-author with Carol Marsh of *La Danse Noble: an Inventory of Dances and Sources* (1992), and has published numerous articles on Baroque music and dance.

MAM  **Michael Marissen** is associate professor of music at Swarthmore College and the editor of *Creative Responses to the Music of J. S. Bach from Mozart to Hindemith* (Lincoln, Nebr., 1998), co-author with Daniel Melamed of *An Introduction to Bach Studies* (Oxford, 1998), and author of *The Social and Religious Designs of J. S. Bach's Brandenburg Concertos* (1995) and *Lutheranism, Anti-Judaism, and Bach's St. John Passion* (Oxford, forthcoming).

DRM  **Daniel R. Melamed** is associate professor of music at Yale University and was director of the Yale Collegium Musicum. He is the author of *J. S. Bach and the German Motet* (1995), editor of *Bach Studies 2* (1995), and co-author of *An Introduction to Bach Studies* (Oxford, 1998).

MM  **Michael Musgrave** is visiting professor of music at Goldsmiths' College, University of London, and lives in New York. He has written, lectured, and broadcast widely on 19th-century German and English music; recent books include *The Music of Brahms* (revised 1994), *The Musical Life of the Crystal Palace* (1995), *Brahms: A German Requiem* (1996), and *A Brahms Reader* (forthcoming). He is a contributor to *The New Grove Dictionary* and the *New Dictionary of National Biography*.

UP  **Ulrich Prinz** studied at the Musikhochschule, Stuttgart, and the University of Tübingen. He took the Ph.D. in 1974 with a dissertation on Bach's instrumentarium (published in 1979), and taught for a time at the Pädagogische Hochschule, Ludwigsburg. Since 1986 he has been head of research at the International Bach Academy in Stuttgart. His numerous other publications have included an exhibition catalogue, *300 Jahre J. S. Bach* (Stuttgart, 1985). His contributions to the present volume were translated by Mary Whittall.

PR-S  **Piotr Rostwo-Suski** is a native of Kraków. He studied at the Jagellonian University, and has taught there since 1989. His research is concentrated on late Baroque English music (especially Handel), and he is working for the Ph.D. on the anthems and services of William Croft. He wrote several entries for the *Encyklopedia muzyczna PWM* and has published numerous articles and reviews. His contribution to the present volume was translated by Teresa Bałuk-Ulewiczowa.

RLS  **Reginald L. Sanders**, born in Knoxville, Tennessee, is a Ph.D. candidate in music history at Yale University. He holds a bachelor's degree in engineering from Princeton University and a master's degree in music history from San Francisco State University.

DS  **David Schulenberg** is assistant professor of music at the University of North Carolina at Chapel Hill. He is the author of *The Keyboard Music of J. S. Bach* and *The Instrumental Music of C. P. E. Bach,* and is a harpsichordist.

MS  **Margaret Steinitz** studied music privately and at Goldsmiths' College, London, where she later held an administrative post for five years. In 1976 she married Paul Steinitz and together they planned and promoted artistic activities centred on the London Bach Society and the Steinitz Bach Players. She founded the annual London Bach Festival in 1990.

RTS  **Russell Stinson** studied at Stetson University and took the MA and Ph.D. in musicology at the University of Chicago. He taught at the University of Michigan and the State University of New York at Stony Brook, and is now associate professor of music and college organist at Lyon College, Batesville, Arkansas. His numerous publications on Bach include two books, *The Bach Manuscripts of Johann Peter Kellner and his Circle* (1989) and *Bach: the Orgel-Büchlein* (1996)

RS  **Robin Stowell** is a professor of music at the University of Wales, Cardiff, and is also a professional violinist, music editor, and author. He has written extensively on the violin and its repertory, and on the conventions of performing early music. His book on *Violin Technique and Performing Practice* was published in 1985 and he has edited *The Cambridge Companion to the Violin* (1992) and *Performing Beethoven* (1994).

# Contributors

JS    **Jeanne Swack** took the Ph.D. in musicology at Yale University, and is associate professor of music at the University of Wisconsin-Madison. Her work has focused on problems of authenticity and style in Bach's chamber music, the music of Telemann, and the north German *Singspiel*. She is also a performer on the Baroque *traverso*.

MT    **Michael Talbot**, FBA, was born in Luton and studied at the Royal College of Music, London, and Cambridge University. He is a specialist in the music of the late Baroque and has a particular interest in Venetian composers, on three of whom (Vivaldi, Albinoni, and Vinaccesi) he has written books. He has been Alsop Professor of Music at the University of Liverpool since 1986.

RT    **Ruth Tatlow** studied music at King's College, London, and clarinet at the Royal Academy of Music. A revised version of her doctoral dissertation was published in 1991 under the title *Bach and the Riddle of the Number Alphabet*. She is a Leverhulme Special Research Fellow at Royal Holloway and Bedford New College researching into 17th- and 18th-century pre-compositional procedures.

YT    **Yo Tomita** took the Ph.D. at Leeds University in 1990 with a dissertation on *J. S. Bach's Well-Tempered Clavier, Book II: A Study of its Aim, Historical Significance and Compiling Process* and has published a two-volume Critical Commentary on that work (1993–5). He is currently a research fellow at The Queen's University of Belfast.

HV    **Henri Vanhulst** is a professor of music at the Université Libre, Brussels, secretary of the Société Belge de Musicologie, and co-editor of the *Revue belge de musicologie*. In 1996 he published the *Catalogus librorum musicorum of Jan Evertsen van Doom* (Utrecht, 1639).

HW    **Harry White** is professor of music at University College Dublin. He is an editor for the J. J. Fux *Gesamtausgabe* and general editor of the series *Irish Musical Studies*. His books include *Johann Joseph Fux and the Music of the Austro-Italian Baroque* (editor) and *Music and Irish Cultural History* (co-editor). He is a national adviser for *The New Grove Dictionary of Music and Musicians*, for which he has written the article on Fux.

PW    **Peter Wollny** studied at Cologne and at Harvard University, where his doctoral dissertation was on Wilhelm Friedemann Bach. He is a research fellow at the Bach-Archiv Leipzig, working on the *NBA* and the *BC* as well as co-editing the *Leipziger Beiträge zur Bach-Forschung*. He also lectures at Leipzig University. He is joint author of a catalogue of the Bach sources in Brussels and has written widely on 17th- and 18th-century topics.

# THEMATIC OVERVIEW

*[entries are arranged alphabetically by headword]*

## Biography and Background

### The Bach Family
Bach family
Bach, Anna Magdalena
Bach, Carl Philipp Emanuel
Bach, Johann Ambrosius
Bach, Johann Bernhard
Bach, Johann Christian
Bach, Johann Christoph (i)
Bach, Johann Christoph (ii)
Bach, Johann Christoph Friedrich
Bach, Johann Elias
Bach, Johann Ernst
Bach, Johann Gottfried Bernhard
Bach, Johann Heinrich
Bach, Johann Jacob
Bach, Johann Lorenz
Bach, Johann Ludwig
Bach, Johann Michael
Bach, Johann Sebastian
Bach, Maria Barbara
Bach, Samuel Anton Jacob
Bach, Wilhelm Friedemann
Genealogy
'Schwarze'
'Windige'

### Earlier Composers (born before 1660)
Ammerbach, Elias Nikolaus
Bassani, Giovanni Battista
Buxtehude, Dietrich
Corelli, Arcangelo
D'Anglebert, Jean-Henri
Drese family
Frescobaldi, Girolamo
Froberger, Johann Jacob
Kerll, Johann Caspar
Knüpfer, Sebastian
Legrenzi, Giovanni
Pachelbel, Johann
Palestrina, Giovanni Pierluigi da
Peranda, Marco Gioseppe
Raison, André
Reincken, Johann Adam
Strungck, Nicolaus Adam
Torelli, Giuseppe

### Bach's Contemporaries

*Composers*
Abel, Carl Friedrich
Albinoni, Tomaso Giovanni
Benda, Franz
Böhm, Georg
Bonporti, Francesco Antonio
Bruhns, Nicolaus
Caldara, Antonio
Couperin, François
Dieupart, Charles
Falckenhagen, Adam
Fasch, Johann Friedrich
Fischer, Johann Caspar Ferdinand
Fredersdorf(f), Michael Gabriel
Fux, Johann Joseph
Graun, Carl Heinrich
Graun, Johann Gottlieb
Graupner, Christoph
Grigny, Nicolas de
Handel, Georg Frideric
Hasse, Johann Adolf
Hebenstreit, Pantaleon
Heinichen, Johann David
Hurlebusch, Conrad Friedrich
Keiser, Reinhard
Krebs family
Kuhnau, Johann
Lotti, Antonio
Marcello, Alessandro
Marcello, Benedetto
Pergolesi, Giovanni Battista
Quantz, Johann Joachim
Scarlatti, Domenico
Stölzel, Gottfried Heinrich
Telemann, Georg Philipp
Vivaldi, Antonio
Wagner, Georg Gottfried
Weiß, Silvius Leopold
Wilderer, Johann Hugo von
Zelenka, Jan Dismas

*Other musicians*
Abel, Christian Ferdinand
Bertouch, Georg von
Brunckhorst, Arnold Matthias
Buffardin, Pierre-Gabriel
Duve, Andreas Christoph
Effler, Johann
Francisci, Jan
Gleditsch, Johann Caspar
Goldberg, Johann Gottlieb
Görner, Johann Gottlieb
Harrer, Johann Gottlob
Hildebrandt, Zacharias
Hoffmann, Melchior
Kauffmann, Georg Friedrich
Kellner, Johann Peter
Kirchhoff, Gottfried
Kropfgans, Johann
Lenck, Georg
Marchand, Louis
Mempell, Johann Nicolaus
Oley, Johann Christoph
Petzold, Christian
Pisendel, Johann Georg
Preller, Johann Gottlieb
Reiche, Gottfried
Reimann, Johann Balthasar
Ringk, Johannes
Rolle, Christian Friedrich
Schemelli, Georg Christian
Schott, Georg Balthasar
Schwanberg, Georg Heinrich Ludwig
Spieß, Joseph
Steindorff, Johann Martin
Stockmar, Johann Melchior
Stricker, Augustin Reinhard
Volumier, Jean Baptiste
Weyrauch, Johann Christian

*Bach's pupils*
Altnickol, Johann Christoph
Bammler Johann Nathanael
Barth, Christian Samuel
Baumgarten, Johann Christoph
Doles, Johann Friedrich
Dorn, Johann Christoph
Dretzel, Cornelius Heinrich
Einicke, Georg Friedrich
Freudenberg, Siegismund
Fröber, Christoph Gottlieb
Geier, Gottlieb Benjamin
Gerber, Heinrich Nicolaus
Gerlach, Carl Gotthelf
Gmelin, Samuel
Gräbner, Christian Heinrich
Haase, Johann Gottlob
Hartwig, Karl
Heinrich, Johann Georg
Homilius, Gottfried August
Kirnberger, Johann Philipp
Kittel, Johann Christian
Koch, Johann Sebastian
Koch, Johann Wilhelm
Köpping, Johann Christian
Kräuter, Philipp David
Kuhnau, Johann Andreas
Ludewig, Bernhard Dieterich
Meißner, Christian Gottlob

# Thematic Overview

Mohrheim, Friedrich Christian Samuel
Müthel, Johann Gottfried
Nagel, Maximilian
Naumann, Gottlieb Daniel
Nichelmann, Christoph
Nicolai, David
Noah, Georg Heinrich
Nützer, Johann Gottfried
Penzel, Christian Friedrich
Raden, Gottlob Ludwig
Ritter, Johann Christoph
Rust, Johann Ludwig Anton
Schemelli, Christian Friedrich
Schimert, Peter
Schmidt, Johann Michael
Schneider, Johann
Schubart, Johann Martin
Schweinitz, Johann Friedrich
Straube, Rudolph
Tischer, Johann Nikolaus
Transchel, Christoph
Trier, Johann
Vogler, Johann Caspar
Voigt, Johann Georg
Wecker, Christoph Gottlob
Wild, Friedrich Gottlieb
Wunsch, Christian Gottlob
Zang, Johann Heinrich
Ziegler, Johann Gotthilf

*Patrons and employers*
August II
August III
Brühl, Heinrich von
Christiane Eberhardine
Christian Ludwig
Ernst August
Ernst Ludwig
Flemming, Joachim Friedrich
Frederick the Great
Friedrich August I
Friedrich August II
Johann Ernst (i)
Johann Ernst (ii)
Keyserlingk, Hermann Carl von
Leopold
Sporck, Franz Anton
Wilhelm Ernst

*Colleagues, friends, and relations*
Apel, Andreas Dietrich
Becker, Johann
Bose family
Breitkopf, Bernhard Christoph
Deyling, Salomon
Eichentopf, Johann Heinrich
Eilmar, Georg Christian
Erdmann, Georg
Ernesti, Johann August
Ernesti, Johann Heinrich

Faber
Feldhaus, Martin
Gesner, Johann Matthias
Geyersbach, Johann Heinrich
Haußmann, Elias Gottlob
Hoffmann family
Krause, Johann Gottlob
Krügner, Johann Gottfried
Lämmerhirt family
Mietke, Michael
Platz, Abraham Christoph
Schmid, Balthasar
Schmidt family
Schübler family
Silbermann, Gottfried
Stählin, Jacob von
Stauber, Johann Lorenz
Treiber family
Walther, Johann Gottfried
Wedemann family
Winckler, Johann Heinrich
Wülcken family
Zimmermann, Gottfried

*Writers, theorists, and librettists*
Adlung, Jakob
Agricola, Johann Friedrich
Birnbaum, Johann Abraham
Clauder, Johann Christoph
Franck, Salomo
Gottsched, Johann Christoph
Heineccius, Johann Michael
Helbig, Johann Friedrich
Helm, Christoph
Hunold, Christian Friedrich
Knauer
Landvoigt, Johann August
Lehms, Georg Christian
Marpurg, Friedrich Wilhelm
Mattheson, Johann
Mizler von Kolof, Lorenz Christoph
Neidhardt, Johann Georg
Neumeister, Erdmann
Niedt, Friedrich Erhard
Picander
Scheibe, Johann Adolph
Sorge, Georg Andreas
Sperontes
Werckmeister, Andreas
Ziegler, Christiane Mariane von

## Places and buildings
Arnstadt
Berlin, Potsdam
Blasiuskirche
Bonifatiuskirche
Carlsbad
Celle
Cöthen
Dornheim

Dresden
Eisenach
Hamburg
Leipzig
Lübeck
Lüneburg
Michaeliskirche
Mühlhausen
Neukirche
Nikolaikirche
Ohrdruf
Paulinerkirche
Saxony
Thomaskirche
Thomasschule
Thuringia
Weimar
Weißenfels

## Offices, institutions, etc.
*Bierfiedler*
*Cammer-musicus*
collegium musicum
consistory
Correspondirenden Societät der Musicalischen Wissenschaften
currency
*director musices*
Hausmann
*Hofcompositeur*
*Kammermusikus*
Kantor
*Kantorei*
*Kapellmeister*
*Konzertmeister*
*Kurrende*
Lateinschule
Mettenchor
*Ratsmusikant*
Rector
*Stadtmusicus, Stadtpfeifer*

## Theology and liturgy
Alt-Gottesdienst
Calov(ius), Abraham
Calvinism
Cantate
Church calendar
Enlightenment
Estomihi
Exaudi
*Florilegium Portense*
*Hauptgottesdienst*
Invocavit
Jubilate
Judica
Laetare
liturgy
Lutheranism
Mariae Heimsuchung

xvi

# Thematic Overview

# Thematic Overview

# Thematic Overview

Swingle Singers
Tilford Bach Society
Tureck, Rosalyn
Werner, Fritz
Whittaker, William Gillies

## Scholarship, reception, and influence

### Later composers and compositions

BACH
*Bachianas brasileiras*
Bennett, William Sterndale
Brahms, Johannes
Busoni, Ferruccio
Clementi, Muzio
Horn, Karl Friedrich
Liszt, Franz
Mendelssohn, Felix
Mozart, Wolfgang Amadeus
Schoenberg, Arnold
Schumann, Robert
Stravinsky, Igor
Wesley, Samuel

### Scholars, editors, and collectors

Anna Amalia
Bitter, Carl Heinrich
Dadelsen, Georg von
Dörffel, Alfred
Dürr, Alfred
Emery, Walter
Forkel, Johann Nikolaus
Hauptmann, Moritz
Kollmann, Augustus Frederic
  Christopher
Marx, Adolf Bernhard
Naumann, Ernst
Neumann, Werner
Poelchau, Georg
Riemenschneider, Albert
Rust, Wilhelm

Schering, Arnold
Schmieder, Wolfgang
Schulze, Hans-Joachim
Schwencke, Christian Friedrich
  Gottlieb
Smend, Friedrich
Spitta, Philipp
Swieten, Gottfried Bernhard van
Terry, Charles Sanford
Wolff, Christoph
Zelter, Carl Friedrich

### Societies and archives

American Bach Society
Bach-Archiv Leipzig
Bach-Gesellschaft
*Bach-Jahrbuch*
Internationale Arbeitsgemeinschaft
  für theologische Bachforschung
Johann-Sebastian-Bach-Institut
museums
Neue Bach-Gesellschaft
Riemenschneider Bach Institute

### Publications

*Bach*
*Bach Compendium*
*Bach Perspectives*
bibliographies
journals, yearbooks, and
  publications in series
*Neue Bach-Ausgabe*
Obituary

### General

Bach, P.D.Q.
canon
chronology
reception and revival
Schübler family

### Technical terms

*Abgesang*
*Abklatschvorlage*

*Accidentien*
*alla breve*
*al rovescio*
*alternativement*
answer
augmentation
*Brustwerk*
BWV
cancrizans
*Clavier-Übung*
countersubject
diminution
*double*
*dramma per musica*
figural music
Galanterie
inversion
invertible counterpoint
*Jahrgang*
*Liedpredigt*
madrigalian verse
*manualiter*
*pedaliter*
*per arsin et thesin*
*per omnes versus*
Phrygian cadence
positive
*Predigtkantate*
*Probe*
*Ratswahl, Ratswechsel*
réjouissance
*Rückpositiv*
*Spruch*
*Stichvorlage*
*Stollen*
stretto
Symbolum Nicenum
*tempus clausum*
*turba*
*Vokaleinbau*
*von Haus aus*
*Vorimitation*
*vox Christi*

MAP OF BACH'S GERMANY

Places where J. S. Bach lived
(with dates) are shown in **bold**

BRANDENBURG

Berlin •

Potsdam •

SAXE-ANHALT

• **Cöthen** (1717–23)

Magdeburg

• Halle

SAXONY

Dresden •

• **Leipzig** (1723–50)

Weißenfels •
• Naumburg

Carlsbad
[Karlovy Vary]

Sangerhausen •

Gera •

• Jena

**Weimar** (1703, 1708–17)

Sondershausen •

Erfurt •

**Mühlhausen** (1707–8)

Gotha •

Dornheim •

**Arnstadt** (1703–7)

THURINGIA

Wechmar •

**Eisenach**
(1685–95)

**Ohrdruf**
(1695–1700)

• Gehren

↑ to **Lüneburg** (1700–2)

Brunswick •

Göttingen •

LOWER
SAXONY

Celle •

Bückeburg •

Kassel •

HESSEN

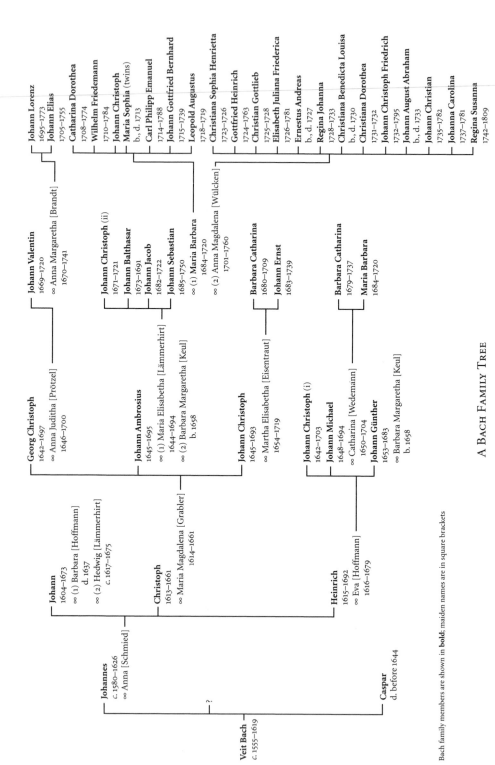

A Bach Family Tree

Bach family members are shown in **bold**; maiden names are in square brackets

# LIST OF ABBREVIATIONS

| | | | |
|---|---|---|---|
| A | alto | | *Johann Sebastian Bach* (5th edn., |
| B | bass | | Kassel and Munich, 1985) |
| BC | H.-J. Schulze and C. Wolff, *Bach* | inc. | incomplete |
| | *Compendium: Analytisch-* | NBA | *Johann Sebastian Bach: Neue* |
| | *bibliographisches Repertorium* | | *Ausgabe sämtliche Werke* |
| | *der Werke Johann Sebastian* | | (Leipzig and Kassel, 1954– ). |
| | *Bachs* (Leipzig, 1985– ) | | See main entry |
| BG | *J. S. Bachs Werke: Gesamtausgabe* | RV | Ryom catalogue (Vivaldi work |
| | *der Bachgesellschaft* (Leipzig, | | nos.) |
| | 1851–99) | S | soprano |
| BJb | *Bach-Jahrbuch* | Schmieder1 | W. Schmieder, *Thematisch-* |
| BDok | *Bach-Dokumente* | | *systematisches Verzeichnis der* |
| | i *Schriftstücke von der Hand* | | *musikalischen Werke von* |
| | *Johann Sebastian Bachs*, ed. W. | | *Johann Sebastian Bach* |
| | Neumann and H.-J. Schulze | | (Leipzig, 1950) |
| | (Leipzig and Kassel, 1963) | Schmieder2 | W. Schmieder, *Thematisch-* |
| | ii *Fremdschriftliche und* | | *systematisches Verzeichnis der* |
| | *gedruckte Dokumente zur* | | *musikalischen Werke von* |
| | *Lebensgeschichte Johann* | | *Johann Sebastian Bach* (2nd |
| | *Sebastian Bachs 1685–1750*, ed. | | edn., Wiesbaden, 1990) |
| | W. Neumann and H.-J. Schulze | Schweitzer | A. Schweitzer, *J. S. Bach*, |
| | (Leipzig and Kassel, 1969) | | English trans. by Ernest |
| | iii *Dokumente zum* | | Newman (2 vols., Leipzig, 1911) |
| | *Nachwirken Johann Sebastian* | Spitta | P. Spitta, *Johann Sebastian* |
| | *Bachs 1750–1800*, ed. H.-J. | | *Bach: His Work and Influence* |
| | Schulze (Leipzig and Kassel, | | *on the Music of Germany,* |
| | 1972) | | *1685–1750*, English trans. C. |
| BWV | *Bach-Werke-Verzeichnis* (see | | Bell and J. A. Fuller-Maitland |
| | main entry) | | (3 vols. in 2, London, 1889) |
| DürrC | A. Dürr, *Zur Chronologie der* | T | tenor |
| | *Leipziger Vokalwerke J. S. Bachs* | Terry | C. S. Terry, *Bach: A Biography* |
| | (2nd edn., Kassel, 1976) | | (2nd edn., London, 1933) |
| DürrK | A. Dürr, *Die Kantaten von* | | |

# NOTE TO THE READER

*Entries* are arranged in letter-by-letter alphabetical order. The exception to this rule is biographical entries, which are ordered letter by letter up to the first punctuation in the headword.

*Cross-references.* These are indicated by SMALL CAPITALS in the text, often preceded by *see*, or *see also*. Cross-references are supplied only when the entry referred to presents further information on, or is closely related to, the article being consulted. Where a person's dates are shown in the body of an article, this may be taken as indicating that there is no article specifically on that person.

BWV *nos.* The standard BWV numbering of *Schmieder2* is used to identify Bach's works; letters following a number (e.g. 243*a*) refer to variant versions of the work in question; figures following a colon (e.g. 243:10) refer to a particular movement or section within a work, as shown in *Schmieder2*. A concordance between the numbering of *Schmieder2* and that of the more recent *Bach Compendium* will be found in the List of Works (Appendix 1).

*Biblical quotations and references* are from/to the Authorized Version of the Bible, except in the case of the Psalms, for which the Book of Common Prayer was used.

*Bibliographies.* The bibliographies appended to certain articles are not intended to be comprehensive. For further information the reader should consult the items listed in the entry BIBLIOGRAPHIES. The following standard reference works have not been included: F. Blume, ed., *Die Musik in Geschichte und Gegenwart* (Kassel, 1949–79; 2nd edn. in progress); S. Sadie, ed., *The New Grove Dictionary of Music and Musicians* (London, 1980; rev. edn. in progress); neither have the *Kritischer Berichte* (Critical Commentaries) of the *NBA*.

*Musical pitches* are indicated as follows (with accidentals as required):

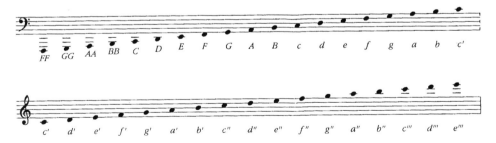

# A

**Abel, Carl Friedrich** (b. 22 Dec. 1723; d. 20 June
1787). Composer and viol player, born in Cöthen,
Thuringia; he was the son of Bach's colleague at
Cöthen, Christian Ferdinand Abel. By the time of
his birth Bach had left Cöthen for Leipzig, but
Abel later had close contact with members of the
Bach family. According to the historian Charles
Burney (1726–1814), he became a pupil of J. S.
Bach in Leipzig, and he no doubt knew Wilhelm
Friedemann Bach at Dresden, where he played
viol in the court orchestra. In London he collaborated with Johann Christian Bach in an import-
ant series of 'Bach–Abel' concerts (1765–81).
Abel's own music consists mainly of orchestral
and chamber works, most of them presumably
composed for his own concerts (the programmes
of which have not survived).

> S. McVeigh, *Concert Life in London from Mozart to
> Haydn* (Cambridge, 1993)

**Abel, Christian Ferdinand** (b. Aug. 1682; d. 3
April 1761). Viol player, born in Hanover. He was
for a time in the service of King Charles XII of
Sweden, and joined the *Kapelle* of Prince Leopold
at Cöthen in 1714. He was evidently a close friend
of Bach, who stood as godfather to his daughter
Sophia Charlotta on 10 December 1720, and it was
possibly for Abel that Bach wrote his gamba sonatas and other viol music. Abel retired in 1737 and
died at Cöthen 24 years later. His sons Carl Friedrich (see above) and Leopold August (1718–94)
were both musicians.

**Abendmusik** ('evening music'). Free public concerts of organ and sacred vocal music begun by
Franz Tunder (1614–67) at the Marienkirche,
Lübeck. Under Buxtehude and his successors they
took place at 4.00 p.m. on the last two Sundays of
Trinity and the second, third, and fourth Sundays
of Advent, and often consisted of a five-part oratorio cycle. (Bach's six-part *Christmas Oratorio*
was likewise devised to span successive feasts, the
six main church services of Christmastide.) The
Lübeck *Abendmusiken* became famous throughout Europe, and Bach is known to have attended
Buxtehude's concerts in 1705. If he was present on
2 and 3 December he must have heard Buxtehude's *Castrum doloris* and *Templum honoris*,
commemorating the death of Leopold I and the
accession of Joseph I as Holy Roman Emperor.
    The term might equally be applied to concerts
which took place in churches elsewhere and (as an
equivalent of the Italian 'serenata') to such occasional civic concerts as the performance of Bach's
secular cantata *Preise dein Glücke*, given in Leipzig's market-place at 9.00 p.m. on 5 October 1734
to celebrate the anniversary of the election of
August III as King of Poland.                    SH

> G. J. Buelow, 'Hamburg and Lübeck', in *Man and
> Music: The Late Baroque Era* (London, 1993),
> 190–215; H. E. Smither, *A History of the Oratorio*, ii
> (Chapel Hill, NC, 1977), 81–102; K. Snyder, *Dietrich
> Buxtehude, Organist in Lübeck* (New York, 1987).

**Abgesang.** The last (B) section in BARFORM
(A–A–B).

**Abklatschvorlage** ('impression model'). A
manuscript copy intended for use in a particular
engraving process. *See* SOURCES, §2.

**Accidentien.** A term used for the incidental payments (for weddings, funerals, etc.) which in
Bach's time, as now, made up a substantial part of
a church musician's income. In his letter to Georg
Erdmann (28 October 1730) Bach remarked that
'my present *station* is worth about 700 thaler, and
if the death-rate is higher than *ordinairement* then
the *accidentia* increase in proportion; but if the air
is healthy they fall accordingly, as last year, when
there was a reduction of over 100 thaler in the
*Accidentien* I would normally receive for funerals'.
Before that Bach had been in dispute over the
*Accidentien* pertaining to services held in the University church.

**Ach Gott, vom Himmel sieh darein** ('O God,
look down from heaven'). Cantata for the second
Sunday after Trinity, BWV2, performed at Leipzig
on 18 June 1724. It belongs to Bach's second *Jahrgang* (1724–5) consisting mainly of chorale cantatas, of which this is one. The history of Bach's
autograph score is of particular interest, and one
that it shares with three other cantatas, nos. 20,
113, and 114. These were among the scores
inherited after Bach's death by his eldest son Wilhelm Friedemann. In 1827 they were acquired,
along with other Bach works, by a Berlin councillor, Carl Philipp Heinrich Pistor (1778–1847), and
they then passed to his son-in-law Adolph August
Friedrich Rudorff (1803–73) and to Rudorff's son
Ernst Friedrich Karl (1840–1916). In 1917 all four
autographs were acquired by the Musikbibliothek
Peters in Leipzig, but in 1945, at the end of World

1

## Ach Gott, wie manches Herzeleid

War II, the archive of this publishing firm was dispersed, part of it going to the Staatsarchiv Leipzig and part into the possession of Walter Hinrichsen (1907–69). Hinrichsen, an American of German origin, took part in administering the American zone of occupation in Germany in 1945–7, and in 1948 he founded the C. F. Peters Corporation in New York. After his death and that of his widow Evelyn (in 1982), their heirs sold some of the autographs (including BWV20 and 113) at Sotheby's in London on 11 November 1982. Cantata 2 was retained by the widow of Walter Hinrichsen's elder brother Max (1901–65).

*Ach Gott, vom Himmel sieh darein* uses the first and last strophe of Martin Luther's hymn of that title, a paraphrase of Psalm 12, for the outer movements; as usual in the chorale cantatas, the central strophes are paraphrased by an unidentified librettist to serve for recitatives and arias. The anonymous melody to which the hymn is sung, published in the *Erfurter Enchiridion* (1524), was used for numerous organ preludes by various composers, including one by Bach himself (BWV741). The text of the cantata calls on God for help in a world where 'the faithful are minished from among the children of men'.

The cantata is scored for unusual forces: SATB, four trombones, two oboes, strings, and continuo. There are six movements (corresponding to the six strophes of Luther's hymn), the first of which is noteworthy for its adoption of the *stile antico*, confirmed by its *alla breve* time signature (¢) and the doubling of the vocal parts by the trombones. Bach returned to this archaic MOTET STYLE in Cantatas 38 and 121 later in the year, and in Cantata 28 the following year. Especially with the cantus firmus in the alto—something which is found in only one other cantata, no. 96—it contrasts sharply with the opening movements of the adjacent cantatas, nos. 20 and 7, and the contrast is underlined by the presence, as a kind of ostinato, of the *passus duriusculus* (a chromatic descent through the interval of a 4th)—a feature also of the earlier Cantata 12:2 and the later Cantata 78:1. It is characteristic of the Bach style that it should be accompanied by its opposite, a chromatic ascent, in a kind of paronomasia, as one might call this juxtaposition of two musical figures similar in structure but different in significance.

The chorale melody is heard again in the two movements that follow. In the first of these, a tenor recitative, lines 1 and 3 are presented, in canon with the continuo bass, in two arioso passages marked 'Adagio'; in the alto aria 'Tilg, o Gott, die Lehren', with violin obbligato, the last line is quoted in the B section (the aria is in modified da capo form). After an accompanied bass recitative (movement 4), ending in arioso, and a

substantial da capo aria, 'Durchs Feuer wird das Silber rein', for tenor with predominantly chordal accompaniment on strings and oboes, the cantata ends with the customary straightforward chorale harmonization in four vocal parts, with *colla parte* instrumental support. AB

For bibliography, *see* CANTATA, §1.

*Ach Gott, wie manches Herzeleid* ('Ah God, how much heart-suffering') **(i)**. Cantata, BWV3, for the second Sunday after Epiphany, first performed on 14 January 1725. The text is anonymous, but based on Martin Moller's chorale (1587) of the same title. The librettist treats the chorale much in the normal manner of the Leipzig cantata texts, using two strophes for the opening chorus and the closing harmonization (movements 1 and 6) and paraphrasing some of the intervening strophes for the inner movements (3–5). The second movement, a chorale harmonization with interpolated recitative, has a composite text combining the second strophe of the original chorale with added text by the librettist. There is little apparent connection between the Gospel for the day (the story of the Wedding of Cana) and the theme of the text, which deals with tribulation and the need for steadfast faith. An autograph score and original performing material survive.

The cantata is scored for SATB, two oboes d'amore, strings, and continuo, with two brass instruments, a trombone and a *corno* (apparently a slide instrument), to double chorale entries in the first and last movements respectively. The work follows the standard six-movement layout shared by many of the Leipzig chorale cantatas. The first movement is a chorale fantasia with the melody in the bass, around which is woven a richly expressive dialogue based mainly on a chromatic subject first given out by the two oboes d'amore in turn and then taken up by the voices. The idea is an elaboration of the descending tetrachord, a stepwise fall through four notes often used as a 'grief' symbol in the funerary chaconnes of Baroque opera (and in Bach's own music). The accompanying parts reinforce the expressive connection with the text through a constant stream of sighing appoggiaturas, and pedal points abound, created by the long-held final notes of the chorale entries.

More unusual in design is the second movement, 'Wie schwerlich läßt sich Fleisch und Blut', which is laid out as a dialogue recitative with all four voices participating. The recitative sections are punctuated by four-part harmonizations of each chorale line in succession, accompanied by an independent instrumental bass line which works out a subject based on a diminution of the first line of the chorale. The following bass aria, 'Empfind ich Höllenangst und Pein', accompanied by the continuo group only, is in da capo form and abounds in writhing chromaticism. The voice part is richly endowed with figures depicting the torments of tribulation and the joys of divine consolation. A simple recitative for tenor, 'Es mag mir Leib und Geist verschmachten', leads to 'Wenn Sorgen auf mich dringen', a duet in da capo form for soprano and alto accompanied by an obbligato line for the two oboes d'amore and violins in unison. Most of the material is based on the opening subject, which is worked out between the voices and obbligato instruments in fugal style. It is suggested in *DürrK* that some of the musical figures are intended to suggest the Cross, particularly in the central section (ending in G♯ minor), in which the accompanying text reads 'Mein Kreuz hilft Jesus tragen' ('Jesus helps to bear my cross').

The cantata ends with a plainly harmonized chorale, setting strophe 18 of Moller's hymn.

DLH

For bibliography, *see* CANTATA, §1.

***Ach Gott, wie manches Herzeleid*** ('Ah God, how much heart-suffering') (**ii**). Cantata, BWV58, for the Sunday after the feast of the Circumcision, first performed on 5 January 1727. The text is anonymous and includes two quoted chorale strophes: strophe 1 of Martin Moller's *O Gott, wie manches Herzeleid* in the first movement, and strophe 2 of Martin Behm's *O Jesu Christ, meins Lebens Licht* in the last. Bach revised the cantata in 1733/4, scrapping the original central aria (movement 3), and substituting a new one; only a single continuo part for the original aria of 1727 has survived. In the later revision Bach also added two oboes and an oboe da caccia (labelled TAILLE) to the first and last movements, where they mainly double the upper strings. The autograph score and original parts survive.

Like BWV153, the other surviving cantata for the Sunday after the Circumcision, Cantata 58 takes its point of departure from the Gospel of the day, which deals with the flight into Egypt and the Massacre of the Innocents, reinterpreting these themes as meditations on the trials of the Christian soul beset by spiritual enemies. Labelled 'Dialogus', the cantata is a duet in which the two voices can be seen as representing God and the Soul, following the usual symbolism of soprano and bass voices in Bach's vocal music. The accompaniment is for strings and continuo (plus the oboes added for the later version), with elaborate solo violin parts in the first and last movements. The work has a symmetrical construction in five movements, with two extended duets (nos. 1 and

5) flanking a central aria (no. 3) and two simple recitatives (nos. 2 and 4).

The first and last movements both take the form of chorale fantasias, with the soprano singing the chorale and the bass an independent poetic text of consolatory character. The instrumental material of the first movement is built round a ritornello in dotted rhythms, giving a *galant* feel to the music which is to some extent a feature of the whole cantata. Since the opposed character of the hymn text and the poetic text makes overall mood-painting difficult, Bach represents the distressed tone of the soprano's chorale by a chromatic descent in the bass line at the opening, and elsewhere gives the movement a bright tone which is in accordance with the other text, 'Nur Geduld, mein Herze' ('Be patient, my heart'). A bass recitative leads to the central soprano aria, 'Ich bin vergnügt in meinem Leiden', which has an obbligato violin part of a distinctly concerto-like character, with a number of *forte* and *piano* markings and detailed bowing indications (including rapid syncopated bowings which preclude a fast tempo). Since the voice part of the 1727 aria has not survived, any suggestion as to why Bach replaced it can only be speculative, but the relatively undemanding voice part of the later aria raises the possibility that the singer may have found the first one too difficult. There follows a second secco recitative for the soprano, with a closing arioso section.

Finally comes a second duet in chorale fantasia form, balancing the first. The soprano's chorale text, 'Ich hab für mir ein schwere Reis' ('I have a hard journey before me'), sounds a note of newfound resolution, to which the interpolated bass text, 'Nur getrost, ihr Herzen' ('Take comfort, ye hearts') provides a counterpoint. In this movement the accompaniment again features an elaborate violin part of some virtuosity, often recalling a quick movement from a concerto. As pointed out in *DürrK*, the ascending triad which opens the instrumental ritornello recalls the first movement of the E major violin concerto, a comparison which gives a good indication of the character of the whole movement.

DLH

For bibliography, *see* CANTATA, §1.

***Ach Herr, mich armen Sünder*** ('Ah Lord, [rebuke not] me, a poor sinner'). Cantata for the third Sunday after Trinity, BWV135, first performed at Leipzig on 25 June 1724. It is a CHORALE CANTATA belonging to Bach's second Leipzig *Jahrgang*. As usual, the anonymous librettist has retained the first and last strophes of the hymn (by Cyriakus Schneegaß, 1597) verbatim, and paraphrased the inner strophes, in this case as two recitative–aria pairs. The hymn itself is a free paraphrase of

# Ach Herr, mich armen Sünder

Psalm 6 but, as Alfred Dürr points out (in *DürrK*, the choice of this hymn was probably prompted by the last verse of the Gospel for the day, 'I say unto you, there is joy in the presence of the angels of God over one sinner that repenteth' (Luke 15:10). The subject of the cantata, then, is repentance at the time of death and joy in the promise of forgiveness.

Musically the cantata is based on the chorale melody by Hans Leo Haßler (1562–1612) popularly known as the PASSION CHORALE because of its association with the *St Matthew Passion*. This is set as a large-scale choral fantasia in the first movement and plainly harmonized in four parts to end the work; phrases from it appear also in three of the central movements. *Ach Herr, mich armen Sünder* is the fourth in Bach's series of chorale cantatas. The first three had all begun with a movement in which the chorale tune was heard as a cantus firmus—in Cantata 20 in the soprano, in Cantata 2 in the alto, and in Cantata 7 in the tenor. Now it is the turn of the bass, but each line of the melody is played first by the upper strings (violins and viola) in unison, and the texture is permeated by a version of the first phrase in quavers, announced at the beginning by the two oboes but soon taken up contrapuntally by the upper strings and the accompanying voices (SAT).

This movement, one of the most impressive among the many fine choruses in Bach's chorale cantatas, is followed by a tenor recitative notable for its dramatic word-painting on 'schnellen' ('rapid') and 'Schrecken' ('terror'). The through-composed tenor aria 'Tröste mir, Jesu' (movement 3), accompanied by two oboes and continuo, begins in a cheerful, almost dance-like vein which seems to belie the sentiments of the text, with its references to 'deep anguish' and death. A quite elaborate melisma on the unimportant word 'aus' ('from') might suggest that the aria makes use of pre-existing music, but appropriate underlining of 'erfreu' ('gladden') and 'stille' ('hushed'), and more especially a thinly disguised reference to the last line of the chorale melody at the final vocal phrase, argue strongly against this.

The alto recitative that follows begins with another reference to the chorale tune, this time to the opening phrase in a highly chromatic Adagio passage expressing the text 'Ich bin von Seufzen müde' ('I am weary with sighing'). The dark sentiments of this brief recitative are dispelled in a bass aria, accompanied by strings and continuo, in which the thrusting quaver arpeggios of the first violin seem to express the opening words, 'Weicht, all ihr Übeltäter' ('Away, all ye evil-doers'). This is cast in modified da capo form, which allows Bach to introduce, towards the end,

a final reference to the chorale melody (this time, to lines 2 and 4) before it is heard in full to end the work.

For bibliography, *see* CANTATA, §1.

## *Ach, ich sehe, itzt, da ich zur Hochzeit gehe*

('Ah, I see now, as I go to the marriage'). Cantata for the 20th Sunday after Trinity, BWV162, first performed in Weimar on 25 October 1716. The text, by Salomo Franck, refers to the Epistle for the day (Eph. 5: 15–21), relating the conduct between a man and his wife in marriage to the spiritual relationship between Christ and his Church.

As it has come down to us, in an incomplete set of parts (Bach's score has been lost), the cantata is scored for four voices (SATB), strings, bassoon, and continuo. The bassoon doubles the continuo in the final chorale and, for the most part, in the first movement as well. When Bach performed the cantata again during his first year at Leipzig, on 10 October 1723, he added a part for *corno da tirarsi* (*see* HORN). This doubles the soprano in the final chorale, but in the opening bass aria it is given a somewhat unusual role, sometimes doubling the viola but for the most part enriching the harmonic texture in a constant ♪ ♫♫ rhythm which (for once) seems designed to allow the player opportunities to breathe. The aria is organized on concerto lines, with a typical FORTSPINNUNGS-TYPUS ritornello in A minor (B minor in the Leipzig version) which recurs twice in related keys during the course of the aria and again at the end.

After a tenor recitative, the soprano sings the D (E) minor aria 'Jesu, Brunquell aller Gnaden'. This is another ritornello aria (again without da capo), and it is obvious from the nature of the ritornello and its relation to the solo line that at least one obbligato part is missing. A reconstruction with two violins has been attempted; two oboes would better complement the wind group in the first and last movements. A simple recitative for the alto follows, and, since neither alto nor tenor has so far been given a lyrical movement to sing, they now join in a C (D) major duet, accompanied by continuo, in which vocal textures fluctuate between free imitation (at the opening), homophony mainly in 3rds and 6ths (at 'die Liebesmacht'), and close canon at the 4th or 5th (at 'der Ehren weisses Kleid').

The quality of this duet and of both the arias is such that the lacunae in the instrumental complement should not be allowed to inhibit performances. The cantata ends with the seventh strophe of Johann Rosenmüller's hymn *Alle Menschen müssen sterben* (1652), plainly harmonized in A (B) minor.

For bibliography, *see* CANTATA, §1.

*Ach, lieben Christen, seid getrost* ('Ah, dear Christians, be comforted'). Cantata for the 17th Sunday after Trinity, BWV114, performed at Leipzig on 1 October 1724. Belonging to Bach's second *Jahrgang*, it is a CHORALE CANTATA based on a hymn by Johannes Gigas (1561) and its associated melody, *Wo Gott der Herr nicht bei uns hält*, by Justas Jonas (1543). The text, which shows no close connection with either of the Bible readings for the day, expresses a philosophy commonly found in the Bach cantatas: that believers should bear punishment and tribulation with patience and fortitude, certain of redemption and comfort in the life to come. The anonymous librettist has included the first, fourth, and last of the seven strophes of the hymn verbatim, paraphrasing the others for two recitatives and two arias (nos. 2, 3, 5, and 6).

The opening chorus is a fine example of the choral fantasias that are the chief glory of Bach's chorale cantatas. The music unfolds on a number of levels. The chorale melody itself is heard, line by line, as a soprano cantus firmus in long notes, with the three lower voices more actively employed, sometimes homophonically, sometimes working out brief points of imitation. Separating the chorale lines, and forming a frame for the whole movement, is an instrumental ritornello composed of various elements: a theme (played at the opening by oboes and first violins) made up of crotchet leaps and stepwise quaver movement; its continuation—repeated staccato quavers in groups of six articulated by a trill (perhaps representing the troubled and trembling Christians who are being addressed); and the omnipresent *figura corta* ( ♪♫♫♪ ), often used to express joy and confidence, played first by second violins and continuo but soon permeating the entire instrumental texture. The movement's structure is determined, of course, by the BAR-FORM (A–A–B) of the chorale melody itself, but Bach is far too inventive a composer merely to repeat the harmonies and figuration of the first two lines for lines 3 and 4.

It is worth remarking, too, how Bach in this cantata, as in others, minimizes the demands placed on his least experienced singers, the trebles of the Thomasschule. The chorale cantus firmus in the opening movement is reinforced (for safety?) by a horn, as is the soprano line of the final chorale (where it is doubled by the two oboes and first violins as well). There is no recitative for the soprano, and in the only aria (no. 4) for that voice, accompanied by continuo, the soloist again sings the same chorale melody, only lightly decorated in the second line. The trebles therefore needed only to learn (and probably already knew) one simple hymn tune.

For the other singers the challenge is greater. In 'Wo wird in diesem Jammerthale' (no. 2) the tenor must not only negotiate some tricky intervals and rhythms but also synchronize with an almost hyperactive flute obbligato, whether suggesting the vale of lamentation at the opening or the joy with which the Christian turns to Jesus for help in the central (Vivace) section of this da capo aria. The other aria (no. 5 in B♭ major), for alto accompanied by oboe, strings, and continuo, is more straightforward and forthright in expression, and again in da capo form. But it is by no means unadventurous in its modulations, which take us into the dark regions of E♭ minor at the words 'es muß ja so einmal gestorben sein' ('one must indeed die one day').

For bibliography, *see* CANTATA, §1.

*Ach wie flüchtig, ach wie nichtig* ('Ah how fleeting, how trivial'). Cantata for the 24th Sunday after Trinity, BWV26, first performed on 19 November 1724. It belongs to the series of chorale-based cantatas which formed the mainstay of Bach's second annual cycle at Leipzig. The foundation of the work is a hymn by Melchior Franck (*c*.1579–1639) on the transitoriness of mortal life. The appointed Gospel reading for this Sunday (Matt. 9: 18–31) relates the raising of Jairus's daughter, but Günther Stiller (*Johann Sebastian Bach and Liturgical Life in Leipzig*, trans. H. J. A. Bouman, D. F. Poellot, and H. C. Oswald, ed. R. A. Leaver (St Louis, Miss., 1984), 246) notes that Bach followed the Leipzig and Dresden hymn schedules which directed that hymns 'Concerning Death and Dying' should be used on this day. Franck's hymn answers the description perfectly, though of course a seemingly fatalistic preoccupation is used to stress the futility of laying up treasures on earth and to remind us of the everlasting life promised to the Christian believer. As usual in Bach's chorale cantatas, unaltered stanzas of the hymn are contained in the opening and concluding sections, while the texts of the intervening recitatives and arias have been paraphrased by an unidentified author from the remaining strophes of the hymn.

The work begins with a sturdy but athletic chorus in A minor, scored for three oboes (with a flute doubling the first oboe), strings, and continuo, and introduced by a vigorous instrumental ritornello. The melody of Franck's hymn, which like the text dates from 1652, is contained in the soprano vocal line, strengthened by a horn. The insistent and rapid upward and downward scale passages, which occur in all strands of the instrumental texture, would seem to evoke the transitory, fleeting nature of mortal life. The da capo aria which follows is a virtuoso piece for tenor, obbligato flute and violin, and continuo. The cascading torrents of semiquavers in the solo instrumental parts are taken up by the voice in a movement which admirably colours the textual imagery of human life seen as water swiftly running down a valley before disappearing. At bar 83 Bach introduces a subtle change in the word-painting to illustrate the textual simile of time disappearing like summer showers ('Wie sich die Tropfen plötzlich teilen'). Here the swirling semiquavers give way briefly to a pattern of descending arpeggios to depict falling raindrops.

An alto recitative reflects on the transitory nature of human aspirations and endeavour. The textual theme is carried forward to the following bass aria where the focus is more specifically on the futility of earthly possessions. In this richly textured E minor movement, in a modified da capo form, the singer is accompanied by three oboes with continuo; the rhythm is that of a bourrée but, as remarked in *DürrK*, this is no merry-making dance but a veritable *Totentanz*, or dance of death. A soprano recitative, to the text of which Bach responds with lively imagination, further considers the transitoriness of a mortal lifespan and leads to the concluding chorale. This is the sixth strophe of Franck's hymn, for which Bach provided a straightforward four-part harmonization with instrumental support. NA

For bibliography, *see* CANTATA, §1.

**'Actus tragicus'.** *See* GOTTES ZEIT IST DIE ALLERBESTE ZEIT.

**Adlung, Jakob** (b. 14 Jan. 1699; d. 5 July 1762). Writer on musical theory and aesthetics, born in Bindersleben, near Erfurt in Thuringia. He studied at Jena University and took organ lessons from Johann Nikolaus Bach (1669–1753). In 1727 he became organist at the Predigerkirche in Erfurt, a post which he retained until his death. His published writings include *Musica mechanica organoedi* (Berlin, 1768); this contains detailed descriptions of over 80 German organs of the time, including some which Bach played. Adlung wrote appreciatively of Bach in his *Anleitung zu der musikalischen Gelahrtheit* (Erfurt, 1758) and gave an account of Bach's aborted contest with Louis MARCHAND which he claimed to have had from Bach himself.

**Affektenlehre** ('theory of the affects'). A term used by 20th-century musicologists to refer to various doctrines concerning expression or the representation of emotion in 17th- and 18th-century music. However, the term 'Affektenlehre' was apparently first used within the context of music by Johann Mattheson, but only for philosophical theories of human emotion in general, with particular reference to that of the French philosopher and mathematician René Descartes (1596–1650). Mattheson elsewhere presented a theory of musical expression which has been revived in recent times by Peter Kivy. Mattheson also published a list which relates keys to particular affects, and he described dances and other types of music (such as the French overture) in ways that seem to associate each genre with particular stereotyped expressive qualities. But, as George Buelow has argued convincingly, musicologists have been wrong to infer from these writings—or those of later 18th-century authors, especially J. N. Forkel—that Bach and his contemporaries adhered to a systematic or universally accepted doctrine of musical expression based on associations between affects and specific musical elements (such as keys).

Nevertheless, Bach is likely to have shared with his contemporaries the Cartesian assumption that human emotions can be classified as a fixed set of affects: unchanging, universally understood and shared emotions, such as fear, exaltation, and joy. Some such principle appears to have been widely recognized in the 17th and 18th centuries, and it finds a parallel in the tendency of Baroque operatic arias, as well as those of Bach's cantatas, to fall into particular types expressive of specific emotions. Yet precise definitions of the resulting categories (such as the 'rage' aria) are hard to come by. Moreover, the view of certain late 18th-century German critics, according to which a musical composition should express only a single affect, is rare or unknown in writings of Bach's time, nor do his musical works provide consistent evidence for the existence of such a doctrine. DS

G. J. Buelow, 'Johann Mattheson and the Invention of the Affektenlehre', in G. J. Buelow and H. J. Marx, eds., *New Mattheson Studies* (Cambridge, 1983), 393–407; P. Kivy, 'Mattheson as Philosopher of Art', *Musical Quarterly*, 70 (1984), 248–65.

*agrémens* (in modern French, *agréments*). A term for ornaments, used (not for the first time) by François Couperin in his *L'Art de toucher le clavecin* (Paris, 1716) for trills, mordents, etc. (*see* ORNAMENTATION). The word is used, somewhat differently, in Bach's English Suites nos. 2 and 3 to designate embellished versions of the sarabandes; these follow the simple (unornamented) dances and were probably meant as alternative versions. In this Bach probably followed the model offered by the 'more ornamented' versions given for several movements in Couperin's *Premier ordre* (1713). DS

**Agricola, Johann Friedrich** (b. 4 Jan. 1720; d. 2 Dec. 1774). Composer and writer on music, born in Dobitschen, near Altenburg. He matriculated at Leipzig University on 29 May 1738. During his three years of study there (1738–41) he was a pupil of Bach. He moved to Berlin in 1741 and became director of the royal *Kapelle* in 1759. He was co-author with C. P. E. Bach of the Obituary of J. S. Bach that appeared in Mizler's *Musikalische Bibliothek* in 1754.

Both in Leipzig and in Berlin, Agricola made many copies of Bach's works, including one of an early version of the *St Matthew Passion*. About 1739 he collaborated with Anna Magdalena Bach in a copy of Part 1 of *The Well-tempered Clavier* and copied out early versions of certain fugues from Part 2, whose genesis was then at an early stage. His annotations to Adlung's *Musica mechanica organoedi* (1768) are of great interest, transmitting Bach's views on organ building, on the lute-harpsichord, and on Silbermann's forte-pianos.                                                  RDPJ

A. Dürr, 'Zur Chronologie der Handschrift Johann Christoph Altnickols und Johann Friedrich Agricolas', *BJb* 56 (1970), 44–65.

***Ah yes, just so, you must your trumpet blow.*** Well-known English version of Momus's aria 'Patron, das macht der Wind' in Cantata 201, *Der Streit zwischen Phoebus und Pan.*

**air, aria.** During the Baroque period the transcription of operatic airs for keyboard led to the use of the term for a suite movement that lacked one of the standard dance rhythms. Examples by Bach are BWV813:4, 815:5, and 830:4—moderately fast binary movements in duple or quadruple time with running semiquavers or quavers. The famous Air 'on the G string' BWV1068:2 is rather more *cantabile* in character, as are the movements that Bach designated 'Aria' in BWV822 and 828 and the Aria on which the Goldberg Variations are based. The *Air pour les trompettes* from the early Suite in A BWV832 is partly modelled on a similarly titled instrumental piece from the opera *Alcide* (1693) by the Frenchman Marin Marais (1656–1728). The concluding Air from the roughly contemporary Partita in F major BWV833, on the other hand, is a keyboard counterpart to a vocal aria, complete with figured-bass ritornellos.

RDJP

For vocal genres, *see* ARIA.

***Air on the G String.*** Title given to an arrangement for violin and piano (or strings) by August Wilhelmj (1845–1908) of the Air from Bach's Orchestral Suite no. 3. In Wilhelmj's arrangement, published in 1871, the melody is designed to be played (at the beginning at least) on the fourth (G) string of the violin.

**Albinoni, Tomaso Giovanni** (b. 8 June 1671; d. 17 Jan. 1751). Italian composer and violinist, born in Venice. An important precursor of Vivaldi in the concerto genre, he was a prolific composer of both instrumental music (sonatas and concertos) and secular vocal music (operas, serenatas and cantatas) from the early 1690s until about 1740. The lucidity of his works and their cool, 'classical' quality appealed to his contemporaries; his instrumental music in particular circulated in print and manuscript throughout northern Europe.

Bach, who appears to have known Albinoni's instrumental music well, had contact with it in three different contexts. First, three early keyboard fugues (BWV946, 950, and 951/951a) take their subjects from movements in Albinoni's *Suonate a tre* op. 1 (1694). Considered as fugues pure and simple, Bach's movements are more developed than Albinoni's, but the latter arguably have a better sense of cohesion and proportion. Bach evidently also knew Albinoni's *Sinfonie e concerti a cinque* op. 2 (1700), since there is a continuo part for the second concerto in Bach's hand in the Musikbibliothek der Stadt Leipzig. This source suggests that Bach was acquainted with the concerto genre long before he encountered Vivaldi's music. Finally, there survives in Berlin a score of the sixth sonata in Albinoni's *Trattenimenti armonici per camera* op. 6 (*c.*1711) copied out with a continuo realization (to which Bach made corrections) by Heinrich Nikolaus Gerber.      MT

G. G. Butler, 'J. S. Bach's Reception of Tomaso Albinoni's Mature Concertos', in D. R. Melamed, ed., *Bach Studies 2* (Cambridge, 1995), 20–46; M. Talbot, *Tomaso Albinoni: The Venetian Composer and his World* (2nd edn., Oxford, 1994).

***alla breve.*** In medieval and Renaissance music the marking 'alla breve' indicated that the unit of musical time (the *tactus*) was to be represented by the breve and not, as normally, by the semibreve; in modern usage it indicates a 2/2 time signature. In Bach's day 'alla breve' had something of the implication of a generic title, referring to a movement in the *stylus gravis*, or STILE ANTICO, the 18th-century inflection of 'Palestrina style' counterpoint expounded by the Austrian theorist and composer J. J. Fux in his *Gradus ad Parnassum* (1725) and taken up by German theorists such as Heinichen, Marpurg, and Kirnberger. Bach's known uses of the marking 'alla breve' all illustrate this point. Variation 22 from the Goldberg Variations treats the bass line of the Aria as a cantus firmus, which is worked in combination with a *soggetto* to create a variety of single and double suspensions on the first beat of almost every bar (Heinichen in 1728 referred to 'beautiful suspensions of consonances and dissonances'). The chorus 'Der aber die Herzen' from the motet *Der Geist hilft unser Schwachheit auf* is an austere

# Allein zu dir, Herr Jesu Christ

double fugue on a large scale in the 'strict' style, in which two conventional subjects are worked out, first separately and then in combination. Finally, the Allabreve in D major for organ BWV589 is a double fugue based on a subject whose underlying pattern is a line of semibreves similar to the subjects set by Fux in *Gradus ad Parnassum*. The execution features a rich crop of learned devices, including stretto entries. In general, the *stile antico* in Bach's music is associated with the 'cut' time signature (₵), notably in 'Credo in unum Deum' and 'Confiteor' from the B minor Mass and the E♭ major organ fugue BWV552:2.     DLH

C. Wolff, *Der stile antico in der Musik Johann Sebastian Bachs* (Wiesbaden, 1968).

***Allein zu dir, Herr Jesu Christ*** ('On thee alone, Lord Jesus Christ'). Cantata for the 13th Sunday after Trinity, BWV33. It belongs to Bach's second annual Leipzig cycle of cantatas and was first performed there on 3 September 1724. The appointed Gospel reading for the day (Luke 10: 23–37) includes the parable of the good Samaritan, but the cantata's anonymous text, based on a 16th-century hymn with its melody (1540) by Konrad Hubert, makes only a fleeting reference to it. The work as a whole is perhaps best understood as both a contemplation of God's love of mankind and an exhortation to the Christian believer to love his fellow human beings accordingly. Both the autograph score, once owned by Mendelssohn, and the original parts have survived.

Adhering to his usual custom in the chorale-based cantatas, Bach begins the piece with an expansive chorale fantasia accommodating the text of the first strophe of Hubert's hymn unchanged. This is introduced by a lively discourse between divided oboes and violins with playful imitation and exchanges of thematic material. The chorale melody is sustained in the soprano line of the four-part vocal texture, while each of the nine lines of the hymn is punctuated by instrumental ritornellos developed from the introductory section, which invests the movement with immense vitality.

A bass recitative with a concluding arioso section envisages Judgement Day and is a confession to God of human frailty. It leads to a da capo aria in C major of sustained beauty. This is scored for alto voice with muted first violins which carry the melody, accompanying pizzicato strings, and a continuo of organ with bass string pizzicato. The text is a continuation of ideas presented in the preceding recitative, but it now envisages the sinner's timid journey towards heaven. Bach's use of musical ideas is economical yet immensely resourceful. Above the simple and delicate accompaniment he has created an alluring melody of broad contours whose expressive warmth and affecting pathos colour the images of the text with the utmost delicacy.

A supplicatory tenor recitative completes what W. G. Whittaker described as 'a triptych of agony' (*The Cantatas of Johann Sebastian Bach* (Oxford, 1959), ii. 367). The second aria, in E minor, is a duet, partly canonic, for tenor and bass with two accompanying oboes and continuo bass. Its text is concerned with both divine love and neighbourly love, and thus converges with the parable of the good Samaritan. The dance-like rhythm and the serenity of a melody which initially recalls the first Trio in the last movement of Brandenburg Concerto no. 1 introduces to the cantata, for the first time, a spirit of sustained optimism. The work concludes with the fourth and last strophe of the hymn, set to Hubert's melody and straightforwardly harmonized by Bach with instruments supporting the four vocal strands.     NA

For bibliography, *see* CANTATA, §1.

**allemande.** A popular DANCE form which appeared in the early to mid-16th century. Among the earliest uses of the term in Germany are certain pieces for cittern published in Strasburg in 1575 by Sixt Kargel and J. D. Lais. The term appears again in ensemble dances published in Hamburg in 1609 by the English composer William Brade, and Hermann Schein (1586–1630) also used it in his *Banchetto musicale* (1617). German keyboard allemandes around 1640 are already stylized beyond the confines of dance accompaniment. Bach appears to have been influenced by Froberger and his followers, whose use of *style brisé*, points of imitation, pseudo-polyphonic texture, and motivic inversion in turn reflects French composers such as Denis Gaultier (1603–72), N.-A. Lebègue (*c*.1631–1702) and Chambonnières (1601/2–72). F. W. Marpurg (*Clavierstücke*, ii (1762), 21) described allemandes as similar to preludes, in that allemandes are often based on a succession of changing harmonies in an improvisatory style. The main difference between the two is that in allemandes the dissonances had to be carefully prepared and resolved. Eighteenth-century writers often described the allemande as serious, grave, or solemn.

Bach's allemandes are all for solo instruments, not for ensembles. All are in duple metre and in BINARY FORM, with the first section consistently ending in a new key. They all begin with an initial upbeat of one or more notes, and exhibit a well worked-out harmony mostly realized in constant semiquaver movement. Technical features often include arpeggiation, motivic development, imitation, and changing numbers of voices.

Of Bach's 37 allemandes, 23 are in keyboard

suites, six in the Cello Suites, and the remainder in the suites or partitas for solo violin, lute, and flute. The allemandes in the English Suites are in a quite strict imitative style, particularly nos. 2–5, and each is preceded by a large-scale prelude. On the other hand, the French Suites, lacking preludes, begin directly with allemandes that show a wide variety of styles. Nos. 1, 2, and 4 use two-voice counterpoint in a prelude-like style which is ornamental and arpeggiated; no. 5 is aria-like and no. 6 uses the hypnotic Italianate violin figurations which have always intrigued listeners. Allemandes in the keyboard partitas BWV825–30 show the greatest variety of all, including arpeggiated style (no. 1), French overture style (nos. 3 and 6), ornamented aria (nos. 4 and 5), and two-voice counterpoint using triplets (no. 5). It is interesting to note that Bach's famous Ouverture in the French Style from *Clavier-Übung II* contains no allemande. The elegant allemandes in the Cello Suites, each preceded by a dramatic opening movement, have been described by Karl Geiringer as 'slow and pensive pieces of great beauty' (*Johann Sebastian Bach* (New York, 1966), 305).

NJ, MEL

R. Hudson, *The Allemande, the Balletto, and the Tanz* (Cambridge, 1986); N. Jenne, 'On the Performance of Keyboard Allemandes', *Bach*, 10/2 (1979), 13–30; V. Mansure, 'The Allemandes of Johann Sebastian Bach: A Stylistic Study' (diss.. University of Oregon, 1992); J. Mráček, 'Inaugurators of Bach's French Style: The Vingt-quatre Violons du Roi and their Contemporaries', in D. Berke and D. Hanemann, eds., *Alte Musik als ästhetische Gegenwart* (Kassel, 1987), i. 355–77. For further bibliography, *see* DANCE.

**Alles nur nach Gottes Willen** ('Everything only according to God's will'). Cantata for the third Sunday after Epiphany, BWV72. As far as we know, Bach wrote four cantatas for this Sunday in the Church calendar; in addition to the present work, performed on 27 January 1726, there are nos. 73 (1724), 111 (1725), and 156 (probably 1729). Since the text of no. 72 is by Salomo Franck, who was active at the Weimar court, and was published in his *Evangelisches Andachts-Opffer* (Weimar, 1715), it has been conjectured that the cantata was composed at Weimar for 27 January 1715 and revived at Leipzig in a totally revised version. It is scored for SATB with two oboes, two violins, viola, and continuo, and divided into six movements (in the *BG* edition and in *Schmieder 1* and *2* the second and third movements are seen as one, making the total five).

The liturgy for the third Sunday after Epiphany includes two readings of particular importance and instruction to Christian worshippers. The Epistle (Rom. 12: 17–21), recalling the words of

Solomon (Prov. 25: 21–2), extols the virtue of charity towards one's enemy. The precept is fundamental to the Christian way of life, and in fact the whole of St Paul's chapter is so charged with exhortation and admonition, and so rich in content, that it might be compared with the Sermon on the Mount in St Matthew's Gospel. The appointed Gospel reading is in fact St Matthew 8: 1–13. It presents Jesus as a worker of miracles in healing the leper and the centurion's servant—a perfect expression of the spirit of charity.

The text of the cantata refers to the biblical readings in a general way, as an act of faith—a testimony to the blind faith that the believer, in good times and in bad times, should place in the Lord. Franck's libretto had designated the opening number an aria, but Bach set it as a chorus in concertante style. It is ternary in form and predominantly imitative in texture, but with passages of chordal writing systematically and symbolically tied to the word 'alles' ('all'), which is repeated almost obsessively. This chorus was later parodied in the *Missa* in G minor BWV235.

The way that Franck constructed the recitative 'O selger Christ, der allzeit seinen Willen' (no. 2) led Bach to organize his setting (for alto and continuo) in three sections: recitative–arioso–recitative. The central arioso brings into prominence the ninefold repetition of 'Herr, so du willt' ('Lord, if thou wilt'), which is set to similar (in the first three cases) or varied melodic phrases. The second recitative section is followed without a break by the alto aria 'Mit allem, was ich hab und bin'; the voice begins immediately, anticipating the instrumental ritornello, which takes the form of a fugato for the two obbligato violins. A final aria, 'Mein Jesus will es tun' (no. 5, for soprano with oboe, strings, and continuo), resolves, with its dance-like (polonaise) character, the dramatic tensions accumulated earlier in the work. The cantata ends with the first strophe of the chorale *Was mein Gott will, das gscheh allzeit* by Margrave Albrecht of Brandenburg (1547) in a straightforward four-part harmonization, with instruments doubling the voices.

AB

For bibliography, *see* CANTATA, §1.

**Alles, was von Gott geboren** ('All that is born of God'). Cantata for the third Sunday in Lent (Oculi), BWV80a, almost certainly performed on 15 March 1716 in the Weimar court chapel, where Bach was organist. A manuscript score, presumably a copy rather than the autograph, was offered for sale in Breitkopf's 1761 catalogue as: 'Bachs, Joh. Seb. Cantate: In Dom. Oculi. Alles, was von Gott geboren. à 1 Oboe, 2 Violini, Viola, 4 Voci, Basso ed Organo' (see *BDok* iii. 161). Although the autograph score and parts, and the Breitkopf copy, of this Weimar cantata are no longer extant, its contents can be fairly accurately reconstructed from its later manifestation as Cantata 80, *Ein feste Burg ist unser Gott*, and Salomo Franck's printed libretto, which appeared in his *Evangelisches Andachts-Opffer* (Weimar, 1715).

Franck's libretto makes use of Luther's hymn *Ein feste Burg ist unser Gott*, commonly used as the Gradual hymn for Oculi. The libretto comprised six movements: three arias, two recitatives, and a concluding chorale. Bach's setting of these movements was in C major (rather than the later D major), with a simple orchestration of strings and a single oboe. The first three movements corresponded to movements 2–4 in Cantata 80. 'Alles, was von Gott geboren' was a bass aria with unison strings and an ornamented version of the chorale melody heard only on the oboe. Movement 2 was a bass recitative ending with an arioso which incorporated marked chromaticisms, appropriately drawing attention to the Cross (the German word 'Kreuz' stands for both 'cross' and the musical sharp sign, ♯). And movement 3 was a tender soprano aria accompanied only by the continuo.

Movements 4 and 5 became nos. 6 and 7 in Cantata 80, and the work concluded with the second stanza of Luther's hymn. The music for this is unknown, but can possibly be identified as the four-part chorale BWV303. RAL

*See also* EIN FESTE BURG IST UNSER GOTT.

For bibliography, *see* CANTATA, §1.

***al rovescio.*** An Italian term meaning 'reversed', or 'upside down', and therefore used in music, especially CANON, to refer to the retrograde or inversion of a theme. Bach used the rubric 'all' roverscio' (*sic*) for the second of the 14 canons he added to his *Handexemplar* of the Goldberg Variations; its solution involves both the retrograde and the inversion of the theme.

***Also hat Gott die Welt geliebt*** ('God so loved the world'). Cantata, BWV68, first performed on Whit Monday, 21 May 1725. It is one of nine with texts by the Leipzig poet Christiane Mariane von Ziegler for the period between Jubilate (third Sunday after Easter) and Trinity Sunday 1725. Together they form a tailpiece to the cycle of chorale cantatas that Bach began on the first Sunday after Trinity in 1724 and abandoned just before Easter 1725. Ziegler based her text on the Gospel reading appointed for Whit Monday (John 3: 16–21), which deals with redemption through faith; its opening words, 'God so loved the world', are taken up in the hymn by Salamo Liscow (1675) which Bach wove in a highly ornamental fashion into the opening chorus. This movement is scored for four-part choir and strings, whose three upper parts are reinforced by two oboes and oboe da caccia, with continuo; in addition, a cornett strengthens the cantus firmus hymn melody by Gottfried Vopelius (1682) in the soprano line. Bach's setting of the hymn in the 12/8 rhythm of a siciliana is outstandingly lyrical, and the lyricism is intensified, as pointed out in *DürrK*, by the introduction and subsequent recurrence of a rising interval (a 6th) with which soprano and bass voices make their entries. The expressive tenderness of the piece is further heightened by Bach's frequent and skilful use of appoggiaturas in the violin and oboe parts.

Both arias of the cantata derive from Bach's earlier Weimar offering in honour of the birthday of Duke Christian of Saxe-Weißenfels, WAS MIR BEHAGT, IST NUR DIE MUNTRE JAGD. The first of them, 'Mein gläubiges Herze' ('My heart ever faithful'), has long been among the handful of Bach's best-known melodies. Its many arrangements, however, with organ, piano, or orchestral accompaniment have tended to ignore the original nature of the piece, which is lightly scored for soprano solo with violoncello piccolo and continuo. With only very small adjustments—the change of the fourth note from C to F is notably effective—Bach transferred the ostinato melody in the continuo of the earlier cantata to the obbligato violoncello piccolo of the present work. The melodically straightforward vocal line of the original, however, is replaced by a completely new one, more complex and ornamental in design. Exceptionally among the arias in his cantatas, Bach added an instrumental ritornello at the end, scored for violin, oboe, violoncello piccolo, and continuo. This trio section, which grows out of the material allotted to the violoncello piccolo and is half as long as the aria itself, is another borrowing from the earlier Weimar piece, where it perhaps served as a separate movement.

The second aria, for bass, prefaced by a short bass recitative, is accompanied by two oboes and oboe da caccia with continuo. The resulting woodwind texture is satisfyingly rich; only Telemann, perhaps, was able to deploy it to comparable advantage. Unlike the previous aria, this one retains the melody of the original, albeit modified and extended.

The cantata ends with a motet-like chorus in the form of a double fugue. To the strings, oboes, and cornett of the opening chorus Bach now adds three trombones which augment the alto, tenor, and bass strands of the vocal texture. The strict contrapuntal discipline of this movement admirably reflects the stern nature of the text: 'he that believeth not is condemned already'. NA

For bibliography, *see* CANTATA, §1.

**Alt-Bachisches Archiv** ('Archive of the elder Bachs'). A collection of music by members of the Bach family owned and probably assembled by J. S. Bach. The estate catalogue of Bach's son Carl Philipp Emanuel (1790) lists 19 vocal works (motets, vocal concertos, and arias) from his father's library under the name 'Alt-Bachisches Archiv'. Some are attributed to Johann Christoph Bach (i), Johann Michael Bach, and Georg Christoph Bach; others are anonymous. C. P. E. Bach also mistakenly included his father's early motet *Ich lasse dich nicht, du segnest mich denn* BWV Anh. III 159. A few family vocal pieces inherited by other Bach children survive, but any family instrumental music that J. S. Bach may have owned is lost. Most of C. P. E. Bach's vocal materials themselves disappeared from the Berlin Sing-Akademie during World War II.

Exactly when and where Bach acquired the music of the Alt-Bachisches Archiv is unknown; there is no evidence for the appealing story that he inherited the whole from his father, Johann Ambrosius. Although writers have cited compositions from the Alt-Bachisches Archiv as specific influences on J. S. Bach's music, there is no evidence that he had any contact with the collection before the last ten years of his life, though the material it contains is representative of the music with which he grew up. He performed four motets by Johann Christoph Bach (i) in the mid- to late 1740s, as well as his St Michael's Day vocal concerto *Es erhub sich ein Streit* (date unknown). C. P. E. Bach also performed several works from the collection, and arranged one of Johann Christoph Bach's motets as the opening movement of a cantata.                      DRM

D. Melamed, *J. S. Bach and the German Motet* (Cambridge, 1995); M. Schneider, ed., *Altbachisches Archiv*, Das Erbe deutscher Musik, ser. 1, i–ii (Leipzig, 1935).

***alternativement.*** A term used in connection with two dances of the same type in a suite, to indicate not (as might be thought) that one should choose between them, but that the first of the two is to be repeated after the second. In Bach's first Orchestral Suite, for example, there are pairs of gavottes, minuets, bourrées, and passepieds intended to be performed in this way, and the practice survived into the Classical period in the minuets and scherzos of such genres as the symphony and the sonata.

***Alt-Gottesdienst*** ('old divine service'). Until 1710 services with music were held at the University church in Leipzig (the Paulinerkirche) only on particular academic occasions and on the principal Church feasts of Christmas, Easter, Whitsun, and the Reformation Festival. Responsibility for the music at these services rested with the Thomaskantor. In 1671 a proposal had been made to institute regular Sunday services, but it was not until 1710 that these were allowed to go ahead, and they were referred to as the *Neu-Gottesdienst* ('new divine service') to distinguish them from those held previously, which became known as *Alt-Gottesdienst*. In 1723 the university appointed J. G. Görner to direct all the services in the Paulinerkirche, which led to a prolonged dispute with the new Thomaskantor, Bach, who was finally granted control of the *Alt-Gottesdienst* and the salary that went with it.

**Altnickol, Johann Christoph** (bap. 1 Jan. 1720; bur. 25 July 1759). Organist and composer, born in Berna, near Seidenberg (now Zawidów, Poland). He matriculated at the University of Leipzig on 19 March 1744 and became Bach's pupil during the same year. On 18 January 1748 he was appointed organist at Niederwiesa, Silesia, but later the same year he moved to Naumburg, being appointed organist at the Wenzelskirche on 30 July 1748, a post he retained until his death. On 20 January 1749 he married Bach's daughter Elisabeth Juliana Friederika (1726–81).

During his period in Leipzig (1744–8) Altnickol assisted Bach as bass singer, string player, and copyist. He collaborated with the composer in the compilation of the 'Eighteen' Chorales, and in 1744 produced a fair copy of the newly completed and revised *Well-tempered Clavier* Part 2. Other important Bach copies of Altnickol's include the Violin Sonatas BWV1014–19, the French Suites, and the *St Matthew Passion*.                      RDPJ

A. Dürr, 'Zur Chronologie der Handschrift Johann Christoph Altnickols und Johann Friedrich Agricolas', *BJb* 56 (1970), 44–65.

***Am Abend aber desselbigen Sabbaths*** ('Then the same day at evening'). Cantata, BWV42, for the first Sunday after Easter (Quasimodogeniti), first performed on 8 April 1725. The unidentified librettist based the text on the opening words of the Gospel reading from St John 20. Although a substantial work in itself, Bach set only one of its seven movements as a chorus. Instead of the kind of elaborate opening chorale fantasia that had characterized almost all the preceding cantatas of the second annual cycle, to which this work belongs, he provided an unusually extended orchestral sinfonia. Alfred Dürr has suggested (in *DürrK*) that Bach deliberately omitted a full-scale choral movement in order to give his choir a well-earned rest after their exacting duties during the Passiontide and Easter festivals.

## Am Abend aber desselbigen Sabbaths

The Sinfonia, in D major, is scored for a concertino group of two oboes and bassoon with strings and continuo, and may derive from a lost instrumental work. Much of the two-part violin writing is in unison, but as the movement unfolds it plays a role of greater intricacy with the woodwind concertino. The piece is in da capo form, with a central section marked 'cantabile'. Here the expressively interwoven woodwind parts, tender and lyrical in character, have led writers to suggest that Bach perhaps intended to evoke eventide and the two disciples' walk to Emmaus with the risen Christ, a recurring motif throughout the cantata.

The first vocal number is a tenor recitative accompanied by a continuo of repeated semiquavers, introducing the words of the appointed Gospel. The ensuing da capo aria for alto with two oboes, bassoon, and strings is concerto-like both in structure and dimension, leading us to speculate whether it might not have once belonged to the same instrumental work from which Bach perhaps borrowed the preceding Sinfonia. This movement, containing the contemplative heart of the cantata, is cast in two distinct sections: an Adagio, which is the more extended of the two, and a brief, effectively contrasting Andante in 12/8 time, which leads to the da capo.

The fourth number is a duet for soprano and tenor accompanied by bassoon, cello, and continuo. The text is based on a strophe from a 17th-century hymn by Jakob Fabricius (1632). In this chorale movement Bach makes fleeting and subtle reference to its associated melody, *Kommt her zu mir, spricht Gottes Sohn*, both in the continuo and in the tenor line. The recitative and aria which follow are for bass. In the concluding bars of the recitative the continuo depicts the impotent rage of Christ's antagonists, while the lively A major aria, scored for two violins (more precisely, a rare case of first violins *divisi*) and continuo with bassoon, contrasts three aspects of Christian belief: the impotence of Christ's enemies is depicted once again, now in restless violin figures, while the vocal line expresses the reassurance imparted by faith, and assertive rhythms in the continuo symbolize persistence and strength.

The cantata ends in F♯ minor with a four-part chorale accompanied by the full instrumental complement. It is made up of two sections joined seamlessly together. The first contains Luther's German translation of the Latin antiphon *Da pacem, Domine* (1529), with its anonymous melody. The second, by Johann Walther (1566), is a prayer for peace and good government traditionally linked with Luther's translation of the antiphon. Its melody, too, is an anonymous one dating from the 16th century.                    NA

For bibliography, *see* CANTATA, §1.

**Amalienbibliothek.** A music collection, including many Bach works, assembled by Princess ANNA AMALIA of Prussia.

**American Bach Society.** An organization dedicated to the preservation and dissemination of Bach's music, as well as to the knowledge and understanding of his life and works through research and performance. It was initially constituted as the American chapter of the Neue Bach-Gesellschaft at a 1972 meeting headed by Arthur Mendel at Princeton University. In 1988 it adopted its present name and in 1992 was reconstituted as an independent organization.

The society publishes a newsletter and holds biennial meetings at which talks, panel discussions, and musical performances are presented, and at which it awards the William H. Scheide Fellowship and the William H. Scheide Prize. These, named after a founder and long-term supporter of the society, respectively support Bach research and honour a recent publication by a young North American Bach scholar. In addition, the society was from 1989 to 1993 affiliated to the Riemenschneider Bach Institute, with which it jointly issued the latter's journal, *Bach*. In 1995 the society began to issue an annual volume of *Bach Perspectives*, containing scholarly articles and reviews, under a rotating editorship.          DS

**Ammerbach, Elias Nikolaus** (b. *c*.1530; bur. 29 Jan. 1597). German organist, born in Naumburg. He served as organist of the Thomaskirche in Leipzig, and died in that city. In 1571 he published a volume of organ music in TABLATURE, *Orgel oder Instrument Tabulatur*, of which Bach owned three copies.

S. Godman, 'Bach's Copies of Ammerbach's "Orgel oder Instrument Tabulatur" ', *Music and Letters*, 38 (1957), 21–7.

*Amore traditore* ('Love, thou traitor'). Italian secular cantata, BWV203, for bass voice and harpsichord. It is an exceptional work, the only one in the Bach catalogue for voice and harpsichord. It probably dates from before 1723 and would therefore belong to Bach's Cöthen years, but the loss of many Bach works, above all secular works linked to a particular occasion, makes it impossible to place this cantata in a context which might suggest the circumstances of its composition. The only thing to be drawn from a reading of the text is that we have here a cantata on an amatory subject: the singer resolves to abjure love, which has brought him only misery. It belongs to a genre much in favour at the time, especially among Italian composers or those with an Italian background.

The cantata was included in catalogues issued by the publishing firm of Breitkopf in 1764 and

1765. Compared with Bach's other Italian cantata, *Non sa che sia dolore*, the text is linguistically more correct, but still defective. The work survives in three 19th-century sources of Viennese provenance which belonged to three different collectors: Franz Hauser (1794–1870), Joseph Fischhof (1804–57), and Aloys Fuchs (1799–1853); the first two are now in the Staatsbibliothek zu Berlin, the third in the Benedictine abbey at Göttweig in Lower Austria.

The authenticity of *Amore traditore*, much discussed especially in the early 20th century (see Schreyer and Schering), seems now to be generally accepted, partly as a result of stylistic analysis but more, perhaps, because of the high quality of the music. The work comprises two arias separated by recitative. The harpsichord is provided merely with a continuo bass for the first aria and the recitative, but in the second aria it is given a fully written-out obbligato part of a virtuoso kind which has no equal in the vast literature of the *cantata da camera*. AB

R. Donington, 'Amore traditore: A Problem Cantata', in H. C. R. Landon and R. E. Chapman, eds., *Studies in Eighteenth-Century Music: A Tribute to Karl Geiringer on his Seventieth Birthday* (London, 1970), 160–76; A. Schering, 'Beiträge zur Bachkritik', *BJb* 9 (1912), 132; J. Schreyer, *Beiträge zur Bach-Kritik* (Dresden, 1910), 22–4.

**Andreas Bach Book.** An important early manuscript source (Musikbibliothek der Stadt Leipzig, III.8.4) for 16 keyboard compositions by Bach, including the Passacaglia in C minor and the 'Little' organ fugue in G minor. Named after one of its former owners, Johann Andreas Bach (1713–79), the manuscript represents an anthology of German keyboard music from around 1700. It contains works by Böhm, Buxtehude, Kuhnau, Pachelbel, and Reincken, as well as keyboard transcriptions of orchestral music by Telemann and the Frenchman Marin Marais (1656–1728). The compiler and principal scribe of the source has been identified as Bach's eldest brother and keyboard teacher, Johann Christoph (ii), who evidently began to assemble the volume about 1708 and completed it about 1713. In copying his brother's music, he probably worked from autographs now lost. The source contains an autograph tablature of the Fantasie in C minor BWV Anh. 205. It is closely related to the MÖLLER MANUSCRIPT, another early source compiled by Johann Christoph Bach. RTS

R. Hill, 'The Möller Manuscript and the Andreas Bach Book: Two Keyboard Anthologies from the Circle of the Young Johann Sebastian Bach' (diss., Harvard University, 1987); R. Hill, ed., *Keyboard Music from the Andreas Bach Book and the Möller Manuscript* (Cambridge, Mass., 1991); H.-J. Schulze,

*Studien zur Bach-Überlieferung im 18. Jahrhundert* (Leipzig, 1984), 30–56.

***Angenehmes Wiederau, freue dich in deinen Auen*** ('Charming Wiederau, take pleasure in your meadows'). Secular cantata to a text by Picander, BWV30a, performed on 28 September 1737. It was designed as a homage cantata for Johann Christian von Hennicke (1681–1752), who had been ennobled in 1728 and was now taking possession of his fief at Wiederau, near Pegau, some 20 km. (12½ miles) south-west of Leipzig. The 'characters' of this *dramma per musica* are Zeit ('Time', soprano), Glück ('Fortune', alto), Elster (the river that flows through Wiederau, tenor), and Schicksal ('Fate', bass). After an opening chorus made resplendent with the sound of three trumpets and drums, the four soloists take turns to praise Hennicke in a series of recitatives and arias.

Like Purcell in his welcome songs, Bach lavished some excellent music on an occasion which was soon to be forgotten—or, rather, to be remembered only because of that music. But shortly afterwards he sought to give his music a wider relevance by adapting the serenata as a church cantata, FREUE DICH, ERLÖSTE SCHAR (no. 30). For this his librettist (possibly Picander again) fitted new words to the opening and closing choruses, four of the arias (nos. 3, 5, 7, and 9) and one of the recitatives (no. 8). Nos. 1 and 5 may also have been used again for an early (lost) version of Cantata 195. The only aria not taken into Cantata 30 was the tenor's 'So wie ich die Tropfenzolle', a ritornello aria in polonaise rhythm accompanied by flute, oboe, strings, and continuo.

For bibliography, *see* CANTATA, §2.

**Anhalt-Cöthen.** A territory in Thuringia which in Bach's time was ruled over by princes whose court was situated at CÖTHEN.

**Anna Amalia,** Princess of Prussia (b. 9 Nov. 1723; d. 30 March 1787). Sister of Frederick the Great, born and died in Berlin. She was a composer and player of keyboard, violin, and flute. Her library, the Amalienbibliothek, was rich in 18th-century music, especially Bach's. Many Bach manuscripts were added to her collection by the Bach pupil J. P. Kirnberger, who became her court musician in 1758. In her will the library went to the Joachimsthalschen Gymnasium in Berlin. From 1914 it was housed in the Berlin Royal Library, and it now forms part of the music collection of the Staatsbibliothek zu Berlin, Preußischer Kulturbesitz.

Anna Amalia's collection included the B minor Mass, the motets, many cantatas, the orchestral suites, the solo violin Sonatas and Partitas, and many keyboard works including *The Well-tempered Clavier* (see the 1783 catalogue in *BDok* iii, no. 887, which lacks the works added from Kirnberger's estate). RDPJ

E. R. Blechschmidt, *Die Amalienbibliothek* (Berlin, 1965); E. R. Wutta, *Quellen der Bach-Tradition in der Berliner Amalien-Bibliothek* (Tutzing, 1989).

**Anna Magdalena Music Books.** Two manuscript volumes presented by Bach to his wife in 1722 and 1725; *see* CLAVIERBÜCHLEIN.

**Ansbach Festival.** A biennial Bach festival held at Ansbach in Bavaria in July. It was founded in 1948.

**answer.** A term used in FUGUE for the second, 'answering' statement of the fugue theme, heard in counterpoint with the continuation of the first voice after it has announced the 'subject'. The answer is normally repeated in alternation with the subject until all the voices have entered. A 'real' answer reproduces exactly the intervals of the subject; a 'tonal' answer alters some intervals, usually preserving the identity of the main tonality, though the practice has its roots in modal writing. The answer is customarily pitched a 5th above or a 4th below the subject, forming a dominant relationship with the subject. However, a subdominant answer (a 5th below the subject) can, on occasion, be more appropriate, as in the organ Fugue in C major BWV531:2. LC

**Apel, Andreas Dietrich** (b. 28 July 1666; d. 14 Jan. 1718). A well-to-do Leipzig merchant. He was the first owner of the 'Königshaus' built in 1705 on the south side of the market-place. The house served regularly as a residence for illustrious visitors, and was used by the Saxon royal family during Bach's time. It was the venue for several of Bach's homage cantatas, or *Abendmusiken*, including *Preise dein Glücke, gesegnetes Sachsen* in 1734.

***Ärgre dich, o Seele, nicht*** ('Do not trouble thyself, o Soul'). Cantata for the seventh Sunday after Trinity, BWV186, first performed at Leipzig on 11 July 1723. This is a reworking of a lost Advent cantata (BWV186a), to a libretto by Salomo Franck, which Bach wrote at Weimar in 1716. In its revised form the text alludes to the Gospel of the day, St Mark 8: 1–9, telling of Jesus's feeding of the four thousand, and dwells on the theme of hunger and its satisfaction as a symbol of Christian acceptance of earthly deprivation in the hope of heavenly bounty. To render the text suitable for the new occasion, the anonymous reviser of Franck's libretto provided words for four new recitatives and lightly altered the words of the arias that became nos. 3 and 5. In its expanded form the cantata was divided into two parts; in accordance

with normal practice, the first would have been heard before the sermon, the second during Communion (*see* HAUPTGOTTESDIENST). Each part ends with a strophe of the hymn *Es ist das Heil uns kommen her* by Paul Speratus (1523), replacing the chorale used in BWV186a.

The complete forces—SATB, two oboes, *taille* (oboe da caccia), bassoon, strings, and continuo—are heard in the opening chorus, a spacious rondo structure, $A^1$–$B^1$–$A^2$–$B^2$–$A^3$, in which the B sections are set apart from the rest by their basically homophonic texture and by having only continuo support. Of the four recitatives, all but one are of the simple type, accompanied by continuo; only movement 7, for bass, has string support. Each one ends with a few bars of arioso, and these constitute some of the most expressive passages in the cantata.

None of the four arias (including one duet) is in the da capo form that was to become a regular feature of Bach's later cantatas. The third, for soprano, is notable for the sinuous chromatic lines of the unison violins that provide the instrumental obbligato; this is one of the arias unaltered from Franck's libretto, and one looks in vain for anything in the text that might explain the presence of those slithery violin semiquavers. The duet (no. 10), on the other hand, gives lively expression to the joy of salvation awaiting those who have not allowed life's tribulations to separate them from Jesus; the dance style, recalling a gigue, is enhanced by the homophonic textures which prevail in the first half of the movement and return for the final vocal phrase and the closing ritornello.

The chorale strophes that end each part of the cantata are set to the same music. Although the setting was presumably newly composed in 1723 (the music would not have fitted the hymn in Franck's text), it is not the plain harmonization with which Bach usually ended his Leipzig cantatas. The chorale melody is heard as a soprano cantus firmus, with the three lower voices entering in shorter note values and mainly in imitative style. Framing the movement, and separating each line of the chorale from the next, is an instrumental commentary in which a turning figure in semiquavers and another consisting of a downward scale passage are playfully passed between the two oboes and the upper strings. One might almost see these movements as a preparation for the great chorale fantasias that were to distinguish so splendidly the cantatas of Bach's second Leipzig *Jahrgang*.

For bibliography, *see* CANTATA, §1.

**aria.** See opposite.

14

# aria

A composition for solo voice and accompaniment, occurring in Bach's music mainly as part of a larger work such as an oratorio or cantata. Arias first became prominent in Italian secular vocal music of the 17th century, especially opera and the chamber cantata, and were introduced into German church music (along with recitative) around 1700 by Erdmann Neumeister.

1. Arias in Bach's vocal music.
2. Scoring.
3. Function.
4. Forms.

1. **Arias in Bach's vocal music.** It is not known how or when Bach became familiar with the conventions for composing arias. However, there undoubtedly were opportunities to hear operas in his native Thuringia and in northern Germany (especially at Hamburg) during his student years. Although Italianate arias of a 'modern' type are rare in Bach's earliest cantatas (*c*.1707–8), they are prominent in vocal works beginning with the first regular series of cantatas, composed in Weimar between March 1714 and December 1716. The role of Cantata 208 (the 'Hunting Cantata'), which dates from the intervening period (probably 1712 or 1713), in the formation of Bach's approach to writing 'modern' vocal solos is especially intriguing (see Whaples).

Bach composed no operas, but arias are found throughout his sacred and secular cantatas, Passions, oratorios, and Latin liturgical works. They are mostly quite demanding, technically and musically, for both vocal soloist and instrumentalists.

2. **Scoring.** Like so many aspects of Bach's music, the scoring of the arias is extremely diverse. The assignment of arias to specific vocal types is often connected with characteristics of their texts. For instance, movements with Jesus as the speaker (the *vox Christi*) are invariably assigned to a bass soloist, following a long-standing tradition in church music. In other cases the use of particular voices was influenced by the affect of the text. For example, supplications and other expressions of humility are typically sung by one of the upper voices, while arias exhibiting anger or defiance are normally taken by the tenor or bass.

While the instrumental ensemble is sometimes restricted to the continuo group alone, it more often includes one or more additional instruments. The solo instruments most frequently used are the violin, flute, oboe, and oboe d'amore. However, more unusual choices such as the viola, violoncello piccolo, recorder, oboe da caccia, bassoon, trumpet, and organ occasionally appear as well. A wide variety of duet combinations is found too, from pairs of violins, oboes, or oboes d'amore to mixtures of strings and winds (e.g. violin and flute or oboe). One of the most common scorings is the string ensemble (usually violins 1 and 2 and viola), often joined by one or more winds. Several of the arias with the largest ensembles (e.g. the tenor aria in Cantata 65, which requires pairs of recorders, oboes da caccia, and horns, in addition to the usual complement of strings and continuo instruments) were composed during Bach's first year in Leipzig (1723–4) and may have been conceived in part as experiments with the extensive instrumental resources available there.

3. **Function.** Arias are the emotional focal points within multi-movement vocal works. In 17th- and early 18th-century operas characters express their thoughts and feelings in arias, while the basic events of the plot are narrated in recitatives. From a dramatic viewpoint, then, arias are moments during which the action is interrupted while a character reflects on something that has occurred. Their aim is to cause the listener to experience a specific affect (e.g. joy, sorrow, or anger) appropriate to a given situation. As composers encountered similar dramatic situations repeatedly, they gradually developed a repertory of aria types. The characteristics of different kinds of arias were described by a number of 18th-century writers, including John Brown (*Letters on the Italian Opera*, London, 1791) who gave them names such as *aria cantabile* and *aria di bravura*.

Although Bach's vocal works are not outwardly dramatic, the arias function similarly to those in contemporary opera: they are vehicles for expressing particular affects. Because of their diversity, Bach's arias are less easily categorized than operatic arias. None the less, striking patterns are observable. For instance, the similarities between the soprano aria 'Zerfließe, mein Herze, in Fluten der Zähren' from the *St John Passion* (expressing the believer's response to Jesus's death) and the alto aria 'Erbarme dich, mein Gott, um meiner Zähren willen' from the *St Matthew Passion* (a poignant plea for mercy following Peter's threefold denial of Christ), both of which employ the imagery of tears, are so extensive as to suggest a sub-category of movements depicting moments of intense sorrow. Among their salient features are the use of high voices, minor mode, slow tempos, metrical structures based on groups of three quavers, passages in which demisemiquaver motion is predominant, and continuo lines which begin with descending scale passages in repeated notes. (The melodic contours of the opening motifs in these two arias are also remarkably similar.) Another group delineated by shared characteristics consists of movements expressing defiance or anger towards evil beings, such as the bass arias 'Höllische Schlange, wird dir nicht bange?' in Cantata 40 and 'Rase nur, verwegner Schwarm' in Cantata 215, and the tenor aria 'Es reißet euch ein schrecklich Ende, ihr sündlichen Verächter, hin' in Cantata 90. All three are powerful compositions in rapid triple metre, with *moto perpetuo* semiquavers, sung by a mature male voice accompanied by strings (with or without one or a pair of oboes) and continuo; and two of them are even in the same key. It would be interesting to investigate thoroughly Bach's settings of texts with similar affective qualities, and to see how far they mirror contemporary operatic practice.

4. **Forms.** Almost all Bach's arias begin with a ritornello, a passage for instruments alone which usually includes the movement's main musical ideas and recurs, either in full or shortened, between vocal sections and at the end. Material from the ritornello is normally taken up by the voice too, and often it is played by the instrumental ensemble while the voice sings an independent line—a technique known as VOKAL-EINBAU ('vocal embedding').

The most important overall pattern for arias during Bach's lifetime was DA CAPO form, whose distinguishing feature is repetition of the opening vocal section after a contrasting middle part, creating a large-scale ternary structure (A–B–A). The quintessential version of this form, however, is actually in five sections ($A^1$–$A^2$–B–$A^1$–$A^2$), excluding ritornellos. In such movements the opening portion of the text is set twice. The first vocal section ($A^1$) modulates from the tonic to the dominant (or relative major) and is followed by a brief ritornello in the new key. The second vocal section (A²) returns to the tonic and is followed by a restatement of the entire opening ritornello, which later concludes the movement as a whole.

While the da capo design is the most common aria form employed by Bach, it occurs much less frequently in his vocal works than in those of his contemporaries (only about a quarter follow this pattern, compared with 90 per cent or more in the works of other German and Italian composers). Instead of returning again and again to the same well-worn path, Bach developed an unusually diverse repertory of formal procedures. One of the most important is the modified da capo form. Although frequently labelled 'free da capo' in the Bach literature, it is 'free' only in comparison with the literal repetition of section A in the so-called strict da capo form. The distinguishing characteristic of modified da capo arias is tonal rather than thematic: the A section ends in a key other than the tonic (usually the dominant). Since the opening part is not tonally closed, it must be modified upon its return. The degree of alteration ranges from the bare minimum required for the movement to end in the tonic to extensive recomposition.

Beyond the obvious similarities between the tonal structures of the modified da capo and the later sonata form, the extent to which these vocal and instrumental genres are related to one another remains unclear. A potentially fruitful line of enquiry, however, is the exploration of the intersection between a number of aria forms (including the modified da capo) and the structures of concertos, especially given the explicit connections drawn by 18th-century theorists such as J. A. Scheibe, J. Riepel, and H. C. Koch. The through-composed forms containing two or three vocal sections but no da capo, which are quite common among Bach's arias, may be meaningfully viewed as vocal equivalents of concerto movements.     SAC

For instrumental arias, *see* AIR, ARIA.

P. Brainard, 'The Aria and its Ritornello: The Question of "Dominance" in Bach', in W. Rehm, ed., *Bachiana et alia musicologica: Festschrift Alfred Dürr zum 65. Geburtstag* (Kassel, 1983), 39–51; P. Brainard, 'The "Non-Quoting" Ritornello in Bach's Arias', in P. Brainard and R. Robinson, eds., *A Bach Tribute: Essays in Honor of William H. Scheide* (Kassel and Chapel Hill, NC, 1993), 27–44; S. A. Crist, 'Aria Forms in the Cantatas from Bach's First Leipzig *Jahrgang*', in D. O. Franklin, ed., *Bach Studies* (Cambridge, 1989), 36–53; S. A. Crist, 'J. S. Bach and the Conventions of the Da Capo Aria, or How Original was Bach?', in P. F. Devine and H. White, eds., *The Maynooth International Musicological Conference 1995: Selected Proceedings, Part One* (Dublin, 1996), 71–85; R. Emans, 'Stylistic Analysis and Text Philology in the Service of "Inner Chronology" Involving Stylistic Analyses of Selected Arias by Johann Sebastian Bach', *Bach*, 26 (1995), 1–14; P. Nitsche, 'Konzertform und Ausdruck: Bemerkungen zu einigen Arien Johann Sebastian Bachs', in H. Danuser *et al.*, eds., *Das musikalische Kunstwerk: Geschichte—Ästhetik—Theorie: Festschrift Carl Dahlhaus zum 60. Geburtstag* (Laaber, 1988), 385–94; M. K. Whaples, 'Bach's Earliest Arias', *Bach*, 20/1 (1989), 31–54; M. K. Whaples, 'Bach's Recapitulation Forms', *Journal of Musicology*, 14 (1996), 475–513.

# Aria mit verschiedenen Veränderungen

**Aria mit verschiedenen Veränderungen** ('Aria with diverse variations'). The title, as it appeared in the original printed edition, of Bach's GOLDBERG VARIATIONS.

**arioso.** A type of heightened declamation in vocal music, somewhere between aria and RECITATIVE.

**Arnstadt.** Town in Thuringia where Bach lived as an organist in 1703–7. Most parts of Thuringia were governed then by several collateral branches of the ducal family of Saxony, but another family, the counts of Schwarzburg, owned three central parts of Thuringia, with Rudolstadt, Sondershausen, and Arnstadt as their capitals. Thus in Arnstadt the castle, Schloß Neideck, acted as a second town centre to the Markt ('market-place').

Arnstadt has two main churches, the Barfüßerkirche (or Oberkirche, 'upper church'), situated south of the Markt, and the Liebfrauenkirche (or Unterkirche, 'lower church') to the west of the town centre. A third church is in the north-east corner of the Markt. In Bach's time this was known as the Neuekirche ('new church') on account of its having been rebuilt in 1676–83 after it had been destroyed by fire in 1581. Formerly the Bonifatiuskirche, it has been called the Bachkirche since 1935.

Arnstadt was one of the first towns 'cultivated' by the Bachs, first of all by a Caspar Bach in the 1620s. Later, two of the three sons of Bach's great-grandfather Johannes held posts there, each of them establishing 'dynasties' of their own. The elder, Christoph, was a *Stadtpfeifer* who passed on the profession to his twin sons Johann Ambrosius (Bach's father) and Johann Christoph. The younger, Heinrich Bach, became organist at the Liebfrauenkirche; his three sons (the 'Eisenach' Johann Christoph (i), Bach's father-in law Johann Michael, and Johann Günther, who continued to live in Arnstadt) were organists too. In Arnstadt some of the most important family reunions took place.

J. S. Bach's first connection with Arnstadt is puzzling. As an 18-year-old court musician at Weimar he was invited to test the new organ in the Neuekirche, built by Johann Friedrich Wender in 1699–1703. How Bach acquired the knowledge to act as an organ expert (which entailed, for example, approving the alloy used for the pipes) is not yet known. Shortly afterwards he became organist at the Neuekirche, beginning his duties there on 14 August 1703 at an annual salary of 84 florins 6 groschen. Parts of Bach's organ are still extant: the original case and seven stops in the church, the console as the principal showpiece in a small collection of Bach memorabilia housed in the Stadtgeschichtliches Museum in the Markt.

Another memorial to the composer is a statue of the young Bach by Bernd Göbel, erected in the Markt itself during the Bach tercentenary year, 1985.

Only a few of Bach's works can be assigned with any degree of certainty to his Arnstadt years. Possibly some of the compositions in the Andreas Bach Buch and the Möller manuscript date from that time: the Prelude and Fugue in G minor BWV535a, for example, as well as some of the keyboard toccatas. Other Arnstadt works probably include the capriccios BWV992–3 and the organ chorale *Wie schön leuchtet der Morgenstern* BWV739.

Bach's time in Arnstadt was overshadowed by three disputes. The first came to light through a trifling incident. On 4 August 1705 Bach was attacked by a senior pupil from the Gymnasium, Johann Heinrich GEYERSBACH, while walking home from the castle late at night, and drew his sword to defend himself. The crux of the matter was brought out in hearings conducted by the consistory. Bach was on very bad terms with the school pupils. Apparently he refused to perform figural music (i.e. ambitious pieces, such as cantatas) with them, declaring that his contract stipulated only that they should sing chorales. The town authorities contradicted this, but indeed in Bach's contract nothing was mentioned beyond his normal duties as an organist.

The second quarrel concerned his visit to the composer and organist Dietrich Buxtehude in Lübeck, for which he was granted four weeks' leave, but extended it to four months. He returned by 7 February 1706, and so his journey must have begun only two months after the Geyersbach incident. It was therefore inevitable that the general problem of performing figural music was revived by the consistory. Another question was raised by the disturbing way in which Bach accompanied chorales in the service. The words recorded by the town scribe suggest that this was not something new, resulting from Bach's visit to Buxtehude, but that it had persisted since his installation. At all events, the distinction between the typical advanced profile of north German organ compositions and the traditional Thuringian style had become apparent in Bach's music. There was also criticism of the length of time his playing occupied (apparently between the lines of the chorales sung by the school pupils). This hearing was therefore concerned mainly with stylistic questions, but it ended with the recurrent charge that Bach refused to perform figural music with the students.

The third dispute, in November 1706, continued where the second left off, but it also brought to light a new complaint: that Bach had

Statue of the young Bach by Bernd Göbel, erected in the market-place at Arnstadt in 1985

allowed a young lady to sing from the organ loft. Perhaps this expressed Bach's new interest in concerted music (in a way which was typical of north German organists), and this would explain why the consistory raised yet again the question of figural music. Some writers suggest that the lady in question was Maria Barbara, Johann Michael Bach's daughter, whom Bach married in 1707.

By the following Easter Bach had auditioned for a post at Mühlhausen, and on 29 June 1707 he returned the organ keys to the consistory and left Arnstadt. His successor there was his cousin Johann Ernst, who earned 15 gulden less than his predecessor. KK

BDok ii, nos. 7–17; K. Küster, *Der junge Bach* (Stuttgart, 1996), 121–50; K. Müller and F. Wiegand, *Arnstädter Bachbuch: Johann Sebastian Bach und seine Verwandten in Arnstadt* (2nd edn., Arnstadt, 1957); M. Petzoldt, *Bachstätten aufsuchen* (Leipzig, 1992), 14–25.

**arrangements.** Numerous precedents for making arrangements of Bach's works were provided by the composer himself. This article is concerned mainly with arrangements by some later composers which involve an element of creativity. Many other arrangements have been made simply to expand the repertory of a particular instrument (such as the guitar) or to exploit the popularity (or potential popularity) of a piece; for some examples, *see* AIR ON THE G STRING; AVE MARIA; JESU, JOY OF MAN'S DESIRING; LOUSSIER, JACQUES; SHEEP MAY SAFELY GRAZE; and SWINGLE SINGERS. For Bach's own arrangements, *see* CONCERTO TRANSCRIPTIONS, HARPSICHORD CONCERTOS, and SCHÜBLER CHORALES.

1. Introduction.
2. 1750–*c*.1900.
3. The 20th century.

1. **Introduction.** Bach made numerous transcriptions between every medium of his output, choral as well as instrumental; his far-reaching extension of the artistic possibilities of transcription merits the broader term 'arrangement'. These arrangements explore the potential of the original either through the addition or substitution of figures more idiomatic to the new medium, or through the redisposition of the texture, sometimes even involving the deletion of material. Bach's arrangements of his concertos for violin and for other instruments as harpsichord concertos in the collection BWV1052–8 or of cantata movements as organ solos in the Schübler Chorales give clear illustration of the process. The purpose of arrangements seems generally to have been functional: the provision of effectively new music by the simplest means, sometimes from practical necessity. But in Bach's youth he applied the same principle to the purposes of study. His arrangements of many works, especially Italian, and notably of Vivaldi, have been credited with influencing his developing style (see, for example, the concerto arrangements BWV592–7, 972–87, and 1065). With the development of more precise textural roles for individual instruments in the Classical era, the scope for such arrangements was reduced. Although a didactic function remained—indeed Bach's own music soon became an object of veneration, seen as representing the summit of a past art of counterpoint—arrangement was directed more towards realizing the music's expressive content. The 19th-century arrangements of Bach's music increasingly sought to 'realize' its content in terms of wider dynamics and added harmonies, a process taken further in the 20th century, largely through the medium of the orchestra.

2. **1750–*c*.1900.** Earlier arrangements were primarily for technical instruction or to broaden the audience. Mozart arranged five four-part fugues from *The Well-tempered Clavier* (K405). It is believed that they were made for the Sunday concerts of the musical antiquarian Baron van Swieten in Vienna which Mozart attended and at which he performed in the years 1782–3. The concerts were devoted to the music of Bach and Handel, and Mozart owed much of his knowledge of these composers to them. Other similar arrangements for string trio, K404a, with new introductions in place of the preludes, are not now regarded as by Mozart and probably emanate from within this circle. The arrangements were doubtless made to reveal the full independence of the counterpoint better than in a keyboard performance. However, Mozart's fuller 'realizations' were directed more towards Handel, notably in the 'additional accompaniments' for orchestra to extensive choral works, including *Messiah* and *Alexander's Feast*.

The role of presenting Baroque instrumental music to the new concert audiences of the 19th century was largely assumed by the piano. SCHUMANN added piano accompaniments to the Sonatas and Partitas for unaccompanied violin and to the six Cello Suites (1852)—works all but unknown at the time—providing support through a discreet realization of the implicit harmony. His arrangement of the best-known movement, the highly demanding Chaconne from the Partita in D minor BWV1004, can be directly compared with that of Mendelssohn, whose accompanied version of this movement is his only Bach arrangement. Mendelssohn is much freer in his interpretation of the implicit harmony and in the creation of accompanimental figures.

The piano alone was the chief vehicle of their contemporary LISZT and successor BRAHMS, though in very different ways. Brahms's three Bach arrangements are nos. 3–5 of the Five Piano Studies published in 1877 without opus number. While his two arrangements of the Presto from the Sonata in G minor BWV1001 realize the harmony in a mirror-like countrapuntal-harmonic left-hand part (the second version reverses the parts between the hands), his purpose in the Chaconne is not expansion but restriction. Here he specified the medium of piano left hand alone in order to impose on the pianist a limitation comparable to that placed on the violinist in music whose expressive power stretches both medium and instrumentalist to the limit. Although Brahms publicly performed major organ works by Bach on the piano, notably the Toccata in F major BWV540, he never published such arrangements, with their need of extended left-hand parts to simulate the pedals. Such arrangements were rather the province of Liszt, who arranged six of the preludes and fugues for organ (BWV543–8) in 1842–50, as well as the Fantasia and Fugue in G minor BWV542 (1863). He also published for organ an 'Introduction and Fugue' taken from Cantata 21, an Andante from Cantata 38, and the Adagio from the Violin Sonata no. 4 in E major BWV1017.

**3. The 20th century.** Liszt's approach was significantly extended into the 20th century by Ferrucio BUSONI, who included a concerto as well as organ, harpsichord, and solo string works in six books of arrangements and editions published as the *Bach-Busoni gesammelte Ausgabe* (Bach–Busoni Edition). His extensive notes and performance markings almost give his editions the status of arrangements. His piano arrangements of the organ works, whether of an intimate or of a public character, present the originals in adaptations of extreme skill. The arrangement of the chorale prelude on *Nun komm, der Heiden Heiland* (BWV659) accommodates both its ornate upper voice and full accompaniment (with pedals) by careful distribution between the hands, while that of the E♭ major Prelude and Fugue BWV552 adds a full array of additional octaves to suggest the effect of the organ, making interesting comparison with a version of the same work for piano by Max Reger (1873–1916), published in 1895, one of his many Bach arrangements for piano solo and duo. Busoni's arrangement of the Chaconne, though beginning like the Brahms, elaborates a virtuoso solo; yet in his arrangement of the D minor Harpsichord Concerto BWV1052 parts of

the solo as continuo are omitted to give a more modern concerto effect. In arrangements by the Russian composer Sergey Rachmaninov (1873–1943) of three movements from the violin Partita in E major BWV1006 (1933), the recompositional process is taken much further, the additional contrapuntal motifs and added chromatic harmonies giving the effect of an original work by the arranger.

It becomes increasingly difficult to distinguish between goals of enhanced sonority and individual recomposition in the orchestral arrangements of the 20th century, which use the resources for great dynamic contrast and textural differentiation. Keyboard music provides the prime source, stimulating such individual responses as the arrangements by Leopold Stokowski (1882–1977) of the D minor Toccata BWV565 and Edward Elgar (1857–1934) of the Fantasia and Fugue in C minor BWV537, as well as Reger's Suite drawn from the keyboard Partitas and English Suites; but orchestral works are also drawn upon, as in the Suite for String Orchestra by Gustav Mahler (1860–1911), based on four movements from Bach's orchestral suites nos. 2 and 3. Although SCHOENBERG claimed that the purpose of his arrangements of two chorale preludes, BWV645 and 667, and the E♭ major Prelude and Fugue BWV552 for organ was to reveal the motivic structure in a way impossible for a single player, the sheer size of his orchestra, which includes, in BWV552, bass wind, a full percussion section, harp, and celesta, brings the music close to some of the aforementioned arrangements in effect (notably to Elgar's final flourish in the C minor Fugue); the 'motivic' scoring of the prelude *Schmücke dich, o liebe Seele* BWV654 is accommodated within a very Romantic sonority.

By contrast, the arrangement by STRAVINSKY of the Canonic Variations on *Vom Himmel hoch, da komm ich her* BWV769 is much closer to the spirit of the original, through the use of an orchestra comprised chiefly of wind (without clarinets), harp, lower strings, and choir. The work might rather be seen as representing a 'commentary' on the original through the composer's extension of its techniques. As well as providing an opening harmonization of the chorale itself (from the *Christmas Oratorio*), not present in Bach's version, Stravinsky adds two more voices, thus making it possible to add new canons to the texture, though the total harmonic effect is none the less entirely in accord with his style: the arrangement was written as a companion piece to the *Canticum sacrum* at its first performance in St Mark's, Venice, in September 1956. The most radical treatment of the orchestra is by Anton Webern (1883–1945) in his orchestration of the six-part

Ricercar from the *Musical Offering* (1933–5), in which, like Schoenberg, he sought to reveal the motivic coherence through orchestration. However, by isolating much shorter motifs throughout the entire texture by orchestral means, he created an entirely different effect—one which is intimately related to his own style as it can be observed in the scoring of his Symphony and Orchestral Variations. MM
*See also* PERFORMANCE STYLES and WISE VIRGINS, THE.

**articulation.** A term referring in musical performance to the degree of separation between successive notes. It was not, in itself, an object of study in Bach's time, but became an issue in performance when, in the latter half of the 20th century, performers on organ and harpsichord began to search for a means of compensating for the lack of dynamic expression on such instruments. With the increasing study of historic instruments and performing techniques, articulation soon became an issue in all media of performance, since the evidence often implied an articulation differing from that intuitively employed on 'modern' instruments.

The issue of articulation has also become significant for the new editions of Bach's music, since close study of the original sources often revealed discrepancies, inconsistencies, or simply incompleteness in the articulation that Bach and his copyists notated in the form of slurs, dots, and, sometimes, strokes. Research into historical instruments and techniques and the study of notated articulation have tended to inform one another in a circular fashion; for instance, the assumption that Bach often conformed to the 'rule of the down-bow' in string playing (where the bowing scheme is engineered to produce a down-bow on important metrical stresses) has often enabled editors to devise plausible solutions to ambiguous string slurring.

Articulation in the performance of Bach's time was doubtlessly as much an unquestioned reflex as it was in 20th-century performance before the advent of historical performance; it is only prominent to us today by virtue of its 'difference'. Recent studies suggest that the 'basic' style of articulation was less overwhelmingly legato than mid-20th-century practice, although this does not necessarily imply the mechanical staccato of some early attempts at historical performance. A 'standard' degree of articulation is particularly evident in the comprehensive keyboard tutors appearing just after Bach's death, such as those by his son Carl Philipp Emanuel and F. W. Marpurg. However, the same point has also been discovered in historical sources on string and wind performance and, most recently, in singing itself, the art which is so often invoked as the model for all other performance (Butt). Perhaps the most essential element of singing technique, from the early 17th century to the end of the 18th, was the improvisation and clean articulation of 'divisions', or 'diminutions'. Much of the melismatic writing, particularly the swifter passage-work in Bach's music, can be understood as an element of diminution and much would thus presumably have been performed with some degree of articulation. While it is unlikely that singers routinely chopped up the musical lines, a seamless legato was probably not the norm, and syllabic writing would, in any case, have been automatically articulated by the consonants and vowel changes of the text.

Diminution treatises often imply that many of the component figures of passages require a particular style of articulation; certainly many of Bach's own markings can characterize certain motifs as 'slurred' (e.g. appoggiaturas and particularly emotive figures such as that opening the *St John Passion*), can delineate component figures within passages (e.g. the fast triplets in the flute part of 'Benedictus qui venit' from the Mass in B minor), or can differentiate the articulation of various figural components (such as the three levels of articulation in the organ prelude 'Vater unser', BWV682, where three distinct levels of articulation—slurred, staccato, and unmarked—are associated with three distinct motivic families).

Another approach is to see 'standard' articulation as linked to the 'grammatical accentuation' of the metre, something which can be traced back to the strong-weak division of the *tactus* and which can be developed on several metrical levels (see Lohmann). Theorists such as Wolfgang Caspar Printz (1641–1717) and J. G. Walther sometimes referred to the variable 'inner' value of the notes as opposed to their external, notated value, and many more writers described the same issue in terms of 'good' and 'bad' notes (long and short, according to their metrical position). A pairing of notes is sometimes inferred from the playing techniques of various instruments: the up- and down-bowing of the strings, the paired syllables for wind and the paired fingers for scale passages on keyboard (*see* FINGERINGS, Ex. 1). However, as performers have become more proficient it seems clear that these techniques do not automatically produce a particular articulation, although they certainly predispose the player to envision a pairing inherent in the music.

Bach seems to have notated articulation in several ways and for several reasons throughout his career: quite often he absent-mindedly included articulation in the very process of composition, particularly for figures customarily associated with a slur; sometimes this compositional slurring might be developed and refined in the course of the composition, just as the very figural material is developed; he added the most articulation marking in parts specifically designed for performance, usually adding more detail in later revisions or in fresh parts for later performances. Sometimes the markings seem advisory, alluding to a particular articulative style for the movement concerned (i.e. generally slurred or, in rarer cases, staccato); at other times, particularly in solo string (and sometimes flute) lines, the articulation is extremely refined and didactic. While a study of articulation is central to the practices of editing and performance, consideration of Bach's own practice often reveals a subtlety and sophistication similar to (and perhaps even part of) that which is evident in his very compositional practice.     JAB

J. Butt, *Bach Interpretation* (Cambridge, 1990); G. von Dadelsen, 'Die Crux der Nebensache: editorische und praktische Bemerkungen zu Bachs Artikulation', *BJb* 64 (1978), 95–112; repr. in G. von Dadelsen, *Über Bach und anderes: Aufsätze und Vorträge 1957–1982*, ed. A. Feil and T. Kohlhase (Laaber, 1983), 144–58; J. R. Fuchs, *Studien zu Artikulationsangaben in Orgel- und Clavierwerken von Joh. Seb. Bach* (Stuttgart, 1985); L. Lohmann, *Studien zu Artikulationsproblemen bei den Tasteninstrumenten des 16.–18. Jahrhunderts* (Regensburg, 1982).

**Art of Fugue, The.** See overleaf.

**Ascension Oratorio** (*Himmelfahrts-Oratorium*). One of Bach's three so-called oratorios, first performed on Ascension Day (19 May) 1735 in one of Leipzig's main churches. BWV11/249b comprises two flanking choruses (with the same scoring as Parts 1, 3, and 4 of the *Christmas Oratorio*), a central chorale, two arias, and recitatives (one developed into a short duet). In style and structure the oratorio differs little from a sacred cantata, and was so classified in the *BG* edition of 1852. It has been published twice in the *NBA*: in 1975, based on the autograph score alone, and in 1983, taking into account the original instrumental and vocal parts made available in Kraków.

The work shares with the other two oratorios not only the ceremonial key of D major, but also a reliance on earlier music. The first chorus, with its ceremonial scoring including trumpets and drums, may have been borrowed from the opening chorus of the lost cantata *Froher Tag, verlangte Stunden* (1732). The alto aria 'Ach, bleibe doch' was based on the aria 'Entfernet euch, ihr kalten Herzen' from a lost wedding cantata, *Auf! süß-entzückende Gewalt* (1725); 'Agnus Dei' in the Mass in B minor is a parody of the same aria but preserves a much simpler and shorter version,

probably reflecting its original state. This suggests that Bach thoroughly revised the aria for inclusion in the *Ascension Oratorio*, although his normal practice was the almost literal transfer of material. Whether parody or not, the music of the second aria, 'Jesu deine Gnadenblicke' (soprano), closely matches the implicit imagery of the text. Christ's bodily departure from Earth is suggested by the absence of a continuo part, but the power of his loving spirit remains and is reflected in the hovering accompaniment for upper instruments (flutes, oboe, violins, and viola). The surviving performing material—which is fairly typical in comprising one copy per part, with one additional copy each for the violins, and includes vocal partbooks containing both the solo and chorus parts—implies that the oratorio was originally performed with forces of around 20.

The text is anonymous and mixes biblical passages for a tenor Evangelist with newly written poetic verses for the choruses, arias, and accompanied recitatives. The judicious biblical compilation (derived mainly from Luke 24: 50–2, and Acts 1: 9–12) provides the work with its narrative thread, really the only major feature to distinguish it from a cantata. The use of biblical passages sung by an Evangelist links the work to the Lutheran tradition of the *historia*, an important forerunner of oratorio, and also to the Passion. Indeed, Bach's treatment of the 'false witnesses' in the *St Matthew Passion* (no. 33) is recalled in the similar texture of the passage in the oratorio (no. 7a) where 'two men in white apparel' reassure the people of Galilee at the moment of Jesus's Ascension. Like the *Easter Oratorio*, the *Ascension Oratorio* is concerned with a single main incident and is essentially contemplative in tone, ending with a chorale-based chorus which looks forward to the Resurrection.     SH

F. Smend, 'Bachs Himmelfahrts-Oratorium', in K. Matthaei, ed., *Bach-Gedenkschrift 1950* (Zurich, 1950), 42–65; repr. in F. Smend, *Bach-Studien: Gesammelte Reden und Aufsätze*, ed. C. Wolff (Kassel, 1969), 195–211.

**Auf Christi Himmelfahrt allein** ('On Christ's Ascension alone'). Cantata for Ascension, first performed on 10 May 1725. The text of BWV128 is by Christiane Mariane von Ziegler (though much altered in the version used by Bach) and was published in Part 1 of her collection *Versuch in gebundener Schreib-Art* in 1728. The two quoted chorales are the first strophe of *Auf Christi Himmelfahrt allein* by Josua Wegelin and Ernst Sonnemann (no. 1) and the fourth strophe of Matthaeus Avenarius's hymn *O Jesu, meine Lust* (no. 5). The text takes its point of departure from the first of these chorales, which is based on biblical texts outlining the theological significance of the

[*cont. on p.26*]

### The Art of Fugue (*Die Kunst der Fuge*)

A collection of fugues and canons, intended as an exemplary set of compositions illustrating various contrapuntal techniques. Although the medium of performance is unspecified, all but one or two movements are playable on a solo keyboard instrument (without pedals), thus following a tradition dating back to the early 17th century of austere contrapuntal music for performance on, or study at, the harpsichord, clavichord, or organ. The complete work is listed as BWV1080; the numbering of the individual movements varies with the edition used.

As it has come down to us, *The Art of Fugue* is unfinished and the intended order of its component movements not entirely certain. Once thought to date from Bach's final years, the work is now known to have been largely completed by about 1742, by which date Bach had written a preliminary version consisting of ten fugues and two canons. Published posthumously in 1751, the work was reissued in 1752 with an expanded preface by F. W. Marpurg. This published version makes numerous alterations to the earlier version (preserved in Bach's autograph manuscript), adding two canons, one complete fugue, and one fragmentary fugue. Also included were an early version of the tenth fugue as well as the chorale fantasia *Wenn wir in höchsten Nöthen sein* for organ and an arrangement for two keyboard instruments of an early version of one of the mirror fugues; but Bach probably did not intend any of this matter for publication.

As published, the fugues—each of which is designated 'Contrapunctus'—appear with each voice on a separate staff. Most are in four parts. The score notation has inspired arrangements for various instrumental ensembles, but the same archaic notation occurs in contrapuntal keyboard pieces by Frescobaldi, Froberger, and other earlier composers that must have served as models for *The Art of Fugue*. For example, the canzonas and capriccios of Frescobaldi and Froberger fall mostly into distinct sections employing variant forms of the main theme, or subject. Moreover, collections of such pieces often follow a systematic plan; thus, in Frescobaldi's 12 fantasias of 1608 the first three are essentially monothematic fugues, the next three double fugues, and so on, culminating in three quadruple fugues. *The Art of Fugue* combines the ideas of variation and contrapuntal culmination by employing versions of the same subject throughout a series of movements all in the same key (D minor) but generally of increasing complexity. Moreover, like that of its models, the style derives from 16th-century vocal polyphony, although distinctly Baroque elements (chromaticism, idiomatic keyboard figuration, etc.) grow somewhat more prominent as the volume proceeds. Indeed, far from being an abstract theoretical work, as it has sometimes been viewed, *The Art of Fugue* is full of variety, virtuosity, and expression, albeit of a somewhat more restrained and subtle type than in Bach's other great collections.

The work's principal subject (referred to henceforth as the 'theme') appears in varied but readily recognizable forms in every movement, save for the fragment of the incomplete fugue. In its simplest form the theme is a rhythmically spare four-bar melody perfectly suited for the austere STILE ANTICO adopted in the first three fugues. Later movements embellish the theme and alter it rhythmically, as well as subjecting it to increasingly complex types of contrapuntal development.

The first four movements are so-called simple fugues, each employing a single form of the subject; except for Contrapunctus 4, which was added for the printed version, these movements are stylistically the most old-fashioned and the closest to the pure *stile antico*, relatively restrained in harmony and expressive content. Contrapunctus 5 continues in this vein, combining the two forms of the subject that have thus far been employed (the original form and its inversion, introduced in Contrapunctus 3). Although superficially alike, even these austere pieces are clearly differentiated: for example, Contrapunctus 2 employs a persistent dotted rhythm, Contrapunctus 3 has a tortuous chromatic countersubject.

Contrapunctus 6 bears the subtitle 'in stile francese', a reference to its use of the pervasive dotted rhythm characteristic of the French overture (also found in the D major fugue from Part 1 of *The Well-tempered Clavier*; slurs in Contrapunctus 2 suggest that the dotted rhythm there is to be less strongly marked). Contrapunctus 6 combines upright and inverted versions of the subject, and these occur with both the original and diminished (halved) note values. The same is true of the following fugue, which adds a third level of augmented (doubled) note values.

Beyond this point the precise order intended by Bach is uncertain. In the printed version Contrapuncti 9 and 10 form a pair of double fugues, each opening with a new subject which is then combined with the main theme. The combinations of the two subjects employ INVERTIBLE COUNTERPOINT at the 12th and 10th respectively; the use of this somewhat abstruse technical device does not prevent Contrapunctus 9 from attaining considerable keyboard virtuosity by virtue of its athletic first subject. (An early version of Contrapunctus 10, included in the printed edition, is sometimes numbered 10*a* and sometimes 14.)

Contrapuncti 8 and 11 are both triple fugues, linked by the use of related secondary subjects and differentiated by the presence of only three voices in Contrapunctus 8. Contrapunctus 11 forms the climax of the extant portion of the work, achieving an extraordinary density of expressively dissonant counterpoint in its final sections.

A pair of mirror fugues follows: four- and three-part pieces respectively, each of which is playable both in its original form and with all voices strictly inverted. Neither is readily negotiable by a single player; Bach's two-keyboard arrangement of the three-part fugue (a lively gigue) adds a free non-inverting part to each version.

The intended place and order of the four canons are uncertain. Although in only two parts, these canons are longer and more idiomatic to the keyboard than those found elsewhere (e.g. in the *Musical Offering*). The simplest (placed second in the printed edition) is a canon at the octave in gigue style. Canons 3 and 4 (added for the printed edition) involve invertible counterpoint at the 10th and 12th respectively, thus correlating with Contrapuncti 10 and 9. Canon 1 employs both augmentation and inversion. Its original version, in Bach's manuscript, is effectively distinct from the printed version and is omitted from many modern editions; both are filled with prickly chromatic figuration.

Bach reportedly intended to cap the work with a quadruple MIRROR FUGUE in four parts, but no such piece survives. Instead, the two existing mirror fugues are followed in the printed edition by a *Fuga a 3 Soggetti*, a triple fugue which breaks off shortly after the exposition of its third subject. The latter's first four notes, Bb, A, C, Bᆗ, correspond, in German nomenclature, to the letters of Bach's name (*see* BACH). Hence, C. P. E. Bach added a comment to his father's autograph manuscript explaining that Sebastian had died 'over [über] this fugue, where the name BACH is brought in as a countersubject [*sic*]'. Subsequent commentators have made much of Bach's apparently leaving unfinished the one piece containing a contrapuntal development of his signature motif. Actually, the third subject of Contrapunctus 11 opens with the same motif, and the notes have been observed in other works (for example, in the bass line of the Second Brandenburg Concerto).

Even in its most complete extant form (the manuscript contains seven additional bars not given in the printed edition), the fragment fails to introduce the main theme of *The Art of Fugue*. But it has been known since the 19th century that it is possible to combine the theme with the fragment's three subjects. Hence it has been proposed that Bach did complete the movement in some form, perhaps including a combination of all four subjects in invertible (mirror) form.

Posthumous reception of *The Art of Fugue* was at first discouraging; it failed to sell, and C. P. E. Bach, who acted as publisher, was forced to dispose of the plates for their copper content. The work continued to circulate in manuscript, however, and the 19th century saw several editions, notably a two-stave keyboard reduction by Beethoven's pupil Carl Czerny (1838). Numerous attempts have been made to complete the fragmentary fugue; Donald Francis Tovey not only completed it but added a four-part quadruple mirror fugue. The 20th century has seen organ arrangements and transcriptions for various instrumental ensembles, including an influential orchestration by Wolfgang Graeser (1927).

Critical evaluations of the work until recently focused on its ingenious technical artifice. Recent writings have sought profound philosophical, autobiographical, and even theological significance in it (often focusing on the BACH subject). Most public performances in the 20th century tended to be in the form of instrumental arrangements, but solo recordings and performances on piano and harpsichord have been gaining the upper hand. DS

*See also* SOURCES, §2.

W. Kolneder, *Die Kunst der Fuge: Mythen des 20. Jahrhunderts* (Wiesbaden, 1977); D. Schulenberg, *The Keyboard Music of J. S. Bach* (New York, 1992), 344–76; D. F. Tovey, *A Companion to 'The Art of Fugue'* (London, 1931); W. Wiemer, *Die wiederhergestellte Ordnung in Johann Sebastian Bachs Kunst der Fuge* (Wiesbaden, 1977); C. Wolff *et al.*, 'Bach's "Art of Fugue": An Examination of the Sources', *Current Musicology*, 19 (1975), 59–77; partly repr. in C. Wolff, *Johann Sebastian Bach: Essays on his Life and Music* (Cambridge, Mass., 1991).

Ascension and expressing confidence that the righteous will join Christ in heaven.

The work is scored for SATB, two horns (the first horn doubling on trumpet in no. 3), two oboes d'amore, oboe da caccia, strings, and continuo. It broadly follows the plan of most of the chorale-based Leipzig cantatas, with one exception which will be discussed below. The first movement, based on the eponymous chorale of the title, is in the normal chorale fantasia form, with the melody given out in the soprano. As usual, the entries of the individual lines of the tune are enriched with lively instrumental counterpoint and separated by ritornello material played by the instrumental forces. This is largely based on a fanfare-like subject related to the first line of the chorale, giving rise to lively interplay between the prominent horns, which lend the required air of jubilation to the music. A simple recitative for tenor leads to the central bass aria, 'Auf, auf, mit hellem Schall', which Bach sets in heroic style with an elaborate trumpet obbligato and accompanying strings. This is unusual in form, incorporating an accompanied recitative which suddenly intervenes in the position of the expected da capo. It is followed by the closing instrumental ritornello to end the movement. Bach achieved this effect by inserting material from the recitative of Ziegler's libretto (originally designed to follow the aria) into the middle of the aria itself.

'Sein Allmacht zu ergründen' (no. 4) is a duet

for alto and tenor with an obbligato line which Bach marked 'organo' in the composing score but, apparently changing his mind, entered in the oboe part (the compass *a* to *a"* indicates that an oboe d'amore is required). Dürr, however, does not discount the possibility (in *DürrK*) that the indication 'organo' could be a later addition. The duet, which is in da capo aria form, strikes a note of subdued tranquillity which contrasts with the generally festive mood of the cantata as a whole. Most of the material is based on the opening subject, which features a characteristic drop of a 5th to depict the word 'ergründen' ('to fathom'). The ritornello theme was used by Max Reger as the basis of his Variations and Fugue on a Theme of J. S. Bach op. 81, dating from 1904. The last movement is a four-part harmonized chorale verse with additional parts for the two horns.          DLH
For bibliography, *see* CANTATA, §1.

***Aufklärung.*** *See* ENGLIGHTENMENT.

***Auf, schmetternde Töne der muntern Trompeten*** ('Sound forth, ringing tones of bright trumpets'). Secular cantata, BWV207a, for the nameday of King Augustus III, Elector of Saxony. The music is mostly parodied from the cantata VEREINIGTE ZWIETRACHT DER WECHSELNDEN SAITEN.

**augmentation.** A term used, particularly in connection with FUGUE, for the device of restating a thematic passage in longer notes than those of the original statement. A striking example is in bars 14–16 of the C minor fugue in Part 2 of *The Well-tempered Clavier*, where the subject appears in its basic quaver movement in the treble and then (freely inverted) in the bass, while the middle part has the same theme simultaneously in crotchets. The opposite process is described as DIMINUTION.          LC

**August II,** King of Poland. The title, as Polish king, of FRIEDRICH AUGUST I, Elector of Saxony.

**August III,** King of Poland. The title, as Polish king, of FRIEDRICH AUGUST II, Elector of Saxony.

***Aus der Tiefen rufe ich*** ('Out of the deep have I called'). Cantata, BWV131, for an unidentified liturgical occasion. As Bach's note on the original score explains, it was commissioned by Georg Christian Eilmar, pastor at the Marienkirche, Mühlhausen, and it must therefore date from the years 1707–8. The text refers to penance, but provides no clue which would help to date the work more precisely.

Like many mid-German sacred concertos from the 17th century, the cantata draws on two textual sources simultaneously. One is the whole of Psalm 130: every number of the cantata takes as its text

one or two verses of this, so that at the end of one movement the text of the next is already anticipated. Also, in two movements Bach uses a strophe from the chorale *Herr Jesu Christ, du höchstes Gut*. In the bass aria 'So du willt' the second strophe ('Erbarm dich mein in solcher Last') is juxtaposed with the psalm; in the tenor aria 'Meine Seele wartet' it is the fifth strophe ('Und weil ich denn in meinem Sinn'). Thus not only the psalm but also the chorale serves to advance the meaning of the cantata. It is interesting that the musical structure of the chorale (A–A–B) affects these two movements in different ways: the tenor aria has a double bar in the middle, so that the music of the first part is repeated in accordance with the form of the chorale melody, while in the bass aria there is only a rough similarity between the solo phrases sung against the two identical chorale lines.

The musical subdivision of the cantata is not easy to describe (and indeed the numbering of the movements differs from one edition or analysis to another). Bach established three or four large units, some of them subdivided into discrete 'movements' with the direction 'attacca' connecting them to the next. The first unit may be said to consist at least of the opening chorus and the bass aria with chorale. But the division between chorus and aria is not the only one in this unit. Bach labelled the opening orchestral passage separately as a 'sinfonia'; it is only in the light of later developments in church music that this could be seen as a ritornello to the chorus that follows. The chorus itself is divided into a slow introduction and a fast continuation ('Herr, höre meine Stimme') with fugal elements. So these opening 'two' movements could easily be described also as a unit made up of four sections. Similarly, the chorus 'Ich harre des Herrn' that follows the bass aria is divided into a slow introduction and a fugue ('Meine Seele harret'). The third unit begins with the tenor aria 'Meine Seele wartet' which ends with a strong cadence and a caesura as if it were an independent movement, but the layout of the score suggests that Bach intended another *attacca* sequence of movements. Therefore, the final chorus (with several changes of tempo) may be understood as part of the same unit as the preceding aria. The chorus ends with a large-scale fugue, 'Und er wird Israel erlösen'.

The *NBA* interprets the pitch of the music differently from earlier editions and prints it a tone higher, in A minor. The difference is due to the relation of CHORTON to CAMMERTON, but it is doubtful whether the modern standard view of Bach's later practice (e.g. in his Weimar cantatas) is directly transferable to his Mühlhausen works.          KK

# Aus tiefer Not schrei ich zu dir

G. Herz, 'BWV 131: Bach's First Cantata', in *Essays on J. S. Bach* (Ann Arbor, 1985), 127–45. For further bibliography, *see* CANTATA, §1.

***Aus tiefer Not schrei ich zu dir*** ('In deep despair I cry to thee'). Cantata, BWV38, for the 21st Sunday after Trinity, first performed on 29 October 1724. The anonymous libretto is based on Luther's chorale of the same title. As usual in the Leipzig CHORALE CANTATA cycle, the first and last movements are taken directly from the original (strophes 1 and 5), while the intermediate movements are freely paraphrased. The libretto also makes reference to the Gospel for the day, especially in its appeal to the uselessness of 'signs and wonders' without the gift of faith.

Cantata 38 is scored for SATB with two oboes, four *colla parte* trombones, strings, and continuo, and is composed in the six-movement form often to be found in the Leipzig cantatas. The opening movement, setting verse 1 of Luther's chorale, is in MOTET STYLE, with each successive line of the tune given out as a cantus firmus in the soprano preceded by imitative treatment of the melodic phrase in the lower voices. The convention, which for the modern listener inevitably recalls the even more elaborate six-part organ setting of the same chorale in *Clavier-Übung III* (1739), serves as an apt symbol for a clamour of entreating voices. Bach varies the order of the entries, employing the order TABS for the first two lines and their repetition as lines 3 and 4, but reordering the voices successively in the last three lines. In the later stages of the chorus he also introduces independent subjects which are worked out together with the main idea. The modality of the chorale, which is a powerful influence on the cantata in general, shows itself in the final PHRYGIAN CADENCE.

After the following alto recitative, the text of which stresses the hope to be found in the grace and forgiveness of Jesus, comes a da capo aria for tenor with two obbligato oboes, 'Ich höre mitten in dem Leiden ein Trostwort'. Much of the material is derived from a predominant four-note figure in the ritornello, which produces anguished suspended dissonances and a maze of serpentine imitative counterpoint with the voice. More word-painting devices occur in the B section (ending in C major), in which 'sein Wort besteht' ('his word endures') is characterized by a long-held note in the voice.

After another recitative, cadencing in D minor, in which the soprano voice laments the weakness of faith, comes not the expected second aria but a 'Terzetto' in fugal style for SAB, 'Wenn meine Trübsal als mit Ketten'. The two vocal sections are marked off by three entries of an instrumental rit-

ornello (for the continuo section only) based on an independent repeated-note figure which is taken up by the voices towards the end of the movement. The opening subject of the vocal material takes its point of departure from the text, with the word 'Ketten' ('chains') characterized by a chain of descending suspensions. Bach paints the word 'Trübsal' ('distress') with a jarring sharp which gives rise to angular diminished 3rds. The second half is based on a more cheerful figure for 'Wie bald erscheint des Trostes Morgen' ('How soon the morning of consolation appears'), and continues with the recall of previous subjects, including the main theme of the opening ritornello. The final chorale harmonization, which again ends in E-Phrygian, sets strophe 5 of Luther's original chorale. DLH

For bibliography, *see* CANTATA, §1.

**authenticity.** A term used, in discussions of Bach's music, either in reference to a work's authorship or to what might be considered the correct way of performing it. *See* PERFORMANCE STYLES.

***Ave Maria.*** The title of an arrangement by the French composer Charles Gounod (1818–93) of the first prelude from Bach's *The Well-tempered Clavier*. It was first published, in 1853, as a purely instrumental piece for violin (or cello) and piano, with organ or cello *ad libitum*, under the title *Méditation sur le Ier Prélude de piano de S. Bach*. In the same year it appeared as a song, with words (*Vers sur un album*) by the French Romantic poet Alphonse de Lamartine (1790–1869). Six years later, in 1859, it was published in the form in which it has become most familiar: as a sacred song to the words of the Latin prayer *Ave Maria*, and with a variety of accompanying instruments. For his arrangement Gounod evidently made use of an edition, probably one in the Czerny tradition, which included the extra bar inserted by C. F. G. SCHWENCKE.

The Bach–Gounod *Ave Maria* has been much disparaged, and it is not hard to see why. At the same time, one can understand why a 19th-century musician, familiar from childhood with the keyboard patterns of Classical accompaniments, might feel that a piece such as Bach's lacked a melodic line; and it would be churlish not to recognize Gounod's success in fitting such a shapely and attractive melody to Bach's harmonies, with only minimal alteration.

In 1889 Gounod brought out a second *Ave Maria*, this time fitted to Bach's C minor Prelude for lute BWV999, but this never achieved the popularity of the first.

# B

**Bach.** Family of musicians. Although there have been many instances throughout the centuries of families whose members have collectively shown unusual talent in music, there has been none in which that talent shone as brightly or as long as it did for several generations in the Bach family. There can be no doubt that by the early 18th century the extraordinary abilities of the Bachs were widely acknowledged by their contemporaries and recognized by the family itself—so much so, indeed, that the word 'Bach' seems to have become synonymous with 'musician' in Thuringia.

For much of the early history of the Bach family we are still dependent on the famous GENEALOGY that J. S. Bach compiled in 1735. From this we learn that the family descended from a certain Veit (or Vitus) Bach (d. 1619), a baker, who left Hungary (or, more precisely, 'Ungarn', which included parts of Moravia and Slovakia) towards the end of the 16th century to settle at Wechmar, near Gotha in Thuringia. Of Veit's three sons, the most important to us was Johannes (d. 1626), the first of the line to earn his living, at least in part, as a musician: he was apprenticed to the *Stadtpfeifer* of Gotha and worked as a town musician.

Johannes also had three sons. The eldest, Johann (1604–73), took the family a step up the professional ladder when he became an organist, first at Schweinfurt and then at the Predigerkirche, Erfurt. The second son, Christoph (1613–61), was a town musician in Erfurt, a calling which he then combined with that of court musician in Arnstadt; his three musical sons included J. S. Bach's father, Johann Ambrosius. Johannes's youngest son, Heinrich (1615–92), achieved prominence as an organist in Arnstadt and fathered two of the most important Bach musicians of the next generation, Johann Christoph (i) and Johann Michael.

The most prominent among the Bachs of the next two generations are allotted separate entries in this Companion. They include, of course, Johann Sebastian himself and his four most renowned sons, Wilhelm Friedemann, Carl Philipp Emanuel, Johann Christoph Friedrich, and Johann Christian. Thereafter the musical torch burnt less brightly, and was soon all but extinguished. The last of Johann Sebastian's direct descendants to follow the calling of a professional musician was his grandson Wilhelm Friedrich

Ernst (1759–1845), who studied with his father, J. C. F. Bach, and his uncle Johann Christian in London, and went on to become music director at Minden and then *Kapellmeister* in Berlin; in 1843 he was present when Mendelssohn unveiled a monument to his grandfather in Leipzig. The last in the line to bear the name 'Bach' were his two daughters (a son and another daughter died in infancy), but the line itself continued through the children of his elder sister Anna Philippina Friederica (1755–1804) and her husband Ernst Carl von Colson (1746–95). At least 15 people living today (the youngest born in 1989) can legitimately claim Johann Sebastian Bach as their great-great-great-great-great-great-great-great-grandfather (see Kock, Tafel III).

K. Geiringer, *The Bach Family: Seven Generations of Creative Genius* (London, 1954; 2nd. edn., 1977); H. Kock, *Genealogisches Lexikon der Familie Bach* (Wechmar, 1995); K. Küster, *Der junge Bach* (Stuttgart, 1996), 13–38; K. Kreuch, *Die Urväterheimat der Musikerfamilie Bach* (Wechmar, 1994); P. M. Young, *The Bachs, 1500–1850* (London, 1970).

**Bach** (née Wülcken), **Anna Magdalena** (b. 22 Sept. 1701; d. 27 Feb. 1760). J. S. Bach's second wife, born in Zeitz. She was a gifted singer and the youngest daughter of a court trumpeter, Johann Caspar WÜLCKEN, who worked at Zeitz and after 1718 at Weißenfels. She was trained in music by her father and her maternal uncle Johann Siegmund Liebe (1670–1742), town and court organist at Zeitz. It is not known when she first made Bach's acquaintance, but it was certainly by 25 September 1721, when both were godparents to Johann Christian Hahn (son of a court servant at Cöthen), who died only two weeks later. Anna Magdalena is referred to in the baptismal registers as 'court singer' and 'chamber musician'.

Following her marriage to Bach at Cöthen on 3 December 1721, Anna Magdalena became stepmother to the four surviving children from his first marriage to Maria Barbara Bach, and gave birth to 13 of her own, five of whom reached adulthood, including the musicians Gottfried Heinrich (1724–63), Johann Christoph Friedrich, and Johann Christian. She received two *Clavierbüchlein* from her husband, one at Cöthen in 1722 and the other at Leipzig in 1725. In Leipzig she was important as a neat and accurate copyist of her husband's music. On Bach's death she received one-third of his estate, which amounted to about half of his yearly earnings. Thereafter she lived mainly on charity and died in poverty.

In 1925 a book, *The Little Chronicle of Magdalena Bach*, purporting to be a transcription of Anna Magdalena's own journal, was published anonymously in London. It proved later to be the work of Esther Meynell and was translated and reprinted many times. It paints a highly romanticized picture of the composer, but the facts it presents are (for its time) remarkably accurate.

RLS

C. Schubart, 'Anna Magdalena Bach: neue Beiträge zu ihrer Herkunft und ihren Jugendjahren', *BJb* 40 (1953), 29–50; R. L. Marshall, 'The Notebooks for Wilhelm Friedemann and Anna Magdalena Bach: Some Biographical Lessons', in L. Lockwood and E. Roesner, eds., *Essays in Musicology: A Tribute to Alvin Johnson* (Philadelphia, 1990), 192–200; G. von Dadelsen, *Bemerkungen zur Handschrift Johann Sebastian Bachs, seiner Familie und seines Kreises* (Trossingen, 1957), 27–37.

**Bach, Carl Philipp Emanuel** (b. 8 March 1714; d. 14 Dec. 1788). The second surviving son of J. S. and Maria Barbara Bach; composer, keyboard player, and writer on music. Once viewed primarily as a link between the late Baroque and the Viennese Classical style, Emanuel Bach is now more generally acknowledged as a major composer in his own right. His roughly 150 keyboard sonatas and 52 concertos reflect his special attachment to strung keyboard instruments, especially the clavichord. He also wrote a two-volume *Versuch über die wahre Art das Clavier zu spielen* (Berlin, 1753–62; Eng. trans. W. J. Mitchell as 'Essay on the True Art of Playing Keyboard Instruments', New York, 1949), which was influential well into the 19th century and remains a valuable source on historical performing practice. His preservation of numerous manuscripts inherited from his father was instrumental in the transmission of the latter's music, and he provided valuable material for J. N. Forkel's biography of J. S. Bach (1802).

Born in Weimar, Emanuel had, by his own account, no teacher of composition or keyboard playing other than his father. He presumably studied the same music as his elder brother Wilhelm Friedemann, including Sebastian's inventions and sinfonias, which provided models for some of his own early compositions. But most early works, such as the 'Solo' in the 1725 *Clavierbüchlein vor Anna Magdalena Bach* (later revised as a sonata movement), reveal a style derived from that of Telemann (his godfather), Hasse, and other *galant* composers.

In 1734 Emanuel began university studies at Frankfurt an der Oder; he then moved to Berlin in 1738, becoming court harpsichordist to Frederick the Great on the latter's accession in 1740. But there is no evidence that any of Bach's music, not even the ten flute sonatas of the 1730s and 1740s, was composed for the king, who is known to have later disapproved of Emanuel's style.

By the late 1730s Emanuel's style had become one based on a two-part texture whose melodic line is characterized by distinctive, sometimes counter-intuitive, types of written-out embellishment and figuration, and by frequently dramatic rhythm and harmony. Particularly in slow movements, Emanuel's style is often reminiscent of recitative—hence modern references to it as 'rhetorical' or 'speaking'; the term 'empfindsamer', referring to its heightened expressivity, is also used. Although these features can be traced to certain works of Sebastian (e.g. the Chromatic Fantasia), Emanuel generally eschewed his father's imitative polyphony. Moreover, he developed his style chiefly in three-movement keyboard sonatas and concertos, both new genres in which he remained active throughout his life. The 1740s saw particularly intense concentration on these genres, including the composition of the 'Prussian' and 'Württemberg' sets of sonatas (published 1742–4) and 21 keyboard concertos.

Perhaps hoping to succeed his father, Emanuel was in Leipzig, probably in early 1750, for a performance of his *Magnificat*, his earliest surviving choral work. Like his father's setting of the same text, it combines contrapuntal movements with references to the Italianate style of Dresden church music. After Sebastian's death, Emanuel saw into print *The Art of Fugue* and housed and taught his young half-brother Johann Christian. Volume 1 of the *Versuch*, concerned with keyboard fingering, ornamentation, and performance style in general, appeared in 1753; volume 2 (published 1762) is devoted to figured bass, accompaniment, and improvisation. Although chiefly concerned with the performance of *galant* and *empfindsamer* music, the book's relevance to Sebastian's keyboard music is plausible in view of the older composer's frequent drawing upon current styles.

Emanuel's compositions after 1750 include an increasing number of relatively accessible keyboard and chamber pieces intended for the growing market for printed music; among these are several sets of pedagogic keyboard works. A new, popular genre is represented by Lieder, of which Bach published several collections beginning in 1758. In their declamatory vocal lines and relatively simple keyboard accompaniments, these mostly strophic settings reveal great sensitivity to the poetry—a trait shared with Sebastian, who could not, however, frequent the brilliant intellectual circles of Berlin and, later, Hamburg in which Emanuel was a regular and valued participant.

Pen and ink drawing of Bach's second son, Carl Philipp Emanuel (centre), with Pastor
Sturm (right) and the artist, Andreas Stöttrup, 1784 (Kunsthalle, Hamburg)

# Bach, Johann Ambrosius

In 1768 Emanuel succeeded Telemann as director of music in the five principal churches of Hamburg. Here he also directed public concerts, performing such works as his oratorio *Die Israeliten in der Wüste* (1769) as well as music by other composers, notably Handel's *Messiah* (in Klopstock's translation) and the Credo from Sebastian's B minor Mass. In addition, he published collections of symphonies, concertos, and keyboard trios, each containing brilliant surprises.

Much of the Hamburg church music, which included 20 Passions, is lost. In the 1770 Passion cantata (based on the previous year's *St Matthew Passion*) the oratorio style of Telemann and C. H. Graun mingles with inventive harmony and occasional contrapuntal movements derived from J. S. Bach. The latter's imprint is also evident in the brief but overwhelming *Heilig* for double chorus and orchestra, which remained popular into the 19th century. The keyboard music published in Hamburg includes six collections subtitled 'für Kenner und Liebhaber' ('for connoisseurs and music-lovers'); these contain, alongside some remarkable sonatas, unparalleled types of rondo and fantasia.

Despite its stylistic independence, the foundation of Emanuel's music lay in the teaching of J. S. Bach, which began with mastery of harmony through figured bass realization. The forms of arias and concerto movements, together with much of their melodic figuration, also derive from Sebastian, as did Emanuel's habit of fully notating melodic embellishments and carefully revising existing works. The view of Sebastian as a conservative composer of primarily contrapuntal music, already encouraged by Marpurg and Forkel, has tended to obscure points that father and son held in common, such as their ability to write music that is both witty and deeply expressive. But Emanuel clearly understood what part of his father's legacy he could best emulate. DS

S. L. Clark, ed., *C. P. E. Bach Studies* (Oxford, 1988); H. G. Ottenberg, *Carl Philipp Emanuel Bach*, trans. P. J. Whitmore (Oxford, 1991); D. Schulenberg, 'C. P. E. Bach', in R. L. Marshall, ed., *Eighteenth-Century Keyboard Music* (New York, 1994), 191–229.

**Bach, Johann Ambrosius** (b. 24 Feb. 1645; d. 24 Feb. 1695). Father of J. S. Bach and twin brother of Johann Christoph Bach (i), born in Erfurt. He was employed as a violinist in Erfurt, and from 1671 until his death as a town musician in Eisenach, where he was also active at the court from 1677. On 1 April 1668 he married Maria Elisabetha Lämmerhirt; their eight children included four sons who made their names as musicians. After his wife's death in 1694, he married Barbara Margaretha Bartholomaei (née Keul), once the wife of

his cousin Johann Günther Bach (1653–83), but he died only three months later.

R. Kaiser, 'Johann Ambrosius Bachs letztes Eisenacher Lebensjahr', *BJb* 81 (1995), 177–82; F. Rollberg, 'Johann Ambrosius Bach, Stadtpfeifer zu Eisenach von 1671–1695', *BJb* 24 (1927), 133–52.

**Bach, Johann Bernhard** (b. 25 Nov. 1700; d. 14 June 1743). Nephew of J. S. Bach, born in Ohrdruf. He studied with Johann Sebastian at Weimar from 1715 to 1717 and at Cöthen, where he also worked as a copyist. In 1721 he succeeded his father, Johann Christoph (ii), as organist of the Michaeliskirche in Ohrdruf.

He should not be confused with another Johann Bernhard Bach (1676–1749), a second cousin of J. S. Bach, who succeeded Johann Christoph (i) as organist of the Georgenkirche, Eisenach, in 1703.

**Bach, Johann (John) Christian** (b. 5 Sept. 1735; d. 1 Jan. 1782). Youngest son of J. S. Bach and his second wife, Anna Magdalena; a composer and keyboard player, and a major figure in music of the mid-18th century. He is best known today for his friendship with and decisive influence on Mozart, but his music deserves to be valued and enjoyed for its own sake.

J. C. Bach was born in Leipzig, where he presumably began his musical studies under his parents and his second cousin Johann Elias Bach. A few short keyboard works by him, possibly composed during the 1740s, survive in a later manuscript collection of pedagogic pieces which somewhat resembles the *Clavierbüchlein* of his mother and that of his elder brother Wilhelm Friedemann. On Sebastian's death in 1750, J. C. Bach inherited a number of music manuscripts (labelled with his nickname 'Christel') as well as a set of three clavichords equipped with a pedalboard (for use in practising organ music).

J. S. Bach's second surviving son, Carl Philipp Emanuel, subsequently took his young halfbrother into his household at Berlin. There Johann Christian composed a number of keyboard sonatas, concertos, and other works in a convincing imitation of the current style of Berlin instrumental music. But in 1755 Bach left Berlin, and by early 1756 he was in Bologna. There he evidently made the acquaintance of Giovanni Battista Martini (1706–84), a priest, composer, and scholar with whom Bach maintained a long correspondence and who served as his mentor and teacher. Under Padre Martini's influence Bach changed both his musical style and his religion; by 1757 he had converted to Catholicism and was composing sacred and instrumental music in the household of Count Agostino Litta of Milan,

Bach's youngest son, Johann Christian; portrait by Thomas Gainsborough (1727–1788)

where in 1760 he obtained a position as cathedral organist.

Martini provided the instruction in strict counterpoint that J. S. Bach (somewhat surprisingly) appears not to have given his pupils. This is reflected in a number of contrapuntal movements in J. C. Bach's sacred works of the period, which include some 30 compositions for the Roman Catholic liturgy. Most movements, to be sure, are in the *style galant* that was fashionable throughout Bach's life; this did not prevent some works, such as the C minor *Dies irae* for double chorus and orchestra, from achieving impressive effects.

In late 1760 *Artaserse*, the first of Bach's ten *opere serie*, was performed in Turin. Two more followed in Naples, and in 1762 Bach moved to London, where, beginning in 1763, he composed five operas and his only oratorio, *Gioas*. Following in the footsteps of Handel (who had died only a few years earlier, in 1759), Bach enjoyed both popular success and royal patronage, becoming music master to Queen Charlotte by 1764. Together with Carl Friedrich Abel, he began that year a series of public concerts (the Bach–Abel concerts) which continued to the end of his life. At one of these concerts in 1768 Bach presented a 'solo' (presumably a sonata) on the fortepiano, the instrument for which most of his solo keyboard works were probably intended; this is often regarded as the earliest public performance of a solo piano work in London. It was also presumably for these concerts that Bach composed most of his 18 published keyboard concertos, several dozen symphonies, and 15 or so symphonies concertantes. Some of his equally numerous chamber and keyboard works may have been performed publicly as well, although these must have been directed primarily towards the rapidly expanding amateur market.

The Mozarts—Leopold and his two children, Wolfgang and Maria Anna—visited London in 1764. Bach made a profound impression on Wolfgang, who reworked three of Bach's piano sonatas as concertos (K107) and for the remainder of his life acknowledged his artistic debt and friendship to the older composer. In 1772 Bach visited Mannheim, home of the best orchestra in Europe, for the performance of his opera *Temistocle*; *Lucio Silla* followed there in 1775. By then he had married the Italian opera singer Cecilia Grassi (apparently in 1773), and in 1779 he visited Paris for the performance of his last opera, *Amadis de Gaule*, based on the French libretto used by Jean-Baptiste Lully almost a century earlier. Returning to London, Bach found that his music had lost much of its earlier popularity. Although he moved in socially and artistically elevated circles—his friends included Thomas Gainsborough

(1727–88), who painted his portrait at least twice—he encountered financial difficulties, and after a year of poor health died on New Year's Day 1782.

Hostility towards Bach for his abandonment of his father's musical style and religion has tended to colour evaluations of his music. Although the music is often disparaged as a pale version of Mozart's, his most substantial works, notably the operas, reveal qualities that we admire in many of Mozart's best compositions, as well as an elegant lyricism which is peculiar to Bach. The operatic works surpass the music of lesser contemporaries in the variety and complexity of their orchestral accompaniments (a feature noted by Burney) and in the expressive use of chromaticism and the minor mode. Although conservative by comparison to the so-called reform works of Gluck, and generally maintaining the traditions of *opera seria*, they reflect the general tendency of the time in such matters as increasing flexibility in scoring and in the use of the da capo aria. The instrumental works, although occasionally facile, share with the vocal music impeccable craftsmanship and a fully formed Classical syntax. They include such dramatic, if atypical, compositions as the C minor keyboard Sonata op. 5 no. 6, whose central movement is a fugue, and the G minor Symphony op. 6 no. 6, as well as three brilliantly scored symphonies for double orchestra.          DS

C. S. Terry, *John Christian Bach* (London, 1929, 2nd edn., ed. H. C. R. Landon, 1967); S. Roe, *The Keyboard Music of J. C. Bach* (New York, 1989).

**Bach, Johann Christoph (i)** (bap. 8 Dec. 1642; bur. 2 April 1703). A first cousin of J. S. Bach's father, Johann Ambrosius, and brother of Johann Michael Bach. Born in Arnstadt, he was briefly organist in the court chapel there, and then spent most of his life as town organist and court organist and harpsichordist in Eisenach, where he was a colleague of Johann Ambrosius Bach, Johann Pachelbel, and Daniel Eberlin. In the Genealogy J. S. Bach described Johann Christoph as a 'profound composer', and C. P. E. Bach later added 'this is the great and expressive composer', presumably to distinguish him from others with the same name. Family lore credited him with the early and daring use of the chord of the augmented 6th, and with improvisation at the keyboard in five or more parts. He is well represented in the ALT-BACHISCHES ARCHIV, and in Leipzig J. S. Bach performed several of his motets, among the finest of the period, and his St Michael's Day vocal concerto *Es erhub sich ein Streit*. His securely attributable organ chorale preludes are craftsmanlike examples of an everyday genre.

Johann Christoph's strong reputation has led to

his being credited with many of the best anonymous or ambiguously attributed Bach family pieces. J. S. Bach's own early motet *Ich lasse dich nicht, du segnest mich denn* BWV Anh. III 159 was long attributed to him; several of the small vocal works in the Alt-Bachisches Archiv attributed simply to 'JCB' may or may not be his; and the two keyboard variation sets in the hand of J. S. Bach's elder brother Johann Christoph (ii) cannot be definitely assigned. But the securely attributable works show that he was indeed a strong and creative composer whom J. S. Bach greatly respected.

DRM

**Bach, Johann Christoph (ii)** (b. 16 June 1671; d. 22 Feb. 1721). Eldest brother of J. S. Bach, born in Erfurt, Thuringia. He studied with Pachelbel at Erfurt and became organist at the Thomaskirche there in 1688. From 1690 he was organist at the Michaeliskirche, Ohrdruf. After the death of his father, Ambrosius Bach, in 1695 his younger brothers Johann Sebastian and Jacob came to live with him at Ohrdruf, where he gave Sebastian his first keyboard lessons. According to C. P. E. Bach, Christoph denied Sebastian a particular manuscript containing compositions by Pachelbel and others, whereupon the younger Bach copied it secretly by moonlight. Christoph became aware of the deception and, to Johann Sebastian's disappointment, confiscated the copy. That the two brothers nevertheless remained close is evident from the fact that two of Christoph's sons later studied with their uncle, Johann Bernhard in Weimar and Johann Heinrich in Leipzig.

Johann Christoph has been identified as the main copyist of two keyboard anthologies, the Andreas Bach Book and the Möller manuscript, which are important sources of Johann Sebastian's early works.

RLS

*See also* OHRDRUF.

R. S. Hill, 'The Möller Manuscript and the Andreas Bach Book: Two Keyboard Anthologies from the Circle of the Young Johann Sebastian Bach' (diss., Harvard University, 1987); H.-J. Schulze, 'Johann Christoph Bach (1671 bis 1721), "Organist and Schul Collega in Ohrdruf", Johann Sebastian Bachs erster Lehrer', BJb 71 (1985), 55–81.

**Bach, Johann Christoph Friedrich** (b. 21 June, 1732; d. 26 Jan. 1795). Son of J. S. Bach, born in Leipzig. He is known as the 'Bückeburg Bach'. He received his musical training from his father and from his second cousin Johann Elias, who lived with the Bach family at Leipzig from 1737 to 1742. J. C. F. Bach studied law at Leipzig University, and then obtained the position of *Cammermusicus* (later *Konzertmeister*) at the Bückeburg court, where he remained for the rest of his life. In 1755 he married Lucia Elisabeth Münchhausen

(1732–1803), the daughter of one of his colleagues at court; their nine children included Anna Philippina Friederica (1755–1804), a gifted keyboard player, and Wilhelm Friedrich Ernst (1759–1845), who was later active in Berlin. In 1778 father and son spent some time in London with Johann Christian Bach, and attended the famous Bach–Abel concerts there.

At Bückeburg J. C. F. Bach enjoyed the friendship of the distinguished pastor, poet, and critic Johann Gottfried Herder (1744–1803), who provided him with librettos for cantatas and oratorios. His other surviving works include symphonies and concertos, as well as a good deal of chamber music and songs.

H. Wohlfarth, *Johann Christoph Friedrich Bach* (Berne, 1971).

**Bach, Johann Elias** (b. 12 Feb. 1705; d. 30 Nov. 1755). Second son of J. S. Bach's first cousin Johann Valentin (1669–1720), born in Schweinfurt. After two years at the University of Jena (1728–30) he returned to Schweinfurt, and then spent the years 1737–42 with the Bach family in Leipzig, where he acted as J. S. Bach's secretary and as teacher of the latter's younger children. For a year he worked as a tutor at Zöschau, near Oschatz, and then returned to Schweinfurt as school inspector and Kantor at the Johanniskirche.

**Bach, Johann Ernst** (b. 8 Aug. 1683; d. 21 March 1739). J. S. Bach's first cousin, son of Johann Christoph Bach (1645–93), born in Arnstadt. He was at school with Sebastian in Ohrdruf, and then studied in Hamburg and Frankfurt. In about 1705 he returned to Arnstadt, and in 1707 he succeeded J. S. Bach as organist of the Bonifatiuskirche there. In 1728 he transferred to a similar post at the Oberkirche and the Liebfrauenkirche.

Of the four other Johann Ernsts in the Bach family, the most important lived from 1722 to 1777. He was the son of Johann Bernhard Bach (1676–1749). He studied with Johann Sebastian in Leipzig, succeeded his father as organist in Eisenach, and was later active as court *Kapellmeister* in Weimar.

**Bach, Johann Gottfried Bernhard** (b. 11 May 1715; d. 27 May 1739). The third surviving son of J. S. and Maria Barbara Bach, born in Weimar. He became organist at Mühlhausen in 1735 and at Sangerhausen in 1737, but left there by 1738 and died shortly after enrolling in 1739 as a law student at the university in Jena. He is reported to have played the flute, and he may have been the copyist of his father's Trio Sonata in G major for two flutes and continuo. Sebastian's letters testify to his proficiency as an organist but also express concern over his debts and disordered life.      DS

**Bach, Johann Heinrich** (b. 4 Aug. 1707; d. 17 May 1783). Nephew of J. S. Bach, son of Johann Christoph (ii), born in Ohrdruf. After attending school in Ohrdruf, he went to the Thomasschule in Leipzig, where he studied music with J. S. Bach and was also among the composer's principal copyists (in which capacity he is often referred to in the earlier Bach literature as Anonymous 2 or *Hauptkopist* C). From about 1728 he assisted his ailing father in Ohrdruf, and in 1735 was appointed Kantor in Öhringen.

Hermann Kock (*see* BACH family) lists eight other family members with the name Johann Heinrich.

H.-J. Schulze, *Studien zur Bach-Überlieferung im 18. Jahrhundert* (Leipzig, 1984), 110–19.

**Bach, Johann Jacob** (bap. 11 Feb. 1682; d. 16 April 1722). Brother of J. S. Bach, born in Eisenach. After his parents' deaths he and Sebastian went to live with their brother Johann Christoph (ii) in Ohrdruf. In 1697 Jacob was apprenticed to the *Kunstpfeifer* Johann Heinrich Halle (1661–1728) in Eisenach. Some years later, probably in 1704, he joined the guard of King Charles XII of Sweden as an oboist, and served in several military campaigns. On one of these, in Constantinople in 1713, he came into contact with the French flautist Gabriel Buffardin, from whom he took lessons. In the same year he joined the Stockholm court as a flautist.

Hermann Kock (*see* BACH family) lists four other family members with the name Johann Jacob.

**Bach, Johann Lorenz** (b. 10 Sept. 1695; d. 14 Dec. 1773). Eldest son of J. S. Bach's first cousin Johann Valentin (1669–1720), born in Schweinfurt. He attended the Lateinschule in Schweinfurt and the lyceum in Ohrdruf (1712–13) before studying with Sebastian in Weimar (1713–17). In November 1718 he was appointed Kantor at Lahm, about 45 km. (28 miles) east of Schweinfurt, and the following year married Catharina Froembes, by whom he had five daughters.

**Bach, Johann Ludwig** (bap. 6 Feb. 1677; bur. 1 May 1731). A distant cousin of J. S. Bach, and the first member of the Bach family to be employed in a leading musical position at a court. He was born in Thal, near Eisenach, and served the ducal court in Meiningen from 1703 until his death, first as a singer and *Pageninformator* (teacher of the court pages), and from 1706, under Duke Ernst Ludwig, as successor to the *Hofkapellmeister* Georg Caspar Schürmann (1672/3–1751). From 1709 onwards he is said to have composed 'operas' (their texts are more like secular cantatas; no music survives). At about the same time he also wrote some influential church cantatas, using a standardized text pattern devised by Duke ERNST LUDWIG. His only extant full-length work, an apocalyptic oratorio in three parts which uses such 'modern' instruments as the chalumeau, was composed in 1724 for the funeral of Ernst Ludwig.

J. L. Bach's music has survived only because of his widespread contacts with other musicians. The extant sources of his sacred cantatas stem possibly from Telemann in Frankfurt, from Heinrich Nikolaus Gerber, and from a Kantor in the Harz region. The most important of these contacts was J. S. Bach, who performed 18 of the cantatas in 1726 and integrated some of their stylistic elements into his own cantata style (see Scheide). In general Johann Ludwig's cantatas seem more short-winded than those of his Leipzig cousin, but J. L. Bach also wrote a number of large-scale motets. The Easter cantata *Denn du wirst, meine Seele* was once thought to be J. S. Bach's earliest extant cantata, and was included as no. 15 in the *BG* edition.

Contacts between the Meiningen Bach family and J. S. Bach in Leipzig are documented especially in the work of J. L. Bach's son Gottlieb Friedrich (1714–85), an artist who portrayed not only his father but also his Leipzig uncle and his cousin C. P. E. Bach.      KK

K. Geiringer, *The Bach Family: Seven Generations of Creative Genius* (London 1954), 102–18; K. Küster, 'Die Frankfurter und Leipziger Überlieferung der Kantaten Johann Ludwig Bachs', *BJb* 75 (1989), 65–106; K. Küster, ' "Theatralisch vorgestellet": zur Aufführungspraxis höfischer Vokalwerke in Thüringen um 1710/20', in F. Brusniak, ed., *Barockes Musiktheater im mitteldeutschen Raum im 17. und 18. Jahrhundert* (Cologne, 1994); W. H. Scheide, 'Johann Sebastian Bachs Sammlung von Kantaten seines Vetters Johann Ludwig Bach', *BJb* 46 (1959), 52–94; 48 (1961), 5–24; 49 (1962), 5–32.

**Bach, Johann Michael** (b. 9 Aug. 1648; d. 17 May 1694). A first cousin of J. S. Bach's father, Johann Ambrosius, and brother of Johann Christoph Bach (i). He was born in Arnstadt, and succeeded his brother as organist in the court chapel there. He then became organist in Gehren, where he spent the rest of his life, serving also as town clerk and as an instrument maker. Of his five daughters, the youngest, Maria Barbara, was J. S. Bach's first wife, and the eldest, Friedelena Margaretha (1675–1729), lived in Bach's household.

Johann Michael is described in the Genealogy as an 'able composer', and he is represented by six vocal works in the ALT-BACHISCHES ARCHIV. He was among the most important motet composers in central Germany, and his many organ chorale

Bach's marriage to Maria Barbara entered in the register at Arnstadt

The church in Dornheim, where J. S. Bach and his first wife, Maria Barbara, were
married in 1707

preludes and variations (strongly represented in the Neumeister collection) demonstrate that he was also among the most influential keyboard composers, particularly on the young J. S. Bach.

DRM

**Bach, Johann Sebastian.** See overleaf.

**Bach, Maria Barbara** (b. 20 Oct. 1684; bur. 7 July 1720). Second cousin and first wife of J. S. Bach, born in Gehren, near Ilmenau in Thuringia. She was the youngest daughter of Johann Michael Bach, town organist at Gehren, and Catharina Wedemann. It appears that after her mother's death in 1704 she went to Arnstadt to live with her uncle, the mayor Martin Feldhaus, in one of whose two guest-houses Bach also took up residence. She may have been the 'frembde Jungfer' ('stranger maiden', or perhaps 'unauthorized maiden') whose music-making in the choir loft of the Neuekirche caused the consistory to charge Bach with a breach of regulations in 1706. Their marriage on 17 October 1707 at Dornheim, near Arnstadt, was facilitated by an inheritance from Bach's maternal uncle Tobias Lämmerhirt. Two of the six children born to them at Weimar died in infancy, but those who reached adulthood include the musicians Wilhelm Friedemann, Carl Philipp Emanuel, and Johann Gottfried Bernhard. Their last child, Leopold Augustus, was born at Cöthen in 1718, but lived less than a year. He was named after his godfathers, one of whom was Prince Leopold of Anhalt-Cöthen. Maria Barbara died prematurely of unknown causes, and was buried while Bach was away with the prince in Carlsbad.

RLS

**Bach, P. D. Q.** A character created by the American composer Peter Schickele (b. 1935). Although Schickele imagined him as 'the last and least of the sons of J. S. Bach', the character of P. D. Q. and the events of his supposed life are to some extent based on those of J. S. Bach himself. Schickele also published music under P. D. Q.'s name, some of which has been recorded and broadcast.

P. Schickele, *The Definitive Biography of P. D. Q. Bach (1807–1742?)* (New York, 1976).

**Bach, Samuel Anton Jacob** (b. 26 April 1713; d. 29 March 1781). Eldest son of J. S. Bach's distant cousin Johann Ludwig, born in Meiningen. After attending school in Meiningen, he studied law at Leipzig University (1732–4) and took lessons from Sebastian. From 1735 to 1761 he was court organist in Meiningen, and also worked as a lawyer and civil servant. He was a talented painter of miniatures. In 1759 he married Maria Catharina Axt (c.1736–97); they had one son, Adam Gottlieb (b. 1764), who lived only a few days, and a daughter, Elisabetha (1766–1806).

**Bach, Wilhelm Friedemann** (b. 22 Nov. 1710; d. 1 July 1784). The first son of J. S. and Maria Barbara Bach; composer and keyboard player. Known in his day primarily as a keyboard virtuoso, he composed a small but distinctive *œuvre* which blends the mid-century *galant* and *empfindsamer* styles with a substantial contrapuntal element usually lacking in the works of his contemporaries, including his younger brothers. He is also famous as the recipient of the *Clavierbüchlein vor Wilhelm Friedemann Bach.* He was, in addition, a teacher and informant of J. N. Forkel, the first biographer of J. S. Bach.

Friedemann was born in Weimar, and after studies with his father, and with the violinist J. G. Graun, he became organist at the Sophienkirche in Dresden in 1733. In 1746 he went to Halle as organist at the Marienkirche. But thereafter he could secure only the honorary title of *Kapellmeister* at Darmstadt in 1762, and two years later he left his Halle position, moving in 1770 to Brunswick and in 1774 to Berlin. He ended his career as a private teacher and keyboard recitalist; among his students was Sarah Levy, great-aunt of Felix Mendelssohn.

Friedemann has been described both as Sebastian's most brilliant son and as a failed imitator of his father who suffered from various defects of character. The small number of surviving works indeed suggests a reticence to commit himself to paper; his Berlin organ recitals evidently consisted mainly of improvisations. But he may also have been affected by changing social conditions that made it difficult for a self-possessed virtuoso to succeed in a church- or court-related position, and he was evidently less willing than most younger contemporaries to compose and publish fashionable, readily accessible music.

At Dresden Friedemann apparently planned the publication of a series of six keyboard sonatas, on the model of Sebastian's six Partitas. He later composed a set of 12 extraordinary polonaises and one of eight *manualiter* fugues, with publication probably in mind. But only two sonatas appeared; the music, especially of the first, in D major, is rich in contrapuntal texture and musical ideas, although difficult to play and to interpret convincingly. Similar observations can be made of the few extant concertos, trio sonatas, organ pieces, and cantatas; these, especially the Halle church works, are sometimes extravagantly difficult, their style, like that of the keyboard music, a remarkable combination of expressive, original ideas with forms and textures derived from those of J. S. Bach.

Much of Friedemann's biography remains elusive; many of Martin Falck's findings have, however, been substantially revised by Peter Wollny.

[*cont. on p.50*]

# Bach, Johann Sebastian

(b. 21 March 1685; d. 28 July 1750). Composer, born in Eisenach in Thuringia.

1. Biographical sketch.
2. Personality.
3. Religion.
4. Income and estate.
5. Library.
6. Portraits.
7. Bach as performer.
8. Bach as teacher.

## 1. Biographical sketch

*(i) Early years, 1685–1708.* J. S. Bach was the youngest child of Johann Ambrosius Bach and his wife Maria Elisabetha (née Lämmerhirt). His mother died in early May 1694, and his father, after remarrying, lived only until February 1695, leaving Sebastian in the hands of his impecunious widow. Both he and his brother Johann Jacob then went to live with their eldest brother Johann Christoph (ii) at Ohrdruf, some 60 km. (37 miles) south-east of their native Eisenach.

In Ohrdruf the young Bach benefited from imaginative teaching at the lyceum and a sound introduction to musical techniques and repertories from Christoph himself. However, there was barely room to house Sebastian in his brother's meagre lodgings, since Christoph's own family was expanding, and when the opportunity arose Sebastian applied successfully for a charitable choral scholarship at the Michaelisschule in Lüneburg, far off to the north-east. Together with an Ohrdruf schoolfellow, Georg Erdmann, he entered that excellent establishment in 1700, at the age of 15.

The date of Sebastian's departure from Lüneburg is unknown, but in July 1702 his successful application for an organist's post at Sangerhausen was blocked by the reigning duke. Except for a brief spell as lackey and musician in Weimar in 1703, his whereabouts are vague until his appointment on 9 August 1703 as organist at the Neuekirche in Arnstadt. There his duties were light, but his behaviour was censured by the consistory and the civic authorities, many of their complaints centring on a visit to Lübeck in 1705–6 when Bach overstayed his leave of absence by about three months. In June 1707 he moved to Mühlhausen as organist of the Blasiuskirche. Despite religious controversies there, he thrived, particularly as a composer of some exciting cantatas, and on 17 October 1707 he married his second cousin Maria Barbara.

*(ii) Weimar and Cöthen, 1708–23.* In June 1708 Bach played to Duke Wilhelm Ernst of Saxe-Weimar, and was immediately invited to serve as his organist and chamber musician in Weimar. There, according to the Obituary, 'the pleasure his Grace took in his playing fired him with the desire to try every feasible artistry in treating the organ', and by 1717 Bach had completed most of the chorales in the *Orgel-Büchlein*, as well as many other organ works. In 1714 he was promoted to the newly created post of *Konzertmeister*, in which capacity he led the main *Kapelle* and was expected to compose a cantata each month (those performed on the intervening Sundays being by his nominal superiors, *Kapellmeister* Johann Samuel Drese and his son Johann

Wilhelm). After J. S. Drese's death on 1 December 1716 and the search for his successor, Bach (who seems not to have been considered for the post) began to look elsewhere, and in August 1717 was formally offered the post of *Kapellmeister* to Prince Leopold of Anhalt-Cöthen. Duke Wilhelm Ernst, however, refused to grant Bach his release, and even placed him in secure detention from 6 November to 2 December.

Grudgingly dismissed from Weimar, Bach embarked on his apparently pleasurable duties in charge of the music at the Cöthen court. Among the works he completed there are the Brandenburg Concertos, Part 1 of *The Well-tempered Clavier*, the Sonatas and Partitas for unaccompanied violin, and the keyboard Inventions. In addition to his duties in Cöthen, he (along with other musicians) accompanied Prince Leopold to the spa of Carlsbad on at least two occasions. On his return from Carlsbad in July 1720 he learnt that his wife Maria Barbara had died. She had borne him seven children, of whom four were still living. On 3 December 1721 Bach took Anna Magdalena Wülcken, a native of Zeitz, to be his second wife. She was to bear him a further 13 children.

Bach probably began to feel restricted by various aspects of artistic life in Cöthen, even before Leopold's marriage to a princess whom Bach later described as an *amusa* (someone indifferent to the arts), and he made steps to seek employment as a church musician in a major centre. In December 1722 he applied for the post of Thomaskantor at Leipzig, left vacant by the death of Johann Kuhnau, but it was not until 22 April 1723, after undergoing the usual *Probe*, and after Telemann and Graupner had declined the post, that Bach was offered it. He and his family moved to Leipzig the following month.

*(iii) Leipzig, 1723–50.* Working with outstanding energy, even for a dedicated Lutheran of his time, Bach set about providing music for the city's four principal churches. By Christmas 1727, or slightly later, he had completed three annual cycles of cantatas, the *St John* and *St Matthew Passions*, the *Magnificat*, and other sacred works. On 12 May 1727 he directed 40 musicians in the performance of a birthday serenade for August the Strong before an audience which included Prince Leopold of Cöthen and Duke Christian of Weißenfels, as well as the elector himself. The kind of music heard on this historic occasion, as well as more intimate chamber works, was to occupy much of Bach's creative energy from 1729 to the early 1740s, when he directed a COLLEGIUM MUSICUM in Leipzig. Also from these years date a number of liturgical works—including the three oratorios, the four *missae*, and the Kyrie and Gloria of what was to become the B minor Mass—based on earlier music, both sacred and secular. This was a period, too, of frequent disputes with the civic authorities and with J. A. Ernesti, installed as Rector of the Thomasschule in November 1734. It was partly to gain support in these disputes that Bach sought in 1733 (and was granted in 1736) a position as composer *von Haus aus* to the Saxon court in Dresden.

The decade from 1739 to 1748 was spent largely in assembling collections of clavier and organ music: Part 2 of *The Well-tempered Clavier*, the Goldberg Variations, *The Art of Fugue*, the Schübler Chorales, the 'Eighteen' chorale preludes, and the Canonic Variations. The *Musical Offering*, resulting from a celebrated audience with Frederick the Great in May 1747, was on sale by late September that year. It is easy to forget, when contemplating these remarkable works, that Bach continued to fulfil his duties as Thomaskantor and *Director chori musici* until at least towards the end of 1749.

Possibly with the dedication of the Dresden Hofkirche in view, he also compiled the later sections of the B minor Mass; indeed, 'Et incarnatus est' and the six-bar introduction to 'Crucifixus etiam pro nobis' may be the last surviving examples of his hand, dating from 1749 or early 1750.

During his last year Bach grew weaker and his sight deteriorated to such an extent that he underwent two debilitating (and unsuccessful) operations at the hand of John Taylor. He had probably slowly developed the then misunderstood and much feared diabetes mellitus, a condition which would have involved sickness, loss of appetite, and violent thirst. But reports of Bach's last illness are vague, and partly fictitious. He died on 28 July 1750, and was buried three days later in the graveyard of the Johanniskirche in Leipzig. *See also* ARNSTADT, CÖTHEN, DRESDEN, EISENACH, HAMBURG, LEIPZIG, LÜNEBURG, MÜHLHAUSEN, OHRDRUF, WEIMAR, and WEIßENFELS.

**2. Personality.** The nature of Bach's personality remains largely a matter for conjecture, since there is little in the way of incontestable evidence to show what he was really like. He seems to have been born industrious, purposeful, and persevering—qualities associated with the Protestant 'work ethic'—but he also displayed a sensitivity and reverence towards his art in society that could result in his vigorously defending his rights, or those of other musicians whom he felt deserving of respect or esteem. His sense of aggrieved surprise when accused and cautioned by the consistory in Arnstadt, his disagreements with the council in Leipzig, and his outrage in disputes over the management of church music with the Rector J. A. Ernesti all testify to this second side of his nature.

Bach's concern for the well-being of his children is amply documented, and was partly rewarded by successes within his own lifetime: Friedemann's in Dresden and Halle, Emanuel's in Berlin, and Christoph Friedrich's in Bückeburg. He was also generous in accommodating more distant relatives, and his modest prosperity made possible the almost continuous protection of a family member to serve as an apprentice in his home from about 1710 onwards. Similar hospitality was extended to other musicians who visited the Bach household from the early Weimar times until the very last years.

The logical rigour of much of Bach's music (including some of his finest works) and its total lack of easy concessions to popular taste might suggest an aloof and unbending figure. But while he was uncompromising on artistic matters Bach was not without a lighter side to his temperament. His love of wine, beer, and tobacco, and the fact that he fathered 20 children is enough to show that he did not scorn life's more sensual pleasures.

**3. Religion.** Lutheran Protestantism was the uncontested religion of Saxony and the Saxon duchies, a region beyond which Bach rarely travelled. When he joined the staff of the Leipzig Thomasschule in 1723, he was interviewed to test his religious motivation and stance, and asked to sign statements confirming his opposition to Calvinism (*BDok* iii, no. 92*a*). However, this official conformity, supposedly upheld by a system of school inspections, could not guarantee dedicated devotion, and it was completely possible for an experienced composer—Telemann is perhaps a good example—to conform to the requirements of the age without actually being more than superficially religious. Indeed it has several times been suggested that Bach's music proceeds only from a studious and professional thoroughness.

Bach in his sixties; portrait by Elias Gottlob Haußmann, 1746

There are good reasons, on the other hand, for believing Bach's religious motivation and stance to have been entirely genuine. In the first place, his German vocal
music was clearly intended to preach, as Luther had instructed, and to do so in the
most subtle and effective ways. The same may be said of much of the organ music,
notably *Clavier-Übung III*. The Latin church music, too, conveys both the details and
the wider meaning and significance of its texts, and seems to centre on a universal
evangelism. Bach's habit of writing inscriptions such as 'J[esu] J[uva]' ('Save, O
Jesu') and 'S[it] D[eo] G[loria]' ('Glory be to God') might seem to result from mere
convention, but they were regularly written on scores or drafts which were mostly for
the composer's personal use.

Other evidence of Bach's genuine piety is seen in his taking of Communion, which
was, according to surviving records, as frequent and dedicated as that of other non-
clerical Lutherans. The fact that he tended to seek Communion at times of emotional
stress (for example, on the deaths of his children) indicates an instinctive supplication to God at times of need. The texts that Bach set in his cantatas and the books
that he possessed in his library have also been adduced as evidence of his religious
sympathies. But in reality he could exercise little or no influence over the choice of
texts, and the use to which he put the books in his library and the value he placed on
them are largely conjectural matters (see §5 below).

Brought up in a tradition of Lutheran Orthodoxy, Bach accepted the use of Latin
in church services, and composed *Magnificat* and mass texts when called upon. In
doing so he was far from embracing Catholicism wholeheartedly, but he lived his life
in situations where traditional religious antagonisms were being relaxed or forgotten. The B minor Mass, which certainly in part, and probably in its entirety, is associated with the Dresden court, provides some evidence that Bach, in his later years,
might even have been happy to succeed Zelenka as 'Kirchen-compositeur' to the
Catholic Polish and Saxon court. Such a move would not have been inconceivable,
and would not by then have indicated a strong leaning towards Catholicism; conditions of appointment at Dresden did not involve interviews or signed declar-
ations.

Attitude and behaviour were never very useful signs of private ambition, private
diplomacy, or even private devotion. Bach does seem to have been consciously
motivated by his beliefs, good-humoured as well as serious, and quite tolerant in his
religious outlook. *See also* LUTHERANISM.

**4. Income and estate.**   Throughout his life Bach derived his income from a number
of sources. In Arnstadt, Mühlhausen, and as *Director chori musici* in Leipzig he was a
public servant accountable to the church; in Weimar and Cöthen he was a private
servant; and as Kantor and Tertius (third schoolmaster) in Leipzig he was a public
servant employed, through the Thomasschule, by the town council. In Arnstadt his
salary was by no means large, but it was at least sufficient to support his needs, and
even to meet some of the expenses incurred in a visit he made to Lübeck in 1705–6 to
meet and hear Buxtehude. He was better paid (and better respected) in the more
senior post as organist of the Blasiuskirche at Mühlhausen.

In Weimar his salary improved again, and his rights to bounties in kind (which
regularly went with salary at the time) also increased. In February 1714 his promotion
to *Konzertmeister* brought another increase, and his work examining newly built and
repaired organs was becoming a profitable sideline. For example, the fee of 20 thaler

which he was paid for trying the rebuilt organ in the Paulinerkirche, Leipzig, in December 1717 was enough to purchase a whole houseful of furniture, and more than enough to buy two good Stainer violins (judging from the official valuation of Bach's possessions after his death; see below).

Bach's house detention at Weimar (see §1, above) probably involved also the termination of his salary there, but this was made good by backdated payments immediately on his arrival in Cöthen as *Kapellmeister* to Prince Leopold. The prince treated Bach and his whole *Kapelle* unusually well; salaries were high, and those of Bach and Anna Magdalena, after their marriage on 3 December 1721, were particularly generous for a small principality like Anhalt-Cöthen. The situation was more variable at Leipzig, where prices fluctuated and Bach's family was becoming more expensive to feed, clothe, and accommodate. Moreover, a substantial proportion of his income as Kantor and *Director chori musici* came from ACCIDENTIEN (occasional payments, such as those for weddings and funerals) which were unpredictable and subject even to vagaries in the weather (as Bach complained in a famous letter to Georg Erdmann).

The inventory of Bach's possessions drawn up after his death (he left no will) presents some evidence as to his acquired wealth, but it raises questions as well as answering them. He clearly owned quite a number of musical instruments, a quantity of theological books (see §5 below) and a fair number of coins and medallions such as he would have been offered as a reward for recitals and other professional services. However, there is no mention of books other than theological ones, or of music paper and writing materials, and Bach's music library, which must have been extensive, is not included. We know, however, that most of his own manuscripts were divided between the two eldest sons, Wilhelm Friedemann and Carl Philipp Emanuel, and that the performing parts of the chorale cantatas were retained by his widow, from whom they passed to the Thomaskirche in Leipzig. The contents of the inventory may be summarized in broad terms as shown in the following table.

| Item | Valuation | |
| --- | --- | --- |
| | Thaler | Groschen |
| Mining share at Klein Vogtsberg | 60 | — |
| Gold and silver coins | 231 | 18 |
| Medallions | 25 | 20 |
| Sums owed to Bach | 65 | — |
| Petty cash | 36 | — |
| Silverware and other valuables | 251 | 11 |
| Musical instruments | 371 | 16 |
| Pewter, copper, and brass | 16 | 22 |
| Clothing | 33 | — |
| Furniture | 29 | 8 |
| Sacred books | 38 | 17 |
| Total | 1,159 | 16 |

Against this are set liabilities amounting to 152 thaler 21 groschen

The musical instruments are of particular interest. They include three claviers with a pedal-board already given to the youngest son, Johann Christian, while Bach was still living (*see* CLAVIER). A valuable veneered harpsichord ('to remain in the family, if possible') and two lute-harpsichords were among the other keyboard instruments Bach owned. A Stainer violin was probably given to him by Prince Leopold, since 'good Tyrolean Stainer violins' had been supplied and charged to the court at Cöthen during the period of Bach's employment there. A lute was valued at 21 thaler (almost three times the value placed on the Stainer violin), but the relatively low values placed on most of the other instruments listed perhaps indicate purchases for family beginners.

5. **Library.** We have no means of knowing the full contents of Bach's library, whether of books or music. The inventory drawn up after his death (see §4 above) includes a list of some 80 volumes of theological writings (among them two copies of Luther's complete works and two complete Bibles with parallel commentaries), and the extent and range of this collection have given rise to much analysis and commentary (see Wilhelmi). However, how far Bach had chosen the books he owned and how they were used (for example for private family devotions and personal enlightenment) is open to conjecture. One reason for listing such books in the mid-18th century was almost certainly to alert the authorities to possible association with proscribed organizations, or with denominations suspected of too much sympathy with the Roman Catholic Church or even with Calvinism.

As well as the books listed in the inventory, we know that Bach owned a copy of Fux's textbook *Gradus ad Parnassum* (Vienna, 1725) in its Latin edition, to which later he must have added Mizler's German translation (Leipzig, 1742). He also possessed several 'ancient' books on music which Carl Philipp Emanuel generously gave to the English historian Charles Burney, but the identities of most of these are unknown. His library must also have contained a good deal of music by his contemporaries and predecessors, in both manuscript and printed form. But we have nothing which might indicate his literary preferences, his favourite poetry, or his attitude towards aesthetics and such important matters as the role of number in contemporary theology, music, and philosophy—topics which scarcely feature in the volumes listed in the inventory.

6. **Portraits.** Bach's portrait was painted in oils by E. G. Haußmann, probably in 1746, and a copy was made by the artist some two years later. The first of these is in the Stadtmuseum, Leipzig; the second is owned by William H. Scheide of Princeton, New Jersey (see p.43). Both have undergone restoration, the Scheide copy rather more successfully than the other. Comparison with other Haußmann portraits suggests that the artist was barely capable of capturing the personality of his sitter—certainly not as capable as Thomas Gainsborough was in his portraits of Johann Christian Bach and Carl Friedrich Abel, for example.

The only other portrait that may be of Bach and done from life was identified as such when it came up for auction in London in January 1978. This is a family picture by Balthasar Denner (1685–1749). The suggestion that the three children in the picture are Emanuel (during his temporary period as a violinist), Johann Gottfried Bernhard (holding a flute) and Gottfried Heinrich (with a half-size violin) is plausible, but the father holds a cello, and for that reason alone is less certainly Johann Sebastian. There is little point in comparing his facial appearance with that in the Haußmann portrait, since the two are separated by about 20 years. The Denner family portrait seems to have more character, even if his Johann Sebastian looks rather avuncular for the busy composer of about 1729.

Two paintings of younger men, often reproduced as Bach portraits in pictorial biographies and on record sleeves, are those by the Weimar court painter Johann Ernst Rentsch (now in the Stadtmuseum, Ehrfurt) and Johann Jakob Ihle (in the Bachhaus at Eisenach). Neither painting has any claim to authenticity as a portrait of Bach. There is, on the other hand, an extensive iconography of post-Haußmann pictures of Bach, which includes inked drawings, pastels, watercolours, engravings, and oil portraits, some freely and others closely copied from Haußmann's originals. A number are reversed in mirror image. A pastel attributed to Gottlieb Friederich Bach (1714–85) or his son Johann Philipp (1752–1846), both of whom were court painters at Meiningen, also shows a clear debt to Haußmann's 1748 painting.

7. **Bach as performer.**   It was as an instrumentalist, and more particularly as an organist, that Bach made his early reputation. His activities in this regard cannot be entirely divorced from his consultancy work in testing and reporting on newly built, rebuilt, or adapted organs. Indeed his early appointment as organist of the Neue-kirche in Arnstadt resulted from his testing the new organ built for the church by J. F. Wender. He continued, with impressive regularity, to be called upon in a similar capacity throughout southern Saxony, and in one case as far away as Kassel, right up to the winter of 1748–9. Such occasions were usually followed by a recital, and these performances soon earned Bach popular and critical acclaim as an executant. He also performed recitals—in Hamburg, Dresden, and Berlin, for example—which were not connected with the appraisal of a new organ. He presumably included in these some of his own organ compositions—we know that he almost certainly played the 'Dorian' Toccata and Fugue at Kassel in 1732—but they would also feature the impro-visations for which he was widely admired. In recalling the Kassel visit in 1743, Kon-stantin Bellermann (1696–1758), then Kantor at Minden, described how Bach could, 'by the use of his feet alone (while his fingers do either nothing or something else) achieve such an admirable, agitated, and rapid concord of sounds on the church organ that others would seem unable to imitate it even with their fingers'.

Several other 18th-century writings attest to Bach's virtuosity on the organ, but he was also an accomplished player of string instruments, and it was arguably the violin rather than the organ that most influenced the style of his mature compositions. His father, Ambrosius, had been a violinist, and C. P. E. Bach reported to Forkel that 'in his youth, and until the approach of old age, [Bach] played the violin cleanly and penetratingly, and . . . understood to perfection the possibilities of all string instru-ments'. Forkel himself stated that Bach took particular pleasure in playing the viola, which placed him, 'as it were, in the middle of the harmony, whence he could best hear and enjoy it, on both sides'.

J. M. Gesner, Rector of the Thomasschule in 1730–4, left us a unique but fascin-ating description of Bach directing (probably at rehearsal) an ensemble of 30 or more musicians, 'giving the right note to one from the top of his voice, to another from the bottom, to a third from the middle of it . . . and although he is executing the most difficult parts himself, noticing at once whenever and wherever a mistake occurs, holding everyone together . . . full of rhythm in every part of his body'. It is clear from this and several other accounts that whenever Bach performed, whether as soloist or in ensemble music, whether as continuo player or as conductor, the occa-sion was likely to be a memorable one.

8. **Bach as teacher.**   Bach was much sought after as a teacher, and more than 80 of his pupils have been identified. At the time the approach to learning and teaching, and

the philosophy behind it, were at an interesting crossroads. The old idea of master and apprentice, rooted in medieval practice, still existed; the apprentice had not only to imitate the master but also to obey and serve him, for example by seeing that instruments were maintained and that livery was in good order when required. The newer approach, a product of Renaissance humanism, required the learner to be to some extent original, and to be self-critical in examining and revising his work.

Bach's approach united elements of the old and the new. It is apparent, for example from the modifications he made to F. E. Niedt's *Musicalische Handleitung* in his own (not fully authenticated) *Vorschriften und Grundsätze* (PRECEPTS AND PRIN-CIPLES), that he avoided any over-prescriptive kind of instruction. Even if we compare his methods with those revealed in the treatises of his son Emanuel or his pupil J. P. Kirnberger, we can see how the sensitive, practical composer of the early 18th century worked to develop the self-criticism of the individual, whereas the still sensitive composer or theorist of the second half of the century attempted to rationalize everything with extensively argued prescriptions.

We have it on Emanuel's authority that Bach's pupils 'had to begin their studies by learning four-part thorough bass [i.e. elaborating passages at the keyboard or on paper from a figured bass]. From this he went to chorales [i.e. the harmonization of chorale melodies]; first he added the basses to them himself, and they had to invent the alto and tenor. Then he taught them to devise the basses themselves . . . . In teaching fugues, he began with two-part ones, and so on. . . . As for the invention of ideas, he required this from the very beginning, and anyone who had none he advised to stay away from composition altogether.'

From this, and from the CLAVIERBÜCHLEIN prepared for and by Wilhelm Friede-mann, it is clear that Bach made no rigid separation between the teaching of composition and that of keyboard playing. He apparently took it for granted that the subject to be learnt was a combination of invention (having 'good ideas'), development (making 'good use' of these), and performance, and that the last of these was to be accurately controlled so that a 'cantabile' style of playing would result. In 1791 E. L. Gerber gave an account of how Bach used his own compositions for instructing Gerber's father, Heinrich Nikolaus, in keyboard playing: 'At the first lesson he [Bach] set his Inventions before him. When he had studied these through to Bach's satisfaction, there followed a series of suites, then *The Well-tempered Clavier*. . . . The conclusion of the instruction was thorough bass, for which Bach chose the Albinoni violin solos.'                                                                                     SFD

*BDok* i–iv; K. Beißwenger, *Johann Sebastian Bachs Notenbibliothek* (Kassel, 1992); H. T. David and A. Mendel, eds., *The Bach Reader: A Life of Johann Sebastian Bach in Letters and Documents* (New York, 1945, 2nd edn. 1966); Y. Kobayashi, 'Zur Teilung des Bachschen Erbes', in *Acht kleine Präludien und Studien über Bach: Georg von Dadlesen zum 70. Geburtstag*, ed. Johann-Sebastian-Bach-Institut, Göttingen (Wiesbaden, 1992), 67–75; R. A. Leaver, *Bachs theologische Bibliothek* (Stuttgart, 1983); H. Löffler, 'Die Schüler Johann Sebastian Bachs', *BJb* 40 (1953), 5–28; A. Mann, *Theory and Practice: The Great Composer as Student and Teacher* (New York, 1987); H. Raupach, *Das wahre Bildnis des Johann Sebastian Bach: Bericht und Dokumente* (Munich, 1983); H.-J. Schulze, 'Zur Überlieferung einiger Bach-Porträts', *BJb* 68 (1982), 154–6; T. Wilhelmi, 'Bachs Bibliothek: eine Weiterführung der Arbeit von Hans Preuß', *BJb* 65 (1979), 107–29; For further bibliography, *see* BIBLIOGRAPHIES.

Bach's eldest son, Wilhelm Friedemann; portrait by Wilhelm Weitsch, *c.*1760
(Staatliche Galerie Moritzburg, Halle)

Thus, for example, the witty concerto for two (unaccompanied) harpsichords is now dated to about 1740; J. S. Bach made a copy of it about two years later. Even the widely reproduced portrait by Friedrich Georg Weitsch (1758–1828) cannot positively be identified as that of the composer, although the sitter's lively, elegant appearance recalls the same painter's portrait of Friedemann's correspondent, the writer Johann Joachim Eschenburg (1743–1820). Friedemann apparently falsified attributions of both his own and his father's music, and is often blamed for dispersing the works of J. S. Bach that he inherited on the latter's death. But it is not known how many works were actually lost as a result.

Friedemann's reuse of his own earlier vocal and keyboard works and his adaptations of several of his father's cantatas differ little from practices also employed by Sebastian and Emanuel Bach. Several of the keyboard fantasias—most, if not all, dating from the years at Berlin, and some probably resembling the improvisations played at Friedemann's recitals there—incorporate substantial passages from earlier pieces. Yet a work like the E minor fantasia (no. 21 in Falck's catalogue) remains a compelling musical drama, effectively juxtaposing fragmentary singing passages and virtuoso arpeggiation with imitations of both simple and accompanied recitative. DS

M. Falck, *Wilhelm Friedemann Bach: sein Leben und seine Werke* (Leipzig, 1913; 2nd edn., 1919); P. Wollny, 'Studies in the Music of Wilhelm Friedemann Bach: Sources and Style' (diss., Harvard University, 1993); P. Wollny, 'Wilhelm Friedemann Bach's Halle Performances of Cantatas by his Father', in D. R. Melamed, ed., *Bach Studies 2* (Cambridge, 1995), 202–28.

**BACH.** In German usage the note B♭ is called B, and B♮ is called H. This allows Bach's name to be expressed as a musical motif, B♭–A–C–B♮, and the composer himself used it in one of the fugue subjects of the final (unfinished) contrapunctus in his *Art of Fugue* (see Ex. 1). Its presence has been observed elsewhere in Bach's works, for example in the first movement of the Second Brandenburg Concerto (bars 109–12, bass) and towards the end of the Canonic Variations for organ; but such instances are not beyond the realm of coincidence, and the four notes are very likely to be found close together when the music veers towards the subdominant in the closing bars of a piece in C major. Bach would certainly have been well aware of the motif's possibilities before he came to write the *Art of Fugue*, however—J. G. Walther referred to it in his *Musicalisches Lexicon* (1732)—but the attribution to him of a Prelude and Fugue in B♭ major on the name BACH, BWV898, is generally considered to be without foundation. The motif appears also on the BACH GOBLET.

Several fugues on the BACH motif were penned by Bach's sons and pupils, and the Bach revival of the 19th century brought a surge of interest in its possibilities for Romantic expression. Schumann, Liszt, Reger, and Busoni all based notable works on it, and the Second Viennese School of Schoenberg and his disciples found it easy to incorporate into totally chromatic, serial works. Not surprisingly, perhaps, a large proportion of the works based on the motif are for organ, and in many cases they take the form of tributes on the occasions of important anniversaries (in 1950 and 1985, for example). The list that follows, which is not claimed to be comprehensive, is arranged alphabetically, and dates, where shown, are of composition or publication.

Acker, Dieter: Canonic Fantasia (1977), flute, alto flute, bass flute, violin, viola, cello, and harpsichord

Aho, Kalvei: Sonata (1973), violin

Ahrens, Joseph: *Triptychon* (1949), organ

Albert, Eugen d': Prelude and Fugue

Albrechtsberger, Johann Georg: Fugue in G minor (c.1781), piano

Allers, Hans-Günther: Introduction and Tarantella op. 16 (1977), wind quintet

Andriessen, Louis: *Mausoleum* (1979), large ensemble; *De materie* [opera] (1989); *De stijl* (1985), large ensemble

Anon.: Fugue in G minor BWV Anh. II 109; Prelude and Fugue in B♭ major BWV898

Aperghis, Georges: *BWV* (1973), voices and large ensemble

Avidom, Menahem: Suite (1962), woodwind, strings, piano, and percussion

Bach, Carl Philipp Emanuel: Symphony in C major H659 (1773), string orchestra

Bach, Johann Andreas: Capriccio in C minor

Bach, Johann Christian: Fugue, piano or organ

Bach, Johann Sebastian: *The Art of Fugue* BWV1080:19

Ex. 1. *Art of Fugue* BWV1080:19

B   A   C   H

Badinski, Nikolai: *Omaggio a Bach* (1977), woodwind, harpsichord, and strings

Barblan, Otto: Chaconne in G minor op. 10 (1902), organ; Passacaglia, Variations and Triple Fugue in G minor op. 24 (1927), organ

Baum, Alfred: Fantasia (1977), organ

Baumann, Herbert: String Quartet in C major (1961)

Baur, Jürg: *Incontri* (1961), alto flute and piano; *Kontrapunkte 77* (1977), flute, oboe, and bassoon; *Ricercare II* (1977), organ; Concerto (1984), organ and string orchestra

Bédard, Pierre Michel: *Un hommage musical* (1984), organ

Bechtel, Helmut: Five Inventions (1960), piano

Becker, Carl Ferdinand: *Choralfuge* (organ)

Beethoven, Ludwig van: *Kühl, nicht lau* woo191 (1825), 3 voices

Behrend, Siegfried: *B–A–C–H* (1981), orchestra of plucked instruments

Behrens, Jack: Fantasy (1985), piano

Benker, Heinz: Toccata and Fugue (1963), organ

Bellermann, Heinrich: Prelude and Fugue op. 8 (1855), organ

Bergmann, Erik: *A propos de B–A–C–H* op. 79 (1980), piano

Bertram, Hans Georg: *Beschwörung: neun Aphorismen* (1976), solo flute; *Du hast meine Klage verwandelt in einen Reigen* (1977), 2 trumpets and 2 trombones; *Konzert mit und ohne b–a–c–h* (1974), violin and string orchestra; Lamento e giubilo (1974), organ

Beutler, Johann Georg Bernhard: Fugue (*c.*1850), organ

Biggs, Richard Keys: Prelude (1944), organ

Blarr, Oskar Gottlieb: *Orgelmesse '58* (Gloria) (1958), organ

Bloch, Waldemar: Ricercar (1952), organ

Blume, Joachim: Sonata no. 3 'Protuberanzen', organ; Sonata no. 4 'Tendenzen' (1977), organ

Boito, Arrigo: Fugue

Bornefeld, Helmut: *Trio mesto* (no. 17 of 30 Inventions), organ

Börner, Hans: *Oboenlied* (1985), alto, oboe, and organ; *Zwiegespräch* op. 34*b* (1985), soprano and alto recorders, four string instruments, and percussion

Borodin, Alexander, and others: *Paraphrases* (1879), piano

Borris, Siegfried: *B–A–C–H, Evolution* op. 134 (1971), 19 wind instruments, 3 double basses, harp, and percussion

Brahms, Johannes: Cadenza for first movement of Beethoven's Piano Concerto no. 4, piano

Brandt-Caspari, Alfred: Prelude and Fugue op. 2

Braun, Peter Michael: *Hommage à Machaut* (1979), piano

Bräutigam, Volker: Concerto (1961), harpsichord and orchestra; 'Johann Sebastian Bach: unbequemer Mann . . .' *Epitaph* (1969), 4–7-voice choir

Bredemeyer, Reiner: *(Cello)²* (1971), 4 cellos

Brehme, Hans: Symphony no. 2 op. 51 (1950), orchestra

Breuer, Franz-Josef: *Immer wieder, ob wir der Liebe Landschaft auch kennen* (1975), female choir

Brewer, Alfred Herbert: *Meditation* (1916), organ

Bruči, Rudolf: *Metamorphoses* (1973), string orchestra

Bruckmann, Ferdinand: Four Studies (1958), piano; 'Bach-Vögel' from *Ornithologische Suite* (1969), 4 recorders and women's voices; Piano Concerto no. 1 (1956); Suite (1967), cello and piano; Symphony no. 1 (1956), string orchestra

Burke, John: *Escher/Bach* (1985), alto flute and harpsichord

Busoni, Ferruccio: *Fantasia contrappuntistica* (1910), piano; *Große Fuge* (1910), piano

Butting, Max: *Festschrift für Bach* op. 77 (1950), flute, cor anglais, bassoon, violin, viola, and cello; String Quartet no. 5 op. 53 (1947); Symphony no. 9 op. 94 (1956), orchestra; Symphony no. 10 op. 108 (1963), orchestra; Two Toccatas op. 88 (1953), piano

Callhoff, Herbert: *Crucifixus* (1984), organ

Casella, Alfredo: *Due ricercari* op. 52 (1932), piano

Christmann, Johann Friedrich: Fantasia (1783)

Christopher, Cyril Stanley: *Soliloquy*

Clementi, Aldo: *B.A.C.H.* (1970), piano; *Esercizio* (1975), mezzo-violin, violin, and viola

Coke-Jephcott, Norman: *Little Fugue* (1956)

Collum, Herbert: Fantasia (1967), choir and chamber orchestra; Fantasia (1969), organ; Suite (1962), organ

Conze, Johann: Organ Sonata

Coulthard, Jean: Variations (1951), piano

Dallapiccola, Luigi: *Quaderno muiscale di Annalibera* (1952), piano; Variations for Orchestra (1954)

DaOoz, Ram: *Lebe wohl B.A.C.H.*, piano

Darmstadt, Hans: '. . . darum hoffe ich noch' (1981), soprano, alto, baritone, choir, and orchestra/organ/piano

Darmstadt, Jean: *Ich steh an deiner Krippen hier* (1967–73), organ

David, Johann Nepomuk: Concerto grosso (1925), orchestra/2 pianos; Partita (1964), organ

Degen, Johannes Dietz: *Die vier Temperamente* op. 30 (1982), string orchestra

Delapierre, André: *Hommage à J. S. Bach* (1950), piano

Delnooz, Henri: Quartet (1969), flute, oboe, violin, and cello

Denhoff, Michael: *Omaggio a Bach, Scarlatti, Händel e Berg* (1984), violin, oboe, and orchestra

Dessau, Paul: Bach Variations (1963), orchestra; *Deutsche Miserere* (1944–7), solo voices, chorus, children's chorus, orchestra, organ, trautonium; *Die Verurteilung des Lukullus* [opera] (1949–50); *Einstein* [opera] (1971–3); *In memoriam Bertolt Brecht* (1957), orchestra; Klavierstück (1948), piano; *Lanzelot* [opera] (1967–9); *Leonce und Lena* [opera] (1978); *Les voix* (1939–41), voice and instruments; *Orchestermusik III: Lenin* (1970) orchestra; String Quartet no. 1 (1932)

Diggle, Roland: *Hommage à Franck*

Dijk, Rudi M. van: Concertante, flute, harp, timpani, and strings

Dittrich, Paul-Heinz: *Cantus I* (1975); Concerto (1978), flute, oboe, and orchestra; *Illuminations* (1976)

Donatoni, Franco: *Voci* (1972–3), orchestra

Dorr, Günter: 'In memoriam', in *Divertimento über B–A–C–H* [collaborative composition] (1984), orchestra

Draht, Theodor: Fantasia op. 9 (1864), organ duet

Dresseler, Rudolf: *Impressionen über b–a–c–h* (1983), organ

Dubitzsky, F.: *Ein feste Burg und B–A–C–H* (1914)

Durkó, Zsolt: *Episodi* (1962–3), orchestra

Egge, Klaus: *Sinfonia sopra B–A–C–H. E–G–G–E*, op. 30 (1967)

Eisler, Hanns: *Das Schlichte*: Recitative and Fugue (1951), voice and piano; *Das Vorbild* (1952), alto and orchestra; *Deutsche Sinfonie* (1947, rev. 1949), orchestra; *Lenin-Requiem* (1936–7), soloists, chorus, and orchestra; *Gegen den Krieg* op. 51 (1936), chorus; Prelude and Fugue op. 46 (1934), string trio

Engel, Paul: Fantasia and Fugue (1942), string orchestra

Engelmann, Johannes: Fantasia, Passacaglia and Fugue op. 28 (1941), organ

Erdmann, Dietrich: *Spectrum* (1975), chamber orchestra

Erdmann, Veit: Canonic Variations (1978), 2 flutes, viola, and harpsichord

Erpf, Hermann: Introduction, Ostinato and Fugue (1928), piano

Etti, Karl: Prelude and Fugue (1972), organ

Eyken, Jan Albert van: Toccata and Fugue op. 38 (*c.*1865), organ

Fackler, Helmut: Toccata and Passacaglia (1977), organ

Fährmann, Hans: Introduction and Double Fugue op. 11 (1902), organ; Sonata no. 3 in B minor op. 17 (1902), organ; Toccata, Introduction and Fugue in C major op. 69 (?1916/1932), organ

Fehres, Wilhelm: *Meditation II* (1980), organ

Feix, Otto: Improvisations op. 106*b*, organ

Fiebig, Kurt: *Drei Kontrapunkte* (1983), organ

Fleischer, Hans: *Kleine Hausmusik* op. 143 (1950), violin and piano

Fodi, John: Concerto grosso op. 74 (1984), orchestra

Forest, Jean Kurt: Fantasy (1950)

Fork, Günther: *Aus tiefer Not* (1976), organ; *Metamorphosen* (1964–5), mixed choir

Forster, Walter von: *Jesu, hilf siegen, du Fürste des Lebens* op. 36 (1936), organ

Fortner, Wolfgang: Fantasia (1950), 9 solo instruments, 2 pianos, and orchestra

Frederichs, Henning: *Tu es Petrus* (1982), soloists, choir, and ensemble

Frickhöffer, Otto: Fantasia (1923), organ

Fritsch, Johannes G.: *Modulation I* (1966), violin, viola, cello, double bass, and piano; *Modulation II* (1967), 13 instruments and electronics

Funk, Heinrich: Passacaglia op. 50*a* (1958), organ [also in other versions]

Gade, Niels Wilhelm: *Rebus* op. 2*a* (?1841), piano

Gebauer, Adolf: Prelude and Fugue (1984), string orchestra

Gellman, Steven: *Overture for Ottawa* (1972), orchestra

Gerber, René: Prelude and Fugue, clarinet

Ginastera, Alberto: Toccata, Villancico and Fugue op. 18 (1947), organ

Godowsky, Leopold: Prelude and Fugue (1930), piano left hand; Sonata in E minor (1911), piano

Goehr, Alexander: Three Pieces op. 18 (1964), piano

Goldmann, Friedrich: *Essays I–III* (1971–3), orchestra; Fantasia (1972), organ; Sonata (1970), piano and wind quintet; String Quartet (1978); Symphony (1972–3), orchestra

Görner, Hans Georg: Fantasia and Double Fugue op. 50 (1972), organ

Graap, Lothar: *Fantasie III (B–A–C–H)* (1985), organ

Gründer, Monika: *Look at Johnny S.* (1985), piano

Gruschwitz, Günter: Toccata and Fugue (1985), organ

Günther, Jens Uwe: *Konfrontationen zu B–A–C–H* (1977), two orchestral groups

Haag, Hanno: *Silences* op. 11*a* (1973), piano; as op. 11*b* (1983), small orchestra

Haager, Max: Symphony no. 7 in D minor (1976–9), string orchestra

Haarklou, Johannes: Prelude and Fugue (1924), organ

Hannemann, Johannes: Symphonic Fantasia, organ, woodwind, and percussion

Hartzell, Eugene: Toccata and Passacaglia (1983), organ

Haselbach, Josef: *Vorspiel* (1973), organ

Hatzis, Christos: *Spring Equinox* (1985), flute, oboe, bassoon, trumpet, trombone, piano, synthesizer, percussion, and string quartet

Heiller, Anton: *Ein wenig über B–A–C–H* (1975), harpsichord

Heilmann, Harald: *Dyogramm über A–S–C–H. B–A–C–H* (1984), organ; *Meditation* (1969), organ; Sonata no. 4 in A major (1979), organ

Heinen, Jeannot: *Partita concertata—Hommage à J. S. Bach* op. 120, violin and harpsichord; Six Inventions op. 42 (1972), organ; String Trio op. 118 (1984)

Heinichen, Johann David: *Kleines harmonisches Labyrinth* BWV591, organ

Helfer, Friedrich August: Canon (1867), organ; Double Fugue (1867), organ

Helmschrott, Robert Maximilian: *Hommage à Albertus Magnus* (1982), organ

Henze, Hans Werner: Symphony no. 2 (1949), orchestra

Herzog, Johann Georg: Fugue (*c.*1858), organ

Hesford, Bryan: *Aria und Litanei in memoriam Dimitri Schostakowitsch* op. 55, organ

Hesse, Adolph Friedrich: Double Fugue, organ

Heussenstamm, George: *Reflections* op. 20 (1972), organ

Hinlopen, Francina: Improvisation (1985), harp and flute

Hlobil, Emil: Concerto op. 61 (1963), organ, strings and timpani

Hoddinott, Alun: Cello Sonata op. 73 no. 2 (1970), cello and piano

Hold, Trevor: *Three Foxtrots* (1975), piano

Holland-Moritz, Thomas: *Sonata breve* (1972), organ

Honegger, Arthur: Prelude, Arioso and Fughetta (1932), piano

Hovland, Egil: *Hymnus auf König Olaf*, 9 wind instruments and organ

Hulse, Camil van: Prelude and Fugue op. 150 (1974), organ; *Ricercata quasi fantasia* op. 56 no. 1 (1949), organ

Hummel, Bertold: *Metamorphosen* op. 40, organ and 11 wind instruments

Hupel, Hans: String quartet 'B–A–C–H' (1950)

Indy, Vincent d': 'Beuron', *Tableaux de voyage* op. 33 no. 11 (1888), piano

Ives, Charles: *Three-page Sonata* op. 14 (1905), piano

Jelinek, Hanns: Fantasia op. 18 (1951), clarinet, piano, and orchestra

Joachim, Otto: Fantasia (1967), organ; *Tribute to St Romanus* (1980–1), organ, 4 horns, percussion

Johner, Hans-Rudolf: Psalm 116 (1984), solo voice and organ

Jongen, Léon: Largo (1956), violin

Jónsson, Thórarinn: Prelude and Double Fugue (1925), violin

Kadosa, Pál: Three Little Piano Pieces (1961)

Kaegi, Werner: *Miniaturen I–VIII* (1959–61), oboe, bassoon, and harpsichord

Kalabis, Victor: String Quartet no. 4 op. 62 (1984)

Karg-Elert, Sigfrid: 'Basso ostinato' in *Acht Charakterstücke* op. 58 (1918), organ; Chaconne op. 73 (1910), organ, 2 trumpets, 2 trombones, 2 tubas, and percussion; Passacaglia and Fugue in B♭ minor op. 150 (1932), organ; Sonata no. 2 in B♭ minor (1912), harmonium

Karkoschka, Erhard: *Triptychon* (1965–7), organ

Kaufmann, Otto: *Zur stillen Nacht* (1980), 3 voices

Kaun, Hugo: *Eisenach: BACH* op. 30 no. 2 (1904), piano

Keijzer, Arie J.: Fantasia (1982), organ

Keller, Ludwig; *Meditation* op. 14 (1940), piano

Kern, Matthias: *De profundis* (1984), organ; *Metamorphosen* (1967), organ

Kersters, Willem: *Meditation* op. 45 (1967), small trumpet, piano, and strings

Klebe, Giselher: 'Dona nobis pacem' from *Missa 'Miserere nobis'* op. 45 (1964), choir and 18 wind instruments

Klein, Bernhard: Passacaglia and Fugue (1965), organ

Knecht, Justin Heinrich: Fugue in B♭ major, organ

Kochan, Günter: *Das Friedensfest, oder Die Teilhabe* [oratorio]; *Klavierstück für D. Sch.* (1975), piano; Mendelssohn Variations (1971–2), piano and orchestra

Koechlin, Charles: *Offrande musicale* op. 187 (1942–6), orchestra

Köhler, Siegfried: *Der gefesselte Orpheus* (1976), orchestra; *Reich des Menschen* [oratorio] (1962); String Quartet no. 1 (1977)

Kokkonen, Joonas: *Sinfonia da camera* (1962), strings

Kolberg, Kåre: *Tonada* (1978), organ, wind instruments, and percussion

Komma, Karl Michael: Piano Concerto no. 2 (1982)

Konarski, Jan M.: Suite (1965), organ

Krebs, Johann Ludwig: Fugue in B♭ major, organ

Krenek, Ernst: *Parvula corona musicalis ad honorem Johannis Sebastiani Bach* (1950), string trio; String Quartet no. 1 op. 6 (1921)

Krol, Bernhard: *Pas de deux* op. 59 (1970), 2 organs

Kropfreiter, Augustinus Franz: Concertino (1963), flute, piano, and strings

Kucharzyk, Henry: *The Art of Mix* (1970), electronic mix

Kühnl, Claus: *Reflexionen* (1982–3), strings

Kukuck, Felicitas: *Meditationen zu 'O Heiland, reiß die Himmel auf'* (1970)

Kuntz, Michael: Fantasia (*c.*1950), organ

Kuntzen, Johann Christian: 36 Organ Pieces

Kvech, Otomar: *Pocta Bachovi* (1971), orchestra

Lampersberg, Gerhard: *Missa per organo* (1974), organ

Lang, Craig Sellar: Fugue op. 64 no. 21 (1953), piano

Lauermann, Herbert: *Verbum II* (1980), violin

Lawall, Georg: *Jonas, der Prophet* (1985)

Lehmann, Hans Ulrich: *Sonata da chiesa*, violin and organ

Leitermeyer, Fritz: *Mutationen in honorem J. S. Bach* op. 82 (1983), orchestra

Leitner, Ernst Ludwig: *Suite breve* (1977), organ

Lerstad, Terje: Fantasia op. 17 (1983), double bass

Leyendecker, Ulrich: String Quartet in One Movement (1978)

Lindeman, Ludvig Mathias: Three Fugues, organ

Linjama, Jonko: *Organum supra B–A–C–H* (1982), organ; Sonatina op. 3 (1961), organ

Linke, Norbert: *Bach-Fragmente* (1985), organ; *Home Joseba*, trumpet and organ; Hommage à J. S. Bach (1985), organ

Liszt, Franz: Prelude and Fugue (1855), organ [various later versions]

Lohmann, Heinz: *Bach-Variationen* (1983), organ; Fantasia in E♭ major (1984), organ; Partita (1983), flute

Mach, Konstantin: Suite op. 27, organ

Machl, Tadeusz: Fantasia and Double Fugue (1942), organ

Maderna, Bruno: Variations (1949), 2 pianos

Majo, Ernest: *Präludium* (1982), 4 trombones; *Rhapsodische Sequenzen* (1983), wind orchestra

Malipiero, Gian Francesco: *Prélude à une fugue imaginaire* (1932), piano

Maros, Miklós: *HCAB–BACH* (1971), piano

Marsh-Edwards, Michael: *Labyrinth* (1963), flute

Medek, Tilo: *B–A–C–H: vier Töne* (1973), organ; *Der große Marsch* (1974), orchestra; *Todesfuge* (1966), soprano and 16-part choir

Meister, Karl: Canon 'Einen Geistes sammeln sie sich in jenem Namen: BACH', in *Klavierheft für Hermann Maria* op. 61 (1969), piano

Mendelssohn, Alfred: Partita, violin

Merkel, Gustav Adolf: Fugue op. 40 (1867), organ

# BACH

Meyer, Ernst Hermann: *Präludium für D. Sch.* (1975), piano; Suite (1944), 2 trumpets, 2 pianos, and percussion

Meyer-Fiebig, Thomas: Prelude and Fugue (1977), organ

Michael, Frank: *De profundis* op. 46 (1977), choir and orchestra; Serenade op. 47 no. 1 (1978), oboe

Middelschulte, Wilhelm: Canonic Fantasie (1906), organ; *Perpetuum mobile* (1933), organ

Mieg, Peter: *L'Aérienne* (1975), cello; Piano Trio (1984)

Moevs, Robert Walter: Prelude, *'B–A–C–H'—Es ist genug* (1970), organ

Moldovan, Mihai: Three Studies (1966), woodwind

Molino, Pippo: *Jeu* (1984), oboe

Moroi, Makato: Fantasia and Fugue (1978), organ

Moser, Toland: *Stilleben mit Glas* (1969–70), tape and electronic sounds

Moulaert, Raymond: *Passacaille* (1932), soprano

Mozetich, Marjan: Capriccio (1984), viola

Muldowney, Dominic: Trombone Concerto (1996)

Naprstek, Gerhard: Fantasia and Fugue (1965), organ

Nathow, Dieter: Variations on B–A–C–H, in *Divertimento über B–A–C–H* [collaborative composition] (1984), orchestra

Nieland, Jan: Fantasia and Fugue (*c.*1943), organ

Nielsen, Riccardo: Ricercar, Chorale and Toccata, piano

Nowak, Hans Peter: *BACH* (1978), voice and piano

Nowka, Dieter: Passacaglia and Fugue, in *Hommages*, piano

Ohse, Reinhard: Concerto (1975), organ, strings, and chorus

Orlinski, Heinz Bernhard: *Fantasia meditativa* (1972), organ

Pachaly, Traugott Immanuel: Fugue (*c.*1848), organ

Pander, Oscar von: Suite, piano duet

Pâque, Désirée: *Fuguette* (1913), organ

Pärt, Arvo: *Collage B–A–C–H* (1964), oboe, harpsichord, piano, and strings; *Wenn Bach Bienen gezüchtet hätte* (1984), harpsichord, electric guitar, prepared tape and instrumental ensemble [also other versions]

Penderecki, Krzysztof: *Passio et mors Domini nostri Jesu Christi secundum Lucam* (1963–5), narrator, solo voices, boys' choir, mixed choir, and orchestra

Pepping, Ernst: Three Fugues (1943), piano

Petzold, Frank: *BACH-Metamorphosen* and Toccata, in *Divertimento über B–A–C–H* [collaborative composition] (1984), orchestra

Pezold, Christian: *Fuga sub diatessaron*, organ

Pfundt, Reinhard: *Inventiones über B–A–C–H* (1985), string quartet

Pikethy, Tibor: Fantasia op. 28 (1949), organ

Piston, Walter: Chromatic Study (1940), organ

Piutti, Carl: *Fest-Hymnus* op. 20 (1890), organ

Plate, Hans Wilhelm: *Fuß-Noten zu B–A–C–H* (1977), 3 flutes, string trio, and harpsichord

Pogojeff, W.: Fugue op. 2 no. 2 (1902), piano

Porfetye, Andreas: Fantasia (1968), organ

Poulenc, Francis: *Valse improvisation* (1932), piano

Radauer, Irmfried: *Perspektivem auf B–A–C–H*, 19 instruments

Raito, Peutti: *Due figure* (1985), orchestra

Ramovš, Primož: *Utrinki ob Bachovem imenu* (1965), piano

Reda, Siegfried: *Laudamus te* (1962), organ

Reger, Max: Fantasia and Fugue op. 46 (1900), organ

Reiche, Johannes: *Sonata per due* (1985), bass clarinet and percussion

Reiner, Karel: *Dialogy* (1978), 2 flutes

Reinhard, August: Fantasia op. 78 (1904), piano duet

Renner, Willy: Six Preludes op. 6 (1914), piano

Rettich, Wilhelm: Trumpet Concerto op. 122 (1970)

Rheinberger, Joseph: Fugue in C major op. 123 no. 3 (1883), organ

Riegel, Friedrich: Six Fugues op. 24 (1890), organ

Rilling, Helmuth: 'Aber wenn der Rilling . . .' in F major (1983)

Rimsky-Korsakov, Nikolay: Double Fugue in G minor (1875), piano; Fugue in E minor op. 17 no. 6 (1875), piano; Six Variations op. 10 (1878), piano

Rinck, Christian Heinrich: Prelude and Fugue (1818), organ

Rössler, Franz Georg: 'Hommage à Béla Bartók' and 'Ritual über zwei Gräben' from *Eisblumen* (1984), recorder and piano; Invention no. 4 (1981), piano

Roland, Claude-Robert: Prelude and Fugue (*In memoriam II*) op. 20 (1984), organ

Rosenfeld, Gerhard: Concerto (1967), cello and orchestra

Rota, Nino: Variations and Fugue (1950), piano

Roussel, Albert: Prelude and Fugue (*Hommage à Bach*) op. 46 (1932–4), piano

Roy, Léo: Fugue, organ

Sarin, Marger Ottowitsch: Variations (?1950), organ

Sawa, Marian: Fantasia (1971), organ

Schellenberg, Hermann: Fantasia (*c.*1850), organ

Schenker, Friedrich: Sonata (1973), wind instruments and percussion; *Sonate für Johann Sebastian Bach* (1977), orchestra

Schilling, Hans Ludwig: *Interludium I* (1978), organ; Partita (1954–64), organ

Schloemann, Burghard: Variations (1981), organ

Schmidt-Walter, Herbert: Divertimento (1969), piano duet

Schnittke, Alfred: Piano Quintet (1972–6); *Preludio in memoriam D. Schostakowitsch* (1975), violin and tape; Violin Sonata no. 2 (1968)

Schoenberg, Arnold: Suite op. 25 (1921–3), piano; Variations for Orchestra op. 31 (1926–8)

Schollum, Robert: *Toccata in Betrachtung des Kreuzwges* op. 96 (1975), organ

Schulze, Manfred: *Improvisation über B–A–C–H* (1983), jazz group

Schumann, Camillo: Organ Sonata no. 2 op. 16

Schumann, Georg: Passacaglia and Finale op. 39 (1905), organ

Schumann, Robert: 6 Fugues op. 60 (1845), organ/pedal piano

Schwaen, Kurt: 'Auf der Straße' from *Ausflug der Kinder*, piano; 'Blut ist durch die Straßen

regenschwer geflossen' from *In den stolzen Städten*;
*Der neue Kolumbus* (1961); Study (1972), piano
Searle, Humphrey: Symphony no. 1 op. 23 (1953)
Seckinger, Konrad: *Votiftafeln* (1985)
Sekles, Bernhard: Passacaglia and Fugue op. 23 (1914),
string quartet
Sermilä, Jarmo: *Cornologia* (1976), 24–44 horns
Sigmund, Oskar: *Contrapuncti organales* (1972),
organ; *In memoriam Joannis Kepleri* (1974), organ;
Passacaglia and Fugue in memoriam J. S. B. (1958),
piano; String Quartet (1975–6); Suite (1975), guitar
Simek, Otto: Ricercar (1972), organ
Smith Brindle, Reginald: Variants (1970), guitar
Sokola, Miloš: *Passacaglia quasi Toccata* (1966), organ;
3 Studies (1972), organ
Soproni, József: Inventions (1970–1), piano
Sorge, Georg Andreas: 2 Fugues BWV Anh. II 107 and
110, organ
Spilling, Willy: *Musik über B–A–C–H* op. 37 (1957–8),
orchestra
Springer, Max: 6 Fughettas op. 14, organ
Stearns, Peter Pindar: Adagio—B–A–C–H (1968),
organ
Steif, Gerhard: *B–A–C–H Zitate* (1985), flute, clarinet,
violin, piano, 2 church bells, and tape
Steinhäuser, Carl: Fugue op. 53 (1895), organ
Stendel, Wolfgang: Variation (1984), in *Divertimento
über B–A–C–H* [collaborative composition] (1984),
orchestra
Sterl, Raimund W.: Arioso (1983), harpsichord;
*Praeambulum, Choral und Ostinato* (1982),
keyboard ad lib; 3 B–A–C–H Studies (1982–3),
organ; Toccata (1985), harpsichord/piano/organ
Stoffers, Erich: *Evolution des B–A–C–H* (1985), organ;
Fantasia (1961), organ; 3 Fugues (1983), organ;
Prelude and Double Fugue op. 149 (1984), organ;
*Triptychon* op. 150 (1985), organ
Stojantschev, Stojan: Bach Variations, in *Divertimento
über B–A–C–H* [collaborative composition] (1984),
orchestra
Stoll, Stephan Michael: Organ Sonata (1984)
Storp, Sigmund Hans: 8 Two-part Inventions (1960),
piano
Stranz, Ulrich: *Contrasubjekte* (1981), 14 string
instruments
Suchon, Eugen: Symphonic Fantasia (1971), organ,
strings, and percussion
Sulze, B.: Prelude and Fugue, organ
Suthoff-Gross, Rudolf: Partita in E major (1965)
orchestra
Szalonek, Witold: *Little B–A–C–H Symphony* (1979),
flute, clarinet, violin, viola, cello, double bass,
piano, and percussion [arranged for orchestra,
1981]
Szathmáry Zsigmond: *Dialog* (1971), organ
Terényi, Eduard: Partita (1967), organ
Thieme, Karl: *Varianti B–A–C–H*, orchestra
Thoma, Xaver: Cantata op. 7 (1974) alto, choir,
strings, timpani, and organ
Tietchens, Asmus: *Studie über B–A–C–H* (1983),
synthesizer

Tremain, Roland: Nine Studies (1965), violin and
viola
Tucapský, Antonín: Sonata (1985), violin
Ulmann, Helmut von: Concerto grosso (1946–7),
chamber orchestra
Varvoglis, Mario: Canon, Chorale and Fugue (1930),
string orchestra
Viitala, Mauri: *Hommage à J. S. Bach* (1976), organ;
Passacaglia (1979–82), organ
Villinger, Alexander: Kyrie and Gloria (1985), soloists,
choir, and orchestra
Voss, Friedrich: *Hommage à J. S. Bach* (1984),
4 saxophones; *Sinfonia humana* (1966–7), orchestra
Wallenstein, René: *Toccata in meditatione* (1980),
organ
Walter, Ludwig: *4 Kanons mit B–A–C–H* (1985),
3 instruments
Weber, Reinhold: Fantasia and Fugue (1981), organ
Webern, Anton: String Quartet op. 28 (1936–8)
Wehrli, Werner: Introduction, Passacaglia and Fugue
op. 41 (1935), organ
Weiand, Werner: *Monstranz* (1979), soprano/choir
and orchestra
Weinstangel, Sasha Alexander: Variations (1968),
soprano, 2 flutes, string quartet, timpani, and
vibraphone
Weiss, Manfred: Concerto (1976), organ, string
orchestra, and percussion
Wellesz, Egon: Partita op. 96 (1965), organ
Wiemer, Wolfgang: *Anläufe* (1972), organ; *Kreuzweg*
(1973–4), organ and slide projector
Wiley, Frank: Fantasia (1983), organ
Wünsch, Gerhard: *Spectrum* (1969), piano
Zbinden, Julien-François: *Hommage à J. S. Bach*
op. 44 (1969), double bass
Zechlin, Ruth: *Hommage à Bach* (1985), choir; *Musik
zu Bach* (1985), orchestra; Organ Concerto no. 1
(1974–5)
Zehm, Friedrich: Toccata (1968), organ
Zerbe, Johannes: Variations (1983)
Zuckmayer, Eduard: B–A–C–H Canon in three parts
(1950)

W. Häcker, 'Erberezeption im Sozialismus: das Ton-
symbol B–A–C–H im Musikschaffen der DDR',
*Beiträge zur Musikwissenschaft*, 31 (1989), 266–78;
S. W. Robinson, 'The B–A–C–H Motive in German
Keyboard Compositions from the Time of J. S. Bach
to the Present' (thesis, University of Illinois at
Urbana-Champaign, 1972); U. Prinz, J. Dorfmüller,
and K. Küster, 'Die Tonfolge B–A–C–H in Kompositionen des 17. bis 20. Jahrhunderts: ein Verzeichnis',
in *300 Jahre Johann Sebastian Bach* (Tutzing, 1985)
[exhibition catalogue], 389–419.

**Bach.** A journal issued bi-annually by the RIE-
MENSCHNEIDER BACH INSTITUTE.

**Bach-Archiv Leipzig.** A research centre for
Bach studies in LEIPZIG.

**Bach Before the Mast.** A keyboard piece by the
harpsichordist and conductor George Malcolm

(1917–97), published in 1954. It treats the well-known *Sailors' Hornpipe* in a Bachian manner.

**Bachbewegung** ('Bach movement'). A term sometimes used for the Bach revival of the 19th–20th centuries. *See* RECEPTION AND REVIVAL.

**Bach bow.** A violin bow with a highly arched stick, designed to enable the player to sound all four strings together and thus to negotiate the multiple stops in such works as Bach's Sonatas and Partitas for unaccompanied violin. One such bow was designed by Rolph Schröder about 1930, and this influenced the Hungarian violinist Emil Telmányi to commission others, notably the 'Vega' bow by the Danish maker Knud Vestergaard. This was fitted with a mechanism allowing immediate tightening or loosening of the hairs. None of these so-called Bach bows had any historical validity, or anything to do with Bach.

D. D. Boyden, *The History of Violin Playing from its Origins to 1761* (London, 1965), 431–5.

**Bach Cantata Club.** An association founded in London in 1926 to promote 'authentic' performances of Bach's choral works. It was supported by C. S. Terry, Albert Schweitzer, W. G. Whittaker, and other Bach enthusiasts, but its activities languished with the outbreak of World War II.

**Bach Choir.** A title adopted by many choral societies (usually preceded by the name of the town in which they are situated: e.g. Swansea Bach Choir) which specialize in the music of J. S. Bach. The best known is that founded in 1875 in London by Arthur Coleridge (1830–1913) and first conducted by Otto Goldschmidt (1829–1907). Later conductors have included C. V. Stanford (from 1885 to 1902), Walford Davies (1902–7), Vaughan Williams (1920–6), Adrian Boult (1926–32), and David Willcocks (1960–98).

**Bach Compendium** (*BC*). A multi-volume reference work edited by Hans-Joachim Schulze and Christoph Wolff. Publication began in 1985, and by 1989 the four volumes of Part 1, covering the vocal music, had appeared. The *BC* is designed to provide comprehensive source-critical and bibliographical information on Bach's entire output, including sketches, drafts, lost works, and compositions of doubtful and spurious authenticity, as well as works from Bach's music library written by other composers. Arranged by genre, each entry in the *BC* concerns a single work, or version of a work, and differs from those of *Schmieder2* in that authorship, dating, revision, and the like are all determined on the basis of particular sources and documents that are directly cited. The selected bibliographical references, mostly from after 1950, direct the reader to the general literature and to further discussions of all aspects of the work. Musical incipits represent each movement's important structural points. Cross-references direct the reader to other arrangements and to parodies, and a concordance of *BC* and BWV numbers is provided.                    RLS

**Bachfest** ('Bach festival'). A term which might be used for any festival featuring Bach's music, but which is associated particularly with the festivals promoted by the Neue Bach-Gesellschaft since its foundation in 1900. As well as performances of music by Bach and associated composers, the festivals usually include a musicological conference. The festivals were held at first triennially, then biennially, and since 1920 annually (with interruptions to the series during the two World Wars). The locations have been:

| | | | |
|---|---|---|---|
| 1901 | Berlin | 1964 | Weimar |
| 1904 | Leipzig | 1965 | Hamburg |
| 1907 | Eisenach | 1966 | Leipzig |
| 1908 | Chemnitz | 1967 | Wuppertal |
| 1910 | Duisburg | 1968 | Dresden |
| 1912 | Breslau | 1969 | Heidelberg |
| | (now Wrocław, | 1970 | Leipzig |
| | Poland) | 1971 | Bremen |
| 1914 | Vienna | 1972 | Leipzig |
| 1920 | Leipzig | 1973 | Nuremberg |
| 1921 | Hamburg | 1974 | Frankfurt an der |
| 1922 | Breslau | | Oder |
| 1923 | Leipzig | 1975 | Leipzig |
| 1924 | Stuttgart | 1976 | West Berlin |
| 1925 | Essen | 1977 | Schwerin |
| 1926 | Berlin | 1978 | Marburg |
| 1927 | Munich | 1979 | Bratislava |
| 1928 | Kassel | 1980 | Mainz |
| 1929 | Leipzig | 1981 | Leipzig |
| 1930 | Kiel | 1982 | Würzburg |
| 1932 | Heidelberg | 1983 | Graz |
| 1933 | Cologne | 1984 | Kassel |
| 1934 | Bremen | 1985 | Leipzig |
| 1935 | Leipzig | 1986 | Duisburg |
| 1936 | Königsberg | 1987 | Prague |
| 1937 | Magdeburg | 1988 | Strasburg |
| 1938 | Leipzig | 1989 | Leipzig |
| 1939 | Bremen | 1990 | Munich |
| 1950 | Leipzig | 1991 | Berlin |
| 1951 | Bremen | 1992 | Brunswick |
| 1952 | Lübeck | 1993 | Bremen |
| 1953 | Leipzig | 1994 | Leipzig |
| 1954 | Ansbach | 1995 | Rostock |
| 1955 | Leipzig | 1996 | Freiburg |
| 1956 | Lüneburg | 1997 | Frankfurt |
| 1957 | Eisenach | 1998 | Köthen |
| 1958 | Stuttgart | 1999 | Cologne |
| 1959 | Mühlhausen | 2000 | Leipzig |
| 1961 | Essen | 2001 | Eisenach |
| 1962 | Leipzig | 2002 | Mannheim |

**Bach-Gesellschaft** (Bach Society). A society founded in Leipzig in 1850 with the primary intention of producing a collected edition of

Bach's works. It grew out of the Bach revival of the early decades of the 19th century that increasingly focused on the composer's great vocal works. These had previously been largely neglected, but several attempts were now made by individuals or publishers to initiate editions of the complete works or of particular groups of works. During the second half of the 18th century Bach's works had been transmitted mainly in manuscript copies, but in the early 19th century, after the dispersion of several great manuscript collections, the need arose to secure his music—now valued as a national heritage—once and for all in reliable editions.

The first mention of a projected society to promote a complete edition of Bach's compositions is found in a letter of J. N. Schelble to Franz Hauser, dating from the early 1830s; many of Schelble's ideas were later incorporated into the by-laws of the society. Other important figures who helped to pave the way for the Bach-Gesellschaft and a complete edition were Moritz Hauptmann, Felix Mendelssohn, and Robert Schumann. An event of particular importance was the foundation in 1843 of the Handel Society in London, with which Mendelssohn was in close contact. The central instigator, however, was the historian and Mozart biographer Otto Jahn (1813–69), who in July 1850, on the occasion of the centenary of Bach's death, published an *Aufforderung zur Stiftung einer Bach-Gesellschaft* ('A Call for the Founding of a Bach Society'; see Kretzschmar, pp. xvi–xvii). Like the London Handel Society, the Bach-Gesellschaft formed a so-called Subskribentenverein ('Association of Subscribers'), which financed the edition solely by the dues of its members (5 Reichstaler annually); the edition was produced by the Leipzig firm of Breitkopf & Härtel. In the early stages of the society Jahn's closest supporters were Carl Ferdinand Becker (1804–77), Siegfried Wilhelm Dehn (1799–1858), Franz Hauser, and Carl von Winterfeld (1784–1852).

According to the society's by-laws (published in Kretzschmar, pp. xviii–xx), the 24 constituting members who had signed the *Aufforderung* in July 1850 voted from among themselves a board of directors, consisting of five persons living in Leipzig, while the others formed a council to the society; the first board consisted of Becker, Hauptmann, Jahn, Ignaz Moscheles (1794–1870), and the firm of Breitkopf & Härtel. The board of directors and council met annually, usually in November or December; their first meeting took place on 15 December 1850, and this date legally marks the society's beginning. The annual meetings were held at the Kleiner Saal of the old Gewandhaus.

Probably the most crucial prerequisite for the planning of the edition, though never published, was Hauser's thematic catalogue of Bach's works, compiled over several decades on the basis of his own and other private manuscript collections, as well as of Bach sources in public institutions. The sequence in which the works appeared was determined mainly by practical considerations, such as the availability of original sources and an attempted regular alternation of vocal and instrumental works.

During the first phase of the edition (up to 1860), its most active editors were Hauptmann and Julius Rietz (1812–77); among the works that appeared in the society's first decade are 40 cantatas, the *Christmas Oratorio*, the B minor Mass, and the *St Matthew Passion*. The second phase of the edition is characterized by the work of Wilhelm Rust, who alone prepared as many as 19 of its total of 45 volumes. In the first years of his editorship Rust set a new standard in the overall quality and scope of critical editing, and much of the high esteem the Bach edition has achieved since then can be credited to his work. In later years, however, because of numerous conflicts with the society's board of directors, Rust's enthusiasm waned and several of his later volumes were harshly criticized, particularly by Philipp Spitta; this ultimately led to his resigning from the editorship in 1882. During the last phase of the edition the remaining volumes were distributed mainly between Alfred Dörffel, Ernst Naumann, Paul Graf Waldersee (1831–1906), and Franz Wüllner (1832–1902). The edition was completed in December 1897 when the 45th volume was presented to the society's board of directors, and in 1899 Hermann Kretzschmar (1848–1924) published an extended report of the society's work during the previous 50 years. Since its primary function—the complete edition of Bach's works—had been fulfilled, the society was dissolved, but immediately a NEUE BACH-GESELL-SCHAFT was founded, which aimed at disseminating Bach's music among a wider public.                                                          PW

H. Kretzschmar, *Die Bach-Gesellschaft in Leipzig: Bericht bei Beendigung der Gesammtausgabe von Joh. Seb. Bachs Werken* (Leipzig, 1899).

**Bach goblet** (*Bach-Pokal*). A glass drinking-vessel, possibly made in Dresden about 1735–6, which was presented to Bach by an unknown friend, colleague, or admirer. It is engraved with Bach's monogram and with three musical 'puzzles', each using four different notes of the chromatic scale. The first four notes spell out Bach's name (*see* BACH); the significance of the others is not known. The goblet is in the Bach museum in Eisenach.

***Bach Goes to Town.*** A piece by the Welsh-born American composer Alec Templeton (1910–63) which exists in several versions and many arrangements. It takes the form of a witty fugue, and is the best-known of a series of pieces by Templeton which parody older composers' styles in a modern, jazzy idiom.

**Bachianas brasileiras.** A series of nine pieces, or sets of pieces, for various combinations of voices and instruments which Heitor Villa-Lobos (1887–1959) composed between 1930 and 1945. In them he sought to explore affinities which he found between Bach's works and the folk music of his native Brazil.

**Bach-Institut, Göttingen.** *See* JOHANN-SEBAS-TIAN-BACH-INSTITUT.

**Bach-Jahrbuch.** A year-book published by the NEUE BACH-GESELLSCHAFT and distributed to its members. It is one of the main regular forums for the dissemination and exchange of information and views on everything to do with Bach and the Bach family. It was founded in 1904 and first edited by Arnold Schering.

**Bach Perspectives.** A volume of essays on topics to do with Bach, issued annually by the AMERICAN BACH SOCIETY.

**Bach-Pokal.** *See* BACH GOBLET.

**Bach Revival.** *See* RECEPTION AND REVIVAL.

**Bach trumpet.** A modern trumpet in A, designed to facilitate the playing of Bach's high, 'clarino' trumpet parts; it was made for the Berlin trumpeter Julius Kosleck, and first used by him in 1884. The name was later used for a smaller D trumpet, but neither instrument had any basis in the instruments of Bach's own time.

E. H. Tarr, 'The Baroque Trumpet, the High Trumpet and the So-called Bach Trumpet', *Brass Bulletin* (1972), nos. 2–3.

**badinerie** ('jesting'). The designation of the final movement of Bach's Orchestral Suite no. 2 in B minor. The word is spelt 'battinerie' in the partly autograph parts that comprise the principal source for the work. The movement is a light binary-form piece in a swift 2/4 metre beginning on the upbeat, much in the manner of a fast gavotte. Badineries also appear in French *ouvertures* by Graupner and Telemann, again in fast tempos and in 2/4 or *alla breve* metre. The presence of an upbeat is not a consistent feature; examples by Telemann include the upbeat (including one example which is essentially a gavotte), while Graupner's do not. It is unlikely, however, that Bach was familiar with these examples.

While the designation 'badinerie' is not common, its Italian counterpart 'scherzo' appears with greater frequency. Bach himself provided an example in the sixth movement of the keyboard

Partita in A minor; like the Badinerie in the B minor Orchestral Suite, this is a light binary movement in 2/4 beginning on the upbeat. That the two movements are so similar in character suggests that Bach considered 'badinerie' and 'scherzo' to be equivalent.                    JS

C. Großpietsch, *Graupners Ouverturen und Tafelmusiken: Studien zur Darmstädter Hofmusik und thematischer Katalog* (Mainz, 1994); A. Hoffmann, *Die Orchestersuiten Georg Philipp Telemanns* TWV55, *mit thematisch-bibliographischem Werkverzeichnis* (Wolfenbüttel, 1969); J. Rifkin, 'The "B minor Flute Suite" Deconstructed: Johann Sebastian Bach, Johann Bernhard Bach, and the Ouverture BWV 1067', in *Bach Perspectives* (forthcoming).

**Baldwin-Wallace College Bach Festival.** An annual festival founded in 1933 by the Bach scholar Albert Riemenschneider and directed by him at the Baldwin-Wallace College, Berea, Ohio. The festival has been particularly active in promoting performances of Bach's major choral works.

**Bammler, Johann Nathanael** (bap. 11 Jan. 1722; d. 8 May 1784). Singer, instrumentalist, and teacher, born in Kirchberg, Saxony. In 1737 he entered the Thomasschule in Leipzig, where he remained for about ten years, becoming prefect of the second choir and, in his last year, of the first choir. In this capacity he deputized for Bach during the latter's absences from Leipzig, and he also acted as one of his copyists; Peter Wollny identified him as the copyist previously known as 'Hauptkopist H'. On 10 May 1748 Bammler enrolled at Leipzig University as a theology student. In 1749 Bach wrote one testimonial and dictated and signed another for him in connection with his application for the post of deputy Rector at the school in Eilenburg. In this he was unsuccessful, and in 1750 he returned to his native town. He succeeded finally in securing a post as Kantor in Elsterberg (Vogtland), where he remained for the rest of his life.

P. Wollny, 'Neue Bach-Funde', *BJb* 83 (1997), 7–50, esp. 36–50.

**Barform.** A term used for a three-part musical structure (A–A–B) consisting of a repeated first section (repeated to different words in the case of a vocal piece) and a final (usually longer) section. The first (A) sections are known as *Stollen*, the final (B) section as the *Abgesang*—terms used by the medieval German Meistersinger, in whose songs *Barform* occupied a central place. In the context of Bach's music *Barform* is to be observed mainly in the CHORALE, and therefore in pieces based on chorales, such as the large-scale choruses that open most of the chorale cantatas of his second Leipzig *Jahrgang*. In these Bach often makes substantial changes to the music of the second *Stollen*, while still retaining the basic *Barform* of the chorale melody itself.

### Barmherziges Herze der ewigen Liebe ('Merciful heart of eternal love').

Cantata for the fourth Sunday after Trinity, BWV185, first performed at Weimar on 14 July 1715, repeated the following year on 5 July, and revised for a Leipzig performance on 20 June 1723. The text, by Salomo Franck, stems from the Gospel for the day, St Luke 6: 36–42, with its admonition, 'Judge not, and ye shall not be judged' (v. 37), and its advice to the hypocrite, 'Cast out first the beam out of thine own eye, and then shalt thou see clearly to pull out the mote that is in thy brother's eye' (v. 42). These verses are paraphrased in the cantata's two recitatives, the first (no. 2) for alto with string accompaniment, the second (no. 4) for bass with continuo support.

The theme of compassion informs the other movements as well. The opening duet for soprano and tenor, above a running bass almost entirely in quavers, is punctuated by successive lines of the chorale melody *Ich ruf zu dir, Herr Jesu Christ* played by the oboe (trumpet in the Leipzig recension). Like most of the other Weimar cantatas, this one is on a modest, intimate scale, and the entire instrumental forces—oboe obbligato, strings, and continuo (with bassoon)—are not heard until the third movement, an appealing Adagio aria for alto with melismatic highlighting of the text at 'reichlich auszustreuen' ('sow in abundance'), 'Ewigkeit' ('eternity'), and 'erfreuen' ('rejoice'). The other aria, for bass (no. 5), is again accompanied only by continuo. The opening words, 'Das ist der Christen Kunst!', are repeated in Franck's text only once, at the end, but Bach chooses to make them, and the simple but memorable musical phrase to which they are first sung, a recurring motif throughout the aria, thereby emphasizing that compassion is 'the Christian way'.

The chorale melody heard in the opening duet returns to end the work, set in four-part harmony to the first strophe of Johann Agricola's hymn (1529), with the violin adding a decorative 'descant'.

K. Hoffman, 'Neue Überlegungen zu Bachs Weimarer Kantaten-Kalender', *BJb* 79 (1993), 9–29. For further bibliography, *see* CANTATA, §1.

### Barth, Christian Samuel (b. 11 Jan. 1735; d. 8 July 1809).

Oboist, born in Glauchau, Saxony. He attended the Thomasschule in Leipzig (*c.*1748–50), where he was taught by Bach, and was later active as an orchestral player and soloist at Rudolstadt, Weimar, Hanover, Kassel, and Copenhagen. His two sons, Philip (1774–1804) and Christian Frederik (1787–1861), were oboists.

### Bassani, Giovanni Battista (b. *c.*1657; d. 1 Oct 1716).

Italian composer of operas, oratorios, church music, and secular cantatas. He worked mainly at Ferrara, but in 1712 moved to Bergamo, where he died. About 1736–40 Bach called upon an anonymous scribe (perhaps his son Gottfried Heinrich, 1724–63) to copy the entire contents of Bassani's *Acroama missale* (Augsburg, 1709), which consisted of six masses, each with Kyrie, Gloria, Credo, and Sanctus. Later, in 1747–8, Bach himself composed *ex novo* the intonation ('Credo in unum Deum') for the fifth of these. This brief composition (16 bars in length) in F major for four voices, instruments, and continuo (BWV1081) follows the style of the collection and introduces the same plainchant intonation that Bach used in the Symbolum Nicenum of his Mass in B minor.

AB

C. Wolff, *Der stile antico in der Musik Johann Sebastian Bachs* (Wiesbaden, 1968).

### basso continuo. *See* CONTINUO.

### bassoon.

A double-reed woodwind instrument; the lowest of the woodwinds in Bach's normal instrumentarium. The terms 'Fagotto' and 'Bassono' both occur in Bach's scores. The former, found in some of the Weimar cantatas, clearly refers to the *Chorist-fagott*, the old dulcian, built essentially in a single piece and notated in CHORTON with the range C to *f'*. 'Bassono' designates the French bassoon, notated in CAMMERTON, with a fully chromatic range from *B♭'* to *a'*. Two four-jointed bassoons by J. H. Eichentopf of Leipzig survive, one in the Oberösterreichisches Landesmuseum, Linz, the other in the Germanisches Nationalmuseum, Nuremberg.

Bassoon parts survive for more than 50 works by Bach, and it can be assumed that the instrument was called for in further works. It was employed not only as reinforcement for the continuo but also independently, for example to serve as the bass of an oboe choir, to provide figural elaboration and rhythmic enhancement in the continuo, or to play obbligato parts in arias; 'Quoniam tu solus sanctus' in the B minor Mass even has parts for a pair of bassoons. The plural form 'Bassoni' is also found in Cantatas 69, 75, 97, 119, and 194, as well as in the *Magnificat*, the *St John Passion*, and the *Christmas Oratorio*, indicating a special weighting of the continuo with double-reed winds. 'If oboes, then also bassoon' is a practice regularly observed, but surviving Bach sources do not confirm it as a general rule. There are works with bassoon but without oboes, and there are a number of cantatas using oboes in which the bassoon, but not the oboes, is specified in certain movements.

# Bauernkantate

The specification 'Bassono grosso' appears only once in Bach's works, on a continuo part of the *St John Passion* with late autograph annotations, and it recalls a similar compound term, 'Violone grosso', used for some other 16′ parts (for example in the First Brandenburg Concerto). The unusually large size that this term obviously denotes might be associated with the double bassoon made by Andreas Eichentopf (*c*.1670–1721) in 1714. UP

K. Brandt, 'Fragen zur Fagottbesetzung in den Kirchenmusikalischen Werken Johann Sebastian Bachs', *BJb* 54 (1968), 65–79; L. G. Langwill, *The Bassoon and Contrabassoon* (London, 1965; 3rd edn., 1975); U. Prinz, 'Zur Bezeichnung "Bassono" und "Fagotto" bei J. S. Bach', *BJb* 67 (1981), 107–22; U. Prinz, ed., *300 Jahre Johann Sebastian Bach: sein Werk in Handschriften und Dokumenten; Musikinstrumente seiner Zeit; seine Zeitgenossen* [exhibition catalogue] (Tutzing, 1985), 317–22.

**Bauernkantate.** See PEASANT CANTATA.

**Baumgarten, Johann Christoph** (bap. 30 Aug. 1687; d. 27 May 1772). Organist, born in Wölfis, near Ohrdruf in Thuringia. He attended the lyceum in Ohrdruf from 1697 to 1703 (Bach was also there during part of that time) and studied music with Johann Christoph Bach (ii) and, possibly in 1708, with J. S. Bach at Weimar. In 1721 he was appointed organist at Schkölen, near Eisenberg, about 40 km. (25 miles) east of Weimar, and in 1727 at Eisenberg itself.

A. Basso, *Frau Musika: la vita e le opere di J. S. Bach*, i (Turin, 1979).

**BC.** Abbreviation for BACH COMPENDIUM.

**Becker, Johann** (b. 1 Sept. 1726; d. 1803). Organist, teacher, and composer, born in Helsa-Wickenrode, near Kassel. He studied with Bach in Leipzig (*c*.1745–8) and taught in Hartmuthsachsen, Bettenhausen, and Kassel, where in 1761 he was appointed municipal organist and in 1770 court organist. He composed mainly church music.

A. Basso, *Frau Musika: la vita e le opere di J. S. Bach*, i (Turin, 1979).

**Benda, Franz** (bap. 22 Nov. 1709; d. 7 March 1786). Bohemian composer, born in Staré Benátky; he was a member of a large family of musicians. He was employed as a violinist in Warsaw between 1729 and 1733, and then entered the service of the future King Frederick the Great, remaining in his employ for the rest of his life (from 1771 as *Konzertmeister*). He was therefore for a time a colleague of Carl Philipp Emanuel Bach. His compositions are almost entirely instrumental, including symphonies, chamber music, and didactic works for his own instrument, the violin.

Benda became acquainted with J. S. Bach at Dresden, and was among those who credited him with the invention of the VIOLA POMPOSA.

**Bennett, William Sterndale** (b. 13 April 1816; d. 1 Feb. 1875). Composer, conductor, and editor, born in Sheffield. He was a child prodigy. He was admitted to the Royal Academy of Music in London to study piano and composition at the age of 10, and at 16 composed a piano concerto which excited Schumann and Mendelssohn during his visits to Leipzig from 1836. He had been taught by the Bach admirer William Crotch (1775–1847), and this, together with Mendelssohn's encouragement, moved him to found the English Bach Society in October 1849. Its aims were modelled on those of the Handel Society founded in 1843, of which Bennett had been a committee member. One result of the society's activities was the first English performance of the *St Matthew Passion*, which Bennett conducted on 6 April 1854; he later published his edition of the work.

Bennett also advocated the study of Bach's music by pianists, and in 1852 initiated an edition of *The Well-tempered Clavier* which, however, was abandoned after his death when 40 of the 48 preludes and fugues had appeared. His piano manual *Classical Practice* (London, 1839) included the complete English Suite in A minor, and he was jointly responsible with Otto Goldschmidt (1829–1907) for *The Chorale Book for England* (1862–4). SFD

***Bereitet die Wege, bereitet die Bahn*** ('Prepare the way, prepare the course'). Cantata, BWV132, for the fourth Sunday of Advent, first performed on 22 December 1715. The text, from Salomo Franck's *Evangelisches Andachts-Opffer* (Weimar, 1715), dwells on Advent themes, the opening aria being built round Isaiah 40: 3 ('The voice of him that crieth in the wilderness, Prepare ye the way of the Lord, make straight in the desert a highway for our God') and the central aria (movement 3) paraphrasing the words of the Jews to John the Baptist 'Who art thou?' (John 1: 19). Franck's text includes a final chorale strophe, 'Ertöt uns durch dein Güte', from Elisabeth Kreuziger's hymn *Herr Christ, der einig Gotts Sohn* (1524), but there is no setting of this in BWV132, at least in the form in which it survives today. Alfred Dürr persuasively suggests (in *DürrK*) that a chorale harmonization was entered on a loose sheet of paper after the third gathering (which was full) and has since dropped out of the score and been lost. There is a parallel with Cantata 163 (*Nur jedem das Seine*), composed a few weeks earlier, in which a similar loss seems to have taken place. The only other cantata for the fourth Sunday of Advent to have survived is no. 147, *Herz und Mund und Tat und Leben*.

BWV132 is scored for SATB, oboe, strings, and continuo (including bassoon). In its present form it consists of three arias flanking two simple recitatives, with all four voices assuming a solo role. The opening da capo aria is in a lilting 6/8 metre with a rhythm suggesting the influence of the LOURE. Most of the material is based on the opening figure, which lends itself easily to dialoguing and overlapping effects. The prominent solo oboe (the compass of the part shows that an oboe d'amore is required) is heard in dialogue with the soprano voice, exchanging figures based on the melismatic word-painting for 'Bahn', which wanders about its winding way in semiquavers. The words 'Messias kommt an!' ('the Messiah is coming!') are proclaimed unaccompanied, throwing them into relief and forming a climax to the aria's middle section.

The following tenor recitative, 'Willst du dich Gottes Kind und Christi Bruder nennen', is interspersed with arioso sections, with vividly descriptive word-painting to reflect the phrase 'Wälz' ab die schweren Sündensteine' ('Roll away the heavy stones of sin'). There follows a bass aria, 'Wer bist du?', the text of which takes as its point of departure the questions addressed by the Jews to John the Baptist (John 1: 19 ff.). The pervasive bass figure in the accompaniment (for continuo only) is related to the main motif of the voice part. Its Buxtehudian character gives the whole movement an old-fashioned air, the cello working out the figure constantly against the background of simplified writing for the other continuo instruments. Also noteworthy are the spectacular chromatic melismata for 'ein falscher heuchlerischer Christ' ('a false, hypocritical Christian'). The following accompanied recitative leads to a third aria, 'Christi Glieder, ach, bedenket', for alto. Exhorting the Christian to meditate on the baptism of Christ, it is in ritornello form with an elaborate violin obbligato. As mentioned above, the final chorale is apparently lacking.                    DLH

For bibliography, *see* CANTATA, §1.

**Berlin, Potsdam.** Berlin was the capital city of Germany from 1871 until 1945, when it was partitioned into East and West Berlin and the West German seat of government moved to Bonn. In 1990 Berlin was designated the capital of a reunified Germany. In Bach's time it was the Prussian capital and the residence of the electors of Brandenburg. Between 1700 and 1750 the city grew in wealth, distinctive character, population, and artistic standing.

The Bach family had had little reason to concern themselves with Berlin and Potsdam before the time of Johann Sebastian. These places would have seemed remote to earlier generations, effectively foreign in dialect, outlook, and even cultural maturity. Direct contact started in 1718 when Bach himself, living in Cöthen, was sent there by Prince Leopold to commission a harpsichord from the workshop of Michael Mietke. He went again in 1719 to collect the instrument, which seems to have given impetus to the final form of Brandenburg Concerto no. 5. It may have been on one of these Berlin visits that Bach met the Margrave of Brandenburg, to whom all six concertos were dedicated. It is also likely that the extended period of study (mid-1720 to April 1721) spent in Berlin by Emanuel Freytag (1698–1779), a violinist in the Cöthen *Kapelle*, sprang from one of Bach's earlier visits.

Bach's next contacts with Berlin arose as a result of his son Carl Philipp Emanuel moving there when his employer, the Prussian crown prince, succeeded to the throne as Friedrich II (Frederick the Great) in 1740. Bach visited his son in Berlin in July–August 1741, as we know from letters written to him by Johann Elias Bach in Leipzig, informing him of the serious illness of his wife Anna Magdalena. Emanuel Bach married in 1744; his first child, Johann August, was born the following year, his second, Anna Carolina Philippina, in 1746, and his third, Johann Sebastian, in 1748. The elder Bach travelled to Berlin to visit the young family on at least one occasion (in 1747), and he also visited the main centres of music there: the new opera house (completed in 1742) and the music rooms at Sanssouci, Frederick the Great's castle in nearby Potsdam. Two highly important works are associated with these visits: the Flute Sonata in E major BWV1035 was perhaps composed for Frederick's flute duet partner M. G. Fredersdorf (*see* FLUTE SONATAS), and the *Musical Offering* certainly resulted from Bach's Potsdam visit of 1747, when he was received by Frederick the Great and given a musical theme on which to demonstrate his powers of improvisation. On this occasion he also played, on 8 May, at the Heiliggeistkirche to an admiring audience of local connoisseurs (see *BDok* ii, no. 554).

Even before Bach's death Berlin had become the residence of a number of his supporters and former pupils. After 1750 the city was for a time the most vital centre for the cultivation of Bach's music, fostered partly by his elder sons and senior pupils, especially J. P. Kirnberger, and partly by new and influential converts. One of these was the organist and *director musices* at the Nicolaikirche in Berlin, Johann Georg Gottlieb Lehmann (d. 1816), whose actress daughter Caroline married the composer Muzio Clementi in 1804; another was Princess Anna Amalia of Prussia, who employed Kirnberger from 1758 and with his help assembled an outstanding Bach library.

In the autumn of 1800 C. F. Zelter succeeded his teacher Carl Friedrich Christian Fasch (1736–1800) as principal conductor of the Berliner Singakademie. Here music by Bach was regularly rehearsed and, as time passed, publicly performed. If this interest in Bach had not been maintained in Berlin, Mendelssohn would most likely not have encountered the *St Matthew Passion*, let alone 'modernized' and performed it with noteworthy success in 1829. This important event in the history of the international Bach revival occurred not in Leipzig or Vienna, but at the Singakademie in Berlin. The relevance of Berlin to Bach studies has continued throughout the 20th century with the location there, at what is now the Staatsbibliothek zu Berlin—Preußischer Kulturbesitz, of the most important collection anywhere of Bach manuscripts, including numerous autographs.                                              SFD

M. Petzoldt, *Bachstätten aufsuchen* (Leipzig, 1992), 26–38.

**Bertouch, Georg von** (b. 19 June 1668; d. 14 Sept. 1743). Composer, born in Helmershausen, near Meiningen. He studied at Jena University (1688–91), where he got to know Bach's second cousin Johann Nicolaus (1669–1753), with whom he made a journey to Italy. He then pursued a dual career as a composer and an officer in the Danish army. He is said to have corresponded with J. S. Bach and to have imitated the layout of Bach's *The Well-tempered Clavier* in a published volume of 24 sonatas, but no exemplars are known. *See also* RECEPTION AND REVIVAL, §11.

**Bethlehem Bach Festival.** The Moravians, who settled in Bethlehem, Pennsylvania, in 1741, brought to the region a religious heritage greatly enriched by music. The Bethlehem Choral Union (renamed the Bach Choir of Bethlehem in 1898) gave the first complete American performances of many of Bach's major choral works during the 1880s and 1890s. The Bethlehem Bach Festival, which began in 1912, takes place in May and each year presents the Mass in B minor and other choral and instrumental works.                       JAB

R. A. Leaver, 'New Light on the Pre-History of the Bach Choir of Bethlehem', *Bach*, 22/2 (Fall–Winter, 1991), 24–34; R. Walters, *The Bethlehem Bach Choir: A History and a Critical Compendium* (Boston, 1923).

**bibliographies.** Few attempts have been made to list completely the vast and ever-increasing number of books, essays, articles and other literature devoted to Bach and his music. It would be beyond the scope of the present volume to attempt such an undertaking, but readers may find it useful to be directed towards some bibliographies which are comprehensive enough to serve as resources of first enquiry. They are:

A. Basso, *Frau Musika: la vita e le opere di J. S. Bach* (Turin, 1979–83). The chapters of this two-volume study are preceded by ample bibliographies covering particular periods and aspects of Bach's life and music.

*Bach-Jahrbuch.* This journal has published bibliographies every five years or so since 1953, and before that in 1905 and 1910; a collected reprint, with supplement and index, edited by Christoph Wolff, was published as *Bach-Bibliographie* (Berlin and Kassel, 1985).

*Die Musik in Geschichte und Gegenwart,* ed. F. Blume (Kassel, 1949–79), i, cols. 1043–7.

D. R. Melamed and M. Marissen, *An Introduction to Bach Studies* (New York and Oxford, forthcoming). This is essentially an annotated bibliography, organized systematically according to topic, and is likely to prove the most important single tool for the serious Bach student and researcher.

*The New Grove Dictionary of Music and Musicians,* ed. S. Sadie (London, 1980), i. 836–40; repr. with additions in *The New Grove Bach Family* (London, 1983), 215–37, and in *Die Bach-Familie* (Stuttgart and Weimar, 1993), 255–86.

A comprehensive Bach bibliography maintained by Yo Tomita at Queen's University, Belfast, is available on the Internet at the following address: http://www.music.qub.ac.uk/~tomita/bachbib. html.

**bicinium.** A term conventionally applied to a vocal or instrumental duo, for either one player or two. In Lutheran educational circles it had strong didactic overtones, being applied to duos composed for teacher and pupil as exercises in sight-singing and musical notation. The *bicinia* of Lassus (?1530–94), as well as compositions in the same style by Caspar Othmayr (1515–53), Michael Praetorius (?1571–1621) and others, were especially popular in Protestant Germany. Bach used the subtitle 'bicinium' for the chorale prelude on *Allein Gott in der Höh sei Ehr* BWV711 and evoked the spirit of the *bicinium* in the four Duetti from *Clavier-Übung III*, which, it has been suggested, are meant to represent the teacher–pupil relationship in the context of the articles of Luther's Short Catechism. Other keyboard works, including the two-part Inventions and chorale preludes in duo form such as *Du Friedefürst, Herr Jesu Christ* BWV1102, also suggest the *bicinium*, although Bach did not use that title for them.                    DLH

D. Humphreys, *The Esoteric Structure of Bach's Clavierübung III* (Cardiff, 1983), 7–18; P. Williams, *The Organ Music of J. S. Bach* (Cambridge, 1980), i. 321–4; ii. 248–9.

***Bierfiedler*** ('beer fiddler'). A somewhat contemptuous term used in Bach's time for a violinist or other instrumentalist without a permanent position, who was not a member of a musicians' guild but accepted casual employment when it was available. J. A. Ernesti, Rector of the Thomasschule in Leipzig from 1734 to 1759, is reported to have expressed his disapproval of boys who spent too much time practising their instruments by saying to them 'So, you want to be a *Bierfiedler* as well?'

**binary form.** A musical structure in which two complementary strains are normally repeated: ||: A :||: B :||. It was standard in Baroque dances and Bach, like other composers of his time, also employed it as an option in sonatas and preludes, and occasionally in concertos.

The first strain usually modulates to the dominant or, in minor-key movements, to the relative major. Occasionally it remains in the tonic, reaching a half-close or (more rarely) a tonic full close. In French dances, such as the bourrées and gavottes from the English Suites, the first strain often exhibits the phrase structure A–A', the opening phrase being repeated with a different cadence (e.g. first time tonic, second time dominant). In Bach's larger, more mature binary structures the modulation to the dominant (or relative major) leads to a substantial period in that key, often displaying some new thematic element or mode of treatment. This expanded design is found in the allemandes of French Suites nos. 5 and 6, in those of the keyboard partitas and in certain preludes from *The Well-tempered Clavier* Part 2.

The second strain often opens with a dominant counter-statement of the original theme, as in Invention no. 6 BWV777 or the slow movement of the Organ Sonata no. 3. In many cases, especially in allemandes and gigues, the inverted original theme forms the subject of the second strain, in which case the direct theme may return before the close to ensure audible coherence, as in the Gigue from Partita no. 6 BWV830. In the gigues from Partitas nos. 4 and 5 the second strain opens with an entirely new theme, which subsequently forms a regular countersubject to the original theme.

A further directly audible link between the two strains is formed by the rhyming close—an exact or near-exact correspondence (except in key) between the final phrases and/or cadences of each half. On occasion this concept is expanded to the extent that the entire closing period of the first half is recapitulated at the end of the second, as in the Gigue from English Suite no. 2.

Bach often used 'rounded binary' form, in which the first strain is recapitulated in its entirety at the end of the second: ||: A¹ :||: B–A² :||. Where the first strain closes in the tonic, it may be recapitulated without change, leading to the simplest type of RONDEAU (and so called when used by Bach's French contemporaries). Two of Bach's early suites, BWV820 and 822, each contain three examples of this form, but it is rare in his mature works: Menuet 2 from French Suite no. 1 and Bourrée 2 from Cello Suite no. 4 are isolated cases. Far more frequently the first strain, closing in the dominant, is recapitulated at the end in a form modified in order to close in the tonic, as in Minuet 2 from English Suite no. 4.

In certain cases a more complete form of symmetry is adopted in which the entire second strain forms a varied reprise of the first: ||: A :||: A' :||, with keys adjusted and thematic material inverted. This form is found in the gigues of English Suites nos. 4 and 5 and in the closing Allegro of the Organ Sonata no. 1.

The large and complex structure of Bach's binary sonata movements appears to have influenced the design of his mature binary preludes and dance movements. Where such pieces end with an extended varied reprise of the first strain (with adjusted keys) the resemblance to an essential feature of the later sonata form is strong, particularly where the return to the tonic during the second strain coincides with a return of the first theme. Examples of this include Invention no. 6 BWV777, the slow movement of the Organ Sonata no. 3, the Sarabande from Partita no. 4, the Corrente from Partita no. 6, and several binary preludes from *The Well-tempered Clavier* Part 2. The analogy with sonata form is still more evident when a clearly defined dominant-key period at the end of the first half is recapitulated in the tonic at the end of the second, as in the Praeludium in G BWV902:1.

Finally, in a number of movements from the Violin Sonatas BWV1014–19 an elaborate binary structure, with contrasting middle section and tonic reprise, is effectively united with fugue.

RDPJ

**Birnbaum, Johann Abraham** (bap. 30 Sept. 1702; d. 8 Aug. 1748). Writer and teacher, born in Leipzig. He taught rhetoric at Leipzig University, and was also a good keyboard player. He became friendly with Bach, and was the latter's principal defender in the dispute engendered by the criticism of Bach's music that J. A. SCHEIBE published in 1737. Birnbaum's pamphlet *Unpartheyische Anmerkungen* ('Impartial Observations') appeared anonymously the following year; it has been suggested that Bach himself had a hand in compiling it. Birnbaum's defence centred on Scheibe's referring to Bach as a 'Musikant' (a term which he argued was belittling) and characterizing Bach's music as 'bombastic and confused'.

***Bisher habt ihr nichts gebeten in meinem Namen*** ('Hitherto have ye asked nothing in my name'). Cantata, BWV87, for the fifth Sunday after Easter (Rogate). This strikingly dark and powerful cantata is one of nine which Bach set to texts by C. M. von Ziegler, a leading Leipzig poet and member of the circle of the Enlightenment poet J. C. Gottsched. During the 1720s her house became a meeting-place for artists and scholars and at this time, when her work was enjoying a considerable reputation, she provided Bach with texts which may be considered among the finest that he set in cantata form. This one is based on verses from St John 16.

Bach first performed the work on 6 May 1725. The brooding, minor-mode key sequence (D minor–A minor–G minor–C minor) remains virtually unbroken until the sixth section, when Bach introduces a B♭ siciliana in 12/8 time, the effect of whose contrasting tonal radiance and carefree dance rhythm is intensified by the dark colours of the preceding sections, before we are returned, once more, to the key of D minor in which the work closes.

The opening section is scored for bass with strings (the upper strands doubled by two oboes and an oboe da caccia) and continuo. The form is that of a fugally inclined arioso—the form which Bach used for the vox CHRISTI, though it is not named as such in the surviving autograph score. Some commentators have remarked on the stern nature of Bach's declamation in this movement but it is perhaps better understood as grave and revelatory. A brief simple recitative for alto, urging the sinner to repent, leads to an alto aria accompanied by two oboes da caccia above a continuo bass of persistent rising semiquaver figures. In this prayer of supplication the work reaches its darkest moments.

The text of the accompanied tenor recitative is not by Ziegler but was perhaps inserted by Bach in order to avoid an unbroken sequence of three arias. In it the sinner requests Christ's comfort and trust, the answer to which is found in the following bass solo with continuo. Like the opening movement, this contains the words of Christ in direct speech, from the 16th chapter of St John's Gospel: 'In the world ye shall have tribulation; but be of good cheer, I have overcome the world.' The text is hopeful, yet the music remains sombre in spirit. Only with the tenor aria, a glorious moment in the cantata, and tonally its focal point, is the gravity of the work dispelled. One of the striking features of this movement is the athleti-

cism with which Bach endows the vocal line. The cantata ends with a strophe from Heinrich Müller's hymn *Selig ist die Seele* (1659), set to Johann Crüger's mid-17th-century melody *Jesu meine Freude*. As usual, the voices are supported by all the available instruments, *colla parte*.  NA

For bibliography, *see* CANTATA, §1.

***Bist du bei mir*** ('If thou art with me'). *Lied* for soprano and unfigured bass, BWV508. One of the best-known items in the 1725 *Clavierbüchlein* for Anna Magdalena Bach, it was formerly attributed to J. S. Bach but is now thought to be the work of G. H. Stölzel.

**Bitter, Carl Heinrich** (b. 27 Feb. 1813; d. 12 Sept. 1885). Statesman, and author of the first full-size biography of J. S. Bach. He was born in Schwedt an der Oder and studied in Berlin and Bonn. In 1835–76 he held posts in the Prussian administration, spending some time in Potsdam, Posen, and Schleswig. From 1879 to 1882 he was minister of finance under Bismarck. His Bach biography appeared in 1865. In some respects it provided the starting-point for Spitta's *Bach*, which came out only a few years later and was much more popular, although Spitta was hostile towards Bitter. In the revised and enlarged edition of 1881, Bitter's book—especially volume 4, a collection of documents and a detailed work-list—was particularly influential. Bitter's research also extended to Bach's sons, especially Wilhelm Friedemann and Carl Philipp Emanuel; he published a biography of them both in 1868.  KK

**Blasiuskirche** (St Blasius's Church). The church in MÜHLHAUSEN, also known as Divi Blasius, where Bach served as organist in 1707–8. It was built between 1240 and 1350.

***Blast Lärmen, ihr Feinde! Verstärket die Macht*** ('Sound the alarm, ye adversaries! Strengthen your forces'). Secular cantata, BWV205a, performed on 19 February 1734 in celebration of the coronation of King Augustus III of Poland. It was parodied by an unknown librettist from the cantata ZERREISSET, ZERSPRENGET, ZERTRÜMMERT DIE GRUFT.

***Bleib bei uns, denn es will Abend werden*** ('Abide with us, for it is toward evening'). Cantata, BWV6, for the second day of Easter, first performed in Leipzig on 2 April 1725. The unidentified librettist based his text on the Gospel reading for the day: St Luke's account of the two disciples' walk to Emmaus with the risen Christ (Luke 24: 13–35). Although this cantata belongs to Bach's second annual Leipzig cycle it does not adhere to a unifying chorale structure as most of the others do, but reverts to Bach's earlier favoured scheme: biblical text–aria–chorale–recitative–aria–chorale.

The opening chorus, in C minor, is scored for two oboes, oboe da caccia, strings, and continuo. This is one of two cantatas (the other is BWV109) for which a harpsichord continuo part exists in addition to that for organ, suggesting that dual accompaniment in Bach's cantata performances was at least an accepted practice, if not a habitual one. The chorus is impressive both for the way that its ternary structure consists of two mainly chordal sections which flank a double fugue, and for the skill Bach shows in affective word-painting. The imploring phrase 'Bleib bei uns' is given urgency by its extensive reiteration, while the subsequent reference to evening and approaching nightfall is tenderly evoked by a persistent falling theme which recalls the concluding chorus, 'Ruht wohl' of the St John Passion. The prevailing mood of the movement is thus one of elegy, described by Albert Schweitzer (*J. S. Bach* (London, 1911), ii. 338) as 'a masterpiece of poetry in music'.

The dance-like aria in E♭ which follows is in 3/8 time and scored for alto, with obbligato oboe da caccia and continuo including pizzicato cello. Here Bach illuminates the text, a plea for Christ's continuing presence, with expressive melodic writing, warm yet sombrely coloured, depicting the encroaching darkness. The oft-repeated claim that this movement is a parody of one belonging to a lost secular cantata (BWV Anh. I 19:2) is unsubstantiated. The third section of the cantata is a chorale for soprano solo, 'Ach bleib bei uns, Herr Jesu Christ', accompanied by a violoncello piccolo, an instrument for which Bach provided an obbligato part in nine cantatas. It was later arranged as the fifth of the Schübler Chorales for organ. Two strophes are sung, the first from a German version of the Latin hymn *Vespera jam venit* by Philipp Melanchthon (1579), the second by his pupil Nikolaus Selnecker (1572). The hymn was one of three for this day included in the Leipzig hymn schedules of Bach's time.

The single recitative of the cantata is for bass and is accompanied only by continuo. It leads to the second of two arias, this one in G minor for tenor with full string accompaniment. The resolute melodic contours of the upper string parts reflect the underlying optimism of the text. The cantata concludes with the second strophe of Luther's hymn *Erhalt uns, Herr, bei deinem Wort*, set to its associated, anonymous melody.     NA

For bibliography, *see* CANTATA, §1.

**Blockflöte** ('fipple flute'). German term for the RECORDER.

**Blithe Bells.** The title of a transcription by Percy Grainger of the aria SHEEP MAY SAFELY GRAZE.

**Böhm, Georg** (b. 2 Sept. 1661; d. 18 May 1733). Organist and composer, born in Hohenkirchen, near Ohrdruf, in Thuringia. In the early 1690s he moved north to Hamburg, and in 1698 became organist at the Johanniskirche in Lüneburg, a post he held until his death. As a pupil at the Michaelisschule, Lüneburg, from 1700 to 1702, Bach no doubt encountered Böhm, but it is not known whether he received direct tuition from him. In a letter to Forkel of 13 January 1775, C. P. E. Bach initially referred to Böhm as his father's 'Lüneburg-ischen Lehrmeister' ('Lüneburg teacher'), but he subsequently deleted the phrase. The two composers must have remained on friendly terms, for in 1727 Böhm sold copies on commission of Bach's second and third keyboard partitas.

During his Hamburg years Böhm not only absorbed the style of the north German school but also encountered the French and Italian styles at the cosmopolitan Hamburg opera. Elements derived from the operatic aria and from French theatrical dance music are evident in his keyboard works. His style thus enriched, and including associated structural features such as ritornello, motto, *petite reprise*, etc., seems to have exerted a strong influence on the young Bach during the period *c*.1703–10/12, notably in the organ chorales BWV718, 1102, and 1114, and in the chorale partitas BWV766–8 and 770.     RDPJ

J.-C. Zehnder, 'Georg Böhm und Johann Sebastian Bach: zur Chronologie der Bachschen Stilentwicklung', *BJb* 74 (1988), 73–110.

**Bonifatiuskirche** (St Boniface's Church). Church in ARNSTADT destroyed by fire in 1581 and rebuilt in 1676–83 as the Neue Kirche. Bach was organist there from 1703 to 1707.

**Bonporti, Francesco Antonio** (bap. 11 June 1672; d. 19 Dec. 1749). Italian composer and violinist, born in Trent. Bach's connection with this talented priest-musician, who published several collections of music in a persistent but vain attempt to gain clerical promotion, is at first sight fortuitous: Alfred Dörffel included four 'Inventions' from Bonporti's op. 10 (1712), a set of sonatas for violin and continuo, in volume 45 of the *BG* edition, misled by their unusual title and by an attribution to Bach in a manuscript. But Bach may indeed have borrowed Bonporti's title (if not its precise significance) for his own keyboard works, just as the 'Ecco' movement in Bonporti's tenth Invention may lie behind the similarly titled movement in the Ouverture in the French Style BWV831.     MT

A. J. B. Hutchings, *The Baroque Concerto* (London, 1961; 3rd edn., 1973).

65

**borea.** Italian form of BOURRÉE, used by Bach as a tempo indication for the last movement of his Partita no. 1 for solo violin ('Tempo di Borea').

**Bose.** A Leipzig family of merchants who stood in close contact with Bach and his family. In the early 18th century the head of the family was Georg Heinrich Bose (1682–1731). Between 1731 and 1742 three of his daughters acted as godmothers to four of Bach's children. The Boses had a lively interest in music and it is quite likely that Bach played regularly at their house; in addition, it has been speculated that the wedding cantata *O holder Tag, erwünschte Zeit* was written to celebrate the wedding between Anna Regina Bose (1716–50) and Friedrich Heinrich Graf (1713–77) in April 1742. Since 1985 the Bose family residence at 16 Thomaskirchhof has housed the Leipzig Bach-Archiv.                    PW

W. Neumann, 'Eine Leipziger Bach-Gedenkstätte: über die Beziehungen der Familien Bach und Bose', *BJb* 56 (1970), 19–31; H.-J. Schulze, 'Anna Magdalena Bachs "Herzens Freündin": Neues über die Beziehungen zwischen den Familien Bach und Bose', *BJb* 83 (1997), 151–3.

**bourrée.** A French dance performed frequently at court balls and in theatrical works during the reign of Louis XIV in France (*see* DANCE); also an instrumental form used in suites by J. S. Bach and numerous other Baroque composers. The bourrée's jaunty rhythm persisted well into the late 18th century and was incorporated into such works as the opening movement of Mozart's Symphony no. 40 in G minor K550.

Bourrées were described by theorists of Bach's time as gay and joyful, to be played lightly (*fort légèrement*). The bourrée is in duple metre, with a minim beat; crotchets and quavers are the rhythmic levels below the beat, and semiquavers are always ornamental. The time signature is normally 2 or ¢. The characteristic rhythmic phrase is eight beats (four bars) in length, with points of repose on beat three and the first half of four, and seven and the first half of eight. An upbeat of a quaver or two semiquavers is characteristic, as are frequent syncopations (for a comparison of bourrée and gavotte rhythms, *see* RHYTHM, Ex. 1). *Notes inégales* (rhythmic inequality) may be applied to conjunct groups of quavers (*see* RHYTHM). Most 18th-century theorists regarded the bourrée's tempo (i.e. the speed of the minim beats) as generally faster than the gavotte (*see* TEMPO). A reasonable tempo range for the bourrée is minim = 80–8, based on evidence from choreographic and other written sources as well as from the pieces themselves.

Twenty-nine titled bourrées by Bach have survived, counting separately the several instances that exist of bourrées in pairs. They are found in several early works for clavier (BWV822, 820, and 832) and for lute (BWV996), the first two English Suites, the fifth and sixth French Suites, all four orchestral suites, Partitas nos. 1 and 3 for solo violin (the latter also for lute), Cello Suites nos. 3 and 4, the Partita for solo flute, the Suite in E♭ major for clavier, BWV819, and the Ouverture in the French Style from *Clavier-Übung II*. The bourrées in the English Suites are probably among the earliest; both consist of a pair of contrasting dances in two-part texture. Long, extended phrases mask the dance structure of those in the A major suite and the first in the A minor suite, but the contrasting bourrée in the A minor suite is in musette style with clear phrases. Dance structure is particularly clear in the bourrées from the French Suites, Partita no. 1 for solo violin (where Bach uses the designation 'Tempo di Borea'), the Cello Suites and the second and third Orchestral Suites. In the other two orchestral suites Bach experiments with syncopations and Italian orchestral practices. In Partita no. 3 for solo violin he employs ambiguity, not in the middle of the piece where one would expect it, but in the very first phrase; the violin uses a broken-chord technique to evoke two- or three-part texture, followed by sequences and echo effects, all of which are far from the French bourrée style. The two bourrées in the Ouverture in the French Style are also unorthodox: Bourrée I is almost a textbook model of the dance style, while Bourrée II has a surprising three-note upbeat and seems to be in the style of a prelude.

The rhythmic pattern of the bourrée frequently occurs untitled in other Bach works, for example the C♯ major fugue from Part 1 and the F minor fugue from Part 2 of *The Well-tempered Clavier*, the organ fugues in C minor BWV537 and G minor BWV542, and the Trio Sonata from the *Musical Offering* (second movement), and in the cantatas, both sacred and secular (for further examples, see Little and Jenne).                    NJ, MEL

For bibliography, *see* DANCE.

**Brahms, Johannes** (b. 7 May 1833; d. 3 April 1897). Composer of piano, chamber, orchestral, solo vocal, and choral music, born in Hamburg, He later settled in Vienna, where he died. Brahms successfully re-established Classical formal principles in a Romantic language and came to be seen as the greatest opponent of the powerful development towards programmatic musical thought and Wagnerian music drama. His enthusiasm for Bach permeated his life as pianist, conductor, and composer. His first public piano recital, at the age of 15 in 1848, included a 'fugue by Bach', and he regularly included in his programmes the Chromatic

Fantasia and Fugue as well as his transcriptions of organ works. A copy of the '48' was often open on his piano and he knew the work intimately.

As a conductor Brahms was a pioneer in performing unknown choral works which were only just becoming available in the *BG* edition, to which he later subscribed. These included Cantatas 4, 8, 21, 34, and 50, as well as the *Christmas Oratorio*. Bachian influence was gradually absorbed more deeply into his own work. Obvious stylistic influence is present in the early organ works and suite movements for piano (published later), and in the chorale-based motets op. 29 no. 1 and 74 no. 2 (published in 1874, but written earlier). The fugal style of the finale of the Cello Sonata in E minor op. 38 is often attributed to Contrapunctus 13 of *The Art of Fugue*, while the slow movement of the String Quintet op. 88 recomposes a Sarabande of 1855 to mask its Bachian provenance completely. The summit of this absorption appears in the finale of the Fourth Symphony, a mighty set of variations on a theme derived, as Brahms acknowledged, from a ground bass in Cantata 150. Bachian models are again to the fore, as might be expected, in the late chorale preludes for organ op. 122.          MM

**Brandenburg, Margrave of.** *See* CHRISTIAN LUDWIG, Margrave of Brandenburg. *See also* BRANDENBURG CONCERTOS.

**Brandenburg Concertos.** See overleaf.

**Breitkopf, Bernhard Christoph** (b. 2 March 1695; d. 23 March 1777). Founder of a Leipzig firm of music printers and publishers, born in Clausthal, in the Harz region, Lower Saxony. He was one of the Leipzig printers to whom Bach turned for the printing of a number of cantata librettos during the 1730s. Breitkopf was primarily a book printer for whom musical editions played only a secondary role. As printer and publisher of the Schemelli Songbook (*Musicalisches Gesangbuch*, 1736), he would have worked in collaboration with the editor, G. C. SCHEMELLI, and Bach as music consultant and contributor. Breitkopf was the printer of the title-page and preface of Bach's last two publications, the *Musical Offering* and *The Art of Fugue* (2nd edition). Breitkopf extended credit to Bach, and on the composer's death there was money owing to the firm for its work on the *Musical Offering*.          GB

G. Butler, 'Breitkopf: The Formative Years', in G. B. Stauffer, ed., *J. S. Bach, the Breitkopfs, and Eighteenth-century Music Trade* [Bach Perspectives, ii] (Lincoln, Nebr., 1996), 159–68; H. von Hase, 'Breitkopfsche Textdrücke zu Leipziger Musikaufführungen zu Bachs Zeiten', *BJb* 10 (1913), 69–127.

**Brich dem Hungrigen dein Brot** ('Deal thy bread to the hungry'). Cantata, BWV39, composed for the first Sunday after Trinity (23 June) 1726. That Sunday had a special significance for Bach: on the corresponding day in 1723 he had entered on his Leipzig post with a performance of *Die Elenden sollen essen*; and on its first anniversary he inaugurated a series of chorale cantatas with *O Ewigkeit, du Donnerwort* (BWV20). In 1725 Bach apparently abandoned the practice of alluding to his installation, and *Brich dem Hungrigen* comes as one in a series of cantatas which extends from February 1726 to the end of September. During this period Bach had recourse to church music originating in the court chapel of Meiningen: to texts written perhaps by Duke Ernst Ludwig, and to compositions by Bach's distant cousin, Johann Ludwig Bach. The first Meiningen text that Bach himself set was one for Ascension, *Gott fähret auf mit Jauchzen*; what was performed on the Sunday after Ascension, at Whitsun, and on Trinity Sunday is unknown, but *Brich dem Hungrigen* was the first text from the series that Bach set for a normal Sunday.

The cantata exemplifies what might be called the standard Meiningen pattern: a movement based on an Old Testament passage (in this case Isaiah 58: 7–8); a recitative and aria; a New Testament text (fourth movement; here Hebrews 13: 16); another aria and recitative (the latter typically having two or more sentences, allowing the composer to set the final part as a chorus, as in most of J. L. Bach's examples); and, finally, one or more strophes of a chorale. The two biblical texts are linked in subject-matter; in this cantata the common theme is that of helping the poor.

Bach modified this structure in two respects. First, he divided the texts into two parts so that the composition could frame the sermon and the words of institution that followed it. Only in *Herr, deine Augen* did he conclude Part 1 with no. 4 (the New Testament extract); in the other works he opened the second part with it, thus beginning each part with a passage from the Bible. Also, he designed the whole poetical unit preceding the chorale as a recitative, rather than a recitative followed by a chorus. For both the poet had used alexandrines, a metre which is uncommon in recitatives of the time. This gives Bach's composition a regularity which appears somewhat old-fashioned.

As in most cases, the opening movement of BWV39 is a chorus. The biblical text is quite long, and Bach set it as a multi-sectional movement (G minor) comprising several fugal parts. As in the other cantatas of the Meiningen type, the second number is a simple recitative, and this is followed by an F major aria, 'Seinem Schöpfer noch auf

[*cont. on p.74*]

# Brandenburg Concertos (*Brandenburgische Konzerte*)

Six concertos, BWV1046–51, which Bach dedicated to Christian Ludwig, Margrave of Brandenburg, in March 1721.

1. Background.
2. Structure and scoring.
3. The individual concertos.
4. The concertos as a set.

**1. Background.** Bach had visited Berlin in 1719 to pick up a 'large harpsichord with two keyboards by Michael Mietke' (*BDok* ii. 95), and the margrave most probably heard him perform at that time. The two may have first become acquainted even earlier, when Bach's employer, Prince Leopold of Anhalt-Cöthen, took six of his musicians, including Bach, and the 'princely harpsichord' (*BDok* ii. 86) on a trip in 1718 to the spas at Carlsbad, an established vacation spot for German nobles (the margrave's presence, however, is undocumented). Bach's wife, Maria Barbara, died in 1720, evidently while he was once again with Leopold's entourage in Carlsbad. Bach's position at Cöthen was becoming less appealing for various reasons: a greater share of the prince's budget was now being allocated to the castle guard; relations between Cöthen's Lutheran and Reformed inhabitants were often strained; and, to make matters worse, Leopold's new bride, Princess Friderica, reportedly did not care much for music. (It should be noted, however, that Bach had been seeking employment elsewhere before she arrived.)

Bach's beautifully calligraphed score of the 'Six Concertos for Several Instruments', with its obsequious dedication in French to Christian Ludwig, may actually represent not so much the fulfilling of a commission as a thinly veiled application for employment in the margrave's musical establishment. There is no record of his response. Because of this and the fact that the concertos were not mentioned among the margrave's effects, it is often suggested that he did not appreciate Bach's efforts. There is, however, no reason why we should expect to see Bach's concertos specified, as the sources in question were meant to document an equal division of Christian Ludwig's estate among his beneficiaries. In the 18th century printed sources of music were considerably more valuable than manuscripts, and most probably for this reason it is the margrave's concerto printed editions, not his manuscripts, that are listed by composer. The Brandenburg Concertos were no doubt kept among his several manuscript collections of 'concertos by diverse masters'.

**2. Structure and scoring.** The formal designs of Bach's concertos owe a great deal to Italian predecessors, including Torelli, Albinoni, and especially Vivaldi. In Vivaldian concertos the alternation between the tutti (entire ensemble) and the concertino (sub-group) involves contrasts in texture as well as in the types of music performed. The tutti plays 'ritornellos' and the concertino 'episodes'. The ritornellos are expository in character, and normally they begin and end in the same key. The episodes are so named because they tend to be much less expository; they are often virtuoso, and normally they begin in one key and end in another. A Vivaldian concerto movement consists mainly of free episode material with occasional returns of part or all of the ritornello.

In his concerto-style works Bach shows a predilection for a Vivaldian ritornello type containing three clearly differentiated segments, a type which modern students of Vivaldi's music have labelled the 'Fortspinnungstypus', or 'Fortspinnung-type'. Its first segment grounds the tonality by focusing on the chords built upon the first and fifth degrees of the scale (tonic and dominant). The second segment follows with short bits of thematic material repeated at different pitch levels (called 'sequencing'); the changes in underlying harmony are marked mostly by successions of chords with fundamental pitches that are five positions apart in the scale. And the third segment brings the ritornello to a satisfying end by way of a closing gesture in the tonic. Many writers refer to these three segments of ritornello with the German terms 'Vordersatz', 'Fortspinnung', and 'Epilog'. 'Fortspinnung-type' will be used here to describe only this specific variety of Vivaldian ritornello, which is featured to varying degrees in all six Brandenburg Concertos. (Bach's other concertos frequently draw on different formal models, some of them also occasionally referred to as being of the *Fortspinnung*-type.)

What makes the structure of Bach's concertos so challenging and rewarding to follow is that they frequently assign conventional ritornello attributes to episodes, and vice versa (e.g. a ritornello will be performed by the concertino, or an episode will incorporate melodic snippets derived from the ritornello). As to scoring, Bach is often credited with bringing brass and woodwind into the Baroque concerto. Recent research, which has been based on the study of concerto manuscripts, not merely of printed editions, has shown that the scorings of Italian concertos were in fact quite varied and that German composers in the generation before Bach wrote for similar combinations of instruments. If Bach's forms and scorings are not, in and of themselves, particularly innovative, his treatments of them are surely unparalleled.

### 3. The individual concertos.

*(i) Concerto no. 1.* This is scored for two hunting horns, three oboes, bassoon, violino piccolo, strings, and basso continuo. It must have made a sensation the first time it was heard. In the first movement the woodwind and strings perform an elegant ritornello with multiple *Fortspinnung* and *Epilog* segments, while loud greeting-calls from the hunting horns—outdoor instruments probably never before heard in the elegant chamber music rooms where Bach's concertos were performed—clash rhythmically and harmonically. Just as the episodes develop clearer identities by becoming thematically less dependent on the ritornello, the horns lose their distinctive identities by giving up the idiomatic fanfares of the ritornello and becoming assimilated (i.e. within the episodes) as true partners to the other instruments' more graceful lines.

The focus in the remaining movements shifts to the role of the violino piccolo (tuned in this case a minor 3rd higher than the regular violin). Bach appears to have designed only the third movement with the violino piccolo in mind from the start. There is no part whatever for the instrument in the early version of the work, the Sinfonia BWV1046a, which lacks both the third movement and the polonaise section of the last movement. (Incidentally, we do not know precisely how the early version read. The oldest surviving copy, a score prepared by C. F. Penzel in 1760, was based on a lost set of parts, and these transmitted revisions that Bach made in 1726 when he reused the first movement as a sinfonia for his church cantata *Falsche Welt, dir trau ich nicht*.) In the Brandenburg version the violino piccolo line is mostly borrowed note for note from the first violin part of the Sinfonia. The violino piccolo doubles the first violin in the opening movement and in the tutti Minuet of the Brandenburg version; and in the second movement Bach gives to the violino piccolo what was originally the first violin part of the sinfonia and writes new filler material for the first violin.

The violino piccolo thus plays a marginal role in the first movement. In the second movement (Adagio)—a sort of triple-concerto passacaglia in which the first oboe, violino piccolo, and continuo instruments constitute the concertino—it becomes a true member of the concertino, often even playing in canon with the first oboe. Only in the third movement (Allegro) does the violino piccolo approach becoming the central soloist. But even here its status appears problematic. At first the solo violin can do nothing but borrow themes from the *Fortspinnung*-type ritornello. In the middle section (from bar 53), as it begins playing distinctive material, other instruments immediately take away the spotlight.

In the fourth movement, a series of dances, the violino piccolo again recedes completely into the background. An elegant French minuet performed by the tutti acts as a sort of ritornello around three different sorts of trios. The first is a minuet scored for the Lullian trio of two oboes and bassoon, the second a polonaise for strings without violino piccolo, and the third a jarring bit of Germanic hunting music for horns (constituting the two upper parts) with the three oboes playing in unison.

Bach used the third movement again, in D major, as the opening choruses in his secular cantatas *Vereinigte Zwietracht der wechselnden Saiten* (in 1726) and *Auf, schmetternde Töne der muntern Trompeten* (in the 1730s). The choruses and the concerto movement may have originated in some still earlier vocal composition in F major, now lost (the high tessitura of the vocal lines in such a work would have presented few problems if it was performed in Cöthen, where Bach wrote other vocal works with similar ranges and where the pitch standard was evidently *tief*-CAMMER-TON). Bach also used the third trio as an independent instrumental movement in the two cantatas just mentioned.

*(ii) Concerto no. 2.* This is scored for trumpet (notated in C, but required to match an ensemble in F), recorder, oboe, violin, strings, and continuo. The soloists represent four different ways of producing sound: brass, woodwind, reeds, and strings—the four categories in which contemporary *Stadtpfeifer* were expected to demonstrate proficiency. Bach writes for the instruments here as if they were interchangeable; furthermore, the remaining string lines, apart from the cello, are written in such a way that, if they were removed, nothing harmonically or contrapuntally essential would be lost.

The first movement starts out in an uncharacteristically four-square manner: a ritornello with twin two-bar *Vordersatz* segments followed by twin two-bar *Epilog* segments, and episodes consisting at first of nothing but a continually quoted two-bar static gesture. Only when the movement switches to the minor mode does the ritornello feature a *Fortspinnung* segment, and from that point the music spins forth in ever more thematically fragmented and harmonically distant ways (i.e. it becomes unmistakably Bachian).

The second movement (Andante) is scored for recorder, oboe, violin, and continuo. This anguished music consists almost entirely of sequencing on a simple two-bar phrase or its counterpoint. Trumpeters must have been grateful for this respite between the ferociously difficult fast movements! The third movement (Allegro assai) is a cheerful fugue for the four solists and continuo with occasional reinforcement from the tutti. The fugue's subject acts as a sort of *Vordersatz*, and the tutti perform connecting *Fortspinnung* and *Epilog* segments. There is very little episodic material.

It is often reported that Penzel's copies (a score and a set of performing parts) represent an early version with horn in place of the trumpet and with a small violone performing at pitch as the only string bass instrument. Careful study of Penzel's manuscripts reveals, however, that his scoring of the bass line is in fact the same as in the Brandenburg version and that the indication 'ô vero Corne da Caccia' was added afterwards to what originally read only 'Tromba', presumably because no trumpeters were available who could negotiate the part or who owned the odd size of trumpet required to match the ensemble.

*(iii) Concerto no. 3.* This is scored for three violins, three violas, three cellos, and continuo (violone and harpsichord). The violins, violas, and cellos perform both as soloists and as an ensemble. The initial section of the first movement features similar thematic material presented in contrasting textures, and a second section (from bar 47) contrasts ritornellos with distinctively episodic material. As a sort of synthesis, a third section (from bar 78) features ritornello and non-ritornello material simultaneously in fugal form. Following the musical equivalent of an 'erasing of the blackboard' (bars 87–90), the movement now propels itself with episodes that move from the earlier distinctive material gradually to become more like the ritornello (at bars 91 and 108).

The second movement, as notated, is only one bar long and consists of only two chords. Some have suggested that the rest of a longer movement must be missing (but this fails to take into account that Bach notated the two chords at the middle of a page in the margrave's score, removing doubts about missing music by providing double lines on either side of the bar). More frequently, others have suggested that Bach expected an improvisation which could close with the two indicated chords. (But then, why is the fermata (⌢) over the second chord instead of the first? If it were over the first it could be understood as a corona, a sign for improvising, identical in appearance to a fermata.) It may be that the movement is not meant to 'work': perhaps it ought to be performed just the way it appears, as an enigma.

The third movement (Allegro) assumes the general character and specific (binary) form of a gigue, but its twelve-bar opening section is structured as a *Vordersatz* with *Fortspinnung* in the tonic, followed immediately by a *Vordersatz*, *Fortspinnung*, and *Epilog* in the dominant. This large block comes back several times in its entirety and thus functions as a sort of ritornello.

In 1729 Bach richly rescored the first movement as the sinfonia for his church cantata *Ich liebe den Höchsten von ganzem Gemüte*, adding new lines for brass, reeds, and strings.

Owing to too perfunctory reading of the sources, it is sometimes reported that Penzel's copies (a score and a set of performing parts) represent an early version with only one cello line. Working from a set of parts and noticing that the three cellos perform mostly in unison, Penzel wrote the three cello lines into one performing part and marked in the occasional *divisi* (indicating where the players should play different notes); he later scored up the work from his own parts and sometimes forgot to include the *divisi* readings. It is possible, however, that there was an earlier version without violone. Bach's title in the margrave's score fails to mention this instrument, and the bottom lines of the three relevant sources offer slightly different readings, which suggests that in each case a new bass part, meant to sound an octave lower, has been derived from the cello lines.

(iv) *Concerto no. 4*. This is scored for violin, two *fiauti d'echo*, strings, and continuo. Terminological, notational, and technical evidence suggests that Bach's *fiauti d'echo* (*see* FIAUTO) were recorders that produced the pitch $f'$ when all their holes were covered. The first movement opens with an enormous minuet-like ritornello (to bar 83) that features multiple *Vordersatz*, *Fortspinnung*, and *Epilog* segments and frequent textural contrasts, making it a sort of concerto within a concerto. The episodes are marked by struggle between the violin and recorders for primacy, the violin through its overt and sometimes empty virtuosity and the recorders through their more solid melodies and counterpoint.

The second movement (Andante) is a sophisticated formal mixture of sarabande and *Fortspinnung*-type concerto with continual echoing of the tutti by the concertino. The third movement (Presto), a driving fugal concerto, is marked by the scoring conflicts of the first movement, now carried even further.

In the 1730s Bach arranged this work as a concerto in F major for obbligato harpsichord, two recorders, and strings.

(v) *Concerto no. 5*. This is scored for flute, solo violin, obbligato harpsichord, and strings (here with only one violin line). The first movement opens with an assertive ritornello of repeated semiquavers somewhat in *stile concitato*. In the initial episodes the soloists work to undermine the affective power of the tutti by taking some of the *concitato* material and restating its pitch content in the form of *affettuoso* slurred couplets in quavers (in Baroque music these styles are polar opposites). The sense of struggle soon focuses on the harpsichord, which becomes increasingly frenetic. With various starts and stops, the instrument moves from its traditional role as continuo, to an obbligato role still somewhat overshadowed by the flute and solo violin, to an obbligato overshadowing the concertino, to a role completely overwhelming the tutti, and finally to one which, during the first section of its famous extended episode (often referred to as a CADENZA), in effect becomes the ensemble. This extraordinarily long episode (which Bach labelled simply 'solo senza stromenti') features extreme departures from the rhythmic and harmonic conventions of concerto style. Some listeners are disturbed by a sense that the closing ritornello is not entirely successful in containing this remarkable outburst.

The second movement (Affettuoso) is an intimate piece of chamber music scored for the soloists alone. None the less, Bach constructs it, too, as a concerto with various ritornellos and episodes. The third movement (Allegro) is designed as a gigue-like fugue. There are stretches of sequential and harmonically more static material, but the organization of the blocks of material is not clearly based on any conventional idea of ritornello form. In fact, even though there are various sections markedly set off for only the concertino members, the structure does not appear to be organized according to any concerto style involving textural contrast as a formative principle.

Two earlier versions of this concerto survive. One of them, transmitted in a set of performing parts in Bach's handwriting, is only marginally different from the version in the margrave's score. The other (BWV1050*a*), still not widely known, has some substantial differences. The scoring of the string bass line is for small violone only (i.e. there is no bass part at the lower octave), and the solo episode preceding the final ritornello of the first movement is much shorter (it more or less corresponds to the concluding part of the Brandenburg version but features even more unconventional harmonies).

It is unlikely that this concerto was designed for the above-mentioned Mietke harpsichord, as none of the versions requires two manuals. Also, Bach's performance part occasionally reproduces notational habits he abandoned in his composing scores well before he acquired the Mietke instrument.

*(vi) Concerto no. 6.* This is scored for two violas, two violas da gamba, cello, and continuo (harpsichord and violone of the gamba type). The grouping of these string instruments in an ensemble creates a striking visual impression, for it sets up a contrast of lower-pitched members of the violin and viola da gamba families. Violas and cellos were normally treated as orchestral instruments with secondary, relatively easy parts to play; gambas, on the other hand, were normally treated as special chamber instruments with difficult parts to play. Here, however, the violas and cello press forward with virtuoso solo parts, while the gambas either amble along with easy, secondary parts (in the fast movements) or are silent (in the Adagio).

It is not readily apparent that the first movement comes from a concerto; textural and thematic contrasts are severely attenuated. On closer consideration, however, the movement is indeed found to be marked by contrasts of ritornello and episode— something easily overlooked, as there are some reversals in syntax: *Fortspinnung*-type organization appears in the episodes, whereas more rambling material marks the ritornello, both categories for the most part proceeding in canon.

The second movement, scored for the members of the violin family and continuo, is an exquisite Adagio which, uncharacteristically, begins and ends in different keys. The third movement, assuming the character of a gigue, opens with a full *Fortspinnung*-type ritornello. What is first presented as a solo theme (from bar 9) is, in fact, a thinly disguised trio variation on the *Vordersatz* segment of the ritornello (bars 9–12 could be superimposed upon 1–4 without clash). Episodic material which is not derived from the ritornello appears only in the middle section (from bar 46).

**4. The concertos as a set.** It is difficult to say whether the disposition of concertos in the collection is itself meaningful. Some suggest it cannot be, because Bach must have composed the works over a long period. Others counter that this is irrelevant, because meaningful sets can be planned out early on but take a long time to realize (e.g. Bach's *Orgel-Büchlein*) or result from careful selection of older materials. The complicated arguments surrounding this issue are explored in interpretative studies by Geck and Marissen. MAM

M. Boyd, *Bach: The Brandenburg Concertos* (Cambridge, 1993); L. Dreyfus, *Bach's Continuo Group: Players and Practices in his Vocal Works* (Cambridge, Mass., 1987); L. Dreyfus, 'J. S. Bach's Concerto Ritornellos and the Question of Invention', *Musical Quarterly*, 71 (1985), 327–58; M. Geck, 'Gattungstraditionen und Altersschichten in den Brandenburgischen Konzerten', *Die Musikforschung*, 23 (1970), 139–52; G. Hoppe, 'Köthener politische, ökonomische und höfische Verhältnisse als Schaffensbedingungen Bachs (Teil 1)', *Cöthener Bach-Hefte*, 4 (1986), 13–62; M. Marissen, *The Social and Religious Designs of J. S. Bach's Brandenburg Concertos* (Princeton, 1995).

Erden', for alto, accompanied by solo violin and oboe. Part 2 begins with a bass aria, 'Wohlzutun und mitzuteilen' (D minor), and continues with a soprano aria ('Höchster, was ich habe', in B♭ major with two recorders) and an accompanied recitative for alto. A chorale strophe, 'Selig sind, die aus Erbarmen' (B♭ major) in straightforward four-part harmony concludes the work. None of the arias is in da capo form, the central one (no. 4) being bipartite (A–A'), the other two having two differentiated sections (A–B).                KK

For bibliography, *see* CANTATA, §1.

***Bringet dem Herrn Ehre seines Namens*** ('Ascribe unto the Lord the honour due unto his name'). Cantata, BWV148, for the 17th Sunday after Trinity, first performed on either 19 September 1723 or 25 September 1725. The anonymous libretto is based on (or possibly an earlier version of) a libretto by Picander, *Weg, ihr irdischen Geschäfte*, which was published in his *Erbauliche Gedancken* (1725) but draws on the Psalter for the opening chorus (taken from Psalm 96: 8–9, or alternatively from Psalm 29: 2). The central theme of the text is drawn from the Gospel for the day (Luke 14: 1–11), which concerns the legitimacy of healing on the Sabbath. The librettist, who on the whole seems in sympathy more with the Pharisees' view of the episode than with the evangelist's, lays a heavy emphasis on the inviolability of the Sabbath consecrated to the praise of God.

Cantata 148 is scored for SATB with trumpet in D, three oboes, strings, and continuo, and follows the six-movement form frequently found in the Leipzig cantatas. The opening chorus, jubilant in tone, is divided into two halves by a central entry of part of the instrumental ritornello (bars 100–9). The chorus parts are partly based on a fugal treatment of the fanfare-like opening figure of the ritornello, which is unusually long and complex, and supplies much of the material for the movement. There is no closing instrumental ritornello, although the final section (bars 114–47) is essentially a rescored repetition.

The second movement, 'Ich eile, die Lehre des Lebens zu hören' ('I hasten to hear the teaching of life'), is a tenor aria in B minor with a florid obbligato for solo violin. The violin part moves with appropriately fleeting motion and makes a feature of arpeggiation across the strings. The aria is in ritornello form, with an effect of recapitulation created by the return to B minor at bar 92. After the subsequent accompanied recitative for tenor, cadencing in G major, there follows a second aria, 'Mund und Herze steht Dir offen', for alto, accompanied by two oboes, oboe da caccia, and

continuo. It is in da capo form and has a placid, pastoral tone imparted by the reed instruments, with much of the material generated by the short, uncomplicated phrases of the ritornello. The central section includes undulating ostinato figures appropriately representing the text 'Glaube, Liebe, Dulden, Hoffen, Soll mein Ruhebette sein' ('Belief, love, endurance, and hope shall be my resting couch').

After a final tenor recitative comes the closing chorale in a plain four-part harmonization. It is untexted, but the melody was associated with two hymn texts, *Auf meinen lieben Gott* and *Wo soll ich fliehen hin*, and presumably a strophe from one of these would have been sung here.                DLH

For bibliography, *see* CANTATA, §1.

***brisé*** ('broken'). *See* STYLE BRISÉ.

**Brühl, Heinrich von** (b. 13 Aug. 1700; d. 28 Oct. 1763). Diplomat and courtier, born in Gangloffsömmern, near Sömmerda in Thuringia. In his youth he served as a page at the courts of Weißenfels and Dresden, and by 1732 rose to high office in the Saxon administration. On the election of King Augustus III in 1734 his career waned for a time, but in 1738 he was appointed minister of civil and military affairs, and in 1746 first minister. He was made first count, then baron, and accumulated considerable wealth, which he lost after the Seven Years War when he was accused of extortion and arrested. Brühl's name appeared on the document notifying Bach's appointment as *Hofkompositeur* to the Dresden court in 1736, and he was influential in securing the appointment of J. G. Harrer as Bach's successor in Leipzig in 1750.

A. Basso, *Frau Musika: la vita e le opere di J. S. Bach*, ii (Turin, 1983).

**Bruhns, Nicolaus** (b. 1665; d. 29 March 1697). Composer and instrumentalist, born in Schwabstedt, near Husum in Schleswig-Holstein. He studied in Lübeck with Buxtehude, and after working for a time in Copenhagen was appointed organist at the Stadtkirche, Husum, in 1689. He remained there until his early death at the age of 32, writing mainly church cantatas and organ pieces, which Bach is said to have known and studied. His main instruments were the organ and the violin, which according to Johann Mattheson he was able to play simultaneously.

**Brunckhorst, Arnold Matthias** (b. 1670; d. 1725). Organist and composer, born in Celle or Wietzendorf. He worked for a time in Hildesheim before being appointed organist at the Stadtkirche in Celle in 1697. In 1720 he was made court organist at Hanover. Bach may have come across him, or his music, while he was at the Michaelisschule in Lüneburg.

**Brustwerk** ('breast division'). A division of organ pipes normally located in the main case over the music rack (just above the organist's head) and played from the uppermost keyboard. The term 'Brustpositiv' is also used. It appeared less frequently after the 17th century because of the tendency of organ builders to abandon spatially separated cases for each of the divisions in favour of a single case. The division was, however, a feature of many instruments with which Bach was familiar (including the organs in the Bonifatiuskirche, Arnstadt, and the Thomaskirche, Leipzig), and he requested that a 'Brustpositivgen' ('little Brustpositiv') be added to the organ at Mühlhausen (1708) consisting of the following stops: Stillgedackt 8′, Fleute douce 4′, Quinta 3′, Octava 2′, Tertia [1⅗′], Mixtur III, and Schalemoy 8′ (*BDok* i. 153). During Bach's time a number of builders scaled the Brustwerk 'keenly but gently' (J. Adlung, *Musica mechanica organoedi* (Berlin, 1768), i. 124 and 190), making it the least assertive division.                                                QF
For bibliography, *see* ORGAN.

**Buffardin, Pierre-Gabriel** (b. *c*.1690; d. 13 Jan. 1768). French flautist, born in Provence and active at the court of Dresden. Early in his career he served as instructor to J. S. Bach's younger brother Johann Jacob in Constantinople. Buffardin was appointed first flautist in the Dresden court ensemble in 1715, returning to France in 1750. He was one of the leading flautists of his time. Marshall has speculated that he was the intended player for the Partita in A minor for solo flute, while Schulze has suggested that he was the flautist in Bach's putative 1736 performance of the Sonata in A major for flute and cembalo.     JS
R. Marshall, *The Music of Johann Sebastian Bach: The Sources, the Style, the Significance* (New York, 1989); H.-J. Schulze, Foreword to *Johann Sebastian Bach: Konzert c-Moll für zwei Cembali und Streichorchester BWV 1062, Sonate A-Dur für Flöte und Cembalo BWV 1032* [facsimile] (Leipzig, 1979).

**burlesca.** A term used by Bach for the fifth movement of Partita no. 3 BWV827. In its original form (in the *Clavierbüchlein* for Anna Magdalena Bach of 1725) the piece was entitled 'Menuet', but when Bach revised it for publication in 1727 he employed the fanciful title 'Burlesca' and paired it with a similarly playful piece in contrasting time (2/4 instead of 3/4) entitled 'Scherzo'. The altered title reflects the fact that the Burlesca is less a dance than a character piece in dance tempo. It may also reflect the movement's somewhat capricious character; J. G. Walther (*Musicalisches Lexi-*

*con*, 1732) described burlesque music as 'comical and amusing'.                                                RDPJ

**Busoni, Ferruccio** (b. 1 April 1866; d. 27 July 1924). Composer and pianist of German and Italian parentage, born in Empoli, near Florence. He wrote chiefly piano, orchestral, and stage works, including the unfinished opera *Dr Faustus*. He was resident in Berlin from 1894 and died there. After early years as a touring virtuoso and teacher, he concentrated on serious composition and advancing his concept of *junge Klassizität* ('young Classicism'). This visionary concept embraced a wide range of elements, including advanced chromaticism and contrapuntal techniques. Bach and Mozart were the key stylistic figures, though Bach's methods and even materials are more clearly to be identified in Busoni's original music (predictably, in view of the large number of his Bach arrangements). These include the *Improvisation über Bachs Chorallied 'Wie wohl ist mir'* for two pianos (1916), *Zwei Kontrapunktstudien nach J. S. Bach* (1917), and *Sonatina brevis in signo Joannis Sebastiani Magni* (1919).

Busoni's greatest instrumental work is the Bach-influenced *Fantasia contrappuntistica*, which exists in four versions. The final version takes the form of variations on the chorale *Ehre sei Gott in der Höhe* (also incorporating the BACH motif), followed by four fugues gradually unveiling subjects from *The Art of Fugue* separated by intermezzos and variations; the work ends with a coda.                                                MM
*See also* ARRANGEMENTS and PERFORMANCE STYLES.

**Buxtehude, Dietrich** (b. *c*.1637; d. 9 May 1707). Composer and organist, the foremost member of the north German Baroque school. He is best known for his organ music, but his sacred vocal compositions are equally important. Both groups of works exerted a profound influence on the young Bach, who visited Buxtehude in Lübeck for three months in 1705–6.

Buxtehude grew up in Helsingør, Denmark, where in 1660 he became organist at the Marienkirche, having previously succeeded his father Johannes as organist at Helsingborg in 1657/8. In 1668 he became organist and *Werkmeister* (administrator) at the Marienkirche, Lübeck, where, following custom, he married Anna Margarethe Tunder, daughter of his predecessor Franz Tunder (1614–67). He continued Tunder's practice of offering public concerts, which under Buxtehude came to be known as ABENDMUSIKEN and included oratorios and other ambitious vocal works.

These works, many of them presumably composed by Buxtehude, are (with one possible exception) lost except for their librettos. Nevertheless, over 100 German and Latin sacred vocal works remain. Often referred to inaccurately as 'cantatas', these include through-composed concertato motets, strophic arias and chorale settings, and cantata-like works combining both types of setting. The organ works include some two dozen praeludia—toccata-like compositions alternating improvisatory and fugal sections—and about 50 works based on chorale melodies. There are also some 25 suites and variation works for clavichord or harpsichord and an important group of 14 sonatas for violins, viola da gamba, and harpsichord, published about 1694–6.

Buxtehude's keyboard music is in the tradition of Frescobaldi and Froberger, but it incorporates elements of more recent Italian and French style as well. His vocal works belong, in general, to the tradition of Heinrich Schütz (1585–1672), placing great emphasis on the vivid line-by-line musical representation of the text but also, in some works, on strict counterpoint—qualities that Bach evidently emulated in his early vocal works. The lost *Abendmusiken* works probably contained echoes of the Hamburg Opera; Buxtehude was on good terms with the opera composer and gambist Johann Theile (1646–1724) and with the Hamburg organist J. A. Reincken. The three are thought to be depicted together in a painting by Johannes Voorhout, now in Hamburg.                      DS

G. Karstädt, *Thematisch-systematisches Verzeichnis der musikalischen Werke von Dietrich Buxtehude* (Wiesbaden, 1974); K. Snyder, *Dieterich Buxtehude, Organist in Lübeck* (New York, 1987); A. Edler *et al.*, eds., *Dietrich Buxtehude und die europäische Musik seiner Zeit* (Kassel, 1990); P. Walker, ed., *Church, Stage, and Studio: Music and its Contexts in Seventeenth-Century Germany* (Ann Arbor, 1990); G. Webber, *North German Church Music in the Age of Buxtehude* (Oxford, 1996).

**BWV.** Abbreviation for Bach-Werke-Verzeichnis ('Catalogue of Bach's Works'), the short title of the *Thematisch-systematisches Verzeichnis der musikalischen Werke von Johann Sebastian Bach* by Wolfgang Schmieder (Leipzig, 1950; 2nd edn. Wiesbaden, 1990). It is by their BWV numbers that Bach's works are usually identified.

# C

**cadenza.** An ornamental passage, often placed immediately before a cadence (in Italian the words for 'cadence' and 'cadenza' are identical). Most cadenzas are for one player or singer only, are unaccompanied (except possibly by a long-held 'pedal' note in the bass), are improvised or improvisatory in style, and are designed above all to display technical virtuosity or power of expression. The usual position for a cadenza is at the end of the last solo (or vocal) section of a movement. This applies particularly to movements in ritornello form and to da capo arias.

Cadenzas may be classed as 'short' or 'long'. Several authorities, including J. J. Quantz (writing in 1752), recommended that the first type, in vocal music, should not exceed the length of a single breath. In the late Baroque, vocal cadenzas are scarcely ever notated; the point for their insertion is typically marked by a fermata ($\frown$), possibly supplemented by a direction such as 'a piacimento'. Their nature was left to individual singers, who, drawing on the rich tradition of diminution and *fioritura*, moulded them to their own voices. Extant transcriptions of vocal cadenzas show that no attempt was made to match them thematically to the rest of the movement. Predictably, Bach rejected such a free-and-easy approach, but elements of cadenza style often occur briefly at climactic points in his movements.

The 'long' cadenza is specifically instrumental. It originated in the early concerto, where, in works written in Italy around 1700 by Torelli and others, it takes the form of repetitive passage-work over a pedal note. Bach applies this formula in the first movement of his Harpsichord Concerto in D minor. In some works Vivaldi took the idea one stage further, performing free-standing and entirely unaccompanied cadenzas in several sections, a few of which survive in notated form (two are paraphrased by Bach in his concerto transcription for organ BWV594). These are the models for the 'capriccios' of P. A. Locatelli (1695–1764) and Giuseppe Tartini (1692–1770), and also for the cadenza for solo harpsichord in the first movement of Bach's Fifth Brandenburg Concerto (*see* BRANDENBURG CONCERTOS, §3 (v)), which, remarkably, manages to accommodate orthodox thematic development alongside virtuoso flights of fancy. This passage of 65 bars, accounting for over a quarter of that movement's length, foreshadows the fully written-out cadenza of the 19th century. MT

P. Whitmore, 'Towards an Understanding of the Capriccio', *Journal of the Royal Musical Association*, 113 (1988), 47–56.

**Caldara, Antonio** (b. ?1670; d. 28 Dec. 1736). Italian composer, born in Venice. He was active in Vienna from 1716 until his death and contributed prolifically to every musical genre (his sacred works alone include about 40 oratorios and some 300 other compositions). In about 1740–2 Bach copied and performed Caldara's *Magnificat* in C major, adding parts for two violins in *stile antico* to the verse 'Suscepit Israel' (BWV1082/243a).

AB

K. Beißwenger, *Johann Sebastian Bachs Notenbibliothek* (Kassel, 1992); C. Wolff, *Der stile antico in der Musik Johann Sebastian Bachs* (Wiesbaden, 1968), 21, 160, 204.

**calendar, Church.** *See* CHURCH CALENDAR.

**Calov(ius), Abraham** (b. 16 April 1612; d. 25 Feb. 1686). An Orthodox Lutheran, exegetic, systematic, and polemical theologian, and prolific author, born in Mohrungen, East Prussia (now Morag, Poland). After teaching and preaching in north Germany, he was called to the University of Wittenberg as professor of theology in 1650. Two years later, in 1652, he was appointed general-superintendent of the Wittenberg churches, a quasi-episcopal position.

Calov was the editor of *Die deutsche Bibel* (in six volumes, bound as three), a commentary on the whole of Scripture edited from the writings of Martin Luther. Bach owned a set of these volumes, and entered manuscript marginalia and underlining in them. He appears to have had high regard for these volumes, since he mentioned them in passing in a book auction receipt of 1742, and they were the first books to be listed in the inventory of his estate drawn up after his death in 1750. RAL

*BDok* i. 199; iii. 636–7; H. Cox, ed., *The Calov Bible of J. S. Bach* (Ann Arbor, 1983); R. A. Leaver, *J. S. Bach and Scripture: Glosses from the Calov Bible Commentary* (St Louis, Miss., 1985); A. C. Piepkorn, 'Calov(ius), Abraham', in J. R. Odensieck, ed., *The Encyclopedia of the Lutheran Church* (Minneapolis, 1965), i. 352–3.

**Calvinism.** The reformed Protestant tradition based on the theology of the Swiss reformer Jean

Calvin (1509–64). Although sharing much with LUTHERANISM, there were significant differences between the two confessions, especially with regard to the nature of law, grace, the Church, worship, the sacraments, and music, which the Calvinists permitted only in the form of congregational psalmody. The Lutheran Saxon Visitation articles of 1593 specifically proscribed the tenets of Calvinism.

Bach endorsed this anti-Calvinist stance: he owned August Pfeiffer's *Anti-Calvinismus* (Lübeck, 1699), and as a Lutheran church musician was required to subscribe to the 1593 Saxon articles. In Cöthen, between 1717 and 1723, Bach served as *Kapellmeister* to a Calvinist court, where there existed no opportunity for concerted religious music, except for such celebrations as the birthday of the duke and New Year. While on friendly terms with his Calvinist employer, Prince Leopold, Bach drew attention to Pfeiffer's *Anti-Calvinismus* on the title-page of the manuscript *Clavierbüchlein* he prepared for his wife Anna Magdalena in 1722.                                    RAL

BDok i. 268; C. Garside, *The Origin of Calvin's Theology of Music, 1536–1543* (Philadelphia, 1979); R. A. Leaver, *Bachs theologische Bibliothek* (Stuttgart, 1983), 133–4; E. A. McKee, 'Context, Contours, Worship', *Princeton Seminary Bulletin*, 16 (new series) (1995), 172–201; F. Smend, *Bach in Köthen*, Eng. trans. J. Page, ed. S. Daw (St Louis, Miss., 1985).

**Cammer-musicus.** *See* KAMMERMUSIKUS.

***Cammerton (Kammerton).*** A general instrumental PITCH standard, usually at $a' \approx 415$ but also commonly at $a' \approx 404$ or $a' \approx 390$ (this last known as *tief-Cammerton*). $a' \approx 415$ had been used by choirs in early 17th-century Germany, but first became associated with instruments on the arrival of the newly developed French woodwinds at about the time that Bach was born. A few *Cammerton* organs began to be built at the beginning of the 18th century, and their pitches agree well with those of contemporary instruments of relatively immovable pitch, like recorders and transverse flutes.

In 1713 Johann Mattheson wrote of 'A- und B-*Cammerton*'. These terms expressed an interval relation to CHORTON rather than absolute pitch frequencies. To produce the note C in the *Cammerton* a major 2nd below *Chorton*, an organist would need to play his B♭ (B in German nomenclature), hence the name B-*Cammerton*. Playing an A produced a C in A-*Cammerton*, a minor 3rd below *Chorton*. The names 'A- und B-*Cammerton*' may also have been used as instructions for notation when parts had to be copied. Since *Chorton* was commonly at $a' \approx 465$ (alias CORNET-TON), A- and B-*Cammerton* were virtually absolute pitch designations (a minor 3rd below 465 is 390, a major 2nd is 414). J. J. Quantz and J. F. Agricola later used the term 'A-*Cammerton*' to mean a specific pitch frequency.                                    BH

**cancrizans.** A Latin term, meaning 'crab-like', used to denote a line or passage which appears in retrograde form, usually along with its original shape. It is most commonly associated with contrapuntal music from the Renaissance onwards, and in particular with CANON. One of the canons in Bach's *Musical Offering* is headed 'Canon 1 a 2 cancrizans'.                                    LC

**canon.** A term commonly used to describe two or more parts of a contrapuntal piece which have the same melody but begin at different points. This, the strictest form of imitation, can begin at the unison or at any other interval, and can also involve more complex processes, such as AUGMENTATION, DIMINUTION, INVERSION, and retrograde (or CANCRIZANS) motion. The canonic process may extend to several parts (as in the numerous and often witty rounds and catches of the 17th century, which can be repeated *ad infinitum*), but in most instrumental examples it involves only two parts. Group canons are also a possibility, in which two or more independent melodies are imitated canonically and simultaneously. In a 'canon 4 in 2', for example, four parts present two melodies, each of them canonically treated.

All these canonic devices were originally used to provide a self-sufficient musical texture. However, despite the immense skill and ingenuity required to solve the problems which composers set themselves, it was not long before they found that the technique could be employed in combination with one or more free parts, and canon developed with ever-increasing complexity from the famous 13th-century Reading Rota (*Sumer is icumen in*) to the intricate and artistic examples in the music of Guillaume de Machaut (*c.*1300–77), Guillaume Dufay (*c.*1398–1474), and others. Palestrina and other 16th-century composers often used the term 'fuga' in their masses to draw attention to the presence of a two-part canon in a larger polyphonic texture (only later did the term come to mean what we now know as 'fugue').

Strictly speaking, the term 'canon' (from the Greek 'kanōn', meaning 'rule') refers to the instruction, explicit or cryptic, according to which the polyphony is to be derived from the single line. A 'puzzle canon' is one for which no such instruction is provided. The emphasis on ingenuity and cerebral activity that has always been associated with canon, despite the artistic ends to which it has been put, is exemplified by the theorist Johannes Tinctorus, who defined the term in his *Terminorum musicae diffinitorium* (1495) as 'a rule which shows the intention of the composer in an obscure way', and by Pier Francesco Valentini (*c*.1570–1654), who published a canon for which there were over 2,000 different solutions.

Few would dispute that the highest point in the history of canon was reached by Bach, whose immense technical expertise in handling it was always balanced by artistic necessity. He took delight (as did many other composers) in setting canonic problems in the personal albums of friends and acquaintances; some of these (BWV1073–5 and 1077–8) have survived (see Schulze). Bach's submission on joining Lorenz Mizler's Correspondirenden Societät der Musicalischen Wissenschaften in 1747 was the Canonic Variations on *Vom Himmel hoch* BWV769. But his use of the device is as varied as it is resourceful, and in connection with chorale settings it can be especially satisfying. *In dulci jubilo*, from the *Orgel-Büchlein*, shows the soprano and tenor using the chorale melody one bar and one octave apart, while the alto and bass almost complete another canon at the same distance, mostly in quaver triplets; two-thirds of the piece might therefore be described as a canon 4 in 2. In *O Lamm Gottes* ('Canone all Quinta'), also from the *Orgel-Büchlein*, the inner voices present the chorale a 5th and two beats apart, while the outer ones weave elaborate free parts around them.

Canon acts as a structural element in a wider sense in the Goldberg Variations, in which every third variation employs canon at a different interval, starting with the unison (Variation 3), and continuing with canon at the 2nd (Variation 6), the 3rd (Variation 9), and so on; all except Variation 27 (canon at the 9th) include an additional free part in the bass. The canons at the 4th and 5th (Variations 12 and 15) proceed by inversion, while Variation 18 (at the 6th) is an example of 'close canon' (for which the term STRETTO is also sometimes used), in which the entry of the second voice follows very closely that of the first (in this case, after a single minim beat).

A more austere use of canon, with no added texture, is found in the 14 canons that Bach entered into his personal copy of the Goldberg Variations (see Kenyon), and is a particular feature of his late works. The four canons in *The Art of Fugue* exemplify canon at the octave, four bars apart; at the 10th, four bars part; at the 12th, eight bars apart; and by augmentation and contrary motion at the 4th, four bars apart. Those in the *Musical Offering* are perhaps the most searching of all. Two of them are puzzle canons, leaving the performer or editor to solve the working-out of a version of the 'Royal Theme' presented to Bach by Frederick the Great. Among the panoply of riches in this work are the canon 4 in 2 by augmentation and contrary motion, and the 'canon 1 a 2 cancrizans'. Symbolism as well as skill is applied to the 'canon 5 a 2 per tonos' in which each repetition of the melody is a tone higher than the previous one; Bach added the Latin motto 'Ascendente . . . modulatione ascendat Gloria Regis' ('As the modulations rise, so may the glory of the king'). In these canons, as in almost the whole of the *Musical Offering* and *The Art of Fugue*, Bach left the instrumentation unspecified, suggesting that the musical ideal (involving the solution of self-imposed problems) took precedence in his mind over matters of practical realization. However, he always wrote with the possibility of performance in mind, and numerous successful realizations of both works have been made.                LC

N. Kenyon, 'A Newly Discovered Group of Canons by Bach', *Musical Times*, 117 (1976), 391–3; H.-J. Schulze, 'Johann Sebastian Bachs Kanonwidmungen', *BJb* 53 (1967), 82–92.

**Canonic Variations on *Vom Himmel hoch*.**
See overleaf.

**cantata.** See p.82.

**Cantate.** In the CHURCH CALENDAR, the fourth Sunday after Easter. It takes its name from the introit to the Mass for that day in the Latin rite, beginning 'Cantate Domino canticum novum'.

***Cantate [en] burlesque*** ('Burlesque Cantata'). An alternative title for the PEASANT CANTATA.

**cantus firmus** ('fixed melody'). A Latin term used, principally in the context of medieval and Renaissance polyphony, for a plainchant in long notes around which newly composed counterpoint was deployed. In the B minor Mass Bach used two plainchants in this way, in 'Credo in unum Deum' and 'Confiteor unum baptisma'; in the *Magnificat* he introduced a psalm tone, *tonus peregrinus*, into 'Suscepit Israel'. In the context of his other music, however, the term 'cantus firmus' is normally used for a chorale tune which is heard in evenly paced notes (mainly minims or crotchets) while the other parts proceed in shorter notes and usually in imitation. In this sense a cantus firmus is present in most of the opening choruses of the chorale cantatas in Bach's second *Jahrgang* and in many of his organ chorales.
*See also* VORIMITATION.

W. Gerstenberg, 'Zum Cantus firmus in Bachs Kantate', in W. Rehm, ed., *Bachiana et alia musicologia*, (Kassel, 1983).

## Canonic Variations on *Vom Himmel hoch*

A set of five variations for organ on the traditional Lutheran Christmas hymn, 'From highest heaven', BWV769. The earliest source is the autograph manuscript, included in a miscellany of organ works which can be dated to the period around 1746–7. Modern research indicates that the original printed version of the collection, engraved, printed, and published by Balthasar Schmid in Nuremberg, appeared only later, although the first stage of the engraving project probably goes back to the period around Easter 1746.

While the version in the autograph is notated in organ score (i.e. on three staves, with the pedal part occupying the lowest one), changes in notational format in the original edition hint at Bach's changing conception of the work. Variations 1–3 seem to have been composed first as a series of highly abstract canons in the context of Bach's work on the 14 canons (BWV1087) he wrote into his *Handexemplar* of the GOLDBERG VARIATIONS some time between 1742 and 1746. BWV769: 1–3 must have been shown in enigmatic notation (i.e. without the imitating voice, or 'comes') in the source from which Schmid prepared his engraver's copy, for this notational format is only slightly altered in the original edition to include the incipits of the *comes*. Variation 5, which was composed next, is notated in organ score in the original edition. The occasion for its composition may have been the service of thanksgiving to mark the signing of the Peace of Dresden, held in the Nikolaikirche, Leipzig, on 25 December 1745. Variations 1, 2, 5, and 3 were entered into the autograph first, possibly during the summer of 1746. Variation 4 was entered only after a considerable break, and it was engraved after the other four variations. This final stage in the genesis of the collection can be viewed in the context of Bach's presentation of the work to Lorenz Mizler's Correspondirenden Societät der Musicalischen Wissenschaften, into which Bach was inducted in June 1747. In the original edition Variation 4 is notated in open score on four staves, perhaps reflecting the recherché notational format adopted for the fair copy of the collection submitted to the society. This last variation was subsequently engraved and the collection published, probably to appear at the Michaelmas fair of 1747. A reprinting seems to have been undertaken by C. P. E. Bach in 1751.

The first part of the printed title reads: 'Einige canonische Veraenderungen über das Weynacht-Lied: Vom Himmel hoch da komm ich her' ('Some Canonic Variations on the Christmas hymn: Vom Himmel hoch da komm ich her'). In the first four variations two voices in canon—at the octave, 5th, 7th, and again at the octave in augmentation—sound against the cantus firmus (the hymn melody) stated in long notes. In Variation 5 the four phrases of the cantus firmus are treated in inverted canon at various intervals successively, the whole culminating in a stretto in diminution.

In Variations 1 and 2 the cantus firmus is presented in the pedal following the entry of the two upper voices in the manuals in canonic imitation at the lower octave and lower 5th respectively. Given the sustained cantus firmus notes, the breaks of a bar (or a bar and a half) between phrases, and the three-part texture, it is not surprising that the canonic voices in both cases proceed for the most part in semiquavers. In Variation 1 the leading voice (*dux*) begins with a scalar descent through an octave which is imitated immediately in the *comes* at the octave below, giving the impression of a downward-sweeping cascade which perfectly suggests the angel's descent from heaven in the first strophe of the chorale. The designation 'alio modo' in the title of Variation 2 suggests a pairing of the first two variations, and indeed the cantus firmus is presented at the same pitch level. However, while the canonic voices in Variation 1 are not derived from the chorale melody, in Variation 2 they begin with a slightly ornamented version of its first phrase.

In the original edition Variation 5, the cantus firmus canon, appears at the end, while in the autograph it is placed as the central axis of the work to give the overall scheme of 1–2–5–3–4. The order in the autograph could not be followed in the printed edition because Variations 1–3 had already been engraved with the end of no. 2 sharing a plate with no. 3. Internal evidence would seem to support the view that the autograph represents Bach's definitive order. Not only are Variations 1 and 2 paired, but they are clearly distinguished from Variations 3 and 4 by a change in texture from three to four voices. It is interesting that the free, fourth voice first enters at the mid-point of Variation 5. In the first half, two distinct canons at consonant intervals (a 6th and a 3rd) are presented, as in Variations 1 and 2, in the two uppermost voices. The accompanying voice in the pedal throughout is in running quavers. In the second half two more distinct canons at dissonant intervals (a 2nd and a 9th) are contrapuntally inverted so that the *dux* becomes the *comes* and vice versa, and they migrate first to the lowest two voices and finally to the outer two. Here, the added fourth voice is in semiquavers throughout. All these features impart to Variation 5 a central, pivotal role in an axially symmetrical disposition. In the closing bars of this variation, various phrases of the cantus firmus are presented in diminution, and then in stretto, over the concluding phrase of the chorale stated in long notes by the pedals.

Like Variation 2, no. 3 begins with an anticipation, more extended this time, of the initial phrase of the chorale melody, here in canon at the upper 7th. The marking 'Cantabile' suggests a slower tempo, and the pervasive use of syncopation, chromaticism, and appoggiatura figures, along with the drawn-out plagal cadence, impart an affect of melancholy. With breaks between phrases of the cantus firmus as long as seven bars, the fourth variation is by far the longest. The canon is presented in the outer voices and, as in Variation 1, at the lower octave. The *dux* is highly florid and convoluted, proceeding for the most part in demisemiquavers. With the notes B♭, A, C, and B♮ (*see* BACH) in the alto voice over the concluding two notes of the cantus firmus, Bach signs his name to this imposing final variation.          GB

*See also* SOURCES, §2.

G. Butler, *Bach's Clavier-Übung III: The Making of a Print* (Durham, NC, 1990), 91 ff.; W. Emery, 'A Note on the History of Bach's Canonic Variations', *Musical Times*, 104 (1963), 32–3; H. Klotz, 'Über Johann Sebastian Bachs Kanonwerk "Vom Himmel hoch, da komm ich her" ', *Die Musikforschung*, 19 (1966), 295–304; F. Smend, 'Bachs Kanonwerk über "Vom Himmel hoch, da komm ich her" ', *BJb* 30 (1933), 1–29; P. Williams, *The Organ Music of J. S. Bach*, ii (Cambridge 1980), 315–27.

# cantata (*Kantate*)

A term rarely used by Bach, but subsequently applied both to works he wrote as *Hauptmusik* ('principal music') for Lutheran Church services and to compositions, mainly of the serenata type, that he provided for secular occasions.

1. Sacred cantatas.
2. Secular cantatas.

1. **Sacred cantatas.** Although Bach himself very rarely used the term 'cantata' for his church pieces, preferring such designations as 'concerto', 'Stück' ('piece'), or simply the 'Musik', German theorists, from about 1700, employed the Italian term for concerted, multi-movement liturgical pieces comprising recitatives and arias to freely composed poetry as well as choral movements with biblical texts and settings of chorale melodies. It was only in the 19th century, notably by Spitta and the editors of the *BG*, that the term 'cantata' was generally applied to the sacred works of Bach, his contemporaries, and his predecessors.

*The Lutheran cantata before Bach.* The roots of the German Lutheran cantata are found in the liturgical reforms of Martin Luther. Two primary elements contributed to its development as a musical homily within Lutheran liturgies: the sung Gospel of the day and congregational song. Luther's understanding of music as proclamation led him to retain, albeit in a modified form, the tradition of chanting the biblical lections, especially the Gospel of the day, in the weekly evangelical Mass. In the *Formula missae* (1523) he encouraged the continuance of the practice of singing the Epistle and Gospel, and in his *Deutsche Messe* (1526) he included specific melodic formulae for these biblical lections. The focal point of the first part of the eucharistic liturgy was the chanting of the Gospel of the day and the sermon, which was an exposition of the Gospel pericope. By the middle of the 16th century a musical counterpart to the chanted Gospel and the sermon on the Gospel lection became common: the *Evangelienmotette* ('Gospel motet') or *Spruchmotette* ('Bible-text motet'). As with other Lutheran practices, this was a development of the Roman Catholic practice of Gospel motets, such as those of Josquin Desprez (*c.*1440–1521) and Orlande de Lassus (?1530–94), in which the key verse (or verses) of the Gospel pericopes were given specific musical settings. But Lutheran practice was more systematic and widespread in that numerous yearly cycles of *Evangelienmotetten* were published between the middle of the 16th century and the end of the 17th. Among the foremost composers were Sethus Calvisius (1556–1615), Andreas Raselius (*c.*1563–1602), Christoph Demantius (1567–1643), Melchior Vulpius (*c.*1570–1615), and Melchior Franck (*c.*1579–1639), and their settings employed from two to eight or more voices.

A distinctive feature of Luther's liturgical reforms was his recovery of the corporate voice of the congregation in vernacular hymnody. His early collaboration with the composer Johann Walter (1496–1570) effectively created the polyphonic *Liedmotette* ('chorale motet'), the cantus firmus setting of a chorale melody. One of the most important functions of the new vernacular hymnody was to prepare for the chanting of the Gospel of the day, since it was sung following the Gradual—that is, between the Epistle and the Gospel. These polyphonic settings by Walter and others were sung by the choir in alternation with the unison congregation at this juncture. Thus the Gospel of the day was effectively framed by suitable 'Gospel' music: the *Graduallied* ('Gradual hymn') of the choir and congregation sung before the chanting of the Gospel, and the *Spruchmotette* of choir alone, after the sermon on the Gospel. In the course of time, after the practice of alternation with the congregation was discontinued, the chorale motet developed independently, and, with the expanded use of instruments (especially the continuo), evolved into the chorale concertato. Michael Praetorius (?1571–1621) composed large-scale polychoral chorale concertatos, especially in his *Polyhymnia caduceatrix* (1619), and J. H. Schein (1586–1630) created smaller-scale solo concertatos in his *Opella nova* (1618–26).

These two elements—freely-composed settings of biblical texts and congregational chorale melodies in their varied manifestations—ultimately became unified within a single form, the *Kirchenstück*, the embryonic cantata, especially with the addition during the 17th century of independent instrumental parts playing sonatas and ritornellos as well as accompanying. Composers of such sacred concertos include Heinrich Schütz (1585–1672) and Samuel Scheidt (1587–1654).

In the third quarter of the 17th century the Darmstadt *Kapellmeister* W. C. Briegel (1626–1712) issued two collections of expanded Gospel motets under the title *Evangelischen Blümengarten* (1666–8). These vocal works, mostly in a simple chordal style, are, like the traditional Gospel motets, settings of the key verses of the respective Gospels for the Sundays and feasts of the Church year. But each one concludes with what Briegel designates an 'aria'. These use neither biblical verse nor chorale stanzas, but free strophic poetry, thus expanding the literary form of the cantata. Other composers of the period who contributed to the evolving genre include Andreas Hammerschmidt (1611/12–75), Franz Tunder (1614–67), Matthias Weckmann (*c.*1619–74), Johann Rosenmüller (*c.*1619–84), Johann Pachelbel, Dietrich Buxtehude, various members the Bach family (notably Johann Michael and Johann Christoph (i)), and J. S. Bach's immediate predecessors in Leipzig, Johann Schelle (1648–1701) and Johann Kuhnau.

The church cantata was further expanded in the early 18th century by the incorporation of the operatic da capo aria form and recitative, both simple and accompanied. This 'reform' type of cantata was advocated by Erdmann Neumeister, an Orthodox pastor in Hamburg, who wrote librettos for J. P. Krieger (1649–1725), a composer at the court of Weißenfels (but *see also* ERNST LUDWIG). Neumeister described the new cantata form as resembling 'a piece from an opera'. Between 1700 and 1717 he issued five annual cycles of librettos, and the complete five-year anthology was published as *Fünffache Kirchen-Andachten* (Leipzig, 1717), with later supplements issued in 1726 and 1752. Neumeister's technique was to put the substance of his sermon on the Gospel for a given Sunday or festival into poetic form, thus underscoring the function of the cantata as the musical counterpart of the sermon, the former being a musical and the latter a verbal exposition of the principal biblical lection of the day. Other cantata librettists were encouraged to write and publish their own annual cycles in accordance with this 'reform' type, and these were set by various composers, among them G. H. Stölzel (1690–1749), Christoph Graupner, Telemann, and J. S. Bach.

*Bach's pre-Leipzig cantatas.* Cantatas form the most substantial part of Bach's total output. He probably composed about 300, of which about 200 are extant. Some older writers suggest that this is a staggering number of works, but many of Bach's contemporaries were more prolific: Graupner, for example, composed almost 2,000, and Telemann about 1,200. However, although Bach's output was numerically smaller, his cantatas cover a wider range of musical style, contrapuntal complexity, and emotional intensity than those of his two contemporaries.

Most of Bach's cantatas were composed during two intensive periods of creativity: between 1713 and 1716 in Weimar, and between 1723 and 1729 in Leipzig. But there was also a modest number of early, pre-Weimar cantatas, each one distinctive in its own way; celebratory cantatas composed at Cöthen that were later reworked for liturgical use in Leipzig; and a relatively small but important group of later Leipzig cantatas.

Bach's earliest cantatas were written in Mühlhausen (though it is possible that Cantata 4 was composed in Arnstadt, following his return from Lübeck, for Easter Day 1706); they are:

| 1707 | BWV: ?4, ?131, ?106, 223 |
| 1708 | BWV: 71, 96 |
| ? | BWV: ?150. |

These cantatas in general follow the late 17th-century form, with librettos consisting of biblical and chorale texts with a limited use of free poetry. Choral movements are in MOTET STYLE and the solo movements are usually short, with a tendency towards word-painting on the key words of the text. The cantatas are usually symmetrically structured, with choruses to begin and end and various solo movements surrounding a central choral movement. Stylistically they are related to the cantatas of Pachelbel and Buxtehude.

Bach became court organist in Weimar in 1708, and by the end of 1713 he had written one or two occasional cantatas. But after his appointment as *Konzertmeister* in March 1714 his duties included the composition and performance of a cantata every four weeks. Their chronology is beset with uncertainties, but the latest research suggests the following:

| 1713 | BWV: ?21*a* |
| 1714 | BWV: 182, 12, 172, 21*b*, 199*a*, 61, ?63, 152 |
| 1715 | BWV: ?18, 54, 31, 165, 185, 163, 132 |
| 1716 | BWV: 155, 80*a*, 161, 162, 70*a*, 186*a*, 147*a*. |

The main librettist for these cantatas was Salomo Franck, court librarian and poet in Weimar, who began writing librettos of the Neumeister type at about the same time that Bach was promoted as *Konzertmeister*. Bach's Weimar cantatas, in contrast to his earlier ones, include simple recitative and da capo arias. But he was also developing his compositional techniques, especially his use of the permutation fugue in choral movements (e.g. Cantatas 21:6 and 11, and 182:2) and investigating French and Italian styles. Thus the Weimar cantatas exhibit a variety of forms and genres: motet (no. 21), fugue and canon (no. 182), ostinato (no. 12), concerto (no. 172), and French overture (no. 61).

As *Kapellmeister* to the Calvinist court of Prince Leopold at Cöthen (1717–23), Bach was not required to write church cantatas, but he was expected to provide appropriate music for the prince's birthday and for New Year celebrations. Although most of these works are not extant, and the evidence is somewhat fragmentary, it is known that many of these pieces were later parodied for liturgical use in Leipzig:

| 1718 | BWV: 66*a*, Anh. 5 |
|------|--------------------|
| 1719 | BWV: 134*a* |
| 1720 | BWV: Anh. 6 and 7 |
| 1721–2 | BWV: ?173*a*, ?194*a* |
| 1722–3 | BWV: 184*a*, Anh. 8. |

Smend (1985) and Dürr (1951, rev. 1977) both agree that Cantatas 145 and 193, together with one movement of no. 120, are most likely parodies of lost celebratory cantatas composed in Cöthen.

*Bach's Leipzig cantatas.* In 1723, almost at the end of his tenure in Cöthen, Bach composed two cantatas (nos. 22 and 23) that were performed in the Thomaskirche, Leipzig, on 7 February as audition pieces for his application for the position of Thomaskantor. They proved to be forerunners of the extraordinary period of creativity in the composition of church cantatas that followed his appointment to the position in May that year.

Bach's first official Sunday in Leipzig was the first Sunday after Trinity, 30 May 1723. A new cantata (no. 75) was composed for the occasion, and for the next three years or so he was composing new cantatas, or rearranging earlier ones, at a rate of one a week; some weeks saw him at work on two or more. In the Obituary it is stated that among his unpublished music there were 'fünf Jahrgänge von Kirchenstücken, auf alle Sonn- und Festtage' ('five annual cycles of church pieces for all the Sundays and festivals': *BDok* i. 86). Although this is a reference to the total extent of Bach's compositions in the genre, the researches of Dadelsen and Dürr have shown that it also reflects his compositional activity, especially in his early years in Leipzig (*see* JAHRGANG). The first annual cycle, *Jahrgang* 1, ran from the first Sunday after Trinity 1723 to Trinity Sunday 1724; *Jahrgang* 2 ran from 1724 to 1725. These first two cycles are fairly complete; *Jahrgang* 3 (1725–6) is less so; *Jahrgang* 4 is difficult to assess with accuracy; and *Jahrgang* 5 is hardly definable at all. It is possible that the 100 or so cantatas no longer extant may have originally been in *Jahrgänge* 4 and 5.

*Jahrgang* 1 included not only newly composed cantatas but also earlier ones that were revived or reworked into newer forms. The sequence of performances is as follows:

1723  BWV: 75, 76, 21, 24, 185, 167, 147, 186, 136, 105, 46, 179, 199*c*, 69*a*, 77, 25, 119, 138, 95, 148, 48, 162, 109, 89, ?163, 194, 60, 90, 80*b*, 70, 61, 63, 40, 64

1724  BWV: 190, 153, 65, 154, 155, 73, 81, 83, 144, 181, 18, 23, 182, 4, 66, 134, 67, 104, 12, 166, 86, 37, 44, 172, ?59, 173, 184, 194, ?165.

In the newly composed cantatas of *Jahrgang* 1 Dürr has identified three variants of a basic structure. The primary form, Type A, is employed in ten cantatas first performed in July, August, and October 1723, and April 1724 (nos. 136, 105, 46, 179, 69*a*, 77, 109, 89, and 104):

biblical text–recitative–aria–recitative–aria–chorale.

Type B, exemplified in six cantatas first performed in October and December 1723, and January and April 1724 (nos. 48, 40, 64, 153, 65, and 67), is a similar structure, but with an additional chorale following the first recitative:

biblical text–recitative–chorale–aria–recitative–aria–chorale.

Type C, found in five cantatas first performed in February and May 1724 (nos. 144, 166, 86, 37, and 44), is a modification of Type B in which one recitative is eliminated and the position of one aria is advanced:

biblical text–aria–chorale–recitative–aria–chorale.

The movements of the newly composed *Jahrgang* 1 cantatas present an astonishingly rich variety of musical forms, compositional techniques, contrapuntal intricacies, breathtakingly beautiful arias, and stunningly inventive obbligato instrumental parts.

The singing of newly composed, complex choruses week after week, with little time to learn them, must have strained the resources of the Thomanerchor, which may have been one of the reasons for the significant compositional change that took place for *Jahrgang* 2. This cycle is distinguished by its high proportion of chorale cantatas, each of which is based textually (and melodically, at least in the outer movements) on a single CHORALE. The opening movement in most of these cantatas is a chorus, with the chorale melody in the soprano supported by imitative counterpoint in the other voices. These choruses were less demanding, certainly for the sopranos, than many of the fugal choruses of *Jahrgang* 1.

*Jahrgang* 2 was apparently extended to include the whole of the Trinity season in 1725:

1724   BWV: 20, 2, 7, 135, 10, 93, 107, 178, 94, 101, 113, 33, 78, 99, 8, 130, 114, 96, 5, 180, 38, 115, 139, 26, 116, 62, 91, 121, 133, 122

1725   BWV: 41, 123, 124, 3, 111, 92, 125, 126, 127, 137, 168, 164, 79.

Since many of the chorales used in these cantatas are the Wittenberg hymns of Luther and others, which began to be published in 1524, it seems highly likely that the cantatas of *Jahrgang* 2, which began in 1724, were intended to celebrate 200 years of Lutheran hymnody.

Four of the cantatas of *Jahrgang* 2 (BWV6, 42, 85, and 79) conform structurally to Type C of *Jahrgang* 1. The chorale cantatas, written and performed between the first Sunday after Trinity 1724 and Easter 1725, share a common form. The opening choral movement is an elaborate setting of the unaltered first strophe of the chorale on which the cantata is based; the following movements—recitatives, arias, duets, etc.— are textual paraphrases of the inner strophes of the chorale; and the final movement is a simple four-part setting of the final strophe. Although the chorale melody is usually in the soprano in the opening movements, it is occasionally found in other voices (e.g. alto in Cantata 96, tenor in no. 7, and bass in no. 3). As in *Jahrgang* 1, Bach employed a variety of musical forms. The opening movements of the first four cantatas, for example, are a French overture (BWV20), a cantus firmus motet (BWV2), a chorale movement with concertante solo violin (BWV7), and a chorale fantasia (BWV135). The chorale cantatas came to an end at Easter 1725, after which Bach turned first to librettos by Christiane Mariane von ZIEGLER. The remaining works in the *Jahrgang* are akin to those of *Jahrgang* 1.

During 1725–6 Bach apparently composed fewer cantatas than in the previous two years:

1725   BWV: 110, 57, 151, 28

1726   BWV: 16, 32, 13, 72, 13, 146, ?129, 39, 88, 170, 187, 45, 102, 35, 17, 19, 27, 47, 169, 56, 49, 98, 55, 52.

Between February and September 1726, instead of composing new cantatas, Bach performed 18 by his cousin J. L. Bach (including the misattributed BWV15). These works, which are less demanding than his own, may indicate that there were problems with Bach's vocal and instrumental resources, or he may have used them to give himself time to work on the *St Matthew Passion*, which was first performed in the following spring 1727. Their use may also mean that he planned to compose the cantatas of *Jahrgang* 3 over a period of two years (1725–7), by which reckoning it would also include:

1727   BWV: 58, 82, 84, 69*a*, 120.

The musical characteristics of *Jahrgang* 3 include instrumental sinfonias, obbligato organ parts, and CHOREINBAU.

*Jahrgang* 4 is perhaps to be identified as the 'Picander *Jahrgang*' since in 1728–9 Bach set librettos by Picander in the following works:

1728   BWV: 149, 188, 197*a*
1729   BWV: 171, 156, 159, 145, 174,

and, moreover, Picander named Bach as the composer of his complete *Cantaten auf die Sonn- und Fest-Tage durch das gantze Jahr* (Leipzig, 1728)—though whether in doing so he was expressing a hope, an intention, or an established fact is not clear.

Later cantatas, some of which may have formed part of *Jahrgang* 5, are: 1730: BWV190, 120, Anh. I 4, and 51; 1731: BWV112 and 140; 1732: BWV177; post-1732: BWV100; 1734: BWV97; pre-1735: BWV158; 1734–5: BWV248$^{\text{I–VI}}$, 14, 11, and 9; post-1738: BWV30 and ?80; and *c*.1742: BWV200. In addition to these cantatas, which were heard as part of the regular worship on Sundays, festivals, and celebrations, there are the funeral and memorial cantatas (BWV157 and 198), and wedding cantatas, which were not necessarily performed in church (BWV34*a*, 195, 120*a*, and 197).

In addition to librettos by unknown poets, Bach is known to have used texts from about 20 different published sources (see *BC* i. 24), including annual cycles by Franck, Lehms, Neumeister, Picander, and Ziegler. Other composers were content to work their way through a *Jahrgang* of librettos by a single author. Bach was more selective in his choice of texts, which he would modify if he felt the need. The fact that the senior clergy in Leipzig, notably Superintendent Deyling, had to approve them in advance does not invalidate the conclusion that Bach was careful in selecting the texts he wished to set. Deyling had the right of veto, but Bach had the right to choose.                               RAL

*DürrC, DürrK*; J. Day, *The Literary Background to Bach's Cantatas* (London, 1961); A. Dürr, *Studien über die frühen Kantaten J. S. Bachs* (Leipzig, 1951; rev. edn. Wiesbaden, 1977); A. Glöckner, 'Zur Chronologie der Weimarer Kantaten Johann Sebastian Bachs', *BJb* 71 (1985), 159–64; R. A. Leaver, 'The Liturgical Place and Homiletic Purpose of Bach's Cantatas', *Worship* 59 (1985), 9–29; K. Hofmann, 'Neue Überlegungen zu Bachs Weimarer Kantaten-Kalender', *BJb* 79 (1993), 159–64; D. R. Melamed, 'Mehr zur Chronologie von Bachs Weimarer Kantaten', *BJb* 79 (1993), 213–16; U. Meyer, *Biblical Quotation in the Cantata Libretti of Johann Sebastian Bach* (Lanham, Md., 1997); W. Neumann, *Handbuch der Kantaten Johann Sebastian Bachs* (Leipzig, 1947; 5th edn. Wiesbaden, 1984); W. Neumann, *Sämtliche von Johann Sebastian Bach vertonte Texte* (Leipzig, 1974); F. Smend, *Bach in Cöthen*, trans. J. Page, ed. S. Daw (St Louis, Miss., 1985); M. P. Unger, *Handbook to Bach's Sacred Cantata Texts* (Lanham, Md., 1996); C. Wolff, 'Wo bleib Bachs fünfter Kantatenjahrgang?', *BJb* 68 (1982), 151–2; C. Wolff, ed., *The World of the Bach Cantatas*, i: *Johann Sebastian Bach's Early Sacred Cantatas*, Eng. trans. C. Bakker and M. Ross-Griffel (New York, 1997).

**2. Secular cantatas.**   The earliest use of the term 'cantata' was for Italian strophic songs with music varying from one strophe to the next; such works are now often referred to as 'strophic variations'. In printed volumes of 'Cantade et arie' by Alessandro Grandi (2nd edn., 1620) and Giovanni Pietro Berti (1624) the term is coupled with another strophic binary form of the time, the aria. With this meaning the term was transferred also to Germany by Heinrich Schütz's pupil Caspar Kittel (1603–39), whose *Arien und Cantaten* were published in Dresden in 1638. The most important developments in the secular cantata during the 17th century took place at Rome, especially in the works of Giacomo Carissimi written between about 1640 and 1672. Many of these consist of a sequence of separate movements, thus establishing one of the characteristics of the later cantata.

Following the contemporary apportioning of musical styles and genres into 'church', 'chamber', and 'theatre' (reflecting the places where the works were usually performed), the secular cantata was often designated a *cantata da camera* ('chamber cantata'). Such cantatas were mostly for one or two singers, and a penchant for mythological subjects soon led to the introduction of elements from contemporary opera. Notable composers of the early secular cantata in Italy included, in addition to Carissimi, Antonio Cesti (1623–69) and Alessandro Stradella (1644–82). Agostino Steffani (1654–1728), remembered particularly for his chamber duets, forms another link to northern musical practice, since he was active mainly at German courts in Munich and Hanover.

The chamber cantatas of Alessandro Scarlatti (1660–1725), numbering over 600 (mainly for solo voice and continuo), form a landmark in the history of the genre. They reflect all the important changes that took place in the history of virtuoso vocal music at the end of the 17th and the beginning of the 18th centuries, such as the gradual abandonment of binary and strophic forms in favour of da capo structures, the development of differentiated texts for recitatives (unrhymed lines of seven or eleven syllables) and arias (rhymed lines of regular and more varied lengths), and the standardization of the structure into pairs of alternating recitatives and arias. This strengthened the expressive element of the cantata because it encouraged the inclusion of contrasting situations and affects within a single work. It was this type of cantata that Handel encountered when he went to Italy in 1706.

In German Protestant regions the purpose of secular cantatas was more clearly defined as part of the celebrations at the princely courts (and sometimes within the aristocracy as well). They show similarities to the contemporary Italian genre in their musical forms (recitatives and arias, sometimes framed by choruses), in duet or 'dialogue' structures (which are much more common than works for solo voice), and in an orientation towards mythology in the choice of subjects, or settings. In several cases the term DRAMMA PER MUSICA is used for them. The work's 'plot', however, is not centred on the particular legend in question, and makes no pretence at dramatic verisimilitude, but is merely converted into an act of homage to the princely person whose birthday or nameday is celebrated. (A commemorative work may follow similar patterns.) A typical example is provided by a cantata, *Stimmet freudig allzusammen!*, performed in Meiningen in 1716 (the music is lost and the composer not named). This is based on the story of 'The Choice of Paris'. Mercurius sets the scene, and all the mythological persons appear—Paris, Juno, Minerva, and Venus—but the sole content of the text is that today, on the duchess's nameday, the situation would be totally different (and the Trojan War would be avoided) because of the duchess's rank. The singers then join in a concluding 'Vivat' without any further allusion to the myth. In other examples of the genre the singers appear one by one with an aria, introduced by recitative, and report something about the princely person; dialogue structures are then established (which bring some slight dramatic element into the work), and the final 'chorus' takes the form of a big ensemble movement expressing adulation.

For all those non-dramatic structures, scenic elements were not absolutely excluded. Sometimes the singers are in motion (e.g. in Bach's Peasant Cantata the two singers are on their way to an inn); sometimes they are represented as having some offering in their hands. But it is important to note that the main 'actor'—the princely person to whom the work is addressed—is silent all the time. Admittedly, this address can be seen as a dramatic event in itself, but an even more static, absolutely non-dramatic structure is possible, too.

This kind of secular cantata was cultivated outside the courts as well, as we see in the few secular cantatas written by Bach without any reference to the 'homage' character (*Der Streit zwischen Phoebus und Pan* and the Coffee Cantata, both performed as public entertainment), but which hardly differ from the contemporary 'court cantatas'. It was, of course, the poets who introduced such non-dramatic elements as the narrator in the Coffee Cantata, but Bach himself was at least aware of different approaches in chamber cantatas composed in Italy. In 1731 he copied Handel's *Armida abbandonata* (1707) for a similar performance.                                    KK

DürrK; K. Küster, ' "Theatralisch vorgestellet": zur Aufführungspraxis höfischer Vokalwerke in Thüringen um 1710/20', in F. Brusniak, ed., *Barockes Musiktheater im mitteldeutschen Raum im 17. und 18. Jahrhundert* (Cologne, 1994), 118–41.

**canzona.** A fugal work in two or more sections, which are often on variants of the same subject. The young Bach was probably acquainted with keyboard canzonas by Frescobaldi, Froberger, Kerll, and Buxtehude. Only one such work by Bach himself survives: the Canzona in D minor BWV588, which dates from his early years (before 1707) and is written in strict counterpoint of a traditional pseudo-vocal type. It is made up of two fugues, of which the second, a double fugue, is based on triple-time variants of the original subject and countersubject.

BWV588 is clearly related in style to other early essays in strict counterpoint: the Alla breve in D major BWV589 and the Fantasia in G minor BWV917. Its technique of thematic variation links it with the praeludia of Buxtehude and with Bach's own early Prelude and Fugue in E major BWV566. Bach returned to this technique in his late period: in the closing fugue of *Clavier-Übung III* (1739), *The Art of Fugue*, and the *Musical Offering*.                    RDPJ

P. Williams, *The Organ Music of J. S. Bach*, i (Cambridge, 1980), 272–4.

**capriccio.** A term applied (1) to three keyboard pieces of various types by Bach, and (2) to cadenza-like passages in certain Baroque works. In the early Baroque, Frescobaldi used the term for multi-sectional fugal keyboard pieces; by the time of Bach's youth it could also apply to a virtuoso keyboard fugue in a single long section. The latter idea persists in Bach's Capriccio in E, composed around 1707 and apparently dedicated to his elder brother Christoph. Also fugal, although

in binary form, is the athletic capriccio that closes Partita no. 2, occupying the place normally taken by a gigue.

Bach's best-known piece under this title is the Capriccio 'sopra la lontananza del fratello dilettissimo' ('on the departure [more properly "absence"] of his most dear brother'), which is thought to commemorate his elder brother Jacob's entrance in 1704 into the service of King Charles XII of Sweden. Presumably modelled on Kuhnau's *Biblische Historien* (1700), the work consists of six linked movements, each bearing a programmatic title. Most notable are the third movement, a lament in F minor consisting of 12 variations over a chromatic chaconne bass, and the closing fugue, whose subjects imitate trumpets and post horns. The precise date and, more recently, the occasion for the piece have been disputed, but it is clearly early and Bach's only substantial programmatic effort.

During the early 18th century the term was also applied to a long unaccompanied solo passage near the end of a quick concerto movement, as in the outer movements of the Vivaldi work that Bach arranged for organ as BWV594. Comparable passages occur in the Fifth Brandenburg Concerto and the Harpsichord Concerto in D minor, but in neither case is the passage labelled 'capriccio'; in an early version of the D minor concerto it is designated 'cadenza all'arbitrario' and a portion is left to be improvised by the player.                    DS

D. Schulenberg, *The Keyboard Music of J. S. Bach* (New York, 1992), 48–50, 65–7; P. Vendrix, 'Zum

Lamento aus J. S. Bachs Capriccio BWV 992 und seinen Vorläufern', *BJb* 75 (1989), 197–201; C. Wolff, 'The Identity of the "Fratro Dilettissimo" in the Capriccio B-Flat Major and Other Problems of Bach's Early Harpsichord Works', in P. Dirksen, ed., *The Harpsichord and its Repertoire: Proceedings of the International Harpsichord Symposium Utrecht 1990* (Utrecht, 1992), 145–56.

**Carlsbad.** A spa town (now Karlovy Vary in the Czech Republic) to which Bach and other musicians from Cöthen accompanied Prince Leopold on at least two occasions, in 1718 and 1720 (*see* BACH, JOHANN SEBASTIAN, §1).

**Carmel Bach Festival.** An annual festival held in Carmel, California. It began as a three-day event in 1935, and has since grown to become a more than three-week festival of performances, concerts, masterclasses, symposia, and educational programmes. Bruno Weil took over as music director in 1992 and the festival now attracts numerous international artists. JAB

**Catechism Preludes.** A set of organ preludes on Catechism hymns included in CLAVIER-ÜBUNG III.

**Celle.** Historic town in Lower Saxony, about 85 km. (53 miles) south-west of Lüneburg. Celle (also known as 'Zelle') was the seat of the reigning dukes of Braunschweig-Lüneburg when Bach was attending the Michaelisschule in Lüneburg in 1700–2.

The Obituary (*BDok* iii, no. 666) refers to Bach's encountering well-managed French music played by the 'then-famous band kept by the Duke of Zelle'. It states that most of the players were actually French—a result of its having been formed by the French duchess of the ducal line, Eléonore Desmier d'Olbreuse (see also *Terry*, pp. 50–1, where the orchestral personnel are named). The duchess retired to her dower house in Lüneburg in 1705, but she had already chosen it by 1700, and it may have been there, or elsewhere in Lüneburg, that Bach heard the orchestra. The assumption made by J. N. Forkel and others that the young Bach actually travelled to Celle is today regarded with scpeticism. SFD

**Cello Suites.** Bach apparently compiled the six suites for unaccompanied cello BWV1007–12 as a sequel to the Sonatas and Partitas for solo violin (1720). This does not imply that the cello pieces were necessarily written later, and indeed some of them might date from the Weimar years (1708–17). The violin solos adapted the texture of classic sonata and partita genres to a single instrument, while still allowing for a certain amount of polyphony; the Cello Suites show a further stage of distillation, since the possibilities for chordal playing on the cello are much more limited.

We still do not know for whom Bach wrote these pieces. The name of Christian Ferdinand Abel, Bach's friend and colleague at the Cöthen court from 1717 to 1723, frequently comes to mind. The earliest source, in the hand of Bach's wife Anna Magdalena, dates from about 1727–31, and H.-J. Schulze (pp. 96–101) has shown that this copy, together with Anna Magdalena's manuscript of the violin works, was probably commissioned by a former pupil in Wolfenbüttel. Several later manuscripts suggest that the suites went through further stages of revision. The *NBA* includes an edition which not only gives the two basic versions of the performance markings but also presents the four major manuscripts in facsimile, so that players can make up their own minds as to how the music should be performed.

Bach expands the core of the traditional Baroque suite (the four 'old' dances: allemande, courante, sarabande, and gigue) with a prelude to open each suite and a pair of dances of the 'modern' kind (minuet, bourrée, and gavotte) placed between the sarabande and gigue. Predictably, the greatest diversity is to be found in the opening preludes: the first and fourth feature a perpetual spinning-out of arpeggios which generate both chords and melodies; the second is a richly developed argument on the opening minor triad; the third presents conjunct lines and arpeggiated figuration intertwined to form a loosely framed fantasia. Perhaps most impressive are the preludes to the last two suites: the fifth is basically a French overture, its stately opening section followed by a fugue in which a single line has to impersonate the multiple voices of a contrapuntal texture. The prelude to the sixth suite is the most extrovert of the set: a brilliant virtuoso piece which seems to evoke something more imposing than a solo cello piece. Of the succeeding movements, the allemande is the one which had been furthest developed from its roots as a vehicle for dance. The examples from the first and sixth suites provide an interesting comparison since their opening gestures are so similar: while the first uses almost continuous motion in semiquavers with a fairly clear-cut phrase structure, the sixth employs an astonishingly wide range of note values.

One of the most renowned movements of the whole set is the Sarabande of the fifth suite. Yet this, without a hint of double-stopping, contains perhaps the fewest number of notes in any movement. The expressive gestures of the melody have to serve as both bass and accompaniment, since the pitch range is so wide. Another 'simple' movement is the second Bourrée of the fourth suite. Here the very absence of the elaborate diminutions of the first Bourrée is conspicuous; we almost hear the dance as a skeleton, the leanest form a bourrée can take. On the other hand, the implied two-part texture of the piece is extremely subtle; in the second half the two voices seem to cross one another—something which would be unusual in 'real' part-writing, since the two would end the piece the wrong way up.

The fifth suite is unusual in requiring SCORDATURA, a tuning of the A string down to G. Although the piece can be adapted for the more conventional tuning, the scordatura allows chordal spacings that would not otherwise be possible, and it also affects the resonance of the instrument, creating a colour distinct from that of the other suites. The last suite is for a five-string instrument (perhaps a violoncello piccolo). Again, the work can be adapted for the modern cello, but it is much more difficult to play without the expanded range afforded by the fifth string.

JAB

R. Efrati, *Johann Sebastian Bach: The Interpretation of the Sonatas and Partitas for Solo Violin and the Suites for Solo Cello* (Zurich, 1979); E. Gruetzbach, *Stil- und Spielprobleme bei der Interpretation der 6 Suiten für Violoncello von J. S. Bach* (2nd and rev. edn., Hamburg, 1981); H. Schenker, 'The Sarabande of J. S. Bach's Suite no. 3 for Unaccompanied Violoncello (BWV 1009)', *Music Forum*, 2 (1970), 274–82; H.-J. Schulze, *Studien zur Bach-Überlieferung im 18. Jahrhundert* (Leipzig, 1984); H. Vogt, *Johann Sebastian Bach's Chamber Music: Background, Analyses, Individual Works*, Eng. trans. K. Johnson (Portland, Oreg., 1988).

**cembalo.** A term in general use by Bach and others for the HARPSICHORD.

**chaconne.** A Baroque dance and instrumental form based on continuous variations of a four-bar phrase. The chaconne has its roots in early 17th-century guitar music, song, and dance in Spain and Italy. It was also a favourite in French theatrical works at the court of Louis XIV and later. Its expanding structure was ideal for large scenes involving both singers and dancers; choreographies survive, however, only for solo or duet performances. As a solo dance the chaconne was associated with a pantomimic performance and subtle expressive gestures; castanets punctuated and enlivened the rhythms. Chaconnes are normally notated with a time signature of 3 or 3/4 and use a tempo slightly faster than a sarabande (*see* DANCE). Many chaconnes are long, complex, emotionally charged pieces using a wide variety of techniques, including strong contrasts in instrumentation, dynamic level, texture, mode and key,

repetition scheme, melody, harmony, rhythm, and occasionally even metre.

Two chaconnes by Bach survive. The concluding piece in Cantata 150 is a 'ciacona' in B minor, 'Meine Tage in dem Leide', performed by the chorus, solo bassoon, two violins, and continuo. It is in 3/2 time, and the ground bass, built on a four-bar rising pentachord, is heard 22 times. Embellishments include ever-changing Italianate figuration in the vocal and instrumental parts, and variations on the ground itself by the bassoon.

The gigantic 'ciaccona' that concludes the second partita for solo violin BWV1004 is Bach's other marvellous contribution to the literature. The four-bar ostinato bass is varied either melodically (to form a chromatic descending tetrachord, a descending diatonic tetrachord, or a variation of the two) or harmonically, as in the first arpeggio section. The overall key structure is D minor–D major–D minor, with variations usually appearing in pairs, and French and Italian styles juxtaposed in a seemingly infinite variety of diminutions, syncopations, dotted rhythms, and ornamentation.

NJ, MEL

For bibliography, *see* DANCE.

**chiastic structure.** A term, derived from the Greek letter *chi* ($\chi$), used to describe the symmetrical ordering of some element (or elements) in a composition—for example, the keys, scoring, or formal types of individual movements or sections—on either side of a central component, which is thus brought into prominence. Chiastic structures have been observed in many of Bach's mature vocal worls. Examples include the 'Herzstück' of the ST JOHN PASSION and a rather more complex disposition centring on the aria 'Aus Liebe will mein Heiland sterben' in Part 2 of the ST MATTHEW PASSION.

**choir.** *See* CHORUS.

**chorale.** See overleaf.

**chorale cantata.** A CANTATA of which the text is (or is derived from) a hymn (chorale), and the music is usually based on the melody to which the hymn is sung. The hymn text may be used verbatim and set strophe by strophe (*per omnes versus*), as in Bach's early cantata *Christ lag in Todes Banden* (no. 4). In the type associated particularly with his second Leipzig *Jahrgang* (1724–5) the outer strophes are retained verbatim, the first set as a large-scale chorale fantasia and the last plainly harmonized, while the intervening strophes are paraphrased in such a way as to make them suitable for musical setting as recitatives and arias.

**chorale partita.** *See* CHORALE VARIATIONS.

# chorale (*Choral*)

The distinctive Lutheran hymn, both text and melody, intitiated by the reformer Martin Luther and his Wittenberg colleagues. This form of congregational song, a synthesis of old and new elements, was as important theologically as it was musically in the Lutheran church. The Augsburg Confession (1530) states that 'in certain places [in the evangelical Mass] German hymns ("teutsch Gesänge") are sung . . . for the instruction and exercise of the people' (Art. 24), and the 'Formula of Concord' (1577) draws attention to Lazarus Spengler's chorale *Durch Adams Fall ist ganz verderbt* (1524; see BWV18, 637, and 705) as the summary of the Lutheran position on the doctrine of original sin ('Solid Declaration', Art. 1).

The earliest chorale melodies were either adaptations of earlier forms, such as plainchant and vernacular religious song, or newly composed. The term 'chorale' indicates the plainchant origin of many of the melodies, being derived from 'choraliter' (applied to monodic unison chant), as opposed to 'figuraliter' (applied to polyphonic music). Thus the melody *Nun komm, der Heiden Heiland* was derived from the Latin *Veni redemptor gentium*, and *Komm, Gott Schöpfer, Heiliger Geist* from *Veni creator spiritus*. Another source was vernacular religious folksong, especially the type known as *Leisen*, whose melodies were taken over with little modification; examples include *Wir glauben all an einen Gott, Nun bitten wir den Heiligen Geist,* and *Christ ist erstanden.* Many of the newly composed melodies were in BARFORM (A–A–B), commonly found in vernacular narrative ballads, *Hofweisen* ('court songs'), and the creations of the Meistersinger; among such melodies are *Ein feste Burg, Es ist das Heil,* and *Wachet auf.* Composers of the late 16th and the 17th centuries continued to show a preference for *Barform.* By the end of the 16th century some melodies from the Calvinist Genevan Psalter were adapted for Lutheran use, among them *O Mensch, bewein dein Sünde groß* (Psalm 36), *Herr Jesu Christ, wahr' mensch und Gott* (Psalm 127) and *Herr Gott, dich loben alle wir* (Psalm 134 = 'Old 100th'). Following the devastations of the Thirty Years War in the early 17th century, a more intimate form of melody was devised, notably by J. G. Ebeling and Johannes Crüger, who consciously modelled his style on Genevan psalm tunes. Around the turn of the 18th century Lutheran Pietists went further still and produced melodies that were simple and direct. The most important Pietist *Gesangbuch* was edited by J. A. Freylinghausen (Halle, 1704 and 1714).

Luther's Latin liturgy, the *Formula missae*, directed that the people should sing vernacular chorales as *Graduallieder* ('Gradual hymns') between the Epistle and Gospel at the Eucharist (*see* HAUPTGOTTESDIENST). At first they were chorales of the season, such as *Nun komm, der Heiden Heiland* (Advent), *Gelobet seist du Jesu Christ* (Christmas), *Christ lag in Todesbanden* (Easter), and *Komm, Gott Schöpfer, Heiliger Geist* (Pentecost). Later the concept was expanded to include all the Sundays and festivals of the Church year, and by the early 18th century a rich repertory of such chorales was in use. The major part of the *Orgel-Büchlein* is made up of settings of the principal chorales of the Church year, and many cantatas employ chorales appropriate to the Sunday or festival for which they were composed.

In the *Deutsche Messe* (1526) Luther introduced the concept of congregational chorales that would be sung either in substitution of, or in sequence after, the traditional parts of the Latin Ordinary. Ultimately particular chorales come into almost universal use throughout Lutheran Germany: *Kyrie, Gott Vater in ewigkeit* (Kyrie),

*Allein Gott in der Höh sei Ehr* (Gloria), *Wir glauben all an einen Gott* (Credo), *Jesaja dem Propheten das geschah* (Sanctus), and *Christe, du Lamm Gottes* or *O Lamm Gottes, unschuldig* (Agnus Dei). Bach composed a number of preludes on the Gloria hymn, *Allein Gott in der Höh sei Ehr* (e.g. BWV711, 715, and 717), and he included a set of organ settings of the Kyrie and Gloria chorale melodies in his *Clavier-Übung III*. He composed preludes on, and at least one vocal setting of, the chorale *Wir glauben* (BWV437, 680, 681, 740, 765, and 1098), and employed both German versions of the Agnus Dei in his vocal music, as *Christe, du Lamm Gottes* in the final movement of Cantata 23, and *O Lamm Gottes, unschuldig* in the opening chorus of the *St Matthew Passion*.

At Sunday Vespers it was customary to teach the substance of Luther's Catechisms and to sing the appropriate Catechism hymns: *Dies sind der heilgen zehn Gebot* (Ten Commandments), *Wir glauben all an einen Gott* (Creed), *Vater unser im Himmelreich* (Lord's Prayer), *Christ unser Herr zum Jordan kam* (Baptism), *Aus tiefer Not schrei ich zu dir* (Repentance), and *Jesus Christus unser Heiland* (Eucharist). These melodies can be found in various compositions by Bach, especially in *Clavier-Übung III*, where there are two complete cycles of organ chorale preludes, one for manuals alone and the other with pedals, corresponding to Luther's 'small' and 'large' Catechisms.

The Lutheran chorale was therefore fundamental in Bach's compositional output; it is found in a variety of forms, but two predominate. First, the organ chorale preludes, whose function was to precede congregational singing. In addition to the *Orgel-Büchlein*, *Clavier-Übung III*, and the Schübler Chorales, there are a further 63 miscellaneous chorale preludes (BWV651–68 and 690–764), as well as the three organ partitas (BWV766–8) (*see* ORGAN CHORALE and CHORALE VARIATIONS). Second, the four-part chorales found in many of the cantatas and in the passions. Almost since they first began to appear in a collected edition, the first part of which was issued in 1765, they established a basic corpus for the teaching of theory and keyboard harmony that continues today. This is because they explore an astonishing variety of harmonic progression with faultless part-writing. For some of these four-part chorales Bach's method was to begin with an existing setting, found in such sources as Gottfried Vopelius's *Neu Leipzig Gesangbuch* (Leipzig, 1682) and the *Geist- und Lehrreiches Kirchen- und Hauß-Buch* (Dresden, 1684), and then to transform completely the inner voices. This probably reflects Bach's teaching method, which was, according to C. P. E. Bach (*BDok* iii. 298), to ground his students' composition studies in the writing of inner parts to chorales.

Even though a good many of the four-part chorales are to be found in modern hymnals, they were not composed for congregational use. Most were originally included in cantatas and Passions, to be sung by the choir, and can be identified with specific works. Presumably a significant proportion of the remainder were written for the 100 or so cantatas no longer extant.

Bach was the music editor for the Schemelli *Gesangbuch* (Leipzig, 1736; *see* SCHEMELLI, GEORG CHRISTIAN), which includes numerous melodies of the Freylinghausen type. He also composed chorale melodies, some written in a freer, post-Pietist style. The following can be attributed to him with reasonable certainty: four melodies in the second manuscript *Clavierbüchlein* for Anna Magdalena Bach, entered after 1725 and before 1733 (BWV452, 512, 514, and 516); the chorale at the end of the motet *Komm, Jesu, komm*, first performed some time before 1732 (BWV229); a chorale in Part 4

of the *Christmas Oratorio* of 1734–5 (BWV248:42); 19 melodies with figured bass in the Schemelli *Gesangbuch* of 1736 (BWV439–40, 443, 449, 453, 462, 466, 468–9, 471, 478–80, 484, 487, 492, 494, 498, and 505); two melodies in the recently discovered Penzel collection (BC F 41 and F 198; see Wiemer); and four other melodies that are unknown except in Bach's settings (BWV357, 384, 400, and 423).                    RAL
*See also* ORGAN CHORALE.

D. Gojowy, 'Kirchenlieder im Umkreis von J. S. Bach', *Jahrbuch für Liturgik und Hymnologie*, 22 (1978), 79–123; R. A. Leaver, 'Bach's "Clavierübung III": Some Historical and Theological Considerations', *Organ Yearbook*, 6 (1975), 17–32; R. A. Leaver, 'Bach, Hymns and Hymnbooks', *The Hymn*, 36/4 (Oct. 1985), 7–13; R. L. Marshall, 'How J. S. Bach Composed Four-part Chorales', *Musical Quarterly*, 56 (1970), 198–221; C. S. Terry, *Bach's Chorals* (Cambridge, 1915–21); W. Wiemer, *Johann Sebastian Bach und seine Schule: neu entdeckte Choral- und Liedsätze* (Kassel, 1985).

**chorale prelude** (*Choralvorspiel*). *See* ORGAN CHORALE.

**chorale variations.** A set of variations (often referred to as 'partitas') based on a chorale melody, usually for keyboard or (as in the case of Bach's chorale variations) for organ.

Bach seems to have shown interest in writing chorale variations only at the beginning and end of his career (the Canonic Variations on *Vom Himmel hoch* BWV769 being virtually his last work composed entirely afresh). Two pieces that show multiple settings of chorale melodies date from the Weimar period (*Christ ist erstanden* BWV627 from the *Orgel-Büchlein* and *O Lamm Gottes unschuldig* BWV656 from the 'Eighteen'), and both of these relate to chorales with three strophes; however, neither could be considered fully-fledged chorale partitas. Several other pieces come close to the genre: *Ach, was ist doch unser Leben* BWV743 and *Aus der Tiefe rufe ich* BWV745, both of doubtful attribution, and the single-strophe bicinium on *Allein Gott in der Höh sei Ehr* BWV711.

Of the chorale partitas (i.e. those with more than three variations), *Allein Gott in der Höh sei Ehr* BWV771 is probably all the work of Nicolaus Vetter (1666–1734). Although the authorship of *Ach, was soll ich Sünder machen* BWV770 has sometimes been questioned, there is no reason to believe that it is not the work of the young Bach, in direct imitation of Pachelbel's variation style. Scholars have often considered the three remaining (and finest) partitas (BWV766–8) to date from Bach's earliest years, perhaps (in the case of the first two, at least) from his time at Lüneburg (1700–2), where he would have encountered Georg Böhm, a prolific composer in the genre. However, in all three works the motivic rigour and consistency of part-writing point towards the

sort of settings that Bach was to achieve in his *Orgel-Büchlein*. Furthermore, the bicinia that come after the opening chorale in each of the three variation sets show a strong family resemblance to independent organ accompaniments in the Mühlhausen cantatas, most specifically the movements with an ostinato bass line in Cantatas 71 and 106.

The chorale variations may have corresponded to specific liturgical practices at Arnstadt and Mühlhausen, such as providing interludes between the strophes of a chorale: the number of variations in *Christ, der du bist der helle Tag* and *O Gott, du frommer Gott* match the number of strophes in their respective chorales. The chorale for *Sei gegrüsset, Jesus gütig* exists in several versions, none of which seems to match the number of variations in Bach's set, but this also survives in a variety of versions. While, as with the other partitas, there seems to be no immediate affective link with the text of the chorale, Bach seems to have gone out of his way to provide a catalogue of variation techniques, presenting diverse changes of mood and texture. This seems to be the most carefully conceived set (Bach presumably made several attempts at a satisfactory ordering) and, as such, may represent his first comprehensive collection of pieces related by theme or genre.      JAB
*See also* CANONIC VARIATIONS.

**Choreinbau** ('choral in-building'). *See* VOKAL-EINBAU.

**Chorton.** A general PITCH designation inherited from the 17th century and preserved in the 18th on most organs, traditional brass instruments, and cornetts. Among organs that were said to be at *Chorton* at the time they were built, and whose original pitches have survived, the level varies from $a' = 437$ to $a' = 486$, but averages $a' = 465$ (which is the frequency of CORNET-TON, a specific type of *Chorton*). An important reason for the existence of organs pitched above *Cornet-ton* was to save tin on pipes; if they were used only with voices, there was no need to tune them to an exact pitch standard.                                    BH

**chorus.** See overleaf.

***Christen, ätzet diesen Tag*** ('Christians, etch this day'). Cantata for Christmas Day, BWV63, composed either in 1714 or 1715 in Weimar, but probably not performed there. Bach used it for his first Christmas in Leipzig, 25 December 1723, again about 1729, and again at a later date. The libretto is an earlier variant of a text that J. M. Heineccius, principal pastor of the Liebfrauen-kirche, Halle, provided for the bicentenary of Luther's Reformation in 1717. Bach was in Halle at the end of 1713, in connection with his unsuccessful bid to become organist of the Liebfrauen-kirche, when he may have encountered the original Heineccius libretto. Perhaps Bach's libretto represents Heineccius's original form, which the author later parodied for the 1717 Reformation Day libretto—or perhaps Bach's and Heineccius's 1717 librettos were both parodies of an earlier Heineccius libretto.

BWV63 is a bright, celebratory cantata with unique features. It employs four trumpets instead of the usual three, a rare occurence in Bach's cantatas; it has no solo aria, no direct biblical quotation, and no concluding chorale; and it contains few allusions to traditional Christmas themes. This might suggest that it was originally a Reformation Day cantata that was later adapted for use on Christmas Day.

The cantata shows a balanced symmetrical structure, typical of many of Bach's works:

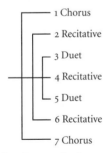

1 Chorus
2 Recitative
3 Duet
4 Recitative
5 Duet
6 Recitative
7 Chorus

It opens with a large-scale da capo movement. The A section is framed by a brilliant orchestral ritornello, within which the chorus declaims 'Christians, etch this day in metal and marble'. In the B section the chorus is punctuated by short orchestral interludes (without trumpets), and there is some sparkling word-painting on 'Strahl' ('ray'). The balancing final movement is also a large-scale da capo form. Section A begins with a brilliant orchestral ritornello, then, after a homophonic statement of the opening words, 'Höchster, schau in Gnaden an' ('Highest one, look in mercy'), the four-part choir begins a double fugue, which for five bars remains unaccompanied.

The recitatives nos. 2 and 6 provide the links between their respective choruses and duets, the first a somewhat lengthy simple recitative with concluding arioso, the other a brief but inventive one accompanied by oboes, strings, bassoon, and continuo.

The first duet (movement 3) is for soprano and bass with an animated oboe obbligato (organ in the later version), in da capo form with canonic imitation. The second duet (movement 5) is for alto and tenor with string accompaniment, a lively 3/8 dance movement in free da capo form.

At the centre of the cantata is movement 4, just 12 bars long. Here Bach contrives, by text repetition, to make the word 'Gnaden' ('grace') appear at the mid-point of the recitative. Further, he emphasizes the word with a melodic figure that is in strong contrast with the basic syllabic style of the recitative as a whole. Therefore the fulcrum on which the whole of this cantata turns is God's grace, the concept that lies at the heart of the celebration of Christmas Day (or of Reformation Day).                                    RAL

W. Neumann, *Sämtliche von Johann Sebastian Bach vertonte Texte* (Leipzig, 1974), 303. For further bibliography, *see* CANTATA, §1.

**Christiane Eberhardine,** Electress of Saxony and Queen of Poland (b. 19 Dec. 1671; d. 5 Sept. 1727). She was the daughter of the Margrave of Brandenburg-Bayreuth. On 1 January 1693 she married Friedrich August I, but when, in 1697, her husband converted to Roman Catholicism in order to accede to the throne of Poland she separated from him and went to live at Pretzsch, near Wittenberg. Her refusal to renounce her Lutheran faith earned her wide respect and affection, and it was in her honour that Bach composed and performed his TRAUER-ODE.

**Christian Ludwig,** Margrave of Brandenburg (b. 24 May 1677; d. 3 Sept. 1734). A patron of the arts and sciences. He was the youngest son from the second marriage of Friedrich Wilhelm of Brandenburg (the Great Elector). The elector's grandson, Friedrich Wilhelm I (the Soldier King, and father of Frederick the Great), was more than a nominal Calvinist and had no interest in promoting music. Soon after assuming the throne he disbanded the musicians, but he did allow his uncle Christian Ludwig to remain in residence at

[*cont. on p.100*]

Christian Ludwig, Margrave of Brandenburg, to whom Bach dedicated his *Six Concerts*;
portrait by Antoine Pesne (1683–1757)

# chorus

The term has two applications in Bach's environment; one is to a group of singers, generally associated with, but not exclusively comprising, pupils of a Lutheran school (sometimes termed a 'Kantorei'); the other is to pieces (other than simple chorale settings) involving all four vocal ranges and (normally independent) instrumental parts. The fact that the same Latin or German word 'chorus' can refer to either of these (while the German 'Chor', like the English 'choir', usually refers only to the body of singers) does not mean that one usage automatically implies the other, although there is obviously a close relationship between them. Bach employed the term 'Chorus' very seldom in his scores and performance parts, mostly to clarify what comes next in a score if this is not immediately obvious (such as at the end of the *Christmas Oratorio*, Part 3, where there is a direction to repeat 'Chorus 1' in the autograph score). In the score of the *St Matthew Passion* Bach used the words 'Chorus' and 'Chori' in a different way, to indicate which of the two groups are to perform; here the word refers to instruments as well as voices and is applied to all musical genres, including recitatives and arias.

Since Reformation times the entire body of resident pupils in Lutheran schools had been divided up to provide singers for a variety of purposes, from street singing (*see* KURRENDEN) to the most complex music that the Kantor was able to promote. In Leipzig the Kantor was required to divide the school body into four choirs (each a 'chorus musicus' or 'Kantorei'), which sang in each of the city's main churches on Sundays and feast-days. He was responsible for directing the first choir and appointing deputies to direct the other three. Bach's famous *Entwurff* (the memorandum he addressed to the Leipzig town council on 23 August 1730) gives a particularly clear picture of the division of pupils: each choir should have at least 12 singers, ideally 16 (i.e. four to a part). Bach makes a further division of the singers into concertists and ripienists, there being ordinarily one concertist per part and at least two ripienists. The concertists were essentially the soloists in modern terminology, ripienists presumably doubling their parts in certain places. (This distinction and terminology can be traced back at least as far as Michael Praetorius, c.1570–1621.)

The only musical genre Bach discusses in relation to vocal scoring is the motet, and, given that most of the motets regularly sung in the liturgy (from an early 17th-century anthology) were in eight parts, he calls for a choir of at least 12 singers, so that if members fall ill (a frequent occurrence, apparently) all eight parts will still be furnished. Here he does not make the distinction between concertists and ripienists, but, if there were normally only four concertists, clearly some parts had to be sung by ripienists alone. Traditionally, it seems, motets of this kind were sung by all competent singers who happened to be present. Webber (pp. 41–2, 177–8) cites several examples from the late 17th century which imply that motets were 'choir music', just as they had been in the late Renaissance. The theorist Wolfgang Caspar Printz (1641–1717) gives perhaps the clearest verbal testimony from the late 17th century, stating that doubling singers are required in motets and at the points marked 'capella' in 'modern' pieces (Butt, p. 112).

One of the most heated debates about the performance of Bach's choral music has centred on whether those movements of the 'Chorus' genre in cantatas and other concerted works were to be sung by all the singers together. While there is no definitive answer in this matter, some light might be shed by considering the genealogy of what we call 'cantata' (Bach, when he gave a generic title, more normally used the term 'concerto'). While it can be traced back to several earlier genres, it is clear that the cantata's most direct line is from the Italian sacred concerto, a genre which stressed solo singing and one which was particularly suitable during and after the Thirty Years War, when performers were thin on the ground.

Webber (pp. 102–6) shows that works of the Buxtehude generation were designed for a fluctuating body of performers. A basic scoring might consist of instruments and solo singers, and this could be amplified both with the addition of extra instruments and with a secondary choir of ripienists (the 'capella'). The sources suggest one, or at most two ripienists per part (thus surprisingly close to Bach's own specifications) and these fleshed out the texture at certain points. However much directors desired more ripienists for the concertos, it seems that they still did not need as many as they required for motets (Webber, p. 77). Buxtehude himself seems to have used a variety of vocal scorings (see K. Snyder, *Dieterich Buxtehude, Organist in Lübeck* (New York, 1987), 360–6). In the larger pieces, employing five or more voices, the *capella* was often added to reinforce the concertino when instruments doubled the voices. But Snyder concludes that Buxtehude most likely performed the majority of works in four vocal parts with soloists alone.

Bach may have composed the cantata *Gott ist mein König* (1708) under the direct influence of Buxtehude's practice of dividing the entire forces into multiple choirs. Here Bach employs four vocal and instrumental choirs; the vocal choir (in only four parts) may be doubled by ripienists at certain points (though not, as with Buxtehude, coinciding directly with the instrumental doubling). That Bach had single concertists and single ripienists in mind is suggested by his title-page, where he lists the number of performers as 'ab 18. è se piace 22' (see Rifkin, p. 747). The ripieno parts tend to double loud exclamations, such as the opening line and its repetitions, and elsewhere provide dynamic shading for the solo parts. Indeed, at one point they even provide a simplified version of the concertists' runs (a unique occurrence in Bach's vocal scoring).

It is clear that, by the beginning of the 18th century, many music directors desired more singers in the *capella*, and that more skilled singers were becoming available. This impression is reinforced by writers, such as the theologian Gottfried Ephraim Scheibel (1696–1759), who objected to the trend towards adding extra voices to vocal lines (see Butt, p. 112). While most scholars agree that Bach had neither the room nor the resources to perform the Weimar cantatas with ripienists, the most intense dispute surrounds Bach's actual and desired scoring for the Leipzig works. It should be stressed that the cantatas belong to the concerto tradition and not to the *stile antico* motet tradition, so a full choir cannot immediately be assumed. Rifkin's intensive study of the performing parts suggests that they conform, more or less generically, with the traditional format of the German sacred concerto tradition. The principal parts are used by soloists alone, who sing every line within their ambitus (there are, for instance, few indications as to where ripienists might join in, while many other performance details are quite precisely notated); doubling singers (where evident) perform from separate copies abstracted from the principal parts. Such parts exist in a few instances (such as the first three Leipzig cantatas and the *St John Passion*), but, assuming these to be the exception rather than the rule, Rifkin concludes that the vast majority of the vocal works were sung by one singer to a part, without ripienists.

Moreover, when there is positive evidence that Bach had more singers available, this does not necessarily mean that they joined in the choruses, or even the chorales; for instance, the bass who sang Pilate in the *St Matthew Passion* had a part in which all the choruses and chorales within its boundaries were marked 'tacet'. Even the score of this Passion seems to add weight to Rifkin's argument: the chorus 'Sind Blitze, sind Donner', running straight on from the previous duet, on the same staves, begins with the vocal designations 'Basso 1 Chori, Basso 2 Chori', for the bass line, and 'due Tenori' for the tenor line, while the continuo line (requiring all the cellos, basses, and organs of both choruses) is marked 'tutti li Bassi in unisono'. Since we know for sure that there were more than two bass instruments on the continuo line, Bach's use of the word 'tutti' is quite predictable, but if there had been more than one singer per vocal part he would have been perverse not to use the same designation.

While no one has explained away evidence such as this, several critics have suggested external reasons why Rifkin's hypothesis might be wrong. For instance, the ripienists might have sung from memory, or countless sets of ripieno parts may simply have gone missing. But if there is one definite thing that we can learn from the hypothesis, it is that the doubling singers sang with the soloists and not vice versa; in other words, the vocal parts of cantata choruses are conceptually solo—often virtuoso—lines that may or may not have been reinforced.

Of course, these issues of vocal scoring make little sense without a consideration of who the singers actually were. According to Bach's contemporary Martin Fuhrmann (1669–1745), a boy's voice might not break until after the age of 18. Thus it is not surprising that Bach was so grateful for the services of his future son-in-law, J. C. Altnickol, as a bass singer in the *chorus musicus*; Bach also notes that the students in the Thomasschule leave too early for their broken voices to reach maturity (*BDok* i. 148–9). We know, too, that Bach's predecessors relied heavily on local students—indeed that Kuhnau resented the fact that many former pupils of the Thomasschule forsook the choir for other musical activities once they became university students. Bach complains of the progressive dwindling funds for these 'extras' in his 1730 *Entwurff*, although Schulze has shown that the funds were not, in fact, declining before 1729 and that in this year Bach's appointment as director of the collegium musicum would have secured a regular supply of students to work for him as both instrumentalists and singers. While the majority of the students who sang would presumably have furnished the tenor and bass parts, we know that at least one of them was an alto (the versatile C. G. Gerlach; see Schulze, p. 50).

Schneiderheinze notes from the school records that pupils who were admitted into the upper four classes entered between the ages of 13 and 15, although quite a few were admitted at 11 and 12, 17 and 18; in exceptional cases, boys were admitted between the ages of 19 and 21. It was these classes that boys joined as boarders and that therefore supplied the principal body of singers. The average entrance age of 13 to 15 is also reflected in Bach's notes on boys admitted to the school in 1729 (*BDok* i. 130–5). Boys were assigned to the four classes by virtue of their level of experience and expertise rather than their age. The majority left the school at the age of 20 or older (24–7, in extreme cases). Going by the sporadic records of the exact disposition of the third choir, boys in all four vocal ranges could be 17 or 18; indeed, they suggest that the age of the boy will give no certain indication of his voice range (although broken voices could not have been much younger than 16). It cannot entirely be discounted that some treble and alto parts were sung by falsettists; there is certainly evidence that falsettists were used to sing alto and soprano parts in Lutheran choirs (Webber, p. 178; Butt, pp. 85 and 203), so Gerlach, who, as a university student, was probably singing alto in 1728 at the age of 24 (Schulze, pp. 47, 50), may not have been the only mature alto singer. However, when Bach in his *Entwurff* refers to the fact that his two predecessors were given extra money to pay for singers from the university body he notes that they thus acquired more vocalists, namely 'a bass, a tenor, and even an alto'; this suggests that the use of falsettists was the exception rather than the rule. Whatever the constitution of the choirs, we can be sure that, with some unbroken voices at the age of 17 or 18, they sounded like nothing that is possible today. JAB

J. Butt, *Music Education and the Art of Performance in the German Baroque* (Cambridge, 1994); A. Parrott, 'Bach's Chorus: A "brief but highly necessary" Reappraisal', *Early Music*, 24 (1996), 551–80; J. Rifkin, 'Bach's Chorus; a Preliminary Report', *Musical Times*, 123 (1982), 747–54; A. Schneiderheinze, 'Bachs Figuralchor und die Chorempore in der Thomaskirche', *Beiträge zur Bachforschung*, 1 (1982), 32–45; H.-J. Schulze, 'Studenten als Bachs Helfer bei der Leipziger Kirchenmusik', *BJb* 70 (1984), 45–52; G. Wagner, 'Die Chorbesetzung bei J. S. Bach und ihre Vorgeschichte; Anmerkungen zur "hinlänglichen" Besetzung im 17. und 18. Jahrhundert', *Archiv für Musikwissenschaft*, 43 (1986), 278–304; G. Webber, *North German Church Music in the Age of Buxtehude* (Oxford, 1996).

the castle and to keep his own *Kapelle*. Probably seeking a position there, Bach dedicated six concertos, now known as the BRANDENBURG CONCERTOS, to the margrave in 1721. MAM

H. Becker, review of *NBA*, VII/ii [Brandenburg Concertos], *Die Musikforschung*, 13 (1960), 115–17; H. Besseler, 'Markgraf Christian Ludwig von Brandenburg', *BJb* 43 (1956), 18–35.

**Christ lag in Todes Banden** ('Christ lay in the bonds of death'). Cantata for Easter Sunday, BWV4. The date of the first performance is unknown, but the work was probably written in 1707/8, and it was subsequently performed at Leipzig in 1725, and probably the previous year as well. It has been suggested that it might have been composed for Bach's audition for the position of organist at Mühlhausen, and that it is his earliest surviving sacred vocal work.

A CHORALE CANTATA, the work is a setting of the seven strophes of Martin Luther's Easter hymn, which derives both text and music from the 11th-century sequence *Victimae paschali laudes*. The popularity of Luther's hymn—Bach set it three times for organ—together with the earnest expressiveness of the cantata have made this one of Bach's better-known early works. The earliest surviving sources are the manuscript parts prepared at Leipzig in 1724–5; these originally called only for four voices and a five-part instrumental ensemble (two violins, two violas, and continuo). Wind parts (for cornett and three trombones) were added in 1725, but these are confined to doubling the voices in movements 2, 3, and 8. The concluding movement, a four-part setting of the chorale melody, appears to have been newly composed in 1724, replacing an earlier setting of stanza 7 now lost. Bach might have borrowed a few details from a similarly scored cantata by Pachelbel on the same chorale, but the latter could not be considered a direct model. Nevertheless, Bach here follows 17th-century tradition in employing the chorale text in every vocal movement, omitting 'madrigalian' movements (recitatives and arias). Also archaic is the five-part instrumental ensemble with two violas.

The brief opening sinfonia for strings and continuo incorporates motifs from the first two phrases of the chorale melody, which recurs in its entirety in each of the seven vocal movements. The tonality, moreover, remains E minor throughout. But the scoring and style of the vocal movements are varied according to a symmetrical arrangement which places four-part vocal writing in *versus* 1, 4, and 7; duets in *versus* 2 and 6; and solos in *versus* 3 and 5. As in many chorales, the melody is in BARFORM. But three *versus* (1, 5, and 6) are through-composed, permitting individual treatment of each line; for example, *versus* 1 distinguishes the significant word 'Leben' ('life') with a lengthy melisma. Moreover, each stanza of the text ends with the word 'hallelujah', which is set off in one way or another in most movements.

*Versus* 1 is scored for the full ensemble, and from the very outset the chorale melody appears as a cantus firmus in long notes in the soprano. As in older chorale fantasias for organ, each phrase receives individual contrapuntal development in the lower voices; the concluding word, 'hallelujah', is repeated at length in a separate fugal section.

*Versus* 2 is for soprano and alto over a quasi-ostinato continuo line; *versus* 3 is for tenor accompanied by a lively descant for unison violins. The central *versus* is scored in MOTET STYLE, without independent instrumental parts. Here the chorale cantus firmus is in the alto, transposed to B minor, although the tonality of the movement as a whole remains E minor; and the three 'free' voices combine lines 1 and 2 simultaneously in counterpoint (likewise lines 3 and 4).

*Versus* 5 sets the bass voice against the string choir, which echoes each phrase of the chorale melody until the final 'hallelujah', in which first violin and bass proceed in close canon (from bar 85). This is perhaps the most rhetorical movement, with the voice singing complementary long notes on 'Tod' ('death', a low note) and 'Würger' ('strangler', high), and an unexpected suspension on 'hält' ('hold'). *Versus* 6 returns to the texture of its symmetrical twin, *versus* 2, but with a more lively rhythm. The work concludes with a four-part chorale setting typical of Bach's later cantatas.                                                    DS

G. Herz, *Bach: Cantata No. 4, Christ lag in Todesbanden: An Authoritative Score—Background—Analysis—Views and Comments* (New York, 1967). For further bibliography, *see* CANTATA, §1.

**Christmas Oratorio.** See p. 104.

**Christum wir sollen loben schon** ('We should give praise to Christ'). Cantata for the second day of Christmas, BWV121, first performed on 26 December 1724. The libretto, by an unknown poet, is based on Luther's Christmas hymn, which is itself derived from the famous 5th-century Latin hymn *A solis ortus cardine*. The poet followed the usual convention for chorale paraphrase cantatas, taking over the first and final strophes of the hymn for the opening and closing numbers of the cantata and refashioning the intervening strophes into two recitatives and two arias to make a six-movement structure. There is little specific relationship between the readings for the day and the cantata text, which dwells on the wonder of the Incarnation (movements 1–3) and the response of mankind worshipping the Christ-child at the manger (movements 4–6).

Cantata 121 is scored for SATB, oboe d'amore,

strings, and continuo, with cornett and three trombones playing *colla parte*. The opening chorus takes the form of a chorale fantasia, with the melody worked out fugally in prefiguring imitative entries in the lower voices before the main entry in long note values in the soprano. Each line of the chorale is worked out in turn. Apart from the chorale itself, the main material consists of a serpentine countersubject figure first used for the word 'loben' ('praise'), which plays an extensive part in the accompanying texture. Bach varies the order of the entries for the four lines as follows:

$$
\begin{array}{llll}
\text{line 1:} & \text{T} & \text{A} & \text{B} & \text{S} \\
\text{line 2:} & \text{A} & \text{T} & \text{B} & \text{S} \\
\text{line 3:} & \text{T} & \text{B} & \text{A} & \text{S} \\
\text{line 4:} & \text{T} & \text{A} & \text{B} & \text{S} \\
\end{array}
$$

so that only line 4 shares the same order as line 1. Although the chorale (as transposed by Bach) is strictly in F♯-Phrygian, the emphasis on E (the opening pitch of lines 1 and 4) produces a bias towards E minor in some portions of the music, despite the two-sharp key signature. The long final note of each line forms a protracted inverted pedal, the final note of line 4 being held for 11 bars over spirited counterpoint in the lower voices.

After this archaic opening number, the following aria, 'O du von Gott erhöhte Creatur', radically changes the tone of the music. It is in da capo form and firmly establishes B minor after the modal ending of the first movement. Most of the material is derived from the opening ritornello melody played by the accompanying oboe d'amore, which then keeps up a flowing dialogue with the voice throughout the course of the aria. The following recitative for alto and continuo lightens the tone further, though the sudden turning away from F♯ minor to C major at the end is boldly expressive of 'zu kehren' ('to turn'). C major is the key of the subsequent bass aria, 'Johannis freudenvolles Springen', the text of which refers to the biblical episode in which the unborn John the Baptist leaps in the womb of his mother Elisabeth at the salutation of Mary (Luke 1: 41). Bach sets this in a spacious concerto-like style with a ritornello of considerable length (19 bars in 4/4 metre). The accompaniment, scored for strings, is based on vigorous violinistic ideas, with the opening leaping figures subjected to close imitation. The aria is in da capo form, with the B section ending in the dominant (G major). Lively syncopated rhythms and an abundance of *forte*, *piano*, and even *pianissimo* markings give the music a taste of the approaching *style galant*. The following soprano recitative, in which the voice rises as high as *b"* at one point, leads back to B minor for the final chorale, an unadorned setting of the melody of

[*cont. on p.106*]

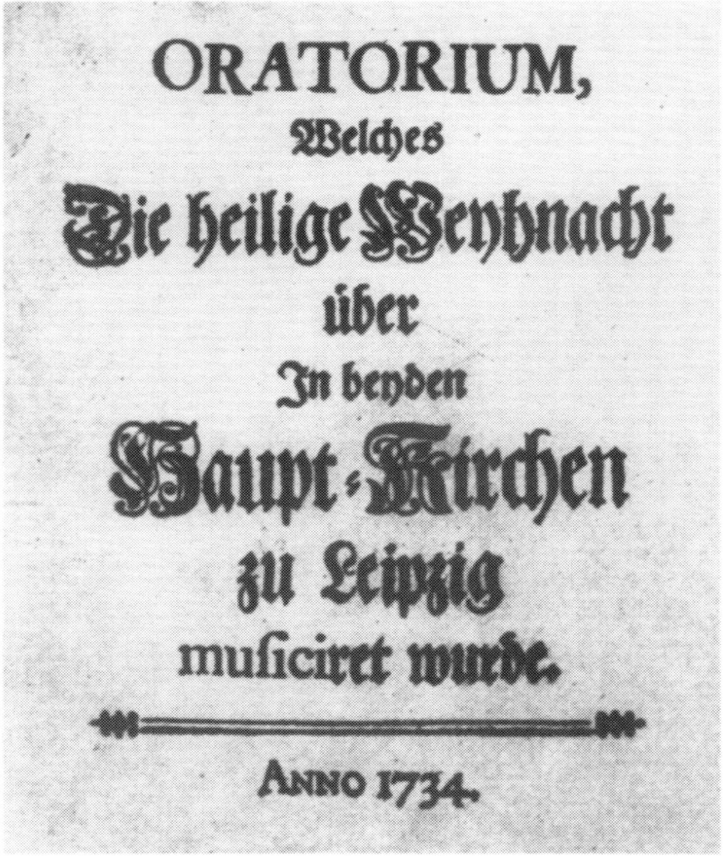

# ORATORIUM,

Welches

## Die heilige Weyhnacht

über

In beyden

# Haupt-Kirchen
## zu Leipzig
musiciret wurde.

ANNO 1734.

---

Am 1sten Heil. Weyhnacht-Feyertage,

Frühe zu St. Nicolai und Nachmittage zu St. Thomae.

Tutti.

Jauchzet! frohlocket! auf! preiset die Tage,
Rühmet, was heute der Höchste gethan.
Lasset das Zagen, verbannet die Klage,
Stimmet voll Jauchzen und Fröhlichkeit an:
Dienet dem Höchsten mit herrlichen Chören
Laßt uns den Nahmen des Höchsten verehren.

Da Capo.

Evang.

A 2

---

Title-page and beginning of the original libretto of the *Christmas Oratorio*

Opening of Bach's *Christmas Oratorio*, autograph score
(Staatsbibliothek zu Berlin, Preußischer Kulturbesitz)

## Christmas Oratorio (*Weihnachts-Oratorium*)

The longest and best known of Bach's three oratorios. BWV248 is not a conventional 18th-century oratorio; its use of biblical passages and an Evangelist link it to the Lutheran *historia* and oratorio Passion. It is cast in the form of six self-contained but linked cantatas and was written for the celebration of Christmas at Leipzig in 1734–5. Each part was given separately as the 'principal music' on the six feast-days between Christmas Day and Epiphany, and replaced the cantatas which would otherwise have been performed. The title-page of the printed libretto indicates that these six cantatas were heard 'in the two chief churches in Leipzig' (the Nikolaikirche and Thomaskirche), but Parts 3 and 5 were given only at the Nikolaikirche. Parts 1, 2, and 3 were for the first, second, and third days of Christmas, Part 4 for the feast of the Circumcision (1 January), Part 5 for the first Sunday in the New Year (2 January 1735), and Part 6 for the feast of the Epiphany (6 January).

Bach did not so much compose the *Christmas Oratorio* as compile it. In common with his two other oratorios and much of his later music for the church, the work is largely based on earlier material. Evidence from surviving instrumental parts for Part 6 shows that it was a parody of a church cantata (BWV248/VIa), now lost. The original sources for the arias and large-scale choruses in Parts 1–5 were a series of three secular cantatas written for the Elector of Saxony and his family: *Herkules auf dem Scheidewege* (1733), *Tönet, ihr Pauken!* (1733), and *Preise dein Glücke* (1734). The recitatives and ariosos, the chorale settings, and the well-known 'Pastoral Symphony' were newly composed. Although Bach rarely parodied the narrative sections of earlier works, the TURBA choruses 'Lasset uns nun gehen gen Bethlehem' (no. 26) and 'Wo ist der neugeborne König?' (no. 45) were probably adapted from 'Ja nicht auf das Fest' and 'Pfui dich' from the *St Mark Passion* (1731).

In Bach's time the reuse of material in this way was entirely usual. Although some scholars have disparaged PARODY technique on such a large scale, it should be remembered that originality *per se* was not the major criterion of artistic judgement that it is today. Bach was on the whole as literal as possible when transferring material from one work to another, and often the change of text was the only major alteration. Although this sometimes led to surprising incongruities—the inappropriate echoes in the aria 'Flößt, mein Heiland' (no. 39) are explained only by the text of its model, 'Treues Echo, dieser Orten' from *Herkules*—Bach was usually careful in his selection of material. The texts for the aria 'Schließe, mein Herze' (no. 31) and the opening chorus of Part 5 directly parallel verses from *Preise dein Glücke* (no. 7) and *Herkules* (no. 13), suggesting that Bach contemplated parodying these latter movements but eventually thought better of it. In both cases he found it necessary to compose the music afresh, and 'Schließe, mein Herze' may well be considered one of the most carefully crafted and compelling numbers in the work.

Parody technique relied heavily on the contribution of the poet. The ease with which 'Schlafe, mein Liebster, und pflege der Ruh' (in which Pleasure beguiles Hercules) was adapted to become 'Schlafe, mein Liebster, genieße der Ruh' (no. 19, a rustic lullaby to Christ in the cradle) suggests that Bach's regular librettist, Picander, may well have been involved. He was an experienced writer of parody texts and the original author of *Herkules auf dem Scheidewege*. If he was indeed responsible for the oratorio text, his collaboration with Bach might have involved material contributions from the composer, and this in turn might explain why he laid no claim to it as his own work in print.

The backbone of the text is provided by the biblical narrative, which charts the Nativity of Jesus up to the coming of the Three Wise Men, using the prescribed Gospel lessons for Christmastide divided into six separate scenes. However, in the interests of dramatic continuity the distribution of the lessons between the six parts does not always follow the division observed in church. Parts 1–4 use verses from St Luke 2: Part 1, vv. 1 and 3–7; Part 2, vv. 8–14; Part 3, vv. 15–20; and Part 4, v. 21. Parts 5 and 6 make use of readings from St Matthew 2: 1–6 and 7–12 respectively. Unlike their accounts of the Passion, neither St Luke's nor St Matthew's description of the Nativity includes much dramatic dialogue between individuals and groups. There are in fact only six sections of direct speech in the Gospel lessons employed, and Herod and the Angel are the only named characters. This throws the emphasis of the oratorio on narration and contemplation rather than action. But the librettist supplied some recitatives of his own. Like the ariosos added to the *St Matthew Passion* they are generally meditative (following a Gospel reading and preceding an aria), but a number go beyond merely commenting on the action. The first bass recitative in Part 2, for instance, actually urges the shepherds to approach the manger and sing the infant Jesus to sleep, thus preparing the way for the following aria, the lullaby 'Schlafe, mein Liebster'. Here, as elsewhere, the transition from free recitative to aria is smoothed by retaining the same orchestral accompaniment.

Bach was not the first to compose an oratorio in several independent parts. Five-part oratorio cycles were a regular feature of the Lübeck ABENDMUSIKEN, which Bach had witnessed as early as 1705. The composer headed his autograph score 'Oratorium', and it is clear that he considered the six cantatas to form a single coherent cycle. Nevertheless, he was involved in a delicate balancing-act between the liturgical necessity of producing six free-standing cantatas appropriate for the individual feast-days of Christmastide, and the artistic desire for a conceptual and integrated whole. Each of the six parts is structurally indistinguishable from many of Bach's cantatas, opening with a full-scale chorus (a sinfonia in Part 2), and concluding with an accompanied chorale or chorale-based chorus in the same key (a da capo of the opening chorus in Part 3). Between these movements the arias are evenly distributed at two per part (in Part 3 one is a duet and in Part 5 one is a trio). Oratorio-like unity is achieved through the continuous Gospel narrative and musically in three main ways: by the use of an overall tonal scheme for the six cantatas revolving around D major (D–G–D–F–A–D); by similar scoring in the three D major cantatas (including three trumpets and drums); and by the structural deployment of the chorale melody 'Herzlich tut mich verlangen' at the beginning and end of the work. In the same way in which Leipzig congregations would have regarded the six major feasts from Christmas Day to Epiphany as one integrated festival, so too the six component parts of the work together form a complete and unified whole.          SH

*DürrK*; W. Blankenburg, *Das Weinachts-Oratorium von Johann Sebastian Bach* (Munich and Kassel, 1982); H. Smither, *A History of the Oratorio*, ii (Chapel Hill, NC, 1977), 158–68; G. Stiller, *Johann Sebastian Bach and Liturgical Life in Leipzig* (St Louis, Miss., 1984).

the final verse of Luther's chorale. As in the opening movement, the final note is spun out to form an inverted pedal—perhaps to be regarded as a piece of word-painting for the final word, 'Ewigkeit' ('eternity')—cadencing on F#-Phrygian as before.                                          DLH

For bibliography, *see* CANTATA, §1.

***Christ unser Herr zum Jordan kam*** ('Christ our Lord came to Jordan'). Cantata for the feast of St John the Baptist (24 June), BWV7, first performed at Leipzig in 1724. It is the second of three surviving cantatas for this feast-day, and its text is based on a baptismal hymn by Martin Luther dating from 1541. Two verses are accommodated in their original form in Bach's scheme, while the remaining five appear in paraphrase by an unidentified author. The hymn focuses on the work of John the Baptist with particular reference to Christ's baptism in the River Jordan and its Christian symbolism. Bach's scoring is modest, consisting of two oboes d'amore, two concertante violins, and ripieno strings with continuo. These instrumental parts, nevertheless, are granted considerable prominence in the opening movement where they provide concerto-like ritornellos between the choral episodes.

Customarily among Bach's chorale-based cantatas of the Leipzig period, the most elaborate writing is to be found in the impressively proportioned opening choruses. In these Bach was able to demonstrate his consummate artistry both in portraying vivid, often colourful images and in unifying disparate musical elements and disciplines. In the present work the opening chorus occupies almost a third of Bach's score. It is an elaborate choral fantasia in which the voices set the scene of Christ's own baptism. A pervasive image of the undulating waters of the Jordan, it would seem, is affectingly evoked by the predominantly flowing quavers of the oboes d'amore set against the restless, lapping semiquavers of the ripieno strings. This extraordinarily subtle movement further incorporates a 16th-century chorale melody by Johann Walther, providing an example of a technique in which Bach's pupil J. P. Kirnberger considered that his master 'excelled all the composers in the world'.

The recitative and arias that follow expand in various ways on the Christian significance of baptism. First comes a continuo aria for bass whose text reflects on the symbolism of the baptismal water. A tenor recitative contains part of the celebrated text from St Matthew 3: 17, 'This is my beloved Son, in whom I am well pleased'. The tenor aria which follows further considers Christ's baptism with particular reference to the Trinity and to the symbol of the holy dove. Bach colours the text here with two concertante violins which soar, bird-like, above the vocal line and the basso continuo. The text of the bass recitative, with string accompaniment, relates to St Matthew 28: 19; in the sixth bar the recitative merges into arioso where the words of Christ's exhortation to his disciples, 'Go ye therefore, and teach all nations' are paraphrased. The text of the last aria, for alto with two oboes d'amore, strings, and continuo, serves as a reminder to mankind that without faith and cleansing by baptism there is no hope of everlasting life. The cantata ends with a straightforward four-part harmonization of the hymn melody by Walther already quoted in the opening chorus.                                          NA

For bibliography, *see* CANTATA, §1.

***Christus, der ist mein Leben*** ('Christ, who is my life'). Cantata for the 16th Sunday after Trinity, BWV95. The appointed Gospel reading relates St Luke's account of the raising from the dead of the young son of the widow of Nain (Luke 7: 11–17). It is clear, in view of both the present work and Bach's three other extant cantatas for this Sunday (nos. 161, 8, and 27), that the story was understood symbolically to represent man's resurrection to eternal life. Bach first performed the piece at Leipzig on 12 September 1723.

The unidentified author of the text incorporates into his scheme single verses from four different hymns, each with its associated melody. Two of these are contained in the opening chorus, an ingenious, experimental, and highly original composition whose complexity of design holds surprises for the unsuspecting ear. It is made up of three component parts forming a pattern of chorus–recitative–chorus. An instrumental opening, in which a syncopated figure in the divided oboe d'amore parts is answered by the upper strings, leads to the first hymn, *Christus, der ist mein Leben* (*c*.1609), whose melody, by Melchior Vulpius, is sustained in the soprano line. The four lines of the strophe are presented in four distinct choral sections whose chordal declamation is broken only once, at the words 'Sterben ist mein Gewinn' ('To die is my reward'). Here, with a sudden change from (implied) *forte* to *piano*, Bach brings in the voices one by one on successive dissonances, arriving at a diminished 7th chord followed by a pause. A bridge is formed between this hymn and the next by an extended declamatory passage for solo tenor made up of arioso and simple recitative, punctuated by instrumental references to the syncopated figure from the previous section. A sequence of key changes (beginning in G major and ending on the dominant of G minor) leads to the second hymn melody, sung to the first strophe of Luther's *Mit Fried und Freud ich fahr dahin* (1524; a paraphrase of the *Nunc dimittis*). The lines of the chorale are separated this time not by independent motivic material, but by *Vorimitation* of the melody on horn and oboes (replacing the oboes d'amore heard previously) over a running quaver bass. The sturdy character of Luther's hymn, and the thematic homogeneity achieved by the presence of its melody in both the vocal and the instrumental strands, give strength and uniformity to this section of the movement.

Following this superbly constructed chorus is a simple recitative for soprano whose text bids farewell to life's transient pleasures. It leads into the third chorale of the cantata, the first strophe of Valerius Herberger's *Valet will ich dir geben* (1613), set to its melody by Melchior Teschner. Bach cast the movement as a trio in which the soprano sustains the cantus firmus, accompanied by two unison oboes d'amore and an ostinato continuo bass. Both the playful character of the oboe d'amore writing and the lively gestures of the continuo give this captivating chorale setting a lyrical, even dance-like quality.

The next two numbers are for tenor, their texts intensifying man's longing for death on earth and eternal life with Christ. After a simple recitative, Bach introduces an aria of outstanding beauty in which the pictorial imagery of tolling bells at the last hour plays a prominent role. While divided oboes d'amore evoke an appropriately swinging rhythm for the bells, the bells themselves are heard, large and small so to speak, in the pizzicato playing of the strings. The urgent, declamatory tenor line, addressed largely to the ultimate tolling of the death knell, remains in a conspicuously high vocal register almost throughout this extended da capo aria in D major.

A bass recitative, merging into arioso, underlines the believer's faith in everlasting life. The cantata ends with the fourth chorale quoted in the piece, the fourth strophe of the hymn *Wenn mein Stündlein vorhanden ist*, with text (1560) and melody (1569) by Nikolaus Herman. Bach's setting includes an independent violin line, providing a fifth voice, soaring above the vocal strands to symbolize the risen Christ.                    NA

For bibliography, *see* CANTATA, §1.

**Chromatic Fantasia and Fugue.** A two-movement keyboard composition, BWV903. The work has generated admiration and astonishment since the 18th century, primarily for the fantasia, which not only contains chromatic modulations that are exceptionally sudden and distant, even for Bach—hence the title—but includes a recitative passage that seems to burst the bonds of ordinary late Baroque keyboard style. The fugue is notable for the free treatment of its highly chromatic sub-

ject and for its somewhat unusual modulatory design.

The two movements did not necessarily originate at the same time, and neither can be precisely dated, although surviving manuscript copies suggest that both may have originated before Bach left Weimar in 1717. Two early versions of the fantasia give divergent readings for the cadenzas that interrupt the opening section. These are probably authentic, but an embellished version of the recitative section, included in the first edition (1819) and repeated in some modern editions, is almost certainly spurious, although its existence presumably reflects continued performance of the work during the second half of the 18th century. Certainly unauthentic is the notorious edition (frequently reprinted) by the pianist and conductor Hans von Bülow (1830–94), which adds numerous interpretative markings and takes flagrant liberties with the notes.

The work's extraordinary qualities were already recognized in the 18th century; more manuscript copies exist of it than of practically any other single Bach work. Some Romantic commentators heard it as a precursor of 19th-century style. Yet the opening arpeggiation is a fixture of the Baroque prelude, and the recitative section would have been suggested by similar passages in works by Johann Kuhnau and Vivaldi. The fantasia probably reflects the style of Bach's improvisations, and although only one other work, the equally adventurous organ fantasia in G minor, comes close to it in this respect, its influence is felt in works by W. F. and C. P. E. Bach from the 1740s and later. The work has invited programmatic interpretation ever since Spitta; it was also the subject of a perceptive analytical study by Heinrich Schenker (1868–1935), whose edition, however, is of little independent value.           DS

D. Schulenberg, *The Keyboard Music of J. S. Bach* (New York, 1992), 114–20; H. Schenker, *J. S. Bach's Chromatic Fantasy and Fugue*, Eng. trans. and ed. H. Siegel (New York, 1984); G. Stauffer, ' "This fantasia … never had its like": On the Enigma and Chronology of Bach's Chromatic Fantasy and Fugue in D minor, BWV 903', in D. O. Franklin, ed., *Bach Studies* (Cambridge, 1989), 160–82.

**chronology.** Scholars have made enormous progress in sorting out the chronology of Bach's music, but the issue, which has become central to Bach research, has led to impassioned debates about our image of the composer and to questions about why scholarship has been so concerned with dating in the first place.

Chronology was not important in the earliest writings on Bach. J. N. Forkel, for example, in 1802 separated the discussion of Bach's music from the treatment of his life, and dating served only to separate the immature music (characterized by useless, even tasteless 'exercises' best forgotten) from mature 'masterpieces'. A work's date went hand in hand with its quality, with the exception of a few early pieces which Bach made worthy by later revision.

Chronology first became central in the biography (published in 1873–80) by Philipp Spitta, who integrated his discussions of Bach's life and works and presented the music largely in what he considered was its chronological order. But there was a problem because, by and large, the autographs and manuscript copies that transmit most compositions do not bear dates, and only a few pieces can be directly connected with events whose dates are known. Much of Spitta's chronology depended instead on the hypothesis that Bach's output corresponded to his duties: organ music when he was an organist, concertos and chamber music when he was a *Kapellmeister*, and sacred vocal music when he was a Kantor. Spitta regarded Bach's appointment as Kantor in Leipzig as the culmination of his career, and saw the CHORALE CANTATA cycle (which he recognized as unified by the paper types in its performing parts and surviving scores) as the culmination of Bach's sustained artistic and theological growth. Spitta dated these works to the years 1735–44.

Spitta's chronological views were challenged in the years after World War II; indeed, chronology became a principal motivator of the source-critical orientation of post-war Bach research. Most influential were Georg von Dadelsen's detailed chronology of Bach's handwriting and Alfred Dürr's study of the papers and copyists, both published in the late 1950s. The focus of both Dürr and Dadelsen was Bach's Leipzig church cantatas. They made an ideal subject because most of them survive in autograph scores or original performing parts, because the pieces can be assigned to specific liturgical occasions, and because patterns of transmission make it possible to reconstruct yearly cycles of cantatas.

By carefully sorting out the papers Bach used (distinguished by their watermarks) and the handwritings of those who copied the original performing parts, and by considering evidence of the liturgical purpose of the works, information on their transmission, and a few explicit dates in the sources, Dürr and Dadelsen produced a substantially complete calendar of Bach's composition and performance of church cantatas in Leipzig.

The creation of these works turned out to be concentrated in his first few years as Thomaskantor, a discovery which suggested a radically new view of Bach's production of church music. A principal challenge to Spitta was the demotion of

his beloved chorale cantata cycle from its place of honour at the end of Bach's life (c.1735–44) to merely the second of three (or five) cycles, composed and performed in 1724–5. A heated debate arose about the 'new image of Bach' articulated by Friedrich Blume that made him out to be less religiously motivated than in Spitta's portrait and demanded a break with the Bach image of the past. Some could not bring themselves to accept the new chronology and its implications: the demolition of old ideas about Bach, for example, led Friedrich Smend to ask 'What remains?' The new chronology is now generally accepted, though the debate about our image of Bach has not been settled.

The diplomatic tools developed by Dürr and Dadelsen also made possible the datings of some later reperformances of cantatas, as well as of other works (Passions, instrumental music, etc.). Since then, the identification of many anonymous copyists by H.-J. Schulze and others has narrowed some datings even further. The close scrutiny of paper, handwriting, and copyists has been continued, especially by Yoshitake Kobayashi, who has extended it particularly to Bach's later years.

The myths shattered by the cantata chronology have led to the healthy questioning of other assumptions, and to some significant redatings of other works. Christoph Wolff's investigations of *The Art of Fugue* revealed that much of its music dates from the late 1730s or early 1740s, and that this contrapuntal project was not Bach's last work, as tradition had it. (Kobayashi's research suggests that the compilation of the Mass in B minor may have been Bach's last project.) Joshua Rifkin's demonstration that the *St Matthew Passion* dates from 1727, and not 1729, made it clear that the so-called Cöthen Funeral Music was a parody of Bach's great sacred drama and not the other way around. The traditional periodization of Bach's output has also come into question; Wolff and Robert Marshall have demonstrated that much of the instrumental music, assigned more or less automatically to Cöthen under the standard model, may well date from Bach's time in Leipzig.

Some repertories were untouched by the new chronology, especially those transmitted only in secondary sources, where datings based on style and biographical assumptions have continued to dominate. The early keyboard music is a particular problem, in which questions of dating and authenticity are intertwined. The success of efforts on the Leipzig church cantatas has led to an idealistic expectation that the same kind of exact dating is possible for other repertories, even when that is unlikely or impossible.

For better or worse, the experience of the cantatas made a search for dates a principal goal of much Bach scholarship. Bach studies have come under fire for being obsessed with facts, and some have gone so far as to suggest that the post-war focus on source studies, chronology, and the production of the *NBA* represented 'safe' ventures for German scholarship in the wake of the nation's experiences under National Socialism.　　DRM

*DürrC*; *Spitta*; F. Blume, 'Outlines of a New Picture of Bach', *Music and Letters*, 44 (1963), 214–27; G. von Dadelsen, *Beiträge zur Chronologie der Werke Johann Sebastian Bachs* (Trossingen, 1958); Y. Kobayashi, 'Zur Chronologie der Spätwerke Johann Sebastian Bachs: Kompositions- und Aufführungstätigkeit von 1736 bis 1750', *BJb* 74 (1988), 7–72; R. Marshall, 'The Compositions for Solo Flute: A Reconsideration of their Authenticity and Chronology', in *The Music of Johann Sebastian Bach: The Sources, the Style, the Significance* (New York, 1989), 201–25; J. Rifkin, 'The Chronology of Bach's Saint Matthew Passion', *Musical Quarterly*, 61 (1975), 360–87; F. Smend, 'Was bleibt? Zu Friedrich Blumes Bachbild', *Der Kirchenmusiker*, 13 (1962), 178–88; C. Wolff, 'Bach's Leipzig Chamber Music', in *Bach: Essays on his Life and Music* (Cambridge, Mass., 1991), 223–38; 'The Compositional History of the Art of Fugue', in ibid. 265–81.

**Church calendar.** In Western Christendom the liturgical year is governed by the two feasts of Easter and Christmas, the first one movable, being linked to the Jewish Passover which is determined by the lunar calendar, the other fixed on 25 December since the 4th century. Christmas is preceded by the four-week preparatory period of Advent. The ensuing major divisions of approximately the first half of the Church year follow the major events of the life of Christ: Christmas (birth), Epiphany (infancy), pre-Lent and Lent (ministry and temptations), Holy Week (Passion and death), Easter (Resurrection), and Ascension. Then follow the festival of Pentecost, commemorating the coming of the Holy Spirit on the Church, and the celebration of the doctrine of the Trinity on the feast of the Holy Trinity. In the remainder of the Church year, designated Sundays after Trinity (now customarily known as Sundays after Pentecost), various themes of Christian life were explored in the Sunday lections of Epistles and Gospels.

In Catholicism the temporal calendar is supplemented by the sanctoral calendar, the celebration of particular saints on specified dates. At the Reformation Luther emphasized the weekly Sunday worship of the temporal calendar and drastically reduced the number of saints' days. He retained the traditional sequence of Sunday Epistles and Gospels and the Lutheran pattern for Sunday preaching was quickly established: at the morning eucharistic HAUPTGOTTESDIENST the sermon was an exposition of the Gospel of the day, and at afternoon VESPERS it was on the Epistle of the day. Luther published two sequences of sermons on the Epistles and Gospels of the Church year, an example followed by many Lutheran theologians and pastors in succeeding centuries. Bach had at least 13 such books of sermons for the Church year in his personal library.

As the cantata was the musical counterpart of the sermon, it was closely associated with these propers, the Epistle and Gospel, on a given Sunday or feast; indeed, the libretto usually contains numerous quotations from these lections, or allusions to them. It was therefore customary for Lutheran composers, including Bach, to specify the day for which the cantata was composed. The Church calendar therefore became an organizing principle for collections of cantatas. With the addition of such celebrations as New Year, the election of the town council, and Reformation Day, about 60 cantatas were required for an annual repertory. There were varieties of practice. In some places, such as the Weimar court chapel, cantatas were performed throughout the seasons of Advent and Lent. In Leipzig, however, while the first Sunday in Advent was celebrated as a festival (the beginning of the Church year), there was no cantata or any other concerted music on the remaining Sundays in Advent, which were designated a *tempus clausum*. Similarly, there was no such music during Lent until almost the end of Holy Week, with the performance of a concerted passion at Good Friday Vespers. This explains why some of Bach's earlier Advent and Lent cantatas were later reworked for other Sundays in Leipzig.

The following is an outline of the Sundays, festivals, and other celebrations of the Church year in Leipzig. The three major feasts of Christmas, Easter, and Pentecost (or Whitsun) were celebrated with special services (and cantatas) on three days. The Latin names used for some of the Sundays, such as those in Lent and after Easter, are derived from the first words of the traditional introits for those days. German names are shown in parentheses where appropriate.

*Sundays and Festivals*
Advent—four Sundays before Christmas
Christmas Day (Weinachtstag)—25 December and
　the two days following
Sunday after Christmas
New Year's Day (Neujahr), also Circumcision
　(Beschneidung Christi)—1 January
Sunday after New Year
Epiphany (Epiphanius)—6 January
Sundays after Epiphany (the length of the Epiphany
　season is variable, depending on the date of Easter)
*Septuagesima—third Sunday before Lent
*Sexagesima—second Sunday before Lent

*Estomihi—Sunday before Lent
*Invocavit—first Sunday in Lent
*Reminiscere—second Sunday in Lent
*Oculi—third Sunday in Lent
*Laetare—fourth Sunday in Lent
*Judica—fifth Sunday in Lent
*Palm Sunday (Palmarum)
*Good Friday (Karfreitag)
*Easter Day (Ostertag) and the two days following
*Quasimodogeniti—first Sunday after Easter
*Misericordias Domini—second Sunday after Easter
*Jubilate—third Sunday after Easter
*Cantate—fourth Sunday after Easter
*Rogate—fifth Sunday after Easter
*Ascension (Himmelfahrt)
*Exaudi—Sunday after Ascension
*Pentecost (Pfingsttag) and the two days following
*Trinity Sunday (Trinitatis)
*Sundays after Trinity (variable in number to a
   maximum of 27, depending on the date of Easter)

*Saints' Days*
St Stephen's Day (Gedenktag des Märtyrers
   Stephanus)—26 December
St John's Day (Gedenktag des Apostels Johannes)—27
   December
Purification (Mariae Reinigung)—2 February
Annunciation (Mariae Verkundigung)—25 March
St John the Baptist's Day (Fest Johannes des
   Täufers)—24 June
Visitation (Mariae Heimsuchung)—2 July
St Michael's Day (Fest des Erzengels Michael)—29
   September

*Other Days*
Inauguration of the town council (Ratswechsel)—last
   Monday in August
Reformation (Reformationsfest)—31 October

Those Sundays and feast-days marked with an asterisk (*) in the above list fall on dates which are dependent on the date of Easter. In calculating these dates for a particular year it should be noted that, while Protestant Germany adopted the Gregorian calendar in 1700, the date of Easter was, until 1776, calculated according to a 'Verbesserte Kalender' ('improved calendar'). As a result there were two years (1724 and 1744) in which Easter Day in Protestant Germany fell a week earlier than in most other Christian countries (including Great Britain, as it happens, since the Julian Easter was on the same day as the Gregorian Easter in those years). This explains why, for example, the first performance of Bach's *St John Passion* took place on 7 April 1724, while most of Christendom observed Good Friday on 14 April that year. After 1776 Protestant Germany came into line with other countries in calculating the date of Easter.
                                                  RAL
Dr Bauermann, 'Chronologie: III. Christliche Zeitrechnung', in H. Gunkel and L. Zscharnach, eds., *Die Religion in Geschichte und Gegenwart* (2nd. edn.,

Tübingen, 1927–32), i, cols. 1671–6; R. A. Leaver, 'Bach's Understanding and Use of the Epistles and Gospels of the Church Year', *Bach*, 5/4 (1975), 4–13.

**ciaccona, ciacona.** Italian forms of CHACONNE.

**clarino.** A term used to refer to the high register of the TRUMPET, and occasionally to a part composed specifically for a trumpet capable of playing in that register.

**Clauder, Johann Christoph** (b. 1701; d. 1779). A teacher at the University of Leipzig. In 1734 he wrote the text for Bach's secular cantata *Preise dein Glücke, gesegnetes Sachsen*, performed on 5 October to celebrate the first anniversary of Friedrich August II's election as King August III of Poland.                                      KK

**clavichord.** A strung keyboard instrument of the late Middle Ages to early 19th century, characterized by a simple action in which the ends of the keys are attached to metal tangents which simultaneously stop and strike the strings. This action permits more immediate physical communication between the player's fingers and the strings than is found on any other type of keyboard instrument, making possible sensitively gradated dynamics and even a type of vibrato. These advantages are offset by a generally soft dynamic level which makes most clavichords unsuited for public performance.

Through most of its history the clavichord was viewed primarily as an inexpensive practice instrument. On the so-called 'fretted' instruments prevalent until the later 18th century, each string, stopped at different points, served for as many as four different pitches, making such instruments awkward in chromatic passages or music in remote keys. Bach was undoubtedly familiar with the clavichord, and indeed J. N. Forkel reported that it was his favourite keyboard instrument, but it seems unlikely that any of his music was composed specifically for it. Nevertheless, German organists sometimes practised on instruments comprised of as many as three clavichords placed atop one another, with a pedal-board attached to the lowest; the account of Bach's estate suggests that he owned such an instrument.

The word CLAVIER, sometimes translated as 'clavichord', acquired that specific meaning only after Bach's death; thus the title 'The Well-tempered Clavier' does not refer specifically to the clavichord. Some movements, however, can be played effectively on it, and the original title of the Inventions, which refers to a 'cantabile style', cites an attribute often associated with the clavichord,

although not every piece in the collection displays
it.                                                                    DS

H. Henkel, *Clavichorde* (Leipzig, 1981) [catalogue of
the Musikinstrumenten-Museum der Karl-Marx-
Universität, Leipzig, vol. iv]; R. Loucks, 'Was the
*Well-Tempered Clavier* Performed on a Fretted
Clavichord?', *Performance Practice Review*, 5 (1992),
247–92; N. van Ree Bernard, *Seven Steps in Clavichord Development Between 1400 and 1800* (Buren,
1987); E. M. Ripin and H. Schott, 'The Clavichord',
in *The New Grove Early Keyboard Instruments* (London, 1989), 141–71.

**clavier.** A term with widely differing uses and
meanings; in the broadest sense it signifies 'keyboard' or 'keyboard instrument'. Derived from
Latin 'clavis' ('key'), it was regularly used from the
early 17th century to the mid-18th or later by
French and German writers in the sense of
'musical keyboard' (as in references to the 'clavier'
of the organ).

In titles and musical scores of Bach and his contemporaries the term may refer either to one or
more keyboard instruments (clavichord, harpsichord, organ) or to the idea of a musical keyboard
in the abstract. But in later 18th-century Germany
it acquired the more specific meaning of 'clavichord' and in the 19th century that of 'piano' (the
usual meaning of the modern German 'Klavier').
Therefore modern translations of titles, and
indeed of all documents containing terms for keyboard instruments, must be carefully scrutinized
to ensure that the original language has not been
misinterpreted; it is wrong, for example, to speak
of the 'Well-tempered Clavichord' (the work is for
'clavier').

Bach would have encountered the term in the
titles and prefaces of keyboard music by Johann
Kuhnau, beginning with the latter's *Neue Clavier-
Übung* (1689–92). Bach's use of the term 'Clavier-
Übung' in several titles, beginning in 1726, clearly
reflected Kuhnau's model, and, like Kuhnau, Bach
must have expected music published under this
title to be played on various instruments, including both organ and harpsichord. Other com-
pounds of 'Clavier-' employed in modern
German, such as 'Klavierstück' ('piano piece') and
'Klavierkonzert' ('piano concerto'), occasionally
appear in verbal documents and in manuscript
copies of Bach's music from the second half of the
18th century, but not all such words were necessarily part of Bach's own vocabulary.

Bach's earliest documented use of the term is in
the autograph manuscript of the two early organ
fantasias on 'Wie schön leuchtet der Morgenstern'
(BWV739 and 764), where the macaronic heading
'a 2 Clav[iere] Ped[aliter]' refers to the use of two
manuals and pedals. Bach used similar headings
in organ works throughout his life; he also used

the abbreviation 'Clav.' alone to refer to the two
keyboards of a double-manual harpsichord (in
the Goldberg Variations) and apparently also to
refer to the two separate instruments called for in
the arrangement for keyboard duo of Contrapunctus 13 in *The Art of Fugue*. In each instance,
'clavier' appears in the title in order to point up
the existence of distinct contrapuntal parts which
are presumably to be played with contrasting
timbres or registrations. Thus, in the organ works
in question, the two manuals either bear equal
parts sounding in the same (usually treble) range,
as in a trio sonata, or one bears a dominant voice
while another furnishes accompanying voices in a
contrasting range (as in a chorale setting), the
pedals bearing the bass line in either case.

It is important to recognize that the term does
not designate a specific instrument in Bach's
usage. In the title 'Das wohltemperirte Clavier'
('The Well-tempered Clavier') it probably refers
to the abstract idea of a keyboard instrument
tuned in a circular or 'well-tempered' system. The
word 'Clavier-Übung' must be translated literally
as 'Keyboard Practice'; the last three volumes
published under this title include subtitles which
clarify the intended medium (organ in Part 3,
double-manual harpsichord in the other two).

Already by the 1740s the term was often understood to mean 'clavichord' (as in a list drawn up
by Zacharias Hildebrandt of instruments built
mainly for Leipzig clients). Thus the '3 Clavire
nebst Pedal' included in Bach's estate might have
been a set of three clavichords fitted with a pedal-
board in order to serve as an ersatz organ for practising (a common arrangement at the time). J. N.
Forkel, however, appears to have used the specific
word 'Clavichord' wherever a distinction was crucial (as in his famous but often questioned assertion that the 'Clavichord' was the instrument on
which Bach best liked to play).                    DS

***Clavierbüchlein*** ('little keyboard book(s)').
Three well-known manuscripts from the Bach
family are customarily referred to by this word:
the *Clavier-Büchlein vor Wilhelm Friedemann
Bach*, presented to Bach's eldest son at Cöthen on
22 January 1720, two months after his ninth birthday; and two manuscripts prepared for Bach's
second wife, Anna Magdalena, the first in 1722
(the year following their marriage) and the second
in 1725. The 1720 manuscript is in the Yale University library, the other two in the Staatsbibliothek zu Berlin. The volumes are sometimes
referred to in German as 'Notenbüchlein' ('little
music books'). The 1720 and 1725 volumes have
been issued in several modern editions and in
facsimile.

# Clavier-Übung

The three manuscripts are invaluable as documents for the teaching of music in the Bach household and as sources for the repertories—mostly simple, semi-popular compositions—employed in musical education in 18th-century Germany. They are also witnesses to J. S. Bach's technique and teaching of composition and to the early musical development of his two eldest sons, Wilhelm Friedemann and Carl Philipp Emanuel.

The 1720 and 1725 books contain mostly short, pedagogical pieces; like similar compositions in comparable manuscripts of the period, these probably played an important role in the teaching of basic technical and theoretical musical skills. It has been suggested that other members of the family, such as Bach's second son Carl Philipp Emanuel, at one time possessed similar books which are now lost.

The 1720 book is almost entirely in the hands of Sebastian and Friedemann Bach, the former having a greater share in the earlier entries, Friedemann in the later ones. Entries were made in appreciable numbers until about 1726, after which Friedemann does not appear to have used the book regularly. Besides introductory matter illustrating the elements of musical notation—in particular, a table of ornament signs—the volume contains chiefly works by Sebastian. Among these are early versions of the two- and three-part Inventions and Sinfonias (here called preludes and fantasias) and of 11 preludes from Part 1 of *The Well-tempered Clavier*, alongside various other preludes and similar pieces. (Some of these recur in the collection known as the Twelve Little Preludes; Bach probably had nothing to do with its compilation.) There are also pieces by Telemann and G. H. Stölzel, as well as what appear to be early efforts by W. F. Bach.

The 1722 book consists entirely of Bach's music: chiefly the early versions—in some movements evidently the first drafts—of a number of the French Suites, as well as a few minuets and other pieces, some fragmentary. A substantial number of pages were deliberately removed from the manuscript at an early date; perhaps these contained rejected drafts or sketches. Most of the extant musical entries are in Sebastian's hand, which suggests that the volume, although apparently a wedding gift for Anna Magdalena, later served as a sketchbook for Sebastian.

The 1725 book, on the other hand, is primarily a collection of pedagogical or recreational music by other composers, presumably used by Anna Magdalena for either her own enjoyment or the instruction of the children, several of whose hands appear within. Although opening with early versions of the A minor and E minor Partitas (in Sebastian's hand), the volume continues with copies of numerous minuets, polonaises, and other short keyboard pieces, mostly anonymous. The polonaises represent a minuet-like version of the dance popular in the 18th century. The famous Minuet in G BWV Anh. 11 114 has been identified as a movement from a suite by the Dresden organist Christian Pezold, and there are also pieces by J. A. Hasse, François Couperin, and C. P. E. Bach, as well as chorales and other vocal numbers. Several pieces are given twice, with different bass lines or otherwise varied; these would have furnished lessons in composition or improvisation, as would some brief rules for figured bass realization included at the end.    DS

D. Schulenberg, *The Keyboard Music of J. S. Bach* (New York, 1992), 128–59, 387–90.

***Clavier-Übung*** ('Keyboard Practice'). A title used by Bach for four sets of keyboard pieces published between 1726 and 1741. They are:

*Clavier-Übung I* (1726–31): the six Partitas BWV825–30;

*Clavier-Übung II* (1735): the Italian Concerto BWV971, and the Ouverture in the French Style BWV831;

*Clavier-Übung III* (1739), consisting mainly of liturgical organ music, BWV669–89 and 802–5; and

*Clavier-Übung [IV]* (1741): the Goldberg Variations.

In calling these works 'Clavier-Übung' Bach was following the example of his predecessor at Leipzig, Johann Kuhnau, who had used it for two volumes of keyboard music published in 1689 and 1692.

***Clavier-Übung III***. The third instalment in Bach's series of *Clavier-Übungen*, published towards the end of September 1739. It was his first published collection of works for the organ and the most ambitious publishing project that he would ever undertake. The first part of the printed title reads as follows: 'Dritter Theil der Clavier Übung bestehend in verschiedenen Vorspielen über die Catechismus- und andere Gesænge, vor die Orgel' ('Third part of the *Clavier Übung* consisting of various preludes on the catechism and other hymns, for the organ'). The heterogeneous collection consists of multiple settings of the German Kyrie and Gloria BWV669–77, pairs of settings for each of the six catechism chorales BWV678–89, and four duets BWV802–5, all framed by the Prelude and Fugue in E♭ major BWV552. The occasion for the composition of the collection is obscure. It has been linked variously with an organ recital given by Bach on the new organ of the Frauenkirche, Dresden, on 1 December 1736 and with celebrations throughout Lutheran Germany marking the bicentenary of the Augsburg Confession on 12 August 1739. It may have grown out of Bach's renewed interest in the chorale as reflected in his involvement in the Schemelli hymn-book project in 1736. The inclusion of pieces in a pointedly modern idiom has also been seen as a musical refutation of J. A. Scheibe's criticism of his former teacher's outmoded style in 1737. Certainly, the catechism was an area of the Lutheran liturgy to which Bach had not previously turned his attention in organ music.

Although no autograph source materials survive, studies based on the original edition suggest that work on the collection goes back to the period about 1735–6, not long after the publication of *Clavier-Übung II*. Demonstrable influences on the works in the collection are varied and wide-ranging, including the compositions of the north German keyboard virtuoso C. F. Hurlebusch, Bach's cousin J. G. Walther, the Dresden lutenist S. L. Weiß, French *Livre d'orgue* collections, and Italian *stile antico* compositions. Bach's guiding principle in this, as in all other such collections, seems to have been the exhaustive treatment of a particular genre, in this case the organ chorale, in order to demonstrate the virtually limitless possibilities for its treatment. As he had done in his 1724–5 cycle of cantatas, he here demonstrates his continuing preference for 16th-century chorale melodies. Their emphasis on the church modes allows Bach to go beyond the harmonic limitations imposed by the major-minor system and explore modal harmony in a systematic way. At the same time, variation procedure comes to the fore for the first time in Bach's late works.

Within the disposition outlined above, a general organizational plan can be discerned. Each chorale tune is treated first in an extended cantus firmus setting *pedaliter*, and then in a short setting *manualiter*. This same principle extends even to the free works: each of the two pairs of *duetti* can be seen as small-scale *manualiter* counterparts to the large-scale prelude and fugue 'pro Organo pleno'.

The Praeludium which opens the collection is unique in Bach's treatment of the genre. It features a juxtaposition of three highly contrasting elements: a massive five-voice French overture module, which acts as a refrain; a light, homophonic *galant* trio module, complete with echo effects; and a fugal module. The Fuga itself, separate from the Praeludium and placed at the very end of the work, is hardly less unusual. It is a double fugue with three subjects in which the second and third subjects, in 6/4 and 12/8 metre respectively, after receiving an initial formal exposition, are each combined in double counterpoint with the opening *stile antico* subject. All three subjects never appear in combination, as in a true triple fugue. Although separated by the remaining movements of the work, the prelude

and fugue are linked, not only through their 'pro organo pleno' designation, but also through their E♭ major tonality and their presentation of three *soggetti*. Both these features are elements of the Trinitarian symbolism which pervades the collection as a whole.

In the German *missa* settings which follow, the Kyrie is first treated in the severe *stile antico* style in *alla breve* metre. In its three settings the cantus firmus in semibreves drops down progressively from soprano, through tenor, to bass voice in the climactic concluding *Kyrie, Gott heiliger Geist* BWV671, which is in five voices, rather than four, and is marked 'cum organo pleno'. In each section the subject is fashioned from the first two phrases of the cantus firmus. In the first it is treated in inversion and in the third in stretto in contrary motion. These processes of technical intensification are supported by increasing rhythmic animation and by climactic chromaticism at the conclusion. The three sections of the *manualiter* setting which follows present free imitative treatments of the incipits of the chorale melodies in 3/4, 6/8, and 9/8 metres respectively.

The first of the three settings of the German Gloria, *Allein Gott in der Höh sei Ehr*, is a straightforward cantus firmus setting employing VORIMITATION. The second is an ingenious trio setting in which the repeat of the *Stollen* is written out with the upper two parts inverted in double counterpoint at the octave. In the *Abgesang* the first two phrases of the chorale melody are treated in canon at the lower octave in the outer two voices, and the concluding phrase is treated in fugal imitation with four entries distributed through all three voices. The concluding *manualiter* setting is a concise double fugue whose two subjects are diminutions of the first two phrases of the chorale melody.

The pairs of settings of each of the six catechism chorales form the core of the collection and are the only settings to be specifically named in the work's title. The large-scale *pedaliter* settings placed first in each pair are organized into two groups of three, in which the outer two in each group present the cantus firmus in canon and the central one is a setting 'In Organo pleno'. All three settings in the first group have free bass parts with firm, regular rhythms, while in the second group the cantus firmus is played by the pedals in each case. In these *pedaliter* settings the emphasis is on variety. The first, *Dies sind die heilgen zehn Gebot* BWV678, is a flowing pastorale-like setting in which the two upper parts (with alternating stepwise semiquaver figuration and quaver appoggiatura figures) and the pedal (with almost constant crotchet motion) enclose the cantus firmus in canon in adjacent inner voices. The next, *Wir glauben all an einen Gott* BWV680, is the only one of these *pedaliter* settings without a cantus firmus, perhaps because the chorale melody in this case is inordinately long. In its place an ostinato bass figure is stated six times below a fugue (sometimes nicknamed the 'Giant') based on the first phrase of the chorale. The last setting in the first group, *Vater unser im Himmelreich* bwv682, is perhaps the most complex rhythmically of any chorale setting by Bach, featuring extended passages in Lombardic rhythm (a stressed short note followed by an unstressed longer one) and long skeins of triplet semiquavers in soprano and first tenor parts. The cantus firmus is heard in canon in the alto and second tenor after extended passages of *Vorimitation*. The pedal part, while extravagantly chromatic, presses forward relentlessly with its constant quaver motion, providing a firm foundation to the rhythmic complexity of the upper voices.

The outer two *pedaliter* settings in the second group, *Christ unser Herr zum Jordan kam* bwv684 and *Jesus Christus unser Heiland* bwv688, are both concertante pieces, and both have three clearly defined rhythmic strata: in the upper two, semiquaver and quaver motion constantly replace each other in discrete units of varying length, while the cantus firmus enters below in long notes. bwv688 is a dance-like setting in 3/4 metre dominated by a striking, disjunct, wedge-shaped motif which usually appears against running semiquaver figuration, but on occasion against an inverted and syncopated version of itself. The axial setting in this group, *Aus tiefer Not schrei ich zu dir* bwv686, is a massive chorale motet setting which is notable for being one of only two keyboard works by Bach in six parts (the other is the six-part Ricercar from the *Musical Offering*). It is also one of Bach's few works for organ with double pedal. Although this feature had precedents in 16th-century German organ music, it was anachronistic by Bach's time, a factor which fits in with the severe *stile antico* of the piece.

An organizational scheme is also to be seen at work in the six 'alio modo' *manualiter* settings of the catechism chorales. In each of the two groups of three, two settings are fugal while the third is a cantus firmus setting. In the first group *Vater unser im Himmelreich* bwv683, like numerous settings in the *Orgel-Büchlein*, presents the cantus firmus unembellished in the soprano, without interludes and with uniform figuration in the lower parts. In the second group *Aus tiefer Not schrei ich zu dir* bwv687 is a Pachelbellian setting with *Vorimitation* in contrary motion and with a stretto, also in contrary motion, over the concluding pedal. Of the four fugal settings, the two in the first group, *Dies sind die heilgen zehn Gebot* bwv679 and *Wir glauben all an einen Gott* bwv681,

are distinctly modern in their use of movement types from the French suite, the gigue and the ouverture respectively. Typical of the gigue, the first employs inversion of the subject, while second treats it in stretto from the outset. Both the fugues in the second group, *Christ unser Herr zum Jordan kam* bwv685 and *Jesus Christus unser Heiland* bwv689, are more abstract. The first presents the subject and countersubject together in double counterpoint right from the start, while in the second (the only one to be entitled 'Fuga' rather than 'Fughetta') the opening line of the chorale melody supplies the subject for a more extended and resourceful fugue employing stretto (at various distances) and augmentation.

Bach scholars have been somewhat at a loss to explain the inclusion of the four duets in the collection, and indeed they were entered in a separate category in *Schmieder1*. As mentioned already, it has been suggested that the Prelude and Fugue bwv552 relates to the four duets just as the large-scale *pedaliter* chorales do to their small-scale *manualiter* counterparts. This is borne out by the grouping of the duets into two pairs of two, in each case a free prelude in triple time followed by a fugue in duple time. At odds with this theory is the fact that the members of each pair are in different tonalities and modes. In fact, this short cycle is organized by a scheme in which the tonality of the works rises by step. While Duetto no. 4 is a fairly straightforward *alla breve* fugue with a rather long subject in which syncopation figures prominently, no. 2 is unusual in a number of respects: it is in da capo form—a rare, but not unique, instance among Bach's fugues—and it features, as well as a rather strict and pervasive use of stretto, a number of extended passages in its middle section which are in strict canon.

*Clavier-Übung III* represents a landmark in Bach's *œuvre*. In some sense it marks a turning inwards, and as such stands on the threshold of the late period. In it are forecast many of the preoccupations which dominate the works of the last decade: a concentration on the techniques of fugue and canon; an adherence to the variation principle; a style-consciousness manifest in the sharp contrast between pieces in the *stile antico* and others in a modern style; an interest in highly abstract, recherché musical thought; and a preoccupation with saying the last word in a given genre with an attendant monumentality of conception.                                                    GB

*See also* sources, §2.

C. Albrecht, 'J. S. Bachs "Clavier Übung dritter Theil": Versuch einer Deutung', *BJb* 40 (1969), 46–66; G. Butler, *Bach's Clavier-Übung III: The Making of a Print* (Durham, NC, 1990); K. Ehricht, 'Die zyklische Gestalt und die Aufführungsmöglichkeit des III. Teiles der Klavierübung von Joh. Seb. Bach', *BJb* 38 (1949–50), 40–56; D. Humphreys, *The Esoteric Structure of Bach's Clavierübung III* (Cardiff, 1983); H. Klotz, 'Bachs Orgeln und seine Orgelmusik', *Die Musikforschung*, 3 (1950), 189–203; U. Meyer, 'Zum Verständnis der zehn großen Liedbearbeitungen in Bachs "Clavierübung dritter Theil" ', *Musik und Kirche*, 41 (1971), 183–9, 297–302; 42 (1972), 17–19, 74–81; R. Tangeman, 'The Ritornello Forms in Bach's Catechism Chorale Preludes', in *Essays on Music in Honor of Archibald Thompson Davison* (Cambridge, Mass., 1957), 235–41; P. Williams, *The Organ Music of J. S. Bach* (Cambridge, 1980–4), i. 184–91, 321–7; ii. 175–225.

**Clementi, Muzio** (b. 23 Jan. 1752; d. 10 March 1832). Composer and many-sided musician, born in Rome but active mainly in London. He is often given credit for his compositional swagger and keyboard virtuosity, but his standing as a commercial musician and critical scholar needs more careful examination. He developed a respectful admiration for Bach's music during his years of training in Dorset (1766–70) but, after 30 successful years as a keyboard soloist and continuo player in London, he decided to concentrate his efforts on developing his instrument factory and a publishing business.

Clementi and his partners issued bulky anthologies of keyboard music, such as the four volumes of *Selected Practical Harmony for the Organ or Piano Forte* (London, 1801–?15) and his *Introduction to the Art of Playing on the Piano Forte* (London, 1801). These were clearly intended to educate their purchasers' taste and extend their repertory—as well as improve their technique—and they included early (in some cases first) editions of Bach's organ Fantasia in G major bwv572, the fugues in A minor bwv944:2 and C major bwv953, the Toccata in D minor bwv913, and the French Suite in G major (printed in A major and with the movements in jumbled order).

Also included were the Fugue in C minor bwv575 (misattributed to C. P. E. Bach), and a version of the C♯ minor Fugue from Book 2 of *The Well-tempered Clavier* which is today unique. These two fugues conclude the *Second Part of Clementi's Introduction to the Art of Playing on the Piano Forte* (London, 1820–1). Since they are preceded by the C major Fugue exactly copied from the source material for *The Well-tempered Clavier* Book 2 now in the British Library, which is headed 'from an Original MS of the author', they create a puzzle. By 1720 Clementi certainly owned the 'London autograph' of Book 2, but it no longer contains any version of the C♯ minor Fugue, or its Prelude.

Clementi assembled manuscript copies of Bach's music during a large part of his lifetime. He often marvelled at its beauty and recalled the high value he had placed on it as learning material. SFD

S. Daw, 'Muzio Clementi as an Original Advocate, Collector and Performer, in Particular of J. S. Bach and D. Scarlatti', in P. Williams, ed., *Bach, Handel, Scarlatti: Tercentenary Essays* (Cambridge, 1985); L. Plantinga, *Clementi: His Life and Music* (London, 1977).

**Coffee Cantata** (*Kaffeekantate*) ['Schweigt stille, plaudert nicht' ('Be silent, don't chatter')]. Like *Der Streit zwischen Phoebus und Pan*, this secular cantata, bwv211, was written not for a courtly occasion but for Bach's collegium musicum. Its 'concert hall' was thus the Leipzig coffee-house of Gottfried Zimmermann, and coffee was therefore a good choice of subject. Leipzig coffee-houses had already a long tradition, and poems about coffee and its dangers were common at the time. So the cantata is a contribution both to the Leipzig coffee mania and to the literary genre. The text is by Picander, who published it as early as 1732, but it was probably not until 1734 that Bach set it to music.

Unlike most of Bach's other secular cantatas, the work begins with a simple recitative; this is addressed to the audience by a narrator (tenor). The text performs the function of a theatre bell: 'Schweigt stille, plaudert nicht und höret, was jetzund geschieht!' ('Be silent, don't chatter, and listen to what happens now!'). It is hard to imagine that the recitative had its intended effect; judging from operatic practices of the time, the audience would have expected it to be preceded by an overture of some kind. The narrator's only remaining duty after this is to introduce the final 'coro' with comments on the preceding plot; during its evolution only two real dramatis personae are present: Herr Schlendrian and his daughter Lieschen (or 'Liesgen'). Schlendrian (bass) is angry because his daughter will not obey him in everything (aria, no. 2); the main problem is revealed only in the following dialogue (recitative, no. 3): 'Tu mir den Coffee weg!' ('You must stop drinking coffee'). But Liesgen (soprano) persists in her mania to drink at least one cup of coffee a day. How strong her desire is demonstrated by her aria (no. 4) with flute and continuo, 'Ey! wie schmeckt der Coffee süße' ('Ah, how sweet the taste of coffee'), a minuet of *galant* character (except, perhaps, in its three-bar phrases). In the following recitative Schlendrian tries to bargain with Liesgen: she will not be allowed to attend marriage parties; she will be forbidden to buy a new crinoline or to look out of the window; and she will not get a silver or golden ribbon for her cap. Liesgen is content with all of this, if only she is allowed the pleasure of drinking coffee. Schlendrian is help-less and sings another aria (no. 6) about the obstinacy of girls. The strangeness of the human character is reflected in the chromatic line of the aria's continuo accompaniment.

Schlendrian suddenly has an idea: he forbids Liesgen to get married. At this she is ready at once to give up coffee. In her second aria (no. 8) she expresses her fervent wish to get married. But we are denied the final happy duet between father and daughter that we might have expected. Instead the narrator reports how Liesgen treats the agreement: in the town she makes it clear that she will only accept a husband who will allow her to indulge her passion. The final moral deals with the incorrigible minds of cats (who persist in catching mice) and girls (who persist in drinking coffee). But it was not Picander's idea to end the story like this; his text extends only as far as Lies-gen's second aria (no. 8). The final twist in the plot was an afterthought, perhaps by Bach him-self.

The only obbligato solo instruments appear in Liesgen's arias: a flute in no. 4 and a harpsichord (extending its continuo function with long chains of semiquavers) in no. 8. The strings are heard only in two of the arias (the first of Schlendrian's and the second of Liesgen's) and the final 'coro'. The scoring might seem unduly modest, but it must have been apt for a work performed in the narrow room of a coffee-house.                               KK

For bibliography, *see* CANTATA, §2.

**collegium musicum.** A term sometimes applied to a professional ensemble (e.g. Prince Leopold's orchestra at Cöthen), but more often to an amateur or semi-professional society which met regularly for practical, and usually informal, music-making.

The collegium musicum tradition in Germany stretches back to the 16th century, and several of Bach's predecessors in Leipzig directed groups of this kind. It was initially an amateur institution, usually associated with university student music-making, which met at least once a week to per-form a selection of fashionable music. Two collegia were active in Leipzig during Bach's resi-dence there: the one he was ultimately to direct, founded by Telemann in 1702, and another founded by J. F. Fasch in 1708.

Telemann's collegium, which became associ-ated with organists at the Neukirche in Leipzig, was in the hands of G. B. Schott before Bach took over in 1729 (*BDok* i. 57). The weekly concerts took place in winter, from 8 to 10 o'clock on Fri-day evenings, in Gottfried Zimmermann's coffee-house on the Catherinenstraße (see picture, p.534), and in summer, on Wednesday afternoons,

in the coffee-garden by the Grimmische Tor; dur-ing the spring and autumn trade fairs the group performed twice weekly. Bach seems to have given up the collegium between 1737 and 1739 while it was directed by his former pupil C. G. Gerlach. He was back in charge from about October 1739, but again relinquished the post during the early 1740s, perhaps after Zimmermann's death in May 1741.

While newspaper announcements testify to the regular activity of the 'Bachische Collegium Musi-cum', they give no information about the pro-grammes. However, we may assume that Bach performed a great deal of his orchestral, chamber, and keyboard music at these meetings, and that his copies of works by other composers, such as Albinoni, Johann Bernhard Bach, Handel, P. A. Locatelli (1695–1764), and Vivaldi, were prepared for these performances. We know rather more about the additional concerts, for special occa-sions, at which many of Bach's secular cantatas were performed. His activity was most intense in this regard around 1733–4, when August II became Elector of Saxony and Bach was keen to show his allegiance to the new ruler and his family (*see* CANTATA, §2). The post certainly brought him much publicity; indeed, the entry on 'Musicum Collegium' in volume 22 of J. H. Zedler's *Großes Universal-Lexicon* (Leipzig 1739), one of the fore-most encyclopedias of the day, notes the particu-lar fame of the 'Bachische Collegium Musicum' (see Casper).

While it has been customary to consider Bach's tenure with the collegium musicum as the Leipzig corollary of the Cöthen years (i.e. the principal arena of his secular music-making), this concep-tion is open to modification (see especially Wolff). First, Bach was involved in some promin-ent public performances in Leipzig before 1729, such as those of Cantata 205 and the *Trauer Ode*. Second, several important instrumental works appear in Leipzig manuscripts before 1729. Fur-thermore, Bach regularly called on the services of university students for performance of his church music before his official appointment as director of the collegium. As Wolff notes, the report of Bach's first cantata performance in 1723, which refers to him as the new 'Kantor and director of the Collegii Musici', might suggest that he was involved with the group from the start (*BDok* ii. 104).

Gerlach again took over the group from Bach in the 1740s, renaming it the 'Neues Concert'; it later became the 'Großes Concert' (formed in 1743 and directed by J. F. Doles). This was the direct ances-tor of the Gewandhaus Concerte and thus represents a crucial stage in the development of the modern concert tradition.                      JAB

W. Braun, 'Die Brüder Nagel und das Collegium musicum J. S. Bachs', in W. Vetter, ed., *Festschrift Max Schneider* (Leipzig, 1955), 167 ff.; S. J. Casper, 'Zum "Bachische Collegium Musicum" ', *BJb* 70 (1984), 175; A. Glöckner, 'Neuerkenntnisse zu Johann Sebastian Bachs Aufführungskalender zwischen 1729 und 1735,' *BJb* 67 (1981), 43–75; J. Rifkin, 'Some Questions of Performance in J. S. Bach's Trauerode', in D. Melamed., ed., *Bach Studies 2* (Cambridge, 1995), 119–53; W. Neumann, 'Das Bachische Collegium Musicum', *BJb* 47 (1960), 13–22; C. Wolff, 'Bach's Leipzig Chamber Music', *Early Music*, 13 (1985), 165–75; repr. in *Bach: Essays on his Life and Music* (Cambridge, Mass., 1991), 223–38.

**concerto.** See overleaf.

**Concerto nach Italiaenischem Gusto** ('Concerto after the Italian Taste'). *See* ITALIAN CONCERTO.

**concerto transcriptions.** Bach's transcriptions of concertos by himself and others were made during two distinct periods of his life, and for very different reasons. At Weimar he made arrangements, some for organ and some for harpsichord, of concertos by Vivaldi and other (mainly Italian) composers. These were done, it seems, at the request of the young Prince Johann Ernst (*see* CONCERTO, §3). Some 20 years later Bach turned again to concerto arrangement, this time reworking concertos, almost all of them by himself, by substituting one or more harpsichords for the original string and woodwind instruments. The purpose this time was to provide music for himself and other keyboard players to perform with the collegium musicum that he directed at Leipzig (*see* HARPSICHORD CONCERTOS).

**consistory.** A judiciary board responsible for the legal aspects of Church government and administration. Lutheran consistories generally followed the Wittenberg model, introduced in 1539, and involved both theologians and lawyers. Their primary function was to oversee the administration of marriage and other ordinances, the employees of the churches, the resolution of disputes, and so on. Thus in 1706 Bach was reproved by the Arnstadt consistory for a prolonged absence in Lübeck and for unusual harmonizations in the chorales (*BDok* ii. 19–22); and the Leipzig consistory dealt with the issue of Bach's non-musical teaching in the Thomasschule in 1724, and a dispute concerning the choice of hymns for Vesper services in 1727 (*BDok* ii. 137–8 and 182).    RAL

**continuo.** The instrumental bass line of a Baroque ensemble composition; also, the specific instrument or instruments that play it. The term is an abbreviation for 'basso continuo'. It has often been conflated both in modern times and in the 18th century with 'thorough-bass', 'figured

bass', and other expressions that refer more specifically to the notation of such a part and its realization by a keyboard player. In the early Baroque the term was limited to the keyboard part accompanying a vocal or instrumental ensemble, and throughout the 17th and 18th centuries it remained possible for a single organ or other polyphonic instrument to serve as the sole continuo instrument, particularly in small ensembles. A fully notated continuo part consists of the bass line to which are attached figures—numerals and other symbols as in the examples on pp.123–4. The player 'realizes' the figures—that is, plays appropriate chords or, in some cases, more elaborate additions. Various types of lute, as well as other instruments, occasionally realized figured basses as well, but their role in Bach's music seems to have been minimal. Because the basso continuo is so ubiquitous in the ensemble music of the later Baroque, during the 18th century (and well into the 19th) the realization of figured bass was regarded as a fundamental skill required of all serious keyboard players and of many other musicians, and its underlying principles are basic to 18th-century German harmonic theory.

Techniques for realization are explained in great detail in a number of contemporary treatises; among the most comprehensive is a work by Bach's son Carl Philipp Emanuel which presumably reflects his father's teaching, *Versuch über die wahre Art das Clavier zu spielen* (Berlin, 1753–62; English trans. W. J. Mitchell, New York, 1949). Among modern studies those by F. T. Arnold and Peter Williams (see bibliography, below) are particularly useful. The rules for figured bass realization included in the second *Clavierbüchlein* for Anna Magdalena Bach are, unfortunately, only rudimentary. A collection of exercises in figured bass which has been edited as a work of Bach's (*see* PRECEPTS AND PRINCIPLES) is taken from a manuscript only indirectly associated with him; it clearly preserves elements of contemporary German teaching, and distills sections from the *Musicalische Handleitung* (Hamburg, 1700–17) of F. E. Niedt, who apparently studied with Johann Nicolaus Bach of Jena.

Modern scores of Bach's ensemble works often include only an unfigured continuo part, as do most of Bach's autograph manuscript scores. But in preparing individual parts for performance Bach generally added figures to the part (or parts) intended for keyboard instruments. He also sometimes produced slightly different parts for other members of the continuo group. Even some autograph scores—notably those for the early cantatas and the Brandenburg Concertos—contain distinct parts for Fagott (bassoon), cello, violone, and keyboard continuo.

[*cont. on p.123*]
117

# concerto (*Konzert*)

An instrumental work in several movements based on the principle of contrast or opposition. From the time of Bach onwards the opposition has usually been between one or more solo instruments and an orchestra, although concertos for non-orchestral forces—in extreme cases a single instrument, as in Bach's Italian Concerto for two-manual harpsichord—or for orchestra without soloists are also possible. The concerto was the only important instrumental genre invented during the late Baroque period and the dominant one in orchestral music during the period 1710–50.

Bach also used the term 'concerto' as a label for many of his church cantatas: *see* CANTATA, §1.

---

1. Origin and early development.
2. The Vivaldian concerto.
3. Bach's concerto arrangements BWV592–7, 972–87, and 1065.
4. Bach's original concertos BWV1041–64.

---

1. **Origin and early development.**   As its etymology (from the Latin 'concertare': 'to compete in a common endeavour') suggests, the term 'concerto' usually denotes an ensemble work in which different elements, at different times, come to the fore. During most of the 17th century, 'concertos' were sacred works for mixed voices and instruments—the ancestors of what we today call church cantatas. However, towards 1700 a progressive offshoot of the sonata, also termed 'concerto', was created in northern Italy. The impetus for its birth was the establishment, in churches, courts, and music societies, of orchestras in the modern sense of the word: ensembles, based on the violin family plus continuo instruments, in which the doubling of parts was treated as normal and desirable. The expression 'concerto grosso' actually means little more than 'orchestra' or, by extension, an orchestral composition. Large ensembles performing in the spacious acoustic of a large church, such as the basilica of San Petronio in Bologna, were best served by a simple, predominantly homophonic style which avoided intricate counterpoint, favoured dialogue between different parts of the ensemble (using the *concertato* technique), and catered simultaneously for the superior skills of the best musicians in the *cappella* and the more modest ones of the rank and file.

Concerto-like features are already evident in many of the sonatas (also called sinfonias) for trumpet and strings produced by the Bologna school from the 1650s onwards. The characteristic trumpet style (broken-chord figures and motifs employing rapidly repeated notes) was taken over and developed further by the nascent concerto; it survives in the ritornello of the first movement of Bach's Fifth Brandenburg Concerto. There is no reason to dispute J. J. Quantz's statement that the earliest concertos were written by Giuseppe Torelli; such works appear alongside sonatas (sinfonias) in his op. 5 (Bologna, 1692) and constitute the entire set in his op. 6 (Ansbach, 1698). These seminal compositions quickly became known on both sides of the Alps. The coincidence of the rise of the concerto with the sudden expansion of music publishing in northern Europe (initially dominated by the Amsterdam firm of Estienne Roger) greatly aided the diffusion of the new genre.

118

Within the orbit of the publishing centres of Bologna and Venice, Torelli had many imitators. The most important of these was the Venetian Tomaso Albinoni, whose first two collections, op. 2 (1700) and op. 5 (1707), proved as influential as Torelli's. After 1700 most concertos came to be cast in three movements (fast–slow–fast). However, the inclusion of sections featuring one or two solo instruments (violins, occasionally cello) remained optional. When present, they fulfilled a decorative rather than a structural role. The fast movements tended to be concise, assembled from a series of 'open' periods (sections beginning and ending in different keys) that were normally introduced by the same head-motif. (The Praeambulum to Bach's Fifth Partita for harpsichord retains this primitive scheme.) The form of the slow movements was (and long remained) less standardized. Some were mere chordal transitions (the middle 'movement' of Bach's Third Brandenburg Concerto is the ultimate reduction of this type), while others gave the soloist lyrical material.

Concurrently with the rise of the concerto in northern Italy, an important sub-type less distinct in form from the parent genre, the sonata, evolved in Rome. The salient characteristic of this variety is its division of the violins into four sections, rather than the usual two or three. Two parts are usually orchestral, belonging to the 'ripieno'; the other two, teamed with a solo cello and separate continuo to form a 'concertino', are for solo players. The most famous works in this tradition are Corelli's *Concerti grossi* op. 6, published posthumously in 1714. Their scoring, and to some extent their style, had some influence on north European concertos (the finale of Bach's Sixth Brandenburg Concerto, for instance, recalls the rhythms of Corelli's jigs), but outside England their form, which scarcely differed from that of Corelli's violin sonatas, found few imitators.

Bach familiarized himself thoroughly with the first generation of Italian concertos. A continuo part for the second concerto in Albinoni's op. 2 copied out in Bach's hand survives in the Manfred Gorke collection of the Musikbibliothek der Stadt Leipzig. His early music often reproduces, in other genres, the thematic and structural features of contemporary Italian concerto movements. Good examples are the first variation of the chorale partita for organ on *Sei gegrüßet, Jesu gütig* and the setting, for tenor solo, violins, and continuo, of the third strophe of Cantata no. 4, *Christ lag in Todes Banden*.

**2. The Vivaldian concerto.**  The concertos of Antonio Vivaldi, which began to appear towards 1710 and burst on the European scene in 1711 with the publication of his op. 3, *L'estro armonico*, ushered in a new phase in the history of the genre. Vivaldi popularized what we know today as RITORNELLO form, based on the alternation of closed (ritornello) and open (episodic) periods. He established the concerto for one instrument, strings, and continuo (the 'solo' concerto) as the dominant species and the prototype for all the others, which included 'double' concertos (for two like or unlike solo instruments), 'ensemble' concertos (for three or more solo instruments), 'chamber' concertos (for three or more solo instruments without orchestra), and 'ripieno' concertos (for string orchestra without solo instruments). To Vivaldi, also, belongs the credit for establishing a clear stylistic difference between sonata and concerto. Henceforth, the sonata becomes in general a repository of conservative musical values (including counterpoint), while the concerto embraces virtuosity, instrumental colour, and 'showiness' of all kinds. The Vivaldian scheme for the concerto remained virtually unchanged for the rest of the Baroque period, subsequently transforming itself by almost imperceptible degrees into the Classical concerto of the Haydn–Mozart period.

The first clear sign of Bach's absorption of Vivaldi's innovations comes in his transcriptions for organ and harpsichord of several concertos by the Venetian, mostly taken from *L'estro armonico*. There is no direct evidence that he had the opportunity to write concertos of his own during his Weimar years, but he certainly perfected the use of ritornello form in other genres. The Prelude to the Third English Suite (? *c*.1715) is an even more convincing re-creation, for keyboard alone, of the first movement of an imaginary solo concerto than that in the much later Italian Concerto. But just as the technique and spirit of Vivaldi's concertos informed Bach's music in almost every genre, so too, in a parallel process, formal and stylistic elements from other (not always Italian) genres flowed into Bach's own concertos. This complex ebb and flow of influences will be examined later.

**3. Bach's concerto arrangements** BWV592–7, 972–87, and 1065. The original stimulus behind Bach's keyboard arrangements of concertos may have been the similar organ transcriptions that his friend and distant cousin J. G. Walther made for the latter's gifted pupil Prince JOHANN ERNST of Saxe-Weimar. But whereas nearly all of Walther's arrangements concern the first (pre-Vivaldian) generation of concerto composers, those by Bach are of works by Vivaldi and his contemporaries. They most likely date from 1713–14, following the return of Johann Ernst from his travels in the Netherlands. In fact, the prince himself figures strongly as a composer in Bach's transcriptions. Of the six concertos transcribed for organ, two (BWV592 and 595) are by Johann Ernst and three (BWV593, 594, and 596) by Vivaldi; BWV597 is by an unknown composer and the transcription is probably not by Bach. Of the 17 for harpsichord, six (BWV972–3, 975–6, 978, and 980) are by Vivaldi and four (BWV592a, 982, 984, and 987—the first and third are alternative versions of BWV592 and 595 respectively) by Johann Ernst; Alessandro Marcello (BWV974), his brother Benedetto (BWV981), Telemann (BWV985), and possibly Torelli (BWV979) each contribute one, leaving untraced the originals for BWV977, 983, and 986.

In making his transcriptions, Bach freely changed the key to suit the instrument's compass, transposed individual lines to facilitate performance, converted the ornamentation into forms more suitable for the keyboard, added harmonic and contrapuntal enrichment, and 'edited' a few details. All in all, however, his adaptations are respectful of the originals in basic matters. While one hesitates to claim, as German scholars once did, that the arrangements offer improvements on the originals, they all contain moments of inspiration which show the presence of an exceptional creative mind.

The arrangement for four harpsichords and strings of Vivaldi's Concerto in B minor for four violins op. 3 no. 10 (BWV1065) falls outside this scheme, since it belongs to the repertory of the Leipzig COLLEGIUM MUSICUM, which Bach directed from 1729. In some ways this is his least successful concerto transcription, tending to dissipate the raw vigour of the original through excessive elaboration.

**4. Bach's original concertos** BWV1041–64. Bach's first complete, free-standing concertos may date from his Cöthen years (1717–23), although many of them draw on material that had existed earlier, in different contexts, in Weimar. It must be remembered that the post of *Kapellmeister* to Prince Leopold of Anhalt-Cöthen was the first to require him to produce concertos as part of his normal duties. At Cöthen Bach probably composed many concertos, but only nine survive in their original state. These are the violin concertos in A minor and E major BWV1041–2, a concerto for two violins in D minor BWV1043, and the set of six Brandenburg Concertos, all for different instrumental combinations, that he sent in 1721 to the Margrave of Brandenburg as a demonstration of his talent. (It should be added here that Christoph Wolff has argued for a possible Leipzig origin for the violin concertos BWV1041 and 1043.)

A second phase of concerto composition and (increasingly) arrangement occurred in Leipzig in connection with Bach's directorship (1729–37 and 1739–41) of the collegium musicum. These concertos have in common the participation of at least one solo harpsichord; they were evidently vehicles for Bach himself, his sons, and his pupils. Only one of them, a concerto for two harpsichords in C major BWV1061, originated with certainty as a keyboard concerto. Otherwise, we have harpsichord versions (transposed down a tone) of the three surviving concertos for one and two violins BWV1058, 1054, and 1062; a similarly transposed version of the Fourth Brandenburg Concerto, with harpsichord replacing violin (BWV1057); a pastiche of earlier chamber works (BWV1044); arrangements for three harpsichords of two lost concertos for three violins (BWV1063–4); four solo harpsichord concertos wholly or partly arranged from lost concertos for violin (BWV1052 and 1056) and for oboe or oboe d'amore (BWV1053 and 1055); and a two-harpsichord concerto in C minor BWV1060, based on a putative original (possibly in D minor) for violin and oboe. Reconstructions of the original versions published in the *NBA* and elsewhere have in some cases begun to rival the 'harpsichord' versions in frequency of performance; the last-mentioned concerto, in particular, is already more popular in its reconstructed form.

These 24 works (not counting two fragments, BWV1045 and 1059, and the Italian Concerto for solo harpsichord) divide into nine solo concertos, four double concertos, nine ensemble concertos, and two chamber concertos. These last—Brandenburg Concertos nos. 3 and 6—are unusual in requiring a large number of obbligato instruments (respectively nine and five) in addition to the continuo, but, since neither work calls for a string ripieno, their classification is not in doubt.

The musical characteristics of Bach's concertos can best be shown by comparing them on the one hand with those of Vivaldi, and on the other with those of German contemporaries such as Telemann. Bach adopts the three-movement plan more consistently even than Vivaldi himself; the slow introductory movement common in Italian 'church' concertos and favoured by Telemann is never found. He seems to follow French-influenced German taste when he appends dance movements to the concerto proper in the First Brandenburg Concerto (though the complex history of that work suggest that it was the Italianate third movement that was the true appendage). Rondo form, extremely rare in Vivaldi, appears in deference to the same taste in the finale of Bach's Violin Concerto in E major, as in many of Telemann's concertos. However, the use of strict da capo form in the first movement of the same concerto and in the finales of Brandenburg Concertos nos. 5 and 6 appears eclectic and experimental.

Bach's application of ritornello form diverges from the Vivaldian model in that it promotes thematic and textural integration above contrast and virtuosity. This is a typically German approach—but one must express admiration at how much virtuosity Bach still manages to pack in despite its relatively low priority! The drive for integration causes the material of ritornellos and episodes, as well as of episodes in relation to one another, to be closely related; indeed, the characteristics of the two types of section interpenetrate to such an extent that, were one to ignore their tonal function, they would often seem equivalent. The accompaniments to the soloist(s) routinely draw on ritornello material: the lean, 'athematic' accompaniments common in Vivaldi are largely eschewed. In comparison with Vivaldi, Bach makes the proportions of ritornellos and episodes more even: there is rarely any sense that the soloist achieves final dominance over the orchestra (the D minor Harpsichord Concerto and the Fifth Brandenburg being exceptions by virtue of their cadenzas). Except in the curiously perfunctory final ritornello of the first movement of the Concerto in D minor for two violins, Bach likes to end his concerto movements with an extended tutti passage which reasserts the primacy of the full ensemble. All his concerto movements have an architectonic, 'planned' quality rooted in an earlier German tradition exemplified by such figures as Heinrich Biber (1644–1704) and Georg Muffat (1653–1704).

The melodic and rhythmic language of Bach's concertos is clearly beholden to Vivaldi—consider, for example, the 'three-hammer-blow' opening of the Violin Concerto in E major—but is frequently overlaid with *galant* elements, as in the central movement of the Fifth Brandenburg Concerto. There is probably also some debt to Torelli. Bach's fondness for 'self-imitating' lines (a *locus classicus* is the first solo episode of the Concerto in D minor for two violins) and for sequences in which the interval of repetition is a 3rd, rather than a 2nd or 4th/5th, has a clear affinity to the older master's preference. Needless to say, the richness of harmony, density of counterpoint, delicately etched lyricism, and perfection of detail in Bach's concertos belong to him alone.

But perhaps the rarest quality of Bach's concertos is their playful aspect. There is scarcely a movement without its *jeu d'esprit*: the horn calls disrupting the ponderous opening of the First Brandenburg Concerto; the improbable cluster of four 'high' solo instruments (pitting the 'soft' recorder against the 'loud' trumpet) in the Second Brandenburg Concerto; the seemingly interminable descent of the bass at the climax of the first movement of the Third Brandenburg Concerto; and so on. No other composer has united science and fantasy as effectively as Bach did in his concertos.

MT

*See also* BRANDENBURG CONCERTOS, HARPSICHORD CONCERTOS, ITALIAN CONCERTO, and VIOLIN CONCERTOS.

P. Drummond, *The German Concerto: Five Eighteenth-Century Studies* (Oxford, 1980); A. J. B. Hutchings, *The Baroque Concerto* (London, 1961; 3rd edn. 1973); H.-J. Schulze, 'J. S. Bach's Concerto-Arrangements for Organ: Studies or Commissioned Works?', *Organ Yearbook*, 3 (1972), 4–13; M. Talbot, *Tomaso Albinoni: The Venetian Composer and his World* (Oxford, 1990); M. Talbot, *Vivaldi* (London, 1978); C. Wolff, 'Bach's Leipzig Chamber Music', *Early Music*, 13 (1985), 165–75; repr. in *Bach: Essays on his Life and Music* (Cambridge, Mass., 1991), 223–38.

Hence the precise constitution of the continuo group varied from work to work—even from one performance to another—and was determined by a number of factors, including local traditions and the composition of the ensemble as a whole. External factors might influence the scoring of the continuo group, as when the organ was out of repair, requiring the substitution of the harpsichord in a church cantata. But Bach appears to have had purely musical reasons for employing various continuo groups, including so-called 'dual' accompaniment (the use of organ and harpsichord continuo simultaneously) in at least a few performances of his sacred vocal works (on this and all aspects of continuo instrumentation, see Dreyfus).

Bach's continuo parts raise a number of problems besides that of their instrumentation. Although the written parts, including the occasional passage in which the bass line is the sole notated part, are usually harmonically self-sufficient, a correct continuo realization was considered indispensable. Yet the highly contrapuntal, frequently chromatic, dissonant character of Bach's harmony makes his figured basses the most difficult to realize of any Baroque composer, requiring much study before any facility can be achieved. His notation of the figures is usually meticulous, but in works for which his figured bass parts do not survive, including many of the cantatas, players find it necessary to study the score carefully or to employ an editorial realization (such as is included in most performing editions). Special preparation may also be necessary for so-called 'continuo arias', such as 'Geduld, Geduld' in the *St Matthew Passion*, in which the figured bass is the sole written accompaniment, leaving the continuo realization particularly exposed. Such movements may call for a realization which possesses some independent melodic interest, particularly in the ritornellos.

The accompaniment of recitative raises questions about the duration of the notes (and chords) of the continuo part. A preponderance of evidence appears to indicate that, except in his earliest works, Bach intended both bass notes and chords in simple recitative to be held only briefly, for roughly the length of a crotchet. This is so despite the fact that he usually wrote the continuo parts of recitatives primarily in sustained notes, specifying their actual short values (with rests following) only when there was a need to avoid misunderstanding, for example by players who might not have been familiar with the convention (as in certain bassoon and organ parts).

On another matter, however, Bach appears to have avoided an unwritten convention: the practice of delaying the last two chords of a full cadence, which emerged in Germany during the 18th century in order to avoid the so-called 'telescoped' cadence of later Baroque Italian recitative. In such cadences the singer's penultimate tonic note clashes with the dominant harmony (Ex. 1). In Bach's recitative, however, 'telescoped' cadences are usually avoided either through explicit rests (Ex. 2) or by a figured bass which directs a realization incorporating the dissonant note (Ex. 3). His accompanied recitatives nevertheless contain distinct clashes, sometimes as an apparent response to the text, as on the word 'Sünder' ('sinner') in Ex. 4. Hence, the notated rhythm of the cadences in Ex. 5 should probably be interpreted literally, although the familiar convention governing singers' appoggiaturas, by which the written *c'* is replaced by the editorial *d'* (shown in small type) probably applies here.

A limited number of works by Bach contain what may be regarded as written-out figured bass realizations, as in the Largo of the B minor flute sonata, the arioso 'Betrachte, meine Seele' in the *St John Passion*, and passages in the harpsichord concertos. The first of these works, with its largely chordal harpsichord part, provides a suggestion of the type of rich harmony that Bach evidently took for granted, recalling J. C. Kittel's report that Bach would intervene to add additional notes whenever the student entrusted to the harpsichord furnished an insufficient accompaniment in a church

Ex. 1. Handel: *La Lucretia*

di ca-sti-gar-mi.     mi     si per - do - ni

# continuo

work. Other examples seem to bear out Lorenz Mizler, who mentioned Bach's improvising accompaniments so intricate that they sounded as if they incorporated written-out obbligato counterpoint.                                              DS

On the relationship of figured bass realization to free improvisation, *see* IMPROVISATION; on the instrumentation of bass lines, *see* ORCHESTRA.

F. T. Arnold, *The Art of Accompaniment from a Thorough-Bass* (Oxford, 1931); L. Dreyfus, *Bach's*

Ex. 2. Bach: Cantata 204

Ex. 3. Bach: Cantata 7

Ex. 4. Bach: Cantata 40

Ex. 5. Bach: Cantata 40

*Continuo Group* (Cambridge, Mass., 1987); P. Williams, *Figured Bass Accompaniment* (Edinburgh, 1970); P. Williams, 'Johann Sebastian Bach and the Basso Continuo', *Basler Jahrbuch für historische Musikpraxis*, 18 (1994), 67–86.

**contrafactum.** A vocal piece in which the text is a replacement for the one to which the music was originally composed. In Bach's music contrafactum overlaps with PARODY. The latter term usually implies some compositional input, but several Bach works to which the term 'parody' is usually applied are simple contrafacta. If the chorus 'Gratias agimus tibi' in the Gloria of the B minor Mass may be said to parody the opening chorus of *Wir danken dir, Gott* (Cantata 29), its reappearance at the end of the Mass to the words 'Dona nobis pacem' is more an example of contrafactum.

**contrapunctus** ('counterpoint'). A Latin term used by Bach as a title for the fugues in the ART OF FUGUE.

**copyists.** *See* SOURCES, §1, (iii).

**Corelli, Arcangelo** (b. 17 Feb. 1653; d. 8 Jan. 1713). Italian composer and violinist, born in Fusignano, near Bologna. He was the first composer specializing in instrumental music to become recognized as a 'classic', and one of the first to show clearly those qualities of restraint, balance, consistency, and attention to detail that one associates with the 18th century. Almost his entire work is contained in six published collections: two of trio sonatas in the 'church' style, opp. 1 and 3 (1681 and 1689); two of trio sonatas in the 'chamber' style, opp. 2 and 4 (1685 and 1694); one of violin sonatas, op. 5 (1700); and one of 'grand' concertos, or *concerti grossi*, op. 6 (1714).

The trio sonatas established a style of fluent counterpoint which was taken as a universal model; the violin sonatas educated violinists everywhere in the essential technique of their instrument; the concertos, laid out in a typically Roman style with separate concertino (two violins, cello and continuo) and ripieno (the same, doubled orchestrally, plus violas), had a limited impact on the development of concerto form, but a stronger one on orchestration (see, for instance, the slow movement of Bach's Fourth Brandenburg Concerto).

Bach wrote a fugue for organ (BWV579) on a subject of Corelli taken from the second movement of op. 3 no. 4. That apart, a general, diffused influence of Corelli is perceptible in his music. A 'walking bass', as used in the B minor Prelude in Part 1 of the *The Well-tempered Clavier*, is a Corellian cliché; another is the half-close (Phrygian cadence) in the relative minor introducing, for

example, the final movement of the Third Brandenburg Concerto. MT

M. Pincherle, *Corelli, his Life and Work*, Eng. trans. H. E. M. Russell (New York, 1956).

**cornett.** A wooden instrument, either curved or straight, of various sizes and with a variable number of finger-holes. Bach was one of the few composers who continued to use the cornett (or *Zink*, as it was known in Germany), together with trombones, to support the vocal parts in his church music at a time when the instrument was becoming antiquated and being replaced by the fashionable Waldhorn. The curved instrument, made of various woods, is hexagonal or octagonal in cross-section with a conical bore, and is blown by means of a cup-shaped mouthpiece. It was this type, known as the *krummer Zink* (see picture overleaf), that Bach wrote for, notating its part in either violin or treble clef, with the compass $c'$ to $d'''$, to sound as written in CAMMERTON or to transpose a whole tone in CHORTON.

Bach used the cornett to support the sopranos in 13 of his Leipzig vocal works, notably in *stile antico* movements in the annual cycle of chorale cantatas (1724–5). It is used as an obbligato instrument in Cantata 25 and in the motet *O Jesu Christ, meins Lebens Licht*. Bach specified two cornetts in his arrangement of Palestrina's *Missa sine nomine*. UP

U. Prinz, *Studien zum Instrumentarium J. S. Bachs mit besonderer Berücksichtigung der Kantaten* (Tübingen, 1979), 186–95; U. Prinz, 'Zink und Posaune: Studien zu Überlieferung, Instrumentenbau und Repertoire', in *Basler Jahrbuch für Aufführungspraxis*, 5 (1981), 11 ff.

***Cornet-ton.*** A specific level of CHORTON at $a' = 465$ (*see* PITCH). All the organs Bach regularly played were at *Cornet-ton*. The name is derived from the standard pitch of cornetts, the majority of which had been made at this approximate frequency for centuries. Most German organs made in Bach's lifetime whose pitches survive are in the range 460–70. Of the 13 organs that were described as in *Cornet-ton* at the time they were built and whose pitch has survived, the range is 450–67, with an average of $a' = 463$. BH

***corno, corno da caccia, corno da tirarsi.*** See HORN.

**corrente.** *See* COURANTE, §2.

**Correspondirenden/Korrespondirenden Societät der Musicalischen Wissenschaften** (Corresponding Society of Musical Sciences). A society founded in 1738 by Lorenz MIZLER, which Bach joined in 1747.

**Cöthen** (in modern spelling, Köthen). A town in Saxony, about 30 km. (19 miles) north of Halle,

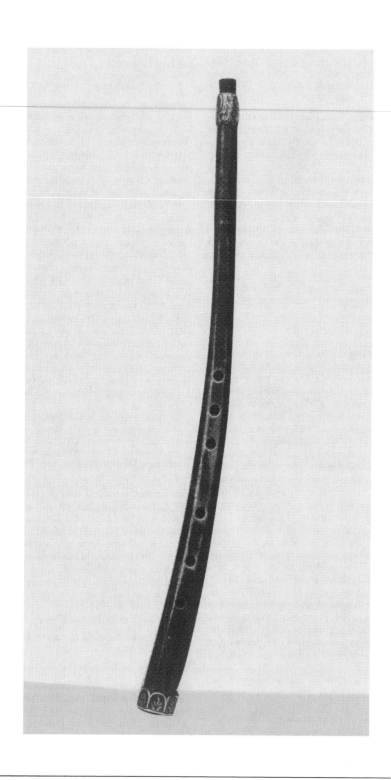

Cornett (*krummer Zink*), 17th–18th century
(Germanisches Nationalmuseum, Nuremberg)

where Bach was employed between 1717 and 1723 as *Kapellmeister* to Prince Leopold of Anhalt-Cöthen. The palace at Cöthen functioned as a princely residence from 1310 to 1847; the part of it where Leopold lived had been added by Prince Ludwig, who ruled from 1600 to 1650. The uppermost floor of this portion of the building was taken up by the mirror-lined throne room, which would have acted as the local courtroom, the meeting-place of the privy council, and the main music room of the palace, the town, and the principality. It was large enough for a small orchestra to play in, and yet small enough for a keyboard instrument to sound well in it. This 'Spiegelsaal' survives today, restored to the condition to which it was modified in the early 1730s by Leopold's brother and successor August Ludwig (1697–1755).

Leopold and his father Prince Emanuel Lebrecht had chosen to adhere to a strictly reformed (Calvinist) persuasion, and Cöthen's hilltop Jacobskirche was a rather elaborate vehicle for this unfestive doctrine in Bach's time. Bach, along with other members of the household (including the widow of Leopold's father), attended the less externally opulent, but in its way no less resplendent, Agnuskirche, which had been dedicated in 1699 when Prince Emanuel had acceded to his wife Gisela Agnes's request to allow celebration of the Orthodox Lutheran rite in the town. The Agnuskirche was closer than the Jacobskirche to the palace, as well as to the smart town house granted to Gisela Agnes after her husband's death. (She seems to have lived the last part of her life in her own Schloß Nienberg on the River Saale, about 50 km. (31 miles) north-west of Cöthen, and it was there that she died, on 12 March 1740.) At times opposition between the pastors of the two churches became openly hostile, and there can be little doubt that such antagonisms caused disquiet in the princely household.

Cöthen was isolated enough to be provincial and even a little old-fashioned in its social life: the court accounts and minutes were kept in German rather than French, and the language spoken at court was also, it seems, largely the vernacular. In the interests of social convention, Prince Leopold, a capable musician, may not have taken part in public concerts himself, but there were certainly regular visiting participants in serious music-making at Cöthen. Some were musical adventurers who journeyed from court to court, earning a living as they went; the lutenist Johann Kropfgans seems to have been one of these. Others included musicians, especially solo singers, from Halle or beyond who were engaged to take part in homage cantatas addressed to Leopold on his birthday (28 November, old style) and

on New Year's Day. One of these singers, the bass Johann Gottfried Riemschneider, sang for Bach with the Cöthen *Kapelle* on 16 December 1718 and for Handel in three operas (*Lotario, Giulio Cesare,* and *Partenope*) in the 1729–30 season at the King's Theatre, London—the only performer known to have been directed by both composers.

Two widely accepted views of Bach's Cöthen period probably stand in need of correction. One is that he specially enjoyed his employment there. He may well have done so to start with, and in a much-quoted letter to Georg Erdmann he glanced regretfully back to it after settling in Leipzig. But the fact that he did leave, that he had in fact applied as early as 1720 (shortly after the death of his first wife Maria Barbara) for a post in Hamburg, and that Prince Leopold's enthusiasm for music may have become less generous when revenues began to dwindle and costs to rise, may all have led to a sense of insecurity. This would have been heightened by disputes in a smallish town which would have felt far less distracting in a larger centre such as Hamburg or Leipzig.

The other probably mistaken view is that all or most of Bach's chamber music (including that sometimes misleadingly referred to as 'orchestral') originated in Cöthen, or was revised and completed there. The portion of his instrumental ensemble music of which this is certainly true is actually quite small. Most of it has surer associations with the activities of the Leipzig collegium musicum, in which Bach's main involvement as director, composer, and arranger was concentrated in the years from 1729 to the early 1740s.

The Cöthen years nevertheless saw the composition of one of Bach's supreme collections of ensemble music, the Brandenburg Concertos. This was the period, too, of the works for solo violin and solo cello and of such didactic keyboard collections as the two- and three-part Inventions and Part 1 of *The Well-tempered Clavier.* SFD

M. Petzoldt, *Bachstätten aufsuchen* (Leipzig, 1992), 61–73; F. Smend, *Bach in Köthen* (Berlin, 1951; Eng. trans. J. Page, ed. S. Daw, 1985).

**Cöthen funeral music.** See KLAGT, KINDER, KLAGT ES ALLER WELT.

**counter-fugue** (*Gegenfuge*). A term used to describe a type of FUGUE in which an inverted form of the subject replaces the normal answer in the exposition. The first chorus of Bach's Cantata 179, *Siehe zu, daß deine Gottesfurcht nicht Heuchelei sei,* and Contrapunctus 5 of *The Art of Fugue* are typical of its most straightforward use. Contrapunctus 6 and 7 of the same work show more involved use of the technique, with answers in diminution and augmentation respectively. LC

**countersubject.** A term used in FUGUE to denote the figure that combines with the answer of the fugue subject, usually but not invariably in INVERTIBLE COUNTERPOINT. This figure usually has a character independent of that of the subject, and is normally also a recurring feature of the fugue. It is frequently invertible at the octave. *The Well-tempered Clavier* contains a high proportion of fugues with recurring and invertible countersubjects, for example the F major Fugue from Part 1.                                    LC

**Couperin, François** (b. 10 Nov. 1668; d. 11 Sept. 1733). French composer, born and died in Paris. Bach's high opinion of Couperin is attested by F. W. Marpurg, who wrote in 1750: 'I can do no more in praise of Couperin than to inform you that the learned Bach regarded him as worthy of approbation' (*BDok* iii, no. 632). Bach seems to have owned a copy of Couperin's *Second livre de pièces de clavecin* (Paris, 1716–17), for the rondeau *Les Bergeries* was copied from it by Bach's wife Anna Magdalena in her *Clavierbüchlein* of 1725, and the Allemande in A major 'à deux clavecins' from the same book was written out by Bach's eldest son Wilhelm Friedemann when he was still a child. The organ arrangement, attributed to Bach (BWV587), of *L'Impériale* from *Les Nations* (Paris, 1726) is of doubtful authenticity.             RDPJ

**courante.** A dance and instrumental form originating in the early 17th century. In Bach's suites, two different types of dances appear as 'courante' and 'corrente'.

---

1. Courante.
2. Corrente.

---

1. **Courante.** This was a slow, stately, aristocratic French dance associated with the courts of Louis XIII and XIV, which spread to England, Germany, and other European countries. It was still taught as a French social dance in Bach's Germany, as described in detail and with several choreographies in Gottfried Taubert's *Rechtschaffener Tanzmeister* (Leipzig, 1717). As an instrumental form it occurred more often than any other dance in 17th-century French harpsichord and lute music. It is stylistically the most ambiguous, employing irregularly recurring beats and aspects of modal harmonies and melodies. It had a reputation as the grandest in style and noblest in character of all the French court dances, and was variously described as serious, noble, and majestic.

The metrical structure is unique in that, as J. P. Kirnberger stated (*The Art of Strict Musical Composition*, Eng. trans. D. Beach and J. Thym (New Haven, 1982), 394–5), both 3/2 and 6/4 metres may occur within the dance phrase, one bar after another in all the parts, or in pitting one part in 3/2 against another in 6/4. Kirnberger cites François Couperin's *ordre* no. 1 from the *Pièces de clavecin* (1713) as an example. Basically, however, a point of repose of some weight occurs at the beginning of each bar and the active, or arsic, high point is typically on the third minim beat of the bar, immediately preceding the thesis on beat 1. The last bar of each strain is in 6/4 time. In Bach's courantes there is less ambiguity than in those of French composers. Bach used mixed metres often, but their elusive effect is softened by clear harmonic progressions that establish a particular metre even when the rhythms do not.

Bach wrote 19 courantes: in an early suite for lute BWV996, each one of the English Suites, French Suites nos. 1 and 3, the Cello Suite in C major, the clavier suites BWV819, 818, and 818a, the Orchestral Suite in C Major, the keyboard Partitas nos. 2 and 4, the lute suite BWV995, and the Ouverture in the French Style for clavier. The courante is not used as a basis for works outside the suites. All courantes are marked 3/2 except in the French Suite no. 3, which has a signature of 6/4. The second courante in the English Suite no. 1 has two *doubles*.

2. **Corrente.** Correntes and *corontos* were danced in Italy, England, and many other parts of Europe in the late 16th and early 17th centuries. The Italian dancing-master Cesare Negri describes in his *Nuove inventioni di balli* (1604) corrente choreographies with numerous hops and springs (see Little and Jenne, ch. 9). It was accompanied by music which could be transcribed in 6/8 or 12/8 time in balanced phrases, sometimes with an upbeat, sometimes not. Bach inherited the corrente from Italian composers such as Corelli. It usually consists of a continuous elaboration in quavers and semiquavers over a bass line in fast triple metre with simple texture, slow harmonic rhythm, phrases of varying length, and a metre sign of 3/4. Its affect is gay and cheerful, and its metrical structure occurs in two ways. One is with a dotted minim beat in phrases of eight bars, divided into three crotchets and then into duple quavers: a major point of repose is on beat 8. The second has a crotchet beat in phrases of four bars, with duple subdivision of quavers and semiquavers; a major point of repose often occurs on beats 10–12 (bar 4). *Notes inégales* (i.e. uneven playing of paired notes of shorter value) are not appropriate to this dance.

Bach's 19 surviving correntes, which include one *double*, are found in the keyboard suite BWV821 and the sonata BWV965, Partitas nos. 1 and 2 for solo violin, Cello Suites nos. 1, 2, 3, 4, and 6, French Suites nos. 1, 4, 5, and 6, and the keyboard

Partitas nos. 1, 3, 5, and 6. There are no correntes in the orchestral works, but there are a few untitled ones in other works, for example the little Prelude in D minor BWV935. NJ, MEL

For bibliography, see DANCE.

**currency.** During Bach's time the following coins were in use: the Reichsthaler (or simply thaler; both forms are also found without the 'h' after the 't'), usually abbreviated as 'Rthlr' or 'Thlr'; the 'gulden', usually shown as 'fl' (= florin); the 'groschen', usually abbreviated as 'gr'; and the 'pfennig', usually abbreviated as 'δ'. One Reichsthaler equalled 24 groschen, while one gulden yielded only 21 groschen; the relationship between the Reichsthaler and the gulden was thus comparable to that between the guinea and the pound sterling in Britain. One groschen equalled 12 pfennige.

The purchasing power of 18th-century money in relation to modern times can only be approximated, since victuals and such luxuries as tobacco, coffee, and alcohol were much more expensive, particularly when compared to the cost of labour. An instructive overview of the value of household equipment, books, and musical instruments can be found in the 'Specificatio of the estate left by the late Mr Johann Sebastian Bach' (*BDok* ii, no. 627), and a recently discovered receipt signed by Bach (see *BJb* 80 (1994), 32–3) reveals the cost of the spirits and tobacco he consumed during a visit to Halle from about 1 to 15 December 1713. Bach's salary as organist rose from 80 thaler in Arnstadt to 85 in Mühlhausen, and further to 150 gulden (i.e. 131 thaler 6 groschen) in Weimar. His salary as *Kapellmeister* at Cöthen was 400 thaler, while it is quite impossible to assess his exact income as Kantor in Leipzig because of the complicated system of benefits established there.

The price of music paper in Bach's time can be gleaned from receipts from his Weimar years (*BDok* ii, no. 71), according to which a ream consisting of 480 bifolios was bought for 2 gulden 6 groschen. The price of printed or engraved music varied according to size and the quality of the paper. A copy of one of the separately issued keyboard Partitas could be obtained for 12 groschen; *Clavier-Übung II* was sold for 18 groschen, while for the voluminous *Clavier-Übung III* the relatively high price of 3 thaler was charged (*BDok* ii, nos. 361, 370, and 456). Music in manuscript was generally much cheaper, but prices varied greatly depending on quality, rarity, and particularly the age of the repertory. In 1741 Bach, through his nephew Johann Elias, offered a copy of a cantata for solo bass (possibly BWV82) to his friend Johann Wilhelm Koch for 12 groschen, while four years later J. G. Walther tried to sell the complete scores and parts of a whole cantata cycle by Johann Schelle for 5 thaler. PW

**Currende.** See KURRENDE.

# D

**da capo.** An Italian term (often abbreviated 'D.C.') meaning 'from the head', placed at the end of a movement or section to indicate that a piece is to be repeated from the beginning until the word 'fine' ('end') or a fermata ($\frown$) is reached. It is a labour-saving device, used to avoid the task of writing out material that has already been presented. In Bach's music it is most frequently found at the end of the middle part of the so-called da capo ARIA as an indication that the entire opening section (including ritornellos) is to be performed again.

The da capo design also appears in a number of choruses. Two prominent examples are the opening movements of the original version of the *St John Passion* ('Herr, unser Herrscher') and of the *Christmas Oratorio* ('Jauchzet, frohlocket, auf, preiset die Tage'). But choruses in da capo form are especially common in the secular cantatas (in fact, the movement that begins the *Christmas Oratorio* is a parody of one from Cantata 214) and many of those in the church cantatas are reworkings of material from earlier secular works.

The term sometimes occurs in instrumental compositions as well. For instance, in the final movements of the Fifth and Sixth Brandenburg Concertos, the return of the opening music towards the end is indicated in the autograph scores by the words 'da capo'. Moreover, da capo designs are also found in works for several solo instruments, including the organ (e.g. the 'Wedge' fugue), harpsichord (e.g. the preludes in the English Suites nos. 2–6), lute (the fugues in BWV997 and 998), and violin (the fugue in the Sonata in C major). In suites containing two dance movements of the same type, the return to the first is frequently indicated by an expression such as 'Gavotte I da capo' or its Latin equivalent, 'Repetatur Gavotte I'. SAC

*See also* ALTERNATIVEMENT.

**Dadelsen, Georg von** (b. 17 Nov. 1918). Musicologist, one of the leading German Bach scholars, born in Dresden. He studied at the Universities of Kiel and Berlin (Freie Universität), where in 1951 he wrote his doctoral dissertation on historicism in 19th-century music. In 1952–60 he worked at the University of Tübingen. Large parts of the former Preußische Staatsbibliothek which had been removed from Berlin during World War II were then in the local university library, allowing Dadelsen access to many Bach manuscript sources. During those years he wrote a study of Bach's handwriting, later the fundamental *Beiträge zur Chronologie der Werke Johann Sebastian Bachs*, his *Habilitation* thesis (1958). In 1960–71 he was professor in Hamburg, and in 1971–84 in Tübingen. From 1962 to 1992 he was director of the Johann-Sebastian-Bach-Institut, Göttingen, and chief editor of the *NBA*, for which he edited such important works as the *Clavierbüchlein* for Anna Magdalena Bach and the two- and three-part Inventions. KK

**dance.** The art of measured bodily movements, usually accompanied by music. Dance in Bach's Germany was a vital concomitant of life on all social levels, and ranged from informal social and recreational dancing to formal social dancing and elaborate theatrical presentations. Many of Bach's compositions have dance titles and numerous other pieces by Bach, both instrumental and vocal, incorporate characteristic dance rhythms. Some of Bach's dance music has choreographic roots in dance styles contemporary with him, while some derives from forms no longer danced.

Germany was still recovering from the severe economic and social disruptions of the Thirty Years War (1618–48) when Bach was born in 1685. Many German courts and cities in which he lived imported culture, including dance, from France and Italy as part of their reconstruction after the war. Although dance appeared in both Italian styles and in native German forms, the predominant dance style in courts and cities, and the style that was most reflected in Bach's music, was French court dancing.

Court dancing in France originated with Louis XIV about the 1660s, and this was the origin of ballet as we know it today. The technical achievements of this style—for example, the turn-out of the legs from the hips, the five positions for the feet, and the calculated opposition of arms to step-units (see Hilton)—were a distinctive, recognizable improvement on other dance styles in Europe. Social dancing at court was done by noblemen, who practised daily under the tutelage of a dancing-master in order to perform at carefully planned ceremonial court balls. Following strict rules of decorum, some dancers performed while an assembled company watched and admired their grace and skill. Ballets were also presented at court at least once a year. They were usually organized around a theme, such as the seven liberal arts, or an event from classical mythology, such as the birth of Venus. Ballets consisted of a series of vocal airs interspersed with dance entries performed by various characters in fanciful costumes. Even the king, Louis XIV, danced in court ballets as a young man.

Numerous French dancing-masters were imported to teach and choreograph in the courts in which Bach moved, including those at Celle, Cöthen, and Dresden, and in free cities such as Leipzig. They taught a graceful and noble carriage of the body, as well as the latest dance pieces from Paris, to aristocrats and middle-class persons alike. Bach may have learnt to dance in this style, though no direct evidence survives. He attended the French court in Celle as a student at times during 1700–2. He visited the Saxon court at Dresden many times while he lived at Cöthen and Leipzig. He also knew personally a number of dancing-masters. One was his friend Pantaleon Hebenstreit, a virtuoso instrumentalist at the Dresden court who was also a dancing-master at the courts of Weißenfels and Eisenach, Bach's birthplace. Another was Jean Baptiste Volumier, violinist and orchestral leader at the Dresden court from 1709 to 1721. Bach probably knew, or knew the work of, Johannes Pasch (1653–1710), who taught French dancing both at the Dresden court and in Leipzig for over 40 years.

Over 300 choreographies of specific dances have been preserved in a special dance notation known as *chorégraphie* (see Little and Marsh). This repertory reveals a large number of bourrées, gavottes, minuets, courantes, and other titled dances of which Bach composed examples. Each of the French court dances exhibited a characteristic affect, rhythm, and tempo which made it easily recognizable to listeners. For example, the gavotte and passepied were often pastoral, sometimes using bagpipe effects (see MUSETTE); the bourrée was joyful and lively; the minuet was in a medium tempo and exhibited only moderate passions; loures and sarabandes were slow, sustained, and serious. In Bach's hands, these dances kept their basic character and rhythmic structure, but grew into sublime musical abstractions in many cases. Some of Bach's greatest elaborations on the French dances appear in the keyboard Partitas, the French and English Suites for keyboard, the solo Cello Suites, the violin Partitas, and the orchestral suites. Untitled French dances freely appear in Bach's cantatas, oratorios, Passions, and organ works (see Little and Jenne, Appendix B).

Bach also composed dances whose choreographic roots were lost in time. Allemandes occur

in almost all his dance suites. Many incorporate prelude-like features such as frequent arpeggiation and an imitative style with changing numbers of voices; some use the emphatic rhythms of the French overture. Sicilianas occur occasionally, most often in arias in the cantatas and Passions, but also in concerto slow movements such as that in the Harpsichord Concerto in E major, where the soulful melody soars above accompanying semiquavers in a slowly rocking 12/8 metre. Polonaises were danced in Bach's time but no direct choreographic evidence is currently available.

NJ, MEL

*See also* ALLEMANDE, BOURRÉE, CHACONNE, COURANTE, FORLANA, GAVOTTE, GIGUE, LOURE, MINUET, PASSACAGLIA, PASSEPIED, POLONAISE, SARABANDE, and SICILIANA.

W. Hilton, *Dance of Court and Theater: The French Noble Style* (Princeton, 1981); M. Little and N. Jenne, *Dance and the Music of J. S. Bach* (Bloomington and Indianapolis, Ind., 1991); M. Little and C. Marsh, *La Danse noble: An Inventory of Dances and Sources* (Williamstown, NY, 1992).

**D'Anglebert, Jean-Henri** (b. 1628; d. 23 April 1691). French composer and keyboard player, born and died in Paris. Bach was presumably familiar with D'Anglebert's *Pièces de clavecin* (Paris, 1689), for he copied out the ornament table from it around 1709–12. D'Anglebert's style of ornamentation and his use of ornament signs appear to have exerted some influence on Bach, judging by the ornaments table in the *Clavierbüchlein* for Wilhelm Friedemann Bach of 1720 and the ornaments in Bach's keyboard works from the 1720s onwards. It is often assumed that the influence extended to the substance of Bach's suites, but this has not been firmly established.

RDPJ

***Darzu ist erschienen der Sohn Gottes*** ('For this purpose the Son of God was manifested'). Cantata for the second day of Christmas, BWV40, first performed in Leipzig on 26 December 1723. Its overall structure follows one of the most common patterns for cantatas: two recitative–aria pairs are flanked by an opening chorus with a biblical text and a concluding four-part chorale. Unusually, however, an additional chorale is interpolated between each recitative and aria, for a total of three chorales: chorus–recitative–chorale–aria–recitative–chorale–aria–chorale. Whether the added chorales stem from Bach or his anonymous librettist is not known. In either case, their inclusion (and the fact that they are all in simple, four-part style) contributes to the unusually 'communal' feeling of this work.

Although the text of the opening chorus (I John 3: 8) is not from the readings appointed for the

# Das neugeborne Kindelein

second day of Christmas, it none the less encapsulates succinctly the opposition between Jesus, who entered the world on Christmas Day, and the Devil, whose works are to be destroyed by the powerful Son of God. The energetic ritornello, which features pairs of horns and oboes as well as strings and continuo, subsequently provides much of the thematic material for the setting of the first clause, 'Darzu ist erschienen der Sohn Gottes'. The destruction of the Devil ('daß er die Werke des Teufels zerstöre') is captured in a rhythmically vigorous passage which coalesces into unison declamation (bar 24) before dissolving into a bold melisma on 'zerstöre' ('destroy'). Following the fugal middle section, in which the entire text is set a second time, the original texture returns for a third setting. Some 25 years later (c.1738–9), Bach reworked the music extensively (while retaining its original key and performing forces) as the concluding movement of the *Missa in F major*.

The tenor recitative (movement 2) is an exhortation to consider the implications of Christ's incarnation. It employs several standard biblical metaphors for Jesus, for example 'the Word who became flesh and dwells in the world', 'the light of the world', 'God's Son', 'the King', and 'the Lord'. The musical pretensions of this movement are modest, and it is accompanied by continuo alone. The only significant departure from the predominantly syllabic setting is a melisma on the word 'bestrahlt' ('illumined', a word suggested musically by quick upward scale motion), which is subsequently imitated in the continuo line.

The bass aria (movement 4) develops the theme of Satan's destruction in imagery drawn from Genesis 3: 15. Since it is addressed to Satan (in the form of a snake), it employs the conventions of a type of movement in contemporary opera known as a 'rage' aria. The attitude of defiance against the 'hellish serpent' is captured by the quick tempo, *moto perpetuo* semiquavers, minor mode, and wide leaps in the melody.

The alto recitative (movement 5) differs from the previous one in several respects. It is accompanied by strings playing a gently undulating arpeggiated figure. The constant semiquaver motion requires a stricter rhythm which lends it the measured character of an arioso. Diminished 7th chords emphasize the word 'Gift' ('poison') in bars 3 and 7, and the tonic minor underscores the meaning of 'betrübter' ('distressed') before a final cadence in the major.

The imagery of the tenor aria (movement 7), in which Jesus is likened to a hen protecting her chicks, is borrowed from the Gospel for St Stephen's Day (Matt. 23: 34–9), traditionally celebrated on 26 December. The instrumentation of this movement, with its strong emphasis on wind instruments (pairs of horns and oboes, plus continuo), is unique among Bach's arias. The tenor part, which includes a number of lengthy melismas on 'freuet' ('rejoice'), is even more difficult than usual. Of particular interest is the lack of a ritornello between the end of the B section and the (modified) da capo. This apparently is related to the fact that the second half of the B section (bars 29–35) was inserted later (in the autograph score it is notated on the bottom two staves). This passage, which was added perhaps in part to give the wind players a chance to catch their breath (only the voice and continuo are active), contains some graphic word-painting, especially on 'erschrecken' ('to frighten'), where rests within the melisma mimic the breathlessness associated with fear.                                   SAC

For bibliography, *see* CANTATA, §1.

***Das neugeborne Kindelein*** ('The new-born child'). Cantata for the Sunday after Christmas, BWV122, first performed on 31 December 1724. It is a CHORALE CANTATA belonging to Bach's second Leipzig *Jahrgang*. The anonymous librettist has, as usual, retained verbatim the first and last strophes of the hymn, by Cyriakus Schneegaß (1597), but in this case he has also used the third strophe for what in the cantata is the fourth movement. The second strophe is paraphrased in movements 2 and 3, and movement 5 elaborates freely on the substance of the hymn, which celebrates the newborn Jesus, who brings both a new year and salvation to mankind. The four strophes of the hymn are thus remodelled to serve the usual six movements of the cantata.

The architecture of the work as a whole is largely determined by the nature of the chorale itself. This is in triple time instead of the more common 4/4 metre, and has only four short lines instead of the usual six or more. As a result the opening chorale fantasia is on a smaller scale than many of the others among the chorale cantatas, and its instrumental scoring is appropriately modest, consisting of two oboes and *taille* in addition to the usual strings and continuo. This ensemble supplies the ritornellos that separate the lines of the chorale itself, the melody of which is heard as a cantus firmus in the soprano, with the other three voices working out points of imitation loosely based (except in the case of the final line) on the chorale tune.

If the rejoicing in this opening chorus seems a little muted, the da capo bass aria that follows, with its chromatically tortured ritornello, seems to dwell more on the 'men who daily sin' than on the 'joy of the angels', despite a long, exuberant melisma on 'Freude' ('joy'). The singer is accompanied here by continuo alone, but in the succeeding recitative (no. 3) the soprano is joined by a choir of three recorders playing a harmonized version of the same chorale melody as in no. 1, representing the angel chorus which fills the air with its sound. The chorale melody is heard again in movement 4 in a very different context. It is sung as a cantus firmus by the alto, doubled by unison violins and viola, to the third strophe of Schneegaß's hymn, while the soprano and tenor weave counterpoints around it to different words and the continuo bass pursues independently its dance-like motifs.

After a bass recitative with string accompaniment which dwells on the joyful message of Christmastide, the final strophe of the hymn is sung in the usual plain four-part harmonization with instruments doubling the voices.

For bibliography, *see* CANTATA, §1.

**Dazu ist erschienen der Sohn Gottes.** *See* DARZU IST ERSCHIENEN DER SOHN GOTTES.

**'Deathbed Chorale'** ('Sterbchoral'). Bach's organ fantasia BWV668 on the chorale *Vor deinen Thron tret ich*, which exists incomplete as the last of the 'Eighteen' Chorales. It was first published complete, in a slightly different form, with *The Art of Fugue*, to which it is not, however, related musically. The latter version bears the title *Wenn wir in höchsten Nöthen sein* and is designated BWV668a. The nickname derives from a notice in the original publication stating that a few days before his death Bach, by this point blind, had dictated the piece to a friend, later identified by J. N. Forkel as J. C. Altnickol.

Both versions appear to incorporate an early chorale prelude which Bach had included in the *Orgel-Büchlein* in an embellished form under the title *Wenn wir in höchsten Nöthen sein* (BWV641). The existence of this version, recently dated to the period 1709–13, casts the 'deathbed' account into question. At the most, the ailing Bach can have 'dictated' only the three-voice sections of BWV668a absent from BWV641; perhaps he merely directed a few small refinements present in BWV668 (but not in BWV668a). Forkel's report cannot be confirmed; the manuscript of BWV668 is not in Altnickol's hand.

For a slightly different account which also considers the legends that have accrued to the story, see C. Wolff, 'The Deathbed Chorale: Exposing a Myth', in *Bach: Essays on his Life and Music* (Cambridge, Mass., 1991), 282–94.    DS

*See also* VORIMITATION.

**Dem Gerechten muß das Licht** ('There is sprung up a light for the righteous'). The earliest version of this wedding cantata, BWV195, belongs to a period between 1727 and 1731. This version has been lost, but two later ones have survived. One of these, dating from about 1742, is incomplete; the other, discussed here, contains fewer sections than the second version but nevertheless may be thought to represent Bach's last intentions, at least in so far as it belongs to the very end of his life, having been revised for performance some time around 1748–9. In this last revision Bach omitted the aria, recitative, and concluding chorus that had constituted the second half of the cantata, sung after the marriage itself, and replaced them with a single strophe from a hymn by Paul Gerhardt, *Nun danket all und bringet Ehr* (1647), set to its associated melody *Lobt Gott, ihr Christen alle gleich*. Alfred Dürr has suggested (in *DürrK*) that Bach's extra-curricular duties of providing occasional music for weddings, university functions, anniversaries, and so forth may have been greater than we realize, and that he was probably in the habit of stockpiling works suitable for such ceremonies, drawing upon them as and when required.

This cantata was evidently performed in 1736 (in Ohrdruf) and again about 1742, but the last performance of which we have definite knowledge was on 11 September 1741. This was at the wedding, almost certainly in the Thomaskirche, Leipzig, of Johanna Eleonora Schütz (daughter of a former pastor at the church and a great-great-niece of the composer Heinrich Schütz (1585–1672)) and Gottlob Heinrich Pipping, a lawyer and burgomaster from Naumburg.

The cantata begins with a chorus of imposing dimensions, sumptuously scored for three trumpets, timpani, two oboes (each doubled by a flute), strings, and continuo. The four-part chorus is also spaciously deployed and divided into solo and ripieno groups—an unusual, though by no means unique, procedure in Bach's sacred cantatas, indicating that he had a large number of singers at his disposal. The movement is in two sections, each consisting of an independent choral fugue; the first, in common time, takes up thematic ideas from the opening instrumental ritornello, while the second, in 6/8 metre, introduces new material. The two sections are based on the 11th and 12th verses of Psalm 97, from which the cantata derives its title.

A bass recitative with continuo accompaniment leads to the single aria of the cantata, also for bass voice. Scored for two oboes d'amore with doubling flutes, strings and continuo, the piece (in da capo form) is of particular interest for the splendid example it affords of Bach's fluency with the emerging *galant*, early Classical style of the period. Among several distinctive features is Bach's adoption, infrequently encountered in his music, of the so-called Lombardic rhythm, or 'Scotch snap', which gives this captivating piece in 2/4 time an airy, dance-like character. The soprano recitative, whose text is closely linked to the marriage service, is elaborately accompanied by pairs of flutes and oboes d'amore with continuo. This leads to the second chorus of the cantata, which is scored similarly to the opening movement; once again the vocal parts are deployed between solo and ripieno groups punctuated by instrumental ritornellos. With this movement the first part of the cantata comes to a close. All that follows in the second part, sung after the wedding, is the chorale for SATB with doubling strings and oboes, accompanied by two horns, timpani, and a pair of unison flutes. The inclusion of horns, which do not otherwise feature in the cantata, suggests that the setting was imported from another work.                                      NA

P. Wollny, 'Neue Bach-Funde', *BJb* 83 (1997), 7–50, esp. 26–36. For further bibliography, *see* CANTATA, §1.

***Der Friede sei mit dir*** ('Peace be with you'). Cantata for the third day of Easter, BWV158, believed to have been written at Leipzig by 1735. Joshua Rifkin, citing musical and textual parallels to works dating from 1726–9, has suggested as possible dates 15 April 1727 and 30 March 1728. A puzzling and rarely performed work, it may be considered, along with Cantatas 56 and 82, a third solo cantata for bass voice, although the second movement includes a chorale cantus firmus for soprano.

In its existing form the work gives the impression of being a fragment, and it has been thought that the two inner movements originated as parts of a lost cantata for bass solo intended for the feast of the Purification. This liturgical designation is retained on the title-pages of the principal manuscript sources, a posthumous score and parts copied by C. F. Penzel. An alternative assignment in Penzel's parts to the third day of Easter is, however, borne out by the anonymous text, which presents parallels to that of Cantata 56, possibly by Picander, and to other works known to be by him.

Among these parallels is the use of a refrain, in this case 'Der Friede sei mit dir', sung three times as an arioso in the first movement, which is otherwise a simple recitative. Inevitably, however, attention focuses on the one extended movement, the aria with chorale that follows. This has been regarded as one of the most accomplished movements of its type, in view perhaps of the expressively florid solo instrumental part. Although assigned to the violin in the sources and modern editions, this obbligato is more appropriate to the

flute and bears certain similarities to that of 'Domine Deus' in the B minor Mass (scored for flute and in the same key, G major).

The chorale tune, Johann Rosenmüller's *Welt ade, ich bin dein müde*, is sung by soprano doubled by oboe, using the first strophe of the text by Johann Georg Albinus (1649). The aria text likewise opens with the words 'Welt, ade' ('World, adieu'), expressing the familiar theme of farewell to the world. The poetic metre of the aria text changes after its fourth line, as it expresses the desire to dwell in heaven. But the change is not reflected in the music and, curiously, at this point the chorale text states the contradictory sentiment, 'World, you are full of conflict and strife'.

The following movement begins as another simple recitative, but in the second half it turns to arioso as it repeats the second part of the preceding aria text. Although no music from the aria is repeated exactly—something Bach had done in Cantata 56—the motivic parallels are unmistakable. Moreover, at this point, as in the aria, the tonality turns to E minor; this modulation, together with the tortured melodic lines and harmonies for the concluding phrase, 'himmlischen Kronen' ('heavenly crown'), might be regarded as pointing towards the Cross. An Easter reference, this passage prepares for the final movement, a four-part setting of the fifth strophe of Luther's *Christ lag in Todes Banden*, in E minor. The *BG*, following Penzel, gives a seemingly imperfect version of this movement; the *NBA* follows the better version from Breitkopf's 1786 volume of Bach's chorale harmonizations.                         DS

J. Rifkin, Notes to *J. S. Bach: Cantatas 56, 82, and 158* (L'oiseau-lyre, 425 822–2). For further bibliography, *see* CANTATA, §1.

***Der Geist hilft unser Schwachheit auf*** ('The Spirit helpeth our infirmities'). Motet for eight-voice double chorus, BWV226, on Romans 8: 26–7. Bach wrote on the score and original parts that the motet was performed at the burial on 20 October 1729 of J. H. Ernesti, a professor at the University of Leipzig and Rector of the Thomasschule. Evidence from Bach's autograph score and from details of the scoring suggests that this work is based, at least in part, on older material; whether or not that was an older motet is unknown.

The motet is in one movement with several contrasting sections, the first two of which may be adapted from an older composition. The buoyant opening section is musically somewhat uncharacteristic for a motet in its use of 3/8 metre and in the tunefulness of its opening material. It also uses the double-choir forces unusually. The tune is presented first in the soprano of choir 1 in duet with the soprano of choir 2, accompanied by the lower voices of both choirs. It is then repeated in the sopranos with the two choirs reversed, then in the altos of the two choirs, and later in the tenors and basses of the two choirs. Presentations of this material alternate with contrasting music, setting the text 'Denn, wir wissen nicht'.

A change of metre and affect takes place in the fugal second section. The abstract first part of the text, 'Sondern der Geist selbst vertritt uns aufs beste' ('but the Spirit itself pleads our cause') is sung to a syncopated subject; the continuation of this line is interrupted with rests illustrating the second part of the text, 'mit unaussprechlichem Seufzen' ('with ineffable sighing'). There are two unusual features in the fugal treatment and in the double-choir writing here: the first is that the imitating voices do not enter alone, but are accompanied by a kind of written-out basso continuo realization in the lower voices of choir 1; the second is that, although there are eight voices, the tenors, the basses, and eventually the altos join together, yielding a five-part texture.

The last section of the motet, in which the two choirs combine, is a double fugue. The first phrase, 'Der aber die Herzen forschet', is presented with one musical subject, the next phrase, 'denn er vertritt die Heiligen', with a second, and then the two are combined, with the final phrase, 'nach dem, das Gott gefället', appearing at the very end.

The original performing parts for the motet—copied by Bach, his son Carl Philipp Emanuel, his wife Anna Magdalena, and other assistants—include instrumental parts: a continuo group (string bass and organ with figures), strings doubling one choir, and woodwinds doubling the other. This is the best evidence we have that Bach performed his motets with basso continuo and *colla parte* instruments.

Nowadays one always hears this motet followed by a four-part chorale, 'Du heilige Brunst', the third stanza of Martin Luther's hymn *Komm, heiliger Geist*. The composition is Bach's, but the chorale is quite probably not part of the motet. It is present in the original vocal parts, so we know that it was sung in connection with the Ernesti funeral, but it does not appear in the instrumental parts. The best guess is that the chorale was performed later in the ceremonies—perhaps at the graveside—but was not part of the motet, and so it should not be performed as if it were the concluding chorale of the kind often found in Bach's church cantatas.                    DRM

M. Geck, 'Zur Datierung, Verwendung und Aufführungspraxis von Bachs Motetten', in *Bach-Studien*, 5 (Leipzig, 1975), 63–71. For further bibliography, *see* MOTET.

**Der Herr denket an uns** ('The Lord hath been mindful of us'). Cantata, BWV196, to a text from Psalm 115: 12–15. Its exact date is unknown, though it is probably among Bach's earliest surviving vocal compositions; nor is its purpose specified, but it may be a wedding composition.

*Der Herr denket an uns* is not transmitted in any original source, but only in a score copied in the early 1730s by Bach's pupil Johann Ludwig Dietel which does not specify an occasion. The work's text—typical for cantatas from the very early 18th century—does not point to any particular liturgical or non-liturgical use. Each of the four psalm verses uses the word 'segnen' ('bless'), and Bach emphasizes this word when it appears. This may suggest that the cantata was for a wedding; indeed, Philipp Spitta suggested that it was for the marriage in Arnstadt of one of Bach's in-laws in 1708, and, despite lack of evidence, this association has persisted.

Even if the cantata was not for this wedding or for another, Spitta's dating, which places it during Bach's time in Mühlhausen, is certainly plausible. The work's organization around successive psalm verses, one to a movement, links it with other early Bach cantatas, especially *Aus der Tiefen rufe ich*, datable to c.1707–8. Certainly the absence of free poetry set as recitatives and arias, and of Vivaldian ritornello structures, suggests that the piece dates from before 1713, by which time both the musical and textual make-up of Bach's church cantatas had changed substantially.

Various musical features point to the stylistic legacy of the late 17th century and suggest as well that the work is early. The first vocal movement is particularly characteristic: Bach breaks the text into short units and presents them in affectively contrasting ways. The first part of the text is sung in imitation by pairs of voices and punctuated with four-voice statements. The next phrase, 'und segnet uns' ('and will bless us'), is presented in a strongly contrasting fashion: slower note values, harmonic stasis, homophonic text declamation, and separate use of voices and instruments. The remainder of the movement is given over to the words 'Er segnet das Haus Israel, er segnet das Haus Aaron' ('He will bless the house of Israel, he will bless the house of Aaron'), presented in a PERMUTATION FUGUE, a type found in Bach's early vocal music.

The other movements are also characteristic of Bach's earliest cantatas. The one aria, in da capo form (a structure not in itself associated with the early period), uses a minimum of text, 'Er segnet, die den Herrn fürchten beide, Kleine und Große', and little musical elaboration—it squeezes into just 19 bars (plus a da capo) an instrumental ritornello, a motto statement, a setting of the first part of the text, the ritornello again, and a harmonically contrasting setting of the second part of the text. The duet 'Der Herr segne euch', with its pairs of violins and voices in imitation, its old-fashioned notation in large values, and its long sequences, could easily be mistaken for a work from a previous generation. The final chorus, like the first, is sectional, and its extended contrapuntal 'Amen' section shows features of the permutation fugue.

The instrumentation of this cantata is modest, calling only for strings and basso continuo. The instruments' most independent role comes in the opening sinfonia, which shares thematic material with the first vocal movement. The three-part string texture is enriched by a cello line which is sometimes independent of the continuo part.

DRM

K. Küster, ' "Der Herr denket an uns" BWV 196: eine frühe Bach-Kantate und ihr Kontext', *Musik und Kirche*, 66 (1996), 84–95. For further bibliography, *see* CANTATA, §1.

***Der Herr ist mein getreuer Hirt*** ('The Lord is my faithful shepherd'). Cantata for the second Sunday after Easter (Misericordias Domini), BWV112, first performed in the Nikolaikirche, Leipzig, on 8 April 1731. It is the last of three cantatas for this Sunday, the others being nos. 104 (1724) and 85 (1725), but it is quite probable, judging from the gap separating these from no. 112, that Bach wrote another work for this occasion which has been lost. Certainly *Der Herr ist mein getreuer Hirt* belongs to the last creative period of Bach's involvement with this particular genre of liturgical music, and the year 1731 seems to have been a specially important one in this regard.

The autograph of Cantata 112 belonged after Bach's death to his son Wilhelm Friedemann, and then passed through various hands until in 1950 it was owned by Mary Flagler Cary (1901–67), whose music collection was donated in 1968 to the Pierpont Morgan Library, New York. The cantata is scored for SATB, two horns, two oboes d'amore, two violins, viola, and basso continuo. A CHORALE CANTATA, it uses all five strophes of the hymn *Der Herr ist mein getreuer Hirt* by Wolfgang Meuslin (1530), a paraphrase of Psalm 23. This accords well with the Gospel reading appointed for the day (John 10: 12–16), portraying the good shepherd ready to lay down his life for the sheep—a potent symbol in Jewish as well as Christian culture. In a society mainly given to sheep farming, it is natural that the shepherd, as master and guardian of the flock, should assume important connotations. The shepherd was recognized as a figure of authority, but also one of protection, dedication, love, and brotherhood—qualities associated with

strength of both body and spirit. It is fitting that it was the shepherds who first adored the Christchild, and that Jesus's disciples were known as the 'little flock'.

The melody associated with Meuslin's hymn—that of *Allein Gott in der Höh sei Ehr* by Nikolaus Decius (1522)—is heard only in the outer movements (nos. 1 and 5). The first is a typical motet-fantasia on the chorale, with the soprano cantus firmus supported by imitative counterpoint in the other voices, and the lines of the hymn separated by instrumental ritornellos; the last is, as usual, a straightforward four-part harmonization with *colla parte* instrumental support. But there are also veiled allusions to phrases from the chorale melody in the three central movements.

Given the subject of the cantata, it is not surprising that the music has a decidedly pastoral character. This is suggested by the pairs of horns and oboes d'amore in the opening movement, but even more by the rustic tone of the two arias: the first of these, 'Zum reinen Wasser er mich weist', is for alto with oboe obbligato; the second, 'Du bereitest für mir einen Tisch', is a duet for soprano and tenor with strings and continuo in the style of a bourrée. Between these two movements the bass sings touchingly of walking 'through the valley of the shadow of death', beginning as an arioso with continuo only and continuing as an accompanied recitative rich in symbolism. AB

For bibliography, *see* CANTATA, §1.

***Der Himmel lacht! die Erde jubilieret*** ('Heaven laughs, the earth rejoices'). Cantata for Easter Sunday, BWV31, first performed at Weimar on 21 April 1715; the scoring was revised for performances at Leipzig in 1724 and 1731, and perhaps later. Some of the original parts survive (in Kraków), but losses have left unclear some details in the complicated history of the work's revisions.

The unusual richness of the Weimar scoring evidently created problems for Bach's later performances, because of differences in notational conventions and PITCH at Leipzig. At Weimar the outer movements encompassed three instrumental choirs: brass (trumpets and timpani), double reeds (exceptionally in five parts: three oboes, *taille*, and bassoon), and strings (also in five parts), with organ continuo. Moreover, the first vocal movement is for five voices, including two sopranos—the only such movement in Bach's regular Sunday cantatas. But the woodwinds, which are usually limited to doubling other parts, may have been an afterthought, possibly added for a second Weimar performance in 1716. Only the top two woodwind parts seem to have been retained at Leipzig, where each was apparently played on the lower oboe d'amore. Moreover, there is some evidence that Bach eliminated one of the two soprano parts after 1731, although no version consolidating the two parts survives. On the other hand, at Leipzig Bach extended the cello's partial doubling of the organ continuo to cover the entire continuo line.

The work, like Bach's previous cantata (BWV18, composed four weeks earlier), opens with a sinfonia in a simple version of ritornello form. As in the similar, and perhaps contemporary, opening movement of the First Brandenburg Concerto, a brass motif is prominent in the ritornello; here it is a trumpet-call, doubled by the entire ensemble, appropriate to a celebration of Christ's resurrection. The triumphal character of the feast is reflected as well in the opening of the following chorus, although Salomo Franck's text subsequently turns to thoughts of earthly mortality. Bach's music reflects this change of character by shifting in later movements to lighter scoring and, in the final aria, an almost elegiac tone.

The first aria text is set as a chorus for the full ensemble in BARFORM. The same melismatic subject, treated fugally, therefore serves for both the opening words, 'Der Himmel lacht', and for 'Der Schöpfer lebt' ('the Creator lives'). There is no opening ritornello, and subsequent text lines receive contrasting musical material, as in a motet. But a closing instrumental passage which repeats the movement's initial phrase serves as a wordless, abbreviated da capo. Three recitative–aria pairs follow, for bass, tenor, and soprano in turn; the last aria includes a chorale cantus firmus, as in a number of Bach's other Weimar cantatas. The plain scoring of the bass movements, for voice and continuo alone, is offset by the imaginative writing of the bass recitative, which alternates between quicker and slower tempos for lines referring to life and death respectively (the same occurs in the latter part of the opening chorus). The bass aria is accompanied throughout by a vigorous dotted motif sometimes associated with Jesus's scourging, but here more plausibly representing his princely power mentioned in the opening line.

The instrumentation of the soprano aria changed several times; at Leipzig the solo obbligato line must have been played by an oboe d'amore, and Bach also added the violins to the violas' unison sounding of the cantus firmus *Wenn mein Stündlein vorhanden ist*. The latter melody—its opening phrase presaged by rising scale motifs which appear prominently at several points in the bass recitative—returns in the closing movement, a four-part setting of the final strophe of Nicolaus Herman's chorale text (1575). To this Bach adds a fifth descant part for the first violin (the doubling

of this very high part by the first trumpet might be a product of copyist error). DS

A. Dürr, 'Neue Erkenntnisse zur Kantate BWV 31', *BJb* 71 (1985), 155–9. For further bibliography, *see* CANTATA, §1.

**Der Streit zwischen Phoebus und Pan** ('The dispute between Phoebus and Pan') ['Geschwinde, geschwinde, ihr wirbelnden Winde' ('Haste, haste, you whirling winds')]. One of Bach's few secular cantatas not written for an aristocratic or princely occasion. It was most probably intended for performance at the concerts of Bach's collegium musicum in 1729.

The cantata, BWV201, deals with the question of good and bad art; good music is represented by Phoebus, bad music by Pan. It has been suggested more than once that the cantata refers directly to problems Bach had during his Leipzig years, such as the quarrel with the Rector of the Thomasschule, Johann August Ernesti. However, Ernesti was active there only from 1734 onwards, and it is perhaps more reasonable to understand the plot from a purely aesthetic viewpoint—that of Bach dealing in a general way with matters affecting his art (as Richard Strauss did in the opera *Ariadne auf Naxos*). While it is perhaps worth mentioning that the cantata was performed again in 1749, the year that Bach entered into dispute with the Freiberg Rector Johann Gottlob Biedermann over a published attack on school music, it should also be noted that the German word 'Streit' does not necessarily mean 'quarrel' or 'dispute', but can also mean 'competition'. The cantata does start with a quarrel, but the plot itself concerns a competition. The text is by Picander, after Ovid, *Metamorphoses*, Book 11.

The cantata begins and ends with large choruses (both in da capo form) which serve only to establish that the plot refers to music. In the opening chorus the emphasis is on expressing the text: the whirling of the winds is heard in the orchestra's triplet semiquavers, and in the middle section Bach alludes to the word 'echo'. The audience is then introduced to the two quarrellers: Phoebus (bass) is offended by Pan's claiming that his singing is more beautiful than Phoebus's; Pan (bass) is offended by Phoebus's opposition to the nymphs' admiration of Pan's singing. The quarrel is interrupted by Momus (soprano), who makes fun of Pan in the aria 'Patron, das macht der Wind', well-known to English-speaking audiences as 'Ah yes, just so'. Then Mercurius (alto) proposes a professional competition between the two 'musicians'. Both elect judges: Tmolus (tenor) is appointed by Phoebus, Midas (tenor) by Pan.

The competition begins. Phoebus sings a beautiful aria, 'Mit Verlangen'; a short recitative leads to Pan's much less refined contribution, 'Zum Tanze, zum Sprunge'. Curiously, Phoebus, the mythological inventor of the kithara, is accompanied by flute and oboe d'amore as obbligato instruments, while Pan, 'inventor of the flute', has only unison violins and continuo. Thirteen years later Pan's music was parodied in the Peasant Cantata as 'Dein Wachstum sei feste', in which a peasant searches for a musical language typical of his social rank. This may reflect Bach's intentions regarding Pan's music as well.

The judges then sing their arias, first Tmolus (again accompanied by oboe d'amore), and then Midas (with unison violins, as in Pan's aria). Both are convinced that the singer they supported was the better one, but mythology teaches that Midas's judgement was false. He is given donkey's ears, and Bach, in his music, imitates a donkey's call with a downward leap an octave and a half on the word 'Ohren' ('ears'). In the following recitative everyone condemns Midas for his judgement. The only singer at this stage to be left without an aria is Mercurius; his movement, 'Aufgeblasne Hitze', is characterized by a bass-like vocal line and accompanied by two flutes. In a final recitative Momus draws the moral—judgements should be justified—before calling on Phoebus to take up his lyre again, an injunction echoed in the concluding chorus.

This work has a special place among Bach's secular cantatas. On the one hand, it has a purely musical design: each character sings one aria, and particular instruments are clearly identified with either the losing faction (violins in unison) or the winning one (strings supported by 'modern' instruments such as flute and oboe d'amore). Consequently a truly dramatic approach might appear to be of secondary importance. But, in contrast to the typical homage cantata centred directly on the occasion to be celebrated, what we have here is a self-contained and independent plot: a story recounted by Picander which is divided into several dramatic units in an operatic way. Thus the work exemplifies a type of 18th-century German secular cantata which can be described as at least semi-dramatic.      KK

For bibliography, see CANTATA, §2.

**Der vergnügte Mensch.** See ICH BIN IN MIR VERGNÜGT.

**Der zufriedengestellte Aeolus** ('Aeolus placated'). See ZERREISSET, ZERSPRENGET, ZERTRÜMMERT DI GRUFT.

**Deyling, Salomon** (b. 14 Sept. 1677; d. 5 Aug. 1755). Theologian and clergyman, born in Weida, near Gera, in Thuringia. He studied at Wittenberg University and after serving as superintendent at Pegau and Eisleben, he went to Leipzig, where he was superintendent and pastor at the Nikolaikirche during the whole period of Bach's Kantorate. At the same time he was also professor of theology at Leipzig University. In his capacity as superintendent he was responsible for overseeing Bach's duties as *director chori musici* and must therefore have been involved in some of the disputes between the composer and the Leipzig authorities. But there seems to have been no animosity between the two men, and Bach's disagreements were, in any case, with the council rather than with the consistory.

**dictum** ('saying'). See SPRUCH.

**Die Elenden sollen essen** ('The poor shall eat'). The first cantata (BWV75) performed in Leipzig after Bach was appointed civic music director and Kantor at the Thomasschule. According to contemporary reports, the composer and his family arrived in Leipzig on Saturday, 22 May 1723, and Cantata 75 was performed the following week, on the first Sunday after Trinity (30 May) 'with great success'. Similarities of overall structure and performing forces make it clear that this work and Cantata 76, for the second Sunday after Trinity (6 June 1723), were conceived as companion pieces.

The anonymous text develops several themes that are related to the appointed Gospel reading, the story of the rich man and poor Lazarus (Luke 16: 19–31). The verse at the beginning (Psalm 22: 26) states that appearances are deceptive. Like Lazarus, those who suffer in this life ('die Elenden') will one day be satisfied. Conversely, riches and worldly pleasures are transitory and can take a person's spirit to hell (movement 2). Through a kind of divine inversion, those who seek heaven on earth will be cursed, while those who overcome hell in this world will find joy in the next (movement 4). Movement 5 refers to Lazarus by name, noting that patient endurance of tribulation results in divine favour. Paradoxically, the way of self-denial leads a person to find both himself and God (movement 11). The key to such a life is unreserved devotion to Jesus (movements 3, 10, 12, and 13). The one who pursues it learns that God does all things well and will bring ultimate comfort (movements 7 and 14).

The opening chorus falls into two sections. The first, with its stately triple metre and dotted rhythms, has the character of a French overture. The first two clauses of the text are set in individual paragraphs preceded and followed by ritornellos. For the third clause, the metre shifts to common time and an elaborate fugue ensues. The fugal subject was clearly influenced by the meaning of the last two words: the longest note value is reserved for the word 'ewiglich' ('eternally'), while an extended melisma illustrates the word 'leben' ('to live').

The vocal parts of the chorale that concludes both halves of the cantata are similar to a normal four-part harmonization. What is novel, though, is the brief, catchy ritornello heard at the beginning and end, and between phrases. Played by the oboes, strings, and continuo no fewer than seven times (all but once in the same key!), it gives this setting an unmistakably joyous quality.

The same chorale tune, played by the trumpet, recurs in the energetic instrumental sinfonia that opens the second part (movement 8). Since the trumpet remains silent until this point, its appearance here and in the bass aria (movement 12) distinguishes the sound of the second half of the work from that of the first.

The distribution of vocal solos is remarkably egalitarian. Each voice type has at least one recitative and aria (the tenor and bass both have a second recitative). All the recitatives are accompanied by the continuo alone except for movements 2 and 9, in which the harmony is filled out by the strings. The arias are notably heterogeneous in their instrumentation, affect, and form. The soprano aria (movement 5), which uses as a solo instrument the newly invented oboe d'amore, has all the traits of the normal Italianate da capo form. The last aria (movement 12), on the other hand—one of a number of Bach arias in which a bass soloist is joined by trumpet, strings, and continuo—is in a modified da capo form (the da capo is recomposed so that it remains in the tonic rather than modulating to the dominant, as did the A section).

The tenor aria (movement 3) has an innovative design which gives the impression of a full da capo, although it is in fact considerably shortened; the second half of the B section (bars 100 ff.) is elided with the da capo. First, the head-motif returns, sung to the final words of the B portion of the text (bars 111–12); next, the opening sentence comes back (bars 113 ff.); the remainder of this vocal section quotes from the end of A in an increasingly literal manner, beginning in the tenor part (bars 115 ff.), then the continuo (bars 118 ff.), and finally the strings and oboe (bars 121 ff.), before the movement concludes with a complete restatement of the opening ritornello. The alto aria (movement 10), while differing in details, manifests a similar fluidity in which the text is treated as an integral whole rather than being separated into two distinct parts.          SAC

E. Chafe, 'Bach's First Two Leipzig Cantatas: A Message for the Community', in P. Brainard and R. Robinson, eds., *A Bach Tribute: Essays in Honor of William H. Scheide* (Kassel and Chapel Hill, NC, 1993), 71–86; S. A. Crist, 'Bach's Début at Leipzig: Observations on the Genesis of Cantatas 75 and 76', *Early Music*, 13 (1985), 212–26. For further bibliography, *see* CANTATA, §1.

***Die Himmel erzählen die Ehre Gottes*** ('The heavens declare the glory of God'). Cantata for the second Sunday after Trinity, BWV76, first performed on 6 June 1723. This was the second cantata Bach performed after taking up his post as Kantor and *director chori musici* at Leipzig, and it shares a number of structural and stylistic features with no. 75, *Die elenden sollen essen*, heard the previous Sunday. The text, loosely based on the Gospel reading for the day (Luke 14: 16–24), calls on Christians to turn from idolatry and bear testimony to the goodness and glory of God.

*Die Himmel erzählen die Ehre Gottes*, like its companion work, is divided into two parts, each with seven movements. The opening chorus, which employs the combined forces of SATB, trumpet, two oboes, strings, and continuo, is cast in the form of a prelude and fugue which incorporates elements of the concerto, both in the ritornello opening and in the contrast between solo voices (accompanied by continuo) and full choir (with orchestral support). It is a spirited setting of Psalm 19: 1 and 3, with the solo trumpet 'striding the blast'. A gentle da capo aria in which the soprano, partnered by a solo violin, calls the people to God and a robust rejection of idolaters in a bass aria accompanied by trumpet and strings are the other main constituents of Part 1, which ends with the first strophe of Martin Luther's hymn *Es woll uns Gott gnädig sein*. Each line of the chorale, plainly harmonized in four vocal parts, is anticipated and then doubled by the trumpet, but what gives the movement its curiously halting gait is, first, the syncopated (even wayward) harmonic writing for the strings and, second, a persistent off-beat rhythmic figure ($\gamma$ $\sqrt{}$ $\sqrt{}$ $\rfloor$) in the continuo. Together with the melody's modal (Phrygian) contours, they produce an effect which the Leipzig authorities, suspicious of anything 'operatic' being heard in church, may have found reassuringly archaic.

Part 2, which was presumably heard during Communion (*see* HAUPTGOTTESDIENST), opens with an instrumental movement for oboe d'amore, bass viol, and continuo: a four-bar Adagio followed by a contrapuntal Allegro. Like the opening chorus, this too may be thought of as a prelude and fugue—though 'prelude and three-part invention' perhaps more correctly suggests its form and texture. Bach used it again as the opening movement of his Organ Sonata in E minor. In Part 1 the soprano and bass were heard as vocal soloists; in Part 2 it is the turn of the other two voices. The tenor aria 'Hasse nur', with continuo, derives much of its energy from the dissonance on which the voice enters to emphasize the word 'hate'; with 'Christum gläubig zu umfassen' the expression relaxes in a long melisma on 'umfassen' ('embrace') and another on 'Freude' ('joy'). The alto aria 'Liebt, ihr Christen', with oboe d'amore and bass viol, is more unified in its gentle meditation on the love of Christ. After the last, and shortest, of the work's six recitatives, the cantata ends with the same chorale setting that concluded Part 1, sung now to the third strophe of Luther's hymn.

For bibliography, *see* CANTATA, §1.

**Dieupart, Charles** (b. ? after 1667; d. *c*.1740). French musician, also known as François Dieupart. He worked mainly in London. His *Six Suittes de clavessin* (Amsterdam, 1701) exerted a significant influence on Bach, who copied them out during the period 1709–16. Unlike his French contemporaries, Dieupart treated the suite as a musical unit containing a series of dances fixed in number and type: ouverture, allemande, courante, sarabande, gavotte, menuet, and gigue. In essentials this is identical with the movement structure that Bach adopted in the English Suites, the Cello Suites, and the keyboard Partitas.

RDPJ

K. Beißwenger, *Johann Sebastian Bachs Notenbibliothek* (Kassel, 1992), 190–5, 200–2, 280–2.

**Die Wahl des Herkules** ('The Choice of Hercules'). A title which is sometimes used (incorrectly) for Cantata 213, LASST UNS SORGEN, LASST UNS WACHEN.

**Die Zeit, die Tag und Jahre macht** ('Time, which makes the day and the year'). Secular cantata, BWV134*a*, for New Year's Day, first performed in homage to Prince Leopold at Cöthen on 1 January 1719. In the original (anonymous) libretto it is designated a serenata. Scored for alto (as Divine Providence), tenor (as Time), and SATB (in the final movement), with two oboes, strings, and continuo, it consists of four recitative–aria pairs, the second aria set as a duet and the last one as a chorus.

When Bach parodied the work in 1724 as the sacred cantata *Ein Herz, das seinen Jesum lebend weiß* (no. 134) he omitted the third aria, 'Der Zeiten Herr', for alto. Possibly he felt its key (G minor) and rather sober dress (the voice is accompanied by continuo only) made it less suitable for an Easter cantata than the three lyrical movements he included: an aria, a duet, and a chorus. Like these, 'Der Zeiten Herr' is in da capo form, but the opening phrase of the introduction returns so many times as almost to make it a ground bass aria.

For bibliography, *see* CANTATA, §2.

**diminution.** A term used in FUGUE for the device of restating the subject in shorter notes than those of the original statement. In Bach's fugues, and probably in those of other composers as well, diminution is employed much less often than its opposite, AUGMENTATION. A rare example occurs in the E major Fugue from Part 2 of *The Well-tempered Clavier*, where diminution of the subject is found in all four parts from bar 27 on.

The term 'diminution' can also denote the elaboration of a melody by replacing long notes by many short ones, while retaining the melody's essential contours. One example of the application of diminution in this sense can be seen in the organ chorale *O Mensch, bewein dein Sünde groß* from the *Orgel-Büchlein*.

***director musices.*** Throughout the Leipzig years (1723–50) Bach usually referred to himself as 'director musices' or 'director chori musici', sometimes, but not always, coupled with 'Cantor' or 'Kapellmeister'. Press reports concerning both Bach and his predecessor Johann Kuhnau also often use the 'director' title. However, official documents from the school and town council nearly always refer to Bach as 'Cantor' as if to insist that this is Bach's official title and role (*see* KANTOR).

In fact, the 'director' title had been appropriated by many Kantors who wished to show they were serious musicians, basically in charge of the music for a town's main churches (if not the town as a whole); even a century before Bach, the Leipzig Kantor J. H. Schein (1586–1630) used the term, and Michael Praetorius (*c*.1571–1621) at the same time described it as a synonym for 'Kantor'. A contemporary of Bach's, Martin Fuhrmann (1669–1745), made it clear in 1715 that there was a distinction between the academic, but musically informed, Kantor and he who must understand the fundamentals of composition; only the latter deserved the title 'director musices'.

JAB

**Doles, Johann Friedrich** (b. 23 April 1715; d. 8 Feb 1797). Kantor, organist, and composer, born in Steinbach, Thuringia. He was a pupil of Bach for four years while a student at Leipzig University (*BDok* i. 272). As Kantor at Freiberg from 1744, he came into contact with the school Rector J. G. Biedermann, who inveighed against music in the educational curriculum. Bach himself was one of several prominent figures involved in the ensuing pamphlet war. Doles became Kantor at the Leipzig Thomasschule in 1755. In 1789, his last year as Kantor, he directed the performance of Bach's motet *Singet dem Herrn* that reportedly made such a deep impression on Mozart. His excellent manuscript treatise on singing may preserve some elements of Bach's own methods.

JAB

H. Banning, *Johann Friedrich Doles: Leben und Werk* (Leipzig, 1939); A. Schneiderheinze, ed., 'Johann Friedrich Doles: *Anfangsgründe zum Singen*', *Beiträge zur Bach-Forschung*, 7 (1989) [entire issue].

**Dörffel, Alfred** (b. 24 Jan. 1821; d. 22 Jan. 1905). Writer and editor, born in Waldenburg, Saxony. He studied with Mendelssohn and Schumann at the Leipzig conservatory. In 1871 he published a catalogue of Schumann's printed works, and in 1884 a book on the history of the Gewandhaus concerts (once directed by Mendelssohn). He also worked for the publishers Breitkopf & Härtel and Peters (e.g. in proof-reading works such as Wagner's *Tristan* and Liszt's symphonic poems) and as a librarian at the Musikbibliothek, Leipzig.

Dörffel edited several *BG* volumes, including Cantatas 111–30 (continuing the series of volumes edited by Wilhelm Rust), Cantatas 171–93, and some of the instrumental music.          KK

**'Dorian'** ('Dorische'). A nickname given to Bach's Toccata and Fugue in D minor BWV538. It derives from the fact that the earliest manuscript copies (there is no autograph) transmit the piece without a key signature of one flat; in medieval theory and practice the Dorian mode, with B♮, was likewise centred on D. It was, however, by no means unusual, even as late as the 18th century, for pieces in D minor to be notated without key signature, and there is nothing modal about the harmonies of BWV538.

**Dorn, Johann Christoph** (b. 5 Sept. 1707; d. 18 April 1785). Organist and schoolmaster, born in Gruna, near Chemnitz in Saxony. He attended the Thomasschule in Leipzig as a day-boy from 1724 and studied with Bach, who supplied a testimonial for him in 1731 when he competed unsuccessfully for the post of organist at the Johanniskirche. The following year he was made deputy organist at Belgern, near Torgau, and in 1744 he was appointed organist and schoolmaster in Torgau itself, where he died.

**Dornheim**. A village near Arnstadt. It was in the small church there, the Bartholomäuskirche, that Bach married his second cousin Maria Barbara Bach on 17 October 1707. Their choice of this church for the wedding probably resulted from their friendship with the pastor there, J. L. Stauber.

M. Petzoldt, *Bachstätten aufsuchen* (Leipzig, 1992), 39–47.

***double***. A French word for a type of variation which follows a dance, in which ornamentation and elaboration are incorporated into the fabric of the original piece while the supporting harmonies remain essentially the same. About a dozen *doubles* by Bach survive. The English Suite

no. 1 is unusual in having two courantes, and the second courante equally unusual in having two *doubles*. In the *double* of the Polonaise from the B minor Orchestral Suite BWV1067 the melody is transferred to the bass, while the flute performs an agile counterpoint above it.          NJ, MEL

**double bass** (*Kontrabaß*). The lowest-pitched member of the violin family. Bach did not use the term 'Kontrabaß' in his scores, preferring to designate his lowest string parts as 'violone', 'violono', or 'violono grosso', terms which might be used for bass string instruments of various sizes and pitches.

**double counterpoint**. A term used for INVERTIBLE COUNTERPOINT in two parts.

**double fugue**. A fugue which uses two subjects simultaneously in INVERTIBLE COUNTERPOINT. The term is used in more than one sense, although the requirements of compositional technique are the same. Bach's 'St Anne' Fugue, BWV552 shows the tripartite form, in which a fugue on one subject is followed by a fugue on another, the two subjects being then combined in invertible counterpoint. A more straightforward type combines the two subjects in invertible counterpoint from the start, as in the Fugue in A minor, BWV551:2. The term has also been applied to any normal fugue which has a distinctive invertible and recurring countersubject.          LC

***dramma per musica***. Italian term commonly employed in the 17th and 18th centuries for an opera libretto. Bach, or his librettists, adopted the term for a number of works which are now known as secular cantatas (BWV201, 205, 205a, 206, 207, 207a, 213, 214, and 215), but which in many ways are more closely related to the contemporary Italian serenata. See CANTATA, §2.

**Dresden**. The main city and capital of Saxony, in Bach's time and today. From 1694 Dresden was also the residence of the kings of Poland, August II (Elector Friedrich August I of Saxony) and his son August III (Elector Friedrich August II of Saxony). The father followed French examples and customs, whereas the son showed also Italianate tastes, including a notable predilection for opera.

From about 1685 the newly rebuilt section of the city on the west bank of the Elbe was enriched and enlivened as a result of the artistically enlightened despotism that made Dresden a cultural citadel open to the public, as well as to the court. The city's many palaces and museums acquired both old and new masterpieces, and the creative and performing arts were put on public display as a demonstration of both affluence and refined taste. The manufacture of Dresden china in imitation of far-eastern porcelain began in 1709 in

Dresden, but was transferred the following year to nearby Meißen. Figurines and decorations on the porcelains depict festive events of the day and provide glimpses into the lavish court life when the city was at its cultural zenith around 1730.

Bach seems to have had a genuine admiration for Dresden. He cast envious eyes at the musical establishment maintained there by the Saxon court, and in the *Entwurff* (1730) he used it as a stick with which to beat his Leipzig employers. He visited the city at least five times, and on each occasion the aristocracy there were made aware of his visit, and his public performances were the subject of journalistic approval. The occasion of his visit in 1717 was the famous keyboard challenge from which Bach's contestant, Louis Marchand, withdrew at the last minute; on 19–20 September 1725 Bach gave recitals at the Silbermann organ in the Sophienkirche; during the week beginning 14 May 1731 he was again heard in the Sophienkirche and at court, and he may also have attended the première of J. A. Hasse's opera *Cleofide* on the 13th; in July 1733 he was in the Saxon capital to present the parts of the B minor *Missa* (Kyrie and Gloria) to the elector; and on 1 December 1736, shortly after his appointment as *Kapellmeister von Haus aus* to the Dresden court, he gave a recital on the recently completed Silbermann organ in the Frauenkirche.

These were doubtless not his only visits to the Saxon capital; according to J. N. Forkel, he took his eldest son, Wilhelm Friedemann, to the opera in Dresden several times. Friedemann's association with the city was eventually even closer than his father's. From 23 June 1733 to April 1746 he served as organist of the Sophienkirche, which was effectively the place of worship for Lutherans in the royal employ throughout this period; he is certain to have had regular dealings with the court's official Lutheran composer, Pantaleon Hebenstreit, during these years.                SFD

G. J. Buelow, 'Dresden in the Age of Absolutism', in *Man and Music: The Late Baroque Era* (London, 1993), 254–95; O. Landmann, 'The Dresden Hofkapelle During the Lifetime of Johann Sebastian Bach', *Early Music*, 17 (1989), 17–30.

**Drese.** Family of musicians from Thuringia who enjoyed a considerable reputation in the 17th–18th centuries. Bach came into contact with at least two of the family members.

Adam Drese (b. c.1620; d. 15 Feb. 1701) was a composer and bass viol player. He was appointed *Kapellmeister* to Duke Wilhelm IV of Saxe-Weimar in 1652, but when the duke died, ten years later, the *Kapelle* was disbanded and Drese sought a similar position with Duke Bernhard at Jena. When Duke Bernhard died in 1678, Drese found yet another post as *Kapellmeister*, this time to the

Count of Schwarzburg at Arnstadt, where he remained for the rest of his life.

When, in 1683, Duke Wilhelm Ernst reconstituted the Weimar *Kapelle*, he appointed Adam Drese's cousin Johann Samuel Drese (b. c.1644; d. 1 Dec. 1716) as his *Kapellmeister*. J. S. Drese was thus in charge of the court music when Bach served as 'lackey' in 1703 and, although inferior to his cousin Adam as a musician, he was still nominally in charge when Bach returned to Weimar as court organist in 1708, though he was by then in rather poor health.

Much to Bach's disappointment, Samuel Drese was succeeded at Weimar by his son Johann Wilhelm Drese (bap. 8 July 1677; bur. 25 June 1745), who had served as vice-*Kapellmeister* since 1704. In 1702 he had spent eight months in Italy, at the duke's expense, with the aim of perfecting himself in composition, but little is known of his activities after Bach left Weimar in 1717. He died in Erfurt.

A. Basso, *Frau Musika: la vita e le opere di J. S. Bach*, i (Turin, 1979).

**Dretzel, Cornelius Heinrich** (bap. 18 Sept. 1697; d. 7 May 1775). Organist and composer, born in Nuremberg, where he appears to have spent his whole life in various organists' posts. He reputedly studied with Bach in Weimar in 1716–17, and his compositions certainly reveal points of contact with Bach's. They include a concerto for harpsichord solo, perhaps modelled on the Italian Concerto, which was once thought to be by Bach; an early version of the slow movement was entered in *Schmieder1* as BWV897:1.

**duetto** ('duet'). Italian term, usually used for a piece for two voices or instruments (with or without accompaniment) or for a two-part piece for a single instrument. Bach used the term for four keyboard pieces in CLAVIER-ÜBUNG III, and their presence there, together with the unusual profiles they present, have given rise to much speculation as to their significance. The four elements, the four cardinal virtues, the four Gospels, the four temperaments, the four major prophets, the four rivers of Eden, the four beasts seated before God's throne in Revelation 4, and the four weeks of Lent are among suggested 'interpretations' (see Basso). David Humphreys links them to the four teaching precepts in Martin Luther's Lesser Catechism.

A. Basso, *Frau Musika: la vita e le opere di J. S. Bach*, ii (Turin, 1983), 595–6; D. Humphreys, *The Esoteric Structure of Bach's Clavierübung III* (Cardiff, 1983), 7–18.

***Du Friedefürst, Herr Jesu Christ*** ('Thou prince of peace, Lord Jesus Christ'). Cantata for the 25th Sunday after Trinity, BWV116, first performed on 26 November 1724. We owe the existence of this fine cantata to the singular fact that in 1724 Protestant Germany celebrated Easter a week earlier than most of the rest of Christendom (*see* CHURCH CALENDAR). Had this not been the case, the Trinity season would have ended with the 24th Sunday that year, and Bach might well have composed a very different work when the 25th Sunday next formed part of the calendar. As it is, Cantata 116 is a CHORALE CANTATA belonging to the composer's second Leipzig *Jahrgang*. Jacob Ebert's hymn (1601) on which the text is based speaks of Jesus as the prince of peace to whom mankind turns in time of trouble. As is customary in the chorale cantatas, the anonymous librettist has retained the original first and last strophes of the hymn, refashioning the intervening strophes as recitatives and arias.

Also as usual, Bach sets the first strophe as an elaborate chorale fantasia, beginning in this case with a 16-bar instrumental ritornello for two oboes d'amore, strings, and continuo, with a concertante part for the first violin. Ritornello material then alternates with the chorale lines sung as a cantus firmus by the soprano, with horn support. What is unusual about the structure of the movement is the treatment of the three lower voices. In the first *Stollen* of this BARFORM movement, and again in the final line of the *Abgesang*, they support the soprano with harmonies in cantional style. For the other lines they work out motifs from the ritornello in imitative counterpoint. In this way the traditional melody of the chorale and the 'modern' material of the ritornello are brought into unusually close union.

In the opening phrases of the alto aria (no. 2) the oboe d'amore has to come to the aid of the singer to express the 'unaussprechlich' distress of the believer at the thought of judgement, which it does in a chromatic, tortuous obbligato. After a brief tenor recitative, each phrase of which is prefaced by a continuo reminder of the chorale melody from movement 1, there follows a terzetto, or trio, in which the soprano, tenor, and bass acknowledge the redemption won by God's son. Trios such as this are something of a rarity in Bach's cantatas, but even more unusual (perhaps unique) is the movement's structure, which may be represented as A–B–A–B'. The first section of this E major movement modulates to the dominant (B major), and the second (B) section closes in the relative minor (C♯) at bar 88. One might then expect a modified da capo of the A section, closing in the tonic, but instead Bach repeats the A section exactly, and then returns to the home key with a modified repeat of the B section. The result is a long movement, but one rich in harmonic and contrapuntal interest which does not overstay its welcome.

After a dramatic recitative, accompanied by strings and continuo, in which the alto pleads for God's assistance in adversity, the cantata ends with the customary simple harmonization of the chorale melody heard at the opening, this time sung to the final strophe of Ebert's hymn.

For bibliography, *see* CANTATA, §1.

***Du Hirte Israel, höre*** ('Hear, O thou shepherd of Israel'). Cantata for the second Sunday after Easter (Misericordias Domini) BWV104, first performed in the Nikolaikirche, Leipzig, on 23 April 1724. Bach was under enormous pressure during his first months as Thomaskantor, since he was contracted to perform sacred cantatas on feast-days and most Sundays of the Church year. Nevertheless, his first Leipzig cycle, which ran from Trinity Sunday 1723 to the Sunday after Ascension 1724, contained at least 36 newly composed works in which he adopted a variety of formal patterns. One such wholly original piece is *Du Hirte Israel, höre*, whose text, by an unidentified author, evokes throughout the image, much cherished by the Christian faith, of Christ the good shepherd. In this respect it bears a close relationship with Cantatas 85 and 112. The score has been lost, but Bach's original parts survive.

We may justly consider the opening chorus, scored for SATB, two oboes, oboe da caccia, strings, and continuo, to be among the very finest in Bach's cantata output. It takes its text from the opening verse of Psalm 80: 'Hear, O thou shepherd of Israel, thou that leadest Joseph like a sheep; shew thyself also, thou that sittest upon the cherubims.' The pastoral imagery is tenderly and imaginatively evoked in the lyrical G major opening chorus in 3/4 time. The gigue-like rhythm, the sighing phrases, and the urgently reiterated supplications, 'höre' ('hear') and 'erscheine' ('appear'), suffuse the movement with a profound melancholy, while the flattened 7th of the instrumental introduction at bar 19 provides yet another moment of expressive intensity in this pastoral elegy. Bach and Telemann, more than any other composers, showed an awareness of the rich sonorities inherent in three-part oboe texture, whose sound was traditionally associated with pastoral subjects.

In the following simple recitative (tenor), which ends in a passage of arioso, Bach takes us from the G major of the preceding movement to B minor for the succeeding tenor aria. The text extends the image of the good shepherd, and this is continued in the aria, which is accompanied by two oboes d'amore whose wide-ranging, somewhat melancholy melodic contours and plangent sonority delicately colour the image of the lost soul in search of the shepherd.

# Durchlauchtster Leopold

The second recitative–aria pair is in D major and scored for bass. The uncertainty expressed in the preceding aria is dispelled as the shepherd gathers his flock. In the aria, in 12/8 metre and with the character of a pastoral dance, Christ's flock is offered a glimpse of heaven and the hope of Christendom. The accompaniment is provided by strings and continuo, with a single oboe d'amore doubling the first violin line. The cantata ends with a metrical verse from Psalm 23. The hymn from which it is taken, by Cornelius Becker, dates from 1598. The melody, straightforwardly harmonized by Bach in the brightly coloured key of A major, is *Allein Gott in der Höh sei Ehr* by Nikolaus Decius (*c*.1485–after 1546). NA

For bibliography, *see* CANTATA, §1.

**Durchlauchtster Leopold** ('Most illustrious Leopold'). Secular cantata, BWV173a, composed for the birthday of Prince Leopold of Anhalt-Cöthen (10 December), probably in 1720 or 1722. Bach called the work 'Serenada'.

During his years in Cöthen Bach's duties included the composition of music for Prince Leopold's birthday and for New Year. Normally music was required for the church services and also for the secular parts of the celebrations, but most of it is lost, or survives only in parodies for church cantatas from Bach's Leipzig years. *Durchlauchtster Leopold* is one of only two congratulatory cantatas which are extant in their complete original state (the other is *Die Zeit, die Tag und Jahre macht* for New Year 1719). The author of the text is unknown; the subject of the eight movements is effectively a paean of praise to the prince.

The cantata is scored for soprano, bass, and strings, with two flutes and bassoon. Neither singer appears as a dramatic figure; most probably even the final 'coro' was sung only by the two soloists. Except for the two recitatives (nos. 1 and 5), the movements are mostly dance-like. Especially remarkable is the duet 'Unter seinem Purpursaum' (no. 4), headed 'Al tempo di menuetto'. The three strophes of the text are set as three distinct sections; their keys follow the circle of 5ths from G major, via D major, to A major, the first being scored for bass, the second for soprano, and the third for both singers.

Perhaps as early as 1723 the text and the original music were parodied as a Whit Monday cantata, *Erhöhtes Fleisch und Blut*; movement 7 also found its way into another work, *Er rufet seinen Schafen mit Namen*. KK

For bibliography, *see* CANTATA, §2.

**Dürr, Alfred** (b. 3 March 1918). German musicologist, one of the most influential Bach scholars of the 20th century, born in Berlin. He studied at the University of Göttingen, where in 1950 he completed his Ph.D. dissertation on Bach's early cantatas. A fellow student was Georg von Dadelsen; both men were working simultaneously on a revision of Spitta's chronology of Bach's vocal works. The results were almost identical; Dürr's work was first published in the *Bach-Jahrbuch* in 1957, and revised and enlarged as *Zur Chronologie der Leipziger Vokalwerke J. S. Bachs* in 1976.

From 1951 Dürr worked at the Bach-Institut, Göttingen, where he was deputy director from 1962 to 1981. From 1953 he served for 20 years as the 'Western' editor of the *Bach-Jahrbuch*, and he also edited some important volumes of the *NBA*: the *Christmas Oratorio* (with Walter Blankenburg), the *St Matthew Passion*, and *The Well-tempered Clavier*, as well as several cantatas. His most widely read publication is *Die Kantaten von Johann Sebastian Bach*, a collection of 'portraits' of every extant Bach cantata, first published in 1971 and several times reprinted. KK

**Du sollt Gott, deinen Herren, lieben** ('Thou shalt love the Lord thy God'). Cantata for the 13th Sunday after Trinity, BWV77, first performed in Leipzig on 22 August 1723. The text is from (? Johann Oswald) Knauer's *Gott-geheiligtes Singen und Spielen* (Gotha, 1720) with some alterations. The first movement quotes Luther's chorale *Dies sind die heilgen zehn Gebot*, while the final chorale (movement 6), which is untexted in the autograph, is based on the melody *Ach Gott, vom Himmel sieh darein*. Suggestions for a text to fit it have included strophe 8 of David Denicke's hymn *Wenn einer alle Ding verstünd* and strophe 8 of the same writer's *O Gottes Sohn, Herr Jesu Christ*, both dating from 1657. The text of the cantata is related to the Gospel of the day (Luke 10: 23–37), in which a Pharisee questions Jesus: 'Master, what must I do to inherit eternal life?', to which Jesus responds by asking him to recall the law, 'Thou shalt love the Lord thy God with all thy heart, and with all thy soul, and with all thy strength, and with all thy mind; and thy neighbour as thyself', and by telling the parable of the good Samaritan. Nothing is known of the performance history of the work after 1723.

Cantata 77 is scored for SATB, slide trumpet, two oboes, strings, and continuo. It is laid out according to the normal six-movement scheme, with an opening chorus, two recitatives and arias (movements 2–5), and a final chorale strophe. The opening chorus is unusual in design. Its structural basis is formed by the chorale *Dies sind die heilgen zehn Gebot*, which is given out line by line in long note values by the instrumental bass. Each line is

144

preceded by an entry, a 5th higher, in normal note values played by the slide trumpet, seeming to 'herald' the augmented main entry. Bach may have intended this for symbolic purposes; it is worth recalling the visual symbolism of the trumpet-playing angel found elsewhere in his church music. The voices, singing in closely imitative texture, work out a rising figure derived from a diminution of the first line of the melody. Bach uses differentiated registers to mark out the main entries of the chorale line, resulting in long *bassetto* passages for the continuo group when the chorale is not playing. The movement ends, after a full restatement of the chorale melody by the trumpet, in G-mixolydian in accordance with the modality of the chorale, but the problems of harmonizing the melody when it is stated in the bass lead to a number of striking harmonic effects, the prominence of repeated notes in the tune resulting in a generally slow rate of harmonic change. The striking B♭ in the last line of the melody clouds the harmonic atmosphere.

A short simple recitative for bass then leads to the first aria, in A minor, 'Mein Gott, ich liebe dich'. It is scored for soprano, with two obbligato parts evidently for oboes (the parts are not labelled in the score). The aria is in a light-weight amatory style with the oboes playing long stretches of music in parallel 3rds—though, as usual, Bach soon introduces some counterpoint into the texture. In ritornello form, the aria includes a single complete restatement of the instrumental ritornello, in E minor, at mid-point, with the oboes' 3rds harmonically inverted to form 6ths. In the following accompanied recitative the tenor prays for the 'heart of a Samaritan'. In the subsequent da capo aria, 'Ach, es bleibt in meiner Liebe', the alto laments his shortcomings in fulfilling the injunction to love one's neighbour. It is a short, relatively simple aria with an accompanying obbligato unusually labelled 'tromba' and apparently for slide trumpet. The instrument's lack of agility forces Bach to keep its part relatively simple, though some short semiquaver runs are present. The simplicity and regular phrasing of the voice part recall the pious songs of the Schemelli Songbook, for which Bach was later to provide harmonizations. As mentioned above, the final chorale has no text in the score.                                                    DLH

G. Herz, 'Thoughts on the First Movement of Johann Sebastian Bach's Cantata No. 77 "Du sollst Gott, deinen Herren, lieben" ', in *Essays on Music* (Ann Arbor, 1985), 206–17. For further bibliography, *see* CANTATA, §1.

**Duve, Andreas Christoph** (bap. 30 July 1676; bur. 5 Nov. 1749). Kantor, born in Brunswick. He was the son of a pastor at the Aegidienkirche and was appointed Kantor at the Martinikirche, Brunswick. He was one of the unsuccessful candidates for the post of Thomaskantor at Leipzig in 1722, performing his test cantata in the Nikolaikirche on 29 November (the first Sunday in Advent). In the older Bach literature he is named as Tufen.

U. Siegele, 'Bachs Stellung in der Leipziger Kulturpolitik seiner Zeit', *BJb* 69 (1983), 7–50.

***Du wahrer Gott und Davids Sohn*** ('Thou true God and son of David'). Cantata for the Sunday before Lent (Estomihi), BWV 23. It is one of two cantatas performed at the *Hauptgottesdienst* in the Thomaskirche, Leipzig, on 7 February 1723 as Bach's audition pieces for the post of Thomaskantor. Earlier in the service Cantata 22, *Jesus nahm zu sich die Zwölfe*, was heard, Cantata 23 being performed during the distribution of communion. In Lutheran worship the Agnus Dei, in either Latin or German, was customarily sung at Communion, and Cantata 23 therefore makes appropriate and significant use of the German Agnus Dei, *Christe, du Lamm Gottes*.

Movement 1 is a duet for soprano and alto—a long and poignant prayer for mercy which is linked both to the blind man's cry for mercy in the Gospel for the day (Luke 32: 31–43) and to the liturgical prayer for mercy, the Agnus Dei. In the following recitative the connection is emphasized in a profound conjunction of parallel ideas, one verbal and the other non-verbal. The text is based on the words of wrestling Jacob in Genesis 32: 26: 'I will not let thee go, except thou bless me.' Here the tenor expresses the request to the Saviour not to leave without imparting a blessing. The non-verbal parallel thought is expressed by the unison oboes and first violins, who together play, in augmentation, the first melodic line of the Agnus Dei, 'Christe, du Lamm Gottes, der trägst die Sünd der Welt, erbarm dich unser' ('Jesus Christ, Lamb of God, that takest away the sins of the world, have mercy upon us'). With this textless use of the German Agnus Dei Bach particularizes the desire for health and salvation expressed in the recitative.

Movement 3 is in a kind of rondo form, in which words from Psalm 145: 15, 'The eyes of all wait upon thee, O Lord', sung by the whole chorus in four parts, alternate with episodes for tenor and bass only. The whole psalm verse, which continues 'and thou givest them their meat in due season', was frequently expounded as a eucharistic reference in homiletic and devotional literature: God feeds the faithful with the body and blood of Jesus Christ. Significantly the chorus is built upon a recurring bass line that follows the contours of the opening melodic phrase of *Christe, du Lamm Gottes*.

The original autograph score of this cantata (now in the Staatsbibliothek zu Berlin) includes only these first three movements; the words 'Il-Fine' are entered at the end of the manuscript. However, the vocal and instrumental parts indicate that for the Leipzig trial Bach added a fourth movement, perhaps only a matter of days before its performance in the Thomaskirche. This concluding chorale movement was, however, not newly composed; instead Bach used a movement he had written some ten years or so earlier in Weimar as part of a Passion setting now lost (see *BC* iii, D1).

In the first three movements the melody of *Christe, du Lamm Gottes* was heard only in the orchestral accompaniment. Now the German Agnus Dei, both text and melody, is given a complete setting to end the cantata. Each time the basic melody of the liturgical prayer is heard, it is given a different musical treatment. The first imprecation is set as a slow, homophonic choral section; for the second the tempo changes to Andante and the mood becomes more confident in a cantus firmus setting where the melody appears in a three-voice canon: soprano, oboes, and first violin; and for the third and final petition of Agnus Dei the melody is heard in the soprano, phrase by phrase, with some imitative counterpoint in the lower voice parts and an independent oboe above. The lack of tension at the end underlines the prayer for peace: 'gieb uns deinen Frieden' ('grant us thy peace'). RAL

L. and R. Steiger, *Sehet! Wir gehn hinauf gen Jerusalem: Johann Sebastian Bachs Kantaten auf den Sonntag Estomihi* (Göttingen, 1992); C. Wolff, 'Bach's Audition for the St. Thomas Cantorate: The Cantata "Du wahrer Gott und Davids Sohn"', in *Bach: Essays on his Life and Music* (Cambridge, Mass., 1991), 128–40. For further bibliography, *see* CANTATA, §1.

# E

**Easter Oratorio** (*Oster-Oratorium*). One of three works for which Bach employed the term 'Oratorium'. It was probably performed on Easter Sunday 1735 in place of the usual cantata in one of Leipzig's main churches. In style, length, and instrumentation BWV249 is similar to many of Bach's secular cantatas, and much of the music was in fact drawn from a lost cantata, *Entfliehet, verschwindet, entweichet, ihr Sorgen*, written for the birthday of Duke Christian of Saxe-Weißenfels on 23 February 1725. Just over a month later, on 1 April, with a parody text possibly supplied by Picander and newly composed recitatives, Bach performed the work as an Easter cantata. The celebratory tone of the music and its festal scoring, including three trumpets and drums, were ideally suited to Easter celebrations. Bach pressed the music into service again on 25 August the following year as a birthday cantata for Count Joachim Friedrich von Flemming entitled *Die Feier des Genius*, BWV249b, again to a text by Picander (the music is lost), and he returned to it for the last time in the early to mid-1730s when he revised the Easter cantata version, retitling it 'Oratorium', replacing the solo oboe with a flute in the second movement of the sinfonia, and reworking the opening duet as a chorus.

Both as a birthday offering and as an Easter cantata, the work's four vocal parts were assigned to named characters. Despite the removal of the names of Mary the mother of James, Mary Magdalene and the Apostles John and Peter in the revisions of 1732–5, the work remains the closest of Bach's three oratorios to the Italianate dramatic form. Biblical recitatives, included in the *Christmas* and *Ascension Oratorios*, are here omitted in favour of a freely invented poetic text (there is therefore no need for an Evangelist), and there are no chorales. The work is essentially contemplative in tone, with little action apart from the discovery of the empty sepulchre on Easter morning.

The oratorio opens with a substantial two-movement introductory Sinfonia. The opening chorus that follows it returns to the style and scoring of the first movement and serves to complete a three-movement (fast–slow–fast) concerto design. The three da capo arias (for soprano, tenor, and alto soloists) are interspersed with simple recitative, blossoming into arioso just before the final aria in contemplation of the risen Jesus. At the centre of the work, both structurally and

musically, is the tenor aria 'Sanfte soll mein Todeskummer'. It is a comforting 'slumber' aria, with a rocking accompaniment for recorders and muted strings, in which the Christian soul celebrates Jesus's power to triumph over death and reduce its pains to mere sleep. A final chorus of praise returns to the style and scoring of the opening. SH

H. Smither, *A History of the Oratorio*, ii (Chapel Hill, NC, 1977), 154–7. For further bibliography, *see* CANTATA, §1.

**echo.** A term used by Bach for the finale of the early Suite in B♭ BWV821, a rondeau (A–B–A–C–coda) consisting largely of single-bar phrases played *forte* in four-part harmony and immediately repeated in three parts as a *piano* echo. In his mature years Bach used the term again for the finale of the Ouverture in the French Style BWV831, a binary-ritornello structure in which the *piano* echoes are mostly elaborations of preceding *forte* phrases rather than literal repeats.

Hercules's aria 'Treues Echo dieser Orten' from the secular cantata *Laßt uns sorgen, laßt uns wachen* (1733) contains an additional vocal part for 'Echo', who merely repeats the words 'nein' ('no') and 'ja' ('yes'); in addition, brief *forte* figures are immediately repeated *piano* in the obbligato oboe d'amore part. In 1735 this movement was adapted to form the aria 'Flößt, mein Heiland' in Part 4 of the *Christmas Oratorio*. RDPJ
*See also* BONPORTI, FRANCESCO ANTONIO.

E. Koch, 'Tröstendes Echo: zur theologischen Deutung der Echo-Arie im IV. Teil des Weinachts-Oratorium von Johann Sebastian Bach', *BJb* 75 (1989), 203–11.

**echo flute.** *See* FIAUTO, FIAUTO D'ECHO.

**editions (original).** *See* SOURCES, §2.

**Effler, Johann** (b. *c*.1635; d. 4 April 1711). Organist. He was town organist at Gehren until 1673, when he succeeded Johannes Bach (1604–73) as organist at the Predigerkirche, Erfurt. In 1678 he left Erfurt for Weimar, where he acted as both organist and financial secretary to the court. He was still there, although in poor health, when Bach was appointed 'lackey' in 1703, and in 1708 Bach succeeded him as *Hoforganist* (court organist).

**Ehre sei Gott in der Höhe** ('Glory to God in the highest'). Cantata, BWV197a, probably composed for Christmas Day 1728. It thus belongs to what may have been Bach's fourth annual cantata cycle at Leipzig. It survives only as a fragmentary autograph score, comprising the last three movements of the cantata and the concluding 19 bars of the alto aria which precedes them. The text, by Picander, is based on verses from St Luke's Gospel but also incorporates, in its closing chorale, a strophe from Caspar Ziegler's Christmas hymn *Ich freue mich in dir* (1697). The missing sections of the work were most likely an opening chorus, followed by an aria and a recitative.

The incomplete aria for alto is scored for a pair of transverse flutes, cello, violoncello piccolo or bassoon (Bach's intention is unclear), and basso continuo. This movement was reconstructed and completed by Diethard Hellmann in 1964 and published by Hänssler-Verlag. A simple recitative for bass follows, leading to a bass aria with oboe d'amore and continuo. Both this delightful piece, in 6/8 metre, and the preceding alto aria were parodied by Bach some years later in his wedding cantata *Gott ist unsre Zuversicht*. In each instance Bach expanded the texture, altered the instrumentation, and changed the vocal disposition, as well as making further small adjustments to his earlier text. The cantata ends with the fourth strophe of Ziegler's *Ich freue mich in dir*, for which Bach harmonized the melody *O Gott, du frommer Gott*.

NA

For bibliography, *see* CANTATA, §1.

**Eichentopf, Johann Heinrich** (b. 1678; d. 30 March 1769). Instrument maker, born possibly in Stolberg in the Harz region. He moved to Leipzig in 1707 and was married there in 1710. He was a leading maker of both woodwind and brass instruments, and would almost certainly have known Bach, although there is no certain evidence to support the tradition that it was Bach who first proposed to Eichentopf the design of the oboe da caccia.

**'Eighteen' Chorales.** 'The Eighteen' is the name popularly given to Bach's manuscript collection of the organ chorales BWV651–68 prepared in Leipzig in the 1740s, probably with publication in mind. The manuscript, now in the Staatsbibliothek zu Berlin (Mus ms Bach P.271), was prepared mainly by Bach himself; his pupil, and later son-in-law, J. C. Altnickol was responsible for the fair copies of BWV666–7, and the last piece (BWV668), which is separated from the other seventeen in the source, was copied by an anonymous scribe who also produced parts for the *St John Passion* and other works. The manuscript now contains also the six Organ Sonatas BWV525–30 and a version of the Canonic Variations BWV769.

Most of the chorales were composed during the Weimar period; the fair copies in P.271 incorporate Bach's later revisions, and an autograph of the Weimar version of BWV660 is in fact appended to P.271. Some of the revisions are minor, others more radical. For example, Bach modernized the layout of *An Wasserflüssen Babylon*, eliminating (except in the last three bars) the archaic double-pedal writing and the five-part texture found in earlier versions. Other preludes have still more complex pre-histories. *Herr Jesu Christ, dich zu uns wend* exists in four progressively revised versions, of which that in P.271 is the last.

The last two chorales, *Komm, Gott Schöpfer, heiliger Geist* BWV667 and *Vor deinen Thron tret ich* BWV668, are both expanded versions of short preludes found in the *Orgel-Büchlein*. For the first of these Bach lengthened the original (BWV631) by adding a further 18 bars, incorporating a second complete entry of the chorale in the pedals and an expansive final pedal point. However, the existence of an earlier copy of BWV667 shows that this version was not prepared specifically for the 'Eighteen', and the possibility cannot be ruled out that BWV631 was in fact extracted from BWV667. *Vor deinen Thron tret ich* is a more complex case. What seems to be the original version is in the *Orgel-Büchlein* with the title *Wenn wir in höchsten Nöthen sein* (BWV641). The expanded and revised version, BWV668, was printed in score with the title unchanged in the garbled first edition of *The Art of Fugue* (1751) as a makeweight, intended as compensation for the incomplete fugue. F. W. Marpurg's preface to the second impression (1752) of *The Art of Fugue* repeated the observation that it was 'dictated extempore by the deceased in his blindness', leading to the romantic mystique of naming it the 'DEATHBED CHORALE'. In converting BWV641 into its later form as BWV668 Bach removed the melodic filigree in the treble and added imitative passages preceding the main statement of each of the four lines, as well as a concluding coda.

The 'Eighteen' are large-scale chorale fantasias with the entries of the chorale lines separated by rests (with the single exception of BWV656). In this they contrast with the concise convention of the *Orgel-Büchlein*. The careful organization of the set reveals itself in the grouping together of different settings of the same chorale, which gives an opportunity to observe the variety and resourcefulness of Bach's technique. The set opens with two settings of the Whitsun chorale *Komm, heiliger Geist, Herre Gott*. The first sets the chorale in the pedal, with the upper voices working out a word-painting figure derived from the first line of the chorale. The second works out each line as a fugato, with imitative preambles culminating in the principal entry in the soprano. Similarly contrasted are the three settings of *Nun komm, der Heiden Heiland*. The first is in a florid (*coloriert*) style, but with prefatory imitations to each line; the second is a trio, and the third a fugue in which the manuals work out a subject based on the first line of the chorale in combination with the complete melody, stated unadorned in the pedals. The three preludes on *Allein Gott in der Höh sei Ehr* stand in a similar relationship to each other.

The two settings of *Jesus Christus, unser Heiland* are in a style apparently suggested by the way chorale improvisations were made during Communion; in this respect they recall BWV689, a prelude on the same chorale in *Clavier-Übung III* which is composed in the same loose-limbed style. Finally, *O Lamm Gottes, unschuldig* (BWV656) is set PER OMNES VERSUS, giving the opportunity for some detailed word-painting and symbolism in verse 3.                    DLH

W. Breig, 'The "Great Eighteen" Chorales: Bach's Revisional Process and the Genesis of the Work', in G. Stauffer and E. May, eds., *J. S. Bach as Organist* (London, 1986), 102–20; P. Williams, *The Organ Music of J. S. Bach*, ii (Cambridge, 1980), 124–74; C. Wolff, 'The Deathbed Chorale: Exposing a Myth', in *Bach: Essays on his Life and Music* (Cambridge, Mass., 1991), 282–94.

**Eilmar, Georg Christian** (b. 6 Jan. 1665; d. 20 Oct. 1715). Theologian, clergyman, and author, born in Windeberg, near Mühlhausen in Thuringia. In 1693 he was made archdeacon of the Marienkirche in Mühlhausen and found himself in conflict with Johann Adolf Frohne (1652–1713), superintendent and pastor at the Blasiuskirche, where Bach was organist (*see* MÜHLHAUSEN). Bach was on friendly terms with Eilmar and his family; Eilmar stood as godfather to Bach's first-born, Catharina Dorothea (1708–74), and Eilmar's daughter Anna Dorothea (1691–1762) performed a similar function at the christening of Bach's eldest son, Wilhelm Friedemann, in 1710. Eilmar may have supplied the librettos for Bach's Cantatas 71 and 131. He succeeded Frohne as superintendent at Mühlhausen in 1713.

***Ein feste Burg ist unser Gott*** ('A strong citadel is our God'). Cantata for the Reformation Festival, BWV80. Especially in its opening chorus, it is one of Bach's contrapuntal masterpieces. The final form is an expansion of a Weimar cantata for the third Sunday in Lent, ALLES, WAS VON GOTT GEBOREN, BWV80*a*. Since cantatas were not customarily performed in Leipzig during Lent, this one had to be adapted for another occasion if it was to be used in the city churches.

The anniversary of the Reformation was celebrated on 31 October each year, commemorating the day Luther posted his 95 theses on indulgences in 1517, the catalytic beginning of the Reformation. As the Weimar Lent cantata, BWV80*a*, made use of Luther's famous Reformation hymn, *Ein feste Burg*, it could therefore be expanded to become a *Reformationsfest* cantata. As such it exists in two forms: an earlier and a later Leipzig version. The early Leipzig version (*BC* A 183*a*) was performed at the 1723 *Reformationsfest*. All that exists of this version are three separate fragments—in Paris, Leningrad, and Princeton—that together constitute the first page of the autograph score, comprising the first movement and the beginning of the second. Watermark evidence establishes that this version was composed in 1723. Its first movement, however, was not the massive chorus of the later Leipzig version, but a four-part chorale. This early Leipzig version thus began and ended with a straightforward four-part chorale harmonization, a rarity in Bach's extant cantatas; the remainder of this earlier version was, presumably, essentially the same as in the later form.

In the later Leipzig version (*BC* A 183*b*), which is the one known and performed today, the opening four-part chorale was displaced by a majestic contrapuntal movement in *stile antico*, 228 bars in length. There is no introductory orchestral ritornello; the movement begins with a tenor statement of the theme, derived from the chorale melody, that generates the movement's vigorous imitative counterpoint. The chorale melody itself is heard as a massive two-part instrumental canon framing the five-part counterpoint of the voices and the continuo, making a texture of seven parts in all. Each line of the chorale canon is played by the oboes and, one bar later and three octaves lower, by the continuo. So that the lower voice of the canon should be heard, Bach took the unusual step of providing what amounts to a double continuo: one undergirding the vocal counterpoint, and the other for the lower voice of the two-part canon. In the oldest surviving manuscript score of the later Leipzig version—which is not an autograph but a copy, dating from 1744–7, in the hand of Bach's pupil and son-in-law J. C. Altnickol—the continuo part is designated 'Violoncello e Cembalo' and the lower voice of the canon 'Violone e Organo'. This indicates that the continuo was intended to sound in the 8′ register and the lower voice of the canon in the 16′ register.

The opening movement of Cantata 80*a* became the second movement of the later Leipzig version, but with the soprano singing the decorated chorale melody with the oboe, stanza 2 of Luther's hymn 'Mit unserer Macht'. Movements 2–5 of the Weimar cantata became nos. 3, 4, 6, and 7 in the later Leipzig version. Bach may, of course, have revised these movements, but without the earlier score it is impossible to know what these revisions might have been. One change is known, however. In movement 7 the obbligato oboe was replaced by oboe da caccia, an instrument unavailable earlier in Weimar.

Movement 5 was newly written in Leipzig, almost certainly for the 1723 version of the cantata. It is a strong movement in which the contrast between the rock-like chorale melody sung by the chorus and the restless agitation of the orchestra, in 6/8 time, is descriptive of stanza 3 of Luther's hymn: 'Should the world be full of devils . . . and the prince of devils . . . a little word will slay him.' The thickening of the orchestral texture by the addition of three oboes appears to be a later revision, and there are reasons for thinking that in the 1723 version the chorale was probably sung by tenors (or tenors and basses) alone, and that the octave unison of all voices was a later decision.

The concluding four-part chorale, the final stanza of Luther's hymn, was probably written for the later Leipzig version, replacing the 1723 setting.

After Bach's death his son Wilhelm Friedemann parodied movements 1 and 5, with added trumpets and timpani, for his Latin cantata *Gaudete omnes populi*, performed in Halle some time after 1750. The *BG* edition incorporated these additional parts into Cantata 80, and they are still frequently heard, but they do not belong to the authentic J. S. Bach cantata.                RAL

W. Blankenburg, 'Musikalische Interpretation der Kantate "Ein feste Burg ist unser Gott" (BWV 80)', in W. Blankenburg and R. Steiger, eds., *Theologische Bach-Studien*, i (Stuttgart, 1987), 127–36; C. Wolff, 'The Reformation Cantata "Ein feste Burg"', in *Bach: Essays on his Life and Music* (Cambridge, Mass., 1991), 152–61. For further bibliography, *see* CANTATA, §1.

**Ein Herz, das seinen Jesum lebend weiß** ('A heart that knows the living Jesus'). Cantata for the third day of Easter, BWV134, first performed at Leipzig on 11 April 1724. It was performed again, with revisions, on 27 March 1731 and, probably some time after that, Bach prepared a new score, writing fresh music for the recitatives. The cantata is a reworking of a secular New Year cantata, *Die Tag, die Zeit und Jahre macht*, written at Cöthen and performed there on 1 January 1719. This much might have been guessed, even if the original had suffered the same fate as many of Bach's other Cöthen cantatas and been lost. The text, singing the praises of the risen Christ, is full of adulatory phrases of a kind that prevails in homage cantatas addressed to earthly princes and potentates; the recitatives are long (except for the first) and shared between two 'characters'; the vocal lines (especially that of the tenor) have a rather high

written tessitura, characteristic of the Cöthen works; the lyrical items (one aria, one duet, and a final *coro*) are all ample da capo structures, with long ritornellos which seem to invite some kind of choreography; and the style of the music, in which major keys prevail, is strongly secular and dance-like in tone.

Like Cantatas 173 and 184, both of which were also fashioned from Cöthen originals, *Ein Herz, das seinen Jesum lebend weiß* has no introductory sinfonia or opening chorus, but begins immediately with a brief recitative which in the original served to introduce the 'characters' Time (tenor) and Divine Providence (alto). The tenor aria 'Auf, Gläubige' and the final chorus are both joyous, dance-like movements in 3/8 metre accompanied by the full instrumental forces of two oboes, strings, and continuo. The alto-tenor duet 'Wir danken und preisen', accompanied by strings with a concertante violin part, is reminiscent of several Brandenburg Concerto movements in its chugging quavers and its figuration.

For bibliography, *see* CANTATA, §1.

**Einicke, Georg Friedrich** (b. 16 April 1710; d. 19 Jan. 1770). Organist and Kantor, born in Hohlstedt, Thuringia. He studied at Leipzig University and with Bach, 1732–7, and was then Kantor in his native Hohlstedt. In 1746 he was appointed to a similar position in Frankenhausen, and in 1757 became *director musices* at Nordhausen, where he remained for the rest of his life. In 1749–50 he was briefly drawn into the controversy between Scheibe and Bidermann regarding the merits of Bach as a composer, acting as go-between on behalf of Bach and his supporters.

**Einige canonische Veraenderungen über das Weynacht-Lied** *Vom Himmel hoch da komm ich her* ('Some Canonic Variations on the Christmas hymn *Vom Himmel hoch da komm ich her*'). The title, in the original printed edition, of the CANONIC VARIATIONS for organ.

**Ein ungefärbt Gemüte** ('An unstained mind'). Cantata for the fourth Sunday after Trinity, BWV24. This is the second of three cantatas that Bach wrote for this Sunday; it was performed on 20 June 1723 along with another cantata, *Barmherziges Herze der ewigen Liebe* (no. 185), which Bach had already performed in Weimar. As always when two cantatas were performed, one was heard before the sermon and the other during Communion (*see* HAUPTGOTTESDIENST). Both works use texts—harking back to Bach's years at the Weimar court—by two of the most respected authors of this type of devotional liturgical poetry: that of Cantata 185 is by Salomo Franck (published in 1715), while Cantata 24 is on a text by Erdmann Neumeister from his *Geistlichen Poesien* (Frankfurt, 1714; repr. Eisenach, 1717). The juxtaposition of these two texts, which differ greatly in structure, was surely not fortuitous; rather it seems to have been done purposely in order to compare two distinct compositional 'models'.

The autograph score, along with many others, belonged at one time to the great Bach collector Georg Poelchau and his heirs; in 1841 it was acquired by the Königliche Bibliothek and is now in the Staatsbibliothek zu Berlin. The work is scored for SATB, clarino (trumpet), two oboes (doubling oboe d'amore), two violins, viola, and continuo. Two points of particular interest in the scoring are, firstly, the unison violins and viola in the opening alto aria and, secondly, the careful concertante vocal scoring, with solo and ripieno markings, in the third movement, 'Alles nun, das ihr wollet', a chorus on words from St Matthew 7: 12.

This chorus, in a rigorous MOTET STYLE, is the high point of the cantata. Is is bipartite in form, in the nature of a prelude and fugue, but in this case the two sections have the same text, as if to demonstrate how two different musical settings can serve for the same passage, interpreting symbolically and metaphorically Jesus's words: 'Therefore all things whatsoever ye would that men should do to you, do ye even so to them.' The commandment serves as a link with the appointed Gospel reading (Luke 6: 36–42), which underlines the concept of divine mercy and grace in a passage from the Beatitudes. The chorus is noteworthy also for its inclusion of an imposing part for 'clarino', identifiable in this case as a trumpet or a natural horn; the instrument is heard also in the final chorale, a four-part setting, with instrumental interludes, of Johann Heermann's *O Gott, du frommer Gott* (1630).

Each of the two choruses is preceded by an aria and recitative. The first aria (no. 1), for alto, is accompanied by unison strings and continuo, as mentioned above; the second (no. 5), for tenor, includes obbligato parts for two intertwining oboes d'amore.                                           AB

For bibliography, *see* CANTATA, §1.

**Eisenach.** Town in Thuringia where Bach was born. Eisenach is situated at the important spot where the old travel route from Frankfurt to Silesia enters the Thuringian basin. To the south is the Thuringian forest; the Wartburg castle, guarding both the town and the route, is situated on one of its hills. It was on the Wartburg that the famous medieval singing contest took place, as recounted in Wagner's opera *Tannhäuser*, and Martin Luther translated the New Testament there in 1521–2.

From 1672 onwards Eisenach was the capital of the Duchy of Saxe-Weimar-Eisenach. All the important official buildings of the town are grouped around the Markt (market-place). The castle is on its northern side (the present building dates from 1742–8); in the north-eastern corner is the old town hall; and in the centre is the Georgenkirche with the font at which Bach was baptized on 23 March 1685. Going west from the main entrance of the Georgenkirche the visitor reaches the former Dominikanerkloster. In its main cloistered building was the Lateinschule that Bach attended from 1692 to 1695, and nearby is the former ducal mint. Going south-east from the Markt one reaches the Frauenplan with the Bachhaus (Bach house) and the Bach monument by Adolf von Donndorf (1883). The Bachhaus was founded in 1907 as the museum of the Neue Bachgesellschaft in the building where Bach was then thought to have been born. This is probably the wrong house, since Bach's father lived at no. 35 Fleischgasse (now Lutherstraße, where the building no longer stands) from 1675 to 1695. The supposition that Bach was born at no. 21 Frauenplan is based on a 19th-century tradition; the building is now a museum with a large collection of musical instruments and documents about music history (and the Bach family) in Thuringia.

Members of the Bach family had lived in Eisenach for only a short time before Bach's birth. In 1665 Johann Christoph Bach (i) (son of Heinrich Bach, 1615–92) came from Arnstadt to Eisenach and was installed as organist at the Georgenkirche; his duties included also playing the organ in the Nicolaikirche, to the north-east of the Markt. For some time he lived in the ducal mint near the Lateinschule. From 1698 onwards he supervised the rebuilding of the organ in the Georgenkirche; only the case is extant. After his death he was succeeded by his nephew Johann Bernhard Bach, whose son Johann Ernst and grandson Johann Georg (1751–97) maintained the Bach tradition in Eisenach almost to the end of the 18th century.

Bach's father, Johann Ambrosius, came to Eisenach in 1671 as *Hausmann*, or director of the *Stadtpfeifer*; a report from Easter 1672 tells us how much he impressed the audience in Eisenach with his playing on the organ, violin, cornett, trumpet, and drums. In addition to his duties in the church, he had to assist on official civic occasions, to play chorales from the tower of the town hall twice a day, and to organize the *Stadtpfeifer* ensemble (which included teaching its junior members). Furthermore, he and his ensemble had the privilege of playing at private festivities in the town, and individual members of the *Stadtpfeifer*-

Interior of the Georgenkirche, Eisenach, where Bach was baptized on 23 March 1685

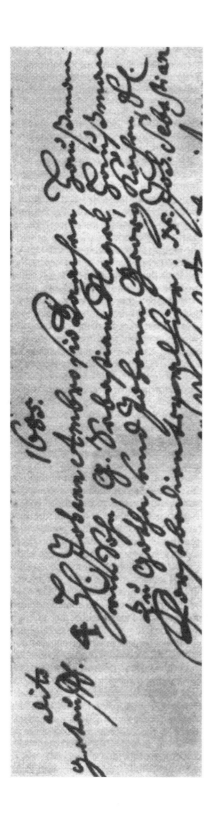

Entry in the register of the Georgenkirche, Eisenach, recording Bach's baptism on 23 March 1685 (Stadtkirchnerei Eisenach)

might be called upon to take part in the ducal court music.

Members of the Bach family were also active in the choir (*Kurrende*) of the Lateinschule: not only the sons of Johann Christoph and Johann Ambrosius, but also Johann Jacob (1655–1718), father of Johann Ludwig Bach. The *Kurrende* was directed by the Kantor Andreas Christoph Dedekind (*c*.1662–1706); he was apparently successful in separating his musical interests from the normal duties of a Kantor, which included teaching at school (especially in Latin and religion). This might have impressed the young Johann Sebastian, who followed the same pattern in his Leipzig years. The repertory of the choir survives in the *Kantorenbuch* established in 1540 by the Eisenach Kantor Wolfgang Zeuner, containing motets by Luther's friend Johann Walter (1496–1570) as well as others by Josquin Desprez (*c*.1440–1521) and Jacob Obrecht (*c*.1450–1505); in 1690 it was still in use. Bach must have become acquainted with this music, as well as with four-part chorales, during his time as a schoolboy in Eisenach; its influence on his later music in the *stile antico* has not yet been properly estimated.

Bach's musical activities in Eisenach did not, however, last long. After his mother's death in 1694 and his father's the following year, Johann Sebastian and his brother Johann Jacob went to live with their eldest sibling Johann Christoph (ii) in Ohrdruf.                                                    KK

K. Küster, *Der junge Bach* (Stuttgart, 1996), 39–61; C. Oefner, *Die Musikerfamilie Bach in Eisenach* (Eisenach, 1984); M. Petzoldt, *Bachstätten aufsuchen* (Leipzig, 1992), 48–60.

**Emery, Walter** (b. 14 June 1909; d. 24 June 1974). Musicologist; the leading British Bach scholar of his time, born at Tilshead in Wiltshire. His experience as organist and music publisher (with the firm of Novello for many years) determined his scholarly interests: above all, Bach interpretation and text-critical problems. He was the first to distinguish clearly between the handwriting of Johann Sebastian and that of Anna Magdalena Bach. His many publications on Bach include 'The Compass of Bach's Organs as Evidence of the Date of his Works', *The Organ*, 32 (1952), 92–100; 'The London Autograph of "The Forty-Eight"', *Music and Letters*, 34 (1953), 106–23; *Bach's Ornaments* (London, 1953); *Editions and Musicians* (London, 1957); *Notes on Bach's Organ Works: Six Sonatas for Two Manuals and Pedal* (London, 1957); and an edition of *Clavier-Übung II* for the NBA (1981).                                               RDPJ

**English Bach Festival.** A festival founded in 1963 by Lina Lalandi and held annually, first in Oxford and then jointly in Oxford and London. Its first aim was to present Bach's music in 'authentic' performances, but it soon extended its coverage to other areas of Baroque music (notably French opera) and commissioned many new works.

**English Suites** (Englische Suiten). Title given to six keyboard suites BWV806–11. The English Suites are distinguished by their opening preludes, which in all but the first suite are extended virtuoso movements whose style recalls the Italian violin concerto. Each prelude is followed by a series of dance movements consisting of allemande, courante, sarabande, and gigue, the last preceded by an additional pair of movements whose type varies from suite to suite.

The English Suites are thought to be the earliest of Bach's three collections of keyboard suites, differing from the probably later French Suites not only in the inclusion of preludes but also in the somewhat larger dimensions and generally more serious style of the dance movements. Despite the title, the dances are in many respects closer to those of Couperin and other French Baroque harpsichord composers than are the dances of the French Suites. Yet they also employ a greater amount of imitative counterpoint than do those of the later set. Thus, for example, in all but the First English Suite the initial theme of the allemande is subsequently exchanged between the hands, as in an invention. The gigues of the last four English Suites are three-part fugues, the second half of each employing the inversion of the subject.

Prototypes for individual movements can be found in suites by earlier composers, but the simultaneous combination of the refined French and the virtuoso Italian styles, and of contrapuntal texture with *galant* melody and traditional dance rhythms, is distinctly Bach's. The original purpose of the works is unknown; the exuberant virtuosity of the preludes suggests public or at least semi-public performance, such as might have occurred in private recitals before patrons or at court. But the intricate and sometimes tortuous counterpoint and part-writing (as in the Allemande of the E minor suite) are not fully manifest except to the student practising alone at the keyboard. That Bach employed such pieces in teaching is evident from comments of E. L. Gerber (1746–1819), who reported that his father, H. N. Gerber, studied 'a series of suites' with Bach after the Inventions and prior to *The Well-tempered Clavier*, and from the numerous manuscript copies made in the 18th century, some by pupils of Bach (among them H. N. Gerber).

The source of the title is unknown, but it was already used by J. N. Forkel (1801), who explained that it refers to an unknown English dedicatee. Forkel might, however, have assumed that Bach followed the common convention of naming works after those who commissioned them. It is unclear whether the presence of extended preludes in orchestral style would have been thought peculiarly English, although there does exist a set of six keyboard suites by Charles DIEUPART, a French harpsichordist active in England, each opening with an ouverture; Bach made his own manuscript copy of that work, which was published at Amsterdam in 1701.

The English Suites were not published until the 19th century, and the loss of essentially all Bach's manuscript material for them makes discussion of their dating and original title speculative. The works may date from as early as 1714 or so and, unlike Bach's other mature keyboard music, underwent relatively little revision thereafter. Still, the collection was probably not assembled into its present form until about 1725.

The principles governing the order of the suites are unclear, although there is a tendency towards more expansive dimensions and greater compositional rigour in the last five suites. The first suite stands apart from the rest, especially as its prelude is essentially a three-part invention; it also includes a second courante with two DOUBLES. The concerto-style preludes of Suites nos. 2–6 recall some of the quick movements from the Brandenburg Concertos in their large da capo forms and the alternation of recurring ritornello material with soloistic passages. The sarabandes of Suites nos. 2 and 3 are provided with alternative embellished versions (*agrémens*); the Sarabande of Suite no. 6 is followed by a *double*. The second Gavotte of Suite no. 3, usually labelled a musette, might be understood as one of Bach's few pictorial keyboard pieces, the alternative title serving not as a genre designation but as a reference to the pastoral bagpipes clearly represented by the drone in the bass. DS

H. Eppstein, 'Chronologieprobleme in Johann Sebastian Bachs Suiten für Soloinstrument', *BJb* 62 (1976), 35–57; D. Schulenberg, *The Keyboard Music of J. S. Bach* (New York, 1992), 231–53.

**engraving.** See SOURCES, §2.

**Enlightenment** (*Aufklärung*). An international cultural movement rooted in 17th-century rationalism which reached its zenith in Germany during the mid- to late 18th century. Essential to Enlightenment thought was the supremacy of reason, which was the key both to human perfection and to the workings of the universe. Not surprisingly, the hegemony of Christianity in thought and belief was challenged, although many religious reforms themselves stressed the importance of human reason and individual accountability. By far the most important literary figure of Bach's time was the Leipzig reformer Johann Christoph GOTTSCHED, who established a school which sought to purge German literature of its apparent bombast and redundant embellishment.

Given that the Enlightenment is usually associated with the 'progressive' in 18th-century culture and thought, and that many Enlightenment principles still form the basis of democratic society, many have striven to portray Bach as an Enlightenment figure. This has also appealed to scholars who seek to purge Bach of an excessively religious disposition and to many scholars in the former German Democratic Republic, because the Enlightenment, according to Marxist theory, was a crucial forerunner of the socialist state.

On the other hand, the fact that Bach was more closely aligned with Orthodox Lutheranism than with the more progressive Pietism, and that he was in protracted dispute with the 'enlightened' Leipzig rector, J. A. Ernesti, suggests that Bach was hardly a natural affiliate of the early German Enlightenment. The matter is not simplified by the fact that the treatment of 'reason' in cantata texts is highly ambiguous (see Chafe, pp. 224–53). Certainly, it may be said that Bach could not have composed as he did without the cultural environment of rationalist thought; yet, as Dreyfus argues, Bach's aesthetic concerns may point well beyond the provinciality of Enlightenment values and anticipate the musical aesthetics of the early 19th century. This was, after all, the most enthusiastic period of Bach reception. JAB

E. Chafe, *Tonal Allegory in the Vocal Music of J. S. Bach* (Berkeley and Los Angeles, Calif., 1991); L. Dreyfus, 'Bach as Critic of Enlightenment', in *Bach and the Patterns of Invention* (Cambridge, Mass., 1996), 219–44; H. J. Kreutzer, 'Johann Sebastian Bach und das literarische Leipzig der Aufklärung', *BJb* 77 (1991), 7–31.

**Entwurff** [in modern German, 'Entwurf'] ('draft', 'sketch'). Short title, often used in the Bach literature in both English and German, for the memorandum (*BDok* i, no. 22) that Bach addressed to the Leipzig council on 23 August 1730: *Kurtzer, iedoch höchstnöthiger Entwurff einer wohlbestallten Kirchen Music* ('Brief but highly necessary draft of a well-appointed church music'). In it he set out what he considered was needed in the way of singers and instrumentalists to maintain the musical services at the four main Leipzig churches, and drew attention to shortcomings in their current provision. The document is a highly important one for various reasons, but its details are sometimes imprecise or conflicting and its interpretation has given rise to misunderstanding and controversy. Ulrich Siegele

has related it to certain political changes taking place in the Leipzig town council at the time.
*See also* CHORUS, LEIPZIG, and ORCHESTRA.

U. Siegele, 'Bachs Stellung in der Leipziger Kulturpolitik seiner Zeit', *BJb* 72 (1986), 33–67.

**Epilog** ('epilogue'). *See* FORTSPINNUNGSTYPUS.

**equal temperament.** *See* TEMPERAMENTS and WELL-TEMPERED CLAVIER, THE.

**Erdmann, Georg** (bap. 19 Feb. 1682; d. 12 Oct. 1736). Diplomat, born in Leina, near Gotha in Thuringia. He was at school with Bach in Ohrdruf from 17 January 1698 and enrolled with him in the Mettenchor of the Michaelisschule in 1700. He went on to study law at Jena University in 1708, and in 1714 joined the Russian army in the service of Prince Anikita Ivanovič Repnin (1668–1726) in Riga. In 1718 he was made Russian representative in Danzig and later a member of the imperial Russian court.

Bach and Erdmann exchanged letters in 1726, and on 28 October 1730 Bach furnished his former schoolfriend with news about himself and his family (*BDok* i, no. 23), outlining the difficulties and drawbacks of his life in Leipzig, and hinting at the possibility of a remove. Erdmann's response, if he made one, has not survived.

G. Pantijelew, 'Johann Sebastian Bachs Briefe an Georg Erdmann: nebst Beiträgen zur Lebensgeschichte von Bachs Jugendfreund', *BJb* 71 (1985), 83–97.

**Erforsche mich, Gott, und erfahre mein Herz** ('O Lord, thou hast searched me out and known me'). Cantata, BWV136, originally performed in Leipzig on the eighth Sunday after Trinity (18 July) in 1723. The anonymous text is a gloss on the appointed Gospel reading (Matt. 7: 15–23), a warning against false prophets. Some manuscript evidence suggests that the alto aria, at least, is based on material which was composed earlier but has been lost. On the other hand, over 20 years later the opening movement was reworked into 'Cum Sancto Spiritu' in the *Missa* in A major BWV234.

The work begins with a choral fugue which falls into two halves, in each of which the entire biblical text (Psalm 139: 23) is set. Preceding the normal fugal opening is a so-called motto (bars 7–8)—an isolated soprano statement of the fugue theme which draws special attention to the first clause. This Italianate feature is more commonly associated with arias. This movement's festive character, though delightful, seems at odds with the reverent (even penitential) tone of the text.

Both recitatives (movements 2 and 4, for tenor and bass respectively) are almost exclusively syllabic and accompanied by continuo only; the concluding bars of the bass recitative shift to arioso style with the introduction of regular quaver motion in the continuo.

In the alto aria (movement 3) the soloist is joined by the analogous member of the oboe family, the oboe d'amore; the structure is ternary (A–B–A'). In an arresting passage in the A section, the lurching rhythms of a pair of melismas on 'erzittern' ('tremble') fittingly depict the terror of hypocrites on the Day of Judgement. The oboe d'amore drops out in the B section, and there is an abrupt change to compound metre and a more rapid tempo (*presto*) in keeping with mention of the power of God's wrath ('seines Eifers Grimm'). Since the middle section of a Bach aria normally modulates, it is striking that this one begins and ends in the same key—a clue that it was added later to a pre-existing movement. Other corroborating evidence includes the unusual tonal plan of the da capo (A': it begins in the dominant rather than the tonic), as well as the fact that the music is very different from that of A, exceeding by far the usual adjustments in the A' section of a modified da capo aria. The testimony of the original performing parts confirms this notion: not only was the B section a later addition in one of the continuo parts, but it also survives in score on two small slips of paper in Bach's own hand (one the composing score and the other a fair copy) included among these materials.

The other aria (movement 5) is a duet for tenor and bass, with unison violins and continuo. The B section begins with an ambitious canon between the two voices (bars 33–9). Additionally, it includes a musical interpretation of a pun: an alternative sense of the word 'allein' (used here as a conjunction meaning 'but' or 'however', but also meaning 'alone') is illustrated by using rests to isolate it from the passage that follows (Bach omitted this word from both subsequent settings of the clause). Also impressive are the lengthy melismas (semiquavers in parallel 3rds and 6ths) that vividly portray the word 'Strom' ('stream').

The concluding four-part chorale offers a refreshing departure from the usual pattern. Violin 1 weaves a pleasing line of its own, predominantly in quavers, instead of joining the horn and oboes in doubling the soprano melody.　　SAC
For bibliography, *see* CANTATA, §1.

**Erfreut euch, ihr Herzen** ('Rejoice, ye hearts'). Cantata for the second day of Easter, BWV66. It is a parody of five movements from the secular cantata *Der Himmel dacht auf Anhalts Ruhm und Glück* (no. 66a), which Bach performed for the birthday of Prince Leopold of Cöthen on 10 December 1718, and to which he added a closing chorale. The sacred version was first heard in

Leipzig on 10 April 1724 and repeated in 1731 and, probably, 1735. The parodied text, by an unknown author, is a joyous hymn of praise to the risen Christ, incorporating dialogue between Fear (alto) and Hope (tenor) which in the original had been between Fame and Happiness. The music betrays its origins in a number of ways: the main movements are all substantial da capo structures in major keys with amply proportioned ritornellos; and much of it is dance-orientated, particularly the bass aria (no. 3), with its passepied rhythms in 3/8 metre.

The opening chorus is also in 3/8 time, and somewhat in the style of the opening chorus of the *Christmas Oratorio*: the voices are supported by the work's full complement of instruments—trumpet, two oboes, bassoon, strings, and continuo—and there is much rushing up and down scales in demisemiquavers. In the original secular version this was the closing movement (like other Cöthen cantatas this one began with recitative), but it is possible that Bach composed a new central section in 1724. At this point the tempo slackens to Andante and plangent chromaticism is introduced to express the words 'das Trauren, das Fürchten, das ängstliche Zagen' ('grief, fear, and anxious trembling'), but there is nothing to invite a comparable change of affect in the original text. The dialogue between Hope and Fear is brought to the fore in a lengthy continuo recitative (no. 4) encompassing a passage of arioso in imitative style, and in the succeeding duet, in which the voices are partnered by a virtuoso violin solo, reminding us that the Cöthen period is particularly associated with some of Bach's most ambitious writing for string instruments.

The plainly harmonized chorale that ends the cantata is the third strophe of the hymn *Christ ist erstanden* (c.1090).

For bibliography, *see* CANTATA, §1.

**Erfreute Zeit im neuen Bunde** ('Joyful time in the new covenant'). Cantata for the feast of the Purification, BWV83, first performed at Leipzig on 2 February 1724. As pointed out in *DürrK*, the Gospel reading for this day, St Luke 2: 22–32, has less to do with the Purification than with Simeon, about whom it was prophesied that 'he should not see death, before he had seen the Lord's Christ'. It is from this passage that the words of the *Nunc dimittis* are taken, and these are quoted in the second movement of the cantata, which sings of death as a joyful liberation (a recurring subject in the Bach cantatas).

The cantata's basic tone of cheerful confidence is established in the opening movement, a generously proportioned da capo aria in which the alto soloist's ecstatic melismas on the 'joyful' words

'erfreute' and 'freudig' compete for attention with a virtuoso solo violin part and accompanying forces consisting of two oboes, two horns, strings, and continuo. Noteworthy in the B section of the aria is the solo violin's *bariolage* with which Bach sounds the death-knell at 'letzten Stunde' ('last hours'). In the second movement the bass intones three verses of the *Nunc dimittis* to a version of the medieval psalm tone no. 8, while strings and continuo weave around it a filigree of two-part counterpoint, mostly in strict canon—almost as if the ancient melody had gathered cobwebs. The first verse is separated from the other two by a section of recitative twice interrupted by reminders of the canon, as though the singer were musing on the biblical text. The movement is quite unlike anything else in Bach's music.

Violin virtuosity returns in the succeeding tenor aria, in da capo form, and once again the singer is called upon to match it with protracted melismas, this time mainly on the word 'treten' to convey the idea of hastening towards the throne of mercy. The text is based on Hebrews 4: 16, and after a brief alto recitative, the cantata ends, appropriately, with Martin Luther's paraphrase of the same verse in the fourth strophe of his hymn *Mit Fried und Freud ich fahr dahin* (1524), which, as usual, Bach set in a plain four-part harmonization with instrumental doubling.

For bibliography, *see* CANTATA, §1.

**Erhalt uns, Herr, bei deinem Wort** ('Sustain us, Lord, with thy word'). Cantata for the second Sunday before Lent (Sexagesima), BWV126, first performed at Leipzig on 4 February 1725. The hymn on which this CHORALE CANTATA is based is a compilation of four strophes by Martin Luther (nos. 1–3 and 6), two by Justus Jonas (nos. 4 and 5), and one by Johann Walther (no. 7); in this form it appeared in the hymn-books of Bach's time. The unknown librettist has retained the first strophe for the opening chorus, interspersed the third with free poetic text (set as recitative in movement 3), and run together the last two for the final movement; the other strophes have been paraphrased for recitative and arias. The cantata calls on God to destroy his enemies and bring peace and salvation to his people.

Even among the jewels of Bach's second cantata cycle (1724–5), the opening chorus of no. 126 shines brightly, if more briefly than in some other works. The chorale tune is set as a soprano cantus firmus, as usual, with the other three voices adding contrapuntal comment, and the instruments (trumpet, two oboes, strings, and continuo) busying themselves with independent ritornello material. The frequent return of the opening four-note trumpet figure (foreshadowing the chorale melody), as well as long-held notes for both the trumpet and the voices, ensure that the words 'Sustain us, Lord' are kept constantly in mind.

The tenor aria 'Sende deine Macht' (no. 2), in a modified da capo form, is accompanied by the two oboes and continuo. The word 'erfreuen' ('to rejoice') and its cognate forms rarely fail to elicit special treatment in Bach's vocal works, and the elaborate melisma which clothes the word here sparkles with 'staccato' semiquavers and roulades of demisemiquavers (bars 34–5), but even this is outshone by the still longer and more elaborate melisma on its rhyme, 'zertreuen' ('to scatter'), which stretches over four and a half bars (39–43). In the other aria (no. 4) the bass is partnered only by the continuo instruments, but the music is no less striking for its forthright leaps in the voice part and its rapid downward scales in the accompaniment, both suggestive of the retribution to be inflicted on the arrogant opponents of Christ.

After a brief tenor recitative, the cantata ends with the four-part chorale combining Luther's *Verleih uns Frieden gnädlich* (1531) and Walther's *Gib unsern Fürsten und aller Obrigkeit* (1566). The first two lines of the melody are virtually identical to those of the chorale used in movements 1 and 3, but the remaining 12 lines are heard here for the first time.

For bibliography, *see* CANTATA, §1.

***Erhöhtes Fleisch und Blut*** ('Exalted flesh and blood'). Cantata for Whit Monday, BWV173. It was probably first performed on 29 May 1724, but Bach may have had it ready for performance in 1723, shortly before he took over his new Leipzig duties.

Strictly speaking, the original sources of *Erhöhtes Fleisch und Blut* exist only from later times. The whole cantata is a parody of the Cöthen cantata DURCHLAUCHTSTER LEOPOLD (1720/2). Bach merely inserted the new text— praising God's goodness towards humankind, with references to the Epistle and Gospel for the day—into the existing score (and, perhaps, into the old parts, too, but they are not extant). But he did not reuse the entire congratulatory cantata; he omitted the sixth and seventh of the original eight movements. It was not until 1728–30 that he commissioned the copyist Christian Gottlob Meißner to make a new fair copy of the work.

The main musical difference between the secular Cöthen and the sacred Leipzig cantata is the vocal scoring. While Bach maintained the keys of the movements and the instrumental layout of two flutes, strings, and continuo, he enlarged the number of soloists from the original two (soprano and bass) to a complete quartet and transformed the original final duet into a chorus. The first two movements, previously for soprano, were allotted to the tenor: the recitative 'Durchlauchtster Leopold' became 'Erhöhtes Fleisch und Blut', and the aria 'Güldner Sonnen frohe Stunden', with its fashionable music, became 'Ein geheiligtes Gemüte'. By a reverse process of transposition the bass aria 'Leopolds Vortrefflichkeiten' became 'Gott will, o ihr Menschenkinder' an octave higher for the alto. The duet for soprano and bass was left unaltered, but the text now quoted from the Gospel for Whit Monday, 'So hat Gott die Welt geliebt' ('God so loved the world'; John 3: 16). Minor changes were necessary to alter the succeeding recitative from an expression of homage to a prince (for soprano and bass) into one of homage to God (for soprano and tenor). The transformation of the final homophonic duet into a chorus demanded only the introduction of two inner voices into a clearly organized harmonic construction. KK

For bibliography, *see* CANTATA, §1.

**Ernesti, Johann August** (b. 4 Aug. 1707; d. 11 Sept. 1781). Theologian, writer, and teacher, born in Tennstedt, Thuringia. He studied at Wittenberg University from 1726, and then at Leipzig University, where he took a master's degree in 1730. In 1731 he was appointed co-Rector at the Thomasschule, and in 1734 he succeeded J. M. Gesner as Rector. In 1759 he was appointed professor of theology at Leipzig University, where he remained until his death.

Unlike his two predecessors at the Thomasschule, Ernesti showed no liking for music, but despite this he and Bach seem to have got on reasonably well at first. Bach composed the cantata *Thomana saß annoch betrübt*, BWV Anh. I 19, for Ernesti's installation (the music is lost), and Ernesti acted as godfather to Bach's last two sons in 1733 and 1735. But the two men were soon at loggerheads, ostensibly over the appointment of prefects at the school, though their differences sprang from irreconcilably opposed views on what constituted a liberal education, and particularly on the place of music in the curriculum.

**Ernesti, Johann Heinrich** (b. 12 March 1652; d. 16 Oct. 1729). Theologian and teacher, born in Königsfeld, near Rochlitz in Saxony. He studied theology and philosophy at Leipzig University and was appointed co-Rector at the Thomasschule in 1680, and Rector in 1684. He was over 70 years old when Bach was appointed Kantor in 1723, and had allowed the school to decline in both numbers and reputation, but Bach had no personal quarrels with him. Ernesti's wife and daughter acted on different occasions as godmother to two of Bach's children, and for Ernesti's funeral Bach composed one of his finest motets, *Der Geist hilft unser Schwachheit auf.*

**Ernst August,** Duke of Saxe-Weimar (b. 19 April 1688; d. 19 Jan. 1748). He was the son of Duke Johann Ernst II (1664–1707) who reigned jointly in Weimar with his elder brother WILHELM ERNST from 1685 (see family tree). A family law of 1629 stipulated that there should be joint rulers in Weimar, and therefore when Ernst August reached his majority in 1709 he reigned jointly with his uncle. He lived outside the elder duke's castle, the Wilhelmsburg, in the Rotes Schloß (Red Castle), which communicated with the main residence through a covered gallery. Although employed by Wilhelm Ernst, Bach took part in music-making at the less puritanical Red Castle, much to the elder duke's dissatisfaction. To mark Ernst August's birthday in 1716 Bach performed the secular cantata *Was mir behagt, ist nur die muntre Jagd,* originally composed for Duke Christian of Weißenfels three years earlier.

E. Wülcker, 'Johann Ernst', in *Allgemeine deutsche Biographie,* xiv (Leipzig, 1881), 360–4.

**Ernst Ludwig,** Duke of Saxe-Meiningen (b. 7 Oct. 1672; d. 22 March 1724). Soldier and ruler, born in Gotha, Thuringia. He served in the imperial army in high military ranks, reigned over the Duchy of Saxe-Meiningen from 1706, and died in Rome. He made a collection of French and German poems (writing some of them himself), wrote sermons and the text of his funeral music (composed by Johann Ludwig Bach), and is said to have written two cycles of church cantata texts. Literary and historical evidence suggests that one of these might be the cycle from which Bach drew in composing Cantatas 17, 39, 43, 45, 88, 102, and 187. The texts were written by 1704 at the latest, when they were set to music by Ernst Ludwig's *Kapellmeister,* Georg Caspar Schürmann (1672/3–1751). With their inclusion of 'madrigalian' verse for recitatives and arias, they anticipate the so-called reform cantatas of Erdmann NEUMEISTER, which were written only some years later. Thus the duke played an important role in

the invention of this new type of cantata, perhaps even as its creator.  KK

K. Küster, 'Meininger Kantatentexte um Johann Ludwig Bach', *BJb* 73 (1987), 159–64.

***Er rufet seinen Schafen mit Namen*** ('He calleth his own sheep by name'). Cantata, BWV175, for the third day of Pentecost (Whit Tuesday), first performed on 22 May 1725. It is notable for the rare use of three recorders in the two opening movements and the final chorale; these lend the cantata a pastoral quality appropriate to its text.

This was Bach's eighth cantata to a text by Mariane von Ziegler; like the sixth and seventh, for the two preceding days of Pentecost (BWV74 and 68), it is in part a parody of previously existing works. The text incorporates two New Testament verses, both from the Gospel of the day (the parable of the good shepherd).

The opening movement, a brief tenor recitative, suggests a quiet affect commensurate with its text (from John 10: 3) through its initial tonic pedal point in the continuo and the recorders' flowing accompaniment. The latter, however, was an afterthought; Bach initially wrote simple sustained chords for the three recorders. The following alto aria, in modified da capo form, is scored for the same instruments and adopts the gentle rhythm of a pastorale, yet it emphasizes yearning (for 'green pastures') through the expressive chromatic lines of all five parts.

A short tenor recitative leads to a tenor aria with violoncello piccolo. As in the previous day's cantata (no. 68), the movement employing this instrument is a parody; an earlier version (using ordinary cello) occurs in the Cöthen cantata *Durchlauchtster Leopold,* written for Prince Leopold's birthday on 10 December, probably in 1720 or 1722. To accommodate the present lengthy text, Bach took the unusual step of fitting lines 3 and 4 to a repetition of the first section of the original aria. The remaining lines were distributed over the two concluding sections; the vocal part had to be rewritten where the prince's name was mentioned, but the two instrumental parts were virtually unchanged. A second recitative opens with verse 6 from St John 10 ('they understood not'),

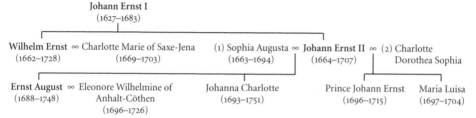

Johann Ernst I
(1627–1683)

Wilhelm Ernst ∞ Charlotte Marie of Saxe-Jena    (1) Sophia Augusta ∞ Johann Ernst II ∞ (2) Charlotte
(1662–1728)        (1669–1703)                    (1663–1694)         (1664–1707)      Dorothea Sophia

Ernst August ∞ Eleonore Wilhelmine of        Johanna Charlotte        Prince Johann Ernst    Maria Luisa
(1688–1748)      Anhalt-Cöthen                 (1693–1751)             (1696–1715)            (1697–1704)
                 (1696–1726)

[Dukes of Saxe-Weimar are shown in **bold**; family members who died before the age of two have been omitted]

sung by the alto in simple recitative; the bass then presents Ziegler's commentary with string accompaniment. A third aria, for bass with two trumpets and continuo, follows; the scoring, unusual for Bach, represents a compromise between the gentle character of the cantata as a whole and the requirements of the present text ('Open your ears'). (Among Bach's other works, only Cantata 59 uses a pair of trumpets, in that case with timpani; normally Bach wrote for either one or three trumpets.)

The trumpets are absent from the B section of this da capo aria and from the final chorale, a setting of the melody *Komm, heiliger Geist*. This was taken from Cantata 59; the recorders take over the partly independent string parts of the original, and the new text is strophe 9 of Johann Rist's poem *O Gottes Geist, mein Trost und Rath* (1651).

DS

For bibliography, *see* CANTATA, §1.

**Erschallet, ihr Lieder** ('Ring out, ye songs'). Cantata for Whit Sunday (Pentecost), BWV172, first performed at Weimar on 20 May 1714. In later performances at Leipzig (in 1724, 1731, and again some time thereafter) the work was given in revised versions. The third of the cantatas that Bach composed as *Konzertmeister* at Weimar, it is notable for the brilliant trumpet writing of the first two aria movements and the intricate combination of dialogue with chorale cantus firmus in the penultimate duet.

The text, probably by Salomo Franck, is similar in form to that in each of Bach's two preceding church compositions. Bach again employs a four-part string choir (two violins, two violas), here joined by a brass choir of three trumpets and timpani and a 'Fagotto' (*Chorton* bassoon) serving as bass of the string choir. The surviving Weimar parts (in C major) include a cello, but this doubles the organ continuo and thus is not part of the string choir as such.

The loss of the autograph score and of many of the manuscript parts prepared for the various performances makes it difficult to ascertain the form in which the work was performed on each occasion, especially at Weimar. Clearly, however, differences in local pitch standards and notational conventions led to revisions that placed the instrumental parts in D major when the work was first performed at Leipzig. Evidently, however, this made some of the parts too high, and for subsequent performances (1731 and later) Bach prepared a new version with vocal and instrumental parts notated in C. For the 1731 performance he also eliminated the repetition of the first movement at the end of the work.

It is uncertain what instrument originally played the chorale cantus firmus in the fifth movement. This was assigned at successive Leipzig performances to oboe d'amore, then (presumably) regular oboe, and finally organ. The organ also took over the bass line, originally entrusted to the cello alone (without keyboard doubling); hence the movement became a trio for two voices and obbligato organ.

The *BG* edition conflates the versions of 1714 and 1731 (the organ version of the duet is given in small type); the *NBA* gives the versions of 1724 and 1731 separately (designated 'D major' and 'C major'), with the later organ scoring of the last aria appearing as an 'ossia' in the C major version.

The grand scoring of the first movement reflects the day's festive character in the Church calendar. This choral aria is in da capo form, like the opening vocal movements of the two previous cantatas, but its A section is now a fully-fledged ritornello structure (the presence of an opening ritornello perhaps explains the absence of a separate instrumental opening movement).

The second movement, a bass recitative, broadens into arioso for the final clause of the text (John 15: 23). This introduces a bass aria in an irregular da capo form, brilliantly scored for three trumpets representing the text's 'heiligste Dreieinigkeit' ('most holy Trinity'); its main motif alludes to a FANFARE THEME found several times in Bach's music. The ensuing tenor aria is in a more orthodox da capo form; as in the opening movement, its A section is composed largely through VOKALEINBAU, the lyrical tenor line combining with a more flowing ritornello theme in the violin. The minor mode presumably expresses desire for, as opposed to attainment of, the text's 'Seelenparadies' ('spiritual paradise').

The duet follows the pattern of other movements in Bach's Weimar cantatas that combine an aria text with an instrumental chorale cantus firmus. But here the aria text takes the form of a dialogue between the Holy Spirit and a believing Soul, represented by alto and soprano; the chorale is Luther's *Komm, heiliger Geist*. The fitting of the chorale against the three stanzas of the aria required free treatment of the melody, which is embellished and rhythmically altered, and its central portion omitted. Moreover, the sense of dialogue is diminished by the fact that the two voices simultaneously present their texts; nevertheless the multi-layered conception of the movement is remarkable.

The five-part chorale movement that closes the work in the latest version is a setting of the melody and fourth strophe of Philip Nicolai's *Wie schön leuchtet der Morgenstern*.

DS

For bibliography, *see* CANTATA, §1.

***Erwünschtes Freudenlicht*** ('Longed-for light of joy'). Cantata for the third day of Pentecost, BWV184, first performed at Leipzig on 30 May 1724 and repeated there in 1731. It is a parody of a secular cantata composed at Cöthen, of which the text is lost and only a few instrumental parts survive among the Leipzig performing material. The main structural difference between the two works is that the penultimate movement of the Cöthen version, a recitative, has been replaced by a plainly harmonized setting of the eighth strophe from Anarg von Wildenfels's hymn *O Herre Gott, dein göttlich Wort* (1526). The anonymous librettist has fitted a new text which relates to the Gospel reading for the day, St John 10: 1–10, telling of Jesus as the good shepherd. The music has a distinctly pastoral character, enhanced by the instrumentation of two flutes, strings, and continuo, and possibly the original text was bucolic.

Cantata 184 betrays its Cöthen origins in other ways, too, for example in the emphasis placed on duet writing and in the dance-like character of much of the music. Also, like several other works of Cöthen origin, it begins not with a chorus or instrumental prelude but with recitative, in this case introduced by a triplet figure on the two flutes which persists throughout, mainly in 3rds and 6ths, except for eight bars of continuo-accompanied arioso towards the end. The duet for soprano and alto that follows is typical of the Cöthen period in the generous proportions of its da capo form and length of its ritornellos, which rather suggests that dancing may have played a part when such works were performed before Prince Leopold. The tenor aria 'Glück und Segen sind bereit' with violin obbligato, though less attractive on its own account, fits perhaps more easily into its new context; it uses the modified da capo structure (A–B–A') that Bach made largely his own in his mature vocal works.

After the chorale (no. 5), the bucolic, open-air atmosphere is resumed in a final chorus—a gavotte in all but name—which seems to have been adapted from a soprano and bass duet, and in fact alto and tenor sing in only 24 of its 94 bars (including the repeat of the A section).

For bibliography, *see* CANTATA, §1.

***Es erhub sich ein Streit*** ('There was war'). Cantata, BWV19, for the feast of St Michael and All Angels (29 September), first performed in Leipzig in 1726.

The vividly pictorial account in Revelation 12: 7–12 of the battle which 'Michael and his angels fought against the dragon [Satan]' has inspired both painters and poets. It also inspired two musicians, both of them members of the Bach family: Johann Christoph (i) and Johann Sebastian. In a

letter to J. N. Forkel dated 20 September 1775, Bach's son Carl Philipp Emanuel wrote of Johann Christoph's cantata *Es erhub sich ein Streit*: 'This composition in 22 parts is a masterpiece. My blessed father performed it once in a church at Leipzig and everybody was surprised by the effect it made.' It is possible that Sebastian Bach's own cantata, partly drawing on the same biblical text, was influenced by that of his illustrious forebear, although his performance of the latter may not have taken place until much later (see D. Melamed, *J. S. Bach and the German Motet* (Cambridge, 1995), 186–8).

*Es erhub sich ein Streit* is the second of three complete surviving cantatas that Bach wrote for the feast of St Michael. The text is an adaptation, by an unknown hand, of a poem published the previous year in Picander's *Sammlung Erbaulicher Gedancken*. The story of the encounter between St Michael and Satan, and the subsequent triumph of good over evil, appealed to the 18th-century mind. The imagery is splendid, inspiring Bach, each time he dealt with the subject (in BWV19, 50, 130, and 149), to respond with music of striking originality.

Nowhere is this more evident than in the opening C major chorus of the present work, scored for three trumpets, drums, two oboes doubling the violin parts, an oboe da caccia (*taille*) doubling the viola, and basso continuo. In this great fugal da capo movement Bach illustrates the conflict between heaven and hell with sustained rhythmic tension and a confrontational vigour which is almost startling in its ferocity. Sometimes the instruments are used thematically, but by and large their function is to provide colour and to deepen images of the battlefield already firmly imprinted by the rhythmic vitality of the four-part vocal writing.

This dramatically charged chorus is followed by a simple recitative (bass) in which the outcome of the battle in favour of the archangel Michael is declared. It leads to an aria for soprano with two oboes d'amore and continuo. Images of the recent encounter linger, but this aria, with its gently imitative writing for voice and instruments, is concerned with the protection offered to humanity by the angelic host. An accompanied tenor recitative also focuses on heavenly protection, and is followed by a lyrical but technically demanding tenor aria in E minor, in the rhythm of a siciliana. Into this movement, containing a plea for heavenly guidance, Bach skilfully introduces a chorale tune: a single trumpet penetrates at intervals the warmly textured string accompaniment with Martin Schalling's melody (1571) associated with the late 17th-century hymn *Herzlich lieb hab ich*

## Es ist das Heil uns kommen her

*dich, o Herr.* Both the hymn and its melody were closely linked with the St Michael's Day worship.

A brief soprano recitative offers praise to the angelic host and the cantata ends with a verse from the early 17th-century hymn *Freu dich sehr, o meine Seele.* Its melody is resonantly harmonized by Bach, who once more introduces the full instrumental arsenal heard in the opening chorus.

NA

For bibliography, *see* CANTATA, §1.

***Es ist das Heil uns kommen her*** ('Salvation has come to us here'). Cantata for the sixth Sunday after Trinity, BWV9, dating from the first half of the 1730s. The text draws on a hymn by Paul Speratus first published in 1523/4.

In textual organization and musical execution *Es ist das Heil uns kommen her* clearly resembles the cantatas of the second annual cycle that Bach composed in Leipzig in 1724–5, and indeed the transmission of its original sources shows that Bach considered it part of that cycle. But the composing score and original performing parts point clearly to a date of composition in the 1730s, indicating that the work was a late addition to the *Jahrgang.* We know why. Bach and his wife were away from Leipzig for the sixth Sunday after Trinity in 1724 (16 July); they were paid on 18 July for a musical performance in Cöthen, though the occasion and identity of the music are unknown. Bach prepared no new cantata for that week, but a decade later he filled this gap in the CHORALE CANTATA cycle with BWV9.

Like all the cantatas from the chorale cycle, BWV9 draws the text of its seven movements from the strophes of a hymn. As is typical, the first and last movements of the cantata use complete stanzas; here the last movement uses stanza 12 (of 14) rather than the usual last strophe (the 13th and 14th stanzas of this hymn are metrical versions of the doxology and the Lord's Prayer). The internal movements of the cantata, alternating recitatives and arias, are derived from the middle stanzas of the hymn. The recitative no. 2 paraphrases portions of stanzas 2, 3, and 4; the aria no. 3 atypically is not derived directly from the chorale; the recitative no. 4 draws on stanzas 5, 6, and 7; the duet no. 5 paraphrases stanzas 8 and 10; and the recitative no. 6 is based on stanzas 9 and 11.

Speratus's hymn, from the earliest years of the Reformation, deals with God's law and the necessity of strong belief in the redeeming power of Jesus's death ('justification by faith'). The cantata addresses these themes, along with ideas from the Gospel for the day (Matt. 5: 20–6, on the Christian way to fulfil the law) and the Epistle (Rom. 6: 3–11, on the belief in freedom from sin through the Crucifixion).

The first movement is cast as an instrumental concerto featuring two solo woodwinds, with strings mostly in the role of the ripieno. The instruments provide opening, closing, and intermediate ritornellos for the presentation of the chorale phrases in long notes in the soprano. The lower voices enter after the soprano, in imitation of each other but with material not related to the chorale phrases they support. The last movement also uses the chorale melody, in a four-part cantional-style setting with instruments doubling the vocal lines.

The first of the two arias, for tenor with violin obbligato, presents its anguished text in a particularly tortured melodic line. The second aria is a duet with a duet obbligato for woodwinds. In the outer sections of this da capo piece the instruments are treated imitatively in the ritornello, anticipating imitation in the voices, and leading to some four-part textures. In the middle section the instruments double the voices (or, more precisely perhaps, 'shadow' them) for a strong textural contrast.

The recitatives are all of the simple type, accompanied by continuo only. The second of them was originally composed for alto, but Bach transposed it down an octave for bass, unusually assigning all three recitatives to this voice. This is probably a reflection of the traditional association of the bass voice with the persona of God, whose law and its fulfilment are the topics of the recitative texts.

There are a few unusual features of Bach's original performing parts for this cantata. The violin obbligato in movement 3 was possibly played by a soloist in a later performance of the work, but none of the other surviving violin parts contains an instruction not to play. The original organ part omits movements 2, 3, 4, and 6 (three recitatives and the solo aria); they were added to the part only for a later performance. A continuo realization was presumably provided some other way, perhaps on a harpsichord, resulting in a timbral contrast between two groups of movements.

DRM

For bibliography, *see* CANTATA, §1.

***Es ist dir gesagt, Mensch, was gut ist*** ('He hath shewed thee, O man, what is good'). Cantata, BWV45, which Bach produced on 11 August 1726 for the eighth Sunday after Trinity. Thus it belongs to his third annual cycle (1725–7) which contains cantatas treated in a variety of ways. The text, according to *DürrK*, may be the work of a writer from Meiningen since the structure resembles those sometimes used by his cousin Johann Ludwig Bach, who was *Kapellmeister* at Meiningen from 1711 until his death in 1731 (*see* ERNST

LUDWIG). In 1726 Bach performed no fewer than 18 of Johann Ludwig's cantatas at Leipzig, and he repeated some of them in later years. The text of the present cantata is one of seven which he set and performed in 1726 from a Rudolstadt textbook, printed in the same year.

Some commentators, among them W. G. Whittaker (*The Cantatas of Johann Sebastian Bach* (Oxford, 1959), ii. 195), have been ungenerous in their assessment of this work. 'In spite of much fine music', Whittaker remarked, '[it] lacks the qualities which are needed to make it one of those cantatas to which we are attracted again and again. The libretto is cold and wanting in imagery, though not devoid of skill.' Nothing could be further from the truth, as Bach unfailingly demonstrates in each and every section of this subtly conceived and powerfully declamatory work.

The opening movement of the cantata is an architecturally complex but magnificent concertante piece in the form of a choral fugue for four-part chorus with pairs of flutes and oboes, strings and continuo. The text focuses on Micah 6: 8, which reminds man of his duty towards God. The brightly coloured key of E major, the frequently reiterated opening words, 'Es ist dir gesagt', and Bach's supple vocal writing contribute to the joyful affirmation of this vigorously declaimed music, in which an older MOTET STYLE is blended with concerto writing of consummate skill.

The unaccompanied tenor recitative underlines the stern yet compassionate teaching of the previous movement, leading to a tenor aria in C♯ minor with strings and continuo. The robust character of this richly textured aria, together with its dance-like 3/8 rhythm, somewhat alleviates the textual severity in which man is warned to prepare himself for the day of reckoning.

Like the other six cantatas from the Rudolstadt textbook, this one is in two sections. Part 2, which would have been sung during Communion, after the sermon and the words of institution (*see* HAUPTGOTTESDIENST), begins with a vividly dramatic A major bass arioso with strings and continuo. This is a setting of St Matthew 7: 22–3, part of the Sermon on the Mount in which Christ vigorously denounces false prophets and those who claim to have worked miracles in his name. Although termed an arioso (a means Bach used to distinguish the *vox Christi* from passages of indirect speech, though he did not usually label it so), the structure is that of a complex aria containing elements of canon, ostinato, and sequence. Its musical gestures breathe the air of the opera house, but we may wonder what Bach's Leipzig congregation made of its stern message delivered in such declamatory, theatrical terms.

The gentle, intimately addressed da capo aria for alto with flute obbligato and continuo which follows provides an effective contrast, both of key (F♯ minor) and spirit. In it man is urged to be God-fearing and to serve him faithfully; this teaching is extended to the alto recitative which leads to the concluding chorale. It is a verse of the hymn *O Gott, du frommer Gott* by Johann Heermann (1630), whose associated melody is straightforwardly harmonized by Bach. Günther Stiller (*Johann Sebastian Bach and Liturgical Life in Leipzig*, trans. H. J. A. Bouman, D. F. Poellot, and H. C. Oswald, ed. R. A. Leaver (St Louis, Miss., 1984), 243) has noted that this hymn was designated for the ninth Sunday after Trinity, rather than the eighth, in the Dresden hymn schedules then in use at Leipzig.                    NA

For bibliography, *see* CANTATA, §1.

***Es ist ein trotzig und versagt Ding*** ('The heart is deceitful above all things'). Cantata for Trinity Sunday, BWV176, first performed on 27 May 1725. The last of nine works on texts by Christiane Mariane von Ziegler, it marked the completion of Bach's second year of cantata composition at Leipzig. One of his shortest cantatas, it was his last completed work prior to his apparent cessation of regular cantata composition.

The opening biblical quotation (Jer. 17: 9) is set as a four-part choral fugue. The verse is too brief to be divided between subject and countersubject but, although it might seem to have presented little musical potential, the contrasting affects suggested by its two adjectives are exploited within the subject. This is divided into a lively triadic portion, with a rising melisma on 'trotzig' ('spiteful'), and a quiet chromatic phrase for 'verzagt' ('despairing'). This division is paralleled in the accompanying strings, which throughout the movement present their own countersubject; the latter opens with a vigorous idea reminiscent of the Fifth Brandenburg Concerto, but this gives way to sustained chords that Bach marked *piano* in the original parts. The top three vocal parts are doubled by two oboes and *taille*. The form is unusual for a Bach choral fugue: two and a half expositions (without ritornellos), each beginning with a bass entry in the tonic (C minor); new counterpoint is added in the second exposition.

A recitative for alto leads to a soprano aria in A–B–B′ form. The text of both movements refers to Jesus's teaching to Nicodemus, subject of the Gospel for the day (John 3: 1–15). The aria sports an easy-going gavotte rhythm, befitting the text's reference to 'unclouded brightness'. *Figura corte* motifs (quaver plus two semiquavers, also found in the Gavotte of the fourth Orchestral Suite) dominate the first half of the ritornello and of the aria as a whole, but these are replaced by flowing triplets in the second half of each.

Another recitative, for bass, concludes with a long arioso setting a Gospel text (John 3: 16). The text is not found in Ziegler's published libretto and is presumed to be Bach's addition. Several expressive melismas dominated by turning motifs emphasize the word 'verloren' ('lost').

The concluding alto aria is in a through-composed three-part form. Odd chromatic appoggiaturas in the ritornello and first vocal section represent the fear and 'shuddering' expressed in the first section. This music recurs in the instrumental accompaniment during the final section, by which point, however, the voice has turned to jubilant diatonic melismas on 'Loben' ('glorification') and 'preisen' ('praise'). These are addressed to the Trinity, represented in the original instrumentation for the three double reeds in unison, but Bach later eliminated the two oboes, leaving only oboe da caccia.

The work ends with a four-part setting of strophe 8 of Paul Gebhart's *Was alle Weisheit in der Welt*, sung to the tune *Christ unser Herr zum Jordan kam*. Bach's harmonization of the tonally ambiguous melody effects a transition from the E♭ major of the previous aria to a C minor conclusion concordant with the opening chorus.　　DS

For bibliography, *see* CANTATA, §1.

***Es ist euch gut, daß ich hingehe*** ('It is expedient for you that I go away'). Cantata for the fourth Sunday after Easter (Cantate), BWV108. Bach concluded his great second cycle of sacred cantatas (1724–5) with an unbroken sequence of nine works set to texts by the Leipzig poet and gifted amateur musician Christiane Mariane von Ziegler. In each of these Bach departed from the concept of the chorale-based cantata with its unifying theme, which characterized the cycle as a whole, reverting to the more heterogeneous patterns of the previous Leipzig cycle. Ziegler included the nine texts in her first published collection of verse, *Versuch in gebundener Schreib-Art* (1728), but the many differences which occur between her verses and those of the actual cantatas suggest that Bach himself may have adjusted them to his particular needs.

This is the second of the Ziegler texts which Bach set; the work was first performed at Leipzig on 29 April 1725. The words are closely associated with the appointed Gospel reading for the day, St John 16: 5–15. In the opening movement the bass voice assumes the role of Christ with a passage of direct speech (John 16: 7). Both the key (A major) and the choice of oboe d'amore as obbligato instrument, with four-part string support, suffuse this piece with radiance, though its dance-like

character is counterbalanced by expressive intensity and melismas in the vocal writing. The movement is an aria in all but name; following a customary procedure in solos containing passages of biblical direct speech, Bach omitted any specific designation.

The tenor aria, taking us into the relative key of F♯ minor, is a response to the words of Christ heard in the preceding movement. The voice is accompanied by a violin obbligato, wide-ranging and with affecting melodic contours over an ostinato bass figure. In this lyrically conceived movement Bach skilfully focuses attention on significant words in the text. One of these occurs in its second section where, entering the key of A major, 'glaube' ('trust') is given emphasis in sustained notes, first over three bars and then over two. Intimate and fervent responses to the text such as this afford Bach's settings of Ziegler's poetry a special place in his legacy of sacred cantatas.

A brief unaccompanied recitative, also for tenor, leads to an energetic choral Vivace in which verse 13 of the Gospel is declaimed in the manner of a fugal motet, with two violins (each doubled by an oboe d'amore) and viola contributing to the contrapuntal texture. The tripartite structure accommodates three fugues, the first of which is striking in its originality and affirmative in its declaration of the faith.

The third and final aria is for alto, strings, and continuo with the first violins playing a prominent role. Once again Bach shows inspired examples of his skill in word-painting in a movement which serves to consolidate the textual message of the Gospel. The cantata ends with a four-part setting of the tenth strophe of Paul Gerhardt's hymn *Gott Vater, sende deinen Geist* (1653) to the melody *Kommt her zu mir, spricht Gottes Sohn*. Although an Ascension hymn, it was nevertheless assigned to the fourth Sunday after Easter in the Dresden hymn-books in use at Leipzig at the time.　　NA

For bibliography, *see* CANTATA, §1.

***Es ist nichts Gesundes an meinem Leibe*** ('There is no health in my flesh'). Cantata for the 14th Sunday after Trinity, BWV25, first performed in Leipzig on 29 August 1723. The anonymous text takes as its point of departure the Gospel reading for the day, the story of the healing of ten lepers (Luke 17: 11–19). Their disease is likened to human weaknesses such as lust, pride, and greed, which are the stains of original sin (movement 2). Continuing the line of questioning initiated at the end of this movement, the bass aria (movement 3) asks where help can be found, then supplies the obvious answer: Jesus, the great physician, 'weist die beste Seelenkur' ('knows the best cure for the soul'). A passionate plea to Jesus for strength, mercy, and spiritual healing (movement 4) finally gives way to jubilant songs of praise and thanksgiving for answering this prayer (movements 5 and 6).

The moments of greatest musical interest are the opening chorus and the soprano aria. The opening chorus is a setting of Psalm 38: 3, in which the psalmist acknowledges his lack of health and peace. An ingenious double fugue is spun out, incorporating a chorale tune and utilizing an unusually large instrumental ensemble of two oboes, three recorders, and a choir of three trombones and cornett, in addition to the usual four-part chorus, strings, and continuo. In the introduction, and again in bars 21–4, the oboes and strings play a series of 'sighing' motifs while the first seven notes of the chorale are presented in long note values in the continuo. The first subject is presented and developed twice in passages that begin as canons between the upper two and lower two voices. When the second subject is introduced (bars 41 ff.), the continuo line breaks into an erratic passage in semiquavers, illustrating unrest: 'und ist kein Friede in meinen Gebeinen' ('and there is no peace in my bones'). In the final set of vocal entries both subjects are used simultaneously; the first is sung by the tenor and alto, the second by the soprano and bass. Meanwhile, throughout the movement a four-part harmonization of the chorale is presented by the trombone choir, one phrase at a time (the melody in the cornett part is reinforced by the recorders). Throughout this contrapuntal *tour de force*, by judicious use of chromaticism and harmonic instability, Bach conveys a vivid sense of the physical and spiritual sickness that are the subject of this work.

The next three movements—a tenor recitative, a bass aria, and a soprano recitative—are as remarkable for the modesty of their performing forces (all three are accompanied by continuo alone) as the opening chorus is for its sonic opulence. The bass aria (movement 3) is dominated by the theme first heard in the opening ritornello, which recurs throughout as a basso ostinato. This movement dispenses with da capo form in favour of a simple through-composed design, presumably because it is unnecessary to repeat the question posed at the beginning, 'Ach, wo hol ich Armer Rat?' ('Ah, where will this poor man find help?'), once Jesus is named as the solution.

In sharp contrast to the spare scoring of the preceding movements, the soprano aria (movement 5) calls for two instrumental choirs (strings and oboes, and recorders) that both alternate and collaborate. Its joyful and dance-like character accords with the believer's anticipation of participating with the angels in the heavenly choir. The final four-part chorale offers praise to God for his gracious aid.                                          SAC

For bibliography, *see* CANTATA, §1.

***Es reißet euch ein schrecklich Ende*** ('A dreadful end awaits you'). Cantata for the 25th Sunday after Trinity, BWV90. It belongs to Bach's first annual Leipzig cycle and was performed on 14 November 1723. The unidentified author of the powerful text took as his basis the appointed Epistle and Gospel, which speak of Christ's second coming. The attendant horror of the Last Judgement was a favoured theme among Baroque artists, and one which, as we can see in several other instances in the cantatas, evoked colourful responses in Bach's imagination.

The cantata begins with one of two da capo arias which, since there is no opening chorus, are its dominant features. It is scored for tenor with strings and continuo and is virtuoso in its writing both for first violins and for the voice. (The autograph score does not specify the instrumentation; oboes may have doubled the violins in this and other movements.) This is a stern aria whose textual warnings are conveyed by Bach in bold passages of chromaticism, wild, upward-swirling demisemiquaver runs in the first violin, vocal coloratura, and almost ferocious declamation.

An alto recitative vividly contrasts God's goodness with worldly ingratitude before we are confronted by the second aria. The robust, supple writing of the previous aria is comfortably matched in this bass aria, whose resonant virtuoso trumpet obbligato provides an additional brilliant dash of colour. Virtuosity penetrates almost every strand of the texture, with cascades of demisemiquavers, menacing passages of repeated semiquavers in the continuo, and, dominating all, the trumpet sounding warrior-like, threatening, and doom-laden calls. In short, Bach has conjured up a scene of dreadful horror, an unforgettable vision of God's anger.

A short tenor recitative anticipates heavenly victory over Satan's brood, and the cantata ends with a verse of Martin Moller's hymn *Nimm von uns, Herr, du treuer Gott* (1584). The melody, affectingly harmonized by Bach, is that which is associated with Luther's vernacular version of the Lord's Prayer, *Vater unser im Himmelreich* (1539).
                                                          NA

For bibliography, *see* CANTATA, §1.

**Estomihi.** In the CHURCH CALENDAR, the Sunday before Lent. It takes its name from the introit to the Mass for that day in the Latin rite, beginning 'Esto mihi in Deum protectorem'.

## Es wartet alles auf dich

*Es wartet alles auf dich* ('These wait all upon thee'). Cantata for the seventh Sunday after Trinity, BWV187, first performed on 4 August 1726. Like *Brich dem Hungrigen*, *Herr, deine Augen*, and others, the cantata is based on a text probably written by Duke ERNST LUDWIG of Saxe-Meiningen. Following the two biblical quotations (movements 1 and 4), the poet focuses on the Lord's power to appease the hunger of all creatures.

Like the other works from the same cycle, it begins with a large chorus (G minor) based on a passage from the Old Testament (Psalm 104: 27–8). Its first part (v. 27) is divided into three sections in imitative style, and serves as a kind of contrapuntal prelude to the main part of the movement, a fugue setting verse 28, 'wenn du ihnen gibest'. In the short third part Bach summarizes the whole movement both textually and musically. The chorus is followed by a recitative–aria pair typical of this type of cantata. The recitative is sung by the bass, the aria, in B♭ major, by the alto accompanied by strings and a single oboe. The aria is in modified da capo form: the music of part A (to the text 'Du Herr, du krönst allein das Jahr mit deinem Gut') leads from the tonic to the dominant, and the tonic is reached again only after the B section of the aria; the conclusion is a variant of the A section.

The cantata is one of several divided into two parts. The second part opens with a G minor movement for bass, unison violins, and continuo, a setting of St Matthew 6: 31–2. Bach formed an aria from it, divided into three sections, each framed by music from the opening ritornello. As in most of the other cantatas in this cycle, the next two movements form an aria–recitative pair. The E♭ major aria for soprano, solo oboe, and continuo consists of a slow 'introduction', 'Gott versorget alles Leben' ('God preserves all that live') followed by a lively second part, 'Weicht, ihr Sorgen' ('Sorrows vanish'). The following accompanied recitative is also for soprano. The final chorale sets two strophes of Hans Vogel's *Singen wir aus Herzensgrund* (1563).

When, in the 1730s, Bach wrote his four 'short' masses he parodied cantata movements for most of the music. Two of the seven Meiningen-type cantatas were of central importance for these works: Bach drew three times on *Herr, deine Augen* and four times on *Es wartet alles auf dich*. He could not, of course, transform the two recitatives and the final chorale into mass movements, but the opening chorus and the three arias offered him ideal possibilities for his parody technique. Almost the entire Gloria of the G minor *Missa* BWV235 is formed from them. After the opening chorus (based on Cantata 72, *Alles nur nach Gottes Willen*), the fourth movement of BWV187 became the 'Gratias agimus' (bass); 'Domine Fili' is a reworking of aria no. 3 (for alto, as in the cantata); the soprano aria (no. 5) was rescored for tenor (still in E♭ major)—the slow first half becoming 'Qui tollis peccata mundi, suscipe deprecationem nostram', and the fast second half 'Quoniam tu solus sanctus'; and, finally, all three parts of the chorus 'Es wartet alles auf dich' were taken over for 'Cum sancto spiritu'.                      KK

For bibliography, *see* CANTATA, §1.

**Exaudi.** In the CHURCH CALENDAR, the Sunday after Ascension. It takes its name from the introit to the Mass for that day in the Latin rite, beginning 'Exaudi Domine vocem meam'.

# F

**Faber.** The unknown dedicatee of Bach's seven-part canon, BWV1078, dated 1 March 1749. The name is spelt out in the four-note ostinato that accompanies the canon—F A B (= B♭) E (Repetatur)—and also (along with Bach's) in the Latin dedication itself: 'Domine possessor Fidelis Amici Beatum Esse Recordari, tibi haud ignotum: iatque Bonae Artis Cultorem Habeas verum amIcum Tuum' ('It can hardly be unknown to the honoured possessor that to recall a faithful friend means happiness; therefore take the cultivator of the good art as your true friend'). The letters I and T refer to Isenaco and Thuringum (Eisenach in Thuringia), Bach's birthplace.

The identity of 'Faber' is not known for certain, but he was obviously close to Bach. Among those who have been suggested as the canon's recipient are the printer and publisher Balthasar SCHMID and the theologian and writer Johann Michael SCHMIDT; 'Faber' is the Latin equivalent of the German 'Schmidt' ('smith').

> H. T. David and A. Mendel, eds., *The Bach Reader* (London, 1945, 2nd edn. 1966), 184 and 406–7; H.-J. Schulze, 'Johann Sebastian Bachs Kanonwidmungen', *BJb* 53 (1967), 82–92.

**Fagott.** German word for BASSOON.

**Falckenhagen, Adam** (b. 26 April 1697; d. 6 Oct. 1754). Lutenist and composer, born near Leipzig. By 1715 he was employed as a musician by the Dieskau family (*see* PEASANT CANTATA) in Merseburg. After attending Leipzig University (1719–20) and studying for a period with S. L. Weiß, he worked as a lute teacher and later as court musician at Weißenfels (1720–7); other court appointments, at Jena and Weimar (1729–32) followed, and in 1734 he joined the musicians of the Bayreuth court, where Margravine Wilhelmina, a sister of Frederick II of Prussia, was an expert lutenist.

Falckenhagen was one of the most distinguished of several lutenists associated with Bach; his own works, several of which were printed, range from simple *galant* pieces to difficult sonatas and concertos. Schulze's suggestion that Falckenhagen (or one of his Bayreuth colleagues) copied the tablature version of Bach's G minor Lute Suite BWV995 is strengthened by the fact that the notation consistently employs Falckenhagen's idiosyncratic system of ornament signs, or Man-ieren, otherwise seen only in his own music.

TTC

> *BDok* ii. 655, 698; H.-J. Schulze, '"Monsieur Schouster"—ein vergessener Zeitgenosse Johann Sebastian Bachs', in W. Rehm, ed., *Bachiana et alia musicologia: Festschrift Alfred Dürr zum 65. Geburtstag* (Kassel, 1983), 243–50; J. Domning, 'Der Lautenist Adam Falckenhagen', *Laute und Gitarre*, 5 (1983), 322–8.

***Falsche Welt, dir trau ich nicht*** ('False world, I trust you not'). Cantata for the 23rd Sunday after Trinity, BWV52. In common with several other cantatas of this period, and especially those for solo voice, it makes use of an earlier concerto movement as an introductory instrumental sinfonia. The work belongs to Bach's third Leipzig annual cycle (1725–7), and was first performed on 24 November 1726, the last Sunday of the liturgical year in this instance. The text, by an unidentified librettist, reflects on the comfort afforded by faith in Christ, while further denouncing the false and treacherous world referred to in its opening line. The cantata is for solo soprano, only the concluding chorale verse being sung by the choir.

The resonant opening sinfonia may at once be recognized in the more familiar context of Brandenburg Concerto no. 1 in F major, where it forms the first movement. Here the piece appears in an earlier version which, together with other movements that also found a place in the concerto, may have been connected with a birthday cantata, *Was mir behagt, ist nur die muntre Jagd*, performed by Bach for the Duke of Saxe-Weißenfels in about 1713 (a hypothesis regarding which many reservations have been expressed, however). The chief difference between the two versions lies in the reworking of the Brandenburg movement to include a violino piccolo. In the cantata the piece is scored for two horns, three oboes, strings, and continuo with bassoon.

The first vocal section of the cantata is an unaccompanied recitative leading to a D minor da capo aria accompanied by violins in two parts, and continuo with organ and bassoon. The text, austere at this point, portrays the soul beset by falsity and worldly hypocrisy, thus relating to the Gospel reading of the day, 'Then went the Pharisees, and took counsel how they might entangle him in his talk' (Matt. 22: 15).

The second recitative, which merges into arioso in its concluding four bars, and the ensuing aria are in strong contrast with the previous pair of movements, and are in the nature of a response to them, both celebrating and expressing confidence in Christ's benevolence. The aria, in 3/4 time and with the character of a polonaise, is an alluring piece whose light-hearted vocal line is accompanied by three oboes, bassoon, and continuo. Only Bach and Telemann, perhaps, fully realized the richly satisfying texture inherent in writing for three oboes. Alec Robertson (*The Church Cantatas of J. S. Bach* (London, 1972), 324) remarks on similarities between this aria and Cleopatra's 'V'adoro, pupille' in Handel's opera *Giulio Cesare*, first performed in London in 1724; Robertson suggests that Bach might have heard it in Hamburg, or have known it in some other way. Although tenuous, this hypothesis is not without interest; the present writer has often been struck by similarities which exist between the concluding trio of Bach's Coffee Cantata and the final *coro* of *Giulio Cesare*.

The cantata ends with the first strophe of a hymn by Adam Reusner, *In dich hab ich gehoffet, Herr* (1533). This is straightforwardly harmonized by Bach, who nevertheless provided independent parts for the two horns heard in the opening sinfonia, while requiring the three oboes, strings, and continuo to double the four vocal strands.    NA

For bibliography, *see* CANTATA, §1.

**fanfare theme** (Fanfarenthema). A term which has been used to refer to a theme found in several works by Bach. Ex. 1 shows it as it appears in Gavotte II from the first Orchestral Suite, and it is quoted in almost identical guise in the opening chorus of Cantata 70. Klaus Hofmann has identified the theme also in BWV20:8, 119:7, 127:4, 143:5, 214:3 and 7, 1046:1, and related works, sometimes in variant forms. He has located it also in works by other composers and has suggested that Bach used it as a symbol for worldly or divine authority. It is present also in BWV130:3 and 172:3, while its inclusion (in the form shown at Ex. 1) in Telemann's cantata *Die Tageszeiten* suggests a possible military origin, perhaps as a reveille call.

K. Hofmann, ' "Großer Herr, o starker König": ein Fanfarenthema bei Johann Sebastian Bach', *BJb* 81 (1995), 31–46; see also M. Boyd, 'Bach, Telemann und das Fanfarenthema', *BJb* 82 (1996), 147–50, and K. Hofmann, 'Nochmals: Bachs Fanfarenthema', *BJb* 83 (1997), 175–9.

**fantasia.** Bach used 'fantasia' with a somewhat unspecific meaning for a freely constructed piece, although the term could also encompass chorale-based compositions for organ. Extended chorale preludes on a large scale are occasionally entitled 'Fantasia' (e.g. BWV651, 695, 713, and 735), in which cases it implies a large-scale treatment with an improvisatory element and often fugal treatment of each line of the melody in turn. The word 'fantasia' could also be used as an alternative to 'prelude' in prelude-and-fugue pairings, often with the vagaries of different scribes playing a part in the casual variation of titles (BWV537 and 562). Bach himself also used the title for early versions of the three-part Inventions (*see* INVENTION). More characteristically, he used the word for a freely constructed keyboard piece with no specific form and often alluding to improvisation. The title is used for two such contrasted pieces as the CHROMATIC FANTASIA AND FUGUE and the C minor Fantasia (and incomplete fugue) BWV906, which is a movement in a distinctly advanced style incorporating crossed-hands effects and textures anticipating the *empfindsamer Stil* of pre-Classical composers.

The Bach canon also includes four uncoupled fantasias, BWV917–20, for keyboard. BWV917 in G minor (attribution dubious) opens with a very brief toccata-like flourish, but continues in the form of a single movement in three-part imitative texture based on a conventional chromatic subject. More unconventional in design is BWV918 in C minor, which is called *Fantaisie sur un Rondeau* in the principal manuscript source. It is a long, somewhat prolix movement in two-part counterpoint throughout. Despite the title, it is not in strict rondo form, though the opening section is recapitulated intact at the end of the movement and motifs from it form the basis of most of the development. The brittle textures, which recall the canons from *The Art of Fugue*, and the constant driving syncopations suggest that this is a late work. The C minor Fantasia BWV919 is a shorter work, also in two-part counterpoint and closely related in style to the two-part Inventions. The G minor Fantasia BWV920 (dubious) is a single movement in improvisatory style. There are arpeggio passages in the manner of the Chromatic Fantasia and Fugue, with some loosely woven fugal secions and toccata-like roulades, which

Ex. 1.

form the basis of the somewhat flimsy content of the movement. The rambling, vapid quality of the music, as well as the ineptitude of some of the part-writing, make the attribution to Bach (which is poorly attested) hard to credit.

In the organ works the use of the title 'fantasia' instead of 'praeludium' normally implies a free construction and an improvisatory character (although the title is not by any means always Bach's own). These elements are particularly marked in the G minor Fantasia and Fugue BWV542, in which the Fantasia features some of Bach's most adventurous chromatic modulations—a true counterpart to the Chromatic Fantasia and Fugue for harpsichord. There are several uncoupled fantasias for organ. BWV570, in C major, clearly an early work, is a short and somewhat uninspired essay in the style of Pachelbel, one of Bach's earliest models. More interesting, though still evidently early, is BWV571 in G major, a three-movement piece with a central Adagio in the relative minor; its final section uses a bell-like repeated bass figure as an ostinato. BWV572 in G major, entitled 'Pièce d'orgue' in the principal source, is also in three sections; it has French tempo markings (Très vitement–Gravement–Lentement) and a majestic central section in five-part writing which perhaps suggests Bach's contact with the music of French organists such as De Grigny. A tantalizing fragment is BWV573 in C major, a fine beginning to what promises to be a fully mature work but which breaks off after 12 bars.　　　　　DLH

D. Schulenberg, *The Keyboard Music of J. S. Bach* (New York, 1992); P. Williams, *The Organ Music of J. S. Bach*, i (Cambridge, 1980).

## Fasch, Johann Friedrich (b. 15 April 1688; d. 5 Dec. 1758). Composer, born in Buttelstedt, near Weimar. He was educated at the Thomasschule and the university in Leipzig, where he founded a collegium musicum in 1708; this functioned in parallel, and no doubt to some extent in rivalry, with the COLLEGIUM MUSICUM founded a few years earlier by Telemann and later directed by Bach. After brief periods of employment in various places, Fasch accepted in 1722 the post of court *Kapellmeister* in Zerbst, having been one of the unsuccessful applicants for the post of Thomaskantor in Leipzig. He remained in Zerbst for the rest of his life.

Fasch was a prolific and widely performed composer. He wrote 12 cantata cycles (i.e. over 700 works) and much other church music, as well as numerous orchestral suites (ouvertures) and concertos. Ouvertures by Fasch were apparently performed by the collegium musicum that Bach directed in Leipzig, though perhaps not by Bach

himself (see Glöckner), and the organ Trio in C minor BWV585, once thought to be a work by Bach and subsequently attributed to J. T. Krebs, is now known to be an arrangement of two movements from a trio sonata by Fasch.

A. Glöckner, 'Fasch-Ouvertüren aus Johann Sebastian Bachs Notenbibliothek?', *BJb* 76 (1990), 65–9.

## Feldhaus, Martin (bap. 9 Nov. 1634; d. 1 Nov. 1720). Councillor and man of property, born at Arnstadt, where he served as burgomaster. On 18 February 1679 he married Margarethe Wedemann, and the marriage brought him into contact with members of the Bach family: one of his wife's sisters, Maria Elisabetha, was married to Johann Christoph Bach (i) and another, Catharina, to Johann Michael Bach. Feldhaus was undoubtedly influential in securing J. S. Bach's appointment as organist at the Neue Kirche in Arnstadt in 1703, and it was probably as a lodger in one of Feldhaus's houses, 'Zur Goldenen Krone' or the 'Steinhaus', that Bach got to know his future wife Maria Barbara.

## *fiauto, fiauto d'echo* ('flute', 'echo flute'). According to Ulrich Prinz, in Bach's usage the terms 'Flauto', 'Flaute', 'Flauti', 'Flaut:', 'Fiauto', 'Fiaut.', 'Fiauti', 'Fiauti à bec', and 'Flöten à bec' always referred to the treble RECORDER. The 'Fiauto piccolo' in the earliest versions of Cantatas 8 and 96 is a sopranino recorder, that in Cantata 103 a sixth flute (descant recorder in D).

The identity of the two 'Fiauti d'Echo' that Bach mentioned in the title of the Fourth Brandenburg Concerto has been the subject of endless speculation. The instruments have a range of $f'$ to $g'''$, usually avoiding the high $f\sharp'''$, which was difficult to obtain on treble recorders. In the solo parts (for violin and *fiauti d'echo*) of the second movement Bach wrote $f$ (*forte*) in the tutti passages and $p$ (*piano*) in the echo-like solo passages. In the staff headings he designated the instruments simply 'Fiauto 1mo' and 'Fiauto 2do'.

There have been two general avenues of approach to the *fiauti d'echo*. First, that Bach had in mind instruments called 'echo flutes'—some size or sizes of the common instruments of the flute family (recorder, flageolet, or flute) or different from them in some special way. There was in fact an echo flute in Bach's day. The French theorist and pedagogue Étienne Loulié (1654–1702) made a puzzling reference to 'deux flûtes d'echo' in his *Éléments ou principes de musique* (Paris, 1696). The French expatriate recorder player James Paisible (*c*.1656–1721) played 'the echo flute', once even 'the small echo flute', in public concerts in London between 1713 and 1719. When Paisible died, however, the inventory of his possessions failed to list echo flutes, only recorders of various sizes. Perhaps the echo flute consisted of two recorders tied together. In 1668 the woodwind maker Samuel Drumbleby showed Samuel Pepys how to do that; and Sir John Hawkins reported that John Banister the younger (1662–1736), a close colleague of Paisible's, 'was famous for playing on two flutes [recorders] at once'.

The second avenue of approach to the *fiauti d'echo*—that Bach simply meant treble recorders and the appendage 'd'echo' referred to an echo effect, either literal or figurative—is better supported by contemporaneous evidence. An aria in *Il fiore delle eroine* (1704) by the Italian composer Giovanni Bononcini (1670–1747) is scored for '2 flauti' and '2 flauti eco'; the four instruments have an identical range (*a′* to *d′′′*), and the *flauti eco* imitate (perhaps offstage) the phrase endings of the normal recorder. As Michael Marissen has shown, there is no need for the instruments in the Fourth Brandenburg Concerto to play soft and loud. In Bach's notational practice the *f* and *p* markings indicated tutti and solo passages to the soloists, playing from parts with minimal rehearsal time. He concludes on this and other grounds that Bach meant a figurative echo.     DL

G. Goebel, 'New Evidence on the Echo Flute', *Galpin Society Journal*, 48 (1995), 205–7; D. Lasocki, 'Paisible's Echo Flute, Bononcini's Flauti Eco, and Bach's Fiauti d'Echo', *Galpin Society Journal*, 45 (1992), 59–66; M. Marissen, 'Organological Questions and their Significance in J. S. Bach's Fourth Brandenburg Concerto', *Journal of the American Musical Instrument Society*, 17 (1991), 5–52; J. Martin, F. Morgan, and M. Tattersall, 'Echoes Resounding', *The Recorder: Journal of the Victorian Recorder Guild*, 10 (1989), 19–24; U. Prinz, 'Studien zum Instrumentarium Johann Sebastian Bachs mit besonderer Berücksichtigung der Kantaten' (diss., University of Tübingen, 1979).

**'Fiddle'.** Nickname for the organ Fugue in D minor BWV539:2. It is an arrangement of the second movement of the Sonata in G minor for unaccompanied violin BWV1001.

**figural music.** A term originally used for contrapuntal music, as distinct from chant. In the context of Bach's music it is often used to refer to concerted music for voices and instruments (especially cantatas), as distinct from simple chorales. At Arnstadt Bach was more than once reprimanded for his unwillingness to rehearse the students there in figural music.

***Figurenlehre*** ('doctrine of [musical] figures'). The 'doctrine of musical figures' belongs to the terminology of early 20th-century scholars. It is a significant part of the general theory that Bach and his predecessors thought of musical composition and performance as analogous to the art of rhetoric.

Virtually anyone who was educated in a German Lateinschule would have learnt something of the ancient classical art of rhetoric. Moreover, German compositional theorists, from the time of Joachim Burmeister (1564–1629) onwards, used rhetorical analogies to describe how compositions worked, particularly in relation to verbal text. How much this analytical method became prescriptive and was actually followed by composers is moot; furthermore, there is little unanimity between theorists. They doubtlessly used rhetoric as a way of justifying music in terms of verbal text. It was no longer of use once the concept of autonomous, 'absolute' music took hold.

Figures relate to the embellishments orators use to make their speech more persuasive and elaborate. Just as a 'figure of speech' is a transgression of the usual linguistic conventions for rhetorical effect, so a musical figure is to some degree an exception to the most basic compositional procedure. However, one composer's exception is often likely to become another's rule, so that, by Bach's time, it is possible to see virtually every aspect of the musical texture as a figure. For example, the very presence of imitation could be described under a number of classical and pseudo-classical labels such as *repetitio* or *anaphora*; likewise simple melodic sequence. One particularly productive definition of figure stems from Christoph Bernhard (1628–92) who influenced Bach's cousin J. G. Walther: the association of figures with dissonance-treatment. Here the sense of 'transgression' is particularly appropriate.

J. G. Walther's description of 'Figura' in his *Lexicon* of 1732 seems to equate the idea of figure with motif. This is an eminently suitable usage for Bach, for whom the entire texture of the music involves the elaboration and integration of figures, a continual play between motifs which are no longer really exceptions but the very stuff of the composition. To some, a knowledge of the figures used and an awareness both of how the musical texture is put together and of the various levels of elaboration are important guides to the interpretation of the music in performance, which is, after all, the final goal of rhetoric.

Rhetoric is not to be confused with semantics. Rhetoric is used to make the oration persuasive, to drive home a meaning or emotion; it is not strictly the meaning itself. Thus the same figure can be used to underline entirely different verbal points, and *Figurenlehre* is therefore not the Baroque equivalent of the Wagnerian *Leitmotif*.

JAB

**fingerings.** The choices of which fingers are to play which notes. Fingerings are given in the manuscript sources of several keyboard pieces by Bach, but rarely if ever in the string music. When the manuscript is in another hand, one may wonder whose are the fingerings; but even those of a pupil might reflect the master's techniques and style of articulation and phrasing.

Ex. 1 is from the first piece Bach wrote down for his eldest son, Wilhelm Friedemann. D. G. Türk (1750–1813) later recalled how Friedemann in his maturity would play certain runs 'with astonishing velocity', using just the third and fourth fingers (3434 . . .). Bach's second son, Carl Philipp Emanuel, suggested in his *Essay on the True Manner of Playing Keyboard Instruments* that 1234 3434 might be smoother than 1231 2345 in a C major scale. Emanuel also said, however, that for his

father the thumb (1) was the 'chief finger'. The scale fingerings given in Emanuel's *Essay* (there is evidence from elsewhere that J. S. Bach never had his own pupils practise mere scales) suggest that this prominence of the thumb was due to its use not only to add profile to a line, as in Ex. 2 (from a piece by J. S. Bach written down on a sheet of Bach's paper by one of his best former pupils), and for inner parts, as in Ex. 3, but also for scale passages where the thumb is used just before or after a finger which plays a sharp or flat: thus (according to Emmanuel) 2132 1432 . . . for the left hand taking an A major scale up from *A*.

Ex. 4, from a manuscript in J. S. Bach's hand, is one of many available illustrations of a tendency to group notes within the bar rather than to connect by legato an upbeat group across the barline to the next downbeat. Bach here also avoided

Ex. 1. Applicatio ʙᴡᴠ994

Ex. 2. Prelude in C major ʙᴡᴠ870

Ex. 3. Prelude in C major ʙᴡᴠ870

Ex. 4. Prelude in G minor ʙᴡᴠ930

Ex. 5. Prelude in C major ʙᴡᴠ870

giving a sharp or flat to the thumb; evidence from elsewhere suggests, however, that he sometimes did play such notes with the thumb.

Ex. 5 (from the same manuscript as Exx. 2 and 3) is one of several available illustrations of a tendency to vary the fingerings in sequential passages. Bach evidently liked a kaleidoscopic array of nuances in his phrasing, as in his melodic and harmonic configurations.                           ML

Q. Faulkner, *J. S. Bach's Keyboard Technique: A Historical Introduction* (St Louis, Miss., 1984); 'Griepenkerl on J. S. Bach's Keyboard Technique: A Translation and Commentary', *American Organist*, 22/1 (Jan. 1988), 63–5; M. Lindley, 'Keyboard Technique and Articulation: Evidence for the Performance Practices of Bach, Handel and Scarlatti', in P. Williams, ed., *Bach, Handel, Scarlatti: Tercentenary Essays* (Cambridge, 1985), 207–43; M. Lindley and M. Boxall, *Early Keyboard Fingerings: A Comprehensive Guide* (London, 1992).

**Fischer, Johann Caspar Ferdinand** (b. *c*.1670; d. 27 March 1746). Composer and *Kapellmeister*, probably from Bohemia and associated with the Baden court, for which he wrote much instrumental and theatre music. He was a major influence in transmitting the Lullian style to Germany. Of his celebrated keyboard collections, the *Ariadne musica neo-organoedum* (1702) is particularly relevant to Bach. The paired preludes and fugues cover no fewer than 19 keys. At least two of Bach's subjects in *The Well-tempered Clavier* Part I suggest the influence of Fischer, and an early version of Bach's collection partly follows Fischer's ordering, with the minor mode preceding the major.                                  JAB

**flauto** ('flute'). A term normally used by Bach and his contemporaries for the RECORDER; 'flauto traverso' or other terms were used for the transverse FLUTE.

**flauto piccolo.** A small, high-pitched RECORDER. Bach included the flauto piccolo in Cantata 96, *Herr Christ, der einge Gottessohn.*

**Flemming,** Count **Joachim Friedrich** (b. 25 Aug. 1665; d. 11 Oct. 1740). Nobleman and cavalry general, from 31 July 1724 military governor of Leipzig, born in Dresden. It was at the Dresden residence of his brother, Count Jakob Heinrich von Flemming (1667–1728), that Bach was to have taken part in the famous contest with Louis Marchand in 1717. Bach wrote, or adapted, three cantatas in homage to the elder Count Flemming: *Verjaget, zerstreuet, zerrüttet, ihr Sterne* BWV249b was performed for the count's birthday in 1726; *So kämpfet nur, ihr muntern Töne* BWV Anh. I 10, for his birthday in 1731; and *O angenehme Melodei*

BWV210a for an unspecified occasion between 1735 and 1740. Some of the music survives in other compositions.

*Florilegium Portense.* A collection of motets for eight to ten voices with organ by German and Italian composers, compiled and edited by the Kantor and theologian Erhard Bodenschatz (1576–1636). It was first published in Leipzig in 1603; an enlarged edition, including in all 115 works, appeared in 1618, to which a second part was added in 1621. It remained in print during Bach's lifetime, and he ordered new copies for use at the Thomasschule in Leipzig.

**flute** (Flöte, Querflöte). In common parlance, a side-blown, treble, woodwind instrument; it was particularly popular in the 18th century. For the instrument that Bach and his contemporaries normally referred to as 'flauto', *see* RECORDER.

We are well informed about the flute of Bach's time, thanks to surviving examples (by J. H. Eichentopf and others), detailed accounts in contemporary sources and instruction manuals, and the illustrations accompanying such texts. In the early part of Bach's career the instrument was constructed as a conical tube in only three sections: the head with mouth-hole, the body with six finger-holes, and the foot, incorporating a key (closed when at rest) as a seventh finger-hole ($d\sharp'$). This type of instrument is illustrated as early as 1707 in Hotteterre. After 1720 the body was divided into two sections, allowing the instrument's pitch to be altered by means of up to six interchangeable upper sections of different lengths.

Bach always called this instrument a *Traversiere* (or used an Italian alternative, and sometimes compound forms such as *flauto traverso* or *flute traversiere*) to distinguish it from the *flauto* (recorder), and furthermore he always notated the latter in the French violin clef in both scores and parts. The transverse flute is the treble woodwind instrument he used most frequently after the oboe. There are very few cantatas specifying transverse flute that do not also require oboes. C. S. Terry, in his book *Bach's Orchestra* (London, 1932), assumed that Bach needed several different types of transverse flute, but more recent research shows that he used only one, with $d'$ as the lowest pitch; he invariably notated its music in the normal violin clef, with a compass of $d'$ to $g'''$ ($a'''$ in BWV1013), and used its full chromatic range. Apparent extension of the range below $d'$ is only ever encountered when parts are doubled by other instruments, and there is no reason to suppose that Bach had instruments capable of playing these lower notes. There are no notes below $d'$ in the autograph flute parts, but there exist a number of written-out adjustments—octave transpositions, alternative readings, or rests—illustrating the ways in which players coped with unplayable notes.

Where the original parts of Bach's works survive, they include separate flute parts, but these contain only the movements for which the transverse flute is specified; the remaining movements usually have tacet markings. Except in Cantatas 96 and 101, there exist no explicit or implicit indications that any of the music is intended for recorders or oboes, while the converse—music for recorder written into oboe parts—occurs in at least five works: BWV46, 69a, 81, 122, and 249. The only plausible interpretation of this state of affairs is that Bach must have employed separate instrumentalists to play the transverse flute in Leipzig, and did not expect them to double as oboists or recorder players. Any statements about the works that survive only in full score are necessarily hypothetical, as is the supposition that one player might have had separate parts for different instruments on his desk.

More than 80 Bach works call for the transverse flute: over half of these employ one flute and the rest two, except for Cantata 206 (which requires three) and the St Matthew Passion (four). When a work was revived, arranged, or transposed, parts originally for oboe or recorder were sometimes given to the transverse flute, and the flute is sometimes replaced by another melody instrument. Also there are over a dozen movements to which Bach later added a flute part, doubling an existing part at the unison or octave, or occasionally contributing a new and independent line (as in 'Et expecto resurrectionem mortuorum' in the B minor Mass and in the final chorus from Cantata 191).

Bach used the D flute as a rule only in keys which, in modern notation, would have a signature of up to four sharps or two flats. Undoubtedly his choice of instrument was to some extent governed by differences between the so-called natural notes and those produced by cross-fingering, as well as by the contemporary debate about tempered versus pure intonation.

Although the sources are fragmentary, it can be shown that Bach already used transverse flutes (two in each case) in the secular cantatas nos. 173a, 184a, and 194a, which he wrote in Cöthen. His earliest specified use of a flute in Leipzig is in the St John Passion, first performed on 7 April 1724. He made positively virtuoso demands of the flautist in arias in 12 cantatas written between 6 August and 19 November 1724, and evidently had an exceptionally expert player in the early Leipzig years—probably his pupil, the law student Friedrich Gottlieb Wild. Bach later recommended Wild

for the post of Kantor at the Jakobikirche, Chemnitz, in a testimonial dated 18 May 1727, laying particular emphasis on his 'well-schooled Flaute-traversiere' (BDok i, no. 57).

Bach's use of the transverse flute can be summed up as follows: it is found far less often doubling other parts (except in chorales) than in an obbligato role; in other words, he used it much more to contribute to the musical substance than to add colour or reinforcement. He most often wrote for one obbligato flute in arias, but for two in choruses and recitatives. Unison playing by two transverse flutes is rare in solo contexts, but it frequently occurs in support of other vocal and instrumental parts, especially in the two Passions. Six arias with transverse flute, but with a bassetto rather than a continuo bass, must be counted among Bach's more unusual sonorities: BWV11:10, 173a:4 (middle section), 215:7, 234:4, 244:27a, and 244:49. Bach gave musical substance to the 'flutes' invoked in the text of three soprano arias of the middle Leipzig period, writing for solo flute in BWV210:6, for two flutes in 214:3, and for three in 206:9.                                                 UP

P. Bate, The Flute: A Study of its History, Development and Construction (London, 1969; 2nd edn. 1979); J. Hotteterre, Principes de la flûte traversière, ou flûte d'Allemagne (Paris, 1707; Eng. trans., 1729); R. L. Marshall, 'J. S. Bach's Compositions for Solo Flute: A Reconsideration of their Authenticity and Chronology', Journal of the American Musicological Society, 32 (1979), 463–98; A. Powell and D. Lasocki, 'Bach and the Flute: The Players, the Instruments, the Music', Early Music, 23 (1995), 9–29; J. J. Quantz, Versuch einer Anweisung die Flöte traversiere zu spielen (Berlin, 1752; 3rd edn. Breslau, 1789; Eng. trans. E. R. Reilly, London, 1966); H.-P. Schmitz, Querflöte und Querflötenspiel in Deutschland während des Barockzeitalters (Kassel, 1952; 2nd edn. 1958).

**Flute Sonatas and Partita.** See overleaf.

**Forkel, Johann Nikolaus** (b. 22 Feb. 1749; d. 20 March 1818). Writer and music historian, usually credited with the earliest biography of Bach. He was born in Meeder, near Coburg in Bavaria, and enrolled at Göttingen University in 1769. In 1770 he took over the post of university organist, and in 1772 began to teach compositional technique. From 1779 he was music director of the university.

Forkel was one of the pioneers who tried to fill the gap between a knowledge of contemporary (i.e. 18th-century) music and what was known about ancient and medieval music from music theory. In his Allgemeine Geschichte der Musik (1788–1801) he wrote about music 'from the beginning' to the mid-16th century; his material for the music of the subsequent 150 years

[cont. on p.176]

# Flute Sonatas and Partita

Bach's extant sonatas for transverse flute comprise the following works: two sonatas for flute and obbligato cembalo, BWV1030 in B minor and BWV1032 in A major; two for flute and continuo, BWV1034 in E minor and BWV1035 in E major; the Trio Sonata in G major for two flutes and continuo BWV1039; and the Trio Sonata in C minor from the *Musical Offering*. To these must be added the Partita in A minor for unaccompanied flute BWV1013 and four works of doubtful authenticity (see below).

The two well-authenticated sonatas for flute and obbligato cembalo, in B minor and A major, both survive in autograph fair copies dating from 1736. Since neither is a composing score, the dates of composition cannot be determined. For the A major sonata the source is a unique 'double manuscript', in which Bach wrote out the Concerto in C minor for two harpsichords and, on the three remaining staves at the bottom of each leaf, the flute sonata (at the end of the harpsichord concerto the sonata continues on all the staves).

For the B minor sonata a later harpsichord part survives in G minor, and this, in conjunction with some copying errors in the autograph involving notes misplaced by a 3rd, confirms the work's origin in that key. The manuscript for the A major sonata is mutilated; Bach excised about 46 bars from the first movement by cutting the bottom three staves from the manuscript. The reason for this is unknown, but enough of the movement remains to provide clues for possible completions. Michael Marissen has speculated that the work originated as a trio sonata in C major for recorder, violin, and continuo.

Both obbligato sonatas, as well as the continuo sonata in E minor, are of a special type: the 'sonata in the concerted manner', a type especially cultivated at the Dresden court. In such works at least one movement, usually the first fast movement, takes on the RITORNELLO structure typical of the Vivaldian concerto. The first movement of the B minor sonata is Bach's most complex and lengthy example of this. The second movement is a heavily ornamented siciliana, with the cembalo part composed in the manner of a written-out continuo realization. The final movement juxtaposes a *stile antico* fugue with a fugal gigue on the same subject, thus presenting movements representing both the *sonata da chiesa* and the *sonata da camera*. The A major sonata presents its allusions to the concerto more overtly, both the first and third movements exemplifying a complex ritornello structure.

The autograph of the Sonata for flute and continuo in E minor is lost. The surviving sources, of which the earliest dates from 1726/7, differ in a number of details regarding pitches, the presence or absence of bass figures, articulation, and the ending figures in the flute in the last three movements. The work combines features of the *sonata da chiesa* and the sonata in the concerted manner. The second movement again presents a Vivaldian ritornello structure.

The principal source for the Sonata in E major with continuo dates from *c*.1800, and bears a still later inscription, 'für den Kämmerier Fredersdorff aufgesetzt' ('for the royal valet Fredersdorf'). Michael Gabriel Fredersdorf was servant and flute duet partner to Frederick the Great in Berlin. It has been speculated that Bach composed the work in conjunction with one of his trips (in 1741 or 1747) to visit his son Carl Philipp Emanuel, who was then employed by Frederick the Great at the Berlin court. The work does present a more modern style for Bach, especially in its employment of copious 'mixed-taste' embellishments and modish triplets in the first movement. For

Frederick's *galant* taste, however, some features, for example the canonic imitation in the Siciliano, must have seemed old-fashioned.

The Partita in A minor represents a technical *tour de force* for the flautist. Again, Bach's autograph has been lost, and the work's unique source, dating from about 1723, is in the hands of two different copyists (the manuscript is appended to a copy of the Sonatas and Partitas for unaccompanied violin). The copy seems to be faulty in places with regard to both pitch and rhythm. The work presents a variant of the typical German ordering of the early 18th-century partita: Allemande, Corrente (in place of a courante), Sarabande, and Bourée angloise (in place of a gigue). While the Allemande, with its nearly unbroken succession of semiquavers and ruthless ascent to a high $a'''$ at the end, has been especially singled out as 'unidiomatic', since it appears to lack breathing-places, the movement does lend itself to successful performance if it is not played too fast, allowing both for unobtrusive breaths and for the movement's complex implied counterpoint to be heard.

Three other sonatas have been attributed to J. S. Bach: those in E♭ major (BWV1031) and G minor (BWV1020) for flute and cembalo, and the Sonata in C major for flute and continuo BWV1033. All three works have been excluded from the volume of flute music in the *NBA*. The sonatas in E♭ major and G minor are both relatively simple examples of the sonata in the concerted manner. The E♭ major sonata appears to derive from a Dresden trio by Quantz: its attribution to Bach is based on two manuscripts from Bach's circle, which, however, are clearly copied from a single parent manuscript. The G minor sonata is probably a work, albeit somewhat anomalous, by C. P. E. Bach. Neither work approaches the sophistication of Bach's secure sonatas in the concerted manner. The C major sonata survives in a manuscript in the hand of the young C. P. E. Bach, copied about 1731, and bears an attribution to his father. The first Menuet is related to the first in a set of variations in a concerto for oboe, obbligato cembalo, and doubling cello by the Merseburg composer Christoph Förster (1693–1745), and suggests that the movements may have had a disparate origin, as does the sudden appearance of an obbligato cembalo part solely for that movement. The work must remain questionable as a work of J. S. Bach.

For Bach's two authentic trio sonatas with flute parts, *see* GAMBA SONATAS and MUSICAL OFFERING. The Trio Sonata in G major for flute, violin (employing scordatura), and continuo BWV1038 is an arrangement of the Violin Sonata in G major, BWV1021, with largely new upper parts written over the old bass part. The work survives in a single unattributed manuscript in Bach's hand, but its authenticity as Bach's own arrangement is doubtful, and Ulrich Siegele has suggested that it is the work of one of Bach's students, perhaps C. P. E. Bach. JS

M. Marissen, 'A Trio in C Major for Recorder, Violin, and Continuo by J. S. Bach?', *Early Music*, 13 (1985), 384–90; R. Marshall, *The Music of Johann Sebastian Bach: The Sources, the Style, the Significance* (New York, 1989); U. Siegele, *Kompositionsweise und Bearbeitungstechnik in der Instrumentalmusik Johann Sebastian Bachs* (Stuttgart, 1975); J. Swack, 'Bach's A major Flute Sonata BWV1032 Revisited', in D. Melamed, ed., *Bach Studies* 2 (Cambridge, 1995), 154–74; J. Swack, 'On the Origins of the *Sonate auf Concertenart*', *Journal of the American Musicological Society*, 46 (1993), 369–414; J. Swack, 'Quantz and the Sonata in E-flat Major for Flute and Cembalo, BWV1031', *Early Music*, 23 (1995), 31–53.

remained unpublished, perhaps because of the lasting shock he received when, after the French occupation of Vienna in 1805, the plates that had been engraved in readiness for his *Denkmäler* edition were melted down.

From Forkel's standpoint the development of music was a permanent improvement, and for him its climax might have been Bach's music. He was in lively contact with Wilhelm Friedemann and Carl Philipp Emanuel Bach, who told him details about their father's life and works; Forkel integrated these into the largely anecdotal biographical accounts of Bach handed down in the music dictionaries of the later 18th century. In this respect his book is not very 'original'; neither was it the first monograph on Bach, since it was preceded in 1801 by Ludwig Siebigke's *Bach* (which did not go beyond the standard information available at the time). But Forkel added aesthetic and analytical reports on Bach's music (occupying nine of its 11 chapters). His work-list reflects the fact that Bach's keyboard music was much more widely known than his vocal compositions in the late 18th century. *Über Johann Sebastian Bachs Leben, Kunst und Kunstwerke* was published in Leipzig in 1802, during the Napoleonic wars. Forkel understood the book also as a means of arousing the national sentiments of the Germans, as is particularly apparent in its final sentences. It was dedicated to Gottfried van Swieten, the friend of C. P. E. Bach, Mozart, and Haydn.                KK

G. B. Stauffer, 'Forkel's Letters to Hoffmeister & Kühnel: A Bach Biographical Source Recovered', *Journal of Musicology*, 5 (1987), 549–61.

**forlana, forlane.** A dance, possibly of Slavonic origin, which came to 18th-century music through its popularity as a Venetian street dance accompanied by mandolins, castanets, and drums. André Campra (1660–1744) popularized forlanas in France by including them in ballets, beginning in the 1690s. The forlana is characterized by balanced phrases with segmented repeats, rondeau form, simple harmonies, a predominantly homophonic texture, and 6/4 or 6/8 metre in a moderate tempo. It frequently uses the lilting *sautillant* rhythm (*see* GIGUE) and begins with an upbeat. Choreographies exist in the French court dance repertory (see Little and Marsh).

The metric structure, when in 6/8 metre, is made up of dotted crotchet beats, with lower levels consisting of quavers grouped in threes and semiquavers in twos. The characteristic rhythmic phrase is 8 beats (4 bars) long, with a primary thesis on beats 7 and 8 and a secondary point of repose on beats 3 and 4.

Bach's single forlana (headed 'Forlane') is in his Orchestral Suite in C Major. It is not in rondeau

form, but simply has two strains, each repeated. A pastoral effect is created by the drone bass, with a simple melody using segmented repeats taken by unison violins and oboes (see MUSETTE).

NJ, MEL

For bibliography, *see* DANCE.

**fortepiano.** A term often used for the early PIANOFORTE to distinguish it from the modern instrument developed in the mid-19th and the 20th centuries.

***Fortspinnungstypus*** ('Fortspinnung type'). A term invented by Wilhelm Fischer to categorize a type of RITORNELLO structure commonly found in late Baroque concertos and other works. Fischer observed its construction in three sections: the *Vordersatz* (V), or opening motif, which established the tonality and, to a certain extent, the character of the movement; the *Fortspinnung* (F), or continuation, which usually involved sequential repetition and moved away from the tonic and dominant harmonies of the *Vordersatz*; and the *Epilog* (E), or conclusion, which ended the ritornello with a well-defined cadence.

There are numerous examples of the *Fortspinnungstypus* among the ritornellos in Bach's works, both vocal and instrumental. An example from the former is the opening chorus, 'Fallt mit Danken, fallt mit Loben', from Part 4 of the *Christmas Oratorio*: V, bars 1–8; F, bars 9–22; E, bars 22–4. From among several instances in concerto ritornellos might be mentioned the first movement of the Violin Concerto in E major: V, bars 1–3; F, bars 4–8; E, bars 9–11.

W. Fischer, 'Zur Entwicklungsgeschichte des Wiener klassischen Stils', *Studien zur Musikwissenschaft*, 3 (1915), 24–84.

**'Forty-eight'.** A popular title for the WELL-TEMPERED CLAVIER.

**Francisci, Jan** (b. 14 June 1691; d. 27 April 1758). Organist and composer, born in Neusohl, Upper Hungary (now Banská Bystrica, Slovakia). In 1709 he succeeded his father as Kantor there before going to Vienna in 1722 and he visited Bach in Leipzig in 1725. He then worked as a church musician in Preßburg (now Bratislava) until 1735, when he returned to Neusohl. In 1737 he resumed his former occupation there and, except for the years 1743–8, remained in it until his death.

**Franck, Salomo** (b. ?6 March 1659; bur. 14 June 1725). Poet, author of cantata texts, born and died in Weimar. He came from a family with old traditions linking its members to the ducal court at Weimar. In 1701, after his studies at the University of Jena, he occupied a government post as consistorial secretary, librarian, and head of the numismatic collection—a post held by members of his family for generations.

Franck was a typical court poet of the German High Baroque. His main output consisted of sacred strophic texts and congratulatory poems, which were of a sufficiently high standard to earn him membership of the illustrious Fruchtbringende Gesellschaft. His sacred texts were at first confined to the types of church concerto typical of the 17th century, combining strophic verses with biblical passages (e.g. in his *Evangelische Seelen-Lust*, 1694). It is notable that in his mid-50s Franck was ready to adopt new poetical principles for his cantata texts, integrating da capo arias and recitatives into his poetry. With these texts a fruitful collaboration between Bach and Franck was established in 1714. As far as is known, all Bach's cantatas written for the Weimar church use texts by Franck except two (by Erdmann Neumeister and G. C. Lehms). Even during his Leipzig years Bach continued to work with Franck's texts, partly by enlarging existing cantatas (e.g. nos. 70 and 80) and partly by composing new ones (72 and 168).　　　　　　　　　　　　KK

**Französiche Suiten.** *See* FRENCH SUITES.

**Frederick the Great** [Friedrich II], King of Prussia (b. 24 Jan. 1712; d. 17 Aug. 1786). The third King of Prussia, from 1740 to 1786. He earned his reputation as a military commander in the War of the Austrian Succession (1740–8) and the Seven Years War (1756–63), and succeeded in extending Prussian territory and making his country one of the strongest political and economic forces in Europe. He was born in Berlin and received a strict upbringing from his father Friedrich Wilhem I, the 'soldier king', who was fundamentally hostile to music and culture. This did not prevent Frederick and his siblings from cultivating the arts, and above all music. Frederick's musical instruction came initially from the Berlin Cathedral organist Gottlieb Heyne, but it was only after he met J. J. Quantz in Dresden in 1728 that he began to master both the flute (which he had enjoyed playing since childhood) and composition.

As testimony to Frederick's compositional gifts we have 121 sonatas for flute and keyboard and four flute concertos, among other things. At Ruppin (from 1732), Rheinsberg (from 1736), and Potsdam (from 1740) he maintained a court orchestra of the first rank. It was at Potsdam, where he died, that the historic encounter between Frederick and Bach took place on 7 May 1747, when Bach was called upon to improvise on the 'forte e piano' a fugue on a theme given to him by the king in person. And it was on this *thema regium* that Bach subsequently based the entire MUSICAL OFFERING, printed by the Schübler brothers and presented with a dedication to the king on 7 July 1747.　　　　　　AB

A. Basso, 'Federico II, re musicista', *Musica e dossier*, 3 (1987), 5–66; E. Helm, *Music at the Court of Frederick the Great* (Norman, Okla. 1960); G. Müller, *Friedrich der Große: seine Flöten und sein Flötenspiel* (Berlin, 1932); G. Thouret, *Friedrich der Große als Musikfreunde und Musiker* (Leipzig, 1898).

**Fredersdorf(f), Michael Gabriel** (b. 1708; d. 12 Jan. 1758). Flautist, born in Garz an der Oder, near Stettin (now Szczecin, Poland). He was a servant and flute duet partner to Frederick the Great. Fredersdorf entered the Crown Prince Frederick's employ in Cüstrin in 1731 and remained in his service until shortly before his death in Potsdam. He initially served Frederick as a soldier, flautist, and oboist, and soon became his friend and valet. Upon Frederick's succession to the Prussian throne in 1740, Fredersdorf was promoted to private secretary. More than a mere servant, he was a trusted confidant to the king.

Both the principal source for Bach's Sonata in E major for flute and continuo (copied *c*.1800) and a 19th-century manuscript (both of which may have been copied from Bach's lost autograph) bear inscriptions attesting to the work's having been written for Fredersdorf. Thus the piece has been connected to Bach's visits to Berlin in either 1741 or 1747.　　　　　　　　　　　　　JS

R. Asprey, *Frederick the Great: The Magnificent Enigma* (New York, 1986); R. Marshall. *Johann Sebastian Bach: The Sources, the Style, the Significance* (New York, 1989); J. Richter, ed., *Die Briefe Friedrich des Großen an seinen vormaligen Kammerdiener Fredersdorf* (Berlin, n.d.).

**French overture.** *See* OUVERTURE.

**French Suites** (Französische Suiten). Title given to six keyboard suites by Bach, BWV812–17. The French Suites lack preludes and consist of what had become by the early 18th century the traditional sequence of allemande, courante, sarabande, and gigue, with additional movements of various types following the sarabande (and possibly the gigue, as in Suite no. 6).

What appear to be Bach's first drafts for several of the suites are found in the 1722 *Clavierbüchlein* for Anna Magdalena Bach, but the set was not completed before 1725 or so. Moreover, portions of the first five suites were probably copied into the 1722 manuscript from earlier drafts. Several of the suites survive in significantly variant versions; two (nos. 4 and 6) even exist in versions with preludes, suggesting that the make-up of the set was for a while fluid as Bach considered including some of these works in the series of suites with preludes—that is, the ENGLISH SUITES.

Despite the title (used by F. W. Marpurg as early as 1762, but not found in any early source traceable to Bach), the style of the works is not particularly close to that of Bach's French contemporaries. Indeed, the dance movements in the English Suites come somewhat closer to dances by Couperin and other French composers. But, like most comparable French works, the French Suites contain relatively little imitative counterpoint and hardly any of the Italianate concerto-style writing found in the preludes of the English Suites.

The first three French Suites (all in minor keys) remain old-fashioned in important respects. Suite no. 1, for example, includes (as do all the English Suites) a French-style courante (in 3/2 time) with an invention-like contrapuntal texture. The Gigue is of the strict fugal type, although it is one of just two examples by Bach in quadruple time (a type possibly familiar to Bach from the suites of Froberger). On the other hand, all but one of the remaining courantes are of the Italian type (in 3/4). The sarabandes of Suites nos. 2–6 employ textures dominated by a singing treble, as opposed to the more strictly homophonic style of the sarabandes in the English Suites. The trend away from complex imitative polyphony suggests an enthusiastic adoption of the *style galant*; this is equally evident in other keyboard works from the period, including many of the little pieces in the 1725 *Clavierbüchlein*. This style is especially pronounced in the last two French Suites, with their tuneful gavottes and bourrées and, in Suite no. 6, a polonaise and a minuet—the latter placed after the Gigue in some manuscripts.

Together with the relatively light textures and the small dimensions of many movements, the frequent hints of *galant* style suggest that, even more than the English Suites (or the later Partitas), the French Suites were written with students in mind. A number of manuscript copies by Bach's pupils survive; these have aided in the identification of several stages in Bach's composition of the pieces, notably the successive revisions of the Allemande and Courante of Suite no. 2 and the addition not only of a prelude but of a second gavotte to Suite no. 4 (both movements seem to have been subsequently dropped, however).

In both 18th-century manuscripts and modern editions the French Suites are often grouped together with similar suites by Bach in A minor and E♭ major (BWV818–19). The A minor suite seems relatively early in style and might have been composed before both the French and the English suites. The one in E♭ major is somewhat more sophisticated and might date from the same period as the later French Suites.

BWV818 and 819 both appear to have undergone the same process of revisions as did the French Suites proper, including the addition of ornament signs and of new movements. Older editions of all eight suites often conflated the various versions, but in the *NBA* and other recent editions the early drafts, the rejected variants, and the more heavily ornamented late versions are clearly distinguished.                    DS

H. Eppstein, 'Chronologieprobleme in Johann Sebastian Bachs Suiten für Soloinstrument', *BJb* 62 (1976), 35–57; D. Schulenberg, *The Keyboard Music of J. S. Bach* (New York, 1992), 254–75.

**Frescobaldi, Girolamo** (b. Sept. 1583; d. 1 March 1643). Italian composer, born in Ferrara. He was one of the most important keyboard composers of the 17th century, and wrote also church music and secular vocal works. As we know from a letter which Carl Philipp Emanuel Bach addressed to J. N. Forkel on 13 January 1775, J. S. Bach was acquainted with Frescobaldi's music from his boyhood years in Ohrdruf, and some of his early chorale preludes for organ reflect certain stylistic traits of Frescobaldi's works, above all his toccatas and canzonas. Bach also possessed a manuscript copy of Frescobaldi's *Fiori musicali* (Venice, 1635), which he signed and dated 1714 (see *BDok* i, Anh. I/5); it was later in the collection of the Akademie für Kirchen- und Schulmusik, Berlin, but was destroyed during World War II. Frescobaldi's mastery in this collection is matched in Bach's *Clavier-Übung III*, which contains two 'organ masses' (consisting of Kyrie and Gloria) and a supplementary series of chorales and free pieces, recalling the three organ masses and other pieces of Frescobaldi's publication.        AB

F. Hammond, *Girolamo Frescobaldi* (Cambridge, Mass., 1983); N. Koptschewski, 'Stilistische Parallelen zwischen dem Klavierwerk Frescobaldis und dem Spätwerk Bachs', in W. Hoffmann and A. Schneiderheinze, eds., *Bericht über die Wissenschaftliche Konferenz zum V. Internationalen Bachfest der DDR in Verbindung mit dem 60. Bachfest der Neuen Bachgesellschaft* (Leipzig, 1988), 437–47.

**Freudenberg, Siegismund** (bap. 20 April 1704). Organist, born in Seifershau, Riesengebirge. He studied with Tobias Volckmar (1678–1756) at Hirschberg and with Bach while reading law at Leipzig University between 1724 and 1728, but he was unsuccessful in his attempts to find employment as an organist in Schweidnitz (1728) and Görlitz (1730). In April 1731 he competed, again unsuccessfully, with J. A. Scheibe and Theodor Christian Gerlach (1694–1768) for the post of organist at Freiberg Cathedral.

*Freue dich, erlöste Schar* ('Rejoice, ye ransomed host'). Cantata, BWV30, for the feast of St

John the Baptist (24 June), first performed between 1738 and 1742. One of Bach's late cantatas, it is a parody of a secular work, ANGE-NEHMES WIEDERAU, FREUE DICH IN DEINEN AUEN, which he performed in September 1737. For the sacred version Bach and his librettist (possibly Picander, who wrote the original text) divided the work into two parts, introduced a chorale (no. 6) to end Part 1, and omitted an aria and recitative towards the end. As a result, the tenor is left as the only solo singer without an aria (the bass has two, as in the secular work). Bach also trimmed the instrumental scoring, removing the three trumpets and drums that had lent brilliance to the secular occasion; the forces required are therefore two flutes, two oboes (one of them doubling on oboe d'amore), strings, and continuo.

What was originally a fulsome serenata to welcome a new landlord was thus turned into an effective cantata to welcome Christ's prophet. The music well suits its new context, and if some of its features—the rondo design of the opening chorus (repeated to different words as a closing number); the syncopated rhythms of that chorus, and of the alto aria 'Kommt, ihr angefochtnen Sünder'; and the Lombardic rhythms of the bass aria 'Ich will nun hassen'—might seem to betray its secular origins, they can all be found in some of Bach's other sacred works as well. And the cantata is sanctified by a new 'figured' recitative for bass, with two oboes and continuo, to open Part 2 and by a strophe from the hymn *Tröstet, tröstet, meine Lieben* by Johann Olearius, plainly harmonized by Bach, to close Part 1.

For bibliography, *see* CANTATA, §1.

**Friedrich II.** *See* FREDERICK THE GREAT.

**Friedrich August I,** Elector of Saxony (b. 12 May 1670; d. 1 Feb. 1733). Elector and Duke of Saxony, born in Dresden. He succeeded his brother Johann Georg IV in April 1694. After his conversion to Roman Catholicism, he was made King of Poland, as August II, in January 1698, and became known as 'August the Strong'. In 1693 he had married Christiane Eberhardine, Margravine of Brandenburg-Bayreuth, for whose commemorative service in 1727 Bach composed the *Trauer Ode*.

Bach is known to have composed at least three secular cantatas in honour of Friedrich August I, but only the texts and a few fragments of music remain. The first of these, *Entfernet euch, ihr heitern Sterne* (BWV Anh. I 9), to a text by Christian Friedrich Haupt, was performed in the garden of Apel's house in Leipzig by over 40 musicians under Bach's direction; it crowned the sumptuous celebrations that took place on the evening of 12 May 1727 to mark the elector's birthday. A few

months later, on 3 August 1727, Friedrich August's nameday was marked by a performance of *Ihr Häuser des Himmels* (text by Picander); some of the music was used three weeks later for the council election cantata *Ihr Tore zu Zion*. Finally, *Es lebe der König, der Vater im Lande* (BWV Anh I, 11; text again by Picander) was performed on 3 August 1732. It seems likely that Bach composed other works, of which we have no information, for the annual celebrations of the sovereign's birthday and nameday. AB

**Friedrich August II,** Elector of Saxony (b. 7 Oct. 1696; d. 5 Oct. 1763). Elector and Duke of Saxony from February 1733 and, as August III, King of Poland from 1734; he was born in Dresden and died there. It was to him that Bach presented the *Missa* in B minor—the Kyrie and Gloria of what was to become the B minor Mass—along with a petition, dated 27 July 1733, requesting a title in the royal *Kapelle*. The request was finally granted on 19 November 1736 (see BDok ii. 388) after Bach had submitted a second petition which has not survived.

A number of secular cantatas by Bach are linked with the sovereign's name: *Schleicht, spielender Wellen*, performed to celebrate his birthday on 7 October 1736 and repeated for his nameday (3 August) in 1740; *Frohes Volk, vergnügte Sachsen* (BWV Anh. I 12; the music is lost) and *Auf, schmetternde Töne* for his nameday in 1733 and (probably) 1735 respectively; *Blast Lärmen, ihr Feinde!*, a parody of Cantata 205 performed on 19 February 1734 on the occasion of his coronation as King of Poland; and *Preise dein Glücke, gesegnetes Sachsen* to mark the first anniversary of his accession as king on 5 October 1734.

In 1737 Bach sought the elector's support in a dispute with the Rector of the Thomasschule, J. A. Ernesti, over the choice of school prefects, but Friedrich August seems to have been unwilling to become personally involved. AB

**Fröber, Christoph Gottlieb** (b. 27 Aug. 1704; d. 14 May 1759). Kantor, born in Langhennersdorf, Erzgebirge. He studied at Leipzig University from 1726 to 1731, and during that time was a pupil of Bach. On Good Friday 1729 a Passion setting by him was performed in the Neukirche in Leipzig, but his application for the vacant organist's post there was unsuccessful the following month. In 1731 he was appointed Kantor at Delitzsch, where he seems to have spent the rest of his days.

**Froberger, Johann Jacob** (bap. 19 May 1616; d. 6/7 May 1667). Composer, primarily of keyboard music, born in Stuttgart. He was a student of Frescobaldi and imperial court organist at Vienna.

The OBITUARY mentions Froberger as one of the composers whose works Bach surreptitiously copied as a boy. C. P. E. Bach later listed him among the 'strong fugue writers' whose music his father 'heard and studied', presumably referring to sections of Froberger's capriccios, fantasias, and ricercares. The open-score notation of these pieces in Froberger's autograph manuscripts resembles, and might have influenced, that of Bach's *The Art of Fugue*. Moreover, a collection in score of 12 of Froberger's capriccios and ricercares—here termed 'fugas'—exists in manuscript copies by (probably) J. P. Kirnberger and J. N. Forkel, and hence appears to have circulated in the Bach circle. In addition, Froberger's highly expressive suites and toccatas, which carry the French and Italian Baroque keyboard styles respectively to Germany, apparently furnished models for similar works by J. A. Reincken and Dietrich Buxtehude that Bach must have known.

DS

**fughetta.** A short FUGUE. The term has been in use since the late Baroque period, but could well be applied to shorter pieces which carry the title 'fugue': for example, those by J. C. F. Fischer and many by Johann Pachelbel. However, the implication of the term 'fughetta' is that it does not pretend to the weightier arguments and extended invention implied by 'fugue'.

In many of his chorale-based pieces called 'fughetta', including those in the Kirnberger collection, Bach shows so many aspects of fugal writing as to make them hardly distinguishable from fugues in matters of construction. The fughetta *Gelobet seist du, Jesu Christ* BWV697, for example, concentrates on the opening notes of the chorale in diminution with a scalic invertible countersubject. In its 14 bars 12 entries of the subject are discernible, with episodic passages totally avoided. In the fughetta *Herr Christ, der ein'ge Gottes-Sohn* BWV698 double-fugue style is used, with both subjects (invertible) entering together. In *Vom Himmel hoch* BWV701 the later chorale phrases in diminution are skilfully interwoven with the subject, which is based on the opening phrase. Many of these fughettas (like those in *Clavier-Übung III*) are for manuals alone, which might give a further clue as to Bach's intention concerning their weight. There are, however, exceptions, such as *Das Jesulein soll doch mein Trost* BWV702.

Outside the genre of the organ chorale, Bach wrote a fughetta as the tenth of the Goldberg Variations, skilfully adapting the binary form imposed by the 'Aria' to the requirements of fugal style.

LC

**fugue.** See opposite.

180

***Fürchte dich nicht*** ('Fear thou not'). Motet for eight-voice double chorus, BWV228, setting Isaiah 41: 10 and 43: 1, and strophes 11 and 12 of Paul Gerhardt's hymn *Warum sollt ich mich denn grämen*. No original sources survive for this motet and there is no record of any of Bach's performances, so it is undatable on documentary grounds. There is no evidence to support the much-repeated speculation that it was composed for a Leipzig funeral in 1726. The theme of the text centres on the second of the passages from Isaiah: 'Fear not: for I have redeemed thee, I have called thee by thy name; thou art mine.'

Several pieces of evidence point to the motet's early origin, probably in Bach's Weimar period: its structural and stylistic similarities to *Ich lasse dich nicht, du segnest mich denn* (ii), known to date from 1712–13 or before (see Melamed); its construction, like *Ich lasse dich nicht*, along the lines of the traditional central German motet; its use of a version of the hymn tune that does not resemble Bach's Leipzig form of the melody; and its stylistic resemblance to two early cantata movements, BWV21:9 and especially sections of BWV63:7.

Instead of the typical single biblical text, *Fürchte dich nicht* employs two different passages from Isaiah, both beginning with the words 'Fürchte dich nicht'. The first is treated in the first half of the motet starting with a striking passage which lands with a dissonance on the word 'nicht'. Bach rounds off the first section of the motet with a return of these words and their musical setting, which also serves as the opening of the second section, making a seamless connection even as the texture is reduced from eight voices to four. At the end of the four-voice section, Bach returns once more to this textual and musical phrase, whose three appearances serve as pillars of the motet's structure.

The motet shows its indebtedness to traditional models, though with clear Bachian twists. The first section, despite its somewhat animated part-writing and modern dissonance treatment, is essentially homophonic and is built from short-breathed phrases in alternating choirs, like the simpler motets of Bach's predecessors and contemporaries. The second section has a texture typical for a motet: a chorale is presented in long notes in the soprano, supported by lower voices singing a biblical text. But Bach's accompanying material here consists, atypically, of three-part invertible counterpoint—three musical ideas that are worked out all the way through the section. (One of the ideas emphasizes the long–short–short pattern known as the *figura corta*, familiar from many of Bach's early compositions both for voices and for organ.)

[*cont. on p.184*]

# fugue

A type of composition in which a melodic idea, the 'subject', is treated imitatively by subsequent voices as they enter, one by one, in a gradual build-up of the texture, each part continuing without interruption until all the voices have entered, so completing what is termed the 'exposition'. (The term 'voice' is commonly used for each strand of fugal texture, even in instrumental examples.) Despite codifications suggested at various times by theorists from Fux to Fétis (1784–1871), not to mention numerous teachers and examination systems, fugue is not really a structure but rather a composition which includes particular aspects of contrapuntal texture and, crucially, an exposition on the lines described above.

Fugue has its historical antecedents in the Renaissance motet, and in instrumental pieces of the 16th and 17th centuries, usually with titles such as 'ricercare', 'canzona', and 'fantasia' (or, in England, 'fantasy' or 'fancy'). Bach, in his more reflective, 'learned' manner, could write a fugue in a style which harks back to the ricercare type, as in the Fugue in C♯ minor in Part 1 of *The Well-tempered Clavier*. Indeed, the *Musical Offering* contains both a Ricercar a 3 and a Ricercar a 6, while BWV588 is an organ Canzona in D minor.

Contrapuntally imitative style in the 16th and early 17th centuries was, of course, used within the conventions and restraints imposed by modality, but most of the contrapuntal features and devices of fugal style were available to these earlier composers. What was not available was the free range of modulation from key to key which evolved with the movement towards the tonal system of the late 17th century onwards. The sequential patterns so beloved of Corelli and Vivaldi, whether or not they were writing contrapuntally, were important not only for the ritornello structure of the Baroque concerto but also for the development of fugue in the hands of masters such as J. S. Bach. Wider explorations of tonal areas became possible in what are termed 'episodes' (those passages in a fugue which normally contain no direct reference to the subject). Bach's mature fugues, notably those of *The Well-tempered Clavier*, were never excelled in this regard, but many of his more youthful organ fugues revert to earlier German styles of fugal treatment.

The earliest use of the term 'fuga' in the 16th century did not, in fact, imply the idiom as we now know it; rather it meant CANON, strictly applied. As imitative contrapuntal idioms evolved from Josquin (c.1440–1521) onwards, the embryonic exposition, common to all pieces that can legitimately be described as 'fugue', also evolved. In the motet, the ricercare, the canzona, and the fantasia a series of quasi-expositions occurs (the different subjects of which may or may not be related to each other), often producing in instrumental pieces a suite-like sequence. In general, the chosen mode does not change or transpose. Some of these features persist in the late 17th-century organ praeludia (in modern terms, preludes and fugues) of Buxtehude, in which the fugal sections, separated by bravura passage-work, are often related, as in his Praeludium in G minor BUXWV149. Some features of Buxtehude's manner remain in Bach's earliest organ fugues, such as the five-section Prelude and Fugue in A minor BWV551.

By the time of the Bach fugue typified by *The Well-tempered Clavier*, certain features can be regarded as established. In the exposition the subject is immediately answered by a second voice (*see* ANSWER) in counterpoint with the first. The answer is most frequently at the pitch (though not necessarily in the key) of the dominant (a

5th higher or a 4th lower than the subject), but sometimes at subdominant pitch (a 5th lower), as in the Prelude and Fugue in C major for organ BWV531. The third voice then enters with the subject in the tonic key, sometimes immediately, but more often after a slight delay, the intervening episodic passage being described as a 'codetta'. Many keyboard fugues remain in three parts, so that the exposition closes after the third entry. In a four- or five-part fugue, further entries (usually alternating subject and answer) will follow. As each voice continues uninterruptedly to the end of the exposition, the contrapuntal density increases until the last voice has entered.

There may or may not be a recurring and invertible COUNTERSUBJECT associated with the answer; Bach was on the whole more consistent in employing one than were many of his predecessors and contemporaries. The answer itself may be 'real' (an exact transposed version of the subject) or 'tonal' (with a slight modification of the early note sequence, usually to substitute the tonic for what in a real answer would have been the supertonic; see * in Exx. 1 and 2). The replacing of a 4th by a 5th (or

Ex. 1. The Art of Fugue: Contrapunctus I

Ex. 2. Cantata 21:11

vice versa) which often results is, of course, also a feature of imitative writing in modal polyphony. A further adjustment of the note sequence in the answer is required in the case of subjects which invite a cadence in, or on, the dominant; without such an adjustment the answer would veer even further towards the sharp side of the tonic. The fugue subject of the final chorus in Bach's cantata *Ich hatte viel Bekümmernis* (Ex. 2) shows both a tonal answer (*) and a modulation adjustment (**).

The generic term 'fugue' has, over the centuries, been applied to any complete composition which contains an exposition, whether or not the same number of voices is used consistently throughout the rest of the piece. Many of J. C. F. Fischer's fugues finish soon after the exposition, and Pachelbel's *Magnificat* fugues are also short. However, the fully-fledged fugue as typified by the mature Bach and continued by masters such as Mozart, Beethoven (1770–1827), Mendelssohn, and Brahms is an extended composition in which a number of other features connected with fugal technique can be expected to occur. A prominent feature of many (perhaps most) fugues is the inclusion of episodes, the first of which normally occurs immediately after the exposition. The type of sequential writing typical of late 17th-century Italian masters such as Corelli and Vivaldi (whether writing contrapuntally or not) enables a harmonic framework to underpin a normally contrapuntal texture which eventually modulates to a closely related key. At this point an entry of the subject occurs, for which an answer is optional.

Two possibilities can delay the appearance of this middle entry: a 'redundant entry' (i.e. a 'second bite of the cherry' by a voice which has already stated the subject or answer), as in the B major Fugue from Part 2 of *The Well-tempered Clavier*; or a 'counter-exposition' (i.e. an extension of the exposition with reordered entries of subject and answer), as in the F major Fugue from Part 1 of the same work. Occasionally treatment of the subject can be so concentrated and episodes so nugatory that middle entries are not easily identified. In other fugues episodes and entries of the subject in related keys alternate freely, with no prescribed pattern. Relative keys, both minor and major, are temporarily defined, and the textural density is normally quite varied. Bach avoids the danger of 'formulae' creeping into the composition of episodes by making figuration grow apparently naturally and spontaneously from material contained in the exposition. The art of development, in the sense applied to that word in the Classical symphony, might be said to have been foreshadowed in the episodes of Bach's mature fugues.

The final structural feature of the typical Bach-style fugue is a final entry in the tonic (which, like the middle entries, may or may not be answered) and frequently a closing passage which may contain an episode and a further tonic entry before the final bars (coda). Within this loose framework there exists an infinite variety of structural possibilities; no two fugues in *The Well-tempered Clavier* follow exactly the same pattern.

Devices occasionally found in fugues include STRETTO, which has tension-raising potential, as does the pedal point (a sustained note, usually the dominant or tonic), which heightens the degree of dissonance between upper voices and the bass. Other possible resources include INVERSION, AUGMENTATION, and DIMINUTION. Recapitulation of episodic material is sometimes found, as in the Fugue in F major from Part 1 of *The Well-tempered Clavier*.

Many movements not entitled 'fugue' combine fugal techniques with other formal and stylistic elements. The French overture typically, and the gigue frequently, involves fugal writing, or at least a fugal exposition, although the continuation may be more informal. In the gigues of, for example, Bach's French and English Suites, interesting combinations of fugal technique with binary structures often occur, as in the French Suite in G major, in which each of the two sections involves fugal exposition, the subject of the second section being the inversion of that of the first. A combination of ritornello structure and fugue is found in many of Bach's instrumental works, such as the finales of Brandenburg Concertos nos. 4 and 5. Fugal idioms abound also in Bach's chorale preludes and fantasias for organ, particularly when a chorale phrase is foreshadowed contrapuntally in diminution, as in the Fantasia a 3, *Christ lag in Todes Banden*, BWV695, with imitative fugal writing in the outer parts and the cantus firmus in the alto. This aspect of organ works involving a chorale harks back to earlier masters such as Buxtehude, and extends to many choral movements in Bach's sacred works.

The pairing of prelude and fugue, which became almost the norm in solo keyboard works after *The Well-tempered Clavier*, does not necessarily exclude the use of fugal devices in the prelude. The E♭ major Prelude in Part 1, for example, is replete with fugal passages.

These examples serve to show how fugue was an almost all-embracing aspect of Bach's compositional technique. If fugue reached it apogee then, it is hardly surprising that its study remained central to the craft of composition in subsequent generations, even if it began to acquire an almost archaic quality in the hands of certain late 18th- and 19th-century composers. LC

*See also* CANZONA, FANTASIA, PERMUTATION FUGUE, PRELUDE AND FUGUE, and RICERCARE.

R. Bullivant, *Fugue* (London, 1971); A. E. F. Dickinson, *Bach's Fugal Works, with an Account of Fugue Before and After Bach* (London, 1956); G. Stauffer, 'Fugue Types in Bach's Free Organ Works', in G. Stauffer and E. May, eds., *J. S. Bach as Organist* (London, 1986), 133–56.

Without the original parts we cannot be sure how Bach performed the piece, but in addition to the broad evidence for the use of basso continuo and *colla parte* instruments in Bach's motets, sources for *Fürchte dich nicht* from C. P. E. Bach include some extra untexted notes in the bass parts. This suggests the presence of a basso continuo part in the original. DRM

For bibliography, *see* MOTET.

**Fux, Johann Joseph** (b. 1660; d. 13 Feb. 1741). Austrian composer and theorist, born in Hirtenfeld, near Graz. As court composer (from 1698), deputy *Hofkapellmeister* (1711–15), and *Hofkapellmeister* (1715–41) to the Habsburg court in Vienna, he came to represent the definitive and final forms of the Austro-Italian Baroque in music. There are perhaps three important points of contact between Fux and Bach which suggest that he was a source of influence on Bach's late style and that he was regarded by contemporary commentators as a composer (as well as a theorist) of comparable significance to Bach.

A letter from C. P. E. Bach to J. N. Forkel of 19 January 1775 attests to Bach's preference for actual music in the teaching of composition as against 'the dry species of counterpoint that are given in Fux and others', but the same letter places Fux at the head of those (contemporary) composers whom Bach most admired: Fux, Caldara, Handel, Keiser, Hasse, J. G. and C. H. Graun, Zelenka (a pupil of Fux's), and Benda.

In 1742 a German translation of Fux's *Gradus ad Parnassum* (Vienna, 1725) was published by Bach's pupil Lorenz Mizler. Bach knew the Latin original well and his personal copy has survived. As Christoph Wolff and Alfred Mann have shown, the *Gradus* stands behind Bach's preoccupation with *stile antico* counterpoint in his late works, but not as a primer of strict counterpoint: it is the aesthetic of Fux's stylistic continuity (as between *stile antico* and *stile moderno*) and Fux's own prowess as a composer (to which the longer excerpts in the *Gradus* bear witness) that influenced Bach's conception and reintegration of *antico* techniques.

F. W. Marpurg's *Abhandlung von der Fuge* (1753–4) advanced Bach's compositional technique as the *locus classicus* of fugal counterpoint: this treatise implicitly recognized Fux's practice as an important precedent for the summation of fugal discourse which Marpurg discerned in *The Art of Fugue*. In this respect Marpurg relies not only on the *Gradus* but also on Fux's actual compositions (as in his quotation of 'Christe eleison' from the *Missa canonica*). This usage deserves to be distinguished from the long afterlife which Fux's *Gradus* enjoyed both as a composition manual and as the source of various treatises based more or less directly upon it. Mattheson remarked in *Der vollkommene Capellmeister* (1739) that the great fugal masters known to him were Bach, Fux, Handel, Johann Krieger (1652–1735), Kuhnau, Johann Theile (1646–1724), Telemann, and J. G. Walther. It is clear that Fux belonged to this distinguished gathering not as a theorist but as a composer, especially given Mattheson's favourable account of his choral writing and his chamber duet style. J. A. Scheibe likewise, in *Der critische Musikus* (1745), ranked Fux alongside Bach, Handel, Telemann, and others as a composer whose command of Italian style was combined with mathematical exactitude.     HW

A. Mann, 'Bach und die Fuxsche Lehre: Theorie und Kompositionspraxis', in R. Flotzinger and J. Trummer, eds., *Johann Sebastian Bach und Johann Joseph Fux* (Kassel, 1985), 82–6; F. W. Riedel, 'Musikgeschichtliche Beziehungen zwischen Johann Joseph Fux und Johann Sebastian Bach', in A. A. Abert and W. Pfannkuch, eds., *Festschrift Friedrich Blume zum 70. Geburtstag* (Kassel, 1963), 290–304; C. Wolff, *Der stile antico in der Musik Johann Sebastian Bachs* (Wiesbaden, 1968).

# G

**Galanterie** (literally, 'gallantry'). A term used (in the plural) by Bach on the title-page of *Clavier-Übung I*, where he describes the movements that make up the partitas as 'bestehend in Praeludien, Allemanden, Couranten, Sarabanden, Giguen, Menuetten, und andern Galanterien'. It is generally assumed that 'Galanterien' refers to the smaller, lighter movements that Bach inserts towards the end of each partita (Rondeaux, Scherzo, Aria, etc.). Bach's wording, however, appears to follow that of J. C. F. Fischer, whose *Pièces de clavessin* (eight partitas op. 2, 1696) are described on the title-page as 'bestehend in unter-shi[e]dlichen Galanterien: als Praeludien, Alle-manden, Couranten, Sarabanden, Bouréen, Gavotten, Menueten, Chaconnen . . .' ('consisting of [such] various *Galanterien* as Preludes, Alle-mandes [etc.]'). 'Galanterien' thus appears to be a collective term for the various movements, of whatever character, that constitute a suite.

RDPJ

**galant style.** *See* STYLE GALANT.

**gamba.** *See* VIOLA DA GAMBA.

**Gamba Sonatas.** Three sonatas, in G major, D major, and G minor, for viola da gamba and obbligato harpsichord, BWV1027–9, recast in Leipzig from earlier works composed for other instrumental combinations. The intended recipients were probably either Carl Friedrich Abel or Ludwig Christian Hesse (1716–72), both renowned gambists in Bach's circle.

Available sources indicate that these sonatas are of mixed origins and were not conceived as a set. Only the G major sonata survives in Bach's autograph, the calligraphy and watermark of which date it to *c*.1740 and confirm that it is a revision of BWV1039 for two flutes and continuo, which may in turn be traced back to an even earlier version, perhaps for two violins. The principal and earliest surviving sources for the D major and G minor sonatas are copies by C. F. Penzel. Dated 1753, these are somewhat lax in detail regarding articulation and ornamentation. Arguments concerning the presumed original version of the D major sonata have ranged from a trio sonata in E♭ major or E major with flute and violin (or in D major with two violins) to an original work for bass viol; some scholars believe the third movement (Andante) to have vocal origins. The three-move-

ment G minor sonata may have originated from a trio sonata or, bearing in mind its external and internal affiliations with Italian concerto structure, a double violin concerto now lost.

The transcriptions for gamba and keyboard are mostly in the nature of trio sonatas, the harpsichord part being in two parts throughout, except for some occasional brief passages of figured bass. BWV1028 is exceptional in that its tessitura requires a seven-string instrument, while the other sonatas scarcely exploit the lower register of the tenor-bass gamba. Although Bach was familiar with the instrument's capability for multi-voiced chord playing, as exemplified in his *St Matthew Passion*, his technical demands in these sonatas are conservative.

The individual movements display remarkable diversity of structure and character. The lyrical, quasi-pastoral opening Adagio of the G major Sonata is followed by a jubilant, concertante-like Allegro, a brief Andante (E minor), and a powerful three-voice fugal Allegro moderato. The D major Sonata adopts a similar external structure, but its short opening Adagio introduces a dance-like binary Allegro of *galant* character. The ensuing Andante (B minor) is a siciliana in all but name, while the concluding Allegro incorporates two virtuoso solo passages at its climax. Both outer movements of the G minor Sonata adopt ritornello structures which open in fugato vein, the melodies, rhythms, and gestures (particularly of the first movement) suggesting those of a concerto rather than a sonata. The poignant central Adagio combines the Italian style of improvised ornamentation (here written out in full by Bach) with the slow triple metre and dignified style of the French sarabande. It is not unlike the slow movements in trio format of the Fifth and Sixth Brandenburg Concertos, in which only the concertino instruments are involved. RS

H. Eppstein, 'J. S. Bachs Triosonate G-Dur (BWV1039) und ihre Beziehungen zur Sonate für Gambe und Cembalo G-Dur (BWV1027)', *Die Musikforschung*, 18 (1965), 126–37; H. Eppstein, *Studien über J. S. Bachs Sonaten für ein Melodieinstrument und obligates Cembalo* (Uppsala, 1966, 2nd edn. 1983); H. Vogt, *Johann Sebastian Bach's Chamber Music*, Eng. trans. K. Johnson (Portland, Ore., 1988); P. Williams, 'Bach's G minor Sonata for Viola da Gamba and Harpsichord BWV1029: A Seventh Brandenburg Concerto?', *Early Music*, 12 (1984), 345–54;

C. Wolff, 'Bach's Leipzig Chamber Music', *Early Music*, 13 (1985), 165–75, repr. in *Bach: Essays on his Life and Music* (Cambridge, Mass., 1991), 223–38.

**gavotte.** A dance performed with various different types of steps and music at least from the 1580s to the 1790s. It was especially well known as a French court dance from the courts of Louis XIV and XV, where it was frequently enjoyed in theatrical works and as a social dance. Both music and dance achieved widespread popularity during the pastoral craze of the 1720s and 1730s, when it was favoured because of the predictable rhyme of its balanced phrases. It was during this period that Bach wrote most of his gavottes.

Many 18th-century writers stated that the gavotte could express a variety of affects, ranging from tender to joyful. J.-J. Rousseau (*Dictionnaire de musique*, 1768) says 'the movement of the gavotte is normally graceful, often gay, and sometimes also tender and slow'. The theorist F. W. Marpurg, an admirer of Bach's music, said that the gavotte could be either sad or joyful. All of these are moderate affects, not extreme ones.

The metrical structure of the gavotte is duple on all rhythmic levels (*see* RHYTHM). The beat is the minim, with crotchet and quaver rhythmic levels below this; smaller note values are ornamental. The time signature is normally 2 or ¢. The characteristic rhythmic phrase is eight beats (four bars) in length, with points of repose on beats four and eight (for a comparison of bourrée and gavotte rhythms, *see* RHYTHM, Ex. 1). *Notes inégales* may be applied to conjunct quavers in performance (*see* RHYTHM). Tempos varied somewhat from fast to slow, though always within the moderate range except in Italian-style pieces. Several theorists stated that gavotte beats move at a slower tempo than those of the bourrée, the rigaudon, and the march.

In instrumental music gavottes appeared in both French and Italian styles, the latter in violin music in a fast tempo and using virtuoso performance techniques, for example in Corelli's op. 4 no. 3. Bach's 'Tempo di Gavotta' from the keyboard Partita no. 6 is probably an example of Italian style (see Little and Jenne, p. 60).

Bach wrote 26 titled gavottes: in an early keyboard suite BWV822; English Suites nos. 3 and 6; French Suites nos. 4, 5, and 6; Partita no. 3 for solo violin (and its lute arrangement BWV1006a); Cello Suites nos. 5 (and its lute arrangement BWV995) and 6; the orchestral suites BWV1066, 1068, and 1069; the E minor Partita for keyboard; the Ouverture in the French Style; and the aria 'Sehet in Zufriedenheit' from Cantata 202.

Among the gavottes that are most French—that is, with the characteristic moderate affect and predictable rhyme and balance—are those from the English Suite no. 6, Cantata 202, Partita no. 3 for solo violin (in rondeau form, and the longest of Bach's gavottes), the Cello Suites, the French Suites, and the Ouverture in the French Style. Among those showing definite Italian influences are Gavotte I from the English Suite no. 3, Gavotte II from BWV815a (the second longest gavotte), and those in the orchestral suites. Untitled gavottes include the aria 'Quia fecit mihi magna' from the *Magnificat*. NJ, MEL

For bibliography, *see* DANCE.

***Gegenfuge.*** *See* COUNTER-FUGUE.

**Geier, Gottlieb Benjamin** (bap. 23 May 1710; bur. 17 May 1762). Church musician, born in Eisleben, Saxe-Anhalt. He studied theology at Leipzig University and was also a pupil of Bach in Leipzig between 1732 and 1737, after which he worked as Kantor in his native town, first at the Annenkirche, and from 1741 at the Nikolaikirche.

***Geist und Seele wird verwirret*** ('Spirit and soul are dumbfounded'). Cantata for the 12th Sunday after Trinity, BWV35, first performed on 8 September 1726. A solo cantata for alto voice, the work is thought to incorporate the outer movements of a lost oboe concerto. These serve as sinfonias, opening the first and second halves of the cantata; the original soloist is replaced by obbligato organ, and two oboes and *taille* are added to the (presumably) original string accompaniment.

This cantata dates from the same Trinity season during which Bach composed at least four others with obbligato organ; two of these are also solo alto cantatas (BWV169 and 170). It is not known for whom these works were written, but the presence of a transposed organ part within the autograph score of the present work suggests that Bach played this part himself from the score. There also survives a manuscript score copied by J. F. Agricola, who may have played in later performances.

The text, like that of Cantata 170, had been published by G. C. Lehms in 1711. It is restricted to MADRIGALIAN VERSE, for recitatives and arias, making it appropriate for a solo cantata. Its theme of rejoicing in God's power perhaps justified the incorporation of two lively concerto movements. Bach later began, but abandoned, an independent arrangement of the concerto as a work for solo harpsichord, oboe, and strings (the fragment BWV1059). The original may have dated from his Weimar years; it seems to have had points in common with the oboe concerto by Alessandro Marcello that Bach transcribed there for solo keyboard as BWV974—for example the binary form of the last movement, which Bach otherwise avoided in concerto movements.

# Gelobet sei der Herr, mein Gott

The second movement of the lost oboe concerto is usually identified with the Sinfonia of Cantata 156, but peculiarities in the second movement of the present cantata, a da capo aria, have been seen as evidence that this too may be derived from a concerto slow movement. If so, it was revised more substantially than were other instrumental movements that Bach is known to have incorporated into his church works. Nevertheless, the aria's siciliana rhythm and expressive chromatic harmony, which are combined with a florid organ obbligato, seem joined somewhat uncomfortably to a text describing the soul's astonishment at God's wonders. This suggests the reuse of older music, except perhaps in a brief passage in the B section which introduces an athletic motif for the word 'Jauchzen' ('rejoicing').

The second aria, accompanied only by organ and continuo, might also be a parody; its abbreviated da capo form unexpectedly connects the last line of the text to a restatement of the first, a device reminiscent of Bach's Weimar arias. Only a brief recitative and a single aria follow the second sinfonia, which would have been heard during Communion, after the sermon and the words of institution (see HAUPTGOTTESDIENST), in the original performance. As in the first aria, the ritornellos of the third employ the rhythm and phraseology of a dance (the minuet), as well as florid organ interpolations.                     DS

For bibliography, see CANTATA, §1.

***Gelobet sei der Herr, mein Gott*** ('Praised be the Lord, my God'). Cantata for Trinity Sunday (or possibly for the Reformation Festival), BWV129; the first performance probably took place in 1726–7 (perhaps on 31 October 1726). This is a CHORALE CANTATA setting the five strophes of Johannes Olearius's chorale of the same title (1655), which opens with three strophes praising the three persons of the Trinity in turn. The uncomplicatedly jubilant tone of the words (the first four strophes all begin 'Gelobet sei der Herr') colours the music and to some extent determines the forms of the cantata, which has no recitatives or da capo arias.

BWV129 is scored for SATB with flute, two oboes, three trumpets, timpani, strings, and continuo (including harpsichord). The opening chorus, set in the usual manner as a chorale fantasia, has the melody of the hymn *O Gott, du frommer Gott* in the soprano as cantus firmus, accompanied with imitative work in the lower voices and instruments. The movement begins with a ritornello (based on lively violin figuration with interpolations from the trumpets), which returns complete at the end of the movement. As usual in movements of this type, Bach uses the gaps in between the lines of the melody to effect most of the major structural modulations, with medial entries of material from the ritornello in A major and F♯ minor. The text is in praise of God the Father.

In contrast to the opulently festive scoring of the first movement, the second is a ritornello aria in A major for bass accompanied by the continuo section only. The chorale strophe is in praise of Jesus, and the music is dominated by the dotted rhythms of the ritornello, which returns between the main vocal paragraphs to articulate the key scheme A–E–F♯ minor–A. The third movement is addressed to the Holy Spirit. Bach sets it as an aria for soprano in E minor, accompanied by flute and violin obbligatos. Longer and more elaborate than the previous movement, it features a persistent semiquaver figure probably meant to suggest the Holy Spirit as a flame, or a 'rushing mighty wind'. The voice part also features other word-painting figures, notably a long melisma for the word 'Leben' ('life') which Bach employs in sequential repetitions. There are four entries of the ritornello, outlining the key sequence E–B–A–E (all minor).

The fourth strophe of the chorale (also beginning 'Gelobet sei der Herr, mein Gott') is set as an aria for alto with oboe d'amore in G major, in a pastoral style suggested by the 6/8 metre. Nature imagery may have been suggested to Bach by the phrase 'den alles lobet, was in allen Lüften schwebt' ('whom all things praise that hover in the air'). Much of the material is derived from the opening rising scale figure, which is constantly heard in dialogue between the voice and the oboe, in overlapping sequences. In its general character the music recalls 'Et in spiritum sanctum' from the B minor Mass. Like that aria, this one is in ritornello form, with medial entries in the dominant and relative minor.

The final strophe, 'Dem wir das Heilig itzt', is set not as the usual plainly harmonized chorale, but with instrumental interpolations in fanfare style which recall the triumphalist tone of the setting of *Nun danket alle Gott* in Cantata 79, the final chorus of the *Christmas Oratorio*. The fanfares of the opening instrumental ritornello, with prominent trumpets, return to punctuate the entries of the chorale lines, which are given out in four-part texture by the choir, with the flute doubling the melody at the upper octave. This movement, an arrangement of which was included in William Walton's ballet *The Wise Virgins* (1940), forms a rousing conclusion to the work.                     DLH

For bibliography, see CANTATA, §1.

*Gelobet seist du, Jesu Christ* ('Praised be thou, Jesus Christ'). Cantata for Christmas Day, BWV91, first performed on 25 December 1724. The text is based on Luther's famous Christmas hymn of the same title. As usual in the chorale paraphrase cantatas, the opening and closing strophes of the hymn are taken over unaltered for the first and last numbers of the cantata respectively (movements 1 and 6). Movements 3–5 set a paraphrase of the intervening strophes by an anonymous poet, while in movement 2 the poetic commentary is interpolated with the second strophe of the chorale itself. Bach revived the cantata in 1731/2 and again after 1735 (probably after 1740); for this final performance he slightly revised movements 5 and 6. For Christmas Day Bach also composed Cantatas 63, 110, and 197*a* (incomplete), as well as Part 1 of the *Christmas Oratorio*, and perhaps also *Gloria in excelsis Deo* BWV191, an adaptation of the opening two movements of the Gloria of the B minor Mass.

BWV91 has a six-movement structure which falls well within the normal convention of the Leipzig chorale cantatas. The text, closely based on Luther's chorale, emphasizes the contrast between the majesty of Christ's heavenly state and the lowliness of his birth for the salvation of mankind. The cantata is scored in an appropriately festive manner for SATB, three oboes, two horns, timpani, strings, and continuo (including bassoon). It opens with the usual concerted chorale setting, with Luther's melody sung by the soprano against jubilant counterpoint from the voices and instruments. The rushing scales from the oboes which open the ritornello are characteristic of Bach's portrayals of angels in other works, and the mood is here reinforced by fanfare writing for the two horns. The following simple recitative for soprano and continuo is interpolated with statements of the four lines of the chorale, given out in arioso style to the accompaniment of entries of the first line in diminution in the bass. This leads to a ritornello aria in A minor, 'Gott, dem der Erdenkreis zu klein', set to the accompaniment of the woodwind (three oboes and bassoon doubling continuo). The ritornello material is based on a sprightly figure in dotted rhythms which gives the music a *galant* air, the regal French 'dotted style' being the normal symbolic representation of kingly majesty in Baroque music from Jean-Baptiste Lully (1632–87) onwards. The movement is in an unusually clear-cut ritornello form, with medial entries in E minor, G major, D minor, and E minor punctuating the main periods in the development of the music. An abundance of dynamic and articulation marks further emphasizes the expressive character of the music.

The following bass recitative, accompanied by the strings, ends in an arioso marked Adagio, featuring extravagant chromaticism prompted by the reference in the text to 'this vale of tears' (there is also a pair of parallel 5ths which were gleefully pointed out in the text of the *BG* edition). The subsequent duet, 'Die Armut, so Gott auf sich nimmt', again uses dotted rhythms, this time in a somewhat Handelian accompanying figure (violins 1 and 2) which persists almost throughout the movement, as though adding substance to the words, which concern the poverty which God takes upon himself for the salvation of mankind. The voices do not participate in the ritornello material, but pursue their own course, singing for much of the movement in close imitation over a Corellian walking bass. The final chorale, which is accompanied by additional parts in fanfare style for the horns and drums, restores the jubilant tone of the opening chorus.                    DLH

For bibliography, *see* CANTATA, §1.

**gematria.** A term sometimes applied to certain aspects of NUMBER SYMBOLISM in the works of Bach.

**Genealogy** (*Genealogie*). A word used in the Bach literature (and throughout the present volume, with an initial capital) to refer to a document, the *Ursprung der musikalisch-Bachischen Familie*, containing brief biographical sketches of members of the Bach family arranged in chronological order. According to C. P. E. Bach, it was his father Johann Sebastian who made the original draft of the document, apparently in or about 1735. This has not survived, but copies were made and additions entered into them to keep the family record up to date. The copy usually quoted in the Bach literature (and twice issued in facsimile: ed. Max Schneider, n.d., and C. S. Terry, 1929) is in the hand of Emanuel's daughter Anna Carolina Philippina (1747–1804).

The Genealogy remains an important source of information about the older members of the Bach family, and several family trees have been compiled from it, including one which C. P. E. Bach sent to J. N. Forkel, along with Anna Carolina Philippina's copy of the Genealogy itself, in 1774. *See also* BACH FAMILY.

H. T. David and A. Mendel, eds., *The Bach Reader* (London, 1945; 2nd edn. 1966), 202–11.

**Gerber, Heinrich Nicolaus** (b. 6 Sept. 1702; d. 6 Aug. 1775). Organist and composer, born and died in Wenigen-Ehrich, near Sondershausen in Thuringia. He matriculated as a law student at Leipzig University on 8 May 1724, and towards the end of the same year became a pupil of Bach's. In 1731 he was appointed court organist to the Prince of Schwarzburg at Sondershausen, a post in which, upon his death, he was succeeded by his son, the music lexicographer Ernst Ludwig Gerber (1746–1819). E. L. Gerber's dictionary of musicians (Leipzig, 1790–2; rev. edn., 1812–14) contains a vivid account of his father's tuition under Bach (see David and Mendel).

Numerous keyboard works by Bach survive in copies made by H. N. Gerber during his Leipzig years (1724–7), including the Inventions and Sinfonias, the French Suites, English Suites nos. 1, 3, 5, and 6, the first two Preludes and Fugues from *The Well-tempered Clavier* Part 1, and some miscellaneous works (BWV818, 819, 914, and 996).     RDPJ

H. T. David and A. Mendel, eds., *The Bach Reader* (London, 2nd edn., 1966), 263–5; A. Dürr, 'Heinrich Nicolaus Gerber als Schüler Bachs', *BJb* 64 (1978), 7–18.

**Gerlach, Carl Gotthelf** (b. 31 Dec. 1704; d. 9 July 1761). Organist, born in Calbitz, near Oschatz, about 50 km. (31 miles) east of Leipzig. He attended the Thomasschule in Leipzig between 1716 and 1723, and probably studied with Bach in the 1720s. In 1727 he enrolled in Leipzig University, and in 1729 was appointed organist of the Neukirche there. Up to that time the organist of the Neukirche had always directed the collegium musicum that Telemann founded in Leipzig in the early years of the century, but in 1729 Bach himself took charge of the collegium musicum. Gerlach, however, took over from Bach for a couple of years between 1737 and 1739.

**Geschwinde, geschwinde, ihr wirbelnden Winde** ('Haste, haste, you whirling winds'). Textual incipit of the secular cantata DER STREIT ZWISCHEN PHOEBUS UND PAN, BWV210.

**Gesner, Johann Matthias** (b. 9 April 1691; d. 3 March 1761). Writer and teacher, born in Roth, near Nuremberg. In 1715 he was made pro-Rector and librarian of the gymnasium at Weimar, during the period when Bach was employed at the Weimar court. He left in 1729 to become Rector of the gymnasium in Ansbach, but the following year he succeeded J. H. Ernesti as Rector of the Thomasschule in Leipzig, thus renewing his friendship with Bach. In November 1733 his wife, Elisabeth Charitas (1695–1761), stood godmother to Bach's son Johann August Abraham, who survived for only one day. In 1734 Gesner took up his final appointment as professor of philology at the University of Göttingen. His library of over 4,000 volumes went to the university library after his death.

During his few years at Leipzig, Gesner instituted some much-needed reforms at the Thomasschule and shared Bach's views about the importance of music in the curriculum and in worship. His edition of the *Institutio oratoria* of Quintilian, published in 1738, includes a famous passage, in Latin, which paints a vivid picture of Bach's versatility as a practical musician (*BDok* ii, no. 432).

**Geyersbach, Johann Heinrich** (bap. 9 July 1682). A student and bassoon player, born in Holzhausen, near Arnstadt. Bach, in the company of a cousin, Barbara Catharina, quarrelled with him in the market-place on 4 August 1705. Geyersbach threatened Bach with a stick, saying he had insulted him by calling him a Zippel Fagottist (usually translated as 'nanny-goat bassoonist'), and Bach drew his sword to defend himself. Both disputants were called before the consistory in a series of hearings which lasted until 21 August and resulted in reprimands. In 1706 Geyersbach left school and enrolled at Jena University.
*See also* ARNSTADT.

**'Giant Fugue'.** Nickname sometimes used for the organ chorale *Wir glauben all an einen Gott* BWV680 from CLAVIER-ÜBUNG III. The name springs from the 'striding' quasi-ostinato bass figure which is played six times on the pedals.

**gigue, giga.** A lively, often complex dance that normally brings a Baroque suite to a close. Gigues by Bach appear to be of three distinct types: the French gigue, and two others for which the Italian form 'giga' is appropriate.

---

1. The French gigue.
2. The *giga*, type 1.
3. The *giga*, type 2.

---

1. The French gigue.   This is the only type for which choreographic roots survive (*see* DANCE). It was described by 18th-century theorists as lively, spirited, and joyful; in his *Dictionnaire* the French lexicographer Sébastien de Brossard (1655–1730) ascribed a skipping quality to it. Its most distinctive feature, however, is a graceful lilt produced by almost constant use of the so-called *sautillant* figure (Ex. 1). The metrical structure of the gigue consists of duple groups of beats, each beat expressed by the *sautillant* figure (Ex. 2a); that is to say, the beat is divided into triple groupings of quavers, and duple groupings of semiquavers below that. Phrases may be balanced, as in groups of four-plus-four beats, or unbalanced, with irregular groupings of beats. Tempo is usually described by theorists as fast in comparison with other French dances of the time.

Only six French gigues by Bach survive: in two early works BWV822 and 823, the Fifth Cello Suite, the Second French Suite, the Suite in G minor for lute BWV995 (based on the Fifth Cello Suite), and the Ouverture in the French Style.

IOHANNES MATTHIAS GESNERVS
natus CIƆIƆCLXXXXI. moritur
ΤΟΠΑΡΟΝΕΥΠΟΙΕΙΝ

J. M. Gesner, Rector of the Thomasschule, Leipzig, 1730-4

**2. The *giga*, type 1.** Along with the other type of *giga*, this joyously expresses the Baroque love of complexity. Neither type appears to have retained choreographic associations by Bach's time. In Bach's hands the first type may have a time signature of 6/8, 9/16, 12/8, 12/16, or even ₵, or ¢. Its metrical structure is made up of dotted minim beats, each of which contains two triple groups of quavers (Ex. 2*b*). Alternatively, it may be notated in 12/16, as in the G major French Suite and the D minor English Suite.

This type of *giga* is the only Baroque dance type which consistently has triple groupings at the lowest metrical level. Its texture is often imitative and sometimes fugal. Phrases are of unpredictable length, and important cadences often appear only at the end of each strain, producing a relentless sense of forward motion.

Of Bach's gigues 15 belong to this type, all of them pieces for a virtuoso soloist. The best known are from the English Suites nos. 2, 3, 4, and 6, and the keyboard Partitas nos. 1, 3, 4, and 6. The one in Partita no. 4 is unique in Baroque dance music in that it uses triple groupings on two of the metrical levels below the beat, with a key signature of 9/16. Another unique but problematic *giga* is in the keyboard Partita no. 6; it has no notated tripleness, but is written in common time with all metrical levels notated as duple (see the discussion in Little and Jenne, pp. 175–84).

Bach's untitled movements of this type include the organ Fugue in G major BWV577; the Prelude in G♯ from *The Well-tempered Clavier* Part 1; the Prelude in A major and the Fugues in C♯ minor and F major from *The Well-tempered Clavier* Part 2; and the chorus 'Lob, Ehr und Preis' from Cantata 192.

**3. The *giga*, type 2.** This is the most complex and exploratory type among Bach's gigues. He notated them mostly in 6/8, as in the *giga* in the French Suite in E major, but he also used 3/8, 12/8, ₵, and ¢. The metrical structure is made up of beats which contain one triple figure of equal quavers or, occasionally, of the *sautillant* figure (see Ex. 2*c*), with semiquavers running along on a lower level.

This *giga* type appears often in the works of French composers, but few Germans except for Bach used it. It has long phrases of unpredictable length, imitative texture, fugal procedures, and few, if any, internal cadences. Even though these are also characteristics of the type 1 *giga*, type 2 is different because it has a different metrical structure, and because pieces of this kind are longer and more complex. They include a fugue in four parts and three in three parts.

The French gigue and *giga* type 2 share several characteristics, including a common metrical structure with tripleness below the rhythmic level of the beat, harmonic changes within this lower level, and a moderate tempo with some ornamentation. They differ in their complexity, and in their use of the *sautillant* figure, which prevails in the French gigue but is only rarely heard in the *giga*.

Twenty type 2 *giga* pieces by Bach survive. They include examples in English Suites nos. 1 and 5; Cello Suites nos. 1, 2, 3, and 6; Partitas nos. 2 and 3 for solo violin; French Suites nos. 1, 3, 4, and 6; the keyboard Suite in A minor (BWV818); keyboard Partita no. 5; and Partita in C minor for lute, which also has a *double*. The intense, problematic *giga* in the D minor French Suite, notated in ₵ or

Ex. 1

Ex. 2

(*a*) 3/8 or 6/8

(*b*) 6/8 or 12/8

(*c*) 6/8 or 12/8

¢, has stimulated much scholarly discussion (see Little and Jenne, pp. 175–84).

Bach's untitled movements of this type include the organ Fugue in A minor BWV543:2; the two-part Invention in A major; the last movements of Brandenburg Concertos nos. 5 and 6; the Sinfonia and 'Kommt, eilet und laufet' from the *Easter Oratorio*; and 'Gloria in excelsis' from the B minor Mass.                                              NJ, MEL

For bibliography, *see* DANCE.

**Gleditsch, Johann Caspar** (b. 1684; d. 20 May 1747). Oboist. He was first oboist with the Leipzig *Stadtpfeifer* from 1719 until his death, and no doubt performed some of the obbligato oboe parts in Bach's church cantatas.

**Gleichwie der Regen und Schnee vom Himmel fällt** ('As the rain cometh down, and the snow from heaven'). Cantata for Sexagesima, BWV18, first performed at Weimar, perhaps in 1713 or 1714 and at the latest on 24 February 1715. Like other Weimar cantatas, it was revived at Leipzig in a revised version first heard probably on 13 February 1724.

The work is one of the few by Bach setting a text by Erdmann Neumeister, from the latter's 1711 *Jahrgang* for the nearby Eisenach court. A setting of the same text by Telemann, who had been at Eisenach in 1708–12, has been dated to 1719. The text is unusual in being built around extracts from the German litany; Bach's setting is unparalleled in both structure and scoring. The early version uses the five-part string writing typical of the Weimar works, but with two violas instead of the usual two violins (i.e. four violas in all). The result is an unusually low, quiet sonority which presumably seemed appropriate to the litany.

At Leipzig Bach added two recorders; this entailed a nominal change of key from G minor to A minor, but the actual pitch must have remained about the same. The recorders merely double the first and second violas at the octave (except in the ritornellos of the Sinfonia, where they are silent). Together with the recorders, these two violas serve as soloists in the opening Sinfonia; the two lower viola parts (along with the Fagott) furnish the ripieno. Separate organ and cello parts provide the continuo; the organ is doubled by violone, which, at least at Weimar, must have played at written pitch. This is, incidentally, the only doubling of any part for which there is documentary justification; a doubling of parts elsewhere (e.g. to produce a solo–ripieno alternation in the vocal movements) would be anachronistic and seems unnecessary.

The Sinfonia resembles the Sixth Brandenburg Concerto in its instrumentation (in both works the solo parts were probably played by violinists).

Like a number of other instrumental movements that Bach composed at Weimar, it combines ritornello and da capo form; moreover, the unison ritornello, with all parts playing in octaves, recalls concerto movements by Bach and Vivaldi, as does the subsequent employment of the ritornello theme as bass line for certain solo passages.

The initial bass recitative sets the simile of Isaiah 55: 10–11 comparing the watering of the earth and the spreading of the word, thereby alluding to the parable of the sower (Luke 8: 4–15, the Gospel for the day). The cantata's central movement, which follows, is built around four extracts from the litany. The archaic traditional melody of the latter, resembling a psalm tone, is initiated each time by the soprano and completed by the full ensemble. These passages are unvaried musically save in the continuo part, which, for example, grows animated when the text calls for preservation from 'Turks and Papists'. Each extract from the litany is preceded by an extensive arioso for tenor or bass, with string accompaniment. These sections are through-composed, alternating between *adagio* and *allegro* to reflect the changing sentiments of the text.

The sole aria is a short but elegant solution to the problem posed by Neumeister's somewhat ungrateful text. The soprano is accompanied by the four violas in unison, doubled at Leipzig by the recorders. The setting is in binary form (A–B), with a unifying ritornello; the second part employs an insistent rising motive ('away with all [temptations]') that contrasts with the more bucolic first part. The cantata concludes with a four-part setting of stanza 8 of the chorale *Durch Adams Fall*.                                              DS

For bibliography, *see* CANTATA, §1.

**Gmelin, Samuel** (b. 1 Nov. 1695; d. March 1752). Musician and schoolmaster, born in Plauen, Vogtland, Saxony. He matriculated at Jena University in September 1715, and studied with Bach in Weimar between then and 1717. In 1719 he was appointed Kantor at Elsterberg, about 15 km. (10 miles) north of Plauen, and in 1726 applied unsuccessfully for a similar post at the Johanniskirche in Plauen itself. Other applications for posts in Schleiz and Gera also came to nothing, and he remained in Elsterberg, where he was made Rector in 1730.

**Goldberg, Johann Gottlieb** (bap. 14 March 1727; bur. 15 April 1756). Composer and keyboard virtuoso, best known for the attachment of his name to Bach's GOLDBERG VARIATIONS. A dearth of dependable biographical information and the small number of available compositions have left many details of his life and work unclear. Born at Danzig, he was a child prodigy. He seems to have been brought by Count Keyserlingk to Dresden in the mid-1730s, and to have served him until 1745 and again from 1749 to 1751. He remained in Dresden until his death, playing in the *Kapelle* of the Saxon prime minister Heinrich von Brühl.

Reports that Goldberg studied with J. S. Bach have never been confirmed; W. F. Bach in 1767 implied that Goldberg had been his own pupil. The influence of both is clear in Goldberg's music, which includes six trio sonatas, at least two preludes and fugues, and two church cantatas. One of the cantatas was apparently performed at Leipzig by J. S. Bach and later at Hamburg by C. P. E. Bach. The Trio Sonata in C major was mistakenly published in *BG* as a work by Sebastian Bach (BWV1037) and is still often listed under his name.

The above-mentioned works employ strict fugal counterpoint and chromatic part-writing directly modelled on those in Sebastian's late works. A keyboard sonata and two keyboard concertos, however, are more in the style of Emanuel or Friedemann Bach, and Goldberg's set of polonaises in all 24 keys recalls Friedemann's series of 12 such pieces. Eighteenth-century reports stressed Goldberg's virtuosity at the keyboard, making plausible Forkel's implication that he was performing the Goldberg Variations for his patron at the age of 13 or 14. His sister Constantia Renata, whom he taught, was praised by the composer and writer J. F. Reichardt (1752–1814) for her 'unbelievable dexterity and strength' in playing Goldberg's works (see Dadder, p. 65).    DS

E. Dadder, 'Johann Gottlieb Goldberg', *BJb* 20 (1923), 57–71; A. Dürr, 'Johann Gottlieb Goldberg und die Triosonate BWV 1037', *BJb* 40 (1953), 51–80 [includes thematic catalogue and survey of works].

## Goldberg Variations. See opposite.

**Görner, Johann Gottlieb** (bap. 16 April 1697; d. 15 Feb 1778). Organist, born in Penig, about 20 km. (12½ miles) north-west of Chemnitz in Saxony. He attended the Thomasschule and the university in Leipzig, and was organist at the Paulinerkirche from 1716 to 1721, at the Nikolaikirche from 1721 to 1729, and then at the Thomaskirche until his death, when he was succeeded by his son Carl Friedrich. From 1723 he also directed the collegium musicum founded in 1708 by J. F. Fasch. He came into conflict with Bach in 1723 over provisions for the ALT-GOTTESDIENST at the university, and again in 1727 over the commissioning and performance of the TRAUER ODE, but there seems to have been no personal enmity between the two men and after Bach's death his widow chose Görner as guardian for her young children. Görner applied unsuccessfully to succeed Bach as Thomaskantor.

*Gott der Herr ist Sonn und Schild* ('The Lord God is a light and defence'). Cantata, BWV79, for the Reformation Festival, 31 October 1725, performed again some time between 1728 and 1731. For the later performance Bach indicated that flutes should be added to the oboes of the earlier version. The librettist is unknown, but since the opening psalm verse, which is echoed in later movements, was Erdmann Neumeister's personal motto, he may have been the author (or possibly the dedicatee). The Reformation Festival was an annual celebration of the Lutheran Reformation, commemorating Luther's nailing of his 95 theses to the door of the castle church in Wittenberg on 31 October 1517. Three of Bach's cantatas are directly associated with the festival: nos. 76 (part 1) and 80, in addition to the present work.

The splendid opening movement begins with an impressive 44-bar integral sinfonia, or prelude, in $A^1$–B–$A^2$ form. The $A^1$ section is characterized by a triumphal theme for obbligato horns undergirded by insistent repeated notes on the timpani, perhaps depicting Luther's hammering. The B section is a three-part fugato on a theme which is then combined with the initial horn theme in the final ($A^2$) section. The voices make their dramatic entrance at bar 45 and sing against the counterpoint of both themes a verse from Psalm 84, 'The Lord God is sun and shield' (to quote the Authorized Version). At the words 'no good thing shall he [God] withhold from them that live a godly life' the chorus sets out on a four-part fugue, employing a modified form of the earlier fugato theme. It is an extremely powerful movement with few rivals among Bach's other cantatas.

Movement 2, an engaging alto aria with oboe (later flute) obbligato, paraphrases the same psalm verse used in the opening movement. Movement 3 employs the third stanza of Martin Rinckart's *Nun danket alle Gott* ('Now thank we all our God', 1636), with its familiar melody. Bach brilliantly accompanies the sturdy chorale with the obbligato horn theme (with timpani) of the opening movement. The close textual and thematic relationship between these three movements has led some to suggest that they must have constituted the earlier form of the cantata, to which movements 4–6 were added later. The argument is persuasive but it remains unsupported by documentary evidence.

The following bass recitative (movement 4) leads to a soprano and bass duet, a prayer for God's continued faithfulness, which is accompanied by a vigorous obbligato for unison violins which derives its energy mainly from octave leaps and repeated quavers. The concluding chorale is a simple four-part setting of stanza 8 of Ludwig

[*cont. on p.197*]

# Goldberg Variations

Aria with 30 variations for two-manual harpsichord, BWV988. The Goldberg Variations (1741) form the fourth and final part of Bach's *Clavier-Übung* cycle, which began with the first keyboard Partita in 1726. Although it is not specifically numbered as part four, the title-page shares the same format as the first three parts, and is likewise dedicated to 'music-lovers'. Bach was clearly concerned to demonstrate the diversity of the keyboard idiom with the four collections, so there is little continuity between them. However, it is striking that each has a movement in French overture style (characterized by majestic writing in dotted rhythm) at its midway point: the opening of Partita no. 4 in *Clavier-Übung I*, the opening of the French overture in *Clavier-Übung II*, the second setting of *Wir glauben all* in *Clavier-Übung III*, and Variation 16 of the Goldberg Variations.

According to his first biographer, J. N. Forkel, Bach composed the variations at the request of J. G. Goldberg, who needed pieces to entertain Count Keyserlingk, the Russian ambassador to the Saxon court and a notorious insomniac who desired music during the night. The story has some plausibility given that Bach was a guest of Keyserlingk in Dresden in November 1741, although this is evidence for Bach's presentation of the new publication rather than for the initial impetus for its composition. But even if Forkel's account is not strictly accurate, it may well be that Goldberg, as a talented pupil of Bach and a virtuoso performer, soon gained a reputation as a performer of these pieces.

With declining health, it is unlikely that Bach himself could play the variations in the last few years of his life. Indeed, he had never composed such demanding music for keyboard and may have been influenced by the *Essercizi* (1739) of the Italian composer Domenico Scarlatti, which likewise contain many hand-crossings and virtuoso figurations. The writing shows the greatest development in Bach's keyboard idiom since his transcription of Italian instrumental concertos for organ and harpsichord, nearly 30 years earlier.

Much controversy has centred on the origins of the Aria on which the variations are supposedly based; Frederick Neumann was one of several scholars who suggested that it could not be of Bach's own composition. While it is very probable that Bach was strongly influenced by at least one French keyboard dance here (see Elster), it is equally certain that most of the details of figuration and melodic line are of his own invention. Certainly it was a popular piece in the Bach household, since Bach's second wife added it to the second of her two famous music books (but probably not until after the Goldberg Variations were published in 1741). None the less, the Aria is hardly the 'theme' as such, since it is the bass line and its implied harmonies that are shared by all the variations; in other words, virtually any of the movements could equally well be taken as the 'theme'. This method of composition, sometimes termed 'composition by variation' (see Schulenberg, p. 320), is perhaps one of the most important of the age (documented, for instance, by F. E. Niedt, some of whose writings Bach possessed). It involves generating pieces of the utmost diversity from a single pattern, even to the extent of obscuring the connection between successive pieces. This not only points to perhaps the primary way Bach learnt to compose—his well-documented tendency to copy and adapt the work of others—but also to a particular philosophical stance: the quest for the greatest diversity within the greatest unity.

The same stance is still more evident in the other aspect of Bach's compositional achievement here: his contrapuntal prowess within extremely tight compositional constraints. Every third variation is a canon: no. 3 at the unison, no. 6 at the 2nd, no. 9 at the 3rd, and so on until no. 27 at the 9th. Unlike many of the late works that examine the possibilities of strict contrapuntal devices, these canons show a remarkably wide range of character, from the supremely lyrical (Variations 3 and 9) to the intensely emotional (Variations 15 and 21) and even the humorous (Variation 27).

The closing variation comes where we would expect a canon at the 10th, but it is in fact a QUODLIBET, a piece which combines fragments drawn from folk melodies. The two melodies are 'Cabbage and beets have driven me away' and 'I have for so long been away from you'. As H.-J. Schulze has noted (*BJb* 62 (1976), 58–72), the latter comes from a *Kehraus*, the final dance of an evening, and is therefore particularly appropriate for the set. While some see the text as heralding the return of the Aria (indeed both texts concern the notion of being 'away'), there is no doubt that Bach's intent was mainly humorous, the combination of the thick four-part texture with the ungainly fragments of traditional tunes poking fun at his own contrapuntal inclinations.

The fact that the Aria returns after Variation 30 suggests that the work has gone full circle, something which is also implied by the canons. Indeed, as far as the canons are concerned the cycle may be said to 'overshoot', since those at the octave and the 9th are analogous to the opening canons at the unison and the 2nd. The variations which immediately precede a canon (mainly duets), on the other hand, show a more progressive sequence, becoming ever more virtuoso. Given that there are some discrepancies in this format—for example, the canon–free variation–duet format does not begin until Variation 3, and in Variations 28 and 29 we have two successive virtuoso pieces—some have suggested (see Breig) that there were originally only 24 variations, built around the first eight canons. Certainly it is becoming increasingly evident that other works, such as the *Clavier-Übung III* cycle that preceded this one, were built up in stages.

In 1974 Bach's own copy (HANDEXEMPLAR) of the printed score was discovered (see Wolff); it contains not only several corrections and more performance markings, but also 14 further canons on the first eight bass notes of the Aria. These do not seem so clearly designed for keyboard performance and are considerably more 'abstract' than the Goldberg Variations themselves. It may be that Bach considered amplifying the collection into a loosely formatted compendium of the arts of canon and variation, somewhat analogous to the *Musical Offering* or *The Art of Fugue*.

Nevertheless it seems clear that Bach strove to unify the work as it appears in the original printed edition: its present format comprises 32 pieces of music, thus complementing the 32 bars of the Aria (and the majority of the variations). Although, as Schulenberg (p. 322) notes, the ordering of many pieces could be shuffled without harming the collection as a whole, there are clearly pieces that cannot be reordered, most notably the canons. There is also some sense of intensification, both within the virtuoso duets (culminating in Variations 28–9) and within the free variations (culminating in the supremely expressive Variation 25). Furthermore, there are often links between successive variations, implying that portions of the work were designed in a continuous sequence; for instance, the head-motif for the first variation is heard in the closing notes of the Aria; the last two upper notes of the final variation seem to anticipate the first two notes of the reprised Aria; the head-motif of Variation 13 first appears in the second half of Variation 12, that for Variation 17 in the second half of Variation 16. Moreover, many variations end on the register appropriate for the succeeding variation; the sequence from Variation 24 to Variation 26 is particularly striking, with a change of mode between each variation. In all, it does seem clear that Bach was concerned with the cyclic aspects of the variations, even if these were taken into account towards the end of the compositional process rather than at the outset.

It is not the pacing of the variations, their contrapuntal ingenuity, nor even their virtuosity which is the most striking aspect of the set: it is the fact that Bach uses virtually every stylistic and affective device at his disposal. He provides a comprehensive, encylopaedic view of his musical world through the narrow focus of a single harmonic form. JAB

*See also* SOURCES, §2.

W. Breig, 'Bachs Goldberg-Variationen als zyklisches Werk', *Archiv für Musikwissenschaft*, 32 (1975), 243–71; G. Butler, 'Neues zur Datierung der Goldberg-Variationen', *BJb* 74 (1988), 219–21; P. Elster, 'Anmerkungen zur Aria der sogenannten Goldberg Variationen BWV 988: Bachs Bearbeitung eines französischen Menuetts', W. Hoffmann and A. Schneiderheinze, eds., *Bericht über die Wissenschaftliche Konferenz zum V. Internationalen Bachfest der DDR . . . Leipzig, 25. bis 27. März 1985* (Leipzig, 1988), 259–67; F. Neumann, 'Bach: Progressive or Conservative and the Authorship of the Goldberg Aria', *Musical Quarterly*, 71 (1985), 281–94; D. Schulenberg, *The Keyboard Music of J. S. Bach* (New York, 1992), 319–37; C. Wolff, 'The Handexemplar of the Goldberg Variations', in *Johann Sebastian Bach: Essays on his Life and Music* (Cambridge, Mass., 1991), 162–77.

Helmbold's *Nun laßt uns Gott, dem Herrn*, with its associated melody; the instruments play *colla parte*, except for the horns, which have independent parts.

Bach later used three movements of this cantata for settings of the Gloria in two of his Lutheran *missae*: nos. 1 and 5 in the *Missa* in G major BWV236, and no. 2 in the *Missa* in A major BWV234. RAL

R. A. Leaver, 'The Libretto of Bach's Cantata no. 79: A Conjecture', *Bach*, 6/1 (Jan. 1975), 3–11. For further bibliography, *see* CANTATA, §1.

**Gottesdienst** ('divine service'). The main service of the Lutheran church is referred to as the HAUPTGOTTESDIENST.

*See also* ALT-GOTTESDIENST and VESPERS.

**Gottes Zeit ist die allerbeste Zeit** ('God's time is the best of all times'). Cantata, or motet, BWV106, probably for a funeral; it is often referred to as the 'Actus tragicus'. The scoring, musical style, and form of both music and text mark it as an early work, composed perhaps at Mühlhausen in 1708. The subtle and poignant treatment of the text and many ingenious compositional features of the music have made this perhaps the most admired of Bach's compositions presumed to date from before his appointment at Weimar (1708), and it was one of the first cantatas to be published (in 1830) after his death.

The text, an anonymous compilation of Bible verses and chorale strophes, leaves little doubt that the work was composed for a funeral. Bach's Erfurt uncle Tobias Lämmerhirt, who died on 10 August 1707, is one of several persons with whom the work has been connected, but all such indentifications remain speculative. No performances during Bach's lifetime are documented, and the earliest manuscript (and source of the title 'Actus tragicus'), by an unidentified copyist, is dated 'Leipzig, 1768'. This, together with all other sources, is thought to derive from a copy owned by the Leipzig publisher Johann Gottlob Immanuel Breitkopf (1719–94), who listed the work in his 1761 catalogue of music manuscripts.

The work is scored for four-part vocal ensemble, with two recorders, two viola da gambas, and basso continuo. Although modern editions divide it into numbered movements, it should probably be understood as an unbroken sequence of short sections performed without substantial breaks (apart from the central fermata).

As in the roughly contemporary Cantata 4, a short instrumental movement (designated 'Sonatina') introduces a symmetrical sequence of vocal movements. The Sonatina is permeated by a drooping 'sigh' motif frequently employed in Bach's early works. The opening vocal section (no. 2a in the *NBA*), for all four voices, sets three contrasting clauses; the textual antithesis of the last two, 'In ihm leben' ('In him we live', Acts 17: 28) and 'in ihm sterben' ('in him we die'), is represented by a shift from quick diatonicism to slow chromaticism. There follow solos in aria style for tenor (no. 2b, 'Ach Herr, lehre uns bedenken', after Psalm 90: 12) and bass (no. 2c, 'Bestelle dein Haus', Isaiah 38: 1). The tenor solo is through-composed, although again permeated with sigh motifs; the much livelier bass section alludes to da capo form in closing with a repetition of the three opening words.

At the centre of the work lies a chorus (no. 2d) combining three distinct strands: a fugal setting of the verse 'Es ist der alte Bund' (Eccles. 14: 18), for the three lower voices; a soprano arioso 'Ja, komm, Herr Jesu' (Rev. 22: 20); and the chorale melody *Ich hab mein Sach Gott heimgestellt* in the instrumental accompaniment. The remarkably original conception of this section includes the dramatic stroke of closing with the soprano's prayer, unaccompanied, followed by a full bar of silence under a fermata (⌢).

Two more solos follow: for alto (no. 3a, 'In deine Hände', Psalm 31: 5), over a quasi-ostinato continuo line, and for bass (no. 3b, 'Heute wirst du mit mir', Luke 23: 43). The former has only continuo accompaniment, but the latter is eventually joined by another chorale, Luther's *Mit Fried und Freud*; the melody is sung by the alto, which remains to conclude the section after the bass has dropped out. The work closes with a setting (no. 4) for the full ensemble of the doxology-like seventh strophe of Adam Reusner's chorale text *In dich hab ich gehoffet, Herr* (1533; the melody is in soprano and recorders). The final line of the chorale is set as a fugue with an exuberant 'amen' countersubject.

Nineteenth-century editions give the work in E♭, modern ones in F. The latter is nominally a more correct interpretation of the original notation, and it eliminates several unplayable notes for the recorders. The sources provide no basis for the 'tutti' and 'solo' indications given in the *NBA*. Performance with more than a single voice or instrument to each part throws off the exquisitely planned scoring of the work; every indication is

that it was conceived for an ensemble of four singers balancing the four melody instruments and supported by continuo (possibly organ alone). DS

For bibliography, *see* CANTATA, §1.

*Gott fähret auf mit Jauchzen* ('God is gone up with a merry noise'). Cantata for Ascension Day, BWV43, first performed on 30 May 1726. From Purification (2 February) onwards that year Bach did not perform his own compositions in the main services at Leipzig, but used cantatas by his Meiningen cousin Johann Ludwig Bach. For Ascension, however, he decided for the first time to compose one of these Meiningen texts himself. The reason might be that for the main ecclesiastical feasts (Christmas, Easter, Ascension, Whitsun, and the Reformation Festival) the Meiningen texts consisted of many sections, and this led Johann Ludwig to write quite short movements which were not very attractive (as in *Denn du wirst meine Seele*, once thought to be J. S. Bach's earliest cantata, BWV15). Bach might have wished to avoid any short-windedness in a cantata for such an important feast as Ascension.

The characteristic feature of this longer form is that the number of movements in the 'standard' Meiningen cantata (*see* BRICH DEM HUNGRIGEN DEIN BROT) is increased by the addition of recitatives and arias after the New Testament passage. In *Gott fähret auf mit Jauchzen* Bach was faced with a poem of six strophes, which he 'modernized' by introducing an alternation of arias and recitatives from movement 5 to movement 10. Furthermore, the division of the text into two parts is here independent of the fact that the first and fourth movements are based on biblical texts, one from the Old Testament and one from the New; the first part now ends with the aria 'Mein Jesus hat nunmehr' (no. 5), the first section of the added strophic poem. Thus the 'traditional' shape of the text is replaced by a general pairing of recitative and aria throughout the cantata.

After the opening chorus (based on Psalm 47: 5–6, which can be understood as an allusion to Christ's Ascension) Bach casts the first recitative–aria pair for tenor. It is important for him to integrate the New Testament passage into this chain of paired movements, and the soprano recitative 'Und der Herr, nachdem er mit ihnen geredet hatte' (Mark 16: 19) is therefore directly linked to the E minor aria 'Mein Jesus hat nunmehr' (also for soprano, with strings and two oboes).

High voices (soprano and tenor) sing the recitatives and arias of Part 1; consequently the next four movements are an accompanied recitative and an aria, 'Er ists, der ganz allein' (with solo trumpet), for bass and a simple recitative and an aria, 'Ich sehe schon im Geist' (with two oboes), for alto. The scoring of the arias in Part 2 is thus dominated by the winds (in Part 1 by the strings); and the keys of the arias in the first part (G major and E minor) are a 5th higher than those in the second part (C major and A minor). As if to compensate for this, the final chorale, 'Du Lebensfürst, Herr Jesu Christ', is in a key (G major) a 5th higher than that of the opening chorus. Thus Bach gave the strict structure of the original libretto a totally different, but equally plausible, shape.                                                                KK

For bibliography, *see* CANTATA, §1.

**Gott ist mein König** ('God is my king'). Cantata, BWV71, for the annual change of administration in the imperial free city of Mühlhausen. It was performed on 4 February 1708 in the Marienkirche. In the following year, when Bach had become court organist at Weimar, the commission for the annual composition was again entrusted to him. Nothing of this second work has remained, although, like *Gott ist mein König*, it was printed at the expense of the council. For more than a century these two works remained Bach's only printed cantatas.

*Gott ist mein König* is a complex blend of traditional and modern elements. Apparently Bach was not yet influenced by elements of modern Italian vocal music such as recitative and the ritornello principle in arias; his model might have been rather Buxtehude's polychoral music as performed in Lübeck. Consequently, Bach designed the music of the opening movement for six 'choruses', as the grouping of the parts in his autograph score shows: four instrumental groups (trumpets and drums, violins and violas, oboes and bassoon, recorders and cello) and two vocal choruses, one of soloists and the other of doubling ripienists. All six groups are employed for the words 'Gott ist mein König'; the remainder of the text is entrusted to the solo voices accompanied by the strings. The result is a sequence of three tutti refrains enclosing two 'verses' for the four soloists.

Similarly, the bass aria, 'Tag und Nacht ist dein', is not a da capo aria, despite its A–B–A form, but another sequence of short, song-like refrains, with a radically contrasting middle section setting a considerable amount of text. The situation of the alto aria, 'Durch mächtige Kraft', is similar to this. Important for the nature of the work was Bach's understanding of his individual position as the leading organist of the city with a broad insight into north German music. This is reflected in the structure of the fugues 'Dein Alter sei wie deine Jugend' (no. 3) and 'muß täglich von Neuem' (in no. 7), which are of the north German PERMU-

TATION type, as well as in two passages for obbligato organ. One of these occurs in the tenor aria 'Ich bin nun achtzig Jahr', in E minor with the G major chorale strophe 'Soll ich auf dieser Welt' sung by the soprano—the same tonal relationship between chorale tune and newly composed music that occurs in the opening chorus of the *St Matthew Passion*. The other brief organ solo is in the final chorus at the text 'Friede, Ruh und Wohlergehen', where the instrumental interludes are passed from the violins to the oboes and the recorders, and then to the organ. Here Bach displays himself as an ideal organist-cum-conductor.

Most of the text is based on Psalm 74 (movements 1, 4, and 6), and the poet drew on other biblical texts for the tenor line in movement 2 and for the chorus 'Dein Alter sei wie deine Jugend' (no. 3). Movements 5 and 7 use specially written verses (Bach ignored the strophic layout of the text for the final chorus in the interests of a richer musical structure), and these introduce into the composition direct allusions to the political situation; for example, the person named Joseph is the emperor—the highest sovereign of the imperial city. This 'free' poetry, normally an indicator for modern cantata forms, appears here in a quite traditional context.

The poet evidently paid homage to burgomasters of considerable age (this being a central idea especially of the biblical texts not belonging to Psalm 74). Indeed, the new principal burgomaster, Adolf Strecker (1624–1708), was 83 years old; his colleague Conrad Meckbach (1637–1712, apparently one of Bach's most important patrons in Mühlhausen) was 70.                    KK

*See also* SOURCES, §2.

For bibliography, *see* CANTATA, §1.

**Gott ist unsre Zuversicht** ('God is our hope and strength'). Wedding cantata, BWV197. Although it belongs to the later years of Bach's life, two of its movements, at least, were originally composed for a Christmas cantata, *Ehre sei Gott in der Höhe*, performed probably in 1728. The present work, however, was produced some time around 1736–7 when, according to Bach's 19th-century biographer Philipp Spitta, it was performed at the wedding of people of rank. Nothing is known about the occasion itself, but the dimensions of the piece (one of only seven to which Bach appended the term 'cantata'), the large assembly of instruments, and the solemn Latin subheading, 'In diebus nuptiarum', would seem to support Spitta's claim.

The libretto, by an unidentified author, has few distinctive features and is constructed in simple, unadorned language. Only the chorale strophes which conclude each part of the cantata come from identifiable sources: the first from Luther's hymn *Nun bitten wir den heiligen Geist* (1524), the second from Georg Neumark's *Wer nur den lieben Gott läßt walten* (1657), on which Bach had earlier based his cantata of the same name. The remaining sections of the cantata's text are concerned with God's providence, omnipotence, and mercy (Part 1), and with an address to the wedded couple in terms of well-wishing (Part 2).

The occasional nature of the cantata is reflected in the vigorous opening choral fugato, in da capo form, with its festive scoring for three trumpets, timpani, two oboes, strings, and continuo. By means of a 24-bar instrumental prelude, scored for the full orchestral complement, Bach effectively provides an introductory sinfonia and chorus in one resplendent movement. A declamatory bass recitative, which merges into arioso, leads to the first of three arias. This tenderly expressive movement, a modified da capo structure in A major scored for alto voice with oboe d'amore, strings, and continuo, affectingly colours and enlivens the directly worded exhortation to trust in God's guidance. A second recitative, again for bass but this time accompanied by string chords, is followed by the third strophe of Luther's *Nun bitten wir den heiligen Geist*, sung to its associated melody. It concludes Part 1 of the cantata.

Part 2, which would have been performed after the wedding ceremony itself, begins with a bass aria, lightly scored for oboe, muted violins in two parts, bassoon obbligato, and continuo. The soft colours of Bach's instrumental palette, the playful dialogue between the oboe, violins, and bassoon, and the freely expressive contours of the vocal writing imbue this captivating aria with a warmth and ardour entirely appropriate to this intimate address to the bridal pair. The piece is a parody of an incompletely surviving alto aria in the Christmas cantata already mentioned.

The following two sections are both for soprano. A simple recitative, which breaks into an extended arioso to illustrate the concluding line of the text, leads to an aria scored for solo violin with two-part oboe d'amore accompaniment and continuo. The 6/8 metre and the unusual use of the oboes d'amore to play off-beat quavers evoke the character of a folk dance; yet in its original context it might be understood as a lullaby or cradle-song, since the piece is another parody of one in *Ehre sei Gott in der Höhe*. One last recitative for bass, this time accompanied by strings and oboes, is followed by the strophe from Neumark's hymn, whose associated melody is straightforwardly harmonized by Bach.                                                    NA

For bibliography, *see* CANTATA, §1.

*Gottlob! nun geht das Jahr zu Ende* ('Praise be to God! The year is drawing to its close'). Cantata for the Sunday after Christmas, BWV28, first performed on 30 December 1725 as part of Bach's third Leipzig cantata cycle. The libretto is by Erdmann Neumeister (1714). The text of movement 2 is the first strophe of *Nun lob, mein Seel, den Herren* by Johann Gramann (1530); movement 3 is Jeremiah 32: 41; movement 6 is the last strophe of *Helft mir Gotts Güte preisen* by Paul Eber (c.1580).

The Sunday after Christmas, which does not occur in every Church year, is the last Sunday of the secular year, and BWV28 takes the passing of the old year and the coming of the new as its principal topic. The opening soprano aria, with its particularly rich concerted texture of strings and three oboes, calls on the soul to recall God's gifts in the previous year, and for a song of thanks in hope of continued blessings in the new year. The second movement, a setting of the chorale *Nun lob, mein Seel, den Herren*, may represent that song of thanks. The chorale melody is presented in long notes in the soprano, with each phrase preceded by 'pre-imitation' in the lower voices. There are no independent instrumental lines; strings, oboes, cornett, and trombones double the vocal parts.

This movement is a motet, and Klaus Hofmann has suggested that Bach used MOTET STYLE, which was understood as retrospective, to invoke the past. But chorale motets, especially on certain chorale tunes like this one, were also a Christmas-season tradition in central Germany, and Bach's use of a motet setting connects it to contemporary practice. The movement may have a history before its appearance in this cantata (the composing score suggests that it already existed), and Bach also reused the movement in a pastiche motet, *Jauchzet dem Herrn, alle Welt* BWV Anh. III 160.

The theme of God's gifts is continued in the third movement, a biblical text in which God speaks of providing for Israel. The movement is for bass, long associated with the voice of God. After the first words 'So spricht der Herr' ('And God said'), Bach presents the text as an arioso supported by a continuo line that dwells on one motif. Movement 4 is a recitative for tenor accompanied by strings continuing the theme of God's generosity. The following continuo aria, a duet for alto and tenor, sums up the themes of gratitude, praise, and wishes for further beneficence. Its text is in anapaestic metre, and Bach responds, as he often does, with a lilting compound musical metre (6/8). Each of the text's three couplets begins in loose imitation between the voices and ends with simultaneous declamation.

The final movement is the last strophe of *Helft mir Gotts Güte preisen*, chosen for its mention of God's goodness and of New Year, in a simple four-part harmonization.                                         DRM

K. Hofmann, 'Alter Stil in Bachs Kirchenmusik: zu der Choralbearbeitung BWV28/2', in D. Berke and D. Hanemann, eds., *Alte Musik als ästhetische Gegenwart: Bach Händel Schütz: Bericht über den internationalen musikwissenschaftlichen Kongreß Stuttgart 1985* (Kassel, 1987), i. 164–9; D. Melamed, *J. S. Bach and the German Motet* (Cambridge, 1995).

**Gott, man lobet dich in der Stille** ('Thou, O God, art praised in Sion'). Cantata for the installation of the Leipzig city council, BWV120. The inaccessibility of the autograph manuscript for a period after World War II—it is now in Kraków, Poland—hindered study of the work, which is now known to be one of Bach's last council election cantatas, performed no earlier than 27 August 1742. It consists largely of movements parodied from earlier compositions, brought together into an imaginative new design.

The work opens with a setting for alto (with two oboes d'amore and strings) of Psalm 65: 1. The restrained scoring and quiet phrase endings were occasioned by Luther's text, 'You are praised, God, in the silence' (the last word appears in neither the Authorized Version nor the Book of Common Prayer). Nevertheless the vocal part is extraordinarily florid, utterly unlike the older duet from which Bach borrowed the ritornello. Musically the movement is a modified da capo form in A major, the second half of the psalm verse being reserved for the B section.

Jubilation follows. The text of the second movement is a da capo form, which Bach follows strictly in a choral setting with three trumpets, timpani, and strings (oboes doubling the violins). The two lines of the A text each receive compact fugal expositions, both subjects having been previously heard in the ritornello: for 'jauchzet' ('rejoice') a rising arpeggio, for 'steiget' ('rise') a climbing melisma.

In a recitative in B minor, addressed to Leipzig itself ('beloved city of lindens'), the bass soloist prays for blessings, which are then the subject of a quietly ecstatic aria in G major. A similar sequence of movements appears in the earlier Cantata 120*a*, which employed a version of the same aria with different text; both versions are for soprano and strings, with a florid solo violin part. An accompanied recitative for tenor, containing a prayer for rectitude, modulates back to B minor, preparing the final movement, a four-part harmonization of the fourth strophe of Luther's German *Te Deum*. The archaic modal melody ensures a thoughtful setting that turns to D major only in the final phrase. Trumpets and drums are silent

here, but the autograph contains a direction to conclude with an 'intrada con trombe e tamburi', perhaps a fanfare or march of some sort; one might substitute the *Marche* attached to Cantata 207 or 207*a*.

The complex parody relationships of this work remain incompletely understood. The first movement, both music and text, appears to have been taken from Cantata 120*b*, which bears the same title; the music of movements 2 and 4 also came from that work, but there they have different texts. BWV120*b* was the second of three cantatas that Bach composed for the 200th anniversary of the Augsburg Confession, observed at Leipzig on 25–7 June 1730. Its music is lost, but Picander's text survives; it corresponds closely in metre and rhyme scheme to that of Cantata 120 (hence strongly pointing to Picander's involvement in the latter).

The music of BWV120*b* cannot have been the original version, however, for the three movements also appear in distinct forms, and in a different order, in HERR GOTT, BEHERRSCHER ALLER DINGE BWV120*a*, a wedding cantata of (probably) 1729. In addition, the soprano aria exists as the third movement of a version of the G major sonata for violin and obbligato keyboard BWV1019*a*, dating from no later than about 1725. Moreover, the chorus common to all three works recurs yet again in a later but apparently independent adaptation as 'Et expecto' in the Mass in B minor.

Hence, all three movements appear to go back, directly or indirectly, to even earlier works that are completely lost. The violin sonata movement was probably arranged from an earlier aria, and the opening alto solo of Cantatas 120 and 120*b* may likewise go back to an earlier aria or duet (Smend's derivation of the movement from a lost concerto depends on his anachronistic view of the 'instrumental' character of the vocal line). In the chorus the scoring (without independent woodwind parts) and the straightforward da capo form seem to point to Bach's pre-Leipzig period. Even the second recitative (movement 5) of BWV120 may have been borrowed, to judge from Bach's alteration of a word in the text (whose final clause seems curiously unrelated to what precedes it).

DS

For bibliography, *see* CANTATA, §1.

**Gottsched, Johann Christoph** (b. 2 Feb. 1700; d. 12 Dec. 1766). Writer and literary reformer, born in Juditten, near Königsberg in Prussia. He was the leading literary figure in Leipzig during Bach's Kantorate, and seminal in the foundation of German as a literary language.

Bach's music survives for only one Gottsched text, the *Trauer Ode* of 1727. Although it is unlikely

## Gott soll allein mein Herze haben

that Gottsched would have approved of the textual alterations, which probably stem from Bach, the two seem not to have clashed; indeed, in 1732 Gottsched sent keyboard pieces by Bach to his future bride. However, the famous attack on Bach by J. A. SCHEIBE (1737) shows every influence of Gottsched's aesthetic theories.     JAB

***Gott soll allein mein Herze haben*** ('My heart shall have God alone'). Cantata for the 18th Sunday after Trinity, BWV169, first performed on 20 October 1726. It is the last and arguably the greatest of the four cantatas for solo alto and, with Cantata 35 of six weeks earlier, one of two incorporating concerto movements arranged for obbligato organ. The opening Sinfonia and the second aria derive from the first two movements of the lost work (possibly for oboe) that Bach later arranged as the E major harpsichord concerto; the final movement of that work became the Sinfonia of Cantata 49, performed two weeks later. Unlike that movement, the present Sinfonia includes three occasionally independent parts for two oboes d'amore and *taille*.

The libretto is anonymous but shows signs of the composer's intervention. The first vocal movement alternates between arioso and recitative, the three arioso sections anticipating the text of the first aria ('My heart shall have God alone') and, through their minuet-like rhythm and mainly diatonic D major tonality, contrasting sharply with the recitative passages. Alfred Dürr (*DürrK*, p. 637) suggests that the arioso passages represent Bach's interpolation into the text to produce an ingenious quasi-dialogue. The aria itself is a straightforward da capo form in D major, with an ornate obbligato organ part; the vocal line is independent of both the organ part and the preceding arioso, despite the common text (the opening motif of the arioso returns here in free inversion).

A recitative leads to the second aria, which, as in Cantata 146, superimposes new vocal writing over the slow movement of the pre-existing concerto, now scored for organ, strings, and continuo (without the oboes). The text, with its irregular prosody and rhyme scheme, must have been written, or at least adapted, specifically for use in the present contrafactum. Its theme of farewell from worldly life ('Die in me, world') is well suited to the underlying instrumental movement in B minor, designated 'Siciliano' in the later harpsichord version. The aria includes a second ritornello absent from the later version; this introduces the second part of the text ('die in me, pride'). At the recapitulation (bar 27) the voice omits the first three words, instead presenting new material that

includes a repeated turning motif emphasizing 'Welt' ('world').

A brief recitative leads to a four-part setting of stanza 3 of Luther's *Nun bitten wir den heiligen Geist*.     DS

For bibliography, *see* CANTATA, §1.

***Gott, wie dein Name, so ist auch dein Ruhm*** ('O God, according to thy Name, so is thy praise'). Cantata for New Year's Day, BWV171. It is probably the last of the five surviving cantatas that Bach wrote for this festival at Leipzig, and was most likely performed on 1 January 1729. The text is by Picander, who in the previous year had published a set of cantata librettos for the entire Church calendar. In this particular cantata Picander focuses on the significance of God's name for all Christians; but he also makes specific reference to the hope of Church and State that God's guidance and protection will attend them throughout the coming year. The text is, furthermore, loosely connected to the appointed Gospel reading (Luke 2: 15–21) and, in the case of the opening movement, more specifically to part of the ninth verse of Psalm 48: 'O God, according to thy Name, so is thy praise unto the world's end.'

The introductory chorus is a joyful one, generously scored for three trumpets, timpani, two oboes, strings, and continuo. It is cast as a vigorous choral fugue in which the woodwind and strings perform a *colla parte* role while the trumpets and drums enjoy greater independence. Bach further delivers a masterstroke by bringing in the first trumpet at bar 23 with a restatement of the fugue subject already presented in each of the four vocal parts. With this resonant gesture and the overall contribution of brass and timpani, the glittering, occasional opulence of the movement is assured. In the 1740s Bach parodied this music for 'Patrem omnipotentem' in the Symbolum Nicenum of his B minor Mass.

From the festive D major of the opening chorus, the tenor aria takes us into A major. Bach's autograph lacks any precise specification for the two imitative obbligato parts, but the usual practice of assigning them to violins seems to be the most likely solution. Voice and instruments play roles of equal importance, resulting in a particularly pleasing texture. An alto recitative provides the link between this aria and the second one of the cantata, a virtuoso D major movement in 12/8 metre, in which the protagonists are soprano voice and solo violin. This is a masterly parody of an aria which Bach had written a few years earlier for a secular cantata, *Zerreißet, zersprenget, zertrümmert die Gruft*. As Alfred Dürr remarked in a note accompanying a recording of the cantata

(*Cantate* 651 209), 'Anyone who has absorbed this aria must find it difficult to believe that the melody which fits the text so effortlessly was ever sung to different words.'

The bass movement that follows is of particular interest for the way in which Bach dovetails elements of accompanied recitative and arioso. It begins with a passage of arioso in 3/8 time accompanied by the continuo; this leads to a section of recitative in which the continuo is joined by two oboes; the concluding six bars, however, revert to arioso, yet retain the oboes of the middle section, thus uniting the disparate elements of this effectively declaimed movement.

The cantata ends with the second strophe of Johann Hermann's hymn *Jesu, nun sei gepreiset* (1593). Bach had previously used this elaborate setting for another strophe of the same hymn in another New Year cantata, no. 41 (1725). While the woodwind and string instruments reinforce the vocal parts, the trumpets and timpani provide fanfare-like interludes between some of the lines of the hymn. A change from duple to triple time takes place in the second half of the stanza, both illuminating the text and emphasizing, by means of a more lyrical song-like declamation, the festive nature of the occasion and its hopeful message. It is with the fifth and last of the fanfares that this resplendent work is concluded.                NA

For bibliography, *see* CANTATA, §1.

**Gould, Glenn** (b. 25 Sept. 1932; d. 4 Oct. 1982). Canadian pianist, composer, and writer, born in Toronto. From the age of 14 he appeared as a solo pianist, both with orchestras and in recitals. He made his USA concert début in 1955 and in the same year his first commercial recording of Bach's Goldberg Variations. From then onwards Bach became the composer with whom Gould was most closely identified. His performances fostered the art of personal communication and his charismatic, idiosyncratic interpretations won for him a wide and loyal following. Gould was seldom dull as either performer or writer, and his secure technique, lucid realization of texture, and musical insight often provided a satisfying counterbalance to his unorthodox interpretations and, at times, bewildering eccentricity.                NA

*See also* RECORDINGS.

**Gräbner, Christian Heinrich** (b. ?1705; bur. 5 Jan. 1769). Organist, born and died in Dresden. He studied with Bach in Leipzig in 1725–6. In 1733 he applied unsuccessfully for the post of organist at the Sophienkirche, Dresden (the appointment went to Bach's eldest son, Wilhelm Friedemann). He assisted his father Johann Heinrich Gräbner (*c.*1665–1739), who was organist at the Frauenkirche, Dresden, and in 1739 he succeeded him there. From 1742 he was organist at the Kreuzkirche.

**Graun, Carl Heinrich** (b. 1703/4; d. 8 Aug. 1759). Composer, born in Wahrenbrück, about 65 km. (40 miles) north-east of Leipzig, in Brandenburg. He was the brother of J. G. Graun. He worked at the Brunswick opera from 1725 and was appointed *Kapellmeister* to the Prussian crown prince (later Frederick the Great) in 1735. He was important above all as an opera composer, but he also wrote instrumental and sacred music, notably the Passion cantata *Der Tod Jesu* (1755). An earlier Passion cantata, *Ein Lämmlein geht und trägt die Schuld*, exists as a pasticcio with additions by Bach, Telemann, and Kuhnau. A score was prepared by J. C. Altnickol and another copyist, but no performance is documented. C. P. E. Bach stated that both Graun and his brother were among the composers that his father 'in his last years esteemed highly'.

J. W. Grubbs, 'Ein Passions-Pasticcio des 18. Jahrhunderts', *BJb* 51 (1965), 10–42; G. Herz, 'J. S. Bach and the Church Music of the Age of Rationalism: A Style-Critical Comparison of Bach's *St. Matthew Passion* and C. H. Graun's *Tod Jesu*', in *Essays on J. S. Bach* (Ann Arbor, 1985), 51–65.

**Graun, Johann Gottlieb** (b. 1702/3; d. 27 Oct. 1771). Composer and violinist, born, like his younger brother Carl Heinrich, in Wahrenbrück. He studied with J. G. Pisendel in Dresden and with Giuseppe Tartini (1692–1770) in Prague. In 1726/7 he was appointed *Konzertmeister* at Merseburg, where he taught the violin to Bach's son Wilhelm Friedemann. He joined the establishment of the Prussian crown prince (later Frederick the Great) in 1732, and in 1740 was made *Konzertmeister* of the Berlin Opera. His compositions, in contrast with those of his brother, are mainly orchestral and instrumental.

**Graupner, Christoph** (b. 13 Jan. 1683; d. 10 May 1760). Composer, born in Kirchberg, about 10 km. (6 miles) south of Zwickau in Saxony. He first established a reputation as an opera composer in Hamburg, and in 1709 moved to Darmstadt as vice-*Kapellmeister* (from 1712 *Kapellmeister*) to the Landgrave Ernst Ludwig. In 1723 he competed successfully for the post of Kantor at the Thomasschule in Leipzig, but the landgrave refused to release him and instead increased his salary, leaving the way clear for Bach's appointment at the Thomasschule. Graupner then remained at Darmstadt, composing prolifically in practically every genre, sacred and secular, vocal and instrumental. A keyboard Allemande and Courante in

### 'Great G minor'

A major once thought to be by Bach (BWV838) is now attributed to Graupner.

**'Great G minor'.** Nickname for the organ Fantasia and Fugue in G minor BWV542, used to distinguish it from the 'Little' Fugue BWV578 in the same key.

**Grigny, Nicolas de** (bap. 8 Sept. 1672; d. 30 Nov. 1703). French organist and composer, born and died in Reims. He was organist of Reims Cathedral, and a leading member of the French Baroque school of organist-composers. De Grigny's only surviving music is his *Livre d'orgue* (1699), of which Bach made a complete copy about 1713. This has naturally led to a search for De Grigny's influence on Bach's own organ music, supported to some extent by C. P. E. Bach's citation of 'some good and old Frenchmen' among the composers whose works Bach had studied in his youth. Attention has focused on two works in particular. Bach's Fantasia (*Pièce d'orgue*) in G major BWV572 has French tempo markings for the three sections in the main source (*Très vitement–Gravement–Lentement*); the central section certainly invites comparison with some of De Grigny's *plein jeu* movements, though on a vastly increased scale. Also probably indebted to French models is the C minor Fantasia BWV562, a majestic essay in five-part counterpoint based on a subject which has been compared with a fugue labelled 'petit plein jeu' from the Gloria of De Grigny's organ mass.

DLH

M. C. Alain, 'Réflexions sur le livre d'orgue de Nicholas de Grigny d'après la copie de J. S. Bach', in D. Mackey, ed., *L'Orgue à notre époque* (Montreal, 1981), 91–105; P. Williams, *The Organ Works of J. S. Bach*, iii (Cambridge, 1984), 60–2, 97–102.

# H

**Haase, Johann Gottlob** (b. *c.*1715; d. after 1755). Organist, born in Profen, about 25 km. (16 miles) south of Leipzig. He attended the Thomasschule in Leipzig from August 1731, and enrolled at Leipzig University in 1735. He studied with Bach for over a year at this time and was a member of his collegium musicum. Bach wrote a testimonial for him which has not survived, but Haase referred to it in a letter, dated 18 November 1756 (see *BDok* i, no. 72), in pursuit of his application for the post of court organist at Zeitz, left vacant after J. L. Krebs moved to Altenburg. He had apparently been living at Zeitz, not far from his native Profen, since at least 1743.

***Halt im Gedächtnis Jesum Christ*** ('Hold in remembrance Jesus Christ'). Cantata for the first Sunday after Easter (Quasimodogeniti), BWV67, first performed in Leipzig on 16 April 1724. Unlike the music Bach had performed during the Easter festival itself, for which he had fallen back on earlier cantatas, *Halt im Gedächtnis* was entirely new. Both in respect of content and formal symmetry the work bears an affinity to five other cantatas scheduled for performance in 1724 on the subsequent Sundays leading up to Whitsuntide. This has prompted some writers to suggest that Bach conceived them as a little cycle within the larger annual one embracing the liturgical year.

The text, by an unidentified author (perhaps the Weimar theologian and poet Salomo Franck), is closely allied to the appointed Gospel reading, St John 20: 19–31, which contains the story of doubting Thomas. The supple, declamatory opening chorus, scored for SATB with *corno da tirarsi*, flute, two oboes d'amore, strings, and continuo, establishes a joyful Easter spirit which is maintained throughout the work. (The exact nature of the *corno da tirarsi* is uncertain, but it is likely that Bach intended a slide trumpet with a modified mouthpiece or other device to produce a sound closer to that of a horn.) The single sentence of the text, from 2 Timothy 2: 8 (in the Authorized Version: 'Remember that Jesus Christ of the seed of David was raised from the dead') serves to emphasize the Gospel reading. The movement is impressive not least for the immediacy of its word-painting, one feature of which is the way that Bach always relates the periodic sustained *corno da tirarsi* notes to the word 'halt' ('hold').

From the chorus key of A major, Bach leads us to E major for the dance-like tenor aria with oboe d'amore and strings. This presents two conflicting emotions, the joy of the Resurrection on the one hand, but doubt concerning its reality on the other. This spiritual vacillation is further emphasized in the ensuing triptych where the first strophe of Nikolaus Herman's affirmative hymn, *Erschienen ist der herrlich Tag* (1560), set to Herman's own melody of the same date, is framed by two simple recitatives for alto, in which the doubts of would-be believers are reflected.

The heart of the cantata lies in the ensuing bass aria with choral interjections, which contains Christ's Easter greeting, 'Friede sei mit euch' ('Peace be unto you'). This A major movement, uniquely constructed among those in Bach's cantatas, takes the form of a dramatic scena for bass solo and three-strand 'chorus' (SAT). In it the bass assumes the role of VOX CHRISTI, repeating at intervals Christ's blessing, while the other voices represent mankind. In this profoundly symbolic section of the work Bach effectively highlights the contrasting elements by adopting a scheme of alternating time signatures, dynamic markings, and instrumental groupings. The *vox Christi*, for instance, in all but the last of the solo sections, where it is supported by woodwind and strings, is accompanied by woodwind alone (flute and two oboes d'amore) in 3/4 time. The three interjecting choral episodes, on the other hand, are in 4/4 time and accompanied by strings. In the last of these episodes Christ's blessing (*vox Christi*) is united with the remaining vocal strands. It is perhaps hardly surprising to find a movement so affecting and so skilfully constructed as this appearing in another context. Bach, in fact, later parodied it in the Gloria of his Lutheran *Missa* in A major.

The joyful concluding chorale is a strophe from a hymn by Jakob Ebert, *Du Friedefürst, Herr Jesu Christ*; both the text and the melody, by Bartholomäus Gesius, date from 1601.          NA

For bibliography, *see* CANTATA, §1.

**Hamburg.** A port in north Germany and a major city in the Hanseatic league. It developed as an important trading centre during the 17th century, and in 1678 it became an important musical centre, too, with the opening in the Gänsemarkt of the first, and for a long time the most important, public opera house in Germany. According to the Obituary, Bach visited Hamburg a number of times during the period he spent at Lüneburg (1700–2) in order to hear the famous organist J. A. Reincken at the Catharinenkirche; whether he also attended the opera is not known. He may have revisited the city in 1706 on his way back to Arnstadt from Lübeck, but the next certain report we have of his presence there comes in November 1720, when, a few months after the death of his wife Maria Barbara in Cöthen, he entered his candidature for the vacant post of organist at the Jacobikirche. He spent two or three days in the city, playing on the fine church organs there and astonishing the aged and revered Reincken with his improvisation on the chorale *An Wasserflüssen Babylon.*

The customary formal *Probe* for the Jacobikirche post was fixed for 28 November, but by then Bach had returned to Cöthen and three of the other seven candidates had also withdrawn from the competition. The reason for this is not far to seek. It had long been the custom at the Jacobikirche for the appointee to make a substantial contribution to the church coffers, and in effect—other things being more or less equal—the post would have gone to the highest bidder. In this case, however, things were not more or less equal, since Bach was by far the most able and distinguished of the eight original candidates. Efforts were therefore made to persuade him to accept the post, but he chose not to, and one may question whether he really had any serious intention of relinquishing his post of *Kapellmeister* to Prince Leopold at Cöthen to officiate again at a church organ—even at the four-manual Schnitger organ of the Jacobikirche. The incident was not forgotten in Hamburg, however, and Johann Mattheson (*Der musicalische Patriot* (Hamburg, 1728), 316) recalled how 'the son of a wealthy tradesman [Johann Joachim Heitmann, d. 1727], who could prelude better with thaler than with his fingers ... was given the post', and how the pastor Erdmann Neumeister, 'who had not consented to the simony ... ended his sermon ... like this: He was quite certain that if one of the angels at Bethlehem had come down from heaven and played divinely to become organist at St J, but had no money, he might just as well fly away again.'

This was Bach's last visit to Hamburg, but the city's association with the Bach family was renewed in 1768 when Bach's son Carl Philipp Emanuel was appointed *director musices* and spent the last 20 years of his life there.

**Handel, Georg Frideric** (b. 23 Feb. 1685; d. 14 April 1759). Composer, born in Halle, Saxony. His early years seemed to prepare him for a career similar to Bach's: he studied with F. W. Zachow

(1663–1712), organist at the Marienkirche in Halle and a composer of church cantatas and keyboard music, and his first appointment was as organist at the Calvinist cathedral in Halle. But he soon began to map out a career as an opera composer, first in Hamburg, then in Italy, and finally, from 1711, in London.

Although born within a few weeks, and quite a short distance, of each other, Bach and Handel never met. In 1719 Bach did travel to Halle in the hope of a meeting, but Handel had left by the time he arrived; again in 1729, when Handel was once more in his native city, Bach sent his son Wilhelm Friedemann to invite Handel to Leipzig, but Handel was unable to make the journey. In a quite extraordinary way the music of these two greatest of late Baroque composers shows few meeting-points either. Bach excelled in genres, such as the church cantata, oratorio Passion, mass, and Vivaldi-type concerto, that Handel barely touched; Handel's greatest achievements were in opera, oratorio, and the Corelli-type concerto—genres uncultivated by Bach. Where their interests did overlap—in the keyboard suite and instrumental sonata—their styles differed greatly. The solo keyboard sonata they left almost entirely to the third member of the 1685 triumvirate, Domenico SCARLATTI.

***Handexemplar*** ('copy in use'). A term used to refer to Bach's personal copies of the printed editions of his works. It is clear that, since Bach was both publisher and distributor of a number of his works, there remained varying numbers of exemplars of each print in his inventory. To qualify as a true *Handexemplar* a personal copy must show more than mere corrections to the musical text in Bach's hand. It must show revisions representing part of the continuing compositional history of the work. There survive true *Handexemplare* for the original editions of *Clavier-Übung I, Clavier-Übung II, Clavier-Übung [IV]*, and the Schübler Chorales. The *Handexemplar* of the Canonic Variations, which is known to have existed, is no longer extant.                    GB

G. Butler, *Bach's Clavier-Übung III: The Making of a Print* (Durham, NC, 1990), 110–11; J. Fuller-Maitland, 'A Set of Bach's Proof Sheets', *Sammelbände der Internationalen Musikgesellschaft*, 2 (1900–1), 643–50; C. Wolff, 'Bach's *Handexemplar* of the Goldberg Variations: A New Source', *Journal of the American Musicological Society*, 29 (1976), 224–41; C. Wolff, 'Bachs Handexemplar der Schübler-Choräle', *BJb* 63 (1977), 120–9; C. Wolff, 'Textkritische Bemerkungen zum Originaldruck der Bachschen Partiten', *BJb* 65 (1979), 65–74.

**Harnoncourt, Nikolaus** (b. 6 Dec. 1929). Austrian cellist, viol player, and conductor, born in

Berlin. He grew up in Graz. In 1953 he and his wife Alice, a violinist, formed the Concentus Musicus, Vienna, an ensemble of period instruments specializing in the performance of Baroque and Classical music. As well as recording the Brandenburg Concertos (1964) and the orchestral suites (1966), which he directed from the cello or viola da gamba desk, Harnoncourt made highly acclaimed recordings of the *St John Passion* (1965), the B minor Mass (1968), the *St Matthew Passion* (1970) and the *Christmas Oratorio* (1972). A major project, shared with Gustav Leonhardt, to record all Bach's sacred cantatas was launched in 1971 and completed in 1990. Each director revealed his own distinctive approach in the series, with Harnoncourt the more demonstrative, exuberant, and mannerist in his musical expression. The enterprise established a landmark in Bach recording, both for its challenging of previously accepted interpretative conventions and for the use of a boy's voice to sing almost all the soprano solos.

NA

*See also* RECORDINGS.

**harpsichord.** The principal strung keyboard instrument in Bach's day, consisting of two or more sets of strings plucked by separate sets of jacks, controlled by one, two, or rarely three keyboards. Although the smaller, cheaper, and softer-sounding CLAVICHORD was often used for private study and enjoyment, all Bach's keyboard works would most frequently have been played on the harpsichord. Even works for organ would have been playable on the occasional harpsichord provided with a pedalboard. The Italian Concerto, the Ouverture in the French Style, and the Goldberg Variations were specifically conceived for two-manual harpsichords. The harpsichord was also used for both continuo and obbligato accompaniment and as a solo instrument in concertos.

Harpsichords were not standardized, especially in Germany, where there was no dominant centre of musical culture and where many makers worked in relative isolation among the various principalities. No harpsichord owned by Bach or proven to have been played by him has survived. There is no record of his preferences, although documented connections between Bach and the makers Michael Mietke and Zacharias Hildebrandt might suggest where his tastes lay. The inventory of Bach's estate lists five harpsichords, but the dearth of details allows only the inference that these ranged from a simple one-manual instrument to a large two-manual. Their variety presumably reflected the variety of harpsichords found in those areas of Germany where Bach lived and travelled. With only a few extant instruments

and a small number of contemporary documents and writings (especially those of Jakob Adlung) to go on, present-day knowledge about harpsichords in Bach's environs remains fragmentary. Nevertheless, recent research has been able to question earlier views that Bach's harpsichords were mainly of Italian and Flemish origin and that the best and most typical German two-manual harpsichords were made in the French style. The discovery of several previously unknown German harpsichords has disclosed the antiquity and vigour of native harpsichord-making traditions.

German one-manual harpsichords usually had a compass of four octaves, *C* to *c'''*, but often, especially in instruments made before about 1700, with a short octave (i.e. lacking the lowest four accidentals). Chromatic-bass keyboards, however, were known as early as the 16th century and are necessary for the performance of almost all Bach's works. Occasionally, there were a few more notes below *C*, typically down to *GG*; sometimes the compass extended up to *d'''*, a limit rarely exceeded on single-manual instruments during Bach's lifetime. Two-manual instruments (all extant examples of which were made after 1700) tended to have somewhat larger compasses. *FF* or *GG* to *d'''* was relatively common, and five octaves, *FF* to *f'''* was not unknown.

In one-manual instruments there were usually two sets of strings at unison (8') pitch, each set being acted upon by a register of jacks that could be turned on or off. Often the tone of one or both stops could be modified by a buff stop—a batten with leather or cloth pads touching the strings, which then produced a lute-like timbre. A fairly common addition to the basic scheme was a third set of jacks plucking one set of strings very close to their ends, resulting in a bright, nasal tone. A third set of strings at octave (4') pitch was also sometimes included.

About half of the extant German two-manual harpsichords have the 'classic' disposition of three stops: 8' and 4' on the lower keyboard, 8' on the upper, and a coupler. Relatively common, however, were more elaborate and varied dispositions with, for example, a third set of 8' strings, nasal or 4' stops on the upper manual, and sub-octave (16') stops. Of considerable interest are documents indicating that Mietke made harpsichords with 16' stops and that a Hildebrandt harpsichord, presumably made in Leipzig before 1750, had a lower manual with 16' and 8', an upper with 8' and 4', plus a nasal 8' in the bass, and a coupler.

Little is known about how the various stops were used in performance. Pedals or knee-levers to change stops while playing were probably unknown. The Italian Concerto and several of the Goldberg Variations require simultaneous use of two keyboards more or less evenly balanced. That playful and elaborate use of different combinations of stops (including the buff and nasal 8′) was not unknown in Bach's circle is shown by the registrations indicated by C. P. E. Bach for his Sonata in D minor (no. 69 in Wotquenne's catalogue, no. 53 in Helm's). JK

H. Henkel, 'Der Cembalo-bau der Bach-Zeit im sächsisch-thüringischen und im Berliner Raum', W. Felix, W. Hoffmann, and A. Schneiderheinze, eds., *Bericht über die Wissenschaftliche Konferenz zum III. Internationalen Bach-Fest der DDR* (Leipzig, 1977), 361–74; H. Heyde, 'Der Instrumentenbau in Leipzig zur Zeit Johann Sebastian Bachs', in U. Prinz and K. Küster, eds., *300 Jahre Johann Sebastian Bach* [exhibition catalogue] (Stuttgart, 1985), 73–88; J. Koster, 'The Harpsichord Culture in Bach's Environs', in *Bach Perspectives* (forthcoming); D. Krickeberg and H. Rase, 'Beiträge zur Kenntnis des mittel- und norddeutschen Cembalobaus um 1700', in F. Hellwig, ed., *Studia organologica: Festschrift für John Henry van der Meer* (Tutzing, 1987), 285–310; J. H. van der Meer, 'Beiträge zur Cembalobau im deutschen Sprachgebiet bis 1700', in *Anzeiger des Germanischen Nationalmuseums* (Nuremberg, 1966), 103–33; G. B. Stauffer, 'J. S. Bach's Harpsichords', in T. J. Mathiesen and B. V. Rivera, eds., *Festa musicologica: Essays in Honor of George J. Buelow* (Stuyvesant, NY, 1995), 289–318.

**Harpsichord Concertos.** See opposite.

**Harrer, Johann Gottlob** (b. 8 May 1703; d. 9 July 1755). Composer, born in Görlitz, about 80 km. (50 miles) east of Dresden in Saxony. He studied law at Leipzig University and found a powerful patron in Count Heinrich von Brühl, in whose Dresden establishment he served from 1731 to 1750. It was largely Brühl's influence that secured him the post of Kantor at the Thomasschule in 1750, in succession to Bach. In fact, on Brühl's recommendation Harrer was allowed to perform a *Probe* in Leipzig as early as 8 June 1749, with a view to a 'future appointment as Kantor . . . in case the *Kapellmeister* and Kantor Herr Sebastian Bach should die'.

Harrer's surviving compositions include liturgical works in Latin (written for Dresden) and German (mostly for Leipzig), as well as numerous instrumental pieces.

*See also* PALESTRINA, GIOVANNI PIERLUIGI DA.

A. Schering, 'Der Thomaskantor Joh. Gottlob Harrer (1703–1755)', *BJb* 28 (1931), 112–46; A. Glöckner, 'Handschriftliche Musikalien aus den Nachlässen von Carl Gotthelf Gerlach und Gottlob Harrer in den Verlagsangeboten des Hauses Breitkopf 1761–1769', *BJb* 70 (1984), 107–16.

**Hartwig, Karl** (b. 18 Aug. 1709; d. 5 Aug. 1750). Organist, born in Olbernhau, about 30 km. (19 miles) south-east of Chemnitz in Erzgebirge. In 1729 he applied unsuccessfully for the post of

organist at the Nikolaikirche in Leipzig, and in 1733 for that of organist at the Sophienkirche, Dresden, where Wilhelm Friedemann Bach was appointed. He studied with J. S. Bach in Leipzig between 1732 and 1735, and was then appointed organist at the Johanniskirche, Zittau, where he was preferred to another of Bach's pupils, J. L. Krebs. In 1741 he acted as agent at Zittau for Bach's newly published *Clavier-Übung III*.

**Hasse, Johann Adolf** (bap. 25 March 1699; d. 16 Dec. 1783). Composer and singer, born in Bergedorf (now Hamburg-Bergedorf). He was active in various Italian cities (principally Venice and Naples) from 1721, was made *Kapellmeister* at the Dresden court in 1731, and travelled widely throughout Europe. He died in Venice.

According to J. N. Forkel, Hasse and his wife, the singer Faustina Bordoni, visited Leipzig several times 'and admired [Bach's] great talents'. No account exists of any direct contact between the two men, but an anonymous contribution to the *Allgemeine deutsche Bibliothek* (1788) stated that Hasse and his wife were among those present when Bach gave an organ recital at the Sophienkirche. This was probably on 14 September 1731; on the previous evening the première took place of *Cleofide*, Hasse's first opera for Dresden. Before that Bach had already 'honoured' the person of Hasse by including his Polonaise in G major (BWV Anh. II 130) in the second *Clavierbüchlein* for Anna Magdalena Bach. There were numerous occasions on which Bach could have attended performances of Hasse's operas in Dresden; he composed about 30 such works for the court there between 1734 and early 1750. One of these, *Alfonso*, received its première on 11 May 1738, just a week before Bach's organ recital in the Frauenkirche.

AB

***Hauptgottesdienst*** ('principal divine service'). A term for the morning eucharistic rite celebrated on Sundays and feast-days in Lutheran Germany. Liturgical usage in Leipzig during the 18th century was somewhat conservative. Details of the Leipzig *Hauptgottesdienst* can be reconstructed from a number of sources, such as the Saxon Agenda (1539/40), the manuscript notes of the Thomaskirche sacristan Johann Christoph Rost (d. 1739), the *Neu Leipziger Gesangbuch* (1682) of Gottfried Vopelius (1645–1715), and a number of lay devotional books such as the *Leipziger Kirchen-Andachten* (1694) and the *Leipziger Kirchen-Staat* (1710). In addition there is the outline of the liturgical order for the *Hauptgottesdienst* that Bach noted on the covers of two Advent cantatas, nos. 61 and 62 (see *BDok* i. 248–9 and 251). The order on the former is headed *Anordnung des Gottes-*

[cont. on p.212]

# Harpsichord Concertos

This article deals with the accompanied concertos for one or more harpsichords. For the solo (unaccompanied) harpsichord concertos, *see* CONCERTO, §3 and ITALIAN CONCERTO.

1. Outline of the repertory.
2. Chronology and purpose.
3. Models, surviving and conjectural.
4. The process of transcription.
5. Musical style.

1. **Outline of the repertory.** The most important body of material is the collection of seven harpsichord concertos BWV1052–8, which survive in a single autograph, together with the fragment of an eighth, BWV1059. This represents Bach's only collection of concertos from the Leipzig era, and finds its only parallel, as a collection, in the six concertos that Bach sent to the Margrave of Brandenburg during the Cöthen years.

Three concertos survive for two harpsichords and strings, BWV1060–2. Of these, BWV1061 in C major was originally conceived for the two harpsichords alone (BWV1061*a*), the strings being later added to supplement the texture; it may thus belong rather more with the Italian Concerto for a single harpsichord than with the concertos for harpsichord and strings. There are two concertos for three harpsichords and strings, BWV1063–4, and one for four harpsichords, BWV1065. Given that the concerto in F major with solo recorders, BWV1057, is regarded as a harpsichord concerto, two other concertos should at least be mentioned within the domain of the harpsichord concerto: the Fifth Brandenburg Concerto and the Triple Concerto BWV1044. In both these cases the harpsichord shares a solo role with a violin and a transverse flute and, indeed, it often dominates the texture.

2. **Chronology and purpose.** Bach seems to have written his first orchestral concerto using solo harpsichord in Cöthen: the Fifth Brandenburg Concerto, which reached its final version in the 1720s. All the concertos for multiple harpsichords seem to belong within the years of his initial involvement with the COLLEGIUM MUSICUM, 1729–37; surviving parts for the Concerto for four harpsichords suggest a date around 1730. Furthermore, if Forkel's testimony that Bach prepared the concertos for three or more harpsichords for performance with his two eldest sons is correct, they would presumably come from before 1733, the date that Wilhelm Friedemann left for Dresden. Nevertheless, other pupils, such as J. L. Krebs, might also have been involved.

The seven solo harpsichord concertos BWV1052–8 are found in an autograph manuscript compiled about 1737–9. This seems to be precisely the time that Bach temporarily relinquished the directorship of the collegium, suggesting that he compiled them for some other project, perhaps for performance and presentation at the Dresden court, where he had held the position of honorary *Kapellmeister* since 1736 (see Schulze). However, given the fact that the manuscript remained in Leipzig, it may well have been used for the performance of harpsichord concertos during Bach's second term as director of the collegium, 1739–*c.*1741. Furthermore, given that all seven are transcriptions of earlier works for solo melody instruments, there is no reason why Bach could not have performed these concertos before compiling the manuscript, embellishing the solo part himself at the keyboard.

3. **Models, surviving and conjectural.** Of the entire body of harpsichord concertos, only three pieces seem clearly to have originated as keyboard solos: the harpsichord part to Brandenburg no. 5, that of the Triple Concerto BWV1044 (the outer movements derive from a harpsichord prelude and fugue, BWV894, the middle movement is related to the slow movement of the Third Organ Sonata BWV527), and the Concerto for two harpsichords in C major BWV1061. All the rest seem to be transcriptions of concertos for melody instruments. In all concertos for which an original model survives, the harpsichord version has been transposed down a tone to suit the compass of the instrument.

The collected harpsichord concertos, together with the Brandenburg Concertos, may well represent Bach's entire concerto output (i.e. he probably arranged every available concerto). On the other hand, there are among the cantatas three slow movements for solo oboe without voice which possibly derive from lost oboe concertos (see Haynes, p. 25). Instrumental models are known for the following harpsichord concertos: Concerto in D major BWV1054, from the Violin Concerto in E; Concerto in G minor BWV1058, from the Violin Concerto in A minor; Concerto in F major, from Brandenburg Concerto no. 4 in G; Concerto for two harpsichords in C minor BWV1062, from the Concerto for two violins in D minor; and the Concerto for four harpsichords in A minor, from Vivaldi's Concerto for four violins op. 3 no. 10. There have been multifarious hypotheses regarding the (lost) models of the remaining concertos; unfortunately, many attempts at recovering oboe concertos from the harpsichord concertos have been conceived with the modern oboe in mind and do not represent the types of instruments that would have been available to Bach. Bruce Haynes, taking into account a variety of factors drawn from his experience with early oboes, concludes that 11 movements from the harpsichord concertos may have originated in concertos for oboe or oboe d'amore: the Concerto in E major BWV1053, the first and third movements of the Concerto in A major BWV1055, the second and third movements of the Concerto in F minor BWV1056, the middle movement of the Concerto in D minor for three harpsichords BWV1063, and the Concerto for two harpsichords in C minor BWV1060 (with violin as the other soloist). The Concerto in D minor BWV1052 is now generally assumed to have been a very early concerto by Bach and almost certainly for violin (it contains many passages suggestive of string-crossing and of figuration based around open strings). If this is indeed the case, it is Bach's most virtuoso violin concerto, and is equally impressive in his arrangement for harpsichord. The two concertos for three harpsichords are doubtlessly transcriptions; given the style and figuration of the D minor concerto, it is not impossible that Bach's sons may have had a hand in the arrangement (the same, incidentally, could be said of the curious orchestration of the Triple Concerto).

Some movements in the third Leipzig cycle of cantatas (1725–7), usually sinfonias, in which the solo line is treated as an organ obbligato, later appeared in the harpsichord concertos. None of these represents the original version of the piece in question; they are, rather, independent keyboard arrangements, cousins of the harpsichord concertos rather than their direct ancestors. Nevertheless, they belong to the same trend for transcribing works from melody instrument to keyboard.

**4. The process of transcription.** Werner Breig has undertaken an extremely penetrating and perceptive study of Bach's compilation of the manuscript of the seven solo harpsichord concertos. He has shown that the first six concertos originally belonged to a separate manuscript and that the manuscript containing the seventh (BWV1058) and the fragment of the eighth (BWV1059) was, in fact, written first. These last two concertos show the simplest form of transcription, the harpsichord taking over the original solo part with the right hand and doubling the basso continuo line with the left. Bach followed more or less the same procedure in the D minor concerto at the beginning of the second manuscript, but added considerably more embellishment to both harpsichord lines. When transcribing the opening movement of the E major Violin Concerto, however, Bach completely rewrote the harpsichord bass line, removing the string bass from many of the solo sections and rewriting the upper string parts in light of the new solo part. In the other movements, and in later concertos, he left the upper string parts more or less untouched, copying these first and then supplying the harpsichord part and, finally, the string bass (largely in the tuttis). In transcribing the Fourth Brandenburg Concerto, Bach reworked the relation between the harpsichord (originally violin) and the recorders, some passages involving an entirely new line for the harpsichord.

**5. Musical style.** Bach's development (and essentially the invention) of the solo keyboard concerto is most crucial to note here, since it proved to be the start of such a long and impressive tradition, passed on directly through his sons. The existence of the C major double concerto in an early version without strings suggests that one of Bach's primary interests was to exploit the keyboard's ability to mimic a large range of textures normally associated with concerted instruments. The same tendency is evident in the way the harpsichord can take over original bass lines and, in the middle movement of the F major concerto, the entire solo texture of violin and recorders. Bach counteracts the lack of sustaining ability and dynamic shading on the harpsichord by embellishing the long lyrical lines of the slow movements. Perhaps the most striking tendency, evident right from the time of Brandenburg Concerto no. 5, is the virtuosity of the keyboard parts, doubtlessly recording on paper something of the performance that Bach himself may have given.

It is quite clear that Bach gave much thought to the process of arrangement; these concertos are not the ephemeral, hasty affairs they are often believed to be. The collected concertos for single harpsichord fit well into the pattern of his later activity, summing up the compositional achievement of his entire career and presenting the works in as developed a form as possible.                                                           JAB

*See also* CONCERTO, §4.

W. Breig, 'Composition as Arrangement and Adaptation', in J. Butt, ed., *The Cambridge Companion to Bach* (Cambridge, 1997), 154–70; B. Haynes, 'Johann Sebastian Bachs Oboenkonzerte', *BJb* 78 (1992), 23–43; H.-J. Schulze, 'Johann Sebastian Bachs Konzerte: Fragen der Überlieferung und Chronologie', P. Ahnsehl, K. Heller, and H.-J. Schulze, eds., *Beiträge zum Konzertschaffen Johann Sebastian Bachs* [Bach-Studien 6] (Leipzig, 1981), 9–26.

*Dienstes in Leipzig am 1 Advent-Sontag frühe* ('Order of Worship in Leipzig for the First Sunday in Advent early [i.e. the eucharistic *Hauptgottesdienst*]'):

1 [Organ] Preluding
2 [Latin] Motetta
3 Preluding on the Kyrie, which is wholly concerted
4 [Collect] intoned before the altar
5 Epistle read
6 The Litany is sung [only in Advent and Lent]
7 Preluding on the chorale [which is then sung]
8 Gospel read
9 Preluding on the principal music [i.e. the cantata, which follows]
10 The Faith [*Der Glaube*] is sung [i.e. the Credal hymn *Wir glauben all an einen Gott*]
11 The sermon [which concludes with confession and absolution, intercessions, and notices]
12 After the sermon, the usual various verses from a hymn are sung
13 Words of institution
14 Preluding on the music. And after which alternating preluding and the singing of chorales until Communion is ended *& sic porrò*.

The reference to the Kyrie (3) indicates a Lutheran *missa*, that is a concerted Kyrie and Gloria. Although it was customary to omit the Gloria during Advent, Advent Sunday itself was considered a major feast of the Church year and therefore a complete *missa*, both Kyrie and Gloria, was required, as the Leipzig liturgical sources direct.

The congregational chorale (7) before the Gospel is the traditional Lutheran *Graduallied* ('Gradual hymn') that was closely linked to the Gospel of the day. Many of the texts and tunes of these hymns are found in the appropriate Bach cantatas.

The cantata (9) immediately followed the reading of the Gospel of the day (8) and was its musical equivalent. On Sundays other than in Advent the Nicene Creed was sung in Latin between the Gospel and cantata, usually to plainchant but occasionally in a choral or concerted form. Whether or not the Latin Creed was included, the German hymn version (10) was always sung.

At principal celebrations, such as Christmas, Epiphany, Easter, Ascension, Pentecost, and Trinity (but not the first Sunday in Advent), the *Sursum corda* and a Latin preface were chanted, leading to the Latin Sanctus, before the words of institution. The Sanctus was sung either in simple monody, or in the six-part setting of Vopelius's *Neu Leipziger Gesangbuch*, or in a concerted setting.

After the words of institution, during Communion, there was *musica sub communionis* (14). This could be either another cantata or the second part of a two-part cantata. After this concerted music Bach notes that there should follow 'alternating [organ] preluding and the singing of chorales until Communion is ended' (14). This singing of eucharistic hymns could also include the Latin Agnus Dei, sung by the choir, and/or the congregational German version *Christe, du Lamm Gottes*. The service concluded with a thanksgiving collect, benediction, and congregational response, sung to the *tonus peregrinus* (see BWV323).     RAL

G. Stiller, *Johann Sebastian Bach and Liturgical Life in Leipzig*, Eng. trans. H. J. A. Bouman, D. F. Poellot, and H. C. Oswald, ed. R. A. Leaver (St Louis, Miss., 1984); C. S. Terry, *Joh. Seb. Bach Cantata Texts, Sacred and Secular, with a Reconstruction of the Leipzig Liturgy of his Period* (London, 1926).

**Hauptmann, Moritz** (b. 13 Oct. 1792; d. 3 Jan. 1868). Composer, theorist, and Thomaskantor. In his home city of Dresden he met the composer and violinist Louis Spohr (1784–1859), whom he accompanied first to Vienna and later to Kassel. Spohr (and Mendelssohn) recommended him to succeed his former Dresden teacher, Theodor Weinlig (1780–1842), as Thomaskantor in Leipzig. Together with the composer Robert Schumann and the writer Otto Jahn (1813–69, remembered for his important biography of Mozart), Hauptmann founded the Bach-Gesellschaft in 1850 and became its first president. As the editor of the first two volumes of cantatas in the *BG* edition (containing nos. 1–20) he was responsible for establishing the far-sighted editorial principles on which this first complete edition of a composer's works was based.     KK

*Hauptmusik* ('principal music'). A term for what is now usually referred to as a CANTATA in the Lutheran service.

*Hauptwerk* ('principal division'). A term used, interchangeably with 'Hauptmanual' and 'Werk'), to denote the primary division of an organ, containing its most prominent stops. Its 'backbone' consists of principal stops at 16′ (possibly), 8′, 4′, 2 2/3′, 2′, and one or more mixtures. In 18th-century Germany the *Oberwerk*, the division played from the upper manual, could be the primary division, and so replace the designation 'Hauptwerk'. Thus in the organ Bach played at Mühlhausen the primary manual was called *Hauptwerk*, while at Arnstadt it was called *Oberwerk*.     QF

**Hauser, Franz** (b. 12 Jan. 1794; d. 14 Aug. 1870). Bohemian singer, born in Krasowitz (now Krasovice), near Prague. He sang in opera throughout Germany and in Prague and London, and later taught in Vienna and directed the Munich Conservatory. He assembled an important collection of music manuscripts, including several Bach autographs, which he left to his son Joseph (1828–99) and which in 1904 was acquired by the Königliche Bibliothek (now the Staatsbibliothek), Berlin. In 1831 he edited two works, BWV574*b* and 769, in a projected but abandoned complete edition of Bach's organ music, and in 1850 he was a member of the first committee of the newly founded Bach-Gesellschaft. His manuscript catalogue of Bach's works, compiled in 1830–3 was destroyed by fire.

Y. Kobayashi, 'Franz Hauser und seine Bach-Handschriftensammlung' (diss., University of Göttingen, 1973).

**Hausmann.** The person in charge of the music provided by *Stadtpfeifer* on civic occasions. Bach's father, Johann Ambrosius, exercised the profession of *Hausmann* at Eisenach from 1671 until his death in 1695.

**Haußmann, Elias Gottlob** (b. 18 March 1695; d. 11 April 1774). Painter, born in Gera, about 50 km. (31 miles) south of Leipzig. He was the official portraitist at Leipzig from 1720, and at the Saxon court from 1723. He painted Bach's portrait, probably in readiness for his admission to Lorenz Mizler's Correspondirende Societät in 1747 (*see* BACH, JOHANN SEBASTIAN, §6), and his other sitters included the trumpeter Gottfried Reiche in 1727.

**hautbois.** A French term (literally, 'loud woodwind') for the OBOE.

**Hebenstreit, Pantaleon** (b. 1667; d. 15 Nov. 1750). Instrumentalist, composer, and dancing-master, born in Eisleben, about 30 km. (19 miles) west of Halle. He is remembered mainly as the inventor of a kind of dulcimer with 185 double strings of metal and gut, which so impressed Louis XIV in Paris that the king decreed that it should be named the pantaleon, after its inventor. Hebenstreit was appointed dancing-master at the Weißenfels court in 1698, and then at the ducal court in Eisenach in 1706, and from 1714 he filled various posts at the Dresden court, finally as director of Protestant church music and privy counsellor. As vice-*Kapellmeister* there in 1733 he was largely responsible for appointing Wilhelm Friedemann Bach as organist. *See also* DANCE.

**Heineccius, Johann Michael** (b. 14 Dec. 1674; d. 11 Sept. 1722). Clergyman, born in Eisenberg, about 50 km. (31 miles) south-west of Leipzig. He was made pastor at the Liebfrauenkirche (now generally known as the Marktkirche), Halle, where he supervised the local church music and wrote cantata texts. The role he played for Bach is a matter of some controversy, and rests on the identity of the cantata performed by Bach after his application to succeed F. W. Zachow (Handel's

teacher) at the Liebfrauenkirche in 1713, and whether or not its text was by Heineccius. There are similarities between the texts written by Heineccius and that for Bach's Christmas cantata *Christen, ätzet diesen Tag*; but Bach left Halle before Christmas. It is possible that Bach's contribution was *Ich hatte viel Bekümmernis*, but the text of that work shows features more typical of Salomo Franck. A third possibility is that Bach and Heineccius collaborated on another, unknown work. KK

M. Petzoldt, ' "Die kräfftige Erquickung unter der schweren Angst-Last": möglicherweise Neues zur Entstehung der Kantate BWV 21', *BJb* 79 (1993), 31–46; P. Wollny, 'Bachs Bewerbung um die Organistenstelle an der Marienkirche zu Halle und ihr Kontext', *BJb* 80 (1994), 25–39; A. Dürr, 'Zu Johann Sebastian Bachs Hallenser Probestück von 1713', *BJb* 81 (1995), 183–4.

**Heinichen, Johann David** (b. 17 April 1683; d. 16 July 1729). Composer and theorist, born in Krössuln, near Weißenfels. He studied music with Johann Kuhnau at the Thomasschule in Leipzig, and then law at Leipzig University. He gave up an incipient career as an advocate to write music, particularly operas, in Weißenfels, Leipzig, Naumburg, and Venice (where he taught music to Prince Leopold, later Bach's employer at Cöthen). In 1717 he was made *Kapellmeister* at Dresden, where he remained for the rest of his life, writing a great deal of music but no longer operas. He is remembered now above all for his informative treatise *Der General-Bass in der Composition* (Dresden, 1728).

Heinichen has been credited with the composition of the *Kleines harmonisches Labyrinth* for organ BWV591, which more recent scholarship tends to regard as an arrangement by Bach of another's work.

**Heinrich, Johann Georg** (b. 10 April 1721; d. after 1744). Organist, born in Merseburg, about 25 km. (15 miles) west of Leipzig. He attended the Thomasschule in Leipzig between 1734 and 1740 and was a pupil of Bach during that time. Bach wrote a testimonial for him in May 1744, when he applied, unsuccessfully, for an organist's post in Torgau.

**Helbig, Johann Friedrich** (b. 19 April 1680; d. 18 April 1722). Writer of church cantata texts, born probably in Neustadt, Thuringia. From 1709 onwards he was active as secretary at the ducal court of Saxe-Eisenach, and in 1718 was also appointed court poet. In this position he wrote an annual cycle of church cantata texts, *Aufmunterung der Andacht* ('Encouragement of Devotion'), published in 1720. Telemann (who perhaps had been his fellow student at Leipzig University) set

213

168 of Helbig's cantata texts. The only text Bach chose from that collection for his Leipzig cantatas is *Wer sich selbst erhöhet*, written in autumn 1726 shortly after his compositions to texts from the Meiningen collection.                                    KK

**Helm, Christoph** (d. 1748). Theologian, churchman, and poet, born probably in Beichlingen, near Erfurt in Thuringia, where his father was a pastor. He studied theology at Jena (1692–5) and worked as Kantor at the Rudolstadt court and, from 1704, as a priest at Berga-Kelbra, near Nordhausen.

In 1977 Walther Blankenburg suggested Helm as the author of texts for cantatas by Johann Ludwig Bach and for seven by J. S. Bach: nos. 17, 39, 43, 45, 88, 102, and 187. Konrad Küster has shown Blankenburg's conjecture to be mistaken, and has suggested Duke ERNST LUDWIG of Saxe-Meiningen as a more likely author.

**Henrici, Christian Friedrich.** One of the most important of Bach's librettists; he wrote under the pseudonym of PICANDER.

**Hercules auf dem Scheidewege** ('Hercules at the Crossroads'). Title of the cantata LASST UNS SORGEN, LASST UNS WACHEN, BWV213.

*Herr Christ, der einge Gottessohn* ('Lord Christ, the only son of God'). Cantata for the 18th Sunday after Trinity, BWV96, first performed on 8 October 1724 in Leipzig. The anonymous text is based on Elisabeth Kreutziger's chorale of the same title, strophes from which supply the text for movements 1 (the opening chorus) and 6 (the final chorale harmonization) of Bach's cantata. As usual, the intermediate movements (2–5) are settings of a poetic paraphrase of the intermediate verses of the chorale in the form of two recitatives and arias. Although originally an Epiphany hymn praising Christ as the morning star, it also has a traditional association with the 18th Sunday after Trinity, since the Gospel of the day (Matt. 22: 34–6) deals in part with Christ's theological questions to the Pharisees as to the meaning of the expression 'son of David'. The text of the cantata reaffirms Christ's status as 'the only son of God'. Bach revived the cantata twice, once in 1734 (or, less probably, 1735) and again some time during the period 1744–7 (*BC* suggests 1 October 1747). Cantata 169, *Gott soll allein mein Herze haben*, was composed for the same liturgical occasion.

BWV96 is scored for SATB, horn (replaced by trombone in the second revival of 1744–7), sopranino recorder (replaced by violino piccolo in the revival of 1734), strings, and continuo and is in the six-movement form that characterizes many of the Leipzig cantatas. It opens with the usual figured chorale, based on the Advent hymn of the

title. The most immediately striking features of the movement are the lilting 9/8 metre and the twinkling figures for sopranino recorder which permeate the whole movement, representing the appearance of the star to the Magi against the background of a pastoral landscape. The chorale is given out line by line in the usual manner, sung by the alto in long note values. The following alto recitative leads to a tenor aria in C major, 'Ach, ziehe die Seele mit Seilen der Liebe', accompanied by obbligato flute. The flute ritornello melody, with its lightly side-stepping appoggiaturas, provides most of the material for the aria, which is light, charming, and *galant* in character. After another simple recitative, this time for soprano, comes a bass aria, 'Bald zur Rechten, bald zur Linken' ('Now to the right, now to the left'), in the *pomposo* style of the Hamburg opera. The text gives much opportunity for word-painting, the antithesis contained in the first line being reflected by short antiphonal phrases played alternately by strings and woodwind. The lurching steps of the misguided soul are represented by rapid switches in the direction of melody and harmony. At the words 'Gehe doch mein Heiland mit' ('Go then, my saviour, with me') Bach introduces quieter conjunct movement and placid rhythm to represent the new-found sense of direction in the guidance of Jesus. Disruptive chromaticism returns for 'Laß mich in Gefahr nicht sinken' ('Let me not fall into danger'). The cantata ends in the usual manner with a straightforward chorale harmonization.                                    DLH

For bibliography, *see* CANTATA, §1.

*Herr, deine Augen sehen nach dem Glauben* ('O Lord, are not thine eyes upon the truth?'). Cantata, BWV102, first performed on 25 August 1726 (tenth Sunday after Trinity). It belongs to the series of works based on cantata librettos from the Meiningen court (*see* ERNST LUDWIG) and follows the same pattern as *Brich dem Hungrigen dein Brot*.

The text of the opening movement is from Jeremiah 5: 3. It consists of many discrete textual units, and in Bach's music their number is further increased. The movement is split roughly into three sections: in the first the chorus enters after an orchestral ritornello for two oboes, strings, and continuo; the imitative second section sets the text 'Du schlägest sie'; and a third, fugal section begins with 'Sie haben ein härter Angesicht'. But the musical substance of each section spills over into the movement as a whole: firstly, Bach reverts to the opening text (and its music) at the end of each section, even at the very end of the movement; secondly, the staccato motif of the imitative second section is anticipated in the homophonic opening section; and thirdly, after the fugue the whole text preceding it is repeated. The musical structure more clearly matches that of the text in the movement's parody as the Kyrie of the G minor *Missa*, where the opening and the fugue form the two 'Kyrie' sections framing 'Christe eleison' based on the central 'Du schlägest sie'.

Unlike Bach's other cantatas to Meiningen texts, the first part of this one consists of four (not three) movements, since it includes the movement (no. 4) based on a passage from the New Testament. A bass recitative leads to the F minor aria 'Weh! der Seele' for alto with solo oboe and continuo. Both the oboe and the voice enter with an impressive, syncopated, and dissonant D♭; when Bach reworked this movement as 'Qui tollis' in the F major *Missa*, its effect was weakened by an additional upbeat note. Following this aria, the first part of the cantata ends with a bass arioso from Romans 2: 4–5, beginning 'Despisest thou the riches of his goodness and forbearance?' Unlike most of the other New Testament passages in these cantatas, this one is not scored simply for voice and continuo (or, as in *Brich dem Hungrigen*, with a single additional line for unison violins) but for the full string orchestra. It uses a kind of da capo structure, which means that the question put at the beginning ends Part 1 of the cantata, thus leading to the Sunday sermon.

The second part of the cantata consists only of a tenor aria, 'Erschrecke doch, du allzu sichre Seele' ('Be startled then, thou overconfident soul'), accompanied by a solo flute, an accompanied recitative for alto and two oboes, and a chorale. In the aria the voice enters with music totally different from that heard on the flute. This may reflect the meaning of the text: the listener is 'startled' by the different music presented by the tenor, and by its disjointed phrases. It is hard to understand why Bach wished to form 'Quoniam tu solus' in the F major *Missa* from this music, an adaptation possible only with a general reworking of the vocal line.

After the publication of two cantatas for the change of administration in Mühlhausen in 1708–9, no Bach cantatas appeared in print until 1830, when A. B. Marx published a set of three, later numbered 101–3. Thus, *Herr, deine Augen* played an important part in the early dissemination of Bach's church music during the 19th century.                                                                    KK

For bibliography, *see* CANTATA, §1.

**Herr, gehe nicht ins Gericht** ('Lord, enter not into judgement'). Cantata for the ninth Sunday after Trinity, BWV105, first performed in Leipzig on 25 July 1723. The Gospel reading appointed for that day was St Luke 16: 1–9, telling the parable of the unjust steward who, about to be dismissed for failing to collect what was due from his master's creditors, rescinded part of their debts in anticipation of future recompense. The anonymous cantata text makes no direct reference to this, however, but is rather a gloss on the final words (v. 13) of the same chapter: 'Ye cannot serve God and mammon.'

A verse from Psalm 143 serves to introduce the trembling and penitent servant, and the poetic text for the two recitatives and arias includes other biblical references, to Psalm 51, Malachi, and St Paul's epistles to the Romans and the Colossians. Bach responds to this with a variety of forms and textures. In the magnificent opening chorus the two clauses of the psalm text are set as a kind of prelude (with independent instrumental support and interludes, deployed over a ceaselessly throbbing quaver bass) and fugue (with instruments doubling the voices, except for one brief phrase for the horn and first oboe). Notable in both sections are Bach's dynamic markings; the fugue is at one point shaded down to *piano* and then *pianissimo*, only to resume *forte* after the next cadence.

The first recitative, for alto, is accompanied only by the continuo instruments, which are then silent in the soprano aria, 'Wie zittern und wanken', that follows. The upper strings accompany with lightly repeated notes (semiquavers for the violins, quavers for the violas), while an expressive oboe obbligato serves to introduce the voice, and then to echo its phrases; later the echoes come closer, at a quaver's distance, like the canon at the opening of the Sixth Brandenburg Concerto. In the second recitative the accompaniment to the bass voice is shared between the three upper strings, reiterating for the most part a simple turning figure in rhythmic unison, and a pizzicato murky bass—by no means common in Bach's music. The tenor aria 'Kann ich nur Jesum mir zum Freude machen' is no less remarkable for the way the instrumental obbligato is shared between horn and first violin, playing sometimes in unison but more often with the violin 'improvising' elaborate diminutions in demisemiquavers. As if reluctant to prolong the comparison, the horn falls silent in the B section of this substantial da capo aria.

Bach seizes every opportunity in the work for expressive word-painting, but nowhere more imaginatively than in the final chorale, Johann Rist's *Jesu, der du meine Seele* (1641), where the upper strings suggest the gradual calming of the sinner's troubled conscience by slowing their accompanying semiquavers to triplet quavers, then to quavers, and finally winding down in a chromatic crotchet phrase while the voices and bass fall silent.

For bibliography, *see* CANTATA, §1.

## Herr Gott, Beherrscher aller Dinge

*Herr Gott, Beherrscher aller Dinge* ('Lord God, ruler of all things'). Wedding cantata, BWV120*a*, probably composed in 1729. Although it consists largely of reworkings of earlier compositions, it was, like the later masses, a significant and imaginative work. Only the concluding portion of Bach's autograph score survives, and of his manuscript performing parts only those for voices, viola, and continuo are fully extant; the others might have been lost after being reused for a parody of the present work. Enough survives to give a reasonably clear picture of its content and its relationship to other compositions, particularly GOTT, MAN LOBET DICH IN DER STILLE (Cantata 120).

The text is anonymous and in the parody movements does not always sit comfortably with the music. It opens with a da capo form fitted to a grand chorus with trumpets, timpani, and strings in D major; the music recurs in the first chorus of Cantata 120 and at 'Et expecto' in the Mass in B minor. Bach's insertion of several bars into the A section permitted choral statements of the opening words in imitative texture; he would use the same procedure later in the mass. As in Cantata 120, a reference to 'goodness and mercy' in the text of the B section reflects the silence here of the trumpets and the modulation to B minor.

A long bass recitative in B minor continues the praise of God begun in the first movement. The recitative is interrupted by a choral setting (doubled by strings) of what appears to be an extract from the chorale *Nun danket alle Gott*, in the key (G) usually associated with that melody. The melody itself, however, is absent, and the text has been plausibly explained as a quotation from Ecclesiasticus 50: 24. The style is archaic, either intentionally or because this music was parodied from a lost early work. The succeeding soprano aria addresses the couple about to be married, using the same music (again in G) later used for the aria 'Heil und Segen' in Cantata 120.

Part 2, which originally followed the exchange of vows, opens with a Sinfonia for organ obbligato and strings. This is an arrangement of the prelude from the E major violin Partita; the subsequent version of the arrangement (with trumpets) in Cantata 29 is better known. A tenor recitative follows; it concludes with all four voices singing a verse from the litany (a device Bach had used at Weimar in Cantata 18). The next movement is, appropriately, a duet for alto and tenor, with strings and two oboes d'amore. Its ritornello is the same as that of the opening movement of Cantata 120, but except for the opening theme the vocal material is entirely different, and unlike that movement this one is in unmodified da capo form. Only in the B section does the bow vibrato, or 'slurred tremolo', of the ritornello become comprehensible; this figure pervades the continuo as the text refers momentarily to 'Furcht' ('fear').

After another simple recitative for bass, the work concludes with the fourth and fifth strophes of Joachim Neander's *Lobe den Herrn* (1679). The setting is taken from Cantata 137 (transposed from C to D major), but the autograph score directs that the trumpets and timpani—which constitute four additional real voices—be withheld until the second stanza.                                    DS

For bibliography, *see* CANTATA, §1.

*Herr Gott, dich loben alle wir* ('Lord God, we all praise thee'). Cantata for the feast of St Michael, BWV130. The Epistle for the feast of St Michael and All Angels (Rev. 12: 7–12), 'There was war in heaven', evidently appealed greatly to Bach. In the four surviving cantatas which he wrote for this festival, an important one in the Lutheran church calendar, his musical responses to the story are varied and strikingly pictorial. The present cantata belongs to Bach's second annual cycle and was performed at Leipzig on St Michael's Day 1724. The unidentified author of the text based his libretto on Paul Eber's hymn *Herr Gott, dich loben alle wir* (1554). This, in turn, derives from the Latin canticle *Dicimus grates tibi* (1539) by Martin Luther's colleague Philipp Melanchthon (1497–1560).

The opening chorus, in C major, resplendently scored for three trumpets, timpani, three oboes, strings, and continuo, is set to the first strophe of the hymn. Its melody, *Or sus, serviteurs du Seigneur* (1551) by Loys Bourgeois (it is better known to English-speaking audiences as the 'Old Hundredth'), is contained in the soprano line, with the three remaining vocal strands contributing to a rich polyphonic texture.

A brief alto recitative leads to the theological kernel of the cantata's text, the confrontation of St Michael and his angels with Satan, evocatively and Miltonically depicted as 'Der alte Drache' ('The old dragon', or 'serpent'), ever planning new mischief. (The opening vocal phrase recalls a heroic FANFARE THEME much used by Bach.) As Alfred Dürr pertinently remarks (in *DürrK*), Luther's angels were not, by and large, those somewhat effeminate portrayals by the Italian Renaissance painters, but sturdy representatives of the Church militant, capable of doing their bit in the struggle against the forces of evil. It is, indeed, a ferocious confrontation which Bach introduces, almost menacingly, with a single, portentous introductory drum beat. This is a C major aria in modified da capo form for bass voice, resonantly accompanied by three trumpets (to the first of which

Bach allots some thrilling concertante writing), timpani, and continuo. Few arias among the sacred cantatas revel in such dazzling colours as these, although (presumably for a later performance) Bach prepared a version for strings and continuo omitting both brass and timpani.

The following accompanied recitative is a duet for soprano and tenor whose light textures in vocal writing of alluring warmth and transparency provide a striking contrast with the warrior-like gestures of the preceding section, and prepare the ground for the ensuing da capo tenor aria. This captivating piece, in G major, is one of several in the cantatas composed between 23 July and 5 November 1724 to include a virtuoso part for transverse flute; we may assume that a particularly talented flautist was available. The text is an invocation to Christ, Prince of Cherubim, whose music—light-footed, airy, and dance-like in the manner of a gigue—is far removed from the scene of the earlier battlefield. The cantata ends with the two concluding verses of Paul Eber's hymn, for which Bach provided straightforward harmonizations of the Old Hundredth melody, accompanied by trumpets, timpani, oboes, strings, and continuo.                                          NA

For bibliography, *see* CANTATA, §1.

**Herr Gott, dich loben wir** ('Lord God, we praise thee'). Cantata, BWV16, for New Year's Day 1726, performed again on the same day in 1731, some time after 1745, and again in 1749. The text, by G. C. Lehms, was published in his *Gottfälliges Kirchen-Opfer* (Darmstadt, 1711) under the heading 'Nachmittags-Andacht auf Neu-Jahrs-Tag' ('Afternoon Devotion for New Year's Day'); the closing chorale of the cantata is not found in Lehms's libretto.

The first movement is similar to the opening movements of Bach's chorale cantatas, except that the text and melody in this case do not, strictly speaking, constitute a chorale. Instead the movement is a setting of the first four lines of Luther's vernacular *Te Deum* in rhymed couplets (1529), with Luther's variant form of the associated plainchant melody. Two years earlier Bach had used the same text and melody in the first two movements of his 1724 New Year's Day cantata, no. 190. The movement is effectively a chorale motet, with the melody in the soprano, doubled by a horn, and close imitation in the lower parts. Rather unusually, it begins with the continuo and is somewhat short, just 34 bars in length.

A brief bass recitative leads into a movement (no. 3) which is remarkable in a number of respects. It takes the form of a modified da capo aria (A–B–A′) in which the outer (A) sections are choral, and in part fugal, without the usual

orchestral introduction. The angular fugal theme is an example of word-painting expressive of 'jauchzen' ('shout for joy'), although what one hears is more like 'lachen' ('laugh'), so exuberant is the celebration of the new year. Counter-motifs of joy are introduced by first violins and then woven throughout the independent orchestral accompaniment. The central (B) section, for solo bass with a single choral interjection, continues the theme of rejoicing, with pictorialism on 'krönt' ('crowns'), a musical figure that resembles a crown in the score. It is an extraordinary movement, almost without parallel in Bach's sacred cantatas.

Movement 4 is an alto recitative that calls for the protection of church and school, the overlapping spheres of Bach's activity in Leipzig and the interconnected institutions necessary for the continuance of the Lutheran tradition of church music. In the only solo aria of the cantata (no. 5), for tenor in da capo form, the mood changes from extrovert rejoicing to introverted prayer. It is a reflective trio for tenor, continuo, and (in 1726) oboe da caccia; for a later performance the obbligato instrument was changed to 'violetta' (viola). With either instrument Bach wanted the darker colours to contrast with the earlier movements and to convey the meditative nature of the text.

The concluding chorale is a straightforward setting of stanza 6 of Paul Eber's *Helft uns Gotts Güte preisen* (*c*.1580) with its associated melody. The instruments play *colla parte*, with the horn again doubling the soprano, as in the first movement.                                          RAL

For bibliography, *see* CANTATA, §1.

**Herr Jesu Christ, du höchstes Gut** ('Lord Jesus Christ, thou highest good'). Cantata for the 11th Sunday after Trinity, BWV113, first performed at Leipzig on 20 August 1724. It is a CHORALE CANTATA belonging to Bach's second Leipzig *Jahrgang*, and is based on a hymn by Bartholomäus Ringwald dating from 1588. The hymn itself is somewhat in the nature of a sermon on the phrase 'God be merciful to me a sinner' from the Gospel reading for the day, St Luke 18: 9–14. The anonymous librettist has retained the first two and the last of the hymn's eight strophes, and also the fourth, which he has glossed with passages that Bach sets as recitative. The remaining four strophes have been paraphrased for a recitative, two arias, and a duet.

There are therefore four movements based on the chorale melody. The first, as usual, is a choral fantasia for the entire forces—SATB, two oboes, strings, and continuo (a flute is called for in no. 5)—but it has some unusual features. In the first place, the melody is not treated as a soprano cantus firmus in long notes supported by more active lower voices, but instead is quite plainly harmonized in triple metre. Also, most of the instruments that play the ritornellos separating the chorale lines fall silent each time the voices enter, leaving only the first violin to maintain continuity with its almost unbroken stream of semiquaver figuration; only for the final chorale line are all the instruments and voices heard together. In movement 2 the chorale melody is heard as a cantus firmus, sung by the alto while unison violins and continuo engage in a kind of *bicinium* around it. In movement 4, as mentioned earlier, the chorale, sung by the bass with active continuo support, is three times halted by passages of recitative. And the final strophe is, as usual, plainly harmonized in four parts.

Of the three paraphrased arias, the first, 'Fürwahr, wenn mir das kömmet ein', is a through-composed ritornello movement close in style to 'Et in Spiritum sanctum' from the B minor Mass. Both are in A major, for bass voice, and are accompanied by two oboes d'amore and continuo; the fact that the cantata aria is in a lilting 6/8 metre, while the Mass aria is in a lilting 12/8, is of little importance. The tenor's 'Jesus nimmt die Sünder aus', in modified da capo form, is chiefly remarkable for its highly virtuoso flute obbligato, while in the continuo-accompanied duet for soprano and alto virtuosity resides entirely in the long melismas attached, like comets' tails, to nuclei formed from phrases in the chorale melody.

For bibliography, *see* CANTATA, §1.

### Herr Jesu Christ, wahr' Mensch und Gott

('Lord Jesus Christ, true man and God'). Cantata for Quinquagesima Sunday (Estomihi), BWV127. Bach first performed this finely wrought cantata at Leipzig on 11 February 1725. Thus it belongs to his second Leipzig cantata cycle and, more specifically, to the body of chorale-based works which are its distinctive feature. Alfred Dürr in his disc notes for a recording of the work, spoke of special care that Bach seems to have devoted to this Sunday in the Church's year. 'Almost all [the cantatas] (with the possible exception of the "test piece", BWV22, which was hastily prepared for Leipzig) bear the mark of specially high artistic skill.'

The appointed Gospel for Quinquagesima, St Luke 18: 31–43, concerns Christ's decision to go to Jerusalem, his third announcement of his Passion, Crucifixion, and Resurrection, and the healing of the blind man near Jericho. Reference to all these events is contained in the text by an unidentified author, who based his work on the hymn *Herr Jesu Christ, wahr' Mensch und Gott* by Paul Eber

(1562). In accordance with the standard pattern of Bach's chorale cantatas of this period, the opening and concluding sections retain stanzas of the hymn in their original form. As Alberto Basso (p.341) has remarked, both the hymn, which Eber wrote on the death of his son, and the melody, adapted from Claude Goudimel (1565), are, in effect, a funeral lament, or 'Sterbelied'.

The opening chorus is an elegiac fantasia of great expressive intensity, scored for two treble recorders, two oboes, strings, and continuo. Bach, with consummate skill, combines the first line of the hymn tune—played first by the oboes and then, consecutively, by the recorders, the continuo, and finally the upper and middle strings—with the beginning of the chorale *Christe, du Lamm Gottes* (the Lutheran Agnus Dei). This is played in long note values first by the upper and middle strings (bars 1–4), then by the oboes (9–11) and the recorders (38–40). The voices enter in imitation, each one drawing on the melody of Eber's hymn. Bach completes this tender evocation of Christ's impending Passion with a quotation (possibly fortuitous, but none the less appropriate) from a third chorale melody, the 'Passion' chorale *Herzlich tut mich verlangen*, contained in bars 6–8 of the continuo part and heard five more times during the course of the movement.

A tenor recitative leads to the first aria of the cantata, scored for soprano with two recorders, oboe, and continuo. The conventional Baroque image of the soul's eager departure from mortal life is treated by Bach with tenderness and emotional restraint. In da capo form, the aria is notable for its limpid texture and subtly conceived imagery. The oboe introduces the melody against a staccato chordal accompaniment of two recorders and a pizzicato basso continuo; the voice takes up the melody of the oboe, with which it maintains a dialogue. In its short middle section, one of alluring beauty, oboe and recorders are joined by pizzicato violins and viola in a passage illustrating the 'Sterbeglocken' ('funeral bells') of the text.

In the accompanied recitative and aria for bass—the two are interwoven in three alternating sections—the intensity of Bach's word-painting is maintained, though its character abruptly changes, focusing on another aspect of the Protestant faith which was of special significance in the Baroque period: the Last Judgement. To illustrate this apocalyptic event Bach introduces a trumpet whose awesome, reiterated calls immediately follow the opening words of the recitative, 'Wenn einstens die Posaunen schallen' ('When finally the trumpets [literally "trombones"] sound'). Furthermore, in the vocal part of each of the three recitative episodes Bach ingeniously quotes the opening line of the chorale melody on which the cantata is founded. The intervening 'aria' passages, in 6/8 time, are fiery and combative in spirit as they illustrate man's rescue from the violent bonds of death. The assertive, declamatory vocal line is accompanied by recurring trumpet blasts and downward flurries of demisemiquavers in the string parts. In its rapid fluctuations of tempo and (by implication) dynamics, its *concitato* string writing, and even to some extent its text, this movement finds an echo in the tenor aria 'Zerschmettert mich, ihr Felsen' that Bach wrote for the 1725 revival of the *St John Passion* a few weeks later.

The cantata ends with a single strophe of Eber's hymn in which the four vocal lines are supported by the instruments of the opening movement.

NA

A. Basso, *Frau Musika: la vita e le opere di J. S. Bach*, ii (Turin, 1983), 340–2; A. Dürr, 'Zum Choralchorsatz "Herr Jesu Christ, wahr' Mensch und Gott" BWV 127 (Satz 1) und seiner Umarbeitung', *BJb* 74 (1988), 205–9. For further bibliography, *see* CANTATA, §1.

***Herr, wie du willt, so schicks mit mir*** ('Lord, as thou wilt, so ordain it unto me'). Cantata for the third Sunday after Epiphany, BWV73, first performed in the Nikolaikirche, Leipzig, on 23 January 1724. The original parts have survived, but Bach's autograph score has been lost. The text, by an unidentified author (Salomo Franck has been suggested), is based on the appointed Gospel reading for the day, which contains the story of Jesus's healing of the leper (Matt. 8: 1–13). The contrasting states of human frailty, on the one hand, and God's will, on the other, which are central to the text, derive from the leper's plea, 'Lord if thou wilt, thou canst make me clean'. Indeed, the initial phrase of the quotation provides the cantata with a leitmotif which, in turn, lends powerful cohesion to the work.

The opening chorus, in G minor, is unusually elaborate in its construction. The scoring consists of divided oboes and violins, viola, obbligato horn or organ, and basso continuo (Bach had a horn player at his disposal for the 1724 performance, but apparently not for a subsequent one in the early 1730s, when he substituted the organ). The movement is introduced by an instrumental ritornello built around a four-note motif, first heard in the horn in the third bar, which persists tenaciously at different pitches and in different keys throughout. The motif itself derives from the opening of the chorale melody around which the fantasia is woven, *Wo Gott der Herr nicht bei uns hält* (1535). The text is the first strophe of Kaspar Bienemann's hymn (1582) from which Bach's can-

tata takes its title. Interspersed with the lines of the hymn, which are homophonically sung, are three passages of recitative for tenor, bass, and soprano in turn. These both reflect and lend emphasis to the conflicting aspects of the textual theology.

Following this subtly constructed and highly original movement is a da capo tenor aria in E♭, accompanied by oboe and continuo. Once again, a strong contrasting element exists between the joyful confidence expressed in the first section and da capo and the faltering belief of frail humanity contained in the poignant chromaticisms of the second section. The simple recitative and aria for bass which follow are both musically and textually linked. Both focus unremittingly on the horror of death, reflecting at the same time on the strength of God's will and the need of the Soul fearlessly to place his trust in him. The aria, scored for strings and continuo, is darkly coloured and profound in its agonized intensity of expression. It reaches a climax in a vividly pictorial episode where a short passage of sombre chromaticism leads first to the dark key of B♭ minor and then to a section of string pizzicato evoking the tolling of the death-knell. Here, and indeed, throughout this profoundly expressive aria, Bach treats the vocal line with wonderful freedom.

The cantata ends with the ninth strophe of Ludwig Helmbold's hymn *Von Gott will ich nicht lassen* (1569), whose associated melody (1571) is simply harmonized by Bach with instruments doubling the four-part vocal texture. The text acknowledges the presence and potency of the Holy Trinity.

NA

For bibliography, *see* CANTATA, §1.

***Herz und Mund und Tat und Leben*** ('Heart and mouth, deeds and life'). Cantata for the feast of the Visitation of the Virgin Mary, BWV147. In its present, extended form it belongs to Bach's Leipzig period, but much of its material originated in Weimar, where, on his appointment as *Konzertmeister* in 1714, Bach was made responsible for providing a monthly cantata for the ducal chapel. *Herz und Mund und Tat und Leben* is made up of music belonging to both the Weimar and the Leipzig periods. In its earlier form Bach intended it for performance on the fourth Sunday of Advent in 1716. This version (BWV147a) lacked recitatives, but included the opening chorus and the four arias incorporated into the later version. For Leipzig Bach added three recitatives and the celebrated chorale movement which concludes each of the two parts. Bach's autograph score of the Leipzig version survives, but only that for the opening movement of the Weimar piece is extant.

The first Leipzig performance of *Herz und Mund und Tat und Leben* took place on the feast of the Visitation (2 July) in 1723. Bach's original designation of the cantata for Advent was inappropriate for Leipzig, where (except on Advent Sunday) concerted music was suspended during this season of the Church year. Nevertheless, Bach retained the text by the Weimar secretary and court poet, Salomo Franck, perhaps adding himself the words of the recitatives, as well as choosing the hymn strophes for the two chorale movements. Franck included a different hymn, the sixth strophe of Johann Kolrose's *Ich dank dir, lieber Herre*, which expresses praise to God in general terms appropriate to almost any church festival. By its inclusion in the recitatives of references to Mary's *Magnificat* from the appointed Gospel reading (Luke 1: 39–56), the Leipzig version of the cantata is specifically linked to the feast of the Visitation.

The cantata begins with a radiant, elaborately constructed chorus in C major framed by a festive, fanfare-like instrumental ritornello introduced by a single trumpet with bassoon and continuo and followed by strings with two oboes doubling the first violin. The vocal element is predominantly fugal and falls into two sections. In the first the four strands enter contrapuntally from the top downwards (S–A–T–B), but in the second Bach reverses the scheme, introducing the bass strand initially and working upwards. The technique is masterly and the taut construction a splendid example of the composer's skill in sensitive, affective deployment of vocal and instrumental resources to create a unified ensemble. The tenor recitative with string accompaniment which follows is a tenderly expressive piece of writing of a strongly contrasting character. Its meditative, intimate quality is shared by the alto aria in A minor, with its vacillating rhythmic patterns and the warm tones of the oboe d'amore, making an early appearance in Bach's music. The bass recitative is accompanied by a busy continuo line which, no less than the vocal part enlivens the textual imagery, for example with repeated semiquavers in *concitato* style at 'obschon vor ihm der Erde Kreis erbebt' ('although before it [God's arm] the round earth trembles'). The soprano aria 'Bereite dir, Jesu', in D minor with violin obbligato, constitutes a lyrically expressive high point in the work. There is a beguiling innocence about the vocal line, while that of the violin, predominantly in triplets, provides an ecstatic accompaniment. The chorale which concludes Part 1 of the cantata is popularly known in English-speaking countries as 'Jesu, Joy of Man's Desiring'. The four-part vocal ensemble declaims the sixth strophe of a hymn (1661) by Martin Jahn, set to a melody (1642) by Johann Schop, in a steady 3/4

metre, with the trumpet reinforcing the soprano melody. Around this Bach has woven an independent accompaniment for strings and oboes in lilting 9/8 quavers; it is loosely based on the first two phrases of the chorale melody.

Part 2 begins with a declamatory F major tenor aria with a lively continuo accompaniment for cello, violone, and organ. The accompanied alto recitative, whose vocal line is gently punctuated by two oboes da caccia, evokes the spirit of some of Bach's Passion recitatives. The remaining aria is for bass, accompanied by trumpet, strings (with oboes doubling each of the two violin parts), and continuo. This resonant C major piece, with passages of vocal coloratura, proclaims Christ's wonders. The melodic contours of the vocal line at times seem to foreshadow the middle section of the alto aria 'Es ist vollbracht' in the *St John Passion* (1724). The cantata ends with the 16th strophe of Jahn's hymn in a setting identical to that which concluded Part 1 of the work.                    NA

For bibliography, *see* CANTATA, §1.

**Hildebrandt, Zacharias** (b. 1688; d. 11 Oct. 1757). Keyboard instrument maker, born in Münsterberg, Silesia. He was trained by Gottfried Silbermann and became an expert tuner. In 1723 Bach composed a cantata (no. 194) for the dedication of Hildebrandt's new organ at Störmthal, and throughout the late 1730s and 1740s Hildebrandt was a colleague of Bach's at Leipzig. He tuned the harpsichords at the Thomaskirche and Nikolaikirche, and built a *Lautencembalo* (*see* LUTE-HARPSICHORD) for Bach about 1739. In 1748 he became overseer of the Leipzig organs. Bach and Silbermann were the advisers for his 53-stop organ of 1743–6 (still extant) in Naumburg, near Leipzig, where J. C. Altnickol became organist in 1748. In describing the organ, Altnickol said that Hildebrandt followed Neidhardt's style of temperament.                    ML

*See also* ORGAN, §3.

**Himmelfahrts-Oratorium.** *See* ASCENSION ORATORIO.

**Himmelskönig, sei willkommen** ('King of heaven, be thou welcome'). Cantata for Palm Sunday or the feast of the Annunciation, BWV182. In March 1714 Bach was appointed *Konzertmeister* to Duke Wilhelm Ernst of Weimar. His new responsibilities included the provision of cantatas for the ducal chapel. Palm Sunday and the feast of the Annunciation coincided in 1714 to fall on 25 March, and since cantatas were not sung during Lent (except when the feast of the Annunciation fell on a Sunday) we may assume that this work, whose original sources have survived complete, was Bach's first such offering to the duke in his new capacity as *Konzertmeister*. Later on, at Leipzig, Bach revived the cantata on at least two occasions, each time making adjustments to it. For the first of the revivals, in 1724, he strengthened the continuo group; for the second, probably in 1728, he added an oboe to the existing instrumentation. This addition can be felt particularly in the introductory instrumental Sonata, where the oboe is substituted for the concertante violin of the original.

The librettist has not been identified, but the Weimar court poet, Salomo Franck, has often been cited as a probable author. The text, which draws on Psalm 40 (vv. 8–9), as well as incorporating a strophe of Paul Stockmann's hymn *Jesu Leiden, Pein und Tod* (1633), is closely related to the appointed Palm Sunday Gospel, in particular to that part of it which describes Christ's entry into Jerusalem.

The cantata begins with a Sonata for treble recorder and violin concertante with a pizzicato accompaniment (in all but the last five bars) of violin, divided violas, cello, and continuo. The dialogue between the concertante instruments is both intimate and lyrical and provides an affecting prelude to the work. The second movement is a skilfully constructed da capo chorus, beginning with a PERMUTATION FUGUE and leading through a texture of canonic imitation to a homophonic conclusion. The single recitative of the cantata is for bass and has a strong arioso element with accompanying cello and organ continuo.

There follows an unbroken sequence of three arias—a scheme only infrequently encountered in the cantatas—in which Bach deliberately dispels any danger of monotony by ensuring effective contrasts in form and colour. The first aria is for bass accompanied by solo violin, divided violas, cello, and continuo. Its text reflects on divine love. The second aria, in da capo form, is for alto with treble recorder obbligato and continuo. The text here urges Christians to have faith in the Saviour. The third aria is again quite different from the other two. Against a busy continuo of cello and organ, the tenor soloist expresses in poignant, declamatory, and suppliant phrases the agony of the *via crucis* (the road to the Cross).

Following the third of the arias comes a fugal chorale fantasia whose style recalls the technique of the late 17th-century German motet. The movement incorporates another strophe from Stockmann's hymn, with the melody by Melchior Vulpius (1609) heard as a soprano cantus firmus supported by recorder and violin. Bach ends the cantata with a short da capo chorus, treated as a permutation fugue in much the same manner as the opening choral movement; its spirit is joyful

and ceremonial, providing an optimistic conclusion to a multifaceted composition.  NA

For bibliography, *see* CANTATA, §1.

***Höchsterwünschtes Freudenfest*** ('Much awaited joyful feast'). Cantata, BWV194, for the dedication of the restored organ in Störmthal near Leipzig, later revised as a cantata for Trinity Sunday. The earliest surviving form of the work (*BC* B 31) is the Störmthal version, which was first performed at the dedication service on 2 November 1723, or possibly on the previous Sunday (31 October). The anonymous libretto, which dwells in an unfocused way on the majesty of God, was of sufficiently generalized content to permit Bach to reuse without modification for the Trinity Sunday version, which was first performed in Leipzig on 4 June 1724, though the use of high choir pitch required some changes to the vocal lines. For a later revival (probably on 16 June 1726) Bach shortened the work (version *BC* A 91*b*), changing the order of the movements and rescoring two of the arias to replace one of the oboes with an obbligato organ. Material has also survived for a still later revival, which took place on 20 May 1731.

Even the Störmthal version was evidently not the original form of BWV194, however. Some instrumental parts (though unfortunately no vocal parts or text) survive for a still earlier version (BWV194*a*, *BC* G 11), which was apparently a secular congratulatory cantata composed during the Cöthen period. This did not include the two chorales (movements 6 and 12) from the Störmthal version, but it did have a closing minuet which Bach jettisoned for the church version. Dürr's reconstruction of it in the *NBA* (Critical Commentary) includes a blank staff labelled 'Singstimme', but despite the title 'Aria' it seems more likely that the movement is an instrumental dance.

For present purposes the Störmthal version will be treated as the 'core' form of BWV194. In this form it has 12 movements, divided into two groups (1–6 and 7–12) which form a *prima* and *secunda pars* (apparently heard, as usual, before and after the sermon). The cantata opens with a grandiose French overture in which the voices enter only at the central section after the double bar. The rapid triple-time section which forms the bulk of the movement is based on the fugal working out of the motif for the opening of the text; it also includes reduced sections for the two oboes and rapid antiphonal writing between the woodwind and strings. The voice parts, which do no more than double the instruments, drop out when the main tempo returns after the central section (indeed, the awkward handling of the voice parts throughout the movement arouses suspicions that they may have been added later to a purely instrumental movement). After a bass recitative, which Bach remodelled for the Leipzig version to lower the range of the voice part, comes the bass aria 'Was des Höchsten Glanz erfüllt', which Bach sets in pastoral 12/8 metre. The accompaniment is for strings and oboe, which Bach replaced by an obbligato organ for the 1726 revival. A soprano recitative leads to a second aria, 'Hilf, Gott, daß es uns gelingt'; this is in da capo form, with a sturdy gavotte-like rhythm which recalls the secular origins of the cantata. Part 1 closes with a plain chorale, 'Heiliger Geist ins Himmels Throne', which Bach added to the original secular cantata for the Störmthal version. It sets the sixth and seventh strophes of Johann Heermann's hymn *Treuer Gott, ich muß dir klagen* (1630).

Part 2 opens with a tenor recitative, followed by an aria, 'Des Höchsten Gegenwart allein', for tenor with continuo alone. Its material, which expands from an initial motto figure in 'regal' dotted rhythms, poses familiar problems in the synchronization of dotted rhythms and triplets. The following recitative–aria pair are scored for a duet combination (soprano and bass). The duet aria, 'O wie wohl ist uns geschehn', is set in a minuet tempo to the gently pastoral accompaniment of two oboes (one of which was again replaced by obbligato organ in the 1726 revival). After a final bass recitative in which the dedication theme of the text receives due emphasis, comes the closing chorale, which Bach again added for the Störmthal version to replace the minuet of bwv194a. It sets strophes 9 and 10 of Paul Gerhardt's hymn *Wach auf, mein Herz, und singe*.

DLH

P. Wollny, 'Neue Bach-Funde', *BJb* 83 (1997), 7–50, esp. 21–6. For further bibliography, *see* CANTATA, §1.

***Hochzeitsquodlibet*** (Wedding Quodlibet). *See* QUODLIBET.

***Hofcompositeur*** ('court composer'). A title which might be granted to a composer (not necessarily one who was resident at court), who was then expected to write music for court functions. In 1736 Bach was granted the title of *compositeur* to the royal *Kapelle* in Dresden. In the court calendars after that date he is referred to as *Kirchencompositeur* ('church composer'), and he frequently signed himself 'Hofcompositeur' in testimonials (e.g. those he wrote for C. G. Wunsch and J. D. Heinrich; see *BDok* i, nos. 78–9), in reports (e.g. those on organs in Zschortau and Naumburg; see *BDok* i, nos. 89–90), and on title-pages (e.g. that of the Canonic Variations for organ). What works Bach provided for the Dresden court in his role of

church composer remains a matter for conjecture. The four *missae* bwv233–6 may have been among them.

**Hoffmann.** Family of musicians whose lives and careers were intimately bound up with those of the Bachs. Close ties between the two families began in 1636, when Johann Bach (1604–73) of Wechmar married Barbara Hoffmann, daughter of the *Stadtpfeifer* Christoph Hoffmann, with whom Johann had studied. Barbara died in childbirth the following year, but the two families were united again in 1640, when her sister Eva (1616–79) married Johann's brother Heinrich (1615–92). Their son Johann Michael married Catharina WEDEMANN, a member of yet another family whose fortunes were tied in with the Bachs', and their daughter Maria Barbara became the first wife of J. S. Bach in 1707.

**Hoffmann, Melchior** (b. 1678/9; d. 6 Oct. 1715). Composer, born in Bärenstein, near Dresden in Saxony. He studied at Leipzig University from 1702, and in 1705 succeeded Telemann there as organist of the Neukirche and director of the collegium musicum that Bach later took over. He was, with Bach, an applicant for the post of organist at the Liebfrauenkirche, Halle. After Bach withdrew, Hoffman accepted the post but resigned soon after. Two cantatas once thought to be the work of Bach and included in the *BG* edition (nos. 53 and 189) are now known to be by Hoffmann.

**'Hohe Messe'** ('High Mass'). A title sometimes used for the Mass in B minor. *See* MARX, ADOLF BERNHARD.

**Homilius, Gottfried August** (b. 2 Feb. 1714; d. 2 June 1785). Composer and organist, born in Rosenthal, Saxony. He studied law at Leipzig University from 1735, becoming also one of Bach's pupils for a number of years. In 1742 he was appointed organist at the Frauenkirche in Dresden, and in 1745 Kantor at the Kreuzschule and *director musices* of the three main Dresden churches His works include numerous cantatas and motets, as well as oratorios and organ pieces. An organ chorale, *Schmücke dich, o liebe Seele* bwv759, once attributed to Bach is now thought to be by Homilius.

**horn.** A brass instrument which in Bach's time was constructed in many different forms, from the *corno da caccia* with mainly cylindrical bore, close-coiled several times, to the large-coil, narrow-bore horn with slightly conical tubing used on the hunting-field (especially in France) and later called a par-force horn, in which the number of coils was variable. There survive both a double-coil horn in F and a triple-coil horn in G ending in a wide flare (227 mm.) by J. H. Eichentopf of Leipzig, who was acquainted with important developments in horn construction taking place in Bohemia. In Bach's instrumental specifications, the term 'corno' (or 'corne') predominates, but he also used 'corno da caccia' (or 'corne du chasse'); 'corne par force' (in BWV14) and 'Waldhorn' (in a testimonial for C. F. Pfaffe, 1745) also occur. Bach used horns in F and G by far the most frequently, but he occasionally required others: in C, D, and E♭ (basso) and in A, B♭, C, and perhaps also D (alto). He specified 'corno da tirarsi' in Cantatas 67 and 162, and 'tromba o corno da tirarsi' in Cantata 46. No example of a *corno da tirarsi* survives, and theoretical writings have not so far yielded any references to it. By analogy with the *tromba da tirarsi* it must have had a straight, cylindrical mouthpipe, in which the air was vibrated by an attached mouthpiece.

When all Bach's horn parts are collated, the range (as in the case of the trumpet) is from the third to the 18th harmonic, and possibly higher depending on the fundamental. The principal register lies between the third harmonic and the eighth. This is the range, for example, of *corno* 3 in Cantata 143; *corno* 2 goes up to the 16th harmonic in the clarino register, and *corno* 1 up to the 18th. Players were expected to show the same virtuosity as trumpet players in the clarino register—which must have required a cup-shaped mouthpiece. On the other hand, in lower registers *corno* 1 and 2 are also asked to play the third harmonic.

The pitches shown below are specified for *corno* 1 (with *C* as the fundamental); trills are found on pitches represented by black notes. Only *corno* 1 plays all these notes; *corno* 2 plays those from from the sixth harmonic to the 11th and no trills are written for *corno* 3. If we also bear in mind that in any kind of tuning suitable for concerted music the seventh harmonic is too low as *b♭′*, the 11th harmonic too high as *f″* and too low as *f♯″*, the 13th harmonic too low as *a″* and too high as *g♯″*, and the 14th harmonic too low as *b♭″*, then it is plain to see that Bach had high expectations of his horn players and trumpeters. There are limits to the degree of correction of 'impure' notes attainable by alteration of lip tension and breath pressure (over- and underblowing). The bell of the instrument was held upwards during play, indicating that the technique of hand-stopping was unknown before the middle of the 18th century.

In some 30 works by Bach orchestral parts for the horn are usually written in violin clef to be transposed. Approximately the same number of parts are notated to sound as written, using violin clef and the prevailing key signature. These are mainly parts providing instrumental support for a vocal cantus firmus, with the chorale melody almost always in the soprano; a concentration of such parts is evident in the chorale-cantata *Jahrgang* (1724–5). The situation is complicated by the fact that there are also cantatas with horn parts in which some sections are to be transposed and others not, and also because some transposing parts that double a vocal cantus firmus include pitches that lie outside the natural harmonic series.

For special festivals in the church year—Christmas, New Year, Epiphany, Ascension, Whitsun, Marian festivals, and Reformation Day—and for secular congratulatory cantatas Bach might enlarge his orchestra with two horns, and sometimes also with two drums as bass support (e.g. in Cantatas 79, 91, and 100; no. 143 has three horns); here again there is a clear analogy with the use of trumpets. The only Bach work to combine three trumpets, two horns, and timpani is Cantata 205, in which the bass aria (no. 11) is accompanied only by brass, timpani, and continuo. The earliest work to include the horn may be the New Year cantata BWV143 (*c.*1708–14), but this does not survive in autograph; or it might be the 'Hunting' Cantata, no. 208, probably performed in 1713 with the Sinfonia BWV1046a as introduction in the same key and for the same forces. Except for these two cantatas and the First Brandenburg Concerto (the dedication copy of which is dated 1721), there is no known work by Bach using horns before he took up his Leipzig post in 1723. A considerable number of works with horn parts after that date are undoubtedly connected with the outstanding skill on brass instruments shown by the celebrated senior *Stadtpfeifer* in Leipzig, Gottfried REICHE.

Cantata 212 (1742) must be one of the last compositions to include a horn part. Parts originally for the horn were often given to other instruments when a work was revived, and Bach sometimes added independent horn parts to new arrangements. There are a dozen chorale movements with obbligato horns and they are also found in some choral fugues, playing either independent lines or fugal parts. Seven cantatas have unison passages for two horns (never as cantus firmus support), and horns were occasionally used also to provide

essential background during rests in the continuo (e.g. in BWV65:5 and 205:15). UP

G. and J. Csiba, *Die Blechblasinstrumente in J. S. Bachs Werken* (Kassel, 1994); R. Dahlqvist, 'Corno and Corno da caccia: Horn Terminology, Horn Pitches and High Horn Parts', in *Basler Jahrbuch für historische Musikpraxis*, 15 (1991), 35–80; P. Damm, 'Zur Ausführung des "Corne da Caccia" im Quoniam der Missa h-Moll von J. S. Bach', *BJb* 70 (1984), 91–105; H. Fitzpatrick, *The Horn and Horn-Playing and the Austro-Bohemian Tradition from 1680 to 1830* (London, 1970); R. Morley-Pegge, *The French Horn: Some Notes on the Evolution of the Instrument and its Technique* (London, 1960; 2nd edn., 1973); U. Prinz, 'Das Corno da Caccia in der h-Moll-Messe', in *J. S. Bach: Messe h-Moll, "Opus ultimum" BWV 232* (Kassel, 1990), 118–31.

**Horn, Karl Friedrich** (b. 13 April 1762; d. 5 Aug. 1830). Organist, teacher, and composer, born in Nordhausen, Thuringia. He studied the organ with C. G. Schröter, and had the good fortune to win the support of the Saxon ambassador to London, Count Brühl, who had known and admired Bach. The count took Horn to London at the age of 20 and introduced him to aristocratic society there. He became the keyboard teacher to Queen Charlotte and later to Princess August Sophia, and played a leading part in the English Bach revival. In 1807 he published 12 Bach fugues in transcriptions for string quartet. The following year he met Samuel Wesley, with whom he collaborated on a number of publications, but in 1823 Horn was appointed to succeed William Sexton as organist of St George's Chapel, Windsor. This was distant enough from London to cause him to sever his contacts with the London Bach circles. Horn's original compositions are mainly small-scale instrumental works. SFD

**Hunold, Christian Friedrich,** pseudonym 'Menantes' (b. 29 Sept. 1681; d. 6 Aug. 1721). Librettist and literary theorist, born in Wandersleben, near Arnstadt in Thuringia. With his libretto *Der blutige und sterbende Jesus*, set by Reinhard Keiser in 1704, Hunold established the Protestant Passion oratorio, and he is also credited with introducing the symbolical 'daugher of Zion', who turns up in several Bach cantatas and the *St Matthew Passion*. Hunold's most important work, the theoretical study *Die allerneueste Art, zur reinen und galanten Poesie zu gelangen* (1707), is, strictly speaking, plagiarism: he based it on the ideas Erdmann Neumeister had developed in his lectures at the University of Leipzig. Most of his career Hunold spent as a teacher of poetry and rhethoric at the University of Halle. In Hamburg he worked as a librettist, sometimes for Reinhard Keiser. During his time in Halle, he wrote the texts for a number of Bach's congratulatory cantatas performed in honour of Prince Leopold of Anhalt-Cöthen (BWV66a, 134a, parts of 204, and Anh. I 5–7) and the congratulatory poem of the *Hofkapelle* in 1719 (see *BDok* ii, no. 97). KK

**Hunting Cantata** (*Jagdkantate*). A title often used to refer to Cantata 208, WAS MIR BEHAGT, IST NUR DIE MUNTRE JAGD.

**Hurlebusch, Conrad Friedrich** (b. *c*.1696; d. 17 Dec. 1765). Composer and keyboard player, born in Brunswick. Although he would seem to have been the sort of 'Klavierritter' ('knight of the keyboard') that Bach clearly despised, he had evidently established a reputation as a keyboard virtuoso by the time he visited Bach in Leipzig, probably some time in 1734. On that occasion he played a piece—in all likelihood the Ouverture which opens Part 2 of his *Compositioni musicali*, recently published in Hamburg—and presented a copy to Bach's sons. Bach himself thought enough of the collection to borrow themes and structural ideas from the Ouverture and one of the five fugues in the work as the basis for the Prelude and Fugue BWV552 which acts as framing pillars in *Clavier-Übung III*. Furthermore, that Bach agreed to act as the Leipzig distributor for Hurlebusch's publication is clear from an entry in *Der eingelauffene Nouvelle* of 5 May 1735, stating that copies 'are to be had right here in Leipzig from Capellmeister Bach at the Thomasschule'. GB

G. Butler, 'Borrowings in J. S. Bach's Clavierübung III', *Canadian University Music Review*, 4 (1983), 204ff.

# I

**Ich armer Mensch, ich Sündenknecht** ('I, a poor mortal and sinner'). Cantata for the 22nd Sunday after Trinity, BWV55, first performed on 17 November 1726. It is Bach's only extant cantata for solo tenor. The singer for whom it was intended is unknown, but it was performed during a season in which Bach composed solo cantatas for soprano, alto, and bass as well. Although not easy to sing, and rising several times to high B♭ (usually avoided in Bach's tenor parts), it lacks coloratura writing and employs modest instrumental forces, and is one of Bach's shorter cantatas; for these reasons it is relatively little known.

The autograph score and the original manuscript parts contain clear indications that only the first two movements were newly composed in 1726. The remainder apparently are revised versions of movements from an otherwise unknown work; Glöckner suggests that they derive from a Passion oratorio which Bach composed in 1717. Nevertheless, in both arias the anonymous text is marked by the inclusion of short lines which recur in the manner of a refrain.

In the opening aria, as in that of Cantata 82, *Ich habe genung* (for which this is in some ways a preliminary study), the refrains within the text made it possible to conflate elements of da capo form with rounded binary form. The aria, in G minor, is scored for the unusual combination of flute, oboe d'amore, and two violins (each doubled), plus continuo; in the ritornello the pairs of woodwinds and violin parts are set off antiphonally. The ritornello combines twice with the voice in VOKALEINBAU, once at the end of the first section, to lines 2–3 of the text, and again at the end of the aria, where the opening verse is repeated. The result is a sort of pun, as the tenor's concluding chromatic line is appropriate for both 'Furcht und Zittern' ('fear and trembling', line 3) and 'armer Mensch' ('poor mortal', the recurring line 1).

A recitative leads to a binary-form aria in D minor with a florid flute part. The subject has turned here from sinful humankind to divine mercy, but the affect remains quiet and expressive, and the chromatic opening motif of the ritornello is also used to set the recurring opening line, 'Erbarme dich' ('Have mercy on me'). In the B section, the second statement of the words 'deinen Zorn . . . stillen' ('still your anger') elicits a sudden silence, making all the more dramatic the following repetition of 'erbarme dich'. These words

return to open the ensuing accompanied recitative; here they are set to a motif close to that used in the alto recitative 'Erbarm es Gott!' in the *St Matthew Passion*. A four-part setting in B♭ of strophe 6 of Johann Rist's *Werde munter, mein Gemüthe* concludes the work.

In a departure from Bach's usual practice, his autograph score gives a later version of the last three movements than do the original performing parts. An appendix in the *NBA* gives the second aria in the earlier version, which is slightly less florid at the beginning of the B section.          DS

A. Glöckner, 'Neue Spuren zu Bachs "Weimarer" Passion', *Leipziger Beiträge zur Bach-Forschung*, i (1995), 33–46. For further bibliography, *see* CANTATA, §1.

**Ich bin ein guter Hirt** ('I am the good shepherd'). Cantata for the second Sunday after Easter (Misericordias Domini), BWV85. The prevailing idea behind this lyrically conceived work, which Bach performed in Leipzig on 15 April 1725, is a pastoral one. More particularly it develops the image of Christ the good shepherd, who gives his life for his flock. It is an image which inspired Bach to write some of his most tenderly expressive music, as we find both here and in his two other cantatas for this Sunday in the Church year, nos. 104 and 112.

In the present work the unidentified librettist has, to a greater or lesser extent, retained the pastoral metaphor almost throughout its six sections, basing his text on the appointed Gospel reading for the day (John 10: 11–16). Bach responded with music whose intimacy, declamatory fervour, and delicately wrought instrumentation reflect with unusual consistency the pastoral images of the text. The cantata begins with a movement in arioso style for bass voice with solo oboe, violins, viola, and continuo. In this sonorous, contrapuntally woven piece the opening bars of the basso continuo are taken up by the bass, who assumes the role of Christ (*vox Christi*). The following aria, for alto voice with a busy violoncello piccolo obbligato, is a meditation on Christ the good shepherd. The structure is in one respect most unusual. Musically the piece is shaped like a free da capo aria (A–B–A'), with a full ritornello fore and aft and a brief recall in the dominant (D minor) after the first A section. But the words of the central (B) section are the same as those of

# Ich bin in mir vergnügt

both A sections. In other words, Bach has here imposed on the brief text a musical design for which it was certainly not intended.

The third movement, for soprano solo, is an elaboration of the chorale melody *Allein Gott in der Höh sei Ehr*, set to a hymn text by Cornelius Becker (1598). The voice is accompanied by two oboes, some of whose material derives from the chorale melody, and continuo. There follows a strongly characterized accompanied tenor recitative—the emphasis on the closing words, 'doch seinen Rachen zu', as the shepherd restrains the menacing wolf 'by its jaws', is splendidly effective—and this leads to the remaining solo number of the cantata. It, too, is for tenor voice and is accompanied by unison violins and viola and cast in a pastoral 9/8 metre. On a deeper level this affecting aria is a profound reflection on the celebration of the Holy Sacrament. The cantata ends with an appropriately chosen strophe, 'Ist Gott mein Schutz und treuer Hirt' ('God is my support and my faithful shepherd'), from a hymn (1658) by Ernst Christoph Homburg, for which Bach supplied an expressive harmonization of its associated melody.                                    NA

For bibliography, *see* CANTATA, §1.

***Ich bin in mir vergnügt*** ('I am in myself content'). Secular cantata for solo soprano, BWV 204, composed in 1726 or 1727. Although neglected, it is a major work, each of its four arias revealing the full art of Bach's mature style. The labour Bach put into it is clear from the large number of alterations in the extant composing manuscript. Although it is not known for what occasion the work was composed, the markedly virtuoso vocal part, which reaches high B♭ at climaxes in all four arias, points to an intended performance by an accomplished singer (presumably female) in a public setting.

The libretto derives from a text published under the title 'Von der Zufriedenheit' ('On Contentment') in a 1713 collection of C. F. Hunold. The outer movements and parts of the seventh were added by an unknown poet and, unlike Hunold's portions, fall into strophic *Lied* form (largely ignored in Bach's setting). Hunold's text, although technically accomplished, is marked by somewhat old-fashioned Baroque rhetoric, and its moralizing theme of satisfaction with one's condition is no longer fashionable, although it was evidently sympathetic for Bach, whose manuscript is entitled 'Von der Vergnügsamkeit' ('On Contentedness'; another source bears the title 'Der vergnügte Mensch'). Cantata 84, dating from the same period, is a sacred treatment of the same theme.

The opening recitative introduces the theme of modesty in contentment, which continues in the first aria, a da capo form in G minor with two oboes. The aria's compositional artifice includes the quasi-fugal development of a ritornello theme whose initial presentation is largely homophonic; the theme even enters in the bass at several points. The occasionally agitated harmony at times seems to contradict the text's opening words, 'Ruhig und in sich zufrieden' ('Quiet and contented'), but the contrast between the dissonant counterpoint and the voice's held notes on 'ruhig' ('quiet') and, especially, 'behält' ('retain') might symbolize the contrast between true happiness and worldly preoccupations.

The latter become the concern of the following accompanied recitative, in which the strings are first heard. The accompaniment becomes momentarily active in a *presto* passage at the mid-point of the movement, marking the 'flying away like dust' of worldly riches. A single solo violin accompanies the following aria, in F major, a modified da capo form again with unusually rich musical development.

The fifth movement, a simple recitative, constitutes the dramatic centre of the cantata. Twice, rapid vocal scales represent the poem's typically Baroque image of an oyster whose opening exposes the pearl inside to the light of heaven. This leads to a modified da capo aria in D minor with flute, even more elaborately developed than the previous one.

Only the first two lines of the final recitative are by Hunold, and these originally constituted the complete text of his *opening* movement. The remainder comprises six stanzas of folklike verse, the last three of which Bach set as an arioso whose relatively simple song style belies the grim words about the unreliability of friends and the imminence of death.

Against this, the closing aria, scored for the full ensemble in B♭ major, sounds as a pleasant relief. The dance-like ritornello has an attractively irregular phrase structure and is heard repeatedly, thanks to the extensive use of VOKALEINBAU. The form is unusual: the two stanzas of text, both in praise of 'Vergnügsamkeit', alternate twice, the second statement of the second stanza being sung to a recapitulation of music earlier used for stanza 1. The final vocal phrase is a cadenza-like passage that contains the soprano's concluding ascent to B♭, representing 'göttliche Vergnügsamkeit' ('divine contentedness'). The movement was parodied in two incompletely preserved cantatas, BWV 216 and 216a.                                    DS

For bibliography, *see* CANTATA, §2.

***Ich bin vergnügt mit meinem Glücke*** ('I am content with my good fortune'). Cantata for Septuagesima, BWV84, first performed on 9 February 1727. A solo cantata for soprano, it might have been written for the same unidentified soloist employed in Cantata 52, performed the previous November. The text is presumed to be by Picander, who included a comparable libretto for the same day (incorporating a few identical or similar verses) in a collection published the following year. The joy-in-moderation preached here was evidently a timely theme; within a year or so, Bach set Hunold's text on the same subject in the secular cantata BWV204.

The two arias are unusually long modified da capo forms with double B sections (A–B–B′–A′); moreover, both employ VOKALEINBAU in most of each A section. The two aria texts might have suggested music of similar expressive character as well, but the opening aria avoids emphasizing any one word, such as 'Glücke' ('good fortune'). Instead it takes on a generalized elegiac tone, or perhaps one of resignation, through its E minor tonality and the florid oboe part (joined by strings) of the ritornello, whose melody is taken up by the voice. The second aria (movement 3), on the other hand, is one of Bach's most exuberant expressions of delight, dominated by the leaping theme of the A section (borrowed from the ritornello, for oboe and solo violin with continuo). It darkens chromatically only briefly in the B section, for the word 'Not' ('need').

The rather long texts of the two recitatives are set somewhat routinely, although the second (accompanied) recitative (no. 4) serves to move the cantata back towards minor keys. This reflects its text's presentiments of death and prepares the concluding chorale, a setting in B minor of the 12th strophe of the hymn *Wer weiß, wie nahe mir mein Ende* (1686) by Ämilie Juliana, Countess of Schwarzburg-Rudolstadt; the melody is *Wer nur den lieben Gott läßt walten*.

As in Cantata 56, Bach's original list of performing forces implies that none of the vocal parts of the chorale was doubled ('à Soprano Solo è 3 Ripieni'). Performance questions arise in conjunction with certain stylistically uncharacteristic articulation markings (slurs and dots) in the two arias, especially the second. These markings are included in modern editions as they are found in the original manuscript parts prepared by Bach's copyists, to which Bach himself added a number of ornament signs. But it is possible that other markings in these parts are spurious later additions, such as are known to have been made in manuscript sources for other works.          DS

For bibliography, *see* CANTATA, §1.

### Ich elender Mensch, wer wird mich erlösen

('O wretched man that I am! who shall deliver me?'). Cantata, BWV48, first performed in Leipzig on the 19th Sunday after Trinity (3 October), 1723. Its point of departure is the apostle Paul's cry of anguish (Rom. 7: 24), in which he bewails the spiritual death that results from the flesh's inclination to sin. This text is set as a choral fugue (movement 1). The principal motif of the opening ritornello is presented in a striking ascending sequence, which may represent a kind of reaching towards heaven. The first complete fugal exposition (bars 31–44) is preceded by a canonic duet between the upper two voices (bars 13–21), similar to a motto opening in an aria. Simultaneously, the trumpet and oboes begin their presentation of the chorale melody *Herr Jesu Christ, ich schrei zu dir*, also in canon, one phrase at a time. Next, the entire complex (ritornello, motto-like passage, fugue) is repeated. This time, however, the order of vocal entries is changed: the two lower voices sing the motto, and then the voices enter in the order alto–soprano–tenor–bass, reversing the previous order. The subsequent course of the movement includes two additional points of imitation. As it draws to a close, the trumpet rounds off the canonic presentation of the chorale tune by repeating the first phrase while the oboe sustains the tonic.

Compared with the brief tenor recitative (movement 5), accompanied by the continuo alone, the alto recitative (movement 2) is quite substantial. The voice and continuo are joined by strings (violins 1 and 2, and viola), which trace in sustained notes the sometimes adventurous harmonic trajectory. Of particular significance is the predominance of sharps (symbolizing the Cross) when the sufferings of this world are compared to the bitter taste of the 'Kreuzkelch' ('Cross's chalice') (bars 10–13). This passage stands out in especially bold relief in a cantata where all seven movements have key signatures of two or three flats.

There are moments of vivid harmonic colour in the next two movements as well. In movement 3, a four-part harmonization of the fourth strophe of the chorale *Ach Gott und Herr*, chromaticism and minor inflection of the tonic and subdominant (bars 2 and 8–9) underscore the meaning of the words 'Straf und Pein' ('punishment and suffering') and 'büßen' ('to atone for'). Likewise, in the alto aria (movement 4), both the lowering of the 3rd in bar 27 and the passage in B♭ minor at the end of the A section (immediately before a cadence in the dominant, B♭ *major*) are surely connected with illustrating the word 'zerstöret' ('destroys').

The boldest harmonic motion, however, is found in the tenor aria (movement 6). Since both the opening ritornello and the A section of this modified da capo aria modulate to the dominant, the da capo (A′) and the concluding ritornello had to be adjusted so that the movement would end in the tonic. More surprising, however, is the sequence of tonalities in the B section. The first vocal passage (bars 45–57) modulates to the supertonic minor (A minor), a move outside the normal range of tonal relationships in Bach's arias. But the medial ritornello (bars 58–63) then confounds all expectations by abruptly modulating a semitone upwards to the mediant, B♭ major. This remarkable passage is nothing less than a musical representation of resurrection, suggested by the words 'Er kann die Toten lebend machen' ('He can raise the dead').

A simple four-part chorale, with the same melody as in the opening chorus, closes the cantata.

SAC

For bibliography, *see* CANTATA, §1.

***Ich freue mich in dir*** ('I rejoice in thee'). Cantata for the third day of Christmas, the feast of St John the Evangelist, BWV133. Its framework is provided by the first and last strophes of a hymn by Caspar Ziegler, *Ich freue mich in dir* (1697). The two remaining strophes were paraphrased by an unidentified author and are accommodated in the intervening sections of the cantata. The text, though making passing reference to the appointed Gospel reading for the day (John 1: 1–14), is a celebration of the Christmas story. Bach first performed the piece at Leipzig on 27 December 1724 (it thus takes its place among the chorale-based cantatas of the second Leipzig cycle) and probably revived it on at least one subsequent occasion.

The cantata begins with a concerto-like movement in D major of enormous rhythmic vitality, in which the eight lines of Ziegler's hymn, set to an anonymous melody, are interpolated between joyfully spirited instrumental ritornellos scored for strings and continuo with oboes d'amore doubling second violin and viola. Six lines of the hymn are presented in straightforward cantional style, while the remaining two (lines 6 and 8) are effectively elaborated in order to emphasize key words in the text. Thus in the sixth choral interpolation Bach highlights the words 'süßer Ton' ('sweet sound') by sustaining the 'Ton' in the soprano line for three and a half bars, while in the last choral phrase he elaborates the vocal texture to underline the 'große' of 'große Gottessohn' ('the mighty son of God'). The chorale cantus firmus is sustained throughout in the soprano line and supported by a cornett.

The alto aria in A major which follows is accompanied by two obbligato oboes d'amore with continuo. Its central textual motif is contained in the word 'Getrost' ('be confident')

which is reiterated with emphasis both in the opening section and in the freely treated da capo. The remainder of the text makes symbolic reference to the appointed Gospel reading, given expressive intimacy and warmth by the oboes d'amore. A tenor recitative, whose concluding Adagio section in arioso style makes reference to the Christ-child, leads to an extended aria for soprano with string accompaniment. Its text contains the Christmas message of the angels that Christ has come to save mankind. This effectively constructed and subtly expressive da capo movement in B minor is introduced by strings and continuo. The melodic idea which dominates the first section of the aria and the da capo is presented by the first violin and taken up with modest elaboration by the voice. At bar 17 a brief passage for solo violin introduces affective and recurring imagery of ringing bells to accompany the words 'Wie lieblich klingt es in den Ohren' ('How sweetly in my ears it rings'). The middle section provides strong contrast: the rhythm changes to 12/8, the tempo is marked 'Largo', and the continuo remains silent. It is a meditation on the name of Jesus in which Bach combats the rock-hard human heart with music of lyrical, intimate tenderness.

A bass recitative, with an arioso section marked 'Adagio', reflects on Jesus's love and protection. The cantata ends with the last strophe of Ziegler's hymn, set to the same anonymous melody that was incorporated into the opening chorus of the work and simply harmonized by Bach with instruments doubling the voices.

NA

For bibliography, *see* CANTATA, §1.

***Ich geh und suche mit Verlangen*** ('I go and seek with longing'). Cantata for the 20th Sunday after Trinity, BWV49, first performed on 3 November 1726. Like a number of other works composed during the 1726 Trinity season, it is a solo cantata (lacking choral movements), with a substantial part for obbligato organ. Moreover, as Bach's title in the autograph score indicates, it is a dialogue, the two vocal parts—soprano and bass—representing the Soul and Jesus respectively. The anonymous poet was possibly the same as for the previous week's Cantata 56, whose solo bass part was presumably sung by the same soloist employed here. Bach himself probably played the organ part.

The cantata opens with a Sinfonia arranged from the final movement of the lost work that Bach later revised as the E major Harpsichord Concerto. As in Cantata 169, which incorporated the first movement of the same concerto and had been performed just two weeks earlier, the organ takes over the solo part. In this cantata Bach also added an oboe d'amore—perhaps a reminiscence of the oboe thought to have served as the original soloist, although in this movement it only doubles the first violin. The sinfonia is in da capo form; its dance-like character, recalling the minuet or passepied, perhaps justified its inclusion in a cantata whose text celebrates a symbolic marriage (with references to the Song of Solomon).

The bass sings first, in an aria accompanied by obbligato organ and continuo (confined to cello and violone, to judge from the surviving manuscript parts). The form is an unusual modified da capo (A–B–A′) in which the second A section is interrupted by a substantial restatement of B, which presents the question posed by Jesus to the Soul: 'Where have you gone?' Following a precedent established in the previous week's cantata, a portion of this aria recurs in a later movement—here, the following accompanied recitative, which turns into a brief love duet as the soprano answers. The soprano continues with an aria in modified da capo form; this is notable for its fugal ritornellos, which are scored for oboe d'amore and violoncello piccolo, with continuo (including organ).

Another dialogue recitative leads to the concluding duet. Here the bass sings a da capo aria text while the soprano intones the seventh strophe of Philipp Nicolai's chorale *Wie schön leuchtet der Morgenstern* as a cantus firmus. Both the bass's principal melody and the ritornello theme (played by the organ in embellished form) derive from Nicolai's melody. DS

For bibliography, *see* CANTATA, §1.

***Ich glaube, lieber Herr, hilf meinem Unglauben*** ('Lord, I believe; help thou mine unbelief'). The central theme of this cantata (BWV109), the conflict between belief and unbelief, is implicit in the Gospel reading for the 21st Sunday after Trinity, the occasion of its first performance on 17 October 1723. The appointed passage (John 4: 47–54) relates an incident in which Jesus's spoken assurance to a royal official leads to the healing of the official's son, and this becomes the occasion for him and his entire family to believe in Jesus. For the first movement, however, Bach's anonymous librettist chose a different text—one that also involves the healing of a man's son, but in which the father verbalizes his inner conflict by exclaiming, 'Lord, I believe; help thou mine unbelief' (Mark 9: 24).

Musical contrasts, emblematic of the polarity between belief and unbelief, are woven into the texture of the entire cantata. In the opening chorus they are manifested in the frequent juxtaposition of smaller and larger groups of instruments in the manner of a concerto grosso. This is heard already in the first bar, where the opening gesture, played in unison by first oboe and first violin, is answered by the entire ensemble (horn, two oboes, strings, and continuo). Similar contrasts are indicated by the markings 'solo' and 'tutti' in the first violin part, as well as by the dynamic indications *piano* and *forte*. Opposition between a portion of the group and the entire ensemble is also seen in the choral writing, which thins to a single part much more frequently than usual.

The struggle between faith and doubt is dramatized at the level of the individual Christian in the next two movements, both for tenor. The recitative (movement 2) contains three pairs of statements: each affirmation of trust in God's loving care, marked *forte*, is countered by an expression of doubt or fear, marked *piano* and prefaced by the words 'Ach nein' ('Ah, no'). (Dynamic markings such as these, common enough in the instrumental parts, are extremely rare in the vocal lines of Bach's works.) In the final passage the anguished cry 'Ach Herr, wie lange?' ('O Lord, how long?'), sung *forte* and in tempo (*adagio*), calls forth a graphic melisma (illustrating the word 'lange'), whose upward melodic motion at the end imitates the proper inflection of a question. Diametrical opposition is represented in the movement's tonal plan as well. The modulation from B♭ major to E minor entails not only a shift to the opposite mode but also root motion from B♭ to E (pitches separated by the distance of a tritone and therefore tonal opposites).

In the tenor aria (movement 3), the agitated mood associated with the Christian's intense doubt and the trembling of his terrified heart is graphically depicted by jagged melodic contours and dotted rhythms as well as by illustrative melismas (triplet semiquavers) on the word 'wanket' ('trembles'). The unusually adventurous harmonic structure of the B section embodies the polarity between belief and unbelief (D minor at bar 32 and F♯ minor at bar 39 are equally remote in opposite directions from the tonic, E minor). The abrupt turn away from the dominant (B minor) towards A minor just before the da capo is also emblematic of psychic uncertainty.

The alto recitative (movement 4) turns from inner struggle to faith by pointing to the sure fulfilment of God's promises. The subsequent aria, in which the alto is joined by a pair of oboes, affirms that the Saviour is aware of his people's struggles and will come to their aid. The predominantly calm mood of this lovely movement is broken only by the virtuoso melismas in the B section, which illustrate the word 'streiten' ('to fight').

Instead of a simple four-part chorale, this cantata concludes with an elaborate concerted setting

of one of the earliest and most famous hymns of the Lutheran Reformation, strophe 7 of Lazarus Spengler's *Durch Adams Fall* (1524).          SAC
    For bibliography, *see* CANTATA, §1.

***Ich habe genung/genug*** ('I am content'). Cantata for the feast of the Purification, BWV82, first performed on 2 February 1727. A solo cantata, it is one of Bach's best-known vocal works and was evidently a favourite of the composer's, existing in a version for soprano as well as the familiar one for bass. Its popularity owes much to the great beauty of its three arias, which trace a path from world-weariness to joyful anticipation of death, a favourite theme in Bach's cantatas.

The earliest version (*BC* A 169*a*), performed in 1727, was already for bass voice with oboe and strings. Yet Bach had initially written the first aria for alto, only then adding a rubric directing transposition of the vocal part down an octave for bass. Bach's change of mind suggests that he did not conceive of Cantata 82 as specially appropriate for the bass voice. Yet the change cannot have been undertaken for want of an alto, for an alto sings in Cantata 83, a work of 1724 which was repeated on the same day in 1727.

Probably four years later, Bach prepared a second version in which a soprano replaced the bass (*BC* A 169*b*, sometimes referred to improperly as BWV82*a*). This version entailed a transposition from the original C minor to E minor, and the replacement of oboe by flute. Of this version only the manuscript parts for voice and flute survive; the *NBA* gives a 'reconstruction', but it omits dynamics and other markings (notably the bass figuration) that Bach would have included in the lost string and continuo parts.

Some time after 1735 Bach altered the clef and key signature in the soprano part of 1731 to produce a C minor version. He also added 'mezo' to the right of the original 'soprano' heading. This has led to a view of this third version (*BC* A 169*c*) as one for mezzo-soprano, although it lies entirely within Bach's usual alto range; the new heading might have been meant only to point to the unusual clef (a C clef on the second line of the staff) in the revised manuscript part. Further revisions were undertaken in 1746/7, when Bach's student Altnickol copied out a new manuscript part for bass voice (possibly for his own use) and Bach wrote a new organ part—a simplified version of the continuo line—and revised the instrumentation of the final aria. Still later, Bach added an oboe da caccia to double the first violin in the second aria, thus producing the final version (*BC* A 169*d*).

It is unknown why or for whom Bach prepared any of these versions. Editors have dealt with them variously. The *BG* gives only the late version, but without the oboe da caccia part and without the 'ripieno' second violin part added in the *forte* passages of the last movement. The *NBA* presents the work three times: in the original C minor version; in the final C minor version, with the solo part designated as 'Basso o Mezzosopran'; and in the reconstruction of the E minor soprano version.

The anonymous text shows signs of Picander's style, including the recurrence of the incipit 'Ich habe genung' at the outset of the second movement. (The spelling 'genug' is a more singable variant already found in the copy by Anna Magdalena Bach mentioned below.) The expansive opening aria is, in principle, of the through-composed binary type (or, rather, A–B–B'), unified by refrain-like recurrences of the opening three words and their expressive motif. The latter is introduced in the ritornello by the oboe only after two opening bars for the strings; this, as well as the written-out melodic embellishment of the oboe part, might have been suggested by the adagios of certain Italian oboe concertos, such as the one that Bach arranged for keyboard as BWV974.

The following recitative makes the cantata's only direct reference to the day's scriptural reading, broadening into imitative arioso at the line 'Let us follow this man'—that is, Simeon, who considered himself ready to die after seeing the infant Jesus in the temple. The ensuing lullaby, in rondo form, is one of Bach's most affecting arias; Anna Magdalena Bach copied a version of it, together with the preceding recitative, into her second *Clavierbüchlein*. The brief recitative that follows ends with a slow (*adagio*) 'good night' to the world in C minor. The subsequent aria in that key is, however, marked 'vivace' and is characterized by extended melismas on 'freue' ('rejoice'). It is a modified da capo form, scored like the first aria for oboe and strings.          DS
    For bibliography, *see* CANTATA, §1.

***Ich habe meine Zuversicht*** ('I have my assurance'). Cantata for the 21st Sunday after Trinity, BWV188, believed to have been first performed on 17 October 1728. One of several cantatas to incorporate organ concerto movements, it is a substantial work on a text by Picander published in 1728 (hence the presumed date of composition). Unfortunately, the autograph composing score was broken up in the 19th century in order to be sold in fragments—some as small as a third of a page! As a result, most of the opening Sinfonia is lost, and the remainder is scattered between European and American libraries and private collections.

Enough of the Sinfonia survives to show that it was a version of the final movement of the lost violin concerto that Bach later arranged for harpsichord as BWV1052. As in Cantata 146, whose first two movements were taken from the same lost concerto, Bach arranged the solo part for organ and added parts for two oboes and *taille*. The Sinfonia is thus a furious virtuoso movement, after which the opening aria, for tenor, oboe, and strings, sounds, appropriately, as a confident respite ('I have my assurance'). In F major, its character falls somewhere between that of a polonaise and a sarabande; it is in da capo form, making a dramatic change of character and texture—with broken chords in the strings—for the B section, 'if all should break and fall'.

An extended bass recitative concludes with an imitative setting of Jacob's words to the angel, 'I will not let thee go, except thou bless me' (Genesis 32: 26); a rising melisma marks the crucial word 'segne' ('bless'). The following alto aria, in E minor with a florid obbligato organ part, contrasts sharply with the previous aria, particularly with its expressive chromatic appoggiaturas in the B section at 'Kreuz und Pein' ('Cross and suffering').

Dramatic repeated string chords—an afterthought in Bach's composing score—introduce a short accompanied recitative for soprano. The cantata ends with a four-part setting of the first strophe of the chorale *Auf meinen lieben Gott*.

DS

R. Schureck, 'The Restoration of a Lost Bach Sinfonia for Organ and Orchestra', *Musicology*, 5 (1979), 205–9. For further bibliography, *see* CANTATA, §1.

### Ich hab in Gottes Herz und Sinn ('I have into God's heart and soul').

Cantata for the third Sunday before Lent (Septuagesima), BWV92, first performed at Leipzig on 28 January 1725. It is a CHORALE CANTATA belonging to Bach's second Leipzig *Jahrgang*, and is based on a hymn by Paul Gerhardt dating from 1647. The unknown librettist has refashioned the 12 strophes of Gerhardt's hymn for a nine-movement cantata, but has retained an unusually high proportion of them intact. The text is not specifically related to either of the appointed Bible readings, but exhorts the congregation to put their trust in God through good and ill.

Of the five hymn strophes retained in their original form, the first is set as a choral fantasia with the chorale melody, *Was mein Gott will, das g'scheh allzeit*, sung as a soprano cantus firmus in long notes. The imitative material in the three lower voices is derived from the ritornellos that separate the lines of the chorale; these employ the full instrumental forces of two oboes d'amore, strings, and continuo. It is a beautifully constructed chorus, containing many subtleties.

What it lacks in dramatic incident is made up for in the succeeding movement, in which the bass's singing of the second hymn strophe is nine times halted by passages of recitative, some of which rouse the continuo accompaniment to vigorous word-painting. In a less frenetic way, movement 7 also alternates chorale lines, this time sung chorally, with passages of recitative sung in turn by the four vocal soloists. In movement 4 the chorale melody appears as a lightly decorated alto cantus firmus, with the oboes d'amore and continuo weaving a kind of three-part invention around it. And the cantata ends, as usual, with a plain four-part harmonization of the same melody with instrumental *colla parte* support.

The first of the three paraphrased arias (no. 3) takes its expressive cue from the opening words, 'Seht, seht! wie bricht, wie reißt, wie fällt' ('See, see! how it breaks, and tears, and falls, what is not held by God's strong arm'), the breaking suggested by the wide leaps and jagged rhythms of the tenor line, the tearing by vigorous *tirades* for the first violin, and the falling by plunging downward arpeggios in the continuo bass. If the bass aria with continuo (no. 6) is in comparison rather routine in its filling of the conventional da capo structure, the soprano's 'Meinem Hirte bleib ich treu' (no. 8) is a wholly delightful aria, both for its ingenuous, dance-like melody and for its lightly sketched accompaniment of oboe d'amore and pizzicato strings.

For bibliography, *see* CANTATA, §1.

### Ich hatte viel Bekümmernis ('I was sore afflicted').

Cantata for the third Sunday after Trinity, and *per ogni tempo* ('for any occasion'), BWV21. This profoundly expressive and beautifully proportioned piece is justifiably considered among Bach's finest contributions to the Lutheran cantata. The work is striking both for its vivid imagery and for its sections of impassioned dialogue but, notwithstanding its compound origins, it also reveals a masterly organization of musical ideas, a cohesive strength, and a dramatic intensity hardly inferior (though on a smaller scale) to that of the two great Passions and the B minor Mass.

The history of the cantata is complex. According to Bach himself, the work was composed for the third Sunday after Trinity in 1714. That was some three months after his employer, Duke Wilhelm Ernst, had appointed him *Konzertmeister* in addition to his existing post as court organist at Weimar. As part of his new responsibilities Bach was required to compose and perform a cantata once a month. Yet it is possible that he had written a shorter version of this work the previous year, performing it as a test piece when applying for the

# Ich hatte viel Bekümmernis

post of organist at the Liebfrauenkirche in Halle. Later performances include one in Hamburg's Jacobikirche in autumn 1720, when Bach transposed the C minor key of the Weimar version to D minor. On this occasion Bach had travelled from Cöthen, where he may also have performed the cantata, in search of a Hamburg post, and also to hear the renowned and by then aged organist Adam Reincken. The last documented performance of the piece took place in Leipzig on 13 June 1723, once again on the third Sunday after Trinity. For Leipzig Bach made some important adjustments, reverting to the key of C minor and adding *colla parte* cornett and trombone parts to the three upper string parts and to the bassoon in the choral ninth section of the work.

Although the score of *Ich hatte viel Bekümmernis* is lost, the surviving autograph parts confirm a performance at Weimar on 17 June 1714. However, Bach's inscription 'Per ogni tempo' on the title-page suggests that he did not initially intend the work for a specific Sunday or festival in the Church year. The text is usually attributed to the Weimar cleric and court poet, Salomo Franck, who based it on verses from the Psalms and from the Epistle for the third Sunday after Trinity: 'Cast[ing] all your cares upon him, for he careth for you' (1 Peter 5: 7). A picture of deep suffering, through which the soul finds heavenly joy, is the central and all-pervading theme of the work.

The scoring of the cantata, in its Leipzig version, is for soprano, tenor, and bass soloists—Bach had previously allowed for alternative solo vocal grouping, perhaps according to circumstance—and a colourful ensemble of three trumpets, timpani, oboe, bassoon, and strings, as well as the cornett and three trombones already mentioned. The opening movement is a poignant Sinfonia (Adagio assai) in the form of a dialogue between oboe and first violin. An especially talented oboe player, Gregor Eylenstein (1682–1749), attached to the young musical Prince Johann Ernst's household, may well have been the oboist. The Sinfonia leads to the first chorus, a bipartite structure containing a fugal motet-like first section with a subject that bears a resemblance to the imitative theme in the last movement of Vivaldi's Concerto in D minor op. 3 no. 11; Bach's solo organ transcription of this work dates from approximately this time. The second section of the chorus is a Vivace in a freely constructed polyphonic style concluding with a brief Andante. The two sections are linked by a single bar, marked 'Adagio', for the word 'aber' ('but'), by which means Bach emphasizes the contrasting nature of the text in each part. The third movement is a poignant soprano aria with oboe obbligato, completing a triptych of profound anguish. This aria,

like the remaining two belonging to the cantata, is in an up-to-date Italian concertante style, drawing sharp contrasts with the older style of the choruses.

The following recitative and da capo aria are for tenor with strings. The aria, in F minor, extends the prevailing mood of agony with affective vocal and instrumental writing, where tears of sorrow, evoked in the A section and its da capo, are contrasted with the B section where images of storms and waves of the sea threaten to submerge the soul, a popular theme in Baroque poetry. Part 1 of the cantata concludes with a declamatory and partly fugal chorus set in MOTET STYLE with frequently alternating sections of solo and tutti vocal textures. The form is bipartite, the madrigalian first part leading to a vigorous fugal conclusion.

The recitative and aria which begin Part 2 are cast as a dialogue between Jesus (bass) and the Soul (soprano). The intimate fervour of the recitative is wonderfully conveyed by Bach in a warmly sustained string accompaniment and in some tenderly affecting intervals; notable among them is that of a 12th in the first violin at the words 'Bei mir? hier ist ja lauter Nacht' ('With me? here there is only night'), and another of a descending interval of a 7th in the soprano line at the close of the same phrase. Bach's vivid sense of theatre is present in both these movements, reflecting perhaps a north German predilection for spiritual and dramatic expression cultivated, for instance, in operas and Passion oratorios in Hamburg. Such fervent dialogue as this furthermore perhaps betrays Pietist influence—although the Pietists would, of course, have disapproved of this kind of music in church.

The skilfully woven contrapuntal choral movement that follows incorporates the melody and two strophes of a hymn (1657) by Georg Neumark for which Bach seems to have had special affection, *Wer nur den lieben Gott läßt walten*. In the first of these (strophe 2 of the hymn) the melody is sustained in long notes by the tenors, while in the second (strophe 5 of the hymn) the melody is similarly sustained by the sopranos with doubling oboe. In the last of the arias, an animated, virtuoso movement for tenor with a lively cello continuo, the mood of the cantata abruptly changes. The Soul, now free from care, rejoices in Christ's protection. The concluding chorus is a veritable *coup de théâtre*. In a dazzling declamatory outburst Bach suffuses his canvas in a radiance of colour, unleashing three trumpets and timpani for their first and only appearance in the cantata. This hymn of praise is in the form of a prelude and fugue whose jubilant, even heroic character brings one of Bach's most powerful cantatas to a resonant concluding 'Alleluia!' Is it possible that Mozart saw this score when he visited Leipzig? And if so, did he recall its final bar when writing the conclusion of his Symphony no. 39 in E♭, K543? NA

M. Petzoldt, ' "Die kräfftige Erquickung unter der schweren Angst-Last": möglicherweise Neues zur Entstehung der Kantate BWV 21', *BJb* 79 (1993), 31–46; J. Rifkin, 'From Weimar to Leipzig: Concertists and Ripienists in Bach's *Ich hatte viel Bekümmernis*', *Early Music*, 24 (1996), 583–603. For further bibliography, *see* CANTATA, §1.

***Ich lasse dich nicht, du segnest mich denn*** ('I will not let thee go, except thou bless me') **(i).** Funeral cantata, BWV157, also performed on the feast of the Purification. It was composed for a memorial service in Pomßen, near Leipzig, for Johann Christoph von Ponickau (1651/2–1726), an eminent court counsellor and appeal lawyer, on 6 February 1727. The printed libretto shows that a second cantata, *Liebster Gott, vergißt du mich*, which appears over the name C. G. Wecker, was performed after the sermon. This is a slightly altered version of a text by G. C. Lehms published in 1711, and its inclusion has led to various theories and speculations about Bach's involvement in the work. It has been suggested that *Liebster Gott, vergißt du mich* was composed by Bach's pupil Christoph Gottlob Wecker, and even that Wecker composed the first cantata as well. Klaus Hofmann has argued that Bach composed both cantatas as revisions and part-parodies of works he originally wrote in Weimar. To complicate matters further, the only sources to survive, prepared by C. F. Penzel after Bach's death, indicate that the work was also used as a cantata for the feast of the Purification (2 February), though there is nothing to show that Bach himself performed it on such an occasion.

Except for the biblical quotation (from Genesis 32: 26) which serves for the opening movement, the text, by Picander, of *Ich lasse dich nicht, segnest mich denn* has nothing in common with that of the motet of the same title (see below). Bach set the Genesis text as a duet for tenor and bass, accompanied by flute, oboe, and violin with continuo. It is a highly contrapuntal movement, in five imitative parts above a bass which moves mainly in purposeful quavers. After an opening instrumental ritornello, the bass and tenor enter with their own material in a seven-bar canon; both the ritornello and the canon are then repeated in the dominant with the flute and oboe parts exchanged and the tenor leading. There being no more words than those already quoted, the movement proceeds contrapuntally over a firm harmonic framework, with the voices and instruments now sharing the same or similar material. The music's effortless flow is impressive; its relevance to the text is harder to fathom.

In the tenor aria 'Ich halte meinen Jesum feste' that follows, the idea of clinging on to Jesus is expressed by several long notes on the word 'halte' ('hold'), but there are also some florid exchanges between the voice and the solo oboe d'amore. The repetition of the first line at the end of the aria text, rather than inviting a da capo repeat of the opening section, precludes it, since in both rhyme and meaning it follows on from the preceding line. Bach responds with an unusually flexible and unpredictable ritornello structure, but even more unusual is the bass aria 'Ja, ja, ich halte Jesum feste' (no. 4) which follows after an accompanied recitative for the tenor. The course of this ritornello aria, brightly accompanied by flute, violin, and continuo, is thrice interrupted, twice by passages of recitative and once by three bars of arioso (Adagio)—an unusual structure for Picander as well as for Bach, and one which supports the conjecture of a parody.

The plainly harmonized four-part chorale that ends this enigmatic, but musically most satisfying, work is the sixth strophe of Christian Keymann's hymn *Meinen Jesum laß ich nicht* (1658).

K. Hofmann, 'Bachs Kantate "Ich lasse dich nicht, du segnest mich denn" BWV 157: Überlegungen zu Entstehung, Bestimmung und originaler Werkgestalt', *BJb* 68 (1982), 51–80. For further bibliography, *see* CANTATA, §1.

***Ich lasse dich nicht, du segnest mich denn*** ('I will not let thee go, except thou bless me') **(ii).** Motet for eight-part double chorus, BWV Anh. III 159, on Genesis 32: 26 (plus the words 'mein Jesu') and strophe 3 of the hymn *Warum betrübst du dich, mein Herz*. The work, dating probably from Bach's years in Weimar and documenting his early cultivation of the motet, was long misattributed to his second cousin Johann Christoph Bach (i).

The oldest source is a fair copy from about 1712–13, partly in Bach's hand and partly in the hand of his pupil Philipp David Kräuter. The damaged score has no composer's name on it, and may never have had one. The score's age is probably what led C. P. E. Bach to include the motet (anonymously) among the compositions of older Bachs in the ALTBACHISCHES ARCHIV. The work was apparently known in Leipzig as J. S. Bach's after his death, and was regarded as his in Berlin Bach circles as well. But it was published in the 1820s under the name of Johann Christoph Bach, a speculative attribution with no foundation but one which has largely persisted, though it has been doubted at times.

The restored attribution to J. S. Bach depends largely on stylistic evidence. The work is in the mould of the traditional central German motet, presenting a biblical text in its first half and a cantus firmus chorale, supported by a repetition of

# Ich lebe, mein Herze, zu deinem Ergötzen

the biblical text, in its second half. In the first section of *Ich lasse dich nicht* the persistent homophony does not suggest Bach's later writing, but the unusual key of F minor and the adventurousness of the harmony—especially the prominant dissonance on 'nicht'—suggest Bach's musical language. The construction of the motet on such a short text, and the thorough working-out of the text and associated musical ideas is also Bachian.

The second half of the motet, though traditional in its presentation of a chorale cantus firmus over the biblical text, is most unusual in its contrapuntal treatment of the lower parts. The accompanying voices present fugal imitation on just two musical ideas, showing a degree both of contrapuntal sophistication and of thematic economy found in no other composer's motets. The only comparable works are J. S. Bach's: his motet *Fürchte dich nicht* and the motet-like chorus 'Sei nun wieder zufrieden, meine Seele' from the cantata *Ich hatte viel Bekümmernis*. The latter is nearly contemporary with the date of copying of *Ich lasse dich nicht*.

The motet is much performed, often under the name of Johann Christoph Bach and in editions that reproduce one of several harmonic 'improvements' made in the 19th century, including one from the *BG*. One source, the earliest printed edition of Bach's motets, includes a four-part chorale at the end; although probably by Bach, it is not clear whether this was his addition to the work or a later accretion.

Nothing is known of the circumstances of the motet's composition; neither the biblical verse nor the chorale would be out of place at a funeral or memorial service.                DRM

For bibliography, *see* MOTET.

***Ich lebe, mein Herze, zu deinem Ergötzen*** ('I live, my heart, for your delight'). Cantata for the third day of Easter, BWV145, first performed probably on 19 April 1729. Picander's text, published in 1728, is in five sections, which in the cantata's 19th-century source are preceded by a chorale, *Auf mein Herz, des Herren Tag*, and a chorus (by Telemann), *So du mit deinem Munde bekennet Jesum*. It seems unlikely that these were performed by Bach, and not only because their texts are more appropriate to Easter Day itself. Possibly the work was copied and performed as a pasticcio some time after Bach's death.

The joyful sentiments of Picander's text, which calls on the believer to be mindful of the salvation that Christ's resurrection has brought, are well matched in Bach's music. Certain features of the score, however, suggest a Cöthen origin, especially for the bass aria, with its dance-like (passepied) character, ample ritornellos, and high tessitura.

The work begins (if we disregard the appendages to Picander's text) with a duet between Jesus (tenor) and the Soul (soprano), accompanied by solo violin and continuo, and this also recalls some of the duets in the Cöthen cantatas; had he been composing it *ex novo*, Bach would in any case have been more likely to represent Jesus by the bass voice.

The succeeding tenor recitative ends with a short Adagio passage referring to the Resurrection, 'Mein Herz, das merke dir!' ('My heart, be mindful of that!'). These words are then taken up in the aria 'Merke, mein Herze', in which the bass is accompanied by the full instrumental forces of trumpet, flute, two oboes d'amore, strings, and continuo. Like the opening duet, it is cast in modified da capo form. After a brief soprano recitative, the cantata ends with the 14th strophe of the hymn *Erschienen ist der herrlich Tag* in a plain harmonization with *colla parte* instrumental support (in which the trumpet does not join).

For bibliography, *see* CANTATA, §1.

***Ich liebe den Höchsten von ganzem Gemüte*** ('I love the highest with my whole heart'). Cantata for Whit Monday, BWV174, first performed in Leipzig on 6 June 1729. Picander's text, published in his *Cantaten auf die Sonn- und Fest-tage durch das gantze Jahr* (1728), stems from the opening words of the Gospel reading for the day, St John 3: 16–21: 'For God so loved the world'. These words are quoted in the tenor recitative (no. 3), but the first aria (no. 2), and indeed the cantata as a whole, is concerned more with the love the Christian should show towards God.

Picander's text is quite short, consisting only of a recitative and two arias in addition to the closing hymn strophe. To add substance to the cantata, therefore, Bach began it with an arrangement of the first movement of Brandenburg Concerto no. 3, the choice of which probably stemmed from his activities as director of the collegium musicum that he had taken over a few months earlier. In adding two horns, three oboes, and a bassoon to the concerto forces of nine-part strings (three each of violins, violas, and cellos) and continuo, he disguised, rather than reinforced, the ritornello structure (which is in any case not strongly articulated in the original) and thus fashioned it more as a sinfonia and less as a concerto.

The only way in which the instrumentation of this movement has affected the rest of the cantata (apart from some doubling of the voices in the final chorale) is in the tenor recitative that separates the two arias; this is accompanied by the three violins (in unison) and the three violas (also in unison) rather than by the customary first and second violins and viola. It is preceded and followed by solo arias of ample proportions, both in da capo form (modified in the case of the second aria). Lilting dotted rhythms in 6/8 metre and intertwining oboes lend a distinctly pastoral air to 'Ich liebe den Höchsten von ganzem Gemüte' (no. 2), for alto, while in 'Greifet zu, faßt das Heil' (no. 4) the bass's call to the faithful to 'grasp salvation with your hands' is expressed in more forthright tones, with unison violins and violas lending active, clean-limbed support.

The chorale that ends the cantata, plainly harmonized in four parts, is the first strophe of Martin Schalling's *Herzlich lieb hab ich dich* (1569).

For bibliography, *see* CANTATA, §1.

***Ich ruf zu dir, Herr Jesu Christ*** ('I cry to thee, Lord Jesus Christ'). Cantata for the fourth Sunday after Trinity, BWV177. Composed in 1732, this was a late addition to the corpus of church cantatas, occasioned by a clash in the Church calendar which took place in 1724, when the fourth Sunday after Trinity coincided with the feast of the Visitation of Mary (2 July). For this occasion Bach composed Cantata 10, *Meine Seel erhebt den Herren*, and he added BWV177 to the cycle in 1732, when the fourth Sunday after Trinity fell on 6 July. The work is a CHORALE CANTATA *per omnes versus*, setting the unaltered text of the chorale of the same title by Johann Agricola (*c*.1530). Bach is known to have revived it at least once, in 1742. The form of the chorale text has an influence on the design of the work in that there are no recitatives, with strophes 1 and 5 of the hymn set as a chorale fantasia and a plain harmonization respectively. Strophes 2–4 are set as arias. The work is scored for SATB, two oboes (one doubling on oboe da caccia), bassoon, concertante violin, strings, and continuo.

In the opening movement the first strophe of the hymn is treated in fantasia style and therefore conforms to the general pattern of Leipzig church cantatas. The melody is given out line by line by the soprano, doubled by the two oboes and accompanied by imitative work in the lower voices; the opening idea of the ritornello, which is prominent in the instrumental interpolations, is derived from the first line of the chorale. The scoring is rich and complex, with the concertante violin and the two oboes prominent. The second movement, 'Ich bitt noch mehr, O Herre Gott' ('I

beg still more, O Lord God'), is an alto aria in ritornello form accompanied by continuo only. The anguished tone of the text is reflected musically in the opening ritornello, which is partly based on a motif joining the *suspirans* figure (a stepwise anacrusis preceded by a rest) to a sighing appoggiatura (see Ex. 1). This figure underpins much of the accompaniment, counterpointed against florid melismas in the voice part.

Next comes a soprano aria, 'Verleih, daß ich aus Herzens Grund', with obbligato oboe da caccia. Despite the 6/8 time signature, this has a minuet-like quality imparted by the oboe's lilting phrases. The music pursues a generally placid course, disturbed only by uneasy throbbing quavers moving in chromatic progression for the words 'wenn Unglück geht daher' ('when misfortune comes along') in the second half of the aria.

The last of the three contrasting arias, 'Laß mich kein Lust noch Furcht', is scored for tenor with obbligato violin and bassoon. Like the other two, it is in ritornello form, with much of the musical interest lying in the elaborate interplay of violin and bassoon. The generally cheerful atmosphere of the music is disrupted only by the line 'die uns errett' vom Sterben' ('which delivers us from death'), which calls forth a dark-hued passage just before the final cadence. Bach depicts it with a long chromatic melisma in the voice, accompanied by a shuddering repeated-quaver bass line with *piano* and *pianissimo* markings in the instrumental parts. The final strophe is set in a plain four-part harmonization.          DLH

For bibliography, *see* CANTATA, §1.

***Ich steh mit einem Fuß im Grabe*** ('I stand with one foot in the grave'). Cantata for the third Sunday after Epiphany, BWV156, first performed probably on 23 January 1729. On a text by Picander, it is, like a number of his other Picander cantatas, a lightly scored 'solo' cantata whose arias reveal Bach's late style at its most subtle.

The opening Sinfonia in F major for oboe and strings derives from a lost concerto movement which Bach later arranged as the Largo of the F minor Harpsichord Concerto. Here it is marked 'adagio' and the solo part is considerably less ornate than in the final harpsichord version. It also ends differently, on the dominant, leading

Ex. 1

## Ich will den Kreuzstab gerne tragen

directly into the following movement, also in F major.

This movement combines a five-line aria text, sung by the tenor, with a six-line chorale cantus firmus in the soprano—the first strophe of *Mach's mit mir, Gott, nach deiner Güt* by Johann Hermann Schein (1586–1630), a predecessor of Bach as Thomaskantor at Leipzig. Although Bach had often used such forms in his Weimar cantatas, the ritornello theme (for strings in unison) has an expressive irregularity characteristic of Bach's later chorale works. Moreover, although the chorale melody is in BARFORM, the repetition of the first section is written out to permit a different continuation. Thus the sustained note at the beginning of the ritornello corresponds with the tenor's entering phrase, 'Ich steh' ('I stand'), whereas the twisting line at the end of the ritornello, with its suggestions of C minor, points to the concluding tenor melisma on 'kranker Leib' ('sick body') in line 2; neither idea returns in the vocal part, however, when lines 3 and 4 of the aria text are sung against the repeated first section of the chorale.

A bass recitative concludes with a brief, somewhat angular arioso to express the anguished words 'the longer here [on earth], the later there [in heaven]'. This is answered by an alto aria, 'Herr, was du willt', in B♭ major, in modified da capo form. The general affect here is decidedly airy, but the lively contrapuntal accompaniment (in three parts, for oboe, violins, and continuo) pauses at the mention of 'Sterben' ('death') in the B section.

A second bass recitative leads to a four-part setting of the opening stanza of Kaspar Bienemann's chorale *Herr, wie du willt* (1582), whose opening line has just been paraphrased in the previous aria.                                      DS

J. Rifkin, 'Ein langsamer Konzertsatz Johann Sebastian Bachs', *BJb* 64 (1978), 140–7. For further bibliography, *see* CANTATA, §1.

***Ich will den Kreuzstab gerne tragen*** ('I will gladly carry the cross-staff'). Cantata for the 19th Sunday after Trinity, BWV56, composed for performance on 27 October 1726. It was one of several solo cantatas composed that season and is probably Bach's earliest for bass; Joshua Rifkin suggests that all three cantatas for solo bass might have been written for Johann Christoph Samuel Lipsius, a student who received payments during this period for performances as a bass singer.

The anonymous text derives from Neumeister's previously published libretto *Ich will den Kreuzweg gerne gehen*, for the 21st Sunday after Trinity. Imagery drawn from the sermons of the 17th-century theologian Heinrich Müller is one of several indications that the present text is by Picander, who drew on Müller's writings elsewhere. Stylistic parallels to the texts of Cantatas 158, 153, and 49 have also been noted.

Both Bach's composing score and the original manuscript parts (which are unusually faulty) are extant. As Rifkin notes, Bach's listing of the vocal forces ('S. A. T. et Basso Conc[ertato]') appears to limit the number of voices in the final chorale to one per part. Two oboes and *taille* join strings in the outer movements.

A *Kreuzstab* ('cross-staff') was an astronomical instrument used in navigation, a forerunner of the sextant (invented in 1731); its mention in the opening line is the first of several nautical metaphors in the text. In the opening aria the chromatically sharpened fourth note of the ritornello theme, used for the word 'Kreuzstab', makes explicit the pun on this word ('Kreuz' means both 'sharp' and 'cross'). The aria develops this theme fugally, not only in the ritornellos but also in the first two vocal sections. Each of these sets two lines of text, which is in BARFORM; the concluding couplet receives a livelier setting employing triplets, reflecting the text's image of laying one's earthly cares in the grave. This text and music are repeated, essentially unchanged, just before the cantata's concluding chorale.

The image of life as a sea voyage, frequently found in operatic librettos of the period, is reflected in the wave-like cello arpeggios that accompany most of the second movement. The following da capo aria, with solo oboe, gives full sonata-form treatment, including a sort of false reprise, to the short A text; the longer but more earthbound B text is treated with greater concision up to its concluding line, which expresses longing for death. The same theme is repeated, after an accompanied recitative, in the concluding chorale, a particularly expressive setting of the sixth strophe of Johann Franck's hymn text *Du, o schönes Weltgebäude* (1653).                    DS

J. Rifkin, Notes to *J. S. Bach: Cantatas 56, 82, and 158* (L'oiseau-lyre, 425 822–2). For further bibliography, *see* CANTATA, §1.

**iconography.** See BACH, JOHANN SEBASTIAN, §6.

***Ihr, die ihr euch von Christo nennet*** ('Ye who call yourselves after Christ'). Cantata, BWV164, for the 13th Sunday after Trinity. The Gospel appointed for the day (Luke 10: 23–37) includes the parable of the good Samaritan, preceded by Jesus's reply to the lawyer who had asked what he must do to inherit eternal life: 'Thou shalt love the Lord thy God'. This reply was taken as the incipit of the first of three cantatas that Bach wrote for this Sunday (no. 77, dated 1723); for the same Sunday the following year he composed Cantata 33, and the present work was performed on 26 August 1725.

The text is from Salomo Franck's *Evangelisches Andachts-Opffer*, published at Weimar in 1715, and the cantata may have been composed that year and performed on 6 September 1716 (cantatas were not performed during August and September 1715 because of the period of mourning for Prince Johann Ernst). At all events, the reworking for Leipzig, if it took place, must have made it in effect a new composition.

The autograph score, included in the sale catalogue of C. P. E. Bach's library (1790), passed first to Georg Poelchau, then to Abraham Mendelssohn, and in 1835 to the Berlin Singakademie before it was acquired in 1854 by the Königliche Bibliothek (now the Staatsbibliothek zu Berlin). The work is scored for SATB, two flutes, two oboes, strings, and continuo, and consists of six movements: aria–recitative–aria–recitative–duet–chorale. The chorus is therefore limited to the final hymn, the sixth and last strophe of Elisabeth Creuziger's *Herr Christ, der einig Gotts Sohn* (1524) with its melody from the *Erfurter enchiridion* (also 1524). Cantatas of similar construction, with only a final chorale in four parts, occur frequently in Bach's first and third annual cycles, but in only five cases in the second *Jahrgang* (1724–5).

The cantata is notable for the variety of its aria forms, which do not include the typical da capo structure. The first one, for tenor with strings and continuo, is in a bipartite form, A–B: A'–B', with a pastoral 9/8 rhythm, anticipating in a sense the affect of the succeeding bass recitative, which includes two passages from the sermon on the mount (Matt. 5: 7 and 7: 7). Movement 3 is an alto aria, 'Nur durch Lieb und durch Erbarmen', with two obbligato flutes in an extended binary form (A–B–B). After a tenor recitative with string accompaniment, there follows a duet for soprano and bass, 'Händen, die sich nicht verschließen', in a four-section structure (A–B–C–A') with extensive use of canon and with all the treble instruments (flutes, oboes and violins) playing in unison.                                                                    AB

For bibliography, *see* CANTATA, §1.

### Ihr Menschen, rühmet Gottes Liebe ('Ye people, make known God's love'). Cantata for the feast of St John the Baptist, BWV167, first performed at Leipzig on 24 June 1723. The text, by an unidentified poet, stems from the Gospel reading for the day, St Luke 1: 57–80, telling of the birth of John the Baptist and including the *Benedictus* can-

ticle of his father, Zacharias. The cantata is on a small scale—two recitatives, two arias (one of them a duet) and a final chorale—and Bach's setting requires only oboe (or oboe da caccia) in addition to the usual strings, with a trumpet to double the melody in the chorale. But the music is consistently interesting, and often inspired.

The opening tenor aria, in G major, is a very clear example of the type of modified da capo structure (A–B–A') that Bach was largely responsible for developing: the first section (A) ends in the dominant key of D major, the second (B) in the mediant minor (B minor), and the final section (A') then repeats the material of the first section but adjusts its tonal course so as to steer the music back to the home key of G major. Among several instances of felicitous word-setting might be mentioned the tenor's imitation of a hunting-horn at 'das Horn des Heils, den Weg zum Leben', referring to v. 69 in the Gospel text.

The ensuing alto recitative is notable for its closing arioso passage, with a semiquaver bass accompaniment idiomatic to the cello. The soprano and alto duet 'Gottes Wort das trüget nicht', accompanied by oboe da caccia and continuo, uses the traditional da capo form (A–B–A), but with the central (B) section sharply differentiated from the first and itself divided into two. In the first of these subdivisions the voices proceed almost entirely in canon, unfolding a long melisma to underline the text 'und vor so viel hundert Jahren' ('and so many hundred years ago'; the number of notes on the first syllable of 'Jahren' actually exceeds 130!); in the second the metre changes to 3/4 and the voices proceed mainly in parallel 3rds and 6ths, cutting a narrow path through the imitative counterpoint of the oboe and bass.

At the end of the bass recitative (no. 4) the words 'und stimmet ihm ein Loblied an' ('and sing to him a hymn of praise') are sung to the first line of the chorale *Nun lob, mein Seel, den Herren*, thus leading naturally into the final movement, which is a setting of the fifth strophe of Johann Gramann's hymn (1549). Bach makes this the climax of the whole cantata, bringing together for the first time the combined vocal and instrumental forces and spacing out the lines of the hymn with independent material dominated by the busy semiquaver figuration of the oboe and first violin.

For bibliography, *see* CANTATA, §1.

### Ihr Pforten zu Zion ('Ye portals of Zion'). *See* IHR TORE ZU ZION.

### Ihr Tore zu Zion ('Ye gates of Zion'). Cantata for the installation of the Leipzig city council,

BWV193, performed on 25 August 1727. A fragment, the work survives only in an incomplete set of original manuscript parts (two oboes, two violins, viola, soprano, and alto). Three movements were parodied from an earlier secular cantata, *Ihr Häuser des Himmels, ihr scheinenden Lichter* BWV193a, of which only the text survives.

BWV193a was a *dramma per musica* for the nameday of the reigning Augustus II, performed at Leipzig on 3 August 1727. The text of its 11 movements, which included solo parts for the allegorical figures Providentia, Fama, Salus, and Pietas (Providence, Fame, Welfare, and Piety) is by Picander, who may therefore have been involved in its sacred parody performed just three weeks later. The manuscript parts for BWV193 show numerous corrections, including a copyist's substitution in the soprano part of the word 'Pforten' ('portals') for the original 'Thoren' ('gates')—hence the identification of the work as *Ihr Pforten zu Zion* in older publications.

The opening movement is a grand D major chorus in compact modified da capo form, parodied from the opening chorus of BWV193a (there sung by a 'Council of the Gods'—a flattering coincidence for any members of the Leipzig council who noticed it!). In addition to the surviving parts, it must have included at least three trumpets, timpani, and continuo, and perhaps two flutes and a third oboe as well.

A soprano recitative leads to a da capo aria in E minor, 'Gott, wir danken deiner Güte', also for soprano, accompanied by oboe and strings. Although parodied from Salus's aria 'Herr! so groß als dein Erhöhen' in BWV193a, its untroubled minuet rhythm and relatively simple formal structure have led to suggestions that both works derive from a lost secular cantata of Bach's Cöthen period. Christine Fröde suggests that the aria was parodied again in a lost cantata for the Thomasschule in 1734. Less clear is the case of the G major alto aria 'Sende, Herr, den Segen ein', which follows a recitative for the same voice. Parodied from Pietas's aria 'Sachsen, komm zum Opferherd' in BWV193a, it resembles the first part of a da capo aria; perhaps there was a B section in some earlier version. The affect is rather neutral, despite the ornate oboe part, which, with continuo, was apparently the sole accompaniment.

The surviving parts indicate that a recitative for tenor or bass followed, the opening chorus then being repeated. The extant material is sufficient to permit a convincing reconstruction, except for the final recitative, which is completely lost. Unfortunately, the version published by Reinhold Kubik (Stuttgart, 1983) requires modern brass instruments and makes other departures from Bach's style.                                                                    DS

C. Fröde, 'Zur Entstehung der Kantate "Ihr Tore zu Zion" (BWV 193)', *BJb* 77 (1991), 183–5. For further bibliography, *see* CANTATA, §1.

***Ihr werdet weinen und heulen*** ('Ye shall weep and lament'). Cantata, BWV103, for the third Sunday after Easter (Jubilate), first performed on 22 April 1725. This was the first of the nine works that Bach composed in spring 1725 on texts by Mariane von Ziegler; all nine librettos were included in 1728 in her first published collection of verse. From the omission of certain rhyming lines and other peculiarities, it appears that Ziegler's originals have been abbreviated and otherwise altered, perhaps by Bach himself.

With BWV103 and the following Ziegler cantatas, Bach completed his second yearly cycle of Leipzig cantatas, one made up mainly of chorale cantatas. Nevertheless, like most of the other works of the 1725 Easter season, Cantata 103 returns to the format of Bach's first Leipzig cycle, lacking an underlying chorale. Most of these works are now regarded as belonging to the third *Jahrgang*, leaving some gaps in the series of chorale cantatas.

The theme of Cantata 103 is announced in its opening movement—a setting of a biblical text, as in most of the works of the 1725 Easter season. The verse (John 16: 20), from the Gospel for the day, proclaims that weeping will turn to joy; unlike Bach's two other Jubilate cantatas (nos. 12 and 146), which also set portions of this verse, *Ihr werdet weinen* employs its full text. This takes the form of two clauses constituting an antithesis; each clause, moreover, is itself an antithesis.

Bach's solution to this problem of musical rhetoric is one of his more intricate and dramatic choral movements. In B minor—a key which Bach employed for some of his most expressive vocal and instrumental writing—it opens with a lively ritornello dominated by a solo part for piccolo recorder in A, presumably representing the idea of rejoicing. (Bach's only other vocal work to use piccolo recorder was the earlier Cantata 96. In each case the instrument was replaced in a later performance—in Cantata 103 by violin or transverse flute—presumably because the requisite player or instrument was unavailable.)

The first clause of the text is set as a four-voice fugue, with tortuous chromatic melismas on the word 'weinen' ('weep'). The second clause, 'but the world shall rejoice', then appears in a sort of episode, set to a motif from the ritornello. But in the subsequent second exposition this motif becomes a countersubject, and the two text clauses are thus combined. Up to this point the movement by and large resembles a common type of choral double fugue especially suited to texts consisting of paired clauses. But now it is interrupted by an accompanied recitative for bass voice, which presents the third clause ('ye shall be sorrowful'). This is answered by a final fugal exposition in which the subjects previously used for the first two clauses are employed for the fourth one. This reuse of the recapitulated music reflects the text's theme of transformation: 'but your sorrow shall be turned into joy'.

The following two recitative–aria pairs continue the antithesis of sorrow to joy. A simple recitative for tenor, concluding with a chromatic melisma on 'Schmerzen' ('sorrows'), introduces an alto aria in the unusual key of F♯ minor; this is accompanied by a florid part for the recorder. The alto then presents a recitative whose final line includes a soaring melisma on 'Freuden' ('joy'). The same word is the basis for an astounding melisma, nearly 100 notes in length, in the latter part of the succeeding tenor aria. This is an exuberant movement, yet its extraordinary trumpet part incorporates recurring non-harmonic notes to represent the text's remembrances of 'betrübte Stimmen' ('troubled voices').

The cantata ends with a four-part setting of the ninth stanza of Paul Gerhart's *Barmherzger Vater* (1653), set here to the melody *Was mein Gott will, das g'scheh allzeit*. In Bach's autograph score this movement appears on the same page as the opening bars of a cantata for the first Sunday after Easter. Apparently never completed, the fragmentary ritornello bears some similarity to that of Cantata 103; it might represent an effort begun for the Sunday two weeks earlier and then rejected in favour of what became Cantata 42.            DS

For bibliography, *see* CANTATA, §1.

**Immortal Bach.** A choral composition by the Norwegian composer Knut Nystedt (b. 1915). It consists mainly of Bach's harmonization of the chorale *Komm, süßer Tod* BWV478 sung very slowly and with each chord overlapping and merging with the next, producing an impression of timelessness.

**improvisation.** Literally, unpremeditated performance. In practice, few performances today are truly without preparation, and the same must have been true in the 18th century, when, however, various types of improvisation held a firmer place in the repertory of skills of serious musicians. This was in part because music remained more an oral tradition than it is today for 'classically' trained musicians. Opportunities for rehearsal in the modern sense were limited, and musicians frequently read their parts at sight even in public performances, no doubt relying on their ear, a strong sense of style, and an ability to improvise their way out of any difficulties that might occur

(as in the presence of errors and lacunae in the hastily prepared manuscript parts that Bach employed for virtually all his performances).

In 18th-century Germany improvisation by amateurs and run-of-the-mill musicians might have been limited to the occasional addition of stereotyped ornaments—trills, mordents, and the like—to written or memorized tunes and orchestral parts. But the training of most professional musicians probably included the impromptu embellishment of melodic intervals, such as is presented in the treatises of Wolfgang Caspar Printz (*Phrynis Mytilenaeus, oder Satyrischer Componist*, 1676–9; 2nd edn. 1696), F. E. NIEDT (1700–17), and J. J. QUANTZ (1752). Moreover, keyboard players would have studied figured bass realization, the impromptu playing of an accompaniment (*see* CONTINUO).

More accomplished musicians, including solo singers and instrumentalists, would have been expected to excel at improvisational skills, especially when performing arias and concertos, in which virtuosos were generally expected to embellish their parts in individual fashion. Embellishment was particularly expected in, but by no means confined to, the slow movements of Italian instrumental music and the repeated sections of da capo arias and instrumental movements. Neither is it clear that improvisation was restricted to soloists, although certain ensembles, in particular the opera orchestra of the French Royal Academy, were noted for their uniform execution and the lack of musical initiative by individual players.

Elsewhere, however, original invention was expected of soloists, especially in the CADENZA, which, as Quantz indicates, in duets might even include simultaneous improvisation in simple imitative style by two soloists. But the highest development of improvisatory skills appears to have been expected of organists, who in auditioning for positions at major churches were sometimes required to invent chorale fantasias and fugues on the spot, and whose public recitals—a tradition in some parts of Europe since at least the early 17th century—may have consisted largely or entirely of improvisation. According to one report, Bach opened his recitals with a written work in order to stimulate his powers of invention. Forkel, on the other hand, describes Bach's practice of impulsively improvising an entire series of different pieces on a single subject, concluding with a fugue, and the story of his unprepared improvisation of fugues on the subject of the *Musical Offering* is well known.

The skills required in such performances were to some degree the same ones called for in continuo realization, and they were apparently developed in part through study of pieces consisting solely of figured bass lines (*partimenti*). Johann Mattheson published an annotated collection of such pieces (*Große General-Baß-Schule*, Hamburg, 1731), and two similar works attributed to Bach, the fantasias and fugues BWV907 and 908, suggest that he and his students applied the skills associated with continuo playing in the improvisation of keyboard music, a practice that C. P. E. Bach later demonstrated in his *Versuch über die wahre Art das Clavier zu spielen* (Berlin, 1753–62).

To what degree such playing was truly improvisatory is difficult to say. Some organists' auditions permitted the applicant to work out fugue subjects on paper ahead of time, and any competent player must have possessed a repertory of more or less fully worked out variations on the standard chorale melodies. Much of the extant keyboard repertory, including Bach's, consists of models for improvisation; preludes, toccatas, chorale settings, and even fugues correspond to types of music that were improvised during recitals and church services, and C. P. E. Bach implied that some of his father's keyboard works grew out of actual improvisations. Moreover, many composers, including Corelli, Vivaldi, Couperin, and Telemann (not to mention Bach himself), wrote both vocal and instrumental works in which ornaments and embellishments that might normally have been improvised were fully written out.

Performers today generally avoid improvisatory additions to Bach's works, apart from the realization of the continuo part. This reflects statements made during his lifetime that he notated all that was necessary to good performance, and it also reflects the complexity of most of Bach's mature compositions, which hardly admit improvisatory additions. Yet Bach's frequent revisions of his own works included the addition of ornaments, embellishments, and even cadenzas which he presumably performed before they were written down. Many works can benefit from at least the occasional addition of ornaments, and further embellishments and even cadenzas (at fermatas) cannot be summarily ruled out for musicians who have mastered the preliminary skill of figured bass realization (which, as Quantz suggested, was essential for all musicians). DS

J. Butt, *Music Education and the Art of Performance in the German Baroque* (Cambridge, 1994); D. Schulenberg, 'Composition and Improvisation in the School of J. S. Bach', *Bach Perspectives*, i (Lincoln, Nebr., 1995), 1–42.

**In allen meinen Taten** ('In all that I do'). Cantata for SATB, two oboes, strings, and continuo, BWV97. It is one of the few Bach cantatas for which the liturgical occasion is unknown (the

others being nos. 100, 117, 192 and the fragmentary nos. 50 and 200). A copy of the score in the hand of C. F. Penzel (? *c.*1760) specifies the fifth Sunday after Trinity (in which case it would have been performed on 25 July 1734), and it has also been suggested that it was composed for a wedding. The date 1734 appears on the autograph, which passed through several hands in the course of the 19th century before it became part of the Herter collection in the Public Library at Lincoln Center, New York, in 1932. The work received two further performances, one soon after 1735 and the other between 1740 and 1747, as indicated by the addition of an organ part for movements 3 and 4, which was then transposed from B♭ to G major.

The text is the complete hymn in nine strophes by Paul Fleming (1642), but the celebrated melody to which these austere verses are sung, *O Welt, ich muß dich lassen* (derived from the secular *Innsbruck, ich muß dich lassen* by Heinrich Isaac, *c.*1450–1517), appears only in the first and last movements. The central movements—four arias, a duet, and two recitatives—make no reference to the melody.

The first movement is a spectacular fusion of a French overture (an instrumental Grave, with repeat, followed by a fugal Vivace in which the voices join) and a cantus firmus motet, recalling Cantatas 75 and 20 from the first and second annual cycles respectively. The six lines of the strophe feature brief but demanding passages of imitative writing for the lower voices, relaxing only in the last line, which is treated homophonically. The four arias employ each voice in turn, proceeding from the lowest to the highest (B–T–A–S); each aria is in the same bipartite form (A–A), the duet 'Hat er es denn beschlossen' (no. 7) being the only movement in the usual da capo structure, albeit in a modified version (A–B–A'). The tenor aria 'Ich traue seiner Gnaden' (no. 4) is particularly interesting for its unusual solo violin writing, which includes both sprightly runs in short note values and strongly syncopated passages and punctuates the discourse with stretches of polyphony (mostly in double stopping) in a style associated with the sonatas for unaccompanied violin.

In sharp contrast to this movement, which symbolically expresses the image of divine grace generously granted to the faithful, is the simple style of the soprano aria 'Ihm hab ich mich ergeben' (no. 8), accompanied by two oboes and continuo, which expresses complete and confident submission to the will of God. The complex network of emblems permeating the work is crowned by the final chorale: three independent string parts are added to the usual four-part chordal harmonization to form a texture made up of seven strands—a number which from time immemorial has served as a symbol for perfection.

AB

For bibliography, *see* CANTATA, §1.

**instrumentation.** See overleaf.

**Internationale Arbeitsgemeinschaft für theologische Bachforschung** ('International Society for Theological Bach Studies'). A relatively small but distinguished society of cross-disciplinary Bach scholars, founded by Walter Blankenburg and Christoph Trautmann at the Berlin Bachfest of 1976. The first working conference took place in Schlüchtern in February 1977, and a sequence of annual conferences ensued. Building on the foundation of such works as Hans Preuß's study of Bach's library, *Bachs Bibliothek* (Leipzig, 1928), Hans Besch's analysis of Bach's piety and faith, *Joh. Seb Bach: Frömmigkeit und Glaube* (Berlin, 1938), and Günther Stiller's work on the Leipzig liturgical context, *Johann Sebastian Bach und das Leipziger gottesdienstlichen Leben seiner Zeit* (Kassel, 1970), the aim was to encourage further research into theological aspects of Bach's life and work. Initially individual papers appeared in the journal *Musik und Kirche* and the *BJb*; later conference papers were published together in an annual bulletin (Heidelberg, 1988– ). In 1983 a series of books, edited by Blankenburg and Renate Steiger, was begun: R. A. Leaver and Elke Axmacher contributed monographs in 1983 and 1984, and in 1987 a volume of essays, *Theologische Bach-Studien I*, was published (Stuttgart, 1987). After Blankenburg's death in 1986, leadership of the society passed to Renate Steiger.

RAL

R. A. Leaver, 'Editor's Introduction', in G. Stiller, *Johann Sebastian Bach and Liturgical Life in Leipzig*, trans. H. J. A. Bouman, D. F. Poellot, and H. C. Oswald (St Louis, Miss., 1984), 11–17, esp. 13–15.

**invention.** A term employed by Bach (in the Latin form, 'inventio') for 15 keyboard pieces in two contrapuntal parts, BWV772–86. The term is often applied also to the similarly organized set of three-part sinfonias BWV787–801. Bach appears to have borrowed it from the *Inventioni da camera* op. 10 (Bologna, 1712) of F. A. BONPORTI. It seems unlikely to have been mere coincidence that in 1723, when Bach made a fair copy of his own Inventions, using that term for the first time, he also assisted a pupil (known as Anon. 5) in copying out four of Bonporti's *Inventioni*.

First drafts of the 15 'praeambula', as they were originally called, together with 15 three-part 'fantasias', were entered in the *Clavierbüchlein* for Wilhelm Friedemann Bach towards the end of 1722 and in early 1723. All the most commonly used keys were represented in the symmetrical order C–d–e–F–G–a–b–B♭–A–g–f–E–E♭–D–c (lower-case letters indicate minor keys). In the autograph fair copy made shortly afterwards (the inscription 'Cöthen, 1723' places it before the move to Leipzig in April of that year) the *praeambula* became 'inventions' and the fantasias 'sinfonias'. In addition, both sets were rearranged in a new key order similar to that of *The Well-tempered Clavier* Part 1, which was given its final form at about the same time: C–c–D–d–E♭–E–e–F–f–G–g–A–a–B♭–b.

The didactic purpose of the Inventions is stated clearly on the title-page of the fair copy, which may be rendered thus: 'Sincere Instruction, In which Lovers of the Keyboard, especially those who are keen to learn, are shown a Clear Method, not only 1) of learning to play clearly in two Parts, but also, after further Progress, 2) of dealing well and correctly with three obbligato Parts. At the same time they are shown not only how to come by good Ideas but also how to develop them well. Above all, however, they are shown how to arrive at a *Cantabile* Style of playing, while also acquiring a strong Foretaste of Composition.' The Inventions are thus designed to further the study of keyboard playing and composition in equal measure. As far as performance is concerned, they foster cantabile playing and help to develop independence of the hands in two- and three-part contrapuntal playing. For the learning composer emphasis is laid on 'gute *inventiones*' and their development. 'Invention' thus means primarily 'idea', the initial musical thought which is subsequently elaborated to form a composition. Elsewhere we learn that Bach regarded the capacity for musical ideas as innate rather than acquired: C. P. E. Bach, writing to J. N. Forkel on 13 January 1775, tells us that 'As for the invention of ideas ("die Erfindung der Gedancken"), [Bach] required this from the very beginning, and anyone who had none he advised to stay away from composition altogether' (*BDok* iii, no. 803). When, therefore, Bach says on the title-page of the Inventions that pupils 'are shown how to come by good Ideas' ('gute *inventiones* zu bekommen'), he must mean that they are provided with models of good ideas (and their development). The ideas are good not merely because they are striking and characterful, but because they are readily susceptible to development; hence Forkel's definition, in his Bach biography, of an invention as 'a musical subject which was so contrived that, by imitation and transposition of the parts, the whole of a composition might be unfolded from it'.

Forkel's definition is obviously applicable to the Inventions based exclusively on a single motif, such as those in C and B♭ major and E minor. But

## instrumentation

Instrumentation (or orchestration, with which the word is practically synonymous) was not studied in Bach's time as a musical discipline in the way that, for example, figured bass, chorale harmony, and fugal counterpoint were. G. P. Telemann's intention, formulated as early as 1717, of writing a treatise on instruments and their characteristics did not come to fruition, and the earliest published works on the subject date from the 19th century, J.-G. Kastner's *Traité général d'instrumentation* (1837) and Berlioz's *Grand traité d'instrumentation et d'orchestration modernes* (1843) being among the first. A Baroque composer's understanding of the capabilities of instruments and his skill at combining them would have been acquired by practical experience and observation, and his choice of which instruments to use for a particular piece would have been decided mainly, and simply, by what was available at the time. One cannot imagine Bach combing Leipzig for *Zinks* as Berlioz was prepared to scour Europe for ophicleides.

The Baroque composer would, of course, have had some broad conventions to guide him as to what was considered suitable for certain occasions or affects. Hunting scenes or images automatically invited the use of horns; rustic and pastoral contexts called for oboes and flutes, funerary texts for recorders and viols. Trumpets (and drums) were particularly associated with royalty and the aristocracy, or with Christ in majesty; they were out of place in a Passion setting, but appropriate to a celebratory *Te Deum* or *Magnificat*. Outside such conventions, composers were ready to transfer music from one instrument to another as occasion demanded, and Bach usually achieved this with minimal alteration to the music's actual fabric. An obbligato part to a cantata aria originally written for flute might be played on a violin when the work was repeated later; a movement from a suite for unaccompanied violin could be turned into an organ obbligato in a cantata sinfonia.

This transference of what is largely a violin-based idiom from one instrument to another (its migration to vocal music is something for which Bach has often been censured) occurred not only in the process of arrangement. The opening pages of Brandenburg Concerto no. 2 present a notorious instance of the recorder and the oboe taking over material which seems to have been conceived with the violin in mind. (The trumpet, one suspects, is excused from the more overtly violinistic figuration only because of limitations imposed by the harmonic series.) The combining of instruments to produce a judicious 'blend', which is so much the concern of modern orchestration manuals, seems not to have entered into Bach's calculations, either in this or in other works. And his writing for a particular instrument seems to have been governed more by what that instrument was capable of than by what, in a 19th-century sense, it could best 'express'.

This is not to say that Bach's music is not without some striking effects of instrumentation. The removal of the almost ubiquitous basso continuo, as in the duet portions of no. 27*a* in the *St Matthew Passion*, is a potent way of expressing deprivation and lack of support, and particularly telling use is made of muted or pizzicato strings in several cantata movements to lend emphasis to something in the text (*see* WORD-PAINTING). But it was surely not simply word-painting, but more the quality of the imagined sound *per se*, that led Bach to imagine the opening of the cantata *Weichet nur, betrübte Schatten*, where the long-held oboe note softly penetrates the rising string arpeggios, like a point of light discerned through a mist. The passage might find a place in any 19th-century orchestration treatise. *See also* ORCHESTRA and articles on individual instruments.

the typical texture of the Inventions is double counterpoint, which frequently involves the combination *ab initio* of a pair of themes of equal importance, as in the Inventions in E♭ and E major, and F and G minor. In such cases both themes combined constitute the *inventio*. Other Inventions are canonic (C minor and F major) or fugal (G and A major, and B minor). In fact, whether or not they open with fugal entries, the Inventions may be regarded as preliminaries to the study of fugue. Such an intention may perhaps be inferred from C. P. E. Bach's remark (loc. cit.) that 'In teaching fugues, [Bach] began with two-part ones, and so on'. Viewed in this light, the Inventions lead, by way of the three-part Sinfonias, to the four-part fugues in *The Well-tempered Clavier*.

On the other hand, the Inventions are perhaps more closely allied in style and technique to some of the preludes of *The Well-tempered Clavier* Part 1 (see, for example, those in C♯, F, and F♯ major), differing only in their strict adherence to two parts only—a limitation maintained despite certain passages which can hardly be described as contrapuntal, such as the central episode (bars 29–42) of no. 6, with its florid solo treble and purely accompanying bass, or the episodic bars 7–8*a* and 16*b*–17 of no. 12, where in effect a single part is divided between the hands.

From this point of view, the Inventions and Sinfonias may be seen as a comprehensive preparation for *The Well-tempered Clavier*. That Bach used them as such is clear from the testimony of E. L. Gerber, who, describing the tuition his father (H. N. Gerber) received from Bach, recounts that 'At the first lesson [Bach] set his Inventions before him. When he had studied these through to Bach's satisfaction, there followed a series of suites, then *The Well-tempered Clavier*' (*BDok* iii, no. 950). The pupil is thus introduced first to strict part-writing, then to free-voiced writing (in the suites), and finally to preludes and fugues in which the two types of texture, together with their associated styles and techniques, are conjoined.

RDPJ

*See also* SINFONIA.

D. Schulenberg, *The Keyboard Music of J. S. Bach* (New York, 1992), 149–56.

**inversion.** In melodic contexts, a term indicating the substitution of falling intervals for the equivalent rising ones, and vice versa. The device is often used in the strict forms of canon and fugue. Contrapunctus 5 from *The Art of Fugue*, for example, uses a version of the work's main theme in both its inverted and its 'original' cast (see Ex. 1).

In modern usage the term can also indicate the removal of the root of a triad-based chord to a higher octave, thus placing the 3rd or 5th etc. in the bass and putting the chord into its first or second, etc. inversion. LC

**invertible counterpoint.** A type of counterpoint in which lower and upper parts are interchangeable without producing faults of musical

Ex. 1

243

grammar. Usually, but not always, each part transposes at the octave. When only two parts are involved the term 'double counterpoint' is applied, as in the relationship between subject and invertible countersubject in a fugue. In 'triple counterpoint' three parts are likewise interchangeable, as in the C minor fugue from *The Well-tempered Clavier* Part 1. The principle applied to four parts produces 'quadruple counterpoint'.

Occasionally in the 16th and 17th centuries double counterpoint was used with invertible relationships at the 5th, 10th, and 12th rather than the octave, and Bach revived some of these practices in such works as the canons BWV1080: 16 and 17 in *The Art of Fugue* (compare, for example the passages starting at bars 9 and 42 in the second of these). LC

**Invocavit.** In the CHURCH CALENDAR, the first Sunday in Lent. It takes its name from the introit to the Mass for that day in the Latin rite, beginning 'Invocabit me, et ego exaudiam eum'.

**Italian Concerto** (*Italienisches Konzert*). The *Concerto nach Italiaenischem Gusto* (Concerto after the Italian Taste) BWV971 was coupled with the Ouverture in the French Style BWV831 to form Part 2 of Bach's *Clavier-Übung*, published by Christoph Weigel (1703–77) of Nuremberg in 1735. This was the second in the great series of keyboard publications by which Bach chose to be represented before the musical public of his time. In it he highlights the contrast between the popular French and Italian styles of his day by juxtaposing complete works in the two styles. Only a few years earlier his friend G. P. Telemann had published a keyboard work based on a similar principle, namely the *Fantaisies pour le clavessin* (Hamburg, 1732–3), which contains three dozen fantasias—the first and third dozen in the Italian style, the second dozen in the French.

In *Clavier-Übung II* the contrast between national styles is reinforced by presenting them in keys at opposite ends of the tonal spectrum: the Italian work in a flat major key (F) and the French in a sharp minor key (B). The chief orchestral genre of each nation—the Italian solo concerto and the French overture-suite—is transferred to the keyboard. On the title-page Bach specifies the two-manual harpsichord ('vor ein Clavicymbel mit zweyen Manualen') in order to allow keyboard imitations of tutti–solo contrasts and of orchestral colour effects.

The Italian Concerto, described by Bach's critic J. A. Scheibe as 'a perfect model of a well-designed solo concerto', has partial precedents among Bach's earlier works in the Weimar concerto transcriptions, in the preludes to the English Suites, and in the Prelude and Fugue in A minor BWV894. But, as far as we know, it remains his only complete, original concerto for solo keyboard. In the outer movements RITORNELLO form operates within an overall A–B–A scheme—the framing ritornellos are in each case identical and, in addition, the finale recapitulates its first two 'solo' episodes towards the end in reverse order. 'Tuttis' are played with both hands on the lower manual (indicated by 'forte'), 'solos' with the leading part *forte* and the accompanying part *piano* (= upper manual), or else with both parts *piano*. In the central slow movement the right-hand part (*forte*) has the character of a highly embellished solo violin melody, while the two left-hand parts (*piano*) simply provide harmonic and motivic support. RDPJ

*See also* SOURCES, §2.

D. Schulenberg, *The Keyboard Music of J. S. Bach* (New York, 1992), 300–4.

# J

**Jagdkantate** ('Hunting Cantata'). A title often used to refer to Cantata 208, WAS MIR BEHAGT, IST NUR DIE MUNTRE JAGD.

**Jahrgang** ('annual series'). A term equivalent to 'volume' when used in connection with annual publications such as the *BJb*. As commonly used in Bach studies, however, it is derived from the statement in the Obituary that among Bach's unpublished works there were 'Fünf Jahrgänge von Kirchenstücken, auf alle Sonn- und Festtage' ('five annual cycles of church pieces [cantatas] for all Sundays and festivals'). In establishing the chronology of these vocal works, Georg von Dadelsen and Alfred Dürr employed the term to designate Bach's annual compositional activity during his early Leipzig years. The first two annual cycles, at least, ran from the first Sunday after Trinity to Trinity Sunday the following year: *Jahrgang* 1 began on 30 May 1723, Bach's first official Sunday as Thomaskantor; *Jahrgang* 2 began on 11 June 1724 with a series of chorale cantatas. *Jahrgänge* 3 and 4 are fragmentary and difficult to define; *Jahrgang* 5 is conjectural, lacking documentary evidence.                    RAL
*See also* CANTATA, §1.

> *DürrC*; G. von Dadelsen, *Beiträge zur Chronologie der Werke Johann Sebastian Bachs* (Trossingen, 1958).

**Jauchzet dem Herrn, alle Welt** ('O be joyful in the Lord, all ye lands'). Composite motet for eight-voice double chorus, BWV Anh. III 160, probably assembled or arranged by J. S. Bach. The first section, for eight voices, sets Psalm 100: 1–2, and is of unknown authorship; the second is a setting for four voices of strophe 5 of Johann Gramann's *Nun lob, mein Seel, den Herren*—an arrangement of a movement from Bach's 1725 cantata *Gottlob! nun geht das Jahr zu Ende* for the Sunday after Christmas; a third section, probably added after Bach's death, is an arrangement of a cantata movement by G. P. Telemann for the third day of Christmas, using the text Revelation 7: 12.

The second section is unquestionably Bach's composition, differing from the cantata movement on which it is based principally in the absorption of the cantata's basso continuo line into the vocal bass. In both the motet and the cantata versions the soprano presents the chorale melody phrase by phrase in long notes, supported by imitative counterpoint in the lower voices largely drawn from the chorale tune—a type of chorale setting dating back to the early 16th century. This movement is probably older than the 1725 cantata in which it appears. The motet version is listed as BWV231, but there is no evidence that Bach ever used it as an independent composition.

The first section was described in one lost source as having been 'improved' by Bach, and the movement shows signs of having been expanded from four voices to eight. The present double-choir version shows some striking similarities to Bach's own double-chorus motets, especially in the second half, where a four-part fugue in one choir is supported by accompanimental material in the other, recalling the motet *Singet dem Herrn*.

The principal source of the motet is a copy by Bach's pupil and son-in-law J. C. Altnickol, which attributes it to Bach. The work is listed in the catalogue of C. P. E. Bach's estate under Bach's name, but the copy referred to is lost. The origin of the second movement in Bach's cantata chorus and the construction of the first movement suggest that the motet is Bach's arrangement of a four-part work of unknown authorship (Telemann is a likely composer) and of his own motet-like cantata chorus.                    DRM

> K. Hofmann, 'Zur Echtheit der Motette "Jauchzet dem Herrn, alle Welt" BWV Anh. 160', in W. Rehm, ed., *Bachiana et alia musicologica: Festschrift Alfred Dürr* (Kassel, 1983), 126–40. For further bibliography, *see* MOTET.

**Jauchzet Gott in allen Landen** ('Praise God in all lands'). Solo cantata for the 15th Sunday after Trinity and other occasions, BWV51, probably composed in 1730 and performed on 17 September. The text does not relate specifically to any feast-day—hence Bach's subheading 'et In ogni Tempo' ('and for any occasion')—but it was later adapted for the feast of St Michael. BWV51 is one of only 12 cantatas which require a single solo voice, and one of only nine without an SATB ensemble or chorus. It is scored for a soprano, obbligato trumpet, and strings, a combination found in Italian cantatas, such as *Su le sponde del Tebro* by Alessandro Scarlatti (1660–1725), but unique among Bach's cantatas, and with few if any direct parallels in the German cantata repertory as a whole.

The style of the solo writing is remarkably flamboyant. The trumpet part requires a performer of outstanding skill, and was probably intended for Bach's regular trumpeter, Gottfried Reiche. The most difficult arias in the Leipzig cantatas were usually assigned to falsettists, tenors, and basses, less often to boy trebles. Although Bach may have intended the cantata as a showcase for an exceptional choirboy—possibly Christoph Nichelmann (1717–62), who arrived at the Thomasschule in 1730—the technical demands suggest that it may have been written with a professional singer in mind. With Leipzig's opera house recently demolished, this may have been one of the Italian-trained sopranos who arrived in nearby Dresden in the summer of 1730, possibly even the most famous of these, the castrato Giovanni Bindi, whom Bach might well have heard on one of his frequent visits to the city. Klaus Hofmann suggested a possible Weißenfels origin for the work, but Uwe Wolf found nothing to support this hypothesis among newly discovered documents relating to the Weißenfels court in the Staats- und Universitätsbibliothek, Göttingen.

*Jauchzet Gott* is similar in structure to the Italian solo motet (da capo aria–recitative–da capo aria, leading into an 'Alleluja'), but Bach added a chorale before the final movement. The opening movement is related to the trumpet arias of contemporary Italian *opera seria*, dominated throughout by fanfare figures and virtuoso word-painting, though its heroic tone is here directed towards the praise of God. Befitting the general style of the vocal writing, the single recitative quickly abandons the simple declamatory style for a highly melismatic arioso. The second aria is in striking contrast to the first, its supplicatory sentiments reflected in a straightforward continuo accompaniment. The usual four-part chorale harmonization is dispensed with in favour of an intimate movement in which the soprano intones the melody of the hymn (strophe 5 of Johann Gramann's *Nun lob, mein Seel, den Herren*) a phrase at a time over a three-part string accompaniment punctuated by substantial ritornellos. It leads directly into the final 'Alleluja', one in a long line of such coloratura movements typical of the Italian motet, frequently used by Bach's Dresden neighbour J. A. Hasse, and eventually by Mozart in *Exsultate, jubilate*. The impressive technical demands include long, complex semiquaver runs and arpeggio figures rising to *c'''*. SH

K. Hofmann, 'Johann Sebastian Bachs Kantate "Jauchzet Gott in allen Landen" BWV 51: Überlegungen zu Entstehung und ursprünglicher Bestimmung', *BJb* 75 (1989), 43–54; U. Wolf, 'Johann Sebastian Bach und der Weißenfelser Hof: Überlegungen anhand eines Quellenfundes', *BJb* 83 (1997), 145–9. For further bibliography, *see* CANTATA, §1.

***Jesu, der du meine Seele*** ('Jesus, thou who [hast rent] my soul'). Cantata for the 14th Sunday after Trinity, BWV78, performed for the first time on 10 September 1724. It belongs to the impressive cycle of chorale-based works which Bach wrote at Leipzig in 1724–5 and with which he made his most original contribution to the Lutheran cantata. It is, furthermore, one of his outstanding achievements in this particular type of cantata composition. The original performing parts survive, but the score is known only from a copy dating from about 1755.

The text, by an unidentified author, is based on a 12-stanza hymn by Johann Rist, dating from 1641. It is concerned with redemption, though only loosely connected with the appointed Gospel reading for this Sunday in the Church year (Luke 17: 11–19). The author incorporated the first and last strophes of Rist's hymn, unaltered, in the opening and concluding sections of the cantata; the others are paraphrased in the intervening sections of the work.

The cantata begins with a profoundly expressive lament in G minor, cast as a passacaglia on a chromatically descending ostinato. The scoring consists of divided oboes and violins, viola, and basso continuo. In addition, a single *corno da tirarsi* (slide trumpet) and a transverse flute support the soprano line in declaiming the eight-line cantus firmus (1663) traditionally associated with Rist's hymn. When Bach revived the piece in the mid-1730s he dispensed with the *corno*, reinforcing the soprano line only with a flute. The melancholy theme, first heard in the instrumental introduction, recurs 27 times, providing the basis for a variety of contrapuntal ideas sustained in the alto, tenor, and bass vocal lines. It is a noble movement, of supple contours and harmonic strength yet containing passages both tender and intimate.

The da capo canonic duet for soprano and alto which follows is of a very different character, yet no less inspired in its expressive vitality. The imagery evoked by the imitative vocal writing is clearly that of the eager disciple following in the path of Christ. The voices are accompanied by an energetic basso continuo supplied by cello and organ with obbligato violone whose part is marked 'staccato e pizzicato'. Since the violone obbligato was written on the back of the *corno* part, it would seem likely that both instruments were played by the same player. The Leipzig *Stadtpfeiferei* (town pipers) were required to be proficient on both brass instruments and violone (see L. Dreyfus, *Bach's Continuo Group* (Cambridge, Mass., 1987), 157). The piece is among Bach's most skilfully and affectionately cast duets; the florid Italianate vocal writing recalls that of Agostino Steffani (1654–1728), an Italian composer who had worked in Düsseldorf and Hanover during the early 18th century, and whose music would have been well known in active centres of German cultural life.

A simple recitative for tenor, which broadens into arioso, contains a prayer for forgiveness of unusual expressive intensity. The marking 'piano' at the opening is one of only two instances in the cantatas where this is found in a continuo recitative; the other is in BWV99 (see Dreyfus, p. 243). The vocal writing is wide-ranging and supported by harmonies which provide subtle shades of colour to reflect contrasting images in the text. The aria in G minor which follows is also for tenor, with an obbligato flute. It would seem that during a four-month period, August–November 1724, Bach was able to call on the services of an exceptionally gifted flautist. Almost all the cantatas performed at this time contain a flute obbligato requiring advanced technical and expressive skill. The present text is concerned with cleansing through faith. Bach provides a lyrical instance of word-painting at 'macht mir das Herze wieder leicht' ('makes my heart light again'), where he makes an almost isolated excursion into the major key, suffusing the image with quiet radiance.

The remaining pair of solo movements are for bass. The accompanied recitative is vividly depictive, reflecting first on the agony on the Cross and then, as it develops into an expressive arioso, on a reconciliation with Christ. The C minor aria, with a busy oboe obbligato and requiring virtuosity from the singer, contains a plea for a quiet conscience. The cantata ends with Bach's simple and affecting harmonization of the hymn melody treated with such consummate artistry in the opening movement.                                    NA

For bibliography, *see* CANTATA, §1.

***Jesu, Joy of Man's Desiring***. Title of a transcription by the English pianist Myra Hess (1890–1965) of the chorale that ends each part of Cantata 174, *Herz und Mund und Tat und Leben*. The hymn text, from which the English title is derived, is Martin Jahn's *Jesu, meine Seelen Wonne*; in the cantata Bach set the sixth and 17th strophes. Hess's transcription was published in 1926 for piano solo and in 1934 for piano duet, but the transcription itself has since been arranged for various instruments and combinations. It is often performed slowly and reverentially, in defiance of the affect suggested by its original scoring, for voices with trumpet, oboes, strings, and continuo.

***Jesu, meine Freude*** ('Jesus, my joy'). Motet for five voices, BWV227, on Romans 8: 1, 2, 9–11 and stanzas 1–6 of Johann Franck's hymn *Jesu, meine Freude*. There is strong evidence that various movements of this motet date from different times in Bach's life, and that the well-known 11-movement version, though most probably of Bach's own making, is a compilation. A student copy of some of the chorale movements suggests a date of this version before 1735, but there is no evidence to support the much discussed hypothesis that it was composed for a 1723 memorial service.

The most striking feature of this, the longest of Bach's motets, is its multi-movement construction alternating biblical and chorale texts. Every analysis points out the work's symmetry, emphasizing the identity of the the first and 11th movements (a four-part chorale setting), the near identity of nos. 2 and 10 (on biblical texts), the correspondence of the fourth and eighth (biblical) movements using upper and lower voices in trios, and the pair of chorales movements nos. 5 (a kind of fantasia) and 7 (an elaborated four-part setting), all centred on the sixth movement, a fugal setting of a biblical text. Certain analyses have sought to demonstrate the organic unity of the motet by linking motivic ideas in the biblical sections to motifs in the chorale melody, and some have found elaborate theological objectives in the selection of texts.

But it is clear that this fearful symmetry is imposed on a heterogenous collection of movements. One is immediately struck, for example, by the motet's beginning and ending with a four-part chorale, despite the five-voice texture of the most important biblical movements and the presence of five-voice chorale movements. Even more striking is the version of the chorale melody used in the ninth movement, which is clearly different from that in the other chorale verses. This movement is also the only one to present the chorale in A minor, all the others being in E minor. The best explanation for these features is that Bach assembled the motet from extant material and possibly from some that was newly composed, integrating older movements into the new work. The chorale movement that stands out, no. 9, uses a version of the hymn more closely (but not exclusively) associated with Bach's earlier years, and could point to a Weimar origin. Among the biblical movements, no. 2, with its 3/2 metre and echoes on the word 'nichts' suggests itself as the oldest.

Despite serious attempts to do so, it is difficult to see a direct textual connection between the verses from Romans and the strophes of *Jesu, meine Freude* of the obvious kind one usually finds in central German motets, including Bach's earlier works. So one wonders whether the earliest layer of the 11-movement motet was perhaps a purely biblical motet consisting of the first biblical movement, 'Es ist nun nichts Verdammliches', perhaps together with the present sixth movement, 'Ihr aber seid nicht fleischlich'. Beginning with this material, Bach apparently constructed the present form of the motet, with the aim of including all the stanzas of Franck's hymn. The tenth movement is clearly a (somewhat awkward) retexting of music designed for no. 2; the other biblical movements may have been originally composed. Among the chorale movements, all but no. 9, to judge from their chorale versions, are either borrowed from Leipzig works or newly composed using the usual Leipzig version of the tune. The ninth movement was apparently an older work, though it is difficult to say whether its *bassetto* texture (the bass is silent) was the result of an adaptation of a vocal and instrumental piece or merely Bach's imitation of one.

The lack of original source material for *Jesu, meine Freude* makes it impossible to go beyond a speculative reconstruction of the work's genesis. Nor do we have any documentation of the work's purpose. An early 20th-century hypothesis that it was composed for a Leipzig memorial service in 1723, without good foundation to begin with, was shattered by the discovery of the printed order of service for the event, which mentions neither the chorale nor the motet. (Theological arguments made since to rescue the association with this event are unconvincing.) We have only a student copy of the chorales, probably made from Bach's original performing parts, to establish 1735 as the latest possible date for the compilation of the motet.                                                             DRM

M. Petzoldt, 'Überlegungen zur theologischen und geistigen Integration Bachs in Leipzig 1723', *Beiträge zur Bachforschung*, 1 (1982), 49–52; M. Petzoldt, 'J. S. Bachs Bearbeitung des Liedes "Jesu, meine Freude" von Johann Franck', *Musik und Kirche*, 55 (1985), 213–25; H.-J. Schulze, ' "150 Stuck von den Bachischen Erben": zur Überlieferung der vierstimmigen Choräle Johann Sebastian Bachs', *BJb* 69 (1983), 81–100. For further bibliography, *see* MOTET.

***Jesu, nun sei gepreiset*** ('Jesus, now be praised'). Cantata for New Year and the feast of the Circumcision, BWV41, first performed on 1 January 1725. It is a CHORALE CANTATA to a text by an unidentified author, inspired by a hymn of the same title by Johannes Herman (1593) sung to a melody published two years earlier in the so-called *Wittenberger Gesangbuch*. The hymn has only three strophes, but they are unusually long, having 14 lines each. As usual, the cantata retains the first and last strophes (as movements 1 and 6) in their original form. The central strophe was used to

close Cantata 190 the previous year and would be used again for the last movement of Cantata 171 in 1729. Here the librettist has paraphrased it as two arias and recitatives (movements 2–5). The text, highly appropriate for New Year's Day, expresses gratitude for past blessings and a hope for future ones.

The autograph score, now in the Staatsbibliothek zu Berlin, previously belonged to the noted Bach collector Franz Hauser, among others. The scoring is typical for cantatas designed for important feasts: SATB, three trumpets, timpani, three oboes, two violins, viola, violoncello piccolo and basso continuo—a true *Festmusik* in fact.

The particular layout of Herman's poem led Bach to devise a unique musical structure (A–A–B–C–A') for the first movement, based on the chorale melody itself; it is of exceptional length (213 bars), even incorporating a repetition of the last two lines. The working-out of the first four lines, each with a different contrapuntal motif, is repeated for lines 5–8, constituting the two *Stollen* (A–A) that make up the first part of a BARFORM structure; the instruments contribute a concertante commentary. There follows an Adagio section (B: lines 9–10) in chordal style and in 3/4 time, with independent accompaniment from the orchestra, and an *alla breve* Presto (C: lines 11–14) in the style of a fugal motet, with the chorale melody as a soprano cantus firmus and with instruments doubling the voices. The final section (A') resets the last two lines in the musical language of the first two (and of lines 5–6), while the last 12 bars are an exact repetition of the music with which the work began.

Following this majestically proportioned chorus, and contrasting with it, is a gentle soprano aria, 'Laß uns, o höchster Gott', in the style of a pastorale, with three oboes lending it a rustic flavour. The other aria, for tenor, 'Woferne du den edlen Frieden', is notable for its violoncello piccolo part, characterized by wide and energetic leaps. A particularly interesting feature of the second recitative (no. 5) is the insertion of a passage from Luther's German litany (1528–9), 'Den Satan unter unsre Füße treten' ('Let Satan be crushed under our feet'), set in chordal style for all four voices. Bach had already set these words as part of a more extensive allusion to the litany in a Weimar cantata, no. 18 (movement 3).

The final chorale uses the trumpet fanfares (with timpani) from the first movement as interludes between the lines of the hymn, while the structure of the movement as a whole also recalls that of the opening chorus.                                AB

E. T. Chafe, '*Anfang und Ende*: Recurrence in Bach's Cantata *Jesu, nun sei gepreiset*, BWV41', in R. Stinson, ed., *Bach Perspectives*, i (Lincoln, Nebr., 1995), 103–34. For further bibliography, *see* CANTATA, §1.

***Jesus nahm zu sich die Zwölfe*** ('He took unto him the twelve'), BWV22. The first of two cantatas performed in the Thomaskirche, Leipzig, on 7 February 1723, the Sunday before Lent. Later in the same service Cantata 23, *Du wahrer Gott und Davids Sohn*, was heard during communion. The occasion was Bach's audition in connection with his bid to become the Thomaskantor. Cantata 22 is known to have been performed again the following year, and possibly in other years during Bach's time in Leipzig. The author of the libretto is unknown, but it is closely related to the librettos of the first two cantatas that Bach composed after becoming Thomaskantor (nos. 75 and 76), and also to the two cantatas that Christoph Graupner performed in Leipzig on 17 January 1723, at his audition for the same post. It therefore seems probable that some local Leipzig poet wrote the librettos of all these cantatas, as well as of the first three movements of Bach's Cantata 23.

*Jesus nahm zu sich die Zwölfe* begins with the opening words of the Gospel for the day (Luke 18: 31–43). The first movement is reminiscent of Passion music in that the text is divided between the Evangelist (tenor), Jesus (bass), and the disciples (choir). The last Sunday before Lent (Estomihi) introduced the forthcoming penitential season and was celebrated as a kind of Passion Sunday, since the Gospel of the day pointed ahead to the Crucifixion, the focal point of Holy Week at the end of Lent. Further, Estomihi was the last day on which concerted music would be heard in the Leipzig churches until the performance of a concerted Passion at Good Friday Vespers. This Passion connection also explains the generally restrained nature of this 'test-piece' cantata as a whole and its simple orchestration for strings and oboe. The first movement is held together by the repeated ritornello, heard at different pitches, over a walking bass, an evocation of the journey to Jerusalem. The choral fugue (marked 'allegro') at the end of the movement contrasts with the setting of the words of Jesus, illustrating the explanation in the Gospel that the disciples did not understand what Jesus had said to them.

The following aria (movement 2), a trio for alto, oboe, and continuo in a modified da capo form, is a poignant declaration of intent to follow Jesus to Jerusalem. The ensuing accompanied bass recitative draws a contrast between the glory of the mount of transfiguration and the humiliation of the hill of crucifixion. At the words 'eine fest Burg' Bach makes a melodic allusion to Luther's famous chorale melody. Movement 4 is another

modified da capo aria in a lilting 3/8 metre. Here the musical exposition stresses the 'ewiges Gut' ('eternal good') and Freude' ('joy') that come by dying to the world. The concluding movement, well known in instrumental arrangements, is an extended chorale over a walking bass that recalls the insistent journeying of the first movement.

RAL

L. and R. Steiger, *Sehet! Wir gehn hinauf gen Jeru-salem: Johann Sebastian Bachs Kantaten auf den Sonntag Estomihi* (Göttingen, 1992). For further bibliography, *see* CANTATA, §1.

***Jesus schläft, was soll ich hoffen?*** ('Jesus sleeps, what should I hope for?'). Cantata, BWV81, first performed in Leipzig on 30 January 1724. While there are three or four cantatas for each of the earlier Sundays after Epiphany, this is one of only two for the fourth Sunday. Since the number of Sundays in the Epiphany season fluctuates from year to year, depending on the date of Easter, not every Church year includes this occasion. Hence Bach apparently managed with just this cantata until 1735, when he added Cantata 14 to his repertory. Cantata 81 is unusual in its almost exclusive concentration on solo vocal movements. While the alto, tenor, and bass have each two solos, the only choral movement is the simple four-part chorale at the end.

The imagery is drawn chiefly from the appointed Gospel reading, St Matthew 8: 23–7, in which Jesus calms a furious storm which threatens to engulf the boat in which he and his disciples are travelling. According to the biblical account, the disciples had to awaken him before he could rebuke the wind and waves. In the opening alto aria, scored for a pair of recorders, strings, and continuo, Jesus's slumber is the dramatic context for a solemn meditation on the terror of death. Here, as in some other works, recorders are associated with the contemplation of death. Although it begins and concludes with a ritornello, and material from the first vocal section returns towards the end, this movement forges a unique pattern, following none of the usual aria forms.

In the tenor recitative (movement 2), accompanied by continuo alone, Jesus's soporific silence leads to a sense of alienation from God. In a series of dark questions reminiscent of passages from the Psalms, God is accused of remaining distant and hiding himself. He is then implored to provide guidance by his 'Augen Licht' (the 'light of [his] eye'), just as the wise men were led by the light of the star.

The tenor aria (movement 3) employs bravura passage-work to evoke the fury of storms, both the literal one in the biblical narrative and a figurative one symbolizing the forces that stand in opposition to Christian faith. The believer's valiant (but ultimately bootless) opposition is portrayed in a remarkable series of three *adagio* passages at the beginning of the B section (bars 47, 51, and 55–6). When Jesus finally speaks, first to his disciples and then to the storm, the *vox Christi* is sung by a bass, in accordance with a long-standing tradition in church music. The words from St Matthew with which Jesus rebukes the disciples for their lack of faith are set in a brief contrapuntal movement labelled 'Arioso' in the autograph score (movement 4). This miniature vocal solo, accompanied by the continuo alone, is followed by a full-length bass aria scored for a pair of oboes d'amore, strings, and continuo: a powerful movement in which Jesus commands the sea, storm, and wind to be silent.

It is surprising that the stilling of the storm receives no direct musical representation. Instead it is implicit in the alto recitative (movement 6), which declares that the storm's fearful effects must retreat at Jesus's word. The concluding four-part chorale sums up the work, expressing assurance of Jesus's protection from all evil.         SAC

For bibliography, *see* CANTATA, §1.

**'Jig'.** Nickname used for the organ Fugue in G major BWV577. It derives from the gigue-like nature of the subject, particularly its opening bar. The attribution to Bach has been challenged, but most scholars accept it as authentic, even if its source is not entirely reliable. The fugue theme itself has a number of features in common with that of Buxtehude's Canzona in C major BUXWV174 (see Williams).

P. Williams, *The Organ Music of J. S. Bach*, i (Cambridge, 1980), 245–7.

**Johann Ernst,** Duke of Saxe-Weimar (b. 22 June 1664; d. 10 July 1707). Younger brother of Duke Ernst August of Saxe-Weimar, born in Weimar. Under a family law of 1629 he reigned jointly with his elder brother. It is in the payment lists of Johann Ernst that Bach's name appears as 'lackey' at the Weimar court in 1703. For a family tree, *see* ERNST AUGUST.

**Johann Ernst,** Prince of Saxe-Weimar (b. 25 Dec. 1696; d. 1 Aug. 1715). Composer and string player, born in WEIMAR. He studied the violin with G. C. Eylenstein (1682–1749) and composition with J. G. Walther, who in 1708 dedicated to him his *Praecepta der musicalischen Composition*. He was the brother of ERNST AUGUST, the co-regent of the duchy of Saxe-Weimar, and was blessed with a precocious and formidable talent for music. Between 1711 and 1713 he was in Utrecht and Amsterdam, where he encountered, through the organist of the Nieuwe Kerk, Johann Jacob Grave

(or Jan Jacob de Graaf, 1672–1738), the practice of transcribing Italian instrumental concertos for keyboard. On his return to Weimar he induced both Walther and Bach to do the same.

Of poor health, the prince died in Frankfurt when he was only 18 years old, leaving—as Walther informs us in his *Lexikon* (1732)—19 compositions. To honour his memory Telemann, who early in 1715, just a few months before the prince's death, had dedicated to him a volume of six sonatas for violin and harpsichord, published Johann Ernst's *Six Concerts . . . Opera I.ma* (Frankfurt, 1718), a volume of six concertos in Vivaldian style. Two of these (nos. 1 and 4) were transcribed for harpsichord by Bach (BWV982 and 987), who also arranged two other concertos by the prince (not included in the publication and now lost), one for harpsichord (BWV984; its first movement exists also in a version for organ, BWV595) and the other for organ (BWV592).         AB

H. J. Schulze, 'J. S. Bach's Concerto-Arrangements for Organ: Studies or Commissioned Works?', *Organ Yearbook*, 3 (1972), 4–13; U. Siegele, *Kompositionsweise und Bearbeitungstechnik in der Instrumentalmusik J. S. Bachs* (Stuttgart, 1975), 89–96.

**Johannes-Passion.** *See* ST JOHN PASSION.

**Johann-Sebastian-Bach-Institut.** Research institute, founded at Göttingen in 1951 as a department of the Bach-Archiv, Leipzig. During the period after World War II when Germany was divided between East and West, these twin organizations co-operated to promote and control the editorial work of the *NBA*. The Bach-Institut is supported by a non-profit-making society which finances research from public and private funds; the editorial work for the *NBA* itself (carried out by members of the Bach-Institut as well as by external scholars, including university teachers and freelance editors) is, however, supervised by an international editorial board.

The Bach-Institut's first president was Hans Albrecht (1951–61); he has been followed by Wilhelm Martin Luther (1961–2), Georg von Dadelsen (1962–92, the period of the main editorial work), and Martin Staehelin. The importance of the Bach-Institut is reflected in the research undertaken there since its foundation by Alfred Dürr and, more recently, by Klaus Hofmann, Yoshitake Kobayashi, and others.         KK

**journals, yearbooks, and publications in series.** A number of periodical publications and series of books specialize in the music of J. S. Bach. The most important are the following:

*Bach*, the journal of the Riemenschneider Bach Institute, Baldwin-Wallace College, Berea, Ohio, published at first quarterly and more recently half-yearly.

*Bach-Jahrbuch*, published annually by the Neue Bach-Gesellschaft, Leipzig, since 1904.

*Bach Perspectives*, a series of books sponsored by the American Bach Society and published by the University of Nebraska Press, Lincoln, Nebraska; the first was issued in 1995.

*Bach Studien*, a series of publications by the Forschungskollektiv 'Johann Sebastian Bach', University of Leipzig; the first was issued in 1922 and the most recent (no. 10) in 1991.

*Bach Studies*, a series of books published by Cambridge University Press; the first was issued in 1989.

*Beiträge zur Bachforschung*, a series of publications by the Nationale Forschungs- und Gedenkstätten Johann Sebastian Bach der DDR, initiated in 1982; the most recent (no. 9–10) was issued in 1991.

*Cöthener Bach-Hefte*, a series of publications relevant to Bach's Cöthen period, begun in 1981; the most recent (no. 6) appeared in 1994.

*Interaction*, the journal of the Tureck Bach Research Foundation, first issued in 1997.

*Tübinger Bach-Studien*, an important series of four studies published in Trossingen between 1957 and 1970.

Further details of all the above publications can be found in D. R. Melamed and M. Marissen, *An Introduction to Bach Studies*, which also lists publications deriving from scholarly conferences (*see* BIBLIOGRAPHIES).

A number of more general music journals frequently include articles on Bach, among which are *Early Music* (quarterly, published by Oxford University Press), *Musik und Kirche* (half-yearly, published by Bärenreiter, Kassel), and the *Organ Yearbook* (yearly, published by Frits Knuf, Buren, Netherlands).

**Jubilate.** In the CHURCH CALENDAR, the third Sunday after Easter. It takes its name from the introit to the Mass for that day in the Latin rite, beginning 'Jubilate Deo omnis terra'.

**Judica.** In the CHURCH CALENDAR, the fifth Sunday in Lent. It takes its name from the introit to the Mass for that day in the Latin rite, beginning 'Judica me Deus, et descerne causam meam'.

# K

**Kaffeekantate.** *See* COFFEE CANTATA.

**Kammermusikus** ('chamber musician'). A court musician, usually someone versatile on a number of instruments and sometimes employed in other capacities as well. At the Weimar court Bach was employed as *Hoforganist* ('court organist') and 'Cammer-musicus' from 1708. The payment lists of the Cöthen *Kapelle* make it clear that, there at least, the *Kammermusikus* stood higher in the musical hierarchy than a simple *Musicus*.

**Kammerton.** *See* CAMMERTON.

**Kantate.** *See* CANTATA.

**Kantor.** A person responsible for the teaching and organization of music in a school or church (usually both). Kantors in the earliest Lutheran foundations were primarily academics who were not necessarily eminent 'practical' composers and performers. Furthermore, other teachers on the staff at Latin schools were often musically proficient, assisting in church services and providing some of the school's musical instruction. This situation still pertained during Bach's tenure (1723–50) as Kantor of the Thomasschule in Leipzig (his official title): he was officially required to teach Latin, and other teachers taught elementary music. Although Bach, in a letter of 1730 (*BDok* i. 67–8), implied that the move from a *Kapellmeister* position (at Cöthen) to a Kantorate involved a loss of status, the Kantorates of Hamburg and Leipzig were clearly attractive enough for Telemann and C. P. E. Bach to apply for these posts during their careers; both held the Hamburg post for many years.

Ulrich Siegele's extensive work on the circumstances surrounding Bach's appointment shows that Bach was never a Kantor in the true sense of the word, since he was permitted to find a deputy for his academic duties in the school. His appointment was clearly seen by many as an anomaly, one that was to be rectified with subsequent appointments. Indeed, the proceedings of the town council at the appointment of his successor refer to him as 'the Kantor . . . or rather the *Capell* Director, Bach' (*BDok* ii. 478–9) and one burgomaster remarked that they required a Kantor and not a *Kapellmeister*. Bach was always sponsored by a 'Kapellmeister' faction on the town council and he went out of his way to retain *Kapellmeister* titles

from various courts throughout his Leipzig career.

JAB

U. Siegele, 'Bachs Stellung in der Leipziger Kulturpolitik seiner Zeit', *BJb* 69 (1983), 7–50; 70 (1984), 7–43; 72 (1986), 33–67; U. Siegele, 'Bach and the Domestic Politics of Electoral Saxony', in J. Butt, ed., *The Cambridge Companion to Bach* (Cambridge, 1997), 17–34.

**Kantorei.** A choir drawn from the resident pupils of a Lutheran school, sent to sing in one of the local churches (*see* CHORUS). The 1723 statutes of the Leipzig Thomasschule seem to use the term interchangeably with *Chorus musicus* and direct that the alumni (those boys resident in the school, as opposed to the *Externe*, who lived outside) be divided into four groups, providing choirs for the four main churches (the Thomaskirche, Nikolaikirche, Neukirche, and Petrikirche). Although the term is traditionally (and in modern German usage) associated exclusively with choral music, Bach noted in his 1730 *Entwurff* (*BDok* i. 60–6) that he had to assign several alumni to instrumental parts on account of vacancies in the instrumental band. Thus there is a sense in which Bach's *Kantorei* also contained instrumentalists. In this same document Bach seems to refer to the entire performing forces as the *Chorus musicus*, and to the specifically vocal component as the *Chor*.

JAB

**Kapellmeister** ('chapel master'). The musician in charge of a *Kapelle*, or musical establishment, at a court. The *Kapellmeister* was usually the most highly paid musician at court. His role was to advise on the appointment of personnel, to rehearse singers and instrumentalists, and to compose and select music for them to perform. In larger establishments he was often assisted by a vice-*Kapellmeister*. Bach acted as *Kapellmeister* to Prince Leopold of Anhalt-Cöthen from 1717 to 1723 (*see* BACH, JOHANN SEBASTIAN, §1), and, as he stated in a letter to Georg Erdmann, he was conscious of the fact that when he accepted the post of Kantor at the Thomasschule in Leipzig 'it seemed at first not at all the right thing to become a Kantor after being a *Kapellmeister*'. For reasons of prestige, therefore, and to bolster his authority, he was careful to solicit the courtesy title of *Kapellmeister von Haus aus*, first from Prince Leopold and, after his death in 1728, from Duke Christian of Saxe-Weißenfels.

Bach's official position at Leipzig from 1723 to 1750 was that of Kantor and *director musices*, but his exercise of the above-mentioned courtesy titles, his activities as director of the collegium musicum founded by Telemann, and his close association, as *Hofcompositeur*, with the Dresden court all served to enhance his profile in the city, to the extent that in 1750 the Leipzig councillor and former burgomaster Christian Ludwig Stieglitz (1677–1758) supported the appointment of J. G. Harrer as Bach's successor with the famous remark, 'the school needs a Kantor, not a *Kapellmeister*'.

> U. Siegele, 'Bach and the Domestic Politics of Electoral Saxony', in J. Butt, ed., *The Cambridge Companion to Bach* (Cambridge, 1997), 17–34.

**Kauffmann, Georg Friedrich** (b. 14 Feb. 1679; d. 24 Feb. 1735). Organist and composer, born in Ostermondra, Thuringia, and a music director at the Merseburg court. He was, with Bach, a candidate for the position of Kantor in Leipzig in 1722–3, and his vocal works were performed there, just prior to Bach's arrival, and also during the 1730s under Gerlach at the Neukirche. Kauffmann was a sophisticated composer who seemed equally at home in *galant* and *stile antico* writing. His most important work was the *Harmonische Seelenlust* (published 1733–6), a collection of organ chorales which apparently had considerable impact on Bach since many of the latter's subsequent organ works show close stylistic and motivic affinities. JAB

> J. Butt, 'J. S. Bach and G. F. Kauffmann: Reflections on Bach's Later Style', in D. R. Melamed, ed., *Bach Studies 2* (Cambridge, 1995), 47–61.

**Keiser, Reinhard** (bap. 12 Jan. 1674; d. 12 Sept 1739). Composer, born in Teuchern, about 8 km. (5 miles) south of Weißenfels. He attended the Thomasschule in Leipzig from 1685 and served at the court of the Duke of Brunswick before being appointed *Kapellmeister* in 1696, and then opera director, at Hamburg. He also served as cathedral Kantor at Hamburg from 1728, and, except for brief periods in Stuttgart and Copenhagen, remained there for the rest of his life.

Keiser is important chiefly for the many operas he wrote for Brunswick and Hamburg. As a church musician he also composed Passions, oratorios, and cantatas. Bach probably became acquainted with Keiser's music when he visited Hamburg during his years at the Michaelisschule in Lüneburg. In Weimar, and again in Leipzig, he performed a *St Mark Passion* by Keiser (*see* PASSION).

**Kellner, Johann Peter** (b. 28 Sept. 1705; bur. 22 April 1772). Organist and composer, born in Gräfenroda, Thuringia. In 1725 he was appointed Kantor at Frankenhain and in 1727 assistant Kantor at Gräfenroda, where he became Kantor in 1732 and remained until his death. Kellner was famous as an organ virtuoso and teacher, and he published several of his own keyboard works.

Whether or not Kellner was a Bach pupil, he was personally acquainted with Bach and, by his own admission, took great pleasure in Bach's music. The two jointly copied the Prelude and Fugue in E minor BWV548. The many manuscripts of Bach's keyboard music prepared by Kellner and members of his circle often represent the earliest surviving source for a composition, and in some cases (e.g. the Prelude in C minor BWV999) the only source. Kellner's copy of Bach's Sonatas and Partitas for violin solo, dated 1726, contains what appear to be early versions of the fugues from the G minor and C major sonatas. Kellner seems to have prepared his own organ transcriptions of the work-complex containing Bach's Sonata in G major for two flutes and continuo and his Sonata in G major for viola da gamba and harpsichord. These arrangements were evidently fashioned not from either of these surviving versions but from lost originals, probably scored for two violins and continuo. RTS

> R. Stinson, ' "Ein Sammelband aus Johann Peter Kellners Besitz": neue Forschungen zur Berliner Bach-Handschrift P 804', *BJb* 78 (1992), 45–64; R. Stinson, 'J. P. Kellner's Copy of Bach's Sonatas and Partitas for Violin Solo', *Early Music*, 13 (1985), 199–211; R. Stinson, *The Bach Manuscripts of Johann Peter Kellner and his Circle: A Case Study in Reception History* (Durham, NC, 1990); R. Stinson, 'Three Organ-Trio Transcriptions from the Bach Circle: Keys to a Lost Bach Chamber Work', in D. O. Franklin, ed., *Bach Studies* (Cambridge, 1989), 125–59.

**Kerll, Johann Caspar** (b. 9 April 1627; d. 13 Feb. 1693). Composer and organist, born in Adorf, Saxony; his career took him to Brussels, Munich, and Vienna. He was equally adept in strict counterpoint and in 'modern' styles, including opera and character pieces for keyboard. While organist of St Stephen's Cathedral, Vienna, he was assisted by Johann Pachelbel. He thus belongs to the pedagogic tradition leading to Bach via the latter's elder brother and teacher, Johann Christoph (a pupil of Pachelbel). Kerll is one of the 'masters' included in the music book that Bach secretly copied at his brother's house (according to the Obituary), and Emanuel Bach listed Kerll as one of the composers whom Bach esteemed highly. Bach reworked the Sanctus from Kerll's *Missa superba* in 1747. JAB

**kettledrums.** *See* TIMPANI.

**Keyserlingk,** Count **Hermann Carl von** (b. 1696; d. 30 Sept. 1764). Diplomat, born in Okten,

Courland, on the Baltic. He was a protégé of Tsarina Anna, Duchess of Courland, and in 1731 was made president of the Academy of Sciences in St Petersburg, and in 1733 Russian ambassador to the electoral court of Dresden. From 1745 he served in a similar capacity in Berlin, Vienna, and again in Dresden, and in 1762 was appointed ambassador in Warsaw, where he died two years later.

Keyserlingk was a noted music-lover and friend of the Bach family. His daughter Juliane Luise was a pupil of W. F. Bach in Dresden, and he himself stood godfather to C. P. E. Bach's son Johann Sebastian (1748–78) in Berlin. He was one of those who signed the document notifying Bach's appointment as Hofkompositeur to the Dresden court in 1736, and he was among those who heard Bach's organ recital at the Dresden Frauenkirche on 1 December the same year. His name is inextricably linked with the creation and performance of Bach's GOLDBERG VARIATIONS.

**Kirchhoff, Gottfried** (b. 15 Sept. 1685; d. 21 Jan. 1746). Composer and organist, born in Mühlbeck, near Bitterfeld, about 30 km. (19 miles) north-east of Halle in Sachsen-Anhalt. Like Handel, he was a pupil of F. W. Zachow (1663–1712). In 1709 he was appointed *Kapellmeister* to the Duke of Holstein-Glücksburg, and in 1711 organist at Quedlinburg. In 1714 he accepted the post of organist at the Liebfrauenkirche (Marktkirche), Halle, that Bach had declined, and remained there until his death.

Kirchhoff wrote mainly vocal music and organ pieces for church use. He may have been the composer of two Fantasias and Fughettas for keyboard attributed to Bach (BWV907–8) on evidence which is not altogether reliable.

D. Schulenberg, *The Keyboard Music of J. S. Bach* (New York, 1992), 385–6.

**Kirnberger, Johann Philipp** (bap. 24 April 1721; d. 26/7 July 1783). Composer and music theorist. A pupil of J. S. Bach between 1739 and 1741, Kirnberger was a violinist at the Berlin court of King Frederick the Great in 1751–4, and from 1758 until his death curator of the music library of Frederick's sister Princess Anna Amalia (now the AMALIENBIBLIOTHEK).

Kirnberger's significance for Bach's music lies in his theoretical writings (which claimed, not implausibly, to transmit elements of Bach's teaching) and in his curatorial work, which included the copying and preservation of numerous manuscript copies of music by Bach, Handel, and others. Kirnberger co-edited an early printed edition of Bach's four-part chorale settings (Leipzig, 1784–7) and published analyses of two movements from *The Well-tempered Clavier*. His annotated manuscripts of the latter constitute, in effect, some of the earliest critical editions of Bach's

music. In a dispute with F. W. Marpurg he was supported by C. P. E. Bach in his claim of being a faithful proponent of J. S. Bach's 'principles'.

DS

J. P. Kirnberger, *Die Kunst des reinen Satzes in der Musik* (Berlin and Königsberg, 1771–9); partial trans. by J. Thym and D. Beach as *The Art of Strict Musical Composition* (New Haven, 1982); W. S. Newman, 'Kirnberger's Method for Tossing Off Sonatas', *Musical Quarterly*, 47 (1961), 517–25; J. Lester, *Compositional Theory in the Eighteenth Century* (Cambridge, Mass., 1992), 231–57.

**Kirnberger Chorales.** A title often used for a repertory of chorale preludes for organ (BWV690–713), which exists in two related late 18th-century manuscripts in the Staatsbibliothek zu Berlin (Am B 72 and 72a) from the library of Princess Amalia of Prussia (the so-called Amalienbibliothek). Neither collection is in fact in the hand of Bach's pupil Johann Philipp Kirnberger, but Am B 72, which was apparently copied from Am B 72a, may have been compiled under his supervision in Berlin, where he worked in the service of Prince Heinrich and Princess Amalia of Prussia from 1758 until his death in 1783. B 72a contains all 24 preludes, as well as two from the *Orgel-Büchlein* (BWV633–4) and five additional miscellaneous preludes BWV740–1 and 759–61. The Berlin manuscripts bear the title *Sammlung von variirten und fugierten Choralen vor 1 und 2 Claviren und Pedal von J. S. Bach*. Much of the Kirnberger repertory also existed as part of a lost collection of 114 chorale preludes formerly in the Gdańsk Stadtbibliothek (Mus MS 4203–4); this was copied between 1754 and 1762, probably with publication in mind. The transmission pattern of the Kirnberger repertory suggests that the collection as a whole originated in Leipzig. Hans Klotz, who edited Bach's miscellaneous organ chorales for the *NBA*, concluded that they were assembled after Bach's death from his papers kept in the cupboards of the Thomasschule.

Bach's miscellaneous organ chorales are highly variegated in character, containing items which were apparently rejected as unsuitable for inclusion in his own collections, the *Orgel-Büchlein* and the so-called 'Eighteen'. A few preludes are of dubious authorship, suggesting that the portfolio may have included some material by other composers; BWV692 and 693 are also attributed to J. G. Walther, BWV710 to J. L. Krebs, and BWV711 to Bernhard Bach). Most of the authentic preludes are on a small scale, many of them for manuals only, and there are several short fugal preludes (labelled 'Fughetta') on the first line of the chorale (BWV696–9, 701, and 703–4). The prelude on *Vom Himmel hoch da komm ich her* BWV701, which works material from the first three lines of the hymn in conjunction with bell-like scales, is a particularly charming example of the fugal type. Even more concise are the two preludes on *Wer nur den lieben Gott läßt walten* BWV690 and 691 and two four-part harmonizations of *Liebster Jesu, wir sind hier* BWV706 and 707, which may have been intended as accompanimental harmonizations to follow the *Orgel-Büchlein* prelude on the chorale (BWV633–4).

There are also a few more extended compositions. The two chorale fantasias, on *Christ lag in Todes Banden* BWV695 and *Jesu, meine Freude* BWV713, are closely related in technique, treating the chorale in an expansive manner in combination with fugal working-out in the accompanying voices. Also related in style are the preludes on *Wo soll ich fliehen hin* BWV694 and *Wir Christenleut* BWV710 (the latter perhaps by J. L. Krebs), which are both trios with the chorale melody in the pedal. The collection also contains one of Bach's finest short preludes in *coloriert* (highly ornamented) style, *Herr Jesu Christ, dich zu uns wend* BWV709, which has an affinity with similar preludes in the *Orgel-Büchlein*. Most of the contents of the Kirnberger collection probably originated in the Weimar period (1708–17), though at least one, the prelude on *Vom Himmel hoch, da komm ich her* BWV700, must be an apprentice work from Bach's teenage years.    DLH

P. Williams, *The Organ Music of J. S. Bach*, ii (Cambridge, 1980), 226–53.

**Kittel, Johann Christian** (bap. 18 Feb. 1732; d. 17 April 1809). Organist and composer, born in Erfurt, Thuringia. He studied with Bach in Leipzig from 1748 to 1750, and was organist in Langensalza (1751–6) and then at the Barfüßerkirche (1756–62) and the Predigerkirche (from 1762) in Erfurt, where he remained for the rest of his life and was influential as a teacher. His surviving works are mainly for the organ.

***Klagt, Kinder, klagt es aller Welt*** ('The whole world laments, children'). Funeral cantata for Prince Leopold of Anhalt-Cöthen, performed on 24 March 1729. On 23 and 24 March that year Bach was in Cöthen, along with his wife Anna Magdalena and son Wilhelm Friedemann, to direct the music for the obsequies of his former employer. Two works were performed, one for the funeral itself on the evening of the 23rd, and the other for a service of mourning in the reformed Stadtkirche the following day. The music of both works is lost, but the text of the mourning cantata, or *Trauer-Music*, by Picander has survived. It is divided into four parts, the first two having seven sections, the last two five, making 24 in all. Except for most, if not all, of the ten recitatives and the two choruses (no. 8, repeated as no. 14), the work was parodied

from movements in the *Trauer Ode* (for nos. 1 and 7) and the *St Matthew Passion* (for nos. 3, 5, 10, 12, 15, 17, 19, 20, 22, and 24).

***Kleine Messe.*** A term sometimes used for a Lutheran German MISSA, consisting of Kyrie and Gloria only.

**Knauer.** Cantata librettist, possibly identifiable as Johann Oswald Knauer (b. 1690) of Schleiz (see Krausse). He wrote the texts of liturgical cantatas performed in Gotha in 1720–1. These are divided into two parts, each consisting of a chorus on a biblical text, normally two recitative–aria pairs, and a concluding hymn strophe. Three cantatas composed by Bach in 1723—nos. 64, 69*a*, and 77—are based on texts from the Knauer cycle. In all of them the division into two parts is abandoned: in BWV64 and 69*a* the second movement with a biblical text is removed (as well as other movements in the centre of the cantatas); for BWV77 only the second part of Knauer's text is used.

It is not known how Bach came into contact with Knauer's texts. Andreas Glöckner has pointed out that Bach composed a Passion cantata for Gotha in 1717, and it seems probable that he had lively contacts with the court there later on as well.    KK

A. Glöckner, 'Neue Spuren zu Bachs "Weimarer" Passion', *Leipziger Beiträge zur Bach-Forschung*, 1 (1995), 33–46; H. K. Krausse, 'Eine neue Quelle zu drei Kantatentexten Johann Sebastian Bachs', *BJb* 67 (1981), 7–22.

**Knüpfer, Sebastian** (b. 6 Sept. 1633; d. 10 Oct. 1676). Composer, born in Asch (now Aš, Czech Republic). After a thorough schooling at the Gymnasium Poeticum in Regensburg, he went to Leipzig, where in 1657 he was appointed Thomaskantor, a position he occupied until his death. He wrote both Latin and German church music and a small number of secular vocal pieces. Bach performed Knüpfer's motet *Erforsche mich, Gott*, originally composed for the funeral in 1673 of the wife of a Leipzig burgomaster.

D. R. Melamed, *J. S. Bach and the German Motet* (Cambridge, 1995), 189–97.

**Koch, Johann Sebastian** (b. 16 June 1689; d. 17 Jan. 1757). Musician, born in Ammern, near Mühlhausen in Thuringia. He was one of Bach's first pupils at Mühlhausen in 1708, and served as choir prefect there until 1710. He matriculated at Jena University in April 1711, and in 1712 was engaged at the court of Schleiz as a bass singer. He was made *Kapellmeister* there in 1727.

**Koch, Johann Wilhelm** (b. 31 Jan. 1704; d. 8 Nov. 1745). Musician and schoolmaster, born in Buttelstedt, about 10 km. (6 miles) north of Weimar. He sang in the court chapel at Weimar in 1720–1, and was then *director musices* at the Gymnasium in Lübeck. In 1725 he matriculated at Jena University, and from 1731 was Kantor at Ronneburg. He studied with Bach in Leipzig between 1738 and 1741. Bach was godfather to Koch's daughter Johanna Helena Sophia, who was baptized on 12 September 1739 (she lived less than a year), but he did not attend the ceremony as he was detained in Altenburg for the inauguration of a new organ at court. Letters to Koch from Johann Elias Bach (*BDok* ii, nos. 434, 448, and 455) bear witness to the close relations between Koch and Bach at this time.

### Kollmann, August Frederic Christopher (b. 21 March 1756; d. 19 April 1829).
Organist, composer, and theorist, born in Engelbostel, near Hanover. He was an important figure in the English Bach revival, and brought out the first English edition of Bach's Chromatic Fantasia (London, 1806). He had previously expounded on the accompanying fugue in *An Essay on Practical Musical Composition* (London, 1799), in which he referred to examples of music by a number of composers, including C. P. E. Bach, Handel, Graun, and Kirnberger, but especially J. S. Bach.

Kollmann served as Kantor, from 1782, and organist, from 1792, at the Royal German Chapel in St James's Palace, London. In his short-lived journal, The *Quarterly Musical Register* (1812), he published the first excerpts in English from J. N. Forkel's study of the life and works of Bach, and later made a complete translation of it (London, 1820). He also assisted Samuel Wesley and K. F. Horn in their 'new and correct' edition of The *Well-tempered Clavier*, providing the main source of their edition.                                    SFD

### Koloff, Lorenz Christoph Mizler von. See
MIZLER, LORENZ CHRISTOPH.

### Komm, du süße Todesstunde ('Come, sweet hour of death').
Cantata for the 16th Sunday after Trinity, BWV161, composed in Weimar to a text by the court poet Salomo Franck. It was first performed probably on 27 September 1716, and revised many years later in Leipzig.

The differences between the Weimar and Leipzig versions are most pronounced in the opening alto aria. Whereas the Weimar draft features a pair of recorders ('quiet' instruments, often used in works with texts about death), in Leipzig it was recast for transverse flutes and violins. In the earlier version, the alto sings an aria text in the normal manner while a chorale melody is played by the organ, one phrase at a time (such movements, known as 'chorale arias', are found in several Weimar cantatas). In the later version the chorale is assigned to a soprano, transforming the movement from a vocal solo into a duet and introducing the additional complication of a second text. The comparison between the sweetness of death and honey from the lion's mouth is an allusion to the strange story of Samson's marriage, in which the carcass of a lion provides food for Samson and his parents (Judg. 14). The plea for death to come quickly—so foreign to modern sensibilities—is not to be understood as a morbid 'death wish', because it is undergirded with the firm belief that passing from life to death makes it possible to 'kiss' the Saviour in heaven.

The next two movements develop this theme further and make it clear that the believer's desire is not for death itself but rather for the glory of being with Christ. In the tenor recitative (movement 2), the world is portrayed as a place of deception: its pleasure ('Lust') turns out to be a burden ('Last'); its sugar is actually poison; what seems to be a joyful light is really a portentous comet; and even beautiful roses bring forth thorns that torment the soul. The 'soul's agony' is intensified by chromaticism on the words 'Seelen Qual'. Similarly, the decadence of 'pale death' ('blasse Tod') is captured by an arresting pair of parallel tritones. Soon thereafter the mood becomes more cheerful and ultimately dissolves into a gentle arioso with continuous semiquaver motion in the continuo, suggested by the pastoral imagery of 'Ich habe Lust, bei Christo bald zu weiden' ('I long soon to be at pasture with Christ').

A salient feature of the tenor aria (movement 3) is the repeated use of a 'sighing' appoggiatura figure (e.g. at bars 2 and 11) in connection with the word 'Verlangen' ('desire'). The two halves of the middle section (bars 60 ff. and 92 ff.) are sharply differentiated by virtuoso melismas on 'zermalmet' ('crushed') and 'prangen' ('to be resplendent'), which occur only in the first half, and by the omission of all but the continuo instruments in the second.

The alto recitative (movement 4), accompanied by a pair of recorders (or flutes), strings, and continuo, includes several memorable passages. An especially tender moment is the gentle imitative arioso (bars 7–11) that evokes the feeling of a lullaby as Christ is described as 'mein sanfter Schlaf' ('my peaceful sleep'). This contrasts markedly with the vigorous semiquaver flourishes in bar 18 to illustrate the word 'auferwekken' ('raise from the dead') and the repeated notes and figures (and pizzicato strings) in the final eight bars, which portray the tolling of the bell that signifies the end of time ('letzter Stundenschlag') and the passage through death to eternal life.

Although they employ the same performing forces (recorders or flutes, strings, continuo, and all four vocal parts), the two choral movements differ greatly from one another. The text of movement 5 is a contemporary poem by Franck, while movement 6 is a setting of a stanza from an early 17th-century chorale. A cantus firmus (the chorale melody *Herzlich tut mich verlangen*) is present in the latter but not the former. The relationship between the two wind parts also is divergent: in movement 5 they act as duetting partners, often at the interval of a 3rd or 6th; in movement 6, on the other hand, they play in unison. The strings double the upper three voice parts in the latter movement, while they are mostly independent in the former. Although the cheerful affect of movement 5 might seem to be at odds with a text about death, again the emphasis here is on the joy of being with Jesus in heaven. The body is viewed as a 'Last' ('weight') to be gladly discarded, while the spirit is considered to be a 'guest' which only temporarily takes up residence in the body and lives eternally in heaven after death. The elaborate, independent contrapuntal line for the winds in the chorale setting, differentiated from the other parts by its higher register and shorter note values (predominantly semiquavers), is both an unusual and an ingenious way of portraying the transcendent glory of the new bodies that Christ will give his people, who 'beautifully transfigured through Christ, will shine as the sun'. SAC

For bibliography, see CANTATA, §1.

**Komm, Jesu, komm** ('Come, Jesus, come'). Motet for eight-voice double choir, BWV229, on stanzas 1 and 11 of a poetic text by Paul Thymich (1656–94). The work, known from a score copied by Bach's pupil Christoph Nichelmann and datable to about 1731–2, probably dates from Bach's Leipzig years, but its exact date and purpose are unknown.

The choice of text is somewhat unusual for a motet. It is chorale-like in that it is a strophic, rhymed metrical poem, but it is not part of the standard hymn repertory, and has no standard melody associated with it. Each strophe ends with a quotation from St John 14: 6 ('I am the way, the truth, and the life'), giving the work a link to the biblical SPRUCH texts typical of motets. The text has a strong Leipzig connection: it was written for the funeral in 1684 of the Rector of the Thomasschule, Jacob Thomasius, and set to music by the then Thomaskantor Johann Schelle (1648–1701). It is not known whether Bach knew this published setting, but he could also have known the text from the so-called Wagner hymnal, *Andächtiger Seelen geistliches Brand- und Gantz-Opfer* (Leipzig, 1697), which was among the books he left at his death.

Also unusual is the way Bach treats this text.

The motet uses the first and last stanzas of the poem. The first is set for eight-part double chorus, but more in the manner of a biblical text than of the chorale that it resembles prosodically. Each textual phrase receives its own musical treatment, with changes of texture, affect, thematic material, and sometimes musical metre—in all, a through-composed setting with no predominant melody. The text is in Barform (A–A–B), characteristic of many chorales, and there is some parallelism between the settings of the two A sections, but the effect is much closer to that of a phrase-by-phrase biblical text setting. The final line (the paraphrase of the verse from St John), is strongly emphasized, receiving an extended treatment in nearly endless sequences.

The last stanza is treated as a separate movement, and receives the kind of setting one would actually expect for such a text. This four-voice movement is mostly homophonic, with a predominant soprano melody. This kind of piece, which Bach and his contemporaries called an 'aria', is often found as the last section of motets from central Germany in the early 18th century, where it usually follows a biblical or biblical-cum-chorale setting. DRM

H.-J. Schulze, *Studien zur Bach-Überlieferung im 18. Jahrhundert* (Leipzig, 1984), 130–45. For further bibliography, see MOTET.

**Kommt, eilet und laufet** ('Come, make haste and run'). Textual incipit of the EASTER ORATORIO.

**Kontrabaß.** *See* DOUBLE BASS.

**Konzertmeister.** In modern usage a term for the principal first violinist in an orchestra: the equivalent of the American 'concertmaster' and the English 'leader'. In Bach's time the *Konzertmeister* was normally the most experienced and highly paid instrumentalist in a musical establishment at court, responsible to the *Kapellmeister* for the conduct of the players (but not of the singers) and often for actually directing performances. That the duties of a *Konzertmeister* could vary, however, is exemplified by Bach's promotion to the rank of *Konzertmeister* at Weimar in 1714, a post which placed him third (after the vice-*Kapellmeister*) in the musical hierarchy and carried with it the obligation to compose and perform a church cantata each month.

**Köpping, Johann Christian** (b. 1704). Curator, born in Groß Bothen, about 30 km. (19 miles) south-east of Leipzig. He studied with Bach in Leipzig between 1723 and 1726 and served as curator at the Thomaskirche. Like several of Bach's other pupils, he acted also as a copyist, and it is to Köpping that we owe the only known score of Bach's Cantata 165, *O heilges Geist- und Wasserbad* (1724).

**Korrespondirenden Societät der Musicalischen Wissenschaften.** *See* CORRESPONDIRENDEN SOCIETÄT DER MUSICALISCHEN WISSENSCHAFTEN.

**Köthen.** Modern name for the town of CÖTHEN in Thuringia.

**Krause, Johann Gottlob** (b. 14 Jan. 1714). School prefect, born in Großdeuben, 15 km. (10 miles) south of Leipzig. His name has been perpetuated in the Bach literature not because of his musical talents, which appear to be have been nugatory, but because he stood at the centre of a dispute between Bach and the Rector of the Thomasschule in Leipzig, J. A. Ernesti. In 1736 Ernesti appointed Krause head prefect, despite the young man's musical incompetence and in breach of the Kantor's longstanding prerogative in choosing the prefects. The matter was of no small concern to Bach, since the head prefect was expected to direct rehearsals and services during the Kantor's absences. The 'battle of the prefects' was fought between the two men for several months and Bach even appealed to the elector for support, but there seems never to have been any definitive settlement to the dispute. Krause left the Thomasschule at Easter 1737 and matriculated at Leipzig University on 7 May; nothing is known of his subsequent activities.

**Kräuter, Philipp David** (b. 14 Aug. 1690; d. 7 Oct. 1741). Organist and teacher, born in Augsburg, Bavaria. He went to Weimar in 1712 to study with Bach, and in his request to the Augsburg authorities to prolong his studies he mentioned the prospect of hearing 'much fine Italian and French music from which I shall be able to profit in the composing of concertos and *ouvertures*' (*BDok* ii, no. 58). In September 1737 Kräuter left Weimar to take up the post of Kantor and *director musices* at the Annenkirche in Augsburg, where he remained for the rest of his life.

**Krebs.** Family of musicians closely connected with Bach. Johann Tobias Krebs (b. 7 July 1690; d. 11 Feb. 1762) was born in Heichelheim, near Weimar. In 1710 he was appointed Kantor and organist at Buttelstedt, near Weimar, and in 1721 he became organist and headmaster at nearby Buttstädt, where he remained until his death. From about 1710 to 1714 Krebs studied in Weimar with Bach's kinsman and colleague J. G. Walther, and from about 1714 to 1717 with Bach himself. Along with Walther he was the main copyist of the manuscript complex P 801–3 (Staatsbibliothek zu Berlin), which contains numerous keyboard com-

positions by Bach. Many of Krebs's copies are the earliest surviving sources for certain works.

Of Krebs's three sons the most important was Johann Ludwig (bap. 12 Oct. 1713; d. 1 Jan. 1780), a renowned performer and prolific composer. He was born at Buttelstedt and studied with his father. From 1726 to 1735 he was enrolled at the Thomasschule in Leipzig, where Bach was Kantor, and from 1735 to 1737 he was a student at the university there. In 1737 he was appointed organist at the Marienkirche, Zwickau, and in 1744 court organist at Zeitz. From 1756 he occupied a similar position at Altenburg, where he remained until his death. While in Leipzig, Krebs was one of Bach's private keyboard pupils, and from 1729 to 1731 he copied performing parts for various church cantatas by Bach. (Like his father, Krebs also appears as a scribe in the manuscript complex P 801–3 mentioned above.) In a testimonial (1735) Bach praised Krebs not only as a performer on keyboard instruments, violin, and lute, but also as a composer. During his university years he assisted Bach at the Thomaskirche and played the harpsichord in the collegium musicum. Despite all his Leipzig connections, Krebs failed in his application to become Bach's successor. Bach allegedly referred to him as 'the only crayfish ["Krebs"] in my brook ["Bach"]'.

Another son was Johann Tobias (b. 16 Nov. 1716; d. 6 April 1782), born in Buttelstedt. From 1729 to 1740 he was at the Thomasschule, and from 1739 to 1742 studied at Leipzig University. In 1746 he was appointed assistant headmaster at the lyceum in Chemnitz. He then moved to Grimma, where in 1751 he was appointed assistant headmaster, and in 1763 headmaster. He remained in Grimma until his death. In 1729, following Krebs's audition at the Thomasschule, Bach judged the 13-year-old as having 'a good strong voice and fine proficiency'.

The youngest son was Johann Carl (b. 12 May 1724; d. 6 Jan. 1759), born in Buttstädt. From 1740 to 1747 he was at the Thomasschule and in 1750 was appointed headmaster at the village school in Buttstädt, where he remained until his death. When, in the 1750s, his father became blind, Johann Carl assisted him with his duties as town organist.                                    RTS

*BC* i/1, p. 228; S. Daw, 'Copies of J. S. Bach by Walther and Krebs: A Study of the Mss. P. 801, P 802, and P 803', *Organ Yearbook*, 7 (1976), 31–58; F. Friedrich, *Johann Ludwig Krebs: Leben und Werk* (Altenburg, 1988); H. Zietz, *Quellenkritische Untersuchungen an den Bach-Handschriften P 801, P 802 und P 803* (Hamburg, 1969).

**'Kreuzstabkantate'** ('Cross Cantata'). Title sometimes used for Cantata 56, ICH WILL DEN KREUZSTAB GERNE TRAGEN.

Das Fürstl.Resident
Schloß zu
Cöthen.

The castle at Cöthen, where Bach was employed from 1717 to 1723; engraving in Matthaeus Merian, *Topographie* (1650)

**Kropfgans, Johann** (b. 14 Oct. 1708; d. after 1769). Lutenist, born in Breslau. He was the son of a prosperous Breslau merchant and a pupil of the renowned lutenist S. L. Weiß at Dresden, and became one of the few lute players to enjoy a degree of success after the death of his former teacher in 1750. Like Weiß, he worked principally in the Saxon capital, where he was employed as a musician in the service of Count Brühl. In 1739 Kropfgans joined Weiß and Wilhelm Friedemann Bach in a memorable extended visit to Leipzig, where, as reported by Johann Elias Bach, they played at Bach's house several times. His own few surviving works are mostly light pieces in an idiomatic *galant* style markedly different from Weiß's, but it is certain that many more have been lost.                                                      TTC

BDok ii. 366; C. J. A. Hoffmann, *Die Tonkünstler Schlesiens* (Breslau, 1830), 269; T. Crawford, 'Contemporary Lute Arrangements of Hasse's Vocal and Instrumental Music', in *Johann Adolf Hasse und Polen*, ed. I. Poniatowska and A Żórawska-Witkowska (Warsaw, 1995), 73–95.

**Krügner, Johann Gottfried** (b. 1684; d. 25 Feb. 1769). Engraver, born in Dresden. His father, Salomon, was a cornett player at the Saxon court in Dresden. Johann Gottfried was apprenticed to Moritz Bodenehr (1665–1748), engraver to the Dresden court, and during the first decade of the 18th century he went to Leipzig to complete his training under Martin Bernigeroth. In 1709/10 he enrolled at Leipzig University, and soon afterwards married Bernigeroth's sister-in-law Marie Sophie Weinig. The Krügner workshop produced original plates for Bach's keyboard Partitas and *Clavier-Übung III*, and for the Schemelli Songbook.

G. Butler, *Bach's Clavier-Übung III: The Making of a Print* (Durham, NC, 1990); G. Butler, 'Leipziger Stecher in Bachs Frühdrucken', *BJb* 66 (1980), 9–26.

***krummer Zink*** ('curved Zink'). *See* CORNETT.

**Kuhnau, Johann** (b. 6 April 1660; d. 5 June 1722). Composer, performer, linguist, lawyer, and novelist, born in Geising, Erzgebirge. He received his early musical education in Dresden and became organist of the Thomaskirche, Leipzig (1684), taking over the post of Kantor at the Thomasschule in 1701 (Bach succeeded him in 1723).

His first two keyboard publications began the trend for using the title *Clavier-Übung*, one which Bach later followed. The last piece in Kuhnau's second volume marks the appearance of the sonata genre in German keyboard writing and he produced many further sonatas, culminating in the *Biblische Historien* of 1700. These are the most ambitious programmatic pieces for keyboard of their age and must have influenced Bach's own 'Capriccio on the departure of his most dear brother'. Indeed, five of the *Biblische Historien* are found in the opening section of the Andreas Bach Book.

Although Kuhnau spoke out against modern operatic church music during his years as Thomaskantor (his position was, for a time, greatly threatened by the activities of the young Telemann), his church cantatas show the absorption of recent operatic styles and are among the most important of the generation directly before Bach. Kuhnau and Bach were fellow examiners of the new organ at the Liebfrauenkirche, Halle, on 1 May 1716, and they were doubtless well acquainted with each other.                                            JAB

**Kuhnau, Johann Andreas** (b. 1 Dec. 1703). Kantor, nephew of Johann Kuhnau, born in Annaberg, Erzgebirge. He studied with Bach at Leipzig in 1723–8, and the following year he was appointed Kantor at Grimma. Like other Bach pupils, he also acted as a copyist. He was, in fact, one of Bach's principal copyists at Leipzig, and was identified in the earlier Bach literature as Anonymous 3, or *Hauptkopist* A.

***Kunst der Fuge, Die.*** *See* ART OF FUGUE, THE.

***Kunstgeiger.*** *See* STADTMUSICUS, STADTPFEIFER.

***Kurrende*** (itinerant choir). A term used to refer to the tradition by which choirs of boys from a Lutheran school sang throughout the streets of a town. The division of the money thus collected was usually stipulated by the school ordinances. Although the tradition survived into the 20th century, it was often, particularly in the later 18th century, stigmatized as a form of beggary. It is likely that Bach, as a boy, sang with the *Kurrenden*; the tradition is well documented in Eisenach, and it was part of the duties for singers with free board in Lüneburg. The Leipzig school ordinances during Bach's Kantorate stipulated that *alumni* in all four of the upper classes should participate.

JAB

***Kurzmesse*** ('short mass'). A term sometimes used for a mass setting consisting only of Kyrie and Gloria. *See* MISSA.

# L

**Laetare.** In the CHURCH CALENDAR, the fourth Sunday in Lent. It takes its name from the introit to the Mass for that day in the Latin rite, beginning 'Laetare Jerusalem: et conventum facite'.

**Lämmerhirt/Lemmerhirt.** A family from Erfurt in Thuringia whose fortunes were closely intertwined with those of the Bach family. Valentin Lämmerhirt (b. 1585; d. 19 Nov. 1665) was a furrier and town councillor at Erfurt. He was twice married. His daughter Hedwig (b. c.1617; bur. 5 Sept. 1675) by his first wife married Johannes Bach (1604–73), brother of J. S. Bach's paternal grandfather and founder of the so-called Erfurt line of the Bach family; his daughter Maria Elisabetha (b. 24 Feb. 1644; d. 1 May 1694) was Bach's mother (the family tree below shows the relationships between the two families). Of Valentin's two sons, the elder, also called Valentin (c.1608–65), was the grandfather of J. G. Walther, Bach's colleague at Weimar; the younger, Tobias (bap. 7 April 1639; d. 10 Aug. 1707), who carried on the family trade as a furrier, took as his second wife Martha Catharina Brückner (d. 10 Sept. 1721), a widow, in 1684. She later stood as godmother to Catharina Dorothea (1708–74), the first child born to J. S. Bach, on 29 December 1708. Tobias and Martha Catharina had no children, and J. S. Bach was fortunate to receive a share of Tobias's estate at the time of his first marriage (1707), and a portion also of Martha Catharina's estate at the time of his second marriage (1721).

In addition to the four children shown in the family tree below, the elder Valentin Lämmerhirt had two other sons, Andreas and Caspar. Caspar's wife, the widow Petri, stood godmother to Ambrosius's daughter Maria Salome (1677–1727), J. S. Bach's aunt.

A. Basso, *Frau Musika: la vita e le opere di J. S. Bach*, i (Turin, 1979); H. Lämmerhirt, 'Bachs Mutter und ihre Sippe', *BJb* 22 (1925), 101–37.

**Landowska, Wanda** (b. 5 July 1879; d. 16 Aug. 1959). Polish harpsichordist, born in Warsaw. Although her early training was as a pianist, her chief interest lay in 17th- and 18th-century music, and she is recognized as the leading figure in the 20th-century revival of the harpsichord. She first played the harpsichord in public in 1903, and in 1912 introduced the two-manual instrument by Pleyel of Paris, the sound of which was to become a distinctive feature of her recordings. In 1909 she published a book on early music, *Musique ancienne*. After World War I she played harpsichord continuo in a performance of the *St Matthew Passion* in Basle. Among her many recordings are a complete version of *The Well-tempered Clavier* made in the early 1950s, and the Italian Concerto and Chromatic Fantasia and Fugue, both dating from 1935. *See also* RECORDINGS.                NA

**Landvoigt, Johann August** (bap. 10 Nov. 1715; bur. 16 Feb. 1766). Lawyer, born in Leipzig, where his father was a gardener. He attended the Thomasschule from 1731 to 1737, and while there he wrote the text of the cantata *Thomana saß annoch betrübt*, performed on 21 November 1734 when the new Rector, J. A. Ernesti, was installed. Only Landvoigt's text is extant. He died in Marienberg, Saale, where in 1758 he had married Sophie Friederike Schlegel, aunt of the famous poet and critic, August Wilhelm Schlegel.                KK

***Langtrompete*** ('long trumpet'). *See* TRUMPET.

***Laß, Fürstin, laß noch einen Strahl*** ('Princess, still let a ray shine'). Textual incipit of the TRAUER ODE.

***Laßt uns sorgen, laßt uns wachen*** ('Let's take care, let's keep watch') [*Hercules auf dem Scheidewege* ('Hercules at the Crossroads')]. Secular cantata, BWV213, to a text by Picander, composed for performance on 5 September 1733 in Gottfried Zimmermann's coffee garden in Leipzig to celebrate the birthday of Friedrich Christian, son of

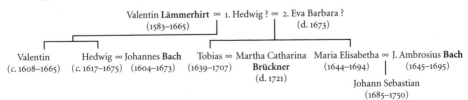

Valentin **Lämmerhirt** ∞ 1. Hedwig ? ∞ 2. Eva Barbara ?
(1583–1665)  (d. 1673)

Valentin (c. 1608–1665)    Hedwig ∞ Johannes **Bach** (c. 1617–1675) (1604–1673)    Tobias ∞ Martha Catharina (1639–1707) **Brückner** (d. 1721)    Maria Elisabetha ∞ J. Ambrosius **Bach** (1644–1694) (1645–1695)

Johann Sebastian (1685–1750)

the Elector of Saxony. The title *Die Wahl des Herkules* ('The Choice of Hercules'), which is sometimes erroneously used, was added by C. F. Zelter to the cover that C. P. E. Bach prepared for the original score and parts. In 1734 the opening chorus and all the arias became part of the *Christmas Oratorio* BWV248 (a similar intention is documented for the concluding chorus, 'Lust der Völker', but its music was replaced by the new 'Ehre sei dir, Gott, gesungen'). None of the arias in the oratorio preserves the original scoring.

In the cantata the 11-year-old prince is compared to the mythological Hercules (alto), who chose the 'right way', suggested by Tugend ('Virtue', tenor), instead of the smooth but wrong path suggested by Wollust ('Pleasure', soprano). A narrator, Mercur (Mercurius, bass) makes clear the link between Hercules and the prince. As in other secular cantatas, it is the dialectic rather than the dramatic component which is stressed, and therefore the interest lies more in Hercules's decision (and how he comes to it) than in the transformation of mythology into action. The recitatives and arias are not, however, divided equally between the singers, the sequence of movements being ruled more by pragmatic and dramatic principles.

In the opening chorus the gods decide to take care of 'our son of a god'; it is not clear whether they are thinking here of Hercules or of the prince (in BWV248 this became the opening chorus of Part 4). Hercules then appears and states in a recitative that he is looking for the 'right way'. Pleasure invites him in an aria (no. 3; no. 19 in BWV248) to follow an easy, enticing path, and the invitation is pressed more urgently in the succeeding recitative (no. 4); but Virtue intervenes. The following aria is sung, however, not by Virtue but by Hercules; he is still in search of the 'right way', but has apparently half decided to reject Pleasure (who is not heard again as a soloist). Hercules's questions in this aria (no. 5; no. 39 in BWV248) are answered by himself, and the replies, 'Yes' or 'No', repeated by Echo (alto).

Again Virtue addresses Hercules with a recitative (no. 6) which this time forms a standard pair of movements with the following aria (in BWV248, no. 41). Another recitative–aria pair leads to Hercules's definitive decision (no. 9; no 3 in BWV248), and all that remains to be achieved is the alliance of Hercules and Virtue. This is prepared by another recitative and sealed by the duet no. 11 (no. 29 in BWV248). The union is commented on by Mercurius in the only accompanied recitative in the work (as in many 18th-century operas, the *accompagnato* appears only at the end of an 'act'), and the final 'coro' is addressed to the young prince by the muses, with a solo for Mercurius in the middle section.

*Laßt uns sorgen* can be seen as a 'modern' cantata, one which reflects the musico-dramatic principles of the time. It is perhaps regrettable that it is so difficult to listen to it now without bringing to mind the sacred versions of the lyrical movements in the *Christmas Oratorio*. For decades this has hampered the individual impression that the cantata can create.                                KK

For bibliography, *see* CANTATA, §2.

**Lateinschule** ('Latin school'). A German school at which Latin was taught, thus preparing the pupil for a career in the learned professions and academia. Many such institutions were founded or refounded during the Reformation era and were often closely connected with one or more of the town churches. The school body was divided into several levels or classes (Prima, the highest level, down to Septima in Leipzig, for instance) to which a pupil was assigned according to his ability rather than age. Although Bach did not go on to a university education, the schools he attended in Eisenach, Ohrdruf, and Lüneburg would have afforded him a thorough grounding in Latin, Greek, Hebrew, mathematics, grammar, logic, philosophy, rhetoric, literary style, and the art of poetry, probably some study of natural sciences and history, and—the keystone of the entire curriculum—theology.

The early Lutheran ordinances show that music was essentially a practical discipline to be taught to boys of all ages. Most of the schoolteachers, including the Rector, were involved to some degree in the practice or teaching of music, although, in the course of the century before Bach, the Kantor often became the supreme musical director. Free boarding places were offered to poor boys who were musically talented and these were allowed to supplement their income by singing at special events: burials, street-singing (KURRENDE) and church services.
                                                JAB

*Laute. See* LUTE.

**Lautenclavecin, Lauten-Clavicymbel, Lautenclavier, Lauten Werck.** German terms for the LUTE-HARPSICHORD.

**Legrenzi, Giovanni** (bap. 12 Aug. 1626; d. 2 May 1690). Italian composer, born in Clusone, near Bergamo. After working in Bergamo and Ferrara, he went to Venice in 1671 and from 1681 until his death he was active at San Marco there, first as vice-*maestro di cappella*, and then as *maestro*.

Bach's Fugue in C minor for organ BWV574 is headed in the Andreas Bach Book 'Thema Legrenzianum. Elaboratum per Joan Seb. Bach. cum subjecto. Pedaliter'. The theme (in reality two themes) that Bach 'elaborated' has been identified as coming from Legrenzi's Trio Sonata for two violins and violone in G minor op. 2 no. 11 (Venice, 1655), entitled *La Mont'Albana*. Bach's fugue is of uncertain date (the autograph, which in 1845 was owned by Karl Wilhelm Ferdinand Guhr (1787–1848), is lost), but it must have been composed before 1708. An earlier version (BWV574*b*) is known, as well as another variant version (BWV574*a*) between this one and the definitive version in the Andreas Bach Book. The work's second theme enters at bar 37; in the final section (bars 70–104) the two themes are combined, and the fugue ends with an extraordinary 14-bar coda in the style of a toccata.                    AB

J. A. Brokaw II, 'The Perfectability of J. S. Bach, or Did Bach Compose the Fugue on a Theme by Legrenzi, BWV 574?' in R. Stinson, ed., *Bach Perspectives*, i (Lincoln, Nebr., 1995), 163–180; R. Hill, 'Die Herkunft von Bachs "Thema Legrenzianum" ', *BJb* 72 (1986), 105–7.

**Lehms, Georg Christian** (b. 1684; d. 15 May 1717). Poet, born in Liegnitz (now Legnica, Poland). He studied at the University of Leipzig and afterwards went to the ducal court of Saxe-Weißenfels before he was appointed poet and librarian at the Darmstadt court. In this position he wrote a great number of cantata texts which were composed by two of his Leipzig fellows, Christoph Graupner and Gottfried Grünewald (1675–1739), who were then active as *Kapellmeister* and vice-*Kapellmeister* at the Darmstadt court. In Weißenfels Lehms would have met the new cantata ideas developed by Erdmann Neumeister and Johann Philipp Krieger (1649–1725).

Almost certainly Bach possessed a copy of Lehms's cycle of cantata texts printed in 1711, since he drew on it at various times. In Weimar in 1714, or even earlier, he composed *Mein Herze schwimmt im Blut* and *Widerstehe doch der Sünde*, and most of the cantatas written at, and immediately after, Christmas 1725 are on texts by Lehms: nos. 110, 57, and 151 for Christmas; nos. 16, 32, and 13 in January 1726. Bach's two remaining Lehms cantatas are solo alto works, BWV35 and 170, written during the following summer.

Some of Bach's cantatas to texts by Lehms are solo or dialogue works. This results from the fact that Lehms had published larger texts for morning services and more intimate ones for afternoon services; among Bach's settings only BWV110 stems from the first part, all the others belonging to the second. Their intimate character is thus reflected occasionally in the vocal scoring.                    KK

***Leichtgesinnte Flattergeister*** ('Frivolous, fickle people'). Cantata for the second Sunday before Lent (Sexagesima), BWV181, first performed on 13 February 1724. It belongs to Bach's first Leipzig cycle of cantatas. The Gospel reading for that day, St Luke 8: 4–15, tells the parable of the sower, and the unidentified author has based his cantata text closely upon it, bringing together the parable itself and the interpretation that Jesus gave his disciples. The 'frivolous, fickle people' of the opening bass aria are the 'fowls of the air' that devour the seed that 'fell by the way side'. They are suggested in the music by the fleeting tempo (Vivace), the fragmented melodic line, the staccato articulation, and the frequent trills. The structure, too, is unusual and somewhat capricious. What promises to be a modified da capo of the first section loses its way after four bars and is transformed into a modified repeat of the second (B) section. This is one of the relatively few cantatas of which the original libretto has survived, and it is obvious from this that it was Bach, not his poet, who was responsible for the aria's unusual, possibly unique, structure. The parts for flute and oboe were not included in 1724, but were added for a later performance; they have no independent line, but double the first violin for much of the time.

An alto recitative with continuo accompaniment (no. 2) relates, in a pictorial manner, the seed that fell on stony ground to hard-hearted unbelievers who die and go below to await Christ's last word, when the rocks will burst asunder and the graves be opened. It is obvious from its melodically inactive opening ritornello that the tenor aria 'Der schädlichen Dornen' (no. 3) was originally accompanied by at least one instrument whose part has been lost; only the continuo bass has survived. The subject is the cares and worldly desires that threaten the Christian life, which are likened to the thorns that choke a growing plant. An uneventful soprano recitative turns from the wasted seeds to those that fell on fertile ground, and the almighty word that prepares fruitful soil in the heart of the believer is celebrated in the final movement, in which the entire forces are heard together for the first time. Flute and oboe again double the first violin (or, in the case of the oboe, occasionally the second violin), but now a trumpet is added to the instrumentation to reinforce the joyous message of the parable, and of the cantata.

For bibliography, *see* CANTATA, §1.

**Leipzig.** A city in Saxony where Bach was employed from 1723 until his death in 1750. It combined an older function as a free imperial city (like Mühlhausen) with that of a garrison and market town. It was in Bach's time larger than the Saxon capital, Dresden, and it was probably older, but although situated at a crossroads of

18th-century Europe, it could boast no navigable river (though the Pleiße was much beloved of its citizens). The population, including those dwelling beyond the city walls, numbered just under 30,000. Leipzig was divided into four *Viertel* ('quarters'), each with its own constabulary subject to the governor; during much of Bach's time in the city the governor was Count Joachim Friedrich von Flemming, to whom Bach dedicated three homage cantatas (BWV210a, 249b, and Anh. I 10). The governor himself, whose headquarters on the Pleißenburg housed a small garrison of Saxon troops, was a token of royal and electoral authority rather than any kind of direct ruler. Civic rule rested in the town council, made up of three burgomasters (or mayors) who each presided over ten assessors (30 in all). Every year on St Bartholomew's Day (24 August) a new burgomaster and ten assessors came into power by rotation.

The university, which had gradually enhanced Leipzig's reputation since its foundation in 1409, was a major influence within the town in matters theological, legal, scientific, and medical. There was no official recognition of music in the curriculum or in the degrees awarded (as there was at both Oxford and Cambridge); most of those who matriculated with any notion of taking up music enrolled as students of law.

The importance of Leipzig in the printing and book trade, together with the tradition of cosmopolitan meetings at the annual book fairs held at Easter, Michaelmas, and New Year, had made Leipzig into a centre of fashion and good manners. With its streets lined with lanterns, and regular patrols made by each quarter's watch, it was an unusually safe place to be, even at night, so that well before 1750 it was being described as a 'kleiner Paris' ('little Paris'). Each *Viertel* had a gate in the city wall through which one gained access to the linden-lined promenades that encircled the old city. Beyond these were the parks and pleasure gardens that added further to the refined reputation of Leipzig, affording rehearsal space on lawns and in amphitheatres for dramatic and musical entertainments, and ensuring that rich and poor alike were able to enjoy the natural delights of plants and birds.

Within the city walls housing was crowded, but there were also open spaces such as the market (reconstructed after the World Wars to recapture its 18th-century appearance), the Thomaskirchhof, and an equivalent space between the Nikolaikirche and its own school. The main thoroughfares were quite wide, and the better houses were built to a height of five storeys, but each *Viertel* had its share of narrower alleys and elbows, mainly of use to pedestrians, such as the appropriately named Stadtpfeifergasse where the

trumpeter Gottfried Reiche lived. Bach and his family occupied rooms in the Thomasschule adjoining the Thomaskirche; the building was extensively reconstructed in 1731–2 with the addition of two storeys, allowing more space for Bach's ever-increasing family (see picture, p.479). It remained virtually unaltered until 1903, when it was demolished.

Bach's official duties as Thomaskantor and *director chori musici* centred on his singers at the Thomasschule and particularly on the first choir, which performed the cantata in the two main churches, the Thomaskirche and the Nikolaikirche, alternately on most Sundays, and at both churches on major feast-days. But there was excellent music at most of the city's other churches too. Morning service at whichever of the two main churches was not favoured with the cantata was provided by Bach's second choir, trained and directed by a prefect under the watchful eye of the school's Connector, or deputy headmaster. A regular musical programme was followed at the university church, the Paulinerkirche, where responsibility lay with J. G. Görner; since festive services were held there only a few times a year (*see* ALT-GOTTESDIENST), Görner was able to work also as organist of the Nikolaikirche (1721–39), and then of the Thomaskirche.

Görner also ran one of Leipzig's two 'town-and-gown' music clubs (*see* COLLEGIUM MUSICUM) which had been founded by musical students (J. F. Fasch and Telemann) early in the 18th century. Bach directed the other from 1729 until after 1740. The locations and times of their meetings were advertised during the Michaelmas and Easter fairs. A later development was the Großes Concert Gesellschaft, a rather more ambitious body capable of performing early Classical orchestral and choral music with soloists. Although Bach himself was not directly involved in this, a number of his pupils and acquaintances, as well as several of the professional *Stadtpfeifer*, lent their services. In contrast with the otherwise comparable town of Hamburg, or the residences at Dresden and Weißenfels, Leipzig failed, after 1709, to support a permanent opera house during the first half of the 18th century.

The burghers of Leipzig witnessed the creation and performance of most of Bach's greatest works (*see* BACH, JOHANN SEBASTIAN, §1), but much of the composer's energy was dissipated in frustrating disputes with his superiors. There was first a dispute with the university authorities over responsibility for the *Alt-Gottesdienst* in the Paulinerkirche, which Bach took as far as the king in Dresden in an attempt to preserve what he saw as his rights. Shortly afterwards there was a ripple of disagreement and misunderstanding over where the *St John Passion* was to be performed on Good Friday 1724, Bach preferring the Thomaskirche but the council insisting on the Nikolaikirche. Four years later there was a dispute with the subdeacon of the Nikolaikirche over who should choose the hymns for Vespers, and in 1730 complaints that Bach was neglecting some of his duties (recalling those levelled against him at Arnstadt) led to his submission to the council of the famous ENTWURFF, in which he set out his ideas and requirements for 'a well-regulated church music'. This was dated 23 August 1730, a clear indication of Bach's hope that the new council taking office the following day might be particularly heedful of his suggestions and requests.

Far from resolving matters, the *Entwurff* seems if anything to have aggravated them, and two months later Bach, in a letter to his former schoolmate Georg Erdmann, spoke of the authorities as 'odd, and little interested in music, with the result that I must live in almost constant vexation, envy and harassment. I shall be compelled, with help from the Most High, to seek my fortune elsewhere.'

Bach was destined, however, to remain at Leipzig for the rest of his life. He made no secret of the fact that, in presenting the Elector Friedrich August II with the *Missa* in B minor, together with a request for a position in the Dresden *Kapelle*, in 1733, he was seeking to bolster his standing in Leipzig. The sought-after title of *Hofcompositeur* ('court composer') was not granted until 1736, by which time Bach had come into conflict with the new Rector of the Thomasschule, J. A. Ernesti, particularly over the appointment of prefects in the school. In March 1739 there was some disagreement over the Good Friday Passion performance, but by then Bach had almost entirely ceased to compose music in his capacity as *director chori musici*. While he continued to discharge the other responsibilities of his post, the outcome of his famous visit to Frederick the Great in May 1747 and his decision to join Lorenz Mizler's Correspondierenden Societät a month later are more indicative of where his interests and sympathies lay during the last decade of his life.

Leipzig has retained its pre-eminence in the performance, publication, dissemination, and study of Bach's music. The Thomanerchor (choir of St Thomas's), under a succession of distinguished conductors, has undertaken foreign tours and made gramophone recordings, and Leipzig has acted as the main host for Bach festivals arranged by the Neue Bach Gesellschaft. The BOSE house in the Thomaskirchhof has been fitted out as a Bach museum, and also houses the Bach-Archiv, a research centre, founded in 1950 by Werner Neumann, which functions as the editorial

office of the *Bach-Jahrbuch* and shares responsibility with the Johann-Sebastian-Bach Institut, Göttingen, for the editing and publication of the *NBA*. SFD

M. Petzoldt, *Bachstätten aufsuchen* (Leipzig, 1992), 74–109; U. Siegele, 'Bach and the Domestic Politics of Electoral Saxony', in J. Butt, ed., *The Cambridge Companion to Bach* (Cambridge, 1997), 17–34; G. B. Stauffer, 'Leipzig: A Cosmopolitan Trade Centre', in G. J. Buelow, ed., *Man and Music: The Late Baroque Era* (London, 1993), 254–95.

**Leipzig Chorales.** A term sometimes used to refer to the 'EIGHTEEN' CHORALES for organ, BWV651–68.

**Lenck, Georg** (b. 7 Nov. 1685; d. 22 March 1744). Musician, born in Reichenbach, Vogtland, Saxony, about 85 km. (53 miles) south of Leipzig; his surname is sometimes spelt Lembke. He was Kantor at Laucha an der Unstrut, near Naumburg, when, in 1722, he competed unsuccessfully for the post of Thomaskantor at Leipzig, which was offered eventually to Bach. In 1725 he was appointed Kantor at Weißenfels, where he remained for the rest of his life.

U. Siegele, 'Bachs Stellung in der Leipziger Kulturpolitik seiner Zeit', *BJb* 69 (1983), 7–50.

**Leonhardt, Gustav** (b. 30 May 1928). Dutch harpsichordist and conductor, born in s Graveland, near Hilversum in the Netherlands. After studying with Eduard Müller in Basle, he made his first recordings of solo harpsichord music by Bach in the early 1950s. These quickly established his reputation as an outstanding Bach interpreter. In 1954, with his Leonhardt Baroque Ensemble, he collaborated with the English countertenor Alfred Deller in a recording of Bach's Cantatas 54 and 170. This early essay in historically aware performance style—the ensemble included his wife Marie and Eduard Melkus (violins), Alice Hoffelner (viola), Nikolaus Harnoncourt (cello), and Michel Piguet (oboe)—may be justly considered an important torch-bearer in the new paths soon to be taken in Baroque interpretation. Since then Leonhardt has performed and recorded all the major solo harpsichord music of Bach. In 1971 he and Harnoncourt jointly undertook a project, completed in 1990, to record all Bach's sacred cantatas. Leonhardt's performances, in which his Leonhardt Consort (formed in 1955, replacing the Baroque Ensemble) provided the orchestral nucleus, are elegantly shaped and often more restrained in expression than those of Harnoncourt. NA

See also RECORDINGS.

**Leopold,** Prince of Anhalt-Cöthen (b. 28 Nov. 1694 (old style); d. 19 Nov. 1728). Bach's employer at Cöthen from December 1717 to April 1723. A great lover of music and a skilled musician, he

Prince Leopold of Anhalt-Cöthen; anonymous painting (Heimatmuseum, Köthen)

most likely made Bach's acquaintance at the wedding of his sister Eleonore Wilhelmine to Duke Ernst August at Weimar in January 1716. Bach enjoyed a most congenial relationship with the prince, and composed several cantatas and the serenade *Durchlauchtster Leopold* in his honour. The prince was a godfather to Bach's short-lived son Leopold Augustus, born on 17 November 1718. For reasons that are not entirely clear, Bach began to seek new employment around 1720. The prince's marriage in 1721 to his cousin Friederica Henrietta, who allegedly did not share his love of music, may have contributed to Bach's desire to work elsewhere. For the prince's funeral Bach composed the 'Trauermusik' *Klagt, Kinder, klagt es aller Welt*. The music is lost, but some of it was most certainly derived from that of the *St Matthew Passion*.                        RLS

> G. Hoppe, 'Köthener politische, ökonomische und höfische Verhältnisse als Schaffensbedingungen Bachs (Teil 1)', *Cöthener Bach-Hefte*, 4 (1986), 13–62; U. Siegele, 'Johann Sebastian Bachs und Fürst Leopolds Auffassungen über das Hofkapellmeisteramt', *Cöthener Bach-Hefte*, 4 (1986), 9–12.

**Liebster Gott, wenn werd ich sterben?** ('Gracious God, when shall I die?'). Cantata for the 16th Sunday after Trinity, BWV8. The foundation of this piece, which belongs to the sequence of chorale cantatas in Bach's second Leipzig cycle (1724–5), is a hymn by Caspar Neumann dating from the end of the 17th century. Its melody, which can be heard in the opening and closing sections of the work, is by Daniel Vetter (b. 1657/8), who had been organist at Leipzig's largest church, the Nikolaikirche, until his death in 1721. Following his normal custom in the chorale-based cantatas of this cycle, Bach used a text, in this instance by an unidentified author, which retains the first and last stanzas of Neumann's hymn in their original form and paraphrases the intervening strophes in the cantata's remaining sections.

*Liebster Gott, wenn werd ich sterben?* was first sung on 24 September 1724. It was a time when Bach seems to have enjoyed the virtuosity of an exceptionally able flautist, since almost all the cantatas he produced between August and November 1724 contain parts for an obbligato flute of a technical and expressive ambitiousness seldom found elsewhere. Yet in this work Bach seems originally to have written several high notes which must have defied even the greatest virtuosos. As a way of getting round the problem he first redesigned the part in the opening movement for a *flauto piccolo*—perhaps a member of the recorder family such as he used in Cantata 103 the following year. Further small adjustments were made for a performance in the late 1730s, and for another, in the mid- to late 1740s, Bach transposed

the music down a tone, to D major, in order to facilitate the flute part of the opening chorus and the bass aria (no. 4). This last solution, though solving one problem, creates another in its distortion of the iridescent tonal palette of the original. Most modern performances follow Bach's first version with minor adjustments.

The transcendently beautiful opening chorus of *Liebster Gott* must rank among Bach's most poetic and alluring fantasias. Several times already he had written profoundly affective music to evoke the death-knell of the human soul's mortal span (in Cantatas 161, 73, and 95) and would do so again (in Cantatas 127 and 198); but nowhere else, perhaps, are the *pizzicato sempre* strings and the flute, with its rapidly repeated notes, sustained with such elegiac tenderness and freedom of imagination as Bach demonstrates in this extraordinarily atmospheric evocation of the *Leichenglocken* ('funeral bells'). The instrumental sections of this opening movement are punctuated by choral ones in which Vetter's expressive melody is proclaimed line by line. Two oboes d'amore, for which Bach provided lyrical music, and a *colla parte* horn reinforcing the soprano vocal line complete this melancholy yet affirmative, and in no sense desolate, picture.

The two arias are effectively contrasted. The first, in C♯ minor, is for tenor with oboe d'amore and pizzicato bass. In this meditation on death the funeral bells once again can be heard, this time by implication in the detached quavers of the vocal line at the words 'Wenn meine letzte Stunde schlagt' ('When my last hour strikes') and in the pizzicato continuo. An accompanied alto recitative prepares the listener for the key of A major and a bass aria accompanied by an animated and wide-ranging flute obbligato with strings. Both the 12/8 metre, in the character of a gigue, and the initial melodic idea recall the concluding movement of the Sixth Brandenburg Concerto. In this aria man's fear of death, so potently expressed in the previous one, is dispelled in a surge of joyful affirmation of the Christian faith. A simple recitative for soprano leads to the concluding chorale and a return to the opening key of E major. A single note in the bass introduces the hymn for which Bach this time provided not his own harmonization, as he was accustomed to do, but Vetter's own—a gesture of appreciation towards a predecessor whom Bach clearly must have respected.                                NA

For bibliography, *see* CANTATA, §1.

**Liebster Immanuel, Herzog der Frommen** ('Beloved Emanuel, Lord of the righteous'). Cantata for the feast of Epiphany, BWV123, first performed on 6 January 1725. The anonymous text is based on Ahasverus Fritsch's chorale of the same name and employs the same technique as most of the other Leipzig chorale cantatas. The first and last strophes of the hymn are taken over for the opening and closing numbers of the cantata (movements 1 and 6) and the remaining movements (2–5) are paraphrased by the poet, so that the cantata as a whole follows the conventional six-movement structure of the Leipzig CHORALE CANTATA. Nothing is known of the performance history of the work after 1725. The text makes little specific reference to the events commemorated during Epiphany, but oblique references to the Gospel for New Year and to the Epistle for Epiphany are pointed out in *DürrK*.

The opening chorus, in the usual chorale fantasia form, is in 9/8 metre, with the melody in the soprano, and takes its central symbol from the first line of the hymn. The presence of nine units in the bar and the constant streams of triplets and three-part chords suggest apparently that Bach interpreted the word 'Frommen' as a reference to the angelic host. The first line of the chorale, which forms the basis of much of the accompanying instrumental material, is treated in chains of imitations and sequential repetitions producing many entries in parallel 3rds (simple and compound) which reinforce this symbolism. The other theme emphasized in the text is the longed-for coming of Jesus ('komm nur bald') which Bach represents by an urgent chromatic build-up over a dominant pedal point. The movement ends with a repeat of the opening instrumental ritornello.

After an alto recitative comes a tenor aria in da capo form, 'Auch die harte Kreuzesreise', accompanied by two oboes d'amore. It has a number of interesting features. The angular ritornello melody (the opening motif of which could perhaps be seen as a version of the Baroque 'cross' figure) represents the 'hard journey of the Cross' with its hard-won ascent through a diminished 7th to a high $a'$; motifs derived from it pervade much of the A section of the aria. As so often in Bach's figural language, the Cross is symbolized by the three sharps in the key-signature (F♯ minor) and by additional sharps as accidentals. For the B section Bach changes the tempo from Lento to Allegro to accommodate the line 'Wenn die Ungewitter toben' ('When the storms rage'), depicting the rumbling of the thunder with an extravagant melisma in the voice part, and he reverts to the main tempo at the next phrase, 'sendet Jesus mir von oben Heil und Licht' ('Jesus sends me salvation and light from above'). After another simple recitative for bass comes the contrasting second aria, 'Laß, O Welt, mich aus Verachtung', in D major with obbligato flute. This also is in da capo

form, and much of the material is generated by the opening phrase, with its characteristic drop of a major 7th at 'Verachtung' ('scorn'). Bach also 'paints' the words 'in betrübter Einsamkeit' ('in troubled loneliness') by chromatic disturbances to the melodic line and by silencing the instruments, leaving the singer momentarily unaccompanied. The flute part abounds in elaborate filigree work and lively semiquaver figures. The B section elaborates on the consolation to be found in Jesus, finally cadencing in the relative minor. As usual, the cantata ends with an unadorned chorale harmonization. DLH

For bibliography, *see* CANTATA, §1.

***Liebster Jesu, mein Verlangen*** ('Dearest Jesus, my desire'). Cantata for the first Sunday after Epiphany, BWV32, first performed at Leipzig on 13 January 1726. The text, by the Darmstadt court poet and librarian G. C. Lehms is a dialogue between the Soul (soprano) and Jesus (bass); it is based on the appointed Gospel reading, St Luke 2: 41–52, telling of the young Jesus preaching in the temple. A passage from this text is quoted in the first, brief recitative, while in the second, with string accompaniment, the soprano sings a passage of arioso to words from Psalm 84, well known from Brahms's setting in his *German Requiem*: 'How amiable are thy dwellings, thou Lord of Hosts! My soul hath a desire and longing to enter into the courts of the Lord.'

The first solo aria, for soprano with oboe obbligato, strings, and continuo, is one of particular beauty. Against an unchanging background of string chords, directed to be played *piano e spiccato* ('quietly and detached'), the oboist and the singer loose a delicate cantilena which, never going back on itself, sounds like some effortless, inspired *improvisation à deux*. The bass aria (no. 3), in which the singer tells of the dwelling-place which the soprano will long for in the arioso to follow, is in a generously proportioned da capo form, graced by an idiomatic, even virtuoso, part for solo violin. In the duet (no. 5), another da capo movement, Jesus and the Soul are at last joined in joyous union, appropriately symbolized by a kind of symbiosis between the two obbligato instruments so far heard separately.

The joyful sentiments of this duet are more simply expressed in the final chorale, sung to the 12th strophe of Paul Gerhardt's hymn *Weg, mein Herz, mit den Gedanken* (1647).

For bibliography, *see* CANTATA, §1.

***Lied*** ('song'). A term used in the Bach literature for two distinct, though related, vocal genres. Most often it is used, in the sense of *Kirchenlied* ('church song'), to refer to a hymn, or CHORALE, typically in BARFORM (A–A–B). But Bach also contributed modestly to the freely composed Baroque continuo *Lied*, or *Generalbaß Lied*, the words of which might be either sacred or secular. Among his examples of the sacred type are BWV511–14 and 516 from the 1725 *Clavierbüchlein* for Anna Magdalena Bach. The best known *Lied* from this collection, *Bist du bei mir*, is now known to be the work of G. H. Stölzel; the five sacred *Lieder* BWV519–23 are of doubtful authenticity. The secular *Lied*, *So oft ich meine Tobackspfeife*, in which the singer compares his state and prospects to those of his pipe, may be a revision by Bach of a *Lied* by one of his sons, possibly Johann Gottfried Heinrich (1724–63). This is also found in the 1725 *Clavierbüchlein*, and, like the sacred *Lieder* from that volume mentioned above, it is in binary form with each section marked for repeat.

G. von Dadelsen, 'Afterword', in *Klavierbüchlein für Anna Magdalena Bach, 1725* [facsimile] (Kassel, 1988).

**Liedpredigt** ('hymn sermon'). A sermon which takes as its 'text' the words of a hymn. It has been suggested that chorale cantatas of Bach's second *Jahrgang* (1724–5) were perhaps designed to be heard in tandem with a series of *Liedpredigten*, though, as Alfred Dürr has pointed out, the modern type of CHORALE CANTATA text favoured by Bach was itself in the nature of a 'sermon'.
*DürrK* 45–6.

**Liszt, Franz** (b. 22 Oct. 1811; d. 31 July 1886). Hungarian composer and pianist, born at Raiding, near Sopron. He wrote a great deal of music for piano (including arrangements), organ, and orchestra, as well as sacred choral music and songs. After early years touring as a piano virtuoso and establishing a technical eminence unique in the history of the instrument, he settled in Weimar in the early 1840s and composed increasingly for orchestra, developing original formal and harmonic concepts which had great influence on successors, not least Richard Wagner. Liszt's considerable attention to the works of Bach as a pianist was very advanced in his time. In the period 1838–48 he included in public recitals the Chromatic Fantasia and Fugue and the Goldberg Variations, as well as fugues from *The Well-tempered Clavier*.

This performing interest shaded directly into his original compositions with Bachian associations. Most striking are his variations on the ground bass from Bach's cantata *Weinen, Klagen, Sorgen, Zagen*, which gradually accumulate drama from the hushed opening. His Prelude and Fugue on the name BACH for organ (which also exists in a different form for piano solo) takes this idiom much further in a dramatic prelude and chromatic free fugue which had great influence on

successors, such as Reger (in his Fantasia and Fugue on BACH, 1900), standing in total contrast to the formal treatment accorded the motif by Schumann. MM

**'Little G minor'.** Nickname for the organ Fugue in G minor BWV578, used to distinguish it from the 'Great' Fantasia and Fugue BWV542 in the same key.

***Little Organ Book.*** See ORGEL-BÜCHLEIN.

**liturgical year.** See CHURCH CALENDAR.

**liturgy.** See CHURCH CALENDAR, HAUPTGOTTESDIENST, MASS, MISSA, and VESPERS.

***lituus.*** A term which has had various meanings in the course of musical history. In classical times it was an instrument used for signalling by the Roman cavalry. In the Baroque era it was variously a cornett, a crumhorn, or a shawm—but also a member of the trumpet or horn family. Bach calls for two *litui* in the motet *O Jesu Christ, meins Lebens Licht*: the title in the autograph score (1736/7) specifies 'Motetto a 4 voci. due Litui. 1 Cornet. 3 Trombone'; when the work was revived in 1746/7, strings and woodwind were added 'se piace'. The *litui* parts were notated in violin clef. The range of *lituus* 1 was $g'$ to $b''$, that of *lituus* 2 $c'$ to $b\flat''$ (sounding a whole tone lower in B♭). They were probably horns in B♭, but southern German tradition would not exclude B♭ trumpets. UP

H. Fitzpatrick, *The Horn and Horn-Playing and the Austro-Bohemian Tradition from 1680 to 1830* (London, 1970), 55–6; C. Sachs, 'Die Litui in Bachs Motette "O Jesu Christ" ', *BJb* 18 (1921), 96–7.

***Lobe den Herren, den mächtigen König*** ('Praise the Lord, the almighty king'). Cantata, BWV137, for the 12th Sunday after Trinity, 19 August 1725. It was apparently the first CHORALE CANTATA of the *per omnes versus* type that Bach had written for almost 20 years, that is since his Easter cantata *Christ lag in Todes Banden* (1708 or earlier). Cantata 137 is based entirely on the five stanzas of Joachim Neander's hymn of 1680 and its associated melody, familiar in English as 'Praise to the Lord, the almighty, the king of creation'. The employment of the text of a chorale without recitatives of biblical orientation or arias of poetic reflection is relatively rare in Bach's total output of cantatas; extremely rare are cantatas, like this one, that employ only the stanzas of the hymn and use the associated melody in every movement. Being closely based on both the text and melody of this hymn of praise meant that the cantata could be used on occasions other than the 12th Sunday after Trinity.

In movement 1, after a lively 16-bar orchestral introduction in triple time, the lower voices of the

# Lobe den Herrn, meine Seele

chorus engage in a three-part fugato on a theme derived from the orchestral introduction, and the sopranos sing the chorale melody. The same sequence is repeated, with orchestral ritornellos, for the second *Stollen* (the repeated A section of the BARFORM chorale melody), which gives way to an emphatic chordal treatment of the *Abgesang* (the B section): 'Kommet zu Hauf, Psalter und Harfen, wacht auf! Laßet die Musicam hören' ('Come in multitudes, psaltery and harps, wake up! Let the music be heard').

Movement 2 (the second stanza of the chorale) is a trio for alto, who sings a decorated version of the melody, obbligato violin, and continuo. It was later transcribed for organ as Schübler Chorale no. 6. In the third stanza the melody appears in two-part imitative counterpoint for soprano and bass, accompanied by two oboes and continuo. Stanza 4 is another trio, this time for tenor, trumpet, and continuo, with the trumpet rather than the tenor carrying the chorale melody. With something of the same ingenuity that he displayed in the opening chorus of the *St Matthew Passion*, Bach here contrives to place a major-key chorale melody in the context of a minor-key movement (in this case A minor). The final stanza is a four-part setting of the chorale, embellished by trumpets and timpani—a movement that was incorporated into the wedding cantata *Herr Gott, Beherrscher aller Dinge*, composed probably in 1729.

Such a useful cantata based on this thanksgiving hymn, that could be used for a variety of different occasions, must have been repeated several times over the years. There is evidence for a performance in 1746/7, when a few modifications were made to some of the instrumental parts.

RAL

For bibliography, *see* CANTATA, §1.

**Lobe den Herrn, meine Seele** ('Praise the Lord, O my soul'). Cantata for the 12th Sunday after Trinity, BWV69*a*, first performed on 15 August 1723. It was revived with alterations about 1727 (probably for 31 August 1727) and underwent a further stage of revision (BWV69) towards the end of Bach's life (probably for 26 August 1748), when it was reused for a council election. The libretto of BWV69*a* is based on the Gospel for the day (Mark 7: 31–7), which recounts Jesus's healing of a deaf and dumb man. An altered version of a text from (? Johann Oswald) Knauer's *Gott-geheiligtes Singen und Spielen* (1720), it expands ideas from the Gospel story, especially in its injunctions to extol the benefits of God 'with a thousand tongues' and in the following passage from the fourth movement: 'my mouth is weak, my tongue mute . . . pronounce thy powerful "Ephphatha" '. The

dominant themes in the text, which expresses thanks to God for his benefits and implores his future help in times of trouble, must have commended the cantata to Bach for a civic occasion. It is scored in festive style for SATB, three trumpets, drums, recorder, three oboes (one doubling oboe da caccia), strings, and continuo.

The enormous first chorus, which is freely composed, can be considered as the centre of gravity of the work. The fanfare-like opening figure is treated quasi-fugally in the ritornello with prominent trumpets. The central section of the chorus (from bar 46) is developed as a double fugue, with two contrasted subjects for the two portions of the psalm verse, 'Lobe den Herrn, meine Seele' and 'und vergiß nicht, was er dir Gutes getan hat' (Psalm 103: 2), developed first separately and then in combination. A modified recapitulation (from bar 127) is followed by a repetition of the opening instrumental ritornello. The following tenor recitative was reworked with a modified text for BWV69. It leads to the first aria, 'Meine Seele, auf, erzähle', scored for tenor with recorder and oboe da caccia. For the 1727 revision Bach transposed this number up a 5th and rescored it for alto with oboe and violin, a change which he retained for BWV69. The aria is in da capo form, with a pastoral flavour imparted by the 9/8 tempo, the scoring, and the lilting melodic figures.

The following movement in BWV69*a* is a simple recitative for alto; for BWV69 Bach replaced this with a more elaborate accompanied recitative, setting a text more appropriate to its new function. The dark hint of future tribulation calls forth rich chromatic harmony and persistent appoggiaturas in the string parts. The aria that follows, 'Mein Erlöser und Erhalter', is in ritornello form, scored for tenor with strings and solo oboe d'amore. Retained unaltered for BWV69, it again implores the Redeemer's aid in times of suffering. The final chorale in BWV69*a* is a plain four-part harmonization of the hymn *Was Gott tut, das ist wohlgetan*. For BWV69 Bach replaced it with a more suitably festive setting of the chorale *Es danke Gott, und lobe dich*, with cadences in the melody underscored by fanfare-like figures for trumpets and drums.

DLH

For bibliography, *see* CANTATA, §1.

**Lobet den Herrn, alle Heiden** ('O praise the Lord, all ye heathen'). Motet for four voices, BWV230, on Psalm 117. There are longstanding questions about the authenticity of this composition and its status as a motet, which stem from the problematic sources that transmit it. A catalogue of the publishers Breitkopf & Härtel from the first years of the 19th century offered copies of the work for sale under J. S. Bach's name. Breit-kopf's source does not survive, but two derivative copies do, one a printed edition (1821) claiming to be made 'from Bach's original manuscript', the other a manuscript copy, apparently one of those sold from the catalogue. The claim that the printed edition was made from an autograph is considered dubious, in light of misidentifications made in the same circumstances, and the manuscript copy attributes the work only to 'Sig. Bach', leaving the exact attribution in question. But the transmission of a Bach work through the Breit-kopf house has precedents; the claimed autograph may have been a copy made by his pupil J. C. Alt-nickol (a similar mistake was made by the publisher with respect to a score of *Ein feste Burg ist unser Gott*), and the musical quality of the work makes Bach's authorship plausible.

The work treats each of the first two phrases of its text ('Lobet den Herrn, alle Heiden/und preiset ihn, alle Völker') in long-breathed fugal imitation, and then combines the two in loose double counterpoint. A predominantly homophonic treatment of the next phrase, 'denn seine Gnade und Wahrheit . . .', is followed by another long-breathed imitative section on the same text. An 'Alleluia' in close imitation in triple metre closes the work.

One distinctive feature of the composition is the presence of a partly independent basso continuo line. This is the only motet of Bach's so provided, and the continuo line has been partly responsible for the suggestion that the piece is actually a movement from a larger work, perhaps a cantata, in which an independent continuo line would be more usual than in a motet. This in turn raises the question of whether Bach really intended the work as an independent motet. Certainly the psalm text is appropriate for one, and the lack of independent instruments points clearly to motet style, even if the movement did originate in a concerted work.

But in the absence of any clear evidence that it did, and of any compelling reason to attribute the work to anyone else, *Lobet den Herrn, alle Heiden* has remained in the canon of Bach's motets, if somewhat uneasily.                              DRM

M. Geck, 'Zur Echtheit der Bach-Motette "Lobet den Herrn, alle Heiden" ', *BJb* 53 (1967), 57–69. For further bibliography, *see* MOTET.

**Lobet Gott in seinen Reichen.** Textual incipit of the ASCENSION ORATORIO.

**London Bach Choir.** *See* BACH CHOIR.

**London Bach Society.** A society founded in 1946 by Paul Steinitz (1909–88), dedicated to the enhancement of Bach scholarship and the performance of his music in period style and in the original language. In 1952 it mounted the first performance in England of the complete *St Matthew Passion* in German, and in 1958–87 the first professional cycle in Britain of the complete sacred and secular cantatas. From 1947 to 1989 the society supported an amateur choir, and it maintains a professional orchestra, the Steinitz Bach Players, founded in 1968. It has also commissioned new works.

Margaret Steinitz has continued her husband's work by extending the membership and founding the annual London Bach Festival in 1990. In 1994 the society hosted the first visit to Britain of the Thomanerchor, Leipzig.                              MS

**Lotti, Antonio** (b. *c*.1667; d. 5 Jan 1740). Italian composer, active mainly in Venice, where he wrote operas, oratorios, secular cantatas, and much church music, and where he died. According to an anecdote recounted by J. A. Birnbaum in 1739 (see *BDok* ii. 441) and referred to elsewhere, a contest in keyboard playing between Bach and Louis Marchand was organized towards the end of September 1717 at the house of Count Jakob Heinrich von Flemming in Dresden. If this account is correct, Bach could on this occasion have met Lotti, who was then in Dresden on leave of absence from Venice to write operas for the Elector of Saxony.

Lotti was among the composers of sacred Latin works whose music Bach made use of (and in part reworked) for church services in Leipzig. The sale catalogue of C. P. E. Bach's estate, under the title 'Works by diverse masters', includes a Sanctus by Lotti (now lost), and the Staatsbibliothek zu Berlin has a score (Mus. ms. 13161), partly in Bach's hand, of a Mass in G minor (Kyrie and Gloria only) for six voices, trumpet, strings, and continuo which Bach used at Leipzig for some liturgical occasion.                              AB

C. Wolff, *Der stile antico in der Musik Johann Sebastian Bachs* (Wiesbaden, 1968).

**loure.** A French court dance appearing in operas and ballets by André Campra (1660–1744), Michel-Richard de Lalande (1657–1726), Jean-Philippe Rameau (1683–1764), and their contemporaries. The music may be thought of as a slow GIGUE and makes frequent use of the *sautillant* rhythm characteristic of the French gigue, but differs because of its 6/4 metre and slower tempo, unbalanced phrase structure, and more contrapuntal texture. Most loures begin with an upbeat.

The affect of the loure is noble and majestic, but languid. Johannes Mattheson (*Der vollkommene Capellmeister* (Hamburg, 1739), p. 228) described them as 'slow and dotted', and said that 'they exhibit a proud and arrogant nature'. This is borne out in the many extant choreographies, in which as many as six steps are set to a bar of music, of a difficulty requiring expert technique (see Little and Marsh). An exception is the popular *L'Aimable vainqueur*, a well-known social dance for one couple, mentioned as late as 1776 by John Hawkins (*A General History of the Science and Practice of Music* (London, 1776), ii. 705).

Bach wrote three loures, one in the G major French Suite, one in the Partita no. 3 for solo violin, and an arrangement of this for lute, placed an octave lower and with different ornamentation. Bach's loures, unlike their French models, show carefully balanced phrases, clear harmonies, and highly ornamented melodies. Loure rhythms occur in the Prelude in C♯ minor from Part 1 of *The Well-tempered Clavier* and in the Fantasia in C minor BWV906.                    NJ, MEL

For bibliography, *see* DANCE.

**Loussier, Jacques** (b. 26 Oct. 1934). French pianist, born in Angers. *See* PLAY BACH.

**Lübeck.** An inland Hanseatic port, some 60 km. (38 miles) north-east of Hamburg. Together with that city and Leipzig, it was a main centre of Lutheran orthodoxy in the time of J. S. Bach.

Easily the most celebrated aspect of musical life in Lübeck in the early years of the 18th century were the ABENDMUSIKEN organized by the Danish organist of the Marienkirche, Dietrich Buxtehude. In October 1705 Bach applied to the ruling consistory in Arnstadt for leave to visit Lübeck, and was allowed an absence of four weeks. This was unrealistic; if, as is reported, he travelled on foot, the journey would have taken two weeks in either direction, without a day's rest or any useful stay in Lübeck. In fact, Bach did not return until late January 1706 and, despite competent deputizing by his cousin Johann Ernst Bach, he was reprimanded and (by implication) threatened with dismissal should he transgress further.

Bach must have spent nearly three months in Lübeck, probably also visiting Lüneburg and perhaps Hamburg. He was probably present at, or even involved in, two occasional works by Buxtehude performed on 2–3 December: *Castrum doloris* and *Templum honoris*, the first occasioned by the death of Emperor Leopold I on 5 May 1705, the second marking the accession of his son Joseph I (1678–1711). Kerala Snyder has suggested that Bach may have been one of the 25 violinists who took part in the second of these works.

Bach must also have been influenced by the organ playing and the organ compositions of Buxtehude, and certainly furnished himself with copies, which he later used for his own teaching and playing purposes. Later on, at Weimar, he had contact with another important collection of Buxtehude's organ music, which had been supplied to

J. G. Walther by Andreas Werckmeister. Between them, Bach's and Walther's collections constitute the earliest surviving sources for more than half of the Danish master's organ works.              SFD

K. F. Snyder, *Dietrich Buxtehude, Organist in Lübeck* (New York, 1987).

**Ludewig, Bernhard Dieterich** (b. 7 Nov. 1707; d. 27 Feb. 1740). Organist, born in Thonhausen, near Ronneburg, about 50 km. (31 miles) south of Leipzig. He studied theology at Leipzig University and was one of Bach's pupils from 1731 to 1737; he also acted as tutor to Bach's younger children. Bach provided testimonials for him in March and October 1737, in which he referred to Ludewig's capabilities in singing and playing various instruments and to his participation in the activities of Bach's collegium musicum. Ludewig was unsuccessful in his applications for posts at Löbau and Zörbig, but on 31 March 1738 he was appointed town organist at Schmölln, not far from his native village. He died two years later, at the age of 32.

**Lukas-Passion.** *See* ST LUKE PASSION.

**Lüneburg.** North German town where Bach attended school in 1700–2. Lüneburg is an old trading centre in Lower Saxony, especially famous for its salt mines. Around 1700 it was one of the principal towns in the duchy of Brunswick-Lüneburg; the duke, Georg Wilhelm, then reigned at Celle.

Lüneburg has three important old churches grouped around the town centre: the Nicolaikirche in the north, the MICHAELISKIRCHE in the west, and the Johanniskirche in the south-east. Important schools were attached to the last two, and the Michaelisschule also had as a neighbour the Ritterakademie, a school for the nobility. Bach entered the highest class of the Michaelisschule around Easter 1700, at the beginning of the summer term.

Both schools had choirs, a small specialist choir (at the Michaelisschule this was the *Mettenchor*, or 'Mattins Choir') and a larger *chorus symphoniacus* which was allowed to sing in the streets (*see* KURRENDE). At the Michaelisschule members of the *Mettenchor* were exempted from paying school fees and earned a small sum of money (between 8 groschen and 1 thaler a month; *see* CURRENCY). The total monthly sum to be divided was about 8 thaler, and eight singers was the minimum composition of the choir (two per voice type). The actual number of singers was from 13 to 15. Only poor schoolboys with good soprano voices were normally accepted as new members of the *Mettenchor*. The monthly records of payments are extant only until May 1700; they give the names of the singers and the fees, but do not specify the voices.

Twice a year the fees for the members of the *chorus symphoniacus* were recorded as well (grouped according to the voices), the last list being from Easter 1700; since this choir included the members of the *Mettenchor*, it is possible to reconstruct the latter's actual make-up at the time immediately preceding Bach's arrival.

The 15-year-old Bach is said in the Obituary (1754) to have been accepted in Lüneburg because of his treble voice, and the same would go for his 18-year-old schoolfellow Georg Erdmann. It is doubtful, however, that they still had treble voices, and in any case when they went to Lüneburg the treble section of the *Mettenchor* was almost overcrowded. On the other hand, only one bass singer (acting at the same time as prefect) was available, and the possibility that Bach and Erdmann entered the choir as basses is supported by documents which show that the Lüneburg schools often filled gaps in the tenor and bass sections with singers from central Germany. Spitta's supposition that Bach, after his change of voice, served the *Mettenchor* as an instrumentalist can therefore be rejected; the money was simply not there to pay a non-singer.

The Kantor of the Michaelisschule while Bach was there was August Braun (d. 1713); he had a wide-ranging repertory of church music at hand. Bach might also have had lessons from the organist of the Johanniskirche, Georg Böhm, a native of Thuringia, who, after studies in Hamburg, had gone to Lüneburg in 1698. Anecdotes refer to journeys that Bach might have made to Hamburg, and these were perhaps recommended by Böhm. Thus, Bach's training, which had been based mainly on Thuringian practices, was developed to include styles typical of north German music. He might have drawn additional experience from performances at the court of Duchess Eléonore Desmier d'Olbreuse, in which he is said to have taken part. They apparently took place not in Celle, but in the castle in Lüneburg itself.

Bach probably stayed at the Michaelisschule until Easter 1702, thus completing the final class of the Lateinschule. In Ohrdruf he had already acquired a more advanced education than earlier members of his family, which suggests that he might have been interested in the specific education he received at Lüneburg rather than entering a purely musical career at a younger age. What he did between spring and summer 1702, when he was elected town organist in Sangerhausen, is not known. What we do know is that the Duke of Saxe-Weißenfels intervened to have Bach's appointment nullified. The next we hear about him is at Weimar in March 1703.          KK

*BDok* iii, no. 666; G. Fock, *Der junge Bach in Lüneburg, 1700–1702* (Hamburg, 1950); K. Küster, *Der junge Bach* (Stuttgart, 1996), 82–117; M. Petzoldt, *Bachstätten aufsuchen* (Leipzig, 1992), 110–26; C. Wolff, 'Johann Adam Reinken und Johann Sebastian Bach: zum Kontext des Bachschen Frühwerks', *BJb* 71 (1985), 99–118.

**lute** (*Laute*). A plucked string instrument characterized, in its Western forms at least, by a vaulted body, flat soundboard, fretted fingerboard, and a distinctive pegbox almost at a right angle to the neck. During the 16th and early 17th centuries it was among the most prominent instruments, both for solo performance and for accompanying the voice. Alongside highly famed virtuosos, who were frequently expert composers, there was a vast number of amateur players, many of great skill. A high proportion of the instrument's repertory survived in manuscript collections by or for amateur lutenists, who frequently (though not exclusively) were members of the aristocracy.

Around the middle of the 17th century the leading centre of lute playing was France, where the famous Gaultiers, François Dufault, and later Jacques Gallot (d. *c*.1690) and Charles Mouton (1617–*c*.1698) were active. By the end of the century the lute had gone out of fashion in Paris, but had become more popular than ever among German musical aristocrats, for many of whom a lutenist (as both performer and teacher) was an essential adornment to their household. Although the main region of activity in lute playing was the Habsburg dominions of Austria and Bohemia (the capitals, Vienna and Prague, in particular), the Silesian capital Breslau (now Wrocław, Poland) also provided many fine players, among them the Brandenburg court lutenist Esias Reusner (1636–79) and the most highly respected of all, S. L. Weiß, whose period of employment at the Dresden court coincided closely with Bach's years at Cöthen and Leipzig.

For some decades after Weiß's death the lute remained popular in Saxony and Prussia—a substantial repertory, approaching 500 solo and ensemble works, was available through Breitkopf's catalogues in the 1760s and 1770s—but it soon suffered a rapid and terminal decline in the face of competition from the newly perfected pianoforte, perceived as a somewhat easier instrument with an even wider range of expressive possibilities.

The lute itself differed from the Renaissance instrument in its tuning and the number of open basses added to the original courses (pairs of strings). Until some time shortly before 1720 the standard instrument was the classic 11-course French model, with the upper six courses tuned to a D minor chord (*f'*, *d'*, *a*, *f*, *d*, *A*) and a diatonic rank of bass courses (strung in octaves) descending to *C*. Scordatura tunings, a common feature of the 17th century, became less used (though they were still known in the 18th century), but the principle of tuning the open bass courses to the diatonic scale of the music's key remained universal.

The ambitus of the bass courses was increased to a full diatonic octave (*AA* to *A*) in the somewhat larger 13-course lute, introduced (possibly at Weiß's instigation) around 1719. A few surviving lutes by German makers, including Bach's Leipzig friend Johann Christian Hoffmann (1683–1750), have an extra 14th course, extending the bass to *GG*.

Lute music was almost exclusively written in TABLATURE, a prescriptive system based entirely on performance indications and ideally suited to the needs of both professionals and amateurs. A number of composers, however, including Andreas Hofer (1629–84), J. F. Fasch, and Bach himself, left lute music written in conventional 'keyboard' notation, which normally needs some adapting to the technical requirements of the instrument.

Two musical characteristics of the lute were praised above all by commentators of all periods: the beauty of its sound and its ability to play expressively, especially in its possibilities of dynamic shading. Baroque lute music has certain idiosyncratic features: a generally low tessitura, seldom rising above *e″*; a bass line containing occasional octave displacements because of the technical difficulty of playing accidentals on the diatonically tuned rank of bass strings; and a characteristically persistent use of chord-breaking (playing *séparée*) whereby the notes of the treble melody and inner parts are frequently rhythmically delayed (referred to as *style brisé* by modern musicologists).

As well as works for solo lute, Bach specified the instrument in three works from the 1720s: the *St John Passion* (no. 31), the early version of the *St Matthew Passion* BWV244b (nos. 56 and 57), and the *Trauer Ode* (which calls for two lutes).    TTC

*See also* LUTE WORKS.

E. G. Baron, *Historisch-theoretische und practische Untersuchung des Instruments der Lauten* (Nuremberg, 1727; Eng. trans. D. A. Smith as *Study of the Lute*, 1976).

**lute-harpsichord.** As its various names—*Lautenclavier, Lauten Werck, Lautenclavecin, Lautencembalo, Lauten-Clavicymbel*—indicate, this was a keyboard instrument with gut strings plucked by a quill mechanism. According to the inventory made at his death (*BDok* ii, no. 627), Bach owned two lute-harpsichords, but not a single original instrument survives, and references to it and its makers are few and far between in docu-

mentary sources of the Baroque period. Makers included J. C. Fleischer in Hamburg (1718), Johann Nikolaus Bach in Jena (after 1720), and Zacharias Hildebrandt in Leipzig (*c*.1740).    UP

H. Ferguson, 'Bach's "Lauten Werck" ', *Music and Letters*, 48 (1967), 259–64; U. Henning, 'The Most Beautiful among the Claviers: Rudolf Richter's Reconstruction of a Baroque Lute-harpsichord', *Early Music*, 10 (1982), 477–86.

**lute works.** Seven of Bach's works (BWV995–1000 and 1006a) are usually listed as being for solo lute, but some of these raise questions about the composer's intended instrumentation, and all of them present textual or technical problems for both editor and performer.

---

1. The works in general.
2. Individual pieces.

---

**1. The works in general.** Bach seems to have made no effort to assemble his lute compositions into a coherent collection, and they evidently represent something of a sideline in his creative output. Three of them are in fact arrangements of works for other instruments. In some cases the intended scoring is not known for certain, but three works (BWV995, 997, and 1000) survive in 18th-century tablature copies by lutenists known to Bach.

While it is unlikely that Bach himself played the lute, he was certainly on close terms with several of Germany's leading lutenists, and was thus familiar with the instrument's sound, idiom, and capabilities. However, nearly all the 'lute works' are not entirely playable in the authentic versions that have come down to us, and they present two particularly serious problems. One is that, because of the diatonic tuning of the bass strings (*see* LUTE), some chromatic notes in the bass line cannot be played without upward octave transposition. Octave displacements in the bass are a normal feature of idiomatic lute music, and their unobtrusive management was an important part of the skill of lute composers and players, the music of S. L. Weiß providing instructive examples. Such displacements do not occur in Bach's copies of his lute music, appearing only in tablature versions, and thus certain bass notes are unplayable at the written octave. The other problem is that certain chord formations occurring either during a sequence of block chords or as a result of polyphonic part-writing are unplayable, given the size, stringing, and tuning of the lute in Bach's time.

Bach may have expected a contemporary player to arrange the lute works idiomatically for the instrument. At first sight, the existence of contem-

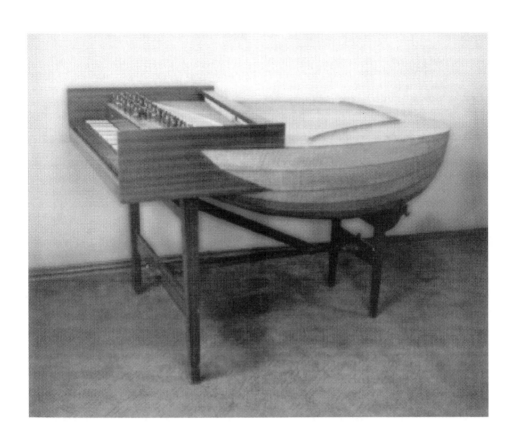

Lute-harpsichord by Rudolf Richter, 1980: reconstruction of a lost instrument by
Johann Christoph Fleischer (*c.*1718) as described by the maker

porary tablature versions of three works written by lutenists with known connections with Bach, seems to provide suitable models. Unfortunately, comparison of these versions with the authentic texts shows that the modifications go somewhat further, and that not all the alterations seem to have been made in the cause of playability. Bach may have accepted that his lute music was not strictly playable on the instrument and tolerated such imperfect solutions, which by and large are musically satisfactory; the textual problems are largely matters of detail. Bach's interest in the lute-harpsichord might be seen as a means of realizing his lute compositions on a 'full-voiced' keyboard instrument with the lute's characteristic sound. Other people—the lutenists Bach knew and admired—may have been permitted to make such adjustments as were necessary, within the bounds of good musical taste.

The problem with this view is that Bach was extremely knowledgeable about the instruments available to him, and it seems uncharacteristic that he should simply abrogate the composer's duty in this way. In a parallel case his music for unaccompanied violin is extremely difficult, but it lies within a tradition of unaccompanied string writing that Bach clearly knew well; the corresponding and related lute tradition was still well alive in his lifetime, and it would have been natural for Bach to draw upon it.

On the other hand, if every note of Bach's lute music is in fact intended to be played and heard as written, then our current understanding of the instrument and its playing technique must be deficient. Thus the door is opened to speculations about the nature of Bach's lute, its tuning(s), and its stringing, about which evidence is rather thinly spread. Such arguments hinge on the question of scordatura tunings and the other varieties of lute-like instruments known to have been available at the time. In other words, they lead to the radical and, on the face of it, unlikely suggestion that Bach himself devised a special type of lute for his own music of which no trace has survived.

The introduction of guitar arrangements of Bach by Francisco Tarrega (1852–1909) and Andres Segovia (1893–1987), including (but by no means restricted to) the lute works, was a partial stimulus for the beginning of the revival of the Baroque lute in Germany in the 1920s. Although the lute works are still most frequently performed on the guitar, often freely arranged, several different performing versions for lute have also appeared. Modern lutenists, such as Nigel North and Hopkinson Smith, following the example of their 18th-century forebears, have also felt free to make versions of other Bach pieces for their

instrument, the unaccompanied violin and cello works proving particularly amenable to arrangement.

2. **Individual pieces.** The Suite in G minor BWV995 is an arrangement of the Cello Suite in C minor BWV1011. It exists both in Bach's autograph (1727–31) and in a tablature version probably prepared not long afterwards by Adam Falckenhagen. There are numerous minor differences between the two lute versions: Bach's requires the low *GG* of the rare 14-course lute, whereas the tablature is for the more normal 13-course lute; the bass line is frequently displaced by an octave; and the tablature version is heavily ornamented with lute *Manieren* in Falckenhagen's style, which are absent from the autograph.

The Suite in E minor BWV996 survives in a copy (Weimar, c.1715) in the hand of J. G. Walther to which a later hand has added the note 'aufs Lautenwerck', possibly implying that this piece was actually intended for the lute-harpsichord in emulation of the lute, rather than for the lute itself. It has an unusually low tessitura, even for lute music, and presents many difficulties for the lutenist, notably some unplayable chords in the Prelude and an unidiomatically dense texture, especially troublesome in the fast movements.

Several manuscript versions of the C minor Suite BWV997 exist in keyboard notation, the earliest from about 1740; an earlier copy (c.1730) of the Prelude (here called 'Fantasia'), Sarabande, and Gigue in lute tablature was made by J. C. Weyrauch. In the keyboard versions the right-hand part is written an octave higher. Suitable transposition of the Fugue and the Gigue's concluding *double*, missing from the tablature version, renders them no less playable than similar movements in Bach's other lute pieces. Thus it is possible that the entire piece was originally intended for lute; however, the Fugue and *double* may be later additions.

Bach's autograph of the Prelude, Fugue, and Allegro in E♭ major BWV998 (entitled 'Prelude pour la Luth ò Cembal') was probably written in the early 1740s. Only the Prelude is easily playable without much alteration. The necessary changes to the Fugue and the Allegro are, however, no more radical than those found in the tablature version of BWV995, although the music is more complex.

The unique source of the Prelude in C minor BWV999 copied by J. P. Kellner carries the title 'Praelude in C mol. pour La Lute. di Johann Sebastian Bach'. It is fully playable on the lute without alteration, and in a characteristic broken-chord style typical of lute preludes in the 18th century, comparable to that of the first prelude in Book 1 of *The Well-tempered Clavier*. (The fact that the prelude ends in the dominant, G major, suggests that it is an extract from a larger work.) The Fugue in G minor BWV1000 is a variant version of the fugue from the G minor Sonata for unaccompanied violin; it was copied in lute tablature by J. C. Weyrauch, perhaps as late as 1740, but as the copyist was a close friend of Bach it is likely to be a sanctioned arrangement.

The Suite in E major BWV1006a, which exists in an autograph dating from the late 1730s, is an arrangement, in keyboard notation, of the E major Partita for unaccompanied violin. The instrument is unspecified, but the arrangement is not idiomatic for the keyboard. Its style and tessitura, the simple diatonic bass line, and the presence of dynamic indications in the Prelude all suggest the lute as a likely candidate, although the harp has occasionally been suggested. Because E major is a rare and difficult key for the lute, the suite is frequently transposed into the more comfortable key of F major.                    TTC

A. Burguete, 'Die Lautenkompositionen Johann Sebastian Bachs: ein Beitrag zur kritischer Wertung aus spielpraktischer Sicht', *BJb* 63 (1977), 26–54; H. Neeman, 'J. S. Bachs Lautenkompositionen', *BJb* 28 (1931), 72–87; H. Radke, 'War Johann Sebastian Bach Lautenspieler?', in *Festschrift Hans Engel zum siebzigsten Geburtstag* (Kassel, 1964), 281–9; H.-J. Schulze, Introduction to *J. S. Bach: Drei Lautenkompositionen in zeitgenössischer Tabulatur* [facsimile] (Leipzig, 1975); H.-J. Schulze, '"Monsieur Schouster"—ein vergessener Zeitgenosse Johann Sebastian Bachs', in *Bachiana et alia musicologia: Festschrift für Alfred Dürr* (Kassel, 1983), 243–50; H.-J. Schulze, 'Wer intavolierte Johann Sebastian Bachs Lautenkompositionen?', *Die Musikforschung*, 19 (1966), 32–9.

**Lutheranism.** The Protestant tradition based on the theology of the German reformer Martin Luther (1483–1546), whose writings formed the basic corpus of Bach's personal library. Lutheran theology, which lays emphasis on justification by faith and on the importance of Scripture, is expressed in the confessional documents, such as Luther's two catechisms (1529), the Augsburg Confession and its Apology (1530), and the 'Formula of Concord' (1577), found in the *Concordienbuch* ('Book of Concord', 1580). Before being confirmed in a church appointment every pastor, teacher, and musician had to give formal and written assent to the doctrines enshrined in the *Concordienbuch*. Thus, before Bach officially became the Thomaskantor in Leipzig, he was given an oral examination in Lutheran theology by Johann Schmid (d. 1731), professor of theology at Leipzig, on or before 8 May 1723 (*BDok* ii. 99–100 and 177). A week later, on 13 May 1723, he was examined again, this time by Salomon Deyl-

ing, professor of theology, superintendent and pastor of the Nikolaikirche, who afterwards wrote in a memorandum to the consistory that the Kantor-elect had specifically endorsed the 'Formula of Concord' (*BDok* ii. 101; iii. 630–1), which implied his acceptance of the theological stance of the *Concordienbuch* as a whole.

Bach wrote music specifically inspired by these Lutheran confessional documents, such as the three cantatas (BWV190a, 120a, and Anh. I 4) celebrating the bicentenary of the Augsburg Confession in 1730, performed in Leipzig on three consecutive days, 25–7 July (much of the music is no longer extant), and the catechism chorale preludes for organ in *Clavier-Übung III* (1739), which appears to have been published to celebrate the bicentenary of the introduction of the Lutheran Reformation into Leipzig.

Although theologically radical, the Lutheran church was liturgically conservative, adapting rather than rejecting traditional forms. Thus the morning eucharistic *Hauptgottesdienst* on Sundays and festivals was an evangelical adaptation of the structure and content of the Catholic Mass. The Lutheran eucharist therefore retained the traditional Sunday and festival Propers—collects, epistles, gospels, etc.—and much of the Ordinary, especially the Kyrie and Gloria (*see* MISSA). Similarly, Lutheran VESPERS was a modified form of Catholic Vespers.

Music was an important and integral element in Lutheran worship. This was in large measure a result of Luther's theological understanding of music as a *donum Dei*, a 'gift from God', rather than a human invention. There are frequent references in the reformer's writings to the close relationship between music and theology, such as: 'I place music next to theology and give it the highest praise'. On the one hand this orientation gave rise to the development of congregational hymnody, the chorale, and on the other hand it promoted what was to become the Lutheran musical tradition, a rich tapestry of instrumental, choral, and vocal sound which included such genres as the chorale prelude and the sacred cantata.

Much of Bach's music is in many respects the culmination of the Lutheran tradition of church music. His organ music (especially the chorale preludes), sacred cantatas, oratorios, passions, *missae*, and even the B minor Mass were self-consciously composed within the ambit of Lutheran theology and practice.

In the later 17th and early 18th centuries Lutheranism was to some degree polarized by Orthodoxy and Pietism. Pietists advocated the simplification of liturgical forms and the elimination of elaborate music; the proponents of

## Lutheran mass

Orthodoxy defended them. Bach, while expressing a piety akin to that of the Pietists, was unsympathetic to their anti-liturgical stance and their opposition to concerted music. Similarly, his disputes with the Rector of the Thomasschule, J. A. Ernesti, a proto-rationalist, would seem to suggest that Bach was part of the mainstream of early 18th-century Lutheranism.                    RAL

J. Bodensieck, ed., *The Encyclopedia of the Lutheran Church* (Minneapolis, 1965); R. A. Leaver, *Bachs theologische Bibliothek* (Stuttgart, 1983); R. A. Leaver, 'Music and Lutheranism', in J. Butt, ed., *The Cambridge Bach Companion* (Cambridge, 1997), 35–45.

**Lutheran mass.** A term often used for a Lutheran German MISSA, consisting of Kyrie and Gloria only.

# M

***Mache dich, mein Geist, bereit*** ('Make thyself ready, my spirit'). Cantata for the 22nd Sunday after Trinity, BWV115. The textual basis of this towering masterpiece is a hymn by the Dresden lawyer and courtier Johann Burchard Freystein (1697). The work belongs to Bach's second annual Leipzig cycle, dominated by chorale-based cantatas, of which this is one; it was first performed on 5 November 1724. The Gospel reading for this Sunday is the parable of the unjust steward (Matt. 18: 21–35), but the unidentified author of Bach's text makes no direct reference to it, providing instead a warning to the soul to be wary of Satan, to pray, and to be prepared for the Last Judgement.

In the opening choral fantasia in G major, both the words of Freystein's hymn and its associated melody, *Straf mich nicht in deinem Zorn* (sometimes attributed to Johann Rosenmüller, *c*.1619–84), are retained. The movement is scored for flute, oboe d'amore, strings, and continuo, with a horn strengthening the stirring melody of the hymn, sustained in the soprano line of the vocal texture. The initial ritornello line is presented by unison upper strings with continuo, then taken up by the flute, oboe d'amore, and the bass, tenor, and alto vocal parts respectively. Only the soprano part remains detached from this material as it sustains the hymn melody throughout this sometimes imitative, sometimes canonic, and always tautly constructed movement.

The suppleness and robust character of the opening chorus provide effective contrast with the aria for alto, oboe d'amore, strings, and continuo which follows. Aptly described by Alberto Basso as an 'aria del sonno' ('sleep aria'), this torpid E minor Adagio in siciliana rhythm paints the subtly varied images of the text with almost hypnotic strength. The piece is initially a cautionary warning to the unwary, slumbering spirit. A brief Allegro, introducing the B section of what is an extended da capo aria, depicts the punishment that lies in store for the unwatchful soul; but this, in turn, gives way to an Adagio, concluding the B section, which prepares the listener, materially and rhythmically, for the da capo. In this short section the text speaks of everlasting sleep—in other words, death.

A bass recitative leads to the second da capo aria of the cantata. The key is B minor and the scoring is for soprano with a translucent accompaniment of flute, violoncello piccolo, and continuo. Marked 'Molto adagio' by Bach, this profound, penitent entreaty for God's understanding and forbearance seems, at times, to break through the conventionally understood boundaries of late Baroque musical expression. The first melody part to enter in this superbly crafted contrapuntal piece is the flute, followed at a bar's interval by the violoncello piccolo, and lastly by the soprano, whose text is a quotation of two lines from the hymn on which the cantata is based. These are supported throughout by a continuo of quavers separated by quaver rests, marking the beats with almost clock-like regularity. A brief tenor recitative leads to the concluding section, a straightforward harmonization in G major of a strophe from Freystein's hymn with its associated melody, supported by the instruments of the opening movement. The very simplicity with which Bach treats this chorale at the close lends emphasis to the inherent strength of a fine melody.                                                                        NA

A. Basso, *Frau Musika: la vita e le opere di J. S. Bach*, ii (Turin, 1983), 323–5. For further bibliography, *see* CANTATA, §1.

**madrigalian verse.** A term often used in the Bach literature, especially as a translation of the German 'madrigalische Dichtung', to refer to the free verse specially designed to be set as recitatives, ariosos, and (sometimes) arias in sacred and secular cantatas and other vocal works. Madrigalian verse is characterized by irregular line lengths and rhyme schemes, and is thus distinguished from biblical passages, strophic arias, and hymn strophes.

**'Magister'** ('Master'). A Latin nickname used by Wagner for a prelude (? and fugue) from Bach's *The Well-tempered Clavier*. In her diary for 4 December 1882 Wagner's wife Cosima wrote: 'In the evening my father [Franz Liszt] plays to us three preludes from the *48 Preludes and Fugues*, among them the "Magister"—or "Magister as Jupiter *tonans*", as R. remarks'. It is not known to which piece she here refers.

M. Gregor-Dellin and D. Mack, eds., *Cosima Wagner's Diaries*, ii: *1878–1883*, Eng. trans. G. Skelton (New York, 1980), 966 and 1152.

***Magnificat.*** A setting of the Latin Vespers canticle (the Song of Mary: St Luke 1: 46–55), written during Bach's first Christmas in Leipzig and performed on Christmas Day 1723. The work survives in two distinct versions, both in Bach's autograph. The first (BWV243a) is in E♭ major, an unusual key for a festive work such as this, with trumpets and drums (possible reasons for Bach's choice of key have been thoroughly examined by Don Smithers). This version includes four Christmas interpolations. Although published by Simrock in 1811, it was omitted from the *BG* edition; it appeared in the *NBA* in 1955. The second version (BWV243), in D major, is the one most familiar today, and it differs in many small matters of detail and instrumentation from BWV243a. It was probably revised about 1732–5 and, shorn of its Christmas movements, could have been used on any major feast-day, and may have been intended for performance on 2 July 1733 when the feast of the Visitation of Mary coincided with the end of national mourning for the death of the Saxon elector, Friedrich August I. In 1786 it was revived by C. P. E. Bach for a charity concert in Hamburg which also included the Symbolum Nicenum from the Mass in B minor.

Although one of the corner-stones of Protestantism was the use of the vernacular, Luther and the early Church Fathers still valued Latin, and during Bach's time at Leipzig there were at least 15 high feasts (including Christmas) on which the *Magnificat* could be sung in Latin. At normal Sunday Vespers the *Magnificat*, in Luther's German version, was usually chanted by the congregation to the plainsong *tonus peregrinus* or sung by the choir in a simple MOTET STYLE, but on high feasts more elaborate settings with instrumental accompaniment were permitted. Furthermore, despite attempts to curb the practice in 1702, a Leipzig Christmas custom favoured the troping of the Latin text with *laudes* (hymns in Latin and German) outlining elements of the Christmas story. Bach's choice of seasonal interpolations in BWV243a was based on the four hymns found in a Christmas cantata written by his immediate predecessor at Leipzig, Johann Kuhnau. *Vom Himmel hoch*, a Lutheran chorale, tells of the angel's appearance to the shepherds; 'Freut euch und jubiliert' announces the angel's message; 'Gloria in excelsis Deo' represents the singing of the heavenly host; and 'Virga Jesse floruit', a late 16th-century Christmas hymn, expresses the joy of Mary and Joseph at the birth of the Saviour.

The overall form of the work, and to some extent its style and scoring, were generated by the text. Like Vivaldi's well-known *Magnificat* RV610, and many other Italian settings, nearly every verse of the canticle was set as a separate movement, alternating between choral and solo forces (see Table 1).

TABLE 1. Structure of *Magnificat* BWV243
(interpolations of BWV243a are shown in **bold** type)

| No. | Text | Scoring | Key (243/243a) |
|---|---|---|---|
| 1 | Magnificat anima mea Dominum | chorus (SSATB), orchestra | I (D/E♭ major) |
| 2 | Et exultavit spiritus meus in Deo salutaris | S2, strings, bc | I (D/E♭ major) |
|  | **Vom Himmel hoch** | chorus (SATB) | I (—/E♭ major) |
| 3 | Quia respexit humilitatem ancillae suae, ecce enim ex hoc beatam me dicent | S1, oboe d'amore, bc (243) S1, oboe, bc (243a) | vi (B/C minor) |
| 4 | Omnes generationes | chorus (SSATB), orchestra | iii (F♯/G minor) |
| 5 | Quia fecit mihi magna, qui potens est, et sanctum nomen ejus | B, bc | V (A/B♭ major) |
|  | **Freut euch und jubiliert** | chorus (SSATB) | V (—/B♭ major) |
| 6 | Et misericordia a progenie in progenies timentibus eum | A, T, 2 flutes, strings, bc (243) A, T, 2 recorders, strings, bc (243a) | ii (E/F minor) |
| 7 | Fecit potentiam in brachio suo, dispersit superbos mente cordis sui | chorus (SSATB), orchestra | IV–I (G–D/A♭– E♭ major) |
|  | **Gloria in excelsis Deo** | chorus (SSATB), strings, oboes, bc | I (—/E♭ major) |
| 8 | Deposuit potentes, et exaltavit humiles | T, violins, bc | iii (F♯/G minor) |
| 9 | Esurientes implevit bonis. et divites dimisit inanes | A, 2 flutes, bc (243) A, 2 recorders, bc (243a) | II (E/F major) |
|  | **Virga Jesse floruit** | S1, B, bc | II (—/F major) |
| 10 | Suscepit Israel puerum suum, recordatus misericordiae suae | S1, S2, A, 2 oboes, bc (243) S1, S2, A, trumpet, bc (243a) | vi (B/C minor) |
| 11 | Sicut locutus est ad patres nostros, Abraham et semini ejus in saecula | chorus (SSATB), bc | I (D/E♭ major) |
| 12 | Gloria Patri, Filio et Spiritui Sancto! Sicut erat in principio et nunc et semper, et in saecula saeculorum, Amen. | chorus (SSATB), orchestra | I (D/E♭ major) |

Despite its expansive formal design, the work is surprisingly concise—less than 600 bars in length without the hymns—since Bach presumably had to adhere to the time limitations imposed by the Vespers service. Compared with his cantatas, the solo movements are not only shorter but, because of the nature of the text, they also avoid da capo form. The festal character of the text is mirrored in the scoring. Bach makes use of the largest orchestra for church music available to him at the time: three trumpets, drums, flutes (recorders in BWV243a), oboes (and oboes d'amore in BWV243), bassoons, strings, and continuo. The choruses are in five parts, with divided trebles, rather than the usual four.

Bach's score demonstrates a clear acquaintance with well-established conventions employed in *Magnificat* settings in both Germany and Italy. The composer was not only familiar with local customs (and possibly Telemann's Leipzig *Magnificat* of about 1704), but also copied out several Italianate works for performance at Leipzig, and may well have known the *Magnificat* in G minor formerly ascribed to Albinoni, which shares several common features with Bach's setting.

Bach's decision to return to the music of the opening in the final chorus at the words 'sicut erat in principio' ('as it was in the beginning') is a traditional musical pun at least as old as Monteverdi (1610). He draws on similar traditions in his attention to word-painting: 'dispersit' is graphically 'scattered'; 'deposuit' and 'exaltavit' descend and ascend appropriately, and (as in the 'Albinoni' *Magnificat*) he detaches the words 'omnes generationes' from the second treble solo to emphasize the weight of 'all generations' with the full chorus. One of the most striking differences between the two versions of the work can be heard in bar 24 of this chorus, where the climactic dominant 9th is sustained in the first version but quickly resolved in the second. As in Telemann's setting, the phrase 'ad patres nostros' from 'Sicut locutus est' seems to have suggested an *a cappella* fugal style which his forefathers would have recognized. The similarly scored 'Freut euch' may actually have been based on a setting of the same text published in 1603 by Sethus Calvisius (1556–1615), one of Bach's predecessors as Thomaskantor. More specifically Lutheran are 'Suscepit Israel' in which the composer employs the *tonus peregrinus*, to which the *Magnificat* was traditionally chanted, and the similar *Vom Himmel hoch*, in which Luther's hymn provides the basis for an old-fashioned *a cappella* cantus firmus motet.                                    SH

R. M. Cammarota, 'The Sources of the Christmas Interpolations in J. S. Bach's Magnificat in E-flat major (BWV 243a)', *Current Musicology*, 36 (1983),

79–99; R. L. Marshall, 'On the Origin of Bach's Magnificat: A Lutheran Composer's Challenge', in D. O. Franklin, ed., *Bach Studies* (Cambridge, 1989), 3–17; U. Meyer, 'Musikalisch-rhetorische Figuren in J. S. Bachs Magnificat', *Musik und Kirche*, 43 (1973), 172–81; D. L. Smithers, 'Anomalies of *Tonart* and *Stimmton* in the First Version of Bach's *Magnificat* (BWV 243a)', *Bach*, 27/2 (1996), 1–59; C. S. Terry, *Bach: The Magnificat, Lutheran Masses and Motets* (London, 1929).

***Man singet mit Freuden vom Sieg*** ('One sings joyfully of the victory'), BWV149. The last of Bach's three complete surviving cantatas for the feast of St Michael and All Angels, first performed at Leipzig either in 1728 or, more probably, on 29 September 1729. The music survives in a score and parts copied by C. F. Penzel; the first 14 bars of the opening chorus also exist in an autograph sketch (*BC* A 182). The text, by Picander, is inspired by the encounter engaged in by St Michael and his angels against the dragon (Satan) and his fiery companions. The story is contained in the Epistle reading for the day and was clearly one that greatly appealed to Bach, since each of his cantatas for this festival, as well as the chorus *Nun ist das Heil* BWV50 (which is all that survives of a fourth cantata for the feast of St Michael), inspired him to write music rich in poetic imagery and instrumental colour.

The scoring of the opening D major chorus is generous, consisting of three trumpets, timpani, three oboes, bassoon, strings, and continuo. The music was not, however, entirely new, since Bach had previously used it at Weimar—though differently scored and in a different key—as the conclusion to his congratulatory cantata *Was mir behagt, ist nur die muntre Jagd*. In 1740 he used the movement once again, this time as the conclusion to his cantata for the town council election, *Herrscher des Himmels, König der Ehren* (BWV Anh. 193), the score of which has not survived. The remaining components of BWV149 may also be parodies of music which Bach had written earlier in his life but, if so, no evidence exists to confirm this.

The continuo aria for bass voice which follows the chorus extends the theme of the conflict between God and Satan. In addition to the keyboard, the continuo line here calls for a violone, or 'violono grosso' as Bach unusually termed it in this cantata. Perhaps, as Laurence Dreyfus has suggested (*Bach's Continuo Group* (Cambridge, Mass., 1987), 254), Bach had thought to use the term having consulted the score to BWV208, whose concluding chorus, parodied here, likewise had called for a 'violono grosso'.

An alto recitative leads to a soprano aria with strings. The 3/8 rhythm and A major tonality of this lyrical, dance-like movement, whose text reflects on the protection afforded by the guardian angels, contribute to the strong contrast it makes, in both colour and affect, to the dark austerity of the preceding B minor aria. A tenor recitative leads to the third aria of the cantata, a duet for alto and tenor with obbligato bassoon whose light-hearted, sinewy, even serpentine figurations—a diverting feature of Bach's writing—are taken up initially by the tenor and alto voices in canon. The cantata ends with a twelve-line stanza from Martin Schalling's hymn *Herzlich lieb hab ich dich, o Herr* (1571), set to its anonymous associated melody (1577). The voices are accompanied by woodwind and strings but, with a startling *coup de théâtre*, Bach introduces the three trumpets and timpani in the concluding two bars, ending the cantata in a blaze of colour.

NA

For bibliography, *see* CANTATA, §1.

***manualiter.*** A term used to indicate that a piece or passage of music (especially organ music) is to be played by the hands. In *Clavier-Übung III*, for example, Bach indicated as 'manualiter' those pieces which were designed to be played without using the pedals. *See also* PEDALITER and TOCCATA.

**manuscripts.** *See* SOURCES, §1.

**Marcello, Alessandro** (b. 24 Aug. 1669; d. 19 June 1747). Italian composer, born in Venice. Like his younger brother Benedetto, he was a *nobile dilettante*: a nobleman who played and wrote music for pleasure alone. Alessandro's small but distinguished musical output includes an oboe concerto in D minor published about 1717 at Amsterdam in a concerto anthology and transcribed by Bach for solo harpsichord (as BWV974), presumably from an earlier manuscript. In the past this fine, typically Venetian concerto has sometimes been attributed to Vivaldi as well as to Benedetto Marcello, but there is no reason to doubt Alessandro's authorship. MT

E. Selfridge-Field, *The Music of Benedetto and Alessandro Marcello: A Thematic Catalogue with Commentary on the Composer, Repertory, and Sources* (Oxford, 1990).

**Marcello, Benedetto** (b. 24 June 1686; d. 24 July 1739). Italian composer, born in Venice. He was the early 18th century's ideal of an aristocratic amateur composer (one of his appellations was 'Princeps musicae'); his austere settings of Italian paraphrases of the first 50 psalms (1724–6) enjoyed in their day a prestige in the vocal sphere as great as Corelli's in the instrumental, though today his music is generally found dry and quirkish. As far as we know, Bach (unlike Telemann) did not share in the encomiums, by professional musicians, of Marcello's art, but he did at least make a keyboard transcription (BWV981) of the second concerto in Marcello's *Concerti a cinque* op. 1 (1708), changing the key from E minor to C minor. MT

E. Selfridge-Field, *The Music of Benedetto and Alessandro Marcello: A Thematic Catalogue with Commentary on the Composer, Repertory, and Sources* (Oxford, 1990).

**Marchand, Louis** (b. 2 Feb. 1669; d. 17 Feb. 1732). One of the most renowned French keyboard virtuosos of his day, born in Lyons. In 1717, during a tour of Germany, he was challenged to engage with Bach in keyboard improvisation at the instigation of the Dresden *Konzertmeister* J. B. Volumier. Accounts differ, but they agree that Marchand failed to appear, having secretly left Dresden before the event was due to begin.

Bach admired Marchand's playing and was acquainted with his *Pièces de clavecin* (Paris, 1699 and 1702), which, according to Jakob Adlung, were played by Bach 'in his own manner; that is, very lightly and with much art'. RDPJ

D. Moroney, Preface to *L. Marchand: Pièces de clavecin*, ed. T. Dart (rev. edn., Monaco, 1987).

**Mariae Heimsuchung.** German term for the feast of the Visitation of the Blessed Virgin (2 July). *See* CHURCH CALENDAR.

**Mariae Reinigung.** German term for the feast of the Purification of the Blessed Virgin (2 February). *See* CHURCH CALENDAR.

**Mariae Verkundigung.** German term for the feast of the Annunciation of the Blessed Virgin (25 March). *See* CHURCH CALENDAR.

***Markus-Passion.*** *See* ST MARK PASSION.

**Marpurg, Friedrich Wilhelm** (b. 21 Nov. 1718, d. 22 May 1795). Composer and writer on music, born near Seehausen, Brandenburg. Active especially from 1749 to 1763 at Berlin as a prolific writer of pedagogic manuals, music theory, and journalistic criticism, Marpurg claimed to have discussed fugue with Bach. He contributed a preface to the second (1752) edition of *The Art of Fugue*; his own writings on fugue frequently quote from Bach's works. After aligning himself theoretically with the French composer and theorist Jean-Philippe Rameau (1683–1764), Marpurg became engaged in a dispute with J. P. Kirnberger and other members of the Bach circle over questions of music theory. DS

F. W. Marpurg, *Abhandlung von der Fuge* (Berlin, 1753–4; facsimile, Hildesheim, 1970); H. Serwer, 'Marpurg versus Kirnberger: Theories of Fugal Composition', *Journal of Music Theory*, 14 (1970),

206–36. For further bibliography, *see* KIRNBERGER, JOHANN PHILIPP.

**Marx, Adolf Bernhard** (b. 15 May 1795; d. 17 May 1866). Composer and musicologist, born in Halle. At first a lawyer, he was later a critic in Berlin and became influential as music director at the University of Berlin. Marx was connected with the German liberalism of the time, and this provided the context for his Bach activities. Thus, against the prevailing taste for C. H. Graun's oratorio *Der Tod Jesu*, he promoted the idea of reviving the *St Matthew Passion*. Three of his Bach editions were of paramount importance: the first vocal scores of the *St Matthew Passion* and the Mass in B minor (for which he created the name 'Hohe Messe', analogous to Beethoven's *Missa solemnis*) and the first Bach cantatas to be printed since 1709 (nos. 101–3), which he published in 1830.        KK

**mass.** In common parlance, a musical setting of the Ordinary of the Latin ritual of the Eucharist as observed in the Catholic Church. Martin Luther (1483–1546) retained much of the Roman liturgy for use in combination or alternation with the vernacular rite. Thus, although the Latin Ordinary became paraphrased in the German congregational chorales of the Lutheran vernacular Mass, all five portions of the Latin Ordinary—Kyrie, Gloria, Credo, Sanctus (with Osanna and Benedictus), and Agnus Dei—were retained in Luther's *Formula missae* of 1523. Two centuries later, when Bach was at Leipzig, parts of the Latin Ordinary were sung in elaborate concerted settings on certain occasions.

By the early 18th century modern concerto and operatic styles were admitted in mass composition, together with the old style of the late Renaissance. While Palestrina's masses were still central to the repertory of the Roman Catholic court chapel at Dresden during Bach's lifetime, the court's extensive repertory of concerted masses from both the Neapolitan school (e.g. those of Alessandro Scarlatti, 1660–1725) and its own resident composers, was undoubtedly a great influence on Bach.

Bach's most celebrated setting of the Kyrie and Gloria, presented to the Elector of Saxony in 1733, eventually became the first part of the complete Mass in B minor. At least two, if not all four, of his other short masses (*see* MISSA) date from the late 1730s, and he performed several settings of the shortened mass by other composers during the Leipzig years. He also performed Sanctus settings, although these always appear independently in the performing material, thus implying that they were never performed together with the Kyrie and Gloria. Of the multiple settings of the Sanctus that Bach performed during the Leipzig years, three

are of his own composition: those in C and D major (BWV237 and 238) date from 1723, the first year at Leipzig, and another in D major, which eventually became the Sanctus of the Mass in B minor, was first performed on Christmas Day 1724.

The only positive evidence for Bach's interest in a polyphonic or concerted setting of the Credo (other than in the Mass in B minor) is in his copy of G. B. Bassani's *Acroama missale* (*c*.1735) where he inserted the first line of the text, 'Credo in unum Deum', into the opening of the vocal parts of the Credo for each mass, thus replacing the solo intonation customary in Catholic practice. Moreover, in the fifth of Bassani's six masses, where the musical setting does not allow room for the new underlay, Bach actually composed a new intonation (*c*.1747–8). He also had complete vocal parts for a *Missa sine nomine* by Palestrina (*c*.1742); however, the fact that he prepared doubling instrumental parts for only the Kyrie and Gloria may suggest that the remaining movements were never used in the liturgy. Bach's only settings of the Osanna, Benedictus, and Agnus Dei are to be found in the Mass in B minor, and signs of uncertainty in the manuscript at this point may suggest that he was unfamiliar with these movements. In all, it seems that Bach could have performed most of the traditional Latin Ordinary within the Lutheran liturgy, but not apparently all at the same time. Given that he gave the title 'Missa' to the 1733 presentation parts of the Kyrie and Gloria in B minor and that the Mass settings of the organ collection *Clavier-Übung III* cover only the Kyrie and Gloria, it is clear that these two texts were the essential element of the Lutheran Mass.        JAB
*See also* MASS IN B MINOR and MISSA.

**Mass in B minor.** See overleaf.

***Matthäus-Passion.*** *See* ST MATTHEW PASSION.

**Mattheson, Johann** (b. 28 Sept. 1681; d. 17 April 1764). Composer, journalist, ambassadorial secretary, and music theorist, born in Hamburg. He was the most prolific writer on music of the age, codifying many elements of the past and anxious to influence the future.

Mattheson stated (in the first printed reference to Bach, published in his *Das beschützte Orchestre*, 1717) that he had seen fine examples of Bach's music, but he criticized Bach's text setting in his *Critica musica* (1725). He often admired Bach's organ performance and fugal writing, sometimes printing his fugue subjects and canons. He repeatedly tried to gather information on Bach for his biographical lexicon of 1740; Bach either never read Mattheson's publications or did not care to provide any information.        JAB

# Mass in B minor

Bach's only complete setting of the Latin Ordinary, BWV232.

---

1. Chronology.
2. The parodied movements.
3. Musical style and structure.
4. Reception history.

---

1. **Chronology.** On 27 July 1733 Bach petitioned Friedrich August II, the new Elector of Saxony, for a court title that would boost his status as the somewhat beleaguered Kantor at the Thomasschule in Leipzig. The 'trifling product' that Bach enclosed was the set of beautifully prepared presentation parts for a *missa*, the Kyrie and Gloria that later became the first part of the Mass in B minor. In scale and idiom the *missa* seems designed for the mass repertory typical of Dresden. Although there is no evidence for a Leipzig performance of the work, it does somewhat fit into a pattern of Latin church compositions that Bach undertook in the 1730s and 1740s (most notably the four further masses consisting of the Kyrie and Gloria only; *see* MISSA).

Bach reused some of the *missa* music in the mid-1740s for the Latin cantata *Gloria in excelsis Deo* BWV191. Gregory Butler (*BJb* 78 (1992), 65–71) has presented a convincing case suggesting that this was put together at short notice to celebrate the Peace of Dresden at the conclusion of the second Silesian War (during which Leipzig had been occupied by the Prussian troops of Leopold of Anhalt-Dessau) at a special academic thanksgiving service in the Leipzig University church on Christmas Day 1745. Coming between the main services in the two principal churches of Leipzig, Bach would have had the use of the two best *Kantoreien* and the Latin text would have been eminently appropriate for an academic occasion. Butler also proposes that the D major Sanctus composed for Christmas 1724 was also performed on this day. Thus the juxtaposition of these two works, related as they are to the Latin Ordinary, may have inspired Bach to compile a *missa tota* in the remaining years of his life, perhaps in response to his first and only personal experience of the horrors of war.

According to Yoshitake Kobayashi (*BJb* 74 (1988), 7–72), the handwriting in the score of Bach's completion of the Mass in B minor—the sections entitled '2. Symbolum Nicenum' (the term Bach uses for the Credo), '3. Sanctus', and '4. Osanna | Benedictus | Agnus Dei et | Dona nobis pacem'—comes from the period August 1748 to October 1749, and thus from the very end of Bach's compositional career. His original score for the Kyrie and Gloria (i.e. the *missa* of 1733), forms the first section of this segmented score. The format seems purposely designed so that each of the four sections could be used separately. Much of this material is clearly arranged from existing works, although the notation of 'Confiteor' shows that this, at least, was a fresh composition; moreover, the many revisions and corrections show that the complete mass was being compiled here for the first time.

While we know that the Sanctus and Cantata 191 were performed in Leipzig (the Sanctus on multiple occasions between 1724 and the 1740s), we have no certain evidence that Bach ever performed the other sections. Hans-Joachim Schulze proposes that the *missa* may well have been performed in Dresden in 1733 on account of the wording on the title-page of the parts and the incredible care with which Bach indicated details of performance (see Prinz, pp. 84–102). C. P. E. Bach's *Magnificat* (finished on 25 August 1749 and possibly performed in Leipzig during his father's last year) contains obvious allusions to 'Gratias agimus tibi' in Bach's *missa* (figuration which is, incidentally, not to be found in the earlier version of this music, in Cantata 29:2) and to the 'Et expecto' of the Symbolum (again, in figuration not to be found in the earlier versions, Cantatas 120 and 120*a*). While Emanuel could have remembered the *missa* material from the time when he helped to copy the parts in 1733, he must have become acquainted with the Symbolum only in 1748–9, something which leaves open the possibility that he witnessed a performance or read-through (see J. Butt, 'Bach's Mass in B Minor: Considerations of its Early Performance and Use', *Journal of Musicology*, 9 (1991), 110–24). Certainly Bach was interested in Credo settings at this time, since he wrote a new Credo intonation for Bassani's fifth mass in 1747–8, and there is recent evidence of an earlier version of the opening 'Credo' movement of the Symbolum (see P. Wollny, *BJb* 80 (1994), 163–9); none of this necessarily proves, though, that any of the Symbolum music was ever performed.

In all, we know of no definite reason for Bach's decision to compile a *missa tota*. There is some circumstantial evidence to link it with further commissions from, or presentations to, the Dresden court (Butt, pp. 20–3) but, bearing in mind Butler's 'war trauma' hypothesis, it is eminently possible that Bach compiled it with no specific occasion or performance in mind, and that it belongs among the increasingly abstract and 'speculative' cycles from his later years, such as *Clavier-Übung III* or *The Art of Fugue*.

**2. The parodied movements.**  Bach drew much of the material for the Mass in B minor from existing works, producing a veritable compendium of all the styles he had employed in the composition of arias and choruses throughout his career. The 'lack' of originality is more than adequately compensated by the skill with which he adapted the material to fit the new context. Furthermore, by abstracting movements from what he evidently considered to be some of his finest vocal works, originally performed for specific occasions and Sundays within the Church's year, he was doubtless attempting to preserve the pieces within the more durable context of the Latin Ordinary.

Even when models survive for specific movements, it is not always certain whether Bach copied the model directly or whether both derive from an earlier, lost version. Alfred Dürr has produced a searching critique of recent attempts at identifying which movements are parodies and of hypotheses regarding their models ('Zur Parodiefrage in Bachs H-Moll Messe: eine Bestandsaufnahme', *Die Musikforschung*, 45 (1992), 117–38). Nevertheless, the only positive evidence of Bach actually composing afresh within the entire score of the mass is in the 'Confiteor' section at the end of the Symbolum.

Christoph Wolff views the opening movement as an original 'Kyrie' which Bach wrote under the influence of several earlier compositions: a Kyrie by J. H. von Wilderer, the opening vocal parts of Bach's *Trauer Ode*, and the Kyrie of Luther's *Deutsche Messe*. Certainly much of the movement—like many others with no known models—seems to have been copied from an earlier version. The first movement for which a previous version survives is 'Gratias agimus', the text of which is virtually synonymous with the German text of the original version, the opening chorus of

Cantata 29, 'Wir danken dir, Gott, wir danken dir'. Bach made considerable alter-ations to the figuration to suit the stress of the Latin words, and this lends greater momentum to the movement as a whole. For 'Qui tollis' Bach drew on the opening chorus of Cantata 46; here again he undertook considerable revisions during the process of transcription and adaptation.

'Patrem omnipotentem' shares much of its material with the opening chorus of Cantata 171 but, given that this too seems to be a parody, 'Patrem' was probably adapted from the lost model for both existing movements. Bach adds a new entry at the beginning and the chordal declamations, 'Credo in unum Deum', but he other-wise follows the cantata version bar by bar. 'Crucifixus' comes from the earliest trace-able model for any movement in the entire mass—the first section of the chorus opening Cantata 12, 'Weinen, Klagen, Sorgen, Zagen', composed in Weimar for 22 April 1714. Here Bach adds the interlocking flute lines, the throbbing crotchet move-ment in the continuo, and the four-bar introduction of the ground bass. The final four bars, with the extraordinary move to G major, are new in 'Crucifixus', perhaps representing Christ lowered into the sepulchre, or the redemption achieved through Christ's death.

Bach had used the music for 'Et expecto' on at least three previous occasions (in the complex of works that make up Cantatas 120, 120*a*, and 120*b*). He basically took the opening section of a da capo movement, removed the opening and closing rit-ornellos, and added a second soprano part throughout. This process of adaptation may provide a clue as to how many of the other movements (for which there are no surviving models) were adapted: elements that might inhibit the momentum of the new sequence of movements are stripped away and the entire texture reworked to accommodate the fifth voice. While the Sanctus derives directly from the earlier ver-sion first performed in 1724, Bach altered the scoring from three sopranos and one alto to two sopranos and two altos (to match the double-soprano format of the work as a whole). 'Osanna' may be a parody of the opening chorus of Cantata 215, or both may derive from a lost model (BWV Anh. I 11). Bach removed the initial instrumental ritornello, presumably so that 'Osanna' can follow 'Sanctus' directly. However, given that the Sanctus is written into an independent manuscript with its own title (i.e. section 3 of the manuscript as a whole) Bach probably did not conceive of 'Osanna' as following 'Sanctus' (which was normally performed separately in Leipzig), although he clearly seems to have left this possibility open. The music for 'Agnus Dei' almost certainly derives from an aria in a lost wedding cantata of 1725. Bach had earlier reused this in Cantata 11, the *Ascension Oratorio*, but this differs markedly from the version in the mass, which, with its simpler melodic line, might reflect the lost earlier version.

**3. Musical style and structure.**   What is most remarkable about the overall shape of the Mass in B minor is the fact that Bach managed to shape a coherent sequence of movements from diverse material. When he presented the B minor *missa* to the Elector of Saxony in 1733, it is unlikely that he considered this to constitute only the first section of an unfinished *missa tota*; clearly he viewed it as a complete and inde-pendent work with its own proportions and unity. The solo numbers utilize all five voices and each instrumental family is represented in turn. The Gloria begins and ends with paired movements, and another paired group is placed just beyond the midway point ('Domine Deus'–'Qui tollis'). 'Domine Deus' also forms the symmetrical centre of the Gloria, surrounded as it is by a pair of choruses, then a pair of arias, and, at the outermost point, by the choruses that begin and end the Gloria. Robin Leaver suggests that another form of symmetry places the theologically crucial 'Qui tollis' (Christ, through his Passion, taking away the sins of the world) at the centre; the liturgical hymn forming the second section of the Gloria (beginning with 'Laudamus te') can be seen as distinct from the first section ('Gloria'–'Et in terra'), the biblical hymn, so that within this second section 'Qui tollis' forms the central focus. The key scheme of the *missa* also seems significant, with the Kyrie covering the triad of B minor (B–D–F♯) and the Gloria based on D major, the key set up by the middle movement of the Kyrie ('Christe eleison') and thus perhaps alluding to the new covenant of Christ.

Like the *missa*, the Symbolum Nicenum (Credo), seems to have its own cohesive structure. Many have observed that it is a superlative example of Bach's concern with symmetry, something which was undoubtedly facilitated by the addition of the independent movement for 'Et incarnatus est' at a late stage in the compilation. With this insertion in place, 'Crucifixus' becomes the central pivot and the centre of the trinity of movements concerning Christ's incarnation, crucifixion, and resurrection. Flanking this are two solo numbers, the duet 'Et in unum' and the aria 'Et in Spiritum sanctum'. The Symbolum begins and ends with pairs of choruses, each consisting of one movement in the *stile antico* (complete with Gregorian cantus firmus) and one in a festal concerted style. This pairing also helps to focus and complement the central choruses, where the contrast of affect between two successive movements could hardly be greater ('Crucifixus'–'Et resurrexit').

Clearly the symmetrical design reflects the doctrinal function of the Credo as the corner-stone of the Christian faith. The use of archaic elements (the references to Gregorian chant and the *stile antico*) underline both the tradition and the 'timeless' qualities behind the text. But Bach is anxious to show the Credo as a living and relevant testimony: he employs modern, almost *galant* idioms ('Et in unum' and 'Et in Spiritum sanctum') and utilizes the most affective and emotional musical means at his disposal for the poignant 'human' components of this ancient text ('Et incarnatus' and 'Crucifixus').

While the sequence of texts from the Sanctus to the Agnus Dei hardly offers the same opportunities for structuring and proportioning the music as the earlier sections of the mass, Bach obviously gave some thought to the sequence of movements. 'Osanna', 'Benedictus', and the repeat of 'Osanna' form a da capo unit, and 'Agnus Dei' and 'Dona nobis pacem' form another unit with two movements of roughly equal length. The striking progression from the flat key of G minor to the festal key of D major is striking, reflecting the textual progression from 'Agnus Dei' (Christ's suffering on behalf of mankind) to the call for peace ('Dona nobis pacem'). As the title-page suggests, Bach considered the movements from 'Osanna' to the end to form a discrete unity: the key scheme D major–B minor–D major–G minor–D major is striking, with the two most 'human' elements ('Benedictus' and 'Agnus Dei') as solo arias in minor keys.

While it is clear that the four manuscripts of the *missa tota* are designed for independent performance, Bach seems to have given considerable thought to the cohesion of the work as a whole. That he had some notion of a cycle of related works is also suggested by the *Christmas Oratorio*, in which the first chorale melody heard in

Part 1 is also that which closes Part 6 (each part being likewise performed on a separate occasion). In the case of the mass, the most obvious cyclic feature is the return of the music of 'Gratias agimus tibi' (from the Gloria) for 'Dona nobis pacem', which closes the entire work. Furthermore, both B minor and D major function as points of reference throughout, and Bach seems to have carefully devised the overall key schemes. For instance, the sequence of keys from the opening 'Kyrie' to 'Gratias' is mirrored by the sequence from 'Confiteor' to the end of the work (the first sequence beginning with a rising B minor triad, the latter with a falling B minor triad).

4. **Reception history.** Bach's score of the mass was inherited by his son Carl Philipp Emanuel, who clearly allowed many scholars and collectors access to it, and who performed at least part of it himself: the Symbolum Nicenum at a charity concert in Hamburg in 1786. By the beginning of the 19th century J. N. Forkel and Haydn possessed copies, and Beethoven made two attempts to acquire a score. During the second decade of the century the Berlin Singakademie rehearsed the entire work, and further performances of parts of it are evident throughout the next two decades. However, there is no firm evidence of a complete performance until that of the Riedel-Verein in Leipzig in 1859.

The comparative lateness of the first complete performance may be partially explained by the fact that there was not a complete edition of the work until 1845, when Simrock completed the edition of which Nägeli had issued a first instalment in 1833. The *BG* produced an edition in 1856, which it reissued a year later after having gained access to the autograph score. Ironically, the first issue was superior in some respects to the second, since it presented many of the detailed readings from the Dresden parts, while the second incorporates some of the readings that C. P. E. Bach added to the autograph in preparation for his 1786 performance of the Symbolum.

With the new editions and first complete performance, many performances were to follow in the latter half of the century, and the work soon became the object of extensive music criticism. Spitta, for instance, tried to unite the Catholic flavour of the work with the essence of Lutheranism, noting that Luther's original intention was to reform rather than to destroy the established Church. He is particularly enlightened regarding the issue of parody, suggesting that Bach chose pieces of appropriate 'poetic feeling', 'precious gems' awaiting a 'new setting'. Schweitzer likewise saw the union of Catholic and Protestant elements, the sublimity of the one sitting beside the intimacy of the other. The first detailed musical analysis of portions of the mass came with Tovey's study in his *Essays in Musical Analysis*, v (London, 1937); he was particularly perceptive of the importance of ritornello form, showing how it works inconspicuously in the opening 'Kyrie' to fulfil the listener's expectations in a way which is not immediately obvious.

The *NBA* produced a new edition in 1954 under the editorship of Friedrich Smend, who drew attention to the structure of the score as four separate manuscripts bound together; he was also a perceptive scholar of Bach's compositional process and his methods of revision and parody. However, the edition soon came in for stern criticism for its faulty evaluation of the sources, such as Smend's use of manuscripts from after Bach's death and his underestimation of the value of the Dresden parts. Many of these shortcomings have been rectified in the recent Peters edition (1994), edited by Christoph Wolff. The mass has become one of the 'key works' in the movement promoting historically informed performance, being central to the recording careers of such directors as Nikolaus Harnoncourt, Joshua Rifkin, Gustav Leonhardt, Andrew Parrott, John Eliot Gardiner, and Philipp Herreweghe. JAB

G. G. Butler, 'Johann Sebastian Bachs Gloria in excelsis Deo BWV 191: Musik für ein Leipziger Dankfest', *BJb* 78 (1992), 65–71; J. Butt, *Bach: Mass in B Minor* (Cambridge, 1991); R. A. Leaver, 'The Mature Vocal Works and their Theological and Liturgical Context', in J. Butt, ed., *The Cambridge Companion to Bach* (Cambridge, 1997), 86–122; U. Prinz, ed., *Johann Sebastian Bach: Messe H-Moll, 'Opus Ultimum' BWV232. Vorträge der Meisterkurse und Sommerakademien J. S. Bach, 1980, 1983 und 1989* (Kassel, 1990); G. B. Stauffer, *Bach: The Mass in B Minor* (New York, 1997); C. Wolff, 'Origins of the Kyrie of the B minor Mass', in *Bach: Essays on his Life and Music* (Cambridge, Mass., 1991), 141–51.

---

***Méditation*** ('Meditation'). The title under which Gounod's AVE MARIA arrangement was originally published.

***Meinen Jesum laß ich nicht*** ('I leave not my Jesus'). Cantata for the Sunday after Epiphany, BWV124, performed on 7 January 1725. It is a CHORALE CANTATA based on a hymn by Christian Keymann (1658) sung to a melody by Andreas Hammerschmidt (1611/12–75). A feature of the hymn text is that the first line, 'Meinen Jesum laß ich nicht', returns as the last line of all six strophes. (Bach had already set the final strophe in Cantata 154 for the same Sunday the previous year, and it was included again in Picander's text for Cantata 157.)

The cantata is scored for SATB, horn, oboe d'amore, strings, and continuo. The autograph score belonged after Bach's death to his son Wilhelm Friedemann, and then to J. G. Nacke (1718–1804), Kantor at Oelsnitz and teacher of C. F. Penzel, who made numerous copies of cantatas and other works by Bach. Penzel's nephew J. G. Schuster (1765–1839, also Kantor at Oelsnitz) acquired it in 1833, and it then passed into the collection of Franz Hauser and, in 1904, was acquired by what is now the Staatsbibliothek zu Berlin.

Unlike the other two extant cantatas for the first Sunday after Epiphany, nos. 32 and 154, the anonymous text of *Meinen Jesum laß ich nicht* makes no reference to the Gospel of the day (Luke 2: 41–52), which tells of the 12-year-old Jesus conversing with the elders in the temple in Jerusalem. Instead it presents a simple declaration of faith in Christ and expounds on the vanity and emptiness of the former lives of all those who have found Christ and followed him. The musical setting reflects the submissive tone of the words: it contains no dramatic episodes, but some *galant* and urbane gestures rare in Bach at his most mystical.

The opening chorus is direct and uncomplicated, in a homophonic style with the soprano cantus firmus doubled by the horn and an instrumental introduction, somewhat in the style of a minuet, which blossoms forth here and there throughout the movement. The oboe d'amore here performs a solo role, and it does again, with string support, in the tenor aria 'Und wenn der harte Todesschlag' (no. 3); this has an interesting and unusual structure, $A^1$–$A^2$–$A^3$ (the sections beginning at bars 9, 35, and 55), with instrumental ritornellos at the beginning, middle (bars 27–34), and end.

The duet for soprano and alto, 'Entziehe dich eilends, mein Herz, der Welt' (no. 5), with continuo accompaniment, is dance-like in character, with the two voice parts proceeding largely in close imitation, and the final chorale strophe is (as usually) plainly harmonized in four parts, with *colla parte* instrumental support. AB

For bibliography, *see* CANTATA, §1.

***Meine Seel erhebt den Herren*** ('My soul doth magnify the Lord'). Cantata for the feast of the Visitation, BWV10, performed on 2 July 1724 as part of Bach's second *Jahrgang* of chorale cantatas, and repeated at least once, some time between 1740 and 1747, with minor revisions. The unknown librettist took over unaltered the text of the German *Magnificat* for movements 1 and 5, and paraphrased the remaining content of the German canticle in movements 2, 3, 4, and 6, with a concluding 'Gloria patri' (in German). For the unaltered words of the German *Magnificat* and 'Gloria patri' Bach used the *tonus peregrinus*, the congregational chant associated with these words in Lutheran tradition.

Movement 1, a celebratory Vivace, is a setting of the first two stanzas of the German *Magnificat*, incorporating the *tonus peregrinus* as the cantus firmus. The opening orchestral ritornello is a trio thematically unrelated to the plainchant, which is given to the sopranos for the first stanza, then to the altos for the second. The ritornello is repeated, with some modification, and then the chorus joins to conclude the movement.

# Meine Seufzer, meine Tränen

In movement 2, an energetic da capo aria, the soprano, representing Mary, sings a paraphrase of the opening of the biblical text. Movement 3 is a chromatic and dissonant tenor recitative, a paraphrase of verses 5 and 6 of the *Magnificat*, with some dramatic pictorialism portraying the proud being blown away like chaff. Movement 4, a bass aria accompanied by continuo, has a distinctive theme in which a shallow incremental ascent is followed by a rapid arpeggiated descent, encompassing two octaves. It is a highly dramatic aria, depicting the unseating of the mighty, the equivalent of 'Deposuit potentes' in Bach's Latin *Magnificat* BWV243, and draws tremendous vigour from the continuo cello's repeated notes and emphatic—almost obsessive—recourse to the instrument's lowest (*C*) string.

Movement 5, a duet for alto and tenor, returns to the unaltered text of the German *Magnificat* with the *tonus peregrinus* chant. Again there are similarities with Bach's Latin *Magnificat*: as in 'Suscepit Israel' in that work, the cantus firmus is instrumental rather than vocal, played by the trumpet in 1724 and by two oboes in the later version. The melody is set against a trio, made up of alto, tenor, and continuo, over a quasi-ostinato bass. Although a relatively short movement it has a sophisticated symmetrical structure (A–B–C–D–C–B–A) and features fugal imitation and invertible counterpoint. An organ transcription of the movement, made perhaps about the same time as the 1740–7 performance of the cantata, was published as no. 4 of the Schübler Chorales.

Movement 6 begins as a simple recitative for the tenor, but at bar 10 the upper strings enter with a gently lapping figure, the ebb and flow of the music depicting the implied waves of the text: 'His [Abraham's] seed must be as great as the sands by the sea'. Movement 7 is what in other cantatas would be the concluding chorale. Here it is a prose rather than a strophic text, the 'Gloria patri' in German, set to the traditional *tonus peregrinus*, which is heard twice in a simple four-part setting.                                      RAL

For bibliography, *see* CANTATA, §1.

***Meine Seufzer, meine Tränen*** ('My sighs, my tears'). Cantata for the second Sunday after Epiphany, BWV13. It belongs to Bach's third Leipzig *Jahrgang* and was first performed on 20 January 1726. The title (or incipit) aptly conveys the affect of the whole text, by the Darmstadt court poet G. C. Lehms. Bach's cantatas not infrequently dwell on the distress and adversity suffered by the faithful Christian, but none is more suffused with pain and sadness than this one. The libretto's only reference to the Gospel reading for the day (John 2: 1–11, telling of Jesus's first miracle

at Cana) is an oblique one, in the first recitative, to the passage 'mine hour is not yet come'. In keeping with the intimate, Pietistic leanings of the text, Bach employs a modest instrumentarium consisting of two recorders and oboe da caccia in addition to the usual strings and continuo.

In the opening tenor aria, to which the woodwind instruments lend a sombre colouring, the singer's sighs and tears are expressed mainly in painful suspensions; beginning in D minor, the tonal course of the music avoids any suggestion of major keys, sinking as far on the flat side as B♭ minor. A complete da capo repeat of the opening section allows the singer to dwell on his suffering. The reason for the distress is revealed in the alto recitative that follows: 'My dear God lets me call in vain'; it closes with a measured, mournful melisma on 'flehen' ('implore').

The arrival at last of a major key (F major) and the entry for the first time of the violins and viola seem to promise a turn to brighter, more optimistic sentiments as the alto, supported in unison by the wind instruments, sings a strophe from Johann Heermann's hymn *Zion klagt mit Angst und Schmerzen* (1636) in long notes while the upper strings separate and accompany the lines with warm, placid, and above all diatonic phrases in quavers and semiquavers. But the text soon turns again to thoughts of 'Traurigkeit' ('sorrow'), and these are intensified in the soprano recitative (no. 4) and still more in the final bass aria, 'Ächzen und erbärmlich Weinen' ('Groaning and pitiful weeping'). Saturated with melodic and harmonic chromaticism, the accompanying instruments (recorders and violin in unison, and continuo) set the mood for what is perhaps the most grief-laden aria that Bach ever wrote. Mention of the 'Freudenlicht' ('joyful light') to be seen by looking towards heaven temporarily relieves the aria of its pall of chromaticism, but a complete subdominant recapitulation of the earlier material (one of Bach's more far-reaching modifications of the traditional da capo form) soon plunges the music into darkness again.

The ninth strophe of Paul Fleming's hymn *In allen meinen Taten* (1641), which ends the cantata, was not included in Lehms's text. It is set by Bach in a straightforward four-part harmonization in B♭ major, but it hardly serves to dispel the disturbing effect of the earlier movements, especially since its melody is inevitably associated in the minds of modern listeners with painful moments in the *St Matthew Passion*.

For bibliography, *see* CANTATA, §1.

***Mein Gott, wie lang, ach lange*** ('My God, how long, ah long'). Cantata for the second Sunday after Epiphany, BWV155, first performed at Weimar on 19 January 1716, and repeated at Leipzig on 16 January 1724. The words are by the Weimar court poet Salomo Franck, and like most of Bach's Weimar cantatas the work is on a small scale, consisting only of two recitatives, a duet, an aria, and a finale chorale. The instrumentation is correspondingly modest, calling only for a bassoon in addition to the normal strings and continuo. The libretto, like that of Cantata 13 for the same Sunday, makes little reference to the Gospel reading for the day (John 2: 1–11), except to dwell on Jesus's statement that 'mine hour is not yet come'. This gives rise to painful feelings that are expressed by the soprano in the opening recitative, accompanied by strings and continuo. Beginning over the repeated quavers of a twelve-bar tonic (D minor) pedal, it ends with elaborate melismatic word-painting for 'Freudenwein' ('wine of joy') and 'sinkt' ('sinks'), as the singer's confidence in God falters.

In the duet (no. 2), for alto and tenor with a remarkably agile bassoon obbligato, the singers answer this despair with a call to trust in Jesus, who will know when the time is right to extend help and comfort, and these sentiments are carried over into the carefully composed bass recitative that follows. Dotted rhythms and wide intervals in both the string accompaniment and the vocal line lend a sprightly character to the soprano aria 'Wirf, mein Herze, wirf dich noch', and confidence is fully restored in the final chorale, a setting in four parts, with instrumental doubling, of the 12th strophe of the hymn *Es ist das Heil uns kommen her* by Paul Speratus (1524).

For bibliography, *see* CANTATA, §1.

**Mein Herze schwimmt im Blut** ('My heart swims in blood'). Cantata for the 11th Sunday after Trinity, BWV199. In 1714 Bach was made *Konzertmeister* at the Weimar court. With this promotion came the responsibility of providing a cantata each month for the Sunday services in the court chapel. Although Bach's surviving Weimar cantatas are comparatively few in number they are none the less striking for their formal, technical, and expressive variety. Some of them, such as no. 21, are expansive in design while others, such as the present cantata, are more modest in their resources and more intimate in expression.

*Mein Herze schwimmt im Blut* was performed at Weimar on 12 August 1714, though in fact it may have been written the previous year. While the Weimar performances were in C minor, Bach transposed the work for subsequent performances at Cöthen and Leipzig into the key of D minor. (For the purposes of this discussion, the Weimar version is considered.) The text, by the Darmstadt court librarian Georg Christian Lehms, is chiefly concerned with repentance and is based on the appointed Gospel reading for the day which tells the story of the Pharisee and the publican (Luke 18: 9–14). The images of torment, though out of tune with modern sensibilities, were in accordance with the Baroque concept of piety. The Darmstadt *Kapellmeister* Christoph Graupner had set the same text two years earlier, and it would appear from resemblances between the two settings that Bach was familiar with Graupner's piece. Although the performance parts of this cantata have long been known, Bach's autograph score was not discovered until 1911, in the Royal Library, Copenhagen.

The cantata is scored for soprano solo with an instrumental ensemble consisting of an oboe, strings, bassoon, and continuo. Its three da capo arias, each preceded by a recitative, are skilfully and affectingly contrasted: the first, with oboe obbligato and continuo, is a poignant, grief-laden supplication in C minor, whose expressive intensity, contained in both the vocal and the instrumental writing, recalls Bach's *Ich hatte viel Bekümmernis*, written only a short while earlier. The second aria, in E♭ major, in which the voice is accompanied by strings and continuo with bassoon, brings Handel to mind with its broad, sweeping gestures. The third, in B♭ major, has the character and rhythm of a gigue and dispels the dark images that dominate the earlier part of the cantata. This one is scored for oboe and strings, bringing the work to a joyful conclusion.

Between the third and fourth recitatives occurs a chorale setting of consummate beauty. Here the soprano declaims the third stanza of Johann Heermann's hymn *Wo soll ich fliehen hin* (1630), set to a melody attributed to Caspar Stieler (1679). The voice is accompanied by an obbligato viola—one of only two instances in the cantatas where the viola is employed in this capacity. An indication of how often Bach performed the work, however, is given by the variety of different instruments he called upon at one time or another to accompany the voice in this chorale. A cello seems to have been used on at least one occasion at Weimar, while a viola da gamba took the part at Cöthen, perhaps reflecting the favoured status enjoyed by an instrument cultivated and played both by Prince Leopold himself and by Christian Ferdinand Abel. At Leipzig a violoncello piccolo was probably the favoured instrument, but we may feel that in this instance Bach's earliest thoughts on the matter offer the most effective solution.                                             NA

For bibliography, *see* CANTATA, §1.

## Mein liebster Jesus ist verloren

**Mein liebster Jesus ist verloren** ('My dearest Jesus is lost'). Cantata for the Sunday after Epiphany, BWV154, first performed on 9 January 1724. In ancient times the feast of the Epiphany was observed with such solemnity that, in answer to the demands of popular devotion, the celebrations were extended for a period of seven days, culminating in a special ceremony which, being eight days away from the feast to which it referred, was known as the octave. This practice, which was of Hebrew origin, became so common—it was observed, for example, at Christmas, Easter, Pentecost, and on many saints' days, as well as at Epiphany—that it led to the idea of bringing together in a special liturgical book the Offices for the octaves that were celebrated in different places and on various occasions. In modern times such celebrations have either been forgotten or have received only nominal observance.

The importance of a feast such as Epiphany, celebrating the manifestation of the Saviour, is reflected in the fact that in the CHURCH CALENDAR the Sundays that follow are numbered from it: the first, second, third, etc. Sunday after Epiphany. The number of Sundays between Epiphany and Septuagesima varies according to the date of Easter, but there are never more than six; cantatas by Bach survive for only the first four.

*Mein liebster Jesus ist verloren* is the earliest of three cantatas by Bach for the Sunday after Epiphany. It was performed again at least once by Bach, probably in January 1737. The autograph score has not survived, but the original parts, which belonged at one time to C. P. E. Bach and then to the Berlin Singakademie, were acquired in 1854 by what is now the Staatsbibliothek zu Berlin. It is scored for SATB, oboe, strings, and continuo. There are reasons for believing it to be a parody of an earlier cantata composed at Weimar before 1717, newly furnished with a text by an unknown author and enriched by the inclusion of two chorale strophes: for no. 3 the second strophe of Martin Jahn's *Jesu, meiner Seelen Wonne* (1661), which uses a melody by Johann Schop (1642); and for no. 8 the sixth strophe of *Meinen Jesum laß ich nicht* by Christian Keymann (1658), to a melody by Andreas Hammerschmidt (also 1658).

If the three arias (nos. 1, 4, and 7) are parodies, the arioso 'Wisset ihr nicht, daß ich sein muß in dem, das meines Vaters ist' is certainly new. In it the bass intones words from the appointed Gospel reading: 'Wist ye not that I must be about my Father's business?' (Luke 2: 49). The text is repeated, as though to unite in the question a reproachful demeanour and feelings of tension and febrile agitation.

It is around this intensely expressive arioso that Bach disposes the other movements of the cantata: the two chorales; the wonderful opening lament for the tenor, with its fragmented ostinato figure in the continuo repeated four times and merging into measured string tremolos before being repeated twice more; the tender alto aria, 'Jesu, laß dich finden', expressly devoid of bold gestures, but with a gentle and subdued melodiousness; and the brilliant duet for alto and tenor, 'Wohl mir, Jesus ist gefunden', with its change of metre to a dance-like 3/8 at the words 'Ich will dich, mein Jesu, nun nimmermehr lassen' ('I shall never again leave thee, my Jesus'). AB

For bibliography, *see* CANTATA, §1.

**Meißner, Christian Gottlob** (bap. 18 Dec. 1707; d. 16 Nov. 1760). Musician, born in Geithain, about 30 km. (19 miles) south-east of Leipzig. He studied with Bach in Leipzig between 1723 and 1729, and during this period he served as one of Bach's principal copyists. He was appointed Kantor at Geithain in 1731, and spent the rest of his life there.

**Mempell, Johann Nicolaus** (b. 10 Dec. 1713; bur. 26 Feb. 1747). Organist, born in Heyda, near Ilmenau, Thuringia. In 1740 he was appointed Kantor at Apolda, where he remained until his death. While in Heyda he may have studied under the Bach devotee Johann Peter Kellner. There is no evidence of a direct connection between Mempell and Bach, but Mempell was one of the main copyists of the so-called Mempell-Preller Collection (located primarily at the Musikbibliothek der Stadt Leipzig), which contains numerous manuscripts of keyboard works by Bach and others. The collection was evidently assembled between 1743 and 1749 by Johann Gottlieb PRELLER (possibly a pupil of Mempell), who added his copies to those made in the 1730s by Mempell himself. RTS

P. Krause, *Handschriften der Werke Johann Sebastian Bachs in der Musikbibliothek der Stadt Leipzig* (Leipzig, 1964), 29–42; H.-J. Schulze, *Studien zur Bach-Überlieferung im 18. Jahrhundert* (Leipzig, 1984), 30–56; H.-J. Schulze, 'Wie entstand die Bach-Sammlung Mempell-Preller?', *BJb* 60 (1974), 104–22.

**Menantes.** Pen-name of HUNOLD, CHRISTIAN FRIEDRICH.

**Mendelssohn (Bartholdy), Felix** (b. 3 Feb. 1809; d. 4 Nov. 1847). Composer, pianist, and conductor, born in Hamburg. Mendelssohn's enthusiasm for Bach's music was deeply rooted in his family. His paternal grandfather, the renowned philosopher Moses Mendelssohn, as well as his maternal grandmother Bella Salomon, had both been students of J. P. Kirnberger. Bella Salomon was a member of the Itzig family, who had been influential patrons of the Bach sons and important collectors of the works of the entire Bach family.

Mendelssohn grew up in Berlin, where, beginning in 1819, he received a solid musical education from C. F. Zelter, the director of the Singakademie. Through the enormous music library of the Singakademie and through Zelter's guidance, Mendelssohn soon became well acquainted with Bach's compositions. While Mendelssohn's name is firmly connected with his famous 'centenary' performance of the *St Matthew Passion* on 11 March 1829, there are numerous other aspects of his reception of Bach's music. Apart from this début, he conducted works by Bach throughout his life, particularly as director of the Leipzig Gewandhaus. As a performer, he regularly played Bach's keyboard concertos on the piano, and as an editor he published several of the organ works. The influence of Bach's music on his own compositions can best be seen in his chorale cantatas. With his practical and scholarly interests, Mendelssohn was one of the most influential figures in the conception of the first complete edition of Bach's works. PW

S. Großmann-Vendrey, *Felix Mendelssohn Bartholdy und die Musik der Vergangenheit* (Regensburg, 1969); F. Krummacher, 'Bach, Berlin und Mendelssohn', *Jahrbuch des Staatlichen Instituts für Musikforschung Preußischer Kulturbesitz 1993*, 44–78; P. Wollny, 'Sara Levy and the Making of Musical Taste in Berlin', *Musical Quarterly*, 77 (1993), 651–88.

**Mer hahn en neue Oberkeet.** Textual incipit of the PEASANT CANTATA.

**Mettenchor** ('Mattins Choir'). The Lüneburg *Mettenchor* was a group of around 12 to 15 singers drawn from pupils at the Michaelisschule who enjoyed free board and lodging for their musical services at the Michaeliskirche. The choir had access to one of the finest Lutheran libraries of the age, containing Italian music dating back to the beginning of the 17th century, together with works by the most up-to-date German figures. Bach entered the choir in March 1700 (together with his schoolfellow from Ohrdruf, Georg Erdmann) and left some two years later. J. N. Forkel, who spent a year in Lüneburg as a chorister, wrote of his disgust at the dissolution of the choir towards the end of the 18th century. *See also* LÜNEBURG. JAB

**Michaeliskirche** (St Michael's Church). Name of the church in Ohrdruf where Bach's eldest brother Johann Christoph (ii) was organist from 1690 to 1721. It was built as an extension of the earlier Bonifatiuskapelle in 1421, and burnt down in 1753. Rebuilt by 1760, it was almost completely destroyed by fire a second time, and again rebuilt, early in the 19th century; finally, an air-raid in 1945 left only the tower standing.

When J. S. Bach left Ohrdruf in 1700 he went from one Michaeliskirche to another, this time at Lüneburg. The Michaeliskirche there was completed in 1415–18. It has the oldest peal of bells in Germany, dating from about 1491.

M. Petzoldt, *Bachstätten aufsuchen* (Leipzig, 1992), 116–24, 159–62.

**Mietke, Michael** (d. 1719). Harpsichord and harp maker, born in Cölln, near Berlin. He was instrument maker to the Prussian court. In 1719 the court at Cöthen, presumably on Bach's recommendation, purchased a large two-manual harpsichord by Mietke. His good reputation in Bach's circle is confirmed by his inclusion as one of the few instrument makers in J. G. Walther's *Musicalisches Lexicon* (Leipzig, 1732, p. 405). Only one harpsichord signed by Mietke is extant, a one-manual instrument of 1710 with two 8′ stops and compass *GG* to *c'''*, now in Sweden. Two unsigned harpsichords in Schloß Charlottenburg, Berlin, one similar to the 1710 instrument, the other with two manuals, are attributed to Mietke. The latter instrument has the standard disposition with 8′, 8′, and 4′ stops, but Mietke or his sons are known also to have made harpsichords with 16′ stops. JK

D. H. Boalch, *Makers of the Harpsichord and Clavichord* (3rd edn., ed. C. Mould, Oxford, 1995); S. Germann, 'The Mietkes, the Margrave and Bach', in P. Williams, ed., *Bach, Handel, Scarlatti: Tercentenary Essays* (Cambridge, 1985), 119–48; H. Heyde, *Musikinstrumentenbau in Preussen* (Tutzing, 1994); A. Kilström, 'The Hudiksvall Mietke', *Harpsichord & Fortepiano*, 5/1 (Oct. 1994), 15–18; D. Krickeberg and H. Rase, 'Beiträge zur Kenntnis des mittel- und norddeutschen Cembalobaus um 1700', in F. Hellwig, ed., *Studia organologica: Festschrift für John Henry van der Meer* (Tutzing, 1987), 285–310.

**minuet.** A dance of French origin popular in the 17th and 18th centuries, and an instrumental form derived from its musical accompaniment (*see* DANCE). The minuet symbolizes more than any other dance the ideals of nonchalance, elegance, subtlety, and nobility of the French court. The earliest forms of both music and dance may be found from the 1660s on at the court of Louis XIV. The wide variety of its styles throughout Europe and the Americas has yet to be fully explored by scholars.

The dance in its classic form, described by Pierre Rameau in *Le Maître à danser* (Paris, 1725), uses minuet step patterns of four tiny steps set to two bars of music in 3/4 time. Several different step patterns were normally employed throughout the dance, resulting in subtle counter-rhythms between the varying patterns of the steps and the music. For example, an emphasis in the dance steps might occur on the third count of a

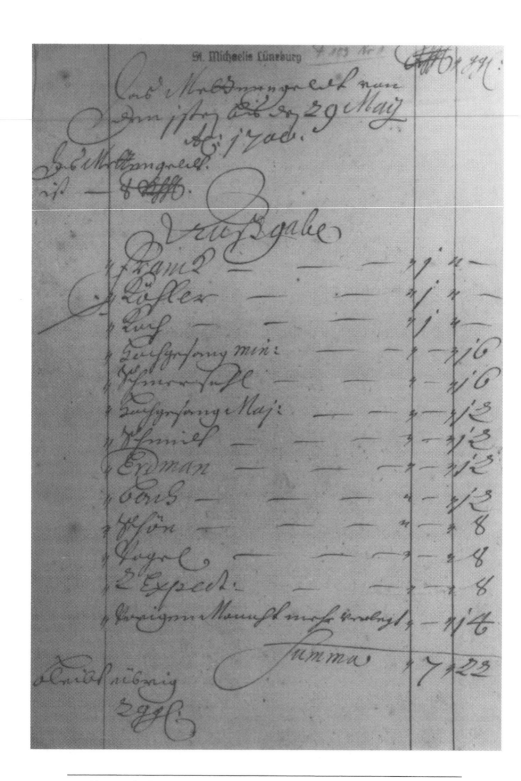

Bach's name (and above it that of Georg Erdmann) in the list of Mettenchor singers at the Michaelisschule, Lüneburg, May 1700 (Stadtarchiv Lüneburg)

Interior of the Michaeliskirche, Lüneburg, where Bach sang as a member of the
Mettenchor; from a painting by J. Burmeister, *c.*1700

bar, forming a counter-rhythm to the downbeat of the following bar in the music.

Floor patterns in the minuet included a 'Z' figure, in which the dancing couple faced each other from opposite ends of a 'Z', passing each other in the middle as they traced the 'Z'. A complete minuet would require 100–20 bars of music, meaning that a single bipartite piece in phrases of, for example, 8 + 8 bars, would not suffice. Thus it was normal practice to use at least two bipartite pieces, repeating them as necessary to complete the performance.

Minuet music is set in bars of 3/4, but the true metre is 6/4, where the beat is the dotted minim, below which move crotchets and duple groups of quavers. Points of repose are on beats two and four. Phrases are balanced in groups of 4 + 4 bars, with frequent use of hemiola, and the tempo is moderate.

Forty-five titled minuets by Bach survive. Early ones appear in an undated (and perhaps inauthentic) flute sonata BWV1033, the keyboard Ouverture in F major BWV820, the Sinfonia in F major BWV1046a (an early version of the First Brandenburg Concerto), and the English Suite no. 4. Later came minuets for solo violin (Partita no. 3), solo cello (Suites nos. 1 and 3), one, or maybe two, in the Clavierbüchlein for W. F. Bach of 1720, the wonderful minuet with its trios which concludes the First Brandenburg Concerto, the pair from the Orchestral Suite in C major, and those in the French Suites nos. 1, 2, 3, 4, and 6. Later minuets include those in the keyboard Partitas nos. 1, 4, and 5, and in the Orchestral Suites in B minor and D major BWV1069.

Most of these minuets are in the French style, with dances in pairs of two to be played ALTERNATIVEMENT. The pairs usually contrast sharply in style, texture, instrumentation, mode, or key, and are based so strictly on a four-bar phrase that they could easily accompany dancing. Conjunct quavers sound well as notes inégales (see RHYTHM). Exceptions are pieces in Italian style, such as the 'tempo di minuetto' of the G major keyboard Partita. It uses ternary groups of quavers instead of duple groups in a prelude-like style, with arpeggio figuration, five feminine cadences and long harmonic sequences. The secular cantata Durchlauchtster Leopold contains a duet for soprano and bass marked 'Al tempo di minuetto'.　　NJ, MEL

For bibliography, see DANCE.

**mirror canon.** A type of CANON which involves the leading voice being played alongside its own retrograde inversion (i.e. upside-down and backwards). The realization from the 'closed' (unrealized) form can be effected by turning the page upside-down, finding a starting-point for the second voice, and beginning its retrograde there alongside the already progressing first voice. The canon a 2 'Quaerendo invenietis' from the Musical Offering, BWV1079: 4i, is a fine example of the process. In its original closed form the alto clef and an upside-down bass clef indicate both the mirror procedure and the appropriate pitches of the voices for the purpose of realization.　　LC

**mirror fugue.** A FUGUE, or rather two fugues, one of which is the mirror image of the other. It is as though a mirror were placed above or below an existing fugue, producing inversions of each interval in each part, as well as inverting the position of the parts within the texture, so that, for example, the topmost part in one fugue is inverted to produce the lowest part in the other. This is well demonstrated by the two four-part fugues of Contrapunctus 12 in The Art of Fugue. The two three-part fugues of Contrapunctus 13 exhibit a similar relationship to each other, but this cannot strictly be called a mirror fugue, since the position of each inverted part is not itself inverted in the texture, SAB becoming not BAS, but BSA.　　LC

**Misericordias Domini.** In the CHURCH CALENDAR, the second Sunday after Easter. It takes its name from the introit to the Mass for that day in the Latin rite, beginning 'Misericordias Domini plena est terra'.

*missa.* See opposite.

*Mit Fried und Freud ich fahr dahin* ('In peace and joy I journey forth'). Cantata for the feast of the Purification, BWV125, first performed on 2 February 1725. The cantata sets an anonymous libretto based on the versification by Luther (1524) of the Canticle of Simeon (Luke 2: 29–32), which forms part of the Gospel for the day. Luther's hymn uses a single verse from the biblical text as the basis for each of its four strophes, and Bach's librettist expanded this into a more suitable format for a six-movement cantata by leaving Luther's first and final strophes unaltered (movements 1 and 6), adding interpolations in recitative style to the second strophe (movement 3), and adding freely constructed material for the intervening movements (2, 4, and 5). Alfred Dürr points to other biblical references in the libretto (in DürrK), notably to St Mark 16: 16 (movement 3) and Romans 3: 25 (movement 4). It is clear from the surviving performance material that a later performance took place some time after 1735. Cantata 125 is one of five known Bach cantatas for the Purification, the others being nos. 82, 83, 157, and 158.

[cont. on p.300]

Latin word for 'mass'. In Lutheran usage by Bach's time it referred to the first two parts of the Ordinary of the mass—the Kyrie and Gloria. Other terms have been employed to distinguish this abbreviated form from the full Roman Ordinary (Kyrie, Gloria, Credo, Sanctus, and Agnus Dei), including 'missa brevis', 'Kurzmesse' ('short mass'), 'Kleine Messe' ('small mass'), and 'Lutheran mass', but these reflect later usage. In the earlier 18th century 'missa' was the common term employed in Lutheran Germany, although 'Kyrie' was sometimes used, as Bach did on the covers of Cantatas 61 and 62 (see *BDok* i. 248 and 250). Here Bach was following the practice of contemporary hymnals that frequently included both Kyrie and Gloria under a single number. For example, in Vopelius's *Neu Leipziger Gesangbuch* (1682) the Kyrie and Gloria appear sequentially together under the heading 'Missa, oder, das Kyrie Eleison'.

Luther's liturgical reform had a bilingual aspect. His *Formula missae* (1523) was an evangelical reform of the Latin Mass. In 16th-century Wittenberg and other places where there were universities or Latin schools the Latin evangelical Mass frequently included polyphonic settings of all five parts of the Ordinary. First generation Lutheran composers generally did not compose mass cycles, since there were numerous examples by Catholic composers readily available, whose continued use posed no theological problem. However, when they did compose mass settings, all five parts of the Ordinary were included, following Catholic models.

Luther's German liturgy, *Deutsche Messe* (1526), introduced the concept of hymnic substitutes for the Ordinary (*see* HAUPTGOTTESDIENST). While the hymnic Gloria and Credo were regularly sung, the Kyrie was sung in a variety of forms and the German Sanctus and Agnus Dei became optional. Later Lutheran liturgical orders were generally conflations of Luther's two liturgical forms, with the first half of the eucharistic liturgy following more closely the Latin *Formula missae* and the second half approximating to the provisions of the vernacular *Deutsche Messe*. Thus the Kyrie and Gloria were retained as a regular feature of the evangelical Mass, and in larger towns and cities were sung in Latin by the choir, after which the congregation sang the hymnic version of the Gloria, *Allein Gott in der Höh sei Ehr*. The congregational credal hymn *Wir glauben all an einen Gott* was always sung, and the German Sanctus and Agnus Dei were options that could be sung during communion. Musical settings of the Latin Credo, Sanctus, and Agnus Dei were used less regularly, and were heard only at festivals or on other special occasions. Thus the regular weekly Lutheran *missa* was effectively reduced to the Kyrie and Gloria.

For normal Sunday use Vopelius included plainchant melodies for the Latin Missa: Kyrie (Vatican XVIII) and Gloria (Vatican XII). On the primary festivals of the Church year, such as Advent Sunday, Christmas, Easter, Ascension, Pentecost, and Trinity, as well as at several other celebrations, a concerted *missa* was customary during Bach's time in Leipzig. Such settings were the culmination of a long tradition of Lutheran *missae* that began with the polychoral concertato style of Hans Leo Haßler (1562–1612), Bartholomäus Gesius (? *c*.1560–1613), and especially the *Missodia* (1611) of Michael Praetorius (*c*.1571–1621) and ultimately led to the Baroque concerted style of Telemann, Bach, and their contemporaries.

Bach is known to have written six *missae* between 1733 and 1747/8, including the fragmentary BWV Anh. II 29. The orchestral and vocal parts of the first of these,

BWV232[1], later incorporated into the MASS IN B MINOR, were sent to the new Elector of Saxony, Frederick Augustus II, with a request, dated 27 July 1733, for the honorary title of Saxon court composer. Bach's purpose was to confirm his rights in a series of disputes with officials in Leipzig concerning his responsibilities in the city. That he sent a Lutheran *missa* to the Catholic ruler might suggest that he originally composed it for performance in Leipzig some time before July 1733. Bach wrote a three-fold Kyrie, following Luther's *Deutsche Messe*, and a jubilant Gloria which uses music parodied from earlier works. Even if these settings had not been incorporated into the B minor Mass, they would still be regarded as the peak of the Lutheran concerted *missa*.

In the decade between 1737–8 and 1747–8 Bach wrote a further five *missae*, BWV233–6, and Anh. II 29. Earlier scholars were inclined to dismiss the four complete Lutheran *missae* as of less value than other vocal music by Bach because they were mostly parodied from other works. But the B minor Mass is also substantially a parodied work, and it has nevertheless been accorded universal praise. The four *missae* are in fact more important than earlier Bach scholarship suggested. Bach worked on them in the period following the creation of the *Christmas Oratorio* (a cycle of six cantatas with many parodied movements) and around the same time that he was working on definitive versions of such works as the Passions and the *Magnificat* and compiling cycles of music such as the Schübler Chorales and the second part of *The Well-tempered Clavier*. They therefore form part of his continuing concern to organize his compositional output into coherent collections of related pieces. But Bach was probably motivated by practical concerns as well. Cantatas composed for the individual Sundays and festivals in the Church calendar were closely associated with the occasion for which they were written and could usually be performed only once in any year. But if movements from various cantatas were reworked into settings of the Kyrie and Gloria, then the music could be performed several times in any year, because such concerted settings were required in Leipzig at the major festivals and other celebrations.

The four *missae* BWV233–66 comprise 24 movements, 19 of which are known parodies from ten cantatas written between July 1723 and January 1727; the first 'Kyrie eleison' of BWV233 was also taken from an earlier work (see Table 1).

TABLE 1. The *Missae* BWV233–6: origins and structure

| Missa | Section | Original version |
|---|---|---|
| Missa in F major BWV233 | 1. Kyrie | Kyrie eleison BWV233a |
| | 2. Gloria in excelsis | ? |
| | 3. Domine Deus, rex coelestis | ? |
| | 4. Qui tollis peccata mundi | Cantata 102:3, 'Weh! der Seele' |
| | 5. Quoniam tu solus sanctus | Cantata 102:5, 'Erschrecke doch' |
| | 6. Cum sancto Spiritu | Cantata 40:1, 'Darzu ist erschienen' |
| Missa in A major BWV234 | 1. Kyrie | ? |
| | 2. Gloria in excelsis | Cantata 67:6, 'Friede sei mit euch' |
| | 3. Domine Deus, rex coelestis | ? |
| | 4. Qui tollis peccata mundi | Cantata 179:5, 'Liebster Gott, erbarme dich' |
| | 5. Quoniam tu solus sanctus | Cantata 79:2, 'Gott ist unsre Sonn und Schild' |
| | 6. Cum sancto Spiritu | Cantata 136:1, 'Erforsche mich, Gott' |
| Missa in G minor BWV235 | 1. Kyrie | Cantata 102:1, 'Herr, deine Augen' |
| | 2. Gloria in excelsis | Cantata 72:1, 'Alles nur nach Gottes Willen' |
| | 3. Gratias agimus tibi | Cantata 187:4, 'Darum sollt ihr nicht sorgen' |
| | 4. Domine Fili unigenite | Cantata 187:3, 'Du Herr, du krönst allein' |

| Missa | Section | Original version |
|---|---|---|
| | 5. Quoniam tu solus sanctus | Cantata 187:5, 'Gott versorget alles Leben' |
| | 6. Cum sancto Spiritu | Cantata 187:1, 'Es wartet alles auf dich' |
| Missa in G major | 1. Kyrie | Cantata 179:1, 'Siehe zu, daß deine Gottesfurcht' |
| BWV236 | 2. Gloria in excelsis | Cantata 79:1, 'Gott der Herr ist Sonn und Schild' |
| | 3. Gratias agimus tibi | Cantata 138:5, 'Auf Gott steht meine Zuversicht' |
| | 4. Domine Deus, agnus Dei | Cantata 79:5, 'Gott, ach Gott, verlaß die Deinen' |
| | 5. Quoniam tu solus sanctus | Cantata 179:3, 'Falscher Heuchler Ebenbild' |
| | 6. Cum sancto Spiritu | Cantata 17:1, 'Wer Dank opfert' |

The four *missae* and the larger-scale 1733 *missa* share a similar structure, conditioned by the theological content of the texts. The four *missae* each begin with a Kyrie movement and continue with a symmetrical, five-movement Gloria in which a central aria (in BWV236 a duet) is framed by two arias and two choruses. The central Gloria movements (including that of BWV232[1]) are settings of 'Domine Fili unigenite', 'Domine Deus, agnus Dei', or its relative clause 'Qui tollis peccata mundi'. The *missae* thus are musical expositions of the traditional Latin texts that focus on the meaning (mercy and forgiveness) of the Eucharist, of which they form an important and integral part. That all these central Gloria movements are parodies of earlier music diminishes neither the creativity of the composer nor the integrity of his liturgical music.

Bach is also known to have composed two separate *missa* movements. In Weimar, some time between 1708 and 1717, he wrote the Kyrie movement BWV233a that also uses the German Agnus Dei, *Christe, du Lamm Gottes*; as Table 1 shows, this Kyrie was incorporated into the *Missa* in F. In Leipzig some time between 1727 and 1732 he composed a setting in G minor of 'Christe eleison' for soprano, alto, and continuo (BWV242) to be inserted into a mass by Francesco Durante.

Bach also performed *missae* by other composers in the worship of the churches in Leipzig. Some time around 1727 he performed the *Missa* in E minor BWV Anh. III 166, composed most likely by Johann Nicolaus Bach (1669–1753); it includes the melody *Allein Gott in der Höh sei Ehr* sung by the second sopranos above a four-part choral fugue with the Latin text 'Gloria in excelsis Deo'. Of particular interest is his use of mass compositions by Durante, G. B. Bassani, and Palestrina, in which he was following a long-standing Lutheran practice of using masses composed by Catholics. Bach copied out the complete score of Palestrina's *Missa sine nomine* about 1742, but only the Kyrie and Gloria were supplied with orchestral parts. This indicates that Bach's practical use of Catholic mass settings conformed to current Lutheran liturgical practice.                                                                                    RAL

*See also* MASS.

R. A. Leaver, 'Parody and Theological Consistency: Notes on Bach's A Major Mass', *Bach*, 21/3 (Winter 1990), 30–3; R. A. Leaver, 'The Mature Vocal Works and their Theological and Liturgical Context', in J. Butt, ed., *The Cambridge Bach Companion* (Cambridge, 1997), 86–122; A. Mann, 'Bach's A Major Mass: A Nativity Mass?', in R. L. Weaver, ed., *Essays on the Music of J. S. Bach and Other Divers Subjects: A Tribute to Gerhard Herz* (Louisville, Ky, 1981), 43–7; A. Mann, ' "Missa Brevis" and "Historia": Bach's A Major Mass', *Bach*, 16/1 (Jan. 1985), 6–11; P. Steinitz, 'Bach's Lutheran Masses', *Musical Times*, 109 (1968), 231–3.

BWV125 is scored for SATB with 'corno' (possibly a slide trumpet), flute, oboe (doubling on oboe d'amore), strings, and continuo. The first of its six movements is in the normal chorale fantasia form, with the melody in the soprano (doubled by the 'corno') accompanied by thematic work in the lower voices. The accompanying material is, as usual, based on the opening ritornello, which sets the tone of the movement in a lilting 12/8 metre which, together with the E minor tonality, inevitably recalls the first chorus of the St Matthew Passion. The opening flute figure, a florid elaboration of an ascending 5th, can be seen as reference to the opening of the first line of the chorale tune. The rest of the material is based on gentle, slurred quaver figures and persistent octave leaps. The high point in the tonal drama comes at the words 'sanft und stille' ('soft and still'), which Bach sets as a sudden slowing-down of the motion, combined with sepulchral low registers in the voice parts and an abrupt turn to the minor, suggested by thoughts of approaching death. The motion slows for a second time at the last line, 'Der Tod ist mein Schlaf worden' ('Death has become my sleep'), which is followed by the final repetition of the ritornello.

The second movement, 'Ich will auch mit gebrochnen Augen', is an aria for alto in B minor, accompanied by obbligato flute and oboe d'amore. It is in ritornello form, with persistent dotted rhythms and sighing appoggiaturas (the latter specifically notated only in the later, revised version) in 3rds and 6ths over a pulsating bass. The following accompanied bass recitative is interpolated with entries of each line of the chorale (strophe 2 in Luther's original), to which the recitative text acts as a commentary. The string accompaniment is mainly dominated by a characteristic 'joy' figure based on a neighbour note and an ascending leap, but at the end of the movement the tone darkens, and the last line, 'im Tod und auch im Sterben' ('in death and also in dying') is set to a writhing chromatic melisma. The fourth movement, 'Ein unbegreiflich Licht', is a duet for tenor and bass with violins and continuo, the violins carrying on a lively trio sonata-like dialogue counterpointed against the voices. A characteristic feature is a long winding melisma on the word 'Kreis' ('orbit'), which forms sequences in parallel 6ths and 10ths between the two voices. The B section of the da capo form (ending in B minor) makes a feature of rapid rebounding imitations suggested by the line 'Es schallet kräftig fort und fort' ('There echoes strongly, on and on'). A short alto recitative leads to the final chorale, strophe 4 of Luther's original, which is set in plain style.

DLH

For bibliography, see CANTATA, §1.

**Mizler von Kolof, Lorenz Christoph** (b. 25 July 1711; d. March 1778). Musical scholar, composer, and littérateur, born in Heidenheim, Württemberg, about 30 km. north of Ulm. He studied at Leipzig University (1731–4) and was a pupil of Bach. In 1736 he founded a periodical, the *Neu eröffnete musikalische Bibliothek*, which survived until 1754, appearing in four volumes with several fascicles. In 1738 he founded a Correspondirenden Societät der Musicalischen Wissenschaften ('Corresponding Society of Musical Sciences') whose members eventually included Telemann, G. H. Stölzel, Handel, C. H. Graun, G. A. Sorge, and 14 others; Leopold Mozart (1719–87) was invited to become its 20th member. Bach joined in 1747, presenting on admission his *Canon triplex* BWV1076 and the Canonic Variations on *Vom Himmel hoch*.

The regulations of Mizler's society, which, like his journal, remained in operation until 1754, required each member to pay an annual subscription of 2 thaler, to remain in correspondence with other members, and to send to the secretary (Mizler) at least once a year a scientific communication following the philosophical principles of Christian Wolff (1679–1754) and the literary style of J. C. Gottsched. The scientific communication could take the form of a speculative musical composition, and members older than 65 were excused it altogether. It was also a requirement of the society that each member should present his portrait in oil (Bach's portrait, painted by E. G. Haußmann in 1746, is the only one known to survive) and bequeath to the society a portion of his estate. The society, for its part, undertook to produce the member's obituary and to furnish the text of an ode or cantata in his honour, both of which would be published, along with his portrait, in the *Musikalische Bibliothek*. Bach's OBITUARY duly appeared in the journal in 1754.

As his own contribution for 1748, Bach sent to the society the *Musical Offering*, and for the following year his composition in lieu of a scientific dissertation was probably to have been what was eventually called *Die Kunst der Fuge* ('The Art of Fugue'). Each of Bach's works connected in one way or another with Mizler's society has strong esoteric and enigmatic connotations and uses variation and contrapuntal rigour as the basis of its construction.

Mizler's interest in the scientific aspects of music extended to methods of tuning. He considered Werckmeister's temperament to be the best of its time, but thought that Neidhardt had subsequently improved on it. As regards Mizler's own music, all that remains are the first three vol-

umes of a four-volume collection of keyboard works entitled *Sammlung auserlesener moralischer Oden* (Leipzig, 1740–6), a unique exemplar of which belonged to Dragan Plamenac (1895–1983).
AB

A. Basso, *L'invenzione della gioia: musica e massoneria nell'età dei Lumi* (Milan, 1994); J. Birke, *Christian Wolffs Metaphysik und die zeitgenössische Literatur und Musiktheorie* (Berlin, 1966); D. Plamenac, Introduction to *Lorenz Mizler: Sammlungen auserlesener moralischer Oden* (facsimile, Leipzig, 1972); F. Wöhlke, *Lorenz Christoph Mizler: ein Beitrag zur musikalischen Gelehrtengeschichte des 18. Jahrhunderts* (Würzburg, 1940).

### Mohrheim, Friedrich Christian Samuel (b. 26 April 1719; d. 1780).

Musician, born in Neumark, about 25 km. (15 miles) south-west of Erfurt in Thuringia. He studied with Bach in Leipzig from 1733 to 1736 and, like other Bach pupils, acted as copyist for him. He was later appointed *Kapellmeister* at Danzig, where he died.

### Möller manuscript.

An important early manuscript source (Staatsbibliothek zu Berlin, Mus. ms. 40644) for 12 keyboard compositions by Bach, including the Capriccio on the Departure of his Most Beloved Brother. Named after one of its former owners, Johann Gottfried Möller (1774–1833), the manuscript represents an anthology of German keyboard music from around 1700. It contains works by Böhm, Bruhns, Buxtehude, Reincken, and F. W. Zachow (1663–1712), as well as keyboard transcriptions of orchestral music by J.-B. Lully (1632–87) and the Italian Agostino Steffani (1654–1728). The compiler and principal scribe has been identified as Bach's eldest brother and keyboard teacher, Johann Christoph (ii). He evidently began to assemble the volume about 1703 and completed it about 1707. In copying the organ chorale *Wie schön leuchtet der Morgenstern* BWV739, he appears to have worked from the surviving autograph. In copying the other J. S. Bach compositions he probably worked from autographs now lost. The anthology, which contains an incomplete autograph of the Prelude and Fugue in G minor BWV535a, is closely related to the ANDREAS BACH BOOK, another early source compiled by Johann Christoph Bach.
RTS

R. Hill, 'The Möller Manuscript and the Andreas Bach Book: Two Keyboard Anthologies from the Circle of the Young Johann Sebastian Bach' (diss., Harvard University, 1987); R. Hill, ed., *Keyboard Music from the Andreas Bach Book and the Möller Manuscript* (Cambridge, Mass., 1991); H.-J. Schulze, *Studien zur Bach-Überlieferung im 18. Jahrhundert* (Leipzig, 1984), 30–56.

**motet.** See overleaf.

### motet style.

A musical style which exhibits features characteristic of a motet. Bach used motet style in choruses in his church cantatas, Passions, and Latin church music. In the cantatas he used motet style for texts that would have been appropriate in a motet proper; in the Passions its use follows a traditional association between motet style and the TURBA chorus; its use in Latin works reflects the musical connections between motet style and the *stile antico*.

Motets and motet-style movements use biblical texts, chorales, or a combination of the two. The most important musical features include large note values (*alla breve* time signature), prominent use of counterpoint, and—most striking in a concerted vocal work—no independent instrumental parts. In most motet-style movements instruments play *colla parte* with the voices, as they often did in motets. Many use cornetts and trombones, which were strongly associated with motet style.

In his church cantatas, Bach often drew on motet style for chorales (BWV2:1, 4:5, 14:1, 28:2, 38:1, 80:1, 121:1, and 182:7); in these pieces the chorale melody is presented as a cantus firmus in one voice, supported by imitative counterpoint based on the chorale in the other voices. Bach chose motet style almost exclusively for the oldest chorale melodies, suggesting that the style held strong historical associations for him.

Bach also used motet style for biblical SPRUCH texts, often abstract theological statements or texts of neutral affect (BWV29:2, 64:1, 68:5, 71:3, 108:4, 144:1, and 179:1). These settings all use imitative counterpoint, often giving each phrase of the text its own musical treatment.

BWV21:9 combines a biblical text and a related chorale in a classic motet. Some cantata movements use motet style for only part of a movement (e.g. BWV76:1, beginning in concerted style and changing to motet style). In others Bach combined motet and concerted styles (e.g. BWV101:1, which embeds a motet-style chorale setting in a concerto texture).

In Bach's mass settings motet style appears alongside the closely related *stile antico*. Some motet-style mass movements are parodies of motet-style cantata movements (e.g. 'Gratias agimus tibi' and 'Dona nobis pacem' in the Mass in B minor). In the *Magnificat* motet style appears both in biblical texts ('Sicut locutus est') and in a chorale interpolation (*Vom Himmel hoch*). In Bach's Passions some of the *turbae* display certain features of motet style, a legacy of older Passion treatments.
DRM

D. Melamed, *J. S. Bach and the German Motet* (Cambridge, 1995).

# motet

A polyphonic composition, or sometimes one for solo voice and accompaniment, usually with a sacred text; the term has been in use since the 13th century for many different types of composition, secular as well as sacred. To a German speaker in Bach's time a motet was a sacred vocal composition using no independent instruments—that is, only basso continuo and perhaps instruments doubling the vocal lines. In French and Italian usage the term came to refer to almost any sacred vocal composition, including those with independent instruments (vocal concertos); Bach used the term a few times in this sense for other composers' works and for his Mühlhausen cantata *Gott ist mein König*.

Bach and his contemporaries understood the term 'motet' to refer not only to modern compositions but also to polyphonic motets of the 16th and 17th centuries (by Orlande de Lassus, Andreas Hammerschmidt, and others); motet style was thus seen as closely related to the *stile antico*, the language of these older pieces. A part of this repertory—mostly for eight-voice double choir—lived on in motet collections such as the *Florilegium Portense*, which remained in print and in liturgical use in Bach's time. The motets of Bach and his contemporaries thus drew on longstanding traditions of biblical motets and polyphonic chorale settings, and probably carried strong historical connotations. Motets were particularly associated with the region of Thuringia where the Bach family lived and worked, and J. S. Bach's ancestors Johann Michael and Johann Christoph (i) were among its most important cultivators.

By Bach's time the motet had been largely eclipsed in the realm of sacred vocal music by the vocal concerto (cantata), from which it differed primarily in its lack of independent instrumental parts, free poetic texts, and solo singing. None the less, German-language motets remained in regular use in smaller towns, especially in the Christmas season, and in larger communities for special occasions.

Motets drew on two types of text: pithy biblical passages known as *Sprüche* or *dicta*, and chorales (together with their melodies). Motets could use one of these types, or both in a combination selected to make a theological point. In motets with combined texts the biblical text is typically presented first, then repeated as accompaniment to a cantus firmus chorale melody in long notes in the uppermost voice. Eight-part double choir motets often contract to four parts in the chorale section.

Bach's earliest surviving motets, *Ich lasse dich nicht* (ii) and *Fürchte dich nicht* (the first and probably also the second from his Weimar years), combine biblical and chorale texts in the traditional manner described above, though with more extensive counterpoint in the chorale sections than was typical. Biblical texts and chorales are combined in alternating movements in the Leipzig-period motets *Jesu, meine Freude* and *Singet dem Herrn ein neues Lied* (ii); in the latter, the chorale is combined with a free text labelled 'aria'. Purely biblical texts are found in *Der Geist hilft unser Schwachheit auf*—the concluding chorale is probably only tenuously related to the motet—and in *Lobet den Herrn, alle Heiden*, whose authenticity and status as a motet are both open to question. A chorale text alone is found in the two versions of *O Jesu Christ, meins Lebens Licht*, where imitative lower voices support a cantus firmus, and a chorale-like poem in *Komm, Jesu, komm*, treated, paradoxically, line by line in the manner of a biblical text.

The extent of Bach's motet output is unclear, but was probably larger than the handful of surviving pieces. Two of his motets known to date from his Leipzig years, *Der Geist hilft unser Schwachheit auf* and *Jesu, meine Freude*, are probably reworkings of older material. Bach's motets were long said all to be Leipzig works, but in fact they span nearly his entire career, from at least 1712/13 (*Ich lasse dich nicht*) to 1746/7 (the second version of *O Jesu Christ, meins Lebens Licht*).

Bach's motets owe their scoring, text selection, overall construction, and dominance of homophonic texture to the tradition of the German motet, but they also show the sophistication of his contrapuntal language, illustrated by the injection of fugal writing in the early motets and the full-blown fugues in others, particularly *Singet dem Herrn*. They also show the influence of other musical types; for example, the multi-movement construction of *Singet dem Herrn* and *Jesu, meine Freude* suggests the structure of the vocal concerto, and the fast–slow–fast organization of the former hints at the Italian instrumental concerto.

The specific purposes for which Bach composed his motets are largely unknown. *Der Geist hilft unser Schwachheit auf* was performed in connection with the burial of a Rector of the Thomasschule in 1729; the text of *Komm, Jesu, komm* suggests a funeral or memorial service as well; and it has been suggested that *O Jesu Christ, meins Lebens Licht* was for a funeral procession. But the speculative assignments of the other motets to Leipzig funerals and to various other occasions—New Year's Day, Weißenfels birthdays, and Reformation Day—are not tenable; we do not know when Bach performed most of his motets.

The performance practice of Bach's motets has been a matter of debate. Contemporary writings and other evidence make it clear that there were several possibilities, of which unaccompanied performance was perhaps the least likely. Basso continuo—keyboard and string bass—was almost certainly used, and there is extensive evidence from Bach's own practice for doubling the vocal lines with instruments. We have Bach's original performing parts for *Der Geist hilft unser Schwachheit auf,* which include *colla parte* strings on one choir and woodwinds on the other, as well as his performing material for a motet by Johann Christoph Bach (i) and one by Sebastian Knüpfer similarly disposed.

Instruments also play a role in the two versions of *O Jesu Christ, meins Lebens Licht*, where they play a brief ritornello and simple accompaniment figures in addition to doubling the voices. Despite the partly independent role of the instruments, Bach clearly labelled the scores of this work 'motet', suggesting that he held a slightly expanded view of the motet compared to his predecessors.

Bach returned to the 17th-century German motet in the last years of his life, copying and performing a work by Sebastian Knüpfer, a predecessor as Leipzig Thomaskantor, and several by an ancestor from his family music collection, the ALT-BACHISCHES ARCHIV. He also used MOTET STYLE in cantata and oratorio movements, and reworked one of his own motet-like cantata movements, together with music by Telemann, into a composite motet, *Jauchzet dem Herrn, alle Welt*.

Bach's own motets, unlike his cantatas, remained in constant use at the Thomasschule after his death, and were among the first of his vocal works to be published (Leipzig, 1802–3) and to be cultivated outside Leipzig, especially at the Berlin Singakademie under Carl Friedrich Zelter.                    DRM

F. Krummacher, 'Textauslegung und Satzstruktur in Bachs Motetten', *BJb* 60 (1974), 5–43; D. Melamed, *J. S. Bach and the German Motet* (Cambridge, 1995); H.-J. Schulze, *Studien zur Bach-Überlieferung im 18. Jahrhundert* (Leipzig, 1984), 174–81.

***motivegeprägtes Accompagnato*** ('accompanied [recitative] imprinted with a motif'). German term for a type of RECITATIVE accompanied by instruments (other than merely continuo) in which the instruments repeat a brief motif while the voice proceeds in a normal recitative style (though inevitably in a stricter tempo than usual). Among many examples in Bach's music might be mentioned the alto recitative 'Ach Golgotha, unsel'ges Golgotha', no. 59 in the *St Matthew Passion*, accompanied by two oboes da caccia, cello, and continuo.

**Mozart, Wolfgang Amadeus** (b. 27 Jan. 1756; d. 5 Dec. 1791). Austrian composer in all the major genres of his time, born in Salzburg. He toured widely as a child keyboard prodigy before settling in Salzburg and building his reputation as a composer. After an uncongenial position in the service of the Archbishop of Salzburg, he lived as a freelance composer in Vienna. His enthusiasm for the music of Bach and Handel was developed through the concerts of Baron van Swieten, for whom he made string arrangements of some of Bach's keyboard fugues, adding preludes of his own. Mozart otherwise had little contact with Bach's music and was as much attracted by the work of Bach's sons. J. S. Bach's music was all but unknown in the Salzburg of Mozart's youth, and his only other documented contact was a visit to Leipzig in 1789, when he heard the eight-part motet *Singet dem Herrn* and played the organ of the Thomaskirche. Works contemporaneous with the Swieten period show striking Baroque characteristics, especially the great Mass in C minor, left incomplete in 1783, notably its 'Kyrie', 'Hosanna', 'Cum Sancto Spiritu', and 'Qui tollis', the last-named built over a descending ground. Keyboard fugues begun in the period also reflect Baroque style, as do the Suite κ399 and the large-scale Fugue in C minor for two pianos κ426.

While many technical features of Mozart's music and its frequent chromaticism can be associated with Bach, they also display a consistent and individual style, sometimes involving contrasted homophony. Thus, to trace the lineage of the fusion of counterpoint and sonata form in the finales of the 'Jupiter' Symphony (no. 41) and the String Quartet κ387 is difficult, not least in light of Baroque influence coming through other sources, such as the fugal finales of Haydn's op. 20 string quartets. Only when a more precise formal parallel can be drawn can one begin to assert the likelihood of Bach's stimulus, as in the case of the duet of the Two Men in Armour in the Act 2 finale of *The Magic Flute* (1791), which is a chorale prelude in organ style whose vocal parts could be played on the pedals. Only in a parallel genre, such as that of the late Fantasia for organ κ608, might a stimulus be reasonably suggested for its concentrated fugal devices and dramatic modulations, the latter finding a striking parallel in Bach's Fantasia in G minor for organ BWV542.                    MM

**Mühlhausen.** Town in Thuringia where Bach was organist in 1707–8. Mühlhausen was an imperial free city, under the control of the emperor himself; its territory included several smaller villages. Following the practice of German town constitutions of the time, the local council changed every year, and the posts of lord mayor, his deputy, and the councillors were filled three times over, so that the officials were active only every third year.

Situated on an incline below which flows the River Unstrut, Mühlhausen has two important churches: in the upper town the Marienkirche, in the lower town the Blasiuskirche. Both churches had schools attached to them, and therefore they each had their own Kantor. They also had their own organists and pastors, but they were not strictly attached to one of the institutions. The pastors held services alternately in both churches; Bach became organist at the Blasiuskirche, but some of his duties were at the Marienkirche. For instance, he was responsible for the cantata per-

View of Mühlhausen, 18th-century engraving (Städtische Bibliothek, Mühlhausen)

formed on the occasion of the annual *Ratswechsel* ('change of council') in the Marienkirche. The reason for this was that in Mühlhausen the leading figure in the town's musical life was one of the organists, not a Kantor as in Leipzig—a tradition dating from the time when Joachim a Burck (1546–1610) was organist at the Blasiuskirche.

Bach's predecessors at Mühlhausen were Johann Rudolf Ahle (1625–73) and his son Johann Georg (1651–1706). Bach was the first member of his family to be active in Mühlhausen. As we know from a letter of J. G. Walther, who also applied for the post, the examination was not confined to playing the organ but included the performance of a cantata. The only known work by Bach which fits the chronological situation is the Easter cantata *Christ lag in Todes Banden*, which means that Bach's examination might have taken place at Easter 1707. His duties there began in July. As in Arnstadt, his contract did not mention any musical duties except those of organist, but Bach composed a number of cantatas in Mühlhausen, including the *Ratswechsel* cantata, *Gott ist mein König*, in 1708 and *Aus der Tiefen rufe ich*. According to his letter of resignation, he might have supervised music in the villages around Mühlhausen as well. During his Mühlhausen years Bach married his cousin Maria Barbara, on 17 October 1707.

As organist of the Blasiuskirche, Bach initiated a complete renovation of the organ by the Mühlhausen builder Johann Friedrich Wender (1655–1729) in 1708–9. The resulting instrument, which had three manuals, pedals, and 37 stops, is not extant, but it was reconstructed in 1956–8 (*see* ORGAN, §2). To save costs, Bach dispensed with the positive organ in the church (the instrument used to accompany music, such as traditional motets, directed by the Kantor) and thereby at the same time assured his own supervision of the music being performed in the Blasiuskirche.

Religious life in Mühlhausen was burdened by quarrels between the two pastors, the superintendent Johann Adolf Frohne (1652–1713), who officiated mainly at the Blasiuskirche, and his colleague from the Marienkirche, Georg Christian Eilmar. Spitta supposed the reason for this to be the Lutheran controversy about Pietism (Frohne) and Orthodoxy (Eilmar), but Petzoldt has shown how little the positions held by Frohne were connected with Pietism. Apparently, it was more a personal quarrel between the two men about the 'proper' interpretation of the Bible. Bach was on good terms with Eilmar; the only extant copy of *Aus der Tiefen rufe ich* was written at Eilmar's request, and Eilmar stood godfather for Bach's first daughter, Catharina Dorothea.

Bach left Mühlhausen around the beginning of July 1708 (he was succeeded by Johann Friedrich Bach (*c.*1682–1730), son of the Eisenach organist Johann Christoph (i) ). His reasons for leaving are obscure. He complained that he had not succeeded in establishing a 'regulated church music', and this could have been because of the theological disputes, or the financial problems of the town (a large part of which had burnt down on 30 May 1707, shortly after Bach's election), but also because of personal considerations. Bach continued to be active for the Reichsstadt. He composed the *Ratswechsel* cantata of 1709, which appears to have been printed, like *Gott ist mein König* the year before, and he was asked to continue supervising the construction of the new organ. In 1735 his son Johann Gottfried Bernhard succeeded Johann Gottfried Hetzehenn (1664–1735), who had been Bach's opposite number at the Marienkirche. KK

K. Küster, *Der junge Bach* (Stuttgart, 1996), 151–81; M. Petzoldt, *Bachstätten aufsuchen* (Leipzig, 1993).

**musette.** A dance-like piece of pastoral character whose style suggests the sound of the musette, a kind of small bagpipe. It is characterized by a drone bass with a melodic line in conjunct motion in a moderate tempo. Various metric structures were used. As a dance of languid and fragile character, it appeared in French ballet as early as *Les Muses* (1703), an *opéra-ballet* by André Campra (1660–1744).

Bach wrote one musette so titled, and several pieces in musette style. Gavotte II 'ou la Musette' from the third English Suite has a continuous bass drone under a lovely melody in quavers in counterpoint with a tenor line in crotchets. The predominantly conjunct melody may be enhanced by the lilt of *notes inégales* (*see* RHYTHM). Pieces in musette style include the second bourrée from English Suite no. 2, the second passepied from English Suite no. 5, the second gavotte from English Suite no. 6, the first minuet from the keyboard Suite in E♭ BWV819, the Passepied in the Ouverture in the French Style, the Forlana of the C major Orchestral Suite, and the second minuet in the solo violin Partita no. 3. NJ, MEL

**museums.** The principal Bach museums, all of them in Germany, are the following:

**Arnstadt.** Stadtgeschichtliches Museum, Haus zum Palmbaum, Markt 3, D-99310 Arnstadt; tel. (03628) 60 29 78. A room devoted to Bach artefacts in the Stadtgeschichtliches Museum includes the organ console which stood in the Neue Kirche during Bach's period as organist there.

**Eisenach.** Bachhaus Eisenach, Frauenplan 21, D-99817 Eisenach; tel. (03691) 20 37 14. In the house once thought to have been Bach's birthplace, the collection includes some notable musical instruments, Bach autographs, the well-known (though not well-authenticated) portrait by Johann Jakob Ihle, and the BACH GOBLET. Information about the Bachhaus is available on the Internet at the following address: http://www.bachhaus.de.

**Köthen.** Historisches Museum, Museumsgasse 4–5, D-06366 Köthen; tel. (03496) 26 27. A section of the Historisches Museum is given over to material on Bach's life and work in Cöthen.

**Leipzig.** Bach-Archiv Leipzig, Thomaskirchhof 16, D-04109, Leipzig; tel. (0341) 9 64 41–0. Formerly the house of Bach's friends, the BOSE family, this houses one of the principal Bach research institutes as well as a museum which contains material relevant to Bach's time in Leipzig and promotes concerts of his music.

**Wechmar.** Bachhaus Wechmar, Bachstraße 4, D-99869 Wechmar; tel. (036256) 2 26 80. Situated in a village near Gotha, this was the house where some of the earliest known members of the Bach family lived. As a museum it concentrates on the Bach family history, with family trees, musical instruments, portraits, artefacts, and a fine display of Bach silhouettes.

*Musical Offering.* See overleaf.

**Müthel, Johann Gottfried** (b. 17 Jan. 1728; d. 14 July 1788). Composer and organist, born in Mölln, about 30 km. (19 miles) south of Lübeck, where his father was organist at the Nikolaikirche. In 1747 he was appointed organist at the court of Mecklenburg-Schwerin, and during a year's leave of absence in 1750 he became for a short time Bach's last pupil at Leipzig. In 1755 he went as *Kapellmeister* to a small musical establishment at Riga, where he remained for the rest of his life. His works are predominantly instrumental. Some show Bach's influence, others are almost wilfully original in style.

*My heart ever faithful.* Title commonly used for the soprano aria 'Mein gläubiges Herze' ('My believing heart'), movement 2 in Bach's Cantata 68, *Also hat Gott die Welt geliebt* (1725). The bass line had previously served for another soprano aria, 'Weil die wollenreichen Herden' in Cantata 208 (?1713); for the sacred cantata Bach composed an entirely new vocal melody, and it is this that has earned the aria its popularity.

## Musical Offering (*Musicalisches Opfer*)

A publication comprising two ricercars, a trio sonata, and ten canons, BWV1079, which Bach printed and dedicated to Frederick the Great, King of Prussia, in 1747. Bach's private concert appearance on 7 May 1747 at the court of Frederick the Great is the most fully documented event in his otherwise unglamorous career. Newspapers throughout German-speaking Europe published descriptions of Bach's visit, and the earliest Bach biographies in turn provided rather more colourful accounts garnered from correspondence with Bach's eldest sons, Carl Philipp Emanuel and Wilhelm Friedemann. On an evening that otherwise would have been spent listening to a recital of flute sonatas performed by the king with C. P. E. Bach at the harpsichord, the Prussian court was treated to a series of improvisations by 'the old Bach' of Leipzig. During the course of the proceedings Frederick provided Bach with a difficult theme on which to improvise a fugue, a genre posing strong challenges even for formal composition. According to the published reports, Frederick, who disliked written-out fugues and other kinds of complicated composition, was astonished by Bach's masterful on-the-spot hand-ling of the 'Royal Theme'. Bach, however, immediately made known his dissatis-faction with his improvisation and announced to the court that he intended 'to set Frederick's exceedingly beautiful theme to paper in a regular fugue and have it printed by means of copper engraving'.

Several months later the *Musical Offering* appeared in print, at Bach's own expense. The work is a collection of pieces on Frederick's theme in diverse genres that add up to a sort of 'art of fugue': two keyboard ricercars (an archaic synonym for 'fugue'); a trio sonata for flute, violin, and continuo (whose two fast movements take the form of fugues); and ten canons (including one structured as a fugue). The complicated transmission problems connected with this edition have occasioned an enormous amount of speculation about the way the collection was put together and the possible significance of its ordering. Recent, closer study suggests, however, that the layout of the complete printed edition essentially corresponded to the description found in a 1747 Leipzig newspaper advertisement, a document unknown to students of Bach's music until the 1970s: 'the Royal Prussian Fugue Theme . . . has now left the press . . . The elaboration consists of 1.) two fugues, one with three, the other with six obbligato parts; 2.) a sonata for transverse flute, violin, and continuo; 3.) diverse canons, among which is a fuga canonica.'

Normally 18th-century printed collections of music were financed by the dedi-catee, included six or twelve pieces in the same genre, and, naturally, corres-ponded to the taste of the recipient. The *Musical Offering* cannot have interested Frederick much, since its complicated, fugal music (which continually confronts the listener with several important thematic strands at once) would not have satisfied his liking for simpler, *galant* music (which comforts the listener with pleasant melodies and unobtrusive accompaniments). Beyond this, it may even have offended the king, since he cannot have failed to notice how the *Musical Offering* occasionally 'baroques' salient features of the *galant* style (consider, for example, the bizarre and unsettling way in which the appoggiatura, a sighing gesture, is lifted from its *galant* context of marking short phrase endings and is presented here in the third movement of the sonata in isolation and repeated extensively at different pitch levels; a breaking-down of *galant* mannerisms can also be found in the three-part fugue). It is difficult to say whether Frederick would have been nonplussed by Bach's ferociously difficult flute part (i.e. for the one- or two-keyed wooden flutes of the 18th century). But Frederick would certainly have understood the entire collection as more than a simple affront to his taste: with its archaic modes of expression and its religious symbolism, the *Musical Offering* embodies a pervasively theological world-view wholly at odds with his enlightened modernity. Such music, as we know Frederick said disparagingly of other works in this style, 'smells of the church'.

It is somewhat peculiar that Bach sent Frederick a printed collection with a German preface. Courtesy, in the original sense of the word, would have required a dedication in French. It is true that the work, although dedicated to Frederick, was published with a wider audience in mind. But J. J. Quantz's *Versuch einer Anweisung die Flöte traversiere zu spielen* (Berlin, 1752), for example, likewise dedicated to Frederick and also intended for a wider audience, was published in two editions, one in German and the other in French. It is known that Frederick was not altogether comfortable with the German language (he once remarked to J. C. Gottsched, 'from my youth I have read not a single German book, and I speak the language like a coachman; now, however, I am an old fellow of 46, and have no more time for it').

At several places the language of Bach's preface suggests a theological tone for the *Musical Offering*. The opening reads: 'Ew. Majestät weyhe hiermit in tiefster Unterthänigkeit ein Musicalisches Opfer' ('To your Majesty [I] consecrate herewith, in deepest submission, a Musical Offering'). It is instructive to compare this with the opening of Quantz's flute book, which, lacking the significant word 'Opfer' and using 'widmen' for Bach's 'weyhen', features similar but much more conventional language: 'Eurer Königlichen Majestät darf ich hiermit, in tiefster Unterthänigkeit, gegenwärtige Blätter widmen' ('To your Royal Majesty, may I herewith dedicate, in deepest submission, these pages'). The expression 'musical offering' may not seem so meaningful in and of itself, but linking 'weyhen' with 'Opfer' in a publication of instrumental music in the 1740s would have sounded rather strange. For Bach to write 'consecrate an offering' makes his collection 'smell of the church' right from the outset.

Towards the end of his preface Bach uses peculiar language that may be especially important for understanding his designs: 'This resolve [to elaborate the Royal theme] . . . has none other than this irreproachable intent, to glorify . . . the glory of a monarch [den Ruhm eines Monarchen zu verherrlichen]'. Both 'rühmen' and 'verherrlichen' mean 'to glorify', and neither one of these words by itself would seem particularly significant. But to use them together, the one as the object of the other, would in the 1740s have seemed linguistically odd, especially in a secular dedication. When Bach's text speaks of 'glorifying the glory' of the king, it presumably refers to different notions of glory.

The opening chorus from the *St John Passion* is helpful for understanding the *Musical Offering*. The chorus sings (my italics): 'Lord [*Herr*], our ruler [*Herr*scher], whose glory [*Ruhm*] is glorious [*herr*lich] in all the lands, show us through your Passion that you, the true son of God, have at all times, *even in the most serious abasement*, been glorified [ver*herr*licht]!' The wording '*Ruhm* . . .

verherrlicht' was presumably adopted deliberately, for the libretto otherwise quotes Psalm 8, which speaks of the glory of God's name ('Name', not 'Ruhm'). The *St John Passion* chorus reflects clearly one of the central ideas in Lutheran theology, the 'theology of the Cross' (the notion that Jesus's glorification as the king of humanity centres on the abasement in his suffering on the Cross).

The canons more than anything else in the *Musical Offering* bespeak Bach's antiquated, Orthodox Lutheran world-view. By the 1740s music in canon was even more strongly criticized than fugue, because it counters the rallying-call of the Enlightenment for freedom of natural expression in art. In canons the various voices are not merely more or less equal in importance, they are equivalent: in the simplest form of CANON subsequent voices imitate the first voice note for note, as in a round. Throughout his career, Bach employed canons to express law in the theological sense ('law' is, in fact, one of the original meanings of the word 'canon'). The procedure is especially well suited for expressing law, as the freedom of the subsequent voices in a canon is restricted by their having, as it were, to follow the commandment of the initial voice. The use of canon in Bach is often tied up somehow with the number ten (in reference to the Ten Commandments of the Hebrew scriptures). There are ten canons in the *Musical Offering*, and at least one of them is linked to a biblical inscription (Matt. 7: 7 or Luke 11: 9) pointing to what Luther called the spiritual or theological function of the law: to become aware of one's sinfulness, and, in repentance, to seek God's mercy and grace.

In the fourth canon (BWV1079:4*d*) Bach musically represents the spiritual glorification of worldly glory in a particularly straightforward way. The dotted rhythms of the bass line point to the French Baroque court style, with its traditional associations of majesty and glory. The realization of the canon, however, calls for augmentation and contrary motion. The line thus becomes 'de-regalized', because at half speed the dotted rhythms can no longer give the aural impression of the French style—the obvious worldly glory of the original line is spiritually glorified by the canonic realization. The inscription 'As the notes increase, so may the fortune of the king' probably has a rather different meaning from what is often suggested (namely, 'Vive le roi!'). The strikingly melancholy *Affekt* and the 'de-regalized' canonic solution link regal fortune (worldly works, glory) not to splendour, might, and fame, but to the theology of the Cross.

Instrumental music with this sort of theological resonance could hardly have appealed to Frederick, who, although tolerant of various religions, was himself strongly anti-Christian. Bach, however, apparently believed that in his compositional ventures, including non-liturgical instrumental music, he was fulfilling the commandment of the New Testament summary of the Law ('love God, and love your neighbour as yourself'). In Bach's understanding, loving neighbours implied imparting one's own God-given knowledge to them. His preface to the *Orgel-Büchlein* reads: 'For the most high God alone to glorify, and for my neighbour, from which to take instruction'. Ultimately the *Musical Offering* is offered not to glorify Frederick the Great, King of Prussia, but to instruct Bach's neighbours and glorify God.                                                                    MAM

*See also* SOURCES, §2.

H. T. David, *J. S. Bach's Musical Offering* (New York, 1945); U. Kirkendale, 'The Source for Bach's *Musical Offering*: The *Institutio Oratoria* of Quintilian', *Journal of the Ameri-*

*can Musicological Society*, 33 (1980), 88–141; M. Marissen, 'More Source-Critical Research on J. S. Bach's *Musical Offering*', *Bach*, 25/1 (1994), 11–27; M. Marissen, 'The Theological Character of J. S. Bach's *Musical Offering*', in D. R. Melamed, ed., *Bach Studies* 2 (Cambridge, 1995), 85–106; C. Wolff, *Bach: Essays on his Life and Music* (Cambridge, Mass., 1991), esp. 239–58, 324–31.

# N

**Nach dir, Herr, verlanget mich** ('Unto thee, O Lord, will I lift up my soul'). Cantata for an unspecified occasion, BWV150. Modern scholarship has been reluctant to accept this work as an authentic item of the Bach canon. Yet, while it is true that the piece contains technical insecurities of a kind not found in Bach's well-authenticated earliest cantatas, there are also features which invite us to consider it as a genuine product of his youth. If we do so, we may assume, both on stylistic grounds and in view of immaturities and curiosities in the part-writing, that this is Bach's earliest surviving cantata. The years 1704–7, when Bach was at Arnstadt, are currently accepted as the most likely period of composition.

No autograph material is known, and the piece survives only in a manuscript copied by C. F. Penzel in 1755, when he was a pupil at the Leipzig Thomasschule. A conspicuous feature of the score lies in the omission of any instrumental middle strand. There is, in other words, no viola part, but instead a polarized scoring for divided violins in the upper register and a bassoon and basso continuo in the lower one. This four-part texture, unique in Bach's cantatas, is matched by four-part vocal writing in the choral movements. The work's concise choral sections, interspersed with solo and ensemble numbers, recall the style of Buxtehude, whom Bach had visited at Lübeck during a four-month absence from Arnstadt beginning in the autumn of 1705.

The text, by an unidentified author, is largely based on verses from Psalm 25. A chromatic, darkly coloured, and poignantly expressive Sinfonia in B minor, the prevailing key of the cantata, leads to the first choral movement, whose harmonic and melodic material, also pervasively chromatic in its opening section, is partly derived from it. The remaining sections of this chorus are governed by a variety of tempo markings partly by which means Bach places emphasis on certain words and images of the text. The reiterated declamation 'Ich hofe' ('I trust') and the repeated 'zuschanden' ('confounded') provide but two instances of vivid word-painting.

The third movement is an aria for soprano, unison violins, and continuo. The text speaks of the steadfastness of the spirit assailed by the storms and flood-waters of misery and torment. Again, instances of lively word-painting, such as the melisma on 'toben' (bluster) and the agitated violin semiquavers accompanying 'Kreuz' ('affliction') and 'Sturm' ('torment'), engage the attention. The fourth section is a chorus whose supplicatory text, 'Lead me forth in thy truth', is given emphasis by frequent verbal reiteration, the opening phrase, 'Leite mich' ('Lead me'), being repeated five times while an unbroken ascending scale threads its way in crotchets from a low *B* through all four voices and the two violins to arrive at a top *e'''* on the word 'Wahrheit' ('truth').

The fifth movement is a terzetto for alto, tenor, and bass voices with bassoon and continuo. The textual imagery is colourful. Christian steadfastness is compared to tall cedars buffeted, damaged, and sometimes broken in the storm. Bach adds further colour with a restless continuo of almost uninterrupted semiquavers and a breezy, swaying 3/4 rhythm. It would be impossible to pass over this continuo line without drawing attention to its similarity to the continuo of the bass aria 'Das Brausen von den rauhen Winden' in a Leipzig cantata of 1725 (BWV92). This piece, like the other, takes as its source of inspiration the nature image of a stormy wind.

The two concluding sections of the cantata are choral. The first is based on words from Psalm 25: 'Mine eyes are ever looking unto the Lord'. In its first section this text is affectingly coloured by a gradually ascending motif in the divided violin parts. The second section, marked 'Allegro' and in contrast with the homophonic opening, is a fugue. The cantata ends with a chaconne or 'ciacona' as it is marked in the score. This supple movement, anguished in its opening phrases, contains both affective chromaticism and striking dissonance. Its continuo bass provided Brahms, one of the subscribers to the 19th-century complete Bach edition, with the outline theme for the chaconne finale of his Fourth Symphony.　　NA

A. Glöckner, 'Zur Echtheit und Datierung der Kantate BWV 150 "Nach dir, Herr, verlanget mich"', *BJb* 74 (1988), 195–203. For further bibliography, *see* CANTATA, §1.

**Nagel, Maximilian** (bap. 22 Nov. 1712; d. 13 April 1748). Lutenist and violinist, born in Nuremberg. From 1732 he attended the Thomasschule, Leipzig, where he rose to be prefect of the first choir and was Bach's pupil. He matriculated at Leipzig University in 1735 and took part in

Bach's performances in church and at the collegium musicum. Two years later he enrolled at Altdorf University. He was appointed lutenist at the court in Ansbach in 1744, and died there four years later at the age of 35.

**Naumann, Ernst** (b. 15 Aug. 1832; d. 15 Dec. 1910). Writer and composer, born in Freiberg. He was the grandson of the composer Johann Gottlieb Naumann (1741–1801), who wrote operas for Dresden and Stockholm. Ernst Naumann studied at the University of Leipzig and received his musical training from the Thomaskantors Moritz Hauptmann and Ernst Friedrich Richter (1808–1879). In 1858 he completed his Ph.D. thesis on the importance of Pythagoras's music theory for contemporary music. In 1878 he was appointed professor; later he became music director of the university and town organist in Jena. For the *BG* Naumann edited the later volumes of organ and harpsichord music as well as Cantatas 151–60.                                                 KK

**Naumann, Gottlieb Daniel** (b. *c.*1710; d. 22 Feb. 1782). Organist, born in Mühlbach, near Chemnitz. He enrolled at Leipzig University in March 1734, and was a pupil of Bach. In April 1740 he succeeded another Bach pupil, B. D. Ludewig, as organist at Schmölln.

**NBA.** See NEUE BACH-AUSGABE.

**Neidhardt, Johann Georg** (b. *c.*1685; d. 1739). Theorist, born in Bernstadt, about 80 km. west of Dresden, and later *Kapellmeister* at Königsberg, where he died. He was particularly interested in unequal temperaments that lend character to the keys without making any key sound harsh. In 1706 he called equal temperament the 'best and easiest' choice; in 1724 he found it the best for a court, but not for anywhere else; in 1732 he found a suitably

unequal temperament always preferable (see Table 1). Mizler, Sorge, and Altnickol all considered Neidhardt's models of unequal temperament, in which $\frac{1}{12}$-comma is the unit of measure, better than Werckmeister's, which use $\frac{1}{4}$- or $\frac{1}{3}$-comma as an indivisible unit. (However, Bach's and Hildebrandt's nuances of tuning, unhampered by any concept of an indivisible unit, may have been even more smoothly controlled than Neidhardt's mathematical models could represent. See TEMPERAMENTS.)                      ML

**Nekrolog.** See OBITUARY.

**Neue Bach-Ausgabe** (*NBA*) ('New Bach Edition'). The most recent complete edition of Bach's works, initiated in 1950. The 'old' Bach edition (*BG*, edited by the BACH-GESELLSCHAFT, 1850–99) was the first attempt to produce a complete edition of a composer's works based on scholarly principles. Its editorial standards, which to begin with were on a very high level, were developed further as the volumes appeared. Subsequently new principles were established, including that of printing the music using modern clefs, rather than the original clefs favoured by the *BG*. Research into the handwriting, not only of the composer himself but also of copyists, and study of the watermarks, altered the image we had of Bach as a composer. Meanwhile, the 'old' edition itself stimulated interest in Bach research, and this in turn led to a pressing demand for copies. During World War II many of these were destroyed, as also were some of the sources themselves (others thought to be lost were rediscovered in Poland after about 30 years; *see* RECEPTION AND REVIVAL, §8). The condition of some sources deteriorated because the iron contained in Bach's ink rusted on the acid 18th-century paper. In short, it became

Table 1. Some characteristics of the theoretical temperaments recommended by Neidhardt in 1724 and 1732

| According to his book of 1724, the best temperament for: | Number of units by which the least and most impure 3rds are tempered: | Largest and smallest semitones (in cents); standard deviation (s.d.) from 100 | According to his book of 1732, the best temperament for: |
| --- | --- | --- | --- |
|  | 2, 10 | 108, 94 s.d.: 5·3 | a village |
| a village | 3, 10* | 108, 94 s.d.: 4·0 | a small town |
| a small town | 4, 10* | 106, 96 s.d.: 3·3 | a large town |
| a large town | 4, 9 | 104, 96 s.d.: 2·3 |  |
| a court | 7, 8* | 100, 100 s.d.: 0 |  |

* for a minor 3rd.

apparent towards 1950 that a new general approach to the sources was necessary.

The *NBA* presents the material in volumes of music and separate *Kritische Berichte* ('Critical Reports') with substantial information about the works in question. The edition is divided into nine series: I: cantatas; II: masses, Passions, and oratorios; III: motets, chorales, and songs; IV: organ works; V: works for clavier and lute; VI: instrumental chamber music; VII: orchestral music; VIII: canons, *Musical Offering*, and *The Art of Fugue*; and XI: addenda (a catalogue of watermarks in the autographs and documentation concerning the development of Bach's handwriting). As a supplement there are also four volumes of *Bach-Dokumente* (*BDok*), the first three consisting of original documents to do with Bach up to 1800, and the fourth a volume of iconography.

The *NBA* is edited by the Bach-Archiv, Leipzig, and the Johann-Sebastian-Bach-Institut, Göttingen; the first volume appeared in 1954. Clearly, its volumes reflect its own history; the very first, Friedrich Smend's edition of the B minor Mass, soon became the subject of controversy, and later volumes have reflected changing approaches to the organ works. But almost from its beginnings the *NBA* was stamped by the CHRONOLOGY of the cantatas established by Georg Dadelsen and Alfred Dürr. For almost four decades it was one of the very few projects which involved intensive co-operation between scholars from Communist countries and the West. KK

**Neue Bach-Gesellschaft** (New Bach Society). The 'old' BACH-GESELLSCHAFT had been founded in 1850 in order to promote and publish a complete edition of the composer's work. With its task completed some 50 years later, the society was dissolved, but it was immediately reconstituted as the Neue Bach-Gesellschaft with the new aim of making the music better known through performances and in other ways. Its main activities during its first 100 years have been: to organize regular festivals of Bach's music in various towns and cities in Germany (and on rare occasions in other countries; *see* BACHFEST); to publish the annual *Bach-Jahrbuch*; to initiate and co-ordinate the work of Bach MUSEUMS; and to encourage the liturgical performance of Bach's cantatas. It has its headquarters at 16 Thomaskirchhof, Leipzig.

**Neu-Gottesdienst** ('new divine service'). *See* ALT-GOTTESDIENST.

**Neukirche** (New Church). One of the four Leipzig churches for the music of which Bach, as *director chori musici*, was responsible. Situated in the north-west district of the city, it resulted from a rebuilding of the 15th-century Barfüßerkirche,

belonging to the Franciscans, which had lain unused since the Reformation. The new church was consecrated on 24 September 1699. The organists there during the period of Bach's Kantorate were G. B. Schott (until 1729) and C. G. Gerlach. The building was destroyed by bombs during World War II.

The BONIFATIUSKIRCHE in Arnstadt was also known as the Neue Kirche.

**Neumann, Werner** (b. 21 Jan. 1905; d. 24 April 1991). Musicologist, born in Königstein, Saxony. He studied at the Leipzig Conservatory and University, where he completed a doctorate with an important dissertation on Bach's choral fugues. His subsequent career was devoted to Bach studies. He founded and directed the Leipzig Bach-Archiv, was co-editor of the *Bach-Jahrbuch* from 1953 to 1974, and edited several volumes of the *NBA*. His publications include a handbook on the cantatas (1947), a pictorial biography (1960), and a compendium of all the texts that Bach set (1974).

**Neumeister, Erdmann** (b. 12 May 1671; d. 18 Aug. 1756). Writer and theologian, born in Uichteritz, near Weißenfels in Saxony. His importance to music history lies in his church cantata texts; he was also a theorist (he lectured on poetry at Leipzig University in 1695; *see* HUNOLD, CHRISTIAN FRIEDRICH) and a pastor, at first for brief periods in minor posts in Saxony and Silesia, and finally for 40 years, from 1715, at the Jacobikirche, Hamburg.

Around 1695 Neumeister wrote his first cantata texts. They belong to the type common in the later 17th century, consisting of biblical verses, strophic arias, and, occasionally, single chorale strophes. In 1700 he published *Geistliche Cantaten statt einer Kirchen-Music* ('Sacred Cantatas in Place of Liturgical Music'), which consist only of recitatives and 'operatic' arias. The title suggests that Neumeister did not intend these as apt for performance during a normal service. It was only in cycles published in 1711 and 1714 and set by Telemann that Neumeister inserted biblical texts and chorales into his cantatas, thus mixing the forms of traditional German church music with those of contemporary Italian opera. But this mixture was already tried out at the Meiningen court in 1704 (*see* ERNST LUDWIG). Thus, *pace* Spitta and many later writers, Neumeister was not the inventor of the type of cantata text so important for the further development of Protestant church music, although he was clearly influential in its adoption.

Bach set five of Neumeister's texts, two (BWV18 and 61) at Weimar, probably about 1714, and three

(BWV24, 28, and 59) during his Leipzig years. That Neumeister supported Bach's application for the post of organist at the Jacobikirche, Hamburg, in 1720 is suggested by the sarcastic comments he made, in one of his sermons, about the simony attached to the election. *See also* HAMBURG.    KK

H. K. Krausse, 'Erdmann Neumeister und die Kantatentexte Johann Sebastian Bachs', *BJb* 72 (1986), 7–31.

**Neumeister Chorales.** A collection of organ chorales by Bach and others (Yale University, MS LM 4708), the discovery of which was announced by Christoph Wolff and Harold E. Samuel in December 1984. The volume was compiled by Johann Gottfried Neumeister (1757–1840) some time after 1790, and contains 82 chorale preludes, arranged in the order of the liturgical year in a similar manner to the *Orgel-Büchlein*. Together with 38 compositions attributed to J. S. Bach, the manuscript contains works by Bach's two cousins Johann Michael and Johann Christoph, as well as music by Johann Pachelbel, F. W. Zachow (1663–1712), G. A. Sorge, and Daniel Erich (c.1660–c.1730). Of the 38 preludes by J. S. Bach, five (BWV601, 639, 719, 737, and 742) were already known in the form found in the Neumeister Collection. The prelude on *Ach Gott und Herr* BWV714 appears in Neumeister with an otherwise unknown introductory section of 37 bars, thematically unrelated to the chorale, while the prelude on *Machs mit mir, Gott, nach deiner Güt* BWV957, which had not previously been recognized as a chorale prelude, has an otherwise unknown closing section giving a simple harmonization of the melody.

The remaining 31 preludes are not known elsewhere, with the exception of *Christe, der du bist Tag und Licht* BWV1096, a shorter version of which is found in another source with a conflicting attribution to Pachelbel (see Krumbach). Krumbach also observed that as many as six of the preludes attributed to J. M. Bach are also ascribed to Pachelbel in other sources, showing that the reliability of Neumeister cannot be accepted without question. One prelude, *In dulci jubilo* BWV751, previously regarded as an *opus dubium* of Johann Sebastian, is attributed to Johann Michael in Neumeister—probably correctly, since the other source identifies the composer merely as 'Sigr. Bach'.

The discovery of the Neumeister Collection was a highly important one for a number of reasons. First, because it has long been apparent that a major collection of chorale preludes by members of the Bach family and copied within the family circle had been lost (the two surviving Bach collections being the ANDREAS BACH BOOK and the MÖLLER MANUSCRIPT). One lost collection of preludes of this type (the so-called Plauen Organ Book) is already documented. The presence in the Neumeister Collection of music by the young J. S. Bach as well as works by his two composing cousins strongly suggests that the compiler had access to at least some of this missing repertory.

Secondly, the design of the Neumeister Collection sheds important light on that of the *Orgel-Büchlein*, which follows the same liturgical order, proceeding through the CHURCH CALENDAR from Advent. It now becomes clear that the plan of the *Orgel-Büchlein* was not unique, but followed that found in at least one other Thuringian chorale collection, having obvious practical uses for a professional Lutheran church organist. The *Orgel-Büchlein* differs from the earlier collection in being larger (164 preludes planned), in being devoted entirely to works by J. S. Bach, and in the greater maturity of the music. Two of the preludes from Neumeister (BWV601 and 639) were also included in the *Orgel-Büchlein*, together with a few others that are known to have come from earlier sources.

Finally, the Neumeister Collection contains valuable music which adds much to our understanding of Bach's early development as a keyboard composer. On grounds of style, some of the preludes seem to be among the earliest surviving music by Bach, probably written before he was 20. Others are slightly more mature in technique, perhaps composed as late as 1710. Few of the preludes specify use of the pedal, and those that do employ it do so only sporadically, not consistently as in the manner of the *Orgel-Büchlein*. The preludes are in general less concise than those of the *Orgel-Büchlein*, working each line of the chorale separately in the manner of the 17th-century chorale fantasia.    DLH

W. Krumbach, 'Sechzig unbekannte Orgelwerke von Johann Sebastian Bach: ein vorläufiger Fundbericht', *Neue Zeitschrift für Musik*, 146/3 (1985), 4–12; 146/5 (1985), 6–18; C. Wolff, 'The Neumeister Collection of Chorale Preludes from the Bach Circle', in *Bach: Essays on his Life and Music* (Cambridge, Mass., 1991), 107–27.

**Nichelmann, Christoph** (b. 13 Aug. 1717; d. 20 July 1762). Composer and keyboard player, born in Treuenbrietzen, Brandenburg, about 55 km. (34 miles) south-west of Berlin. He attended the Thomasschule in Leipzig and was Bach's pupil there from 1730 to 1733, sometimes assisting him as copyist and earning admiration for his treble voice. After some years in Hamburg and elsewhere, he went to Berlin to complete his studies under Quantz and C. H. Graun, and in 1745 he became one of the court harpsichordists (the other being C. P. E. Bach). In 1756 he left the king's service, but he remained in Berlin for the rest of his life. Nichelmann's extant compositions are mainly for keyboard and other instruments, and include 16 harpsichord concertos. He also wrote an influential treatise, *Die Melodie, nach ihrem Wesen* (1755).

H.-J. Schulze, 'Der Schreiber "Anonymus 400": ein Schüler Johann Sebastian Bachs', *BJb* 58 (1972), 104–17.

**Nicolai, David** (b. 22 Feb. 1702; d. 25 Nov. 1764). Organist, born in Görlitz, about 90 km. (56 miles) east of Dresden. He studied with the organist C. L. Boxberg (1670–1729) in Görlitz, and at Leipzig University from 1727 to 1729, and was a pupil of Bach during that time. In 1729 he approached Bach for a testimonial in support of his application to succeed Boxberg as organist at the Petrikirche in Görlitz, and was appointed there the following year. His son David Traugott Nicolai (1733–99), also a musician, succeeded him in 1764.

**Niedt, Friedrich Erhard** (bap. 31 May 1674; d. 13 April 1708). Theorist and composer, born in Jena, Thuringia. He studied (probably law) at Jena University, and also music with J. S. Bach's relative Johann Nicolaus Bach (1669–1753). He applied unsuccessfully for an organist's post in Copenhagen in 1704, but apparently remained there nevertheless. Little of his music survives, but he is remembered for his *Musicalische Handleitung* (1706–13), parts of which Bach commandeered in his own thorough-bass method (*see* PRECEPTS AND PRINCIPLES).

P. L. Poulin, ed., *J. S. Bach's Precepts and Principles for Playing the Thorough-Bass or Accompanying in Four Parts* (Oxford, 1994), pp. xv–xvii.

**Nikolaikirche** (St Nicholas's Church). The principal church in Leipzig, where many of Bach's sacred vocal works were heard for the first time. It dates from the 13th century, but has been many times modified and restored. Like the Thomaskirche, it had its own school attached to it, but it was the Thomaskantor who was responsible for the music at the Nikolaikirche and for providing the singers and players to perform it. During Bach's period at Leipzig the Nikolaikirche was the official town church, used for important civic occasions such as the service to celebrate the council election.

***Nimm von uns, Herr, du treuer Gott*** ('Take from us, Lord, thou true God'). Cantata for the tenth Sunday after Trinity, BWV101, first performed on 13 August 1724. It is a CHORALE CANTATA belonging to Bach's second Leipzig *Jahrgang*

(1724–5). The text is a reworking by an unknown librettist of Martin Moller's chorale (1584), the primary hymn assigned to this Sunday in Leipzig. Movements 1 and 7 are the unaltered stanzas of the hymn; movements 3–6 include unaltered lines from the central stanzas and also paraphrase their content; and movement 2 is freely written. The chorale melody associated with Moller's text in Leipzig was Luther's *Vater unser im Himmelreich*, which is heard in all the movements except the second. Its use therefore emphasizes the concept of prayer on which the whole cantata is based, but also, since Luther's Lord's Prayer hymn was very familiar to those who first heard Bach's cantata, the melody would recall such lines as 'Break Satan's power, defeat his rage; preserve your church from age to age', and 'Curb flesh and blood and every ill that sets itself against thy will'.

The Gospel for the day was St Luke 19: 41–8, which tells of Jesus prophesying the doom of Jerusalem and weeping over the impending destruction. In Leipzig it was customary to read the fulfilment of the prophecy, the Jewish historian Josephus's harrowing account of the destruction of Jerusalem in AD 70, at Vespers on this Sunday. The cantata therefore was heard in both contexts, first in one of the two principal churches at the morning *Hauptgottesdienst*, then again in the other church at afternoon Vespers. The Gospel and Josephus readings account for the rather sombre mood of the magnificent opening chorus.

This austere and grave chorale fantasia is almost unique among Bach's vocal works. The closest to it is the motet *O Jesu Christ, meins Lebens Licht* BWV118, which shares a similar repeated motif, heard here in the upper strings, above a pedal point. The chorale melody in augmentation in the soprano, with the flute at the octave above, contrasts with the dark colours of the orchestral accompaniment and the trombones that double the other voice parts.

The second movement opens up a ray of hope that enlightens the dark presence of judgement. The lightness of the flute obbligato (replaced at a later performance, probably some time after 1735, by a violin) seems to be completely at variance with the tenor, who prays for God to deal kindly with the sinner and not in the way that Jerusalem was treated: the tenor expresses the fear of judgement but the flute (or violin) answers with the hope of grace and forgiveness. The dialectic of law and grace set up in this second movement continues throughout the remainder of the cantata.

In movement 3 ornamented lines of the chorale melody alternate with simple recitative. Move-

Interior of the Nikolaikirche, Leipzig, c.1785

ment 4 stands at the centre of the cantata's chiastic structure:

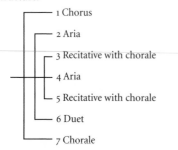

1 Chorus
2 Aria
3 Recitative with chorale
4 Aria
5 Recitative with chorale
6 Duet
7 Chorale

The anger of God is depicted in the Vivace accompaniment to this bass da capo aria. Only the first line of the chorale melody is heard; it is marked Andante and *piano*, and contrasts sharply with the agitated pace of the movement as a whole.

Movement 5 is a recitative with chorale, following the pattern of movement 3. In movement 6, a poignantly beautiful soprano and alto duet, fragments of the chorale melody are used to create a musical prayer for mercy. The concluding chorale prays that 'our town' may be blessed, in contrast to the fate of Jerusalem.                    RAL

For bibliography, *see* CANTATA, §1.

***Nimm, was dein ist, und gehe hin*** ('Take that thine is, and go thy way'). Cantata for Septuagesima, BWV144, first performed on 6 February 1724 as part of Bach's first annual cantata cycle in Leipzig. The author of the libretto is unknown. The text of the first movement is St Matthew 20: 14, from the Gospel for the day (the parable of the labourers in the vineyard); movement 3 is the first strophe of *Was Gott tut, das ist wohlgetan* (Samuel Rodigast, 1674); movement 6 is the first strophe of *Was mein Gott will, das g'scheh allzeit* (Albrecht von Brandenburg, 1547).

Like *Ich bin vergnügt mit meinem Glücke*, also for Septuagesima, BWV144 takes contentment with one's lot as its topic. This is the theme of the parable whose moral is quoted in the *Spruch* that opens the cantata (no. 1), of the two arias (nos. 2 and 5) and recitative (no. 4), and of the four-part chorales (nos. 3 and 6).

Perhaps the most striking movement is the first, with its brief and essentially affectless *Spruch* text, 'Take that thine is, and go thy way'. Bach sets this as a motet, with all the features of the style and genre. The time signature is the characteristic *alla breve*; there are no independent instruments—the strings, oboes, and continuo play *colla parte* with the voices; and the movement is constructed in imitative counterpoint. The principal subject, setting the whole text, is a syllabic theme in minims

and crotchets. For contrast Bach provides a countersubject built on a repeated motif of two quavers and a crotchet and using only the words 'gehe hin, gehe hin'. This motif, which also migrates to the partly independent bass line, provides a rhythmic drive that animates the surface of the movement's typically slow harmonic rhythm. Bach works out exhaustively three imitative subjects: the opening idea, the crotchet-and-quaver motif, and a slow minim rendition of 'gehe hin'.

The two arias are contrasted in many ways. Movement 2, for alto accompanied by strings (and perhaps also oboes), is cast as an expressive minuet in characteristic triple metre and regular four- and eight-bar phrases, using mostly syllabic text declamation. In the outer sections of this da capo piece, the voice is used mostly as an addition to the orchestral texture, often doubling the melody line in the first violin. In the middle section the instruments enter mostly to punctuate vocal cadences. Movement 5, for soprano with obbligato oboe d'amore, shows none of the regularity of phrasing of the alto aria. Its syntax, both in the ritornello and the vocal part, is that of the instrumental concerto's *Fortspinnung* type. The relationship between the voice and obbligato instrument is different as well; here, the two form a contrapuntal duet, a texture only hinted at in the alto aria.

This cantata, especially its first movement, was particularly well known after Bach's death. Writing in 1759, F. W. Marpurg cited the first movement as an example of admirably clear text declamation in a fugal texture (*BDok* iii, no. 701). In the 1770s the author of a dictionary article on metre cited an example from the triple-time alto aria (*BDok* iii, no. 766). That author was probably J. P. Kirnberger, who owned a copy at least of the first movement, as documented by a manuscript in the collection of his pupil Princess Anna Amalia of Prussia (*BDok* iii, no. 887).                    DRM

For bibliography, *see* CANTATA, §1.

**Nitzer, Johann Gottfried.** *See* NÜTZER, JOHANN GOTTFRIED.

**Noah, Georg Heinrich** (b. 1721; d. 1762). Musician and schoolteacher, born in Tennstedt, Thuringia. He studied with Bach at Leipzig in 1740–3, and like several other Bach pupils he also assisted his teacher as a copyist. In 1743 he was appointed Kantor in his native town and was promoted to assistant Rector in 1759.

***Non sa che sia dolore*** ('He does not know what it is to grieve'). Italian secular cantata for soprano, flute, strings, and continuo, BWV209. Its principal source is a copy made about 1800 by J. N. Forkel, now in the Staatsbibliothek zu Berlin, and its authenticity has been much discussed. It was conceived perhaps as a farewell cantata on the departure of a teacher. J. M. Gesner has been suggested as the recipient. He was a native of Roth, near Ansbach, and became assistant Rector of the gymnasium at Weimar, from where he proceeded first to Ansbach as Rector of the gymnasium there (an event which might be the subject of the present cantata) and then to Leipzig as Rector of the Thomasschule from 1730 to 1734.

The cantata uses a composite text by an unknown author (perhaps a German); it includes passages from G. B. Guarini's 'Partita dolorosa' (madrigal no. 41 from his *Rime*, published in Venice in 1598) and Pietro Metastasio's opera *Semiramide riconosciuta* (Act 2, scene 6) and his *azione teatrale Galatea*, together with other verses probably freely invented. It is not known why Bach had recourse to an Italian text which is, among other things, somewhat irregular and disconnected, showing an incomplete mastery of the language. Moreover, it is worth stressing that the predominant taste in Leipzig was not for things Italian; bourgeois society there preferred to follow French modes, unlike Dresden, which was a great consumer and producer of Italian art.

The text explicitly (albeit ungrammatically and with poor scansion) addresses the town of Ansbach ('Ma chi gran ti farà più che non fusti | Ansbaca, piena di tanti Augusti'), where the court was particularly inclined towards Italian music, and in whose theatre were performed operas by Italians from Francesco Cavalli (1602–76) to Antonio Draghi (1634/5–1700) and from Antonio Cesti (1623–69) to Alessandro Scarlatti (1659–1725), while an important role in instrumental music was filled (if only for a brief period towards the end of the 17th century) by Giuseppe Torelli. Taking into account the biographical facts at our disposal, and accepting the cantata as a genuine Bach work, there might seem to be no other way of explaining the reference to Ansbach except as an allusion to the episode in the career of Gesner already mentioned. Gesner was an excellent philologist and a good friend of Bach, whose outstanding gifts as a keyboard player and conductor he praised in his commentary on the *Institutiones oratoriae* of Quintilian (1738). And yet the evidence is too slender to be accepted as testimony that the cantata was composed in Gesner's honour. The text seems rather to be addressed to a young man leaving for military service ('La patria goderai, | A dover la servirai', no. 3), and in two separate passages makes reference to the sea ('Varchi or di sponda in sponda. | Propizi vedi il vento e l'onda', no. 3; 'Qual nocchier . . . in su la prora | Va cantando in faccia al mar', no. 5). All this sug-

gests that the cantata relates to the departure from a port (Hamburg, perhaps?) of a young marine officer.

At all events the text has served for an excellent musical work consisting of a sinfonia, two recitatives (nos. 2 and 4) and two arias (nos. 3 and 5). The Bach style is everywhere in evidence, beginning with the Sinfonia, which takes the form of a single-movement concerto in a da capo structure. The protagonist is the flute, which is heard also in a virtuoso role in the two arias. The first of these displays a decidedly military character in its central section, while the second indulges in descriptive effects. AB

L. Ansbacher, 'Sulla cantata profana N. 209 "Non sa che sia dolore" di G. S. Bach', *Rivista musicale italiana*, 51 (1949), 97–116; P. Berri, 'Sulla cantata profana N. 209 di Bach', ibid. 306–9; K. Hofmann, 'Alte und neue Überlegungen zu der Kantate "Non sa che sia dolore" BWV 209', *BJb* 76 (1990), 7–25. For further bibliography, *see* CANTATA, §2.

***Notenbüchlein*** ('little music book'). A term often used to refer to the CLAVIERBÜCHLEIN that Bach prepared for his son Wilhelm Friedemann and the two similar volumes that he gave to his second wife, Anna Magdalena. It is often mistranslated as 'little notebook'; 'Noten' is the usual German term for written (or printed) music.

**number symbolism.** See overleaf.

***Nun danket alle Gott*** ('Now thank we all our God'). Cantata, BWV192, for an unidentified occasion, perhaps a Reformation festival or a wedding. Bach's original manuscript parts date probably from autumn 1730; these are the sole source, and at least one part, that of the tenor, is lost (the *NBA* includes Alfred Dürr's reconstruction of the tenor part).

A chorale cantata, BWV192 sets only the three stanzas of Martin Rinckart's text (1636); in this it resembles several other late chorale cantatas that similarly lack recitatives or arias. The opening chorus is a chorale fantasia of the type familiar from the 1724–5 cycle of chorale cantatas. But whereas those works usually present the cantus firmus (text and melody) one line at a time, here the first two phrases of the chorale melody, in the soprano, are preceded by an extended fugal exposition of their text by the three lower voices, using an essentially unrelated subject. Following a repetition of the same music for phrases 3–4, the *Abgesang* (phrases 5–8) is treated in similar fashion. Throughout, the orchestra of two flutes, two oboes, and strings provides a contrapuntal accompaniment derived from the opening ritornello.

## number symbolism

In music, the use of numbers, or number alphabets, to convey an esoteric meaning or to determine an element in the structure of a melody, section, or piece. Number symbolism in Bach's music is based on the work of three German scholars: Arnold Schering, Martin Jansen (1885–1944), and Friedrich Smend. Their work is a series of ideas illustrated by examples and interpretations, rather than being a single historically consistent theory. Many musicologists have since adopted and freely adapted their ideas, creating an ever-expanding mesh of numerical processes, popularly (and falsely) classified as 'numerology'. Behind the superficial complexity and diversity of recent numerical examples lies the same common procedural core found in the earlier works of Schering, Jansen, and Smend. It consists of four stages: enumeration, operation, translation, and interpretation.

In the first stage, enumeration, the numbers are usually generated from information found in Bach's scores, by counting: the notes in a melodic line, fugal entry, full score of short section, etc.; the bars in a work, movement, section, phrase, etc.; the movements in a work; repetitions of a phrase, figure, word, entry, etc.; or the words in a section, movement, etc. The work's date can also be transformed into a number, as can the words of an epitaph, a dedication, or the names of people.

In the second stage, operation, the number arrived at in the first stage frequently undergoes some kind of mathematical procedure, such as: dividing it by another significant number (such as 3, 7, or 10); the addition or subtraction of a significant number; reading it as a triangular number (in the sequence 1, 3, 6, 10, 15, 21, etc.); finding the square or cube root; putting it and other numbers into a magic square (see H. Dieben, 'Getallenmystiek bij Bach', *Musica sacra*, 5 (1954–5), 21–3, 47–9); and translating it into letters by means of a number alphabet. There are many different number alphabets, but the most frequently used is the natural order number alphabet (A=1, B=2, C=3 . . . I/J=9 . . . U/V=20 . . . Z=24), first proposed by Henk Dieben in 1943 and published by Smend in 1947.

In the third stage, translation, the numbers are translated in many different and frequently unique ways, into: traditional biblical symbols, with 3 representing the Trinity and 10 the Commandments; words expressing faith, such as 'Credo', 'Christus', 'Kyrie', and 'S. D. G.'; numbers in the Bible, such as 153 (fish) and 12 (disciples); aspects of the structure of the Bible, such as the 27 books of the New Testament and psalm numbers; names of people, such as Bach, Johann Sebastian Bach, and Faber; and words from epitaphs.

When we reach the fourth stage, interpretation, the possibilities range far and wide, but interpretations frequently claim to show something very specific about Bach or his method of composing, for example that he was: making a specific declaration of faith (see, for example, Smend, 1947–9, iv. 13); embedding his signature secretly in the structure (ibid. 17); embedding the dedicatee's name in the structure (ibid. iii. 10); enhancing the theological content of the text by a numerical reference (for example, using 365 notes to enforce the meaning of 'I will be with you every day': see M. Jansen, 'Bach und das Jahr', *Allgemeine Musikzeitung*, 70 (1943), 1).

The four stages are illustrated in Smend's example of the first two movements, 'Credo in unum Deum' and 'Patrem omnipotentem', from the Symbolum Nicenum in the B minor Mass. Together these have 129 bars (enumeration), which can be read as 43 + 43 + 43, or 43 × 3, hence C (3) + R (7) + E (5) + D (4) + O (14) = 43 (operation), which translates into 'Credo, Credo, Credo' or 'Credo' multiplied by the triune God (translation). This, Smend claims, signifies that there is no true belief other than the Trinitarian confession (interpretation).

To make his case even more persuasive, Smend observes that the next two movements, 'Et in unum Dominum' and 'Et incarnatus est', also have a total of 129 bars, and that there are two further instances of 129-bar totals in this section of the mass. It almost makes one's fingers itch to reach for the nearest score and begin counting! And that is precisely the effect his work had on his readers. Without further proof it was now generally accepted that Bach had hidden religious and autobiographical words in the structure of his compositions. Outmoded were the weightier studies of the analyst Wilhelm Werker (1873–1948) and others who had noticed symmetry and architectural features within sections. The repetition of 129 bars was no longer simply a proportional device, but a credal statement.

The lack of evidence from Bach's manuscripts and contemporary treatises for number symbolism should have prevented the subject gaining so much popularity. There are descriptions from Bach's time of musical puzzles, playful cryptographic messages being hidden in pieces of music, and methods for non-musicians of composing by throwing dice, but not of number symbolism as described by Smend.

It is initially puzzling how an eminent musicologist with a great interest in primary sources could have presented such ideas and examples without adequate historical evidence. A close look at his family and educational background shows that he inherited a view of Bach weighted heavily in favour of Bach the church musician. Having studied theology, he knew from Church history that the Church Fathers had written about the symbolic use of biblical numbers. Knowing also that Bach's society was steeped in the Lutheran faith and that Bach himself had a large library of theological books, Smend was perhaps justified in looking for these symbols in Bach's music. His later introduction of number alphabets from cabbalistic gematria, however, is less easily explained, particularly as Christian cabbalism was frowned upon by the Lutheran church in Bach's time. How Smend overlooked this may be explained by the research restrictions during World War II. It would have been unwise, and even dangerous, for Smend to be found poring over Jewish religious literature at this time when he was working at the Prussian State Library.

Smend did not develop his ideas on number symbolism after 1950, and was saddened to see the direction the subject took. In spite of the paucity of historical evidence, number symbolism is still an attractive analytical tool today, as it promises a direct path from the musical scores into the heart and mind of the composer. By locating the correct numbers, operating and translating them accurately, it is possible to create a beautiful interpretation of Bach's thought-world. This has been done both successfully and absurdly.

For the subject to move forward it must reject much of its past. The priority is to establish the historical plausibility that Bach used numbers as a tool when he composed. Only then will it be clear which forms of enumeration, operation, and translation he used, and only then will analysts deciphering his compositional process be able to make valid interpretations.                                                                RT

M. Jansen, 'Bachs Zahlensymbolik, an seinen Passionen untersucht', *BJb* 34 (1937), 98–117; A. Schering, *Das Symbol in der Musik* (Leipzig, 1941); F. Smend, *Bach-Studien: gesammelte Reden und Aufsätze*, ed. C. Wolff (Kassel, 1969); F. Smend, *Johann Sebastian Bach: Kirchen-*

*Kantaten erläutert* (Berlin, 1947–9, 2nd edn. 1950); R. Tatlow, *Bach and the Riddle of the Number Alphabet* (Cambridge, 1991).

The ritornello of the second movement, a duet, opens with several short fragmentary phrases of the type favoured by *galant* composers (including C. P. E. Bach). These later provide an affecting accompaniment to the more sustained lines of the soprano and bass soloists, whose parts employ the quasi-fugal imitations typical of Italian operatic duets of the time. The movement falls into a highly regular binary symmetry, the second half presenting almost precisely the same material as the first even though the long note of the opening vocal subject, on 'ewig' ('eternally'), no longer accords with the text, 'uns' ('us').

The work closes with a second, considerably more compact, choral fantasia setting the chorale's doxology-like final strophe. The ritornello theme is reminiscent of the gigue from the third Orchestral Suite (probably performed, if not composed, during the same period). DS

For bibliography, *see* CANTATA, §1.

***Nun komm, der Heiden Heiland*** ('Come now, Saviour of the heathen') **(i)**. Cantata for the first Sunday in Advent, BWV61. This, one of the best known of all Bach's cantatas, was composed at the end of 1714 and first performed in the Weimar court chapel on Advent Sunday, 2 December 1714. The libretto is by Erdmann Neumeister, pastor in Hamburg and the main architect of the reform cantata incorporating simple recitative and da capo arias characteristic of Italian opera. The text was published three years later in Neumeister's *Fünffache Kirchen-Andachten* (Leipzig, 1717). The cantata is therefore one of Bach's earliest expositions in the new cantata form, and the first one he is known to have composed to a libretto by Neumeister. The text quotes and paraphrases Luther's Advent hymn *Nun komm der Heiden Heiland*, the primary Advent hymn in Lutheran tradition.

The cantata is simple in concept, requiring the modest resources of three vocal soloists and a four-part chorus accompanied by strings (including two violas), with bassoon strengthening the basso continuo. It was composed at a time when Bach was exploring French and Italian musical styles.

The first Sunday of the Advent season is also the first Sunday of the Church year, and Bach therefore began this cantata with an overture. The opening chorale movement, based on Luther's adapted plainchant melody, is a splendid French overture with an A–B–A (*grave*–fugue–*grave*)

structure, incorporating the lines of the chorale melody. The following tenor recitative (movement 2), outlining the significance of the Incarnation, leads to a da capo aria, also for tenor—a movement closely related to the two that follow it. In the tenor aria (movement 3) the request is made: 'Come, Jesus, come to your Church.' The response (movement 4) is a direct quotation of the words of Christ in Revelation 3: 20: 'Behold, I stand at the door, and knock.' The bass represents the voice of Jesus, as elsewhere in Bach's cantatas and Passions, and the knocking of the Saviour is depicted with pizzicato string chords, a typical example of Bach's inventive word-painting. Movement 5 represents the individual—in contrast to the corporate 'Church' of movement 3—responding to the invitation of the Saviour. Again as in other cantatas, the individual Soul is represented by the soprano voice. In a beautiful flow of melody, supported only by continuo instruments (which have an ostinato figure in the main section of the da capo form), the Soul opens its heart to the Saviour.

The cantata ends on a note of joy with the final section (*Abgesang*) of the final stanza of Philipp Nicolai's *Wie schön leuchtet der Morgenstern* (1599), set to its soaring melody, with obbligato violins. It is a striking cantata which Bach was happy to repeat during his early years in Leipzig, probably for his first Advent Sunday there in 1723, and perhaps in other years as well. RAL

For bibliography, *see* CANTATA, §1.

***Nun komm, der Heiden Heiland*** ('Come now, Saviour of the heathen') **(ii)**. Cantata for the first Sunday in Advent, BWV62. This was Bach's second CHORALE CANTATA based on Luther's Advent hymn, the first being the Weimar cantata BWV61. The present work belongs to Bach's second Leipzig *Jahrgang*, and was first performed on Advent Sunday, 3 December 1724. Bach is known to have performed it again some time during the period 1732–5. The libretto, by an unknown poet, uses stanzas 1 and 8 of Luther's hymn as the opening and closing movements, with stanzas 2–7 paraphrased in movements 2–5.

The opening chorus, in a spirited 6/4 metre, is framed by an orchestral ritornello in which the opening melodic line of the chorale melody is first heard in the continuo and then echoed in the upper strings and oboes. Altos, tenors, and basses enter in imitation with a variant form of the melody in diminution before the sopranos, with the horn in unison, sing the chorale line by line. The ritornello is also repeated between the lines of the chorale melody. The tenor da capo aria 'Bewundert, o Menschen' (movement 2) is a joyful 3/8 dance movement celebrating the coming of Christ, with florid vocal passages and word-painting on 'höchster Beherrsche' ('highest ruler').

A bass recitative (movement 3), leads to the bass aria 'Streite, siege, starker Held'—a da capo aria accompanied, unusually for Bach, by all the string instruments in octaves (marked in the score simply 'sempre col continuo'). The extended ostinato, which somewhat resembles the theme of the two-part Invention no. 14 in B♭ major, depicts the 'conquering hero' of the text. Not many of Bach's preliminary sketches have survived, but there is one for this movement; it is an earlier form of the extended ostinato, which was clearly composed before the voice part. Movement 5, an allusion to Christ as the light that shines on this dark world, is a delightful accompanied recitative for soprano and alto in which the two singers move almost entirely in 3rds and 6ths and throughout in rhythmic unison.

The cantata concludes with a 'simple' four-part chorale, enhanced by Bach's chromatic harmonies and with the soprano again doubled by the horn.

RAL

R. L. Marshall, *The Compositional Process of J. S. Bach: A Study of the Autograph Scores of the Vocal Works* (Princeton, 1972), i. 151–2; ii, no. 40. For further bibliography, *see* CANTATA, §1.

**Nur jedem das Seine** ('To each only his due'). Cantata for the 23rd Sunday after Trinity, BWV163, first performed at Weimar on 24 November 1715. The text is drawn from Salomo Franck's *Evangelisches Andachts-Opffer* (1715) and refers to the Gospel for the day (Matt. 22: 15–22), which deals with the Pharisees' questioning of Jesus as to the legitimacy of paying tribute to Caesar. The libretto takes up the theme suggested by Jesus's reply. The heart is the 'coin of tribute' rightfully due to God, but a false image is often stamped upon it. (It is worth recalling that Franck was a numismatist in charge of the ducal coin collection at Weimar.) Since no original parts survive to supplement Bach's composing score, information about possible later performances is lacking, but it seems likely that Bach would have revived the cantata in Leipzig as he did most of the other Weimar cantatas. The work is scored for SATB with strings (the third movement has two independent cello

parts) and continuo, and has something of the chamber-music character of many of the Weimar cantatas. (The first violin part is wrongly labelled 'oboe d'amore' in the *BG* edition.)

Somewhat unusually, BWV163 opens with a da capo aria. The opening motto motif, 'Nur jedem das Seine', can be seen as a paraphrase of Jesus's famous injunction to 'render unto Caesar the things which are Caesar's' and forms the basis of much of the material of the movement, treated in dense imitation by the instruments. The following simple recitative for bass features chromaticism for the phrase 'Ach, aber Ach, ist das nicht schlechtes Geld?' ('Ah, but is that not bad money?'). It leads to a bass aria, 'Laß mein Herz die Münze sein', in ritornello form and uniquely accompanied by two obbligato cellos which play material of almost concerto-like elaboration. The parts break into triplets over a long-held pedal point for the D major cadence at 'so komm doch und erneure'. Also unusual in design is the following movement, a duet recitative in arioso style for soprano and alto with continuo. Successive ideas in the text are treated in elaborate imitative style, with sections marked off by tempo markings, 'Un poco allegro' and 'Adagio' (the latter presumably implying a return to the original tempo). The following movement, 'Nimm mich mir und gib mich dir', is a chorale fantasia, with the upper strings (two violins and viola) giving out the chorale verse line by line to the accompaniment of an independent duet for soprano and alto.

The final chorale is lost except for the figured bass, which is all that appears in Bach's composing score. The libretto shows that it was a setting of the last strophe of Johann Heermann's chorale *Wo soll ich fliehen hin* (1630). DLH

For bibliography, *see* CANTATA, §1.

**Nützer, Johann Gottfried** (b. 30 March 1709; d. 2 Dec. 1780). Musician and teacher, born in Bitterfeld, about 30 km. (19 miles) north of Leipzig. He attended the Thomasschule in Leipzig from 1724 to 1731 and studied with Bach during that time; in the ENTWURFF Bach included him (as 'Nitzer') among the more accomplished of the school's singers. He found employment as a schoolteacher in Delitzch, not far from his native town, and Bach was godfather there to his son Johann Heinrich August on 9 December 1734, although he was not able to attend the christening in person.

# O

**O angenehme Melodei** ('Oh pleasing melody'). Secular cantata, BWV210a, in homage to Duke Christian of Saxe-Weißenfels. Between 9 and 17 January 1729 Duke Christian paid a visit to Leipzig, and it was during this visit, on 12 January, that Bach performed this cantata. This was not its only performance. It was repeated between 1735 and October 1740 in honour of Count Joachim Friedrich von Flemming, and again on at least one other occasion. Only the solo soprano part of this version has survived (in the Biblioteka Jagiellońska, Kraków), but Bach also adapted the work, with minimal alterations, as a wedding cantata, O HOLDER TAG, ERWÜNSCHTE ZEIT, some time during the 1740s, and in this version it survives complete.

H. Tiggemann, 'Unbekannte Textdrucke zu drei Gelegenheitskantaten J. S. Bach aus dem Jahre 1729', *BJb* 80 (1994), 7–23.

**Oberwerk.** An organ division played from the upper manual. In 18th-century Germany the term frequently signified the organ's primary division (*de facto* its HAUPTWERK), as in the organ Bach played at Arnstadt. Alternatively it might be a secondary division, as in the Silbermann organ at the Dresden Sophienkirche (where Bach performed three organ concerts in 1725 and 1731, and where his son Wilhelm Friedemann was organist from 1733 to 1746); that organ had two manuals: *Hauptwerk* and *Oberwerk*. QF

**Obituary** (Nekrolog). The only substantial obituary of Bach was that included in the final issue of Lorenz Mizler's periodical, *Musikalische Bibliothek*, and even that did not appear until four years after the composer's death, in 1754. It is often referred to (as in the present volume) simply as 'the Obituary', and, although not correct in every detail, it remains an important source of information about Bach and his music. It was published anonymously, but the authors are known to have been Bach's son Carl Philipp Emanuel and his pupil J. F. Agricola; the last four sentences were added by Mizler himself.

BDok iii, no. 666; H. T. David and A. Mendel, eds., *The Bach Reader* (London, 1945; 2nd edn., 1966), 214–24.

**oboe.** A double-reed woodwind instrument much used by Bach, especially as an obbligato instrument in his sacred vocal works. A process of fundamental technical change in the construction of woodwind instruments, and hence changes in the sounds they made, originated in France in the second half of the 17th century. The tube of the oboe, with its slightly conical bore, was now made in three sections. The wood was usually box, more rarely prunus. It was equipped with six frontal finger-holes, the third, and quite often the fourth also, taking the form of a pair of smaller holes. The construction of the keys demonstrates something about playing technique, since the position in which the instrument was held was not yet standardized: the little-finger open key ($c'$) in the centre of the instrument is usually in the shape of a swallow-tail with two 'wings', and the lateral $e^{b\prime}$ closed key is often symmetrically installed on each side of the instrument in the early period, which means that the player could operate the keys at the lower end of the instrument either with the right hand (as the player of the modern instrument does) or with the left, as illustrated in the engraving in J. C. Weigel's *Musicalisches Theatrum* (Nuremberg, c.1720), plate 8. Oboes with three keys are, as a rule, older than those with two (see Bate, pp. 41–2). The best known Leipzig instrument maker of Bach's day was J. H. Eichentopf, who made both woodwind and brass instruments. Altogether 29 of his instruments survive.

Among wind instruments, Bach gave pride of place to the oboe family, and called for the treble, in particular, in more than 160 works composed over the whole course of his career. The term 'hautbois' can refer also to other, lower-pitched oboes—the OBOE D'AMORE and OBOE DA CACCIA. He notated treble oboe parts in violin clef, and employed the instrument's full chromatic range from $c'$ to $d'''$. As Baroque oboes have neither a hole nor a key designated for the semitone above the fundamental pitch ($c\#'/d^{b\prime}$), this pitch can be produced only by partly closing the open $c'$ key, which brings problems of intonation in its wake. When the oboe is doubling another part (e.g. the violin) this note occurs frequently, and there are numerous movements in which special expedients to avoid $c\#'/d^{b\prime}$ can be observed, in the form of changes to the parts for example. When oboes are required to play *colla parte* with violins or singers, the part is not usually written out on a separate staff in the score. Oboe parts were frequently copied from violin parts, on Bach's instructions, with the result that they sometimes go down to *g*. This requirement to go lower than the oboe's compass

An oboe by Jacob Denner (1681–1735)

shows that the copyists worked mechanically and that Bach did not always check their work carefully enough. The players will have coped in these cases, either by omitting the notes they could not play or by playing them an octave higher; or Bach may have given them alternative instructions by word of mouth. Comparable things occur in parts for the two lower-pitched members of the oboe family.

The original parts show that in a majority of works the players had to change instruments from one movement to the next and that sometimes it was more than a simple matter of alternating between two. In addition to the lower-pitched members of the oboe family, an oboist was called upon to play recorder and transverse flute, and in one case (a revival of Cantata 199) viola and cello as well. These changes are not always indicated verbally, but often by a change of clef: the French violin clef signals a change to the recorder, the alto clef a change to the oboe da caccia, and the normal violin clef a return to the oboe, sometimes confirmed by the direction 'Hautbois l'ordinaire' or something similar. Using one oboe is characteristic of the earlier cantatas, and several solo cantatas. Two is the usual number. Three—often two 'ordinary' oboes and an oboe da caccia or *taille*—are used pre-eminently in works for major festivals in the Church year, elections of a new city council, homage cantatas, or works composed for the dedication of a new organ; on such occasions the ensemble usually included also a complement of trumpets and drums. Four oboes are required in the *St Matthew Passion*.

All imaginable ways of using the oboe as an obbligato instrument in arias (and recitatives) are to be found, in three- to five-part writing, with the strings, or with the whole orchestra. To such soloistic use should be added the purely instrumental trios without continuo (two oboes and bassoon) on the French model—for example in the last movement (Trio I) of the First Brandenburg Concerto and of the Sinfonia BWV1046a; in the first movements (middle sections) and Bourrées of the Orchestral Suites nos. 1 and 4; and in the trio sections of Cantata 97, first movement. And there are also, of course, the oboe concertos. It is hard to arrive at the exact number of these, as the original sources are lost and we cannot do more than reconstruct hypothetical versions, for example from the various keyboard arrangements. In chorales the oboes usually double the cantus firmus in the soprano; sometimes the second oboe doubles the alto. The doubling of vocal parts in arias is the exception rather than the rule; it is more common for the violins to be supported. The oboe's lower register and limited compass, in comparison to the recorder and transverse flute, mean that it is almost never required to provide octave doubling. Nevertheless, the source materials contain numerous unusual sonorities—for instance when Bach has doubling oboes rest in the vocal sections of arias, or exploits registral nuances or dynamic gradations, ripieno shadings, or echo effects. Last, but not least, Bach often uses the oboe family as a means of evoking a pastoral milieu, notably in the shepherds' music in the *Christmas Oratorio* but also in association with references to Christ as the good shepherd in some of the cantatas, for example nos. 85, 92, 104, and 112.                UP

P. Bate, *The Oboe: An Outline of its History, Development and Construction* (London, 1956; 3rd edn. 1975); B. Haynes, 'J. S. Bachs Oboenkonzerte', *BJb* 78 (1992), 23–43; H. Heyde, 'Der Instrumentenbau in Leipzig zur Zeit Johann Sebastian Bachs', in U. Prinz, ed., *300 Jahre Johann Sebastian Bach: sein Werk in Handschriften und Dokumenten; Musikinstrumente seiner Zeit; seine Zeitgenossen* [exhibition catalogue] (Tutzing, 1985), 73–88; E. Nickel, *Der Holzblasinstrumentenbau in der Freien Reichsstadt Nürnberg* (Munich, 1971); W. Waterhouse, *The New Langwill Index* (London, 1993).

**oboe da caccia.** A tenor member of the oboe family, known to Bach as an *hautbois da caccia* or *taille (de hautbois)*. It survives in four different forms, with a straight or curved tube, and with a flared or pear-shaped bell; the bell may be of wood or brass. The flared brass bell was evidently a speciality of the Leipzig instrument maker J. H. Eichentopf, who made outstanding wind instruments, both wood and brass. Two of his oboes da caccia survive, both of 1724.

Bach used the instrument in its full chromatic range, from $f$ to $a^{b''}$, usually notating its part in the alto clef, to sound as written. The oboe da caccia can appear alone or in pairs, or partnering higher-register oboes; 'taille' is given as a designation of the register only when the instrument is used alongside two oboes. Oboe da caccia and *taille* are each specified in some 30 works, used in ways described elsewhere (*see* OBOE), with the additional function as 'Bassätchen' (*bassetto*), for example in the soprano aria 'Aus Liebe will mein Heiland sterben' in the *St Matthew Passion*. Interesting conclusions about the ability of individual players can be drawn from the original parts, for instance when the oboe da caccia obbligato in an aria is included in the first oboe part.

In modern performances, prior to the revival of interest in period instruments, oboe da caccia parts were regularly played on the cor anglais.                UP

R. Dahlqvist, 'Taille, oboe da caccia and corno inglese', *Galpin Society Journal*, 26 (1973), 58–71; C. Karp, 'Structural Details of Two J. H. Eichentopf

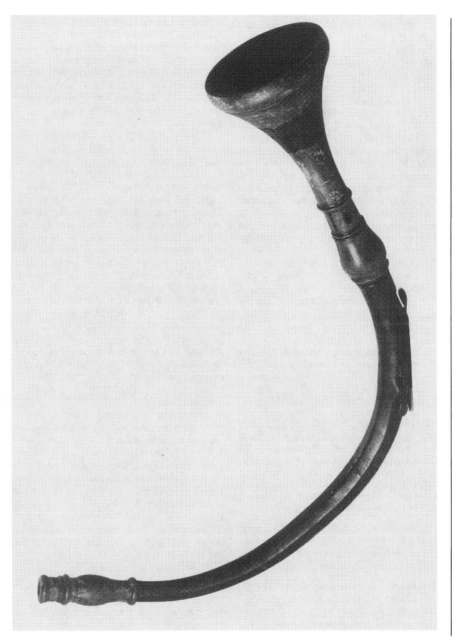

An oboe da caccia by M. Deper, c.1750 (Germanisches Nationalmuseum, Nuremberg)

Oboi da Caccia', *Galpin Society Journal*, 26 (1973), 55–7; U. Prinz, *Studien zum Instrumentarium J. S. Bachs mit besonderer Berücksichtigung der Kantaten* (Tübingen, 1979), 161–84.

**oboe d'amore.** A double-reed woodwind instrument, known in Germany from about 1720 as the 'hautbois d'amour'. It is pitched a minor 3rd lower than the normal oboe, and its tube ends in a characteristic pear-shaped bell. Surviving examples by the Leipzig instrument maker J. H. Eichentopf include some with two or three keys. Several of Bach's contemporaries, notably Christoph Graupner, G. H. Stölzel, and Telemann, used the oboe d'amore frequently. Bach himself used it for the first time in Cantata 23, one of his test pieces for the Leipzig Kantorate, performed on Quinquagesima Sunday 1723. He used the full extent of the instrument's chromatic range, from *a* to *c♯'''* (or *d'''*). Five different methods of notating pitch and fingering are to be found in works of 1723, because a standard notation had not yet been settled on at that date, only a few years after the instrument had been invented.

Bach required players to alternate between oboe and oboe d'amore in over two dozen works, and in four of them to play the oboe da caccia as well. This is not always stipulated in words in the original parts, and the players must draw their own conclusions from the clef, the key, and the compass. With its fundamental pitch of *a*, the oboe d'amore is particularly suited to playing music in keys with several sharps. It is distinctive in timbre and highly expressive, and Bach used it in about 100 works, as a soloist and also in pairs, or partnered by the *taille* or two oboes da caccia.

UP

W. Breig, 'Zur Gestalt von J. S. Bachs Konzert für Oboe d'amore', *Tibia*, 18 (1993), 431–48; D. Jones, 'Über die Herstellung von Reproduktionen barocker Oboi d'amore und Oboe da caccia', *Tibia*, 9 (1984), 13–20; U. Prinz, ed., *300 Jahre Johann Sebastian Bach: sein Werk in Handschriften und Dokumenten; Musikinstrumente seiner Zeit; seine Zeitgenossen* [exhibition catalogue] (Tutzing, 1985), 309–11.

**Oculi.** In the CHURCH CALENDAR, the third Sunday in Lent. It takes its name from the introit to the Mass for that day in the Latin rite, beginning 'Oculi mei semper ad Dominum'.

***O ewiges Feuer, o Ursprung der Liebe*** ('O eternal flame, o fount of love'). Cantata for Whit Sunday, BWV34, first performed about 1746. Most of the music has been derived from a wedding cantata with the same title (BWV34a) written about 20 years earlier, evidently for the nuptials of a Leipzig clergyman. Bach was probably inspired to make the adaptation by a reference in the opening chorus of the wedding piece to the 'himmlische

Flammen' ('heavenly flames'); the Epistle reading for Whit Sunday (Acts 2: 1–13) tells of the 'cloven tongues like as of fire' which appeared to the apostles and 'sat upon each of them'. These are represented in the music by crackling semiquaver figuration for the first violins, anticipating Loge's music in Wagner's *Ring of the Nibelung*, while the 'ewiges' ('eternal') flame is expressed in long-held notes for both voices and instruments. Trumpets and drums add a festive note to this expansive movement in da capo form (A–B–A); the other instruments are two oboes, strings, and continuo.

The text of the cantata as a whole, however, springs not from the Epistle but from the Gospel reading appointed for the day, St John 14: 23–31, in particular v. 23: 'If a man love me, he will keep my words: and my Father will love him, and we will come unto him, and make our abode with him.' The adaptation required only minimal changes to the wedding text, which the anonymous librettist achieved by removing references to the bridal pair in the three concerted numbers and by inventing two new recitatives to connect them. Thus, in the alto aria 'Wohl euch, ihr auserwählten Seelen' the 'chosen sheep whom a faithful Jacob loves' become 'the chosen souls whom God selected as his dwelling'. Nevertheless, this beautiful aria, with its reticent accompaniment of flutes and muted strings, still conveys a feeling of tender affection in a key (A major) closely associated in Bach's music (as in Mozart's) with expressions of human love. The modified da capo structure is nowhere more convincingly or imaginatively deployed.

A second brief recitative (bass), emphasizing once again the main message of the Gospel, ends with a reference to the motto that God has inscribed in the hearts of men, and it is with the motto itself, 'Peace over Israel', that the final chorus begins. The imposing, rather Handelian chords to which it is set serve to introduce a jubilant movement in two sections, in each of which thanksgiving to God is expressed first by the orchestra alone (with, once again, trumpets and drums to the fore) and then by voices and instruments together.

For bibliography, *see* CANTATA, §1.

***O Ewigkeit, du Donnerwort*** ('O eternity, thou thunderous word') **(i).** Cantata, BWV20, for the first Sunday after Trinity, first performed on 11 June 1724. The anonymous libretto is based on Johann Rist's chorale (1642), with the twelve strophes of the hymn condensed and adapted to form an eleven-movement cantata. Strophes 1, 8, and 12 are retained verbatim, and the others paraphrased in the usual manner of Bach's Leipzig

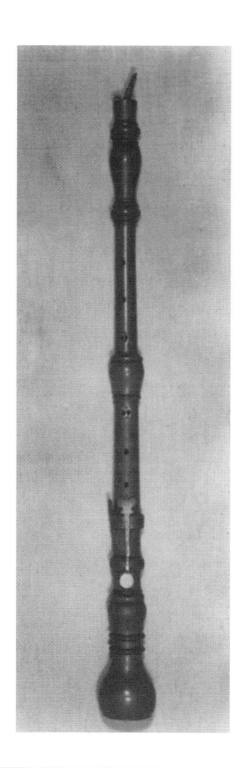

An oboe d'amore by J. H. Eichentopf, after 1720
(Koninklijk Musiekconservatorium Instrumentenmuseum, Brussels)

# O Ewigkeit, du Donnerwort

cantata librettos. The text dwells on the awesome prospect of eternity, stressing the justice of God, the pains of the damned, and the urgent need for repentance, making passing reference in movement 10 to the Dives and Lazarus story (Luke 16: 19–31), which forms the Gospel for the day. The cantata is in two parts, with movements 8–11 inscribed 'seconda parte' and presumably designed to be performed during Communion in the usual manner (*see* HAUPTGOTTESDIENST). BWV20 is scored for SATB with trumpet (doubling slide trumpet), three oboes, strings, and continuo.

Like BWV61 (*Nun komm, der Heiden Heiland*), BWV20 opens with a chorus in which the first strophe of the chorale is combined with a French overture. Lines 1–3 of the chorale form the opening Grave section of the overture, with lines 4–6 (which repeat the melody of lines 1–3) set to the rapid triple-time second section (marked 'Vivace'). Here the chorale lines are combined with a freely constructed double fugue, with a chromatically descending subject perhaps suggested by line 5, 'Ich weiß vor großer Traurigkeit' ('I know not, for great sorrow'). The return of the main tempo for lines 7 and 8 is marked by a dramatic pause chord with chromaticism and a sudden disintegration of texture. This, too, is a response to an idea in the text: 'Mein ganz erschrocknes Herz erbebt' ('My wholly terrified heart trembles').

After a simple recitative for tenor comes a tenor aria with strings and continuo, 'Ewigkeit, du machst mir bange', setting a text which dwells gloomily on the fear of damnation and the torments of the damned. Word-painting ideas include long-held notes for 'Ewigkeit', semiquaver melismas for 'Flammen, die auf ewig brennen' ('flames that burn for ever'), and sighing paired appoggiaturas. After another simple recitative, the bass sings a da capo aria, 'Gott ist gerecht', scored with three oboes and continuo. Much of the material is based on the opening arpeggio figure and its florid semiquaver continuation. Another aria, 'O Mensch, errette deine Seele', follows immediately, without introductory recitative. Scored for alto with strings and continuo, it is in an unusual form (A–A′–B–B′), with the outer statements scored for instruments only and the inner ones doubled by the singer. It makes extensive use of hemiola and features rich chromatic harmony. Part 1 ends with a harmonization of the chorale in plain style.

Part 2 is livelier in tone, concentrating on the need to renounce sin and undertake appropriate action for the amendment of life. It opens with a bass aria, 'Wacht auf, wacht auf', accompanied by strings and woodwind, with a prominent solo trumpet part. The ritornello begins with an unaccompanied trumpet call, followed by *tirades* from the oboes and strings, and the aria continues in similar vein with more than a suggestion of the dotted French style. The only darkening of the atmosphere occurs at the phrase 'vor das Gerichte ruft' ('calls to trial'), where the prospect of final judgement elicits a sudden turn to the minor. After a simple recitative for alto comes a duet in ritornello form for alto and tenor, 'O Menschenkind, hör auf geschwind', in which mankind is again exhorted to leave his sinful ways. The voice parts are elaborately imitative in character, including word-painting for 'ein Tröpflein Wasser' ('a little drop of water'); it is here that the reference to Dives and Lazarus occurs. The work ends with the same four-part harmonization of the chorale that concluded Part 1. DLH

For bibliography, *see* CANTATA, §1.

***O Ewigkeit, du Donnerwort*** ('O eternity, thou thunderous word') **(ii)**. Cantata, BWV60, for the 24th Sunday after Trinity. On the folder containing the original performing parts is the following notation, in Bach's own hand: 'Dominica 24 post Trinit: Dialogus Zwischen Furcht u. Hoffnung'. From it we learn of the work's liturgical occasion, which in 1723, the year of its première, fell on 7 November. Bach's choice of the word 'dialogus' instead of 'concerto' (his preferred term for sacred vocal works of this type) reflects its unusual concentration on pairs of voices: none of the movements employs just one vocal soloist, and all four voices are required only for the concluding chorale. Additionally, the inscription discloses the identities of the two main partners in the dialogue: the allegorical figures Furcht ('Fear') and Hoffnung ('Hope').

The subject of this work is the fear of death. Rather than a detached intellectual treatment, it is a gripping dramatization of existential angst. The opening movement is a duet in which the alto and tenor assume the roles of Fear and Hope respectively. The alto (doubled by the horn) sings a chorale stanza (the same one that opens Cantata 20) likening eternity to a 'thunderous word'. Its contemplation engenders both emotional and physical distress. It feels like a 'sword that bores through the soul', brings 'great sadness' and confusion, and causes trembling and a dry mouth. After the alto has presented the first sentence, the tenor (Hope) counters with a simple expression of trust: 'Herr, ich warte auf dein Heil' ('I wait for thy salvation, O Lord': Genesis 49: 18, also Psalm 119: 166). Musical means are employed for illustrative purposes throughout this movement. For instance, the sustained notes in the continuo at the beginning (and analogous passages) and the lengthy melismas in the tenor represent the passing of time associated with 'Ewigkeit' ('eternity') and 'warte' ('wait'). Similarly, it is no accident that the final word in the alto part ('klebt'), used to describe the tongue sticking to the gums, is held out for no fewer than three and a half bars! Moreover, the terrifying sound of eternity's thunderous word is evoked by dissonant clusters of repeated notes in the strings (e.g. beat 3 of bars 1 and 3).

A feature of the first recitative (movement 2)—a dialogue between Fear and Hope—is that the two voices never sing simultaneously, even when the recitative twice gives way to arioso. Hope offers a response to each of Fear's three complaints, lengthy melismas illustrating the words 'martert' ('tortures') and 'ertragen' ('endure') at bars 8–11 and 21–6 respectively. (The meaning of 'martert' is also underscored with chromaticism.) It is worth observing, too, that the first few notes of the recitative quote from the beginning of the chorale in the previous movement (the third and fourth notes are raised by a semitone, however).

Movement 3, an aria for two solo instruments (oboe d'amore and violin) and two vocal soloists (alto and tenor) plus continuo, embodies the principle of contrast. The characteristic profile of the oboe d'amore part, defined by the incessant dotted quaver–semiquaver rhythm, is strongly differentiated from that of the violin, which involves rapid scale motion. Moreover, in each of three pairs of contradictory statements, the vocal soloists first sing separately—the alto expressing the viewpoint of Fear, the tenor the opposite perspective of Hope—before joining together. (As in the previous movement, however, Hope has the last word.) A different mode of contrast is found at the end of the last vocal section (bars 76–80), where the uniform dotted rhythms in all three instrumental parts punctuate the lengthy melisma sung by the tenor.

The dramatic turning-point occurs in movement 4, a recitative in which Fear (alto) is confronted three times by a heavenly voice (bass), which sings, in arioso style, progressively longer fragments of Revelation 14: 13 ('Blessed are the dead, which die in the Lord from henceforth'). At first Fear speaks of death as the enemy of hope, and then worries about the fate of the soul and the decay of the body. By the end of the movement, however, Fear is vanquished and both the body and soul receive encouragement and refreshment. The relatively settled tonality of the arioso sections stands in marked contrast to the harmonic peregrinations of the recitative passages (e.g. bars 14–17).

The final movement, a four-part setting of the chorale *Es ist genung*, includes a number of bold harmonic progressions, for example the outlining of a tritone in the first two bars of the soprano line and intense chromaticism in bars 15–16, illustrating the words 'großer Jammer' ('great misery')—a harmonization made famous by its incorporation into Alban Berg's Violin Concerto (1935). It is a remarkable expression of trust, which functions both as summary and conclusion of the work, as well as response and application for the believer.

SAC

For bibliography, *see* CANTATA, §1.

***O Haupt voll Blut und Wunden.*** Hymn by Paul Gerhardt (1656). *See* PASSION CHORALE.

***O heilges Geist- und Wasserbad*** ('O holy bath of spirit and water'). Cantata for Trinity Sunday, BWV165, first performed on 16 June 1715. It was probably repeated on Trinity Sunday (7 June) the following year, and it was revived in Leipzig, possibly on Trinity Sunday (4 June) 1724. Like other Weimar cantatas it is on a modest, intimate scale, with four voices accompanied by strings, continuo, and bassoon (which, however, has no independent part). The text, by Salomo Franck, stems from the Gospel reading for Trinity Sunday, St John 3: 1–15, and particularly from Jesus's words to the Pharisee Nicodemus: 'Except a man be born of water and of the Spirit, he cannot enter into the kingdom of God.'

The first movement, for soprano with all the instruments accompanying, is unusual in structure. The seven lines of the verse are set in five phrases of 2 + 1 + 2 + 1 + 1 lines; each phrase is for the most part melodically independent of the others (the second starts as an inversion of the first, and the last recalls the words and music of the first) and each one starts from a different key centre, but the whole is held together mainly by recurrent motifs from the fugal ritornello heard at the opening and repeated in full at the end. A similar flexibility in the shaping of the vocal line can be seen in the alto aria with continuo, 'Jesu, der aus große Liebe', and more especially in the tenor's 'Jesu, meines Todes Tod', with unison violins and continuo. Separating these from the first aria and from each other are two bass recitatives. The first, with continuo accompaniment, is by no means inexpressive, but the second, accompanied by strings and bassoon, is in many ways the most striking movement in the work. The instruments sometimes sustain long-held chords, but at other points they play a more active role. Their most telling contribution, however, comes at the very end when, after the bass has sung 'wenn alle Kraft vergehet' ('when all strength fails'), the upper strings cannot find the energy to play the expected final chord, leaving only the bass instruments (without continuo harmony) to sound a quiet low

G. Bach was to do something similar, to no less telling effect, at the end of 'Esurientes implevit bonis' in the *Magnificat*, where the 'hungry are sent empty away'.

A simple four-part setting of the fifth strophe of Ludwig Helmbold's hymn *Nun laßt uns Gott, dem Herrn* (1575) ends the cantata. *See also* KÖPPING, JOHANN CHRISTIAN.

For bibliography, *see* CANTATA, §1.

***O holder Tag, erwünschte Zeit*** ('O glorious day, longed-for time'). Wedding cantata, BWV210, for an unknown occasion. It is scored for soprano solo, flute, oboe d'amore, strings, and continuo. The surviving performance material, in the hands of J. S. Bach and J. F. Agricola, points to the last decade of Bach's life, and the following marriages during that time in Leipzig have been suggested as possible occasions for the cantata: 3 April 1742, between Friedrich Heinrich Graf (1713–77) and Anna Regina Bose (1716–50); 6 February 1744, between Zacharias Richter and Christina Sibylla Bose (1711–49); and 11 August 1746, between Friedrich Gottlieb Zoller and Johann Catharina Amalia Schatz. The music, however, derives from a much earlier homage cantata, O ANGENEHME MELODEI, dating from 1729. The original arias (nos. 2, 4, 6, 8, and 10) and most of the final recitative (no. 9) have been retained, with modifications to their texts where appropriate, and new recitatives have been composed for nos. 1, 3, 5, and 7. As refashioned, the text is addressed primarily to the bridegroom, meditating on the place of love and music in his future life.

As is usually the case with wedding cantatas, this one is divided into two sections, the first to be performed before the exchange of vows, the second afterwards. The virtuosity of the first aria, 'Spielet, ihr beseelten Lieder' and its high written tessitura (reaching $c\sharp'''$ at one point) suggest a mature and accomplished singer—possibly Bach's wife Anna Magdalena if the wedding ceremony was performed at home. In this aria the oboe d'amore doubles the first violin throughout; in 'Ruhet hie, matte Töne' (no. 4), a slumber aria in a languorous 12/8 time, the two instruments are given separate obbligato parts. Both arias are followed in the 1729 libretto by the unusual rubric 'S'il plait D[a] C[apo]' (in the case of no. 4, 'D. C. s'il plait'); Bach responded with a literal da capo in no. 2 and a modified da capo in no. 4. After a third recitative, which again takes the singer to a high $c\sharp'''$, a solo flute begins an aria ritornello in B minor, only to be interrupted after one bar by the soprano's 'Schweigt, ihr Flöten, schweigt, ihr Töne' ('Be silent, flutes, cease your sounds'); the flute must then complete its ritornello after the singer's motto opening, but it continues to adorn

the music with decorative filigree in defiance of the words.

With the next recitative (no. 7) the power of music and its place in the forthcoming marriage are at last asserted. The text of 'Großer Gönner, dein Vergnügen' (no. 8) addresses the bridegroom as a beneficent music-lover. Bach set it as a C$\sharp$ minor aria in polonaise rhythm, ignoring the 'Da Capo' indication in the original text (even though it was not in this instance followed by 's'il plait'). The aria appears also, a tone lower, in Cantata 30*a*, *Angenehmes Wiederau, freue dich in deinen Auen*. Bach was able to retain the accompanied recitative (no. 9) with minimal alteration, adding six bars at the end to express good wishes for the future of the bridal pair, a sentiment carried over into the final movement—a high-spirited da capo aria in A major, accompanied by all the instruments, which again calls for some virtuoso singing.

H. Tiggemann, 'Unbekannte Textdrucke zu drei Gelegenheitskantaten J. S. Bach aus dem Jahre 1729', *BJb* 80 (1994), 7–23. For further bibliography, *see* CANTATA, §2.

**Ohrdruf.** Town in Thuringia where Bach lived from 1695 to 1700. Ohrdruf was the capital of the small county of Gleichen. The local school was of some importance: pupils came not only from distant parts of Thuringia, but also from Hesse.

Bach was a successful pupil at the school and lived with his brother Johann Christoph (ii), who had gone to Ohrdruf when only 18 as organist at the MICHAELISKIRCHE (destroyed in World War II). Ohrdruf organists normally served also as teachers at the school, but, perhaps following the example of the Eisenach Kantor A. C. Dedekind (*c*.1660–1706), Christoph tried to confine his duties to music. But he could not live that way (he earned only 40–50 florins a year), a fact which he grasped too late. In 1696 he was elected organist in Gotha, but the consistory at Ohrdruf refused his release and demanded his promise of lifelong service. It was only in 1700 that he took up the additional teaching duties. Probably Johann Sebastian was influenced by these impressions in mapping out his own musical career as an organist (at a socially higher level).

Johann Christoph is said to have been Bach's first keyboard teacher—perhaps a quite authoritarian one. In the Obituary it is reported that Sebastian copied by moonlight a volume of clavier works which Christoph kept in secret; when Bach's 'innocent deceit' was discovered, the copy was taken from him. Apparently, in the long run relations between the brothers were quite friendly. They stood godfather to each other's children, and from Johann Christoph's family two important musical sources survive (the Andreas Bach

Book and the Möller manuscript), containing several of Bach's early keyboard works.

In 1697 a new Kantor was appointed, Elias Herda (1674–1728). He had studied theology at the University of Jena with great success and was a respected teacher at the school. His duties were not primarily musical, and in the services he was responsible only for the singing of chorales. Before his university studies he had attended the Michaelisschule in Lüneburg, where Bach went when he left Ohrdruf towards Easter 1700. The reason for Bach's departure is given in the school reports as 'ob defectum hospitiorum'. This might indicate that the top class of the school was overcrowded; a further six pupils were dismissed for the same reason in 1698–1700. It meant that Bach had lost his entitlement to attend the school at low (or no) cost, and might be explained by his change of voice (*see* LÜNEBURG). KK

BDok iii, no. 666; K. Küster, *Der junge Bach* (Stuttgart, 1996), 62–81; H.-J. Schulze, 'Johann Christoph Bach (1671 bis 1721), "Organist und Schul Collega in Ohrdruf": Johann Sebastian Bachs erster Lehrer', *BJb* 71 (1985), 55–81.

### O Jesu Christ, meins Lebens Licht ('O Jesus Christ, light of my life'). Motet for four voices and instruments, BWV118/231, on Martin Behm's hymn (?1608), known in two versions that differ in their instrumentation. Bach clearly called this work a motet despite its limited use of independent instruments, but modern observers have stubbornly resisted his designation.

In both versions the chorale melody is presented phrase by phrase as a long-note cantus firmus in the soprano. Each cantus firmus phrase is introduced and then supported by imitative counterpoint in the lower voices based on the phrases of the chorale; this is classic chorale motet texture. At the beginning of the motet, and between chorale phrases, the principal group of instruments plays ritornello-like interludes based on a limited amount of musical material; when the voices sing, these instruments double the vocal lines. Two additional instruments (*litui*) participate in the ritornellos, but mostly play non-thematic harmonic filler. All this occurs over a continuous pulsating bass line.

The two versions differ in their instrumentation. The first calls for a cornett and three trombones (strongly associated with motet style), with no basso continuo; the second, two violins, viola, and continuo, with the optional addition of three oboes and bassoon, presumably doubling the vocal lines. Both versions call for a pair of instruments that Bach calls 'lituo' (*see* LITUUS). To judge from their range and from historical uses of the term, this probably refers to a B♭ horn of some kind. The two versions probably also differ in

their performing pitch; the first (brass) version is Bach's only Leipzig work notated in *Chorton*, whereas the second (string) version, notated at the same level, probably sounded a step lower at *Cammerton* pitch.

From source evidence, the first version can be dated to about 1736–7, the second version to about 1746–7, but for neither performance is the occasion known. The lack of stationary instruments, including continuo, in the first version has led to the suggestion that it was for outdoor performance, perhaps at a funeral or during a funeral procession. The provision of repeats for the performance of more than one stanza may support this theory.

There remains the question of genre. The partly independent instruments have led commentators to regard the composition as a vocal concerto (cantata): the *BG* published it among the church cantatas, and it was given a BWV number accordingly. But Bach labelled both autograph scores 'Motetto', a term he used in limited senses, and we need to take that label seriously. In most respects *O Jesu Christ, meins Lebens Licht* has the textual and musical features of a motet: it sets a chorale as a contrapuntally supported cantus firmus in large note values. Its first version uses trombones, strongly associated with MOTET STYLE, and they are mostly *colla parte* with the voices. The independent instrumental sections are unusual for a motet, but they are limited in their thematic material in the ritornello sections, and entirely subservient to the voices (limited to harmonic filler) otherwise. Bach apparently held a slightly expanded view of what a motet could be. DRM

T. MacCracken, 'Die Verwendung der Blechblasinstrumente bei J. S. Bach unter besonderer Berücksichtigung der Tromba da tirarsi', *BJb* 70 (1984), 59–89; H.-J. Schulze, ' "O Jesu Christ, meins Lebens Licht": On the Transmission of a Bach Source and the Riddle of its Origin', in P. Brainard and R. Robinson, eds., *A Bach Tribute: Essays in Honor of William H. Scheide* (Chapel Hill, NC, 1993), 209–20. For further bibliography, *see* MOTET.

### Oley, Johann Christoph (bap. 3 June 1738; d. 20 Jan. 1789). Organist and composer, born in Bernburg, near Cöthen. In 1755 he was appointed organist at Bernburg, and in 1762 he became organist and assistant schoolmaster at the reformed church in Aschersleben, where he remained until his death. Oley was a renowned performer and prolific composer. Despite claims to the contrary, there is no documentary evidence that he was a Bach pupil. He did, however, prepare manuscript copies of several keyboard works by Bach, including an early version of the Italian Concerto. Oley also owned a copy of the original printed edition of the Schübler Chorales, to which

he added revised readings found in Bach's *Hand-exemplar*, as well as variant readings found in no other source.                                               RTS

K. Beißwenger, 'An Early Version of the First Movement of the *Italian Concerto* BWV 971 from the Scholz Collection', in D. Melamed, ed., *Bach Studies 2* (Cambridge, 1995), 1–19; H. Löffler, 'Die Schüler Joh. Seb. Bachs', *BJb* 50 (1953), 5–28; R. Sietz, 'Die Orgelkompositionen des Schülerkreises um Johann Sebastian Bach', *BJb* 32 (1935), 33–96; C. Wolff, 'The Clavier-Übung Series', in *Bach: Essays on his Life and Music* (Cambridge, Mass., 1991), 189–213.

**oratorio.** A musical work on a sacred text, usually with some dramatic element but not normally designed for theatrical or liturgical performance. J. G. Walther, in his *Musicalisches Lexikon* (1732), defined it as 'the musical conception of a sacred history'. Extended vocal settings of biblical stories were particularly popular during the 17th and 18th centuries and owed much to contemporary operatic styles. In Italy from the early 17th century oratorios were written for the edification of religious confraternities during Lent and were performed in oratories attached to major churches. By the 18th century they were sung in a wide variety of contexts (palaces, conservatories, and theatres), often as a Lenten substitute for opera. In England the oratorio was a commercial genre, and concert performances of Handel's oratorios (usually in theatres) were given almost exclusively for the entertainment of paying audiences.

During the early 18th century German oratorio was developed in parallel with opera in Hamburg (by Keiser, Mattheson, and Telemann) and Dresden (by Hasse), and was well established in the *Abendmusiken* at Lübeck. The subject-matter was usually biblical, and although some use was also made of actual texts from the Bible (often in choruses), the librettos were predominantly poetic. Although chorales were often included and choruses were prominent, the works otherwise owed much to Italian opera and oratorio in their regular succession of recitatives and arias. Oratorios were performed at concerts, on ceremonial occasions, and occasionally within the liturgy; Mattheson's oratorios substituted for cantatas on feast-days at Hamburg Cathedral and were later heard in public concerts.

In their final form Bach's *Christmas, Easter,* and *Ascension Oratorios* seem to have been conceived together to cover the most important festivals of the Church year in 1734–5. The 1730s witnessed a marked decline in Bach's output for the Church and an interest in revising and reusing earlier music. All three oratorios are parody works strongly indebted to the cantata. The *Christmas Oratorio* is actually a series of six self-contained but linked cantatas based on secular cantatas written for the Dresden royal family (BWV213–15) and Count Jakob Heinrich von Flemming (BWV Anh. I 10) in 1731–4.

Partly because of their parody nature, Bach's oratorios are hybrids, combining musical elements of the cantata with literary features of the oratorio Passion and the *historia* (Passion, Easter, and Christmas stories with biblical texts performed in church). Like his Passions, the *Christmas* and *Ascension Oratorios* make use of biblical narrative assigned to an 'Evangelist', together with poetic texts (for arias, choruses, and some recitatives) and Lutheran chorales. The narrative thread, mostly from the Gospels, is really the only major feature to distinguish them from cantatas. The *Easter Oratorio*, without biblical texts or chorales but with a freely invented libretto, most closely approaches the style of the Italianate oratorio. Compared with those of his European contemporaries, the main distinguishing feature of Bach's oratorios was one of function rather than style. Even among his fellow countrymen, Bach was one of the few composers whose oratorios were specifically intended for liturgical performance on important feast-days when the Lutheran church permitted oratorios to be given in place of the usual cantatas.

Although the label 'Oratorium' was applied to a wider range of works in Germany than elsewhere in Europe, Bach's so-called oratorios are unique. Why he or his librettist employed the term is not clear, though in view of the indebtedness of the works to the cantata they may have followed Neumeister's narrow definition of the oratorio propounded in his Leipzig lectures on poetry in 1695. For him the oratorio was a literary companion of the cantata which coupled pre-existing texts (biblical passages and chorales) with newly written poetic verses (exemplified by two cantata texts of his own in *Die allerneueste Art* of 1707). The use of the all-embracing term 'Oratorium' to encompass the six Christmas cantatas may have been suggested by the five-part oratorios performed over the five days which constituted the Lübeck *Abendmusiken*.                                               SH

*See also* ABENDMUSIK, ASCENSION ORATORIO, CHRISTMAS ORATORIO, and EASTER ORATORIO.

S. Daw, *The Music of Johann Sebastian Bach: The Choral Works* (Rutherford, NJ, 1981); H. Smither, *A History of the Oratorio*, ii (Chapel Hill, NC, 1977).

**orchestra.** The size, and to some degree the make-up, of Bach's instrumental ensemble in his various places of employment has been the subject of much scholarly debate. In many ways the problems of determining who played in Bach's orchestra parallel those of determining who sang in Bach's chorus. The controversies centre on the number of performers available to Bach, the number of surviving parts in the original performance material, and how many players were likely to have read from each part. This is most crucial in the case of the strings, which formed the core of the instrumental ensembles.

Schulze posits the likely instrumental forces available in each place of Bach's employment, as well as in courts and towns that he is known or thought to have visited. Very little is known about ensembles available to Bach in Arnstadt or Mühlhausen. In Weimar the core of the instrumental contingent apparently consisted of three violinists, from 1714 two cellists, one bassoon, and two trumpets, with an additional ensemble supplying five more trumpet players and a timpanist (the Weimar Easter cantata *Der Himmel lacht! die Erde jubiliert* (1715) also requires three oboes and oboe da caccia).

In Cöthen Bach had a *Kapelle* of about 18 musicians, which did not include regular horn players. Schulze speculates that extra players were brought in to augment the resident ensembles in both Weimar and Cöthen, and that the string parts were intended to be doubled. But, as Rifkin points out, in hardly any pre-Leipzig work does a surviving set of parts include more than one string part for each musical line (i.e. one first violin part, one second violin part, one or two viola parts, and one or more bass parts). There is no evidence that more than one player played from each physical part (as is the usual practice for string players today); thus, the number of surviving string parts seems to correspond to the number of players listed on official personnel lists. Bach's famous ENTWURFF of 1730 appears to specify '2 or even 3 for violin 1; 2 or 3 for violin 2; 2 for viola 1; 2 for viola 2; 2 for violoncello; 2 for the violone; 2, or sometimes 3 according to need, for the oboe; 1 or 2 for the bassoon; 3 for the trumpets; 1 for the timpani; a total of at least 18 people. NB: if a cantata also needs flute, either recorders or transverse flutes (these often alternate), then we need at least 2 more people. This makes altogether 20 instrumentalists.'

Whether Bach intended that the desired number of string players would all play together in a single work, or that they would make up a roster from which the string players for individual pieces would be chosen (in the same way that the total number of singers specified in the *Entwurff*, as Rifkin has convincingly argued, does not mean that they were all to sing together in the same piece) is unclear. In Leipzig sets of sacred cantata parts usually included two first violin and two second violin parts, while the instrumental works and secular cantatas in small scorings still maintained one-to-a-part strings. While Schulze posited lost string parts for some of these works, Rifkin has presented evidence to show that most surviving sets are complete. Thus, the instrumental ensemble in Leipzig was still quite small: one to a part for smaller secular works, and essentially one to a part (except for the violins, for which there is a single doublet each) in almost all of his sacred music and secular cantatas in larger scorings. In all cases, no more instruments should necessarily be presumed than there were actual parts, and enough sets of parts survive to infer Bach's general practice with regard to instrumental doubling.

As far as the scoring of Bach's bass lines is concerned, Dreyfus lists 28 vocal works with surviving parts for the bassoon. In only six of these is the bassoon part identical with the continuo part. An additional 16 vocal works indicate the bassoon on the score. The participation of the bassoon in works with no indication of its presence has been debated; according to Dreyfus, the bassoon was a regular member of Bach's ensemble only in Weimar, but it was used, probably more irregularly, in Leipzig. In pre-Weimar works the cello should probably be used only when explicitly called for. The vocal works from Weimar and Cöthen consistently specify the use of the cello; in Leipzig the bass parts are usually labelled simply 'continuo' but the participation of a cello on this part is likely. The word 'violone' referred in Bach's time to a variety of string instruments at either 8′ or 16′ pitch: a small violone in G at 8′ pitch, a 16′ contrabass (double bass) in D, and a four-string 16′ contrabass tuned in 4ths with the lowest string C. Just which instrument Bach meant by 'violone' varied with the place of his employment.

A further question concerns Bach's use of the word 'Orchestre' itself. As Marshall has pointed out, his known use of this word occurs only once in his musical and prose sources: in the letter accompanying his submission of the Kyrie and Gloria of the Mass in B minor to the Elector of Saxony, dated 27 July 1733. Here Bach promised his 'untiring zeal in composing church music as well as for the Orchestre'. Marshall speculates that by 'Orchestre' Bach may have meant opera, citing J. G. Walther's *Musicalisches Lexikon* (Leipzig, 1732), where 'Orchestre' is defined as 'nowadays that part of the theater where the instrumentalists are located'. As a second explanation Marshall offers the use of the term broadly to mean the musicians who performed the secular music at the Dresden court. Rifkin cites Telemann's regular use of the word 'Orchester' in Hamburg to refer to both singers and instrumentalists who together form a musical ensemble for the performance of ceremonial works. This supports Mashall's second explanation, while ruling out the use of the word 'Orchestre' to refer to opera. JS

L. Dreyfus, *Bach's Continuo Group: Players and Practices in his Vocal Works* (Cambridge, Mass., 1987); R. Marshall, *Johann Sebastian Bach: The Sources, the Style, the Significance* (New York, 1989); J. Rifkin, 'Bach's Orchestre', *Early Music*, 14 (1986), 566–7; J. Rifkin, 'More (and Less) on Bach's Orchestra', *Performance Practice Review*, 4 (1991), 5–13; J. Rifkin, 'Some Questions of Performance in J. S. Bach's Trauerode', D. Melamed, ed., *Bach Studies 2* (Cambridge, 1995), 119–53; H.-J. Schulze, 'Johann Sebastian Bach's Orchestra: Some Unanswered Questions', *Early Music*, 17 (1989), 3–15.

**Orchestral Suites.** Four works, BWV1066–9, modelled on the type of overture-suite widely cultivated in Germany as entertainment music during the second quarter of the 18th century. This instrumental genre, also known as OUVERTURE, probably developed from suites of excerpts from French operas and ballets, which became popular in arrangements for lute, melody instruments, and harpsichord at the end of the 17th century. Its opening overture was followed by a number of character dances, mostly of the variety known then as *galanteries*: gavotte, minuet, bourrée, and lighter movements not in a specific dance rhythm. German court composers wrote such suites to satisfy their employers' French tastes. Fasch, Graupner, and Telemann were among the most prolific composers in the genre, Telemann's 135 surviving examples representing only a fraction of those he is known to have written. The Suite in G minor BWV1070, sometimes attributed to Bach, is a spurious work.

The small proportion of Bach's orchestral suites to survive in autograph suggests that these works were not conceived as a set. Our principal sources are copies of the Leipzig period, some written or corrected by Bach himself, and recent research suggests that the works themselves, with the possible exception of no. 1, originated during his Leipzig years. No. 1 exists in a set of parts copied out by C. G. Meißner in 1724/5. An original set of performing parts for no. 2 (including autograph parts for the flute and viola) has been dated to 1738/9, while no. 3 was copied to make a set of performing parts around 1730, alongside two Ouvertüren for smaller ensembles by Johann Bernhard Bach. J. S. Bach himself wrote out the parts for the first violin and the basso continuo, the remainder being contributed by his son Emanuel and his pupil J. L. Krebs. An early version of no. 4, with two main choirs of instruments (strings; oboes and bassoons), became the basis of the first movement of Cantata 110, *Unser Mund sei voll Lachens*, composed for Christmas Day 1725, with additional parts for three trumpets and drums. The final, enlarged version of the whole suite, with trumpets and timpani added also to Bourrée I, the Gavotte, and the Réjouissance, probably dates from about 1730.

Each of Bach's four suites begins with a movement in the French overture mould, comprising a fairly slow majestic opening section, often employing dotted notes and rapid scale figures to grand effect, a central fast contrapuntal section, bringing together fugal and ritornello procedures and isolating passages for soloists, and a modified reprise of the opening section by way of conclusion. After this reprise, the central and final sections are marked for repeat. Bach's marriage of the popular Italian concerto style with that of the French suite, especially in the overture, considerably enriched the genre. While the overture of the first suite most closely approximates to examples by J.-B. Lully (1632–87), with two oboes and a bassoon performing the solo function in its various episodes, that of the second is more like a concerto for solo flute, while various concertante groups occur in the two D major suites, nos. 3 and 4, especially in their overtures.

A group of dances, most with a strong French element but varying in number and kind, follows each overture, the infrequent appearance—or even total absence—of some of the customary dances of the suite emphasizing Bach's comparatively free approach to the genre. The allemande (or German dance), almost omnipresent in Bach's keyboard and string suites, is a notable absentee; the courante appears only in the first suite and the sarabande only in no. 2. Only the bourrée is common to all four orchestral suites, and there is a preponderance of *galanteries*, such as the forlane and gavotte, and lighter movements without strict dance affinities, such as the badinerie of no. 2 and the réjouissance of no. 4.

The first suite, in C major, is arguably the most conservative of the four, with its orthodox scoring (two oboes, bassoon, strings, and continuo), its direct harmonic manner, its inclusion of a courante, and its four sets of dance-pairs to be played *alternativement*. This practice, which required the first dance to be repeated after the somewhat less flamboyant second, dates back to Lully and was becoming unfashionable in France by about 1715. The French Courante, in 3/2 metre and with its characteristic dotted rhythms, adopts a traditional, asymmetrical binary structure. Of the Italianate binary-form gavottes, the second features the wind instruments over a texture in which unison violins and violas intone a FANFARE THEME identical to one that punctuates the opening chorus of Cantata 70. Bach's only example of the forlane follows. A lively dance (perhaps of Slav origin) taken over into the French court tradition, its most characteristic features are its anacrusic opening, its dotted rhythms, and its use of repeated phrases within sections; but Bach's inner string parts here impart an unusual, contrasting linear element through their use of quavers slurred in pairs. Menuet I is for the full ensemble, while the more subdued Menuet II involves only strings and continuo. Similarly, the second bourrée, the only movement in the minor mode, is given to the wind instruments alone. Two passepieds complete the work. The melody of Passepied I is played by unison first violins and oboes; for Passepied II the violins and violas repeat this melody in the lower octave, while the oboes weave new counterpoints above it.

Somewhat more fashionable for its time was Bach's second suite, in B minor. Featuring a solo transverse flute, which was becoming an extremely popular instrument in the 1730s, it exploits the new 'scientific' approach to music popularized by Lorenz Mizler in Leipzig—for example, versions of the same theme in quadruple and then in triple metre are presented in the two Grave sections of the overture. The recipient of the solo flute part is unknown, but may have been Dresden-based Pierre-Gabriel Buffardin. Following the overture, in which the flute either doubles the first violin or takes over the role of soloist, comes a Rondeau, whose opening phrase recurs after each of two episodic passages. The slow, stately Sarabande features a canon at the 12th between the flute (with first violins) and the bass. The lively Bourrée I, founded on a four-note ostinato pattern, is succeeded by a second bourrée in which the flute is given solo passage-work over a light, syncopated accompaniment. In the Polonaise the flute doubles the melody at the octave and is allotted an ornate solo role above the main dance theme in the ensuing DOUBLE. As with the Bourrée, the original dance is then repeated. A short, graceful Menuet in a four-part texture with the flute doubling the first violins is followed by a jocose Badinerie in which the solo flute contribution brings the work to a brilliant conclusion.

The third and fourth suites involve oboes, trumpets, timpani, strings, and continuo, and are centred, appropriately, in D major. The oboes are seldom treated independently and mostly double the first or both violins; it has, in fact, been suggested that the third suite was originally scored for strings alone (see Rifkin). Following the overture, in which the first violins undertake a quasi-concertante role in two episodes, no. 3 continues with the popular Air, a binary movement for strings and continuo in which Bach achieves remarkable emotional tension through dissonance, and transforms, through skilful inner part-movement, what appears to be a harmonic background to the florid melody into a delicately balanced counterpoint. Two gavottes, paired *alternativement*, are scored largely for oboes, strings, and continuo with occasional interjections from the trumpets and (in Gavotte I) timpani. Gavotte II, in the same key and with its prevalent rhythmic motif essentially a reversal of that in Gavotte I, displays some subtle contrasts: the timpani are silent, the trumpets play largely in unison, the violas provide the bass of a three-part texture for approximately half the dance, and the first trumpet sounds a short, independent motif three times. The Bourrée follows the expected binary pattern and is scored more fully, the oboes uniting with the first violins, and the violas and bass instruments, like the trumpets and timpani, interjecting a rhythmic figure that seems rooted in the Gavotte. A lively Gigue of asymmetrical binary design provides a brilliant and rousing conclusion.

Of the four dance-types in the fourth suite, the two bourrées, paired *alternativement*, give prominence to the woodwind, Bourrée II (in B minor) being led by the oboes above the bassoon's flowing ornamental version of the bass line. Oboes and bassoons are also treated independently in the ensuing Gavotte, while the strings come to prominence in the second of the menuets. Strings and woodwind play in unison in the first part of the Réjouissance but are more independently employed in the second section, to which the trumpets and drums contribute more fully, emphasizing the joyous nature of this radiant finale.                                                                    RS

M. Bernstein, 'The Chronology of the Orchestral Suites BWV 1066–1069', in *Report of the Eighth Congress of the International Musicological Society, New York, 1961* (Kassel, 1962), ii. 127–8; C. Floros, 'Die Thematik in Johann Sebastian Bachs Orchestersuiten', *Studien zur Musikwissenschaft*, 25 (1962), 193–204; J. Rifkin, 'Besetzung—Entstehung—Überlieferung: Bemerkungen zur Ouvertüre BWV 1068', *BJb* 83 (1997), 169–76; H. Schmidt, 'Bach's C major Orchestral Suite: A New Look at Possible Origins', *Music and Letters*, 57 (1976), 152–63.

**orchestration.** *See* INSTRUMENTATION and ORCHESTRA.

**Oregon Bach Festival.** A summer music festival, which originated in 1970 in workshops by the organist and conductor Helmuth Rilling at the University of Oregon at Eugene, Oregon. Known since 1981 under its present name, it has expanded to include concerts with internationally known operatic and instrumental soloists; the repertory includes 19th- and 20th-century works as well as those of Bach.                                                    DS

**organ.** See overleaf.

# organ

A keyboard instrument that generates sound by means of wind under pressure being channelled through pipes. The instrument reached a tonal and mechanical high point in Western Europe during Bach's lifetime.

1. The German organ of Bach's time.
2. The 'Bach' organs.
3. Surviving instruments associated with Bach.

1. **The German organ of Bach's time.** Although Bach's travel was limited to areas in northern Germany (Lüneburg, Lübeck, and Hamburg) and central Germany (Thuringia and Saxony), he was familiar with a number of organ types.

*Thuringia.* An imposing example of the type of organ encountered in Thuringia during the first half of the 18th century is the 58-stop Sterzing organ in the Georgenkirche, Eisenach, where Bach spent the first ten years of his life. He had left Eisenach before the instrument was begun in 1696, but his distant cousin Johann Christoph Bach (i) designed the organ, and was organist there from 1665 to 1703. Its stoplist was:

| *Manualbrustwerk (first keyboard)* | |
|---|---|
| Grobgedackt | 8′ |
| Kleingedackt | 4′ |
| Principal | 2′ |
| Supergemshörnlein | 2′ |
| Sifflöte | 1′ |
| Sesquialtera, from *g–e″[′]* | II |

| *Manualhauptwerk (second keyboard)* | |
|---|---|
| Bordun | 16′ |
| Principal | 8′ |
| Violdigamba | 8′ |
| Rohrflöte | 8′ |
| Quinte | 6′ |
| Oktave | 4′ |
| Flöte | 4′ |
| Nasat | 3′ |
| Sesquialtera *c g e[′]* | 4′ III |
| Mixtur | 2′ VI |
| Cymbel | III |
| Trompete | 8′ |

| *Manualoberseitenwerk (third keyboard)* | |
|---|---|
| Quintatön | 16′ |
| Großoktave | 8′ |
| Gemshorn | 8′ |
| Gedackt | 8′ |
| Principal | 4′ |
| Flöte douce | 4′ |
| Hohlflöte | 4′ |
| Hohlquinte | 3′ |
| Superoktave | 2′ |
| Blockflöte | 2′ |
| Sesquialtera (*c′, g′, e″*) | 2′ III |
| Scharf | IV |
| Vox humana | 8′ |

| *Manualunterseitenwerk (fourth keyboard)* | |
|---|---|
| Barem | 16′ |
| Stillgedackt | 8′ |
| Quintatön | 8′ |
| Principal | 4′ |
| Nachthorn | 4′ |
| Spitzflöte | 4′ |
| Spitzquinte | 3′ |
| Oktave | 2′ |
| Rauschquinte | 1½′ |
| Superoktave | 1′ |
| Cymbel | III |
| Regal | 8′ |

| *Pedal* | |
|---|---|
| Großer Untersatz | 32′ |
| Principal | 16′ |
| Subbaß | 16′ |
| Violon | 16′ |
| Oktave | 8′ |
| Gedackt | 8′ |
| Superoktave | 4′ |
| Flöte | 4′ |
| Bauerflöte | 1′ |
| Mixtur | V |
| Posaune | 32′ |
| Posaune | 16′ |
| Trompete | 8′ |
| Cornet | 2′ |
| Glockenspiel | 2′ |

*Auxiliary stops*
two ventils for the manuals
three tremulants
two stopknobs for the Cymbelsterns
coupler *Hauptwerk* to *Pedal*
manual compass: *C* to *e′″*
pedal compass: *C* to *e′*

The 18th-century Thuringian organ is characterized by an increasingly generous number of 8′ flue stops, including string stops of delicate but incisive timbre, with a slight purr or sizzle, and with a characteristic initial speech suggesting the bowstroke of a string instrument. The 8′ flue stops, together with an ample number of 16′ and 32′ stops, provide gravity of tone. Spatially separated and encased divisions are rejected in favour of a broad and deep chest layout (often on the same level), fronted by a single large façade of pipes. The *Rückpositiv* is gradually abandoned. There are relatively few reed stops, especially manual reeds. Pedal divisions often do not contain mixtures and other high-pitch stops (in this regard the organ at Eisenach was exceptional). Mixtures are increasingly likely to contain 3rd-sounding pipes.

*North Germany.* The stoplist of the organ at the Catharinenkirche, Hamburg, serves as an example of the imposing instruments Bach encountered on his trips to the north. His pupil J. F. Agricola stated that Bach admired certain features of this instrument, in particular the prompt speaking of the 32′ pedal Principal and Posaune and the rich and varied supply of reed stops (16 in all, over 25 per cent of the total number of stops). Its stoplist was:

| *Werck* | | | Sesquialtera | II |
|---|---|---|---|---|
| Principal | 16′ | | Scharff | VIII |
| Quintadena | 16′ | | Regal | 8′ |
| Bordun | 16′ | | Baarpfeiffe | 8′ |
| Octava | 8′ | | Schallmey | 4′ |
| Spitzflöte | 8′ | | | |
| Querflöte | 8′ | | *Brust* | |
| Octava | 4′ | | Principal | 8′ |
| Octava | 2′ | | Octava | 4′ |
| Rausch-Pfeiffe | III | | Quintadena | 4′ |
| Mixtura | X | | Waldpfeiffe | 2′ |
| Trommete | 16′ | | Scharff | VII |
| | | | Dulcian | 16′ |
| *Oberwerk* | | | Regal | 8′ |
| Principal | 8′ | | | |
| Hohlflöte | 8′ | | *Pedal* | |
| Flöte | 4′ | | Principal | 32′ |
| Nasat | 3′ | | Principal | 16′ |
| Gemshorn | 2′ | | Sub-Baß | 16′ |
| Waldflöte | 2′ | | Octava | 8′ |
| Scharff | VI | | Gedact | 8′ |
| Trommete | 8′ | | Octava | 4′ |
| Zincke | 8′ | | Nachthorn | 4′ |
| Trommete | 4′ | | Rauschpfeiffe | II |
| | | | Mixtura | V |
| *Rückpositiv* | | | Cimbel | III |
| Principal | 8′ | | Groß-Posaun | 32′ |
| Gedact | 8′ | | Posaune | 16′ |
| Quintadena | 8′ | | Dulcian | 16′ |
| Octava | 4′ | | Trommete | 8′ |
| Blockflöte | 4′ | | Krumhorn | 8 |
| Hohlflöte | 4′ | | Schallmey | 4′ |
| Quintflöte | 1½′ | | Cornet-Baß | 2′ |
| Sifflet | 1′ | | two tremulants | |

The north German instruments are characterized by fewer and less colourful 8′ stops, large, prominent mixtures, and a generous supply of high-pitch stops. String stops are rare. Encased and spatially separated divisions are the rule, and each division has its own façade. A large *Rückpositiv* is a prominent feature of most sizeable organs. Reed stops are plentiful and varied, in both manual and pedal. The pedal is a large division (often the largest), and contains a full complement of mixtures and high-pitch stops.

Bach never had such an organ at his constant disposal. The north German instruments, however, constitute an important organ type which Bach must have become intimately familiar with during his formative years as an organist.

*Saxony.* Bach performed three concerts on the Gottfried Silbermann organ in the Sophienkirche, Dresden, in 1725 and 1731, and his eldest son Wilhelm Friedemann was organist there from 1733 to 1746. Through his many organs in Saxony and his apprentices who carried on his work, Silbermann decisively influenced all aspects of the organ in Saxony for generations after his time. The stoplist of the Sophienkirche organ was as follows:

| *Hauptwerk* | | | *Quintatön* | 8′ |
|---|---|---|---|---|
| Bordun | 16′ | | Octave | 4′ |
| Principal | 8′ | | Rohrflöte | 4′ |
| Spitzflöte | 8′ | | Nasat | 3′ |
| Rohrflöte | 8′ | | Quinte | 1½′ |
| Octave | 4′ | | Octave | 2′ |
| Spitzflöte | 4′ | | Octave | 1′ |
| Quinte | 3′ | | Mixtur | III |
| Octave | 2′ | | Vox humana | 8′ |
| Terze | [1³⁄₅′] | | | |
| Cornet | | | *Pedal* | |
| Mixtur | IV | | Principal | 16′ |
| Cimbel | III | | Subbaß | 16′ |
| Trompete | 8′ | | Posaune | 16′ |
| Clairon | 4′ | | Trompete | 8′ |
| | | | | |
| *Oberwerk* | | | *Auxiliary stops* | |
| Quintatön | 16′ | | tremulant for the *Hauptwerk* | |
| Principal | 8′ | | *Schwebung* for the *Oberwerk* | |
| Unda maris (from *a* up) | 8′ | | coupler, *Hauptwerk* to *Pedal*, with | |
| Gedackt | 8′ | | separate pallets | |

Silbermann's apprenticeship with his brother Andreas in Strasburg resulted in a number of characteristics in his instruments that were novel in Germany, in particular the powerful cornets and reed stops of considerable brilliance. Yet his style also exhibits prevailing central German traits, such as broad and deep chest layouts, the absence of a *Rückpositiv*, and a pedal weak in high-pitch stops. The Silbermann organ type has at times been identified as the ideal Bach organ. Bach's pupil J. F. Agricola criticized Silbermann's organs on three counts, however: for their too-uniform stoplists, their idiosyncratic temperament and their too-weak mixtures (see J. Adlung, *Musica mechanica organoedi* (Berlin, 1768), i. 212). Agricola also praised the organs' superb workmanship, simplicity of design, magnificent voicing, and light playing actions. Limitations imposed by temperament and pedal compass render the performance of Bach's organ works problematic on Silbermann's instruments.

In 1747, towards the end of his life, Bach visited Potsdam and became familiar with yet another organ type when he played instruments by the Berlin builder Joachim Wagner (1690/1–1749) at the Heiliggeistkirche, Garnisonkirche, and Nicolaikirche. He was also introduced to the French organ through involvement with the music of De Grigny and other French composers; his acquaintance with that organ type, however, cannot have been more than marginal.

**2. The 'Bach' organs.** Documentation attests to Bach's involvement with a number of organs during his career, as consultant, examiner, or recitalist. As resident organist he regularly performed on three instruments during his lifetime—at Arnstadt, Mühlhausen, and Weimar; in addition he probably had access to various instruments in Leipzig, particularly those in the Thomaskirche, during the years of his Kantorate.

*Bonifatiuskirche, Arnstadt.* The organ was built by Johann Friedrich Wender (1655–1729) of Mühlhausen, completed on 3 July 1703, and tested by Bach. The console (altered somewhat) is in the Museum der Stadt (town museum) in Arnstadt, and seven stops (marked * below) survive. Its stoplist, according to the memorandum drawn up by Wender, was:

| *Oberwerk* | | | |
|---|---|---|---|
| Principal | 8′ | Principal | 4′ |
| Viol Di Gamb:* | 8′ | Spielpfeiffe | 4′ |
| Quinta dena* | 8′ | Nachthorn* | 4′ |
| Grobgedackt* | 8′ | Quinte | 3′ |
| Gemshorn* | 8′ | Sesquialtera doppelt | |
| Quinta | 6′ | Mixtur | III (altered |
| Octava* | 4′ | | to IV) |
| Mixtur | IV | | |
| Cymbel | II (altered | *Pedal* | |
| | to III) | Sub Baß | 16′ |
| | | Principal Baß | 8′ |
| Trompet | 8′ | Posaunen Baß | 16′ |
| tremulant | | Cornet Baß | 2′ |
| Zymbel Stern | | manual coupler | |
| | | pedal coupler | |
| *Brustwerk* | | | |
| Stillgedackt* | 8′ | | |

*Blasiuskirche, Mühlhausen.* The organ was rebuilt by J. F. Wender in 1708–9, following a report by Bach. A new organ, in accordance with Bach's recommended disposition, was built by the Potsdam firm of Alexander Schuke in 1956–8. The stoplist was given in J. Adlung, *Musica mechanica organoedi.*

| *Ober- und Hauptwerk* | | | |
|---|---|---|---|
| Quintatön | 16′ | *Rückpositiv* | |
| Principal | 8′ | Gedackt | 8′ |
| Violdigamba | 8′ | Quintatön | 8′ |
| Oktave | 4′ | Principal | 4′ |
| Gedackt | 4′ | Salcional | 4′ |
| Quinte | 3′ | Oktave | 2′ |
| Oktave | 2′ | Spitzflöte | 2′ |
| Sesquialtera | II | Quintflöte | [1⅓′] |
| Mixtur | IV | Sesquialtera | |
| Cymbel | II | Cymbel | III |
| Fagott (C–c′) | 16′ | *Baßlade (Pedal)* | |
| *Brustwerk* | | Untersatz | 32′ |
| Stillgedackt | 8′ | Principal | 16′ |
| Flöte | 4′ | Subbaß | 16′ |
| Principal | 2′ | Oktave | 8′ |
| Terz | 1⅗′ | Oktave | 4′ |
| Quinte | 1⅓′ | Mixtur | IV |
| Mixtur | III | Posaune | 16′ |
| Schallmey | 8′ | Cornetbaß | 2′ |
| | | Rohrflötenbaß | 1′ |

*Schloßkapelle, Weimar.* The organ was rebuilt in 1714 by Heinrich Nikolaus Trebs (1678–1748), who did further work on it in 1719–20 and 1726. The stoplist was given in G. A. Wette, *Historische Nachrichten von der berühmten Residenz-Stadt Weimar* (Weimar, 1737).

| Ober Clavier | | Klein Gedackt | 4′ |
|---|---|---|---|
| Quintadena | 16′ | Wald-Flöthe | 2′ |
| Principal | 8′ | Sesquialtera ('aus 3 und 2 Fuß') | IV |
| Grobgedackt | 8′ | Trompete | 8′ |
| Gemsshorn | 8′ | | |
| Octava | 4′ | **Pedal** | |
| Quintadena | 4′ | Groß Untersatz | 32′ |
| Mixtur | VI | Violon Baß | 16′ |
| Cymbel | III | Sub-Baß | 16′ |
| Glockenspiel | | Principal Baß | 8′ |
| | | Posaun Baß | 16′ |
| *Unter Clavier* | | Trompete Baß | 8′ |
| Principal | 8′ | Cornet Baß | 4′ |
| Viol di Gamba | 8′ | tremulant (both manuals) | |
| Gedackt | 8′ | Cymbelstern | |
| Octava | 4′ | | |

3. **Surviving instruments associated with Bach.** It is clear from the Obituary that Bach never had at his regular disposal an instrument that he considered first-rate. Among the organs that survive today, only two would satisfy the three criteria needed for inclusion in such a category, namely: substantial tonal resources, capable of rendering adequately the most ambitious of Bach's organ works; documentary evidence that Bach found the instrument to be successful; and preservation either in its original state or with enough original substance intact to permit tolerably accurate restoration. The two instruments in question are in Altenburg and Naumburg, both in the vicinity of Leipzig.

*Court chapel, Altenburg.* The organ was built by Tobias Heinrich Gottfried Trost (1673–1759) in 1735–9.

| Hauptwerk | | Nasat | 3′ |
|---|---|---|---|
| Quintatön | 16′ | Octave | 2′ |
| Flötetraversiere | 16′ | Waldflöte | 2′ |
| Principal | 8′ | Superoktave | 1′ |
| Rohrflöte | 8′ | Cornet | V |
| Bordun | 8′ | Mixtur | IV–V |
| Spitzflöte | 8′ | Vox humana | 8′ |
| Violadagamba | 8′ | | |
| Octave | 4′ | **Pedal** | |
| Gedackt | 4′ | Principalbaß | 16′ |
| Quinte | 3′ | Violonbaß | 16′ |
| Superoktave | 2′ | Quintatönbaß* | 16′ |
| Blockflöte | 2′ | Flötetraversiere* | 16′ |
| Sesquialtera | II | Octave | 8′ |
| Mixtur | 2′ IX | Bordun* | 8′ |
| Trompete | 8′ | Superoktave* | 4′ |
| Glockenspiel, from c′ to c‴ | | Mixtur* | VI–VII |
| | | Posaune | 32′ |
| *Oberwerk* | | Posaune | 16′ |
| Geigenprincipal | 8′ | Trompete | 8′ |
| Hohlflöte | 8′ | *from the *Hauptwerk* by transmission | |
| Lieblichgedackt | 8′ | | |
| Quintatön | 8′ | *Auxiliary stops* | |
| Vugara [Fugara] | 8′ | tremulant for both manuals | |
| Gemshorn | 4′ | *Schwebung* for the Vox humana | |
| Flötedouce | 4′ | pedal coupler | |
| (two pipes per note on a common toeboard) | | coupler between the two manuals | |

Bach visited and played the organ about the time it was completed; he praised both the durability of the workmanship and the character of the individual stops. After major alterations during the 19th century, the organ was restored to its original condition in 1974–6.

Altenburg is an extreme example of the Thuringian organ type: five colourful 8′ flue stops on each manual, including two strings; four 16′ flue stops and a 32′ pedal Posaune; relatively few reed stops; a rudimentary pedal (augmented by stops brought from the *Hauptwerk*); mixtures containing prominent 3rd-sounding ranks. The instrument's tone is weighty and solid without forgoing brilliance and incisiveness.

*Wenzelskirche, Naumburg.* The organ was built between 1743 and 1746 by Zacharias Hildebrandt.

| Hauptwerk | | Rückpositiv | |
|---|---|---|---|
| Principal | 16′ | Principal | 8′ |
| Quintatön | 16′ | Quintatön | 8′ |
| Oktave | 8′ | Violdigamba | 8′ |
| Spitzflöte | 8′ | Rohrflöte | 8′ |
| Gedackt | 8′ | Prästant | 4′ |
| Oktave | 4′ | Fugara | 4′ |
| Spitzflöte | 4′ | Rohrflöte | 4′ |
| Quinte | 3′ | Nasat | 3′ |
| Oktave | 2′ | Oktave | 2′ |
| Weitpfeife | 2′ | Rauschpfeife | II |
| Sesquialtera | III | Cymbel | V |
| Cornet | IV | Fagott | 16′ |
| Mixtur | VI– | | |
| | VII– | *Pedal* | |
| | VIII | Principalbaß | 16′ |
| Bombart | 16′ | Violonbaß | 16′ |
| Trompete | 8′ | Subbaß | 16′ |
| | | Oktave | 8′ |
| *Oberwerk* | | Violon | 8′ |
| Bordun | 16′ | Oktave | 4′ |
| Principal | 8′ | Nachthorn | 2′ |
| Unda Maris (*a* to *c‴*) | 8′ | Mixtur | VII |
| Hohlflöte, of metal | 8′ | Posaunenbaß | 32′ |
| Prästant | 4′ | Posaunbaß | 16′ |
| Gemshorn | 4′ | Trompete | 8′ |
| Quinte | 3′ | Clarino | 4′ |
| Oktave | 2′ | | |
| Waldflöte | 2′ | *Auxiliary stops* | |
| Terz | 1⅗′ | tremulant for the Rückpositiv | |
| Quinte | 1½′ | four ventils | |
| Sifflöte | 1′ | Cymbelstern | |
| Scharf | V | manual compass C–*e‴* | |
| Vox humana | 8′ | pedal compass C–*e′* | |

Bach was asked to appraise the organ that preceded this one in the Wenzelskirche; it is quite possible that he recommended his friend Hildebrandt to build the new one (in the existing case). Together with Silbermann, Bach examined the newly completed instrument and found it successful; several years later Bach's son-in-law J. C. Altnickol was chosen as organist (on Bach's recommendation). After drastic changes during the 19th and 20th centuries, including the removal of many stops and the installation of an electric console (the original keyboards are intact but disconnected), the organ is, at the time of writing, being thoroughly restored.

The Naumburg organ is an eclectic instrument: rich in colourful 8′ stops (including an Unda Maris, a Principal tuned slightly sharp so as to undulate when drawn with the *Oberwerk* 8′ Principal); it is well supplied with 16′ stops, but also with sizeable mixtures and a full complement of high-pitch stops, including mutations; and it has a large *Rückpositiv* and a complete pedal, both unusual for this organ's time and place. Adlung wrote of this organ, 'It is a successful instrument, whose beautiful tone can scarcely find an equal' (*Musica mechanica organoedi*, i. 264).

Although both the Altenburg and the Naumburg organs were much altered during the 19th and 20th centuries, in each case enough of the organ's substance has been preserved (winding system, chestwork, and many pipes) to make a tolerably accurate restoration to its original state. It is curious to reflect on why these two large instruments, both praised by Bach, still exist. It cannot be because of Bach's approval; otherwise other organs that he was known to have admired would have been preserved. Bach's reputation was hardly sufficient during the first 100 years after his death to restrain the forces of fashion and modernization.

These organs survived, in the first place, because they are well built, durable, and tonally successful. They were widely admired during the 18th century (by Adlung and Agricola, for example), and continued to elicit the admiration of succeeding generations. Even more interesting, though, is the fact that both are, in decisive ways, progressive and forward-looking. They embody characteristics of future organs up to the beginning of the 20th century (including ample, stable winding, multiple colourful 8′ stops, mixtures with 3rd-sounding ranks, and gravity of tone), so that there was no pressing need to alter them beyond recognition or to replace them.     QF

*See also* REGISTRATION.

H. T. Blanchard, *The Bach Organ Book* (Delaware, Oh., 1985); U. Dähnert, 'Organs Played and Tested by J. S. Bach', in G. Stauffer and E. May, eds., *J. S. Bach as Organist: His Instruments, Music, and Performance Practices* (London, 1986), 3–24; L. Edwards, 'The Thuringian Organ 1702–1720', *Organ Yearbook*, 22 (1991), 119–50; P. Williams, *A New History of the Organ: From the Greeks to the Present Day* (London, 1980), 111–18.

## organ chorale

1. Definition and function.
2. History.
3. Classification.

**1. Definition and function.** The term 'organ chorale' can refer to any solo organ piece based on a Lutheran chorale melody or part of one. The genre probably had a wide range of functions (for a comprehensive survey, see Williams). It could provide the introduction to a congregational chorale (whether accompanied or unaccompanied), the elaborated accompaniment of a chorale, or the interlude between the verses of a chorale; it could also introduce a concerted work (most typically the cantata, but perhaps also canticles such as the Magnificat) or form a component in an organ recital. This last function was possibly more important than many historians, unduly concerned with seeing the genre in a purely religious context, realize. Bach's improvising on the chorale *An Wasserflüssen Babylon* for half an hour in front of the ageing Reincken may point to his standard practice in organ concerts (see *BDok* iii. 84). Given that Bach knew of Reincken's famous fantasia on the same chorale, it may also be that certain notated organ chorales were valued for their

musical quality rather than for their specific liturgical function. At the other end of the spectrum, it is likely—in view of complaints by the Arnstadt consistory about his introducing 'strange notes' into the chorales (*BDok* ii. 19–20)—that some of Bach's earlier settings were little more than notated accompaniments. These might include those settings which are relatively simple, sometimes with short interludes between the lines (for a selection, see May, p. 85); Bach's German *Te Deum, Herr Gott, dich loben wir* BWV725, is unique in providing accompaniment for each successive verse. We can be less certain as to whether the organ provided accompaniment in Weimar and Leipzig, and Bach was, in any case, the Kantor rather than an organist at Leipzig. But it is highly likely that his notated repertory of organ chorales, at least up to the Weimar years, may represent only the tip of a vast improvised iceberg.

Other functions, particularly in the Leipzig years, might include presentation (Bach presented the Canonic Variations on *Vom Himmel hoch* to Mizler's Societät der Musicalischen Wissenschaften) and publication for home use. This latter purpose may have been served by at least the smaller settings of *Clavier-Übung III*, which seems to be aimed at more or less the same 'Kenner und Liebhaber' as the three *Clavier-Übung* volumes

Autograph of the organ chorale *Wir Christenleut* bwv612 from the *Orgel-Büchlein*, showing completion in organ tablature (Staatsbibliothek zu Berlin, Preußischer Kulturbesitz)

designed specifically for the harpsichord. Perhaps the most valuable function of all, to Bach's contemporaries and to us today, is the pedagogical role of notated chorales—something Bach made explicit on the title-page of the *Orgel-Büchlein*. He probably notated a large number of his chorales both to develop organ technique (such as the obbligato pedal in the *Orgel-Büchlein*) and to provide compositional models.

**2. History.** The predominance of liturgical pieces in German sources from the Reformation years suggests that the organ played an important role in church services. It is likely that the organist continued to provide pieces for the Ordinary, Propers, and Offices in the Lutheran rite (presumably as introductions, *alternatim*, or substitution for the sung settings). Pieces with German titles appear only sporadically in the first half of the 16th century. August Nörmiger's tablature of 1598 is the first comprehensive chorale book for keyboard, providing settings for the Church year, Catechism, and other Lutheran celebrations. The genealogy of Bach's organ chorales can be traced most directly to J. P. Sweelinck (1562–1621), an organist who, ironically, worked almost entirely in the domain of Dutch reformed Calvinism, while possibly remaining a Catholic. His chorale variations take over some of the virtuoso traits of the English virginal school and were undoubtedly designed for public secular performance. Sweelinck's style was adopted by two major Lutheran pupils, Samuel Scheidt (1587–1654) and Heinrich Scheidemann (c.1595–1663), the latter developing the free chorale fantasia which he passed on to Reincken. Most significant among Bach's immediate predecessors are Buxtehude, who developed the short but intensively worked setting of a chorale melody, his distant cousin Johann Christoph Bach (i) of Eisenach, who wrote chorale fughettas, and Johann Pachelbel (teacher of Bach's elder brother Johann Christoph (ii) of Ohrdruf), who was important specifically in developing the cantus firmus setting with pre-imitation of each line of the chorale. Our knowledge of Bach's immediate models (especially Johann Michael Bach) and of his own early attempts in the genre has been greatly enhanced by the discovery of the Neumeister Collection.

**3. Classification.** Ernest May provides the most comprehensive classification of Bach's chorales. First there is the traditional chorale motet and its derivatives. In its purest form this presents successive lines of the chorale in imitation and cantus firmus, exemplified in the mature works by *Aus tiefer Not* BWV686 from *Clavier-Übung III*. The freer form developed by Scheidemann, with virtuoso elements, is the chorale fantasia, represented

by three early Bach works including *Wie schön leuchtet der Morgenstern*, which survives in one of the composer's earliest autographs. Rather more examples survive for the chorale fughetta, a much briefer version of the chorale motet without cantus firmus, presumably to introduce a sung version of the chorale. May separates from the above genres the free chorale fugue, which follows the idea of the chorale motet but falls more into the category of fugue (although the subject does not necessarily appear in the pedals); the earliest example is the fine fugue on the *tonus peregrinus* of the Magnificat, *Meine Seele erhebet den Herren* BWV733.

The second main family of organ chorales is the chorale variation in the Sweelinck–Scheidt tradition. Bach would doubtless have known excellent examples by Pachelbel and, particularly, by Georg Böhm of Lüneburg. However, he seems to have given little attention to this genre after the early years (with the exception of the late Canonic Variations). May's remaining categories are the short and long chorale preludes. The short version is most clearly exemplified in the *Orgel-Büchlein*; Russell Stinson (*Bach: The Orgelbüchlein* (New York, 1996), 62–75) adopts May's subdivisions of melody chorale, ornamental chorale, and chorale canon, and includes two one-off genres (melody in the alto and a unique chorale fantasy). May divides the long chorale into those without independent structure in the chorale-free parts (including the long cantus firmus chorale and the long ornamental chorale) and those with independent structure in the chorale-free voices (e.g. invention, trio, and ritornello structure). Some works, such as the large setting of *Vater unser im Himmelreich* BWV682, present an extremely challenging combination of forms: trio sonata and chorale canon.

Classifications of various chorale forms do not automatically account for stylistic elements or for Bach's developments of style. For instance, chorale motets belong to the earliest and the latest phases of his compositional development and show an increasing concern with the pure counterpoint of the *stile antico*. In other words, Bach's style in this form begins as relatively 'modern' (or at least up-to-date for the early 18th century) and seems to become more 'ancient' towards the end of his career. This trend towards purer counterpoint was itself a wider fashion of the 1730s and 1740s, one that was complemented by a trend towards more modern, *galant* idioms. Most interesting in this regard are the late Schübler Chorales, most of which are direct transcriptions of movements from cantatas. Similar works by G. F. Kauffmann and J. L. Krebs suggest that there was a vogue for organ pieces mimicking or transcribing instrumental textures and idioms. JAB

*See also* CHORALE VARIATIONS, CLAVIER-ÜBUNG III, 'EIGHTEEN' CHORALES, KIRNBERGER CHORALES, NEUMEISTER CHORALES, and ORGEL-BÜCHLEIN.

E. May, 'The Types, Uses, and Historical Position of Bach's Organ Chorales', in G. Stauffer and E. May, eds., *J. S. Bach as Organist* (London, 1986), 81–101; P. Williams, *The Organ Music of J. S. Bach*, ii (Cambridge, 1980), iii (Cambridge, 1984).

**Organ Concertos.** Six concertos for solo organ, BWV592–7, which Bach arranged from works by Vivaldi, Johann Ernst, and one unknown composer. *See* CONCERTO.

**organ mass.** A setting of the Mass in which the organ, alternating with the choir, replaces portions of the text with short pieces. Bach was familiar with organ masses by Frescobaldi and 17th-century French composers, but to refer to his CLAVIER-ÜBUNG III as an organ mass, as is sometimes done, is inaccurate and misleading.

**Organ Sonatas.** Bach compiled his manuscript of the six sonatas BWV525–30 for two keyboards and pedal (often termed the 'Organ Sonatas' or the 'Trio Sonatas') during the late 1720s, and a copy was soon made by his second wife, Anna Magdalena, and his eldest son Wilhelm Friedemann. According to J. N. Forkel's biography (1802), Bach prepared these pieces for Friedemann, so they seem to fit into the pedagogic series of keyboard works that began with the *Clavierbüchlein* designed for Friedemann in 1720. Having acquired a thorough keyboard technique with works such as the Inventions and Sinfonias, and the first book of *The Well-tempered Clavier*, the sonatas would have helped to consolidate Friedemann's organ technique, particularly the co-ordination of hands and feet. His work on the sonatas presumably paid off, since he acquired his prestigious first post as organist of the Sophienkirche, Dresden, in 1733 and was subsequently well known for his virtuosity at the organ.

The sonatas evidence another trend within Bach's compositional development: his eagerness to transfer styles and idioms from one instrument or ensemble to another (particularly the keyboard). In the Weimar years he made a practice of transcribing Italian concertos for organ and harpsichord, and he was subsequently to develop the keyboard concerto (with and without orchestra) and the sonata for melody instrument and keyboard obbligato. The organ sonatas continue this trend by transferring the Italianate trio sonata texture to the organ. In their technical difficulty, intensity of construction, and distance from the most common idioms for the instrument, these

sonatas may also be considered a corollary to the collected works for unaccompanied violin and cello.

Given the wide manuscript dissemination of the sonatas among Bach's pupils from the middle of the 18th century, it seems likely that these works were well known and well used within services and recitals by members of the Bach circle. J. L. Krebs, in particular, produced many organ works of his own in a similar 'instrumental' style, showing that the idiom remained in vogue after Bach's death. Their easy contrapuntal mastery and their clear-cut motivic gestures are such that these sonatas were among the few Bach works that were widely admired in the latter part of the century; in 1788 the anonymous author (possibly C. P. E. Bach) of a comparison between Handel and Bach noted that they are so *galant* that they still sound very good (*BDok* iii. 441).

Bach did not compose all the sonatas at the time of their compilation in the late 1720s. The Andante of Sonata no. 4 may well date from his earliest years as an organ composer; it betrays the short-breathed motivic style of 17th-century German music, but also some of the pathetic gestures of contemporary Italian opera, notably the chord of the Neapolitan 6th, which occurs at the conclusion of each sequential segment. Early versions also survive for the opening movement of Sonata no. 1 (a fragment), all the movements of nos. 3 and 4, and the Largo of no. 5 (as the middle movement of an early version of the Prelude and Fugue in C major BWV545). The fact that the opening movement of Sonata no. 4 began life as the Sinfonia to the second part of Bach's Cantata 76 (scored for oboe d'amore, viola da gamba, and continuo), one of his very first Leipzig compositions, suggests that some of the other movements may have been originally composed for instrumental trio. Bach's manuscript shows that he rewrote several of the movements as he made the compilation; certainly he seems not to have been certain of the order of the sonatas even as he began penning the manuscript (see Butt). Both the manuscript evidence and the style of the music suggest that the Sixth Sonata was written specifically for organ near to the time that Bach made the compilation. The opening Vivace is in a 'modern' concerto-sonata style with several non-contrapuntal sections; the Lento is strikingly reminiscent in motif and gesture to certain arias in Bach's Passions and cantatas (most notably 'Erbarme dich' from the St Matthew Passion of 1727).

The three-movement form relates more to the concerto than to the sonata, and the ritornello structure of the Vivace of Sonata no. 2, the Allegros of no. 5, and the Vivace of no. 6 was something

# Orgel-Büchlein

Bach owed directly to the concertos of Vivaldi. With movements such as the Allegro of Sonata no. 2, Bach seems to have moulded several normally discrete genres into a unique structure: the piece is simultaneously in fugal, modified da capo, and ritornello forms. Furthermore, while the opening fugal exposition bears some of the severity of traditional counterpoint, the new subject opening the central section is modern, if not *galant*, in idiom. That this, too, is treated in an imitative manner is typical of Bach's tendency to thwart the conventional categories of his age.     JAB

  J. Butt, 'Bach's Organ Sonatas BWV 525–530: Compilation and Recomposition', *Organ Yearbook*, 19 (1988), 80–90.

***Orgel-Büchlein*** ('Little Organ Book'). A collection of 46 organ chorales, BWV599–644. Most pages of the autograph manuscript are blank except for the title of a chorale, revealing that Bach intended to include 164 chorales. Along the lines of a comprehensive Lutheran hymnal, the first 60 titles follow the order of the Church year, while the remainder are appropriate for any liturgical season. The emphasis on early Lutheran hymnody is remarkable: 70 per cent of the proposed chorales date from the 16th century, and most of the others are from no later than 1650. Bach may well have been influenced in this regard by Johann Gottfried Olearius (1635–1711), an eminent hymnologist and deacon of the Neue Kirche in Arnstadt when Bach served there as organist in 1703–7. The concept of the *Orgel-Büchlein* was probably also inspired by such central German organ chorale collections as Johann Pachelbel's *Choral-Fugen durchs gantze Jahr* and also the *Choraele zum Praeambuliren*, a set of 44 fughettas by Johann Christoph Bach (i).

  *Helft mir Gotts Güte preisen*, the fragment *O Traurigkeit, o Herzeleid*, and the revised versions of *Christus der uns selig macht* and *Komm, Gott Schöpfer, Heiliger Geist* date from Bach's Leipzig years (1723–50). Otherwise, all the works were written while he was organist at the Weimar court (1708–17). Most were composed directly into the autograph (see picture, p.345).

  In creating the *Orgel-Büchlein* Bach took pre-existing chorale types and elevated them to their highest possible artistic level. The vast majority of the settings exemplify the melody chorale, in which the tune appears in the soprano voice as a continuous, unornamented melody. These works are distinguished from the melody chorales of such central German composers as Pachelbel, J. G. Walther, and Johann Michael Bach by their use of an obbligato rather than an *ad libitum* pedal part, and by motivic figuration in four rather than three voices.

Three settings (*Das alte Jahr vergangen ist*, *O Mensch, bewein dein Sünde groß*, and *Wenn wir in höchsten Nöten sein*) are ornamental chorales, in which the tune appears in the soprano as a continuous but highly embellished melody. Bach's models for these works were north German, most notably the ornamental chorales of Dietrich Buxtehude. In all three examples Bach indicated that the soprano be played on a separate keyboard, while in the 31 melody chorales he did so in only three pieces. Clearly, he was making a bow to the north German tradition of performing ornamental chorales *à due clav.*

  No fewer than nine settings are canons, in which the chorale tune is set canonically. Along with the many examples by Bach's Weimar colleague J. G. Walther, these are among the earliest examples of this chorale type. Of special interest is the double canon *In dulci jubilo*, which contains a canonic accompaniment.

  The ways in which the *Orgel-Büchlein* evolved reveal a clear stylistic development. Most of the settings in the early compilation phase, for example, are melody chorales in four parts, and several of these contain a 'walking' bass line. In the middle compilation phase four-voice melody chorales continue to predominate, but the bass lines are virtually all motivic. In the late compilation phase Bach tended to look beyond the melody chorale, and he experimented with placing the tune in voices other than the soprano and with thickening the texture beyond four parts. Included in this phase are the fantasia-like *In dir ist Freude*, where the chorale melody constantly migrates from one voice to the next and where the texture ranges from one to five voices, and *Christum wir sollen loben schon*, the only non-canonic work in the collection where the chorale tune appears exclusively in a voice (alto) other than the soprano. With regard to canonic writing, the earliest canons (e.g. *In dulci jubilo*) are at the octave, while the latest (e.g. *Liebster Jesu, wir sind hier*) tend to be at the more difficult interval of a 5th. As the *Orgel-Büchlein* evolved, then, its musical style became at once less strict and more complex.

  According to the title-page of the autograph, which Bach inscribed during his years in Cöthen (1717–23), the *Orgel-Büchlein* is intended to give guidance 'to a beginning organist in how to set a chorale in all kinds of ways, and at the same time to become practised in the study of pedalling'. This links the *Orgel-Büchlein* to such didactic keyboard collections from Bach's Cöthen period as the Inventions and Sinfonias and Part 1 of *The Well-tempered Clavier*.

  The purpose of the *Orgel-Büchlein*, though, clearly extends beyond pedagogy. With respect to composition, it may be thought of as an exercise book which allowed Bach to hone his skills as a composer of certain types of organ chorales. It also provides the first glimpse of Bach's tendency to write numerous examples of a particular genre within a relatively short period—and to achieve within narrow confines a remarkable level of diversity and individualization. This procedure would lead to such works as (in approximate chronological order) the Inventions and Sinfonias, *The Well-tempered Clavier*, the French and English Suites, the Sonatas and Partitas for solo violin, the Cello Suites, the Leipzig chorale cantatas, the Partitas for harpsichord, *The Art of Fugue*, the Goldberg Variations (and the Goldberg canons BWV1087), and the *Musical Offering*.

At the same time, the *Orgel-Büchlein* is a very pragmatic work, intended to furnish Bach with music for services at the Weimar court. Perhaps more than any keyboard collection by Bach, it is *Gebrauchsmusik*. Finally, the collection also has religious significance, as the title-page contains the dedicatory couplet: 'For the highest God alone honour; for my neighbour, that he may instruct himself from it'. The *Orgel-Büchlein* thus has both a divine and a worldly purpose, in accordance with Christ's summary of the Law in St Matthew 22: 37–40: 'Thou shalt love the Lord thy God . . . and . . . thy neighbour as thyself.'            RTS

R. A. Leaver, 'Bach and Hymnody: The Evidence of the *Orgelbüchlein*', *Early Music*, 13 (1985), 227–36; H.-H. Löhlein, *Johann Sebastian Bach: Orgel-Büchlein* (facsimile edn., Leipzig, 1981); E. May, 'The Types, Uses, and Historical Position of Bach's Organ Chorales', in G. Stauffer and E. May, eds., *J. S. Bach as Organist: his Instruments, Music, and Performance Practices* (London, 1986), 81–101; R. Stinson, *Bach: The Orgel-Büchlein* (New York, 1996); R. Stinson, 'The Compositional History of Bach's *Orgel-Büchlein* Reconsidered', *Bach Perspectives*, i (1995), 43–78; P. Williams, *The Organ Music of J. S. Bach*, ii (Cambridge, 1980), 3–102.

**ornamentation.** See overleaf.

**Orthodoxy.** Following the doctrinal controversies of the later 16th century, the boundaries of Lutheran theology were established in the *Concordienbuch* ('Book of Concord', 1580), the anthology of Lutheran confessional documents (*see* LUTHERANISM). Strict adherence to this doctrinal standard became the mark of authentic or Orthodox Lutheranism during the 17th century. Among the leading Orthodox theologians of this formative period were Martin Chemnitz (1522–86), Johann Gerhard (1582–1637), and Abraham Calov—authors whose writings could be found in Bach's personal library. In the later 17th and early 18th century 'objective' Orthodoxy was challenged by the rise of 'subjective' PIETISM, but retained its

adherence to traditional liturgical forms and elaborate church music. Although Bach's cantata librettos breathe a piety similar to that of the Pietists, the music he wrote for them, with its operatic da capo arias and recitatives, expresses the ideals of Orthodoxy rather than Pietism. Further, Bach's association with such Orthodox pastors as G. C. Eilmar of Mühlhausen, Erdmann Neumeister of Hamburg, and Johann Gottlob Carpzov (1679–1767) of Leipzig, suggests that he had at least moderate Orthodox sympathies.

Another challenge to Orthodoxy in the 18th century came from the new thinking of rationalism, the *Aufklärung* (*see* ENLIGHTENMENT), of which J. A. Ernesti, Rector of the Thomasschule, was an early pioneer. Ernesti, a classical philologist rather than theologian, argued that the text of Scripture should be treated in the same way as any other writing from classical antiquity. This ran counter to the Orthodox understanding of Scripture as revealed truth, the word of God with its own validity and integrity. Again, Bach's cantata librettos express more the ethos of Orthodoxy than of proto-rationalism.            RAL

R. A. Leaver, *Bachs theologische Bibliothek* (Stuttgart, 1983); P. S. Minear, 'J. S. Bach and J. A. Ernesti: A Case Study in Exegetical and Theological Conflict', in J. Deschner *et al.*, eds., *Our Common History as Christians: Essays in Honor of Albert C. Outler* (New York, 1975), 135–55; J. Pelikan, *Bach Among the Theologians* (Philadelphia, 1986); M. Petzoldt, 'Zwischen Orthodoxie, Pietismus und Aufklärung: Überlegungen zum theologiegeschichtlichen Kontext Johann Sebastian Bachs', in R. Szeskus, ed., *Bach und die Aufklärung* [Bach-Studien 7] (Leipzig, 1982), 66–107.

***O sacred head sore wounded.*** See PASSION CHORALE.

***Oster-Oratorium.*** See EASTER ORATORIO.

**ouverture.** A type of French operatic overture developed by Jean-Baptiste Lully (1632–87). It opens with a slow section (A) in duple or quadruple time with stately dotted rhythms, closing in the dominant. A repeat of this leads to a fast fugal section (B), often in triple or compound time, which may lead to a return of the slow introductory material (A'); this second section is then usually repeated. The overture as a whole thus takes the form ‖: A :‖: B–(A') :‖.

Overtures of this type, together with the ballet dances that ensued, were often extracted from operas and performed independently as overture-suites (designated simply 'ouverture'). This practice led to the composition of original overture-suites for instrumental ensemble. Both the operatic and the independent type were
[cont. on p.354]

## ornamentation

A term used in music in two related ways: to refer to the symbols a composer such as Bach employed to indicate specific ornamental formulae (e.g. a trill or a turn); and to refer to free embellishment (sometimes termed 'diminutions' or 'passages') that might be improvised by the performer or indicated prescriptively (or as a suggestion) by the composer.

The very term 'ornamentation', and the French and German equivalents current in Bach's time ('agréments' and 'Manieren'), may suggest that the topic is one of only secondary, cosmetic importance. Frederick Neumann, in by far the most informed and intellectually challenging study of Bach's ornamentation (1978), insists that performers be alerted to the dichotomy of the structural and the ornamental in music—in other words that they be aware of the relative importance of each note to its neighbour. While he acknowledges that there can often be a merging of the categories 'structure' and 'ornament', or a fluid interplay between the two, he insists that the performer internalize the notion that the structural implies weight and importance, while ornament suggests lightness and easy flow.

Yet the intensity of Neumann's writings, and the remarkable degree of bigotry that the subject of ornamentation (particularly Bach's) seems to evince, often give the impression that there is no subject of greater importance to the satisfactory performance of Bach's music. Moreover, there is evidence that certain composer-performers of Bach's age were equally prescriptive: François Couperin's injunction that players should neither add nor take away from what he indicated in the notation (*Troisième livre*, 1722) is well known, and C. P. E. Bach's proscriptions (1753: no pre-beat appoggiaturas, no main-note trills beginning on the beat) are perhaps better known than his many perceptive suggestions. Finally, we have J. A. Scheibe's criticism (1737) of Bach himself: the assertion that Bach indicated every little note—normally the prerogative of the performer—in the notation itself (*BDok* ii. 286–7).

Scheibe was almost certainly referring to the wider area of improvised embellishment, not to the narrower context of ornaments indicated by specific symbols (mostly of French origin). In a certain sense, Bach's notated music is suffused with ornamentation; if one attempts to apply Neumann's conceptual dichotomy of structure and ornament, it is often difficult to distinguish the two; one ornament can be 'structural' in relation to another, and if one succeeds in finding something 'structural' (and such a notion is often rather more subjective than many 'objective' analysts would like to admit) it is not necessarily of particular musical interest. In short, the very subtlety of Bach's music may lie in the notion that everything can be ornamental and structural simultaneously; the ornamented texture is the music, and thus as essential as anything one can hope to find. Furthermore, even in Neumann's sense, the ornamental is not necessarily lighter than that which it elaborates. After all, the most basic function of musical ornament, the controlled and expressive use of dissonance, draws attention to itself and, as with a figure of speech, cuts across the grain of the 'dull' norm (*see* FIGURENLEHRE).

F. W. Marpurg, writing some time after Bach's death, refers to the above sense of ornamentation (i.e. diminution, whether notated by the composer or improvised by the performer) as 'willkürlich' ('optional') ornamentation. The more usual use of the term 'ornamentation' today refers to Marpurg's 'wesentlich' ('essential') ornaments—those indicated by specific symbols or added analogously by the performer. Clearly, there is some interplay between the two categories—the appoggiatura (or 'Accentus' in German terminology) as a one-note grace is both the simplest level of diminution and the simplest ornament indicated by a symbol—but usually the symbol will refer to something that cannot exactly (or even consistently) be indicated in regular notation.

Two pieces of evidence are most often cited as the guide to Bach's ornament symbols: the *Explication* that he wrote at the beginning of the *Clavierbüchlein* for the 9-year-old Wilhelm Friedemann Bach (1720) and the chapter on ornamentation from the keyboard treatise of Bach's second son, Carl Philipp Emanuel (1753), who repeatedly records his indebtedness to his father's methods. Several other tables of ornaments are sometimes noted: those found in the Möller manuscript and the Andreas Bach Book (the earliest significant Bach sources, compiled by his elder brother Johann Christoph) and the copy of J.-H. D'Anglebert's comprehensive table that Bach himself included in his copy of organ and harpsichord music by Nicolas de Grigny and Charles Dieupart. Neither of Christoph's manuscripts was copied while Bach was actually a pupil of his brother; the three tables rather imply that the Bach circle became acquainted with the French system of ornament symbols during the period spanning Bach's Arnstadt and Weimar years (the fact that Bach included the table at the end of his Grigny copy might suggest that he still needed it at that time, *c.*1709–12).

Bach's *Explication* apparently derives from D'Anglebert's system, and its principles seem to accord with those later offered by C. P. E. Bach: all trills begin on the upper note and may or may not conclude with a suffix; appoggiaturas begin on the beat and normally take up half the length of the main note. However, many writers have noted that the *Explication* provides only the most rudimentary guide to ornaments, and that the realization of such ornaments in practice will require an approach far more flexible than whatever can be indicated in notation. Frederick Neumann and, more recently, Paul Badura-Skoda have argued at length that Bach took a flexible (though not, apparently, a liberal) approach to ornamentation, allowing main-note trills and pre-beat appoggiaturas, and that the player should take a wide range of factors (such as dissonance treatment, part-writing, and melodic line) into account when deciding how to interpret an ornament. Two of the opinions that Neumann expresses throughout his writings are among the most valuable in the entire field of historical performance: that there was never uniformity of practice spanning many decades and locations, and that treatises and tables need to be used with caution, taking into account who designed them, for whom, and when. As he stresses with regard to the *Explication*, 'the table tells us that the graces in question *may* have the shapes indicated, but not that they *must* have these shapes which . . . are often disqualified by musical evidence' (Neumann, p. 127).

Neumann is right to draw attention to the fact that the evidence from German theoretical and notational sources of the late 17th century shows a wide range of applications for the one-note grace (*Accentus*), and that the on-beat *Vorschlag* (a 'grace' note preceding the main note) is a French import, evident, for instance, in Walther's *Musicalisches Lexicon* of 1732 (but clearly not as a replacement for all the other applications). Another figure close to Bach is his predecessor in Leipzig, Johann Kuhnau, who coined the concept of the Clavier-Übung with his two publications of 1689 and 1692. Not only does the notation of these publications show a wide range of *Accentus* ornaments (indicated by dashes), many of which can be interpreted as nothing other than the pre-beat *Nachschlag* (a 'grace' note following the main note), but the dashes are extremely profuse, far exceeding the norm for Bach's notated appoggiaturas (something which Neumann does not readily acknowledge). Kuhnau's notation, incidentally, has something in common with English keyboard sources of the 17th century, where the dashes imply a performance highly nuanced by graces—almost indiscriminately at times, it seems. In Kuhnau's two later publications these are not indicated, since Kuhnau assumed the performer to have assimilated the practice and to be able to use his own judgement. Clearly, he sees the ornaments as belonging to the performer's style, and his notated suggestions do not seem to be the issue of profound thought. It is likely that Bach was brought up in this tradition of free, performer-orientated ornamentation, however his practice later developed.

The German tradition shows that the nearly standard main-note trill of the 17th century was still viable well into the next century, and that the influence of the French upper-note trill began at a comparatively late stage (about 1696, according to Neumann). Furthermore, most 17th-century sources of keyboard music with written-out trills (following the Frescobaldi–Froberger tradition) show them beginning on the main note; so, again, Bach's upbringing would almost certainly have begun with this approach to trills. Badura-Skoda, moreover, affirms that the simple *Pralltriller* first described by C. P. E. Bach—the short trill with a single oscillation (i.e. the inversion of the mordent)—should often be applied to Bach's music even if it is not specified in the sources of his time.

Much of the justification Neumann and Badura-Skoda offer with regard to their revolution against the orthodoxy of performance practice is based on apparent problems of part-writing, particularly parallel octaves and 5ths. Peter Williams takes a refreshingly liberal approach to all these issues and, believing that 'ornamentation is a subject that attracts a certain kind of evangelistic pedantry' (Williams, p. 225), asserts that consecutives are simply not a major consideration when it comes to ornamentation, since the ear seldom detects them unaided by the eye. Certainly, a similar opinion is expressed by Bach's own cousin, J. G. Walther, in his *Praecepta* (1708), where he quotes J. G. Ahle's assertion that an ornament can neither cause a compositional lapse nor mitigate one. Thus, although Neumann and Badura-Skoda may well be right in claiming that there was more variability in ornaments practice than modern orthodoxy affirms, their motives might rather be their own personal preference that every element of ornamentation be subject to all the laws of harmony. Moreover, neither seems prepared to countenance the idea that Bach may have been brought up to ornament profusely, if not somewhat indiscriminately.

David Schulenberg (*The Keyboard Music of J. S. Bach*, New York, 1992) sees Bach's attitude towards ornamentation as progressively hardening, suggesting that in the course of many years of teaching 'what were originally offered as suggestions might have gradually become prescriptions' (p. 132). Thus, Emanuel's treatise may be seen as the end of a process that Bach began with the ornaments table of 1720. Neumann might then exaggerate when he paints Emanuel as the 'villain' who led us astray, since the hardening attitude seems already to have begun in France, to have become prevalent in Germany during the 1730s and 1740s, and to have been fostered by Bach

Ex. 1

**appoggiatura (accento, Accent)**

rising

*or*

falling

*or*

**trill (trillo, Pralltriller)**

*or* *or*

**mordent (Mordant)**

**turn (Cadence)**

**slide**

*or* *or*

**appoggiatura and trill**

*or*

**trill and mordent (trillo und Mordant)**

**slide and trill (Doppelt-cadence)**

**slide, trill and mordent (Doppelt-cadence und Mordant)**

**appoggiatura and mordent (Accent und Mordant)**

353

himself. However, Neumann's assertion that the Berlin school, of which Emanuel was a part, was acting under the influence of Prussian militarism and proclaiming a 'categorical imperative of ornamental ethics' (p. 39) is a challenging thought, and one that could also be directed to the absolutism of the French court. Moreover, Bach seems to have progressively aligned himself with the royalty of the Saxon court and, towards the end of his life, the Prussian court, suggesting that he was part of the growing absolutist tide. He does indeed seem to have become increasingly prescriptive, frequently adding ornaments to the instrumental and vocal parts of his cantatas, and he evidently took great care in preparing the *Clavier-Übung* engravings, giving particular attention to the correction of ornaments in his personal copies.

Several questions seem to come to the fore here. Was Bach as a performer as precise with his ornaments as he attempted to be on paper and as a teacher? Should we try to mimic the apparent progression from liberal ornamentation to controlled, 'hardened' categories according to the period from which any particular piece comes? If we were sure we knew them, should Bach's ornamental habits be unquestioningly followed in any case?

The behaviour of ornament pedants today and the evidence of many writers of Bach's time (who set down prescriptions on paper while emphasizing that the correct style can only be attained through the imitation of good performers) perhaps reveal the nearest we get to a fundamental truth regarding ornamentation. It is a question of style, of identifying with a particular fashion. Thus something seemingly insignificant in one environment becomes a social gaffe in another; to play a wrong ornament at court is as bad as wearing the wrong dress at court. The ornamental indeed becomes 'structural' (i.e. of paramount importance). The uniformity against which Neumann railed was not so much the historical style that its proponents supposed as a matter of class identity in performance of the late 20th century—an identity that has (from even before Neumann's death in 1995) become more diverse and open to change.

For a comprehensive table of all the symbols Bach employs, see Klotz, pp. 26–7, and Badura-Skoda, pp. 307–8. Ex. 1 transcribes and expands Bach's ornament table for Friedemann, which, it must again be stressed, gives only the most basic of guides. The most significant omissions from the original table are the appoggiatura (as indicated by a small note, often with a slur, and roughly synonymous to Bach's *Accentus* following D'Anglebert's notation) and the slide.                                                    JAB

C. P. E. Bach, *Essay on the True Art of Playing Keyboard Instruments*, i, Eng. trans. W. J. Mitchell (London, 1949); P. Badura-Skoda, *Interpreting Bach at the Keyboard*, Eng. trans. A. Clayton (Oxford, 1993); H. Klotz, *Die Ornamentik der Klavier- und Orgelwerke von J. S. Bach* (Kassel, 1984); F. Neumann, *Ornamentation in Baroque and Post-Baroque Music, with Special Emphasis on J. S. Bach* (Princeton, 1978); P. Williams, *The Organ Music of J. S. Bach*, iii (Cambridge, 1984).

known to Bach. Around 1729–30 he copied out and performed, with the Leipzig collegium musicum, the ouverture *La Tempête* from the opera *Il zelo di Leonato* (1691) by the Italian composer Agostino Steffani (1654–1728) and four (possibly five) concert ouvertures by a relative, the Eisenach organist Johann Bernhard Bach. Bach's own four ouvertures BWV1066–9, popularly known as ORCHESTRAL SUITES, belong to the same genre.

French overture-suites were frequently transcribed for keyboard around 1700. The Möller manuscript and the Andreas Bach Book—collections compiled in the first decade of the 18th century by Bach's elder brother Johann Christoph (ii)—contain transcriptions of such overture-suites from the opera *Briseide* (Hanover, 1696; sometimes attributed to Steffani) and Marin Marais's *Alcide* (Paris, 1693). Concert overture-suites, too, were often transcribed for keyboard—a keyboard version of Telemann's Ouverture in E♭ TWV55:Es 4 is found in the Andreas Bach Book—and this practice led to the composition of original overture-suites for keyboard. The young Bach's Ouverture in F major BWV820 is present in the Andreas Bach Book alongside Georg Böhm's Ouverture in D major, and another such work by Bach, the Ouverture in G minor BWV822, is transmitted elsewhere.

It is clear that the mature Bach retained an interest in the keyboard overture-suite, for in (or after) 1723 he used a work of this type, the Partita in G minor by G. H. Stölzel, as part of the musical education of his son Wilhelm Friedemann. And in 1735 his own recently composed Ouverture in C minor, transposed to B minor, became the representative of the French style in the keyboard publication *Clavier-Übung II*.

In addition, Bach employed the French overture in various other contexts. In the keyboard Partita no. 4 (1728), following Charles Dieupart's example (he had copied out Dieupart's *Six suittes de clavecin* in about 1709–16), he used it to introduce a keyboard suite of the standard type, and a French overture serves to introduce the second half of the so-called Goldberg Variations.

Particularly striking is the use of the French overture for the introductory choral movement of a number of cantatas. In each case its use symbolizes either 'introduction'—the first of a series of events—or 'festivity', as demanded by a special occasion: the first Sunday in the Church year (Cantata 61); a change of town council (no. 119); an organ consecration (no. 194); the beginning of a new *Jahrgang* (no. 20); or Christmas Day (no. 110). (The occasion for no. 97 is unknown.) Three of these overture-choruses (in Cantatas 20, 61, and 97) are based on chorale melodies. No. 194, which seems to be a reworking of a lost Cöthen secular cantata, is designed rather like an overture-suite, for the arias are in the style and metre of the gavotte, gigue, minuet, etc. The overture to BWV110 is a masterly choral adaptation of the opening movement of the Ouverture (Orchestral Suite) in D major BWV1069.          RDPJ

**Ouverture in the French Style** (Ouverture nach französischer Art). An overture-suite for keyboard, BWV831. It exists in an early version, in C minor, copied out by Bach's wife Anna Magdalena in the early 1730s. The revised, definitive version, in B minor, was coupled with the ITALIAN CONCERTO to form *Clavier-Übung II*, published in 1735. In this the chief orchestral genre of each nation is transferred to the two-manual harpsichord.

The Ouverture in the French Style has precedents among Bach's earlier works in the overture-suites BWV820 and 822 and in the Ouverture to the keyboard Partita no. 4 in D major. But it appears to be his only complete, mature overture-suite for solo keyboard. Its constituent movements are: Ouverture, Courante, Gavottes I and II, Passepieds I and II, Sarabande, Bourrées I and II, Gigue, and Echo. The opening and closing movements combine ritornello form with, respectively, fugue and binary dance form. Passages that correspond to orchestral tuttis are to be played on the lower manual of the harpsichord, which is indicated by 'forte'. 'Solo' passages, on the other hand, are marked 'piano', indicating the upper manual. 'Piano' is used for the 'solo' episodes of the fugal section of the overture, for the second of the paired dances (which are designed to be played *alternativement*), and for the echoes of the finale, which are subtle elaborations of preceding *forte* figures.          RDPJ

*See also* BONPORTI, FRANCESCO ANTONIO; ECHO; SOURCES, §2; and SUITE.

# P

**Pachelbel, Johann** (bap. 1 Sept. 1653; bur. 9 March 1706). Organist and composer, born in Nuremberg, the Bavarian city to which he returned in 1695. He lived for a short while in Vienna, where, as deputy organist of St Stephen's Cathedral, he was closely associated with J. C. Kerll. He was organist at the Predigerkirche in Erfurt (1678–90), during which time he taught Bach's elder brother Johann Christoph (ii).

Pachelbel's surviving vocal and instrumental music shows him to have been fully conversant with the wider field of German music. His systematic exploitation of virtually every chorale genre of the age and his comparatively large number of publications suggest that he may also have been concerned with amassing a body of pedagogic material—music which could be a model for his younger contemporaries. Bach's chorale preludes often follow the formats established by Pachelbel, and he would no doubt have been impressed by Pachelbel's rigorous, yet lyrical, development of motifs, particularly in his splendid variation sets. According to Bach's Obituary, Pachelbel was one of the contemporary masters represented in the book that Bach secretly copied at his brother's house. Emanual Bach also referred to Bach's study of Pachelbel's music in a letter to J. N. Forkel.

JAB

**Palestrina, Giovanni Pierluigi da** (b. 1525/6; d. 2 Feb. 1594). Italian composer, born probably in Palestrina, near Rome. He is remembered chiefly for his sacred music, which included over 100 masses, about 375 motets, and many other works.

Among the compositions by other composers that Bach became involved with, Palestrina's *Missa sine nomine* occupies a special place, since Bach's reworking of it exemplifies a process which was becoming widespread in Germany. For example, J. G. Harrer, Bach's successor as Thomaskantor in Leipzig, had already furnished the same mass with parts for two oboes, three violins, two violas, bass, and continuo (harpsichord and organ). In his youth Harrer had travelled to Italy at the expense of his protector, Count Heinrich von Brühl, and had brought to Dresden a considerable number of sacred works by Italian masters, Palestrina in particular; the *Missa sine nomine* was one of at least six Palestrina masses that Harrer 'restyled'.

Bach's involvement with the work, which first appeared in the *Missarum liber quintus* published in Rome by Francesco Coattino in 1590, is datable to about 1742–5. He provided *colla parte* instrumentation for two cornetts, four trombones, organ, harpsichord, and violone. Only the last three parts are autograph in the Berlin source, the others being in the hand of the so-called *Hauptkopist* I. It is particularly significant that Bach provided instrumental accompaniment only for the Kyrie and Gloria, the two sections constituting the MISSA in the Lutheran liturgy of the time, and it is reasonable to assume that only these sections were performed under Bach's direction. It is nevertheless logical to conclude that the other sections of Palestrina's mass were copied with the precise intention of showing the musicians active in the Bach circle the importance of the *stile antico*.

AB

A. Basso, 'Bach e Palestrina', in L. Bianchi and G. Rostirolla, eds., *Atti del II Convegno Internazionale di Studi Palestriniani* (Palestrina, 1991), 409–19; G. Fellerer, 'J. S. Bachs Bearbeitung der "Missa sine nomine" von Palestrina', *BJb* 24 (1927), 123–32; A. Schering, 'Der Thomaskantor Joh. Gottlob Harrer (1703–1755)', *BJb* 28 (1931), 112–46; C. Wolff, *Der stile antico in der Musik Johann Sebastian Bachs* (Wiesbaden, 1968).

**Palmarum.** Palm Sunday. *See* CHURCH CALENDAR.

**parody.** A term with at least three possible meanings when applied to music. In Renaissance polyphony it is used to denote the incorporation of existing music (usually from a motet or madrigal) into another work (usually a mass). More generally, the term can denote the imitation or adoption of a musical style for humorous or satirical effect; elements of parody in this sense can be observed in Bach's Peasant Cantata. However, in the 18th century 'parody' was understood primarily as the fashioning of a new poem on the model of an extant one. It is now taken to mean the retexting of a vocal composition, and more generally the production of a new vocal work based on the music of another piece. The concept is important in Bach studies because so much of the composer's vocal music appears in more than one guise.

Bach's parodies fall into two broad categories. The first is the reworking of most or all of a vocal composition into a piece for a new occasion.

These parodies clearly began with the production of a parody text based on the structure, diction, rhyme, and metre of the original. Musically, this kind of parody most often involved revisions to choruses and arias, and the composition of new simple recitatives. Most of the compositions Bach treated this way had been performed only once, including many of the secular cantatas for royalty, nobility, and the university. The parody version was sometimes a work that could be used every year, such as a weekly church cantata or oratorio (e.g. BWV30 and 36) and sometimes a work for another special occasion (BWV205a, 207a, and 210a). The most important example of this type of parody is the CHRISTMAS ORATORIO, fashioned largely from three secular cantatas (nos. 213–15).

The second broad category of Bach's parodies consists of works assembled movement by movement from various sources. Almost all are Latin liturgical works, including the four short masses, the Dresden *missa*, and most of the music added to it to form the Mass in B minor. These parodies are largely musical creations, in the sense that existing music is adapted to an existing text, rather than a new text being fitted to existing music. Bach evidently searched out movements from his cantatas whose text and music lent themselves to adaptation for particular sections of the fixed Mass text. He also occasionally parodied works by other composers, for example partly retexting a work of J. C. Kerll for the Sanctus BWV241.

Parodies must often have been executed in close collaboration with a librettist, and parody was apparently a particular skill of the Leipzig poet C. F. Henrici (Picander). Picander wrote the text for the lost memorial service music for Prince Leopold of Anhalt-Cöthen derived from his own *St Matthew Passion* and from the *Trauer Ode*; he and Bach clearly constructed the new work around the existing music. They may have planned the lost *St Mark Passion*, thought to have consisted largely of parodies, in the same way. Picander was possibly also the librettist of the *Christmas Oratorio*, whose text was assembled with specific parody models in mind.

It is often noted that many of Bach's parodies remain in the realm either of the sacred or of the secular; those that cross over are transformations from secular works to church compositions, never the other way round. It is unclear, though, whether the direction of these transformations reflects Bach's ideas about sacred versus secular music, or whether it is merely the consequence of his tendency to parody pieces usable only once (most of the secular works fall into this category) as works for recurring occasions (such as liturgical pieces).

The detection of likely parodies by the close comparison of texts has proved to be one of the most useful tools in the reconstruction of lost works, especially where sources of extant pieces suggest that their surviving text was not the original. There are also some texts that correspond so closely to others with extant music by Bach that they suggest a parody relationship. The search for textual parallels has risks—it can only suggest parody, not prove it—and the method of identifying poetic correspondences has led to occasionally far-fetched claims that Bach set certain texts to music now lost.

Over the years the extent and technique of Bach's parody procedure have come to be well understood, but this understanding has not resolved long-standing questions of why Bach made parodies, and what it means that he did. On one side of this controversial issue is a sense of discomfort with parodies, stemming largely from Romantic and modern aesthetics that place a premium on originality and novelty. (The continued agonizing over Handel's 'borrowings' presents a parallel case.) On the other side is the pragmatic view that parody represents Bach's efficient use of hard-won musical material, and that we should focus on the musical and textual significance of Bach's particular parody choices rather than on their morality. For the moment, the pendulum has swung towards the latter view, but this is the sort of aesthetic question that will never be fully resolved.                                                    DRM

A. Mann, 'Bach's Parody Technique and its Frontiers', in D. O. Franklin, ed., *Bach Studies* (Cambridge, 1989), 115–24; W. Neumann, 'Über Ausmaß und Wesen des Bachschen Parodieverfahrens', *BJb* 51 (1965), 63–85; A. Schering, 'Über Bachs Parodieverfahren', *BJb* 18 (1921), 49–95; F. Smend, *Bach in Köthen* (Berlin, 1950; Eng. trans., St Louis, Miss., 1985); H.-J. Schulze, 'The Parody Problem in Bach's Music: An Old Problem Reconsidered', *Bach*, 20/1 (1989), 7–21.

**partita** (Partie). A term used to refer to either a suite of dances or a set of variations. *See* CHORALE VARIATIONS, FLUTE SONATAS AND PARTITA, PARTITAS, SONATAS AND PARTITAS FOR SOLO VIOLIN, and SUITE.

**Partitas.** Six keyboard suites, BWV825–30, published by Bach himself under the collective title 'Clavier Übung'. They appeared first in separate editions between 1726 and 1730, and then in a collected edition as 'Opus 1' in 1731. Early versions of nos. 3 and 6 were dedicated to Bach's second wife Anna Magdalena, forming the opening items in her *Clavierbüchlein* of 1725. Still earlier versions of the Corrente and Tempo di Gavotta from no. 6 are found as keyboard and violin solos in the Sonata in G major for violin and obbligato cembalo

BWV1019*a*, which was completed in 1725. No. 1, whose minuets exist in early versions, was in autumn 1726 dedicated to the newborn son of Prince Leopold of Anhalt-Cöthen.

The *Clavier-Übung*, which initiated a series under that title (*see* CLAVIER-ÜBUNG), was Bach's first major publication (preceded only by two Mühlhausen cantatas, BWV71 and a lost work). It was clearly modelled on two sets of keyboard suites published in 1689 and 1692 by his predecessor as Thomaskantor at Leipzig, Johann Kuhnau. From him Bach adopted the overall title 'Clavier Übung' ('Keyboard Practice'), the individual title 'Partita' (Kuhnau used 'Partie'), and the concept of a set of suites whose key notes represent degrees of the diatonic scale. In accordance with this key scheme, Kuhnau published seven *Partien* in each set; and we know from a Leipzig press announcement of 1 May 1730 that Bach, too, originally intended to publish seven partitas. Kuhnau's scheme, however, rises by step from C and assigns major and minor modes to separate sets—Part 1: C, D, E, F, G, A, B♭ (all major); Part 2: C, D, E, F, G, A, B (all minor). Bach's starts from B♭ (where Kuhnau left off, as it were), intermingles major and minor, and is more elaborate though no less symmetrical, alternating rising and falling intervals: B♭, c, a, D, G, e, [F] (lower case indicates minor keys). It is not known why he failed to publish (or compose) a seventh partita in F major. Did it perhaps turn into the Italian Concerto, the opening item in *Clavier-Übung II* of 1735?

In Kuhnau's *Partien* the standard scheme of movements is Praeludium, Allemande, Courante, Sarabande, and Gigue. Bach adopts the same scheme, except that he inserts 'andern Galanterien'—relatively lightweight dances of optional type. His conception of the number of optional dances to be included in each partita appears to have changed: no. 2 (if we exclude the Capriccio, which stands in lieu of a gigue) and the early versions of nos. 3 and 6 have only one, but nos. 4 and 5 and the printed versions of nos. 3 and 6 have a contrasting pair. Only in no. 1 does Bach return to his former conception of a like pair to be played *alternativement* (as in the English Suites and Cello Suites).

According to the title-page, the Partitas were 'composed for music-lovers, to delight their spirits'. With this musical public in mind, Bach clearly attempted to make them as attractive as possible by means of vivid stylistic contrasts. Diversity of style and content, reflected in colourful movement titles, becomes a structural principle. Moreover, the conjunction of the popular French and Italian styles of the day is highlighted, as in the solo violin Partitas, by linguistic differentiation ('Courante', for example, alternates with 'Cor-

rente'). The preludes all belong to different types: 'Praeludium', akin to certain preludes in Part 1 of *The Well-tempered Clavier*; 'Sinfonia', a term borrowed from the introductory movements to the cantatas; 'Fantasia', the original name of the three-part Inventions; 'Ouverture', the Lullian type transferred to keyboard; 'Praeambulum', cast in Torellian short ritornello form; and 'Toccata', a compact toccata and fugue like the E♭ major Prelude from Part 1 of *The Well-tempered Clavier*.

The contrast between specimens of any one dance type is often enormous: compare, for example, the brilliantly athletic Allemande from Partita no. 1 with the highly elaborate and lyrical Allemande from no. 4. And the boundaries of the traditional dance types are inevitably stretched and occasionally even transgressed—for example in the sarabandes of nos. 3, 5, and 6, all of which open with an anacrusis. In recognition of this freedom of treatment, Bach sometimes modifies a dance title using the formula 'tempo di . . .', as in the solo violin Partitas, or else dispenses with it altogether: the optional dance in no. 2 is entitled 'Rondeaux', and a 'Capriccio' takes the place of the usual gigue finale; the Menuet of no. 3 was subsequently altered to 'Burlesca' and a 'Scherzo' was added.

With the musical public at large the Partitas established Bach's reputation as a keyboard composer. According to J. N. Forkel, 'This work made in its time a great noise in the musical world. Such excellent compositions for the clavier had never been seen and heard before. Anyone who had learnt to perform well some pieces out of them could make his fortune in the world thereby.' On the other hand, it is clear from comments by Johann Mattheson (1731), Louise Gottsched (1732), and Lorenz Mizler (1738) that the Partitas soon gained a reputation for their technical difficulty. Neither here nor anywhere else did Bach make any concession to the huge 18th-century demand for easy music for amateurs.　　RDPJ
*See also* SOURCES, §2.

G. Butler, 'The Engraving of J. S. Bach's *Six Partitas*', *Journal of Musicological Research*, 7 (1986), 3–27; W. Emery, 'Bach's Keyboard Partitas: A Set of Composer's Corrections?', *Musical Times*, 93 (1952), 495–9; R. D. P. Jones, 'The History and Text of Bach's Clavierübung I' (diss., Oxford University, 1988); G. Kinsky, *Die Originalausgaben der Werke Johann Sebastian Bachs* (Vienna, 1937); C. Wolff, 'Text-Critical Comments on the Original Print of the Partitas', in *Bach: Essays on his Life and Music* (Cambridge, Mass., 1991), 214–22.

**partite diverse.** *See* CHORALE VARIATIONS.

**passacaglia.** A term originally used for a ritornello in 17th-century Spanish song; in 18th-century

Germany it denoted a set of continuous variations on a repeated short theme. Only one work by Bach, the Passacaglia in C minor for organ bwv582, bears the title, although he wrote other works on ground bass patterns. Bach seems to have drawn a clear distinction between the passacaglia and the CHACONNE, using the latter title for the last movement of the D minor Partita for unaccompanied violin, which has an open-ended bass four bars long and an implied chord sequence. It seems clear that for Bach the title 'passacaglia' implied a harmonically complete eight-bar melody, and also an emphasis on the theme itself, which is strictly maintained throughout and sometimes transferred to the treble. The C minor Passacaglia was copied by about 1708 into the Bach family keyboard anthology now known as the ANDREAS BACH BOOK by the main scribe of the collection, Bach's elder brother Johann Christoph (ii). Although the work is highly mature in most respects, an early date is confirmed by the use of a cadential formula (the supertonic rising to the mediant before falling to the tonic) which largely disappeared from his music after this time. In 1802 J. N. Forkel expressed doubts as to whether the organ was indeed the intended instrument, but they are largely overruled by the early manuscript sources, in which the Passacaglia is labelled 'organo' (and in one case 'organo pleno').

The Passacaglia is based on an eight-bar theme, the first half of which is the same as that of a *passacaille en trio* from an organ mass by the French composer André RAISON. The French Bach scholar André Pirro (1869–1943) claimed Raison's composition as the model for Bach's, and this has been supported by many later writers, but it is hardly beyond coincidence that the two composers might have hit on the same eight-note formula, especially since ground bass subjects were highly conventionalized and restricted in style. Certainly Raison's flimsy little piece has nothing else in common with Bach's Passacaglia. A more illuminating comparison can be made with the three chaconnes by Buxtehude, in C minor, D minor, and E minor (BUXWV159, 161, and 160)—works which Bach seems to have studied closely before beginning work on bwv582 (see Williams, p. 257). The subjects of the Buxtehude works are all related to that of bwv582, but Bach expanded them to eight bars and made the subdominant fourth note a feature of his own theme. Much of the figuration used by Bach is also related to Buxtehude's, although Bach's conception as a whole has an architectural grandeur and a cumulative sweep which makes Buxtehude's handling of similar material seem stiff by comparison.

Bach's Passacaglia has 20 variations, followed by a fugue (labelled 'Thema fugatum'). It applies a wide variety of conventional Baroque keyboard figures to the subject, and these are developed successively in the course of the work. The greater unity of Bach's conception in comparison with Buxtehude's results partly from the unobtrusive merging of one set of figures into the next, ensuring an effect of continuity which eludes Buxtehude. The central portion of the work features a gradual thinning of the texture through trio and duo variations into trellis-like arpeggios (variation 15) before full-textured writing returns, heralding the ascent to the final climax. Various viewpoints regarding the overall architecture of the variations (and therefore the shaping of any interpretation) are considered by both Williams and Wolff.

The fugue, which does not correspond to anything in Bach's models, is another demonstration of his superiority over his great predecessor. In it the first half of the passacaglia theme is combined with a countersubject in pairs of repeated quavers. The work contains one final surprise in the form of a shattering Neapolitan 6th chord, which breaks the continuity of the music just before the final cadence. DLH

Y. Kobayashi, 'The Variation Principle in J. S. Bach's Passacaglia in C minor BWV 582', in D. R. Melamed, ed., *Bach Studies 2* (Cambridge, 1995), 62–9; P. Williams, *The Organ Music of J. S. Bach*, i (Cambridge, 1980), 253–66; C. Wolff, 'The Architecture of the Passacaglia', in *Bach: Essays on his Life and Music* (Cambridge, Mass., 1991), 306–16.

**passepied.** A French court dance and instrumental form popular especially in the 18th century. The dance is lively and uses MINUET steps, but, unlike the minuet, it is playful, flirtatious, and even frivolous in character. The tempo is a little faster than that of the minuet, and the dancers present many more elaborate figures than the simple 'Z's of the minuet, including various types of circles around one another, parallel circles holding hands, and angular moves towards and away from one another in many different directions. The music is usually set in 3/8 time, with phrases in a length divisible by four bars; an upbeat is characteristic, as are long phrases, strongly accented hemiolas in unexpected places, and the rhythmic figure ♩♪♫. Conjunct quavers may be played unequally.

Bach's seven passepieds include a set of two in his Orchestral Suite BWV1066, two in the Fifth English Suite, one in the keyboard Partita no. 5, and a pair in the Ouverture in the French Style. All exploit the hemiola idea, with long, elegant phrases replete with opportunities for off-balance

**Passion**

rhythmic effects. In Passepied I from the Ouverture in the French Style a trill on the opening dissonant harmony in bar 1 propels the music into the succeeding dance phrases. This contrasts strongly with Passepied II, which features a drone bass in musette style.                    NJ, MEL

For bibliography, *see* DANCE.

**Passion.** As the Reformation was established across Germany, various church orders included provisions for the observance of Holy Week. The Passion story as related by St Matthew was commonly retained as the Gospel for Palm Sunday and that of St John as the Gospel for Good Friday. In the Catholic Mass these Passions had been customarily sung to the plainchant of the old Latin Passion tones, or in responsorial settings that alternated plainsong with homophony and polyphony. Such *a cappella* settings continued to be sung in Lutheran churches, but more often in German than in Latin. The two Passions (*St Matthew* and *St John*) dating from the second quarter of the 16th century and attributed to Johann Walter (1496–1570), Luther's musical collaborator, are of this type. They were enormously influential and became the primary responsorial Passions sung in the Lutheran liturgy from the middle of the 16th century until well into the 18th; even the three Passions of Heinrich Schütz (1585–1672) did not displace them. The two Walter Passions were included in Gottfried Vopelius's *Neu Leipziger Gesangbuch* (Leipzig, 1682), and were customarily sung as the respective Gospels for Palm Sunday and Good Friday throughout Bach's Kantorate in Leipzig.

From the middle of the 16th century through-composed settings of the Passions by Lutheran composers began to appear alongside the simpler responsorial type, usually in German, though sometimes in Latin, and some continued to employ the traditional chant as a cantus firmus. Composers include Balthasar Resinarius (c.1485–1544), Bartholomäus Gesius (c.1558–1613), Leonhard Lechner (c.1553–1606), and Christoph Demantius (1567–1643). Both the responsorial and the through-composed Passions were settings of biblical narrative alone and were sung *a cappella* (without instruments). The oratorio Passion that began to appear before the end of the 17th century—the earliest (1641) may be that of Thomas Selle (1599–1663)—differed from these types in its use of accompanying instruments and the inclusion of chorales and non-biblical, reflective, or devotional texts. Notable examples of 17th-century oratorio Passions include, in addition to Selle's, those of Johann Sebastiani (1622–83) and Johann Theile (1646–1724). After 1700, following Erdmann Neumeister's incorpor-

ation of operatic elements into his cantata librettos, oratorio Passions began to include simple recitative and da capo arias. One of the earliest examples of this type was Reinhard Keiser's *St Mark Passion* (c.1710), which Bach performed in Weimar in 1713, or earlier, and to which he added a few movements of his own. The introduction of the oratorio Passion came late to many city and town churches; for example, the earliest known concerted or oratorio Passion to be heard in the main Leipzig churches was the *St Mark Passion* of Johann Kuhnau, first performed in 1721; a Passion of this type by an unknown composer had, however, been performed four years earlier at the Neukirche.

Bach was actively involved in composing and performing various Passion settings for practically the whole of his time in Leipzig. According to the Obituary, he composed 'five Passions, of which one is for double chorus' (*BDok* iii, no. 666). 'Double-chorus' here almost certainly refers to the *St Matthew Passion*; of the other four, two must have been the *St John* and *St Mark Passions*, and two are uncertain, though the anonymous *St Luke Passion* may have been intended, and possibly a fragment of a Weimar Passion, movements of which were later used in versions of the *St Matthew* and *St John Passions*. The following chronological table lists those Passions composed by Bach (or which incorporated movements composed by him) and performed during his time in Leipzig (N = Nikolaikirche; T = Thomaskirche):

| | |
|---|---|
| 7 April 1724 | *St John Passion*, first version (N) |
| 30 March 1725 | *St John Passion*, second version, with a number of movements from the presumed earlier Weimar (?*St Matthew*) Passion (T) |
| 19 April 1726 | Keiser's *St Mark Passion*, including movements composed by Bach, first performed in Weimar in 1713 or earlier; additional chorales were included for this Leipzig performance (N) |
| 11 April 1727 | *St Matthew Passion*, earlier version (T) |
| 15 April 1729 | *St Matthew Passion*, ?earlier version (T) |
| 7 April 1730 | anonymous *St Luke Passion* BWV246, including at least one movement by Bach (N) |
| 23 March 1731 | *St Mark Passion*, with music parodied from the *Trauer Ode* and other cantatas (T) |
| ? 11 April 1732 | *St John Passion*, third version, omitting the additional movements of the second version (1725) and restoring those of the first version (1724) (N) |

| 30 March 1736 | St Matthew Passion, later version (T) |
| [1739 | revision of St John Passion begun] |
| ? 23 March 1742 | St Matthew Passion, later version (T) |
| ? 16 April 1745 | anonymous St Luke Passion, later version (N) |
| ? 12 April 1748 | pasticcio, incorporating music by Handel and Keiser (T) |
| 4 April 1749 | St John Passion, fourth version (N). |

The large-scale concerted oratorio Passions were written for performance at Vespers in the two principal churches in Leipzig in alternate years. Good Friday Vespers in Leipzig had a simple liturgical structure:

Hymn: *Da Jesus an den Kreuze stund*
Passion, Part 1
Sermon
Passion, Part 2
Motet: *Ecce quomodo moritur* by Jacob Handl (1550–91)
Collect
Benediction
Hymn: *Nun danket alle Gott.*                      RAL

E. Axemacher, 'Aus Liebe will mein Heiland Sterben': Untersuchungen zum Wandel des Passionsverständnisses im frühen 18. Jahrhundert (Stuttgart, 1984); R. A. Leaver, 'Passion Music', in P. F. Bradshaw and L. A. Hoffman, eds., Passover and Easter: the Liturgical Structuring of a Sacred Season (forthcoming); R. A. Leaver, 'The Mature Vocal Works and their Theological and Liturgical Context', in J. Butt, ed., The Cambridge Bach Companion (Cambridge, 1997), 86–122; G. Stiller, Bach and Liturgical Life in Leipzig, Eng. trans. H. J. A. Bouman, D. F. Poellot, and H. C. Oswald, ed. R. A. Leaver (St Louis, Miss., 1984); B. Smallman, The Background of Passion Music: J. S. Bach and his Predecessors (London, 1957; 2nd edn., New York, 1970).

**Passion Chorale.** A name often used for the chorale *O Haupt voll Blut und Wunden* (usually sung in English to the words 'O sacred head sore wounded'). The melody is that of a love song, *Mein G'Müt ist mir verwirret*, by Hans Leo Haßler (1562–1612), which was adapted first to the words *Herzlich tut mich verlangen* (1613), and later to Paul Gerhardt's hymn *O Haupt voll Blut und Wunden* (1656). It owes its name of 'Passion Chorale' to Bach's five-fold use of it in the ST MATTHEW PASSION, but the melody was sung to several other texts as well, and appears also in the *Christmas Oratorio* (twice), and in Cantatas 135, 159, and 161.

**Pastorella/Pastorale.** A piece for organ in F major, BWV590, usually known as 'Pastorale', but entitled 'Pastorella' in the sources. It is a short four-movement work apparently connected with the Leipzig Christmas liturgy, although its exact place in the service remains obscure. The attribu-

tion of the *Pastorella* to Bach is no longer regarded as dubious, and fingerprints of *galant* style in the writing show that it was composed late in his career. The first two movements feature the characteristic *piffero* style (see below), with the drone basses and skirling melodies conventionally associated with shepherds. The aria-like third movement uses the triple symbolism often associated in Bach's music with angels (three flats in the key-signature, $3 \times 3$ units in the bar), and may have been intended to depict the angels' appearance to the shepherds as described in St Luke 2: 8–15. The final movement is a fugal gigue based on a subject which, as Christoph Wolff has pointed out, is a florid version of the medieval hymn *Resonet in laudibus*, appropriate as a portrayal of the rejoicing shepherds.

The *piffero* convention exemplified in the *Pastorella*, and used by numerous other Baroque composers, originated as an Italian Christmas folk ritual in which bagpiping shepherds processed to major cities bearing gifts in imitation of the shepherds who travelled to Bethlehem to visit the Christ-child. The music of the *piffero* usually features two melody voices, often playing in parallel 3rds or simple canon, supported by a bass line which plays a drone or keeps to simple harmonic formulae based on the tonic, subdominant, and dominant triads.

Bach also used the *piffero* convention in the introductory Sinfonia to Part 2 of the *Christmas Oratorio* and at the opening of the chorale prelude on *Dies sind die heilgen zehn Gebot* BWV678, where it apparently symbolizes the paradisal state of mankind before the Fall. It also occurs in the prelude on *In dulci jubilo* BWV751, which, however, is more convincingly attributed to Johann Michael Bach in the Neumeister manuscript. Arias in siciliana rhythm expressing more generalized pastoral sentiments occur occasionally in the cantatas, for example in the opening aria of Cantata 151, *Süßer Trost, mein Jesus kömmt.*                      DLH

G. Stauffer, 'Bach's Pastorale in F: A Closer Look at a Maligned Work', Organ Yearbook, 14 (1983), 44–60; P. Williams, The Organ Music of J. S. Bach, i (Cambridge, 1980), 277–81.

**Paulinerkirche** (St Paul's Church). In Bach's time, the university church in Leipzig. It was consecrated by the Dominicans in 1240 and later altered and restored several times. The organist there during Bach's Kantorate was Johann Christoph Thiele (1692–1773). Several Bach works, including the *Trauer Ode*, were performed there for the first time. The church survived the bombing in World War II, but was demolished in 1968 to make way for extensions to the Karl-Marx Universität.

# Peasant Cantata

**Peasant Cantata** (*Bauernkantate*) ['Mer hahn en neue Oberkeet' ('We have a new régime')]. Secular cantata, BWV212, to a libretto by Picander, also known as 'Cantate [en] burlesque'. It was written to mark the inauguration of the rule of Carl Heinrich von Dieskau (1706–82) over certain villages in the immediate surroundings of Leipzig. One of these was Klein-Zschocher, probably the place of the cantata's first performance on 30 August 1742.

1. Text and music.
2. Borrowed material.

**1. Text and music.** The whole 'action' is deployed in a sequence of recitative–aria pairs, in this case sung by two persons, Mieke (soprano) and her unnamed male companion (bass). As is common in homage cantatas, there is no proper dramatic content. After an instrumental introduction, the two singers state that a new lord has arrived; the Man says he will dance with Mieke at the feast in an inn (no. 2), but Mieke is anxious. They discuss the lord's character and note that it is only his administrator who is unfriendly towards the country people (nos. 3–6); the new lord is the best they could have. In evidence of this they mention his open-mindedness and the character of his wife; furthermore, the village was exempted from the last military conscription (nos. 7–12). The recitative no. 13 indicates that Mieke and her companion are still on their way to the inn; Mieke decides that before dancing she wants to serenade the new lord. They then compete with each other in praising him, and try to find a proper 'accent' for this—not too urbane nor too rustic (nos. 14–20). In the final movements (nos. 21–4) they both set off for the inn.

The final sections make it clear that the cantata reflects the difference between the town and the countryside. But allusions to this are even stronger in the music. The use of the 'Folies d'Espagne' for no. 8 (the first song in praise of the new 'Kammerherr') introduces a certain gaucheness intended to reflect the naivety of the two *dramatis personae*. The same is true of the lullaby for the third 'serenade' (no. 18), which is inserted by Mieke only to show her companion a style of music inappropriate for the occasion. Furthermore, parts of the text are in Saxon dialect, especially the opening duet which sets the scene: 'Mer hahn en neue Oberkeet' means 'Wir haben eine neue Obrigkeit' ('We have a new régime'); in subsequent movements the use of dialect is restricted to single words. Finally, Bach supports the contrast between courtly and rustic elements by his instrumentation. Mieke's aria 'Klein-Zschocher

müsse' (no. 14), which is described by her companion as 'too clever, and in the style of music played in the town', is accompanied by an obbligato flute, a prominent aristocratic instrument of the time. This courtly aria is in a rudimentary da capo form in which the material of the outer sections is expanded by numerous melodic variations; in the contrasting bass aria (no. 16) the form is reduced to its elementary components, a simple A–B–A structure.

Among socialist music-lovers the Peasant Cantata has always been a favourite piece, since it might appear that Bach has composed a work about the interests of the lower classes. In the context of Leipzig and its surrounding villages, matters can be seen differently; Bach, as a proponent of sophisticated music, was probably making ironic comment on the music of country folk. Attempts have been made to put on stage performances of the Peasant Cantata. Such efforts are questionable, since the piece contains even less action than a number of other secular cantatas by Bach, such as *Der Streit zwischen Phoebus und Pan*, *Was mir behagt*, and *Laßt uns sorgen*. It is a mere dialogue between only two people, and the 'action' is confined to the interruption of their walk to the inn.

**2. Borrowed material.** It has long been known that the Peasant Cantata is not only composed in a deliberately 'rustic' style but actually quotes a number of popular tunes of the time. A sufficient number of such quotations have come to light to suggest, perhaps, that Bach based his entire work on existing music, possibly at Dieskau's request.

No. 1. The opening sinfonia (untitled in the autograph manuscript) is a potpourri of dance tunes, any one of which could be a true folk melody. The tune immediately following the opening Presto is very similar to certain examples of the so-called 'Heyducken Tanz' popular in Germany and Poland, and the central Adagio section is an excellent example of a true polonaise. A number of other movements from the cantata are in Polish style, which may have had a strongly pastoral connotation for the composer.

No. 2. The duet 'Mer hahn en neue Oberkeet' is based on a variant of a rustic bourrée in a German keyboard manuscript from 1693–6 (St Petersburg, Academy of Sciences, the Michael Hansch MS, fo. 71) and also in a Polish tablature for an unspecified plucked instrument from the early 18th century (Warsaw, Biblioteka Narodowa, MS 2088, fo. 1v). In an early 18th-century Dutch collection, *Oude en nieuwe Hollantse Boerenlietjes en Contredansen* (Amsterdam, 1700–16 [facsimile, Amsterdam, 1972], Part 4, p. 16, no. 287), it is called 'De lustighe Boer' ('The jolly farmer').

No. 3. In the recitative 'Nu, Miecke, gib dein Guschel immer her' the strings quote two popular dance tunes. The second of these was also cited by Bach in the final Quodlibet of the Goldberg Variations, and is a version of the traditional 'Großvater Tanz', which has survived with a variety of song texts. In Picander's libretto, responding to the Man's advances, Mieke sings: 'I know you, you saucy devil; later you'll only want to go further and further!' Bach may have expected his audience to supply for themselves one of the best-known 'Großvater-Tanz' texts at the end of their dialogue: 'You and me together to the feather bed, you and me together to the straw'.

No. 4, 'Ach es schmeckt doch gar zu gut', is clearly another tune in polonaise style; a closely related lute piece (entitled simply 'Allegro') survives in a copy of a lost 18th-century German lute manuscript transcribed in the 19th century (Venice, Fondazione Cini, Chilesotti papers).

No. 8. The strings announce the well-known tune 'Folies d'Espagne' at the beginning of 'Unser trefflicher lieber Kammerherr', and it recurs throughout the aria. However, this is not merely a set of variations; the vocal melody itself sounds like a different popular tune, yet to be identified.

No. 12. The aria 'Fünfzig Taler bares Geld' uses a polonaise tune in mazurka rhythm that appears in two tablature manuscripts from the mid-18th century (Nuremberg, Germanisches National-Museum, MS 274, fo. 8; Leipzig, Musikbibliothek der Stadt, MS III.12.18, no. 22) as well as in a collection of Polish dances for violin from 1742 (Martin, Matica Slovenská, 'Uhrovec' MS, fo. 6ᵛ).

No. 14. The opening phrases of the 'courtly' aria, 'Klein-Zschocher müsse', closely resemble the beginning of a minuet from Gregorio Lambranzi's *Neue und curieuse theatralische Tantz-Schul* (Nuremberg, 1716), part 2, p. 51.

No. 16. The 'aria col corne de chasse', 'Es nehme zehntausend Dukaten', uses a very well-known hunting song, originally French, popular all over Europe, and said to have been introduced to Germany by Count Franz Anton Sporck.

No. 20. 'Dein Wachstum sei feste' is a parody of Pan's aria 'Zu Tanze, zu Sprunge' in another of Bach's secular cantatas, *Der Streit zwischen Phoebus und Pan* (BWV201:7).

No. 22, 'Und daß ihrs alle wißt' was probably based on a student song (see Spitta, iii. 178, n. 331); a version of the piece without text, but called 'Aira' (*recte* 'Aria') can be found in the Polish tablature mentioned above (Warsaw, Biblioteka Narodowa, MS 2088, fo. 29).     KK (§1), TTC (§2)

Spitta, iii. 176–81; T. Crawford, 'Bach's Sources for the Peasant Cantata, BWV212', *BJb* (forthcoming); H.-J. Schulze, 'Melodiezitate und Mehrtextigkeit in der Bauerkantate und in den Goldbergvariatio-

nen', *BJb* (1976), 58–72. For further bibliography, *see* CANTATA, §2.

*pedaliter.* A term used in organ music to indicate that a piece of music includes a part to be played by the feet. It appears, for example, in the title of Bach's Prelude and Fugue in G minor BWV535a. *See also* MANUALITER and TOCCATA.

**Penzel, Christian Friedrich** (b. 25 Nov. 1737; d. 14 March 1801). Kantor, teacher, and composer, born in Oelsnitz, Vogtland, Saxony, where he received his first musical training from Johann Georg Nacke (1718–1804). In 1749 he entered the Leipzig Thomasschule and became one of Bach's last pupils. After studying law at Leipzig University, he made an unsuccessful attempt in 1762 to obtain his father's position as sexton at Oelsnitz, and in 1765 he became Kantor at Merseburg, where he stayed until his death. Today Penzel is remembered mainly as one of the most reliable copyists of Bach's works. His Bach copies (from exemplars at the Thomasschule and from sources in the possession of W. F. Bach) are mainly of cantatas, but include also instrumental music. His manuscript collection was inherited by his nephew Johann Gottlob Schuster (1765–1839), who sold most of it to Franz Hauser in 1833; the remainder was acquired by the Leipzig publisher C. F. Peters.     PW

Y. Kobayashi, 'Franz Hauser und seine Bach-Handschriftensammlung' (diss., University of Göttingen, 1973); K. Lehmann, 'Bachiana unter "Tabak & Cigaretten": die Bach-Sammlung des Leipziger Verlages C. F. Peters in der ersten Hälfte des 19. Jahrhunderts', *BJb* 82 (1996), 49–76; K. Lehmann, 'Neues zur Vorgeschichte der Bach-Sammlung Franz Hausers', *Beiträge zur Bachforschung*, 6 (1988), 65–81.

**Peranda, Marco Gioseppe** (b. *c.*1625; d. 12 Jan. 1675). Italian composer, born in Rome or Macerata. He went to Dresden as a court singer in the 1650s and rose to become *Kapellmeister* in 1663 and principal *Hofkapellmeister* in 1672. He wrote mainly church music, including a *St Mark Passion* once thought to be by Heinrich Schütz (1585–1672). The performing material for a Kyrie in C major by Peranda was copied for Bach's use in Weimar.

*per arsin et thesin.* A term used, especially in connection with canon and fugue, in two different senses. Early theorists, including Thomas Morley (1557/8–1602) in his *A Plaine and Easie Introduction to Practicall Musicke* (1597), employed it for the inversion of a theme; thus canon *per arsin et thesin* would mean canon by inversion, as in the 'Canon perpetuus' in Bach's *Musical Offering*, BWV1079:4h. The term is more commonly used for the entry of a fugue theme (often in stretto) in which strong accents replace weak ones and vice versa by virtue of its positioning in relation to the natural accentuation implied by the barlines; an example can be seen in the B♭ minor Fugue in Part 2 of *The Well-tempered Clavier*, at bar 33 in the outer parts. LC

**performance styles.** See opposite.

**Pergolesi, Giovanni Battista** (b. 4 Jan. 1710; d. 16 March 1736). Italian composer, born in Iesi. He was active mainly as a composer of operas, among which the intermezzo *La serva padrona* achieved particularly wide popularity.

Pergolesi's music was already well known in German-speaking countries when his *Stabat mater* (1735), which was circulated widely in both manuscript copies and printed editions, attracted Bach's attention in about 1745–7. Bach's arrangement (BWV1083/243a) is a parody which sets an anonymous rhymed paraphrase in German of Psalm 51, *Tilge, Höchster, meine Sünden*. Designated a 'Motetto a due Voci, 3 Stromenti e Cont.', the score (partly autograph) follows scrupulously Pergolesi's original, in 14 sections, although numerous modifications to both the vocal and the instrumental parts were necessary in order to adapt the music to the new text. It is significant that the only two sections without such changes—no. 9 and the concluding 'Amen' (no. 14)—are those written in the *stile antico*. AB

F. Degrada, 'Lo "Stabat Mater" di Pergolesi e la parodia di Bach', in W. Osthoff and R. Wiesend, eds., *Bach und die italienische Musik/Bach e la musica italiana* (Venice, 1987), 141–69; A. Dürr, 'Neues über Bachs Pergolesi-Bearbeitung', *BJb* 54 (1968), 89–100; E. Platen, 'Eine Pergolesi-Bearbeitung Bachs', *BJb* 48 (1961), 35–51.

**periodicals.** *See* JOURNALS AND YEARBOOKS.

**permutation fugue** (Permutationsfuge). A type of FUGUE or fugal passage in which the subject is followed by a number of countersubjects which then combine with each other somewhat in the manner of a canon, or round, though usually more freely. Permutation fugues are found in Bach's earliest cantatas. In no. 71, *Gott ist mein König*, for example, the theme shown in the music example serves for a four-part permutation fugue to the words 'Dein Alter sei wie deine Jugend' (no. 3). The three limbs of the theme are 'permutated' among the four voices beginning as follows (x = free material):

| | | | | | | | | |
|---|---|---|---|---|---|---|---|---|
| S: | — | — | S | CS1 | CS2 | x | x | S |
| A: | — | — | — | S | CS1 | CS2 | S | CS1 |
| T: | S | CS1 | CS2 | x | — | S | CS1 | CS2 |
| B: | — | S | CS1 | CS2 | S | CS1 | CS2 | x |

bar nos.: 1–2  3–4  5–6  7–8  9–10  11–12  13–14  15–16

An even tighter permutational structure can be found in other works, for example in the first chorus of Cantata 182, *Himmelskönig, sei willkommen*.

Bach has sometimes been credited with the invention of the permutation fugue, but in fact it is found in earlier music, both instrumental and vocal (see Walker).

W. Neumann, *J. S. Bachs Chorfuge: ein Beitrag zur Kompositionstechnik Bachs* (Leipzig, 1938; 3rd edn., 1953); P. Walker, 'Die Entstehung der Permutationsfuge', *BJb* 75 (1989), 21–41; Eng. trans. in *Studies in the History of Music*, iii: *The Creative Process* (New York, 1993), 51–91.

***per omnes versus.*** A term used for a type of chorale setting which treats the hymn and its associated melody strophe by strophe in a kind of variation form. Bach's *Christ lag in Todes Banden* BWV4 is an example of a cantata *per omnes versus*. The term may also be used for a set of purely instrumental chorale variations.

**Petzold/Pezold, Christian** (b. 1677; d. ? May–June 1733). Organist and composer, born in Königstein, Saxony. He was organist at the Dresden court, and from 1703 at the Sophienkirche. In 1709 he was appointed court organist and chamber composer. Anna Magdalena Bach copied two
[*cont. on p.367*]

Subject (S)_____ Countersubject 1 (CS 1)_____

Dein Al - ter  sei wie dei-ne Ju - gend, und __ Gott ist mir dir in  al-len, das  du

___ Countersubject 2 (CS 2)_____

tust,  und Gott ist mit dir in  al - len,  in al - - - len

## performance styles

The question of how Bach performed his music became fundamental to performance style only in the latter half of the 20th century. While there is sufficient information to make plausible hypotheses about some of the general conditions and predispositions of performance practice in Bach's time, the question of how Bach related to these norms is extraordinarily complex. After all, judging Bach's music according to the conventions of his day does not necessarily reveal his strengths as a composer, and we know very little about how he approached his own performances. Certainly it seems clear that as a teacher he became increasingly prescriptive, but this does not automatically imply that his performance style changed (see Schulenberg). Did he respond to the many stylistic influences and developments of his age, and did he do so consistently? Did he follow the rules of his own notation? We know that he was aware of various national styles of composition and performance, as he stated in his complaint to the town council in 1730 (*BDok* i. 60–4), but does this mean that he always made conscious distinctions between national elements in his own music, or that he knew enough about foreign idioms to do so? After all, much of his compositional activity is characterized by a blending of diverse elements and styles.

If the manuscript transmission is anything to go by, it seems that the considerable coterie of organists who had studied with Bach attempted to preserve his style within their local environments during the latter half of the 18th century. Yet, just as a J. L. Krebs sought to preserve Bach's compositional style but was inevitably influenced by the idioms of his day, so it is unlikely that Bach's own performance styles were preserved intact; indeed, certain minor alterations of articulation and ornamentation in the manuscripts may indicate a subtle shift towards the more strongly differentiated gestures of early Classical and *galant* performing styles.

More conscious adaptations towards Classical practice are evident in what we know of Mozart's performance and his transcriptions of Bach fugues for string trio and quartet. Not only are these mediums, like the fortepiano, more appropriate to the 'naturalistic' inclination of the age, but there is a more rationalistic approach to the logic of the counterpoint, with the fugal entries strongly profiled (see Dirst). The trend towards rational order and 'natural' simplicity is also evident in J. N. Forkel's distaste for the 'frivolous' ornamentation he sometimes found in Bach's music.

Matthew Dirst, in a perceptive study of the reception of *The Well-tempered Clavier*, shows that the much-maligned edition by Carl Czerny (1791–1857) in fact preserves something of the Viennese tradition passing through Mozart and Beethoven, particularly in its profiling of subject entries and its consistency and clarity of interpretation. Critics such as A. B. Marx and Schumann objected to Czerny's didacticism, affirming that Bach's music should be purely transmitted in notation so that it can be freely and personally interpreted in performance.

Czerny's publication was clearly designed to present Bach to a wider readership, with the music conveniently pre-interpreted for the amateur. The popularization of Bach was most spectacularly effected by the success of the amateur choral society in Germany. Most significant of all was the Berlin Singakademie, directed from 1800 to 1832 by C. F. Zelter, which not only performed many of Bach's choral works with massed forces for the first time, but also used and adapted Bach's own performing materials, many of which it had acquired. It was this institution that presented Mendelssohn's famous revival of the *St Matthew Passion* in 1829, in a shortened form with 'updated' orchestration.

The Bach Gesellschaft edition, begun in 1850, attempted to present Bach's music in its purest form, as if it were a sacred text requiring the most up-to-date philological methods. Nevertheless, this was precisely the age when composers and performers most freely adapted Bach's music to their own needs: Schumann saw fit to add piano accompaniments to the unaccompanied music for violin and cello; Liszt made free arrangements of Bach pieces and composed several original works on Bach themes; and Gounod made his famous arrangement of the first Prelude in Part 1 of *The Well-tempered Clavier* (*see* AVE MARIA). The fact that Liszt's pieces often went through several versions suggests that much of the thinking behind them came from the improvisational practices of the day. However, despite the 'unfaithfulness' of the transcriptions, this attitude to pre-existing music was not unlike that of Bach's own age, when composers adapted their own and others' music to the needs of the moment.

With the turn of the 20th century, Busoni was continuing the Lisztian tradition of writing works based around Bach, but he also made his own editions of the keyboard music which show some of the performance priorities of the age. As a composer who resolutely believed in the legitimacy of transcription, Busoni strove for the utmost pianism and had no qualms about rearranging Bach's material and omitting pieces and movements that did not seem relevant.

Schoenberg likewise sought to emphasize those elements of Bach's music that came closest to his own priorities and compositional practice, particularly contrapuntal complexity and motivic integrity. His orchestrations of Bach organ works do not, like Mozart's transcriptions, emphasize anything as 'superficial' as thematic entries; rather, his priority is to reveal motivic connections through the differentiation of instrumentation, register, dynamics, phrasing, and articulation. Webern's arrangement of the six-part ricercar from the *Musical Offering* perhaps represents an extreme in Bach performance. The music is orchestrated in accordance with Webern's own compositional style, with the lines splintered into fragments to emphasize the motivic connections between different voices.

While the many 20th-century arrangements of Bach (particularly the popular orchestrations of Leopold Stokowski) preserve something of the 19th-century symphonic tradition, Schoenberg and Webern, their instrumentation notwithstanding, illustrate the fanatical fidelity to the original text that was to become so important for the historical performance movement. Another influence came from the antiquarian climate of the late 19th century, epitomized by the work of Arnold Dolmetsch (1858–1940). Bach scholars such as Albert Schweitzer and Arnold Schering were soon to call for a return to the sonorities and smaller vocal forces of Bach's own era. The work of Schweitzer was also fundamental to the organ reform movement which sought to restore European organs to their original state.

With World War II many manuscripts, instruments, and other musical artefacts were lost for ever. It is surely no accident that the 1950s saw the birth of many new collected editions, beginning with Bach's—a belated attempt to preserve and interpret the original sources before any further disaster occurred. Organs were restored and rebuilt, and increasing attention was given to historical harpsichords. By the

1960s Bach's entire instrumentarium was being researched and recreated. Schweitzer's call for the smaller vocal forces of Bach's time was also being answered in the USA, Europe, and particularly England, where the indigenous cathedral and collegiate tradition was very easily turned towards the historical performance of early music.

The project by Nikolaus Harnoncourt and Gustav Leonhardt to record the complete Bach cantatas, lasting from 1971 to 1989, has proved to be the backbone of the historical performance of Bach, although it is interesting that their approaches are often strikingly different. This suggests that, just as was the case throughout the history of Bach performance, contemporary performers tend to interpret the music according to their own tastes and their own view of the historical evidence. Moreover, whatever the rhetoric of 'authenticity', there is really no means of knowing if historical accuracy has been achieved. Nevertheless, historical evidence has often inspired performers to rethink their musical reflexes and to work with new constraints, which, at their best, engender new interpretative insights.

Perhaps the most extreme historical hypothesis is that of Joshua Rifkin (from the early 1980s), who has concluded that most of Bach's choral music was sung with only one voice to a part (*see* CHORUS). It may be that this shocked historically minded performers into allowing that perhaps not everything Bach may have done, or even desired, is automatically the most satisfactory solution today. Certainly, the late 1980s and the 1990s showed a certain liberalization within the historical performance of many repertories. Anner Bylsma used a Stradivarius cello in 'modern' set-up for his second recording of the Cello Suites, and Harnoncourt did not hesitate to use women's voices in Bach choral works; moreover, many 'historical' recordings of the 1990s seemed to give more attention to richness of sonority than to historical accuracy. Nevertheless, there are still many performers who adhere as strictly as they can to what they believe to be Bach's own practice. In sum, the historical performance practice movement, rather than causing musical performance to conform to one monotonous style (as many of its detractors still affirm), has perhaps, together with new developments in 'mainstream' performance, contributed to a diversity of performing styles that had not before obtained. JAB

*See also* RECORDINGS.

J. Butt, 'Bach Recordings Since 1980: A Mirror of Historical Performance', in D. Schulenberg, ed., *Bach Perspectives*, iv (Lincoln, Nebr., forthcoming); M. Dirst, 'Bach's Well-Tempered Clavier in Musical Thought and Practice, 1750–1850' (diss., Stanford University, 1996); D. Schulenberg, 'Versions of Bach: Performing Practices in the Keyboard Works', in *Bach Perspectives*, iv (Lincoln, Nebr., forthcoming); G. Stauffer, 'Changing Issues of Performance Practice', in J. Butt, ed., *The Cambridge Companion to Bach* (Cambridge, 1997), 203–17.

minuets, in G major and G minor, by Petzoldt into her 1725 *Clavierbüchlein*, and these have often been published under Bach's name. Petzoldt acted as an agent for the sale of Bach's keyboard Partitas.

G. Hempel, 'Johann Sebastian Bach und der Dresdner Hoforganist Christian Petzold', *BJb* 43 (1956), 156–64; H.-J. Schulze, 'Ein "Dresdner-Menuett" im zweiten Klavierbüchlein der Anna Magdalena Bach', *BJb* 65 (1979), 45–64.

**Pfingsttag** (Whit Sunday), **Pfingsten** (Whitsuntide). *See* CHURCH CALENDAR.

**Phoebus and Pan.** See DER STREIT ZWISCHEN PHOEBUS UND PAN.

**Phrygian cadence.** A cadence which might be defined (using modern terminology) as a first inversion subdominant chord (IVb) followed by a dominant chord (V) in a minor key. It takes its name from the third of the eight medieval church modes—the only one in which the final (in modern terms the 'tonic') was preceded by a note a semitone above. It therefore retained its distinctive character, and its name, when the modal system was replaced by the modern tonal system in the 17th century, the other modal cadences being subsumed into major and minor.

In late Baroque sonatas and concertos a Phrygian cadence was often attached to the end of a slow movement, presumably in order to create a feeling of continuity and expectancy; it was usually decorated with trills and divisions, either improvised or (for example in Bach's Fourth Brandenburg Concerto) written out. The Adagio of the Third Brandenburg Concerto, as notated in Bach's score, consists of a Phrygian cadence and nothing more.

**pianoforte.** What was to become the favourite domestic instrument of the late 18th and the 19th centuries was still in its infancy when Bach died. The invention of the pianoforte (or fortepiano as the early type is usually called) is credited to the Italian Bartolomeo Cristofori (1655–1731), whose earliest examples were made in the first decade of the 18th century. In Saxony some 25 years later Gottfried SILBERMANN began making pianos with actions modelled on Cristofori's. Frederick the Great possessed some, which Bach played on his Berlin visit in 1747. The three-part Ricercar from the *Musical Offering* is arguably the only music that Bach conceived with the sound and touch of the piano in mind, though Eva Badura-Skoda has raised the question of whether some at least of his Leipzig keyboard concertos might have been played on such an instrument.

E. Badura-Skoda, 'Komponierte J. S. Bach "Hammerklavier-Konzerte"?', *BJb* 77 (1991), 159–71.

**Picander.** The pseudonym of one of Bach's most important poets, Christian Friedrich Henrici (b. 14 Jan. 1700; d. 10 May 1764). Born in Stolpen, near Dresden, he studied law at Wittenberg University and began his career as a poet in Leipzig in 1721, at first with erotic poems and dramas. His relations with Bach were perhaps only casual at first. In 1725 Picander wrote the texts for Bach's secular cantatas *Entfliehet, verschwindet* BWV249a and *Zerreißet, zersprenget*, but as early as 1723 Bach's sacred cantata *Bringet dem Herrn Ehre* was based on Picander's strophic poem *Weg, ihr irdischen Geschäfte*, and in 1726 *Es erhub sich ein Streit* was based on a similar poem. Both are printed in Picander's collection of shorter (and tamer) poems published in 1724–5 as *Sammlung erbaulicher Gedancken*. The volume was dedicated to Count Franz Anton Sporck, who was also in con-

tact with Bach and may have acted as intermediary between poet and composer.

Collaboration between Picander and Bach later intensified. All five volumes of Picander's *Ernstschertzhaffte und satyrische Gedichte* (Leipzig, 1727–51) contain texts set to music by Bach, including those for the *St Matthew Passion* (and its associated funeral music for Prince Leopold of Anhalt-Cöthen) and the *St Mark Passion*. In the preface to the third volume (1732) Picander claimed that Bach set a whole cycle of his cantata texts in 1729. This has been a matter of speculation, however, since only nine of Bach's settings are known; they include the cantatas for Christmas (*Ehre sei Gott in der Höhe*), New Year (*Gott, wie dein Name*), Whit Monday (*Ich liebe den Höchsten*), and the feast of St Michael (*Man singet mit Freuden*). These compositions were spread widely over the liturgical year, and it is therefore possible that Bach did in fact set all the texts, even if the compositions are lost. But it is doubtful that these 'Picander' cantatas were Bach's principal sources for parodies, as Klaus Häfner argued. Picander's third volume also contains an interesting numerical paragram (see Tatlow).

Picander also wrote the texts for Bach's *Der Streit zwischen Phoebus und Pan* and *Laßt uns sorgen*; his Coffee Cantata was perhaps not written expressly for Bach. The last text of a Bach cantata published by Picander is that of the Peasant Cantata (1742), printed in 1751. Picander was then serving as Assessment and Liquor Tax Collector, Wine Inspector and Vizier, a post he held from 1740 until his death.                          KK

K. Häfner, *Aspekte des Parodieverfahrens bei Johann Sebastian Bach: Beiträge zur Wiederentdeckung verschollener Vokalwerke* (Laaber, 1987); R. Tatlow, *Bach and the Riddle of the Number Alphabet* (Cambridge, 1991).

**Pietism.** Lutheran Pietism was a movement, begun in the later 17th century, dedicated to ecclesiastical reform and spiritual renewal. It was preceded by the lively strand of *Erbauungsliteratur* ('devotional literature') within Lutheranism that owed much to the medieval mysticism of Bernard of Clairvaux (1090–1153), Johannes Tauler (1300–61), and Thomas à Kempis (1379/80–1471) among others. Luther respected such authors, as did the 17th-century Orthodox theologian Johann Gerhard (1582–1637) and the so-called pre-Pietists Johann Arndt, Philipp Nicolai (1556–1608), and Heinrich Müller (1631–75). A common theme in these writings is the Bride–Bridegroom metaphor, taken from the *Song of Songs*, depicting the relationship between the individual Soul and Christ. Arndt's influential and widely-read *Wahres Christenthum* and Gerhard's *Schola pietatis*, together with four or five titles by Müller, were found in Bach's personal library, and Bride–Bridegroom (Soul–Jesus) imagery is found in a number of cantatas, such as BWV21 and 140.

Specific Lutheran Pietism is to be dated from the publication of the *Pia desideria* (1675) of Philipp Jakob Spener (1635–1705), which effectively became the movement's manifesto. Spener called for Church reform based on practical rather than theoretical Christianity, in which there would be much Bible study and prayer, a lay partnership with the clergy in the affairs of the Church, sermons that were simple and effective rather than scholarly and erudite, and disputed questions resolved more by prayer and irenics than by contentious polemics. August Hermann Francke (1663–1727), who taught Hebrew in Leipzig between 1684 and 1690, underwent a conversion experience in 1689 and began to hold *collegia pietatis*, conventicles for prayer and Bible study. The term 'Pietist' appears to have been coined by Joachim Feller (1628–91), professor of poetry at Leipzig, in poems written that year. At first Francke was influential, not least on Erdmann Neumeister, later cantata librettist and bitter opponent of Pietism. But the Orthodox professor of theology, Johann Benedikt Carpzov *junior* (1638–99), detected un-Lutheran tendencies and bitterly opposed Francke's Pietist teachings and practices. In 1691 Francke was called to Halle, as professor of oriental languages, where he founded charitable and other institutions and effectively made the city the centre of Lutheran Pietism. Orthodoxy bitterly opposed the Pietist insistence that Luther's Reformation was incomplete and the clergy ill-equipped for ministry, and that Lutheran liturgy and music needed to be greatly simplified. Although Bach had a volume each of Spener's and Francke's sermons, in simple terms he cannot be regarded as a Pietist, because Pietists did not approve of the kind of concerted music in worship that Bach composed and directed. However, the melodies he contributed to the Schemelli *Gesangbuch* (1736) owe something to the freer style of hymnody advocated by the Pietists. RAL

R. A. Leaver, *Bachs theologische Bibliothek* (Stuttgart, 1983); R. A. Leaver, 'Bach and Pietism', *Concordia Theological Quarterly*, 55 (1991), 5–22; J. Pelikan, *Bach Among the Theologians* (Philadelphia, 1986); M. Petzoldt, 'Zwischen Orthodoxie, Pietismus und Aufklärung: Überlegungen zum theologiegeschichtlichen Kontext Johann Sebastian Bachs', in R. Szeskus, ed., *Bach und die Aufklärung* [Bach-Studien 7] (Leipzig, 1982), 66–107; M. Schmidt, 'Pietism', in J. Bodensieck, ed., *The Encyclopedia of the Lutheran Church* (Minneapolis, 1965), iii. 1898–906.

**Pisendel, Johann Georg** (b. 26 Dec. 1687; d. 25 Nov. 1755). Violinist and composer, born in Cadolzburg, near Nuremberg. He served in the Ansbach court orchestra (*c.*1703–9), taking violin lessons with Giuseppe Torelli, but moved to Leipzig in 1709 to study law, making Bach's acquaintance in Weimar *en route*. He joined the Dresden court orchestra in 1712, touring widely with his royal patron, the electoral prince, and studying with Vivaldi and Francesco Montanari (d. 1730). He later succeeded J. B. Volumier as *Konzertmeister* in Dresden (1728–55), improving further the standards of orchestral playing (especially in collaboration with J. A. Hasse) and introducing not only the instrumental works of Italian composers such as Vivaldi and Tartini but also those of central and north German musicians such as Telemann, Quantz, and the Bendas and Grauns, many of whom he had known and taught in Leipzig.

Pisendel studied composition with J. D. Heinichen. His seven violin concertos and two sonatas represent the best of his extant work, and his Sonata for unaccompanied violin possibly provided the inspiration for Bach's solo violin works. RS

H. R. Jung, 'Johann Georg Pisendel (1687–1755): Leben und Werk' (diss., University of Jena, 1956).

**pitch.** A term often used, as here, to mean 'pitch standards'. The subject is of special interest in relation to Bach because he lived at a time when several pitch standards were used simultaneously (none of which was at the level of standard modern pitch, $a' = 440$ Hz), and the choice of pitch affects the sonorities of his music and the techniques of singers and instrumentalists who perform it. The pitch factor can be a useful tool in dating and editing the music, and in understanding the performing situations of Bach's works, since so many combinations and relations are represented. It is fairly easy, on the basis of written texts, to discover the names of the pitch standards Bach used: *Cornet-ton*, *Chorton*, and *Cammerton*. The pitch distance between these standards (a major 2nd or minor 3rd) is also clear from the notation of the music, and recent research on the original pitches of instruments of the time (cornetts, transverse flutes, recorders, and organs) has made it possible to link frequency values to the standards.

In this and associated articles the expression '$a' = 415$' means that the note $a'$ sounds at a frequency of 415 Hz (or cycles per second). When the pitch is merely approximate (to an accuracy of a quarter-tone), it is expressed as '$a' \approx 415$'.

1. Introduction.
2. Specific works.
3. Transposition.
4. Modern editions of Bach's works.

# pitch

## 1. Introduction.

For obvious practical reasons, the principle of standard pitch was generally accepted in Bach's day, and standards were in widespread use throughout Europe. However, musicians did not pretend, as they do today, that there was a universal 'A'. Several different standards, some quite specific and others more general, were recognized and used simultaneously, taking their names by association from musical functions or instruments (e.g. chamber pitch, opera pitch, cornett pitch, and choir pitch).

A more-or-less standard universal pitch did exist in the centuries before Bach's birth. The pitches of original instruments in the 16th and early 17th centuries cannot be described as uniform, but they are remarkably consistent at one principal level, about $a' = 465$, called (among other things) *mezzo punto, corista di Lombardia, ton d'écurie,* and *Cornet-ton*. Part of the reason for this relative uniformity was that instrument making was centralized; the best woodwinds came from Venice, the best brass from Nuremberg, and those instruments were played all over Europe.

The name CORNET-TON remained connected to this frequency even into the 18th century, since cornetts did not change pitch. Michael Praetorius in 1618 wrote about 'Cornettenthon', but he preferred another name for the same frequency: 'CammerThon', which meant (and still means) standard instrumental pitch. Praetorius's *CammerThon*, however, was not at the same frequency as Bach's *Cammerton*, because in the mean time instruments themselves had changed dramatically.

In the 1670s and 1680s, as a result of a general interest in French culture and the music of Jean-Baptiste Lully (1632–87), a revolutionary new French instrumentarium was adopted all over Europe. The pitch levels of these new instruments, being based on Parisian *ton d'opéra* and *ton de chambre*, were much lower than the traditional German instrumental pitch at $a' \approx 465$. Throughout this period pitch standards underwent important realignments that lasted almost exactly the duration of Bach's lifetime. The new French pitches, since they had become the most common levels for instruments, naturally appropriated the name CAMMERTON.

But 18th-century churches were equipped with 17th-century organs, which were too venerable to replace merely because of a pitch change. A significant expense was also involved in lowering an organ's pitch, as pipes would have to be added to the bottom of each stop (and these were of course the biggest pipes). Nor was there room for larger pipes in organ cases, often highly prized in themselves. Until such time as old organs had to be replaced, church music maintained its own separate pitch. This pitch was known generically as CHORTON. In order that 'figural' instruments (woodwinds, horns, and often strings) at *Cammerton* could be used in the church, however, organs were purposely tuned at a convenient interval to *Cammerton*, so that the two types could, through transposition, function together when desired. The intervals between them were a major 2nd or minor 3rd.

## 2. Specific works.

Determining the original pitch of a specific piece by Bach is usually a question of knowing where he wrote it. The organs he normally had at his disposal were at *Cornet-ton* (the specific type of *Chorton* at $a' \approx 460$–70). His chamber and orchestral works were performed at *Cammerton* ($a' \approx 415$, 404, or 390, depending on the place). Most of his vocal works, since they involved both organ and other instruments, were conceived in a combination of the two levels.

German composers of the early 18th century who were faced with the problem of writing in 'German' and 'French' pitches simultaneously developed an *ad hoc* system of notation to accommodate them. Since *Cammerton* instruments sounded lower, the common factor in this system was that their parts were always written higher than the organ's. There are many examples of pieces written in keys separated by a minor 3rd or major 2nd by, among others, Vincent Lübeck (1654–1740, Stade), F. W. Zachow (1663–1712, Halle), Tobias Volckmar (1678–1756, Breslau), J. L. Krebs (Altenburg), J. F. Fasch (Zerbst), J. D. Heinichen (Dresden), Christoph Graupner (Darmstadt), and G. P. Telemann (Frankfurt and Hamburg).

Bach solved the question of notating *Cornet-ton* and various levels of *Cammerton* in different ways at the various places he worked. The most complex situation was the one at Weimar. The Positiv organ built by Samuel Bidermann (b. 1600) in the court chapel in Weimar where Bach was *Konzertmeister* was documented as in 'Cornet Thon'. During the first year he wrote cantatas (1714), Bach wrote parts for a single 'Oboe' notated a major 2nd above the other parts (organ, voices, and strings). The strings must therefore have been tuned up to *Cornet-ton*, and the 'Oboe' must have sounded a tone below the organ (and therefore at the highest form of *Cammerton*, $a' \approx 415$). But the 'Oboe' disappears at the end of 1714, to be replaced by an instrument consistently called 'Hautbois', whose parts differed a minor 3rd from the organ and strings. From this time Bach also notated certain other instruments at the interval of a minor 3rd, like the 'Basson' and the 'Flaut'. Since the organ did not change pitch, these instruments must have been at *tief-Cammerton*, or $a' \approx 390$. All the remaining works written for the Weimar chapel show this relationship.

The parts to Bach's music written at Cöthen are much simpler: they are all in the same key. Presumably, then, all the instruments were at the same pitch. But there is reason to think the prevailing pitch at Cöthen was a form of *tief-Cammerton* at $a' \approx 403$ or 390. The voice ranges of cantatas written there are unusually high, for instance, and when he used material from Cöthen later at Leipzig, Bach sometimes performed it at 'tief-Cammerthon'. The problematic trumpet part to the Second Brandenburg Concerto would be significantly easier on an original instrument at *tief-Cammerton* rather than at $a' \approx 415$.

At Leipzig the performing materials for the great majority of Bach's vocal works indicate that the strings, voices, and woodwinds were at *Cammerton* and the organ and brass were a major 2nd higher. Bach's predecessor at Leipzig, Johann Kuhnau, had specified in 1717 that the pitch of the organs at the Thomaskirche and the Nikolaikirche was *Cornet-ton*.

Kuhnau used figural instruments at intervals of both a 2nd and a minor 3rd below *Cornet-ton*, 'depending', as he said, 'on which is the more convenient' (i.e. for finding mutually satisfying keys). He had woodwinds available, in other words, at both normal *Cammerton* and at *tief-Cammerton* ($a' \approx 415$ and $a' \approx 390$). Since string instruments sounded best in tonalities with open strings, and appropriate tonalities were critical for unkeyed woodwinds, the presence of woodwinds tuned a semitone apart was extremely practical; it offered Kuhnau a greater choice of keys in which to compose.

During Bach's first year and a half at Leipzig, he took advantage of this option by writing several pieces at *tief-Cammerton*: Cantatas 22, 23, 63, and 194, and the first version of the *Magnificat*. (Cantatas 22 and 23 were his trial pieces and were performed together; no. 63 had been conceived some years earlier, probably for performance at *tief-Cammerton*, and was performed on the same day as the *Magnificat*—which, with Cantata 194, had antecedents in Cöthen.) The last known date that Bach used the *tief-Cammerton* option with his regular winds is 4 June 1724. In the late 1740s he performed a Pergolesi *Stabat mater* and a motet by Johann Christoph Bach (i) at *tief-Cammerton*. He revised the *Magnificat* for performance in the 1730s, transposing it from Eb to D, probably because *tief-Cammerton* woodwinds were no longer available.

**3. Transposition.** For a composer, choice of key was circumscribed by a number of interrelated factors. Four general performing groups were

affected by transposition: the voices, the string band, the organ, and the woodwinds.

Because Bach's vocal ranges are normally close to the possible extremes, changes of key can be critical. Transposition shifts the position of register breaks and alters tone quality and range. Given the primary role of the voice, considerations of transposition must begin with their effect on singers.

Examples of string instruments tuned up to *Chorton* are common in the early 18th century. Many of the instruments in use were made in previous centuries, when the usual instrumental pitch was $a' = 465$ (*mezzo punto* in Cremona). As late as c.1780 in Salzburg, string sections were tuned up to the high brass and organ pitch, while oboes ('hautboys') and bassoons sounded a step lower. It often worked better to retune string instruments than to transpose to keys that shifted their open-string resonances or affected the sonorities of specific notes. With a band of strings, the effect was multiplied. Especially important were the sound of open-string chords (which Bach exploited, for example, in Cantata 161). Strings were regularly retuned as much as a whole tone up or down in this period. When Kuhnau did not want to transpose his organ parts down to remote tonalities, for instance, he had his string players tune up a step.

As far as the organ is concerned, many sources indicate that transposition was considered an essential skill of a good organist, developed for dealing with the common situation of differing pitch standards.

The range of tonalities that functioned well on the essentially keyless woodwinds of Bach's day was limited. The different placement of the forked fingerings and half-holes that produced the accidentals gave each tonality its own particular character, technique, and intonation. Trills and other ornaments were often played with special fingerings; some were easy, others nearly impossible. Various tonalities therefore offered the 18th-century woodwind player particular technical ease or difficulty in choice of fingerings. Transpositions had to be made with care, for musical as well as practical reasons. Another more obvious problem was that of range. Original woodwind parts at *Cammerton* are sometimes transposed down a major 2nd or minor 3rd in modern editions (*BG*, for instance) to match the other instruments notated at *Chorton*. When this occurs, they often include notes below the compass of the instruments (in some cases modern as well as original ones).

Given that the standard transpositions were a major 2nd or a minor 3rd (these intervals were valid both for instruments at different pitch standards and for the transposing 'd'amore' instruments), it was still possible to combine different keys without resorting to equal temperament. 'Regular' meantones (i.e. those in which all the 5ths except one are the same size) accommodate standard transpositions, since intervals are identical in most keys (although the problem of choosing between flats or sharps—C♯ or D♭, for instance—remains). Considerations of temperament applied only to the keyboard instruments, since singers and other instruments made appropriate *ad hoc* tuning adjustments.

The question of what effect transposition had on key character is not straightforward. Bach rewrote pieces for other instruments or situations, changing the key for what often appear to be functional rather than aesthetic reasons. An example is the oboe ('hautboy') aria BWV102:3, once in F minor and once, in BWV233:4, in C minor. The violin concertos BWV1041–3 and 1049 are notated a major 2nd lower in Bach's arrangements for harpsichord, primarily because of range. Bach would not, then, appear to have taken the affective properties of keys very seriously. If the special sound of a particular key is a consideration, a special colour is also produced by the combination of two different keys played simultaneously. That effect is lost, of course, when the piece is reduced to a single key.

**4. Modern editions of Bach's works.** When a work by Bach involves the simultaneous use of different keys, editors of modern editions are faced with a difficult decision. If they choose a single universal tonality, it may be necessary to 'un-transpose' the music, and the result might be unintentionally to alter the original effect. When Bach's cantatas were first published at the end of the 19th century by the *BG*, the transposition factors discussed above were no longer obvious. The editors solved the question of part transpositions in a way that must have seemed quite reasonable at the time: they normally kept to the key of the greatest number of parts. The *BG* remained the definitive edition of Bach's cantatas for about a century, and as a result some of them continue to be misunderstood and difficult to perform.

The pieces that have suffered are the early ones composed at Weimar. Bach reworked a number of those cantatas for later use at Leipzig. Where the difference in notation between the parts was a major 2nd (i.e. Cantatas 12, 21, 172, and 199), his usual practice was to transpose the voice and string parts up a step to the key of the *Cammerton* woodwinds. In this way the sounding pitch remained the same, since the strings and voices were notated at *Cornet-ton* at Weimar and *Cammerton* at Leipzig. Converting the cantatas

notated with a difference of a minor 3rd was more difficult because of the remote keys involved. Bach adapted five of them for Leipzig (31, 155, 161, 182, and 185), putting all the parts in the same key (except, of course, the organ), but in the process much more transposition was necessary, and some parts had to be eliminated or replaced by other instruments.

Notational and transpositional questions caused by pitch differences affect the following works by Bach: BWV12, 18, 21, 22, 23, 31, 63, 70*a*, 71, 80*a*, 106, 131, 132, 147*a*, 150, 152, 155, 161, 162, 172, 182, 185, 186*a*, 194, 199, 208, and 243*a*. Most, but not all, of these questions are addressed by the *NBA*. For a detailed discussion, see Haynes (1995), pp. 299 ff.                                    BH

W. Cowdery, 'The Early Vocal Works of Johann Sebastian Bach: Studies in Style, Scoring and Chronology' (diss., Cornell University, 1989); U. Dähnert, 'Organs Played and Tested by J. S. Bach', in G. Stauffer and E. May, eds., *J. S. Bach as Organist* (London, 1986), 3–24; A. Dürr, *Studien über die frühen Kantaten Johann Sebastian Bachs* (Wiesbaden, 1977); B. Haynes, 'Johann Sebastian Bach's Pitch Standards: The Woodwind Perspective', *Journal of the American Musical Instrument Society*, 9 (1985), 55–114; B. Haynes, 'Pitch Standards in the Baroque and Classical Periods' (diss., University of Montreal, 1995); E. L. Rimbach, 'The Church Cantatas of Johann Kuhnau' (diss., University of Rochester, 1966).

**Platz, Abraham Christoph** (b. 1658; d. 15 Sept. 1728). Leipzig councillor and, from 1705, burgomaster. He was the chief spokesman for those supporting the appointment of a Kantor, rather than a *Kapellmeister*, to succeed Johann Kuhnau as Thomaskantor in 1722–3. He has often been ridiculed and vilified for his remark, made at a council meeting on 9 April 1722, that 'since the best cannot be engaged, we must accept a "mittlere" [someone of middling ability]', the inference being that 'the best' referred to Telemann and Graupner and the 'mittlere' to Bach. It is clear from the context, however, that Platz was not referring to Telemann and Graupner, and that for the *mittlere* he had in mind the Kantor at Pirna, Christian Heckel (1676–1744).

U. Siegele, 'Bachs Stellung in der Leipziger Kulturpolitik seiner Zeit', *BJb* 69 (1983), 7–50, esp. 44–5.

**Play Bach.** The name of a trio formed in 1959 by the French pianist Jacques Loussier (b. 1934) to perform works by Bach in 'jazzed-up' arrangements. The trio toured widely until about 1974 and made several recordings.

**Poelchau, Georg** (b. 23 June 1773; d. 12 Aug. 1836). Music collector, editor, and librarian, born in Kremon, near Riga. From 1792 he studied at the University of Jena and made his first musical appearances as a solo tenor. The year 1799 was important for him in two respects: he went to Hamburg, where he entered circles that had been in touch with Carl Philipp Emanuel Bach; and he met Carl Friedrich Zelter. At about this time Poelchau began to collect music; in 1813 he moved to Berlin, became member of the Singakademie, and, after Zelter's death in 1832, the director of its library.

Poelchau's own collection contained manuscripts of works by Haydn, Mozart, and Beethoven, a huge amount of printed music from the 16th and 17th centuries, and above all many important Bach manuscripts. He acquired many of them from collectors who, in 1790, had bought them from C. P. E. Bach's estate; others were found by lucky chance—a copy of the Sonatas and Partitas for solo violin as wrapping-paper in a butter shop in St Petersburg. From his own collection Poelchau prepared the earliest complete editions of the *Magnificat* BWV243 in 1811, and the *Missae* in A major and G major in 1818 and 1828 respectively. Poelchau left his collection to the Königliche Bibliothek, Berlin, where it served as the basis of that famous music library.　　KK

K. Engler, *Georg Poelchau und seine Musikaliensammlung: ein Beitrag zur Überlieferung Bachscher Musik in der ersten Hälfte des 19. Jahrhunderts* (Göppingen, 1974).

**polonaise.** A French word for dances and instrumental pieces embodying Polish characteristics. Polish dances appeared in European music in 16th-century keyboard tablatures, and Polish influence was still clearly evident in Bach's Germany. Friedrich II, King of Saxony, was also king of Poland, fostering many relationships between the peoples of these two contiguous areas. One report of a court polonaise danced at Dresden tells of musicians playing in the galleries of a great reception hall, while an assembly of splendidly dressed dancers processed below to a martial-sounding music. Unfortunately, no choreographies have survived.

As an instrumental piece, the polonaise in Bach's time was usually recognized by strong rhythms, including ♫ and ♫ ♪, which emphasize the beats; in addition, a cadence or thesis bar may be specially accented with a feminine cadence using the rhythm ♫♫ ♩. Most polonaises lack an upbeat. According to J. P. Kirnberger, the tempo was somewhere between that of the sarabande and that of the minuet.

Three titled pieces by Bach have survived, one for keyboard and two for orchestra (the polonaises in the 1725 *Clavierbüchlein* of Anna Magdalena Bach are not by J. S. Bach). The Polonaise from the Sixth French Suite, entitled 'Menuet

polonoise' in the Gerber manuscript, features strongly accented beats using the characteristic rhythms mentioned above, with no upbeat. The 'Poloinesse' in the First Brandenburg Concerto is actually one of the 'couplets' in a minuet in rondeau form which brings the concerto to a close (*see* MINUET); Bach writes a first violin part with semiquavers bowed in pairs, supported by a musette-style drone bass in the lower strings. The Polonaise from the B minor Orchestral Suite may embody the ceremonial yet festive dances of a grand assembly accompanied by gallery musicians, as described above. A fairly slow tempo is mandated by the inclusion of a *double* with ornamental demisemiquavers, and the melody is full of sharply dotted rhythms and feminine cadences which create an affect of strength and exuberance.　　NJ, MEL

*See also* PEASANT CANTATA.

For bibliography, see DANCE.

**Posaune.** *See* TROMBONE.

**positive** (*Positiv*). A small organ, usually with a single keyboard and no pedals and having a Principal no lower than 2′ (see J. Adlung, *Anleitung zu der musikalischen Gelahrtheit* (Erfurt, 1758), 551). Its name, from the Latin 'positum' ('stationary') and originally intended to distinguish it from the medieval portative (a small, hand-held portable organ), is misleading; although the organist normally remained stationary and seated while playing it, a positive could be carried from place to place, and this was its advantage over a larger organ. It enjoyed popularity as a solo instrument until the mid-17th century, but by Bach's time it served primarily as a continuo instrument for church and court, and as a domestic instrument in the homes of the well-to-do. A number of Bach's compositions, such as the *manualiter* settings in the *Clavier-Übung III*, are suitable for performance on such an organ. A secondary division within a large organ might also be called a 'positiv' (e.g. *Brustpositiv* and *Oberpositiv*).　　QF

R. Quoika, *Das Positiv in Geschichte und Gegenwart* (Kassel, 1957).

**Potsdam.** *See* BERLIN, POTSDAM.

**praeludium.** *See* PRELUDE.

*Precepts and Principles.* Short title for the treatise *Vorschriften und Grundsätze zum vierstimmigen spielen des General-Baß oder Accompagnement* ('Precepts and Principles for Playing the Thorough-bass or Accompanying in Four Parts'). Its only surviving source is a manuscript copy in the Brussels Conservatory, dated 1738 and ascribed to Bach. Bach's authorship has been questioned, however, but H.-J. Schulze's identification of the Bach pupil C. A. Thieme as the scribe of the title-page and several corrections to the text at least places the treatise in the Bach circle. It includes instruction, with worked examples, in four-part harmonization of a figured bass, and is more a written harmony primer than a textbook on continuo playing. The first nine chapters are closely based on Part 1 of F. E. Niedt's *Musicalische Handleitung* (1700).

> Spitta, iii. 315–47; P. L. Poulin, *J. S. Bach's Precepts and Principles for Playing the Thorough-Bass or Accompanying in Four Parts, Leipzig, 1738* (Oxford, 1994); H.-J. Schulze, ' "Das Stück im Goldpapier": Ermittlungen zu einigen Bach-Abschriften des frühen 18. Jahrhunderts', *BJb* 64 (1978), 19–42.

**Predigtkantate** ('sermon cantata'). A term which has been used to denote a cantata, such as no. 163, *Nur jedem das Seine*, the text of which dwells on moral precepts to be drawn from a Gospel narrative. Bach's cantatas in general have often been looked upon as the musical equivalent of the sermon in the *Hauptgottesdienst*.

**Preise dein Glücke, gesegnetes Sachsen** ('Praise your good fortune, blessed Saxony'). Secular cantata, BWV215, performed on 5 October 1734 in homage to Elector Friedrich August II. He and his family were in Leipzig to visit the autumn fair. As usual, they stayed in the Apel house on the south side of the market-place; the performance took place in front of the house and was heralded by a torch-light procession of 600 students. Apparently the ceremony had to be organized at short notice, since the visit was planned only three days before. On the face of it, this left very little time for writing the text (by Johann Christoph Clauder) and composing the music of the cantata (not to speak of rehearsing it). If this was indeed the case, it might seem that the preparation of BWV215 replaced Bach's original intention of performing, on 7 October 1734 (the elector's birthday), another cantata, *Schleicht, spielende Wellen* BWV206, whose text (later altered) seems to allude to the political situation of that autumn. This hypothesis, however, is not supported by the watermarks and handwriting in the sources of BWV206, which point to 1736 (for which year a performance is documented). The text may have been altered for a later revival, possibly in 1740.

It is, in any case, possible that Bach had originally planned to perform a cantata on 5 October 1734, as this was the first anniversary of Friedrich August's election as King of Poland and Grand Duke of Lithuania. It was common to celebrate such princely feasts with works addressed to the (mostly absent) person in question, and Bach performed a number of such works with his collegium musicum. It may, therefore, be the case that he planned BWV215 for this occasion much earlier, but the unexpected presence of the elector in per-

son altered the location and nature of its performance. The instrumental scoring of *Preise dein Glücke* is identical to that of another homage cantata, *Tönet, ihr Pauken*, performed ten months earlier: three trumpets, drums, two flutes, two oboes (d'amore), strings, and continuo. The only difference (though a remarkable one) in their vocal scoring is the use of a double chorus in the opening movement of BWV215. These lavish resources seem intended for an extraordinary occasion, and the carefully composed accompanied recitatives (no. 2 with oboes, no. 6 with flutes, and no. 8 with strings) are further evidence to suggest that Bach's preparation did not begin just a few days before the performance.

Bach called the cantata a 'Drama per musica overo Cantata gratulatoria'. It is not really 'dramatic', but a mere act of homage to the person addressed. After the opening chorus, the tenor, bass and soprano soloists sing a recitative and aria each, expressing their indebtedness to the Saxon elector (although in view of the occasion it is as King of Poland that he is addressed). All three join in a final recitative and arioso, and the work ends in a jubilant, dance-like chorus.

Two movements of the cantata were parodied in later works by Bach. The soprano aria 'Durch die vom Eifer entflammeten Waffen' (no. 7), probably a parody itself, became 'Erleucht auch meine finstre Sinnen' in the *Christmas Oratorio*; the vocal part was adapted for bass and the orchestral scoring reduced from two flutes, oboe d'amore, violins, and viola to a single oboe d'amore. The opening chorus, adapted from the cantata *Es lebe der König* (1732) for the nameday of Friedrich August I (1732), was used again for 'Osanna in excelsis' in the B minor Mass.

The royal and electoral family listened to the complete performance and took pleasure in it, according to the chronicler Salomon Riemer. But for Bach the memory of the performance must have been overshadowed when Gottfried Reiche, the chief *Stadtpfeifer*, died the following day from the strain of playing the trumpet surrounded by the burning torches. KK

> S. A. Crist, 'The Question of Parody in Bach's Cantata *Preise dein Glücke, gesegnetes Sachsen*, BWV215', in R. Stinson, ed., *Bach Perspectives*, i (Lincoln, Nebr., 1995), 135–61. For further bibliography, *see* CANTATA, §2.

**Preise, Jerusalem, den Herrn** ('Praise the Lord, O Jerusalem'). Cantata for the inauguration of the Leipzig town council, BWV119. Bach had already composed at least one cantata, in 1708, to celebrate the inauguration of the new town council at Mühlhausen. *Preise, Jerusalem, den Herrn*, however, was his first to honour the Leipzig council. He performed it on 30 August 1723, just four months after he had taken up his appointment as Kantor of the Thomasschule and the city's *Director musices*. The unidentified librettist based his text on verses from Psalm 147, further incorporating a strophe from Luther's vernacular version of the *Te Deum, Herr Gott, dich loben wir* (1529). Its main theme is the celebration of Leipzig, the city and its people, seen as a new Jerusalem. Commonplace though such sentiments may seem, Bach's music, together with some pleasing local references to Leipzig itself, raise the cantata on to a much higher level. Indeed, the splendour of the instrumental scoring in the opening chorus—four trumpets (as opposed to the customary three in *Festmusik* of this kind), timpani, two recorders, three oboes (two doubling oboe da caccia), and a continuo group consisting of an organ, two cellos, two bassoons, and two violones—outshines that of almost all Bach's other sacred cantatas.

*Preise, Jerusalem, den Herrn* begins with a chorus cast in the manner of a French overture, the ceremonial form *par excellence* of the late Baroque. In the opening and closing sections, with their distinctive and characterstic *saccadé* rhythm, the voices remain silent, but they assume a vital and exhilarating role in the vigorous 12/8 Allegro, with its somewhat instrumentally contoured melody. This was neither the first nor the last occasion on which Bach adapted—we might even say elevated—the fundamentally orchestral form of the French overture to accommodate the human voice, always blending creative genius with absolute technical virtuosity.

A tenor recitative leads to the first of two arias in the cantata. This lyrical movement for tenor solo, with two oboes da caccia, is an alluring celebration of Leipzig's once famous boulevards of lime trees. The manner in which the voice makes its first entry with the word 'Wohl' ('fair') is as subtle as it is beguiling. The ensuing bass recitative is elaborately heralded by the four trumpets and timpani. These interrupt the voice only once, after its first entry; thereafter the vocal line is accompanied by pairs of recorders and oboes da caccia which give way to the brass and timpani in the concluding two bars.

The second aria of the work is for alto accompanied by a pair of recorders in unison. Its 6/8 rhythm complements the lyrical character of the previous aria, though the text at this point is beginning gradually to place emphasis on the spiritual rather than temporal aspects of government. A soprano recitative leads directly to a choral movement of imposing dimensions. Similarly scored to the opening chorus, it is introduced by a resonant brass fanfare in which the third and fourth trumpets play a motif found elsewhere in Bach's music, notably in the opening chorus of Cantata 70, *Wachet! betet! betet! wachet!*, and in the Orchestral Suite in C major (*see* FANFARE THEME). Following the elaborate instrumental introduction, the voices enter fugally with a bold and resolute subject; this is taken up by the accompanying instruments which further provide punctuating passages between the blocks of choral writing. An alto recitative separates this spaciously laid out chorus from the concluding chorale, the fourth strophe of Luther's *Herr Gott, dich loben wir*, in a straightforward harmonization of the traditional plainchant. The cantata, which opened in a blaze of sound, is thus concluded modestly and in a spirit of contemplative prayer.    NA

For bibliography, *see* CANTATA, §1.

**Preller, Johann Gottlieb** (b. 9 March 1727; d. 21 March 1786). Organist, born in Oberrossla, near Apolda in Thuringia. In 1750 he matriculated at the University of Jena and in 1753 was appointed Kantor at Dortmund, where he remained until his death. While in Oberrossla, Preller might have studied under the Bach devotee Johann Nicolaus Mempell or the Bach pupil Johann Tobias Krebs. There is no evidence of a direct connection between Preller and Bach, but Preller is one of the main copyists of the so-called Mempell-Preller Collection (located primarily at the Musikbibliothek der Stadt Leipzig), which contains numerous manuscripts of keyboard works by Bach and others. Preller evidently assembled the present collection between 1743 and 1749 by adding copies to those made in the 1730s by Mempell.    RTS

P. Krause, *Handschriften der Werke Johann Sebastian Bachs in der Musikbibliothek der Stadt Leipzig* (Leipzig, 1964), 29–42; H.-J. Schulze, *Studien zur Bach-Überlieferung im 18. Jahrhundert* (Leipzig, 1984), 69–88; H.-J. Schulze, 'Wie entstand die Bach-Sammlung Mempell-Preller?', *BJb* 60 (1974), 104–22.

**prelude.** Strictly speaking, a piece played before the main part of a performance, establishing the key, and perhaps the effect, of what follows. Like other Baroque composers, however, Bach employed the prelude not only as a preface to a fugue or dance suite but as an independent piece, either freely composed or chorale-based.

The preludes and fugues of Bach's early years are in certain cases (BWV532, 551, and 566) contained within a large toccata-like, multi-sectional structure, as in the *praeludia* of Buxtehude and other north German composers. But more frequent is the PRELUDE AND FUGUE structure that subsequently became the norm. Since preludes were often improvised in the 17th and 18th centuries, it is not surprising to find that notated preludes, like the closely related toccatas and fantasias, are often pseudo-improvisatory in character. This type—highly idiomatic to the keyboard and sometimes virtuoso, rhythmically free, and thematic only in a loose manner—is found frequently among Bach's early works (examples include BWV533, 535, and 543). But within the same period he also composed more structured preludes in figurative and/or imitative style (e.g. in BWV531, 536, 545, 549, and 550)—a type which tends to predominate in later years.

Preludes of small dimensions were used by Bach for teaching purposes, representing a stage more advanced than figured bass or chorale harmonization, but less so than the dance suite or fugue. Most elementary are the arpeggio preludes (e.g. BWV846–7, 851, 872, 924, and 926), in which the student is taught how to elaborate on improvised chord sequences. At a further stage, Bach demonstrates how to build a two- or three-part contrapuntal structure around a single distinctive motif—the underlying principle of the Inventions (which were themselves originally entitled 'praeambula', a synonym for 'preludes'). This motivic-contrapuntal type is found not only in many of Bach's 'Little Preludes' (BWV924–30 and 933–43) but also in many of the preludes from The Well-tempered Clavier. Such pieces are often constructed largely in double or triple counterpoint (see e.g. BWV848:1, 862:1, and 864:1) and in some cases they resemble small fugues (e.g. BWV859:1 and 864:1).

Other forms, in addition to the 'invention' type, are represented among Bach's mature preludes. One illustration of this is the variety of titles he gave to the preludes of the keyboard Partitas: Praeludium, Sinfonia, Fantasia, Ouverture, Praeambulum, and Toccata. Among the most prominent structural types is RITORNELLO form, which is employed in BWV894, in the preludes to the English Suites nos. 2–6 (combined with the A–B–A structure of the da capo aria and, in nos.

5–6, with fugue), and in a number of large-scale organ preludes (those of BWV544, 546, 548, and 552). Preludes to dance suites occasionally take the form of French overtures, as in BWV828, 996, and 1011. The Preludes in E♭ and B♭ major from Part 1 of The Well-tempered Clavier are toccatas, the former in fact comprising toccata and fugue, a type which recurs in the prelude (entitled 'Toccata') of Partita no. 6. Elaborate Italianate adagios form preludes to the fugues in the two sonatas after J. A. Reincken BWV965 and 966, and in the three Sonatas for unaccompanied violin. Similarly, florid slow movements are in certain cases employed as preludes in both parts of The Well-tempered Clavier (for example in BWV849, 853, 861, 867, 873, and 883). Binary form with repeats—derived at least as much from the Italian sonata as from the French dance suite—is encountered in BWV902:1 and 933–8, in the last prelude from Part 1 of The Well-tempered Clavier, and in ten of the preludes from Part 2. RDPJ

See also ORGAN CHORALES and PRELUDE AND FUGUE.

**prelude and fugue.** See opposite.

**printing.** For a description of the printing methods employed in Bach's published works, see SOURCES, §2.

***Probe*** ('trial', 'rehearsal'). The examination to which a candidate was subject when applying for a post as organist, Kantor, or *director musices* at a Lutheran church or school. It usually took the form of writing, rehearsing, and performing a cantata; for a Kantor's post it might include also a test of the candidate's competence as a teacher. Bach underwent his *Probe* for the post of Kantor and *director musices* at Leipzig on 7 February 1723, when he performed Cantatas 22 and 23.

# prelude and fugue

Bach vastly altered and developed the form of the prelude and fugue he inherited from precursors such as Dietrich Buxtehude, and wrote examples of the genre unsurpassed in their mastery and variety.

1. Preludes and fugues for organ.
2. Preludes and fugues for other instruments.

1. Preludes and fugues for organ.   In the course of a composing career of nearly half a century Bach developed the prelude and fugue from a form indistinguishable from the multi-sectional north German TOCCATA to one consisting of two movements of more or less equal weight. Unfortunately, the process by which this occurred is obscured by a number of factors. First of all, titles are sometimes subject to the vagaries of 18th-century scribes, who were also not averse to interfering with the musical text. Secondly, some works, including BWV534, 565, and the fugue of 536, are the subject of disputes over attributions and, if spurious, will obscure our understanding of Bach's development as a composer. Finally, and perhaps of greater importance, there is the fact that Bach kept his work in a constant state of revision, so that the possible existence of lost early versions has to be borne in mind. The process by which a work reached the form in which it is known today is not always clear.

This is particularly true of the 20 or so freely constructed works for organ described as preludes and fugues (or cognate forms) in the sources. For the earliest works there is little point in distinguishing prelude and fugue forms from toccatas, which share much the same structure, especially as few of them survive in autographs which would establish Bach's original designation. The earliest group, most of them probably composed during Bach's period at Arnstadt (c.1704–7), includes BWV531 (C major), 533 (E minor), 535a (G minor), 551 (A minor), and 566 (E major). (The so-called Toccata and Fugue in D minor BWV565 is highly uncharacteristic of Bach at any stage of his career, and is now regarded as probably spurious.) The works in this group feature squat, stiffly constructed canzona fugues in the north German tradition that Bach inherited from Buxtehude and others, embedded in contrasting sections in flamboyant toccata style. The clearest example of the multi-sectional toccata is BWV566, which features two internal fugal sections based on variants of the same subject; Bach's authorship of this inept work has been disputed. Of the other works in the group only BWV533, in most respects a rudimentary work, conforms at all to the later concept of the prelude and fugue, but only in the sense that no toccata-like coda follows the fugue. However, the abruptness of the ending arouses suspicions that further sections may have been excised by the scribes. BWV535a, which survives in an incomplete autograph, was later revised to form the work now known as BWV535, but unfortunately the loss of the end of the earlier versions forces us to reserve judgement on its characteristics.

To this group could be added two fragmentary works which present textual problems. BWV543:1a (A minor) is a single toccata section which Bach later revised (BWV543), adding a masterly fugue in his mature manner. Whether BWV543:1a originally had a different fugue of its own is not known. BWV536 (A major) seems also to have been an uncompleted toccata section to which a fugue was added later, though in this case bibliographic and stylistic evidence suggests that a second composer may have been responsible for it. BWV536:1 shows a distinct stylistic advance on the other works from this group and may have been composed in the Weimar period (it may be no accident that the pedal part rises to $e'$, a note which was available on the pedalboard of the organ in the Schloßkirche, Weimar, but not on the instruments that Bach regularly played in Arnstadt and Mühlhausen in 1707–8).

A group of three works (BWV550, 532, and 564) which probably date from early in the Weimar period (c.1708–12) show a transitional stage in Bach's development. All of them have conservative features, with the fugues still influenced by the old-fashioned permutation fugue as practised by Buxtehude and the traditional virtuoso pedal solos introducing figuration which is then broken up and developed in subsequent *manualiter* sections. On the other hand, an enormous advance in freedom and developmental power can be seen, and the fugues are now fully developed and separate large-scale movements. All of them feature whimsical fugue subjects, which interact wittily with countersubjects in dialogue form, rather in the manner of some of Buxtehude's fugues. BWV550 (G major) may be the earliest of the three, opening with a short and distinctly Buxtehudian toccata section, but the following fugue has a rounded key-scheme and an extended scale in which Bach's new power is already evident. BWV532 (D major), which exists in two versions, is famous for its serpentine fugue subject and flamboyant virtuosity. The C major Toccata BWV564 (despite its title) also deserves to be considered with this group of works. The unusual compass ($C$ to $d'''$) suggests that it was not composed for an instrument which Bach regularly played, and therefore perhaps for an *Orgelprobe* such as the one in which Bach is known to have participated in his former church on the newly restored organ in Mühlhausen in 1709. Other features of the work are also consistent with an occasion of this type. The usual pedal solo (of unusual length and elaboration) is preceded by a flamboyant demonstration of virtuosity on the manual, and the work features a central Adagio in the relative minor which would have shown off the instrument's solo effects to advantage.

The remainder of Bach's freely constructed organ works date from after about 1713, when his compositional style underwent radical change, partly as a result of his contact with the concertos of Vivaldi. His treatment of the prelude and fugue form from this point takes on its mature form, and his idiom loses many of the vestiges of the Buxtehudian tradition. The fugues now exhibit fully developed key schemes and exhaustively worked out ideas, while the preludes become fully organized movements of weight and substance, though in some cases they may have been added later to what was originally an unattached fugue. The next group of works includes BWV545 (C major), as well as two fine examples of the toccata and fugue, BWV540 (F major) and 538 (D minor). Both of these integrate north German pedal virtuosity into the far more highly organized developmental methods of Bach's mature years. The 'Great' G minor Fantasia and Fugue BWV542 may have been played by Bach in the Catherinenkirche, Hamburg, in 1720 (see *Spitta*, ii. 23), but there is no certain evidence for this; quotation of the fugue subject in Johann Mattheson's *Der vollkommene Capellmeister* (1739) is one indication of its fame in Bach's day, but posterity has been equally attracted by the extraordinary chromatic excursions in the Fantasia.

A final series of organ works in prelude and fugue form date from Bach's final period in Leipzig (1723–50). Composed probably over a long period, they hardly form an integrated group, but they nevertheless have certain characteristics in common. The extrovert virtuosity of many of the Weimar works is generally pruned down, and the fugues acquire a mighty architectural breadth together with a new emphasis on contrapuntal complexity. The works concerned are BWV541 (G major), 544 (B minor), 546 (C minor), 547 (C major), 548 (E minor), and 552 (E♭ major). The first of these is thought to have been composed for Bach's eldest son Wilhelm Friedemann to play at his audition for an organist's post at the Sophienkirche, Dresden, in 1733. BWV546 has a complex pre-history; one copy of the fugue suggests that it had previously been linked with the Fantasia *a* 5 BWV562, which itself had been attached to a still earlier fugue which remained unfinished. BWV552, which Bach published in *Clavier-Übung III* in 1739, incorporates numerical symbolism referring to the Holy Trinity, including an elaborate triple fugue in which all the major external parameters are governed by the number 3. BWV539 in D minor has a fugue transcribed from the fugue from the G minor Sonata for unaccompanied violin.

**2. Preludes and fugues for other instruments.** Bach's best-known pieces in prelude and fugue form are, of course, those in the two volumes of *The Well-tempered Clavier*. Other works to be considered include BWV894–902, which are mostly early and in some cases dubiously attributed. BWV895 (A minor) and 896 (A major), in particular, have the appearance of early works, both featuring squat repeated-note subjects in traditional style. BWV898 (B♭ major, of doubtful authenticity) has a fugue based on the motif BACH. Some of the works incorporate material which later found its way into better-known works. BWV894 (A minor) was later reused for the outer movements of the Triple Concerto in A minor for violin, flute, and harpsichord, while BWV901 (F major) and 902 (G major) both contain fugues (titled 'fughetta') which Bach later used in revised form with new preludes in the '48'. These are mainly small- to moderate-scale works which form a relevant background to *The Well-tempered Clavier*.

The idea of encompassing the 24 major and minor keys in chromatic succession was anticipated to some extent by earlier keyboard collections, notably J. C. F. Fischer's *Ariadne musica* (1702), which includes preludes and fugues in 19 of the 24 keys. The music of Bach's first book varies widely in character. Some of the preludes are arpeggiated or patterned pieces which clearly suggest a didactic purpose. Others are in two-part invention style, and still others incorporate elements of the concerto and dance types. The E♭ major Prelude has the character of a self-contained toccata in an old-fashioned manner; external evidence suggests that it may pre-date the main body of the set. The fugues are equally variegated. The number of voices varies from two (E minor) to five (B♭ minor, C♯ minor), with some of the more archaic movements suggesting older ricercare forms.

In the 22 years that elapsed between the fair copy of Book 1 (1720) and the earliest known copy of Book 2 (which in most sources no longer bears the sobriquet 'Das wohltemperierte Clavier') Bach's fundamental style had changed little, but the second set nevertheless contains a number of new features. Some of the preludes, particularly those in remote keys, show the influence of new *galant* and *empfindsam* conventions. The F minor Prelude contains affective melodic sighs and extreme harmonic effects, combined with a radical simplification of Bach's normal contrapuntal methods, which clearly point forwards to a later convention than most of the other movements. The G♯ minor Prelude includes *forte* and *piano* markings and simplified melody and accompaniment features, as well as an air of tearful melancholy which calls to mind C. P. E. Bach. Both these movements would be effective on the early fortepiano or the 18th-century clavichord. The driving syncopations and brittle two-part counterpoint of the B minor Prelude suggest a late work. The fugues, while also including reworkings of earlier music, are generally more uniform in character than those of the first book, but there are some notable exceptions. The E major Fugue is a radical exercise in *stile antico* counterpoint, based on a tag which also appears in the E major Fugue from Fischer's *Ariadne musica*, from which Bach may have taken the idea. There are also some notable contrapuntal *tours de force*; for example, the G minor Fugue features invertible counterpoint at the octave, 10th, and 12th, while stretto and augmentation are prominent in the C minor, C♯ major, and B♭ minor fugues. To this extent, the second book of the '48' suggests the last period of Bach's life, characterized by an increasing preoccupation with contrapuntal artifice which ultimately led to the *Musical Offering* and *The Art of Fugue*.          DLH

*See also* PRELUDE, FUGUE, and WELL-TEMPERED CLAVIER, THE.

D. Schulenberg, *The Keyboard Music of J. S. Bach* (New York, 1992); G. Stauffer, *The Organ Preludes of Johann Sebastian Bach* (Ann Arbor, 1980); P. Williams, *The Organ Music of J. S. Bach*, i (Cambridge, 1980).

# Q

**Quantz, Johann Joachim** (b. 30 Jan. 1697; d. 12 July 1773). Flautist, flute maker, writer, and pedagogue, born in Oberscheden, Hanover. He received his early training in Merseburg, and began his musical career first as an oboist, then as second flautist (to Buffardin) at the court of August the Strong and Friedrich August II in Dresden, where he most likely met Bach. Quantz first met Crown Prince Frederick of Prussia in 1728, and began instructing him twice a year in flute playing. In 1741 he became a member of Frederick's court in Berlin, and remained in the king's service until his death in Potsdam. In Dresden Quantz composed numerous trio sonatas, three of which are sonatas in the concerted manner and may have served as models for some of Bach's sonatas. In Berlin he was a musical colleague of C. P. E. Bach (albeit better paid).      JS

J. Swack, 'On the Origins of the *Sonate auf Concertenart*', *Journal of the American Musicological Society*, 46 (1993), 369–414; J. Swack, 'Quantz and the Sonata in E-flat Major for Flute and Cembalo, BWV 1031', *Early Music*, 23 (1995), 31–53.

**Quasimodogeniti.** In the CHURCH CALENDAR, the first Sunday after Easter. It takes its name from the introit to the Mass for that day in the Latin rite, beginning 'Quasimodo geniti infantes'.

**Querflöte.** A transverse FLUTE.

**Quintilian, Marcus Fabius** (b. *c*.35; d. *c*.100). Roman rhetorician, born in Calagurris (now Calahorra), Spain. He practised as an advocate and became well-known as a teacher. He is remembered mainly for his *Institutio oratoria*, of which Bach's friend and colleague J. M. GESNER published an edition. Ursula Kirkendale suggested that Bach designed his MUSICAL OFFERING to correspond to the sections of a forensic oration as set out by Quintilian.

**quodlibet.** A composition based on a collage of pre-existing and usually familiar melodies. The earliest uses of the term in a musical sense date from the 16th century. There are two main types: the centonization quodlibet, in which fragments of the melodies are heard successively in the same voice, and the combinative quodlibet, in which two or more melodies are heard in combination in different voices. Quodlibet singing was especially popular in Germany, where it seems to have been associated with festive occasions such as Christmas and New Year, but equivalent forms also existed in Spain (the *ensalada*), France (the *fricassée*), and England (the medley).

Classic collections of quodlibets which could have been known to Bach include those by Wolfgang Schmeltzl (1544) and Melchior Franck (1622). A collection in a rather different style from near Bach's own time is the *Augsburger Tafelkonfekt* (1733–46). Bach's interest in quodlibet singing is mentioned by J. N. Forkel (1802), who relates that improvised quodlibets consisting of a *mélange* of 'partly comic and partly improper' words were sung at the annual reunion of the Bach family in various towns in Thuringia.

Two compositions, one certainly and the other probably by Bach, are in quodlibet form. The Quodlibet (Variation 30) from the Goldberg Variations combines the bass line and harmonic matrix of the Aria on which the work is based with jumbled fragments of two tunes, which can be identified from a manuscript addition in a copy owned by Bach's pupil J. P. Kirnberger, as *Ich bin so lang nicht bei dir gewest* and *Kraut und Rüben* (the latter being a version of the traditional bergamasca dance tune). It has been suggested that the movement serves a symbolic function in relation to the set as a whole, representing the Saturnalia or New Year celebrations that mark the ending of the annual cycle.

The other, more problematical work in quodlibet form is the so-called *Hochzeitsquodlibet* BWV524. First published in 1931, soon after its discovery, it is in Bach's hand but, since the bifolium containing both the beginning and the end of the piece is missing, we cannot ignore the possibility that this is a copy made by Bach of a work by another composer. Scored for SATB with continuo, it sets a series of short texts, many of them comic verses. They contain references to places in the Arnstadt district and to a number of individuals, some of whose names correspond to those of members of the Bach family. Other texts are simply homely proverbs or bawdy jokes. The manuscript is written on the same paper type as the autograph of Cantata 71, composed for performance in Mühlhausen on 4 February 1708, and further evidence for a dating around the beginning of 1708 comes from one of the texts, which reads 'In diesem Jahre haben wir zwei Sonnenfinsternisse' ('This year we have two solar eclipses'), referring to an astronomical phenomenon which was indeed visible over north Germany during that year. DLH

M. Neumann and G. Kraft, Introductory essays, in *Johann Sebastian Bach: Hochzeitsquodlibet 1707* [facsimile] (Leipzig, 1973); H.-J. Schulze, 'Notizen zu Bachs Quodlibets', *BJb* 80 (1974), 171–5; C. S. Terry, 'Bach's Quodlibet', *Music and Letters*, 14 (1933), 1–17.

# R

**Raden, Gottlob Ludwig** (b. 19 April 1718; d. 1 June 1764). Organist, born in Zeitz, about 40 km. (25 miles) south-west of Leipzig. He enrolled at Leipzig University in July 1737 and was a pupil of Bach. In 1742 he was appointed organist at the Michaeliskirche in Zeitz, and in 1756 he succeeded J. L. Krebs at the Schloßkirche there.

**Raison, André** (d. 1719). French composer. He was organist of the abbey church of Sainte Geneviève and the college of the Jacobins de St Jacques, Paris. The first of Raison's two published books of organ music (1688), consisting of five masses, includes a *Trio en passacaille* based on an eight-note subject which corresponds to the first half of the ground bass of Bach's C minor Passacaglia for organ; the Raison passacaglia forms the 'Christe eleison' in the *Messe du deuziesme ton*. The resemblance to Bach's theme was first noted by Alexandre Guilmant and André Pirro in their edition of Raison's organ music (*Archives des maîtres de l'orgue*, 1899). However, the Passacaglia shows far stronger evidence of Bach's study of Buxtehude's three chaconnes in C minor, D minor, and E minor, and the suggestion that his theme was based on Raison's can hardly survive an application of Occam's razor, especially since there is no other evidence that Bach was familiar with Raison's music. *See also* PASSACAGLIA.    DLH

**Ratsmusikant.** A musician employed by a town or city council (*Rat*) to provide music on civic occasions. He might be a *Stadtpfeifer* or a *Kunstgeiger*. *See* STADTMUSICUS.

**Ratswahl, Ratswechsel** ('council election', 'change of council'). It was customary in Bach's time to inaugurate a newly elected town or city council with a special service at the Stadtkirche, the official town church. In Leipzig, where a third of the council members were elected each year, the *Ratswechsel* service normally took place in the Nikolaikirche on the last Monday in August, and Bach was expected to perform a special cantata for the occasion. Such works are frequently referred to as *Ratswahl* or *Ratswechsel* cantatas, and five from Bach's Leipzig period have survived: nos. 119 (1723), 193 (?1727, incomplete), 120 (?1728/9), 29 (1731), and 69 (?1748, a reworking of an earlier cantata for the 12th Sunday after Trinity). There are also some for which only the text is known: *Wünschet Jerusalem Glück* (BWV Anh. I 4, ?1727,

1741), *Gott, gib dein Gericht dem Könige* (BWV Anh. I 3, 1730), and *Herrscher des Himmels, König der Ehren* (BWV Anh. 193, 1740).

In Mühlhausen the *Ratswechsel* service was held on 4 February each year. Bach's Cantata 71 was performed on that occasion in 1708, and he wrote another cantata, now lost, for the service the following year. They were the only cantatas to be printed during Bach's lifetime.

*DürrK.*

## reception and revival. See overleaf.

**recitative.** A type of solo vocal writing, originating in Italy around 1600, that imitates the natural rhythms and inflections of speech. It began to appear in German church music in the early 18th century, owing to the influence of Erdmann Neumeister and others. With the exception of a handful of works composed in Mühlhausen in 1708 or earlier, recitative is found in virtually all Bach's sacred and secular cantatas. It also appears throughout his oratorios and Passions (e.g. the narrative portions sung by the Evangelist), but not in Latin liturgical works (the masses and the *Magnificat*) or in motets. In operas of the 17th and early 18th centuries the basic events of the plot unfold in recitative, while the thoughts and feelings of individual characters are expressed in arias. Bach's vocal music follows this general pattern. However, in his church cantatas the recitatives are more often didactic (e.g. summaries of doctrine or Christian experience) rather than outwardly dramatic.

The stylistic scope and expressive depth of Bach's recitatives far exceed the norm for vocal music in the late Baroque. The most common type of recitative, both in Bach's works and more generally, was widely known as *recitativo semplice*; the term 'secco' ('dry') did not come into use until the late 18th century. 'Simple recitative' (the term employed throughout the present volume) is accompanied by the continuo group alone: chords suggested by the figured bass are played on instruments such as the organ or harpsichord (or both), while the bass line itself is strengthened by others (e.g. cello, violone, or bassoon). This kind of recitative often served primarily as a vehicle for traversing narrative portions of the libretto and had little inherent melodic interest, but in Bach's hands even simple recitative sometimes contains

[*cont. on p.407*]

# reception and revival

English-language accounts of how Bach's music has fared in performance, publication, and scholarly research and the impact it has made on societies and cultures since the composer's death in 1750 have, quite naturally, concentrated on its reception and revival in Germany, Austria, and Great Britain. This article attempts to widen the perspective and, although it has not been possible in the time and space available to cover every country (or even every continent), the brief surveys that follow might serve to indicate the wide acceptance that Bach's music has found, and the impact it has made on different national traditions. For a general introduction to the topic, see M. Zenck, 'Bach Reception: Some Concepts and Parameters', in J. Butt, ed., *The Cambridge Companion to Bach* (Cambridge, 1997), 218–25. *See also* PERFORMANCE STYLES.

1. Austria.
2. France.
3. Germany.
4. Great Britain.
5. Italy.
6. Japan.
7. Low Countries.
8. Poland.
9. Portugal.
10. Russia and Ukraine.
11. Scandinavia.
12. Spain.
13. United States of America.

**1. Austria.** The reception and revival of Bach's music in Austria has not yet received systematic study, and the relatively few documents known at present may not be representative. We cannot be certain, for example, when Bach's compositions first became known in Austria. It is possible that copies of the printed editions (or at least the librettos) of Bach's two celebratory cantatas for elections of the town council in Mühlhausen (BWV71 and another cantata, now lost) were sent to the Viennese court, but no documentary proof of this has come to light.

The oldest Austrian source of a composition of Bach's is a copy of the keyboard fugue BWV904:2 from the collection of Gottlieb Muffat (1690–1770), probably dating from about 1740. Muffat's pupil Georg Christoph Wagenseil (1715–77) is supposed to have taught his own students 'the preludes and fugues of Sebastian Bach'. A manuscript at the Staats- und Universitätsbibliothek Hamburg which contains several keyboard works by Bach and is dated 1738 bears the *ex libris* of Johann Anton Graf, organist at Mattsee, near Salzburg. Other Austrian manuscript sources still need to be examined.

Bach himself had contact with several noblemen from the Habsburg empire. Noteworthy is his remark on the original score of the Sanctus BWV232[III], stating that he had lent the parts to Count Franz Anton Sporck in Bohemia. Other documents point to his acquaintance with Count Johann Adam von Questenberg (1678–1752) and Count Eugen Wenzel Joseph von Wrbna, who studied with him at Leipzig in 1747.

Rather more documents and sources relating to the reception of Bach's music in Austria, particularly Vienna, are known for the last quarter of the 18th century. The importance of Baron Gottfried van Swieten has long been established, while the music collection of Franz Joseph von Heß (1739–1804) has only recently been retrieved. Other important members of the Viennese aristocracy who collected and performed Bach's works are Fanny von Arnstein and Cäcilie von Eskeles, both of them daughters of the Itzig family in Berlin, who were great admirers of Bach's music and stood in direct contact with his two eldest sons. Another admirer of Bach was Count Karl Alois von Lichnowsky (1761–1814), a friend and patron of Beethoven; Lichnowsky acquired manuscript copies of Bach's compositions during his student days in Göttingen, where he was probably in contact with Bach's biographer J. N. Forkel.

The three great Viennese masters, Haydn, Mozart, and Beethoven, were all well acquainted with Bach's music, particularly with his keyboard works. Haydn owned a copy of the B minor Mass, while Mozart, on his trip to Leipzig in 1789, came to know Bach's motets through a performance of the Thomaner choir under the direction of J. F. Doles. Beethoven, who got to know *The Well-tempered Clavier* through his studies with Christian Gottlob Neefe (1736–1809) in Bonn, was deeply influenced by Bach's late works, which he became acquainted with through Johann Georg Albrechtsberger (1736–1809). *The Art of Fugue* in particular is reflected in the style of Beethoven's last string quartets.

In two printed catalogues of 1799 and 1804 the Viennese music dealer Johann Traeg offered an astonishingly large number of Bach's works for sale, including sacred vocal music, keyboard works, and ensemble compositions, some of which may stem from the music library of van Swieten. The famous *Œuvres complettes* edition of Hoffmeister & Kühnel, begun in 1802, was available in Austria through the Vienna branch of the firm. Finally, new editions of the treatises of F. W. Marpurg and J. P. Kirnberger, which were published in Vienna around 1800, served to foster a broader understanding of the style and significance of Bach's music.

A new phase in the revival of Bach's music was entered through manuscript collectors such as Franz Hauser, Aloys Fuchs (1709–1853), Joseph Fischhof (1804–57), and Raphael Georg Kiesewetter (1773–1850); the last-named especially, through his historic concerts, helped to establish a new public interest in the music of the previous century. The continuing fascination that Bach's music has held for other composers bore particular fruit in the works and activities of the second Viennese school of Arnold Schoenberg and his pupils Alban Berg (1885–1935) and Anton Webern (1883–1945). Schoenberg was able to find his way forward in serial music by adopting contrapuntal procedures familiar to him from the works of Bach, whom he declared to be, along with Mozart, his principal teacher. Both he and Webern made arrangements of Bach works, and introduced the motif BACH into some of their original compositions. Berg, who had studied Bach's chorale harmonizations with Schoenberg, went even further in paying homage to Bach by introducing into his Violin Concerto the chorale *Es ist genung* in the harmonization from Cantata 60.     PW

*See also* SWIETEN, GOTTFRIED BERNHARD VAN and SCHOENBERG, ARNOLD.

O. Biba, 'Bach-Pflege in Wien von Gottlieb Muffat bis Johann Georg Albrechtsberger', in A. Reichling, ed., *Mundus organorum: Festschrift Walter Supper zum 70. Geburtstag* (Berlin,

1978), 21–34; I. Fuchs, ed., *Johann Sebastian Bach: Beiträge zur Wirkungsgeschichte* (Vienna, 1992) [including essays by Y. Kobayashi, O. Biba, W. Dürr, R. Flotzinger, and H. Krones]; K. Hofmann, 'Johann Sebastian Bach und der deutsche Süden: eine Bestandsaufnahme', in H.-J. Schulze and C. Wolff, eds., *Johann Sebastian Bach und der süddeutsche Raum: Aspekte der Wirkungsgeschichte Bachs* (Regensburg, 1991), 61–74; Y. Kobayashi, 'Franz Hauser: seine Bach-Handschriftensammlung' (diss., University of Göttingen, 1973); A. Plichta, 'Johann Sebastian Bach und Johann Adam Graf von Questenberg', *BJb* 67 (1981), 23–30 [including a *Nachwort* by C. Wolff]; R. Schaal, *Quellen und Forschungen zur Wiener Musiksammlung von Aloys Fuchs* (Graz, 1966); E. F. Schmid, 'Beethovens Bachkenntnis', *Neues Beethoven Jahrbuch*, 5 (1933), 64–83; U. Wolf, 'Die Musikaliensammlung des Wiener Regierungsrats Franz Joseph Reichsritter von Heß (1739–1804) und ihre Bachiana', *BJb* 81 (1995), 195–201; M. Zenck, 'Tradition as Authority and Provocation: Anton Webern's Confrontation with Johann Sebastian Bach', in D. O. Franklin, ed., *Bach Studies* (Cambridge, 1989), 297–322.

2. **France.** During the reign of Louis XVI (1774–93) the Bach family was not unknown in France. Works by J. C. Bach were performed at the Concert Spirituel, and C. P. E. Bach corresponded with Denis Diderot (1713–84) and his daughter, who played the harpsichord. 'Sébast. Bach, père de tous les Bachs' was mentioned in a review published in Paris in 1780 (see Baffert), at a time when examples of his work were beginning to circulate (see Cyr). Even during his life Bach came into contact with French musicians, among them J. B. Volumier and P.-G. Buffardin. In Paris, where he was staying in 1746, F. W. Marpurg recalled the ignominy suffered by the keyboard player Louis MARCHAND when he failed to turn up for a contest with Bach in 1717; among those who heard Marpurg was J. H. Ferrand, who included an account of it in his memoirs. In the same document (published in the *Revue et gazette musicale de Paris*, 1845, but unfortunately overlooked by Bach researchers) Ferrand testifies to having heard organ works by Bach played in Bordeaux by Franz Ignaz Beck (1734–1809), a German composer and instrumentalist who spent most of his working life in France.

Teaching methods at the Paris Conservatoire, a beneficiary of the French Revolution, began gradually to consecrate the contrapuntal genius of Bach. Instrumental tutors and other writings published in Paris cited passages from his works, and very soon the Belgian theorist Jérôme-Joseph de Momigny (1762–1842), resident in Paris, showed himself to be both an admirer and an able analyst of Bach's music. In 1801 *The Art of Fugue* and *The Well-tempered Clavier* were published in Paris.

The first generation of French Romantics viewed these 'models' as merely scholastic. Faced with the acerbic criticism of Berlioz, and despite the 'evangelistic' visits of Mendelssohn to the French capital, few musicians and music-lovers were prepared to risk accusations of pedantry by promoting a Bachian aesthetic. The exceptions included A. P. F. Boëly (1785–1858), who went as far as to complete the unfinished contrapunctus of *The Art of Fugue* (a work which his pupil Saint-Saëns was later to perform on the piano), and the artist J. B. Laurens (1801–90), who made various pilgrimages to Germany, sometimes in the company of the German organist J. C. H. Rinck (1770–1846), who presented him with a manuscript (formerly thought to be autograph) of the *Partite diverse* BWV768. Mention must also be made of pianists such as Stephen Heller, Liszt, Chopin, and Valentin Alkan, who included Bach's works in their recitals, and of intellectuals such as L.-N.-A. Tonnellé (1820–58), Adolphe Guéroult (1810–72), and Adolphe Pictet (1799–1875)—not forgetting the musicologist F.-J. Fétis (1784–1871).

During the years of the Bourbon Restoration (1814–30) and the July Monarchy (1830–48) there was a marked interest in musical antiquarianism, but it was above all Palestrina and Handel who profited from the pioneering efforts of an Alexandre Choron (1771–1834), while Fétis's Concerts Historiques (from 1832) established the myth of 'historical colour' as a somewhat sombre ideal. It was in this climate of antique blandness that an aria from the *St Matthew Passion* was heard at the Concerts du Conservatoire in Paris in 1840—without enthusiasm.

A bourgeois academicism prevailed during the Second Empire (1852–70); Gounod's AVE MARIA (1853) and its immediate success is one sign of it, no less than the contemporary fashion for gavottes and musettes. In 1868, when a performance at the Panthéon of the *St Matthew Passion* under J. E. Pasdeloup (1819–87) was hailed by the Parisian public as a 'première' (in fact, only extracts were given), the concert ended with … the *Ave Maria*. Bach's Protestantism was evidently an obstacle to his acceptance by the French public. Even members of the French organ school, though regenerated by the Bachian tradition recovered by J. N. Lemmens (1823–81) from his teacher A. F. Hesse (1809–63), were mostly unsympathetic towards Bach's Lutheran inspiration.

After 1870 an increase in the number of public concerts, in the provinces as well as in the capital, encouraged a more complete awareness of Bach's works; Alexandre Guilmant (1837–1911) at the organ of the Trocadéro, Charles Lamoureux (1834–99) and other conductors of various choral and orchestral societies (Bourgault-Ducoudray, Concordia, Concerts Colonne, Société Nationale, etc.) did not spare their efforts. At the same time some biographers (Félix Grenier in 1876, Ernest David in 1882, and William Cart in 1885), rejecting the *feuilleton* style that had prevailed until then, made cautious attempts to summarize Bach's career, often drawing on out-of-date German studies. In 1888 the first complete performance in France of the *St Matthew Passion* took place in Paris, and in 1895 that of the *St John Passion*. In between, in 1891, the Mass in B minor was performed at the Conservatoire. Bach was at last heard—but it was the 'gothic' Bach, representing the completion of a slow 'canonization' of 'notre Saint-Père Bach', the model of virtue and artistic humility, and the corner-stone of a 'religion of art' influenced by Wagner's *Parsifal*.

Towards the end of the 19th century a return to the 'letter' was manifest: on the one hand through a concern for greater authenticity in performance (for example in Brussels by F.-A. Gevaert, and in Paris by the Société des Instruments Anciens and, in the period before World War I, the Société Bach de Paris, the harpsichordist Wanda Landowska, etc.); on the other hand through an interest in the symbolical meaning and the 'poetic' aesthetic of Bach's music embodied in the influential books of two of Charles-Marie Widor's disciples, André Pirro (1906) and Albert Schweitzer (1905). Their 'programmatic' approach was contested in the inter-war years by supporters of a more abstract view of pure, de-Romanticized music such as Boris de Schloezer, whose *Introduction à J. S. Bach* (Paris, 1947) argued for a new 'retour à Bach'.          WC

J.-M. Baffert, 'Vier unbekannte Bach-Erwähnungen in Druckschriften des 18. Jahrhunderts', *BJb* 74 (1988), 191–3; W. Corten, 'Le Procès de canonisation de Sébastien Bach en France au 19e siècle' (diss., Université Libre, Brussels, 1978); M. Cyr, 'Bach's Music in France: A New Source', *Early Music*, 13 (1985), 256–9; E. Kooiman, *Jacques Lemmens, Charles-Marie Widor en de Franse Bach-Traditie* (Amsterdam, 1988); E. Lichtenhahn, 'Zum Französischen Bach-Bild des 19. Jahrhunderts', *Basler Jahrbuch für historische Musikpraxis*, 6 (1982), 61–86; H. Schützeichel, 'Albert Schweitzer und die Bach-rezeption in Frankreich', *Musica*, 42

(1988), 141–8; M. Vignal, 'Frühe Bach-Pflege in Frankreich', in I. Fuchs and S. Antonicek, eds., *Johann Sebastian Bach: Beiträge zur Wirkungsgeschichte* (Vienna, 1992), 167–77.

## 3. Germany.

*(i) Before 1750.* During his lifetime Bach was appreciated mainly as an exceptional keyboard virtuoso, while his stature as a composer was fully established only after his death. Few works, mostly for keyboard, were published before 1750; the vocal and instrumental ensemble music was merely transmitted in manuscript form and became known only to a relatively small circle of Bach connoisseurs. It is noteworthy, however, that some of the unpublished keyboard works circulated widely, particularly in Thuringia and Saxony. Also, it is documented that Bach himself frequently lent the performance materials of vocal works to students, friends, and patrons (see, for example, *BDok* i, no. 20; ii, no. 484; and iii, p. 638), and a considerable number of instrumental and vocal works were performed between 1734 and 1738 by the collegium musicum of Frankfurt an der Oder under the direction of the young C. P. E. Bach.

Although Bach is mentioned as a composer in a relatively large number of contemporary treatises (some with references to both published and unpublished works), a comparison with the reception of a master like Telemann puts these documents into perspective. Only a few documents relate Bach's works to the aesthetic discussions of the time; while Johann Mattheson praised his contrapuntal skills in 1731 and 1739, J. A. Scheibe harshly criticized his style of composing in 1737, and Lorenz Mizler emphasized the conservative style especially of his cantatas in 1739.

*(ii) 1750–1800.* While it was formerly believed that after 1750 Bach's music was almost entirely forgotten until well into the 19th century, recent research has proved the contrary. In fact, the large number of Bach's pupils ensured that the works of their teacher were propagated throughout Germany. Particularly important sites of an early Bach reception are Halle, where at the Sunday services in the Liebfrauenkirche W. F. Bach performed cantatas by his father on a regular basis, and Hamburg, where C. P. E. Bach incorporated a great number of vocal works (including parts of the B minor Mass and the two Passions) into his repertory of church music, as well as into his private concerts. While at Halle Bach's works were heard more or less in their original versions, at Hamburg they were used mostly in the form of pasticcios.

The most important centre of Bach reception during the second half of the 18th century, however, was Berlin, where there lived at various times three of his sons (Carl Philipp Emanuel, Johann Christian, and Wilhelm Friedemann) and a number of his former pupils (J. F. Agricola, J. P. Kirnberger, F. W. Marpurg, and Christoph Nichelmann). Bach's works had a regular place in private musical societies (such as that of Princess Anna Amalia), but were apparently also heard occasionally in churches. Other important figures of the Berlin Bach revival were the copyist and collector J. F. Hering and the harpsichordist Sara Levy (née Itzig, 1761–1854). Bach's works were thoroughly discussed in theoretical writings, the most crucial being Kirnberger's *Die Kunst des reinen Satzes in der Musik* (1771–9). The Bach reception in Vienna began about 1770–80, and in its early stages was heavily influenced by the Berlin circle.

After 1750 several music dealers offered a large number of Bach's works in manuscript form; particularly noteworthy are J. G. I. Breitkopf in Leipzig, J. C. Westphal in

Hamburg, J. C. F. Rellstab in Berlin, and Johann Traeg in Vienna. Plans to publish selected keyboard works could not be realized until after 1800.

*(iii) 1800–1850*. The decades after 1800 are characterized by the publication of J. N. Forkel's Bach biography (Leipzig, 1802), which represented the first complete account of the composer's life after the Obituary of 1754; by ambitious editing projects of the keyboard works such as the *Œuvres complettes de Jean Sebastien Bach* (1801–4) undertaken by the Leipzig firm of Hoffmeister & Kühnel; and by an increasing number of public performances of sacred vocal works, particularly in Leipzig and Berlin. While the Bach reception of the early Romantic movement, in which the writer and composer E. T. A. Hoffmann (1776–1822) played a part, concentrated almost exclusively on the keyboard works, after 1820 the focus shifted—coinciding with a new trend towards nationalism—to the great choral works.

By 1800 many of Bach's autographs were in private manuscript collections; the steadily increasing value of these on the antiquarian market forms an interesting aspect of Bach reception. The most important collectors were Georg Poelchau, the Counts of Voß, Aloys Fuchs, J. N. Forkel, Franz Hauser, C. S. Gähler, C. H. P. Pistor, and C. F. Zelter. During the second half of the 19th century most of these collections were acquired by large public libraries that took over the role of preserving Bach's heritage, the most notable being the Königliche Bibliothek (now the Staatsbibliothek Preußischer Kulturbesitz) at Berlin.

*(iv) Since 1850*. The founding of the Bach-Gesellschaft in 1850 marked an important caesura in the history of Bach reception. With the regular appearance of the volumes of the complete edition, Bach's musical profile (particularly as a composer of vocal music) gradually became visible to a larger audience. A companion piece to the edition is Philipp Spitta's monumental Bach biography, published in two volumes in 1873 and 1880, which superseded all previous biographical writings (those by Forkel, 1802; C. L. Hilgenfeldt, 1850; and C. H. Bitter, 1865). Yet, while between 1850 and 1899 all Bach's known works became available, this did not result in an increasing number of performances; indeed, during the 1870s, when the number of subscribers had dropped to little more than 300, completion of the edition was for some time in doubt.

The Neue Bach-Gesellschaft, founded in 1900, was thus proclaimed to popularize and promote Bach's music and to encourage scholarly discussion. This task was approached by establishing an annual Bach-Fest (since 1901) and by founding a scholarly journal, the *Bach-Jahrbuch* (since 1904). Important German Bach scholars of the early 20th century are Arnold Schering, Max Schneider, and Bernhard Friedrich Richter. After 1933 the more popular reception of Bach's music was increasingly influenced by national socialist ideology (particularly noteworthy in this context is the Reichs-Bach-Fest of 1935), while the *BJb* remained remarkably neutral.

Bach scholarship since 1945 has been characterized by the initiation of the Neue Bach-Ausgabe in 1950 and the founding of two research institutes, the Johann-Sebastian-Bach-Institut at Göttingen, and the Bach-Archiv Leipzig. In the course of a new evaluation of the sources, during the 1950s a new chronology of Bach's works was established (by Alfred Dürr and Georg von Dadelsen), which resulted in a completely new conception of Bach's Leipzig period. Through the publication of the *Bach-Dokumente* (edited by Werner Neumann and H.-J. Schulze), traditional views of

Bach's reputation during his lifetime and the first decades after his death were significantly altered.

PW

*See also* ANNA AMALIA; HAUSER, FRANZ; MENDELSSOHN, FELIX; POELCHAU, GEORG; and ZELTER, CARL FRIEDRICH.

F. Blume, *Johann Sebastian Bach im Wandel der Geschichte* (Kassel, 1947; Eng. trans. as *Two Centuries of Bach*, London, 1950); C. Dahlhaus, 'Zur Entstehung der romantischen Bach-Deutung', *BJb* 64 (1978), 192–210; B. Faulstich, *Die Musiksammlung der Familie von Voß: ein Beitrag zur Berliner Musikgeschichte um 1800* (Kassel, 1997); L. Finscher, 'Bach in the Eighteenth Century', in D. O. Franklin, ed., *Bach Studies* (Cambridge, 1989), 281–96; H.-J. Schulze, *Studien zur Bach-Überlieferung im 18. Jahrhundert* (Leipzig and Dresden, 1984); H.-J. Schulze *et al.*, eds., *Bericht über die wissenschaftliche Konferenz anläßlich des 69. Bach-Festes der Neuen Bachgesellschaft, Leipzig, 29. und 30. März 1994* (Hildesheim, 1995); G. Stauffer, ed., *Bach Perspectives*, ii (Lincoln, Nebr., 1996); G. Wagner, ed., *Jahrbuch des Staatlichen Instituts für Musikforschung Preußischer Kulturbesitz 1995* (Stuttgart, 1995); P. Wollny, 'Wilhelm Friedemann Bach's Halle Performances of Cantatas by his Father', in D. Melamed, ed., *Bach Studies 2* (Cambridge, 1995), 202–28; P. Wollny, 'Zur Überlieferung der Instrumentalwerke Johann Sebastian Bachs: der Quellenbesitz Carl Philipp Emanuel Bachs', *BJb* 82 (1996), 7–21.

**4. Great Britain.** Bach's activities were hardly noticed in Great Britain during the composer's lifetime. The religious reformer John Wesley twice passed through Leipzig in 1738 and was well enough organized to arrange meetings with all three English speakers listed as such in the city's annual register, but he made no mention at all of Bach in his journal. Later, as he became familiar with the chorale settings, he began to regard Bach as a sensitive musical artist, and it seems likely that this attitude influenced his sons Charles and Samuel, but by that time Bach was long dead. No Englishman is known to have studied with Bach, and such fragments of his music as came to England before 1750 apparently did so by chance.

Perhaps the first English mention of Bach in print is in John Casper Heck's *The Musical Library and Universal Magazine of Harmony* (London, c.1775; *BDok* iii, no. 811a), where the author comments on Bach's contrapuntal skill in examples from the Canonic Variations and *The Art of Fugue*. A second mention occurs in John Hawkins's *A General History of the Science and Practice of Music* (London, 1776); Hawkins refers to the last, incomplete fugue from *The Art of Fugue* and to the BACH motif as referred to in J. G. Walther's *Musicalisches Lexicon* and demonstrated to Hawkins by Bach's son Johann Christian.

J. C. Bach arrived in England in 1762; in 1764 he was joined by Carl Friedrich Abel in the service of Queen Charlotte. In 1765 the two men began their joint concert series which ran until the year of J. C. Bach's death, 1782. The music they played was drawn from an international repertory, but there is no evidence that their programmes ever included music by J. C. Bach's father (C. F. Abel's godfather). Indeed, there is no evidence at all of J. C. Bach performing, copying, or advocating his father's music in Great Britain, but by the time of his death things were changing in this respect. First to attract attention was the organ music, played by A. F. C. Kollmann at the Royal German Chapel in St James's Palace, by K. F. Horn at the Portuguese Embassy Chapel, and by Samuel Wesley, assisted by the double bass player Domenico Dragonetti (1763–1846), at various London locations.

Bach's keyboard works began to circulate in Great Britain from about 1790 (often in manuscripts copied from poor sources), and Queen Charlotte owned one of the earliest manuscript copies of the B minor Mass, extracts from which were performed by Samuel Wesley. In 1806 Kollmann published the Chromatic Fantasia (without the Fugue); Horn and Wesley jointly published the six Organ Sonatas in 1809; both parts of *The Well-tempered Clavier* were issued by the firms of Lavenu (in ?1809) and Robert Birchall (in 1810); and Muzio Clementi's publishing firms were actively engaged in issuing Bach's music during the first two decades of the 19th century. Into old age Clementi consistently advocated Bach's music, especially the fugues, as a means of acquiring flexible musicianship. In this he was followed by other Bach enthusiasts such as J. B. Cramer (1771–1858) and Ignaz Moscheles (1794–1870).

In April 1829, shortly after his 'centenary' performance of the *St Matthew Passion* in Berlin, Mendelssohn made the first of several visits to Great Britain. In 1837 in Birmingham he performed the Prelude and Fugue in E♭ major from *Clavier-Übung III* in a concert which included also the first extracts from the *St Matthew Passion* (nos. 38*b* and 39) to be heard in the country. In the second half of the century Bach's choral works began to receive increasingly regular performances. Even as early as 1815 Samuel Wesley and Benjamin Jacob (1778–1829), organist of the Surrey Chapel in London, had contemplated founding a Bach Choir, and in October 1849 Sterndale Bennett founded the English Bach Society, with performances of the *St Matthew Passion* as its main aim.

The example of this society was widely followed during the next 60 years or so, and affordable vocal scores in English translation of the cantatas, oratorios, and Passions were issued by the firm of Novello as a principal resource of the Bach revival being enacted by the larger provincial and metropolitan choral societies of late Victorian Britain. In 1876 Otto Goldschmidt (1829–1907), founder of the London Bach Choir, conducted the first complete performance in England of the B minor Mass. Ebenezer Prout's stated opinion that Bach's vocal counterpoint was 'ill-suited to the voice and to good singing' (*Musical Times*, 17, 1876) began to sound unconvincing to singers and audiences confronted with Wagner's music dramas.

The volumes of the *BG* edition, which served as the basis for nearly all British editions issued between 1900 and 1954, served to make available virtually the whole of Bach's output to conductors, performers, and concert promoters. While some societies, for example W. G. Whittaker's Bach Choir in Newcastle upon Tyne, continued to perform the cantatas and other works in English, some more enterprising ones began to promote the singing of them in the original German. Two organizations particularly influential in this respect have been the BBC and the LONDON BACH SOCIETY. Another facet of BBC enterprise was the commissioning of the Welsh organist Geraint Jones (b. 1917) to play Bach on surviving historical organs in Europe after World War II; his recordings fundamentally challenged and reformed the public perception of what a Baroque organ (and *ipso facto* Bach's organ music) should sound like.

Meanwhile at the Leith Hill Festival, founded in 1905, the composer Vaughan Williams (1872–1958) continued to conduct works by Bach, notably the *St Matthew Passion*, in performances which showed little or no regard for 'authenticity' in the interpretation of Baroque music. The use of period instruments and scholarly editions has, on the other hand, been a watchword of the London Bach Festival, founded in 1990 by Margaret Steinitz. Among other festivals devoted wholly or largely to Bach's music, the English Bach Festival, directed from 1963 by Lina Lalandi, was originally based in Oxford but soon extended its activities, both geographically and in terms of the music performed. The Bath Bach Festival has likewise presented Bach's works in the context of other music, while other provincial festivals, such as that organized annually by the Gwent Bach Society (founder Lloyd Davies), have focused more directly on their eponymous composer.

English writers have made some notable contributions to Bach scholarship. Spitta's biography of the composer (1873–80) was translated into English by Clara Bell and J. A. Fuller-Maitland, and published in 1889 by Novello & Co. It served as a basic source of information for a host of subsequent English biographies, among which that of Hubert Parry (1909) was particularly influential. C. S. Terry's biography (1928) embodied the results of much original research in Germany, and Terry also made notable contributions to the study of the chorales, the cantata texts, and Bach's orchestra, as well as writing dependable handbooks on various individual works and genres. Walter Emery worked on aspects of Bach interpretation (his book on *Bach's Ornaments* was published in 1953) and text-criticism, and also as an editor for the *NBA*. Peter Williams's three-volume study of the organ music (1980–4) soon established itself as a standard work on the subject. Among younger scholars, Ruth Tatlow has written authoritatively on Bach and number symbolism, and John Butt's various writings have united careful scholarship with practical experience as an organist and conductor.                                                              SFD

*See also* BENNETT, WILLIAM STERNDALE; CLEMENTI, MUZIO; HORN, KARL FRIEDRICH; KOLLMANN, AUGUSTUS FREDERIC CHRISTOPHER; and WESLEY, SAMUEL.

H. Redlich, 'The Bach Revival in England (1750–1850)', *Hinrichsen's Musical Year Book*, 7 (1952), 274 ff., 287 ff.

**5. Italy.** A letter dated 14 April 1750 from the celebrated musician and writer Padre G. B. Martini (1706–84) to Johannes Baptist Pauli, *Kapellmeister* at Fulda, bears witness to the esteem that Bach enjoyed in Italy during his lifetime. Martini writes: 'I consider it unnecessary to describe the singular merit of Sig. B[ach], since he is too well known and admired not only in Germany but all over our Italy' (*BDok* ii, no. 600). How true this was, however, is difficult to say, since Italian archives and libraries contain no trace of Bach manuscripts dating from the 18th century, but we know that Padre Martini possessed an exemplar of the *Musical Offering*, sent to him by Pauli along with other Bach items in March 1750, and also a portrait of the composer—the engraving by S. G. Kütner (see *BDok* iv, plate B 13), which he received from the conductor and composer J. G. Naumann (1741–1801) in 1774 (*BDok* ii, no. 597*a*).

Johann Christian Bach must, of course, have helped to make his father's works known in Italy. He went there about 1754, and after staying some time in Naples he travelled to Bologna, where for a year (1756) he studied with Martini. He was then active in Milan from January 1757 to June 1762 (though he made his début as an opera composer in Turin, where his *Artaserse* was produced at the Teatro Regio in December 1760). It is worth recalling, too, that a son of Carl Philipp Emanuel Bach, called after his grandfather Johann Sebastian (1748–78), was active as a painter in Rome, and died there. The only other evidence concerning Bach reception in Italy in the 18th century is a letter in which the art historian Christian Theodor Weinlig, describing a visit to the Benedictine abbey of Montecassino in October 1768, mentions hearing the local organist playing some of Bach's music (*BDok* iii, no. 750).

It was probably Mendelssohn who introduced Bach's name to wider musical circles in Italy when he visited various Italian cities between autumn 1830 and summer 1831. In Rome he came into contact with, among others, the *abbé* Fortunato Santini (1778–1861), to whom, on his return home, he sent scores of the six cantatas (nos. 101–6) published in Bonn in 1830 and of the *St Matthew* and *St John Passions* published in Berlin in 1830 and 1831. Santini, who already possessed the first version of the *Magnificat* (published by Simrock in 1811) and the motets (Leipzig, 1802–3), set himself the task of translating into Latin (rather than Italian!) the texts of both the motets and the Passions (of which only the *Passio Domini Jesu Christi secundum Johannem* survives). These translations were made for his friend the Duke de La Valle di Napoli, and for musical circles in Rome.

Among the pioneers of Bach reception in Rome must be mentioned the violinist Tullio Ramacciotti (1819–1910), founder of the Società del Quartetto (1852). There were only five people in the audience for his first concert, which included a violin sonata by Bach, but he was in close contact with Liszt during the famous pianist's Roman sojourn (1861–70) and applied himself seriously to making Bach's music known. He was active in preparing the ground for Uberto Bandini (1860–1919) and Alessandro Costa (1857–1953), who in 1895 founded the Società G. S. Bach, which remained active until 1905. The society gave 19 concerts in the Sala Costanzi, which was equipped with an organ by the firm of Vegezzi-Bossi in order to perform Bach's works.

Before this, some attempts to import Bach's music had been made by musicians and others whose main interest was to promote the cause of chamber and symphonic music. At Turin, for example, the composer Carlo Rossaro (1827–78), Count Vittorio Radicati di Marmorito (1831–1923), who in 1869 had married Schumann's third daughter, and the cellist Carlo Casella (1834–96), father of the composer Alfredo Casella, were all active in this way. It is nevertheless significant that among the 652 subscribers named in the final volume (1899) of the *BG* edition, there are only five Italian institutions and three individuals, Arrigo Boito (Milan) and the Neapolitan librarians Francesco Florimo and Rocco Pagliari.

In his last years Verdi also took to Bach's music, acquiring in 1896 the score of the Mass in B minor. Ferruccio BUSONI is, of course, a special case; his dedication to Bach had a wholly German stamp and was effected outside his native Italy. A number of piano teachers, however, set out to make Bach's music known to their pupils, among them Beniamino Cesi (1845–1907), Bruno Mugellini (1871–1912), Alessandro Longo (1864–1945), and Gino Tagliapietra (1887–1954); and prestigious composers such as Respighi and Casella made orchestral transcriptions or reworkings of works now well known.

It was only at the beginning of the 20th century that the large-scale works of Bach began to be known in Italy, sometimes through the participation of foreign artists. Thus, the first performance in Italy of the *St Matthew Passion* was put on in Milan by the Società del Quartetto on 22 April 1911 under the direction of Volkmar Andreae, who conducted an orchestra of 60 players from La Scala, the Gemischte Chor of Zürich, singers from Milan Cathedral, and five soloists. It was again in Milan that the *St John Passion* received its Italian première, on 1 May 1913; Georg Schumann conducted the Berlin Philharmonic Orchestra and Singakademie. While the instrumental music, both solo and ensemble, became known quite quickly, the cantatas made less headway. In the 1930s, however, this repertory, too, began to be taken into account. At Turin, for example, Pier Giovanni Pistone (1885–1962) performed Cantatas 34, 106, 138, 140, and 186 with the Stefano Tempia Choir, and after World War II Vittorio Gui gave numerous performances of the cantatas and Passions, especially with orchestras and choruses of the RAI. In 1994 the society I Concerti del Quartetto, in collaboration with the Commune of Milan, initiated a ten-year project to perform all the cantatas, together with other large-scale Bach works.

The two most substantial Italian contributions to the Bach literature have also been made in the late 20th century: Alberto Basso's two-volume *Frau Musika: la vita e le opere di J. S. Bach* (Turin, 1979–83) and the more polemical *Bach* (Milan, 1985) by Piero Buscaroli.                                                                          AB

K. G. Fellerer, 'Bachs Johannes-Passion in der lateinischen Fassung Fortunato Santinis', in W. Vetter, ed., *Festschrift Max Schneider zum achtzigsten Geburtstag* (Leipzig, 1955), 139–45; V. Frajese, *Dal Costanzi all'Opera: cronache, recensioni e documenti* (Rome, 1977), ii. 182–8 [calendar of the concerts given by the Società G. S. Bach]; L. F. Tagliavini, 'Johann Sebastian Bachs Musik in Italien im 18. und 19. Jahrhundert', in W. Rehm, ed., *Bachiana et alia musicologica: Festschrift Alfred Dürr zum 65. Geburtstag* (Kassel, 1983), 310–24; I. Valetta, 'L'organo della Società G. S. Bach a Roma: l'esecuzione sull'organo a quattro mani', *Gazzetta musicale di Milano*, 52 (1895), supplement.

**6. Japan.** During Bach's lifetime, and for more than 100 years after his death, Japan's isolationism meant that his works had no influence on the country's musical culture. After the Meiji Restoration (1868), the Japanese government encouraged a rapid Westernization, and European music was introduced into the Japanese educational system. The Music Study Committee, founded in 1879 and renamed the Tokyo Music School in 1888, was the centre for musical Westernization, and at the same time for Bach reception until about 1930. As early as 1890 students from this institution performed 'Crucifixus etiam pro nobis' from the Mass in B minor with 'unexpected success'. The earliest Bach recital, which included the Chaconne from the Partita no. 3 for unaccompanied violin, was given by Nobu Koda (1870–1946) on 29 January 1896 at the Tokyo Music School, and the first pipe organ was inaugurated in the Nanki Concert Hall, Tokyo, on 22 November 1920, when Akira Tanaka gave a recital which included a Bach prelude in D minor. Meanwhile the Concerto for three harpsichords in C major, played by Paul Schulz, Miyaji Takaori, and Ryutaro Hirota, had been included in a concert at the Tokyo Music School on 28 May 1916, and the Third Brandenburg Concerto was performed there for the first time on 12 July 1920, in a programme conducted by Gustav Krone which included also the cantata *Bleib bei uns, denn es will Abend werden*. The Japanese première of the Fifth Brandenburg Concerto, by the New Symphony Orchestra conducted by Hidemaro Konoe, followed on 18 December 1927.

In the 1930s the Bach movement in Japan began in earnest. Eizaburo Kioka played many of the organ works on a pipe organ in the Mitsukoshi department store in Tokyo. The B minor Mass was performed by the chorus and orchestra of the Kunitachi Tokyo Conservatory (now the Kunitachi College of Music), conducted by Keikichi Yatabe, on 18 March 1931, and on 15 July 1935 the Tokyo Music School celebrated the 250th anniversary of Bach's birth with a programme which included the Second Brandenburg Concerto, the cantata *Lobet Gott in allen Landen*, the Harpsichord Concerto in D minor, the Prelude and Fugue in E♭ major arranged for orchestra by Schoenberg, and the *Magnificat*. The conductor was Klaus Pringsheim, who also directed the first performances of the *St Matthew Passion* on 19 July 1937, and of the *St John Passion* on 25 May 1943.

After World War II Japanese musical life developed rapidly. Noboru Toyomasu played the complete keyboard works in a series of recitals in 1950, and Takahiro Sonoda recorded some of the important ones. Historical harpsichords are made today by Japanese builders, including Eizo Hori, and players of international repute include Michio Kobayashi, Motoko Nabeshima, Nobuo Watanabe, Mayako Sone, and Shinichiro Nakano. There are now more than 500 pipe organs in Japan, played by excellent organists such as Goki Taketo, Tsuguo Hirono, Masaaki Suzuki, and Yuko Hayashi. The unaccompanied string works have been recorded by the violinists Teiko Maehashi and Yuko Shiokawa, the cellist Tsuyoshi Tsutsumi, and the Baroque cellist Hidemi Suzuki, among others. The flautist Masahiro Arita conducts his Tokyo Bach–Mozart orchestra playing on period instruments. The vocal works are frequently performed. According to the journal *Church and Music*, there are 33 Japanese choral groups that specialize in Bach's works and 31 others that sing them very often; these include the Tokyo Bach Chorus (conductor Emiko Omura), the Bach Collegium Japan (Masaaki Suzuki), the Kyoto Bach Solisten (Yoshihiro Hukunaga), and the Nissho Academy Chorus (Ryuichi Higuchi).

Japanese musicology began to include research on Bach at an early stage; the periodical *Ongaku Zasshi* in 1890 printed a short biography of Bach by an anonymous author. The many critical biographies by Japanese authors include those of Shoichi Tsuji (1955, rev. 1982), Ichiro Sumikura (1963), Ryuichi Higuchi (1985), Tadashi Isoyama (1985), and Yukio Miyake (1992). Yoshitake Kobayashi has made contributions of supreme importance to the study of Bach manuscript sources, and both he and Higuchi participate in the international project of the *NBA* as editors. Important sources in Japanese libraries include the autographs of the chorale *Aus der Tiefen rufe ich* BWV246/40*a*, the Prelude, Fugue, and Allegro in E♭ major for lute or harpsichord, and the Lute Suite in E major, as well as an exemplar of the original edition of the Canonic Variations for organ. In 1985 an exhibition to mark the 300th anniversary of Bach's birth (supervised by Werner Felix and Higuchi) was held in Tokyo, and a 15-volume anthology of writings on Bach together with recordings of his complete works on 158 CDs is scheduled for completion by Shogakukan in 1999.          RH

R. Higuchi, 'Bach, Berg, Vienna and Tokyo: an Aspect of Japanese Reception of Western Music', in *Austria 996–1996: Music in a Changing Society* (Vienna, forthcoming).

### 7. The Low Countries.

*(i) Belgium.* The earliest Belgian mention of Bach in the 19th century occurs in an 1804 catalogue of the Brussels music dealer Weissenbruch, which includes the 'Art de la fugue' and other works of 'Bach'. The writer F.-J. Fétis (1784–1871) considered the composer to be the absolute authority in the domain of organ music and fugue. He cited Bach in numerous writings and devoted several bio-bibliographical articles to him, one of which is the important entry in the *Biographie universelle* (1835–44). Fétis included seven Bach chorales in his *Science de l'organiste*, an anthology which remained unpublished, though the proofs of it survive. As director of the Brussels Conservatory, Fétis engaged the German Christian Girschner to be professor of organ and in 1849 replaced him with J. N. Lemmens (1823–81), whom he had earlier sent to Breslau to complete his studies with Adolf Hesse (1809–63), a pupil of J. N. Forkel.

Thanks to Lemmens and others at the Brussels Conservatory, Bach's music found a place in the programmes undertaken by students on various instruments. Lemmens played Bach's music in concerts and established throughout Belgium and France a particular manner of playing his organ works: he adopted slow tempos and a generally legato style known as the 'style lié'. So that he could have at his disposal an adequate instrument, he furnished advice to the famous organ builder Cavaillé-Coll (1811–99). Lemmens took Bach's work as an example to regenerate the music of the Catholic church, and this led him to create the École de Musique Religieuse at Mechelen in 1879.

In 1869 the pianist Louis Brassin (1840–84) included the Italian Concerto in one of his recitals, and other pianists performed Bach's music during the second half of the 19th century. The vocal music was made known at the Concerts du Conservatoire de Bruxelles, directed from 1871 by F.-A. Gevaert (1828–1908), where Cantata 106 (the *Actus tragicus*) and excerpts from the *St Matthew Passion* were performed. After the installation of a Cavaillé-Coll organ in the concert hall, the programmes regularly included both vocal and instrumental works by Bach (the vocal works in French versions). In 1897 Gevaert published an edition of the *St Matthew Passion*, with some amendments to the score and with a French translation which conformed to the Bible.

In 1908 the violinist A. Zimmer founded in Brussels a Société Bach with the aim of performing only Bach's works, both vocal and instrumental. This initiative, supported by the aristocracy and upper-middle classes and subsidized by the state, resulted in the first performances in Belgium of about 15 cantatas, the *St John Passion* (in 1910), and some of the instrumental sonatas and harpsichord concertos (performed mostly on the piano). While the Concerts Spirituels at Brussels (1920–35) allotted a relatively modest place to Bach's music, present-day concert societies and those responsible for music festivals are always ready to include his works in their programmes, the more so since several Belgian artists—among them the Kuijken brothers, Philippe Herreweghe, and René Jacobs—have won international renown in the Baroque repertory.

*(ii) The Netherlands.* Towards the end of the 1830s several organists in the Netherlands, some of whom had been trained in Germany, occupied important posts in various towns where they were also active as teachers. The concerts they promoted centred on music in the strict style; in this they were influenced by the physician and amateur musician Florentius Cornelis Kist (1796–1863), who founded the journal *Caecilia* in 1844. In 1837 Kist put on a historical concert in The Hague which included extracts from the *St John Passion*.

From about 1845 Bach's organ music was regularly played by J. A. van Eijken, who in 1854–6 published at Rotterdam some pieces from *The Well-tempered Clavier* transcribed for organ, and by Johannes Gijsbertus Bastiaans (1812–75). Bastiaans was the first organist to dedicate a whole recital to Bach's music, and he also adapted the Goldberg Variations for his instrument. Extracts from vocal works also began to appear in programmes: in 1868 at Rotterdam items from the *St John* and *St Matthew Passions* were interspersed with organ pieces. Programmes of Bach's organ music were frequently given by Marius Adrianus Brandts Buys (1840–1911), Samuel de Lange (1811–84) and his son of the same name (1840–1911), J. B. Litzau, and Willem Nicolaï (1829–96), and after 1870 such recitals became commonplace.

From about 1840 Bach's keyboard works furnished pieces for piano competitions and figured also in recitals. In 1847 the Concerto for three harpsichords BWV1063 was performed at Groningen and the third Orchestral Suite was heard the following year at Amsterdam. Performances of the violin music, with or without piano accompaniment, are known from 1856. The chamber music was often introduced to audiences by foreign instrumentalists on tour.

Performances of Bach's vocal works were undertaken mainly by the Maatschappij ter Bevordering der Toonkunst, and particularly by the society's secretary Jan Pieter Heije (1809–76). The Rotterdam section of the society performed Cantata 144 in their 1843–4 season and in 1860 planned to give the *St Matthew Passion*, but this project was put off until 1870, when their *Kapellmeister* Woldemar Bargiel (1828–97) conducted a performance with some cuts and some reorchestration. In 1872 the composer and conductor Johannes Verhulst (1816–91) performed Cantata 106 (the *Actus tragicus*) with the Amsterdam section of the society. The first complete performance of the *St Matthew Passion* in the Netherlands did not take place until 1926, at Rotterdam. By then the *St John Passion*, the *Christmas Oratorio*, and the B minor Mass had all received performances, in Rotterdam (1876), Utrecht (1880), and Amsterdam (1891) respectively.

In 1850 Bastiaans and van Eijken had founded a Bach Society which had only a short life. The idea was taken up again in 1868 by Samuel de Lange, and this time it met with more success, resulting in concerts given in Haarlem and Rotterdam. The Nederlandse Bach-Vereniging was founded in 1912 by the organist J. Schoonderbeek. The Low Countries are rich in historic organs which are today regularly used for recordings of Bach's music, and Gustav Leonhardt and Ton Koopman especially are internationally renowned for their interpretations of both the instrumental and the vocal music.                                                                                          HV

J. ten Bokum, *Johannes Gijsbertus Bastiaans (1812–1875)* (Utrecht, 1971); W. Corten, 'Le Procès de canonisation de Sébastien Bach en France au 19e siècle' (thesis, Université Libre de Bruxelles, 1978); J. Ferrard, 'La *Science de l'organiste* de Fétis: première anthologie moderne de musique d'orgue', *Revue belge de musicologie*, 50 (1996), 217–48; F. C. Kist, 'Het onthaal van Johann Sebastian Bach's werken in Nederland', *Caecilia*, 7 (1850), 181–3; F. Peeters and M. A. Vente, *The Organ and its Music in the Netherlands, 1500–1800* (Antwerp, 1971); J. D. C. Van Dokum, *Honderd jaar muziekleven in Nederland: een geschiedenis van de Maatschappij ter Bevordering der Toonkunst* (Amsterdam, 1929); H. Vanhulst, 'Le Conservatoire Royal de Musique de Bruxelles: origine et directorat de François-Joseph Fétis', in A. Bongrain and Y. Gérard, eds., *Le Conservatoire de Paris, 1795–1995: des Menus-Plaisirs à la Cité de la musique* (Paris, 1996), 201–17.

**8. Poland.** The first occasion in Poland to be graced by the music of J. S. Bach was the coronation of Augustus III, held in Kraków in January 1734. To mark this event the Leipzig Kantor prepared a secular cantata, *Blast Lärmen, ihr Feinde!* However, all the indications suggest that the first performance of this work did not take place until a month later, when the coronation was celebrated in Dresden.

Bach's music had to wait well over a century before it began to acquire a permanent place in the Polish musical firmament. Although in the early decades of the 19th century Bach was not a performed composer or a widely known one, there were, among those who had received a good musical education, some who knew and valued the chief cycles of keyboard works. These admirers included both of Chopin's music masters, Wojciech Żywny and Józef Elsner, thanks to whom the young genius remained profoundly sensitive to the appeal of *The Well-tempered Clavier*. Chopin gave numerous testimonies of his personal attention to Bach, and in his own music he left palpable traces of the inspiration he drew from the German master, for example in some of the technical details and in the systematics of the Preludes, op. 28, or in the extremely Bachian Fugue in A minor (op. posth.).

In the musical life of Poland, a country carved up between three partitioning powers, Bach's works began to appear only in the 1840s. At first their scope was limited to the organ compositions, performed mainly in the Lutheran church at Warsaw by its organist of long standing, August Freyer (1803–83). Educated at Leipzig, this distinguished virtuoso and composer brought up several generations of Polish organists, passing on his own fascination for Bach to his students. It took somewhat longer for Bach's music to reach Polish concert halls. Throughout the 1850s, 1860s, and 1870s Polish music-lovers could occasionally hear some of his works for keyboard or violin, mainly at guest performances by virtuosos from abroad. The Warsaw performance in 1859 of one of the two concertos for three harpsichords and orchestra (played, of course, on pianos) was no doubt a singular event.

The inclusion of the cantata *Weinen, Klagen, Sorgen, Zagen* in the programme of one of the Bach music concerts given at Lwów in 1876 suggests that interest in his art was significantly broadening in scope. This was perhaps the first Polish performance of a Bach church cantata. The 1880s were marked by events such as a performance of the *St Matthew Passion* by the Towarzystwo Muzyczne w Warszawie (Warsaw Music Society); this was probably the first such performance in Poland, and was acclaimed by the musical press as 'an event of exceptional importance'. The chronicles of Polish concert life in the first decade of the 20th century mention several performances of this work in Warsaw and Lwów. In 1892 the Music Society of Kraków gave in that city a performance billed as the Mass in B minor (consisting perhaps of excerpts, or of the Kyrie and Gloria only). Shortly before World War I the Polish harpsichordist Wanda LANDOWSKA embarked on her international career, reviving interest in an instrument which had been forgotten in the 19th century. Landowska was the first modern performer to play Bach on the harpsichord in public, heralding a series of great changes in the interpretation of his keyboard works.

During the inter-war period, in a now restored Polish State, concert life acquired the attributes of modernity, chiefly through the energetic efforts of the Polish philharmonic institutions, the conservatories, and the leading music societies. The major centres for the dissemination and promotion of Bach were Warsaw and Lwów. The *St John Passion* had entered the concert repertory by 1929 at the latest; and in 1930 there was a performance of the *Christmas Oratorio* in Lwów (its Polish première, as a reviewer stated, though it probably consisted of a selection from the full six-part work, or of some of the cantatas only). The *Magnificat* (probably the D major version) also made its appearance in concert programmes. Now and again orchestras presented some of the orchestral suites and Brandenburg Concertos, which were hardly ever performed by Polish musicians before 1920. In the 1920s and 1930s Polish pianists, like their counterparts throughout Europe, often performed Bach in arrangements by Ferruccio BUSONI.

During the second half of the 20th century Bach's work in most genres became standard in Polish concerts and recordings, though performances of the cantatas remained quite rare. Polish performers of Bach in the post-war period included a handful of first-rate organists, such as Feliks Rączkowski, Jan Jargoń, Joachim Grubich, Józef Serafin, Julian Gębalski and Andrzej Białko; the contralto Jadwiga Rappé became one of the most admired interpreters of Bach in Europe; and several Polish harpsichordists, such as Elżbieta Stefańska, Bogumiła Gizbert-Studnicka and Władysław Kłosiewicz, won worldwide acclaim for their Bach playing. Polish interest in performing on period instruments has, however, been slow to gather pace, and the more conservative traditions in Bach interpretation seem to have exerted a stronger influence on musical education, as exemplified in the study sessions held in the 1980s–90s by the Academy of Music in Kraków in collaboration with the Internationale Bachakademie Stuttgart, under the leadership of Helmut Rilling.

Music studies in Poland have not yet produced a major research specialist on the work of Bach. The only Polish academic book devoted to the composer has been *Bach: muzyka i wielkość* ('Bach: Music and Greatness') (Kraków, 1972), in which the author, Bohdan Pociej, examines Bach's style from an aesthetic and philosophical viewpoint. Pociej's *Bach* (Kraków, 1973) is addressed to a wider readership. The entry on Bach by Elżbieta Dziębowska in the *Encyklopedia muzyczna PWM: Część biograficzna* (Kraków, 1979) is marked by a high level of scholarly achievement. The outstanding Polish novelist and poet Jarosław Iwaszkiewicz has portrayed the composer in a biography, *Jan Sebastian Bach* (Warsaw, 1951), which reveals the author's love and knowledge of Bach's music.

The Biblioteka Jagiellońska in Kraków now houses a number of important Bach autographs which were formerly in what is now the Staatsbibliothek zu Berlin, including the scores of Cantatas 99 (not listed in *Schmieder2*), 111, 120, 121, and 123.

PR-S

**9. Portugal.** The first Portuguese allusion to Bach's work comes, in an indirect way, in João Domingos Bomtempo's *Elementos de música e método do tocar piano-forte* (London, 1819), which includes 24 preludes in all the keys. In the second part of his incomplete and unpublished *Traité de composition musicale* he included examples from *The Well-tempered Clavier* and *The Art of Fugue.*

One must wait until the mid-1870s for the first public manifestations of a Bach movement in the Portuguese concert world. The periodical *A arte musical* (no. 26, 1874) mentions a concert given by the Sociedade de Concertos Clássicos which included works by Mendelssohn, Beethoven, and Steibel, and the 'Souvenir de jeunesse' of (? J. S.) Bach. Most instrumentalists of this period were trained in Germany, and the cultivation of Bach's music was largely in the hands of bourgeois musiclovers such as José Relvas, who admired performances of Bach's music in Leipzig and, in 1905, included it in some of the private concerts at his palace of Alpiarça. Instrumentalists at the Conservatório Nacional de Música in Lisbon also taught Bach to their students, and one of these teachers, the violinist Francisco Benetó, was accompanied at a recital in 1905 by António Lamas on the harpsichord, a year before Wanda Landowska was heard in the capital. Another conservatory teacher, the pianist Alexandre Rey Colaço, initiated a series of historical concerts in 1898, and usually included Bach's music in his programmes.

In 1889 the Spanish violinist Enrique Fernández Arbós (1863–1939), a pupil of the famous Joseph Joachim, introduced Bach's music to the Orpheon Portuense, an amateur society in Oporto. Its organizer, Bernardo Moreira de Sá, who was also a violinist, was personally committed to making known 'the most colossal of Beethoven's predecessors', and in March 1898 he too embarked on a series of historical violin recitals that included Bach works. From 1904 several European artists, including the Busoni–Kreisler duo, were invited to play at the Oporto concerts, always performing music by Bach. Moreira de Sá's approach to Bach derived from Schumann, but in the notes he provided for a concert on 9 November 1911 he quoted from several Bach authorities, including Spitta, Pirro, and Schweitzer.

Bach's orchestral music was sporadically featured in concerts, from 1891 at least, given by such orchestras as those of the Real Academia de Amadores de Música and the Sociedade de Professores de Música (the latter was under the artistic direction of Moreira de Sá). The choral music, however, made little headway among the few Portuguese amateur choirs. The pianist José Viana da Mota (1868–1948), who played the Italian Concerto in Oporto in 1895, was considered by Schweitzer to represent, along with Busoni, the new school of Bach interpretation. He published articles on Bach performance in the *Neue Zeitschrift für Musik* (1904) and *Der Klavierlehre* (1907).

Two notable events in the history of Bach reception in Portugal were the first performance of the *St Matthew Passion*, sung in Portuguese in the Basilica da Estrela, Lisbon, on 7 May 1934, conducted by Ivo Cruz, and the first complete performance of *The Well-tempered Clavier* at the conservatory in Oporto, performed by Maria Helena de Sá e Costa (granddaughter of Moreira de Sá), with analytical commentaries by the composer Cláudio Carneiro (1895–1963). The bicentenary of Bach's death was marked by a concert on 6 May 1950 at the Teatro Tivoli, Lisbon, conducted by Fernando Lopes-Graça, which included two cantatas (nos. 67 and 79).      TC

### 10. Russia and Ukraine.

*(i) Introduction.* The processes of Bach reception in Russia and Ukraine can hardly be separated: the isolated encounters with Bach's music in the 18th century, the growing interest (developed mainly by professional musicians) throughout the 19th century, and the widespread (and still increasing) appreciation by the musical public in the 20th century are equally typical of both parts of the former Russian Empire and the former USSR, which were politically and culturally united.

The sale of a manuscript copy of one volume of *The Well-tempered Clavier*, advertised in a Moscow newspaper in 1794, and a shortened Russian translation of the famous Obituary (*BDok* iii, no. 666), published in a St Petersburg literary miscellany for music-lovers in 1795, are merely formal evidence of the beginnings of Bach reception. It is very likely that Bach's name and his music were known to some people in Russia much earlier. At least three of them knew the composer personally: H. C. von Keyserlingk, the Russian ambassador in Dresden, for whom Bach composed the Goldberg Variations; Georg Erdmann, Bach's schoolmate in Ohrdruf, who became a Russian diplomat in 1714; and Jacob von Stählin, a member of the Russian Academy of Science, who in the 1730s played the flute in performances by the Leipzig collegium musicum directed by Bach.

*(ii) Performance.* The earliest performers of Bach's keyboard music in Russia included three German musicians who settled in the country: W. C. Bernhard (1760–87), who died in Moscow; J. G. W. Palschau (1741–1815), who was taught by Bach's pupil J. G. Müthel and, according to Stählin, played in the manner of Bach; and J. W. Häßler (1747–1822), who was a pupil of Bach's pupil J. C. Kittel. Their

audiences must have been limited to members of the nobility (only in their houses might one find harpsichords) and the congregations of Catholic and Protestant churches (the only places for organs). The impossibility of performing Bach's music in Orthodox churches made it difficult for the choral works to be accepted into Russian musical culture. For this reason the instrumental music acquired a certain prominence that may be considered a distinctive feature of Russian Bach reception.

After settling in Russia in 1803, John Field (1782–1837) played many of Bach's keyboard works at his concerts and taught them to his numerous Russian pupils. On 15 April 1815 he took part in a performance of the Concerto for four harpsichords (in this case, pianos) and orchestra BWV1065 at St Petersburg—the first public performance of Bach's music mentioned in the Russian press. One of his pupils, V. F. Odoevsky (1804–69), an influential figure in Russian Romantic literature, philosophy, and music, became the most important figure in the Russian Bach revival. His devotion to Bach's music, expressed in numerous critical articles and in the novel *Sebastian Bakh* (1835), with its romanticized portrait of the composer, was shared by most prominent Russian musicians of the 19th century, beginning with Glinka and Sergey Taneyev (1856–1915), the greatest admirer of Bach among the Russian composers and an outstanding counterpoint scholar. Tchaikovsky, Taneyev's teacher, was more moderate (though quite respectful) in his attitude towards Bach. The members of The Five, in their young years, were inclined to look on Bach as old-fashioned and mathematical, but later some of them became converts, especially Rimsky-Korsakov. Certain features of Bach's music made an impact even on the works of such a nationalistic composer as Musorgsky.

In the 1850s Bach's music began to appear more frequently at concerts. Anton Rubinstein (1829–94) often played Bach's works at his piano recitals, and on 19 November 1864 he conducted—for the first time in Russia—choral extracts from the *St Matthew Passion* in St Petersburg. On 25 March 1883 Heinrich Stiel (1829–86), a teacher at the St Petersburg Conservatory, introduced the complete work to Russia, conducting a choir from Reval (Tallinn) in the Swedish Church, and on 3 February 1876 parts of the Mass in B minor were given by the choir of the St Petersburg Free Musical School, with Rimsky-Korsakov as conductor.

Bach reception in Ukraine during the 19th century is connected particularly with two men: Gustav Hesse de Calvé (b. 1784), whose treatise on music theory (Kharkiv, 1818) contained many examples from Bach's works, and Mykola Lysenko (1842–1912), the most important Ukrainian composer of the time, who was an enthusiast for Bach's music.

In the first quarter of the 20th century numerous Bach concerts were organized by the conductors A. I. Ziloti (1863–1945), Serge Koussevitzky (1874–1951), and V. A. Bulychiov (1872–1959), the last named being responsible for the first complete performance of the Mass in B minor on 27 and 28 March 1911 in Moscow. The complete *St John Passion* was conducted by L. F. Gomilius in the Lutheran Church of St Peter and St Paul at St Petersburg on 9 March 1904. During these years almost every genre of Bach's music was represented in the programmes, and Bach became a real hero of the Russian musical public. Later on this process was (and still is) supported by numerous Russian and Ukrainian musicians of international repute.

(*iii*) *Other aspects.* Bach's name did not disappear from the pages of the Russian musical press after the 1830s. The critics A. N. Serov (1820–71), V. V. Stasov

(1824–1906), and G. A. Larosh (1845–1904) constantly stressed his importance in their reviews. However, the first two Russian monographs on Bach (by S. A. Bazunov and S. L. Khalyutin) did not appear until 1894 and proved to be rather superficial. The first serious Russian monograph (Moscow, 1911) was by E. K. Rozenov (1861–1935), and Bach studies eventually became an important branch of Russian musicology. The foundation was laid by the innovative ideas of B. L. Yavorsky (1877–1942), who began his researches in Ukraine (Kiev) and continued them in Russia (Moscow). Many musicologists of the Soviet period made essential contributions to various aspects of Bach scholarship: they include B. V. Asafiev (1884–1949), I. A. Braudo (1896–1970), Y. N. Tyulin (1893–1978), A. N. Dolzhansky (1908–66), and (to mention only authors of full-length monographs) A. G. Chugayev (1924–90), M. S. Druskin (1905–91), Y. S. Druskin (1902–80; author of the first book on Bach in Ukrainian), M. A. Etinger (b. 1922), G. N. Hubov (1902–81), T. N. Livanova (1909–86), Y. I. Milshteyn (1911–81), A. P. Milka (b. 1939), V. V. Protopopov (b. 1908), and K. I. Yuzhak (b. 1934).

There are four Bach autographs in Russian archives: a letter to Georg Erdmann of 28 July 1726, in the Arkhiv Vneshnej Politiki Rossii Istoriko-diplomaticheskogo Upravlenija Ministerstva Inostrannykh Del, Moscow; another of 28 October 1730, in the Tsentralnyj Gosudarstvennyj Arkhiv Drevnikh Aktov, Moscow; and two musical sketches in the Russian National Library, St Petersburg—one of 25 bars from Cantata 80, the other of seven bars from Cantata 188.

Bach's multiform influence on 20th-century Russian composers found its most valuable expressions in the neo-Baroque style developed by Igor Stravinsky in the 1920s, and in Shostakovich's 24 Preludes and Fugues (1950–1), inspired by the 200th anniversary of Bach's death. The recognition of Bach's greatness by Russian culture as a whole may be illustrated by the fact that the closeness of Bach's name to the word 'God' (in Russian conversational pronunciation, 'Bokh') became almost a commonplace in Russian modern poetry (for example that of Joseph Brodsky).

BK

L. A. Federowskaja, 'Bachiana in russischen Bibliotheken und Sammlungen: Autographe, Abschriften, Frühdrucke, Bearbeitungen', *BJb* 76 (1990), 27–35; T. N. Livanova and V. V. Protopopov, eds., *Russkaya kniga o Bakhe: Sbornik statej* (2nd edn., Moscow, 1986) [Collection of essays on Russian Bach reception including a bibliography of writings, 1795–1985]; K. Shamayeva, 'Tvorcheskoye naslediye I. S. Bakha na Ukraine v XIX–nachale XX veka', in *I. S. Bakh i sovremennost*, ed. N. A. Gerasimova-Persidskaya (Kiev, 1985), 44–54 [On Ukrainian Bach reception].

**11. Scandinavia.** The Scandinavian countries have traditionally had close political and cultural relations with Germany, of which not the least important evidence is the adoption of the Lutheran Reformation for the state Churches of Denmark (which at the time embraced Norway and Iceland) and Sweden (including Finland) in the early 16th century. Understandably, Denmark's geographical position and complicated political involvement in what is now northern Germany, notably the incorporation of the duchies of Schleswig and Holstein under the Danish crown (terminated by Bismarck in 1864), ensured that exchanges between Germany and Denmark in particular have been a matter of course. As a consequence, though the Scandinavian countries shared to an extent in the general susceptibility to Italian and French taste in the age of Enlightenment, the traditional ties with north German culture were not abandoned.

In so far as a country's musical environment can be assessed from the musical taste of its leading musicians, it would seem that Bach has never been entirely out of favour in Scandinavia. Georg von Bertouch and J. A. Scheibe, both of whom spent many years in the service of the King of Denmark, represent a more or less direct line of connection between Bach and Scandinavia during his lifetime. Bertouch was military governor in Norway from 1719, but he continued to compose and maintained contact with German musical life through correspondence with both Johann Mattheson and Bach (*Spitta*, iii. 235–6); as for Scheibe, who came to Denmark in 1740, his exaggerated notoriety as a critic should not obscure the admiration he also expressed for the Leipzig master on several occasions.

After Bach's death the influence of his pupil and advocate J. P. Kirnberger was strongly felt in Scandinavia. The Norwegian I. G. Wernicke (1755–1838), who came to Denmark in the 1770s and astonished the court by playing 'the most difficult pieces of Sebastian Bach', went to Berlin to study with Kirnberger. Wernicke in turn taught Ole Andreas Lindeman (1769–1857), from whom the Bach tradition passed to his son Ludvig Mathias (1812–87), the most important Norwegian church musician of the 19th century. Kirnberger was also the teacher of J. A. P. Schulz (1747–1800), who became court conductor in Copenhagen in 1787. There he was friendly with F. L. A. Kunzen (1761–1817), who succeeded him in 1795, and the teacher of C. E. F. Weyse (1774–1842), both of whom attested to Schulz's enthusiasm for Bach's music, which they shared. Weyse's pupil Hans Matthison-Hansen (1807–90), organist at Roskilde Cathedral, is credited with introducing Bach's organ works to Denmark. He was ably assisted by his son Gottfred (1832–1909), who taught his friend Edvard Grieg to play Bach on the organ in 1866. Weyse enjoyed a position of authority in Danish musical life in the first half of the 19th century and his veneration of Bach is reflected in the Bach performances of J. P. E. Hartmann (1805–1900), who was his successor as organist of Copenhagen Cathedral, as well as in the contrapuntal studies of the composer J. F. Frøhlich (1806–60), whose manuscript copy of Bach's *The Well-tempered Clavier*, made in 1825, survives among the papers of his friend Hartmann.

At about the time that Schulz went to Copenhagen, a musician representing a rather different tradition went to the Swedish court in Stockholm. This was the *abbé* Georg Joseph Vogler (1749–1814), remembered today (like Scheibe) as, among other things, a presumptuous critic of the great Bach. He travelled extensively in Scandinavia as an organ recitalist and also enjoyed a reputation as a learned theorist, though he was a controversial figure in both capacities. On leaving Stockholm in 1798 he settled for a time in Copenhagen and it was there that his *Choral-System*, in which he criticized and 'improved' Bach's chorale harmonizations, was printed in 1800. In Stockholm his conception of music—and lack of appreciation of Bach—was opposed by J. C. Haeffner (1759–1833), who had inherited both the Bach tradition and a disapproval of Vogler's ideas from his teacher J. G. Vierling. In 1801 Haeffner succeeded in getting the Musical Academy in Stockholm to take subscriptions for the publication of Bach's instrumental works, which began with *The Well-tempered Clavier* in 1804. In 1806 he included three works by Bach in a concert programme—probably the first time that music by Bach was played at a public concert in Sweden.

It is interesting to note that, although Haeffner's programme included two choruses from Handel's *Messiah* and C. P. E. Bach's *Heilig*, J. S. Bach was represented only by instrumental pieces: an 'Ouverture', a 'Fuga', and a 'Sinfonie with oblig. violin and violoncello' (Johnsson *et al.*, *Musiken i Sverige*, ii. 439). As Spitta observed (iii. 234), Bach's reputation was first of all that of an incomparable organist; when he became known as a composer it was principally for his instrumental works, the vocal works being only seldom encountered. A striking, though perhaps not entirely representative, demonstration of the delay in appreciation of Bach's vocal music in Sweden is provided by the response provoked by an article about Mozart (in *The Century*, Nov. 1897) in which Grieg had ranked Bach, Beethoven, and Wagner among the greatest of all composers. To this Gustav Wennerberg (1817–1901), a composer and influential cultural personality, replied in a personal letter to Grieg: 'Let me hear Bach on the organ, the "klavier" or the violin, Beethoven with the piano, the string quartet or the symphony, Wagner in the orchestra; but let me hear Handel, Gluck, and Mozart in oratorio and opera!' (Johnsson *et al.*, *Musiken i Sverige*, iii. 48).

Nevertheless, a number of Bach's vocal works are in Weyse's important music library, now in the Royal Library, Copenhagen, which incorporated material inherited from Schulz and from contacts close to C. P. E. Bach in Hamburg (see Hahne, pp. 11–16, for a survey of the Bach works contained in this and two other 19th-century Danish collections). Here can be seen a copy of the final chorus of the *St Matthew Passion* which bears the inscription 'Copenhagen, 19 January 1788', though it is not known if this refers to a performance directed by Schulz.

The first complete performances of the *St Matthew Passion* were not heard in Scandinavia until many years later, however; appropriately, the first was conducted by Mendelssohn's friend and protégé from Leipzig, Niels W. Gade (1817–90), in Copenhagen in 1875. It was given for the first time in Norway at Bergen in 1884, for the first time in Sweden at Stockholm in 1890. Other large choral works followed soon after: Frederik Rung conducted the Cecilia Society in the Mass in B minor in Copenhagen in 1892 and the *St John Passion* in 1893, which latter work was heard in Christiania the following year. Nevertheless, the music of Bach still seemed to N. O. Raasted (1888–1966), a pupil of Karl Straube and Max Reger, to be insufficiently appreciated when he became organist of Copenhagen Cathedral in 1925. He accordingly founded a Bach Society in that year which organized many important performances before being dissolved in 1945, when it was felt that its particular function was no longer required. JB

N. Grinde, *A History of Norwegian Music*, Eng. trans. W. H. Halvorson and L. B. Sateren (Lincoln, Nebr., 1991); G. Hahne, *Die Bachtradition in Schleswig-Holstein und Dänemark* (Kassel, 1954); L. Johnsson *et al.*, eds., *Musiken i Sverige* (Stockholm, 1992–4), ii–iii.

**12. Spain.** No specialized study of Bach reception in Spain has so far been made, and only a preliminary approach to the subject can be offered here, outlining the conditions that made possible the dissemination of Bach's music from the 19th century to the mid-20th. The public reception of Bach's music in Spain is essentially related, from the 1880s, to two important features of Spanish musical culture of the second half of the 19th century: Wagnerism and the choral movement, which ensured a secular reception of Bach's music as part of the Austro-German musical canon. But already, from the mid-19th century, Bach was a familiar name to Spanish pianists, who appreciated the value of his keyboard works for developing an accomplished polyphonic performing style. On the other hand, the diffusion of the great organ works was hindered by the technical limitations of the traditional Iberian organ and had to await the introduction of modern instruments equipped with pedal-boards during the second half of the 19th century. Even so, some works were known through piano transcriptions, as is shown by two interesting Spanish editions of the 'Great' G minor Fantasia and Fugue and the Prelude and Fugue in A minor BWV543 arranged by Fernando Aranda and published in Madrid in 1877.

The historical dimension of the composer was already well known to Spanish music historians, mainly through the circulation of modern historical reference works such as the *Biographie universelle* (1835–44) by the Belgian scholar F.-J. Fétis. Felipe Pedrell's characterization of the Spanish Renaissance organist Antonio de Cabezon (1510–66) as 'el Bach español' at the end of the 19th century is perfectly representative of this historiographical trend. Earlier references to 'Bach' in Spanish 18th-century historiography refer, of course, to Johann Christian Bach, as might be expected from the substantial Italian influence on Spanish musical culture of the time.

Bach reception in Spain received an important stimulus in Catalonia from the lectures and organ recitals given in 1908 by Albert Schweitzer in Barcelona. This visit started a fruitful collaboration with the Orfeó Catalá, a choral society founded in 1891 by Luis Millet and Amadeu Vives. Years later, in 1911, a complete performance of the B minor Mass was given by the same choir and the Orquesta Simfonica de Barcelona. In the same year Millet was present at the Three Choirs Festival in Worcester, England, where several oratorios, including Bach's *St Matthew Passion*, were performed. A performance of this work, adapted and translated into Catalan by Francesc Pujol and Vincenc de Gibert and, with Schweitzer at the organ, took place on 27 February 1921 at the Palau de la Música Catalana, a concert hall erected by the Orfeó in 1908 with a façade which exhibited a bust of Bach in between Palestrina, Wagner, and Beethoven—a clear sign of the Wagnerian atmosphere in which the reception of Bach was taking place. The Orfeó contributed also to the dissemination of Bach's vocal repertory in other Spanish cities, including Madrid and Zaragoza, where parts of the B minor Mass were performed in 1912. In the Basque country performances by the Orfeon Donostiarra and the Sociedad Coral de Bilbao in the first decade of the 20th century included also works such as the *Christmas Oratorio.*

Spanish guitarists such as Francisco Tarrega (1852–1909) and, especially, Andres Segovia (1893–1987) played and published transcriptions of Bach's works for solo violin from the beginning of the 20th century, increasing the composer's popularity in Spain. Undoubtedly the greatest Spanish contribution to the Bach renaissance of the 20th century was made by the Catalan cellist Pablo Casals (1876–1973). His legendary recordings of the solo Cello Suites in London and Paris during the Spanish Civil War (1936–9) recovered these works for the modern concert hall, setting the seal on a long involvement with them which started in 1890 in Barcelona. Commemorating the bicentenary of Bach's death, the great Spanish writer and critic Adolfo Salazar (1890–1958) published in 1950 the first complete Spanish translation of J. N. Forkel's Bach biography, and the following year two books of his own on Bach.     JJC

**13. United States of America.** Many pioneers in the Bach movement in America were either German-born or studied in Germany. Charles Theodore Pachelbel (1690–1750), son of the famous Johann Pachelbel, emigrated to America in the 1730s. As Bach's elder brother Johann Christoph was a pupil of the elder Pachelbel, and as

J. S. Bach had established a considerable reputation by the 1730s, it seems likely that the younger Pachelbel at least knew of the Leipzig Bach. Similarly, Henry Melchior Muhlenberg, 'the father of American Lutheranism', probably knew about Bach, since he was ordained in Leipzig in 1739. But it is an open question whether either the younger Pachelbel or Muhlenberg knew much of Bach's music.

(i) *Performance.* Towards the end of the 18th century there was an interest in England in Bach's keyboard works that had some influence in America. Muzio Clementi included the Polonaise from the Sixth French Suite in his *Introduction to the Art of Playing on the Piano Forte* (London, 1801), and this was reprinted in the *Rudiments of the Art of Playing on the Piano Forte* (Boston, 1806) edited by Gottlieb Graupner (1767–1836), who had emigrated from Hanover to America, via London, in the 1790s. This is the earliest known publication of any music by Bach in North America.

The publication of the *BG* volumes from 1851 proved influential in promoting Bach's music in America. In the 1850s public performances were sparse, but each decade saw significant increases. Kroeger (p. 36) concludes that 'during 1875 there were more than twice the number of performances of Bach's works than occurred during the entire decade of the 1850s and almost as many in that single year as during the whole of the 1860s'.

Performances of Bach's organ works post-date the appointment of the Englishman Edward Hodges (1796–1867) as organist of Trinity Church, New York, in 1839. But it was the American John Knowles Paine (1839–1906), who had studied in Berlin between 1858 and 1861 and come into contact with the Bach revival in progress there, who did most to make Bach's organ works known in the recitals he gave in the 1860s and 1870s. Other keyboard works were championed by the German-born Otto Dresel, who gave the first performances of keyboard concertos and recitals of other keyboard music in Boston between 1853 and the mid-1860s, and William Mason (1829–1908), son of the composer and conductor Lowell Mason, who similarly included Bach's music in his recitals and concerts from the 1870s.

The German-born conductor Theodore Thomas (1835–1905) gave many first American performances of Bach's orchestral works in New York, Boston, Philadelphia, Cincinnati, and Chicago between 1865 and 1887, including an orchestral suite (1867), the Third Brandenburg Concerto (1874), and the Concerto for two violins (1875), as well as transcriptions of organ works. But Thomas also conducted the American premières of some choral works, including the motet *Ich lasse dich nicht* (1869), the *Magnificat* (1875), Cantata 80 (1880), Cantata 11 (1882), and 11 movements from the B minor Mass (1886). He also conducted the *St Matthew Passion* in 1882, three years after its American première by the Haydn and Handel Society of Boston in 1879.

The most influential conductor of Bach's choral works at the turn of the century was Fred Wolle, who had studied with Rheinberger in Munich. Wolle conducted the first American performance of the *St John Passion* in 1888 by the Bethlehem Choral Union, and the *St Matthew Passion* in 1892. After the demise of the Choral Union, Wolle conducted parts of the *Christmas Oratorio* with his Moravian Church Choir in Bethlehem in 1894. Four years later he founded the Bach Choir of Bethlehem and in March 1900 gave the first complete American performance of the B minor Mass, a performance which eventually gave rise to the annual BETHLEHEM BACH FESTIVAL.

Other Bach groups, societies, and festivals have been founded during the 20th century, among them the Chicago Bach Chorus (1925), the Bach Choir of Pittsburgh (1934), the CARMEL BACH FESTIVAL (1935), the Bach Aria Group (1946, founded by William H. Scheide, a leader in the post-war American interest in Bach), and the OREGON BACH FESTIVAL (1970), as well as the more recent early music festivals of Boston and Berkeley that regularly focus on the music of Bach.

*(ii) Scholarship.* Editions of Bach became increasingly numerous following A. N. Johnson's inclusion of 16 four-part chorales in his *Instructions in Thorough Base* (Boston, 1844). Oliver Ditson of Boston published important editions of Bach, including *The Well-tempered Clavier* (1850), an edition of chorale settings (1856), and the *St Matthew Passion* (1869). The Griepenkerl-Roitzsch edition of the organ works was published by Peters in New York (1852), and in the latter part of the century vocal scores of cantatas and larger choral works in the Novello 'Octavo Editions' were available in New York, as were the German vocal scores published by Breitkopf & Härtel.

Studies of Bach's life and works published in America really begin with the first volume (1851) of the influential periodical *Dwight's Journal of Music*, which included a short article. Over the next 30 years—the active life of the journal—there was hardly a volume that did not contain reviews of Bach performances or publications, or such substantial articles as the serialization of J. N. Forkel's biography in English. Much 20th-century American Bach scholarship has flowed from the work of Arthur Mendel of Princeton University. His documentary biography, *The Bach Reader* (1945; 2nd edn. 1966), with Hans T. David, his practical and critical editions of the *St John Passion* (1951 and 1974), and his work on the editorial board of the *NBA* contributed in large measure to the vigorous nature of contemporary American Bach studies and performances.

Many of Mendel's students, such as Robert L. Marshall, have become influential musicologists who have guided another generation of students in Bach studies, many of whom are contributors to the present *Companion*. Most of them, together with such German-born scholars as Gerhard Herz, Alfred Mann, and Christoph Wolff, are active in the AMERICAN BACH SOCIETY, originally a chapter of the Neue Bach-Gesellschaft, but since 1988 an independent body.                    RAL

J. B. Clark, 'The Beginnings of Bach in America,' in J. R. Heintze, ed., *American Musical Life in Context and Practice to 1865* (New York, 1994), 337–51; G. Herz, *Bach-Quellen in Amerika/ Bach Sources in America* (Kassel, 1984); K. Kroeger, 'Johann Sebastian Bach in Nineteenth-Century America', *Bach*, 22/1 (Spring–Summer 1991), 33–42; R. A. Leaver, 'New Light on the Pre-History of the Bach Choir of Bethlehem', *Bach*, 22/2 (Fall–Winter, 1991), 24–34; A. Mann, 'Zum mährischen Bachpflege in Amerika', in W. Rehm, ed., *Bachiana et alia musicologica: Festschrift Alfred Dürr zum 65. Geburtstag* (Kassel, 1983), 178–82; R. Walters, *The Bethlehem Bach Choir: A History and a Critical Compendium* (Boston, 1923).

moments of high drama (e.g. the earthquake scenes in the *St John* and *St Matthew Passions*).

The other main category is *recitativo accompagnato*, for which the terms *recitativo stromentato* and *recitativo obbligato* are also used; in the present volume it is referred to as 'accompanied recitative'. This type, in which instruments are used in addition to the continuo, is more emotional and lyrical, and is often employed at points of special dramatic intensity. In the most frequent instrumentation for accompanied recitative, the strings (violins 1 and 2 and viola) join the continuo, but many other combinations occur as well. Bach especially favoured a pair, or trio, of woodwind instruments (recorders, transverse flutes, oboes, oboes d'amore, or oboes da caccia), either alone or in conjunction with the strings. In addition, several movements feature less common groupings of woodwinds, such as pairs of recorders and oboes da caccia (BWV119:4), transverse flutes and oboes d'amore (BWV195:4), or oboes d'amore and oboes da caccia (BWV183:3 and two of the bass recitatives in Part 2 of the *Christmas Oratorio*).

The cantatas composed in Weimar (1714–16) are especially rich in accompanied recitatives (see Buelow). But two of the most impressive movements are found in works dating from Bach's Leipzig years. The alto recitative 'Der Glocken bebendes Getön' from the *Trauer-Ode*, first performed at the memorial service for the Electress Christiane Eberhardine on 17 October 1727, calls for an unusually large ensemble (pairs of flutes, oboes, violas da gamba, and lutes, in addition to the usual strings and continuo) in its brief but graphic portrayal of funeral bells; especially effective is the gradual entrance and departure of the instruments, one at a time, at the beginning and end. Of even grander proportions is the last recitative in the cantata *Preise dein Glücke* (no. 215), a lengthy movement for soprano, tenor, and bass, plus three trumpets and timpani, pairs of flutes and oboes, strings, and continuo, which alludes to recent military victories on the part of royalty visiting Leipzig in early October 1734. The tenor sings first, accompanied by the strings and continuo in long note values. After the bass takes over (bar 9), the dramatic impact of the bellicose imagery, 'Zu einer Zeit, da alles um uns blitzt und kracht' ('At a time when there is lightning and thunder all around us'), is heightened by trumpet fanfares and similar passage-work in the strings and continuo. The sustained accompaniment is transferred to the woodwinds when the soprano sings (bars 24–6), and the piece concludes with a vocal trio accompanied by the continuo alone.

Of particular interest in the last section of this movement is the marking 'a tempo' (bar 28) and the initiation of an active continuo line that moves predominantly in quavers. Although the term is not used here, this passage is an arioso, an intermediate vocal style between recitative and aria. (Alternatively, 'arioso' sometimes refers to free-standing solo vocal movements of more modest proportions than normal arias. Mostly these are settings of biblical quotations, especially the words of Jesus, rather than the usual poetic aria texts.) Many of Bach's recitatives end in arioso style, which is characterized by increased lyricism and metrical regularity. Arioso passages also differ from recitative in allowing for some repetition of portions of the text and occasional melismas, as opposed to the through-composed and exclusively syllabic approach to text-setting characteristic of recitative itself.

The tenor and soprano recitatives (nos. 2 and 6) in Cantata 215 deserve brief mention as well, for they typify another important category of accompanied recitatives. Known in the German Bach literature as *motivgeprägtes Accompagnato*, these movements are organized around a brief motif (five notes in each of the present cases) that permeates the upper instrumental parts. Although the continuo line consists of the usual long note values, the presence of the repeated motives necessitates a stricter rhythmic approach than in other kinds of recitative.

Correct performance of Bach's recitatives involves knowledge of several conventions not reflected in the notation. Although written in normal values, the rhythm must follow the declamation of the text rather than a strict metrical interpretation of the notes. Moreover, it is customary for the singer to add occasional appoggiaturas, especially at the final cadence. Finally, the tied semibreves and minims in the typical continuo line of simple recitative are to be played as crotchets followed by rests until the next change of harmony, in accordance with the 18th-century convention of 'short accompaniment' (see Dreyfus, ch. 3). SAC

R. Bertling, *Das Arioso und das ariose Accompagnato im Vokalwerk Johann Sebastian Bachs* (Frankfurt, 1992); G. J. Buelow, 'Expressivity in the Accompanied Recitatives of Bach's Cantatas', in D. O. Franklin, ed., *Bach Studies* (Cambridge, 1989), 18–35; L. Dreyfus, *Bach's Continuo Group: Players and Practices in his Vocal Works* (Cambridge, Mass., 1987); H. Melchert, *Das Rezitativ der Kirchenkantaten Joh. Seb. Bachs* (Frankfurt, 1958); H. Melchert, *Das Rezitativ der Bachschen Johannespassion* (Wilhelmshaven, 1988); H. Melchert, *Symmetrie—Form im Rezitativ der Bachschen Matthäuspassion* (Wilhelmshaven, 1995).

**recorder** (Blockflöte). A type of fipple flute with seven finger-holes and a thumb-hole. In Bach's day recorders appeared in chamber music for amateurs or orchestral music for professionals. These latter parts were usually performed by court musicians or *Stadtpfeifer* whose principal instrument was the oboe, as is evident, for example, from Bach's original performing parts for oboe/recorder in Cantatas 69a, 46, 81, 122, and the *Easter Oratorio*.

Bach wrote for professionals, and he used the recorder in ways that correspond to those in the vocal music of his contemporaries: for pastoral themes in Cantatas 13, 46, 175, 180, and 208; for sorrow in Cantatas 13, 46, 103, and the *St Matthew Passion*; and for death in Cantatas 81, 106, 127, 161, and the *Easter Oratorio* (and possibly Cantatas 8 and 198). Unlike his contemporaries, however,

Bach did not employ the recorder for natural sounds (birdcalls), but he did take interpretative stock of the instrument's low status within the musical hierarchy (in Cantatas 18, 39, 71, 119, 122, 182, and the *Magnificat* in E♭ major).

Certain problems continually come up in studies of Bach's recorder parts. Is the work by Bach (BWV142, 189, and 217 are not)? What is the nomenclature in Bach's sources ('flauto' by itself means 'recorder')? To which version of a work does the recorder part belong (a vexing problem for Cantata 182, and problematic also for nos. 8, 18, 69, and 161)? What clef is used (the only recorder lines not notated in French violin clef—i.e. with $g'$ on the lowest line of the staff—are in the 1724 versions of Cantatas 8 and 182)? Towards what fingering is the part orientated (the players evidently always read as if they were fingering an instrument in $f'$, whatever its actual size or tuning)? And what is the pitch standard of the overall ensemble (in Bach's pre-Weimar cantatas recorders were notated a tone higher than the rest of the ensemble, because there they were tuned to CAMMERTON, while the strings, organ, and voices were in CHORTON; in his Weimar church cantatas a minor 3rd higher, because there the recorders were in *tief-Cammerton*, while the strings, organ, and voices were in *Chorton*; in his Leipzig church cantatas the recorders, strings, and voices were notated at the same pitch—all *Cammerton*—while the organ, there in *Chorton*, was notated a tone lower).

Bach's pre-Weimar works include Cantatas 106 and 71; those composed at Weimar include (in chronological order) Cantatas 208, 182, 152, and 161; all subsequent new recorder parts in vocal works were written during Bach's first five years in Leipzig: BWV46, 69*a*, 25, 119, 243*a* (*Magnificat* in E♭), 65, 81, 18, 182 (new version), 96, 180, 122, 127, 249 (*Easter Oratorio*), 103, 175, 13, 39, and the *St Matthew Passion*. The Second and Fourth Brandenburg Concertos were probably composed at Cöthen, and Bach arranged the Concerto in F major, BWV1057, from the Fourth Brandenburg Concerto at Leipzig. Lost versions of Cantatas 195 and 198 may have had recorder parts.

Most works are scored for a pair of $f'$ instruments. Single $f'$ instruments are found in Cantatas 69*a*, 152, 182, and the Second Brandenburg Concerto; a single $f''$ recorder is used in Cantata 96 and a $d''$ in Cantata 103 (and a single *flauto piccolo* in Cantata 8). Three $f'$ instruments are found in Cantatas 25, 122, and 175. Two lines for $f'$ recorders, each of them performed by more than one player, appear in Cantata 46 and the *St Matthew Passion*.

Bach's parts frequently place demands that go further than those addressed in contemporary woodwind tutors. The treatises were designed to help amateurs with their unassuming repertory of published music. Bach's players were taught not from treatises but through master–apprentice relationships in guilds of professional musicians who performed more difficult, typically unpublished music. Study of the original manuscripts, not today's printed editions, shows that Bach had a remarkably keen understanding of advanced recorder technique; for example, he employs $f\sharp'''$ only in certain contexts and breaks slurring patterns when moving from $e'''$ to $c\sharp'''$ or from $d''$ to $f'''$ (for details, see Marissen, 1991). Coming from a respected family of *Stadtpfeifer*, he almost surely played the instrument himself.          MAM

R. Griscom and D. Lasocki, *The Recorder: A Guide to Writings about the Instrument for Players and Researchers* (New York, 1994); M. Marissen, 'Organological Questions and their Significance in J. S. Bach's Fourth Brandenburg Concerto', *Journal of the American Musical Instrument Society*, 17 (1991), 5–52; M. Marissen, 'Bach and Recorders in G', *Galpin Society Journal*, 48 (1995), 199–204; U. Prinz, 'Flauto', 'Flauto piccolo', in 'Studien zum Instrumentarium Johann Sebastian Bachs' (diss., Tübingen University, 1979), 109–34; M. Ruëtz, 'Die Blockflöte in der Kirchenmusik Johann Sebastian Bachs', *Musik und Kirche*, 7 (1935), 112–20, 170–86.

**recordings.** See overleaf.

**Rector.** The head of a Lutheran LATEINSCHULE. In the course of the century before Bach, Rectors became increasingly academically orientated. As the Kantor reciprocally took over the directorship of music, assuming supreme control over the furnishing of church choirs, there was increasing tension between Rector and Kantor.

Bach seems to have enjoyed cordial relations with the first two Rectors he encountered in Leipzig, J. H. Ernesti and J. M. Gesner; indeed the latter praised Bach highly. However, with the appointment of J. A. Ernesti in 1734, a progressive intellectual who opposed the dominance of music in the curriculum, Bach was plunged into some of the worst political turmoil of his entire career.

JAB

**registration.** A term used in music mainly to refer to the selecting and combining of organ stops for a particular piece or passage. Since there is a great variety of organ types, and of stops within a type, registration is a complex but essential skill for an organist. Little information about registration is available directly from J. S. Bach or from his musical scores; the most reliable indications about his registration practice stem from sources within the Bach circle (sons, students, and close colleagues) and from sources contemporary and co-regional with Bach. In the Obituary,

[*cont. on p.416*]

# recordings

**1. Introduction.** Any claim that historically aware performance of early music is a product of the late 20th century is as inaccurate as the oft-repeated assertion that Bach's music was forgotten after his death until its rediscovery by Mendelssohn in the 19th century. It was in the late 1880s that Arnold Dolmetsch (1858–1940) first came across the precious legacy of English consort music in London's Royal College of Music and the British Library. Already interested in Renaissance and Baroque music, he began to perform it with a declared aim to approach, as nearly as he was able, the performing practices of the time in which it was written. Dolmetsch, like musicians after him who have pursued similar aims, had both adherents and detractors. Many of the former have been largely forgotten, since they neither wrote profusely on the subject nor were able, by and large, to transmit their ideas to posterity through the medium of a recording industry that was much smaller and more élite than it is nowadays. Fortunately there were notable exceptions, and it is the recordings of these artists during the 1930s and 1940s that provide a starting-point for the present survey.

In these decades interest in Bach as a composer focused on only a minute part of his creative output. Ralph Vaughan Williams (1872–1958) once remarked in a BBC broadcast (*c.*1950) that the 'average English parlour contained *The Soul Awakening* framed on the wall, *The Way of the Eagle* on the bookshelf, and the *St Matthew Passion* on the pianoforte'. Vaughan Williams, as it happened, was one of the most eloquent detractors of historically aware performance, but his observation, though exaggerated, was not entirely invalid. To the *St Matthew Passion* of his average English parlour we should undoubtedly add some or all of the 48 preludes and fugues that make up *The Well-tempered Clavier,* the Goldberg Variations, the Italian Concerto, and perhaps a Partita or a French Suite—not forgetting, of course, a piano arrangement of *Jesu, Joy of Man's Desiring.* Little or nothing else by Bach would have found a place either on the piano or inside the piano stool. It would have been to the gramophone cabinet that we turned to find the Brandenburg Concertos, orchestral suites, violin concertos, or the occasional 'piano' concerto.

**2. Keyboard and organ music.** Recordings of Bach's keyboard music during the 1930s and 1940s were dominated by a handful of eminent virtuosos and gifted amateurs whose performances, for various reasons, enjoy a lively following today. Albert SCHWEITZER and Wanda LANDOWSKA were the chief early representatives of the organ and harpsichord respectively, though we should not overlook the contribution made to the harpsichord and clavichord revival during the 1920s by the English musician Violet Gordon Woodhouse. Edwin Fischer and Myra Hess were admired exponents of Bach on the piano, while in Germany Helmut Walcha (organ) began to make important contributions to Bach interpretation during the late 1940s. Of these it would probably be true to say that only Landowska and Walcha had any concern for historically informed performance; Schweitzer, though one of the prominent Bach scholars of his generation, was not much concerned with purist considerations, preferring to demonstrate the unique character of his chosen instruments, above all those of his native Alsace.

Landowska's earliest Bach recordings were made in the 1930s. The sound made by harpsichords in those days bore little relation to that of restored instruments of the 17th and 18th centuries or the fine copies of them available to today's performers. Yet her championship of the harpsichord in the early days of its revival sometimes consorts uncomfortably with her Romantic concept of Bach's music and an over-indulgence of sentiment, for example in her playing of Variation 25 of the Goldbergs, which she referred to as her 'black pearl'. Only since about 1975, perhaps, have ideas regarding the interpretation of this chromatic piece significantly changed. Landowska's most satisfying contribution to Bach recordings is one she made of *The Well-tempered Clavier* at her home in Connecticut in the early 1950s. Although she takes rhythmic and other liberties with the music, there is a nobility in the playing which betrays her affection for the work and her understanding of it.

Edwin Fischer recorded *The Well-tempered Clavier* during the early to mid-1930s on a 20th-century grand piano. He was an artist of rare sensibility, though no stranger to sudden lapses in technique. His Bach performances were rated too Romantic by some critics, even in his own lifetime, yet his light articulation and restrained use of the sustaining pedal to achieve clarity of line and transparency of texture are among many enduring qualities in his playing. In the early 1950s the French pianist Marcelle Meyer and the Romanian Dinu Lipatti, both with stronger techniques, demonstrated a similar skill in preserving textural clarity while at the same time revealing the lyrical content of Bach's melody.

With the advent of the long-playing (LP) record, audiences were given greater opportunity than ever before to choose between different performances of the same work. Bach's music, in particular, was given sharp focus by the Archiv Produktion division of Deutsche Grammophon established in 1947. In that year the blind organist Helmut Walcha made his first Bach recordings in Lübeck's Jacobikirche, and he went on to record virtually complete editions of Bach's organ music, twice over. After World War II musicians, scholars, and antiquarians in Germany felt a necessity to document German musical culture, an endeavour which led to the examination and recording of the country's finest surviving cathedral and church organs. During the 1950s and 1960s organists such as Geraint Jones and Ralph Downes demonstrated a new awareness of effective, style-conscious playing, and in the years since then many complete surveys of Bach's organ music have been recorded, notably by Walter Kraft, Lionel Rogg, Marie-Claire Alain, Wolfgang Rubsam, Peter Hurford, and Ton Koopman.

The touchstone of harpsichord playing since the mid-1950s has been provided by Gustav LEONHARDT. Although he was preceded in the post-war years by Ralph Kirkpatrick, George Malcolm, Ruggero Gerlin, and many others, Leonhardt has probably influenced our present taste in harpsichord playing more than anyone else. His interpretations can be severe and lacking in geniality but the learning behind them is profound, the feeling for stylistic propriety unassailable, and his passionate response to Bach's music often thrilling in its eloquent shaping of phrases, rhythmic tautness, and scrupulous but always pertinent detail. Leonhardt has recorded the greater part of Bach's solo harpsichord music and his version of *The Well-tempered Clavier*, his thrice-recorded Goldberg Variations, his illuminating exposition of *The Art of Fugue*, with an important essay accompanying it, his twice-recorded Partitas, as well as the French and English Suites, are a testimony to this artist's fluent understanding of the composer's rhetoric, craftsmanship, and expressive nuances.

A lively and ever-growing interest in historically aware performance has done little or nothing either to demote or to devalue Bach's music played on a modern piano. Three names, in particular, have become closely associated with Bach on the piano during the second half of the 20th century: Rosalyn Tureck, Glenn GOULD, and Andras Schiff. Both Tureck and Gould have fostered the art of personal communication, unashamedly offering idiosyncratic interpretations of Bach's music. Gould's 1955 début recording of the Goldberg Variations is provocative, entertaining, and lively. How different from his last recording of the work, in 1981, which, by contrast, is stripped of personality, mechanical, and expressively bland. Gould has nevertheless been accorded legendary status by pianists and many harpsichordists alike. Schiff has had at least part of Gould's mantle bestowed upon him by contemporary audiences. He is a communicative exponent of Bach's music, fastidious over articulation, skilful in the preservation of textural clarity, and restrained in his use of dynamics.

**3. Instrumental music.** At about the same time that Landowska was making her earliest recordings of Bach in the 1930s, artists on other instruments were making comparable contributions to Bach performance on disc, and some of them have also taken up permanent residence on the slopes of Mount Parnassus. Georges Enescu and Yehudi Menuhin were universally acclaimed for their recordings of the unaccompanied Violin Sonatas and Partitas and the three violin concertos. Pablo Casals, who first brought Bach's Cello Suites to the attention of modern audiences in the early years of the 20th century, went on to make recordings of them during the 1930s. These were landmarks in the history of the gramophone and went unchallenged until the advent of the LP record in the early 1950s. The rapid growth which has taken place in the recording business since then has provided listeners with an ever-increasing choice of interpretation, each decade producing its own 'legendary' performances. The violinist Nathan Milstein and the cellist Pierre Fournier were among the finest interpreters of Bach's unaccompanied string music during the 1950s and 1960s. Fournier, a generation younger than Casals, had taken the older musician's place in the celebrated trio with Pierre Thibaud and Alfred Cortot, and was known above all as a Romantic cellist, but his intellectually rigorous, expressive, and rhythmically controlled playing of the Cello Suites BWV1007–12 shows him to be an ideal Bach interpreter as well. Indeed, we might even venture the opinion that, overlooking technical details of the instruments themselves and the discrepancy in pitch, Fournier's performance of the Cello Suites comes closer to the ideals of the historically aware than the later of two recordings of the same pieces by the doyen of Baroque cellists, Anner Bylsma.

Bach's chamber music for two or more players hardly attracted the attention of recording companies before 1950. Since then there has been no clear line of interpretative thought, with conventional, mainstream performances on modern instruments holding their own against practitioners on period instruments. The American flautist Julius Baker and harpsichordist Sylvia Marlowe were the first to record all Bach's flute sonatas (*c.*1956), while Wolfgang Schneiderhan and David Oistrakh were among the earliest violinists to record the Sonatas for violin and harpsichord. These performances, however, are all but forgotten today, which perhaps reflects the status of the music itself in public perception as much as the intrinsic merit of the performances. The choice of historically aware performances of this repertory on disc is still surprisingly limited, though August Wenzinger (viola da gamba), Sigiswald Kuijken (violin), Frans Brüggen (flute), Barthold Kuijken (flute), and Gustav Leonhardt (harpsichord) have made significant and characteristically thoughtful contributions.

4. **Music for large ensembles.** No area of Bach's recorded music reveals a wider range of performing styles than the six Brandenburg Concertos and the four orchestral suites. The generally accepted point of departure for these works are the recordings made in 1935 by the Busch Chamber Players under Adolf Busch. Yet Alfred Cortot had recorded all the Brandenburgs in Paris three years earlier, and it is these performances that should rightly be considered as the earliest complete recording. Neither Busch nor Cortot (nor Boyd Neel, who recorded several of the Brandenburgs shortly afterwards) made concessions towards a growing awareness of earlier instruments. Keyboard continuo and solo, for example, were played on a modern piano by Cortot himself, and by Rudolf Serkin in the Busch set. Flutes were used rather than recorders, and cellos instead of viols.

All this was to change in the early 1950s when August Wenzinger and the Schola Cantorum Basiliensis began to explore the possibilities of performing Bach, and other composers, with historical awareness. As early as 1950 a small group of German musicians had made a recording of chamber music by Telemann for Archiv Produktion using a pitch of $a' = 415$ Hz; although this was slow to catch on, further gestures towards historical awareness were made by Karl Haas and Wenzinger, whose performances of Bach's Brandenburg Concertos were among the first on record to feature at least some of the instruments for which Bach wrote. Shortly after, a gesture towards historical propriety came from an unexpected source. In 1953 Jascha Horenstein recorded the Brandenburgs with small forces and, as with the two sets mentioned above, included a few of the less common instruments that Bach specified. Cellos are supplanted by gambas in the Sixth Concerto—one of these, furthermore, being played by a very young Nikolaus Harnoncourt—and the harpsichord takes its rightful place as solo and continuo instrument.

More sustained thought on the instrumentation and performance of the Brandenburgs was provided by Thurston Dart, who was closely involved in two distinct recordings of the concertos during the late 1950s and early 1970s. Some of his conclusions were novel—the use of flageolets as opposed to recorders in the Fourth Concerto, and the substitution of a French horn for the trumpet in the Second Concerto are but two examples—but the approach was and remains stimulating, provocative, and characteristically individual.

Although interesting and in some respects successful, such historically aware performances as these remained an exception to the rule throughout the 1950s and 1960s. They were not, however, without followers. Rudolf Baumgartner and the Lucerne Festival Strings recorded the Brandenburgs in 1959, featuring all but one of Bach's specified instruments: the violino piccolo required for Concerto no. 1 was omitted in favour of a standard violin. It was the 'Urtext' of its time, but was to be supplanted, first in 1964 by a recording with Harnoncourt's Concentus Musicus of Vienna, and soon afterwards by another with the Collegium Aureum, in which Gustav Leonhardt (who was to direct his own highly regarded set in 1976) played both solo and continuo harpsichord. Harnoncourt's performances caused quite a stir, for here was an ensemble which claimed to play instruments hardly (if at all) modified since Bach's own time. Period wind-instrument playing has advanced with colossal strides since 1964 and the set, as a whole, would no longer satisfy audiences that have grown accustomed to the polished performances of the 1990s. The string playing in the Sixth Concerto, however, is of a calibre that testifies to the extraordinary accomplishment of this orchestra in its infancy.

Conventional performances of the Brandenburgs and the orchestral suites remain popular, but ensembles of period instruments have found ever-widening audiences. For some listeners the choice may be determined by little other than the dictates of fashion, while for others the rich kaleidoscope of instrumental colour and nuance, the lighter articulation, and the generally brisker tempos, refresh an aural palette that perhaps became acquainted with this music through weightier, historically unconcerned performances to which there were at one time few alternatives. The parting of the ways between mainstream performance of Bach's music and that of the historically aware has inevitably caused a degree of friction between the opposing factions, and it has become difficult to find Bach programmes in the concert hall performed on other than period instruments. Yet some modern instrumentalists and ensembles (the Amsterdam Bach Soloists being one example) have made themselves aware of the arguments for and against 'historical' performance, and have capitalized on the virtues held by each school of thought. Any notion that period instrument ensembles a priori deliver more illuminating performances than a similarly sized ensemble of modern, style-conscious players is patently absurd.

5. **Vocal music.** The rediscovery of Bach's vocal music through the recording medium was given sustained impetus in the early 1950s by the advent of the LP. A small number of earlier recordings, however, are now recognized as important landmarks in the evolution of Bach performance on disc. Among these is a complete recording of the *St Matthew Passion* under the baton of Willem Mengelberg (1939) and another, with substantial cuts, by the Thomaskantor Günther Ramin (1941). The Evangelist in both recordings was the tenor Karl Erb. Ramin, furthermore, engaged two other singers of distinction, the baritone Gerhard Hüsch, who sang the role of Christus, and the soprano Tiana Lemnitz. A version in English, conducted by Reginald Jacques, was issued in 1949. Perhaps the most notable recording of a Bach cantata in the pre-LP era was that of *Ich habe genug* by the bass-baritone Hans Hotter, with the Philharmonia Orchestra conducted by Anthony Bernard (1950). Hotter is remembered chiefly for his Wagnerian roles, but his early training in church music served him well in a performance that was stylish in its time and is still greatly admired.

The 1950s witnessed a surge of interest by conductors and record companies in the performance of Bach's vocal music, with Leipzig, Vienna, and Berlin as the most active centres. Between 1950 and his death in 1956 Ramin recorded some 25 sacred cantatas with the choir of the Leipzig Thomaskirche and members of the Gewandhaus Orchestra. He was an effective and popular choirmaster and the results he achieved with the boy choristers were impressive. His successor as Thomaskantor,

Kurt Thomas, both duplicated and added to Ramin's discography, but with less conviction. Thomas's direction is lifeless beside that of the other, a weakness that becomes especially apparent in performances of the secular cantatas and the larger vocal pieces. Neither conductor was entirely well served by the solo voices, though a very young Agnes Giebel (soprano) makes a single appearance in the Ramin cycle.

In most respects the recordings of Fritz Lehmann in Berlin and Felix Prohaska and Hermann Scherchen in Vienna do fuller justice to Bach's vocal music. Their choirs were of mixed voices, male and female, and were mostly larger than the vocal groups of the present day; but the soloists, especially in the Lehmann recordings, were of a higher calibre than the Leipzig singers, and included the tenor Helmut Krebs. His light, individually coloured voice and articulate textual declamation lend distinction to both the cantatas and the *Christmas Oratorio*, during the recording of which Lehmann was taken ill, to be replaced by Günther Arndt.

Scherchen and Prohaska drew upon singers from the Vienna Staatsoper for their recordings, with varying results. The sopranos Anny Felbermayer and Teresa Stich-Randall, contraltos Hilde Rössl-Majdan and Dagmar Hermann, tenors Hugues Cuenod and Anton Dermota, and bass Hans Braun proved themselves sympathetically expressive Bach singers, while others, like the tenor Waldemar Kmentt, seemed unable to adjust their technique from the conventions and technical requirements of grand opera.

Few aspects of performing styles in Bach's vocal music distinguished the 1950s from the 1960s. Choirs remained large and conductors continued to engage soloists of disparate vocal disciplines and with varied backgrounds of experience. The major cantata projects which dominated the 1960s were those of Karl RICHTER and Fritz Werner, based in Munich and Pforzheim respectively, and another which drew upon the expertise of a variety of German Kantor-conductors, notably Wilhelm Ehmann, Wolfgang Gönnenwein, Helmut Kahlhöfer, and Diethard Hellmann, and which was loosely connected with the editorial work of the *NBA*. In 1958 Richter had recorded a *St Matthew Passion* with Fritz Wunderlich as the Evangelist, Kieth Engen as Christus, and the baritone Dietrich Fischer-Dieskau. The performance was widely acclaimed, and Richter was hailed as one of the leading young interpreters of Bach's vocal music. Throughout the 1960s and 1970s he recorded some 75 cantatas, the B minor Mass, the two Passions, and the *Christmas Oratorio*; but early promise was not fulfilled, and the recordings of the 1970s became rhythmically ponderous and increasingly anachronistic in the light of the burgeoning stylistic revolution of Harnoncourt and Leonhardt.

Fritz WERNER, who recorded about 55 cantatas between the mid-1950s and the early 1970s, was never able to match Richter's excellence as a choirmaster; but, notwithstanding the younger musician's fine team of soloists, among them the soprano Edith Mathis, contraltos Hertha Töpper and Anna Reynolds, tenor Peter Schreier, and baritone Dietrich Fischer-Dieskau, Werner often achieved more satisfying results. His soloists included the sopranos Agnes Giebel and Ingeborg Reichelt, contraltos Claudia Hellmann and Barbara Scherler, tenors Helmut Krebs and Georg Jelden, and basses Jakob Stämpfli, Barry McDaniel, and Erich Wenk. In the later recordings some of these singers were replaced by others trained at the Schola Cantorum Basiliensis, among whom the soprano Hedy Graf and the tenor Kurt Huber were especially effective. Werner was more scrupulous than Richter in his observance

of Bach's precise instrumental requirements and often proved himself more susceptible to changing taste in Bach performance. Both conductors were able to draw
upon accomplished instrumentalists but, while Richter's performances show the
greater technical discipline and declamatory nobility, it is perhaps Werner who had
the more engaging approach to dance rhythms and who more effortlessly and with
less contrivance reached the contemplative heart of the music.

With the launch, in 1971, by Harnoncourt and Leonhardt of a complete sacred
cantata repertory, almost all previously held convictions about performing Bach's
vocal music were thrown into the melting-pot. At the same time a marked polarity of
interpretative thought became apparent, in which the ideas of Harnoncourt and
Leonhardt were either largely ignored by conductors such as Richter, or openly
opposed by others, notably the Stuttgart-based conductor Helmuth RILLING. Side by
side with the historically informed performances of Harnoncourt and Leonhardt,
Rilling set about recording his own complete edition of Bach's cantatas, creating, as
he himself once put it, 'a synthesis between the historical and Romantic approaches'.
Rilling's approach, in concept at least, hardly differs from the mainly traditional
performances of Werner or the musicologist Hans Grischkat, who recorded a substantial amount of Bach's vocal music, including the B minor Mass, during the 1950s
as well as a small number of cantatas in the years leading up to his death in 1977. As
matters stand, Rilling, Hans-Joachim Rotzsch (who sang tenor under Ramin and
enjoyed a successful solo career prior to his appointment as Thomaskantor in 1973),
and Peter Schreier are among the last directors of Bach cantata series to have
attempted a *rapprochement* between traditional values and those that are shaping
historically based performances exemplified in yet another cantata series begun by
Ton Koopman in 1995.                                                          NA

*See also* PERFORMANCE STYLES.

J. Butt, 'Bach Recordings Since 1980: A Mirror of Historical Performance', in D. Schulenberg, ed., *Bach Perspectives*, iv (Lincoln, Nebr., forthcoming); M. Elste, *Bachs Kunst der Fuge
auf Schallplatten* (Frankfurt, 1981).

---

C. P. E. Bach and J. F. Agricola write: 'He . . .
understood the art of . . . combining the stops . . .
in the most skilful manner' (*BDok* iii. 88), and J.
N. Forkel in 1802 related an anecdote about Bach's
astonishing way of combining stops. These tell us
nothing, though, about actual practice, and precise indications in the Bach manuscripts—for
example in *Gottes Sohn ist kommen* in the *Orgel-
Büchlein*, and in the Vivaldi concerto transcription BWV596—are extremely rare. The source
closest to Bach that offers a reasonably complete
view of registration practice is an article by Bach's
student J. F. Agricola in F. W. Marpurg's *Histor-
isch-kritische Beyträge*, vi (Berlin, 1758), 502–5.

Agricola begins with a recipe for the 'Volles
Werk' (*plenum*, or full organ), prescribing the
exclusive use of Principals without any other flue
stops (a conservative practice). Other contemporary sources call for the use of a 16' pedal reed stop
as part of the *plenum*, but Agricola allows the addition of 16', 8' and 4' Trumpet stops to the manual
as well, 'if they are well in tune'. Many Bach prelude and fugue scores, as well as scores of the
bolder chorale settings, call for a *plenum* registration, probably without change of manuals unless
specifically indicated (see Stauffer, 1986, pp.
203–7). Agricola also specifies the presence of 16'
stops in the *plenum*. The predilection for full, sonorous organ tone is not unique to Agricola; it is
characteristic of most other contemporary
sources as well. In fact, Agricola censures the use
of a 4' stop without an 8' foundation unless 'one
intends to play very rapid florid passages on it'.

Agricola labels flutes and strings as *galanterie*
stops, perhaps thereby suggesting a more
imaginative approach to their registration (in
contrast to the more strictly prescribed *plenum*).
Such stops were commonly used to register
quieter chorale settings. The variety of his suggested stop combinations, together with the wide

pallette of colourful flute and string stops in organs most familiar to Bach, suggests an adventurous approach to quieter registrations. Agricola allows the combination $8' + 2\frac{2}{3}' + 1\frac{3}{5}' + 1'$ for rapid arpeggios, but calls the sound $8' + 2'$, without $4'$ in the middle, 'far too hollow, especially when playing full chords'. He dismisses earlier sanctions by praising the combined tone of four $8'$ flute and string stops (a markedly progressive idea) as producing 'a strange and beautiful effect'. Agricola and other contemporary sources suggest that reed stops were used in the same imaginative ways as *galanterie* stops, but were normally combined with an $8'$ flue stop to muffle their rattle.

Agricola's interest in French registration practice reflects 18th-century German enthusiasm for French culture, an enthusiasm also evident in Bach's music. The types of organs available to Bach preclude his intimate familiarity with French practice, but his fondness for the sound of the characteristically French Cornet combination $(8' + 4' + 2\frac{2}{3}' + 2' + 1\frac{3}{5}')$ is reflected in its inclusion in the new *Brustpositiv* division of the organ at Mühlhausen (*BDok* i. 153), an instrument whose two existing manual divisions were already supplied with Cornet combinations.

Agricola's remarks, as well as those from other contemporary sources, suggest that Bach's 'astonishing way of combining stops' is more likely to apply to non-*plenum* than to *plenum* registrations. In contrast to the codified French approach to combining stops, German practice seems to have been more free; Jakob Adlung (*Musica mechanica organoedi* (Berlin, 1768), i, § 231) posits a few commonsense restrictions and then suggests experimenting with all available possibilities. The detailed and imaginative registrations provided in the *Harmonische Seelenlust* (Leipzig, 1733–6), a collection of chorale settings by the Merseburg organist and probable Bach acquaintance G. F. Kauffmann, reflect this freer practice.

The greatest hindrance to understanding Bach's registration practice is the present unavailability of the type of organ he knew most intimately: the Thuringian organ of the first half of the 18th century. These organs were quite progressive, exhibiting features that became common throughout Germany only in the 19th century: multiple flue stops at $8'$ pitch (including string stops) on all manuals, the availability of many colourful $8'$ and $4'$ stops (often including a Glockenspiel), ample winding, weighty $16'$ manual stops, spacious and deep cases, and mixtures with prominent 3rd-sounding ranks through their compasses. No instrument of this type has been built since the 18th century; all surviving examples are found exclusively in central Germany, and most are as yet unrestored.                QF

Q. Faulkner, 'Information on Organ Registration from a Student of J. S. Bach', *Early Keyboard Studies Newsletter*, 7/1 (Jan. 1993); Q. Faulkner, 'Die Registrierung der Orgelwerke J. S. Bachs', *BJb* 81 (1995), 7–30; G. Stauffer, 'Bach's Organ Registration Reconsidered', in G. Stauffer and E. May, eds., *J. S. Bach as Organist* (London, 1986), 193–211; G. Stauffer, *The Organ Preludes of J. S. Bach* (Ann Arbor, 1980), 155–71; P. Williams, *The Organ Music of J. S. Bach*, iii (Cambridge, 1984), 154 ff.

**Reiche, Gottfried** (b. 5 Feb. 1667; d. 6 Oct. 1734). Trumpeter and composer, born in Weißenfels, Thuringia. He went to Leipzig in 1688 and worked his way up through the ranks of *Stadtpfeifer* and *Kunstgeiger* to become senior *Stadtmusicus* in 1719. In 1696 he published *Vier und zwanzig neue Quatricinia* for cornett and three trombones; his numerous other compositions have not survived. He was the first performer of many trumpet parts in Bach's cantatas and other works, and he died aged 67 after being overcome by torch smoke during a performance of the cantata *Preise dein Glücke, gesegnetes Sachsen*. A portrait by E. G. Haußmann shows him at the age of about 60 holding a coiled trumpet.

D. L. Smithers, 'Gottfried Reiches Ansehen und sein Einfluß auf die Musik Johann Sebastian Bachs', *BJb* 73 (1987), 113–50.

**Reimann, Johann Balthasar** (b. 14 June 1702; d. 22 Dec. 1749). Organist, born in Breslau-Neustadt (now Wrocław, Poland). He visited Bach in Leipzig in 1729 and left an enthusiastic account in the autobiography he wrote for Johann Mattheson (*BDok* ii, no. 429). In the same year he was appointed organist at the Gnadenkirche, Hirschberg, where he remained until his death.

**Reincken, Johann Adam** (d. 24 Nov. 1722). Composer and organist, born possibly in Deventer, in the Netherlands. His date of birth, usually given as 27 April 1623, has been challenged by Ulf Grapenthin, who suggests December 1643 as a possible alternative. Reincken spent a large part of his career as organist of the Catharinenkirche, Hamburg. He was also instrumental in founding the celebrated Hamburg opera in 1678, and his instrumental suites show his close relationship with the burgeoning collegium musicum tradition. The most celebrated work from his remarkably small surviving output, the enormous Fantasia on *An Wasserflüssen Babylon*, provides a compendium of most of the styles, techniques, and figurations available to a German composer of the mid- to late 17th century.

It was on this very same chorale that Bach improvised in front of Reincken, just before the latter's death at an advanced age. Bach had, in fact, been intimately acquainted with Reincken's music some years before, when he based a fugue and two sonatas for keyboard on pieces drawn from Reincken's *Hortus musicus* (1687). These provide an extremely productive window into Bach's compositional practice, his transcriptions ranging from embellishment to entirely independent pieces based on Reincken's subjects.        JAB

W. Breig, 'Composition as Arrangement and Adaptation', in J. Butt, ed., *The Cambridge Companion to Bach* (Cambridge, 1997), 154–70; U. Grapenthin, 'Johann Adam Reincken: Leben und Werk' (diss. University of Hamburg, forthcoming); C. Wolff, 'Bach and Johann Adam Reincken: A Context for the Early Works', in *Bach: Essays on his Life and Music* (Cambridge, Mass., 1991), 56–71.

**réjouissance** ('rejoicing'). A common movement title in the overture-suites of G. P. Telemann (see A. Hoffman, *Die Orchestersuiten Georg Philipp Telemanns* (Wolfenbüttel, 1969) ). It was employed by Bach in a similar context—for the finale of the Orchestral Suite no. 4 in D major—and also by Handel in the *Music for the Royal Fireworks* (1749). The name merely indicates the affect, having no necessary bearing on the piece's metre or mode of rhythmic movement.        RDPJ

**Reminiscere.** In the CHURCH CALENDAR, the second Sunday in Lent. It takes its name from the introit to the Mass for that day in the Latin rite, beginning 'Reminiscere miserationum tuarum, Domine'.

**revival.** See RECEPTION AND REVIVAL.

**rhetoric.** See FIGURENLEHRE.

**rhythm.** The grouping of musical sounds by patterns of motion and repose. According to the Greek writer Aristoxenus (b. *c.*370 BC), the term describes an activity, not a thing. Plato (*c.*429–370 BC), in Book 2 of the *Laws*, defined rhythm as 'order within movement'. Thus, to apply rhythm to something is to bring it to life in a distinctive way by giving it organization, shape, and form. Rhythm in Baroque music may be discussed by considering first the rhythm of beats, which are those places in a line of music corresponding to a conductor's beat. During the Baroque period such rhythm was generally perceived as either strict or free. In a strict rhythm, beats proceed at a more or less uniform speed, whereas in a free rhythm they fluctuate in speed.

A free application of rhythm to beats was especially popular in Europe in the late 16th and early 17th centuries in the new declamatory Italian style, which generously incorporated tempo fluctuation. In the Preface to Frescobaldi's *Toccate e partite* (1615–16) and in Monteverdi's Eighth Book of Madrigals (1638) performers were instructed to alter the regular flow of the beats according to the passion of the text in vocal music or the harmonic patterns in a purely instrumental piece. Bach used free rhythms in the recitatives of his cantatas, oratorios, and Passions, in the free sections of his toccatas, fantasias, and some preludes, and probably in many affective slow movements, both instrumental and vocal.

A strict, or measured, grouping of beats nevertheless predominates in Bach's music, exhibiting both Italian and French influence: Italian in the virtuoso, driving rhythms of the organ and keyboard concertos; French in the use of dance rhythms. French dance rhythms consist of regularly recurring patterns of beats which form a recognizable *Gestalt* for each of the characteristic French dances (*see* DANCE). A gavotte, for example, was not easily confused with a bourrée because, even though both dances employed the same duple metre, their rhythmic organization of the minim beats was quite different (see Ex. 1). The basic eight-beat bourrée rhythm has a *thesis* (point of repose) on beat 3 and the first half of beat 4, and on beat 7 and the first half of beat 8, the whole preceded by a short upbeat. The gavotte rhythm is also eight beats in length, but the *thesis* is on beats 4 and 8; beat one is not an upbeat, but the first beat of the phrase. The tempos of these two dances are also contrasted: the bourrée beats move a little faster than those in the gavotte, and this heightens the contrasting patterns of motion and repose to distinguish further the two dances (*see* TEMPO).

In rhythmic organization below the level of the beat, several notational idiosyncrasies in Baroque music may affect performance in some works by

Ex. 1 (T = *thesis*)

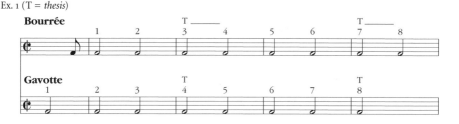

Bach. Among the conventions, which still cause controversy among scholars, are: a form of rhythmic alteration known as *notes inégales*; the practice of over-dotting in certain situations; and the alignment or resolution of duplets with triplets.

*Notes inégales* refers to the altering of note values within the beat. They are applied to a line of conjunct quavers or semiquavers that make up the second metrical level below the beat; for example, if the beat is the minim, *notes inégales* may affect conjunct quavers. The practice is to perform the notated even notes in an uneven fashion by alternating long and short values, keeping the beat steady. This practice arose in France and spread to other countries, including Bach's Germany, and may be applied to Bach's pieces in French style. Bach assimilated and employed Italian, French, and other national styles in his works; he not only copied French music, but experienced it at first hand in performances by French musicians and dancers in many of the areas in which he lived. Thus, one may reasonably apply *notes inégales* to Bach's music in appropriate places, for example to conjunct quavers in minuets, bourrées, gavottes, chaconnes, courantes, and sarabandes in 3/2 time, and to conjunct semiquavers in passepieds, sarabandes in 3/4 time, and some gigues. They are not appropriate in *correntes*, which are Italian in origin, nor in dances in an obvious Italian style such as the Tempo di Gavotta in the keyboard Partita in E minor and the Tempo di Minuetto of the keyboard Partita in G major.

Over-dotting is the convention of holding dotted notes, in some situations, longer than actually notated, so that ♩♪, for example, might be rendered as ♩.♪. Georg Muffat (1653–1704), explaining the French style to German musicians in his *Florilegium primum* (1695) and *Florilegium secundum* (1698), wrote about lengthened dotted notes and shortened succeeding notes in slow, march-like pieces, in noble, stately pieces such as the French overture, and in dances with characteristic dotted rhythms such as the gigue. The workings of this convention are clear in the two versions of the opening movement of the Ouverture in the French Style; the version published in *Clavier-Übung II* (in B minor) fairly consistently uses longer long notes and shorter short notes than the earlier manuscript version (in C minor). Some at least of these changes may be revisions rather than elucidations, but one may reasonably assume that over-dotting would similarly apply in works such as the Ouverture to Cantata 61, *Nun komm, der Heiden Heiland* (i).

Alignment or resolution of notated duplets with simultaneously notated triplets is another recurring situation in Bach's music which is sometimes heatedly discussed by scholars (see Fuller, Hefling, and Schwandt). Lacking definitive rules, each situation must be dealt with individually for an appropriate musical result. Often the short note of a dotted duple figure sounds best when it coincides with the last note of a triplet, as in the *Corrente* of the keyboard Partita in B♭ major, or the Sarabande of the keyboard Partita in D major. In pieces such as *In dulci jubilo* BWV608, however, a duplet figure against a triplet enlivens the overall rhythm and sounds well played exactly as written. According to J. F. Agricola (*Allgemeine deutsche Bibliothek*, 1769, i. 242–3), Bach taught his pupils to align duplets and triplets only in fast tempos.                                  NJ, MEL

P. Aldrich, *Rhythm in Seventeenth-Century Italian Monody* (New York, 1966); M. Little and N. Jenne, *Dance and the Music of J. S. Bach* (Bloomington and Indianapolis, 1991); D. Fuller, S. Hefling, and E. Schwandt, 'Rhythmic Alteration', *Performance Practice Review*, 7 (1994), 120–49.

**ricercare** (Ricercar). A term described by the 18th-century theorist F. W. Marpurg as indicating a strict fugue, art fugue, or master-fugue: a tightly thematic fugal construct that makes copious use of the various contrapuntal artifices (stretto, invertible counterpoint, etc.). Marpurg placed most of the fugues of Bach in this category, contrasting them with the free fugue cultivated by Handel (see *BDok* iii, no. 655).

The imitative ricercare developed in the 16th and 17th centuries as a keyboard counterpart to the motet. Accordingly it was written in a conservative, traditional style rooted in Renaissance polyphony. Bach was acquainted with ricercares of this type by the Italian composer Girolamo Frescobaldi, as well as by certain German composers who came under Frescobaldi's influence— Froberger, Pachelbel, and Johann Krieger (1652–1735). Bach's *alla breve* fugues, such as those in C♯ minor and B♭ minor from *The Well-tempered Clavier* Part 1, belong to this tradition. But his only known use of the term 'ricercar' (to use his own spelling) occurs in the *Musical Offering*, whose six-part Ricercar displays the antiquated, motet-like characteristics of the type.

The three-part Ricercar from the *Musical Offering*, on the other hand, is quite different in character. Its loose, fantasia-like structure suggests that it transmits the substance of Bach's improvisation at the Potsdam court of Frederick the Great in May 1747. It thus recalls the original meaning of 'ricercare' as a preludial piece in improvisatory style, a searching-out (the literal meaning) or testing-out of the tuning or key. That this meaning was still known in the 18th century is clear from Walther's *Musikalisches Lexicon* (Leipzig, 1732), where the ricercare is described as an extempore 'searching for harmonic . . . patterns that might be used in the finished product'.

RDPJ

C. Wolff, 'Apropos the Musical Offering: The Thema Regium and the Term *Ricercar*', in *Bach: Essays on his Life and Music* (Cambridge, Mass., 1991), 324–31.

**Richter, Karl** (b. 15 Oct. 1926; d. 15 Feb. 1981). Conductor and organist, born in Plauen, Saxony. He was the pupil of three great Kantors, Karl Straube and Günther Ramin at Leipzig, and Rudolf Mauersberger at Dresden. In 1949 he was appointed organist of the Leipzig Thomaskirche. Two years later he moved to Munich, where he founded the Bach Choir and Orchestra with which he remained associated for the rest of his life. Richter's concert tours and Bach recordings in which he appeared as both keyboard recitalist and conductor, spanned a period of almost 30 years. Between 1958 and 1970 his interpretations of Bach's vocal music were especially admired for their discipline, rhythmic tautness, and expressive intensity, but with the growing interest in historically aware performances during the 1970s Richter's values were questioned. He made no concessions towards newly emerging ideas about performing practice, yet, partly because of declining health, he was unable to sustain the fresh vigour that characterized his earlier concerts and recordings. A victim of passing fashion and changing taste, he died an embittered man.    NA

*See also* RECORDINGS.

**Riemenschneider, Albert** (b. 31 Aug. 1878; d. 20 July 1950). American scholar, teacher, and collector, born in Berea, Ohio. He was director of the music department at the Methodist Episcopal Deutsches Wallace Kollegium in Berea from 1897 and continued as head when this was merged with Baldwin University to form the Baldwin–Wallace College Conservatory of Music in 1913. He retired in 1947. His edition of *371 Harmonized Chorales and 69 Chorale Melodies with Figured Bass* (New York, 1941) has made his name familiar to several generations of music students. *See also* BALDWIN–WALLACE COLLEGE BACH FESTIVAL and RIEMENSCHNEIDER BACH INSTITUTE.

**Riemenschneider Bach Institute.** An institute founded in 1969 to administer the Bach collection of Albert Riemenschneider, which had been presented to Baldwin–Wallace College, Berea, Ohio, in 1951, following Riemenschneider's death. The institute also publishes a journal, *Bach*, founded in 1970 as a quarterly and now issued twice a year. From 1989 to 1993 the journal was issued in affiliation with the AMERICAN BACH SOCIETY.

**Rilling, Helmut** (b. 29 May 1933). Conductor and organist, born in Stuttgart. He studied choral conducting with Hans Grischkat in Stuttgart and the organ with Fernando Germani in Rome. He founded his first choir, the Gächinger Kantorei, in 1954 and the Stuttgart Bach-Collegium in 1965. He has conducted Bach concerts throughout the world, and in 1972 began his complete recorded cycle of Bach's sacred cantatas, drawing on the services of the Frankfurter Kantorei, the Gächinger Kantorei, and the Stuttgart Figuralchor. Firmly eschewing the historically aware path of Nikolaus Harnoncourt and Gustav Leonhardt, his approach to Bach performance inclines strongly towards a traditional interpretation, which he believes both clarifies and strengthens the meaning of Bach's music for the contemporary listener.    NA

*See also* RECORDINGS.

**Ringk, Johannes** (b. 25 June 1717; d. 24 Aug. 1778). Organist, born in Frankenhain, Thuringia. He studied with J. P. Kellner (who may have been a Bach pupil) in Gräfenroda and with G. H. Stölzel in Gotha, and from about 1740 he held various posts in Berlin, including that of organist at the Marienkirche from 1755 until his death. Ringk was responsible for copies of several organ and keyboard works by Bach, including the famous, but not wholly authenticated, Toccata and Fugue in D minor BWV565. It is also to Ringk that we owe the preservation of the wedding cantata *Weichet nur, betrübte Schatten*.

R. Stinson, *The Bach Manuscripts of Johann Peter Kellner and his Circle* (Durham, NC, 1990).

**ritornello.** A passage written for the full complement of instruments (and sometimes voices) that recurs in various guises during the course of a movement. The word is Italian and can be rendered literally as 'little return'. It has been used in musical history with various specialized meanings—during the Baroque period it also denoted the second section in binary form—but the definition given above is the only one discussed here. Ritornellos are employed in concerto movements cast in the standard Vivaldian fast-movement form (appropriately termed 'ritornello form') and in arias, both da capo and monosectional; additionally, they can occur in almost any other kind of large-scale movement—a chorus, chorale, prelude, sonata movement, toccata, prelude, even a fugue—regardless of whether their use is traditional in that context.

Superficially, a ritornello resembles the refrain of a rondo (*see* RONDEAU/RONDO). It usually frames the movement (although episodic preambles to the first ritornello are not unknown), and there are normally intermediate statements spaced more or less evenly. There is no historical connection between the two devices, however, since the ritornello traces its ancestry back to the motto openings used in early concerto movements. Unlike a rondo refrain, which appears in unaltered form on each statement (except for the kind of decorative variation found in the movement entitled Rondeaux in Bach's keyboard Partita no. 2), a ritornello is subject to alteration (abbreviation, expansion, reordering of elements, paraphrase, etc.) every time it returns. Moreover, intermediate statements of ritornellos are nearly always placed in foreign keys, so acting as tonal landmarks. Ritornellos are nearly always 'closed' musical periods—tonal plateaus that prolong the keys reached immediately before. This does not prevent them, however, from containing within themselves a considerable amount of transitory modulation; this sometimes reproduces in miniature the modulatory course of the whole movement.

The typical character and style of treatment of ritornellos was established in the early concertos of Vivaldi, written around 1710. As many German composers, including Bach, showed through the evolution of their music in those years, the ritornello principle was taken up with enthusiasm in northern Europe (more so, in fact, than in Italy, where older structural models stubbornly persisted). Many of Vivaldi's favourite musical formulae in ritornellos, such as weighty string unisons and the three-hammer-blow opening, became common currency. However, German composers recoiled from some of the extreme features of Vivaldi's treatment of ritornellos. Where an initial ritornello comprises several elements, German composers usually repeat or develop them all more or less equally, rather than omitting some and emphasizing others, as very often happens in Vivaldi. The Germans also tend to reduce the length of ritornellos after the first less drastically than Vivaldi does.

There is no fixed number of ritornellos. In a slow movement there may be merely two, both in the tonic, framing the main section; in the A sections of a da capo aria (A–B–A) there are usually three, the central statement being in the principal subsidiary key; and in a concerto fast movement there are usually four or more. One characteristic of Bach's movements in any form is their tendency to visit, one by one, each of the five keys most nearly related to the home key. This means that in a ritornello structure the number of ritornellos is often unusually large (in the first movement of the Second Brandenburg Concerto there are ritornello statements in seven different keys). Another peculiarity of Bach's use of ritornellos—in great contrast to Telemann's—is his fondness for development and variation, as opposed to simple restatement. Because material from his ritornellos permeates the intervening episodes (in arias these are the vocal sections), and because solo instruments sometimes have independent lines within the ritornellos, it can sometimes prove difficult to determine where sections begin and end, but an examination of the tonal structure always settles the issue.

One great virtue of ritornello form is the ease with which it can be superimposed on, or combined with, other forms. In the opening chorus of the *St Matthew Passion*, for instance, it absorbs structures derived from the chorale fantasia, the fugue, and the *concertato* dialogue. In the fourth movement of Cantata 140, *Wachet auf* (later arranged for organ as the first of the Schübler Chorales), the beguiling ritornello theme captures the listener's attention so completely that it appears as if the cantus firmus is the accompanying voice, rather than the opposite. The way in which Bach first absorbed the ritornello principle thoroughly and then creatively applied it in previously unimagined contexts is a measure of his mastery as a composer.                        MT

P. Drummond, *The German Concerto: Five Eighteenth-Century Studies* (Oxford, 1980); A. J. B. Hutchings, *The Baroque Concerto* (London, 1961; 3rd edn., 1973).

**Ritter, Johann Christoph** (b. 1715; d. 25 Jan. 1767). Organist and composer. He studied with Bach in Leipzig around 1740, at which time he made copies of *Clavier-Übung I* and *II*. In 1744 he was appointed organist at Clausthal, where he remained for the rest of his life. Of his own works only three keyboard sonatas, published in 1751, are extant.

E. R. Jacobi, 'Johann Christoph Ritter (1715–1767), ein unbekannter Schüler J. S. Bachs, und seine Abschrift (etwa 1740) der "Clavier-Übung" I/II', *BJb* 51 (1965), 43–61.

**Rogate.** The fifth Sunday after Easter; Rogation Sunday. *See* CHURCH CALENDAR.

**Rolle, Christian Friedrich** (b. 14 April 1681; d. 25 Aug. 1751). Composer and teacher, born in Halle. He studied law at Halle University. He was appointed town Kantor at Quedlinburg in 1709 and in April 1716 joined Bach and Johann Kuhnau to examine a new organ at the Liebfrauenkirche in Halle. On 13 January 1722 he took up the post of Kantor at Magdeburg, and later that year competed for the post of Kantor at Leipzig but eventually withdrew his candidature. He was later made city music director at Magdeburg, where he was succeeded in 1751 by his son Johann Heinrich

# rondeau/rondo

(1716–85), a composer of oratorios and other works, both vocal and instrumental.

**rondeau/rondo.** After binary form, the most commonly used structure for French dances in the Baroque period, and one frequently employed in other genres as well. The term 'rondeau' was favoured in French contexts and used as a title for several pieces or movements by Bach. The first section of a rondeau closes in the tonic and acts as a refrain, being repeated after each episode, or *couplet*. The structure differs from RITORNELLO form (which is also based on the refrain-like repetition of opening material) mainly because the rondeau refrain returns always in the home key, usually in full, and unaltered in substance.

The type of rondeau with a single episode, A–B–A, occurs in the keyboard suites BWV820 and 822 (there are three examples in each), 823 (*Sarabande en rondeau*), and 812 (Menuet 2). More common is the rondeau with two episodes, A–B–A–C–A, which is found in BWV810, 821 ('Echo', in which a coda replaces the final refrain), 822, 1011, and 1067. Rondeaux with three episodes, A–B–A–C–A–D–A, occur in BWV823 (Prélude, built on a chaconne bass) and 826 (entitled simply 'Rondeaux', since it lacks a specific dance rhythm). The well-known *Gavotte en rondeau* from the solo violin Partita in E major and the finale of the violin concerto in the same key are both rondeaux with four episodes (A–B–A–C–A–D–A–E–A). The most complex of all Bach's rondeau structures is the keyboard *Fantaisie sur un rondeau* BWV918, a mature piece of unknown date.

Bach also employed rondeau form in his vocal works. A comparison of the last chorus of the *St Matthew Passion* (A–B–A) with that of the *St John Passion* (A–B–A–B′–A) shows that the rondeau may be viewed as an expanded da capo form. This type, usually associated with dance rhythm, is found in the closing choruses of Bach's Leipzig congratulatory cantatas nos. 205, 206, 213, and 215, and in the vocal trio that closes the Coffee Cantata. Instances in the sacred cantatas are rare: the opening choruses of no. 186a (1716; adapted as BWV186 in 1723) and no. 30 (based on the secular cantata, BWV30a of 1737) and the remarkable extended chorus 'Aller Augen warten, Herr' (A–B–A–C–A–D–A–E–A) from the first of Bach's two audition cantatas for the Leipzig Kantorate, *Du wahrer Gott und Davids Sohn* (1723). An exceptional case of an aria in rondeau (or rondo) form is the well-known 'Schlummert ein' (A–B–A–C–A) from the solo cantata *Ich habe genung* (1727). RDPJ

***Rückpositiv*** ('positive [organ] at the back'). A division of organ pipes normally located behind the organist's back, on the edge of a gallery, and played from the lowest keyboard. The division appeared less frequently after the 17th century because of the tendency of central German organ builders to abandon spatially separated cases for each of the divisions, in favour of a single case. Bach's use of the *Rückpositiv* is reflected in the indications found in scores, for example in those of various concerto arrangements for organ (BWV592–5). J. F. Agricola's insistence on the value of the *Rückpositiv* (see J. Adlung, *Musica mechanica organoedi*, ii (1768), 8 and 19) suggests that his teacher, Bach, might have held similar views, as does the substantial *Rückpositiv* in the organ of the Wenzelskirche, Naumburg, whose plan Bach probably influenced. QF

**Rust, Johann Ludwig Anton** (b. 12 Dec. 1721; d. Oct. 1785). Registrar and violinist, born in Reinstedt, near Bernburg, about 50 km. (31 miles) north-west of Leipzig. He enrolled at the University of Wittenberg in October 1740, and at Leipzig University in November 1744. At Leipzig he was a pupil of Bach and took part as a violinist in performances of his music. His younger brother, Friedrich Wilhelm Rust (1739–96), reportedly played Part 1 of *The Well-tempered Clavier* from beginning to end at the age of 13, and studied with Wilhelm Friedemann Bach in Halle. Both Rusts owned important manuscripts of works by J. S. Bach.
*BDok* iii, no. 811.

**Rust, Wilhelm** (b. 15 Aug. 1822; d. 18 Apr. 1892). One of the most influential editors of the 'old' Bach edition (*BG*). Born in Dessau, he worked from 1849 in Berlin, mainly as a music teacher and organist. He went to Leipzig as organist at the Thomaskirche in 1878, and in 1880 succeeded Ernst Friedrich Richter (1808–79) as Thomaskantor.

Rust was a member of the *BG* editorial team from 1853, and his activity reached its peak in 1858 when he became the principal editor. He edited all the cantata volumes appearing between 1855 and 1876 (BWV21–110), as well as the *Christmas Oratorio*. Controversies with Philipp Spitta forced him to retire from his post, and even from the editorial board, in 1888. Spitta criticized Rust for arbitrarily altering details of the music (even in the sources themselves); Rust, on the other hand, was perhaps the only scholar who was Spitta's equal in handling philological techniques, and was thus able to criticize Spitta's theories regarding chronology. In his preface to volume 28 of the *BG* he developed his own view of Bach, which was polemical but far-sighted. KK

G. v. Dadelsen, *Beiträge zur Chronologie der Werke Johann Sebastian Bachs* (Trossingen, 1958); R. L.

Marshall, 'Editore traditore: ein weiterer "Fall Rust"', in *Bachiana et alia musicologica: Festschrift* *Alfred Dürr zum 65. Geburtstag* (Kassel, 1983), 183–91.

# S

**'St Anne'.** Nickname for the Prelude and Fugue in E♭ major, BWV552. It derives from the similarity between Bach's fugue subject and the first line of the hymn tune 'St Anne', probably by William Croft (1678–1727), to which *O God, our help in ages past* is commonly sung. There is nothing to suggest that Bach was familiar with the hymn; several other contemporary themes have a similar outline. *See also* CLAVIER-ÜBUNG III.

**Saint-Donat Bach Festival.** An annual festival devoted to Bach's music, held in July–August at Saint-Donat sur l'Herbasse, Drôme. It was founded in 1961 by Henri Lemonon, and its concerts, with which the Swiss conductor Michel Corboz has been particularly associated, centre on the medieval church at Saint-Donat.

**St John Passion.** See overleaf.

**St Luke Passion** (*Lukas-Passion*). An anonymous setting of the Passion story from St Luke's Gospel by one of Bach's contemporaries. Although accepted as a genuine Bach work by Philipp Spitta, included in the *BG* edition (vol. xlv/2), and assigned a catalogue number by Wolfgang Schmieder (BWV246), the *St Luke Passion* is now considered spurious on stylistic grounds. The score, copied by Bach and his son Carl Philipp Emanuel, was probably prepared for performance at the Nikolaikirche, Leipzig, on Good Friday 1730. Leipzig liturgical practice required the division of the Passion into two halves, and it is possible that the instrumental introduction to Part 2 and the orchestration of the following recitative were written by Bach to provide a more convincing opening at the point where he decided to divide the work.                                        SH

A. Glöckner, 'Bach and the Passion Music of his Contemporaries', *Musical Times*, 116 (1975), 613–16. For further bibliography, *see* PASSION.

**St Mark Passion** (*Markus-Passion*). Bach's last setting of the Passion, BWV247, probably performed at the Thomaskirche, Leipzig, on Good Friday (23 March) 1731. The score has been lost, but the libretto by Picander was published among the poet's collected works in 1732. Although neither this text nor the setting advertised in Breitkopf's catalogue in January 1764 mentions Bach, his authorship and compositional method have never been in doubt. As early as 1873 Wilhelm Rust realized that the Passion must have been a large-scale PARODY work, since five stanzas of the libretto mirrored the poetic structure of the main choruses and arias that Picander had written earlier for Bach's *Trauer-Ode* (1727).

Picander's libretto shows that the work was constructed along similar lines to Bach's two earlier Passions: divided into two parts with substantial opening and closing choruses, 6 arias and 16 chorales. The Gospel narrative (Mark 14–15) was assigned to an Evangelist, sections of dialogue to named characters, and the interjections of the crowd to the chorus. Bach's practice in similar parody works was to retain the original scoring where possible, and Breitkopf's catalogue lists forces for the Passion which are almost identical to those of the *Trauer-Ode*: SATB, 2 flutes, 2 oboes, gambas, and strings.

In addition to the three arias from the *Trauer-Ode*, 'Falsche Welt' (the third aria) was drawn from the cantata *Wiederstehe doch der Sünde* (c.1714), and 'Angenehmes Mord-Geschrei' (the fifth aria) probably parodied 'Himmlische Vergnügsamkeit' from *Ich bin in mir vergnügt* (1726–7). The model for the final aria, 'Welt und Himmel', is less certain, but may have been either 'Leit, o Gott' from *Herr Gott, Beherrsche aller Dinge* (c.1729), or an adaptation of 'Himmel reiße' which was added to the *St John Passion* in 1725 but later discarded. Bach would have written the narrative sections of the work afresh in 1731. Although the recitatives are entirely lost, the *turba* choruses 'Ja nicht auf das Fest' and 'Pfui dich' possibly survive in the *Christmas Oratorio*. Enough of the original music exists (albeit in other forms) to allow partial reconstruction of the work. Several performing versions have been published, including those by Diethard Hellmann (1964, with spoken narratives) and G. A. Theill (1984, with pastiche recitatives). The versions by A. H. Gomme (University of Keele, 1993) and Simon Heighes (The King's Music, 1993) both include recitatives and *turba* choruses from Reinhard Keiser's *St Mark Passion*, which Bach is known to have performed.                                        SH

A. Glöckner, 'Bach and the Passion Music of his Contemporaries', *Musical Times*, 116 (1975), 613–16; F. Smend, 'Bachs Markus-Passion', *BJb* 37 (1940–8), 1–35; G. A. Theill, 'Die Markuspassion von Joh. Seb. Bach (BWV 247)', in *Beiträge zur Musikreflexion*, 6 (1978), 11–91.

## St John Passion (*Johannes-Passion*)

A setting of the Passion story from St John's Gospel, BWV245, first performed on 7 April 1724. The oratorio PASSION—a genre in which the standard Passion narrative was embellished with freely composed verse and chorales, and employed Italian operatic genres—had been familiar in several north German cities since the middle of the 17th century. However, it was a novelty in conservative Leipzig, the first performance being in the Neukirche in 1717. The innovation evidently met with sufficient approval for it to be adopted at the Thomaskirche in 1721, two years before Bach's arrival.

The oratorio Passion evolved around the sermon at one of the most important services of the Lutheran year. Preachers traditionally combined commentary on the Passion narrative with meditation on each event, usually vivid and pictorial poetry in the first person. This inspired a rich heritage of devotional writing, some of which was designed for a musical setting, thus occasioning yet another dimension in the exegesis. The resulting oratorio (which included all the biblical narrative too) was sung in two parts on either side of the sermon at Vespers on Good Friday. Among the most celebrated Passion librettos was B. H. Brockes's *Der für die Sünde der Welt gemarterte und sterbende Jesus*, and it was this that an anonymous librettist adapted for several of the arias in Bach's *St John Passion*.

When Bach composed the *St John Passion* in 1724 there was, according to the town council minutes of 3 April, some confusion over the venue: the new Kantor had apparently ignored their decision to perform the Passion that year in the Nikolaikirche (thereafter alternating between the two principal churches), and had printed librettos for use in the Thomaskirche. Bach complied only after additional room had been provided in the choir loft at the Nikolaikirche and the harpsichord had been repaired (*BDok* ii. 139–40).

In 1725 Bach performed the work again, with several modifications to its content. The fact that half of these involve the addition of chorale-based movements suggests that this performance was somehow associated with the cycle of chorale cantatas he composed that year. He performed it again in about 1732, this time returning to the first version, but omitting the two insertions from St Matthew's Gospel (the scenes concerning Peter's remorse and the supernatural events directly following Jesus's death).

When Bach returned again to the *St John Passion* towards the end of the 1730s he began to prepare a calligraphic score. This he seems to have intended as a definitive version of the work, since it contains many refinements, but he broke off after 20-odd pages and the score was finished ten years later by a copyist. It is not certain why Bach abandoned the new score; most likely the hiatus relates to a report in the council minutes of 17 March 1739: a clerk had been dispatched to prohibit performance of the Good Friday music until permission was granted. Bach replied that 'it had always been done so; he did not care, for he got nothing out of it anyway, and it was only a burden; he would notify the Superintendent that it had been forbidden him; if an objection were made on account of the text, it had already been performed several times' (*BDok* ii. 338–9; translation from H. T. David and A. Mendel, eds., *The Bach Reader* (London, 1945; 2nd edn. 1966), 162–3).

The council's reservations may also relate to the somewhat mixed text of the *St John Passion*, and its opinions may well have influenced Bach's changes in the earlier versions (for instance, the excisions of the *St Matthew* texts in the 1732 version may reflect official distaste at mixing Gospel texts merely for greater dramatic effect). Perhaps the Baroque poetry in the Brockes tradition was also going out of fashion; certainly the fourth and final version of the Passion (1749) contains alterations to three aria texts which remove some of the more pictorial language.

The council may also have been swayed by local opposition to the oratorio style. In 1732 the Pietist writer Christian Gerber (1660–1731) complained of the recent introduction of theatrical Passion music in Saxony, stating that many people had been shocked by the development and knew not what to make of it; 'if some of those first Christians should rise, visit our assemblies, and hear such a roaring organ together with so many instruments, I do not believe that they would recognize us as Christians and their successors' (translation from Stiller, p. 265).

The free verse of Bach's *St John Passion* is intensely concerned with the theology of the Gospel. *St John* does not belong to the narrative tradition of the first three Gospels, the so-called synoptic Gospels; rather, John's foremost intention is to provide a cosmic explanation for the phenomenon of Christ, one clearly influenced by the classical philosophic tradition. Luther himself favoured this Gospel on account of its specific theological message and its clear interpretation of Christ's purpose on earth. Christ, like his father, must exist eternally, standing outside human conceptions of time. Christ's earthly office is a sign of God's presence as 'the Word made flesh'; all his activities are designed to prove his ambassadorial position as the Son of God. Within this deterministic scheme, the murder of Christ is the mechanical device by which the Son returns to the Father. John's account omits much of the suffering which Christ must have experienced as a human being; rather, every adverse event is turned into a celebration of the fulfilment of the plan: in death, Christ—who knows everything in advance—exclaims 'Es ist vollbracht' ('It is fulfilled'; 'finished' in the Authorized Version). The darker side of John's ideology is his view of the Jews as eternally damned: they are placed on a lower level, outside Pilate's judgement hall, and it is they who coax this seemingly benevolent governor to kill their impostor 'king'.

The free poetry of the opening chorus establishes the Johannine theme of the work: Christ is portrayed as the eternal and omnipresent ruler. The poet implores him, as the true son of God, to show how he becomes glorified even in the lowliness of his passion. The same pairing of opposites (interestingly, also linked with a modified da capo structure) is evident in the lament 'Es ist vollbracht', where the central section portrays Christ as victor. For many, the pivotal point of Bach's Passion and the most significant distillation of its message is the pseudo-chorale 'Durch dein Gefängnis' (actually an aria text by Heinrich Postel), which again exploits a contradiction: we receive freedom through Christ's captivity. That Bach considered this, the central point (which Friedrich Smend appropriately called the *Herzstück*, the 'heart', of the Passion), to be important seems clear from the surrounding choruses, which fan out symmetrically from it (e.g. 'Wir haben ein Gesetz', before this, and 'Lässest du diesen los', after it, share the same music). Another symmetrical pattern centres on 'Es ist vollbracht', the climax of the narrative, which is surrounded by two strophes of the Passiontide chorale 'Jesu Kreuz, Leiden und Pein' (the strophe 'Er nahm Alles wohl in Acht' coming before, and 'Jesu, der du warest tot' coming after as part of the aria 'Mein teurer Heiland').

Bach may have devised the symmetrical pacing to be analogous to the structure of the Vesper liturgy in which his Passions were performed: this began and ended with a chorale, and centred on the sermon which, in turn, was surrounded by the two parts of the Passion. The Passion, like the cantata which would normally come before the sermon, was clearly closely associated with the sermon, both as an elaborated reading of the Gospel and also as a poetic and theological interpretation of the story.

Given Bach's careful pacing of choruses and the use of symmetrical structures, many writers have sought further elaborate symbolic structures within the *St John Passion*. Certainly such orders are not atypical of the intellectual and religious climate of the time. Eric Chafe has examined the tonal allegory, drawing particular attention to the symbolism of sharp and flat keys and the general flow of tonality within the course of the piece. What comes across in performance is the relentlessness of the events; everything takes place almost with a clockwork precision, in direct and necessary fulfilment of a preordained—indeed prophesied—order. The trial scene is the central point of the Johannine narrative, since it is here that Christ's kingship is judged by the Jews (wrongly, so that it can be shown to be right). Whether or not the musical connections between the crowd choruses (especially those derived from the first, 'Jesum von Nazareth') point to another symbolic dimension, the first listeners must have experienced an increasing sense of inevitability as the piece progressed, since so many choruses would already sound familiar.

Some critics maintain that the *St John Passion* lacks the refinement of its more illustrious sister, the *St Matthew*. The text is something of a mongrel, drawing on Chapters 18 and 19 of St John's Gospel, two small interpolations from St Matthew's Gospel (excised in the third version), extracts from Psalm 8 in the opening chorus, chorale verses (including one with an aria text, Postel's 'Durch dein Gefängnis'), and Passion poetry drawn from Christian Weise, Postel, and especially Brockes's libretto. Certainly the *St John Passion* is not as evenly paced as the later Passion, lacking the almost doctrinaire successions of narrative–arioso–aria which accord to the latter the flavour of a spiritual exercise. But the central trial scene would lose its impact if it were punctuated with ariosos and arias. Both the intense musical colouring of the recitatives (Peter's lament and the scourging of Christ are far more vivid than their counterparts in the *St Matthew Passion*) and the incisive figuration of the choruses (almost a latter-day adaptation of Monteverdi's 'warlike', *concitato* style) recall the idioms of the late 17th century, when Lutheran music followed the very grain of the text. Only the arias and the opening and closing choruses display the distilled, affective style of Bach's mature writing.

Of all Bach's larger works, the compositional history of the *St John Passion* is by far the most complex: no single source transmits the work as a unique and perfect masterpiece. The 20 pages that Bach completed of the 1739 score contain many refinements, but he does not seem to have given much attention to the remainder of the score. However, the similarity between the first and last versions might betray his preferred conception of the work (to the extent that he had a definitive version in mind). Arthur Mendel produced perhaps the most complex critical commentary on the sources in the entire *NBA* series. For his edition he followed the 1739–49 score for the most part, as representing Bach's final intentions, while providing the alternative versions as an appendix and listing all the minor differences in the commentary.

No score and only a few of the parts survive for the first version, and it is not known, for instance, to what extent Bach employed the flutes; the only significant difference between this and the last version is the absence of the earthquake scene at Christ's death (an interpolation from St Matthew's Gospel added in versions 2 and 4). The 1725 version (performed on 30 March) departs most radically from the others, with five pieces replacing or augmenting numbers in the 1724 version; some suggest that these originated in Weimar and may have been part of a lost *St Matthew Passion* (see *BC*). The new opening chorus, 'O Mensch, bewein dein Sünde groß', later became the closing chorus to Part 1 of the *St Matthew Passion* (transposed up a semitone); Bach inserted the bass aria with chorale 'Himmel reiße, Welt erbebe' into the scene where Christ appears before the high priest, replaced the tenor aria 'Ach, mein Sinn' with 'Zerschmettert mich', and also replaced the bass arioso 'Betrachte, meine Seel' and the tenor aria 'Erwäge' with the tenor aria 'Ach windet euch nicht so'. He also replaced the concluding chorale with a more elaborate chorale setting, 'Christe, du Lamm Gottes'.

The third version (probably performed on 11 April 1732) is incomplete, like the first, but enough material survives to show that Bach removed the substitute numbers of version 2. A lost sinfonia filled the place of the earthquake scene, the arioso 'Mein Herz', and the aria 'Zerfließe, mein Herze', which all centre on an interpolation from St Matthew's Gospel. The earlier interpolation (Peter's weeping) and the accompanying aria were also removed and replaced with a lost aria. This was the only version of the Passion to end with the chorus 'Ruht wohl' without a concluding chorale. Organ and muted violins replace lute and violas d'amore in 'Betrachte, meine Seel', and muted violins replace violas d'amore in 'Erwäge, wie sein blutge-färbter Rücken' in the performance parts to both the third and fourth versions. The fourth and final version (4 April 1749) restores the interpolations from *St Matthew*. Many of the changes that Bach made in the later versions imply that he was aiming at 'improvement' rather than merely adapting to circumstances. Among these are the numerous refinements to the notes (particularly in the incomplete score), the muted violin added to the flute in 'Zerfließe, mein Herze' and the 'bassono grosso' indicated for choruses, chorales, and at certain points in four arias and ariosos.

Bach's use of the harpsichord in church music has been a subject of controversy (*see* CONTINUO). The 1749 version is one of the few works for which a part is actually labelled 'cembalo' and thorough-bass figures are added for every movement. Bach's complaints about the state of the harpsichord for the first performance further sug-gest that the harpsichord always belonged with the forces of this work. However, the case of the obbligato part to 'Betrachte, meine Seel' is ambiguous, since this is notated in both harpsichord and organ parts. That additions in the latter are penned in Bach's aged hand suggests that the organ had priority in the final version.

The *St John Passion* is one of the few works for which Bach supplied ripieno chorus parts, suggesting that he may have combined the first two *Kantoreien* (as he did in the *St Matthew Passion*, which requires two separate choirs). While the matter of how many concertists and how many ripienists Bach had singing at any one time is still a matter of considerable debate (*see* CHORUS), it is clear that this Passion required larger choral forces than was the weekly norm.                                    JAB

E. T. Chafe, *Tonal Allegory in the Vocal Music of J. S. Bach* (Berkeley and Los Angeles, Calif., 1991); A. Dürr, *Die Johannes-Passion von Johann Sebastian Bach* (Kassel, 1988); A. Mendel, 'Traces of the Pre-history of Bach's St John and St Matthew Passions', in W. Gerstenberg *et* al., eds., *Festschrift Otto Erich Deutsch zum 80. Geburtstag* (Kassel, 1963), 31–48; F. Smend, 'Die Johannes-Passion von Bach: auf ihren Bau untersucht', *BJb* 23 (1926), 105–28; repr. in F. Smend, *Bach-Studien: gesammelte Reden und Aufsätze*, ed. C. Wolff (Kassel, 1969), 11–23. For further bibliography, *see* PASSION.

**St Matthew Passion.** See overleaf.

**sarabande.** A dance and instrumental form of the 17th and 18th centuries. From probable Spanish origins, it appeared in Italy as a colourful, tempestuous, exotic dance, accompanied by castanets with one or several guitars playing continuous variations on a series of harmonies, the chords punctuated by fiery *rasgueado* strumming. The sarabande was taken over by French dancing-masters at the court of Louis XIV, who transformed it into a more restrained theatrical and social dance in the French style. Several writings of the period hint at a passionate or mannered performance expressed in pantomimic gestures.

As instrumental music from the late 17th century on, the sarabande is serious, sometimes tender, but always with intensity of expression. Variation techniques are important to its soloistic style. The most common metrical sign is 3/4, where crotchets represent the beat; when the time signature is 3/2, minims represent the beat. Rhythmic levels below the beat are normally duple (i.e. quavers and semiquavers in 3/4, crotchets and quavers in 3/2). *Notes inégales* may be applied to the lowest level in either metre (*see* RHYTHM). The rhythmic phrase is 12 beats (4 bars) in length with a *thesis* (point of repose) on beat 10 (the beginning of bar 4) which diminishes further (becomes more thetic) into beat 12. A typical sarabande rhythmic module is shown at Ex. 1.

Bach wrote 42 sarabandes; among the dances they are second in quantity only to minuets if we include the *doubles*. They occur in five early keyboard and lute works, BWV821, 823, 832, 965, and 966; all six English and French suites, as well as the suites in E♭ major BWV818 and A minor BWV819; all six keyboard Partitas; the Ouverture in the French Style; Partitas nos. 1 and 2 for solo violin; all six solo Cello Suites, and the lute version of no. 5; the Partita for solo flute; the C minor Partita for lute; and the Orchestral Suite in B minor.

Bach experimented with a wide variety of technical features in his sarabandes. He wrote them with and without upbeats, and no two upbeat figures are the same; he wrote short sarabandes (BWV832, 965, and 1007) and very long ones (BWV 1013); he wrote a sarabande in which the first strain is repeated da capo (BWV823), one with a written-out *petite reprise* in the *double* (BWV818), stately sarabandes (BWV825 and 1008), lyrical sarabandes (BWV810), sarabandes with constant dotted rhythms which recall the French overture or *entrée grave* (BWV818a, 819, and 1010), and many which present elaborate and harmonically complex dance stylizations. Only one ensemble piece contains a sarabande, and the dance is thus in Bach's hands essentially a piece for a soloist, who has the freedom to use subtle performance techniques not available to larger groups.

Untitled sarabandes include Prelude no. 8 from *The Well-tempered Clavier* Part 1, the Aria of the Goldberg Variations, the Largo in the trio sonata from the *Musical Offering*, and numerous choral movements.                                                                 NJ, MEL

For bibliography, *see* DANCE.

**Saxony.** An area of Germany bordered on the north and east by Prussia, on the south by Bohemia (now the Czech Republic), and on the west by Thuringia and Bavaria. Saxony became an electorate in the mid-13th century. After the death of Frederick II in 1464 it was divided between his sons Albert and Ernest, and after many struggles the Albertine line acquired the electorate, the Ernestine line becoming dominant in the Saxon duchies to the west. In 1697 the elector FRIEDRICH AUGUSTUS I became King of Poland, a move which enhanced the prestige of the electorate but which eventually proved to be a drain on its resources. He was succeeded by his son FRIEDRICH AUGUSTUS II, who ruled from 1733 to 1763. The union with Poland was dissolved in 1763 when Frederick the Great conquered Saxony during the Seven Years War.

[*cont. on p.434*]

Ex. 1

## St Matthew Passion (*Matthäus-Passion*)

A setting of the Passion story from St Matthew's Gospel, BWV244, probably performed on Good Friday 1727. The *St Matthew Passion* is by any standard a remarkable composition—one of the most complex of all Bach's vocal works and for many the most profound. Mendelssohn considered it to be 'the greatest of Christian works', and many other superlatives have continued to be accorded this emotionally powerful music, which almost every choral group aspires to perform.

1. Genesis and early performances.
2. Text and music.
3. Neglect and revival.

1. **Genesis and early performances.**   Until 1975 it was thought that the *St Matthew Passion* was originally composed for Good Friday 1729, but modern research strongly suggests that it was first performed two years earlier. Like the *St John Passion*, the *St Matthew* went through an evolutionary process of composition, the evidence for which is fragmentary, since the earliest manuscript score and parts date from 1736. But it seems that an earlier version of the work was performed on Good Friday (11 April) 1727, and it was almost certainly performed again in the same form in 1729. In 1736 the work was revised and a new score and parts prepared for performance that year. It was substantially in this later form that it was performed again some time around 1742.

Evidence found in scores and parts of other works suggest that Bach was planning this ambitious Passion setting at least as early as 1725. The fourth movement of Cantata 127, *Herr Jesu Christ, wahr' Mensch und Gott*, first heard on the Sunday before Lent (11 February) 1725, contains a 'pre-echo' of the chorus 'Sind Blitze, sind Donner' from the Passion. Although it is difficult to be absolutely certain, a comparison of the two uses of the same thematic material suggests that the chorus in the *St Matthew Passion* was written before the bass aria of Cantata 127. If this is correct, it means that Bach had begun to compose the *St Matthew Passion* by the beginning of 1725. It also means that it was begun during the year, 1724–5, when Bach was composing his second *Jahrgang* of chorale cantatas, and therefore raises the possibility that the composer conceived the *St Matthew Passion* as a kind of 'chorale Passion'. There is some substance in this possibility. Compared with the *St John*, the *St Matthew Passion* makes slightly greater use of four-part chorales, as well as including extensive chorale movements, such as those that open and close Part 1. In the event, it would seem that the composition of such a large-scale work was more time-consuming than the composer anticipated, and it was clear that it would not be ready for performance on Good Friday 1725. Indeed, it would be another two years before it was ready. This protracted compositional process is probably the reason why Bach repeated his 1724 *St John Passion*, with some substitute chorale movements and other changes, in 1725, and it is also possibly why he performed Reinhard Keiser's *St Mark Passion* in 1726.

Another piece of evidence is found on the *verso* of the viola part of the Sanctus BWV232[III] (later incorporated into the B minor Mass) in the set of parts prepared for Count Franz Anton Sporck towards the end of 1726. At the bottom right corner of this manuscript, upside down, is found a sequence of notes that occurs in several places in the first violin part of the aria 'Mache dich, mein Herze, rein' in the *St Matthew Passion* (no. 65). The notes have been crossed out, but the sheet was saved for later use. Although the struck-through draft has, of course, no associated text, the fact that the Passion text of 'Mache dich' is somewhat unusual makes it extremely unlikely to have been associated with other words. As this aria appears towards the end of the work, and as Bach's practice was to compose his cantatas in a linear fashion, working from movement to movement in sequence, Joshua Rifkin has argued that the early version of the *St Matthew Passion* was almost complete at the end of 1726. Eric Chafe, on the other hand, thinks it unlikely that Bach would have composed such a complex work in sequence, and that completion of the *St Matthew Passion* may therefore have taken a few more months.

A further indication that 1727 was the year of the first performance is provided by a Passion libretto by Picander that appeared among the instalments of cantata librettos issued during the liturgical year 1724–5. The complete anthology of librettos was reissued in book form in 1725 with the title *Sammlung Erbaulicher Gedancken über und auf die gewöhnlichen Sonn- und Fest-Tage*. Picander also wrote the libretto for Bach's *St Matthew Passion*, and in it he included three items (nos. 39, 49, and 68) that are poetic parodies of movements from the 1725 Passion libretto, sharing with them vocabulary, imagery, and rhyme schemes. In her researches into the background of the *St Matthew Passion* Elke Axmacher discovered that for approximately half the arias Picander was heavily indebted to various prose passages in a series of eight Passion sermons by the Rostock theologian Heinrich Müller (1631–75), appended to the author's posthumous collection of sermons entitled *Evangelisches Praeservativ wider den Schaden Josephs, in allen dreyen Ständen* (1681). Bach owned a copy of Müller's sermons, and it seems likely that he drew Picander's attention to it. Given the other evidence of the early beginnings of his second Leipzig Passion, the strong suggestion is that Picander worked closely with the composer during the first half of 1725 in creating the libretto for the *St Matthew Passion*, utilizing elements from the recently published 1725 Passion libretto, and drawing on the Passion sermons of Müller. This later libretto, created specifically for Bach, was subsequently published in Picander's *Ernst-Schertzhaffte und Satyrische Gedichte, Anderer Theil* (Leipzig, 1729).

Although the evidence is fragmentary, the fragments together make a persuasive case for concluding that the early version of the *St Matthew Passion* was first performed on Good Friday 1727. Confirmation of this date is found in the movements of the Passion that were parodied for a memorial service for Prince Leopold of Anhalt-Cöthen, Bach's former employer, held on 23–4 March 1729 in Cöthen (*see* CÖTHEN FUNERAL MUSIC).

The manuscript score and parts of this early version of the *St Matthew Passion* are no longer extant, but much of it can be determined in detail from the following important sources: Picander's libretto, published in 1729; a manuscript score in the hand of Bach's pupil and son-in-law J. C. Altnickol, written some time between 1744 and 1748 (BWV244b); and an incomplete score copied some time after 1741 by J. F. Agricola, another Bach pupil. Comparison of these scores with the 1736 autograph reveals many revisions and adjustments. Particularly noticeable is the strengthening of the continuo and various changes made to the instrumentation. A more significant change is found at the end of Part 1, which had originally concluded with a simple four-part chorale, a stanza of Christian Keimann's *Meinen Jesum laß ich nicht*. In the 1736 version this chorale was dropped in favour of the magnificent chorale fantasia *O Mensch, bewein dein Sünde groß*, which had been composed in Weimar (see *BC* iii, D1), employed as the opening movement of the temporary second version of the *St John Passion* in 1725, and now found its final place in the *St Matthew Passion*.

2. **Text and music.** Although a large-scale concerted setting, the *St Matthew Passion*, like the earlier *St John*, was not composed as an independent Passion oratorio, but as an elaborate musical meditation on the content and meaning of the biblical narrative, to be heard in a specific liturgical context (Good Friday Vespers) that included congregational hymns, preaching, and prayer (*see* PASSION).

The *St Matthew Passion* begins with a large-scale chorale fantasia for double chorus, each choir with its own orchestral support: 'Kommt, ihr Töchter, helft mir klagen. Sehet den Bräutigam. Seht ihn as wie ein Lamm' ('Come, O daughters, help my crying. See the bridegroom. See him like a lamb'). At bar 30 the chorale melody *O Lamm Gottes unschuldig*, sung by ripieno sopranos, soars above the combined choral and orchestral texture. The text of the chorale is the metrical paraphrase of the Agnus Dei that had been sung at the end of the morning *Hauptgottesdienst* on Good Friday. This large-scale movement, therefore, sets the stage for the drama that is about to be unfolded, and it is not until the theological statement has been heard, 'Behold the Lamb of God, which taketh away the sin of the world', that the details of the biblical narrative of the Passion can then be recounted. Similar to 16th-century altarpieces that depict the Lamb of God at the foot of the Cross, Bach's profound musical meditation on the Crucifixion flows from this emphatic and emblematic use of the paraphrase of the Agnus Dei: 'O Lamm Gottes unschuldig'.

The unhurried progress through the details of the Passion story is frequently presented in a repeated pattern of biblical narrative, comment, and prayer. First, there is the biblical narrative, sung primarily by the Evangelist, but with the various *dramatis personae* represented by other voices, and groups of people by one or other (or both) of the choruses. Then, before the narrative is continued, a recitative (more in the nature of an arioso) makes some kind of reflective comment on the biblical narrative that has just been heard. Finally, the substance of the comment is transformed into a prayer in an aria that follows. Examples of this pattern, which recurs throughout the *St Matthew Passion*, include the following:

| | |
|---|---|
| Narrative (no. 4e) | Evangelist: 'Da das Jesus merkete' |
| Comment (no. 5) | Recitative: 'Du lieber Heiland' |
| Prayer (no. 6) | Aria: 'Buß und Reu' |
| Narrative (no. 11) | Evangelist: 'Er antwortete und sprach' |
| Comment (no. 12) | Recitative: 'Wiewohl mein Herz in Tränen schwimmt' |
| Prayer (no. 13) | Aria: 'Ich will dir mein Herze schenken' |
| Narrative (no. 21) | Evangelist: 'Und ging hin ein wenig' |
| Comment (no. 22) | Recitative: 'Der Heiland fällt vor seinem Vater nieder' |
| Prayer (no. 23) | Aria: 'Gerne will ich mich bequemen' |

A fourth element in the varied texture of the Passion lies in the chorales that punctuate the narrative. Their primary function is to draw the attention of those who are listening to the meaning of the juncture that has been reached in the unfolding story. For example, the melody of the so-called PASSION CHORALE is heard five times, and each time it follows directly from the biblical narrative (nos. 15, 17, 44, 54, and 62).

The one exception is the chorale (no. 40) that follows the aria 'Erbarme dich', a prayer for mercy and reflection on Peter's tearful repentance. Here the chorale underscores a primary theme of the Passion—repentance and prayer for mercy—that is expressly heard in the German Agnus Dei of the first movement, in the concluding movement to Part 1, 'O Mensch, bewein dein Sünde groß', and in the final chorus, 'Wir setzen uns mit Tränen'.

The *St Matthew Passion* is somewhat different from the *St John*, primarily because the respective biblical narratives each supply a particular perspective on the details of the basic story of the Passion. Although not as tightly structured as the *St John*, the *St Matthew Passion* shows signs of a concern for symmetry. In a way that is analogous to the central quasi-chorale 'Durch dein Gefängnis, Gottes Sohn' in the *St John Passion*, the *St Matthew* is focused on the aria 'Aus Liebe will mein Heiland sterben':

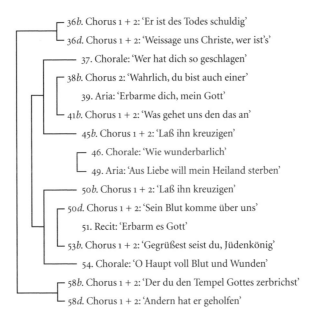

36*b*. Chorus 1 + 2: 'Er ist des Todes schuldig'
36*d*. Chorus 1 + 2: 'Weissage uns Christe, wer ist's'
37. Chorale: 'Wer hat dich so geschlagen'
38*b*. Chorus 2: 'Wahrlich, du bist auch einer'
39. Aria: 'Erbarme dich, mein Gott'
41*b*. Chorus 1 + 2: 'Was gehet uns den das an'
45*b*. Chorus 1 + 2: 'Laß ihn kreuzigen'
46. Chorale: 'Wie wunderbarlich'
49. Aria: 'Aus Liebe will mein Heiland sterben'
50*b*. Chorus 1 + 2: 'Laß ihn kreuzigen'
50*d*. Chorus 1 + 2: 'Sein Blut komme über uns'
51. Recit: 'Erbarm es Gott'
53*b*. Chorus 1 + 2: 'Gegrüßest seist du, Jüdenkönig'
54. Chorale: 'O Haupt voll Blut und Wunden'
58*b*. Chorus 1 + 2: 'Der du den Tempel Gottes zerbrichst'
58*d*. Chorus 1 + 2: 'Andern hat er geholfen'

**3. Neglect and revival.** The *St Matthew Passion* represents the culmination of the Lutheran tradition of liturgical Passions, and was written specifically for Good Friday Vespers. After Bach's time the performance of such works moved outside the confines of the worship of the church; indeed, elsewhere in Germany non-liturgical oratorios on the Passion story were already being composed and performed.

Although members of Bach's family, some of his former pupils, and other Bach enthusiasts remained aware of the work, it was not performed after the composer's death. Musical taste had changed and a simpler style was in vogue. For example, J. F. Doles, Bach's former pupil and another Thomaskantor (from 1755), was of the opinion that old-fashioned counterpoint as epitomized in the works of Bach was inappropriate for contemporary church music. Decades later C. F. Zelter, director of the Berlin Singakademie, obtained a copy of the score of the *St Matthew Passion*, and in the early 1820s rehearsed some of the choral movements in private. Among his singers were Fanny and Felix Mendelssohn, who thereafter sought to give a public performance of the work. Despite Zelter's strong dissuasion (for he thought that the work was inappropriate for public hearing), Mendelssohn gave the first modern performance, in an abbreviated form, with the Singakademie in Berlin in 1829, marking what was thought to be the centenary of its first performance. The Berlin performances were followed by others directed by Mendelssohn in major cities in Germany over the following decade or so. The amazing impact of this work on those who heard it kindled an interest in Bach's other vocal works. This led in turn to the publication of the mature choral works, the formation of Bach choirs across Germany and elsewhere in Europe, and the founding of the Bach-Gesellschaft in 1850. For the general musical public it was this work in particular that inspired the Bach revival of the 19th century, and it remains at the pinnacle of the choral art alongside the B minor Mass.                                                                          RAL

E. Axemacher, 'Aus Liebe will mein Heiland sterben': Untersuchungen zum Wandel des Passionsverständnisses im frühen 18. Jahrhundert (Stuttgart, 1984); E. Chafe, 'J. S. Bach's St Matthew Passion: Aspects of Planning, Structure, and Chronology', Journal of the American Musicological Society, 35 (1982), 49–114; E. Chafe, Tonal Allegory in the Vocal Music of J. S. Bach (Berkeley, 1991); J. Rifkin, 'The Chronology of Bach's Saint Matthew Passion', Musical Quarterly, 61 (1975), 360–87. For further bibliography, see PASSION.

---

Political authority in electoral Saxony during the first half of the 18th century was shared between the elector and the Estates, and the power struggle between the two inevitably impinged on Bach's life in Leipzig, and indeed on the way he was chosen as Kantor and *director musices* there in 1723 (see Siegele). *See also* DRESDEN and LEIPZIG.

U. Siegele, 'Bach and the Domestic Politics of Electoral Saxony', in J. Butt, ed., *The Cambridge Companion to Bach* (Cambridge, 1997), 17–34.

**Scarlatti, Domenico** (b. 26 Oct. 1685; d. 23 July 1757). Italian composer, born in Naples. In his early composing career he followed in the footsteps of his illustrious father Alessandro (1660–1725) by writing operas, cantatas, and church music in Naples and Rome. His most characteristic works, however, are a remarkable series of over 550 harpsichord sonatas, most of them composed after 1720 in the service of Princess (later Queen) Maria Barbara (1711–58) in Portugal and Spain. He thus excelled in the only Baroque genre left virtually untouched by both of his great contemporaries, Bach and Handel.

It is not known for certain whether Bach was familiar with any of Scarlatti's music, though some features of the Goldberg Variations suggest that he could have known the *Essercizi* (30 sonatas) for harpsichord published in London in 1739. Almost certainly he would have known something about Scarlatti himself, if only through the lutenist Silvius Leopold Weiß, who had been a colleague of Scarlatti in the service of Queen

Maria Casimira (1641–1716) in Rome and was friendly with Bach in Leipzig.

***Schauet doch und sehet, ob irgend ein Schmerz sei*** ('Behold, and see if there be any sorrow'). Cantata, BWV46, first performed in Leipzig on the tenth Sunday after Trinity (1 August) 1723. The scoring is unusual: in addition to the normal four-part choir and strings (violins 1 and 2, and viola), it requires pairs of recorders and oboes da caccia, and a slide trumpet (the heading on the original performing part is 'Tromba. ô Corno da Tirarsi'). The cantata's subject-matter is closely related to the appointed Gospel reading (Luke 19: 41–8), in which Jesus predicts the destruction of Jerusalem.

The opening chorus, whose Old Testament text (Lam. 1: 12) articulates the pain of contemplating the Day of Judgement, is quite lengthy and falls into two main sections. Bach uses the ensemble in many different ways. The opening ritornello, in D minor (bars 1–16), is played by just the recorders, strings, and continuo. When the voices enter (bars 17 ff.), first the alto and tenor are paired (the tenor imitates the alto at the lower 5th), then the soprano and bass (the bass follows the soprano at the lower 12th). When the trumpet and oboes da caccia finally enter (bars 30–2), each doubles one of the three upper voices. The beginning of the second section (bars 67 ff.) is marked by a thinner texture (initially just voices and continuo) and a quicker tempo (indicated by the heading 'un poc' allegro'). The first three participants in the long series of fugal entries are the alto, tenor, and bass. When the soprano enters (bar 86), it is doubled by the first violin. The remaining instruments are then woven into the increasingly complex contrapuntal texture: first the recorders, then oboe da caccia 2 and viola, oboe da caccia 1 and violin 2, and finally the trumpet. Throughout the second section, key words—for example 'Jammers' ('misery'), 'grimmigen' ('furious'), and 'Zorns' ('wrath')—are emphasized with melismas. The affective quality of these words also inspired a remarkable modulation to the remote key of F minor (bars 116 ff.). A quarter of a century after its première the first part of this chorus was reworked into 'Qui tollis peccata mundi' for the B minor Mass.

The tenor recitative (movement 2) is addressed to Jerusalem, described as 'zerstörte Gottesstadt' ('destroyed city of God') and 'armer Stein- und Aschenhaufen' ('poor heap of stone and ashes'). The city is enjoined to weep, as a sign of repentance. Throughout the movement, a brief motif played by the recorders in parallel 3rds and 6ths is superimposed on a harmonic backdrop of sustained chords in the strings and detached bass notes in the continuo. The motif serves as a unifying element and also necessitates a steadier tempo than is usual in recitatives. The chromaticism near the end of the continuo line is clearly motivated by the imagery of the text.

The bass aria 'Dein Wetter zog sich auf von weiten' (movement 3) graphically depicts God's judgement on Jerusalem in the form of a terrible storm that gathered from afar and has now broken loose. The storm's fury is suggested by pervasive dotted rhythms, repeated semiquavers (depicting thunder), and descending scales (lightning). Although other bass arias are scored for trumpet, strings, and continuo, the trumpet seems especially appropriate here in view of its traditional associations with the Day of Judgement. The B section is constructed around a striking ascending chromatic line in the continuo in the first half (bars 45 ff.), followed by descending chromatic motion in the second (bars 67 ff.). While the chromaticism is connected with general notions of judgement and doom, the downward descent embodies the meaning of the word 'Untergang' ('downfall').

In the alto recitative (movement 4), accompanied by continuo alone, the discourse becomes more personal; it is addressed not to the city of Jerusalem, but to the individual sinner. As in the two previous movements, the extensive chromatic motion in the continuo line is connected with the terror of God's judgement. The alto aria (movement 5) is at the opposite pole to the bass aria: it employs those instruments (the woodwinds) that

were not used in the earlier movement; it is in the minor key with two flats (G minor), as opposed to the major (B♭ major); and it projects a mood of calm instead of fury. The reason for these contrasts is that this movement unveils a marvellous surprise: instead of judgement, Jesus brings mercy. The text employs both masculine and feminine imagery: Jesus is portrayed as the great Shepherd gathering the devout to Himself 'als seine Schafe' ('like his sheep'), and as a hen gathering her chickens (Matt. 23: 37). Of particular significance is the omission of the normal basso continuo in favour of a line played by the oboes da caccia in unison. The so-called *bassetto* (a high-pitched, unfigured bass line, omitting the low bass instruments) is used fairly infrequently by Bach, usually when something 'unearthly' is depicted. The only departure from the movement's gentle pastoral tone occurs at the beginning of the B section (bars 45 ff.). The mention of 'Wetter der Rache' ('storms of vengeance'), recalling the imagery of the bass aria, is reflected in temporarily increased agitation: arpeggiated figures and virtuoso melismas in the vocal line, disjunct motion and syncopation in the recorder parts, and pulsating repeated notes in the *bassetto*.

In the final chorale (movement 6) the choir sings in unremarkable four-part harmony. However, the instrumental ensemble is handled in novel ways. Although the strings and continuo double the voice parts, they provide a more active rhythmic profile by dividing the crotchets into repeated quavers (the trumpet, on the other hand, simply reinforces the melody). Meanwhile, the recorders weave independent contrapuntal lines that erupt into spectacular semiquaver roulades between phrases, while the voices and other instruments are silent. These extrovert recorder parts aptly express the joy associated with the knowledge that God's wrath has been averted by Jesus's death.                    SAC

For bibliography, *see* CANTATA, §1.

***Schau, lieber Gott, wie meine Feind*** ('See, dear God, how my enemies'). Cantata, BWV153, first performed in Leipzig on the Sunday after New Year's Day (2 January) 1724. This is a modest but highly effective work. It contains no elaborate choruses; instead the choral writing is limited to three simple four-part chorales. Similarly, the instrumental ensemble includes only strings (violins 1 and 2, and viola) with continuo. Moreover, all three recitatives are accompanied by the continuo alone. These modest demands are probably accounted for by the work's place in the calendar: this was the fifth cantata that Bach's musicians had to prepare in just over a week (the others were for the three days of Christmas and New Year's

Day). The anonymous libretto treats the theme of spiritual opposition. Its point of departure is the appointed Gospel reading (Matt. 2: 13–23), which relates the story of the Holy Family's flight to Egypt under the threat of death by the wicked King Herod. The first two movements take the form of prayers. The opening chorale is a plea for God to take note of the great power and cunning of the world, the flesh, and the devil, which can so easily bring ruin. The succeeding alto recitative continues in this vein, asking specifically for his mercy and help.

God's loving response comes already in movement 3, a setting of Isaiah 41: 10. Accompanied by the continuo alone, it employs a bass soloist, traditionally used in church music to represent the voice of God. The heading 'Arioso' is found in several manuscripts that were probably copied from the autograph score, which has not survived; in the present context it refers to a small vocal solo. Like most arias, it begins and ends with a ritornello (which also functions as a *basso ostinato*) and includes modulations to several closely related keys. There are, however, no breaks in the vocal line; the entire text is presented, one clause at a time, without interruption. In the tenor recitative (movement 4) it becomes clear that God's words of comfort have not yet fully penetrated the believer's heart. After a perfunctory acknowledgement of God's comfort, the desperate and plaintive tone of the earlier movements returns. The present recitative is far more substantial than the first: it is over twice as long; it contains several notable instances of word-painting (e.g. chromaticism in bar 3 for 'Leiden' ('suffering') and in bar 13 for 'sterben' ('die'), and a melismatic flourish on 'Bogen' ('bows') in bar 9 to illustrate the trajectory of the arrows aimed at him); and it concludes with a brief arioso passage.

After a chorale that reiterates God's promise to accompany his people through their trials (movement 5), the point of greatest dramatic intensity is reached: a tenor aria (movement 6) that employs the imagery of a raging storm to portray affliction, misfortune, and spiritual warfare. The tempest is represented by rapid scale figures in demisemiquavers, dotted rhythms, and disjunct motion (including octave leaps in the continuo). The surging of the flood is brilliantly depicted by a whirling sequential figure on 'wallt' ('rush'), sung and played in unison in all five parts (bars 9 and 13). A more sedate feeling temporarily intervenes, beginning on the word 'Ruh' ('peace', bar 23), which, characteristically, is sustained through a full bar and beyond. The texture thins to a duet (bars 24–5), then a trio (bars 26–9), before returning to the full-blooded intensity of the beginning.

The bass recitative (movement 7) is the only movement that refers explicitly to the Gospel reading; it urges the believer to remember that Jesus too suffered at an early age, when King Herod tried to kill him. Ultimately, though, the best way to endure hardship is to look to heaven. This idea appears at the end of the bass recitative and also pervades the succeeding alto aria (movement 8), which declares that the Christian's tribulations will end in heaven, where Jesus will transform them into joy. For this aria Bach wrote jaunty music in triple metre, in the style of a minuet. The form is quite unusual. The opening ritornello and first vocal section each present virtually identical melodic and harmonic material, which falls into three four-bar phrases and modulates from the tonic to the dominant, in the manner of the repeated antecedent of a Baroque binary form. The 24-bar instrumental passage (exactly twice the length of the first section) functions as the consequent, and completes the harmonic cycle by modulating from the dominant back to the tonic. The second vocal section begins like a repetition of the consequent, but it diverges after eight bars. In the setting of the last two lines, when the verse metre changes from trochaic to amphibrachic tetrameter, the tempo quickens to *allegro* (bars 71 ff.), and the movement concludes with a shortened version of the consequent.

The final chorale (movement 9), in which the believer expresses his resolve to bear suffering gladly and asks for God's help in this task, is unique, being the only one in all Bach's cantatas in which three full stanzas are sung.          SAC
For bibliography, *see* CANTATA, §1.

**Scheibe, Johann Adolph** (b. 5 May 1708; d. 22 April 1776). Composer and writer on music. His father, Johann (*c*.1680–1748), was an organ builder; Bach tested the instrument he made for the Paulinerkirche, Leipzig, in 1717. After attending the Nikolaischule in Leipzig, Johann Adolph began to study law at Leipzig University, but had to withdraw for financial reasons. He then turned to music as a career, but failed to secure any of the several posts as organist for which he applied. In 1736 he went to Hamburg, where he worked as a critic and composer, and the following year he founded a fortnightly journal, the *Critische Musikus*, which in 1737 included a famous article critical of Bach's music. In it he found Bach's compositions to be 'bombastic' and 'confused', overladen with (written-out) ornamentation, inimical to the voice, and generally in conflict with nature. Scheibe was expressing an Enlightenment view which prized simplicity, directness, and appealing melody as music's most desirable attributes; elsewhere in the *Critische Musikus* he wrote appreciatively of some of Bach's music. Bach did not respond in print, but others, including J. A. Birnbaum, Lorenz Mizler, and C. G. Schröter, took up the case for the defence.

In 1739 Scheibe left Hamburg, and the following year he was appointed *Kapellmeister* to the Danish court in Copenhagen. When King Christian VI died, in 1747, Scheibe retired to Sønderborg, where he continued to write and compose. Most of his music has not survived; that which has includes masses, cantatas, chamber music, and keyboard works.

BDok ii, no. 400; G. J. Buelow, 'In Defence of J. A. Scheibe Against J. S. Bach', *Proceedings of the Royal Musical Association*, 101 (1974–5), 85–100; H. T. David and A. Mendel, eds., *The Bach Reader* (London, 1945; 2nd edn., 1966), 237–52; G. Wagner, 'J. A. Scheibe—J. S. Bach: Versuch einer Bewertung', *BJb* 68 (1982), 33–49.

**Schelble, Johann Nepomuk** (b. 16 May 1789; d. 6 Aug. 1837). Singer and conductor, born in Hüfingen, about 50 km. (31 miles) east of Freiburg in Baden-Württemberg. He was active in Stuttgart and in Frankfurt, where, with his Cäcilienverein, he performed Bach's *St Matthew Passion* in May 1829, only two months after Mendelssohn's famous revival of the work in Berlin.

**Schemelli, Christian Friedrich** (b. 30 Oct. 1713; d. 27 Oct. 1761). Son of G. C. Schemelli, born in Treuenbrietzen, about 60 km. (38 miles) southwest of Berlin. He studied at the Thomasschule in Leipzig, 1731–4, but by all accounts he was a ne'er-do-well. Yet Bach wrote a favourable testimonial for him in 1740, possibly at the insistence of the boy's father. After completing his studies in Leipzig he may have taken up a position in the court *Kapelle* at Zeitz, where he succeeded his father as Kantor in 1758. GB

**Schemelli, Georg Christian** (b. *c*.1676; d. 5 March 1762). Musician, born in Herzberg, Elster. Early in 1727 he took up the post of court Kantor at Zeitz. Bach's second wife, Anna Magdalena, was from Zeitz and Bach may therefore have first come into contact with Schemelli while on a family visit to the town. Alternatively, contact may have been made through Schemelli's son Christian Friedrich, who was at the Thomasschule from 1731 to 1734, during which time he studied with Bach. Georg Christian's only known publication, the *Musicalisches Gesangbuch*, popularly referred to as the Schemelli Songbook, was printed and published in Leipzig in 1736 by B. C. Breitkopf. Of a decidedly Pietistic bent, it contains the texts of 954 hymns and includes engraved plates giving melody, figured bass, and first verse or text incipit for 69 of these. Bach seems to have acted as musical consultant for the project. Three melod-

ies from the collection have been attributed to him: *Dir, dir, Jehova* (autograph in Anna Magdalena's Music Book of 1725); *Komm, süsser Tod* (attributed to Bach on stylistic grounds); and *Vergiss mein nicht* (headed 'di S. Bach D. M. Lips.'). All are arias rather than chorales. The preface indicates that all 69 melodies had 'in part, been newly composed completely, also, in part, improved in the basso continuo by Bach'. This is borne out by the presence of Bach's hand in the reproduction engravings from the collection (*see* SOURCES, §2), either throughout a given setting, in the bass only, or in isolated passages in the bass.
GB

G. Butler, 'J. S. Bach and the Schemelli Gesangbuch Revisited', *Studi musicali*, 13 (1984), 241–57; F. Hamel, 'Die Kompositionen J. S. Bachs im Schemellischen Gesangbuch', *Zeitschrift für Musikwissenschaft*, 12 (1929–30), 232–7; G. Kinsky, *Die Originalausgaben der Werke Johann Sebastian Bachs* (Vienna, 1937), 34 ff.; A. Schering, 'Bach und das Schemellische Gesangbuch', *BJb* 21 (1924), 105–24; W. Wiemer, ed., *Johann Sebastian Bach: Denket doch ihr Menschenkinder* (Kassel, 1984); W. Wiemer, ed., *Johann Sebastian Bach und seine Schule: Neu entdeckte Choral- und Liedsätze* (Kassel, 1985).

**Schering, Arnold** (b. 2 April 1877; d. 7 March 1941). Scholar and writer on music, born in Breslau. He was educated at the Kreuzschule, Dresden, and between 1898 and 1902 at the universities of Berlin, Munich, and Leipzig. His Ph.D. thesis on Vivaldi and his predecessors as concerto composers (1902, revised and published three years later) did much to arouse interest in the Baroque concerto. In 1907 he completed his *Habilitation* thesis on the early oratorio. After teaching at the Leipzig Conservatory from 1909, he was appointed professor at the University of Leipzig in 1915, and then at Halle (1920) and Berlin (1928).

Schering's work on Bach was particularly important in four respects: as editor of the *Bach-Jahrbuch* from its foundation in 1904 until his death, he acted as a bridge between the increasing amount of Bach research and the vigorous Bach movement among the music-loving public; as a musicologist he contributed to Bach research with valuable articles, from an early essay on the treatment of text (1900) to studies of the parody problem (*BJb* 1922) and symbols in music (*BJb* 1925); as editor of numerous Eulenburg pocket scores of concertos and cantatas, he helped in the dissemination of a good deal of Bach's music which had previously been available only in vocal scores or expensive performing material; and as an author he made an important contribution to the Bach literature in two monographs which offered fresh insight into Bach's Leipzig years. His *Johann Sebastian Bachs Leipziger Kirchenmusik* (1936) is a pioneering attempt to understand Bach's cantatas in the context of the original performing conditions, dealing with such matters as the organization of musical and ecclesiastical institutions, organs, and church architecture. In 1926 and 1941 the second and third volumes of *Musikgeschichte Leipzigs* (begun by Rudolf Wustmann in 1909) were published; they help to place Bach in the musical history of the locality from 1650 to 1800.

KK

**Schimert, Peter** (b. 1712; d. 1785). Organist. He studied with Bach between 1733 and 1738, after which he lived in Hermannstadt for the rest of his life. He was appointed organist and *director chori musici* there in 1745 and cathedral organist in 1757.

**Schleicht, spielende Wellen, und murmelt gelinde** ('Flow, playful waves, and murmur softly'). Secular cantata, BWV206, to celebrate the birthday and nameday of the elector.

When Augustus the Strong died in 1733 he was succeeded by his son, Elector Friedrich Augustus II. Like his father, the young elector also became King of Poland, and as such was known as Augustus III. *Schleicht, spielende Wellen, und murmelt gelinde*, Bach's *drama per musica*, was composed in October 1734 as part of the birthday celebrations for the new elector, who was visiting Leipzig at the time. The work, however, was not heard until two years later when, on 7 October 1736, Bach performed it on the same elector's birthday. The concert took place in Gottfried Zimmermann's coffee-house at 8 o'clock in the evening, when Bach himself directed 'eine solenne Music unter Trompeten und Paucken' ('a solemn music with trumpets and drums') with members of his collegium musicum. Some years later, probably on 3 August 1740, he gave a second performance of the piece, this time to celebrate the nameday of the same Friedrich Augustus.

The unidentified author of the libretto—it might have been Picander—chose for his subject a bland and somewhat inconsequential dispute between the four principal rivers of the countries under Augustus's rule, which compete for the special affection of the monarch. The River Pleiße, which flows through Leipzig, is sung by a soprano; since Augustus and his consort are staying in a palace nearby, it claims a special relationship with the sovereign, eventually acting as arbitrator in the dispute. The River Danube (Donau in German) is an alto role; it associates itself with Augustus's consort, the Austrian Archduchess Maria Josepha. The River Elbe is sung by a tenor; its homeland is chiefly Saxony where it flows through the capital city, Dresden. Lastly there is the River Vistula (the Weichsel in German) which flows

through Warsaw, capital of the Polish kingdom ruled by Augustus; this is a bass role.

This unlikely panegyric falls into the customary late Baroque pattern of alternating recitatives and (mainly da capo) arias, with two choruses providing an opulent, richly textured framework. Bach's scoring is colourful and generous, and includes three trumpets, timpani, three flutes, two oboes, two oboes d'amore, strings, and continuo. The opening *da capo* chorus in D major is softly introduced by flutes and strings, but they are joined after eight bars by oboes, drums, and the three trumpets which lend brilliance and splendour to the movement in 3/8 time. Here Bach skilfully unites an evocation of the flowing water of the rivers, softly and in torrent, with a jubilant, occasional spirit.

Following the opening chorus, each river stakes its claim in turn with a recitative and aria. The Vistula pays homage to Augustus in a robust, even swaggering, aria in A major, with full string accompaniment and more than a hint of the dance. The Elbe is more lyrical in praise of the monarch; in a B minor aria in 6/8 metre, the singer embarks on coloratura passages—perhaps reflecting the sophisticated courtly milieu of Dresden—accompanied by an obbligato solo violin. Then it is the turn of the Danube. In an F♯ minor aria, accompanied by two oboes d'amore, it champions the queen, the Habsburg Maria Josepha, now married to Augustus. Boldly (we might even say imprudently) it singles out the reigning Austrian kaiser, Charles VI, for special praise. At last the Pleiße has its say. It weighs up the merits of its friendly rivals and, in a spirited, *galant* G major aria (the only solo item in the cantata not in strict da capo form), urges them to flow in harmony like the three flutes that accompany the voice. In the following recitative each river, in turn, falls in with Pleiße's wishes. Simple recitative gives way to a section of string *accompagnato* as Pleiße, delighted by the harmonious outcome of this rivalry, proposes a chorus of praise. In a lightly-flowing 12/8 gigue in D major, in rondo form (A–B–A–C–A), trumpets and drums once more join the voices, woodwind, and strings. This colourful colloquium brings the aquatic discourse to a close in a spirit of rejoicing.

NA

For bibliography, *see* CANTATA, §2.

**Schmid, Balthasar** (b. 20 April 1705; bur. 27 Nov. 1749). Music engraver, printer, and publisher, born in Nuremberg, the son of a comb maker. He was employed as an organist in various churches in that city and for more than a decade was the head of a successful music-engraving, printing, and publishing firm there. He served his apprenticeship as a music engraver in Nuremberg, where he is mentioned as such in church records in 1726, and is almost certainly the same 'Balthasar Schmid' who enrolled in Leipzig University on 13 March 1726, for he appears as engraver of the musical text of J. S. Bach's keyboard Partitas nos. 1 (1726) and 2 (1727); *see* SOURCES, §2. This is further supported by Ludwig Gerber's attribution of the success of these works to Schmid's engraving.

While in Leipzig Schmid honed his engraving skills as a journeyman and may have studied with Bach. After his return to Nuremberg and the first documented publication of one of his works on 7 August 1729, Schmid engraved, printed, and published a work of his own composition almost yearly for the next decade. In 1734 he engraved the title-page of Bach's *Clavier-Übung II*. After he was articled as a publisher in 1738, Schmid began to bring out the works of other composers until 1748, when his health seems to have failed. One of his first commissions as an articled music publisher must have been the title-page for *Clavier-Übung III*. Soon after, Bach turned to him for the completion of the engraving and printing of that collection, which had been interrupted. As Bach's preferred music engraver until 1748, Schmid acted as engraver, printer, and publisher of the Goldberg Variations and the Canonic Variations on *Vom Himmel hoch*.

Renowned as a music engraver of consummate skill throughout Germany, Schmid was also important in promoting the works of composers from J. S. Bach's circle, including C. P. E. Bach (the 'Prussian' sonatas, keyboard concertos, trio sonatas, and a sinfonia), J. L. Krebs (sonatas for violin and obbligato keyboard, and miscellaneous keyboard works), Christoph Nichelmann (12 keyboard sonatas), and F. W. Marpurg (six keyboard sonatas). It has been suggested that Schmid is the dedicatee of one of Bach's occasional canons, the so-called 'Faber' canon BWV1078, dated 1 March 1749. After Schmid's death in November 1749 his widow Maria Helena Volland (1710–91) carried on the firm's business and it was under her direction that the first edition of *The Art of Fugue* was printed. The firm continued to be important for the publication of works by the Bach family, principally C. P. E. Bach, during the 1750s.   GB

G. Butler, 'The Engraving of J. S. Bach's Six Partitas', *Journal of Musicological Research*, 7 (1986), pp 3 ff.; G. Butler, 'Neues zur Datierung der Goldberg-Variationen', *BJb* 74 (1988), 219–23; G. Butler, *Bach's Clavier-Übung III: The Making of a Print* (Durham, NC, 1990); H. Heussner, 'Der Musikdrucker Balthasar Schmid in Nürnberg', *Die Musikforschung*, 16 (1963), 348–62; C. Wolff, Commentary, in *Johann Sebastian Bach, Clavier-Übung Teil I–IV* [facsimile] (Dresden, 1984); W. Wörthmüller, ed., *Die Nürnberger Musikverleger und die Familie Bach* (Nuremberg, 1973).

**Schmidt.** Family whose fortunes were mixed up with the Bachs' in the second half of the 17th century. In 1671 J. S. Bach's father, Ambrosius, succeeded the recently deceased Christoph Schmidt as *Hausmann* in Eisenach. Five or six years earlier Schmidt's eldest daughter, Anna Margaretha, had married Ambrosius's first cousin Johann Christian Bach (1640–82), and in 1674 Johann Christian's brother Johann Egydius (1645–1716) married Anna Margaretha's sister Maria Susanna (c.1654–c.1684).

**Schmidt, Johann Michael** (b. 16 Jan. 1728; d. 8 April 1799). Theologian and writer, born in Meiningen. He studied at Leipzig University and was probably a pupil of Bach's in 1749–50. From 1754 he was active in Naumburg and in 1762 he was appointed Rector at the Lateinschule in Marktbreit, Lower Franconia, where he died. His *Musico-theologia*, published in Bayreuth and Hof in 1754, contains several commendatory references to Bach. It was possibly to him that Bach dedicated his FABER canon BWV1078.

Alberto Basso lists three other musicians by the name of Schmidt who may have studied with Bach: Johann Schmidt (1674–1746), organist at the Blasiuskirche, Zella; Johann Christian Jacob Schmidt (c.1707–68), his successor at Zella; and Johann Christoph Schmidt (b. c.1696), copyist and organist at Harzgerode from 1719.

A. Basso, *Frau Musika: la vita e le opere di J. S. Bach*, i (Turin, 1979), 25–6; H.-J. Schulze, 'Johann Sebastian Bachs Kanonwidmungen', *BJb* 53 (1967), 82–92.

**Schmieder, Wolfgang** (b. 29 May 1901; d. 8 Nov. 1990). Musicologist and author of the *Bach-Werke-Verzeichnis* (*BWV*), born in Bromberg (now Bydgoszcz, Poland). He attended school in Eisenach and studied at the University of Heidelberg, where he worked as assistant lecturer in 1927–30. In 1931 he completed a supplementary course of study to qualify as a librarian; in 1933–42 he was custodian of the music library of the publishers Breitkopf & Härtel, Leipzig, and in 1943 he founded the music library at the University of Frankfurt, which he directed until 1962.

Building on work already done by Johannes Wolgast and Paul Ruthardt, Schmieder began in 1937 to compile his catalogue of Bach's works; in spite of losing much of his material during World War II, he succeeded in publishing the *BWV* in 1950. He finished a revised edition (Wiesbaden, 1990) shortly before his death in Freiburg.   KK

***Schmücke dich, o liebe Seele*** ('Adorn thyself, O dear soul'). Cantata for the 20th Sunday after Trinity, BWV180, first performed on 22 October 1724. It belongs to Bach's great Leipzig cycle of chorale-based cantatas (1724–5). The autograph score has passed through the hands of many musicians and collectors, notably Bach's eldest son, Wilhelm Friedemann, Mendelssohn, and Pauline Viardot (1821–1910), the celebrated mezzo-soprano and friend of the Russian novelist Ivan Turgenev (1818–83). Viardot had once been a piano pupil of Liszt, and it is he who may well have first interested her in Bach's music. Mendelssohn and Schumann, furthermore, are known to have admired Bach's organ Prelude BWV654, which is based on the same chorale melody as the cantata.

The text of the cantata, by an unidentified author, is a revised version of a communion hymn, *Schmücke dich, o liebe Seele* (1649), by Johann Franck (1618–77); three of its stanzas (nos. 1, 3, and 7 in the cantata) are retained in their original form. The appointed Gospel reading (Matt. 22: 1–14) relates the parable of the marriage feast for the king's son, while the hymn reflects on the symbolic significance of the heavenly wedding feast. Alberto Basso (*Frau Musica: la vita e le opere di J. S. Bach*, ii (Turin, 1983), 321) suggests that the story gave Bach the opportunity of producing a score resembling a eucharistic *musique de table*; certainly the work bears an affinity to a Baroque dance suite in which, as Alfred Dürr remarked (in *DürrK*), the rhythms of a gigue, a bourrée, and a polonaise are represented.

The opening chorus is one of Bach's most translucently textured chorale fantasias. It incorporates the first strophe of Franck's hymn, whose melody, by Johannes Crüger (1598–1662), is sustained in the soprano line. The character and 12/8 rhythm of the movement, in F major, is that of a gigue, whose softly spoken instrumental accompaniment—a pair of treble recorders, oboe, oboe da caccia, strings, and continuo—creates a sound-picture of intimacy and enchantment. The virtuoso tenor aria, with its comparably virtuoso transverse flute obbligato, is also in dance measure, this one a bourrée. Flute writing such as this strongly suggests that Bach was able to call upon the services of an exceptionally gifted player at this time.

The two following sections are cast in recitative. The first, for soprano, is the more elaborate of the two; here Bach uses a combination of simple recitative and arioso. In the lyrical arioso the voice weaves an elaboration of Crüger's melody, set to the fourth strophe of Franck's hymn, while a violoncello piccolo provides an accompaniment of virtually continuous semiquaver arpeggios. The second recitative, for alto, is accompanied by two treble recorders, which provide a delicately shaded *sostenuto*.

For the second da capo aria Bach returns once again to a dance measure, this time a polonaise in

Bb major whose carefree character and warm texture pleasingly complement the affirmative text, 'Lebens Sonne, Licht der Sinnen' ('Life's sun, light of the senses'). A simple recitative for bass follows, and the cantata ends with the seventh stanza of Franck's hymn. The four vocal strands are supported by *colla parte* instruments, which, however, were not specified in this instance in Bach's score.                                                                NA

For bibliography, *see* CANTATA, §1.

**Schneider, Johann** (bap. 17 July 1702; d. 5 Jan. 1788). Organist and violinist, born in Oberlauter, near Coburg in Bavaria. He grew up in Saalfeld and became a keyboard pupil of Bach's, perhaps around 1720. He also studied the violin under J. G. Graun and Johann Graf (1684–1750). In 1721 he became court organist and chief violinist at his home town of Saalfeld. From 1726 he was employed as a violinist in the Weimar court orchestra, and on 23 December 1729 was appointed organist at the Nikolaikirche, Leipzig. Lorenz Mizler, writing in 1747 (see *BDok* ii, no. 565), mentions him as a fine organist, and adds: 'his preludes on the organ are of such good taste that in this field, except for Mr Bach, whose pupil he has been, there is nothing better to be heard in Leipzig'.

The possibility that Schneider is identical with the Bach pupil known as Anon 5, who made numerous copies of Bach's keyboard works under the composer's supervision between about 1720 and 1725, has been raised by Marianne Helms (see *NBA* V/7, *Kritische Bericht*, pp. 183–95).         RDPJ

**Schoenberg, Arnold** (b. 13 Sept. 1874; d. 13 July 1951). Austrian composer, principally of instrumental, orchestral, and choral music, and of several dramatic works including the unfinished opera *Moses und Aron*. After becoming regarded as the most extreme radical in his native Vienna and later in Berlin through his expressionistic works (often called 'atonal' without his consent), he left Europe for the USA, and eventually settled in Los Angeles, where he died.

Bach held a key position in Schoenberg's view of the development of musical language and of the background to his 'method of composition with 12 tones', as revealed in his voluminous writings (including the article 'Bach' of 1950). He saw Bach as standing at the beginning of a new phase which eventually culminated in his (Schoenberg's) method. He defined the period 1750–1900 with the term 'homophonic/melodic', in which motivic development provides the coherence and variation previously ensured by contrapuntal means. He summarized Bach's influence on his own development as including (in his special sense of the term) 'contrapuntal thinking, that is the art of inventing musical figures that can accompany themselves [and] the art of developing everything from one basic germ motive and leading smoothly from one figure into another'. However, a purely 'stylistic' relation to Bach is very difficult to identify in his works, since Schoenberg's complex chromatic language absorbed many stimuli deeply.

Schoenberg's many arrangements of older music included orchestrations of two chorale preludes (BWV631 and 654) and the Prelude and Fugue in E♭ major BWV552 by Bach.        MM
*See also* PERFORMANCE STYLES.

**Scholze, Johann Sigismund.** Poet, best known under his pen-name of SPERONTES.

**Schott, Georg Balthasar** (b. 22 Oct. 1686; bur. 26 March 1736). Organist and composer, born in Schönau, about 10 km. (6 miles) south-east of Eisenach in Thuringia. He studied at the University of Jena from 1709 and at Leipzig University from 1714, and in 1720 was appointed organist of the Neukirche in Leipzig. Two years later he applied for the post of Thomaskantor, but was unsuccessful at his second *Probe* on 2 February 1723. Schott also directed the collegium musicum that Telemann had founded in the city; he gave this up to Bach when he left Leipzig to become Kantor at Gotha in 1729. He remained at Gotha for the rest of his life.

**Schubart, Johann Martin** (b. 8 March 1690; d. 2 April 1721). Organist, born in Geraberg, near Ilmenau in Thuringia. He studied with Bach in Mühlhausen, and followed him to Weimar, living there as a member of his household until 1717. When Bach left Weimar for Cöthen in that year, Schubart was appointed *Kammermusicus* and court organist in his place, at a much lower salary, but he died only four years later at the age of 31.

**Schübler.** Family of artisans from Zella in the Thuringian forest. Their stock-in-trade was iron cutting, the incising of ornamental designs on gun barrels, trivets, and the like. The incising method used was closely related to the *Abklatschvorlage* method employed by the family in their music engraving (*see* SOURCES, §2). The patriarch, Johann Heinrich Schübler, was a gunstock carver. By the age of 10 the youngest son from his second marriage, also named Johann Heinrich (1728–1807), had been instructed by his elder brother Johann Georg (b. *c*.1725) in music and drawing, and by his eldest brother (in reality his half-brother from his father's first marriage) Johann Jakob Friedrich in iron cutting and engraving. To judge from his music engraving, Johann Jakob Friedrich seems to have been the master engraver of the clan, and he must also have

instructed the middle brother in the art. Johann Georg studied music in Leipzig with Bach at the beginning of the 1740s and became an organist and schoolteacher in Mehlis. Probably as a result of this contact, Bach turned to his former pupil for the engraving of the *Musical Offering* in the spring of 1747. The hands of all three brothers can be seen in the plates, and the last page of the six-part ricercar is signed 'J. G. Schübler sc:'.

For Bach, engaging the Schüblers made good sense practically, for they were close at hand, thus facilitating the sending of plates back and forth. They were also obviously able to take on this first project at short notice. Since Bach's preferred engraver, Balthasar Schmid of Nuremberg, was no longer available by 1748, Bach turned to the Schüblers again in that year for the engraving of his *Sechs Choräle* for organ. Johann Georg is named as publisher of the collection on the title-page, and this has led to the appellation 'Schübler Chorales' for the collection. There are strong grounds for identifying Johann Heinrich, the youngest son, as the engraver of *The Art of Fugue*. At Bach's death there remained on account with a 'Herr Schübler' a debt of 2 thaler 16 groschen to be settled, probably as payment for work on the engraving of the collection. The Schüblers were also active as music engravers for Bach's sons. W. F. Bach's Sonata in E♭ major (1748) and the 'Achtzehn Probe-Stücke' that appeared with the first part of C. P. E. Bach's treatise *Versuch über die wahre Art das Clavier zu spielen* (1753) are the work of Johann Heinrich Schübler.        GB

G. Butler, 'J. S. Bach's Musical Offering: New Perspectives from the Original Edition' (forthcoming);
W. Wiemer, 'Johann Heinrich Schübler, der Stecher der Kunst der Fuge,' *BJb* 65 (1979), 75–96.

**Schübler Chorales.** A name usually given to the *Sechs Chorale von verschiedener Art* ('Six Chorales of Various Kinds') for organ BWV645–50, issued by Bach about 1748 (an approximate dating can be supplied from information on the title-page and by comparison with other engravings of Bach's music, such as that of the *Musical Offering*). The title 'Schübler Chorales' derives from the engraver and publisher Johann Georg Schübler, who is named on the title-page. The set contains six preludes for an organ with two manuals and pedal, at least five of them transcribed from movements in Bach's church cantatas, as follows:

| BWV645 | Wachet auf, ruft uns die Stimme | Cantata 140 (1731) |
|---|---|---|
| BWV646 | Wo soll ich fliehen hin? | ? lost cantata |
| BWV647 | Wer nur den lieben Gott läßt walten | Cantata 93 (1724) |

| BWV648 | Meine Seele erhebet den Herren | Cantata 10 (1724) |
| BWV649 | Ach bleib bei uns, Herr Jesu Christ | Cantata 6 (1725) |
| BWV650 | Kommst du nun, Jesu, vom Himmel | Cantata 137 (1725) |

Since no source has been found for BWV646, most scholars have drawn the natural conclusion that the source cantata is one of the 100 or so believed to have been lost. Certainly the trio scoring of the movement suggests that the original may have been for violin, or possibly violins and violas in unison (right hand), and continuo (left hand), with the chorale (pedal) sung by soprano or alto (one of a number of autograph additions to Bach's own copy indicates a 4′ foundation pitch giving a compass of $e'-d''$).

At first sight it seems strange that Bach should have gone to the trouble and expense of securing the services of a master engraver to produce a collection of note-for-note transcriptions of this kind. The fact that he did so indicates that he did not regard the Schübler Chorales as a minor piece of hack-work, but as a significant public statement, worthy of the same serious consideration as his other engraved collections of keyboard music. Most commentators have reasonably seen the Schübler Chorales in the context of the debate opened up by J. A. Scheibe's famous critical article on Bach, published in the sixth issue of his periodical *Der critische Musikus* in May 1737. Scheibe's reservations about Bach's music mainly concern his concerted works, which he criticizes as turgid ('schwülstig') and over-elaborate. This criticism should itself be seen against the background of Scheibe's discussion of the three styles (high, middle, and low) in music, the so-called 'turgid' style being seen as a corrupted form of the 'high' style. Bach's defence against Scheibe's strictures had a number of planks, including two pamphlets written and published by his supporter, the Leipzig University professor of rhetoric, J. A. Birnbaum. Another was almost certainly the Schübler Chorales, in which Bach presented six movements of approachable character from his cantatas through the more marketable medium of keyboard transcriptions.

The music makes a strong contrast with the complex but austere contents of *Clavier-Übung III* or the intricate counterpoint of the Goldberg Variations and the Canonic Variations, being uniformly light-textured and tuneful. Four of the preludes are genuine trios, and the entries of the individual lines of the chorale are widely spaced out so that the texture reduces to two parts when the melody is not playing. The simplicity and charm of these pieces has ensured them a wide public following, which has eluded preludes from some of the other collections despite the fact that the transcription from florid string parts makes the Schübler Chorales awkward for the player.

BWV645 merits special attention as the first item in the collection, and also because the source cantata was composed several years later than the others. When the cantata was first performed on 25 November 1731, Bach had recently returned from a visit to Dresden, where he would have encountered the younger school of musicians and may have been a member of the audience at the first performance of J. A. Hasse's opera *Cleofide* on 13 September. Cantata 140 is unmistakably influenced by the early *galant* style, the melody of the obbligato voice being packed with unprepared appoggiaturas, acciaccaturas and *alla zoppa* rhythms which indicate the influence of the gradual change of taste overtaking music in northern Germany. Another indicator is the simplicity of the bass line, which does not share in the motivic material of the upper voice. As Malcolm Boyd points out (*Bach* (London, 1983), 54), the counterpoint is exceptionally bald and dissonant, the effect being exacerbated in the organ transcription by the absence of a keyboard continuo. The thematic combination of the chorale and the obbligato melody hardly 'works' in the conventional sense, producing a number of loose and unresolved dissonances. It may be, therefore, that Bach's tribute to the new *galant* style is two-edged, reflecting what we know to have been an ambivalent attitude to the music of the rising generation of composers.

The other five preludes are more traditional in style, naturally enough in view of the earlier date of the source cantatas. Attempts by some writers to see the set as some kind of programme related to the subject-matter of the chorales do not carry conviction, though it may be pointed out that most of the texts are appropriate to Advent. It is difficult to believe that Bach had any overall scheme in mind beyond the general character of the movements as lightly textured trios, and in contrasted keys. The light tone of the Schübler Chorales may also suggest the influence of engraved collections by other composers, notably G. F. Kauffmann's *Harmonische Seelenlust* (1733–6) and G. A. Sorge's *Drittes halbes Dutzend Sonatinen* (1744) (not chorale-based), which are dedicated to Bach in flattering terms. DLH

P. Williams, *The Organ music of J. S. Bach*, ii (Cambridge, 1980), 103–23; M. Bighley, 'The Schübler Chorales as Cycle: A Liturgical and Theological Perspective', *Organ Yearbook*, 22 (1991), 97–118.

**Schulze, Hans-Joachim** (b. 3 Dec. 1934). German musicologist and Bach scholar, born in Leipzig. From 1952 to 1957 he studied musicology in

Leipzig at the Hochschule für Musik and at the university, taking his diploma in 1957 and completing his doctorate at Rostock University in 1977. In 1957 he became research assistant at the Leipzig Bach-Archiv, and its acting director in 1974. This position was discontinued when, in 1979, the Bach-Archiv was absorbed as a subdivision of the newly founded Nationale Forschungsund Gedenkstätten Johann Sebastian Bach der DDR. With the restitution of the Bach-Archiv in 1990, Schulze again became its director. In 1993 he was appointed honorary professor at the Leipzig Hochschule für Musik.

Most of Schulze's research focuses on recovering and evaluating the biographical sources relating to Bach and his circle, as well as on the transmission and reception of Bach's music in the 18th century. His identification of several previously unknown copyists in the sources has been of enormous value to Bach studies. His most important publications are the three volumes of *Bach-Dokumente* (1963–72, volumes 1 and 2 in collaboration with Werner Neumann) and his seminal *Studien zur Bach-Überlieferung im 18. Jahrhundert* (Leipzig, 1984). In 1975 Schulze assumed, together with Christoph Wolff, the co-editorship of the *Bach-Jahrbuch*, and in 1985 he began publication (again in collaboration with Wolff) of the *Bach Compendium*. PW

**Schumann, Robert** (b. 8 June 1810; d. 29 July 1856). Composer of a wide variety of music, born in Zwickau, Saxony. His early compositions were devoted to the related genres of piano and song composition, reflecting a literary imagination in which striking characterizations mirrored the composer's own various creative personae. Later years were given over to larger-scale works for chamber ensemble, orchestra, and chorus.

Schumann's deep interest in Bach has received less acknowledgement than that of his contemporary Mendelssohn, and it was manifest in less obvious ways. Yet Schumann claimed Bach and the poet Jean Paul [Richter] (1763–1825) as the two greatest influences on his early music. His library included many Bach works, and he was one of the founders of the Bach Gesellschaft. Although stylistic and structural influence is most obvious in his formal compositions, for example in the six Fugues on the name BACH for pedal piano (1845), a more imaginative stylistic debt is to be found in freer contexts: the fourth movement of the 'Rhenish' Symphony builds successive contrapuntal variations on a Baroque figure, strikingly used by Bach in the C♯ minor Fugue and the E♭ major Prelude from Part 1 of *The Well-tempered Clavier*—a reminder that Schumann regarded these pieces as tone pictures. In short piano

pieces, too, Bachian shapes often appear transformed to new purposes, for example in the angular *Verrufene Stelle* (*Waldszenen* no. 4), which is akin to the fugue subject from the Toccata of the keyboard Partita in E minor. MM

**Schwanberg, Georg Heinrich Ludwig** (bap. 10 March 1696; d. 15 Dec. 1774). Violinist and organist, born in Helmstedt, Lower Saxony. He was employed for most of his working life as a chamber musician at the Brunswick court in Wolfenbüttel, where he died. According to the *Leipziger Zeitung* of 19 September 1727 (see *BDok* ii, no. 224), he sold copies on commission of Bach's keyboard Partitas nos. 2 and 3. From November 1727 he spent at least a year in Leipzig as a pupil of Bach's, subsequently resuming his employment at Wolfenbüttel. On 10 October 1728 he stood godfather to Bach's daughter Regina Johanna. Anna Magdalena's copies of Bach's solo violin and cello works were possibly made especially for Schwanberg (see Schulze, 1984). Their title-pages are in his hand, as is the earliest surviving violin part of the Sonatas for violin and clavier BWV1014–19. RDPJ

H.-J. Schulze, 'Ein "Dresdner Menuett" im zweiten Klavierbüchlein der Anna Magdalena Bach. Nebst Hinweisen zur Überlieferung einiger Kammermusikwerke Bachs', *BJb* 65 (1979), 45–64; H.-J. Schutze, *Studien zur Bach-Überlieferung im 18. Jahrhundert* (Leipzig, 1984), 96–101.

**'Schwarze'.** According to Jacob von STÄHLIN, J. S. Bach's son Carl Philipp Emanuel was referred to in the family circle as 'der Schwarze' ('the dark one').

***Schweigt stille, plaudert nicht.*** Incipit of the COFFEE CANTATA.

**Schweinitz, Johann Friedrich** (b. 16 June 1708; d. 10 July 1780). Organist and Kantor, born in Friedebach, Thuringia. He studied at Leipzig University, 1732–5, and may have been a pupil of Bach. In October 1735 he enrolled at the University of Göttingen, where he founded a collegium musicum on the Leipzig model and worked as Kantor and *director musices* at the Johanniskirche. In 1745 J. M. Gesner supported his application for a Kantorate at the Lateinschule in Celle. He died in Pyrmont.

*BDok* ii, no. 541.

**Schweitzer, Albert** (b. 14 Jan. 1875; d. 4 Sept. 1965). Christian theologian, musician, author, and medical doctor, born in Kayserberg, Alsace. Schweitzer's involvement with J. S. Bach's music lay in four areas. His writings on 18th-century organ building gave decisive impetus to the *Orgelbewegung* (Organ Revival) of the early 20th century. His 1906 pamphlet *Deutsche und französische*

*Orgelbaukunst und Orgelkunst* (Leipzig, 1906) advocated a return to slider chests, mechanical action, lower wind pressures, and spatially separated divisions—ideas that heralded the eventual shift to historically informed organ-building practices. Schweitzer's biography of Bach was published in 1905 in French, and in 1908 in a much expanded German version which was then translated into English and other languages. The work is noteworthy for its aesthetic appreciation of Bach's compositional style, in particular its pictorial and symbolic aspects, as well as its attention to the theological significance of Bach's work.

Schweitzer's third sphere of Bach involvement was a performing edition of the organ works; the free works were published in 1912–13 in collaboration with his teacher Charles-Marie Widor (1844–1937), and the chorale settings followed in 1954–7, in co-operation with Edouard Nies-Berger). Based on the *BG* edition, this one is free of editorial performance markings, but each of the eight volumes contains a preface treating aspects of performing practice and interpretation.

Finally, there are Schweitzer's recitals and recordings of Bach's organ works. The recitals, given throughout Europe, were undertaken in the decades after 1913, the year in which he began his work as a missionary doctor in Africa, and were intended to raise funds to support his hospital. The recordings were made on the organ of the parish church in Gunsbach, Alsace, an instrument that Schweitzer designed and that he believed to be ideal for the performance of Bach's works.

QF

E. R. Jacobi, *Albert Schweitzer und die Musik* (Wiesbaden, 1975); M. Murray, *Albert Schweitzer, Musician* (Aldershot, 1994); L. I. Phelps, 'A Short History of the Organ Revival', *Church Music*, 1 (1967), 13–30.

**Schwencke, Christian Friedrich Gottlieb** (b. 30 Aug. 1767; d. 27 Oct. 1822). Pianist and composer, born in Wachenhausen, Harz. He was a child prodigy as a pianist, and in 1815 went to study in Berlin with F. W. Marpurg and J. P. Kirnberger, and in 1787–8 was a student at the universities in Leipzig and Halle. In 1788 he succeeded C. P. E. Bach as town Kantor in Hamburg, where he remained for the rest of his life. He wrote for the *Allgemeine musicalische Zeitung* and founded a musical academy. He owned a number of Bach manuscripts, including the autograph score of the *St Matthew Passion*, which were subsequently acquired by the great Bach collector Georg Poelchau.

Schwencke wrote numerous compositions—oratorios, cantatas, concertos, sonatas, and songs—but his most frequently performed piece of work is without doubt bar 23 of the first prelude

in Book 1 of Bach's *The Well-tempered Clavier*, which he added to his edition published in 1801 and which has been perpetuated in many other editions since then.

**Schwingt freudig euch empor** ('Soar joyfully aloft'). Cantata, BWV36, which is known in five different versions, of which three are secular and two sacred. The complex history of the work is perhaps indicative of Bach's own high regard for it. The earliest version, *Schwingt freudig euch empor* BWV36c, was written in 1725 to a text probably by Picander, and performed as a birthday tribute to a Leipzig academic. His identity has not been confirmed, but the Bach scholar Werner Neumann suggested that the recipient might have been Johann Burckhard Mencke (1675–1732), a professor at the university who celebrated his 50th birthday that year.

In 1726 Bach revived the piece for the birthday of Princess Charlotte Friederike Wilhelmine of Anhalt-Cöthen (1702–85), the second wife of Prince Leopold. Once again the text was by Picander, *Steigt freudig in die Luft* ('Rise joyfully into the air') BWV36a; the text was published the following year in Picander's *Ernst-Scherzhaffte und Satyrische Gedichte*. Almost ten years later, in 1735, Bach performed the music a third time, on this occasion as a birthday offering to the Leipzig University professor Johann Florens Rivinus (1681–1755). The text was again rewritten, perhaps by Picander, this time as *Die Freude reget sich* ('Joy rouses itself') BWV36b.

Meanwhile, some time between 1726 and 1730 Bach had prepared from some of this existing material a cantata for Advent Sunday, BWV36(1). While retaining the title of the original, the text was adapted by an unidentified hand and cast into five numbers. Evidently the result was not entirely satisfactory to Bach for, in 1731, he expanded the work and made several major structural changes. The most important of these were the addition of three chorale arrangements of Luther's celebrated Advent hymn *Nun komm, der Heiden Heiland* (1524) and the division of the cantata into two parts. Bach, however, retained the concluding chorale of the earlier Advent cantata, the last strophe of Philipp Nicolai's hymn *Wie schön leuchtet der Morgenstern* (1599), but he set instead the previous strophe and used it to round off Part 1 of the new work. In this highly effective revised form (BWV36(2)), consisting of eight sections as opposed to the earlier five, it was performed on Advent Sunday (2 December) 1731. Each of these two sacred parodies has in common its opening chorus and its three arias, all of which are to be found in the earliest secular version; but, as so often with Bach, the music of the 1731 revision was subjected afresh to close scrutiny and improved upon in many details. Its alternating pattern of aria and chorale is unique among his cantatas.

The joyful opening chorus in D major is scored for two unison oboes d'amore (all previous versions call for only one), strings, and continuo. The voices enter in imitation from the bass upwards, illustrating the opening words of the text. In the second half of the movement, clear though unspecific reference is made to the appointed Gospel text relating Christ's entry into Jerusalem. The chorus is followed by the first strophe of the Lutheran hymn *Nun komm, der Heiden Heiland*, which Bach treats as a duet for soprano and alto (each voice supported by a doubling oboe d'amore), with continuo. The setting is both fervent and intimate and one in which Bach's use of the hymn's associated melody in all three strands of the texture is as ingenious as it is inspired. The single aria in Part 1 of the cantata is for tenor with oboe d'amore obbligato. In da capo form, it is a tender evocation of the entry into Jerusalem in which Christ is personified as the bridegroom of the soul. A single strophe of the resonant hymn *Wie schön leuchtet der Morgenstern*, with instruments doubling the voices, concludes the first part of the work.

Part 2 begins with an aria in D major for bass, with violin and string accompaniment. In spirit it harks back to the opening chorus, with its text of welcome to Christ and a plea that he may enter Christian hearts. It is followed by the sixth strophe of *Nun komm, der Heiden Heiland*. The chorale melody is this time stated in long notes by the tenor alone, while dialogue between the two oboes d'amore provides a lively accompaniment, along with a busy continuo. The third and final aria is for soprano with a muted violin obbligato. In the earliest secular version of the work Bach had given the part to a viola d'amore, and he was later, in the third secular version, to give it to a flute. Delicate, echo-like figures both within the violin part and between voice and violin, complementing the text's simply expressed faith in Christ, and an alluring 12/8 rhythm create a picture of considerable enchantment. This extended da capo number leads directly to the concluding chorale. Unlike the two previous chorale arrangements of *Nun komm, der Heiden Heiland*, this, the seventh strophe of the hymn, is straightforwardly harmonized by Bach, with instruments reinforcing the four vocal strands, bringing the work to a close in the key of B minor.                                   NA

For bibliography, *see* CANTATA, §1.

**scordatura.** An Italian term designating the use of a tuning other than the normal, established tuning of a string instrument. Scordatura was fre-

quently used in 16th- and 17th-century lute music and in violin music of the 17th and 18th centuries, composers being attracted to the new colours, timbres, and sonorities offered by the different tuning and the consequent tension changes of the relevant strings. It could also offer new harmonic possibilities, extend the range of the instrument, or make easier or possible certain passage-work.

Up to the beginning of the 18th century, scordatura for bowed string instruments was most extensively employed by German violinists, particularly by Heinrich von Biber (1644–1704). The method of notation accorded with the disposition of the fingers, not the resultant pitch, and presupposed that the player would use open strings and first position unless otherwise indicated, accidentals in key signatures applying only to the specific note and not to its octave above or below. Bach's Fifth Cello Suite represents his solitary fully authenticated example of scordatura, the *a* string being tuned down a tone to *g*. His motives in requiring scordatura have long puzzled scholars and performers, since they have little to do with timbre or greater digital facility. It seems most likely that he was intentionally reviving a tuning which had been standard in the early history of the cello, and which had been used occasionally later as a 'discordatura', for example by Luigi Taglietti (*Suonate da camera* op. 1, 1697) and Jacob Klein *le jeune* (Sixth Duet for two cellos op. 2, c.1720).

Scordatura is employed also in the Trio Sonata in G major BWV1038, where the two highest strings of the violin are both tuned down one tone. The authenticity of this version of the work (which also exists as BWV1021 and 1022) is, however, in doubt.                                   RS

D. D. Boyden, *The History of Violin Playing from its Origins to 1761* (London, 1965); A. Moser, 'Die Violin-Skordatur', *Archiv für Musikwissenschaft*, 1 (1918–19), 573–89; T. Russell, 'The Violin "Scordatura"', *Musical Quarterly*, 24 (1938), 84–96; R. Stowell, *Violin Technique and Performance Practice in the Late Eighteenth and Early Nineteenth Centuries* (Cambridge, 1985), 232–9.

**Sechs Choräle von verschiedener Art.** *See* SCHÜBLER CHORALES.

**Sehet, welch eine Liebe hat uns der Vater erzeiget** ('Behold, what manner of love the Father hath bestowed upon us'). Cantata for the third day of Christmas, BWV64, first performed on 27 December 1723 as part of Bach's first annual cantata cycle in Leipzig. The libretto is a revised version of a text by J. O. Knauer published in 1720. The text of the first movement is I John 3: 1; movement 2 is strophe 7 (the last) of Martin Luther's

## Sehet, wir gehn hinauf gen Jerusalem

hymn *Gelobet seist du, Jesu Christ* (1524); movement 4 is strophe 1 of the hymn *Was frag ich nach der Welt* by G. M. Pfefferkorn (1667); and movement 8 is strophe 5 of *Jesu, meine Freude* by Johann Franck (1650).

The *Spruch* that serves as the text of the first movement, a theologically important but affectively neutral statement of doctrine, is set as a motet. As is characteristic, there are no independent instrumental lines; strings double the vocal parts, as do a quartet of cornett and trombones, instruments closely associated with MOTET STYLE. The basso continuo is partly independent, offering the possibility of occasional five-part textures. The voices are in imitative counterpoint, using a subject that begins syllabically in crotchets and minims ('Sehet, welch eine Liebe hat uns der Vater') and ends in a long quaver melisma ('erzeiget'). Among the various contrapuntal combinations of the subject, Bach exploits the contrast between its two halves; in two passages, for example, two voices present fragments of the first part of the subject in close imitation, while the other parts extend the melismatic second part in long sequences. The rhetorically strongest aspect of the text is its opening exordium, 'Sehet', which Bach sets as a block homophonic exclamation by all four voices before beginning successive imitative entrances.

The four-part chorale that follows echoes the words of the first movement, speaking of God's showing his love ('sein groß Lieb zu zeigen an'); here the librettist has used a strophe from a seasonal hymn to amplify the biblical text. The recitative and four-part chorale that follow form a unit. They are textually connected, in that the recitative text introduces the chorale, ending with the anticipatory words 'Thus I say with a hopeful spirit:' that set up the immediate appearance of the chorale. The recitative's topic of the worthlessness of worldly possessions is again affirmed in the chorale, which asks 'What do I need of this world?' The recitative and chorale are musically linked as well: in the recitative the vocal line is punctuated not by chords but by semiquaver scale figures in the continuo, and at the end of the recitative they lead directly into the four-part chorale and to almost continuous quaver figuration in the continuo.

The two da capo arias that follow, separated by a simple recitative, each deal with the worthlessness of worldly things compared to heavenly ones. The first, for soprano, is cast in the rhythm of a gavotte (with its characteristic double upbeat) and is accompanied by strings with a virtuoso violin part. The second aria, for alto, calls for an oboe d'amore obbligato. A third four-part chorale closes the cantata; its text, a farewell to earthly life

and its sinfulness, sums up the sentiments of the work.                    DRM

For bibliography, *see* CANTATA, §1.

***Sehet, wir gehn hinauf gen Jerusalem*** ('Behold, we go up to Jerusalem'). Cantata for the Sunday before Lent (Estomihi), BWV159. It sets a libretto that Picander published in his *Cantaten auf die Sonn- und Fest-Tage durch das gantze Jahr* (Leipzig, 1728), and was therefore almost certainly first performed on the Sunday before Lent (27 February) 1729. Estomihi was observed as a Passion Sunday (see JESUS NAHM ZU SICH DIE ZWÖLFE). There are therefore links between this cantata and Bach's Passions.

The first movement is a dialogue of questions and answers between Jesus (bass) and the Soul (alto), based on the words of Jesus at the beginning of the Gospel for the day (Luke 18: 31). Three passages of arioso to biblical words are each followed by accompanied recitative—a meditation on what lies ahead in Jerusalem. Movement 2 follows on directly and intertwines an alto aria with a chorale. The Soul declares its intention of following Jesus, while stanza 6 of Paul Gerhardt's *O Haupt voll Blut und Wunden* with its associated melody, *Herzlich tut mich verlangen*, is heard, line by line, as a soprano cantus firmus. This is the well-known PASSION CHORALE that Bach employed a number of times in the *St Matthew Passion*, a work which members of Bach's congregation might have heard only a few weeks later.

Of particular significance in the Passion narrative found in St John's Gospel are the words that Jesus uttered immediately before his death: 'Es ist vollbracht' ('It is finished'). In the *St John Passion* the meditation on these words is the astonishingly beautiful alto aria with viola da gamba obbligato. The fourth movement of the cantata, a bass aria with oboe obbligato, is a meditation on the same words as poignant and beautiful as the earlier aria in the *St John Passion*, and among Bach's finest vocal creations.

The cantata concludes with a chorale, the penultimate stanza of Paul Stockmann's *Jesu Leiden, Pein und Tod*, which Bach used three times in the *St John Passion* (four times in the 1725 version), as well as in Cantata 182 for Palm Sunday.      RAL

For bibliography, *see* CANTATA, §1.

***Sei Lob und Ehr dem höchsten Gut*** ('Let there be praise and honour to the highest good'). Cantata for an unspecified occasion, BWV117. In addition to the great series of chorale-based cantatas of 1724–5, Bach wrote a small number in which the hymn text is retained unaltered *per omnes versus* ('verse by verse') throughout. Cantata 117, dating from the period between 1728 and 1731, is such a piece, in which Bach set the nine strophes of the hymn *Sei Lob und Ehr dem höchsten Gut* (1675) by Johann Jakob Schütz. Each strophe, furthermore, ends with the same line of text: 'Gebt unserm Gott die Ehre!' ('Give honour to our God!'). This provides one of several unifying elements in the cantata. Another of importance lies in the musically identical treatment of the first and last sections of the work, by which means, as Alfred Dürr has remarked, 'Bach has created a majestic framework which encloses the remaining sections' (*DürrK*). The hymn tune, quoted in full in the first and last sections of the cantata as well as in the centrally placed chorale (no. 4), is not that by Johann Crüger, frequently sung with this hymn, but an anonymous 15th-century melody associated with the hymn *Es ist das Heil uns kommen her* but, according to *DürrK*, generally used for Schütz's hymn, too, in the Leipzig of Bach's day.

*Sei Lob und Ehr dem höchsten Gut* bears no designation for a particular Sunday in the Church year. Indeed, we cannot be certain that Bach ever performed it in the context of his regular duties as Kantor at Leipzig. More likely, perhaps, it was intended for a wedding or other special festival. The opening chorus, to the first strophe of the hymn, is scored for flutes, oboes, and violins (each in two parts), viola, and continuo. The movement is in Bach's most impressive and appealing concertante manner. Choral sections, always with the hymn melody sustained in the soprano line, are accompanied by, or juxtaposed with, animated, even playful instrumental ritornellos which permeate each strand of the texture. In this way Bach achieves a pleasing contrast between the stricter vocal polyphony on the one hand and the altogether more light-hearted concertante element on the other. Movement 2 is a simple recitative for the bass, which develops into a lively arioso in the last line of the text, and this is followed by a tenor aria accompanied by two oboes d'amore and continuo. In this piece the dark tone-colour of the oboes and of the key (E minor) is offset by a return to the dance-like 6/8 metre of the opening chorus. The fourth strophe is set as a simple harmonization of the melody on which the cantata is based. It is worth noting that in some modern editions the same music, setting the last stanza of the hymn, provides the conclusion to the cantata instead of the recapitulation of the opening chorus. This does not, however, follow Bach's own directions in the autograph score.

Movement 5 is an alto recitative accompanied by two-part violins, viola, and continuo which at the eighth bar broadens into arioso. There, as the voice takes up a quotation of the chorale melody, the violins and viola are silent, and the sole accompaniment is provided by the continuo, which also quotes the hymn in close imitation of

the voice. An arresting link exists between this section and the following bass aria with violin obbligato, for here Bach introduces another, even subtler reference to the chorale melody at the words 'Gebt unserm Gott die Ehre!' (bars 42–53). This tender aria is followed at once by 'Ich will dich all mein Leben lang' for alto with flute, strings, and continuo, the most extended and the most lyrically conceived of the cantata's three arias.

A short tenor recitative leads to a recapitulation of the music of the opening chorus, though now incorporating the text of the ninth and last stanza of Schütz's hymn. It brings one of Bach's most strikingly varied cantatas to a close.                NA

For bibliography, *see* CANTATA, §1.

***Selig ist der Mann*** ('Blessed is the man'). Cantata for the second day of Christmas, BWV57, first performed in Leipzig on 26 December 1725. As well as being the second day of Christmas, 26 December was also the feast of St Stephen, and Bach's librettist, the Darmstadt court poet G. C. Lehms, here dwells on Stephen's martyrdom as an example of the rewards that await the suffering believer beyond the grave. The text is constructed as a dialogue between the Soul (soprano) and Jesus (bass) and, as in operas of the period, the discourse is carried forward in recitative while the arias expand on the thoughts and feelings raised. The voices are accompanied by a relatively modest instrumental ensemble of two oboes, *taille* (oboe da caccia), strings, and continuo.

As the 'text' of his cantata Lehms took a passage from James 1: 12: 'Blessed is the man that endureth temptation: for when he is tried, he shall receive the crown of life'. Bach set it as an aria—more a kind of extended arioso—for bass, accompanied by the full instrumental forces; with typical resourcefulness, Bach incorporates the quaver figure played by the first violin at the opening into nearly every bar of the music, sometimes in inversion and sometimes in conjunction with a falling chromatic scale which throws a dark shadow over the music, though it is never sung. The gloom of this aria is, if anything, intensified in the soprano's 'Ich wünschte mir den Tod' ('I should wish for death'), a modified da capo aria in which the Soul, with string accompaniment, sings of the torments to be endured without Christ's love.

Members of the Leipzig congregation still intent on celebrating Christmas must have welcomed the change that comes over the music after the brief recitative that follows. With a string accompaniment dominated by the first violin's repeated semiquavers (somewhat in the manner of the first movement of Brandenburg Concerto no. 5), Jesus calls on the Soul to cease its weeping and to look towards a brighter morrow, and this lighter mood is prolonged in the soprano's second aria, despite its minor key. The most dramatic moment in the cantata is reached when this aria comes to a sudden end with the question 'What is your gift to me?', which the four-part chorus, heard for the first and only time, answers with the sixth strophe of Ahasverus Fritsch's hymn *Hast du denn, Jesu, dein Angesicht* (1668): 'Direct yourself according to my wishes, and know that I shall for ever remain your Soul's friend.'

For bibliography, *see* CANTATA, §1.

**serenata** ('serenade'). Italian term for a type of musical work performed in the evening, usually in the open air in celebration of a particular occasion or to pay homage to a particular person. An equivalent German term is 'Abendmusik'. Several of Bach's so-called secular cantatas are works of this type; the libretto of BWV215 described that work as 'eine Abend-Musik'. *See* CANTATA, §2.

**service** (*Gottesdienst*). For the Lutheran order of service in Bach's time, *see* HAUPTGOTTESDIENST and VESPERS.

**Sheep may safely graze.** English title of the soprano aria 'Schafe können sicher weiden' from Bach's Cantata no. 208, *Was mir behagt, ist nur die muntre Jagd*. Both the title and the music itself were made popular through instrumental arrangements, particularly one for piano solo by Mary Howe published in 1937 (her two-piano version had appeared two years earlier). Howe's arrangement actually begins with the preceding recitative, but she could hardly have called it *Will Pales's offering here be the last then?* An idiosyncratic transcription of the aria alone, under the title *Blithe Bells*, was made by the Australian-born composer and pianist Percy Grainger (1882–1961), in versions for piano solo, two pianos, and various orchestral forces. *See also* WISE VIRGINS, THE.

**short mass.** A term sometimes used for a MISSA consisting only of the Kyrie and Gloria.

**siciliana.** A type of song or instrumental piece, particularly of the 17th–18th centuries, characterized by a lilting, often dotted rhythm in 6/8 or 12/8 time. Bach used the term (interchangeably with 'siciliano' and 'alla siciliana') for slow movements of this type in sonatas and concertos, including the Sonata no. 1 for unaccompanied violin, the Violin Sonata in C minor, BWV1017, the Flute Sonatas in E♭ major and E major, and the Concertos for harpsichord in E major and for three harpsichords in D minor. Slow movements not so titled nevertheless often share the same characteristics, for examples those in the Organ Sonatas nos. 1 and 6, the Gamba Sonata no. 2, the Flute Sonata

in B minor, and the Harpsichord Concerto in A major.

Movements of siciliana type are also common in Bach's vocal works. Some of these are quite simple, dance-like pieces in moderate time, recalling Quantz's characterization of the siciliana as 'an imitation of a Sicilian shepherd's dance' (those in Cantatas 29:5, 68:1, 107:7, 174:2, 197:8, and 211:8, as well as the pastoral Sinfonia and closing chorale in Part 2 of the *Christmas Oratorio*). Others are slow, expressive, and elaborate pieces, more akin to the above-mentioned sonata and concerto slow movements: Cantatas 19:5, 35:2, 87:6, 101:6, 120:1, 140:3, 169:5, and (best-known of all) the alto aria 'Erbarme dich, mein Gott' from the St Matthew *Passion*.                                                      RDPJ

D. Finke-Hecklinger, *Tanzcharaktere in Johann Sebastian Bachs Vokalmusik* (Trossingen, 1970), 78–81.

**Siehe, ich will viel Fischer aussenden** ('Behold, I will send for many fishers'). Cantata for the fifth Sunday after Trinity, BWV88, first performed on 21 July 1726. The text, by an unidentified author, is organized in an unusual but effective way, corresponding with several texts of cantatas by Bach's distant cousin Johann Ludwig, who was *Kapellmeister* at Meiningen. In 1726 Bach performed no fewer than 18 of Johann Ludwig's cantatas at Leipzig, and repeated some of them in later years. Bach was evidently attracted by formal aspects of his cousin's cantatas, adopting them in several of his own, including the present work. Customarily divided into two parts, the layout was as follows: Old Testament passage (chorus)—recitative—aria—New Testament passage—aria—recitative—chorale. At least seven of Bach's own cantatas of 1726 adhere to this scheme, allowing for minor variations (*see* ERNST LUDWIG).

Part 1 of *Siehe, ich will viel Fischer aussenden* begins, however, not with a chorus but with an aria—the only one of Bach's cantatas modelled on those of his Meiningen cousin to do so. The text is Jeremiah 16: 16: 'Behold, I will send for many fishers, saith the Lord, and they shall fish them; and after will I send for many hunters, and they shall hunt them from every mountain, and from every hill, and out of the holes of the rocks.' These two contrasting images drew vividly pictorial responses from Bach, in striking contradiction to the generally observed Baroque rule of allowing one affect only to colour a single aria (a rule observed less strictly by Bach than by many other composers, perhaps). The piece is scored for bass voice with divided violins (each doubled by oboe d'amore), viola (doubled by *taille*), basso continuo, and, in the second part of the aria, two horns. In the first part Bach illustrates the image of the fishermen by means of an undulating wave-like motif in 6/8 time. This changes abruptly when, in a second section (¢, Allegro quasi presto) two horns—instruments customarily associated with the chase in Baroque music—are introduced into the texture, announcing, so to speak, the arrival of the huntsmen of the text. The striking effect of this sudden change of instrumental colour, tempo, and metre matches the bold originality of the aria's bipartite design.

A tenor recitative reflects on God's powers of forgiveness, but questions his strength against that of Satan. Doubt is immediately resolved with the first words of the tenor aria 'Nein, Gott is allezeit geflißen, uns auf guten Weg zu wißen' ('No, God is always careful to show us the good path'), which follows without an introductory instrumental ritornello. This unusually constructed piece—a spacious A–B–B′ design to which is added an instrumental tailpiece, with an obbligato oboe d'amore assuming the role of the voice in what amounts to a varied repeat of the first (A) section—brings Part 1 to a conclusion.

The second part begins in the manner of an oratorio, with the tenor acting as narrator in a two-bar burst of accompanied recitative. There follow Christ's words, sung by the bass in an extended arioso over a quasi-ostinato continuo: 'Fear not; from henceforth thou shalt catch men' (Luke 5: 10). The duet in A major (no. 5) for soprano and alto is accompanied by unison oboes d'amore and violins. This movement, too, has striking features, among them the lively invention of the fugal writing in the two voice parts. In a simple recitative for soprano the text bids the faint-hearted go joyfully onwards, and the cantata ends with the last strophe of Georg Neumark's hymn *Wer nur den lieben Gott läßt walten* (1657), which, in the Leipzig hymn schedule, was designated for the fifth Sunday after Trinity.    NA

For bibliography, *see* CANTATA, §1.

### Siehe zu, daß deine Gottesfurcht nicht Heuchelei sei ('See that thy fear of God is not hypocrisy').
Cantata for the 11th Sunday after Trinity, BWV179, first performed at Leipzig on 8 August 1723. The anonymous librettist took the words of the opening chorus from Ecclesiasticus 1, but the cantata as a whole is closely based on the Gospel reading for the day, St Luke 18: 9–14 (the parable of the Pharisee and the publican), the subject of which is also hypocrisy. Bach set the Apocrypha *Spruch* in MOTET STYLE for SATB with *colla parte* strings. The first phrase of the text is set to a fugue subject (bass, and later soprano) which is answered by inversion (tenor and alto). The continuation, 'and come not unto him with a double heart', brings a new fugal subject, with a falling

chromatic phrase for 'falschem' ('false', 'double'), and the two subjects are then heard in combination. Bach had no difficulty in adapting this movement as the Kyrie of his *Missa* in G major.

The tenor aria 'Falscher Heuchler Ebenbild' that follows after a simple tenor recitative was also used in the G major *Missa*, as 'Quoniam tu solus sanctus' in the Gloria. In the *missa* the voice is accompanied only by oboe and continuo; in the cantata Bach used two oboes and first violin for the obbligato part and included also parts for second violin and viola. Possibly this says something about the respective tenor soloists, or about the buildings in which they performed. A bass recitative, which four times subtly merges into a measured arioso style to highlight particular phrases in the text, is followed by a soprano aria, 'Liebster Gott, erbarme dich', in modified da capo form. This is the publican's 'God be merciful to me a sinner', an expressive setting which found an appropriate place as 'Qui tollis peccata mundi' in the *Missa* in A major, where the music is transposed from A to B minor and the two oboes da caccia of the cantata are replaced by flutes.

The imprecatory tone of this aria is carried over into the final four-part chorale, the first strophe of Christoph Tietze's hymn *Ich armer Mensch, ich armer Sünder* (1663), set to one of Bach's favourite chorale melodies, *Wer nur den lieben Gott läßt walten*.

For bibliography, *see* CANTATA, §1.

### Sie werden aus Saba alle kommen ('All they from Sheba shall come').
Cantata for Epiphany, BWV65, first performed at Leipzig on 6 January 1724. Epiphany, the feast of the manifestation of Christ, marks the end of the Christmas season. The unidentified librettist of this cantata skilfully conflated Old and New Testament Scripture to create a text which retains all the symbolic importance of the original, at the same time providing Bach with pictorial images that lend themselves especially well to musical treatment. At the heart of the text is the appointed Gospel reading (Matt. 2: 1–12), which contains the story of the visit to Bethlehem of the three wise men bearing gifts of gold (for a king), frankincense (for prayer), and myrrh (for the Cross). This is linked with the German epistle for Epiphany (Isaiah 60: 1–6), in particular with the words 'all they from Sheba shall come: they shall bring gold and incense; and they shall shew forth the praises of the Lord'. The symbolism of the three wise men, the Magi, or the three kings was prominent in the Lutheran celebration of Epiphany, and in this cantata Bach paints an indelible picture in music of their journey to Bethlehem.

449

## Sie werden euch in den Bann tun

The textual layout is concisely and clearly organized into three groups, each of two movements, with a concluding chorale. The first group illustrates and reflects upon the words of the Epistle and Gospel, while the second and third focus more on the gift of heart and soul to Christ. The concluding chorale acts as a confirmation of this gift.

The opening choral movement is a thrilling picture of the gathering hosts of the Gentiles, bearing gifts and glorifying the Saviour's name. Bach's wonderfully colourful scoring of this piece for two horns, two treble recorders, two oboes da caccia, strings, and continuo resonantly underlines the majesty of the occasion, while the dance-like 12/8 rhythm reflects the joyful fulfilment of the Old Testament prophecy. Bach's ingenuity seems almost boundless in this superbly crafted chorus, whose expressively light-hearted canonic opening section leads to another, more strictly fugal exposition before returning, in a concluding section, to material based on the instrumental introduction.

The resplendent opening chorus is followed by the third strophe from the 16th-century hymn *Ein Kind geborn zu Bethlehem*, the German version of *Puer natus in Bethlehem* (1545). According to Günther Stiller (*Johann Sebastian Bach and Liturgical Life in Leipzig* (St Louis, Miss., 1984), 237), this hymn was regularly sung in Latin and German at Epiphany and on preceding festival days. The four-part vocal texture is supported by unison recorders and divided oboes da caccia. A bass recitative, which leads to passages of arioso, is followed by a bass aria with divided oboes da caccia. The opening melodic motif in the oboes is a persistent one throughout the piece and is taken up by the voice. The second recitative–aria pair is for tenor: the recitative leads to a richly scored aria in which all the instruments of the opening chorus play a prominent role: divided recorders, horns, oboes da caccia, and violins, with viola and basso continuo. The piece is a joyful dance in 3/8 time, with playful figures in the wind and violin parts which both accompany and punctuate the tenor line. Neither aria in the cantata is in conventional da capo form, but rather in one adhering to the scheme A–A–B.

The cantata ends with a straightforward harmonization of the fourth strophe of Paul Gerhardt's *Ich hab in Gottes Herz und Sinn* (1647), set to the melody *Was mein Gott will, das g'scheh allzeit* (1529). NA

For bibliography, *see* CANTATA, §1.

***Sie werden euch in den Bann tun*** ('They shall put you out of the synagogues') **(i).** Cantata for the Sunday after Ascension (Exaudi), BWV 44, first performed in Leipzig on 21 May 1724. The work treats the themes of suffering and persecution, taking as its point of departure the appointed Gospel reading (John 15: 26–16: 4), a passage from a discourse in which Jesus warns his disciples that they will be persecuted because of their relationship with him. The text of movements 1 and 2 is taken from this passage (John 16: 2). The first sentence is set as a duet for tenor and bass. It begins with a long ritornello for two oboes and continuo (bars 1–22) which features the lively imitative interchange and overall character of a trio sonata. When the voices enter, it simply expands to a quintet; the relationship between the two vocal lines is similar to that of the oboes. The texture thins only occasionally, most notably, of course, between statements of the text (bars 40 ff. and 55 ff.). The movement concludes with a ritornello (much briefer than the first), and moves without a break into the next movement, in which the second sentence is set. Both the vocal and instrumental ensembles expand to encompass all four voices and strings (the oboes double the violin lines, while the viola has its own part), and the metre also changes from triple to *alla breve*. A notable feature of movement 2 is the concerted relationship between the choir and instrumental ensemble, in which they first alternate (e.g. bars 1–5 and 13–17), then join together. Also noteworthy is the chromatic melisma illustrating the word 'tötet' ('kills'), which first appears in the bass and continuo lines (bars 6–7 and 18–19), but later spreads to the other vocal parts as well (bars 27–30).

Each of the four voices is assigned a solo in the succeeding sequence of movements. First the alto has a da capo aria (movement 3), accompanied by oboe and continuo. Here it is stated that Christians can expect 'Marter, Bann und schwere Pein' ('torment, ban, and severe suffering'). The gravity of this message is underscored by the persistence of the minor mode throughout the movement. Characteristically, the words 'Marter, Bann und schwere Pein' are illustrated with chromaticism (bars 55–60 and 68–70). Movement 4 is a brief but highly effective setting of a chorale, scored for tenor and continuo alone, which reiterates the idea that following Christ entails hardship. The tenor sings the melody, one phrase at a time, with little embellishment. This diminutive movement derives its expressive power primarily from the tortuous chromaticism, illustrating the words 'Herzeleid' ('heartache') and 'trübsalvoll' ('full of sorrow'), that pervades the relentless continuo line.

The bass recitative (movement 5) also is accompanied by the continuo instruments only. The first five bars contain a high density of diminished and augmented intervals, which clearly symbolize its subject-matter, the ultimate persecution of the Antichrist. Here also is the first hint of the transformation of suffering into consolation. Christians are likened to the branches of palm trees, which grow even higher when they are weighted down ('Allein, es gleichen Christen denen Palmenzweigen, die durch die Last nur desto höher steigen').

The soprano aria (movement 6) picks up this theme, observing that 'Gott vor seine Kirche wacht' ('God watches over his Church') and that trials give way to joy in the same way that the sun comes out after a storm. This movement is supported by the full instrumental ensemble (oboes, strings, and continuo). Its joyful affect is briefly interrupted in the first half of the middle section (bars 34 ff.), where the gathering of storm clouds, emblematic of affliction, is represented by a remarkably graphic set of ascending chords formed by pairs of semiquavers, coupled with agitated melismas in the soprano part. The laughing of the 'Freudensonne' ('joyful sun') also is illustrated with melismas in triplet semiquavers (bars 43–4 and 52–3).

The simple four-part chorale that concludes this work, an exhortation to trust God because of his infinite wisdom, uses the same melody as the unforgettable setting of 'Wer hat dich so geschlagen' from the *St John Passion*, which had received its première just a few weeks earlier, on Good Friday (7 April). SAC

For bibliography, see CANTATA, §1.

**Sie werden euch in den Bann tun** ('They shall put you out of the synagogues') **(ii)**. Cantata for the first Sunday after Ascension (Exaudi), BWV183, first performed on 13 May 1725. The work is little known on account of its unusual instrumentation, its lack of choral movements (apart from the final chorale), and the demands made on both vocal and instrumental soloists. It is, however, a thoroughly accomplished work with a strong dramatic profile. It is the fifth of the cantatas that Bach composed on texts by Christiane Mariane von Ziegler, and it opens with the same New Testament verse as did his Exaudi cantata from the previous year (BWV44). This explains its modern listing as setting 'ii' of this text, although the two works are otherwise musically and textually distinct.

Bach's initial thought for setting the opening scriptural text (John 16: 2) was as a bass aria that would have opened with an unusual fugal ritornello over a chromatic continuo line. (Bach's rejected draft was overlooked in the *NBA*; see

Sketch 116 in R. L. Marshall, *The Compositional Process of J. S. Bach* (Princeton, 1972).) Bach abandoned this idea in favour of a brief accompanied recitative, retaining only the extraordinary accompaniment of two oboes d'amore and two oboes da caccia, with continuo. Bach later used this instrumentation to pastoral effect in Part 2 of the *Christmas Oratorio* (1734), but here the dramatic five-part sonority, with its mid-range double reeds, seems associated with the fear that is the text's initial concern. (Paired oboes da caccia are used several times to similar effect in the *St John* and *St Matthew Passions*.) Luther's translation of the opening verse uses an idiom ('they shall banish you') that is more vivid than that of Jerome or the King James version ('they shall put you out of the synagogues', i.e. the assemblies). But in any case Bach does not 'paint' any words here, save perhaps for 'tötet' ('kill'), where the vocal phrase outlines a diminished 7th chord.

The work's theme is that fear of persecution will be allayed by the 'comforter', that is the Holy Spirit, alluded to in the concluding aria. Hence the work's two recitative–aria pairs present contrasting affects. The quiet scoring of the first aria, for tenor and violoncello piccolo (marked 'molt'-adagio' in the original continuo part), might reflect the negative element in the text—'I fear *not* death's terrors'—but the tortured melodic line of both ritornello and soloist surely represents fear as such. The eight-line text, in da capo form, is divided unequally; the last six lines are fitted into the B section, where a florid melisma on 'ich folge' ('I follow') in line 4 is complemented by a quiet sustained note on 'es mag beruh'n' ('let it rest') in line 8.

A second accompanied recitative, for alto, follows. Its text opens with the same words, 'Ich bin bereit ('I am ready') and virtually the same motif as the second movement of Bach's Ascension cantata BWV128, performed just three days earlier. The scoring is even more remarkable than in the first movement; the four oboes take up the vocal motif, while the upper strings—heard here for the first time—provide a halo of sustained chords. The movement ends with a sudden enharmonic modulation that prepares the C major of the final aria.

This movement, for soprano, is accompanied by the two oboes da caccia (in unison) and strings. The first half of this two-part aria ends with a lively melisma (borrowed from the ritornello) for 'wandeln' ('travel'). But its exuberance seems somewhat shaken by the sudden shift to minor keys at the beginning of the B section, 'hilf meine Schwachheit' ('aid my weakness'). This anticipates the key of the closing chorale, a setting in A minor of the tune *Helft mir Gotts Güte preisen*; the text is the fifth strophe of Paul Gebhardt's *Zeuch ein zu deinen Thoren* (1653).     DS

For bibliography, *see* CANTATA, §1.

**Silbermann, Gottfried** (b. 14 Jan. 1683; d. 4 Aug. 1753). Builder of keyboard instruments, especially organs, born in Kleinbobritzsch, near Freiberg in Saxony. Beginning around 1701, he worked with his brother Andreas (1678–1734) in Strasburg. In 1710 he returned to Saxony, where he spent the remainder of his life. He died in Dresden, while at work on his organ in the Hofkirche.

Bach performed on Silbermann's organs in Dresden, even though he disliked their mean-tone temperament. In 1746 the two men jointly inspected an organ in Naumburg. Bach also performed on Silbermann's pianos, most notably in 1747 at the court of Frederick the Great, and he helped sell the instruments as well. His criticisms of Silbermann's early pianos prompted the builder to improve his design, and the revised disposition met with Bach's 'complete approval'.

RTS

*See also* ORGAN, §1.

E. Badura-Skoda, 'Komponierte J. S. Bach "Hammerklavier-Konzerte"?', *BJb* 77 (1991), 159–71; W. Müller, *Gottfried Silbermann: Persönlichkeit und Werk* (Leipzig, 1982); C. Wolff, 'Bach und das Pianoforte', in W. Osthoff and R. Wiesend, eds., *Bach und die italienische Musik* (Venice, 1987), 197–210.

**sinfonia.** An Italian term used in various periods, and with a variety of applications, mainly for instrumental pieces. Bach used the term chiefly in the sense of an instrumental introduction to his cantatas. The sinfonias of the earliest cantatas are short pieces for strings and continuo (BWV4, 150, and 196, dating from about 1707–9). Those of the late Weimar years (1714–17) are of disparate character, being related to the chaconne (BWV18), the prelude and fugue (BWV152), or the concerto slow movement (BWV12 and 21).

Examples of sinfonias in the cantatas of Bach's Leipzig years (1723–50) are rare (see BWV75, 76, 209, 212, and Part 2 of the *Christmas Oratorio*), except during a specific period, 1725–31, when he frequently adapted existing concerto movements for the purpose. For Cantata 52 he used the first movement of Brandenburg Concerto no. 1 (in its early version, BWV1046a, itself entitled 'Sinfonia'); for Cantata 174 the first movement of Brandenburg Concerto no. 3; and for Cantatas 29 and 120a the Preludio from the solo violin Partita in E major, which is here transformed into a concerto Allegro for solo organ and orchestra. The presumed concerto models for the sinfonias of Cantatas 42, 249, and 249a are unknown. In the case of

Cantatas 35, 49, 146, 156, 169, and 188 the violin or oboe concerto models are lost, but survive in later adaptations as solo harpsichord concertos. The outer, fast movements are here adapted for solo organ and orchestra, except in BWV156, where the slow movement of BWV1056 is employed in its possibly original scoring for solo oboe, strings, and continuo.

Bach also used the term 'sinfonia' in the 1723 autograph of the three-part Inventions BWV787–801, which had formerly been entitled 'fantasia' (*see* INVENTION). Finally, he used the term for the prelude to the second keyboard Partita, which exhibits the sectional scheme Grave Adagio–Andante–Allegro, an expansion of the slow–fast scheme of the sinfonias to Cantata 152 and Part 2 of Cantata 76 (later reused in the Organ Sonata no. 4).     RDPJ

***Singet dem Herrn ein neues Lied*** ('O sing unto the Lord a new song') **(i)**. Cantata for New Year's Day, BWV190, first performed on 1 January 1724. The loss of the first portion of Bach's autograph score and of most of his manuscript instrumental parts (only the two violins survive) has left movements 1 and 2 incomplete. Enough remains, however, to reveal a distinctive and significant festal work and to permit hypothetical reconstructions of both movements (see below). The losses apparently resulted from Bach's removal of portions of his score and parts to another work, a cantata for the first day of Leipzig's celebration of the 200th anniversary of the Augsburg Confession (25 June 1730). Bach's music for that work, known as BWV190a, is entirely lost, but Picander's printed libretto shows it to have been a parody of the earlier one, substituting new recitatives, new aria texts, and a different final chorale.

The first movement combines verses from Psalms 149 and 150 with the first two phrases of the Gregorian *Te Deum* (in Luther's German version, *Herr Gott, dich loben wir*). Bach's setting appears to have been similar to the first movement of Cantata 69a, *Lobe den Herrn, meine Seele*, the only other work with three trumpets, timpani, and three oboes from his first Leipzig *Jahrgang*. Despite their psalm texts, each movement is conceived as a large choral aria, opening with a grandly scored ritornello that furnishes motivic material for the vocal entries, which in both works include fugal sections. In Cantata 190 the fugue stands at the centre of the movement, where it is used for the verse beginning 'Alles, was Odem hat' ('all that hath breath'). This is framed by the *Te Deum* phrases, sung by the chorus in unison; Bach would use this rare vocal scoring again for the chorale *Ein feste Burg* in the Leipzig version of

Cantata 80. (C. P. E. Bach echoed it more precisely, using the *Te Deum*, in his double-chorus *Heilig* of about 1776.)

The *Te Deum* returns in the second movement, where four of its phrases, now sung in four-part harmony, alternate with recitative. Although the *BG* suggests full scoring, it is more likely that the trumpets and drums, and perhaps the oboes as well, were silent here.

The remainder of the work is more fully preserved. The aria for alto and strings, 'Lobe, Zion, deinen Gott', has a simple dance-like style and form that have encouraged suggestions of a Cöthen origin; the score, however, appears to have been first drafted at Leipzig. A recitative for bass leads to a duet for bass and tenor, accompanied by an unspecified instrument, probably oboe d'amore as in the second aria of Cantata 69*a*. Every line of the text opens with the name 'Jesus', replaced in Cantata 190*a* by the word 'selig' ('blessed'); curiously, Bach makes nothing of the repeated invocation, giving this text, like that of the aria, an unusually concise setting.

An accompanied recitative for the tenor leads to a setting for the full ensemble of the second strophe of Johannes Herman's New Year chorale *Jesu nun sei gepreiset* (1593). For this, Cantata 190*a* substituted the final stanza of Luther's *Es woll uns Gott gnädig sein* (1524), perhaps in the same setting that concludes Cantata 69 (a late version of bwv69*a*). The trumpet interludes in Cantata 69 are far more imaginative than the strangely repetitious ones of Cantata 190. Bach must have remembered the latter, however, for the same motif pervades the first movement of the following New Year's cantata, bwv41.

A reconstruction (often questionable) of movements 1 and 2 has been made by Walter Reinhart (Zurich, 1948), and one of BWV 190*a* (with the first movement identical to that of bwv190) by Diethard Hellmann (Wiesbaden, 1972).     DS

For bibliography, *see* CANTATA, §1.

**Singet dem Herrn ein neues Lied** ('O sing unto the Lord a new song') (ii). Motet for eight-part double chorus, bwv225 on Psalm 149: 1–3; stanza 3 of Johann Gramann's hymn *Nun lob, mein Seel, den Herren* and an anonymous poetic text; and Psalm 150: 2 and 6. Source evidence permits the dating of the composition to 1726–7, but the work's purpose and occasion are unknown, despite extensive speculation.

*Singet dem Herrn ein neues Lied* is without equal in the motet repertory in the scope of its conception, its musical complexity, and its virtuoso demands on performers. Like Bach's *Jesu, meine Freude*, it is a multi-movement work, but

whereas *Jesu, meine Freude* was probably assembled partly from existing musical material and relies on the architectural symmetry of a collection of diverse movements, *Singet dem Herrn* shows the composer's concern from the start for the effect of a succession of varied but coherent movements. The sequence of movements (fast–slow–fast, with a stretto effect in the last section) is carefully planned, and calls to mind the outline of the Italian instrumental concerto.

*Singet dem Herrn* shows a combination of traditional motet elements and innovations. Its use of eight voices in a double chorus is typical (the two choirs combine for the last section, in four parts), but the use of one choir to accompany a fugal exposition in the other (first movement) is apparently unprecedented. The motet uses both biblical and chorale texts, typical of motets, but in separate movements rather than together. It makes use of the poetic and musical choral 'aria' type, often found at the end of central German motets, but integrated into the motet itself (second movement). The motet makes use of counterpoint, typical of the genre, but in true fugues rather than mere points of imitation (first and third movements). Outside these fugal sections, the central German motet tradition's tendency to homophony and sequence still makes itself felt, even with Bach's brilliant part-writing.

Perhaps the most extraordinary section is the four-part fugue on the text beginning 'Die Kinder Zion sei'n fröhlich'. The long fugue subject is presented in the order S–A–T–B in choir 1, with accompanimental material in choir 2 using text and music from the opening section ('Singet dem Herrn'). Beginning with the bass entrance, the voices re-enter with the subject in reverse order (T–A–S), this time in both choirs simultaneously, with accompanying material distributed among the fugally unoccupied voices of both choirs. The accumulating voices in the fugue, together with the gradual merging of the corresponding voices in each choir, creates a powerful climax.

The slow middle movement presents a four-part chorale harmonization in one choir and an 'aria' (the term is Bach's), more lyrical and more contrapuntally accompanied, in the other. The origin of this free poetic text is not known, nor is the significance of Bach's possible quotation of a chorale excerpt in its accompaniment. Bach specified in the autograph score that a second strophe of this movement was to be sung (presumably referring not to the chorale but to the aria, a kind of text that more often appeared in multiple stanzas in a motet) with the choirs reversed, but the original performing parts, which Bach helped to prepare, do not reflect this instruction.

The third movement returns to the animated homophony of the opening, and leads to a concluding four-voice fugue with the two choirs combined, culminating in perhaps the best-motivated high soprano B♭ in the entire choral repertory.

The dating of the autograph composing score and original parts to the years 1726–7 eliminated several speculative occasions for which it had been proposed Bach composed *Singet dem Herrn*, but we still do not know its purpose. A connection with the regular Leipzig liturgy seems extremely unlikely, and the work seems out of character for a funeral to modern ears. Recent hypotheses include a connection with Reformation Day or with birthday celebrations in Weißenfels, but Bach's greatest motet remains unassigned.

DRM

For bibliography, *see* MOTET.

**slide trumpet.** *See* TRUMPET.

**Smend, Friedrich** (b. 26 Aug. 1893; d. 10 Feb. 1980). Musicologist, librarian, and theologian, born in Strasburg. His father, Julius Smend (1857–1930), was an eminent theologian interested in Protestant church music; he co-founded the journal *Monatschrift für Gottesdienst und kirchliche Kunst*. Friedrich Smend had similar interests, receiving a licentiate in theology from the University of Münster in 1921, and maintaining a lifelong interest in church music. While holding appointments on the academic staffs of Münster University Library (1921–3) and the Prussian State Library (1923–5), he published almost 20 articles on Bach's works, and, through an extensive correspondence with Martin Jansen (1885–1944), developed ideas on NUMBER SYMBOLISM in Bach's music. The Berlin Hochschule appointed Smend a lecturer (1945), director of the library (1946), and then Rector (1954–5). He retired in 1958.

Smend's publications are wide-ranging, and reflect his special interest in number symbolism, the parody problem, and Bach's secular music. They include books on Luther and Bach (1947), Bach's church cantatas (1947–9), and Bach in Köthen (1951). Smend's edition of the B minor Mass for the *NBA* (1954) aroused wide controversy. His final work, on the original version of the *St John Passion*, was never completed. RT

A. Dürr, 'Friedrich Smend (1893–1980)', *Die Musikforschung*, 33 (1980), 129–30; R. Elvers, 'Bibliographie Friedrich Smend', in *Festschrift für Friedrich Smend zum 70. Geburtstag* (Berlin, 1963), 98–100; R. Tatlow, *Bach and the Riddle of the Number Alphabet* (Cambridge, 1991), 6–36 and Appendices 2 and 3.

**Societät der Musicalischen Wissenschaften** (Society of Musical Sciences). A society founded in 1738 by Lorenz MIZLER, which Bach joined in 1747. Its full title was Correspondirenden Societät der Musicalischen Wissenschaften (Corresponding Society of Musical Sciences).

**sonata.** A piece of music, usually for one or a few instrumentalists and in three or four movements. Bach used the term chiefly in the sense of *sonata da chiesa* ('church sonata'). Thus most of his sonatas exhibit the classical Corellian four-movement order (slow–fast–slow–fast), with a fugal Allegro in second place and the third movement in a contrasting key (usually the relative minor or major). Like many of his contemporaries, Bach no longer observed the traditional distinction between *sonata da chiesa* (mainly abstract movements) and *sonata da camera* ('chamber sonata', essentially a dance suite). Works made up of dance movements are termed by Bach not *sonata da camera* but 'partia' (BWV1002, 1004, and 1006), 'suite' (BWV1007–12), or 'solo' (BWV1013). Mixtures of dance and abstract movements are rare (BWV1023: [Allegro]–Adagio ma non tanto–Allemanda–Gigue; BWV1019, first version: Vivace–Largo–[Corrente]–Adagio–[Tempo di gavotta]–Vivace), although sonata slow movements are often sicilianas and finales are frequently in gigue rhythm.

In the six Organ Sonatas, the Gamba Sonata BWV1029, and the Flute Sonata BWV1032 Bach adopted the three-movement (fast–slow–fast) design of the Vivaldian concerto, with the middle movement in a contrasting key. From the same source derives his frequent use of the RITORNELLO in his sonata Allegros. Typically, the ritornello is deployed within an overall da capo scheme (A–B–A), a procedure that is also found in his concertos and in the preludes to the English Suites. Binary form with repeats, characteristic of the dance, is also common in the abstract movements of Bach's sonatas, not just in those based on dance rhythms.

Bach contributed both to the solo sonata and the trio sonata with continuo. But the greater number of his sonatas are without continuo, and in this respect they rank among his most innovatory compositions. His sonatas of 1720, BWV1001, 1003, and 1005, are written 'a Violino Solo senza Basso', a type but little explored by his contemporaries. In addition, he modified the traditional trio sonata texture in two different ways. In BWV525–30 all three parts are played by one player on one instrument (organ or pedal harpsichord), the upper ones forming a duet between the two manuals while the bass is played on the pedals. In other works the solo violin, gamba, or flute plays a duet with a fully written-out obbligato part for the right hand of the harpsichord, while the left hand (optionally doubled by gamba) takes the bass.

The early fugues on themes by Legrenzi, Corelli, and Albinoni suggest that the young Bach had an extensive knowledge of the late 17th-century Italian sonata repertory. With one exception, however (the Fugue for violin and continuo BWV1026, dating from c.1710), no chamber music of Bach's survives from this period. He used the term 'sonata', instead, for certain early keyboard works—BWV963 and 967, written about 1704 under Johann Kuhnau's influence; and BWV965–6, keyboard adaptations of sonatas from J. A. Reincken's *Hortus musicus* (Hamburg, 1687)—and for the introductory movements to certain early cantatas (nos. 31 and 182; the introduction to no. 106 is termed 'Sonatina').

It was formerly assumed that most of Bach's chamber music originated in the Cöthen years, 1717–23. Of the sonatas, however, only those for unaccompanied violin (1720) and possibly part of the set for violin and harpsichord BWV1014–19 date from that period. In the early Leipzig years, when BWV1014–19 were completed (in 1725), Bach's knowledge of the 'modern' Italian violin sonata is documented by pupils' copies, with additions by Bach himself, of extracts from Bonporti's *Invenzioni* op. 10 (Bologna, 1712) and Albinoni's *Trattenimenti* op. 6 (Amsterdam, c.1712).

In the late 1720s the musical education of Bach's eldest son Wilhelm Friedemann apparently occasioned the compilation of the Organ Sonatas BWV525–30. A similarly didactic aim may be imputed to the Violin Sonata BWV1021 (1732/3), whose bass was reused by Bach pupils in BWV1022 and 1038. The compositional training of Bach's son Carl Philipp Emanuel apparently led to the sonatas BWV1020, 1031, 1033, and 1036, which may have been written, at least in part, by father and son in collaboration. Additional incentives towards sonata composition in Leipzig were no doubt provided by Bach's directorship of the collegium musicum (1729–41), his acquaintance with such notable soloists as the Dresden musicians J. G. Pisendel and P. G. Buffardin, and his contact with the Potsdam court of Frederick the Great, for which his last two extant sonatas, the Flute Sonata in E major BWV1035 (?1741) and the trio sonata from the *Musical Offering* (1747), were both written. RDPJ

*See also* FLUTE SONATAS, GAMBA SONATAS, ORGAN SONATAS, SONATAS AND PARTITAS FOR SOLO VIOLIN, and VIOLIN SONATAS.

H. Eppstein, 'Grundzüge in J. S. Bachs Sonatenschaffen', *BJb* 55 (1969), 5–30; H. Vogt, *Johann Sebastian Bach's Chamber Music*, Eng. trans. K. Johnson (Portland, Ore., 1988); C. Wolff, 'Bach's Leipzig Chamber Music', in *Bach: Essays on his Life and Music* (Cambridge, Mass., 1991), 223–38.

**Sonatas and Partitas** for solo violin. A set of three sonatas and three partitas for unaccompanied violin, BWV1001–6, which Bach completed in 1720 at Cöthen. They represent the culmination of Baroque polyphonic writing for a string instrument, surpassing in musical interest and technical demands works by J. P. von Westhoff (1656–1705), H. I. F. von Biber (1644–1704), J. J. Walther (c.1650–1717), and J. G. Pisendel, which may have provided Bach's initial inspiration. First published complete in 1802, four years after the appearance of the Fugue from Sonata no. 2 in Jean-Baptiste Cartier's *L'Art du violon*, they survive in an autograph fair copy dated 1720 with the title 'Sei solo a Violino senza Basso accompagnato Libro Primo' (the Libro Secondo was apparently the six Cello Suites). Several copies, including one by Anna Magdalena Bach, evidently derive directly from this autograph but some incorporate remarkable discrepancies and variants, notably that by J. P. Kellner (1726), thus leaving much for scholars and performers to contemplate.

Bach may have begun work on his sonatas and partitas at Weimar, where he was more active as a violinist. Their intended recipient is unknown—Pisendel, J. B. Volumier, and Joseph Spieß have all been conjectured in this role—but whoever it was must have been an outstanding executant, for Bach's technical demands, though thoroughly idiomatic, are formidable and exacting. Particularly significant are his lavish use of multiple stopping to sustain a complete polyphonic texture and his exploitation of 'polyphonic melody', in which a single line is made to suggest a fuller texture by constantly shifting between implied voices. Such textural experiments have sometimes caused the works to be misunderstood. Schumann and Mendelssohn, for example, each considered the sustained passages of unaccompanied melody somewhat stark and provided piano accompaniments by way of 'improvement'; while Arnold Schering and Albert Schweitzer, convinced that Bach's multiple stopping could only properly be executed with a bow whose hair was capable of being slackened and tightened by the player's thumb, unwittingly assisted in introducing the so-called Bach bow, a prototype totally unknown to Bach and foreign to his principles.

Sonatas alternate with partitas in Bach's original order. Common to all three sonatas is the four-movement slow–fast–slow–fast sequence of the *sonata da chiesa*. The first two movements comprise largely an improvisatory prelude and an extended fugue, the latter continually alternating between strict polyphony and single-line passage-work. Bach (or perhaps someone else) transcribed the Fugue of no. 1 (G minor) for organ and for solo lute; that of the Second Sonata (A minor) is more expansive, and its two-bar subject is worked out with remarkable resource. The movement culminates with the gradual fusion of the subject and its inversion, after which rushing demisemiquavers provide the final flourish. The insistent dotted rhythms of the Adagio of the Third Sonata (C major) evoke a serious, peaceful mood with which the imposing fugue, based closely on the chorale melody Komm heiliger Geist, Herre Gott, provides striking contrast. Comprising four separate sections of thematic entries, the second in stretto and the third with the theme in inverted form, the movement culminates in a final statement of remarkable polyphonic density. The third movements of these sonatas release the tension and provide welcome tonal relief, while the Allegro or Presto finales share the symmetrical plan of a typical binary suite movement, adopting a free-flowing style devoid of multiple stopping.

The three partitas ('Partia' in the manuscript) are essentially suites of more varied and unorthodox design. No. 1 (B minor) comprises four movements (Allemanda–Corrente–Sarabande–Tempo di Borea), each of which incorporates a simple variation (double), usually in a faster tempo. The five-movement D minor Partita adopts initially a more conventional Allemanda–Corrente–Sarabanda–Giga sequence but concludes with the celebrated Ciaccona, whose vast structure is based on 64 variations of a single open-ended four-bar phrase built around the descending tetrachord (as used by Biber in his Passacaglia). Two sections in the minor enclose a central passage in the major, and the movement displays almost every resource of Bach's and the violinist's art, culminating in a grand restatement of the main thematic material, unadorned, but with new harmonies towards its close. The Third Partita (E major) includes only one of the four dances that form the nucleus of the normal suite, incorporating instead a long prelude and some of the optional, lighter movements sometimes inserted after the Sarabande. Unlike the first two partitas, which (apart from the Sarabande of no. 1), employ Italian designations, the dances in no. 3 are mostly of French origin. The second movement provides a rare example of the loure, which, with its gentle, lilting dotted rhythms, represents a peaceful foil to the brilliance of the Preludio (transcribed by the composer for organ and orchestra in Cantatas 29 and 120a), while the additional description, 'en rondeau', to the Gavotte indicates that the initial dance melody alternates with brief episodes. Menuets I and II (played alternativement), almost Classical in outlook if somewhat statelier in con-

tent, are succeeded in turn by a lively Bourrée and an energetic Gigue. RS

R. Erfrati, Treatise on the Execution and Interpretation of the Sonatas and Partitas for Solo Violin and the Suites for Solo Cello by Johann Sebastian Bach (Zurich, 1979); G. Hausswald, 'Zur Stilistik von Johann Sebastian Bachs Sonaten und Partiten für Violine allein', Archiv für Musikwissenschaft, 14 (1957), 304–23; A. Moser, 'Zu J. S. Bach's Sonaten und Partiten für Violine allein', BJb 17 (1920), 30–65; D. Stevens, 'Bach's Sonatas and Partitas for Violin', in Y. Menuhin and W. Primrose, eds., Violin and Viola (London, 1976), 221–30; R. Stowell, 'Building a Music Library: Bach's Violin Sonatas and Partitas', Musical Times, 128 (1987), 250–6.

**Sonnenkalb, Johann Friedrich Wilhelm** (bap. 22 April 1732; d. 20 March 1785). Organist, born in Triptis, about 45 km. (28 miles) south-east of Weimar in Thuringia. He attended the Thomasschule from 1746 to 1754, and was on friendly terms with Bach and his family. In 1754 he enrolled at Leipzig University, but in the same year he was appointed organist and schoolmaster at Herzberg, near Torgau. He was then Kantor at nearby Dahme from 1759 to 1761, and died at Waldheim.

**Sorge, Georg Andreas** (b. 21 March 1703; d. 4 April 1778). Organist, composer, and, most notably, theorist, born in Mellenbach, Thuringia. His references to Bach show that they were friends; he composed three fugues for organ on the name BACH, and joined Lorenz Mizler's Corresponding Society of Musical Sciences in 1747, just a month after Bach himself.

Sorge's writings on thorough-bass and harmony are very competent, and his theoretical grasp of unequal temperaments excelled even that of J. G. Neidhardt (though still, unfortunately, taking $\frac{1}{12}$ comma as an indivisible unit of measure). He cited Bach as 'witness' that regular $\frac{1}{6}$-comma meantone temperament was inadequate to 'modern' harmony, and he dismissed J. P. Kirnberger's schemes of temperament as 'no good'. ML

See also SCHÜBLER CHORALES.

**sources.** See opposite.

**Sperontes.** Pen-name of the poet Johann Sigismund Scholze (b. 20 March 1705; d. 28 Sept. 1750), born in Lobendau, near Liegnitz (now Legnica, Poland). He settled in Leipzig in the 1720s and published his Singende Muse an der Pleiße there in 1736, following it with three further volumes in 1742–5. In all, the publications contain 250 poems with simple musical settings, depicting scenes and activities from everyday life. Bach has been credited (somewhat unconvincingly) with two of the settings: Ich bin nun wie ich bin and Dir zu Liebe, wertes Herze, BWV Anh. II 40 and 41.

# sources

1. Manuscript sources.
2. Printed editions.

1. **Manuscript sources.** Most of Bach's works are transmitted in manuscript (i.e. handwritten) form. On the whole, manuscript sources reflect clearly the biographical circumstances surrounding the production of scores and parts, and can also provide reliable evidence concerning issues of authenticity, chronology, and the process of composition and revision.

*(i) Classification.* The manuscript sources are usually categorized as either 'primary' or 'secondary'. Among the most valuable are the autograph manuscripts and the copies made under Bach's direct supervision (which sometimes contain specific performance-related marks). Together with the printed works published during the composer's lifetime, these are referred to as primary sources. Among the surviving manuscripts (particularly those transmitting Bach's keyboard repertory), however, the majority are secondary sources, that is manuscripts not written by Bach or under his supervision.

The extensive autograph manuscripts may be divided into early drafts, composing scores, and fair copies, reflecting the various stages of composition. The early drafts are the least numerous, probably because Bach destroyed most of them when they were no longer needed. The surviving drafts are mostly found as sketches in the marginal spaces of other pieces. Composing scores attest to the process of compositions being worked out on the sheet, and are particularly numerous in the cantatas of the early Leipzig period, when Bach was under heavy pressure to cope with the weekly production of new pieces. A typical composing score is written in hasty handwriting and contains many major corrections. Fair copies are the ones intended at the time to stand as a neat and definitive version of the work. They are normally written in meticulous calligraphic script and contain very few corrections.

By scrutinizing his calligraphy, one can arrive at an understanding of Bach's commitment and inspiration at the time of writing the manuscripts, and it is therefore useful to classify them from an aesthetic perspective as well. It has become standard practice to describe Bach's manuscripts in terms which take account of both these criteria (the compositional and the calligraphic), resulting in source descriptions such as 'calligraphic fair copy', 'inspired composing score', and so on.

*(ii) What the manuscripts reveal.* Manuscripts are a treasure-house of information about compositions in their historical context. This information can be gleaned in several different ways, such as studying the handwriting and notational practice, and applying scientific methods used in other disciplines.

The study of handwriting is very rewarding, for it illuminates some of the most interesting aspects of Bach's working habits, methods, and procedures. Particularly fruitful is the analysis of corrected passages and notational peculiarities. When the study covers an extensive spectrum of Bach's creative output, it is possible to trace the development of his script over the years, which helps in dating the sources and, to some extent, the composition as well. Chronological information is also contained in some elements of Bach's notation; for example, he stopped using flat signs (♭) to cancel sharps (♯) about 1713, and from about 1736 he began using double-sharp signs (×).

A still more precise dating of manuscripts is possible by applying some of the rigorous scientific methods commonly employed in diplomatics. In musicology this area of study has concentrated on examination of the paper's date and origin, and how it was used by the scribe. In particular, the watermarks and handwriting in all the primary sources have been studied meticulously, most notably by Wisso Weiß and Yoshitake Kobayashi; see *NBA*, IX/1 (1985) and IX/2 (1989). Most of the papers used by Bach are now dated and their origins ascertained.

Moving closer to the composer's activities, one can scrutinize the way Bach handled paper, observing especially how the paper was prepared before the actual music was written. This entails a study of how the staves were ruled, and of the physical arrangement of sheets—important matters for Bach to consider, especially when writing fair copies. He customarily used a rastrum—an implement for drawing more than one line at a time—to prepare his manuscript paper. No rastra from Bach's household survive, but from the way the staves were drawn we can infer that his apparatus held five nibs, and each rastrum was unique in terms of the width and spacing of individual lines. The implement was apparently very fragile, and so it was replaced whenever one of the nibs became defective. Thus it is theoretically possible to conduct systematic research work to reconstruct the continual process of its use and replacement. Bach usually prepared a supply of paper in advance by ruling the same number of staves indiscriminately. On occasion, however, he planned the layout of the score scrupulously, estimating carefully the space required on each sheet. He sometimes used two rastra of different sizes on a single page to accentuate a particular part; for example, the harpsichord part in the Fifth Brandenburg Concerto was written on much wider staves than were used for the other parts.

The fascicle structure (commonly referred to as the gatherings of a manuscript) likewise reflects the initial plan of the layout, taking into consideration the total length of the piece, and the space reserved for the title-page. The ink used can also be subject to scientific analysis, and can provide strong supporting evidence to a study of the handwriting where an accurate judgement of revised passages is needed. Most studies are currently done with the naked eye. Some more rigorous methods have already been tried and will probably be employed even more in the future, utilizing either chemical analysis (by taking a sample of ink from the manuscript) or spectroscopic analysis, using, for instance, an infrared reflectographic technique.

*(iii) Bach's copyists.* Bach used many copyists; the preparation of performing parts was one of their main roles. Also, his pupils needed to make their own copies when they began their study with him. There is evidence to suggest that Bach did not himself enjoy copying music, especially if he saw it as a mechanical task. The partial autograph of the *St John Passion* provides one example of this: Bach stopped copying the music at the end of page 20 and handed the task over to an assistant, probably because a planned performance had been cancelled.

The identification of a copyist often plays a decisive role in dating a manuscript. Bach's copyists were usually family members, colleagues, or the pupils who were studying under him at the time. His second wife, Anna Magdalena, is particularly interesting: her handwriting so closely resembled her husband's that many of her copies were mistaken as genuine autographs until the 1950s. Among the best known of Bach's copyists outside the family members are J. G. Walther, J. T. Krebs, and J. C. Vogler from the Weimar period; H. N. Gerber and J. L. Krebs from the early Leipzig period; and J. F. Agricola, J. C. Altnickol, J. N. Bammler, and J. C. Kittel from the later Leipzig period. The copyists that Bach employed for the performing parts of his Leipzig cantatas include J. A. Kuhnau, C. G. Meißner, and Bach's nephew Johann Heinrich Bach.

(iv) *Dispersal of the autograph manuscripts.* Bach's autographs are now widely dispersed all over the world, and many are considered lost. This fact reflects, to some extent, the way his estate was distributed after his death in 1750. Precise details remain unclear, since the inventory of Bach's effects, while listing the more obviously valuable items such as musical instruments, did not include manuscripts (see *BDok* ii. 490–1 and 498–9).

It is thought that most of the important music was divided between the two eldest sons, Wilhelm Friedemann and Carl Philipp Emanuel. While Friedemann sold much of what he inherited for his own survival, Emanuel looked after his portion carefully (see the list of Bach's manuscripts in his estate: *BDok* iii. 489–90). After his death in 1788 a portion of this went to C. F. G. Schwencke, his successor as Kantor in Hamburg, and some to J. N. Forkel. Many of these manuscripts were eventually acquired by Georg POELCHAU, and after his death most of them went to the Berlin Singakademie. In 1854 this organization found itself in financial difficulties and sold the works to the Königlichen Bibliothek (now the Staatsbibliothek) in Berlin. There were also many individuals who collected Bach manuscripts to treasure or to protect their national heritage.

It was mainly from these Berlin sources that the *BG* editions (1851–99) were prepared. At the outbreak of World War II many precious items (including those from the Hochschule für Musik, Berlin) were transferred to other locations for safe-keeping. Unfortunately few written records of these transfers survive, and post-war musicological studies have suffered (and still do) from the destruction or loss of some sources, while others still unaccounted for are collectively labelled 'Kriegsverlust' ('war loss'). In the late 1970s some of these reappeared in the Biblioteka Jagiellońska, Kraków (Poland), and this raised renewed hope for further discoveries. Today the major portion of the surviving sources is held at the Staatsbibliothek zu Berlin Preußischer Kulturbesitz. The Thomaskirche in Leipzig also possesses many of the original performing parts; these are now on deposit in the Stadtarchiv Leipzig.

The fact that many autograph manuscripts survive to this day owes much to the care of generations of successive owners who inherited or purchased them. In general it seems that the more beautiful and precious they are, the better have been their prospects of survival. Book 1 of *The Well-tempered Clavier* is a classic example of fortunate preservation, as it is most likely that the hapless Wilhelm Friedemann inherited it; no autographs survive of the earlier versions of the preludes and fugues it contains, other than those in the *Clavierbüchlein* for W. F. Bach.

Although many autograph manuscripts, including Part 1 of *The Well-tempered Clavier*, survived intact, some did not. Perhaps the most regrettable loss is that of a leaf which (if it did, in fact, once exist) contained a sketch of the concluding section of the last, incomplete fugue from *The Art of Fugue*. At any rate, it is fortunate that the surviving primary sources cover most of Bach's major works, and these are conveniently listed in *Schmieder2* and *BC* (and in more detail in the critical commentaries to the *NBA* volumes). One area of Bach's output which suffers most from the lack of autograph manuscripts is his youthful organ works. Many of them are known from manuscript anthologies such as the ANDREAS BACH BOOK and the MÖLLER MANUSCRIPT, the two most important sources for Bach's early keyboard works. However, where doubtful pieces contain unfamiliar idioms, the establishment of authenticity becomes harder. The NEUMEISTER CHORALES are a case in point: not all of those that have been attributed to Bach can be accepted without reservation, and many other mainly minor pieces still await authentication. YT

*DürrC*; G. von Dadelsen, *Beiträge zur Chronologie der Werke Johann Sebastian Bachs* (Trossingen, 1958); G. von Dadelsen, *Bemerkungen zur Handschrift Johann Sebastian Bachs, seiner Familie und seines Kreises* (Trossingen, 1957); U. Hertin, 'Zur Überlieferung der Autographe und Handschriften J. S. Bachs', in R. Elvers *et al.*, eds., *Die Handschrift Johann Sebastian Bachs* [exhibition catalogue, Staatsbibliothek Preußischer Kulturbesitz, Berlin] (Wiesbaden, 1985), 31–44; G. Herz, *Bach Sources in America* (Bärenreiter, 1984); R. L. Marshall, *The Compositional Process of J. S. Bach: A Study of the Autograph Scores of the Vocal Works* (Princeton, 1972); H.-J. Schulze, *Studien zur Bach-Überlieferung im 18. Jahrhundert* (Leipzig, 1984); C. Wolff, 'From Berlin to Łódź: the Spitta Collection Resurfaces', *Notes*, 46 (1989–90), 311–27.

**2. Printed editions.** Only ten works (or collections) by Bach were printed during the composer's lifetime (or, in the case of *The Art of Fugue*, shortly after his death), but a close study of the surviving exemplars can reveal a great deal about their origins and compositional history.

*Engraving, printing, and distribution.* With one exception, those of Bach's works printed during his lifetime were etched (the term 'engraving', although not technically correct, is commonly used) on copper plates. Two different techniques were employed. In freehand engraving the musical text was transcribed directly on to the plate as engraver's copy from the composer's fair autograph. This was done either by reproduction engravers (J. G. Krügner, for example), who reproduced the mirror-image of the musical calligraphy as they would a portrait, or by mechanical engravers (Balthasar Schmid, for example), trained musicians who transcribed from their own personally prepared engraver's copy, often using mechanical aids such as a straight-edge and punches. The other technique was the *Abklatschvorlage* method. The composer's manuscript pages, written on one side only, were soaked in oil to render them transparent, reversed, and then applied directly to the prepared plate by artisans (the Schübler brothers, for example) to make a mirror-image tracing which they then used as guide for the actual engraving.

Once the engraving was complete, the plates were pulled in small copper presses by the *Kupferdrucker* (copper plate printer). For virtually all of those works printed in Leipzig the plates were pulled on cut, single half-sheets in oblong format, while those printed in Nuremberg were pulled on folded double sheets or single half-sheets in upright format. After proof-reading by the composer (in principle), the plates were corrected by the engraver and pulled in a main printing-run of a specified number of exemplars. In fact, Bach must have found correction of the actual plates too troublesome, too time-consuming, or simply too costly an undertaking. More often than not, the necessary corrections were entered directly into the printed exemplars either from errata lists or from uncorrected control copies, not by Bach but by his assistants. Once corrected, the leaves were collated and the work was published, to be distributed either by professional booksellers or by the composer and his agents in other centres. They were sold unbound, and a few of these unbound exemplars have survived. The annual trade fairs, particularly those held three times a year in Leipzig, were for Bach the main venue for publication. Bach often gave complimentary copies to close personal friends.

*Gott ist mein König.* The cantata *Gott ist mein König* has the distinction of being the earliest printed work by Bach to have survived, the only vocal work printed during his lifetime, and the only work not engraved. Its parts were printed, as was customary for such works, by means of movable type in a book press. The work was composed for the annual changing of the Mühlhausen town council on 4 February 1708, during Bach's tenure as organist at the Blasiuskirche. The parts are in upright folio format and are the work of a local printer, T. D. Brückner. The following year, after he had moved to Weimar, Bach was commissioned to compose a second work for the same occasion and it was duly printed, but no exemplar has survived.

*Partitas BWV825–30.* The six keyboard Partitas were published singly by Bach between 1726 and 1730. Two different engravers were responsible for the musical text, the first for Partitas nos. 1 and 2, the second for nos. 3–6. The first of these was the Nuremberg engraver Balthasar Schmid, who registered as a student at the University of Leipzig on 13 March 1726. An aspiring organist, it is likely that he studied with Bach during his time in Leipzig, and the fact that Bach had a journeyman printer among his pupils may have prompted him to undertake the engraving of the First Partita as a limited in-house project to 'test the waters'. Possibly Schmid's work on the engraving of the first two partitas served in lieu of the normal fee, the *Studienhonorar*, that Bach charged his students. It is likely that one of Schmid's principal aims in coming to Leipzig was to further his technical skill as an engraver; his lettering and numbering in the first two partitas are clumsy and unsightly, and he may have wished to improve this important aspect of his craft. Schmid seems to have been back in Nuremberg by 1728 at least, since he engraved and published a collection of minuets in that year. Partitas nos. 1 and 2 were published at the Michaelmas fairs of 1726 and 1727 respectively, so it seems that Schmid worked on the engraving during the preceding summers, when he had free time to devote to the task.

The engraver of Partitas nos. 3–6 was also a musician and engraver-in-training, Johann Gotthilf Ziegler, *Director musices* and organist at the Ulrichskirche, Halle. He had studied with Bach in Weimar for about a year around 1711–12 and they must have remained on close terms, for Bach's first wife, Maria Barbara, was invited to stand as godmother to Ziegler's daughter Christiana Renata in 1718. His work for Bach may have been done in Halle, but the available evidence suggests that the project was carried out under Bach's supervision in Leipzig. Ziegler was a less skilled engraver than Schmid, and his lettering and numbering are even messier. This may be why most of the titles and page numbers are the work of two Leipzig master engravers—in Partitas nos. 3 and 4 Johann Benjamin Brühl, in nos. 5 and 6 the elder Johann Gottfried Krügner. J. G. Walther reports in his *Musicalisches Lexicon* (Leipzig, 1732) that Ziegler had 'taken instruction in copper engraving and etching', so it is possible that he was studying the craft in the shops of Brühl and Krügner during the periods in question. Another piece of evidence placing Ziegler in Leipzig at this time is that he seems to have instructed C. P. E. Bach in music engraving. His hand appears prominently in Emanuel's maiden effort, his *Menuet pour le clavessin* (1731). (The change of shops between 1728 and

1730 suggests that Ziegler was not in Leipzig during this period and may explain the hiatus in the publication of the series.)

Bach presented his former employer, Prince Leopold of Anhalt-Cöthen, with an exemplar of Partita no. 1, complete with a dedicatory poem. For nos. 2 and 3, both published for the Michaelmas fair of 1727, Bach economized by reusing the plate for the title-page of Partita no. 1 with the number altered and the date erased and re-engraved. (The inclusion of a date on the title-page of each partita, and of *Clavier-Übung I*, is unusual in Bach's original editions.) He sought to extend his potential audience by enlisting the aid of agents in Augsburg, Dresden, Halle, Lüneburg, Nuremberg, and Wolfenbüttel. The separate partitas are the rarest of all Bach's original editions, with an average of four surviving for each print. There is not a single surviving exemplar of Partita no. 6, so the date of publication is not known. However, it is generally considered to have been in the same year as Partita no. 5 (1730), and thus almost certainly the same title-page would have been reused.

The six Partitas were brought out as opus 1 in a collected edition entitled *Clavier-Übung* in 1731. The plates of the original issues were used, renumbered and with newly engraved individual titles at the top of the first page of each work and a handsome new title-page. At the foot of the page in a number of exemplars there appears engraved the note: 'Leipzig, in Commission bey Boetii Seel: hinderlasene Tochter, unter den Rath: hause'. Thus it seems that Bach gave over a part of the edition to the Leipzig copper printer and book dealer Rosine Dorothee Boëtius, the wife of Krügner. Given that Krügner was responsible for engraving the added titles, the new page numbers, and the new title-page, it seems likely that his wife was the printer of the collection. There seems to have been a later reprinting, for the exemplar in the Staatsbibliothek zu Berlin shows an engraved letter pagination.

*Clavier-Übung II.* The second instalment of Bach's series of *Clavier-Übungen* was brought out four years later for the Easter fair of 1735 by the Nuremberg publisher Christoph Weigel (1703–77). Weigel, the son of a well-known Nuremberg engraver and art dealer, had left the family firm the previous year to set up his own business, and this was one of his first projects. He was frequently in Leipzig during the fairs to display his latest publications, and it was probably during such a visit that he and Bach became acquainted. It was perhaps at Bach's suggestion that Weigel turned to Balthasar Schmid for the engraving of the title-page. Schmid would most likely have been the composer's first choice for engraving the music as well, but he had not yet been articled as a music engraver in his home town and so was not available. The project was therefore divided between two closely associated Nuremberg engravers, one of whom had connections with Leipzig. The one in charge of the project, responsible for engraving all of the Italian Concerto as well as the page numbers throughout, was Johann Georg Puschner, a prolific Nuremberg engraver active since at least 1716. His precise, mechanical engraving is accomplished, bold, and clean, but he was not a musician and there are numerous errors in the transcription of the text. The Ouverture in the French Style was the work of a team of three engravers led by an associate of Puschner, Johann Christoph Döhne (or Jean Christoph Dehné, as he signed himself). This same team was responsible for much of the music engraving in Sperontes's *Singende Muse an der Pleiße* (1737). The most skilled among Döhne's two assistants may have been his son Johann Friedrich, who studied with his father and found employment in Leipzig in the early 1740s. Bach himself may have had dealings with one or both members of the Puschner-Döhne partnership earlier, in 1731, in connection with his involvement in the publication of Walther's *Musicalisches Lexicon* (1732), for the numerous tables of which these two engravers prepared the plates.

Like the earlier engraving for Walther's treatise, that for *Clavier-Übung II* must have been carried out in Nuremberg. Had it been done under Bach's watchful eye there would not have been so many engraving errors. In fact, problems with the engraving of the Ouverture necessitated the publication of a second, improved edition which, besides correcting numerous errors, involved the re-engraving of pages 20–2 so that Gavotte II in the Ouverture could be played without a page turn. That these corrections go back to Bach himself is clear from his corrected hand copy, one of three exemplars in the British Library. However, not all Bach's corrections appear on the plates; here, as in the other original prints, handwritten corrections in ink form a distinct layer in the editorial process.

*Schemelli Songbook.* Bach seems to have been involved as music consultant in the *Musicalisches Gesang-Buch* edited by G. C. Schemelli and published for the Easter fair of 1736. According to the foreword to the collection, the melodies of the 69 engraved settings were 'in part entirely newly composed by Bach, in part also improved by him in the basso continuo'. Scholars are divided on how many melodies can be attributed to Bach. No. 32, *Dir, dir, Jehova will ich singen* appears in the *Clavierbüchlein* for Anna Magdalena Bach of 1725, and no. 44, *Vergiß mein nicht*, is inscribed 'di J. S. Bach etc.'. However, the vast majority of the diminutive plates were engraved by a team of reproduction engravers from the shop of J. G. Krügner—the same shop that was responsible for engraving the Leipzig portion of *Clavier-Übung III* (see below). Since they faithfully reproduced the *ductus* (continuation) signs at the end of staves in the *Vorlage* (the fair copy used for the engraving), Bach's hand may be traced in the process. Of the 69 plates 63 are the work of the Krügner team and Bach's hand appears in at least 28 of these, either in both cantus and bass, in bass only, in corrections to the bass, or in various minor revisions to a few other settings.

*Clavier-Übung III.* Published by Bach in Leipzig for the Easter fair of 1739, this is the longest and most ambitious of all his printed works. The original printed edition is unique in a number of respects. No fewer than two proof copies, one preliminary and one final, have survived, and the distribution of papers in them, as well as in the exemplars of the main printing-run, reveal that about two-thirds of the plates (section L) were pulled in Leipzig, probably by Boëtius, while the remaining third (section N), all engraved by Schmid, were pulled in Nuremberg. This indicates that work on the engraving, begun in Leipzig by the Krügner team responsible for most of the Schemelli Songbook, was broken off and then completed subsequently by the Nuremberg engraver. A number of the plates engraved by Schmid are printed on the Leipzig paper used for the printing of section L, and it is likely that this, his first work on the collection, was completed while he was in Leipzig, possibly during the Easter fair of 1739. The plates for section N were almost certainly printed in his copper press.

Details in the engraving, such as the erasure and re-engraving of page numbers, indicate that the short *pedaliter* settings did not figure in Bach's original concept of the collection, and that the Prelude and Fugue in E♭ major was included only during the latest stage in the production of section L. Bach's decision to include these works (and probably the four duets as well) at a rather late stage may have been geared towards enhancing the saleability of the collection. This expansion of its scope may have been responsible for Krügner's abandoning the project; it certainly led to a delay in publication.

The leaves have been variously trimmed, but their format, like the dimensions of the plates engraved by the Krügner shop, are consistent with those in *Clavier-Übung I*, indicating that the Leipzig engraver was responsible for the overall design of the print. As mentioned above, Krügner was a highly skilled reproduction engraver, and his rendering of Bach's hand in some of the earlier plates in this printing is almost photographic in its uncanny resemblance to the composer's *Vorlage*. For this reason it was thought for many years that Bach had actually contributed to the engraving of this collection, a wholly untenable proposition. The dimensions of the 34 plates of music engraved by Schmid are consistently smaller. Unlike Krügner, Schmid, as a practised composer and mechanical music engraver, would have prepared his own engraver's copy instead of transcribing directly from Bach's autograph score. In fact, pages 26–9 in the later of the two proof copies of section L may be in Schmid's own hand, a remnant of his personally prepared engraver's copy.

*Goldberg Variations.* Any announcement of the date of publication for *Clavier-Übung [IV]* is lacking and the date occurs nowhere in the original printed edition, but recent research indicates that the work appeared at the Michaelmas fair of 1741. Balthasar Schmid was not only the engraver and printer of the collection, but for the first time he acted as publisher as well. The title-page is headed simply 'Clavier Ubung', without the designation 'vierter Teil', possibly because Schmid did not want to make his début as Bach's publisher with the concluding instalment in the series.

The title-page, with its late Baroque cartouche and immaculate engraving, is striking, and the engraving of the work as a whole seems to have been done with extreme care. Although there is no hard evidence linking the work with J. G. Goldberg, house cembalist to Count von Keyserlingk, as suggested in Forkel's biography, we know that Bach was a guest in Keyserlingk's house in November 1741, at which time he may have presented his Dresden patron with a dedicatory copy of his latest publication.

Bach's *Handexemplar* of *Clavier-Übung [IV]*, now in the Bibliothèque Nationale, Paris, is particularly important in that it contains not only corrections and supplementary material for the Goldberg Variations, but also, on the recto face of the blank leaf 18, an appendix comprising 14 canons (BWV1087) which until 1975 were overlooked. Their presence may suggest that Bach was planning a second edition, but there is no evidence that this project ever came to fruition.

*Miscellaneous canons.* Only two of Bach's various occasional canons appeared in print during his life. These are the so-called Hudemann Canon BWV1074, almost certainly printed in 1727 but for which no exemplar survives, and the *Canon triplex à 6 Voc.* BWV1076, of which two exemplars are extant. The printed edition itself, consisting of a single leaf of small dimensions, can be dated some time during 1747. It was Bach's contribution to the fifth circulating packet of Lorenz Mizler's Corresponding Society of Musical Sciences of which Bach became the 14th member in June 1747. The autograph manuscript, no longer extant, which served as the *Vorlage* for the unknown engraver must have been prepared by 1746, since it served as the basis for the leaf of music held by Bach in the Haußmann portrait of the composer dating from that year.

*The Musical Offering.* Bach had publicly set himself a deadline for bringing out his *Musical Offering*, and the taking on of such an extended and complicated project at short notice by any of the overworked Leipzig engravers was almost certainly out of the question. It was probably largely because of time pressure that Bach turned to the engraving shop of J. G. Schübler in Zella, a town not far from Leipzig in the Thuringian forest. The close proximity of the Schübler shop must have greatly facilitated the sending back and forth of proofs and the process of correction, and this allowed Bach to control all aspects of the production of the edition. Schübler had been a pupil of Bach's, like Ziegler, and the two would thus have been on close terms. The use of the *Abklatschvorlage* method of music engraving by this shop was probably an outgrowth of its specialization in the craft of gunstock engraving and the incising of trivets and gun barrels. For this method Bach had to prepare the engraver's copy himself, transcribing his music on one side of each sheet whose dimensions and ruling of staves corresponded with that on the plates prepared by Schübler.

The *Musical Offering* is unique among the original printed editions of Bach's works. It is the only one to carry a dedication, and the dedicatory copy sent to Frederick the Great in two separate instalments has survived. Further, it is to be singled out for its heterogeneity of scoring and printing formats. Of its five printing units, three are in oblong format. These are: the title-page and dedication, printed by the renowned Leipzig printer Bernhard Christoph Breitkopf by means of movable type in a letter press; the three-part Ricercar in keyboard score; and the six-part Ricercar in open score. Both ricercars were engraved by J. G. Schübler. The remaining two printing units are in upright format. They are: a folio containing the nine canons and canonic fugue in enigmatic notation, engraved by Johann Georg's younger brother Johann Heinrich; and the trio sonata in parts, engraved by the same two engravers in collaboration with their elder stepbrother, Johann Jakob Friedrich. The famous RICERCAR acrostic was printed, probably by means of a woodblock, on paper strips which were glued to the empty recto face of the first page of the canons.

The distribution of papers indicates that the printing was carried out in two stages: in the first the title-page, three-part Ricercar, all but one plate of the six-part Ricercar, and the canons were pulled; in the second the rest of the collection. The first stage in the project was probably complete by about July 1747, the second stage somewhat later. At least the first instalment was printed in Leipzig, probably by one of the *Kupferdrucker* attached to the Breitkopf firm; to judge from the papers, the second instalment may have been printed in nearby Halle.

Exceptionally, we know that the first print-run of the three-part Ricercar comprised 100 exemplars. In a letter to his former secretary, Johann Elias Bach, the composer speaks of his intention of having this printing unit (which had gained a certain notoriety and seems to have been in short supply) reprinted, and recent paper studies indicate that this was indeed done. Twice as many copies of the title-page and dedication were printed, not, it seems, in anticipation of a second printing of the collection but because the work was not necessarily sold complete. Any number and combination of the music printing units could be purchased along with the title-page and dedication.

*Canonic Variations.* The Canonic Variations for organ on *Vom Himmel hoch*, Schmid's second and last publication of a work by Bach, was brought out in Nuremberg towards the end of 1747 or the beginning of 1748. Like *Clavier-Übung [IV]*, this collection was printed in upright format on folded double leaves; its dimensions are about the same as those of *Clavier-Übung [IV]* and the quality of the engraving is on the same high level. Details in Schmid's engraving style indicate that Variations 1–3 and 5 were engraved at the same time (around mid-1746), while Variation 4 (the augmentation canon) was not completed until at least a year later—a detail which is supported by source evidence from Bach's autograph. Bach, or even Schmid, who was an organist, seems to have changed the format of Variations 1–3 at the engraving stage to bring them into line with that of Variation 5. Paper studies point to a second printing of the collection by Schmid's widow in 1751.

*Schübler Chorales.* Recent research suggests that the so-called Schübler Chorales appeared in 1748. The collection was engraved, printed, and published by J. G. Schübler in Zella, and on the title-page Bach and his sons Carl Philipp Emanuel and Wilhelm Friedemann are named as distributors. The engraving is quite unsightly, even by the standards set in the *Musical Offering*, and there are numerous engraving errors which have been corrected in Bach's *Handexemplar* (now in the Scheide Collection of Princeton University Library). It is hard to reconcile the considerable number of errors with the *Abklatschvorlage* engraving technique known to have been used by the Schübler shop, but the music text nevertheless closely resembles that in the *Musical Offering* and *The Art of Fugue*.

*The Art of Fugue.* This was the last original edition of a work by Bach. It was published posthumously in 1751 and reprinted with a new title-page and foreword in 1752. Source studies indicate that the preparation of the engraver's copy was carried out in three distinct instalments. The first, consisting of Contrapuncti 1–10, was the work of a team of five scribes, among them Bach and his son Johann Christoph Friedrich. In the second, comprising Contrapuncti 11–17, J. S. Bach took over the copying with minimal contribution by his son. The third instalment was the work of a single anonymous scribe not among the original team of five. It includes the works added at a late stage, probably after Bach's death: the unfinished *Fuga a tre soggetti*, the earlier version of Contrapunctus 10, the arrangement for two keyboards of the three-part mirror fugue, and the concluding setting of *Wenn wir in höchsten Nöthen sein.*

The engraving is the work of J. G. Schübler. Both its layout and the presence of erased page numbers indicate that Contrapunctus 14, the augmentation canon, was intended by Bach to follow the other three canons as pages 57–9. One hypothesis is that the original gap, comprising pages 45–50 and now filled by the earlier version of Contrapunctus 10 and by Contrapunctus 14, would have been occupied by the unfinished quadruple fugue. Exceptionally, the three leaves of Bach's personally prepared engraver's copy of the augmentation canon, with music text on one face only and rendered transparent through having been soaked in oil as part of the *Abklatschvorlage* process, have survived as *Beilage* (Appendix) 1, along with the autograph materials, in Mus. ms. Bach P 200 of the Staatsbibliothek zu Berlin. Paper studies indicate that the first edition was printed not in Leipzig but in Nuremberg. C. P. E. Bach may have arranged for it to be printed by Schmid's widow, Maria Helena, at about the same time as his own latest publication, *Zwey Trio*—that is before July 1751. He subsequently brought out the work for the Michaelmas fair later the same year. Apparently, sales of the first edition were disappointing. The second edition was printed in Leipzig, probably by Breitkopf, who printed the title-page and foreword and who appears as agent. When it appeared six months later at the Easter fair of 1752 the original foreword had been replaced with a new one by F. W. Marpurg with a view to making the work more saleable. The plates, kept by C. P. E. Bach, were later sold for scrap.                                                                                                    GB

G. Butler, 'Leipziger Stecher in Bachs Frühdrucken', *BJb* 66 (1980), 9–26; G. Butler, 'Ordering Problems in J. S. Bach's *Art of Fugue* Resolved', *Musical Quarterly*, 69 (1983), 44–61; G. Butler, 'J. S. Bach and the Schemelli Gesangbuch Revisited', *Studi musicali*, 13 (1984), 241–57; G. Butler, 'The Engraving of J. S. Bach's *Six Partitas*', *Journal of Musicological Research*, 7 (1986), 3–27; G. Butler, 'J. S. Bach's Einige canonische Veraenderungen: The View from the Original Print', *Bach* 20/2 (1989), 4–37; G. Butler, *Bach's Clavier-Ubung III: The Making of a Print* (Durham, NC, 1990); G. Butler, 'The Engravers of Bach's Clavier-Übung II', in P. Brainard and R. Robinson, eds., *A Bach Tribute: Essays in Honor of William H. Scheide* (Kassel and Chapel Hill, NC, 1993), 57 ff.; G. Butler, 'J. S. Bach's "Hudemann" Canon BWV 1074: A Note on the Engraving and Printing History', *Bach*, 25/1 (1994), 5–10; G. Butler, 'J. S. Bach's Musical Offering: New Perspectives from the Original Edition' (forthcoming); H. Heussner, 'Der Musikdrucker Balthasar Schmid in Nürnberg', *Die Musikforschung*, 16 (1963), 348–62; G. Kinsky, *Die Originalausgaben der Werke Johann Sebastian Bachs* (Vienna, 1937); C. Wolff, Commentary in *Johann Sebastian Bach: ClavierÜbung Teil I–IV* [facsimile] (Dresden, 1984); C. Wolff, 'New Research on Bach's Musical Offering,' *Musical Quarterly*, 57 (1971), 379–408; repr. in *Bach: Essays on his Life and Music* (Cambridge, Mass., 1991), 239–58.

**Spieß, Joseph** (bur. 2 July 1730). Violinist. He served as first violinist at the Berlin court from about 1711, and was employed as principal *Cammermusicus* by Prince Leopold at Cöthen after the Prussian King Friedrich Wilhelm I had disbanded his orchestra in 1713. It has been conjectured that Bach wrote his violin concertos for Spieß, and that he may have been partnered in the Double Concerto by his former colleague in Berlin, Martin Marcus. Spieß has also been suggested as the recipient of Bach's Sonatas and Partitas for solo violin, but there is no documentary support for any of these suppositions.                                            RS

E. van der Straeten, *The History of the Violin* (London, 1933), i. 308.

**Spitta, Philipp** (b. 7 Dec. 1841; d. 13 April 1894). Music historian, born in Wechold, near Hoya in Lower Saxony; one of the most important Bach scholars. He studied classical philology in Göttingen, and wrote his Ph.D. thesis on syntax in Tacitus. From 1866 he was a teacher in Reval (now Tallinn). As early as 1864 he presented a lecture on Bach, but it was probably only after his move to the 'Bach country' (Sangerhausen, in Thuringia) in 1867 that he began work on his monumental biography. The first volume of *Johann Sebastian Bach*, covering the years up to 1723, appeared in 1873. In 1874 he became a teacher at the Nikolaischule in Leipzig; again in a Bach environment, he hoped to finish the second volume, covering Bach's Leipzig years. But only a year later he was invited by the Prussian government in Berlin to become a member of the Königliche Akademie der Künste, reader in music history at the conservatory, and professor at the university. Nevertheless, he kept in touch with Leipzig, especially as a supervisor of the highly active Leipzig Bach-Verein. The Bach biography was finished in 1880.

Spitta was convinced that Bach could not be understood without deep insight into the historical context of 17th-century music, and it was this that led him to establish a proper basis for Schütz research; his edition of Schütz's works was finished only a few days before his death. He also edited Buxtehude's organ works (among other music) and supported the *Denkmäler Deutscher Tonkunst* founded in 1892. His activities are also reflected in the dissertations of his pupils: Emil Vogel on Monteverdi and the Italian madrigal, Max Seiffert on Sweelinck. His interest in music of the 19th century (as an ardent anti-Wagnerian) is documented not only in his letters to composers like Brahms, Bruch, and Heinrich Herzogenberg, but also in his articles on Schumann and Weber in *Grove's Dictionary* (1883–9).                    KK

U. Schilling, *Philipp Spitta: Leben und Wirken im Spiegel seiner Briefwechsel* (Kassel, 1994).

**Sporck,** Count **Franz Anton** (b. 9 March 1662; d. 30 March 1738). Bohemian nobleman, born and died in Lysá nad Labem. He is remembered above all as a munificent patron of the arts. A free thinker and libertine (wrongly credited with introducing Freemasonry into Bohemia), he was a fervent Catholic capable of marrying Jansenism with Lutheran Pietism. Among the numerous activities he promoted were some connected with the theatre. He built theatres at his Kuks residence and also in Prague, in which, between 1724 and 1735, the Venetian company of Antonio Denzio (? c.1690–after 1763) presented some 60 operas as well as numerous intermezzos. Sporck maintained contacts with Vivaldi (some of whose operas were performed) and Bach. As we learn from an annotation in the autograph score, Bach sent him the performing material of the Sanctus that was later incorporated into the B minor Mass; he evidently did not return the parts. AB

A. Basso, *L'invenzione della gioia: musica e massoneria nell'età dei Lumi* (Milan, 1994), 480–2, 485–6; D. E. Freeman, *The Opera Theatre of Count Franz Anton von Sporck in Prague (1724–1735)* (Stuyvesant, NY, 1992); P. Nettl, 'Franz Anton Graf von Sporcks Beziehungen zur Musik', *Die Musikforschung*, 6 (1953), 324–35.

**Spruch** ('saying', 'aphorism'). A term used (in the sense of *Bibelspruch*) for a passage of Scripture occurring as part of the text of a cantata or motet; the term 'dictum' is also used in the same sense. A feature of the cantatas by Bach to librettos from the Meiningen court (nos. 17, 39, 45, 88, 102, and 187) is their division into two parts, each one beginning with a *Spruch*. When the *Spruch* is a saying of Jesus it is commonly set as a bass arioso (*see* VOX CHRISTI); other *Sprüche* often invite the use of MOTET STYLE.

**St** Contraction of 'Saint', and elsewhere treated alphabetically as such.

**Stadtmusicus, Stadtpfeifer** ('town musician', 'town piper'). Titles for a German musician employed by a town council to provide music for civic occasions, church services, and any other regular or occasional festivities requiring music. Town musicians often fought fiercely to preserve their monopoly on musical performance within a certain area. While they were ranked below the principal organists and Kantors of the town, they were none the less respected musicians; indeed, many members of Bach's family had been *Stadtpfeifer*.

Bach's *Entwurff* of 1730 sheds some light on the situation in Leipzig and the terminology used. Eight musicians were regularly engaged for church music, four of them *Stadtpfeifer* (wind players), three of them *Kunstgeiger* (string players), and one an apprentice. Bach's glowing testimonial for Carl Friedrich Pfaffe (d. 1773) in 1745 (*BDok* i. 147) upon his promotion from apprenticeship indicates both the looseness of terminology (Bach uses both terms, *Stadtmusicus* and *Stadtpfeifer*) and the incredible versatility demanded of such players: Pfaffe was qualified on

violin, oboe, flute, trumpet, horn, and 'bass instruments'. JAB

**Stählin, Jacob von** (9 May 1709; d. 25 June 1785). Writer and historian, born in Memmingen, Swabia. He studied at Leipzig University and became friendly with the Bach family there. He took part in the activities of Bach's collegium musicum and played 'flute duets' (possibly pieces for flute and continuo) with Johann Gottfried Bernhard Bach. In 1735 he left for Russia, where he spent the rest of his days. In a letter to his son Peter dated 20 July 1784 he mentioned the nicknames that were used for Carl Philipp Emanuel Bach ('der Schwarze') and his brother Johann Gottfried Bernhard ('der Windige').

H.-J. Schulze, 'Vier unbekannte Quittungen J. S. Bachs und ein Briefauszug Jacob von Stählins', *BJb* 59 (1973), 88–90.

**Stauber, Johann Lorenz** (bap. 12 June 1660; d. 8 April 1723). Clergyman, born in Arnstadt, Thuringia. He officiated at the wedding of Johann Sebastian and Maria Barbara Bach at Dornheim on 17 October 1707, and some eight months later he himself was married to Maria Barbara's aunt Regina WEDEMANN. This was his second marriage; his first wife, Anna Sophie (d. 1707), was a member of the HOFFMANN family, also closely associated with the Bachs. Spitta suggested that Bach wrote the cantata *Der Herr denket an uns* for Stauber's second marriage, but there is no certain evidence for this.

**Steindorff, Johann Martin** (b. 18 March 1663; d. 3 May 1744). Musician, born in Teutleben, between Eisenach and Gotha in Thuringia. He was Kantor at Zwickau. In 1722 he entered his candidacy for the vacant post of Thomaskantor in Leipzig, but did not get as far as the first *Probe* and remained in Zwickau for the rest of his life.

**'Sterbchoral'.** German nickname for Bach's organ chorale *Vor deinen Thron tret ich* as printed in the first edition of *The Art of Fugue. See* 'DEATHBED CHORALE'.

**Stichvorlage** ('engraving model'). Any manuscript source serving as a model for the music engraver in the etching process. In the case of the mechanical and freehand engraving techniques, engravers who are trained musicians prepare their own *Stichvorlage* from the composer's autograph copy. Two leaves from an exemplar of *Clavier-Übung III* in the British Library (Hirsch III. 39) are thought to be part of the *Stichvorlage*, in Balthasar Schmid's hand, on which Schmid based his engraving. In both the reproductive and *Abklatschvorlage* methods of music engraving the engraver works directly from the composer's manuscript. *See* SOURCES, §2. GB

G. Butler, *Bach's Clavier-Übung III: The Making of a Print* (Durham, NC, 1990).

***stile antico*** ('ancient style'). An Italian term used to refer to the modern application of a musical vocabulary and syntax associated with the past, particularly with 16th-century polyphony. In the course of the 17th and 18th centuries what came to be known as the 'stile alla Palestrina' ('Palestrina style'), and was referred to by theorists in such unequivocal terms as 'antiquus', 'vetus', 'gravis', or 'severus', went on being used in sacred music, including that of the most orthodox Lutheranism. A plethora of synonyms was used for the *stile antico*: the Latin *stylus* (or *contrapunctus*) *ecclesiasticus*, *moteticus*, *canonicus*, or even *praenestinus*; and the Italian *stile a cappella* or *stile osservato*.

Because so many of the works are lost, it is not easy to estimate the impact of the *stile antico* on the music of Bach's early period. As far as the cantatas are concerned, an *antico* MOTET STYLE may be observed in nos. 71:3 (1708), 4:5 (*c*.1709), 21:9 (1714), and 182:7 (1714), and some instrumental compositions of the Cöthen years betray archaic compositional methods. But it was during Bach's Leipzig years that archaic procedures assumed greater consistency and importance, as can be seen in many cantata movements written during his first years as Thomaskantor: nos. 64:1 and 179:1 (1723); nos. 2:1, 38:1, 101:1, 121:1, and 144:1 (1724); and nos. 28:2, 68:5, and 108:4 (1725). The same might be said of certain sections in the first version of the *Magnificat* (1723). Later sacred works to exemplify the *stile antico* include Cantata 29:2 and some parts of the B minor Mass, such as the second 'Kyrie eleison' (1733) and 'Credo in unum Deum', 'Crucifixus etiam pro nobis', and 'Confiteor unum baptisma' from the Symbolum Nicenum (*c*.1748–9).

Bach's new interest in the *stile antico* must surely have had something to do with his greater engagement with the motet—not so much in the composition of his own motets as in the use he made of a more traditional type of motet. It is well known that in 1729 he acquired a copy of Erhard Bodenschatz's *Florilegium Portense* (first published in Leipzig in 1603, enlarged in 1618, and followed by a second volume in 1621), and that a second copy was acquired for use at the Thomasschule in 1737 (*BDok* ii, nos. 271 and 407). Firmly anchored in the Leipzig choral tradition, Bodenschatz's collection had long been used in the principal churches of the city, and continued in use until 1770, since it furnished a repertory of 271 pieces mostly in Latin (less than a tenth of the motets are in German). They were used, following the regulations in force, as introits and communion pieces at *Hauptgottesdienst* and also during afternoon Vespers. Bach certainly made ample use of them in the four churches for which he had to supply choristers.

The *stile antico* occupies a special place in the music of Bach's last decade, when the art of variation (particularly canonic variation) occupied his mind, leading him to compose works of an eminently speculative, scientific, and hermetic quality. After the experience of *Clavier-Übung III* (already substantially archaic in style), came the Goldberg Variations, Part 2 of *The Well-tempered Clavier*, the partial 'instrumentation' of Palestrina's *Missa sine nomine*, the Canonic Variations for organ, the canons and ricercars of the *Musical Offering*, and the Contrapuncta of *The Art of Fugue*—all works in which *ars combinatoria* and *sonus numeratus* seem to strive to replace *musica practica* with an esoteric sound world.

In view of the seminal importance of Christoph Wolff's 1968 study, it should be mentioned that Wolff defines the *stile antico* rather more narrowly than is the case here; he applies it to a much stricter form of dissonance treatment than is found, for instance, in *The Art of Fugue*, and specifically to the period following Bach's acquaintance with Fux's writings.                    AB

*See also* FUX, JOHANN JOSEPH.

A. Basso, 'Bach e Palestrina', in L. Bianchi and G. Rostirolla, eds., *Atti del II Convegno Internazionale di Studi Palestriniani* (Palestrina, 1991), 409–19; C. Wolff, *Der stile antico in der Musik Johann Sebastian Bachs* (Wiesbaden, 1968).

**Stockmar, Johann Melchior** (b. 1698; d. 17 March 1747). Musician, born in Naundorf, near Grimma, about 25 km. (15 miles) south-east of Leipzig. He studied theology at Leipzig University, and in 1728 was appointed Kantor at the Matthäikirche in nearby Leisnig. Eight texts set by Bach were among those used for cantatas performed at the church during Stockmar's Kantorate; whether any of them were performed with Bach's music cannot be ascertained with certainty.

W. Neumann, 'Über die mutmaßlichen Beziehungen zwischen dem Leipziger Thomaskantor Bach und dem Leisniger Matthäikantor Stockmar', in W. Rehm, ed., *Bachiana et alia musicologica: Festschrift Alfred Dürr zum 65. Geburtstag* (Kassel, 1983), 201–8.

**Stollen** ('strophe'). A term used for the first and second sections of a piece (or part of one) in BARFORM.

**Stölzel, Gottfried Heinrich** (b. 13 Jan. 1690; d. 27 Nov. 1749). Composer, born in Gründstädtel, near Schwarzenberg in Saxony, about 30 km. (19 miles) south-east of Zwickau. He studied at Leipzig University, 1707–10, and for the next ten years travelled widely, teaching and composing in Breslau, Halle, Italy, Prague, Bayreuth, and Gera, and refusing several offers of permanent employment. In 1719 he married and the following year was appointed *Kapellmeister* at Gotha, where he remained for the rest of his life. In 1739 he joined Lorenz Mizler's Correspondirenden Societät der Musicalischen Wissenschaften, of which Bach was later a member. Stölzel was a prolific composer in nearly every genre of his time. Bach included a *Partia* in G minor by him in the *Clavierbüchlein* for W. F. Bach, and Stölzel has been credited with the composition of *Bist du bei mir*, one of the best-known items in the 1725 *Clavierbüchlein* for Anna Magdalena Bach.

**Straube, Rudolph** (b. 5 Dec. 1717; d. 1785). Lutenist and harpsichordist, born in Elstertrebnitz, near Leipzig. The son of a church warden, he enrolled at the Thomasschule in January 1733. Like others among Bach's better pupils, he was entrusted with music-copying, and his hand has been identified in the performance parts over the following three years for several cantatas, including sections of the *Christmas Oratorio*. He entered Leipzig University in 1740, and soon afterwards may have worked for Carl Heinrich von Dieskau, Bach's patron for the Peasant Cantata, to whom Straube dedicated his *Due sonate* in 1746. In the following year he was engaged as *Cammer-musicus* at the Cöthen court.

In the 1750s Straube, like many other German musicians, moved to London, where he led an increasingly precarious existence as harpsichordist, lutenist, and teacher of the fashionable 'English' (actually German) guitar, for which he published some music in his adopted city. He was one of the eminent musicians whom the artist Thomas Gainsborough persuaded to give him lessons; William Jackson tells an amusing anecdote about their encounter.                    TTC

BDok ii. 372–3, 408; iii. 123, 479, 721; T. Crawford, Introduction to *Rudolph Straube: Due sonate a liuto solo* (Leipzig, 1746), facsimile (Monaco, 1981); W. Jackson, *The Four Ages of Man, together with Essays on Various Subjects* (London, 1798), 151–2; H.-J. Schulze, *Studien zur Bach-Überlieferung im 18 Jahrhundert* (Leipzig, 1984), 120, 212–13.

**Stravinsky, Igor** (b. 17 June 1882; d. 6 April 1971). Composer in all the major traditional genres, born in Oranienbaum (now Lomonosov), near St Petersburg, Russia. He later lived variously in Switzerland and France before settling in the USA in 1935 and becoming an American citizen in 1945. By nature a highly individual transformer of the ideas of others, his music falls into three phases: a Russian period, both Romantic and expressionistic; a neo-classical period; and a late

period, often exploring serial structures. Stravinsky's wide knowledge of music repertory (which included an unusual access to German music from his youth) included a great enthusiasm for Bach, whose style became a key component of his neo-classicism, *The Well-tempered Clavier* being observed at one period as his 'daily fare'.

Stravinsky claimed to have 'steeped himself' in studies of Bach, Beethoven, and Brahms in preparation for his solo Piano Concerto (1923–4). His most overtly Bach-influenced work is the Concerto in E♭ entitled 'Dumbarton Oaks' (1937–8), which he described as 'a little concerto after the Brandenburgs', scored for a similar ensemble and drawing in motifs from Brandenburg Concerto no. 3. A wide range of Bachian idioms can be identified in Stravinsky's neo-classical works, from the rocking accompaniment figure of the slow movement of the Violin Concerto (1931) to the ornate woodwind writing in the second movement of the Symphony of Psalms (1930)—links which continue less obviously into his late works. His arrangements include one for chorus and orchestra of Bach's Canonic Variations (1955–6), and another for strings and woodwind of two preludes and fugues from *The Well-tempered Clavier* (c.1969).                    MM

**stretto.** A term used in fugal composition for close imitation in which two or more statements of the subject (or answer) overlap. The dovetailing procedure may be continued through all the voices of the texture, producing a 'stretto maestrale'. Stretto does not normally occur in the exposition, despite exceptions such as the A major Fugue from Book 1 of *The Well-tempered Clavier*, but rather as a means of increasing tension at later stages in the composition, as in the C major fugue from the same collection; each of these works might, for slightly different reasons, be described as a 'stretto fugue'. The B♭ minor Fugue in Book 2 of *The Well-tempered Clavier* shows a splendid instance of stretto in the outer parts at bars 33–7, where the subject is imitated at the interval of a 9th and at a distance of one beat. Again at a distance of one beat is an almost undetectable example of stretto between the subject (bass) and its inversion (alto) at bars 89–93 of the same fugue.                    LC

**Stricker, Augustin Reinhard** (b. c.1675; d. after 1720). Composer, born possibly in Berlin, where he was employed at court as a violinist and singer from 1702. From 1714 to 1717 he was Bach's predecessor as *Kapellmeister* at Cöthen; his wife was also employed there, as a singer. After leaving Cöthen, Stricker entered the service of the Elector Palatine in Neuberg an der Donau.

**Strungck, Nicolaus Adam** (bap. 15 Nov. 1640; d. 23 Sept. 1700). Composer and instrumentalist, born in Brunswick. He studied at Helmstedt University, and in 1660 was appointed violinist at the court in Wolfenbüttel, moving shortly afterwards to Celle and then to Hanover. He was active mainly as an opera composer in Hamburg and Leipzig, and as vice-*Kapellmeister*, and then *Kapellmeister*, at Dresden. In reply to an enquiry from Bach's biographer J. N. Forkel, C. P. E. Bach wrote in 1775 that Strungck was one of the composers whose music his father had loved and studied.

**Stück** ('piece'). A term frequently used in Bach's time to refer to a church CANTATA.

**style brisé** ('broken style'). A modern term applied to a style of much French Baroque keyboard and lute music in which an essentially chordal texture is notated in a pseudo-polyphonic manner that precisely indicates the arpeggiation of the chords and the holding out of their constituent notes. First widely attested in 17th-century French lute pieces, the style also appears in keyboard music by J.-H. D'Angelbert, François Couperin, and others. Bach adopted it in numerous movements, particularly the allemandes of his suites (e.g. the Allemande in the French Suite no. 2). DS

    D. Buch, 'Style brisé, Style luthé, and the Choses luthées', *Musical Quarterly*, 71 (1985), 52–67, 220–1.

**style galant.** A term applied to various types of late Baroque and early Classical music of the 18th century. During Bach's day the French word 'galant' and its derivatives were used to describe dances and other fashionable pieces; the title-pages of Bach's keyboard Partitas describe their individual movements as 'galanteries' (*see* GALANTERIE). By the mid-century the word had acquired a more specific meaning in German writings as referring to the homophonic texture and relaxed dissonance treatment of up-to-date dances, arias, and other such compositions, as opposed to the rigorous contrapuntal texture of fugues and other more old-fashioned works.

Modern writers have used the expression for the music of Couperin, Telemann, Pergolesi, the Bach sons, and others active in the early and mid-eighteenth century whose works avoid complex contrapuntal textures, favouring singing melodies with simple accompaniments in only one or two real parts. Melodic lines are often concatenated from numerous short motifs, although in the music of later composers, such as Johann Christian Bach, a more sustained melodic style is often cultivated. The simplified textures of the *style galant* led to the invention of new types of scoring,

eventually resulting in the rich variety of accompanimental patterns and types of motivic development employed in the Classical style. In modern usage the term frequently connotes a light, even trivial, expressive effect. The opposite was true during the middle and late 18th century, when the focus on melody was thought to facilitate a more immediate, 'natural' form of expression, as opposed to what was viewed as the artificial counterpoint and musical rhetoric of the Baroque. DS

    D. Sheldon, 'The Galant Style Revisited and Re-Evaluated', *Acta musicologica*, 47 (1975), 240–70; D. Sheldon, 'The Concept *galant* in the 18th Century', *Journal of Musicological Research*, 9 (1989–90), 89–108.

**stylus fantasticus/phantasticus** ('fantastic style'). An expression applied historically to two somewhat different types of keyboard music. As used by Athanasius Kircher (1601–80) in his *Musurgia universalis* (Rome, 1650), it described fantasias and other keyboard pieces of J. J. Froberger characterized by a great variety of contrapuntal devices. Since Mattheson (*Der vollkommene Capellmeister*, Hamburg, 1739) the term has referred to the free, virtuoso writing especially characteristic of the praeludia of Buxtehude and of related works by Bach, particularly the toccatas and the more improvisatory organ preludes. In modern usage the term implies a combination of free form, extravagant modulation (often chromatic), and arpeggiated passage-work, often with references to recitative style; notable examples by Bach include the organ Fantasia in G minor and the Chromatic Fantasia for harpsichord. DS

    C. Defant, *Kammermusik und Stylus phantasticus: Studien zu Dietrich Buxtehudes Triosonaten* (Frankfurt, 1985), 89–114; F. Krummacher, 'Bach's Free Organ Works and the *Stylus Phantasticus*', in G. Stauffer and E. May, eds., *J. S. Bach as Organist* (London, 1986), 172–89; K. Snyder, *Dieterich Buxtehude: Organist in Lübeck* (New York, 1987), 248–57.

**suite.** In the context of Baroque music, a collection of instrumental dances, sometimes introduced by a prelude of some kind. The term 'partita' is also used in the same sense. Within the German tradition the suite was made up essentially of four often interrelated dances in the same key: Allemande, Courante, Sarabande, and Gigue (A, C, S, and G), an order that became standard around 1680. To this scheme an opening prelude and one or more optional dances were often added. As a clearly defined musical unit, this German suite differs significantly from the traditional French type, a loose collection of dances in the same key from which a selection could be made at will.

## Süßer Trost, mein Jesus kömmt

In Johann Kuhnau's *Neuer Clavier Übung* (Leipzig, 1689 and 1692), which exerted an obvious influence on Bach's early suites, one of the four standard dances is often replaced by an alternative (menuet, aria, bourrée, etc.), a procedure adopted by the young Bach in the keyboard suites bwv821 (Prélude, A, C, S, Echo), 832 (A, Air, S, Bourrée, G), and 833 (Prélude, A, C, S + *double*, Air). bwv832, though it does not include a prelude of any kind, contains clear echoes of an overture-suite, known to Bach in keyboard transcription, from Marin Marais's opera *Alcide* (Paris, 1693). This type, in which a French overture introduces a series of French dances, became popular in Germany about 1700. The young Bach was probably acquainted with overture-suites for ensemble by J. A. Coberg (1649/50–1708), J. C. Pez (1664–1716), and Agostino Steffani (1654–1728) and for keyboard by Georg Böhm, G. E. Pestel, and G. P. Telemann. Bach himself contributed to the genre in both garbs: for keyboard in bwv820, 822, and 831; for ensemble in the four Ouvertures, popularly known as orchestral suites, bwv1066–9.

The German suite was in Bach's hands constantly enriched by direct French influence. He knew the first books of *Pièces de clavecin* by both N.-A. Lebègue (1677) and Louis Marchand (1699), and copied out Charles Dieupart's *Six suittes de clavessin* (1701) between about 1709 and 1716. He may also have encountered at Weimar, through J. G. Walther, suites by J. J. de Neufville (1684–1712), Gaspard Le Roux (d. *c*.1706), J.-H. D'Anglebert, and J.-F. Dandrieu (*c*.1682–1738); and by 1725 at the latest he was acquainted with François Couperin's *Second livre de pièces de clavecin* (1717). The most French of Bach's keyboard suites are perhaps bwv806 and 823. In the latter a Prélude in chaconne-rondeau form is followed by a *Sarabande en rondeau* and a Gigue in the rhythm of a *canarie*. bwv806, the first of the English Suites, has two courantes, just like Lebègue's suites and the earlier of the two published by Marchand. The remaining English Suites and all the Cello Suites exhibit the movement order Prélude, A, C, S, Bourrée/Menuet/Gavotte/Passepied I and II, G—closely allied to the standard scheme of Dieupart, who seems to have been the first Frenchman to treat the suite as a musical unit of fixed structure. In his French Suites Bach omitted the prelude and increased the number of optional dances in the course of both composition and revision (nos. 2–5, in revised form, have three; no. 6 has four), expanding the range of dance types to include the air, anglaise, loure, and polonaise. Closely associated with these works in the manuscripts of Bach's pupils are the Suite in A minor bwv818 (A, C, S + *double*, G; revised as bwv818*a*: Prélude, A, C, S, Menuet, G) and the Suite in E♭

major bwv819 (A, C, S, Bourrée, Menuet I and II).

The three Partitas for solo violin belong to a different tradition: the Italian instrumental dance suite or *sonata da camera*, hence the Italian dance titles of nos. 1 and 2 (Allemanda, Corrente, Sarabanda, Giga, etc.). In no. 3, however, a 'Preludio' is followed by a series of French dances. Thus a clear overlap is evident in this set (as also in the related Solo for unaccompanied flute bwv1013: A, Corrente, S, Bourrée anglaise) between the Italian and the French traditions.

Such an overlap is still more pronounced in the similarly titled Partitas for keyboard, where French and Italian headings are deliberately juxtaposed and used in alternation, such as 'Courante' and 'Corrente'. In both the violin and the keyboard partitas Bach uses the formula 'Tempo di …', which reflects the somewhat looser stylization of dances within the Italian tradition. In movement structure the keyboard Partitas follow the English and Cello Suites, except that the *alternativement* pair occurs only in no. 1 (Menuet I and II). The optional dances are otherwise very freely handled, and as often Italian as French. Recognizable dance rhythm is altogether absent from certain movements, such as the Capriccio in no. 2 or the Scherzo in no. 3.

Of Bach's suites for lute or lute-harpsichord, bwv995 (*c*.1730) is an arrangement of the Fifth Cello Suite, and bwv1006*a* (*c*.1735–40) an arrangement of the solo violin Partita no. 3. The Weimar Suite 'aufs Lauten Werk' bwv996 displays the movement order Prélude, A, C, S, Bourrée, G, and the Partita in C minor bwv997 (*c*.1740) has an abridged order reminiscent of the early Suite in F minor bwv823: Prelude and Fugue, S, G + *double*.

RDPJ

See also CELLO SUITES, ENGLISH SUITES, FRENCH SUITES, ORCHESTRAL SUITES, PARTITAS, and SONATAS AND PARTITAS FOR SOLO VIOLIN.

A. Dürr, 'The Historical Background and Composition of J. S. Bach's Clavier Suites', *Bach*, 16/1 (1985), 53–68; H. Eppstein, 'Chronologieprobleme in Johann Sebastian Bachs Suiten für Soloinstrument', *BJb* 62 (1976), 35–57.

**Süßer Trost, mein Jesus kömmt** ('Sweet comfort, my Jesus comes'). Cantata for the third day of Christmas, bwv151, to a libretto by the Darmstadt poet and court librarian G. C. Lehms. Bach had set two of Lehms's texts while still at Weimar, and for the Christmas, New Year, and Epiphany festivals at Leipzig in 1725–6 he based six more cantatas on librettos by his former Darmstadt contemporary, who had died in 1717.

*Süßer Trost, mein Jesus kömmt*, for which Bach's autograph score and original parts have survived, was first sung on 27 December 1725. Lehms's libretto has no apparent link with the appointed Gospel reading but instead provides a reflection on the Christmas Epistle (Hebrews 1: 1–14), focusing on the coming of Christ and the joyful hope of salvation. In common with most of the other cantatas that Bach performed in the period immediately after Christmas, this one dispenses with an elaborate opening choral movement, perhaps enabling some of the choirboys to enjoy a well-earned rest. However, one of them at least must have spent some time preparing the G major aria with which the work begins, and which can justifiably be regarded as one of Bach's most sublime creations for the solo voice. Marked both 'molto adagio' and 'sempre piano', it is lightly and translucently scored for soprano, with flute, violins (an oboe d'amore doubling the first violin), viola, and basso continuo. The text meditates on the significance of Christ's birth, and Bach, focusing on its opening words, 'Süßer Trost', suffuses it with an ethereal inner radiance. In the two outer sections of this extended da capo aria the flute weaves playful arabesques around the lyrical vocal cantilena. The middle section changes from 12/8 metre to a contrasting 4/4 *vivace* in E minor, colouring the words 'Herz und Seele freuet sich' ('heart and spirit rejoice').

A bass recitative, reflecting on the coming of Christ and his suffering for man's salvation, leads to the second aria of the cantata, in E minor. This is in a modified da capo form and is scored for alto voice with solo oboe d'amore, unison upper strings, and continuo. The text is symbolically related to that of the first aria and is concerned with the hope of salvation through Christ's meekness and humility. A simple recitative for tenor follows and the cantata closes with the eighth strophe of the hymn *Lobt Gott, ihr Christen allzugleich* (1560) by Nikolaus Herman, who also wrote the melody. The hymn was listed as appropriate to the third day of Christmas in both the Leipzig and Dresden hymn schedules, and is here straightforwardly harmonized by Bach with *colla parte* instrumental support.                    NA

For bibliography, *see* CANTATA, §1.

**Swieten, Gottfried Bernhard,** Baron **van** (b. 29 Oct. 1733; d. 29 March 1803). Musical patron, born in Leiden; he moved with his family to Vienna in 1745. He became a diplomat for the Austrian government and served in Brussels, Paris, England, Warsaw, and between 1770 and 1777 as ambassador in Berlin. It was in Berlin that he became acquainted with Bach's music, probably through Princess Anna Amalia of Prussia. He also was in contact with C. P. E. Bach, from whom in 1773 he commissioned a series of six sinfonias for string orchestra, and he is the dedicatee of the third set of *Clavier-Sonaten . . . für Kenner und Liebhaber*, published in 1781. After returning to Vienna in 1777, van Swieten was of central influence in promoting the works of the Bach family and of Handel in the Habsburg capital. The weekly soirées in his house, where only music by Bach and Handel was played, are known through letters by Mozart. It was for van Swieten that Mozart made string arrangements of some of Bach's keyboard fugues.

Van Swieten's large music library was auctioned shortly after his death; although the sale catalogue is lost, it seems likely that many of the items were acquired by the music dealer Johann Traeg, whose published catalogue of 1804 contains a remarkable number of works by J. S. Bach, including many cantatas, the *Magnificat* and the *Christmas Oratorio*. A number of Viennese copies of Bach's keyboard works now at the Staatsbibliothek zu Berlin were formerly attributed to van Swieten's collection (see Holschneider), but in fact belonged to Franz Joseph von Heß (1739–1804; see Wolf).                    PW

*See also* MOZART, WOLFGANG AMADEUS.

A. Holschneider, 'Die musikalische Bibliothek Gottfried van Swietens,' in *Bericht über den Internationalen Musikwissenschaftlichen Kongreß Kassel 1962* (Kassel, 1963), 174–8; U. Leisinger, *Joseph Haydn und die Entwicklung des klassischen Klavierstils* (Laaber, 1994); U. Wolf, 'Die Musikaliensammlung des Wiener Regierungsrats Franz Joseph Reichsritter von Heß (1739–1804) und ihre Bachiana', *BJb* 81 (1995), 195–201.

**Swingle Singers.** A French ensemble of eight singers, with double bass and percussion, formed in 1962 by Ward Lemar Swingle and Christiane Legrande. They performed and recorded scat arrangements of mainly Baroque music, including several pieces by Bach. The group disbanded in 1973. It has since been reconstituted, but places less emphasis than formerly on Bach's music.

**Symbolum Nicenum.** A term used by Bach for the Credo of the B minor Mass, and occasionally by other composers (e.g. J. D. Zelenka's 'Credo, sive Symbolum Nicaenum').

# T

**tablature.** A means of notating instrumental music using letters and/or figures, together with rhythmic signs, rather than the notes and lines of staff notation. A major difference between tablature and staff notation is that the former (like Tonic Sol-fa for vocal music) usually conveys little or no visual idea of the rise and fall of a musical line. Rather it indicates where the player's fingers should be placed on the fingerboard or keyboard to produce the required pitch. Bach made occasional use of tablature for organ music, and some pieces by him survive in lute tablature.

1. Lute tablature.
2. Organ tablature.

1. **Lute tablature.** This indicates the finger positions necessary to produce the notes by a system of ciphers, together with a separate indication of the rhythm. Lute tablature existed in several national variants; the 'French' version was in general use in Germany after about 1620. The fingerboard frets are represented by letters: *a* stands for the open string, *b* for the first fret, and so on. These letters are placed on a six-line 'staff' representing the six stopped courses of the lute, with additional letters or numbers underneath for the bass courses, which are usually played open (i.e. unstopped). The rhythm is indicated by signs derived from conventional notation placed above the staff. Three of Bach's works survive in 18th-century lute-tablature copies (*see* LUTE WORKS).

Since lute tablature cannot specify precise durations of notes in polyphonic voices, its interpretation is largely subjective and can give rise to controversy. But it is an ideal notation for the lutenist, although (since laborious transcription is necessary for the non-player) it has severely impeded the general understanding of the significance of the extensive lute repertory by music historians.

2. **Organ tablature.** Although commonly referred to in the context of Bach's music as 'organ tablature', this system of notation was in use, by German musicians in particular, for all keyboard instruments throughout the 15th and 16th centuries and for much of the 17th. By Bach's time its use was becoming rare, and he used it principally in his mature years to save space and avoid using a new sheet of paper to conclude a piece. In the ORGEL-BÜCHLEIN, for example, the titles of the individual preludes were entered before the music was composed, leading Bach to use tablature in some cases where the length of a piece had been miscalculated (see picture, p.345). He also used it occasionally in the composing scores of his vocal works, for example in the E♭ major version of the *Magnificat*.

In the form of organ tablature used by Bach, notes are represented by their letter names: C, D, E, and so on for the lowest octave of notes beginning below the bass staff in conventional notation; lower-case letters are used for the next octave, and a short horizontal line is added above the letter for each additional upward octave transposition. The duration of a note is indicated by a vertical line representing a semibreve, with horizontal strokes indicating each diminution: one stroke for a minim, two for a crotchet, and so on. By Bach's time, numbers standing for the number of such strokes were sometimes substituted for the rhythm signs. Apart from the general distinction between the notes B and B♭ (consistently written as H and B respectively in all periods in Germany), chromatic inflections are specified by the addition of a suffix, '-is', to the letter name to indicate the use of a black key. Thus the key for both D♯ and E♭ is represented by the tablature 'Dis'; enharmonic distinctions are not possible. The suffix appears in various forms in manuscript tablatures, sometimes as a mere squiggle, and the universal use of old German *Kursiv* orthography can make the reading of tablature manuscripts difficult and tedious.

By contrast with lute tablature, organ tablature was recognized to be an inconvenient system for the player, and laborious to write, although the saving of space, together with the fact that part-writing can be clearly expressed by the arrangement of the tablature on the page, was seen as a compensating advantage. In addition, since it forced the user to be aware of the names of the notes, it was a useful pedagogic tool for the training of composers. This form of tablature was also frequently used for the writing of scores of music for voices or instruments, to which it was as well suited as for keyboard music. TTC

R. Hill, 'Tablature versus Staff Notation: Or, Why did the Young J. S. Bach Compose in Tablature?', in P. Walker, ed., *Church, Stage, and Studio: Music and its Contexts in Seventeenth-Century Germany* (Ann Arbor, 1990), 349–59; D. Kilian, 'Zu einem Bachschen Tabulaturautograph', in W. Rehm, ed., *Bachiana et alia musicologica: Festschrift Alfred Dürr zum 65. Geburtstag* (Kassel, 1983), 161–7.

**taille** ('tenor'). A French term used generally for any voice or instrument which plays a middle, or tenor, part. In Bach's scores 'taille' usually indicates an oboe da caccia.

**tamburi** ('drums'). An Italian term which Bach usually used for TIMPANI.

**Telemann, Georg Philipp** (b. 14 March 1681; d. 25 June 1767). Composer, born in Magdeburg. He contributed prolifically to practically every musical genre of his time.

Bach's personal connections with Telemann were numerous. He first met him while Telemann was *Konzertmeister* (later *Kapellmeister*) in Eisenach, at the same time that Bach was court organist in nearby Weimar. A manuscript, dating from *c*.1709, of Telemann's Concerto in G major for two violins, Kross 2 V.G(1), survives in Bach's hand, and Bach also arranged Telemann's G minor Violin Concerto, Kross V.g, for keyboard in about 1713. In 1714 Telemann, by this time in Frankfurt, stood godfather to C. P. E. Bach (hence the second name, 'Philipp'). Bach was made Kantor in Leipzig in 1723 only after Telemann, by then director of music in Hamburg, and Graupner turned the post down. In 1729 Bach took over the directorship of the Leipzig collegium musicum founded by Telemann while a student at the university in 1702. Telemann was succeeded in Hamburg by his godson C. P. E. Bach.

Bach's interest in, and respect for, Telemann's music is described by C. P. E. Bach in a letter to J. N. Forkel: 'In his last years he esteemed highly: Fux, Caldara, Händel, Kayser, both Grauns, Telemann, Zelenka, Benda, and in general everything that was worthy of esteem in Berlin and Dresden. Except for the first four, he knew the rest personally. In his younger years he was often with Telemann, who also held me at my baptism.' Bach performed various cantatas by Telemann in Leipzig (some of which were mistakenly included in the *BG* edition); performances of two of Telemann's Passions have been posited but not confirmed. Bach's name appears among the subscribers to Telemann's 'Paris' quartets (1738), and works by Telemann survive in several keyboard manuscripts from the Bach circle. Bach supplied a puzzle canon for Telemann's music magazine *Der getreue Music-Meister* (1728–9). Telemann was probably the first German composer to apply ritornello form to the sonata and the concerted French *ouverture*, genres taken up by Bach, and was the first to set Neumeister's cantata texts, which served as a model for Bach's cantata librettists. Bach also shared Telemann's interest in combining national styles and genres.

JS

K. Beißwenger, *Johann Sebastian Bachs Notenbibliothek* (Kassel, 1992); H.-J. Schulze, ' "Fließende Leichtigkeit" und "arbeitsame Vollstimmigkeit": Georg Philipp Telemann und die Musikerfamilie Bach', in W. Siegmund-Schultze, ed., *Telemann und seine Freunde: Kontakte–Einflüße–Auswirkungen* (Magdeburg, 1986), i. 34–40; H.-J. Schulze, 'Telemann—Pisendel—Bach: zu einem unbekannten Bach-Autograph', in G. Fleischhauer, W. Hobohm, and W. Siegmund-Schultze, eds., *Die Bedeutung Georg Philipp Telemanns für die Entwicklung der europäischen Musikkultur im 18. Jahrhundert* (Magdeburg, 1983), ii. 73–7; J. Swack, 'On the Origins of the *Sonate auf Concertenart*', *Journal of the American Musicological Society*, 46 (1993), 369–414.

**temperaments.** Tunings of the scale in which most of the consonances are systematically made a little impure so that none will be sour.

---

1. Equal temperament.
2. Unequal temperament.

---

1. **Equal temperament.** Modern theorists sometimes use this term for divisions of the octave into various numbers of equal parts, but as far as Bach might be concerned, it was a matter of 12 equal semitones, as normally on the piano today. There is, alas, an acoustical defect in such a scale. Its minor 3rds ($\frac{3}{12}$ or $\frac{1}{4}$ octave) and major 3rds ($\frac{1}{3}$ octave) are somewhat impure.

(To reckon the impurities, consider that an acoustically pure consonance has a simple ratio of sound-wave frequencies: 2:1 for an octave, 3:2 for a 5th, etc. For a pure major 3rd the ratio is 5:4. Going up that amount three times—say, from A♭ to C to E to G♯—one arrives at an overall interval, A♭ to G♯, whose ratio is 5:4 × 5:4 × 5:4, that is, 125:64; but since 2:1 = 128:64, this G♯ is 125:128 shy of an octave above the A♭. Meanwhile, a traditional ratio for a whole tone (reckoned as the difference between the sum of two pure 5ths and an octave) is 3:2 × 3:2 × 1:2, i.e. 9:8, which is the same as 90:80 or 135:120; so the 128:125 discrepancy between our pure G♯ and A♭ is about $\frac{3}{15}$, or $\frac{1}{5}$, of a whole tone. In equal temperament this overall discrepancy in every chain of three major 3rds making an octave is distributed equally among them, so they are each impure by $\frac{1}{3}$ of approximately $\frac{1}{5}$ of a whole tone, i.e. something like $\frac{1}{7}$ of a semitone—a palpable amount but not enough to make us plug our ears. Other reckonings can show that the 5ths in equal temperament are tempered smaller than pure, but only by about $\frac{1}{7}$ as much as the major 3rds are tempered large, and that the minor 3rd, being the difference between a major 3rd and a 5th, is tempered small by the sum of the amounts of tempering for the 5th and the major 3rd.)

An advantage gained at the cost of these impurities is that 12 major and 12 minor keys are rendered tolerable. Bach's *The Well-tempered Clavier*, with its preludes and fugues in 24 keys, shows how important this advantage was to him (for another view, *see* WERCKMEISTER, ANDREAS). Another characteristic of equal temperament, however, is that the keys are uniformly impure. Whether he found *that* an advantage is dubious.

**2. Unequal temperament.** For people like Bach, Zacharias HILDEBRANDT, G. A. SORGE, Lorenz MIZLER, J. C. ALTNICKOL, and J. G. Neidhardt this was a kind of tuning in which the average sizes of the intervals were the same as in equal temperament but, for the sake of nuances amongst the various keys, the semitones were of various different sizes and some 3rds were less impure than others. Fig. 1 shows the overall pattern. Among the semitones, E to F was about 10 per cent larger than in equal temperament, C to D♭ about 10 per cent smaller. The smallest major 3rd, C to E, was tempered about half as much as in equal temperament or a little less; the largest one, D♭ to F, was tempered less than half again as much as in equal temperament.

The evidence that Bach preferred such a tuning (at least until the mid-1740s) is elaborate and subtle. He never contributed directly to the writings of his day about tempered tuning, but was sometimes mentioned in them. The best hints are in his compositions. The asymmetrical aspects of Fig. 1

are borne out by the fact that in his organ music D♭ major or C♯ major triads are not used as saliently as F♯ major or G♭ major triads. Most of the musical and acoustical evidence is more intricate, depending as it does on the exact ways in which particular notes are used in contexts that are easier to appreciate by ear than to describe. Upon hearing how a subtly unequal temperament (in which each key has its own nuances but none is downright harsh) such as that represented in Fig. 1 heightens the expressive value of Bach's harmony, while mitigating the 'mechanical' quality of the harpsichord and organ, most listeners become convinced that Bach not only accommodated, but positively exploited, the nuances of such tuning.

There is some contrary evidence. The ricercar which concludes the *Musical Offering* sounds best in equal temperament, as it makes use of 'extreme' flats (like D♭) in very straightforward harmonies. This fact can be accommodated by supposing that Bach in his last years accepted equal temperament. Other evidence, however, comes from before the late 1740s: his occasional transposing of entire movements or pieces from one key to another. Sometimes he would change the composition to accommodate the new key, as when he transposed a D major prelude to D♭ for Book 1 of *The Well-tempered Clavier*, and changed the right-hand's initial F♯ to A♭ rather than to F. Yet he did not make such adaptations when transposing the entire *Magnificat*.

Two modern writers have proposed rigidly specified mathematical models for Bach's style of unequal temperament. Herbert Kelletat's suggestion that Bach used an acoustically inept but easy-to-tune scheme invented in the 1760s by J. P. Kirnberger has gained some acceptance (by poor tuners), even though Kirnberger admitted that it

Figure 1

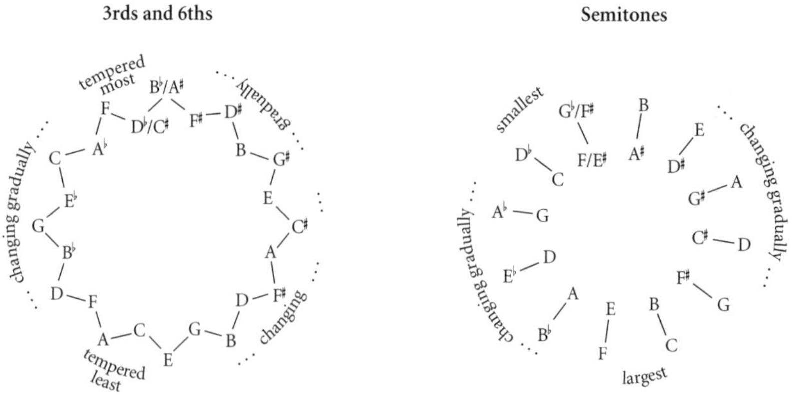

3rds and 6ths

Semitones

was contrary to Bach's instructions to him. Kirnberger's theory of tempered tuning was bluntly criticized by G. A. Sorge, and indeed no 18th-century German musician seems to have had a good word to say for it, though it appealed to some dilettantes such as the Swiss theologian and lexicographer J. G. Sulzer (1720–79). H. A. Kellner has patented a somewhat better scheme and proves—with arguments like those which show that Francis Bacon wrote Shakespeare's plays—that it was Bach's own secret.                ML

*See also* WERCKMEISTER, ANDREAS.

H. Kelletat, *Zur musikalischen Temperatur, insbesondere bei J. S. Bach* (Kassel, 1960); H. A. Kellner, *The Tuning of my Harpsichord* (Frankfurt, 1980); M. Lindley, 'A Quest for Bach's Ideal Style of Organ Temperament', in *Bericht des Musikinstrumentenbausymposiums 'Stimmungen im 17./18. Jahrhundert: Vielfalt oder Konfusion'?* (Michaelstein, 1996), forthcoming; M. Lindley, 'Bach's Harpsichord Tuning', *Musical Times*, 102 (1985), 721–6; M. Lindley, 'Stimmung und Temperatur', in F. Zaminer, ed., *Geschichte der Musiktheorie*, iv (Darmstadt, 1987), 109–331.

**tempo.** The speed at which a musical performance proceeds; the rate of speed of a succession of musical units, which might be expressed in a conductor's beats. A paramount issue in determining tempo is to ascertain the metrical level that represents the beat (i.e. the level at which a conductor would beat time); for example, in a piece in 3/4 metre, the level of the beat might be a dotted minim or a crotchet. A secondary issue is whether the beats proceed at a more or less steady rate (in 'strict' or 'measured', rhythm) or at a fluctuating rate (in 'free' rhythm); *see* RHYTHM. Tempo has been a contentious subject throughout music history, even after the invention of the metronome in the early 19th century. For Bach's music it is probably unwise for performers to make tempo decisions solely on the basis of scholarly research. Rather, information from at least four areas may help to determine tempo in particular cases: the notation; instructions in the score; dance rhythms; and external considerations.

**Notation.** In Bach's music tempo is related to affect. As stated by J. P. Kirnberger, Bach's famous student and disseminator of his art of composition, 'tempo, meter, and rhythm give melody its life and power. *Tempo* defines the rate of speed, which by itself is already important since it designates a lively or quiet character' (Kirnberger, p. 375). Put another way, although Bach's music may be played at various speeds, its character may change considerably in response to the tempo applied; a French overture may sound majestic and serious at one tempo, but militant and even frantic when played just a little faster. J. J. Quantz advised: 'Never lose your composure. For everything that is hurriedly played causes your listeners anxiety rather than satisfaction' (Quantz, ch. 12, §11).

Another tempo determinant is the amount of musical activity notated by the composer. Bach often wrote interesting musical material on two or three metrical levels at once. For example, in his famous 'Jesu, joy of man's desiring' (Cantata 147:6 and 10), with its steady 3/4 chorale harmonization for the voices in minims and crotchets and its 9/8 instrumental melody in lilting, dance-like quavers, one or other level may be rendered ineffective if the chosen tempo is too slow or too fast. The situation is somewhat analogous to a great Baroque church, such as the Benedictine abbey in Ottobeuren, Bavaria, in which grandiose architectural gestures as well as minute details on columns all contribute to the overall impact. Quantz and other 18th-century writers advised performers to consider the smallest note values when determining the tempo of a piece, so as to be sure that such passages are clear and intelligible.

Time signatures, although inconsistently used and not always perfectly understood even in Bach's time, usually carry significant information regarding tempo. Kirnberger (ch. 4), citing many examples by Bach, ties specific metrical indications with specific tempos; for example, 2/2 (*alla breve*) is 'serious and emphatic', 6/16 is 'lighter and faster than 6/8', and 3/2 is 'ponderous and slow'. Valuable scholarly discussions of metre continue to enlighten performers (see Houle, ch. 2, and Williams).

**Instructions in the scores.** Research has found clues to tempo in specific markings by Bach, such as 'allegro', 'adagissimo', and 'presto'. Marshall (p. 267) identified at least 45 different tempo and affect indications in Bach's scores; he concluded that each one offered a relative, rather than an absolute, significance for tempo and affect. Don Franklin has shown that Bach used the fermata sign (⌢) to indicate a change of tempo from one piece to another in a series (e.g. from a prelude to a fugue), and similarly in a set of variations or a suite of dances. A fermata at the end of a piece in a suite indicates a new tempo in the next piece. Conversely, where there is a proportional connection between the tempo of one piece and that of the next the fermata will be absent. Franklin notes that some modern Bach editions wrongly add or delete fermatas, apparently without realizing their significance.

**Dance rhythms.** Kirnberger (pp. 376–7) believed that each dance type had a characteristic tempo, which he called 'tempo giusto', or 'natural tempo'. Performers could learn about these 'natural tempos' by 'diligent study of all kinds of dance pieces. Every dance piece has its definite tempo, determined by the meter and the note values that are employed in it'. In terms of dance choreography, Hilton (p. 266) sets forth a narrow tempo range for the dance types because of the physical limitations of dance style and technique.

**Other considerations.** Some decisions about tempo are made because of the location of the performance (whether in a large church or a small salon), the function of the piece (whether part of a church service or to accompany dancers), and the instruments used. In vocal music the nature of the text obviously plays a part in determining the tempo.                                              NJ, MEL

D. Franklin, 'The Fermata as a Notational Convention in the Music of J. S. Bach', W. J. Allanbrook, J. M. Levy, and W. P. Mahrt, eds., *Convention in Eighteenth- and Nineteenth-century Music: Essays in Honor of Leonard G. Ratner* (New York, 1992), 345–81; W. Hilton, *Dance of Court and Theater: The French Noble Style, 1690–1725* (Princeton, 1981); G. Houle, *Meter in Music, 1600–1800* (Bloomington and Indianapolis, 1987); J. P. Kirnberger, *The Art of Strict Musical Composition*, Eng. trans. D. Beach and J. Thym (New Haven, 1982); M. Little and N. Jenne, *Dance and the Music of J. S. Bach* (Bloomington and Indianapolis, 1991); R. Marshall, 'Tempo and Dynamics: The Original Terminology', in *The Music of Johann Sebastian Bach: The Sources, the Style, the Significance* (New York, 1989), 255–69; J. J. Quantz, *On Playing the Flute*, Eng. trans. E. Reilly (New York, 1966); P. Williams, 'Two Case Studies in Performance Practice and the Details of Notation, 1: J. S. Bach and 2/4 Time', *Early Music*, 21 (1993), 613–22.

***tempus clausum*** ('closed season'). A Latin term used for penitential seasons in the CHURCH CALENDAR during which figural music (i.e. cantatas) was not permitted in church. In Bach's time in Leipzig the six Sundays in Lent were a *tempus clausum*, as also were the second, third, and fourth Sundays in Advent.

**Terry, Charles Sanford** (b. 24 Oct. 1864; d. 5 Nov. 1936). Historian and writer, born in Newport Pagnell, Buckinghamshire. He studied history at Cambridge University and taught the subject at Newcastle upon Tyne and then at Aberdeen, where he was made professor in 1903. He retired in 1930. He cultivated music, and particularly Bach's music, first as a sideline but with increasing seriousness from about 1915, when he published a short book on the B minor Mass. His Bach biography of 1928 incorporated the fruits of much personal research, while his monograph on Johann Christian Bach (1929) was of pioneering importance. Of his other Bach publications the most

influential have been *Bach's Orchestra* (1932) and his edition of the four-part chorales (1929).

**Thomaskirche** (St Thomas's Church). In Bach's time, the second church in Leipzig after the Nikolaikirche. It was built in the late 14th and the 15th centuries on the site of an earlier church dating from 1150, and was consecrated in 1496. It was in the Thomaskirche that the Bach family worshipped, and it was at its elaborate stone and marble font, constructed in 1614–15, that 12 of Bach's 20 children were baptized.

**Thomasschule** (St Thomas's School). A school situated in Leipzig on the western side of the Thomaskirchhof, next to the Thomaskirche. It was founded as an Augustinian convent in the early years of the 13th century. After the Reformation it was taken over by the city council as a LATEINSCHULE, and was extended and reconstructed in 1553 and again in 1732, when Bach celebrated its reopening with the cantata (now lost) *Froher Tag, verlangte Stunden*. As Kantor, Bach came third in the school hierarchy, after the Rector and Conrector. He and his household occupied part of the Thomasschule on three floors for about 27 years. The building was demolished in 1902.

**Thuringia.** An area of central Germany which includes the Harz mountains and the Thuringian forest, and which extends from Arenshausen in the west to Gera and beyond in the east. It was the cradle of Lutheranism. *See also* ARNSTADT, EISENACH, MÜHLHAUSEN, and WEIMAR.

***tief-Cammerton.*** *See* CAMMERTON.

**Tilford Bach Society.** A society founded in 1952 in Tilford, Surrey, by Denis Darlow. Its amateur choir and professional orchestra were formed to promote Bach's choral works, including the cantatas, but the society has also performed and commissioned new pieces. Since 1973 the choir and orchestra have participated in an annual Bach in London Festival which has included liturgical performances of the *St Matthew Passion*.

***Tilge, Höchster, meine Sünden*** ('Take away my sins, O most high'). A parody, BWV1083/243a, of Pergolesi's *Stabat mater*, set to a German paraphrase of Psalm 51. *See* PERGOLESI, GIOVANNI BATTISTA.

**timpani.** The standard Italian term for 'kettledrums'; the German word is 'Pauken'. The theorist Sebastian Virdung illustrated the kettledrum in his *Musica getutscht* (Basle, 1511) as a military instrument with a screw mechanism, but it took a long time for the instrument to be admitted to art music as the bass partner of the trumpets, with its own part written in the score. It is known that trumpets and drums were used in sacred music in

Schwach del 1780.

*Tomas Pforte . II .*

*Stadt von Leipzig*

The Thomaskirche and, to the right, the Thomasschule, Leipzig; 18th-century engraving (Stadtgeschichtliches Museum, Leipzig)

the 17th century by composers such as Michael Praetorius (?1571–1621) and Heinrich Schütz (1585–1672), but no separate timpani parts from the period survive.

Most of Bach's timpani parts use the old-fashioned collective term 'tamburi'. He included them in large orchestras appropriate to major Church festivals, weddings, council elections, feasts, homages, and university ceremonies. There is always a pair of drums, tuned to the tonic and dominant, usually a 4th apart, notated in the bass clef, and sounding either as written or transposed. Timpani can serve to underpin the horns as well as the trumpets, although there are many works with two horns but no supporting drums. There are a few instances of rolls notated as trills (for example, at bar 5 of the opening section of the *Christmas Oratorio*), but not before the 'final cadence', where theorists stipulate their use.     UP

J. E. Altenburg, *Versuch einer Anleitung zur heroisch-musikalischen Trompeter- und Pauker-Kunst* (Halle, 1795; repr. Amsterdam, 1966); U. Prinz, *Studien zum Instrumentarium J. S. Bachs mit besonderer Berücksichtigung der Kantaten* (Tübingen, 1979), 217–36; C. S. Terry, *Bach's Orchestra* (London, 1932), 50–61.

**Tischer, Johann Nikolaus** (b. 1707; d. 3 May 1774). Composer and instrumentalist, born in Böhlen, about 15 km. (10 miles) south of Leipzig. He travelled widely throughout Germany in his youth, studying with Bach in Leipzig in 1726, and in 1728 was appointed regimental oboist and violinist to Duke August Wilhelm of Brunswick. Three years later he was made town organist at Schmalkalden and shortly afterwards *Konzertmeister* to the Duke of Saxe-Coburg-Meiningen. Before 1732 he wrote mainly church music, after that date mainly works for keyboard and for instrumental and orchestral forces.

**toccata.** Any of several types of solo keyboard composition from the late Renaissance and the Baroque, all originating in or inspired by improvisation, usually displaying aspects of what is known as the STYLUS FANTASTICUS. Bach composed three or four *pedaliter* organ works usually designated toccatas, as well as seven *manualiter* toccatas (BWV910–16); the first movement of Partita no. 6 in E minor is also designated a toccata.

Except for this partita movement, which dates from as late as 1725, the *manualiter* toccatas are early works, close in style and design to pieces by Dietrich Buxtehude, J. A. Reincken, and other north German organist-composers. None of the works is precisely datable, but an early version of the Toccata in D major BWV912 is found in a manuscript copy by Bach's elder brother Johann Christoph of around 1707, and the other works were probably composed by 1714.

Unlike other familiar sets of Bach keyboard works, the toccatas were never put into a coherent series of numbered pieces organized by key. A few manuscript copies survive in the hands of Bach pupils, who do not appear, however, to have studied the pieces systematically. Instead the works were handed down individually, like the preludes and fugues for organ, which they resemble. It is possible that the sections of some of the toccatas were composed separately and brought together later; the fugue of the E minor toccata survives alone in some manuscript copies and was apparently modelled on an anonymous fugue known from an early 18th-century Italian manuscript, with which it shares its subject and several subsequent passages.

The forms of the toccatas resemble the through-composed sectional designs of many 17th-century instrumental sonatas, of which they are the keyboard equivalents. Except for the G major Toccata, whose three-movement design is superficially comparable to that of a concerto, each work opens with a section in improvisatory style. One or more fugues follow, usually after an intervening Adagio or Allegro. The Adagios include florid written-out melodic embellishment; the Allegros contain suggestions of ritornello form (as does the opening Allegro of the G major Toccata). Both elements are characteristic of early 18th-century Italian style, but the fugues are firmly in the German keyboard tradition, emphasizing expressive or virtuoso effects rather than strict counterpoint *per se*. Only in the G minor Toccata is there a hint of recurring material—a brief flourish from the opening that returns at the end.

The organization of the Toccata from the E minor Partita follows different principles, but it refers to the traditional design through arpeggiated figuration in its outer sections and a fugue at the centre.

The intended medium of the toccatas has been a subject of dispute. Robert Marshall has argued that the term 'manualiter', found in the manuscript copies of some of the pieces, was used in opposition to 'pedaliter' and therefore implies use of the organ. If so, these works might have been played in church as parts of organ recitals, public harpsichord recitals being almost, if not entirely, unknown in the 18th century. Marshall's argument, however, has been countered by assertions of the specifically harpsichord-orientated style of the *manualiter* toccatas.

The free opening sections of the *manualiter* toccatas imitate many aspects of the *pedaliter* organ toccata and praeludium. But in 18th-century manuscripts the works sometimes appear alongside both *pedaliter* organ pieces and suites for the harpsichord, which remains at the very least a plausible medium for the seven early pieces and is explicitly demanded in the partita. *See also* PRELUDE AND FUGUE DS.

R. Marshall, 'Organ or "Klavier"? Instrumental Prescriptions in the Sources of the Keyboard Works', in *The Music of Johann Sebastian Bach: The Sources, the Style, the Significance* (New York, 1986), 271–93; R. Marshall, 'Johann Sebastian Bach', in *Eighteenth-Century Keyboard Music* (New York, 1994), 73–86; G. Pestelli, 'Bach, Handel, D. Scarlatti and the Toccata of the Late Baroque', in P. Williams, ed., *Bach, Handel, Scarlatti: Tercentenary Essays* (Cambridge, 1985), 277–91; D. Schulenberg, *The Keyboard Music of J. S. Bach* (New York, 1992), 74–89.

***Tönet, ihr Pauken! Erschallet, Trompeten!*** ('Sound, ye drums! Ring out, ye trumpets!'). Secular cantata, BWV214, celebrating the birthday of the Electress Maria Josepha of Saxony, performed for the first time in Leipzig on 8 December 1733, probably at Gottfried Zimmermann's coffee-house.

The autograph score is headed 'Drama p[er] Musica', but a dramatic character is much less in evidence than in other works of this kind. Four figures appear: Irene ('Peace', tenor), Bellona ('Art of War', soprano), Pallas (alto), and Fama (bass). Irene sings only a recitative (after the opening chorus); the other three have an aria and a recitative each, so that a chain of recitatives and arias is formed until Fama's recitative leads to the final chorus. The contributions of the four characters are not related dramatically, but merely form a sequence of movements. It is only in the final chorus that the four 'meet': Irene, Bellona, and Pallas begin the musical units with soloistic phrases, and when Fama enters the tutti section is reached.

Today most of the movements (excluding the recitatives) are better known as parodies in the CHRISTMAS ORATORIO, composed a year later. In the cantata the text of the opening movement is directly expressed in the instrumentation (drums and trumpets; the continuation mentions the string instruments as well). This close correspondence between text and instrumentation is inevitably lost at the beginning of the *Christmas Oratorio*, where the musical layout is heard only as a general opening gesture, without any specific allusion to the text that is sung when the voices enter. Pallas's aria, 'Fromme Musen! meine Glieder!', accompanied by a solo oboe d'amore, was parodied in the oratorio as 'Frohe Hirten, eilt, ach eilet' (for tenor, with solo flute), and Fama's aria, 'Kron und Preis gekrönter Damen', became 'Großer Herr, o starker König'. Only Bellona's aria found no place in the *Christmas Oratorio*. Perhaps this was because of the extravagant, mod-

ern, and almost *galant* character of the music, with its prominent syncopations and accompaniment of two obbligato flutes. Its omission might suggest that Bach did not (as has sometimes been asserted) compose the cantata with the idea already in his mind of transferring the movements to a sacred work. Bellona's aria suggests that the idea of parodying other movements came later, and that the cantata was planned and composed independently. KK

For bibliography, *see* CANTATA, §2.

**Torelli, Giuseppe** (b. 22 April 1658; d. 8 Feb. 1709). Italian composer and violinist, born in Verona. He remained there until 1681, and then went to Bologna, where he died. For a short time in 1698–9 he was active at the court of the Margrave of Brandenburg-Ansbach, where his *Concerti musicali* op. 6 were published. He published in all eight collections of instrumental music; many other works (sinfonias, concertos, sonatas, etc.) remain in manuscript.

Torelli was the probable author of a violin concerto in D minor which Bach transcribed for harpsichord (BWV979, in B minor) at Weimar in about 1714. Torelli's name appears on a manuscript of the original version discovered in 1958 in the Österreichische Nationalbibliothek, Vienna, by the Belgian musicologist Albert vander Linden. In 1967 the Swedish scholar Peter Ryom came across a manuscript of the same work, bearing the name of Antonio Vivaldi, in the collection of Christian Wenster of Lund. On stylistic grounds the attribution to Torelli seems to be the correct one, and this is supported by the concerto's four-movement structure: [Adagio]; Allegro–Adagio–Allegro–Adagio; Andante–Adagio; and Allegro. AB

J.-C. Zehnder, 'Giuseppe Torelli und Johann Sebastian Bach: zu Bachs Weimarer Konzertform', *BJb* 77 (1991), 33–95, esp. 79–81.

**Transchel, Christoph** (b. 12 June 1721; d. 8 Jan. 1800). Keyboard teacher, born in Braunsdorf, near Weißenfels, Sachsen-Anhalt. He entered the Gymnasium at Merseburg in 1731 and enrolled as a student of philosophy and theology at Leipzig University in 1742. He also studied with Bach, and in 1755 established himself as a keyboard teacher in Dresden, where he died.

**transcriptions.** *See* ARRANGEMENTS.

**'Trauermusik'** ('mourning music'). A title sometimes used for the cantata FALSCHE WELT, DIR TRAU ICH NICHT.

***Trauer Ode*** (Mourning Ode). Cantata, BWV198, on the death of Christiane Eberhardine, Electress of Saxony, beginning 'Laß, Fürstin, laß noch einen Strahl'. When Christiane Eberhardine died, on 5

# Trauer Ode

September 1727, the state mourned no ordinary queen. For when, in the closing years of the previous century, her husband, Augustus the Strong, had converted to Catholicism in order to gain the throne of Poland, she remained true to the indigenous Lutheran faith, something which won her the hearts of all Saxony. An enterprising noble student, Hans Carl von Kirchbach (1704–57), commissioned two of the most eminent men in Leipzig, the poet J. C. Gottsched and the Kantor and composer J. S. Bach, to write an ode of mourning.

The occasion was not without its problems: the performance was to take place in the university church (the Paulinerkirche), and the director of music there, J. G. Görner, complained of the infringement of his prerogative. Kirchbach refused to change the terms of his commission and Bach refused to sign a document stating that his activity in the Paulinerkirche was 'purely a favour and not to set any precedent'. In the event Bach finished the score on 15 October 1727 (according to his inscription on the autograph) and the performance went smoothly on 17 October, attended by many important town and university officials. According to a report in C. E. Sicul's *Das thränende Leipzig*, 'there was shortly to be heard the mourning music which Kapellmeister Johann Sebastian Bach had composed in Italian style, with harpsichord, which Herr Bach himself played, organ, violas di gamba, lutes, violins, recorders, flutes, etc., half sounding before, half after the oration of praise and mourning'.

Gottsched was not only a notable poet in the locality of Leipzig, he was one of the greatest reformers of the German language of all time, someone of seminal influence in establishing German as a respectable literary language. His ode consisted of nine stanzas, each with eight lines, all symmetrically balanced and ordered with an ear to the sounding and sequence of syllables. Bach's choice of what was observed as 'Italian style'—i.e. a sequence of choruses, arias, and recitatives—patently ignored the ode structure of Gottsched; furthermore, the stanzas were spread over the divisions of the musical movements. This, and the fact that Bach apparently changed some of the words themselves to create a more pictorial text, shows clearly that the composer was thinking entirely of the musical potentialities of the text; he showed no respect for the literary style *per se* and, indeed, probably had little conception of Gottsched's importance as a poet.

As Sicul's report on the occasion mentioned, Bach employed an unusual instrumentarium for the *Trauer Ode*: the viols are typical in Bach's settings of mournful texts—they are included, for example, in the *Actus tragicus* and the two Passions—but it is highly unusual to find him employing two lutes as well. Joshua Rifkin has outlined some of the problems concerning the scoring of this work that arise, given that Sicul's report and Bach's autograph do not fully agree, the performance took place outside Bach's usual venues, and the original parts are missing.

While he ignored much of the structural integrity of Gottsched's verses, Bach devised his own system in constructing the music: within the tripartite frame of choruses, the solo voices enter in turn (in descending order), each having a recitative and aria except the bass, who has a sequence of recitative–arioso–recitative. Each instrumental family is represented in the scoring of the arias. Bach included most of the idioms appropriate to the 'Italian style': the dense concerted texture of the opening movement, the accompanied recitative (nos. 2, 4, 6, and 9), the simple recitative at the beginning of no. 9, the astonishingly pictorial recitative depicting funeral bells (no. 4), the fugue which apparently depicts the queen as the 'example for great women' (no. 7), and the closing dance-like choral movement. This contains a rare example of the entire chorus singing in unison, at the lines 'Sie ist der Tugend Eigentum, Der Untertanen Lust und Ruhm' ('She has been virtue's property, Her loyal subjects' joy and fame'), clearly underlining the special status Christiane had earned herself. The first aria, 'Verstummt, ihr holden Saiten', calling for the silencing of the 'charming strings', contains the most energetic string writing in the piece, which breaks off when the soprano enters—a typically Bachian pun. The alto aria, 'Wie starb die Heldin so vergnügt', undoubtedly represents the heart of the piece with its obbligato of two gambas accompanied by two lutes.

The opening chorus echoes the final chorus of the *St Matthew Passion*, which Bach had performed for the first time earlier the same year; indeed, he reused this and movement 7 in a cantata mourning the death of Leopold I of Cöthen in 1729—a piece which was essentially a contrafactum of parts of the *St Matthew Passion*. Most of the arias and choruses of the *Trauer Ode* he reused in the ST MARK PASSION, something which confirms the Passion-like nature of the *Ode*, which should perhaps be appreciated on equal terms with the two surviving Passions.　　　JAB

L. Dreyfus, 'Bach as Critic of Enlightenment', in *Bach and the Patterns of Invention* (Cambridge, Mass., 1996), 219–44; J. Rifkin, 'Some Questions of Performance in J. S. Bach's Trauerode', D. Melamed, ed., *Bach Studies 2* (Cambridge, 1995), 119–53; A. Schneiderheinze, 'Über Bachs Umgang mit Gottscheds Versen', in W. Felix, W. Hoffmann and A. Schneiderheinze, eds., *Bericht über die Wissenschaft-*

liche *Konferenz zum III. Internationalen Bach-Fest der DDR, Leipzig, 18./19. September 1975* (Leipzig, 1977), 91–8.

***traversa, traversière*** ('transverse'). Terms (the first Italian, the second French) used for the transverse FLUTE to distinguish it from the downward-held recorder.

**Treiber.** Family of writers and musicians centred in Arnstadt and friendly with the Bach family there. Johann Philipp Treiber (b. 26 Feb. 1675; d. 9 Aug. 1727), a scholar, writer, and composer, studied music with Adam Drese and in 1704 published a manual on thorough-bass, *Der accurate Organist*. He was probably the composer of the four-act opera *Die Klugheit der Obrigkeit in Anordnung des Bierbrauens* ('The Wisdom of the Authorities in the Regulation of Brewing Ale'), at one time thought to be the work of Bach. The music is lost; the words were by Treiber's father, Johann Friedrich (b. 21 Aug. 1642; d. 15 April 1719), who has also been credited with the text of the wedding quodlibet BWV524. This, however, may have been a collaborative compilation.

**Trier, Johann** (b. 2 Sept. 1716; bur. 6 Jan. 1790). Organist and composer, born in Themar, about 12 km. (7½ miles) south-east of Meiningen in Thuringia. He studied theology at Leipzig University, and was probably Bach's pupil, during the early 1740s. By May 1746 he took over the direction of the collegium musicum that Bach had directed in the city, and in 1750 he applied unsuccessfully to succeed Bach as Thomaskantor. Four years later he was appointed organist and *director musices* at the Johanniskirche in Zittau, where he remained until his death. His works include keyboard music and two *Jahrgänge* of church cantatas.

**trio sonata.** The type of instrumental sonata most widely cultivated during the Baroque period, using a texture of three independent musical strands and calling usually for four players. The most common combination was one of two violins and continuo (usually a string bass and a keyboard instrument), as in the trio sonatas opp. 1–4 by Corelli. Bach wrote only one trio sonata of this type, that for flute, violin, and continuo in the MUSICAL OFFERING, but the term 'trio sonata' might be (and has been) applied to the sonatas for flute, violin, and bass viol with obbligato harpsichord, in which the second melody line is taken by the keyboard player's right hand, and to the Organ Sonatas, where all three parts are taken by one player. *See also* GAMBA SONATAS, FLUTE SONATAS AND PARTITA, ORGAN SONATAS, and VIOLIN SONATAS.

***Tritt auf die Glaubensbahn*** ('Walk in the path of faith'). Cantata for the Sunday after Christmas,

BWV152, first performed at Weimar on 30 December 1714. The text, by Salomo Franck, is one of several which present an allegorical dialogue between Jesus (bass) and the Soul (soprano). The subject of their discourse goes to the very heart of the Lutheran religion: faith, as the Rock of Ages which never fails and which will bring redemption and salvation. As in most of Bach's Weimar cantatas, the instrumental ensemble is on an intimate scale, consisting of recorder, oboe, viola d'amore, viola da gamba, and continuo.

The instruments are heard alone in the opening movement, consisting of a brief slow section (four bars) followed by a contrapuntal—indeed fugal—Allegro on a theme which bears more than a passing resemblance to that of the fugue in Bach's Prelude and Fugue in A major for organ BWV536. The shape of the movement as a whole is also indebted to some extent to organ music, for example in the way that the bass instruments (behaving like organ pedals) are silent during a central episode before re-entering with the fugue subject. A feature of this cantata is that it includes no movements in da capo form. There is no going back along the path of faith, and the opening bass aria, with oboe obbligato, that calls on the Soul to tread that path fills its ritornello structure with purposeful music. The bass recitative that follows opens with a clear reference to a verse from the appointed Gospel reading (Luke 2: 33–40): 'Behold, this child is set for the fall and rising again of many in Israel.' Bach responds with one of his most famous passages of word-painting—a deep plunge to a low D♯ for 'Fall' and a return to the bass's normal tessitura for 'Auferstehen' ('resurrection'). This is not, however, the most remarkable feature of the recitative, which ends with a carefully worked-out arioso passage: 'Whoever builds his faith on this corner-stone will find redemption and salvation.'

The symbol of the corner-stone, or Rock of Ages, is taken up in the soprano aria 'Stein, der über alle Schätze', elaborately accompanied by flute, viola d'amore, and continuo; the word 'Stein' ('stone') occurs three times, and each time Bach sets it to a single, long-held note to suggest unwavering firmness. A no less telling, though perhaps subtler, example of word-painting occurs towards the end of the succeeding recitative where, in a reference to the blind leading the blind, Bach causes the bass soloist to stumble from one key to another. The final duet (there is no chorale) unites Jesus and the Soul (and, symbolically, the upper instruments in unison) in the path that leads through tribulation to the crown of life.

For bibliography, *see* CANTATA, §1.

***tromba; tromba da tirarsi*** ('trumpet'; 'slide trumpet'). *See* TRUMPET.

**trombone** (Posaune). A brass instrument existing in various sizes and pitches, used by Bach in his church music. The trombone already had a slide in the 15th century, and is thus the oldest brass instrument capable of playing the full chromatic range. Called the 'trombona' by Bach, it was one of the traditional members of the *Stadtpfeifer* ensemble, and as such was used to sound forth from towers as well as in church music. The Leipzig musicians usually had access to municipal instruments kept in the town hall tower. From inspection reports, as well as the clefs used in the parts, it is apparent that there were treble, alto, tenor, and bass instruments. Trombones by the Leipzig instrument maker J. H. Eichentopf survive.

In Bach's original parts from the Leipzig period trombone parts are notated in CHORTON, like the organ parts. Bach used trombones primarily in his first two years in Leipzig, especially in the annual cycle of chorale cantatas (1724–5); there they appear in motet movements in *stile antico* and in chorales, where vocal lines are supported by treble trombone (or cornett), alto, tenor, and bass trombones, and the effect of this sonority is archaic. Using them as an ensemble is the rule in about a dozen works; using a single trombone to support a vocal line is the exception, seen in Cantatas 3, 96, 133, and 135. UP

P. Bate, *The Trumpet and Trombone* (London, 1966; 2nd edn., 1978); R. Gregory, *The Trombone: The Instrument and its Music* (London, 1973); U. Prinz, *Studien zum Instrumentarium J. S. Bachs mit besonderer Berücksichtigung der Kantaten* (Tübingen, 1979), 196–216.

**trumpet.** There were at least four types of trumpet in Bach's day. The long trumpet, coiled just once, was mainly cylindrical: the mouthpipe, middle tube, and bell were straight sections connected by the U-shaped upper and lower bends, or 'bows'. The German slide trumpet (*Zugtrompete*) differed from the former only in that the mouthpipe could be lengthened by a slide (an extendable tube) to which the mouthpiece was attached: Bach called this the 'tromba da tirarsi'. The tubing of the circular coiled trumpet was the same diameter as that of the long trumpet, but was coiled several times, like a horn; an instrument made in 1697 by Heinrich Pfeiffer is of this type, as is the one shown in the well-known portrait of the Leipzig *Stadtpfeifer* Gottfried Reiche, which dates from 1727. The tubing of the double-coiled short trumpet was again the same diameter as that of the long trumpet, but it was easier to handle because it was more compact, like the circular instrument, and gave a more secure attack.

Nuremberg and Leipzig were the leading centres of brass instrument making. Reproductions of various types of historical trumpet are made nowadays, including some with overblow holes to allow even- or odd-numbered harmonics to be suppressed, and a transposition hole to shorten the vibrating column of air as a convenient means of correcting the 'impure' harmonics (7, 11, 13, and 14). It is important to note that so far not a single example of a trumpet with 'fingerholes' incontrovertibly dating from the Baroque era has been discovered!

In the Bach sources the instrument is most often called 'tromba', but in six cases the old registral designations 'clarino 1', 'clarino 2', and 'Principale' are used. These terms do not refer to instruments of different tuning or construction: at most they indicate small differences in the bore. The Principale ranges approximately from the 3rd to the 8th harmonic, the clarino from the 8th harmonic upwards. Collating all the parts that Bach wrote for trumpet results in a range from the 3rd harmonic to the 20th, that is (assuming a fundamental of C) the pitches shown below.

If the notes played when Bach specifies trills (on the pitches shown in black in the example below) are included, one can appreciate the considerable demands that Bach made on his players, with respect to notes outside the natural harmonic series, exceptionally high notes, and trills. As *transitus*, or lower note of a mordent, Bach calls for notes that can be produced only by over- or underblowing. One notices a considerable increase in the demands Bach made on his players in the Leipzig compositions compared with those of the Mühlhausen period, particularly in third trumpets parts (in which the 12th harmonic is required frequently and exceeded in nine works), but also in second trumpet parts (which require the 15th and 16th harmonics in nearly 20 works)—a clear indication of the high standard of clarino playing among the Leipzig *Stadtpfeifer*.

This statement can only be made in the light of an objective correlation between the compass and the notes available to individual instruments or required in individual compositions; *Chorton*

serves here as the basis for such a correlation. The most favoured tuning, whether for a soloist or in a group, was the '*Chorton* C trumpet', followed by the B♭ trumpet; the early version of the *Magnificat* (BWV243*a*) is an exception. *Cammerton* notation is found in four works: the second Brandenburg Concerto in F, the orchestral suite no. 3 in D, and Cantatas 21 and 63 in C. Trumpet parts are usually notated to be transposed; parts sounding as written are also frequently encountered, with the appropriate key signature, but these occur mainly in the doubling of chorale melodies. These were intended to be performed on a slide trumpet—the *tromba da tirarsi*; the change in notation gave the player a clear indication of a change in musical function (and of instrument, too, if need be). On the other hand, the slide trumpet might also play a part written for the 'tromba' with a very slight adjustment of the slide, as the example of Cantata 77 demonstrates; this is notated at sounding pitch in movements 1 and 6, where the trumpet plays the cantus firmus, but it transposes in the trio section of the contralto aria (movement 5), where the trumpet part is obbligato.

For special occasions, such as major festivals in the Church calendar, council elections, homage cantatas, and university ceremonies, Bach augmented his orchestra with a choir of three trumpets together with their bass support, a pair of timpani which he calls 'tamburi'. Exceptions are the four trumpets required in Cantatas 63 and 119, and the two in Cantatas 59 and 175. Like his contemporaries, he always placed the music for this choir of trumpets and drums at the top of his scores. Is this perhaps a reflection of the social standing of the players? Trumpeters and drummers were, after all, members of an exclusive guild which jealously guarded its privileges and mandates. There was no royal household in Leipzig, but the Thomaskantors performed music with trumpets and drums quite often in the 17th and 18th centuries, and not only in church. So it is reasonable to assume that the trumpet-playing Leipzig *Stadtpfeifer*, who were paid by the city council and the churches and sometimes also held the post of watchman, insisted on an item in Article 10 of their extended charter of 1653: 'As far as concerns students and watchmen, however, these shall not play trumpets outside the churches and towers, and also at academic ceremonies and convocations, unless it is the case that no trumpeter is available *in loco*, or unless the authorities pay the watchmen as trumpeters too' (J. H. Zedler, *Universal-Lexicon*, xlv (Leipzig and Halle, 1745), col. 1126). UP

D. Altenburg, *Untersuchungen zur Geschichte der Trompete im Zeitalter der Clarinblaskunst 1500–1800* (Regensburg, 1973); J. E. Altenburg, *Versuch einer Anleitung zur heroisch-musikalischen Trompeter- und Pauker-Kunst* (Halle, 1795; repr. Amsterdam, 1966); G. and J. Csiba, *Die Blechblasinstrumente in J. S. Bachs Werken* (Kassel, 1994); D. L. Smithers, *The Music and History of the Baroque Trumpet before 1721* (London, 1973; 2nd edn., 1988); D. L. Smithers, 'Gottfried Reiches Ansehen und sein Einfluß auf die Musik J. S. Bachs', *BJb* 73 (1987), 114–50; D. L. Smithers, 'Kritische Anmerkungen zum gleichnamigen Aufsatz von Th. G. MacCracken', *BJb* 76 (1990), 37–51.

**Tue Rechnung! Donnerwort** ('Make a reckoning! Word of thunder'). Cantata for the ninth Sunday after Trinity, BWV168, first performed probably on 29 July 1725. The text, based on the parable of the unjust steward (Luke 16: 1–9), is by the Weimar court poet and librarian Salomo Franck. It is therefore possible that Bach first set it to music during his years as *Konzertmeister* at Weimar (1714–17) but, as pointed out in *DürrK*, the autograph score points clearly to a Leipzig origin for the work in the form in which it has come down to us. The vocal and instrumental forces required are also typical of the Leipzig norm: SATB, two oboes d'amore, strings, and continuo.

Less in keeping with Bach's normal Leipzig practice is the fact that none of the movements is in da capo form. The opening bass aria, a dramatic interpretation of the text with peremptory dotted rhythms in the strings and rumbling melismas for the singer's 'word of thunder', employs a structure in which only the opening ritornello is restated exactly. An eventful tenor recitative is accompanied by continuo and the two oboes d'amore, which then join together in unison for the succeeding tenor aria, 'Capital und Interessen'. This uses basically the same ritornello structure as the first aria. A simple recitative for the bass separates it from the duet for soprano and alto, 'Herz, zerreiß des Mammons Kette' ('Heart, break asunder Mammon's chains'—there is a long, interlocking melisma for 'Kette', of course), accompanied by continuo only. This takes the unusual form (in Bach's cantatas, at least) of a freely deployed ground bass; what is essentially a descending octave scale is repeated in the bass eight or nine times at various pitches, while the two voices, in contrast, constantly renew their matching of music to text.

The cantata ends with a straightforward four-part setting, with *colla parte* instrumental support, of the eighth strophe of the hymn *Herr Jesu Christ, du höchstes Gut* by Bartholomäus Ringwaldt (1688).

For bibliography, *see* CANTATA, §1.

**Tufen, Andreas Christoph.** *See* DUVE, ANDREAS CHRISTOPH.

**tunings.** *See* TEMPERAMENTS.

***turba*** ('crowd'). A Latin word used in the context of Baroque sacred music for a short chorus, especially in PASSION settings, in which a biblical passage is uttered by a group of people. Bach treats the *turbae* in his Passions with imagination and resource, but they are mostly of two basic types. First there are those set in a simple homophonic style, sometimes with insistent text repetition and often with busy instrumental support (in particular, much rushing about in semiquavers for the first violins and other high instruments); among many examples might be mentioned 'Jesum von Nazareth' (nos. 2*b* and 2*d*) in the *St John Passion* and 'Ja nicht auf das Fest' (no. 4*b*) in the *St Matthew*. The other main type, found especially when there is a point to be argued or a law (canon) to be enjoined, uses imitative counterpoint to stir up the tension, with *colla parte* support more or less in MOTET STYLE; examples include 'Wir haben ein Gesetz' ('We have a law', no. 21*f*) in the *St John Passion* and 'Herr, bin ich's?' (no. 9*e*) in the *St Matthew*. Sometimes both styles are employed in the same chorus, and at least one *turba* is of a totally different kind: in the *St Matthew Passion* Bach gives universal expression to the passage 'Truly this was the son of God' by setting it almost in chorale style for both choirs, despite its being uttered only by 'the centurion, and they that were with him'.

**Tureck, Rosalyn** (b. 14 Dec. 1914). American pianist and harpsichordist, born in Chicago. After studying with Sophia Brilliant-Liven and Jan Chiapusso, and at the Juilliard Graduate School from 1931 to 1935, she made her name as a pianist, specializing above all in the music of Bach. She has toured widely and recorded all Bach's major keyboard works on both the piano and the harpsichord. She has also published editions, articles, and books, including *Performance of Bach* (1959) and *Authenticity: A Monograph* (1994), and has been awarded doctorates by four American universities and by Oxford University.

In 1966 she founded the Tureck Bach Institute, with its headquarters in New York, and in 1995 she established in Oxford the Tureck Bach Research Foundation, which sponsors an annual Bach symposium and publishes the proceedings in a journal, *Interaction*, first issued in 1997. *See also* RECORDINGS.

# U

**Unser Mund sei voll Lachens** ('Then was our mouth filled with laughter'). Cantata for Christmas Day, BWV110, first performed on 25 December 1725. The libretto is from Georg Christian Lehms's *Gottgefälliges Kirchen Opffer* (1711) and is the only item from the 'morning cycle' from this collection which Bach is known to have set. The date 1725, which was established on the basis of paper studies in the 1950s, invalidates Arnold Schering's conjecture that the cantata was composed for the end of the War of the Polish Succession in 1734. Lehms's text, which praises God for the Incarnation, takes the form of alternating Bible verses and arias, with a closing chorale strophe. BWV110 has also become famous for its connection with the Orchestral Suite no. 4: the French overture from the suite appears (with added text) as the opening chorus of the cantata. The link between the two works poses some musicological problems, for although it cannot be doubted that the instrumental version came first, alterations to the trumpet parts in the autograph score of BWV110 show that they were composed especially for the cantata itself. It is therefore believed that the suite may once have existed in an earlier version, pre-dating 1725, which lacked the trumpet and drum parts found in the version we know today. The cantata is scored for SATB with three trumpets, drums, three oboes, strings, and continuo. Bach revived it at least once, some time in the period 1728–31.

The enormous first movement can be considered as the centre of gravity of the whole work. Bach performed the task of adapting the overture for voices by leaving the opening section untexted and delaying the chorus entries until the lively middle section (which is more appropriate to the sentiments of Psalm 126: 2–3). The voice parts have 'con ripieni' and 'senza ripieni' markings in Bach's hand, which were, however, probably added for a later revival, thus limiting their relevance to controversies concerning 'one-to-a-part' performance of Bach's sacred vocal music (*see* CHORUS). The long central section, which is mainly developed from the opening triplet motif, contains reduced episodes, one for the three upper voices and one for bass (marked 'senza ripieni' in both cases), with lighter instrumental scoring. The main tempo returns with the tonic cadence at bar 169, at which point the voices drop out and the coda is scored for the instruments alone.

The second movement, 'Ihr Gedanken und ihr Sinnen' ('Ye thoughts and senses'), is an aria for tenor with two flutes and continuo (including a bassoon part marked 'piano sempre'). The poet's invitation to his thoughts and feelings to leave earthly concerns and rise to the contemplation of heavenly things is depicted by the rising flute figures which dominate much of the ritornello. There follows a brief accompanied bass recitative which leads to the second aria, 'Ach, Herr, was ist ein Menschenkind', scored for tenor with obbligato oboe d'amore. The design of the aria is straightforward, with a single medial entry of the ritornello in the dominant (C♯ minor), but it poses problems of the rhythmic alignment of dotted rhythms, semiquavers, and triplets which are only too familiar to students of Baroque performance practice. The Bible returns with the fifth movement, a setting for soprano and tenor of the angelic greeting to the shepherds from St Luke 2: 14, 'Glory to God in the highest', which makes an interesting comparison with the better-known setting of the same text in the *Christmas Oratorio*. In the cantata the sections of the text are marked off by an instrumental ritornello which defines the principal tonal centres (A major–E major–F♯ minor–A major) and underpins much of the vocal writing, in which imitation and close canon predominate. Next comes the last of the three arias, 'Wacht auf, ihr Adern und ihr Glieder', scored for bass with accompanying strings and woodwind, in addition to a solo trumpet part. The aria, in an extended modified da capo structure, is heroic in style, anticipating 'Großer Herr und starker König' from Part I of the *Christmas Oratorio*, with its opening fanfare and florid continuation. The final harmonized chorale, the last strophe of Kaspar Füger's *Wir Christenleut habn jetzund Freud* (1592), is set in plain style.                DLH

For bibliography, *see* CANTATA, §1.

**Ursprung der musicalisch-Bachischen Familie** ('Origin of the musical Bach family'). *See* GENEALOGY.

# V

**variations.** The principle of variation plays an important role in Bach's music, particularly that of his earliest and latest periods. To the early period belong the *Partite diverse* BWV766–8 and 770—chorale variations written partly under the influence of Georg Böhm—and the *Aria variata* BWV989, whose subtitle, 'all[a] man[iera] Italiana', indicates Italian influence. In addition, the young Bach, following the example of Buxtehude and others, used 17th-century techniques of thematic variation in the Prelude and Fugue in E major BWV566 and the Canzona in D minor BWV588 for organ, and explored the principle of continuous variations over an ostinato bass in the well-known Passacaglia in C minor, in the Prélude to the keyboard Suite in F minor BWV823, and in several early cantatas (BWV12:2, 18:1, and 150:7).

No variation sets survive from Bach's middle years, apart from the unfinished Air and Variations BWV991, of which there is a sketch in Anna Magdalena's *Clavierbüchlein* of 1722. The DOUBLE, or dance variation, is present in several suites and explored systematically in Partita no. 1 for unaccompanied violin (1720), and the *basso ostinato* or ground bass type in the famous Chaconne from the Second Partita in the same set, and also in the opening chorus of Cantata 78.

The Goldberg Variations from Bach's later years (1741) form the *ne plus ultra* of the typically Baroque type built around a constant harmonic framework. Canonic variation, employed in every third movement of this work, is explored further in the set for organ on *Vom Himmel hoch* (BWV769) and in the 14 canons that Bach added to his *Handexemplar* of the Goldberg Variations in about 1747–8, as well as in the *Musical Offering* and *The Art of Fugue*. Thematic variation in a fugal context—an underlying principle of *The Art of Fugue*—is foreshadowed in the above-mentioned Prelude and Fugue in E major and Canzona in D minor and in the mature Fugue in E♭ major from *Clavier-Übung III* (1739). A further link between the early and late periods is the reworking of the chaconne 'Weinen, Klagen' from Cantata 12 (1714) as 'Crucifixus etiam pro nobis' in the Mass in B minor (1748–9).          RDPJ

*See also* CANONIC VARIATIONS, CHORALE VARIATIONS, GOLDBERG VARIATIONS, and PASSACAGLIA.

**Vereinigte Zwietracht der wechselnden Saiten** ('United discords of quivering strings'). Secu-lar cantata, BWV207, composed for the installation of Gottlieb Kortte as professor of jurisprudence at Leipzig University on 11 December 1726. Kortte, a young and much respected academic, was born on 27 February 1698 in Beeskow, about 60 km. (38 miles) south-east of Berlin. He took his doctorate at Frankfurt an der Oder in 1724, and was only 28 at the time of his installation in Leipzig, playing the part of the absent-minded professor by leaving the script of his inaugural address at home and having to present it from memory. The libretto of Bach's cantata, by an unknown author, is described as a *dramma per musica*, but there is precious little drama in it. Fleiß ('Industry', tenor), Ehre ('Honour', bass), and Glück ('Happiness', soprano) take it in turns to pay homage to the new don, and Dankbarkeit ('Gratitude', alto) approves of their efforts, adding its own tribute.

The opening chorus is familiar as the third movement of Brandenburg Concerto no. 1, but there are a number of differences. The key of the concerto movement is F major, that of the cantata chorus D major; the concerto includes parts for two horns, three oboes, and bassoon, the cantata has three trumpets, drums, two oboes d'amore, *taille* (oboe da caccia), and flutes doubling the oboes; the music of the solo violino piccolo in the concerto is allotted to the chorus in the cantata; and the cantata chorus is four bars longer than the concerto movement. Brandenburg Concerto no. 1, dating at the latest from 1721, is earlier than Cantata 207 by at least five years and nine months, and the cantata version has often been praised as one of Bach's most successful parodies. But there are reasons for thinking that both the concerto and the cantata may have been adapted from a still earlier model, possibly from one of the lost Cöthen cantatas.

Whatever the truth of this, the chorus makes a festive opening for this celebratory cantata. It is in modified da capo form (a structure associated more with vocal music than with the concerto), and Bach employs this form for the first tenor aria as well. Some of the melismas here are attached to relatively unimportant words, further suggesting an earlier origin for the music. The remaining lyrical items (a duet, a second aria, and a final chorus) are all in full da capo form, the end of the duet being attached to an independent 'ritornello' which again is found in Brandenburg Concerto no. 1, differently scored as the final trio of the

Menuet. Noteworthy in Gratitude's aria 'Ätzet dieses Angedenken' ('Engrave this reminder', no. 7) is the repetitive dotted rhythms of the unison violins and viola, suggesting the hammer chipping away at the 'hard marble'; clearly this aria was either composed afresh or adapted from one with a similar text.

Unfortunately, Gottlieb Kortte did not survive to enjoy the years of retirement that Happiness had promised him in the final recitative (no. 8) of the cantata. He died in Leipzig less than five years later, on 7 April 1731, at the age of 33. A few years after this Bach reused the music, composing afresh all the recitatives except the final *accompagnato* (no. 8), in a homage cantata, *Auf, schmetternde Töne der muntern Trompeten* (BWV207a), for the nameday of King Augustus III, Elector of Saxony. The author of the new text is again unknown. A possible date for the performance of this version is 3 August 1735, and it was probably on this occasion that a March, included with the original material of the cantata, was performed at some point in the ceremony.

For bibliography, *see* CANTATA, §2.

***Vergnügte Ruh, beliebte Seelenlust*** ('Delightful repose, favoured longing of the soul'). Cantata for the sixth Sunday after Trinity, BWV170, first performed on 28 July 1726. It is the second of Bach's four cantatas for solo alto and the first of the three he composed in 1726 incorporating movements with obbligato organ. Unlike the two later ones (nos. 35 and 169), it has no opening instrumental sinfonia. It would have required a second keyboard instrument to furnish the continuo realization, and it was possibly in order to avoid this complication that Bach reassigned the obbligato part in the last movement to the flute when the work was repeated in 1746 or 1747.

The text, by G. C. Lehms, had been published in 1711; it has been described as particularly appropriate to a cantata performed during Communion. Indeed, Bach appears to have performed the cantata *Ich will mein Geist in euch geben* by Johann Ludwig Bach of Meiningen on the same day in 1726. This was presumably heard before the sermon, the present work during Communion (*see* HAUPTGOTTESDIENST).

All three arias are dominated by their opening ritornellos, the alto part being composed largely through VOKALEINBAU, that is, as free counterpoint to the previously heard instrumental material; this is especially true of the last two arias. The opening movement is a D major aria in modified da capo form, scored for strings with oboe d'amore doubling the first violin. The theme of spiritual peace, cited at the outset of the text, is represented by the gentle, slurred repeated quavers of the strings (an indication for 'bow vibrato'). But the chromaticism that enters during the last part of the ritornello reflects the references to sin and bodily weakness in lines 2–4.

These concerns dominate the ensuing recitative and aria, which move to the distant 'sharp' domain of F♯ minor. The aria, 'Wie jammern mich doch die verkehrten Herzen', is scored for organ without continuo, the bass line being taken by violins and viola in unison; the device here represents fear or uncertainty. Except in a few brief passages where the organ is silent, this could almost be a movement from an organ trio sonata; the two hands, playing on separate manuals, move within the upper register, engaging in numerous voice-crossings and exchanges of material. The ritornello, moreover, takes the form of a fugal exposition that recurs, through the use of *Vokaleinbau*, in each of the three main vocal sections. The twisting, chromatic subject, which is confined to the organ, reflects the opening text ('how the sinful hearts lament'). Twice, however, it gives way to running diatonic figuration, in which the voice joins. Bach ingeniously disposes the text so that the livelier music falls first on the mention of 'Rach und Haß' ('vengeance and hatred') in line 4, then in the middle section on the words 'frech verlacht' ('impudently deride'). Moreover, by reusing the imitated music for the final vocal section, Bach assimilates Lehms's text, with its brief one-line da capo, to a complete (if modified) musical da capo form.

An accompanied recitative leads back to D major for the final movement, a da capo aria whose text expresses 'disgust' with life ('Mir ekelt mehr zu leben'). This rather extreme sentiment is represented by the tritone that opens the ritornello, but the mood is happy, with playful echoes and lively figuration for the solo instrument.

DS

G. Stiller, ' "Mir ekelt mehr zu leben": zur Textdeutung der Kantate "Vergnügte Ruh, beliebte Seelenlust" (BWV 170) von Johann Sebastian Bach', in W. Rehm, ed., *Bachiana et alia musicologica: Festschrift Alfred Dürr zum 65. Geburtstag* (Kassel, 1983), 293–300. For further bibliography, *see* CANTATA, §1.

**Vespers.** Lutheran Vespers was an early afternoon service, a revised form of the pre-Reformation office of Vespers with the addition of congregational hymnody and preaching. On the eves of special days, and on the afternoons of Sundays and major feasts, Vespers was expanded to include additional material, such as extended prayer, teaching of the catechism, and special music. These services were variously known as *Betstunde* ('Prayer Hour'), *Katechismusexamen* ('Catechism Teaching'), *Vesperpredigt* ('Vesper

# viol, viola da gamba

Sermon'), *Vespergottesdienst* ('Vesper Worship'), etc.

Lutheran Vespers had a considerable musical content, in which traditional plainchant continued to play a part. From the 16th century the Latin *Magnificat* was sung by choirs throughout the year at Lutheran Vespers in all eight psalm tones. The ninth tone, the *tonus peregrinus*, was reserved for the German *Magnificat*, 'Meine Seel erhebt den Herren', which was sung congregationally. Bach used this congregational *Magnificat* melody in a number of works, including the cantata *Meine Seel erhebt den Herren* and the *Fuga sopra il Magnificat* for organ BWV733. By the 18th century concerted *Magnificat* settings had become the norm for festivals and special occasions, Bach's festive *Magnificat*, with trumpets and timpani, being the most notable example.

In Leipzig during Bach's time it was customary to include a cantata at Sunday Vespers in an alternating practice: the cantata that had been sung in the morning in one of the two principal churches (the Thomaskirche or the Nikolaikirche) was repeated in the other church at Vespers. Leipzig Vespers had the following structure:

> Organ Prelude
> Motet
> Cantata
> Hymn
> Pulpit Hymn
> Sermon
> Intercessions and announcements
> Magnificat
> Collect
> Benediction
> Hymn
> Organ Postlude

On Good Fridays Vespers were arranged differently to incorporate a musical setting of the PASSION story.                                                    RAL

R. A. Leaver, 'Lutheran Vespers as a Context for Music', in P. Walker, ed., *Church, Stage, and Studio: Music and its Contexts in Seventeenth-Century Germany* (Ann Arbor, 1990), 143–61; G. Stiller, *Johann Sebastian Bach and Liturgical Life in Leipzig*, Eng. trans. H. J. A. Bouman, D. F. Poellet, and H. C. Oswald, ed. R. A. Leaver (St Louis, Miss., 1984); C. S. Terry, *Joh. Seb. Bach: Cantata Texts, Sacred and Secular, with a Reconstruction of the Leipzig Liturgy of his Period* (London, 1926).

**viol, viola da gamba.** A family of string instruments, built in various sizes in the 16th century, with a fingerboard which narrowed towards the top, a mostly flat back sloping towards the neck, ribs flush with the belly and back, C-shaped soundholes and a rosette on the belly, and often a carved head rather than a scroll. It had six strings tuned in 4ths with a 3rd midway, and seven chromatically ordered frets (according to Praetorius's *Syntagma musicum*, 1619). The addition of a seventh string (*AA*) is variously ascribed to Marin Marais (1656–1728) and Sainte-Colombe (d. *c*.1696).

Bach wrote for both the six-string instrument and the seven-string tenor-bass gamba, tuned to *AA*, *D*, *G*, *c*, *e*, *a*, and *d'*; the seven-string instrument is required for the D major Sonata BWV1028 and the *St Matthew Passion*, most notably for the three- to six-part chords in movements 34, 56, and 57 in the Passion. Bach is known to have been friendly with the Leipzig instrument maker J. C. Hoffmann; a seven-string gamba (1725) by him is in the Bachhaus, Eisenach, and a six-string gamba (1731) in the Musikinstrumenten-Museum, Leipzig University. A gamba was also listed in the inventory made at Bach's death.

Bach used the viola da gamba throughout his career, from 1707 to the end of his life (in a revival of the *St John Passion*). He wrote for one instrument in Cantatas 76, 152, 199 (revival), and 205, the *St Matthew* and *St John Passions*, and the three sonatas BWV1027–9; and for two instruments in Cantatas 106 and 198, the Sixth Brandenburg Concerto, and the *St Matthew Passion* (last revival, where the two instruments are heard separately). He notated the music in the alto, tenor, and bass clefs; the compass, when all the parts are collated, exceeds three-and-a-half octaves, from *AA* to *e"*, using the full chromatic range. Alternation between tenor and alto clefs can occur within a movement, perhaps because the compass is large (*AA* to *c"* in the *St Matthew Passion*, movement 57, for example) or as a means of distinguishing between functions: for example in the aria 'Es ist vollbracht' in the *St John Passion* the obbligato part in the two Adagio sections is written in the alto clef, the middle section in the bass clef.

Bach calls for the viola da gamba primarily as an obbligato instrument, in arias in three- to five-part texture, in recitatives, and in choral movements. In purely instrumental movements (e.g. BWV76:8, 106:1, 152:1, and 1051:1 and 3) it is used along with other 'quiet' instruments (recorder, oboe, and viola d'amore) in three- to six-part 'chamber music' textures characteristic of Bach's sound ideal before he went to Leipzig in 1723. A preference for melodic, non-chordal writing is characteristic of the pre-Leipzig works, both in obbligato parts and when the instrument doubles vocal and instrumental lines. Arpeggios and chordal textures are, of course, especially well suited to the gamba, with its low bridge and its underhand bowing, but Bach did not make use of these specific possibilities until late in the Leipzig period, when he revised the *St Matthew Passion* and altered the original scoring from continuo (in

Bass viol and bow by Martin Voigt, 1726 (Victoria and Albert Museum, London)

movements 34 and 35) and lute (in movements 56 and 57) to viola da gamba. The direction 'pizzicato' is given for both violin and viola da gamba in movement 4 of the *Trauer Ode*, imitating the 'dying sound' ('Sterbegläut') in a manner typical of Bach's response to words, as can be seen when we compare this with the realism in his setting of comparable passages of text in Cantatas 8:1, 73:4, 95:4, 105:4, 127:3, and 161:6.                    UP

C. Döbereiner, 'Über die Viola da Gamba und ihre Verwendung bei Joh. Seb. Bach', *BJb* 8 (1911), 75–85; H. Le Blanc, *Défense de la basse de viole contre les entréprises du violon et les prétensions du violoncel* (Amsterdam, 1740; repr. 1975); A. Otterstedt, *Die Gambe: Kulturgeschichte und praktischer Ratgeber* (Kassel, 1994); U. Prinz, *Studien zum Instrumentarium J. S. Bachs mit besonderer Berücksichtigung der Kantaten* (Tübingen, 1979), 96–107; J. Rousseau, *Traité de la viole* (Paris, 1687; repr. 1965).

**viola.** *See* VIOLIN FAMILY.

**viola d'amore.** A string instrument with a varying numbers of strings, invented in England in the 17th century. In structure it is related to the treble gamba, with sloping shoulders, flat back (except for the slope towards the neck), soundholes in the shape of flames and a rosette on the belly, and a head instead of a scroll at the pegbox. The shapes of individual instruments vary greatly. The number of strings varies between four and seven, with the same number of sympathetic (resonating) strings usually made of brass or steel. J. F. B. C. Majer (in his *Museum musicum*, 1732) speaks of 14 different tunings of his six-string instrument as pure major or minor chords; in other words, it could be tuned to the key of the piece being played. An engraving in J. C. Weigel's *Musicalisches Theatrum* (*c*.1720) shows a 'viol d'amour' with 12 pegs. J. P. Eisel (*Musicus autodidactos*, 1738) describes the tuning and fingerings for seven-string instruments.

Bach wrote for the viola d'amore in Cantatas 36*c*, 152, and 205, and in the *St John Passion*. The inadequacy of the sources makes it difficult to say very much about the instrument he had in mind: the original viola d'amore parts do not survive, so nothing certain is known about their written fingering, musical notation, or exact tuning. The scores of the three cantatas are autograph, but that of the Passion is autograph only up to movement 10; the movements in which the viola d'amore plays (nos. 19 and 20) are in a copyist's hand, while the original parts for the third version (1732) and the fourth (1749) document the substitution of two muted violins. Arpeggiated chords, from which it might be possible to deduce the probable tuning of the instrument occur only in the Weimar cantata no. 152. Bach writes at the instrument's sounding pitch in the scores, using the

violin, soprano, and alto clefs in *Cammerton*, with a complete chromatic compass from *d* to *c♯'''*. The viola d'amore is used exclusively as an obbligato instrument in a three- to five-part 'chamber music' texture.                    UP

W. E. Köhler, 'Beiträge zur Geschichte und Literatur der Viola d'amore' (diss., University of Berlin, 1938); U. Prinz, *Studien zum Instrumentarium J. S. Bachs mit besonderer Berücksichtigung der Kantaten* (Tübingen, 1979), 86–95; W. Schrammek, 'Die Viola d'amore zur Zeit J. S. Bach', in *Bach-Studien*, 9 (Leipzig, 1986), 55–66.

**viola pomposa.** A string instrument resembling a large viola, played on the arm. At least six documents dating from 1766–90 refer to J. S. Bach as the inventor of the viola pomposa: see *BDok* iii, nos. 731 (two references), 820, 856, 939, and 948. Five-string instruments by Bach's friend J. C. Hoffmann have survived, two of them dated 1732 and 1741 (in the Musikinstrumenten-Museum, Leipzig) and one undated (in the Musée Instrumental, Brussels). Equating the viola pomposa with the VIOLONCELLO PICCOLO has given rise to many misunderstandings and controversies, especially as the latter is named in the Bach sources, while the viola pomposa is not.                    UP

F. T. Arnold, 'Die Viola pomposa', *Zeitschrift für Musikwissenschaft*, 13 (1930–1), 141–5; see also ibid. 13 (1930–1), 325–8 and 14 (1931–2), 35–8 and 178–9; F. W. Galpin, 'Viola pomposa and Violoncello piccolo', *Music and Letters*, 12 (1931), 354–64; H. Husmann, 'Die Viola pomposa', *BJb* 33 (1936), 90–100. For further bibliography, *see* VIOLONCELLO PICCOLO.

**Violin Concertos.** Bach wrote three violin concertos, two (in A minor and E major) for violin and orchestra, BWV1041–2, and one (in D minor) for two violins and orchestra, BWV1043. They are generally thought to have been composed at Cöthen in 1717–23, but autograph material (incomplete) exists only for the A minor and D minor concertos, and Christoph Wolff has suggested the possibility of a later, Leipzig origin for these two works. Bach is believed to have written several more violin concertos at Weimar and Cöthen, and it is likely that many of his HARPSICHORD CONCERTOS were arranged from earlier violin versions which have since been lost; thus, the violin concertos in G minor BWV1056R and D minor BWV1052R and the D minor Concerto for violin and oboe BWV1060R are the conjectural originals of works which have come down to us as harpsichord concertos. The Triple Concerto for flute, violin, and harpsichord is also a reworking (*c*.1730) derived from BWV894 (outer movements) and BWV527 (slow movement), and Brandenburg Concertos nos. 1, 2, 4, and 5 include prominent parts for solo violin (violino piccolo in the case of no. 1).

Although it is conceivable that Bach intended his solo violin concertos for J. G. Pisendel or J. B. Volumier, their most likely recipient (if a Cöthen origin is accepted) was Joseph Spieß, who may have been partnered by Martin Friedrich Marcus in the Concerto for two violins. The three works represent some of the fruits of Bach's enduring attraction to the Italian concerto style, especially the concertos of Vivaldi, many of which he transcribed for keyboard. Bach was especially influenced by Vivaldi's coherent, well-defined ritornello plans, his striking themes featuring short motifs ideally suited to soloistic elaboration, and his use of long cantilenas underpinned by repeated bass ostinato figures in the slow movements. However, Italianate features are fully assimilated into Bach's unique musical language, in which counterpoint and motivic elaboration transform the simple solo–tutti juxtaposition of the Italian concerto into a richer and more cohesive texture. Apart from the slow movements, where the accompaniment is restricted to simple chordal support underpinned by a quasi-ostinato bass figure, the orchestra of strings and continuo participates in the musical argument practically throughout in the solo concertos, the consistent four-voice texture undergoing constant variation and elaborate organization while preserving the soloist's independence. The orchestral contribution in the Double Concerto is generally less complex, occasionally being reduced merely to continuo accompaniment.

Bach's more varied and adventurous harmonic idiom is also noteworthy, as well as his introduction into the ritornello pattern of features normally associated with other forms. The first movement of the E major concerto, for example, follows the design and tonal scheme of the da capo aria stereotype, while the opening ritornello of the Double Concerto is a fully-fledged fugal exposition and the finale of the A minor concerto imbues a ritornello structure with the driving energy of a gigue.

The first movement of the A minor Concerto, which includes two main solo episodes (bars 25–51 and 85–142), is characterized by extensive development of its opening ritornello material, which incorporates five principal motifs (bars 1–4, 4–8, 8–14, 15–19, and 20–4). The first solo entry brings a new idea, derived from the ritornello's head-motif, which frequently appears in an accompanying role thereafter, the long developmental second episode, for example, being punctuated by strong orchestral references to it (bars 101–5 and 122–6). The third ritornello motif makes significant structural contributions at bars 59–67 and 146–54, and the second motif is the subject of solo sequential figuration, serving to emphasize fur-

ther the structural integration of the movement. The violin is predominant in the lyrical Andante (C major), singing its often chromatic cantilena above the steady tread of the ostinato bass, but it is given only two extended solo passages in the concise, gigue-like Allegro assai (A minor). Beginning in fugato style, the movement gathers momentum as the soloist's contribution increases in virtuosity. After a climactic passage and a pause, the dance is resumed, the soloist indulging in a remarkable passage of slurred *bariolage* before the final ritornello.

The first movement of the E major concerto is a da capo, aria-like structure based largely on the four constituent ideas of its opening ritornello. Its initial triadic motif is unmistakably of Italian stock, but Bach treats it contrapuntally, the soloist's first statement being echoed in the bass and accompanied by an idea originally presented by the violins in bar 2. This motif is also used extensively as an accompaniment to solo figuration, sometimes imitatively treated, particularly in the developmental central episode (C♯ minor), where the upper strings introduce new lyrical material (bar 57). It is prominent even when the soloist develops the ritornello's second motif in double stopping (bars 95–101) and plays its part in effecting a forward-looking false reprise (bars 106–7). After a climax and cadence, two descending expressive Adagio bars for the solo violin provide the link to the actual reprise. As in the A minor concerto, the expressive slow movement is in the relative key and is based largely on an ostinato which, apart from the serene central section, frames and underpins the meditative solo part. The final Allegro assai, with its 16-bar refrain which rounds off (unchanged) each of the soloist's four excursions, is a rondeau in the French tradition. The solo episodes, increasing in intensity and technical demand, are also 16 bars long, except for the last (32 bars), which, having wandered far from the tonic, is brought firmly home to roost in E major.

The opening Vivace of the Double Concerto smacks of Torelli in that its first idea is introduced fugally by the orchestra. This fugal exposition, whose four-bar subject provides the pillars on (or between) which the three solo sections are built, links straight into the first episode, in which the soloists introduce a new theme, characterized by its wide leaps and light accompaniment. The second solo episode introduces another new idea, while the final section incorporates material from the two earlier solo sections. The central slow movement (F major) is a flowing, melodious duet, its two-bar opening melody passed gently from one soloist to the other. A further idea (bar 16), likewise exchanged, together with material from the first section, leads to the reprise of the opening melody, first in A minor and eventually in the tonic key. Unlike the finales of the solo violin concertos, the stirring Allegro has little affinity with the dance. Its opening three-note figure is a recurrent feature of the orchestral contribution, recalling a similar orchestral motif in the opening movement (bars 63–8), while the contrasting pulse between the soloists (3/4) and the orchestra (2/4) and the soloists' close canon at the unison emphasize its restless character. It gains increased urgency from an unaccompanied triplet semiquaver figure for the soloists (in 6ths), which returns at significant points. The first episode brings a contrasting idea for the soloists, who later play a sequence of broad four-part chords, sounding almost like an organ, over a unison orchestral statement of the ritornello's head-motif. The solo idea returns in A minor, leading first to a partial statement of the ritornello and then to a new episode. An abortive ritornello entry in G minor is followed by the return of material from the first episode; similarly, an entry in D minor is curtailed by the four-part chordal sequence, after which the ritornello returns complete to bring the movement to its close.                                                    RS

H. Besseler, 'Zur Chronologie der Konzerte Johann Sebastian Bach', in W. Vetter, ed., *Festschrift Max Schneider zum achtzigsten Geburtstag* (Leipzig, 1955), 115–28; H.-J. Schulze, 'Johann Sebastian Bachs Konzerte: Fragen der Überlieferung und Chronologie', in P. Ahnsel, K. Heller, and H.-J. Schulze, eds., *Beiträge zum Konzertschaffen Johann Sebastian Bachs* (*Bach-Studien*, 6) (Leipzig, 1981), 9–26; C. Wolff, 'Bach's Leipzig Chamber Music', in *Bach: Essays on his Life and Music* (Cambridge, Mass., 1991), 223–41. For further bibliography, *see* CONCERTO.

**violin family.** A family of string instruments of the violin type which forms the core of Bach's orchestra. The structural development of this family reached its peak in the 17th century. String writing in five string parts—2 violins, 2 violas, and continuo—is found in some of Bach's Mühlhausen and Weimar cantatas, but four parts (with only one viola part) becomes the rule in the Cöthen and Leipzig compositions. C. P. E. Bach wrote of his father, in a letter of 1774, that the instrument he most liked to play was the viola, 'balancing its *forte* and *piano*. In his youth, and up to the approach of old age, he played the violin with a pure and penetrating tone . . . He perfectly understood the possibilities of all the violin family. His solos for violin and cello without bass [accompaniment] bear witness to this.' The inventory taken at Bach's death shows that the instruments he owned included a 'Stainerische Violine'—a violin probably by the Austrian maker Jacob Stainer (?1617–83) or his less famous countryman Markus Stainer (*c.*1633–93). Bach is known to have been friendly with J. C. Hoffmann, the important Leipzig maker of violins and lutes, to whom he entrusted the maintenance of the instruments in the city's two principal churches in 1734. The church accounts reveal that viols belonging to the two churches were kept there for use by the *Kunstgeiger*. A violin and a cello by Hoffmann are in the collection of the Thomaskirche.

The Bach sources show that the violin was used exclusively in the tuning *g′, d′, a′, e″*, with full chromatic range from *g* to *a′′′*, usually notated in the violin clef but also in the alto and twice even in the bass clef. As a rule the original performing material for pre-Leipzig compositions includes only single copies of the violin parts, indicating one desk to each part; in the case of the Leipzig works there are usually two copies of each violin part, perhaps indicating at least three players to a part (but *see also* ORCHESTRA). Bach used the viola (*da braccio*, as distinct from the viola da gamba) in the tuning *c, g′, d′, a′*, with the range *c* to *g″*. The music is usually notated in the alto clef, but the tenor clef is used for the second viola in eight early cantatas, as an indication of its function in the musical texture.

In normal Baroque usage bass parts are designated simply 'continuo', and in Bach's music, as a rule, this refers to the cello, violone, bassoon, and organ or cembalo. There are some 50 explicit references to the cello in original sources: as the heading of a part, as a label for an individual staff in a score, in an annotation, in the list of instruments on a title-page or at the top of the first page of music, or in conjunction with 'tacet' and 'senza' marks. The cello was tuned *C, G, d, a* (with a fifth string, *e′*, in the Sixth Cello Suite) and its music was normally notated in the bass clef, even when its compass extended up to *a′*. A change to the tenor or alto clef is to be understood as indicating its function as as *basso seguente* (or *bassetto*).                                                    UP

*See also* SCORDATURA.

D. D. Boyden, *The History of Violin Playing from its Origins to 1761* (London, 1965); K. Marx, *Die Entwicklung des Violoncells und seiner Spieltechnik bis J. L. Duport 1520–1820* (Regensburg, 1963); Y. Menuhin and W. Primrose, *Violin and Viola* (London, 1976); U. Prinz, *Studien zum Instrumentarium J. S. Bachs mit besonderer Berücksichtigung der Kantaten* (Tübingen, 1979); M. W. Riley, *The History of the Viola* (Ann Arbor, 1980; 2nd edn., 1993); M. M. Smith, 'Certain Aspects of Baroque Music for the Violoncello' (diss., Flinders University of South Australia, 1983).

**violino piccolo.** A string instrument mentioned in Michael Praetorius's *Syntagma musicum* (1619) as a 'Klein Discant Geig' ('small treble fiddle'), tuned *c′*, *g′*, *d″*, *a″*; it appears in J. G. Walther's *Musicalisches Lexicon* (1732) as 'violino piccolo' with the same tuning. Walther became the rock, therefore, on which a large part of the earlier Bach literature was built. Yet the instrument used by Bach is tuned *bb′*, *f′*, *c″*, *g″*, as is evident from the notation (transposed down a minor 3rd) and the compass in the three works in which he used the instrument: the First Brandenburg Concerto (dedicatory copy 1721), Cantata 140 (1731), and the revised version of Cantata 96 (1734, replacing the flauto piccolo of the 1724 original).

These three works have two things in common: they require first and second violins in addition to the violino piccolo, and in the surviving sources (both scores and parts) the violino piccolo part is written in the violin clef a minor 3rd below the sounding pitch, with the appropriate key signature. As in some oboe d'amore and oboe da caccia parts, this allows the player to employ his customary violin fingering, without needing to transpose. The sounding compass is *bb* to *g‴*, corresponding to *g* to *e′″* in the notation; the lowest open string is thus required for the lowest note and fourth position for the highest. If this is compared with what Bach requires of violinists playing the normal instrument—on which he regularly requires fourth position (*e′″*), but seventh position (*a′″*) is not unknown—it is apparent that his quite rare use of the violino piccolo was more for reasons of sonority than for anything to do with playing technique.        UP

A. Moser, 'Der Violino piccolo', *Zeitschrift für Musikwissenschaft*, 1 (1918–19), 377–80; U. Prinz, *Studien zum Instrumentarium J. S. Bachs mit besonderer Berücksichtigung der Kantaten* (Tübingen, 1979), 61–7; C. S. Terry, *Bach's Orchestra* (London, 1932), 125–7.

**Violin Sonatas.** Bach's extant violin sonatas comprise six works for violin with fully composed keyboard parts, BWV1014–19, sometimes known as 'accompanied sonatas', and two sonatas for violin and continuo, BWV1021 and 1023, in which the keyboard player spontaneously completes the harmonies from a figured bass line.

J. N. Forkel, in his Bach biography of 1802, stated that Bach composed his 'accompanied sonatas' at Cöthen. However, the earliest source of these works—the original keyboard part copied largely by Johann Heinrich Bach and completed by the composer himself—dates from 1725, about two years after Bach's move to Leipzig. Although the first five sonatas may have been completed at Cöthen, only the first two movements (and possibly the fourth) of the Sixth Sonata may have existed at that stage, the remainder being added in 1725. Indeed, Hans Eppstein has suggested that its first, second, and fourth movements may have been transcribed from a lost trio for flute, violin,

and continuo; and various movements in the other sonatas may have been derived from lost trio sonata or concerto movements.

Bach's 'accompanied sonatas' are arranged in a subtly symmetrical overall key scheme (B minor; A major; E major; C minor; F minor; G major) and form a carefully planned and integrated set. The first, second, and fourth movements regularly remain in the basic tonality, while the slow inner movement is always in the parallel key (although in the Fifth Sonata this is established only at the very end of the movement, the greater part of which is in the dominant minor key). True to the title of a copy in the hand of J. C. Altnickol—'Sechs Trios für Clavier und die Violine'—these works are largely in the nature of trio sonatas, the two imitative upper 'solo' parts being taken by the violinist and the keyboard player's right hand, accompanied by a bass part which provides harmonic support and contributes occasionally to the contrapuntal texture. But Bach varies his approach throughout; the keyboard, for example, is especially prominent in the opening movement of the Fifth Sonata, but generally plays a subservient continuo role in the slow third movements.

The first five sonatas adopt the four-movement, slow–fast–slow–fast sequence of the *sonata da chiesa*, their individual movements embracing a wide variety of ritornello, binary, da capo, and through-composed structures. Fugal elements also feature prominently, notably in the second movements of nos. 1 and 2, while the third movement of no. 2 is an effortless canon between the two upper parts over a bass mostly in staccato semiquavers; the equivalent movement of no. 3 is a modulating chaconne. The only other movement with dance connections in these five sonatas is the Siciliano, stylized as a Largo, that opens no. 4. The original version of the Sixth Sonata comprises six movements, incorporating the novel element of a pair of dances—the first a keyboard solo, the second a violin solo (later transcribed by Bach for his keyboard Partita in E minor BWV830)—and concluding with a repeat of the opening Vivace. Available sources suggest that Bach revised the six sonatas twice during his Leipzig period. The modifications made to the first five were minor, but the sixth was radically transformed on both occasions. Bach first replaced its two dance movements with a large-scale slow movement, an instrumental version of a soprano aria with violin obbligato which he reused twice in Leipzig cantatas of 1729–30. In his final version, which may date from as late as the 1740s, this variant was itself replaced by a substantial binary Allegro in E minor for solo keyboard, with a more elaborate, expressive Adagio substituting for the original Adagio. A new 6/8 Allegro in da capo form replaced the former literal repeat of the first movement as a finale.

The two authentic 'continuo sonatas' are probably of later origin than the six 'accompanied sonatas'. The only source of the Sonata in E minor BWV1023 is a Dresden manuscript of about 1730. It combines aspects of both church and chamber sonata in its four movements, all of which are in the tonic key. Its brilliant opening toccata-like movement, in which the continuous semiquavers of the violin are supported by an unbroken tonic pedal, leads straight into an Adagio, in which an improvisatory element is suggested in the violin's chromatic decorations. An elegant Allemande and a lively Gigue, both in binary form, complete the work.

The Sonata in G (BWV1021) also survives in a single source, copied by Anna Magdalena with Bach's assistance in about 1733. Of comparatively small dimensions, it adopts the traditional *da chiesa* structure of four movements, alternating slow and fast tempos. Its opening binary Adagio and its Largo feature an ornate violin line with accompaniment, while the Vivace, in the manner of a courante, and the final contrapuntal Presto treat the two instruments more as equal partners. This sonata later spawned two others of doubtful authenticity, one for flute, violin, and continuo, BWV1038 (*see* FLUTE SONATAS), and one for violin and harpsichord, BWV1022.                    RS

H. Eppstein, *Studien über J. S. Bachs Sonaten für ein Melodieinstrument und obligates Cembalo* (Uppsala, 1966, 2nd edn. 1983); H. Eppstein, 'Zur Problematik von J. S. Bachs Sonate für Violine und Cembalo G-dur (BWV1019)', *Archiv für Musikwissenschaft*, 21 (1964), 217–42; K.-H. Köhler, 'Zur Problematik der Violinsonaten mit obligatem Cembalo', *BJb* 45 (1958), 114–22; H. Vogt, *Johann Sebastian Bach's Chamber Music*, Eng. trans. K. Johnson (Portland, Ore., 1988).

**violoncello.** *See* VIOLIN FAMILY.

**violoncello piccolo.** A type of cello with a smaller soundbox than the regular instrument, and with a fifth string, tuned to *e'*, which extends its treble range. It was played in an upright position, like the normal cello.

There is substantial evidence that Bach had a good working knowledge of the instruments of his time. His friendship with celebrated instrument makers, including Gottfried Silbermann, J. C. Hoffmann, and J. H. Eichentopf, contributed to the interest he took in new sonorities and to his readiness to experiment with novelties such as the oboe d'amore, which he wrote for immediately after its invention, and the Leipzig type of oboe da caccia. The violoncello piccolo can be regarded as another such experiment.

Bach wrote obbligato parts for what he always termed the 'violoncello piccolo' in Cantatas 180, 115, 41, 6, 85, 183, 68, and 175, composed between October 1724 and May 1725, and one more, on 3 November 1726, in Cantata 49. This concentration on the instrument during such a short period indicates that the circumstances were unusual, and this is reflected in the differing styles of notation. There is no consistency in the clefs Bach uses, either in the separate parts or in the relationship of parts to scores. There are instances of notation in the violin clef (to be transposed an octave) as well as in alto, tenor, and bass clefs; the required compass extends from *C* to *c"*. In the surviving performance material there are separate violoncello piccolo parts for Cantatas 85, 183, 68, 175, and 49, while those for Cantatas 41 and 6 are written in the first violin parts. This tells us only that a violinist played the solo part, but not which instrument he played it on.

This is the starting-point for all the confusion and misunderstandings that persist to the present day. First and foremost, it is wholly misleading to equate the violoncello piccolo with the VIOLA POMPOSA. Bach's friend J. C. Hoffmann built both instruments and dated examples have survived, but one is to be held 'da gamba' ('on the leg') and the other 'da braccio' ('on the arm'). Secondly, Bach's musicians were not as specialized or limited to one instrument as players are today. The *Konzertmeister* (leader) of Bach's orchestra in Leipzig (a *Stadtpfeifer*, formerly a *Kunstgeiger*), had in this capacity to be competent not only on the violin but also on woodwind, brass, and bass instruments, as Bach's testimonial of 1745 for Carl Friedrich Pfaffe (1723–73) confirms. To that extent, we can assume that the violoncello piccolo was played by an experienced professional musician when it made its début in Leipzig; the assumption gains support from Bach's own statement (1730) that he always had to have cello parts played by pupils, and the cello parts in the works in question are not marked 'tacet', as the regular continuo forces are specified in the relevant passages of three- or four-part writing.

The original performance material of Bach's works contains several pieces of evidence to show that solos were entrusted to the most experienced players. In the third movement of Cantata 5 the obbligato viola line is written in the alto clef in the first violin part, while the viola part itself is marked 'tacet' in the corresponding place. Oboe da caccia obbligatos are treated similarly: for example, in the parts for Cantatas 74, 87, and 101, the obbligatos are not notated in the oboe da caccia or *taille* part, but in that of the first oboe in every case.                    UP

U. Drüner, 'Violoncello piccolo und Viola pomposa bei J. S. Bach: zu Fragen von Identität und Spielweise dieser Instrumente', *BJb* 73 (1987), 85–112; A. Dürr, 'Philologisches zum Problem Violoncello piccolo bei Bach', in D. Berke and H. Heckmann, eds., *Festschrift W. Rehm zum 60. Geburtstag* (Kassel, 1989), 45–50; U. Prinz, 'Violoncello, Violoncello piccolo und Viola da gamba im Werk J. S. Bachs', in *Bachfestbuch* [programme book of the 53rd Bachfest] (Marburg, 1978), 159–63; W. Schrammek, 'Viola pomposa und Violoncello piccolo bei J. S. Bach', in W. Felix, W. Hoffmann, and A. Schneiderheinze, eds., *Bericht über die Wissenschaftliche Konferenz zum III. Internationalen Bach-Fest der DDR, Leipzig, 18./19. September 1975* (Leipzig, 1977), 345–54.

## Violoncello Suites. *See* CELLO SUITES.

**violone.** The lowest-pitched member of Bach's string ensemble. Its musical function places it with the violin family, though it originated as a member of the viol family. The manifold forms in which it was constructed, even at an early stage, place it in an intermediate position. The string bass is found in both viol and violin form, with and without frets, and in various sizes, especially as the technique of overspinning strings made it possible to build smaller instruments with the same compass. The number of strings varied from three to six, and the tuning was also variable—in 4ths (with a 3rd midway) like the viola da gamba family, or in 5ths like the *viola da braccio* family.

The existence of the '16-foot Contra-C' is expressly confirmed in M. H. Fuhrmann's *Musicalischer Trichter* (1706), J. P. Eisel's *Musicus autodidactos* (1738), and I. F. X. Kürzinger's *Getreuer Unterricht* (1763). Their descriptions are consistent with the great majority of Bach's violone parts, which have a written compass of C to *e'* (higher in isolated cases). (The pitches C and C♯ are avoided in the Fourth and Fifth Brandenburg Concertos, but not in the early version of the latter, BWV1050a.) An inventory of the instruments belonging to the Cöthen *Hofkapelle* lists a 'Contra Violon' by the Leipzig violin maker J. C. Hoffmann. The purchase of a 'großen Violon aus der Auction' ('large violone at auction') was made by the Thomasschule in Leipzig in 1735.

As is the case with the cello and the bassoon, only a relatively small number of Bach's continuo parts (50 or so) expressly specify 'violone', or one of the alternative forms: 'violono', 'violon', 'violone in ripieno' (BWV210, 1047, and 1049), 'violone grosso' (BWV149, 205, 208, 241, 1046, and 1048), and the plurals 'violoni' and 'violons' (although there is no work for which more than one violone part exists). In as early a piece as Cantata 71, composed for the election of the Mühlhausen town council in 1708, Bach assigns the bass parts very precisely to separate 'choirs', bracketing the groups together and naming them before the brace: 'Trombae è Tamburi | Violae [i.e. first and second violins and viola] è Violono | Hautbois è Basson | Flauti è Violoncello | Voci | Organo'.

From the presence of separate systems in the scores, notes with both upward- and downward-pointing stems, annotations in continuo parts, and tacet markings, differences between violone parts and those for other continuo instruments can be discerned. Separate violone parts are only ever notated in the bass clef, they never include music for other instruments of any kind, and they include all the movements as a rule, showing that the instrument is intended to play throughout. Differentiations are none the less made: for example, when the violone is scored to play in ritornellos but not during the vocal sections of an aria (e.g. in Cantata 210), or when the violone differs from other bass parts by being given longer note values or rests (in BWV1069:1). In Cantata 78, after all the parts had been written out, Bach enhanced the instrumentation, using the blank verso of the horn part to write a separate violone part for the second movement, in which crotchets, marked 'staccato e pizzicato', punctuate the continuous quaver motion in the continuo. For a revival of Cantata 100, too, Bach made insertions in the 'Continuo pro Violone' part which result in a changed sonority. UP

S. Bonta, 'From Violone to Violoncello: A Question of Strings', *Journal of the American Musical Instrument Society*, 3 (1977), 64–99; L. Dreyfus, *Bach's Continuo Group: Players and Practices in his Vocal Works* (Cambridge, Mass., 1987); A. Planyavsky, *Der Barockkontrabaß* (Salzburg, 1989); A. Planyavsky, *Geschichte des Kontrabasses* (Tutzing, 1970; 2nd edn., ed. H. Seifert, 1984).

**Vivaldi, Antonio** (b. 4 March 1678; d. 27/28 July 1741). Italian composer and violinist, born in Venice. A prolific writer of both instrumental and vocal music, he earned European renown for his concertos, of which those published as op. 3 (*L'estro armonico*, 1711) and op. 8 (*Il cimento dell'armonia e dell'invenzione*, 1725) circulated most widely. Vivaldi's concertos confirmed the three-movement scheme as standard. They also pioneered ritornello form, which became the normal structure used for the fast movements of concertos.

Equally influential was Vivaldi's style, heavily indebted both to the tradition of virtuosity in Italian string music and to the expressive but deliberately simplified musical language of the opera house. Vivaldi is commonly seen as a prime mover in the 'flight from counterpoint' that ushered in the *galant* style. This view needs qualification, but it remains true that it was the most radically simple features of Vivaldi's concertos that proved influential in their day.

The *BG* edition of ten Vivaldi concertos in Bach's transcriptions for solo harpsichord (BWV972, 973, 975, 976, 978, and 980), solo organ (BWV593, 594, and 596), and four harpsichords with strings (BWV1065) launched Vivaldi's own modern revival. J. N. Forkel's belief that Bach transcribed the works to improve his command of musical form is no longer accepted; far more likely is that he arranged them (leaving aside BWV1065, a later work) at the behest of his patron Johann Ernst of Saxe-Weimar. Nor are the small changes made to the original in the course of their transcription to be understood necessarily as 'improvements'; most arose, rather, from a wish to make the concertos effective in their new medium.

The transcriptions for solo keyboard date from about 1713. Five (to be joined later by BWV1065) came from concertos for one or two violins in Vivaldi's op. 3; the remaining four were of concertos circulating in manuscript, versions of which later appeared in opp. 4 and 7. Bach soon began to imitate Vivaldi in his own compositions. The English Suites of about 1715 contain many Vivaldian features; indeed, the Prelude of the Third Suite is a perfect specimen of ritornello form. Bach also imported Vivaldian style and structure into other genres, vocal and instrumental. Even the episodes of Bach's fugues often draw inspiration from the solo portions of Vivaldi's concertos. A great master in his own right, Vivaldi was perhaps the only non-German to leave a strong mark on Bach as a composer. MT

*See also* CONCERTO *and* RITORNELLO.

H.-J. Schulze, 'Bach's Concerto-Arrangements for Organ: Studies or Commissioned Works?', *Organ Yearbook*, 3 (1972), 4–13; L. F. Tagliavini, 'Bach's Organ Transcription of Vivaldi's "Grosso Mogul" Concerto', in G. Stauffer and E. May, eds., *J. S. Bach as Organist* (London, 1986), 240–55; M. Talbot, *Vivaldi* (London, 1978; 3rd edn., 1993).

**Vogler, Johann Caspar** (b. 23 May 1696; d. 1 June 1763). Composer, born in Hausen, near Arnstadt in Thuringia. He studied with Bach in Arnstadt, 1706–7, and again in Weimar from 1710 to 1714. He was appointed organist in Stadtilm in 1715 and moved to Weimar as court organist in 1721. In 1729 he applied for the post of organist at the Nikolaikirche, Leipzig, but was unsuccessful; according to the report of his *Probe*, he played too fast and confused the congregation. He also applied unsuccessfully for posts elsewhere, but was destined to remain in Weimar for the rest of his life. He was elected deputy burgomaster there in 1735 and burgomaster in 1739, and from 1755 was employed as harpsichordist, under Johann Ernst Bach (1722–77), at the ducal court. Few of his compositions remain except for a printed volume of organ music, *Vermischte musikalische Choral-Gedanken* (1737). He has been identified as the Bach copyist previously known as Anonymous 18.

**Voigt, Johann Georg** (b. 12 June 1728; bur. 5 May 1765). Organist, born in Ansbach, Bavaria. His father of the same name (*c*.1689–1766) worked as an oboist, first at the Weimar court and then, from 1729, at the court of Ansbach. The son studied with Bach in Leipzig around 1740–3 and was appointed organist at the Gumbertuskirche, Ansbach, in 1752.

*Vokaleinbau* ('vocal in-building'). A term used for a device often found in Bach's arias (and less often in those of his contemporaries) whereby the opening ritornello, or part of it, is repeated during the course of an aria while the singer incorporates new material into it. Two examples among many occur in the alto aria 'Mit allem, was ich hab' from Cantata 72: five bars of instrumental ritornello (bars 5–9) are repeated at bars 19–24 and again at bars 45–50, each repeat being combined with the same new melodic material (although not the same text) from the singer. When the technique is employed in a chorus—as, for example, in bars 98–114 in the opening movement of the same cantata—it is usually referred to as 'Choreinbau'.

**Volumier, Jean Baptiste** (b. *c*.1670; d. 7 Oct. 1728). Violinist, composer, and dancing-master of Flemish origin, probably born in Spain. Educated at the French court, he served the Elector of Brandenburg in Berlin (1692–1708), first as a violinist and later as *Konzertmeister* and court dancing-master. His appointment as violinist, and subsequently *Konzertmeister* (1709), to the Dresden court, where he cultivated Friedrich August I's favoured French taste, led to a marked rise in orchestral standards there. A close friend of Bach, he initiated a keyboard competition in 1717 between Bach and Louis Marchand, from which Marchand withdrew. Volumier died in Dresden. His numerous ballets and works for violin have not survived. RS

*Von der Vergnügsamkeit / Zufriedenheit. See* ICH BIN IN MIR VERGNÜGT.

**von Haus aus** ('from outside the house'). A term used in connection with a courtesy title for someone who served a court establishment from outside, but did not live and work there. When Bach left Cöthen for Leipzig in 1723 he retained the title of *Kapellmeister von Haus aus* to Prince Leopold, and from 1729 to 1736 he was similarly honoured by the court at Weißenfels. Such a title laid few, if any, obligations on the holder beyond that of composing music for the court from time to time.

**Vordersatz.** *See* FORTSPINNUNGSTYPUS.

**Vorimitation** ('fore-imitation'). A device, common in Bach's music both vocal and instrumen-tal, whereby the lines of a cantus firmus (i.e. a chorale melody) are anticipated contrapuntally in the other voices, usually in shorter note values. An instrumental example is provided by the famous 'Deathbed Chorale', in which inversion plays a part in the *Vorimitation* (see Ex. 1). The motets, and cantata movements in motet style, present many examples of vocal *Vorimitation*, among which might be mentioned the chorus 'Jesu, deine Passion' in Cantata 182.

**Vorschriften und Grundsätze.** Short title for the treatise *Vorschriften und Grundsätze zum vier-stimmigen spielen des General-Baß oder Accom-pagnement* ('Precepts and Principles for Playing

Ex. 1

the Thorough-bass or Accompanying in Four Parts'). *See* PRECEPTS AND PRINCIPLES.

**Voß-Buch,** Count **Otto Carl Friedrich von** (b. 1755; d. 1823). Music collector. He acquired at auction a number of Bach manuscripts previously belonging to Wilhelm Friedemann Bach. The collection was left to his son Carl Otto Friedrich von Voß-Buch (1786–1864) who added to it other manuscripts from Carl Philipp Emanuel Bach's estate. The Voß-Buch collection was bought by the Königliche Bibliothek (now the Staatsbibliothek zu Berlin) in 1851.

B. Faulstich, *Die Musiksammlung der Familie von Voß: ein Beitrag zur Berliner Musikgeschichte um 1800* (Kassel, 1997).

***vox Christi*** ('voice of Christ'). A Latin term used to denote biblical passages spoken by Jesus. In Bach's two great Passions the role of Christ is allotted to a bass, accompanied in the *St John Passion* by continuo, and in the *St Matthew* by the string instruments (except in Jesus's last utterance from the Cross) and continuo. In the cantatas, too, the *vox Christi* is taken by a bass, and his words are usually set in arioso style.

# W

**Wachet auf, ruft uns die Stimme** ('Awake, the voice calls to us'). Cantata for the 27th Sunday after Trinity, BWV140, first performed on 25 November 1731. A CHORALE CANTATA, it is one of Bach's best-known church works, thanks to the popularity of the tune and poem, both by Philipp Nicolai (1599), on which it is based, and to the chorale's and the cantata's theme of the symbolic marriage between the individual soul and Christ. Although Bach's autograph score is lost, his original manuscript performing parts are extant; the existence of several later manuscript copies of the score suggests that the work was relatively well known during the 50 years after Bach's death, and it was one of the first of the cantatas to appear in print (in 1847).

There can be a 27th Sunday after Trinity only when Easter falls between 22 and 26 March; this happened only five times during Bach's lifetime, and only twice during his time at Leipzig—in 1731 and 1742. Hence, like Cantata 14 of 1735, the present work was composed to fill a gap in the series of chorale cantatas composed in 1724–5. These two works stand apart from several other late chorale cantatas whose texts are drawn entirely from the stanzas of the chorale. This was impossible in Cantata 140, as Nicolai's chorale has only three stanzas; all are used, alongside two recitatives and two arias by an unknown author who, like Nicolai, depended heavily on references to *The Song of Solomon*. Both arias are dialogues, the soprano and bass soloists representing the bride and the bridegroom respectively.

The work is scored for four vocal parts, with double-reed and string choirs (two oboes, *taille*, two violins, and viola); a 'corno' doubles the chorale cantus firmus in the outer movements. The continuo includes separate bassoon ('bassono') and organ parts, and the principal first violin is a violino piccolo tuned a minor 3rd higher than the normal instrument.

The opening chorale-fantasia movement, for the full ensemble, places the cantus firmus in the soprano; the rising opening phrase of the chorale tune is alluded to in the second of two motifs that dominate the ritornello (bar 4). The first motif, a dotted rhythm passed between the string and woodwind choirs, probably does not represent royalty, as is sometimes supposed, for the movement lacks other features of the French overture—for one thing it is in triple, not common, time—although it does shift to fugal texture for the ecstatic ninth line of the chorale (the single word 'Alleluja').

The soprano–bass dialogue is preceded by a short tenor recitative. The ensuing duet, using a modified da capo structure, derives its character from the violin's floridly embellished siciliana line, which was perhaps occasioned by the soprano's references to the flickering oil lamps. The two vocal parts share similar motivic material, but each sings its own text, entering and cadencing independently of the other. Only in the second duet (movement 6, in regular da capo form), with solo oboe, do the two voices join in the parallel 3rds and 6ths and chains of suspensions conventionally employed in contemporary operatic love duets, reflecting the union of the bride and groom.

The second duet is preceded by an accompanied recitative (movement 5) for the bass. At the centre of the cantata (movement 4) is the second strophe of the chorale, sung by the tenor against a ritornello theme for the strings, playing in unison (without violino piccolo). The ritornello melody, characterized by *galant* 'sigh' motifs, seems strangely unrelated to the chorale melody, although it arguably reflects the text's reference to the nightwatchmen's joy or their singing. The movement was transcribed for solo organ as the first of the six Schübler Chorales, and its popularity has been extended through numerous arrangements.

The closing movement of the cantata presents the final stanza of the chorale in a 'simple' four-part setting; exceptionally for Bach, it is notated in 'cut' time (¢), with the minim as the basic unit of movement. This gives the music an archaic appearance, although the style is not notably old-fashioned. DS

G. Herz, ed., *Bach: Cantata No. 140* [Norton Critical Scores, includes analytical commentary] (New York, 1972). For further bibliography, *see* CANTATA, §1.

**Wachet! betet! betet! wachet!** ('Watch and pray, pray and watch!'). Cantata for the 26th Sunday after Trinity, BWV70, first performed in Leipzig on 21 November 1723. Most of the music is derived from a lost Weimar cantata to words by Salomo Franck, probably performed on the second Sunday in Advent (6 December) 1716. The last three Sundays in Advent being a *tempus clausum* in Leipzig, the work was adapted for its new occasion by an unknown librettist, who added four recitatives and a further chorale strophe and divided the work into two parts, the first to be performed before the sermon and the second during Communion (*see* HAUPTGOTTESDIENST). The subject of the work, however, remains the same: the coming of Christ and the Last Judgement. It is one to which Bach responded, especially in the Leipzig recension, with some of the most dramatic music in all his cantatas.

Even in Weimar the opening of the work must have made a striking effect, with the solo trumpet sounding forth its FANFARE THEME over the busy semiquavers of the oboe and strings. This distinctive motif, which occurs in several other works by Bach and his contemporaries and was no doubt well known to his congregations in Weimar and Leipzig, is repeated 14 times in all during the course of the movement—12 times by the trumpet, once by the oboe, and once by both instruments—and always at the same pitch. No less colourful is the bass recitative that follows, with its *concitato* string semiquavers (in which the trumpet and oboe join) and its elaborate, virtuoso melisma on the word 'Freude' ('joy'). In the context of such movements as these it is not surprising if the two arias in Part 1—the first for alto with cello obbligato, the second for soprano with first violin (doubled intermittently by second violin and viola)—make less of an impression, despite their elegant craftsmanship and adept text interpretation.

Part 1 ends with the fifth strophe of the hymn *Freu dich sehr, o meine Seele*, straightforwardly harmonized in four parts and, in accordance with Bach's normal Leipzig practice, given *colla parte* support by the whole instrumental ensemble. The tenor's 'Hebt euer Haupt empor' that opens Part 2 is perhaps the most melodically attractive aria in the work, and the bass's 'Seligster Erquickungstag' (no. 10), with its sharply contrasting middle section, the most dramatic. But it is the accompanied recitative separating these two movements that remains longest in the memory. In this remarkable evocation of the Last Judgement the terrors of the event are vividly represented by the *concitato* bass, the reiterated chords and rushing demisemiquaver scales of the strings, with the trumpet punctuating the confusion with the phrases of *Es ist gewißlich an der Zeit*, a chorale melody which during the Thirty Years War had achieved the status of a kind of *Dies irae*. The tumult subsides as the singer turns his thoughts to Christ's compassion, but music such as this cannot have commended itself to those among Bach's superiors

who were suspicious of operatic inroads into church music.

The final chorale, the fifth strophe of Christian Keymann's *Meinen Jesum laß ich nicht* (1658) was already present in the Weimar version of the cantata, and is harmonized with independent parts for the three upper strings.

For bibliography, *see* CANTATA, §1.

**Wagner, Georg Gottfried** (b. 5 April 1698; d. 23 March 1756). Kantor and composer, born in Mühlberg, Saxony. He attended the Thomasschule in Leipzig from 1712 to 1718, when he began to study theology at the university there. In 1722 he applied unsuccessfully for the post of Kantor at the Michaeliskirche in Zeitz. He assisted Bach in Leipzig as a string player and bass singer, and in 1726 Bach wrote in support of his application for the post of Kantor at the Johanniskirche in Plauen, in which he was successful. He remained there for the rest of his life.

Wagner was the composer of the motet *Lob und Ehre und Weisheit und Dank*, which was published in 1819 as a work of Bach (BWV Anh. III 162). Only one other composition by him has survived.

***Wahrlich, wahrlich, ich sage euch*** ('Verily, verily, I say unto you'). Cantata for the fifth Sunday after Easter (Rogate), BWV86, first performed in Leipzig on 14 May 1724. The Gospel reading for that day was St John 16: 23–30, and the anonymous librettist used part of that lesson as the text for the opening movement of the cantata: 'Verily, verily, I say unto you, Whatsoever ye shall ask the Father in my name, he will give it you.' Bach set it as something between an arioso and an aria, allotting the *vox Christi*, as usual, to a bass soloist and accompanying him with a carefully composed four-part texture of strings and continuo.

What follows is in the nature of a meditation on this biblical text. The alto aria (no. 2) is accompanied by a violin solo as pretty as the roses to which the words refer, and this is followed by a chorale, the 16th strophe of Georg Grünwald's *Kommt her zu mir, spricht Gottes Sohn* (1530), sung by the soprano as a cantus firmus with two decorative oboes d'amore, sometimes answering each other in imitation, at other times proceeding in mellifluous 3rds and 6ths. The tenor follows a brief recitative with an attractive aria which gives robust expression to the repeated claim that 'Gott hilft gewiß' ('God's help is sure'), and one of the least problematic of Bach's cantatas ends with the 11th strophe of the hymn *Es ist das Heil uns kommen her* (1523) in a simple four-part harmonization.

For bibliography, *see* CANTATA, §1.

**Walther, Johann Gottfried** (b. 18 Sept. 1684; d. 23 March 1748). Organist, composer, and theorist, born in Erfurt, Thuringia. In 1702 he was appointed organist at the Thomaskirche in Erfurt, and in 1707 he became organist at the Stadtkirche in Weimar, where he remained until his death.

Walther was a distant relative of Bach—his maternal grandfather, Valentin Lämmerhirt (*c.*1608–65), was the son of Bach's maternal grandfather, another Valentin Lämmerhirt (1585–1665)—and from 1708 to 1717 Walther and Bach were colleagues in Weimar. During this period Walther prepared manuscript copies of numerous keyboard compositions by Bach, and many of these represent the earliest surviving source for a work. The two jointly copied a mass by the 17th-century composer Johann Baal. Bach also reportedly gave Walther some 200 pieces of music, including works by himself and Buxtehude. In 1712 Bach stood godfather to Walther's son. They shared a common pupil, Johann Tobias Krebs, who studied with Walther from about 1710 to 1714 and with Bach from 1714 to 1717. Another pupil of Walther was Prince Johann Ernst, who, as a member of the ruling family at the Weimar court, was one of Bach's patrons. Around 1713–14 the prince may have commissioned Bach and Walther to transcribe concertos for the organ. They not only shared a strong interest in puzzle canons, but were among the first to compose chorale canons for organ, in several instances setting the same melody (perhaps in friendly competition). Spitta proposed Walther as the dedicatee of Bach's four-part canon BWV1073, dated 1713, but there is no direct evidence for this. J. N. Forkel reported that Walther played a trick on Bach to cure him of bragging about his prowess as a sight-reader.

Contrary to what Spitta maintained, Bach and Walther appear to have been on friendly terms well after Bach left Weimar. In 1735, for example, Bach negotiated on Walther's behalf with a Leipzig publisher; he served as a sales agent in Leipzig for Walther's *Musicalisches Lexikon* (1732), and may even have assisted in its completion. The entry on Bach in the *Lexikon*, although brief, refers to Bach's 'excellent' keyboard works and represents the first biographical note on the composer. RTS

K. Beißwenger, 'Zur Chronologie der Notenhandschriften Johann Gottfried Walthers', in *Acht kleine Präludien und Studien über BACH: Georg von Dadelsen zum 70. Geburtstag* (Wiesbaden, 1992), 11–39; S. Daw, 'Copies of J. S. Bach by Walther and Krebs: A Study of the Mss. P 801, P 802, and P 803', *Organ Yearbook*, 7 (1976), 31–58; K. Küster, 'Bach als Mitarbeiter am "Walther-Lexikon"?', *BJb* 77 (1991), 187–92; E. May, 'J. G. Walther and the Lost Weimar Autographs of Bach's Organ Works', in R. L. Marshall, ed., *Studies in Renaissance and Baroque Music in Honor of Arthur Mendel* (Kassel, 1974), 264–82; H.-J. Schulze, 'Johann Sebastian Bachs Kanonwidmungen', *BJb* 53 (1967), 82–92; H.-J. Schulze, *Studien zur Bach-Überlieferung im 18. Jahrhundert* (Leipzig, 1984), 146–73; H. Zietz, *Quellenkritische Untersuchungen an den Bach-Handschriften P 801, P 802 und P 803* (Hamburg, 1969).

***Wär Gott nicht mit uns diese Zeit*** ('Were God not with us at this time'). Cantata for the fourth Sunday after Epiphany, BWV14. Bach first performed this chorale-based cantata on 30 January 1735. The Gospel reading for the day, St Matthew 8: 23–7, relates Christ's calming of the storm at sea, and the unidentified librettist has effectively blended its central theme—God's protection—with that of the hymn which provides the framework of the text, Luther's three-strophe paraphrase of Psalm 124, *Wär Gott nicht mit uns diese Zeit* (1524). No less than the Gospel, Luther's hymn was closely associated with this Sunday in the Church year, both in Leipzig and in Dresden. The structure of the cantata text follows that which Bach favoured for the chorale cantatas of his great second cycle (1724–5); but in 1725 Easter fell early (on 1 April) and therefore there was no fourth Sunday after Epiphany. It seems likely, therefore, that Bach deliberately reverted to the earlier pattern in order to fill a gap in his second cycle caused by the timing of Easter.

He did not, however, begin the work with the kind of imposing chorale fantasia in ritornello form favoured in the 1724–5 *Jahrgang*. Cantata 14 opens with the first strophe of Luther's hymn set in a stern, highly complex MOTET STYLE, with affective chromaticisms. The anonymous melody belonging to Luther's hymn is heard as a textless cantus firmus played in unison by a horn and two oboes, each line anticipated by a paraphrase of the melody worked out in imitation (and inversion) by the four voices supported by *colla parte* strings. The music has an awesome character, but there is no evidence to support the idea put forward by Spitta, and taken up by some other commentators, that its severity reflects the privations suffered by Saxony during the War of the Polish Succession (1733–8). Alfred Dürr has remarked (in *DürrK*) on the similarity that exists between this movement and the opening chorus of another Luther-based cantata, *Ein feste Burg* (no. 80). Although the genesis of *Ein feste Burg* belongs to Bach's Weimar years, the chorus in question was composed much later, and perhaps, Dürr surmises, at the same period as the work under discussion.

The opening chorus is followed directly by the first of two arias, each of which is in modified da

## Warum betrübst du dich, mein Herz?

capo form (A–B–A'). The character of this piece, in B♭ major for soprano voice, is determined by an obbligato horn (*corno da caccia*) whose high-lying part, with four-strand string texture, gives it an immediately arresting brilliance. The musical imagery contained in Bach's writing reflects the textual reference to the wrathful enemy and calls for technical bravura from singer and horn player alike. A tenor recitative, with a colourfully depictive continuo accompaniment, paraphrases the second strophe of Luther's hymn, and leads to an aria for bass with two obbligato oboes. The A section here is less radically modified on its return than in the previous aria. It is a strongly delineated and declamatory movement in which the text focuses on God's intervention and taming of the forces of evil.

The cantata ends with the third strophe of Luther's hymn with its associated melody, now straightforwardly harmonized. NA

For bibliography, *see* CANTATA, §1.

***Warum betrübst du dich, mein Herz?*** ('Why troublest thou thyself, my heart?'). Cantata for the 15th Sunday after Trinity, BWV138, first performed on 5 September 1723. It departs from the usual pattern for cantatas composed during Bach's first year in Leipzig. In the spirit of the second cycle (the so-called CHORALE CANTATA *Jahrgang* of 1724–5), its structural scaffolding includes the first three stanzas of *Warum betrübst du dich, mein Herz?* a chorale that originated in Nuremberg in the 16th century.

The overall theme of the work concerns moving beyond temporal, earthly worries to trust in God. In this respect it is closely related to the appointed Gospel reading (Matt. 6: 24–34), a passage from the Sermon on the Mount in which Jesus instructs his disciples not to fret about food and clothing. Fundamental to the first three movements is the tension between faith and fear. The perspective of faith, expressed in the words of the chorale, affirms that earthly things are merely temporary. Since God has created everything on earth and in heaven, he knows what we need, he will stand by us and not leave us, and we should trust him. The perspective of doubt, verging on despair, is articulated in the recitatives.

The experimental mode of this work is evident already in movement 1, which juxtaposes the two perspectives. Each of the first three lines of the chorale (expressing faith) is set according to the following pattern: the strings and continuo begin the ritornello, and subsequently are joined by the oboes d'amore; the first oboe d'amore begins with a phrase of the chorale tune (similar to *Vorimitation* in organ chorales), while the second plays a doleful, descending chromatic line; next, the tenor

presents a line of the chorale with an independent melody that incorporates the head-motif of the ritornello; finally, the voices sing a four-part setting of the chorale phrase (the melody is doubled by the oboes d'amore, the bass line by the continuo). The next section of the movement is an alto recitative that expresses the darkest despair (bars 31–42); here the strings and continuo accompany in sustained notes, while the oboes d'amore punctuate the passage with semiquaver figures in parallel 6ths and 3rds. Thereafter, the last two lines of the chorale (representing a return to the perspective of faith) are set straightforwardly, with instrumental doubling.

The bass recitative (movement 2) is an unremittingly bitter tirade, which continues in the same vein as the alto recitative of the previous movement. Both passages include many diminished intervals and much chromaticism, in keeping with their subject-matter. Especially striking examples in the bass recitative are found in bar 7, at 'bittern Kelch der Tränen' ('bitter chalice of tears'), and in bar 10 (parallel tritones).

Movement 3, another chorus, follows the bass recitative without a break and involves a similar kind of juxtaposition to that in movement 1. The voice of faith speaks first: the first three lines of the chorale are set rather simply, with the four vocal parts doubled by the strings and continuo and the oboes d'amore providing brief semiquaver punctuation between phrases. The chorale is again interrupted by a recitative with a tone of desperation, sung this time by the soprano and accompanied by the strings and continuo. This passage ends with a question: 'Wo ist jemand, der sich zu meiner Rettung findt?' ('Where is there someone who will strive for my deliverance?'). The answer is provided by the last two lines of the chorale, which are set in an elaborate, motet-like polyphonic style, with the melody doubled by the oboes d'amore: 'Dein Vater und dein Herre Gott, Der dir beisteht in aller Not' ('Your father and the Lord your God, Who stands by you in every need'). A second recitative passage, sung by the alto and accompanied by the continuo only, ends with a similar question: 'Wer steht mir denn in meinem Kummer bei?' ('Who will stand by me then in my sorrow?'). It is answered identically, with a reprise of the last two lines of the chorale.

After the intensity of all the previous recitatives, the tone of movement 4—a tenor recitative expressed in predominantly major and diatonic rather than minor and chromatic sonorities—comes as a breath of fresh air. Its musical qualities reflect the gradual infiltration of faith, the dawning realization that God will soon come to our aid: 'Hilft er heute nicht, so hilft er mir doch morgen' ('If he does not help today, he will surely help me tomorrow'). This movement again flows without a break into the bass aria (movement 5), accompanied by strings and continuo, an outspoken declaration of trust and faith in God's providential care. In most respects it follows the usual pattern for modified da capo arias. After the opening ritornello, the first sentence (lines 1–2) is set in the A section, which modulates from the tonic to the dominant and is followed by a shortened version of the ritornello in the new key. The other two sentences (lines 3–4 and 5–7) are set in two sections (B and B') which modulate to the submediant and mediant respectively. Between them, however, is not only the expected ritornello in the submediant (bars 74–81) but also a reprise of the opening bars of the A section in the *tonic* (bars 82–90 = 21–9). The return of the beginning of A in the tonic, both here and immediately upon the conclusion of B' (the ritornello that usually occurs here is omitted), along with its confident, dance-like triple metre, lends the movement something of the flavour of a rondeau. In the late 1730s Bach adapted it for use in his *Missa* in G major bwv236.

After a brief and unremarkable alto recitative (movement 6), the cantata closes with an uncharacteristically elaborate setting of the third stanza of the same chorale that was heard earlier, in movements 1 and 3. While the voices present the chorale one phrase at a time in slightly more intricate four-part harmony than usual, the instrumental ensemble plays an ornate ritornello featuring brilliant demisemiquaver passages in the violins and parallel motion in the oboes d'amore. The joyous tone of this movement is far removed from the distress of the beginning, and a fitting conclusion for the journey from despair to trust.

SAC

For bibliography, *see* CANTATA, §1.

***Was frag ich nach der Welt*** ('What do I ask from the world'). Cantata for the ninth Sunday after Trinity, bwv94, first performed on 6 August 1724. The basis for the anonymous libretto is Balthasar Kindermann's chorale of the same name (1664). The librettist retained strophes 1, 7, and 8 of the chorale verbatim, expanded strophes 3 and 5 by interpolations in recitative style, and reworked strophes 2, 4, and 6 as arias. The libretto is only loosely connected to the readings for the day, though it does contain echoes of the warnings against apostasy found in the Epistle, and also recalls the statement found in the Gospel (the parable of the unjust steward from St Luke 16) that 'the children of this world are in their generation wiser than the children of light'. Bach revived the cantata some time in the period 1732–5, and a further performance took place in Leipzig in the

1750s, directed by Bach's successor there, Johann Gottlob Harrer. bwv94 is scored for SATB with flute, two oboes, strings, and continuo.

The cantata has eight movements instead of the usual six. It opens in the manner normal for the Leipzig cantatas, with a chorale fantasia, based on the melody of the hymn *O Gott, du frommer Gott*, which is heard in the soprano to the accompaniment of thematic work in the lower voices. Much of the subsidiary material is based on the opening ritornello, which features an elaborate flute solo of some virtuosity springing from a motif derived from the opening line of the chorale. It has been noted that many of the cantatas of this period (around 1724) contain important flute parts, probably pointing to the presence of a player of exceptional ability in the Leipzig musical establishment at the time, though it remains true that the fluttering flute solos may also stand for the shadowy, fleeting nature of the world. The second movement is an aria, 'Die Welt ist wie ein Rauch und Schatten', in da capo form for bass with continuo only. Much of its material is derived from the four-square figure heard in the bass in the opening ritornello. Less conventional in design is the following movement, 'Die Welt sucht Ehr und Ruhm', which sets the third strophe of the chorale with interpolations in recitative style. The successive lines of the chorale are paraphrased in 3/8 time with accompanying figures for two oboes, the recitative passages adding a commentary on the preceding line in each case. The fourth movement, 'Betörte Welt', is an alto aria accompanied by a florid solo flute part. The form can be thought of as a modified da capo structure (A–B–A'), with the second A tonally adjusted to end in the tonic. In the central section the tempo increases to Allegro at the text-phrase 'Du magst den eitlen Mammon zählen' ('You may count the worthless lucre'), slowing again to Adagio to point the contrast with the following phrase, 'Jesus soll allein meine Seele Reichtum sein' ('Jesus alone shall be my soul's wealth').

There follows a second interpolated chorale, this time for bass and continuo, designed in a similar manner to the third movement. Here again the strophe is sung line by line with recitative interpolations. Another unifying feature of the movement is a persistent chromatic bass line, apparently intended to paint the words 'bekümmert sich' ('grieves') in the text. The sixth movement is another aria, 'Die Welt kann ihre Lust und Freud', for tenor with strings and continuo, also in modified da capo form. Its prevailing dotted rhythms, aligned with triplets in the instruments, suggests a slow type of gigue. The third and last aria, 'Es halt es mit der blinden Welt', for soprano with obbligato oboe d'amore in F♯ minor, is in ritornello form, with a medial entry of the ritornello in the relative (A) major. A feature of the aria is a long-held note for 'halt' ('hold'), which recurs several times. The final chorale, *Was frag ich nach der Welt*, is set in plain style and played twice to accommodate the last two strophes of the chorale.

DLH

For bibliography, *see* CANTATA, §1.

***Was Gott tut, das ist wohlgetan*** ('What God does, that is well done') **(i).** Cantata for the 15th Sunday after Trinity, BWV99, first performed on 17 September 1724. It is the earliest of three cantatas associated with the hymn of that title by the 17th-century writer Samuel Rodigast, and belongs to the great series of chorale-based cantatas which Bach produced during his second year at Leipzig. Although the text of the hymn has no specific relationship to the appointed Gospel reading (Matt. 6: 24–34: part of the Sermon on the Mount), its content, perfectly summarized in the opening line, is wholly complementary. Following the customary procedure in Bach's chorale cantatas, the librettist has left the opening and closing strophes of Rodigast's hymn unchanged, paraphrasing the intervening strophes to suit the requirements of recitative and aria. Bach's autograph score, until recently thought to have been lost during World War II, survives (with some leaves missing) in the Staatsbibliothek zu Berlin, and original performing parts are also extant.

The opening chorus places the chorale melody, by an unknown hand, in the soprano line of the four-part vocal texture and strengthens it with a single horn. The eight lines of the stanza are presented in irregular choral blocks interspersed with orchestral tuttis translucently scored for transverse flute, oboe d'amore, strings, and continuo. The tuttis are of substantial proportions, giving the movement, as pointed out in *DürrK*, something of the character of an instrumental concerto. Indeed, in this respect the construction of the piece bears an affinity with the opening chorus of Cantata 133, *Ich freue mich in dir*, which Bach wrote some three months later for the Christmas festival.

This festive G major opening movement is followed by a bass recitative which ends with three-and-a-half bars of arioso for the word 'wenden', effectively expressing the idea of God 'turning away' the singer's misfortune. In the E minor da capo aria which follows, the tenor is partnered by a virtuoso flute obbligato, a recurring feature in the cantatas that Bach wrote at this time, over a period of four months between August and November. The aria, however, is no less remarkable for the expressive subtlety with which the composer highlights contrasting aspects of the text: the chromatically coloured 'verzagte Seele' ('disconsolate spirit') on the one hand; the strong, affirmative declamatory gestures for God as 'weiser Arzt und Wundermann' ('wise physician and performer of miracles') on the other. The alto recitative (no. 4) follows the pattern of the earlier tenor recitative in its three concluding bars of arioso. It leads to a duet in B minor for soprano and alto with obbligato flute and oboe d'amore, and basso continuo. In this movement, where both vocal and instrumental lines proceed for the most part in imitation, Bach reaches ever greater heights of expressive subtlety. Contrasting themes of suffering and triumph over adversity, or, more specifically, the conflict between the spirit and the flesh, are held in the balance with the utmost delicacy.

This beautifully proportioned cantata ends with a plainly harmonized setting of the sixth strophe of Rodigast's hymn, with *colla parte* instrumental support.

NA

For bibliography, *see* CANTATA, §1.

***Was Gott tut, das ist wohlgetan*** ('What God does, that is well done') **(ii).** Cantata for the 21st Sunday after Trinity, BWV98, performed for the first time in Leipzig on 10 November 1726. This is the second of three cantatas with this title based on the hymn by Samuel Rodigast (1674), but unlike the other two it is in no sense a CHORALE CANTATA. It does, however, begin with a chorale fantasia in which the melody is heard as a soprano (and first oboe) cantus firmus, with more active lower voices (ATB) doubled by other wind instruments, and in which the lines of the chorale are separated by string ritornellos with an animated, if not exactly virtuoso, part for the first violin.

The two recitative–aria pairs, shared between the four vocal soloists, that make up the rest of the cantata are, however, related not to the hymn but to the Gospel of the day, St John 4: 47–54, which tells of the nobleman from Capernaum who believed when Jesus told him that his sick son was healed. As W. H. Whittaker succinctly expresses it, 'the tenor [recitative] pleads for rescue from misery, the soprano [aria] bids her eyes cease from weeping, since God the Father lives, the alto [recitative] breathes a message of solace and the bass [aria] declares that he will never leave Jesus' (*The Cantatas of Johann Sebastian Bach* (London, 1959), i. 548–9). The two arias are well contrasted: the first in C minor, 3/8 time, with oboe obbligato, is in ritornello form; the second in B♭ major, ¢ time signature, with unison violins, is in a modified da capo form.

There is, rather unusually, no concluding chorale, but, as pointed out in *DürrK*, Bach bases the initial phrase of the final bass aria 'Meinen Jesum laß ich nicht' on the opening of the hymn of that name by Christian Keymann (1658).

For bibliography, *see* CANTATA, §1.

***Was Gott tut, das ist wohlgetan*** ('What God does, that is well done') (**iii**). Cantata for an unspecified occasion, BWV100. Bach wrote three cantatas with this title which were linked, in varying degrees, to the hymn beginning with the same words by the 17th-century writer Samuel Rodigast. This is the last of them, and the one most closely related to Rodigast's text. Although in some measure representative of Bach's innovative chorale-based cantata output, this work neither belongs to the great series of such pieces he produced for his second annual Leipzig cycle (1724–5) nor conforms to it structurally. Instead, it belongs to a small group of cantatas (the others being nos. 97, 117, and 192) written during the late 1720s and early 1730s in which the hymn text is retained throughout, unaltered *per omnes versus*. Sometimes, as in nos. 97 and 117, Bach adheres to the alternating pattern of recitative and aria within a choral framework. In the present work, however, as in the perhaps fragmentary Cantata 192, recitative is entirely dispensed with in favour of arias and chorale movements. A feature common to all the works in this group is the absence of any designation for a particular occasion or feast in the Church year. It is of interest to note, however, that Johann Christoph Rost, the sexton at the Thomaskirche from 1716 until his death in 1739, linked the four hymns on which these cantatas are based to wedding services. Günther Stiller (*Johann Sebastian Bach and Liturgical Life in Leipzig*, trans. H. J. A. Bouman, D. F. Poellot, and H. C. Oswald, ed. R. A. Leaver (St Louis, Miss., 1984), 246) has also remarked that where Cantata 100 is concerned, a designation for the 21st Sunday after Trinity might have been intended. The Dresden hymn schedules of about 1750 suggest 'Hymns of Lament and Comfort' for this Sunday, among which is listed Rodigast's *Was Gott tut, das ist wohlgetan*. Cantata 100 was probably first performed some time about 1732.

The joyful opening chorus in G major was taken over by Bach from an earlier cantata of the same name (no. 99; see above); but the addition of two horns and timpani for the later version gives the piece an altogether more festive, occasional character. Each strophe of Rodigast's hymn begins with the same words, 'Was Gott tut, das ist wohlgetan'. The second strophe is set as a duet in D major for alto and tenor. Bach ensures further contrast between this section and the richly scored chorus which precedes it by supporting the voices with nothing more than basso continuo,

which provides a quasi-ostinato accompaniment to the imitative vocal writing. Movement 3 is a soprano aria in B minor whose florid and virtuoso flute obbligato suggests that Bach had an unusually accomplished player at his disposal. The music returns to G major for the fourth strophe, a bass aria accompanied by divided violins, viola, and continuo; this is a robustly expressive movement whose syncopated rhythms lend emphasis to its fundamentally dance-like character. The fifth strophe is again in the rhythm of a dance but the key (E minor), the 12/8 time signature, and the softly spoken inflections of an obbligato oboe d'amore evoke an altogether more contemplative, inner spirit of rejoicing.

For the concluding section of the work Bach reused a setting of the chorale melody with which he had ended each part of Cantata 75, *Die Elenden sollen essen*, performed as an inaugural piece on his arrival in Leipzig in 1723. The scoring of this later version, however, is enriched by additional parts for two horns, timpani, flute, and oboe d'amore. NA

For bibliography, *see* CANTATA, §1.

***Was mein Gott will, das g'scheh allzeit*** ('What my God wills always comes about'). Cantata for the third Sunday after Epiphany, BWV111, first performed at Leipzig on 21 January 1725. It belongs to the composer's great cycle of chorale-based cantatas which unfolded, almost without interruption, from the first Sunday after Trinity 1724 until Palm Sunday 1725. Bach's autograph score, previously held in Berlin, was once thought to have been destroyed during World War II, but in fact survives in the Biblioteka Jagiellońska in Kraków, Poland.

The text, by an unidentified author, is a remodelled version of the hymn *Was mein Gott will, das g'scheh allzeit* (1547) by Margrave Albrecht of Brandenburg. According to Günther Stiller (*Johann Sebastian Bach and Liturgical Life in Leipzig* (St Louis, Miss., 1970), 238), this hymn had been sung in Leipzig on the third Sunday after Epiphany 'from time immemorial'. In accordance with Bach's usual practice in the cantatas of this cycle, hymn strophes in their original form are retained in the opening and closing movements.

The cantata begins with a tautly constructed chorus introduced by a 16-bar instrumental statement for divided oboes and violins, viola, and basso continuo. The eight lines of the hymn stanza are sung in long notes by the sopranos, who sustain a melody by Claudin de Sermisy (*c.*1495–1562), published by Pierre Attaingnant in about 1530. The remaining three vocal parts are deployed imitatively, and this sturdy, energetic A

# Was mir behagt, ist nur die muntre Jagd

minor movement is concluded by a repeat of the instrumental introduction.

The first of two arias is for bass with continuo. The resolute character of the music, introduced by the continuo and taken up by the voice, reflects, albeit austerely, the textual declamation which acknowledges God as the source of hope and strength on earth. As so often in the chorale cantatas, an ornamented quotation of the hymn melody in the vocal line—in this case it is twice heard at the words 'Gott ist dein Trost und Zuversicht und deiner Seele Leben'—is a feature both unifying and affecting. An alto recitative warns against ignoring God's authority, promising happiness to those who obey him. This exhortation is further developed in the radiant G major duet for alto and tenor which follows. Here, the central theme of the cantata—the salvation of the soul through death—is presented expressively in a surging 3/4 dance: 'So geh ich mit beherzten Schritten' ('So I go with fearless steps'). Fear and doubt are dispelled by the exuberant, profoundly optimistic character of this extended da capo movement, with its *saccadé*, or dotted, rhythms. Bach's canonic writing for the two voices, the melodic lyricism, and certain structural features remind us of the legacy left by Italian composers, notably perhaps by Agostino Steffani (1654–1728), who spent much of his life in Germany.

After the duet, a dazzling jewel in the cantata, there follows a soprano recitative accompanied by two oboes with continuo. This prayer for everlasting life reaches an expressive climax in a closing arioso section, marked 'Adagio': 'O seliges, gewünschtes Ende!' ('O blessed, longed-for end'). The cantata closes with a second strophe of Margrave Albrecht's hymn, straightforwardly harmonized with *colla parte* instrumental support.

NA

For bibliography, *see* CANTATA, §1.

***Was mir behagt, ist nur die muntre Jagd*** ('The cheerful hunt is all that pleases me') ['Jagdkantate' ('Hunt Cantata'; 'Hunting Cantata')]. Secular cantata, BWV208, for the birthday of Duke Christian of Saxe-Weißenfels (23 February), probably composed in 1713 when Bach was paid for a series of concerts in Weißenfels. It is his first 'modern' cantata, including both da capo arias and recitatives. However, the main sections of the arias have only very brief texts, and Bach often relinquishes simple recitative in favour of a more arioso style. The text is by Salomo Franck.

As usual in secular cantatas, the courtly celebration takes precedence over classical accuracy, but the use of mythological names for the solo voices at least guarantees some slight dramatic action. Four singers are employed: Diana and Pales (both soprano), Endymion (tenor), and Pan (bass). At first, only Diana, the goddess of hunting (a sport for which the duke had an extraordinary passion), appears 'on stage'. After an opening recitative, which was presumably preceded by an instrumental movement (the Sinfonia BWV1046a has been suggested, possibly for a later revival of the cantata), Diana praises hunting as the passion of gods and heroes. Then Endymion appears; he feels rejected by his beloved Diana who at the moment is concerned only with hunting. Endymion expresses his feelings in another recitative–aria pair. Then Diana and Endymion join together in a short dialogue about the reasons for her behaviour, in which Diana explains that today her action is focused on Duke Christian's birthday. At once Endymion accepts this excuse, and they both decide to join in the duke's celebration.

The recitative–aria pattern is repeated with the appearances of Pan and Pales who, unlike Diana and Endymion, praise the duke unreservedly. A short recitative for Diana leads to the first 'chorus' (strictly speaking, an ensemble; the upper parts are for two sopranos, and there is no alto part). This is followed by a succession of arias without recitatives. First Diana and Endymion fulfil their promise to serenade the duke in a duet; then Pales and Pan each sing another aria, and the work ends with a second 'chorus'.

The shape of the cantata is obviously determined by musical rather than dramatic considerations: each singer has an aria before the first chorus and another aria (or duet) before the second. In the first half each aria is preceded by recitative which pushes the 'action' forward, while the aria itself expresses the character's feelings on a higher musical level. Such characterization as there is based on the role the person has in classical mythology, and some of the 'players' carry appropriate belongings. Diana is provided with an arrow (mentioned in her opening recitative), and Pan lays down his shepherd's crook in front of the duke. Both 'props' suggest that the cantata may have been performed in at least a semi-staged manner. Other attributes are suggested by the music. Diana's aria is accompanied by two 'hunting' horns, the first aria of Pales (the goddess of cattle and herdsmen) by two recorders.

Any criticism of the duke was, of course, excluded. Thus it is that Pales, in her first aria, the well-known 'Schafe können sicher weiden' ('Sheep may safely graze'), expresses admiration of the duke as a solicitous ruler, despite the fact that only a few years later Duke Christian was arraigned before the *Reichsgericht* (the supreme court) because of his squandermania, especially as far as hunting was concerned.

With slight alterations the cantata was repeated

some years later for a birthday of Duke Ernst August of Weimar (only the duke's name had to be changed), and again in 1742 for the nameday of the Saxon elector, Friedrich August II. In 1725 Bach incorporated the music of nos. 7 and 13 into Cantata 68, *Also hat Gott die Welt geliebt*, and in 1728/9 the final chorus became the opening chorus of Cantata 149, *Man singet mit Freuden vom Sieg*. Thus the Hunt Cantata was an example of Bach's early vocal music that he was pleased to draw on throughout his further career.                KK

M. Marissen, 'On Linking Bach's F-Major Sinfonia and his Hunt Cantata', *Bach* 23/2 (1992), 31–46. For further bibliography, *see* CANTATA, §2.

***Was soll ich aus dir machen, Ephraim*** ('How shall I give thee up, Ephraim?'). Cantata for the 22nd Sunday after Trinity, BWV89, first performed at Leipzig on 24 October 1723. The Gospel appointed for the day, St Matthew 18: 23–35, deals with forgiveness, exhorting Christians to show the same mercy towards others that God shows towards them, and this in general is the theme of the cantata. But the anonymous librettist has chosen an Old Testament passage, Hosea 11: 8, to stand at the head of his text: 'How shall I give thee up, Ephraim? how shall I deliver thee, Israel? how shall I make thee as Admah? how shall I set thee as Zeboim? mine heart is turned within me, my repentings are kindled together.' Although it is Jehovah, not Christ, who is speaking, Bach set this sombre passage, as he so often did the *vox Christi*, as a bass solo in a manner which lies somewhere between arioso and aria. Following the arioso tradition, each clause of the text is set to new material, while the accompaniment of two oboes, horn, strings, and continuo (the cantata's full instrumental complement) is tightly constructed, with recurring motifs and a formal ritornello at the beginning and end.

Two recitative–aria pairs follow, the first for alto, the second for soprano. Both recitatives are accompanied only by continuo, and so too is the alto aria 'Ein unbaumherziges Gerichte'. This is remarkable above all for its unusual structure. Basically ternary (A–B–A'), in so far as the two opening lines of text are repeated at the end, the first (A) section ends in the dominant (A minor), leading us to expect eventually a modified da capo; but the middle (B) section closes in the distant key of C minor, practically ensuring a thorough reorganization of the final (A') section so as to regain the tonic key (D minor). The term 'free da capo', often somewhat indiscriminately applied to Bach's arias of this basic type, is here for once appropriate. The soprano aria 'Gerechter Gott, ach rechnest du?', in a more straightforward ritornello form and with oboe obbligato, sounds a

note of optimism, and the cantata ends with a four-part setting of the seventh strophe of Johann Heermann's hymn *Wo soll ich fliehen hin* (1630) in cantional style, with *colla parte* instrumental support.

For bibliography, *see* CANTATA, §1.

***Was willst du dich betrüben*** ('Why troublest thou thyself'). Cantata for the seventh Sunday after Trinity, BWV107, composed for 23 July 1724. The structure is unusual in its uninterrupted succession of four arias which are not punctuated by recitatives. Such apparent lack of variety would have been unusual in a specially written poetic libretto, but the text was actually taken directly from Johann Heermann's early 17th-century chorale *Was willst du dich betrüben*. The centrality of the chorale was typical of the cantatas of Bach's second *Jahrgang* (1724–5), which were conceived as a unified cycle in which each work was based closely on one main chorale (*see* CHORALE CANTATA). Usually only the first and last strophes of the hymn were set verbatim, the central stanzas being paraphrased and reversified by Bach's librettist to provide more suitable material for recitatives and arias. BWV107, however, is unique among the cantatas of the second *Jahrgang* in reverting to the 17th-century *per omnes versus* design incorporating the entire chorale, a procedure also seen in such early pieces as *Christ lag in Todes Banden* and in a number of later Leipzig works.

*Was willst du dich betrüben* was one of the less familiar hymns for the seventh Sunday after Trinity, and may have been chosen only because Bach had already employed the standard hymn of the day, *Warum betrübst du dich, mein Herz*, in the cantata of that name written for the 15th Sunday after Trinity in 1723. The choice of chorale was related to the prescribed Gospel reading (which usually preceded the cantata), in this case the miracle of the feeding of the four thousand (Mark 8: 1–9). Heermann's chorale makes no direct reference to the incident, but expands upon the doubt expressed by the disciples and the ultimate restoration of their faith; the main moral message—the value of trust and faith in the Lord—is announced at the outset and clarified in the second strophe (the only recitative).

Although the limitations of employing rigidly structured hymn verse for free recitative are apparent (though ameliorated by a passage of arioso), the concise and at times vivid language of the hymn writer proved a suitable vehicle for Bach's music. The four arias (for bass, tenor, soprano, and again tenor) are well contrasted, though they are all fairly short and, perhaps because of the nature of the text, avoid da capo form. The first tenor aria reflects the Lutheran delight in describing the wiles of Satan, and Bach responds with a version of the stock operatic 'rage' aria, complete with devious runs and leaps (falling 9ths depicting Satan's infernal abode below). The second tenor aria provides a strong contrast, and unison flutes help sustain a mood of happy assent to the will of God. It is one of many such movements with important flute parts which appear in a group of cantatas written between July and November 1724.

Whereas in *Christ lag in Todes Banden* the hymn tune permeates every verse, in the present work the composer adopts the same approach as in the other cantatas of his second cycle, limiting the melody in the main to the first and last choruses. The opening chorus is an expansive chorale fantasia in B minor with a treble cantus firmus (reinforced by a corno da caccia), while the final four-part harmonization of the chorale, decked out with ritornellos, takes on the character of a siciliana. There is a single clear-cut quotation from the last line of the chorale at the end of the B minor soprano aria, where it is used to elevate the repetition of the concluding line, 'God's wishes shall come to pass'.                                    SH

For bibliography, *see* CANTATA, §1.

**watermarks** (*Wasserzeichen*). Watermarks are of major importance in the scientific study of musical sources, particularly as an aid to dating and chronology. Their importance was well known to Philipp Spitta, who included several examples of watermarks to be found in the Bach sources in the appendixes to his Bach biography (1873–80). The most extensive modern study of the Bach watermarks has been undertaken by Wisso Weiß and Yoshitake Kobayashi, whose two-volume *Katalog der Wasserzeichen in Bachs Originalhandschriften* (*NBA* IX/1) was published in 1985.

**Wecker, Christoph Gottlob** (b. 1706; d. 20 April 1774). Kantor and flautist, born in Friedesdorf, Silesia, where his father was an organist. He studied jurisprudence at Leipzig University, and was a pupil of Bach, between 1723 and 1729. In 1727 Bach recommended him for the post of Kantor at the Jacobikirche in Chemnitz, but his application was unsuccessful; two years later he was appointed to a similar post at the Dreifaltigkeitskirche in Schweidnitz, Silesia.

Wecker's name appears at the end of the printed libretto of the cantata *Liebster Gott, vergißt du mich*, performed in 1727 at the same memorial service as Bach's ICH LASSE DICH NICHT, DU SEGNEST MICH DENN. It cannot, however, be assumed that Wecker composed the music.

F. Feldmann, 'Chr. Gottlob Wecker, ein Schüler Bachs als schlesischer Kantor', *BJb* 31 (1934), 89–100; K. Hofmann, 'Bachs Kantate "Ich lasse dich nicht, du segnest mich denn" BWV 157: Überlegungen zu Entstehung, Bestimmung und originaler Werkgestalt', *BJb* 68 (1982), 51–80.

**Wedemann.** A family from Arnstadt in Thuringia, closely tied to the Bach family by marriage and friendship. Johannes Wedemann (1611–84) was town clerk and treasurer at Arnstadt. His wife Maria (née Müller) bore him five daughters. Maria Elisabetha married Johann Christoph Bach (i) in 1667. Catharina (1650–1704) married Johann Michael Bach in 1675; their children included Maria Barbara, who in 1707 became J. S. Bach's first wife. Of the other daughters, Regina (1660–1730) became the second wife of Johann Lorenz STAUBER, the clergyman who officiated at the marriage of J. S. Bach and Maria Barbara Bach in 1707; Margarethe married the Arnstadt burgomaster Martin FELDHAUS; and Susanna Barbara married Johann Gottfried Bellstedt of Arnstadt, brother of Johann Hermann Bellstedt, one of the Mühlhausen councillors responsible for Bach's appointment as organist of the Blasiuskirche there in 1708.

**'Wedge'.** Nickname for the Prelude and Fugue in E minor for organ BWV548. The name describes the shape of the fugue subject, the intervals of which gradually widen from the tonic (E) to an octave B on either side of it.

***Weichet nur, betrübte Schatten*** ('Depart, gloomy shades'). Secular cantata, BWV202, for solo soprano, oboe, strings, and continuo. Beyond the fact that it was composed for a wedding at springtime, which is evident from the text, nothing is known of the occasion for which this cantata was composed. As long as it was thought to date from the Cöthen years (1717–23), it was possible to suggest Bach's second wife Anna Magdalena as the original soprano soloist. The work does indeed have some features associated with the Cöthen cantatas—the dance-like character of the last two arias, for example, and the generously proportioned ritornellos they contain—and the aria 'Phoebus eilt mit schnellen Pferden' (no. 3) has a thematic kinship with a movement in the Violin Sonata in G major BWV1019, which is usually considered to be a Cöthen work. But Alfred Dürr has argued strongly (in *DürrK*) for an earlier, Weimar origin, chiefly on notational evidence in the source (a copy by Johannes Ringck dating from 1730) and on the literary style, which suggests the Weimar court poet Salomo Franck as the librettist.

The cantata begins with one of Bach's most poetic inspirations. Quietly rising string arpeggios suggest the 'gloomy shades', the winter mists, which are then penetrated by a warming ray of light from the oboe's first, long-held note, presaging the soprano's entry; the central part of this da capo aria, in a contrasting metre and tempo, sings of the delights of spring. The cantata then proceeds in a regular alternation of recitative and aria (nine numbers in all), which sing of springtime as the season when even the gods turn towards love. As winter's shades are forgotten, the tone gradually lightens and the cantata concludes with a brief (perhaps too brief) gavotte.

For bibliography, *see* CANTATA, §2.

***Weihnachts-Oratorium.*** *See* CHRISTMAS ORATORIO.

**Weimar.** A town in the electorate of Saxony where Bach was employed briefly in 1703 and again in 1708–17. His first period of employment was as a lackey with additional musical duties (probably as a violinist) between about March and August 1703. The duke of Weimar was then Johann Ernst; at his death on 10 July 1707 he was succeeded by his elder son Wilhelm Ernst, Bach's employer from 1708 to 1717. A second palace, known as the 'red palace', stood between Bach's lodgings and Wilhelm Ernst's residence, and this was inhabited by another filial branch of the ducal family—Duke ERNST AUGUST, who shared a portion of responsibility for Bach's employment, and his brother Prince Johann Ernst. Johann Ernst was not physically robust, but he possessed unusually promising musical talent, which made Bach especially pleased to serve him.

Weimar was a small, compact provincial town, about half the size of Erfurt, or a third the size of Leipzig. The main palace, the Wilhelmsburg, was much smaller than the ducal residence, designed by Goethe, which succeeded it; of the original building only the imposing clock-tower and gatehouse survive today. The court chapel, known as the Himmelsburg ('castle of heaven'), lay at its heart on three storeys; a small loggia in the centre of its roof housed the organ and the seating for singers and instrumentalists newly added during Bach's period of employment.

The market-place and the Stadtkirche, dedicated to St Peter and St Paul, were only a short walk from the palaces. The Elephant Hotel had stood in the market-place for over three centuries, just a few paces from the home of the court singer Adam Immanuel Weldig (1667–1716), with whom the Bachs lodged until Weldig left for Weißenfels in 1713. Where the growing Bach family lived after that is not known. Their number was increased when Bach's nephew Johann Bernhard (1700–43) joined him as an apprentice in 1715.

It was almost certainly at the request of the young Prince Johann Ernst that Bach made the arrangements for harpsichord and for organ of concertos by Vivaldi and other composers (including Johann Ernst himself) that date from this period. In this enterprise he was partnered by his distant relative J. G. Walther, organist at the Stadtkirche. The original compositions of Bach most associated with Weimar are the early mature organ works and the first extended series of cantatas. It was at Weimar that he wrote most of the pieces in the *Orgel-Büchlein*, and his promotion to *Konzertmeister* in 1714 carried the obligation of providing a cantata for the court chapel each month. About 20 cantatas from this period survive, some of them only in later Leipzig recensions.

Bach's productivity—in this direction at least—seems to have come to a temporary halt after he was passed over in the search for a successor to J. S. Drese, who died on 1 December 1716 after serving as Duke Wilhelm Ernst's *Kapellmeister* since 1683. During the months that followed, Bach's personal relationship with the duke deteriorated to the point where Wilhelm Ernst refused to grant him permission to take up a new appointment with Prince Leopold at Cöthen, and even placed him under arrest for 'too stubbornly insisting on his discharge'. Bach seems never to have returned to Weimar after his dismissal (following four weeks of detention) in December 1717. The town retained its rather proud, insular stance for many years—indeed until Goethe began to raise its profile internationally. Passing through in 1737 on his way to Herrnhut in northern Saxony, the founder of Methodism, John Wesley, found it an odd, smallish town with an idiosyncratic reigning duke (Ernst August) whose inspection he had been subjected to before proceeding to Leipzig. From 1919 to 1933 the town served as the administrative capital of Germany's ill-fated Weimar Republic. Today it seeks to attract visitors for its associations with Goethe and Schiller, rather than with Bach. SFD

A. Glöckner, 'Gründe für Johann Sebastian Bachs Weggang von Weimar', in W. Hoffmann and A. Schneiderheinze, eds., *Bericht über die Wissenschaftliche Konferenz zum V. Internationalen Bachfest der DDR in Verbindung mit dem 60. Bachfest der Neuen Bachgesellschaft* (Leipzig, 1988), 137–43; H. R. Jung, *Johann Sebastian Bach in Weimar 1707 bis 1717: Tradition und Gegenwart* (Weimar, 1985); M. Petzoldt, *Bachstätten aufsuchen* (Leipzig, 1992), 167–89.

***Weinen, Klagen, Sorgen, Zagen*** ('Weeping, wailing, lamenting, fearing'). Cantata for the third Sunday after Easter (Jubilate), BWV12, first performed on 22 April 1714 at Weimar, and revived at Leipzig on 30 April 1724. The cantata is best

The castle at Weimar, where Bach was employed in 1703 and again in 1708–17

known for its first vocal movement, whose A section Bach later arranged as 'Crucifixus etiam pro nobis' in the Mass in B minor. Both the autograph score and portions of the Weimar and Leipzig performing materials survive in Berlin; there is some evidence that at Leipzig the work was performed in a version that was notated a tone higher than at Weimar.

The text is presumed to be the work of the Weimar court poet Salomo Franck, whose somewhat old-fashioned Baroque rhetorical style is evident in the opening line, which lists four nouns of similar meaning. The overall design, with its limited use of recitative and four brief, somewhat irregular, arias—only the first is set by Bach as a regular da capo form—is comparable with the texts of Bach's other early Weimar cantatas.

This was the second of the cantatas composed after Bach's appointment as *Konzertmeister* at Weimar, four weeks after Cantata 182. The scoring and the musical forms of the individual movements resemble those of the other early Weimar cantatas; the upper strings are in four parts, with two violas, and the three arias lacking a complete da capo nevertheless allude to that form by restating the opening words of the text in the last part of the movement. The written-out melodic embellishment of the oboe part in movements 1 and 4 reflects Bach's mastery of the style of the Italian Adagio; comparable writing occurs in his concerto transcriptions, which have been dated to the previous year.

Although less ambitious than the adjacent works, BWV182 and 172, Cantata 12 evinces a similar enthusiasm for inventing original musical forms that closely reflect the meaning and affect of the text. For example, the last vocal entrance in the alto aria combines lines from the A and B sections of the text—a departure from convention reflecting the composer's apparent interest in achieving maximum rhetorical effect.

Although scored for four-part vocal ensemble, the first vocal movement is textually and formally a da capo aria. Its A section is a passacaglia built on twelve statements of a descending chromatic bass line, a traditional lamenting figure. Vivaldi's alto aria 'Piango, gemo, sospiro e peno' (RV675:1) has been named as a possible model, but despite the somewhat similar text the two movements have little in common, and Bach had already written at least one comparable movement (the 'Lamento' in the keyboard Capriccio BWV992). The following accompanied recitative for alto (a setting of Acts 14: 22) counterpoints tortured harmonies and melodic writing with a straight C major scale in the first violin. The meaning of the latter is spelt out when the alto likewise sings a rising scale to the words 'into the kingdom of God'.

In the subsequent aria the tortuous character of both alto and oboe lines reflects the 'Kreuz' element of the text ('Cross and crown are united'). The ritornello is combined with the voice through *Vokaleinbau;* although not unidiomatic, the oboe line derives from arpeggiation and must reflect the organist Bach's keyboard improvisations of expressively embellished Italianate melodies. The next aria, for bass, represents the 'comfort' ('Trost') of its text in its major mode and the diatonic principal thematic idea, again a rising scale figure. This is treated imitatively to represent its text, 'ich folge Christo nach' ('I imitate Christ'), and it returns briefly at the end in another reference to da capo form.

The final aria text is combined with a wordless chorale cantus firmus ('Jesu, meine Freude') assigned to the 'tromba' and accompanied by a quasi-ostinato bass. The cantata closes with a four-part setting of the last stanza of Samuel Rodigast's chorale text 'Was Gott tut, das ist wohlgetan' (1674), to which Bach adds a fifth, descant part, probably intended for the first violin (the designation of this part for 'oboe o tromba', as in BG and BC, or with trumpet doubling, as in the NBA, is an editorial guess). DS

For bibliography, *see* CANTATA, §1.

**Weiß, Silvius Leopold** (b. 12 Oct. 1686; d. 16 Oct. 1750). Lutenist and composer, born in Breslau (now Wrocław, Poland). His father Johann Jakob (1662–1754) and brother Johann Sigismund (c.1690–1737) were also lutenists of distinction, and Weiß himself was the leading German lutenist of his age, and one of the greatest players of all time.

By 1706 Weiß was working at the Palatine court at Düsseldorf, and there he began to compose lute music. In 1708 he was engaged by the former Polish queen, Maria Casimira, as a musician in the service of her son Prince Alexander, who travelled to Rome to join her there in that year. In 1714 Weiß returned to Germany and briefly served at the Hesse court at Kassel. In 1717 he first played at Dresden, where he was engaged to join the famous orchestra of the Saxon elector and King of Poland, August the Strong, remaining there for the rest of his life.

Weiß's skill as a player and accompanist was legendary, as were his powers of improvisation. In this he was even compared with J. S. Bach, though it is doubtful whether they actually formally competed in improvisation, as has been suggested. During 1739 Weiß stayed in Leipzig for four weeks, together with W. F. Bach and his own pupil

Johann Kropfgans, and he visited the Bach house frequently; Johann Elias Bach reports that the music he heard then was 'extra-special'. Bach's Suite for violin and harpsichord in A major BWV1025, recently identified as an arrangement of one of Weiß's lute sonatas, may owe its origin to one of these legendary meetings.

More music by Weiß has survived than by any other composer in the history of the lute. Over 600 pieces, mostly organized into suites or 'Suonaten' (Weiß's own term), for solo lute have come down to us in a variety of tablature manuscripts. Nothing of his originally extensive repertory of chamber music, lute duets, and concertos has survived in complete form; in every case the parts that accompany the solo lute are lost.

Weiß's music is characterized by a unique understanding of the capabilities of his instrument, its strengths and its weaknesses; like Bach's, it represents the culmination of a high Baroque style a little at odds with the more progressive aspirations of his younger contemporaries. Weiß was also in demand as a teacher. His many aristocratic pupils included the young Frederick the Great and his sisters Wilhelmena (later Margravine of Bayreuth) and Anna Amalia, Princess of Prussia, and his other pupils included the lutenists Adam Falckenhagen and Johann Kropfgans.

It is often suggested that Bach's lute music was written for Weiß, or even commissioned by him, but there is no concrete evidence for this, despite the musical and personal links between the two men. Bach was connected with a circle of professional and amateur lute players in Leipzig, and Weiß, as a fine composer, is unlikely to have felt the need to ask Bach to write for him. On the other hand Bach would undoubtedly have known Weiß's music through playing it on his lute-harpsichord, probably in transcriptions like the one he made as the basis for the BWV1025 arrangement. It is hard to believe that Weiß did not return the compliment in some way.                                TTC

BDok ii. 290, 366, 387, 410; iii. 7, 186–7, 281, 351, 655; W. S. Newman, *The Sonata in the Baroque Era* (Chapel Hill, NC, 1959; 3rd edn., 1972), 276–7; K.-E. Schröder, 'Zum Trio A-Dur BWV 1025', *BJb* 81 (1995), 47–59; D. A. Smith, 'Sylvius Leopold Weiss: Master Lutenist of the German Baroque', *Early Music*, 8 (1980), 47–55; C. Wolff, 'Das Trio A-Dur BWV 1025: eine Lautensonate von Silvius Leopold Weiss bearbeitet und erweitert von Johann Sebastian Bach', *BJb* 79 (1993), 47–67; *BJb* 81 (1995), 60.

**Weißenfels.** A town on the River Saale, some 30 km. (19 miles) south of Halle. In 1656 the death of the Saxon Elector Johann Georg I occasioned the partition of eastern Saxony in such a way as to make his second surviving son, August, Prince of Merseburg and Duke of Weißenfels. Two gener-

ations later, in 1712, Johann Georg's grandson Christian (1682–1736) succeeded as Duke of Weißenfels. Bach served Duke Christian by composing a homage cantata for him in 1713, and some time after the death of the Weißenfels *Kapellmeister* Johann Philipp Krieger (1649–1725)—possibly after spending a few days at Weißenfels in February 1729—he was appointed composer *von Haus aus* to the duchy, an appointment which in effect made him ineligible, until 1736, for a similar honour at the royal and electoral court in Dresden.

Weißenfels had close ties with Halle, where indeed the court was originally established, and it was during a visit with his father to Weißenfels that the boy Handel's organ playing attracted the attention of Duke Johann Adolph I (reigned 1680–97). Another important figure with Weißenfels connections was the cantata librettist Erdmann Neumeister, who was pastor there in 1704–6. During the reigns of Duke Christian (1712–36) and his successor Johann Adolf II (1736–46), Weißenfels was famed as a centre for touring and home-produced opera, and also as a centre for trumpet-playing. Two sisters of Anna Magdalena Bach, themselves daughters of a court trumpeter at Zeitz, married court trumpeters at Weißenfels, and both Gottfried Reiche, who served Bach as senior *Stadtpfeifer* in Leipzig, and J. E. Altenburg (1734–1801), who published an important history and tutor for the natural trumpet in 1795, came from Weißenfels.

Even today Weißenfels is dominated by the elevated palace in which the dukes lived, and of which the chapel and its organ survive intact and restored. But the extension which housed the theatre where opera performances were given was built on insecure foundations and had collapsed by the mid-18th century.                                SFD

A. Schmiedecke, 'Johann Sebastian Bachs Verwandte in Weißenfels', *Die Musikforschung*, 14 (1961), 195–200.

***Well-tempered Clavier, The.*** See opposite.

**Werckmeister, Andreas** (b. 30 Nov. 1645; d. 26 Oct. 1706). Theorist and organist, born in Benneckenstein, Thuringia. He received his musical training in various Thuringian towns and in 1664 was appointed organist at Hasselfelde, near Blankenburg. His final post, from 1696 until his death, was that of organist of the Martinikirche in Halberstadt. His numerous and influential treatises reflected his wide reading and his view of music as an art 'prescribed by God himself for his service'—a view which he supported with speculation on the relationship between music and mathematics.

[*cont. on p.518*]

### The Well-tempered Clavier (*Das Wohltemperirte Clavier*)

The title of two sets of 24 preludes and fugues in all major and minor keys, BWV846–93, popularly known as the '48'.

1. Genesis and purpose.
2. The preludes.
3. The fugues.
4. Dissemination and influence.

**1. Genesis and purpose.** *The Well-tempered Clavier* was clearly modelled on J. C. F. Fischer's *Ariadne musica*, a set of 20 short preludes and fugues in a chromatic key order ascending from C to B. Bach adopted an identical overall plan, adding the five keys missing from Fischer's set, C♯, d♯ (e♭), F♯, g♯ (a♭), and b♭ (lower-case letters indicate minor keys). Numerous thematic correspondences further attest to the importance of the older composer's example. *Ariadne* first appeared in 1702, but it seems likely that Bach knew it only from the 1715 reissue: preliminary work on Part 1 of the '48' was probably carried out during the period 1715–20.

An early version of Part 1 seems to have been completed by about 1720. The fugues are here entitled 'fughetta', and half of the preludes are considerably shorter than in the definitive versions. All but one of the first 12 preludes are found in early versions (in two series: C–c–d–D–e–E–F; and C♯–c♯–e♭–f) in the *Clavierbüchlein* for Wilhelm Friedemann Bach, begun in 1720. The whole of Part 1 was thoroughly revised about 1721–2, and Bach made a beautiful calligraphic fair copy (today in the Staatsbibliothek zu Berlin) in 1722–3. The many subsequent marks in this copy—corrections, revised readings, and additional ornaments—bear witness to its continued use during the Leipzig period (1723–50).

Bach finished compiling Part 2 in about 1742, roughly 20 years after completing Part 1. This later collection was, in part, based on a set of five preludes and fughettas in C, d, e, F, and G (BWV870a and 899–902), which dates from the 1720s or before, and on a set of four fughettas in C, c, D, and d, transmitted by the Bach pupil J. F. Agricola. The autograph manuscript of Part 2, compiled from separate sheets with the help of Bach's wife Anna Magdalena between about 1739 and 1742, formerly belonged to the composer Muzio Clementi (1752–1834) and is today in the British Library. A revised version was finished by 1744, when Bach's pupil and later son-in-law J. C. Altnickol made a complete copy—entitled 'Des Wohltemperirten Claviers Zweyter Theil'—under the composer's direct supervision. Subsequent revision of this manuscript in Bach's own hand indicates that he continued to make minor improvements to the work after 1744.

From a theoretical standpoint *The Well-tempered Clavier* demonstrates the range of key that becomes possible using what were then relatively modern methods of tuning, or 'temperament'. The epithet 'well-tempered', which is found in the theoretical works of Andreas WERCKMEISTER, was generally used to mean 'appropriately tuned'. It is not known for certain which type of tuning Bach had in mind, but for Werckmeister and other leading German theorists of the time the 'appropriate tuning' for a work employing all 24 keys was equal temperament.

Bach's use of the generic term 'clavier' (keyboard) leaves unspecified the precise instrument to be used. This—in conjunction with the deliberately circumscribed keyboard compass (in Part 1, *C* to *c'''*, only occasionally exceeded in Part 2)—suggests that the work was designed to be universally accessible to keyboard players regardless of the particular type of instrument (harpsichord, clavichord, or organ) that they might have at their disposal.

The title-page of Part 1 discloses its dual purpose: 'For the use and profit of the musical youth desirous of learning and for the pastime of those already skilled in this study'. *The Well-tempered Clavier* became for Bach's pupils their prime vehicle for advanced study. H. N. Gerber, for example, who studied under Bach in Leipzig between 1724 and 1727, learnt the master's works in the order Inventions, suites, and *The Well-tempered Clavier*. Bach is said to have played the work through for him three times 'on one of his splendid instruments'. From what we know of Bach's teaching methods and from the substance of the work we can deduce that it was employed in the study of both keyboard playing and composition. Keyboard students are taught to read and play in all keys and in a wide range of styles and textures; composition students are instructed how to handle all the essential contrapuntal techniques and are provided with a comprehensive collection of compositional models in both strict and free forms.

**2. The preludes.**   The prelude evolved remarkably as a genre in the course of Bach's work on *The Well-tempered Clavier*. The short preludes used for the tuition of his son Wilhelm Friedemann, then aged about 11, form a progressive course of study, starting with arpeggiated preludes (in C, c, and d) and studies for the right hand or left hand (D and e), moving on to two- and three-part inventions (E, F, and C♯), and culminating in elaborate pieces in an expressive *cantabile* style (c♯, e♭, and f). After these pieces had been incorporated in *The Well-tempered Clavier*, Bach presumably found them inadequate as partners for the demanding fugues in those keys, for he expanded them by interrupting the final cadences and inserting reprises (D and f), prestos (c and e), cadenzas (D and d), or passages in toccata style (C♯). The preludes not included in the *Clavierbüchlein* significantly include, alongside pieces of similar types, two toccatas (E♭ and B♭), which would have no doubt been beyond the technical scope of the young Friedemann. The last prelude in Part 1 (b) breaks new ground with its quasi-trio sonata texture (one can readily imagine it played on two violins and continuo) and its binary dance structure.

Binary dance form with repeats comes into its own in Part 2, where almost half the preludes are so structured. A certain affinity can be felt here with many of the sonatas of Bach's Italian contemporary Domenico Scarlatti (it is not known whether Bach was acquainted with them), particularly where keyboard brilliance occupies the foreground (D and B♭). In addition, the preludes of Part 2 are in general on a considerably larger scale than those of Part 1, being fully commensurate with the scale and substance of their companion fugues. Where old pieces were reused (C and d), they had to be greatly expanded to fit the requirements of the work. While certain preludes are constructed in pure two- or three-part counterpoint (a and b♭), idiomatic free-voiced textures are far more common than in Part 1. And the largely homophonic texture and gentle pathos of certain minor-key pieces seem to reflect the *empfindsamer Stil* of Bach's eldest sons (f and g♯). A further novel element is concerto-ritornello structure (F♯ and A♭), which to some extent gives rise to the imitation of tutti–solo contrasts, as in the Italian Concerto and the English Suites.

**3. The fugues.** The gradually enlarged conception of the prelude is not paralleled in the fugues. Two fugues from Part 1 were originally one bar shorter (G and b♭), but otherwise the revision of which we have evidence is a matter of detail. In Part 2 five fugues underwent considerable expansion (C, C♯, e, G, and A♭), but of these all but one were early fughettas which had to be drastically reworked in accordance with the enlarged dimensions and increased complexity of Bach's late style.

The fugues of *The Well-tempered Clavier* offer a characteristically encyclopaedic compendium of all known styles and methods. Contrapuntal techniques employed in Part 1 include the systematic use of stretto (C, d♯, F, a, and b♭); of double counterpoint (e and F♯), triple counterpoint (c, C♯, c♯, g♯, and B♭), and quadruple counterpoint (f); and of inversion (d, d♯, f♯, G, a, and B) and augmentation (d♯). These techniques are also represented among the fugues of Part 2, but to augmentation is here added diminution (C♯); and as well as including a triple fugue (f♯) as a counterpart to that of Part 1 (c♯), it contains four double fugues in Bach's maturest contrapuntal style (c♯, g♯, B, and b). Fugal styles in Part 1 range from the *alla breve* ricercar *a* 5 (c♯ and b♭) to the *stile francese* (D) or a 'modern' Italianate manner (G). In Part 2 Bach's stylistic range is further extended in both historical directions, in keeping with his growing interest both in 16th-century vocal polyphony and in music written 'in accordance with the latest taste'. Part 2 thus includes, on the one hand, a series of stretto fugues *a* 4 in pseudo-vocal style (D, E♭, and E), culminating in the pure *stile antico* of the E major fugue; and, on the other hand, a group of fugues *a* 3 whose episodes (in the case of f, F♯, and b) or codas (C and e: significantly, late additions), however contrapuntally based, have the surface appeal of homophony. In this regard it is worth noting that, while the closing fugues of each half of Part 1 (f and b) are monuments to Bach's contrapuntal art (distilling the key span of the entire work in their partly or wholly chromatic subjects), those of Part 2 illustrate the aesthetic aims of the more progressive styles of the day: natural grace, elegance, and simplicity.

**4. Dissemination and influence.** *The Well-tempered Clavier* remained unpublished during Bach's lifetime. Single preludes or fugues appeared in theoretical treatises and musical journals during the second half of the 18th century, but the work was otherwise disseminated in often incorrect manuscript copies until complete editions appeared in 1801–2. These pioneering publications were edited by C. F. G. Schwenke (for Simrock: Paris and Bonn), H. G. Nägeli (1773–1836) (published by Nägeli himself: Zurich), and J. N. Forkel (for Hoffmeister & Kühnel: Leipzig and Vienna). The first critical editions were those of Franz Kroll (1820–77) for C. F. Peters (Leipzig and Berlin, 1862) and for the *BG* (1866).

After Bach's death in 1750 the '48' continued to be studied by keyboard and composition students, particularly in central Germany. The partly subliminal influence of the work on Bach's sons should not be underestimated. But the decisive moment in its posthumous history arrived when Mozart was introduced to it by Baron van Swieten in 1782. Thereafter it influenced the contrapuntal writing of countless composers (notable 20th-century examples being Hindemith and Shostakovich) and it has formed a fundamental part of the training of virtually every musician in keyboard playing, composition, analysis, and general musicianship.            RDPJ

*See also* SCHWENCKE, CHRISTIAN FRIEDRICH GOTTLIEB and TEMPERAMENTS.

W. Breckoff, *Zur Entstehungsgeschichte des zweiten Wohltemperierten Klaviers von J. S. Bach* (Tübingen, 1965); A. Dürr, *Zur Frühgeschichte des Wohltemperierten Klaviers I von Johann Sebastian Bach* (Göttingen, 1984); W. Emery, 'The London Autograph of "The Forty-Eight" ', *Music and Letters*, 34 (1953), 106–23; D. O. Franklin, 'Reconstructing the *Urpartitur* for *WTC* II: A Study of the "London Autograph" ', in *Bach Studies* (Cambridge, 1989), 240–78; H. Keller, *Das Wohltemperirte Klavier* (Kassel, 1965; Eng. trans. L. Gerdine, London, 1976); Y. Tomita, *J. S. Bach's 'Das Wohltemperierte Clavier II': A Critical Commentary* (Leeds, 1993–5); D. F. Tovey, Commentaries to *J. S. Bach: The Well-Tempered Clavier*, ed. R. D. P. Jones (London, 1994).

In his *Musicalische Temperatur* (?1686–7; 2nd edn., 1691) Werckmeister offered a tuning—not to be confused with equal temperament—which enabled harpsichordists and organists to play in all the major and minor keys. It may have been this type of tuning to which the title of Bach's *The Well-tempered Clavier* refers (but *see also* TEMPERAMENTS and WELL-TEMPERED CLAVIER, THE). The many parallels (even in phraseology) between Werckmeister's *Orgelprobe* (1681; 2nd edn., 1698) and Bach's organ reports show that Bach used this treatise in testing organs. RTS

P. Williams, 'J. S. Bach—Orgelsachverständiger unter dem Einfluß Andreas Werckmeisters?', *BJb* 68 (1982), 131–42; P. Williams, 'Noch einmal: J. S. Bach—Orgelsachverständiger unter dem Einfluß Andreas Werckmeisters?', *BJb* 72 (1986), 123–5; P. Williams, *The Organ Music of J. S. Bach*, iii (Cambridge, 1984), 139–54.

**Wer da gläubet und getauft wird** ('He that believeth and is baptized'). Cantata for Ascension, BWV37, first performed in Leipzig on 18 May 1724. In the Gospel reading appointed for this occasion (Mark 16: 14–20), the account of Jesus's ascension into heaven is preceded by the command to his disciples, 'Go ye into all the world, and preach the gospel to every creature', and the promise that 'He that believeth and is baptized shall be saved'. Instead of focusing on the event of Jesus's ascension, Bach's anonymous librettist (who may well have been a theologian or cleric, judging from the dogmatic and didactic tone of the text) took this passage as the point of departure for a brief treatise on the power of Christian faith. The work opens with a setting of Jesus's promise (Mark 16: 16) just quoted. The next movement declares that belief is a kind of guarantee of Jesus's love. Movement 4 reminds us that, even though it is God's will for Christians to do good works, justification and salvation result from faith alone. In movement 5 faith is said to give wings to the soul, which allow it to soar to heaven. And the concluding chorale is a prayer asking God for the gift of faith in Jesus Christ.

The most substantial movement is the opening chorus. It begins with a lengthy ritornello (bars 1–26) played by the entire instrumental ensemble (a pair of oboes d'amore, strings, and continuo). This is the only passage in which the instruments play alone; once the voices enter (bar 27), they sing through to the end of the movement. The entire text of St Mark 16: 16 is set four times. In the first two passages (bars 27 ff. and 40 ff.), the voices enter one at a time in imitation. The third and fourth sections are distinguished by a thinning of the choral texture to two parts (the upper two in bars 63 ff., the lower two in bars 71 ff.).

Movement 2, a pleasant but unremarkable tenor aria in da capo form, has come down to us in an apparently incomplete state. Neither the autograph score nor the relevant performing part for the first violin has survived. But judging from the unmelodic qualities of the continuo line, the original scoring of the aria probably included solo violin (see Dürr). On the other hand, there is no reason to think that the instrumental ensemble of the next movement ever extended beyond the continuo group; the energetic continuo line stands on its own quite successfully. This movement is a setting for soprano, alto, and continuo of a stanza from Philipp Nicolai's famous chorale *Wie schön leuchtet der Morgenstern* (1599). The individual motifs of the ritornello are woven into a virtually seamless strand. Superimposed on this foundation are the two vocal lines, which are treated as equals. For instance, in the setting of the first phrase, the soprano begins and the alto imitates two beats later (bars 3 ff.), but in the setting of the second phrase, whose melody is identical to the first, the alto takes the lead and the soprano follows (bars 14 ff.). The third phrase of the chorale tune begins with two repeated motifs that are divided equally between the soprano and alto: the first, on the word 'Eia', is sung first by the soprano, then the alto; in the second, on the words 'himmlisch Leben', the order is reversed (bars 25 ff.). Characteristically, Bach composed elaborate, extended melismas on the words 'erfreuet' ('delight') and 'loben' ('praise'). In keeping with his extraordinary sensitivity to nuances of the text, he also elongated the original note values of the chorale melody to emphasize the meaning of 'ewig' ('eternally') (bars 6–7).

The bass recitative (movement 4), accompanied by strings and continuo, moves away from the major mode that has prevailed until now (movements 1 and 2 are in A major, movement 3 in D major) to the closely related key of B minor. The aria that follows is in the same key and has the same scoring, except that the first violin is doubled by an oboe d'amore. The text is not in da capo form, but divided into three segments of two lines each, which Bach sets in three musical paragraphs (A–B–C) separated by brief ritornellos in closely related keys.

The cantata ends with a simple four-part setting, with instrumental doubling, of a stanza from a chorale dating from the early years of the Lutheran Reformation, Johann Kolrose's morning song *Ich dank dir, lieber Herre*.　　　　SAC

A. Dürr, 'Verstümmelt überlieferte Arien aus Kantaten J. S. Bachs', *BJb* 47 (1960), 28–42. For further bibliography, *see* CANTATA, §1.

***Wer Dank opfert, der preiset mich*** ('Whoso offereth me thanks, he honoureth me'). Cantata, BWV17, for the 14th Sunday after Trinity. It was performed on 22 September 1726 as the last composition to result from Bach's encounter with church music from the ducal court of Saxe-Meiningen (*see* BACH, JOHANN LUDWIG and ERNST LUDWIG). Following the typical pattern of these cantata texts, the work is shaped by two corresponding passages from the Bible, one from the Old Testament and one from the New. The text of movement 1 is from Psalm 50: 23; the fourth movement is based on the passage in St Luke 17: 15–16 which tells of the Samaritan who, alone among the ten lepers that Jesus cured, returned to give thanks. The main subject of the cantata is therefore gratitude.

Unlike most of those in the other cantatas of this type, the opening movement (A major) is not multi-sectional, but rather, since the text is only a short one, it consists of a single large choral fugue. It is followed first by a short simple recitative for the alto, and then by a soprano aria with two solo violins, 'Herr, deine Güte reicht'. Contrary to the normal construction of these cantatas, the text of this movement is, strictly speaking, not based on 'free poetry' but on another quotation from the Bible (Psalm 36: 6): 'Thy righteousness standeth like the strong mountains.' This verse serves for the first part of the aria, which then continues with a 'free' strophe. The movement as a whole is given a tonal shape such as might be found in a Baroque concerto movement, with ritornellos in

the tonic (E major), the dominant (B major), the relative minor (C♯ minor) and finally again in the tonic.

With no. 4, 'Einer aber unter ihnen', the second part of the cantata begins. The biblical text is cast as a simple recitative, not as an aria or arioso (as in all Bach's other 'Meiningen' cantatas except *Gott fähret auf*). The reason for this might be that the Gospel *Spruch* is not like the text for a sermon, but a plain biblical narrative which can be entrusted to an Evangelist. This approach, however, is not maintained in the aria that follows, 'Welch Übermaß der Güte schenkst du mir' ('What abundance of goodness thou givest me'). Apparently Bach understood this 'individual' statement as a direct allusion to the Gospel account of the thankful Samaritan, and the words of the aria might be those of the Samaritan himself. Both the biblical narrative and the aria are sung by the tenor. After another simple recitative for the bass, the cantata ends with the third strophe of the hymn *Nun lob, mein Seel, den Herren* by Johann Gramann (1530).

When Bach wrote his four 'short masses' in about 1738–9 he reused the opening chorus of *Wer Dank opfert* for the concluding 'Cum Sancto Spiritu' of the Gloria in the G major *Missa* BWV236, to which its fugal form is well suited. He transposed the music down one tone and replaced the orchestral ritornello with a homophonic vocal introduction.　　　　KK

For bibliography, *see* CANTATA, §1.

**Werk.** *See* HAUPTWERK.

***Wer mich liebet, der wird mein Wort halten*** ('If a man love me, he will keep my words') (i). Cantata for Whit Sunday, BWV59. Once considered, by Spitta, C. S. Terry, and others, to have been a product of Bach's Weimar period, this work is probably among the composer's earliest Leipzig cantatas. While the parts indicate that a performance was given on Whit Sunday (28 May) 1724 at the University Church (the Paulinerkirche), Bach's autograph score had clearly been prepared the previous year. It seems likely, therefore, that the first performance of the piece took place in the same church in 1723, when Whit Sunday fell on 16 May. If this is indeed so, the work may be considered among the very first cantatas that Bach performed at Leipzig, pre-dating by one week the ratification of his position as Thomaskantor.

The text of the cantata is mainly the work of the Hamburg poet and theologian Erdmann Neumeister, whose first volume of *Geistliche Cantaten* (1700) gave the Lutheran cantata new definition. It is contained in the fourth part of the *Geistliche Cantaten* (1714) and is closely linked with words from the Whit Sunday Gospel reading (John 14: 23), which form the text for the opening movement. Bach did not, however, set Neumeister's poem complete, using only three of its six stanzas together with a single stanza from Luther's hymn *Komm, heiliger Geist, Herre Gott* (1524).

The cantata begins not with the customary chorus but with a duet in C major for soprano and bass, accompanied by a colourful instrumental group consisting of two trumpets, timpani, strings, and continuo. The textual heart of the movement is contained in the words 'Wer mich liebet' ('He who loves me'). Each of the five vocal periods begins with these words; four of them are treated canonically while in the fifth and concluding period the two voices enter together. Structurally, this duet owes something to the Italian chamber concerto, though the fluent contrapuntal ideas are unmistakably Bach's own.

An accompanied soprano recitative, developing into an expressive arioso in the last five bars, leads to the first strophe of Luther's Pentecostal hymn already cited. The four-part vocal setting is straightforward, and is accompanied by independent parts for divided violins and viola with basso continuo. In 1725 Bach used this setting once more in his Whitsuntide cantata *Er rufet seinen Schafen mit Namen*, but on this later occasion the independent string parts were given to a recorder trio and the strings assigned to supporting the voices. The cantata ends with a lively and song-like bass aria in C major accompanied by solo violin and continuo. The anticipation of heavenly bliss expressed in the text is beautifully reflected in this skilfully composed movement. Both this number and the opening duet were adapted by Bach in 1725 for use in a more extended cantata of the same name (no. 74) and for the same festival.

Whether or not Bach intended to conclude Cantata 59 without the customary chorale is open to question. One surviving source, dating from 1731 but not authorized by Bach, led Spitta to presume that Bach used another stanza from Neumeister's poem to round off the cantata. Another suggestion, offered by the old *BG* edition, is that Luther's chorale should be repeated to the text of a different strophe. Since Bach's autograph score contains the inscription 'Chorale segue' in the bass part of the concluding aria it would seem almost certain that he intended to end the work with a choral movement of some kind or other.

NA

For bibliography, *see* CANTATA, §1.

**Wer mich liebet, der wird mein Wort halten** ('If a man love me, he will keep my words') (ii). Cantata for Whit Sunday, BWV74, first performed on 20 May 1725. The text is one of nine by Christiane Mariane von Ziegler which Bach set between the third Sunday after Easter and Trinity Sunday 1725. It has the same title as Cantata 59 (to words by Neumeister) because both authors chose the same quotation from the appointed Gospel reading (John 14: 23) as the focal point of their texts. But there is a significant divergence in their treatment of it. While Neumeister addresses the Christian believer in collective, congregational terms, Ziegler is more concerned with personal, individual responses to faith (see Day, pp. 40–2). The two cantatas, however, share more than textual relationship since the first two movements of no. 74 are reworkings of the opening duet and bass aria of no. 59.

The cantata begins with a four-part chorus in C major, scored for a colourful instrumental ensemble of three trumpets, timpani, oboes, oboe da caccia, strings, and continuo. The joyful message of Whitsuntide is reflected both in the 'occasional' splendour of Bach's orchestration and in the carefree agility of the vocal writing. The first of the four arias in the cantata is for soprano with oboe da caccia obbligato and continuo. In the earlier cantata Bach had written this number in C major for bass, with an obbligato violin; here it is transposed to F major, and the lyrical oboe da caccia writing contributes towards a greater intimacy and expressive warmth.

An alto recitative leads to the second aria of the cantata, the text of which is based on a verse from the Gospel reading: 'I go away, and come again unto you. If ye loved me, ye would rejoice . . .' (John 14: 28). The *vox Christi* is entrusted to a bass soloist supported by an attractive, quasi-ostinato continuo part. In the first half of the aria Ziegler's text places emphasis on the phrase 'Ich gehe hin' ('I go away'), while in the second half the emphasis lies firmly on the word 'freuen' ('rejoice'), which Bach illustrates with vividly effective vocal melismas. This E minor aria leads directly to a tenor aria in G major accompanied by obbligato violin and strings. Ziegler's text proclaims the Whitsun story joyfully, while Bach's music, declamatory and dance-like, and in the character of a concerto movement, illustrates it with vocal and instrumental virtuosity. This vital aria is followed by a short bass recitative accompanied by a rich trio texture of two oboes and oboe da caccia with continuo. The text is based on Romans 8: 1: 'There is therefore now no condemnation to them which are in Christ Jesus . . .'. The significance of these words is emphasized and effectively enhanced by the pointed character of the supporting oboes.

The concluding C major aria for alto, in da capo form, retains the three-part oboe texture of the preceding recitative, with the addition of a solo violin, strings, and continuo. In his virtuoso writing for the concertante violin Bach indulges in some splendidly colourful word-painting to illustrate Satan's empty rattling of hell's chains. The song-like melodic contour of the vocal line begins boldly, even with a defiant swagger as Satan is mocked, but there is a contemplative, supplicatory passage leading to the da capo. This dramatic, highly charged movement is followed by the second strophe of Paul Gerhardt's hymn *Gott Vater, sende deinen Geist* (1653). Its associated melody, *Kommt her zu mir, spricht Gottes Sohn* (1630), is simply harmonized by Bach with *colla parte* instrumental support.                     NA

For bibliography, *see* CANTATA, §1.

**Werner, Fritz** (b. 15 Dec. 1898; d. 22 Dec. 1977). Conductor and organist, born in Berlin. Descended from a family of musicians, he studied the piano, organ, violin, and composition in Berlin. He was organist at Potsdam until the outbreak of World War II, when he left Germany and became a music director of the German radio in occupied France. After the war he returned to Germany, taking again a post as organist, this time at Heilbronn, where in 1947 he founded the Heinrich Schütz Choir. With this ensemble and the Pforzheim Chamber Orchestra he recorded over 50 of Bach's sacred cantatas, as well as the two Passions, the *Christmas* and *Easter Oratorios*, the B minor Mass, and the motets. Werner's Bach recordings are uneven in quality, but his finest performances show him to have been a thoughtful, scrupulous, and effective interpreter. He was discerning in his choice of soloists and outstandingly well served by his instrumentalists. *See also* RECORDINGS.    NA

***Wer nur den lieben Gott läßt walten*** ('Who only the loving God lets rule'). Cantata for the fifth Sunday after Trinity, BWV93. In its symmetry of design, its effective musical structure, and, above all, its sheer strength of expression, this work affords a notably fine example of Bach's trenchant originality in the composition of a CHORALE CANTATA. The piece is anchored firmly and with unusual consistency to a hymn by Georg Neumark assigned to the fifth Sunday after Trinity in the Leipzig hymn schedules of Bach's time. Neumark's hymn has seven stanzas, three of which are incorporated into the cantata in their original form. A fourth is used complete, but interspersed with recitative, while the remaining three are adapted by the unidentified librettist to accommodate the requirements of recitative and aria. The hymn text and melody occur, in part or in full, in each of the cantata's seven movements. The melody (which is Neumark's own) would seem to have been a favourite of Bach's; as well as

basing the present cantata on it, he quoted it in at least six others (nos. 27, 84, 88, 166, 179, and 197), composed four chorale preludes for organ on it (BWV642, 647, 690, and 691), and included an ornamented version of it in the *Clavierbüchlein* (1725) for his second wife, Anna Magdalena.

Bach first produced this cantata on 9 July 1724. Thus it belongs to his great annual cycle of chorale cantatas which began in June that year. Only a continuo part for four of the seven movements has survived from this performance, the cantata being known to us through a set of parts prepared for use in 1732 or 1733, when Bach may have recast it.

The Gospel reading for this Sunday (Luke 5: 1–11) tells the story of the disciple Peter's fishing expedition by night and of the miraculous draught that he landed towards dawn. This provides the underlying theme of Bach's cantata—man's surrender to God's guidance. The opening chorus, which retains the first strophe of Neumark's hymn, is in C minor and is scored for Bach's customary four-part vocal forces (SATB), with oboes, strings, and continuo. Pairs of oboes, which introduce the melodic material in close imitation, and violins provide a four-strand instrumental concertante in the short introduction, thereafter sharing an intricate relationship with the remaining instruments and with the voices. The six lines of the hymn, with the cantus firmus always sustained in the soprano, are treated more or less chordally but interspersed, line by line, with concertino episodes of vocal fugato. Thus the first and second lines are each introduced by a section for soprano and alto, the third and fourth lines by others for tenor and bass, and the fifth and sixth lines by sections for all four voices. The subtle interrelationship of all parts in this complex fantasia, together with the consummate skill with which the chorale melody is deployed, reveals a creative and technical virtuosity of the highest order.

The opening chorus is followed by an effective juxtaposition of chorale and simple recitative for bass. The recitative provides commentary on the hymn, while the hymn melody itself is presented with judicious ornamentation in the vocal line with Neumark's unaltered text. The dance-like tenor aria that follows is accompanied by strings and is striking for its paraphrase of the chorale melody substantially in the major key (E♭); as in the preceding movement, the melody itself is embellished. The duet for soprano and alto (no. 4) provides the cantata with a centrepiece of alluring beauty. It is a setting of the fourth strophe of Neumark's hymn, in which the melody is presented by violins and viola in unison while the two voices weave a lyrical fantasy deriving from it.

The movement was later arranged as one of the Schübler organ chorales (BWV647).

The fifth movement, for tenor, is constructed in a manner similar to the earlier one for bass, and consists of alternating passages of recitative with lines of hymn text set to an embellished chorale melody. The second aria of the cantata is for soprano with obbligato oboe; the two parts develop independently of each other. Although the chorale melody occupies a less prominent position than in the remaining sections of the cantata, Bach nevertheless works brief quotations from its last two lines into the vocal part.

The cantata ends with the seventh strophe of Neumark's hymn, straightforwardly harmonized by Bach with *colla parte* instrumental support.

NA

For bibliography, *see* CANTATA, §1.

**Wer sich selbst erhöhet** ('Whosoever exalteth himself'). Cantata for the 17th Sunday after Trinity, BWV47, first performed on 13 October 1726. In length and expressive weight it is dominated by the opening movement, one of Bach's most imposing fugal choruses.

The text was published in 1720 by the Eisenach court official Johann Friedrich Helbig. Telemann set many of Helbig's texts (including this one) in his capacity as Eisenach *Kapellmeister von Haus aus*, but this is Bach's only work based on a text by this poet, whose verses here betray a simplistic directness close to doggerel.

The opening chorus, in G minor, is a setting of St Luke 14: 11. The two halves of the verse, which constitute a rhetorical antithesis ('whosoever exalteth himself shall be abased; and he that humbleth himself shall be exalted'), are set respectively as subject and countersubject of the fugue, which begins with the entry of the voices. The rise and fall of each subject reflects the text, with upward melismas on the recurring word 'erhöhet' ('exalts'). A further reflection of the text's rhetorical form might be seen in the order of the vocal entries in the two expositions, which ascend from tenor to soprano in the first exposition, and then reverse the process in the second (the bass is the last voice to enter in each case). The choral fugue is preceded by an unusually elaborate ritornello in which the two oboes play antiphonally against the strings. The ritornello theme—which is distinct from the subject of the fugue—recalls the opening of the C minor organ Praeludium BWV546 (probably composed at Leipzig in the 1720s); each opens as a series of dissonant appoggiaturas, treated antiphonally. Not only is the idea of antithesis within the subject of the fugue thus anticipated, but in the course of the ritornello the first of the 'erhöhet' melismas is introduced as a motif,

receiving a quasi-fugal development. The entire ritornello recurs at the end of the movement, joined through *Choreinbau* with a restatement of the complete text.

The accompaniment of the first aria, a da capo form in D minor, is given to the organ in the composing score, from which Bach must originally have played it himself (a second keyboard instrument furnishing the figured bass realization). Bach later assigned the solo part to violin for a performance in 1736 or later (the *NBA* gives the original organ part in an appendix; the part designated 'organo obligato' in the *BG* edition is in fact the later violin version). The aria has a rather odd structure, as the closing ritornello of the A section repeats not only the entire opening ritornello but also an ornate instrumental tag that follows the voice's initial motto entrance. Perhaps for this reason the ritornello material is present in the B section only in the continuo part, where the solo instrument is restricted to a sort of written-out figured bass realization in two-part chords (adapted to the violin in the later version).

The association of pride with the Devil, introduced in the aria's B section, is maintained in the accompanied bass recitative that follows it. The stentorian tone of this recitative, which is marked by numerous harsh dissonances, is mollified in the concluding bass aria in E♭ major. The ritornello theme, introduced in fugal imitation by solo violin and oboe, is taken up by the voice. In the autograph Bach initially wrote the opening motif of the theme as two descending quavers; he later embellished these as semiquavers but retained the original form when the motif returns for the final, pleading entry of the voice with the words 'gieb mir' ('grant me'). This section constitutes an altered recapitulation of the first vocal section, despite the through-composed form of the text.

The cantata concludes with a four-part setting of strophe 11 of the chorale *Warum betrübst du dich, mein Herz*.

DS

For bibliography, *see* CANTATA, §1.

**Wer weiß, wie nahe mir mein Ende** ('Who knows how near my end is') Cantata, BWV27, written for, and performed on, the 16th Sunday after Trinity (6 October) 1726. It belongs to the third of Bach's Leipzig annual cycles. The unidentified author of the text has drawn on unusually diverse sources, through which he has sought to reflect the appointed Gospel reading (Luke 7: 11–17), telling of Christ's raising from the dead the son of the widow of Nain. The cantata text focuses on the approaching hour of death, not as an end but as the beginning of a happier life, though not entered without sorrow at leaving earthly associations behind.

The opening chorus, in C minor, is a profound, elegiac lament in 3/4 time into which Bach has woven the melody associated with Georg Neumark's hymn *Wer nur den lieben Gott läßt walten*, itself the basis of an earlier Trinity cantata (no. 93, 1724) bearing its title. The movement is intricately and lyrically constructed a four-strand vocal choir, divided oboes (whose intertwining lines, embellished with appoggiaturas, contribute much to the elegiac spirit of the movement) and violins, viola, and continuo. In addition, the soprano vocal line, which sustains the cantus firmus (the hymn melody), is reinforced by a single horn. At three points in the chorus the six lines of the hymn are interrupted by sections of accompanied recitative sung in turn by soprano, alto, and tenor; the words, unconnected to the hymn, are somewhat in the nature of a commentary on it. The instrumental writing and the established metre of the text, however, remain unimpeded; as Dürr remarks, these sections provide 'the only example of recitative in 3/4 time in the whole of Bach' (*DürrK*). The hymn text of this movement is by Ämilie Juliane, Countess of Schwarzburg-Rudolstadt (1656).

A tenor recitative leads to the first of two arias, for alto with an obbligato accompaniment of oboe da caccia and harpsichord with continuo bass. For a later performance, probably in about 1737, Bach substituted an organ for the obbligato harpsichord. The first two lines of the text seem to hark back to a hymn (1700) by Erdmann Neumeister. The carefree character with which Bach endows both vocal and instrumental parts is an apposite reflection of words that anticipate heavenly joy.

An accompanied soprano recitative, expressing an ardent longing for heaven, leads to the second aria of the cantata: 'Gute nacht, du Weltgetümmel' ('Farewell, thou world of turmoil'). In this piece, scored for bass with violins, viola, and continuo, Bach arrestingly depicts the contrasting, alternating images of the valedictory 'Gute nacht' and the tumultuous world. The first is given the character of a drowsy sarabande, the second suddenly enlivened by busy semiquaver motifs of rapidly repeated notes and scale passages.

The concluding chorale, exceptionally among those in Bach's cantatas, is in five parts (SSATB), rather than the customary four. The text is the first strophe of a hymn by Johann Georg Albinus: *Welt, ade! ich bin dein müde* (1649). Both the melody and the harmonization of this tenderly expressive closing piece are by Johann Rosenmüller, who had been a teacher at the Leipzig Thomasschule and, during the early 1650s, organist of the city's Nikolaikirche.    NA

For bibliography, *see* CANTATA, §1.

**Wesley, Samuel** (b. 24 Feb. 1766; d. 11 Oct. 1837). English composer and organist, born in Bristol. He came from a musical family which included his uncle, John Wesley (1703–91), the founder of Methodism. Samuel and his brother Charles (1757–1834) were musical prodigies; Samuel, in particular, was an outstanding organist from a very young age. In 1778 the family moved to London, but, although he almost certainly became the finest organist in England, Samuel failed to obtain the vacant post of organist at the Foundling Hospital in 1798, and thereafter tried, with varying success, to make his way as a freelance musician.

From an early period Wesley played the music of J. S. Bach. Organ music on three staves was then almost inaccessible to organists in England, where organ pedals were rare, and it was quite usual to play such music with a melody or a bass string instrument. Since Wesley played the violin, as well as keyboard instruments, and the double bass virtuoso Domenico Dragonetti (1763–1846) sometimes assisted by playing the pedal line, newly available copies of Bach's music could easily be tried and repeated.

A group of London musicians, headed by Wesley and including K. F. Horn, Benjamin Jacob (1778–1829, organist of the Surrey Chapel), and Vincent Novello (1781–1861, organist of the Portuguese Embassy chapel), introduced Bach's music in church services (as voluntaries) and later in special concerts. Wesley particularly admired Horn's playing of the Organ Sonatas, which the two men published jointly in 1809. They also published a 'new and correct edition' of *The Well-tempered Clavier* in 1810–13. Wesley could also boast that he had converted the composer William Crotch (1775–1847) and even the less enthusiastic music historian Charles Burney (1726–1814) to the advocacy of Bach's music, and he lived long enough to discuss it with the young Mendelssohn in 1837.

Wesley was probably the first English-born musician to appreciate the variety and power in Bach's music. He always showed sympathy for religious Latin texts, and it is fitting that he and Horn organized and participated in the first British performance of parts of the B minor Mass.

SFD

E. Wesley, ed., *The Bach Letters of Samuel Wesley* (2nd edn., London, 1878; repr. 1981).

**Weyrauch, Johann Christian** (b. 13 Jan. 1694; d. 1 April 1771). Lutenist and organist, born in Knauthain, near Leipzig. He probably learnt to play the lute at an early age; his father was Kantor in the same village where his lutenist contemporary Adam Falckenhagen was raised. In 1717 he entered Leipzig University, where he studied law.

For some years he aspired to a musical career, applying several times for posts as organist, without apparent success; from 1730 he seems to have made his living as a lawyer.

In 1730 Bach provided a testimonial to Weyrauch's skill 'on various instruments' and as a singer. A further testament to their close friendship is the fact that Bach acted as godfather to Weyrauch's son, Johann Sebastian, in 1743, the other godfather being the lute and violin maker J. C. Hoffmann. Weyrauch was apparently a gifted performer and composer; his lute pieces were known to be difficult, but none has survived. He arranged two of Bach's works for the lute (BWV997 and 1000); the tablature copies in his hand are now in the Musikbibliothek der Stadt Leipzig.                                                     TTC

BDok ii. 135–6, 192, 201, 223, 407–8, 449, and 555; H.-J. Schulze, 'Wer intavolierte Johann Sebastian Bachs Lautenkompositionen?', Die Musikforschung, 19 (1966), 32–9; H.-J. Schulze, ' "Monsieur Schouster"—ein vergessener Zeitgenosse Johann Sebastian Bachs', in W. Rehm, ed., Bachiana et alia musicologica: Festschrift für Alfred Dürr (Kassel, 1983), 243–50.

**Whittaker, William Gillies** (b. 23 July 1876; d. 5 July 1944). Conductor, writer, and composer, born in Newcastle upon Tyne. He studied science at university, but soon turned to music and in 1929 was made professor of music at Glasgow University and principal of the Royal Scottish Academy of Music. In 1915 he founded the Newcastle Bach Choir, with which he performed the Bach cantatas in translation. The experience resulted in a number of specialist books and articles, of which Fugitive Notes on Certain Cantatas and the Motets of J. S. Bach (1924) was the first. The two-volume The Cantatas of Johann Sebastian Bach, Sacred and Secular was published posthumously in 1959, by which time it had been largely superseded by new research and new perspectives. It is likely to be consulted now mainly for its English translations of the cantata texts.

**Widerstehe doch der Sünde** ('Stand firm, then, against sin'). Cantata, BWV54, probably written in 1715, a year or so after Bach's promotion to Konzertmeister at the court of Duke Wilhelm Ernst in Weimar. According to the libretto it was intended for the third Sunday of Lent (Oculi), which in 1715 fell on 24 March. The libretto was drawn from Gottgefälliges Kirchen-Opffer (1711), the first cycle of cantatas published by G. C. Lehms, originally intended for the two Darmstadt Kapellmeisters Christoph Graupner and Gottfried Grünewald (1675–1739). It exhorts the believer to hold firm against sin and the subtle wiles of Satan.

Of Bach's 200 or so surviving church cantatas,

Widerstehe doch der Sünde is one of only twelve which require a single solo voice, and one of only nine without an SATB ensemble or chorus; there is therefore no concluding chorale. It is scored simply for an alto soloist and a five-part string ensemble (with two violas) typical of the early cantatas. The tessitura is particularly low for the alto voice, though the range is wide (f to c"). Both the libretto and the music reflect an acquaintance with contemporary Italian practice. In dividing the poetic text into clear-cut arias and free recitative, Lehms was following the lead given by the poet and theologian Erdmann Neumeister, who was in turn indebted to the Italian genres of secular cantata and opera seria.

Structurally the cantata is one of Bach's least complicated, consisting of just two arias separated by a simple recitative. The first aria is in da capo form, and has long been admired for its harmonic richness, particularly the startling unprepared dissonances of the opening bars (dominant 7th chords reiterated over a tonic pedal), and the arresting deceptive cadences at bars 45 and 51. Bach later returned to the aria when compiling his St Mark Passion in 1731, using it as the parody model for the aria 'Falsche Welt'. The final aria promises that if the believer stands firm, Satan will back down. It is actually a three-part chromatic fugue (with a winding semiquaver countersubject) between voice, unison violins, and violas over a free bass, presumably symbolic of the twisted workings of the Devil. It employs a free da capo design, with a written-out and modified reprise, found in several other cantatas written at Weimar, but much more common in the Leipzig cantatas.                                                     SH

For bibliography, see CANTATA, §1.

**Wie schön leuchtet der Morgenstern** ('How beautifully the morning star shines'). Cantata for the feast of the Annunciation of the Blessed Virgin Mary, BWV1, performed on 25 March 1725. The Annunciation was an important event in the Lutheran Church calendar, but the date on which it fell (25 March) nearly always occurred during Lent, a tempus clausum in Leipzig, during which music in the churches was not allowed. If, however (as was the case on three occasions during Bach's Leipzig Kantorate), the Annunciation fell during Holy Week, it was celebrated on Palm Sunday, when the ban on music was lifted and a cantata was sung to celebrate the festival. On two occasions during Bach's Leipzig tenure (in 1725 and 1736) the Annunciation actually coincided with Palm Sunday, and it was for the earlier of these occasions that he wrote and performed this cantata. It was also with this work that Bach brought to a close his great cycle of chorale-based cantatas which he had begun on the first Sunday after Trinity the previous year.

The unidentified librettist took one of the best-known Lutheran hymns, Philipp Nicolai's *Wie schön leuchtet der Morgenstern* (1599), as the basis of his text. In the Leipzig and Dresden hymn schedules it is closely associated with the 20th Sunday after Trinity, but it was used in a much wider context by many German Baroque composers, including Bach. Following the customary layout of the 1724–5 chorale cantatas the first and last sections contain stanzas of the hymn in their original form.

The opening movement, in F major, is a masterly chorale fantasia in which the future birth of Christ, and the journey of the three kings who will follow the star to Bethlehem, is serenely envisaged. The piece is scored for SATB with two oboes da caccia, two concertante violins, two ripieno violins, viola, and continuo. The presence, in addition, of two horns with independent parts evocatively highlights the ceremonial and processional implications of the text, while the concertante violins and oboes da caccia reflect its more intimate message. All this is set within a lively 12/8 dance measure in which the stirring and radiant hymn melody is stated in long notes by the soprano vocal line, supported by the first horn, with the remaining parts weaving a richly contrapuntal texture around it. The movement is a veritable *tour-de-force* in which Bach's consummate skill and inspirational genius are a source of wonder and satisfaction.

Following a short, declamatory simple recitative for tenor comes the first of two arias. This warmly expressive piece is for soprano with oboe da caccia obbligato. Like the opening chorus, it might be said to have something of the character and spirit of a dance, and its common-time metre is enlivened by a pizzicato string bass in the continuo. A simple recitative for bass makes symbolic reference to the 'morning star' of the text and leads to the second aria of the work. Bach here draws on the two concertante violins and the ripieno strings to provide the accompaniment to the tenor soloist. These effectively and appositely colour the 'Ton der Saiten' ('sounding strings') to which reference is made in this extended da capo movement.

The cantata ends with another strophe of the hymn by Philipp Nicolai. The scoring is festive and colourful, with doubling parts for the oboes da caccia, strings, and the first horn, which once more reinforces the soprano melody. The second horn, however, has an independent part, further underlining the 'occasional' character of the work.

NA

For bibliography, *see* CANTATA, §1.

**Wilcke, Wilcken.** *See* WÜLCKEN.

**Wild, Friedrich Gottlieb** (b. 14 Aug. 1700; d. before Aug. 1762). Organist, born in Bernsbach, Erzgebirge. He studied law at Leipzig University from 1723 and was a pupil of Bach between 1726 and 1735. In 1727 Bach wrote a testimonial in support of Wild's application for the post of Kantor at the Jacobikirche in Chemnitz, in which he mentioned the assistance that Wild had given as flautist and keyboard player. The application was unsuccessful, and in 1735 Wild was appointed organist of St Peter's Church, St Petersburg. *See also* FLUTE.

**Wilderer, Johann Hugo von** (b. 1670/71; bur. 7 June 1724). Composer and court musician, born in Bavaria; he held posts in Düsseldorf, Mannheim, and Heidelberg. He was active as a composer of operas, oratorios, and church music. Bach's copy of the Kyrie from Wilderer's *Missa brevis* in G minor, which was apparently made for performance in Leipzig, has survived. Christoph Wolff has pointed to its resemblance to the design of the Kyrie of Bach's Mass in B minor.          DLH

C. Wolff, *Das stile antico in der Musik Johann Sebastian Bachs* (Wiesbaden, 1968); C. Wolff, 'Origins of the Kyrie of the B Minor Mass', *Bach: Essays on his Life and Music* (Cambridge, Mass., 1991), 141–51.

**Wilhelm Ernst,** Duke of Saxe-Weimar (b. 19 Oct. 1662; d. 26 Oct. 1728). He was the son of Duke Johann Ernst I (d. 1683), and was born in Weimar. He succeeded his father as duke in 1683. An early marriage to Princess Charlotte Marie of Saxe-Jena (1669–1703) ended in separation after seven years; there were no children. Wilhelm Ernst led a severe, regimented existence inside his castle, the Wilhelmsburg, in Weimar, dedicating himself principally to religious devotions. But he was also keenly interested in literature, painting, and music. He employed Bach as chamber musician and court organist in 1708, and promoted him to *Konzertmeister* in 1714; in 1717 he placed him in detention before finally allowing him to proceed to Cöthen as *Kapellmeister* to Prince Leopold. *See also* WEIMAR. For a family tree, *see* ERNST AUGUST.

**Wilhelmsburg.** The name of the castle in WEIMAR where Duke WILHELM ERNST held court.

**Winckler, Johann Heinrich** (b. 12 March 1703; d. 18 May 1770). Classicist and schoolmaster, born in Wingendorf in Upper Lusatia. He wrote the text of Bach's lost cantata *Froher Tag, verlangte Stunden*, performed to celebrate the reconstruction and extension of the Thomasschule building in Leipzig on 5 June 1732. Winckler was then *collega quartus* (teacher of the fourth class, i.e. the eighth

Duke Wilhelm Ernst, Bach's employer at Weimar. Engraving, 1716
(Bildarchiv Preußischer Kulturbesitz, Berlin)

and seventh year before the final examination) at the Thomasschule. In 1739 he became a professor at Leipzig university. KK

**'Windige'.** According to Jacob von STÄHLIN, J. S. Bach's son Johann Gottfried Bernhard was referred to in the family circle as 'der Windige' ('the good-for-nothing').

***Wir danken dir, Gott, wir danken dir*** ('Unto thee, O God, do we give thanks, yea, unto thee do we give thanks'). Cantata for installation of the Leipzig city council, BWV29, first performed on 27 August 1731; further performances on 31 August 1739 and 25 August 1749 are documented. The cantata is best known for its opening sinfonia, an arrangement of the Preludio from the unaccompanied violin Partita in E major, and for its first chorus, which Bach reworked as 'Gratias agimus tibi' in the *missa* of 1733, subsequently incorporating it into the Mass in B minor, where the same music is also used for 'Dona nobis pacem' (actually, all three choral movements appear to derive independently from a lost earlier work).

Cantata 29 is one of at least six works that Bach wrote for church services that accompanied the annual election and membership rotation of the Leipzig city council. The sumptuous scoring of this and other such *Ratswahl* cantatas—here including three trumpets and timpani, two oboes, strings, and continuo—reflected the aristocratic pretensions of the city's ruling body. Exceptionally, parts were prepared for four ripieno singers, who doubled the four soloists in the opening and closing vocal movements; there is also a second fully figured copy of the continuo part, presumably for a harpsichordist.

The author of the text is unknown. Both the autograph score and the original manuscript parts survive. The Sinfonia constitutes an independent section of Bach's score and might have been added to the work as an afterthought; it was derived from that of the wedding cantata *Herr Gott, Beherrscher aller Dinge* (no. 120*a*, probably from 1729); only the brass and timpani parts were newly composed. The movement is essentially an organ transcription of the original, now transposed to D major (the key of the cantata), with purely accompanimental parts added for strings and winds. Bach later arranged the entire violin Partita for keyboard or lute as BWV1006*a*.

The first chorus, also in D major, is for the full ensemble, the two clauses of its text (Psalm 75: 1) corresponding with the two subjects of a double fugue in *stile antico*. A tenor aria with solo violin follows; the entire A section ('Hallelujah . . .') of this da capo form returns as the penultimate movement of the cantata.

A recitative for bass leads to a soprano aria

(with oboe and strings) that gives every indication of being derived from a pre-existing slow movement or dance (siciliana); the A section of this da capo structure is in binary form, the voice entering in *Vokaleinbau* for the repetition of each half. The succeeding alto recitative ends with a brief entry for all eight singers on the word 'Amen'; this is followed by the reprise of the tenor aria, with alto substituting for tenor and obbligato organ for violin.

The cantata closes with a four-part setting, with brass obbligato, of the fifth stanza (published in 1549) of Johann Gramann's chorale text *Nun lob, mein Seel, den Herren*. DS

L. Dreyfus, 'The Metaphorical Soloist: Concerted Organ Parts in Bach's Cantatas', *Early Music*, 13 (1985), 237–47; H.-J. Schulze, *Johann Sebastian Bach: Ratswahlkantate, Wir danken dir, Gott, wir danken dir (BWV 29)* (facsimile, Leipzig and Neuhausen-Stuttgart, 1985). For further bibliography, *see* CANTATA, §1.

***Wir müssen durch viel Trübsal in das Reich Gottes eingehen*** ('We must through much tribulation enter into the kingdom of God'). Cantata for the third Sunday after Easter (Jubilate), BWV146. The date of its first performance is unknown, but it was most likely either 12 May 1726 or 18 April 1728. The cantata includes Bach's reworking of the first two movements of the same lost violin concerto that later served as the basis for the D minor harpsichord concerto BWV1052; the concerto's third movement was used in Cantata 188 (probably of 1728).

The work survives only in late sources, including a manuscript copy by Bach's pupil J. F. Agricola (who copied most of Bach's other vocal music with organ obbligato as well). If it was indeed performed in 1726, it would be Bach's earliest known cantata to open with an organ concerto movement; three more followed within the next six months (nos. 35, 169, and 49). Its second movement, moreover, would have been Bach's first vocal composition to include a fully fledged obbligato organ part. Laurence Dreyfus argues that Bach himself is the most likely person to have performed the organ parts in these works.

In keeping with the liturgical character of the day for which it was written, the text traces a spiritual path from grief to rejoicing. It is unclear how the opening instrumental sinfonia fits into that plan; as a lengthy and somewhat difficult solo movement it might represent worldly 'labour' or even 'tribulation', but it may also simply be an instance of the then accepted practice of incorporating 'secular' movements into sacred works. This movement and the next represent a somewhat more literal transcription of the original concerto than does BWV1052, although in both works the keyboard player's right hand usually appropriates the original violin part, and here Bach also adds two oboes and *taille*. A few solo passages require the use of both hands, and at these points the bass line might be played on the pedals; another instrument might have furnished a continuo realization. The opening chorus is grafted on to the slow movement of the concerto, a juxtaposition perhaps suggested by the tortuous ritornello theme, an ostinato bass line heard six times in the course of the movement. The organ adds the solo line, with its expressive written-out embellishments, in the four central entries, to which are now also joined the voices' repetitions of the biblical text (from Acts 14: 22). Unlike Bach's earlier setting of the same verse (in Cantata 12), the movement focuses single-mindedly on the text's 'Trübsal' ('troubles'), notably through sustained dissonances on that word.

The sources do not specify the solo instrument that accompanies the following alto aria; the part could be played on either violin or organ. Rising scales in the A section reflect the passage to heaven that went unrepresented in the preceding movement. But dissonance again pervades the following accompanied recitative for soprano. This introduces a soprano aria whose text refers to Psalm 126: 6 (v. 5 in the Bible version: 'They that sow in tears . . .'). Despite its minor mode and potentially mournful text, the aria (scored for flute and two oboes d'amore) has a galant, almost Telemannesque cheerfulness.

After a tenor recitative, the final aria text (in da capo form) is set as a duet for tenor and bass. Its relatively simple style and construction set it apart from the rest of the cantata; it might be a parody of an older (possibly secular) movement. But both the opening motif and its sequential, imitative treatment have been presaged in the B section of the first aria. As in the initial chorus, *Vokaleinbau* is the prevalent compositional technique in the present A section; the written instrumental parts (two oboes and strings) drop out in the B section, but the organist might improvise a solo in one passage for continuo alone.

The sources fail to include the text for the last movement, a four-part harmonization of the chorale melody 'Werde munter, mein Gemüte'. Scholars have differed on the appropriate text, selecting from at least three different chorale stanzas.                                                    DS

L. Dreyfus, *Bach's Continuo Group: Players and Practices in his Vocal Works* (Cambridge, Mass., 1987), 63–8. For further bibliography, *see* CANTATA, §1.

**Wise Virgins, The.** Ballet, based on the parable of the ten virgins in St Matthew 25: 1–13, with choreography by Frederick Ashton and music arranged by William Walton (1902–83) from the works of Bach. It was first produced at Sadler's Wells Theatre, London, on 24 April 1940. The score consisted of nine numbers, six of which Walton abstracted for an orchestral suite with the following titles:

1. 'What God hath done is rightly done': from the opening chorus of Cantata 99 (or 100), *Was Gott tut, das ist wohlgetan*, used for nos. 3 and 8 in the ballet;
2. 'Lord, hear my longing': from the organ chorale *Herzlich tut mich verlangen*, BWV727, used for no. 4 in the ballet;
3. 'See what his love can do': from the tenor aria 'Seht, was die Liebe tut' in Cantata 85, transposed to D major, used for no. 5 in the ballet;
4. 'Ah! how ephemeral': from the opening chorus of Cantata 27, *Ach wie flüchtig, ach wie nichtig*, used for no. 6 in the ballet;
5. 'Sheep may safely graze': from Pales's recitative 'Soll dann der Pales Opfer hier das letzte sein' and aria 'Schafe können sicher weiden' in Cantata 208, *Was mir behagt ist nur die muntre Jagd*, used for no. 7 in the ballet; and
6. 'Praise be to God'; from the final movement of Cantata 129, *Gelobet sei der Herr, mein Gott*, used for no. 9 in the ballet.

In addition, the ballet itself included the final chorale from Cantata 140, *Wachet auf, ruft uns die Stimme* (no. 1) and the bass aria 'Dein Geburtstag ist erschienen' from the spurious Cantata 142, *Uns ist ein Kind geboren* (no. 2).

**Wo gehest du hin?** ('Whither goest thou?'). Cantata for the fourth Sunday after Easter (Cantate), BWV166, performed for the first time on 7 May 1724 in Leipzig. The question 'Whither goest thou?' that serves as the entire text of the opening movement comes from the first verse of the Gospel appointed for the day, St John 16: 5–15. It is the question which the disciples had failed to put to Jesus, but, as it is actually spoken by Jesus himself, Bach sets it for bass solo in a manner somewhere between arioso and aria, with *Vokaleinbau* as a unifying principle. The *vox Christi* is here accompanied by the whole of the modest instrumental ensemble: oboe, strings, and continuo.

The rest of the text, by an unknown librettist, may be understood as a response to this question on the part of Christians for whom the path to follow leads to the grave and to the life beyond. The tenor aria 'Ich will an den Himmel denken', in full da capo form, has an accompaniment for oboe and continuo which one might well think to be complete, but which evidently lacks a violin part, recoverable in part from an arrangement (not by Bach) for organ, BWV584. The movement that follows might also be considered as a candidate for organ arrangement, in the manner of the Schübler Chorales: the soprano sings the third strophe of the hymn *Herr Jesu Christ, ich weiß gar wohl* as a cantus firmus in long notes, while the unison violins and violas are given a flowing counter-melody above a continuo bass. The only recitative in the work, for bass with simple continuo support, leads to another da capo aria, this time for alto and the entire ensemble of instruments. Its predominantly homophonic texture and its merry melismas on the word 'lacht' ('laughs') make light of the text's stern warning that worldly good fortune can swiftly change, a sentiment taken up in the final four-part chorale. This is the first strophe of the hymn *Wer weiß, wie nahe mir mein Ende* (1686) which Countess Ämilie Juliane of Schwarzburg-Rudolstadt wrote to one of Bach's favourite chorale melodies, Georg Neumark's *Wer nur den lieben Gott läßt walten* (1657).

For bibliography, *see* CANTATA, §1.

**Wo Gott der Herr nicht bei uns hält** ('If the Lord himself had not been on our side'). Cantata for the eighth Sunday after Trinity, BWV178, first performed on 30 July 1724. It is a CHORALE CANTATA belonging to Bach's second Leipzig *Jahrgang*, and is based on a hymn by Justus Jonas (1524) which in turn is based on Psalm 124, treating of God's support in times of human conflict. The unknown librettist has retained an unusually large number of hymn strophes intact, and as a result Bach, in turn, had greater recourse than usual to the chorale melody, which he treated in a variety of ways.

The opening movement, for the combined forces of SATB, two oboes, strings, and continuo, is one of the most impressive of all Bach's chorale fantasias. As usual, the chorale tune is sustained as a cantus firmus by the sopranos, with more active, often imitative writing for the lower voices, and with independent, highly charged participation from the instruments, which both accompany and separate the lines of the hymn. In two of the movements (nos. 2 and 5) the chorale lines alternate with recitative, but in very different ways. In no. 2, the chorale melody is sung in minims by the alto, while the continuo accompanies with the same material in quavers; in no. 5 the melody is harmonized in what might be called normal four-part chorale style, while the recitative interpolations are taken in turn by each of the voices except the soprano. Perhaps on 30 July 1724 Bach had no boy chorister he could rely on for soprano solos; even in movement 4, which surrounds the chorale tune with a contrapuntal working-out of a single motif by two oboes d'amore and continuo,

it is a tenor, not a soprano, that sings the melody.

Only in the two arias, nos. 3 and 6, do the chorale text and melody find no place. No. 2 is a simile aria, such as is found in numerous operas of the period, likening a soul disturbed by the wrath of an enemy to a storm-tossed ship at sea. It is a text which gave Bach ample opportunity for word-painting, and he responded with turbulent semiquaver figures for the unison strings and continuo, agitated melismas for the bass soloist, and some disorientating harmonic excursions. Even more disturbing, though, is the tenor's 'Schweig nur, taumelnde Vernunft', with its syncopations and its disjointed, declamatory phrases for both the singer and the accompanying strings.

Chorale cantatas normally end with the final hymn strophe in a straightforward setting in four parts with *colla parte* instrumental doubling. In this case the treatment is extended to the penultimate strophe as well.

For bibliography, *see* CANTATA, §1.

**Wohl dem, der sich auf seinen Gott** ('It is well for him who on his God'). Cantata for the 23rd Sunday after Trinity, BWV139, performed for the first time on 12 November 1724, and repeated at least twice, in 1732–5 and 1744–7. The autograph score is lost, and the work is known only from the separate parts which once belonged to the Thomasschule and are now in the Bach-Archiv, Leipzig. These parts, however, do not permit the reconstruction of a complete score which is entirely faithful to the original, since the tenor aria 'Gott ist mein Freund' (no. 2) lacks the second obbligato instrument (a part for second violin was provided by William H. Scheide in 1975), while in the bass aria 'Das Unglück schlägt auf allen Seiten' one of Bach's pupils has introduced an obbligato violin part alongside those for two oboes d'amore, whereas the original string part was perhaps for violoncello piccolo.

The author of the text is unknown, but the first and last of the work's six movements use strophes 1 and 5 respectively of the hymn *Wohl dem, der sich auf seinen Gott* (1692) by Johann Christoph Rube, who was then still alive (he died about 1748). It is sung to the melody *Mach's mit mir, Gott, nach deiner Güt* by J. H. Schein (1586–1630); Bach used it again in Cantata 156 (1729). Strophes 2–4 of the hymn are paraphrased in the second, fourth, and fifth movements of the cantata, while movement 3, the recitative 'Der Heiland sendet ja die Seinen', is newly invented. It refers to the Gospel for the day, St Matthew 22: 15–22, which tells of the Pharisees' questioning of Jesus regarding tribute to Caesar, and his famous riposte, 'Render therefore unto Caesar the things which are Caesar's; and unto God the things that are God's'.

The opening movement is a compelling example of the kind of carefully planned architectonic one finds so often in Bach's cantata choruses. On to the basic *Barform* (A–B–B) of the chorale itself, sung as a cantus firmus by the sopranos, is grafted a discourse in which voices and instruments share the same melodic material in a concertante manner. There are three sections, each 24 bars in length, but the third section is organized differently from the first two. The two A sections are made up of ten instrumental bars and two five-bar vocal episodes setting respectively lines 1–2 and 3–4 of the hymn, with an instrumental ritornello separating them; the third (B) section is shared equally between voices and instruments, with six bars for each vocal episode. The structure may be summarized schematically as follows:

A (bars 1–24)
- 10 bars: instrumental
- 5 bars: line 1
- 4 bars: instrumental
- 5 bars: line 2

A (bars 25–48)
- 10 bars: instrumental
- 5 bars: line 3
- 4 bars: instrumental
- 5 bars: line 4

B (bars 49–72)
- 4 bars: instrumental
- 6 bars: line 5
- 6 bars: instrumental
- 6 bars: line 6
- 2 bars: instrumental

The bass aria (no. 4) merits particular attention for its rondo form, with about ten changes of tempo (for the most part alternating between Andante and Vivace) and with changes of metre from 4/4 to 6/8 and back.               AB

W. H. Scheide, 'The "Concertato" Violin in BWV 139', in R. Eller and H.-J. Schulze, eds., *Bach-Studien*, 5 (Leipzig, 1975), 123–37. For further bibliography, see CANTATA, §1.

***Wohltemperirte Clavier, Das.*** See WELL-TEMPERED CLAVIER, THE.

**Wolff, Christoph** (b. 24 May 1940). Musicologist, born in Solingen, Westphalia. He was educated in Berlin and Erlangen, and has held positions at the University of Toronto, Columbia University, Harvard University, and the University of Freiburg. His principal research has been on the music of J. S. Bach, and he has made particularly strong contributions to the study of Bach's cultivation of 16th-century counterpoint (the *stile antico*), the original printed editions of Bach's music, his canonic and contrapuntal works, and his early organ music. He is the editor of several volumes in the *NBA* and co-author of the *Bach Compendium*, and since 1975 he has co-edited the *Bach-Jahrbuch*.               ***

**word-painting.** The use of music to depict the meaning of words in vocal compositions. It is found in many different kinds of music from all periods, but is especially prevalent in European art music of the 16th–18th centuries.

Word-painting is an important strand in the complex web of interrelationships between text and music that pervade Bach's vocal works. It is difficult to locate a precise dividing line between word-painting and more sophisticated varieties of musical symbolism. However, the term normally refers to the localized representation of specific words rather than devices used throughout a section or ways of capturing the affect of an entire movement. While many of Bach's word-painting techniques are similar to those that are routinely encountered in virtually any vocal music of the period, others bear the unmistakable marks of Bach's incisive and original musical imagination. A complete catalogue of them would doubtless run to thousands of entries. This article will present an outline of some of the devices that are encountered quite frequently, and then examine the use of word-painting in one particular work.

Among the most common are extended melismas, which occur in many different contexts. They are used for words of motion, for example 'gehen' ('to walk'), 'laufen' ('to run'), 'wandern' ('to travel'), 'fliehen' ('to flee'), and 'eilen' ('to hurry'). They can illustrate a variety of elemental phenomena, such as water: 'Ströme' ('rivers'), 'Wellen' ('waves'), and 'waschen' ('to wash'); fire ('Feuer'): 'Flammen' ('flames'); and even life itself: 'Leben' and the verb 'leben' ('to live'). Melismas are also associated with vivid sensory images, especially bright light: 'Engel' ('angels') and 'scheinen' ('to shine'); and vigorous music: 'Gesang' ('song'), 'Chöre' ('choirs'), and 'schallen' ('to ring out'). They often appear in connection with words of jubilation, such as 'preisen' and 'loben' ('to praise'), 'jubilieren' ('to rejoice'), 'lachen' ('to laugh'), and 'Freude' ('joy'), but are frequently used as well for words of destruction, including 'zerschellen' ('to smash'), 'zerschmettern' ('to shatter'), 'toben' and 'rasen' ('to rage'), 'drohen' ('to threaten'), and 'streiten' ('to fight'). Finally, melismas are associated with words of desire, such as 'verlangen' ('to ask for') and 'flehen' ('to plead').

Second, the traditional association of chromaticism with painful or unpleasing affects is employed extensively in Bach's music as well. It is often found in connection with words describing physical or emotional distress, for example 'hungrig' ('hungry'), 'bange' ('afraid'), 'weinen' ('to cry'), 'ächzen' ('to groan'), 'Leiden' ('suffering'), 'Qual' ('agony'), and 'Kreuz' ('the Cross'). But chromaticism occurs in other situations too, such as depictions of spiritual blindness, as in expressions such as 'törichten Welt' ('foolish world') or 'falschem Herzen' ('false heart').

Certain special instrumental techniques are invariably associated with word-painting. For example, the use of a mute for the solo violin part in the soprano aria 'Auch mit gedämpften, schwachen Stimmen' ('Even with muted, weak voices') from Cantata 36 was obviously suggested by the words. Likewise, pizzicato chords depict images such as Christ knocking at the heart's 'door', in the bass recitative 'Siehe, ich stehe vor der Tür und klopfe an' ('Behold, I stand at the door and knock') from Cantata 61, or the sound of funeral bells, for example in the arias for tenor in Cantata 95, for bass in Cantata 73, and for soprano in Cantata 127. An additional layer of symbolism is present in the opening chorus of Cantata 8 and the alto recitative of the *Trauer Ode*, where the pizzicato string parts are joined by one or a pair of recorders, an instrument traditionally associated with death.

Finally, there is a large and heterogenous group of techniques in which properties of the notes match the meanings of words in fairly literal ways. For instance, words with directional connotations influence the contours of melodies: the vocal line typically moves upwards on words such as 'Himmel' ('heaven') or 'höher' ('higher') and downwards on 'Abgrund' ('abyss'), 'tief gesunken' ('sunk low'), and the like. Extremely wide downward leaps represent such things as the fall of Israel ('zum Fall' in the first bass recitative of Cantata 152) or the tomb in which Jesus was buried ('und Grab' in the bass recitative of Cantata 78). Similarly, sustained notes are frequently used for words involving length: 'lang' ('long') or 'ewig' ('eternal'); continuation: 'bestehen' ('to continue to exist'); or tranquility: 'Ruhe' ('peace'). More sophisticated devices also occur from time to time, such as the use of imitation to portray the idea of following Christ, for example bars 5–6 of the bass aria 'Ich folge Christo nach' from Cantata 12, or bars 16–17 of the soprano aria 'Ich folge dir gleichfalls' from the *St John Passion*.

This is just one of a number of vivid examples of word-painting in the *St John Passion*. In a passage of Scripture that precedes the portions set by Bach, Jesus predicts that Peter will deny him three times before the cock crows (John 13: 38). In the recitative that narrates Peter's third denial of Jesus, the brief upward arpeggio in the continuo immediately following the word 'Hahn' ('cock') obviously mimics the crowing of the bird. Then,

in a singularly gripping passage, Peter's profound grief is made audible in a pair of lengthy melismas on the word 'weinete' ('wept'). The unstable aspects of this emotional upheaval are intensified by the rhythm, which makes liberal use of syncopation. Moreover, the affective quality of the word 'bitterlich' ('bitterly') is reinforced by thoroughgoing chromaticism in both the vocal and the continuo lines.

An equally powerful scene is the horrific depiction of the scourging of Jesus. In the recitative that recounts this event, the motion of a whip is suggested by rapid triplets in a long melisma on the word 'geisselte' ('whipped'), coupled with jagged contours and dotted rhythms in the continuo line.

Another highly dramatic moment is the account of the earthquake after Jesus's death on the Cross. The tearing of the curtain in the temple 'from top to bottom' ('von oben an bis unten aus') is graphically portrayed by a rapid, downward scale in the continuo that spans a full two octaves. The motion of the tremors is then captured by tremolos on low notes (an idea that is picked up by the upper strings in the next movement, the tenor arioso 'Mein Herz, indem die ganze Welt'). Especially since this scene is interpolated into the libretto of the *St John Passion* from the Gospel of St Matthew, it is worth noting that Bach employed similar techniques when he set the same words a second time in the *St Matthew Passion*.

These illustrations demonstrate Bach's attentiveness to the meaning of individual words and provide a sample of the kinds of correspondences between verbal and musical icons that appear throughout his vocal works.                    SAC

**worship.** *See* CHURCH CALENDAR, HAUPTGOTTESDIENST, and VESPERS.

***Wo soll ich fliehen hin*** ('Where shall I fly to'). Cantata for the 19th Sunday after Trinity, BWV5, first performed on 15 October 1724. It belongs to Bach's ambitious cycle of chorale cantatas, each based on a unifying theme, which he produced at Leipzig in 1724–5. The autograph score, once in the collection of the Austrian essayist and poet Stefan Zweig (1881–1942), is now in the British Library.

In common with all the chorale-based cantatas of Bach's second Leipzig cycle, the author of the text for this piece is unidentified. It derives from a hymn (1630) by the 17th-century writer Johann Heermann and, as usual with the chorale cantatas of this period, the librettist has included strophes in their original form in the opening and concluding sections of the work. In the Dresden hymn schedules for this Sunday in Trinity, Heermann's text was listed under the heading 'Hymns Concerning Repentance and Confession' (G. Stiller: *Johann Sebastian Bach and Liturgical Life in Leipzig* (St Louis, Miss., 1970), 246). The five intervening sections incorporate paraphrased strophes of Heermann's hymn. The Gospel appointed for the day (Matt. 9: 1–8) recounts the story of the man healed of the palsy and from this derives the central theme of the cantata, drawn both from the Gospel and from the hymn text itself: 'Thy sins be forgiven thee.'

The scoring of the opening chorale fantasia in G minor engages the instruments which formed the standard orchestra of Bach's time: divided violins, viola, basso continuo, and a pair of oboes. The vocal writing is in four parts of which the uppermost (soprano) sustains the hymn melody, *Auf meinen lieben Gott*, supported by a single *tromba da tirarsi* (slide trumpet). The instrumental ritornellos pursue a restless semiquaver pattern by which means Bach skilfully illustrates the questing subject of the text; the orchestral writing furthermore develops at the outset material contained in the first bars of the chorale melody, giving the movement a strongly unified structure characteristic of the cantatas in this cycle.

A bass recitative introduces an extended tenor aria in E♭ major, breaking for the first time the prevailing G minor tonality of the preceding movements. This tenderly expressive piece in da capo form, which focuses on the healing power of the divine springs of water, is one of only two instances in the entire cantata canon when Bach calls on a viola to play an obbligato part, in this instance a particularly dense one. Here the words 'Ergieße dich reichlich, du göttliche Quelle' ('Pour forth abundantly, thou divine spring') are skilfully evoked by the almost constantly flowing viola semiquavers. To some extent these are taken up by the tenor, whose line nevertheless contains phrases of greater lyricism, often lingering at the words 'göttliche Quelle'.

The second recitative is for alto but, although essentially unaccompanied, it is given an added dimension by the presence of an oboe which intones a section of the hymn melody to which the cantata is anchored. The remaining aria of the work is a robust declamatory piece in B♭ major, cast in da capo form. The accompanying instruments consist of a high trumpet with strings and two oboes, both of which double the first violin line. In this aria Bach effectively underlines the

command 'Verstumme' ('Be silent') by placing a quaver-beat rest immediately before and after it. The G minor key of the simple recitative for soprano is carried forward into the concluding chorale. This is the 11th strophe of Heermann's hymn sung in a straightforward four-part harmonization with *colla parte* instrumental support.     NA

For bibliography, *see* CANTATA, §1.

**Wülcken.** A Thuringian family of musicians closely connected to the Bachs. The name is found in a number of other forms, including Wilcke, Wilcken, and Wuelcken. Johann Caspar Wülcken (b. *c*.1662; d. 30 Nov. 1731), the son of a Schwerstedt musician by the name of Stephan, was employed as a court trumpeter in Zeitz from 1686; in 1718 he moved to a similar position in Weißenfels. In 1686 he had married Margarethe Elisabeth Liebe (*c*.1666–1746), who was also from a musical family: her father Andreas was organist at Frießnitz, near Weida in Thuringia, and one of her brothers, Johann Siegmund (*c*.1670–1742) was an organist at Zeitz from 1694 until his death.

Johann Caspar Wülcken and his wife had five children. Anna Katharina (b. 25 Nov. 1688; d. 24 Dec. 1757) married Georg Christian Meißner, a court trumpeter at Weißenfels. Johann Caspar the younger (b. 12 July 1691; d. 24 March 1766) was from 1717 court trumpeter at Zerbst; in 1729 Bach stood godfather to one of the sons born to him and his first wife Dorothea Maria Longolius, who died later the same year. Johanna Christina (b. 4 Jan. 1695; d. 1 Jan. 1753), a singer, married a Weißenfels court trumpeter, Johann Andreas Krebs (d. 1748) in 1716; along with her elder sister Anna Katharina and her brother Johann Caspar, she stood godmother to Bach's daughter Regina Johanna in 1728. Erdmuthe Dorothea (b. 18 Sept. 1697) married another Weißenfels court trumpeter, Christian August Nicolai (d. 1760).

The last of the five children, Anna Magdalena, became Bach's second wife in 1721; *see* BACH, ANNA MAGDALENA.

A. Basso, *Frau Musika: la vita e le opere di J. S. Bach*, i (Turin, 1979), esp. 534–7.

**Wunsch, Christian Gottlob** (b. 17 Dec. 1720; d. 1754). Organist, born in Joachimstein, near Radmeritz. He studied with Bach in Leipzig in 1742–3, and in 1743 was an unsuccessful candidate for a post as court organist at Zeitz. In 1753 he was appointed organist at Glogau (now Głogów, Poland), where he died the following year.

# Y Z

**yearbooks.** *See* JOURNALS, YEARBOOKS, AND PUBLICATIONS IN SERIES.

**Zang, Johann Heinrich** (b. 13/16 April 1733; d. 18 Aug. 1811). Organist and composer, born in Zella St Blasii, near Gotha in Thuringia. He probably studied with Bach in Leipzig in 1748–9, and was appointed organist at Hohenstein Castle the following year. In 1752 he became Kantor at Mainstockheim. He composed two cycles of church cantatas, as well as keyboard and organ music, none of which survives. His publications include an interesting treatise on organ design (1798), and he was active also as a painter, chemist, and writer.

**Zelenka, Jan Dismas** (bap. 16 Oct. 1679; d. 23 Dec. 1745). Czech composer, born in Louňovice, where his father worked as an organist. In 1710 he joined the court orchestra in Dresden as a violone player, and in 1715–19 spent much of his time in Italy and Vienna. He then returned to Dresden and composed a good deal of church and other music, but was passed over in favour of J. A. Hasse on the death of the *Kapellmeister* J. D. Heinichen in 1733. He remained in Dresden as *Kirchen-compositeur* until his death.

We know from a letter from C. P. E. Bach to J. N. Forkel, dated 13 January 1775, that J. S. Bach was personally acquainted with Zelenka and admired his music.

**Zelle.** *See* CELLE.

**Zelter, Carl Friedrich** (b. 11 Dec. 1758; d. 15 May 1832). Composer, born in Berlin. He was first trained as a mason and only later was able to pursue his musical interests, which he developed under the guidance of Carl Fasch (1736–1800), whom he succeeded as conductor of the Berlin Singakademie. During the 1790s Zelter, who was an admirer of C. P. E. Bach and had been personally acquainted with W. F. Bach, became interested in J. S. Bach's music, which he cultivated extensively during his 30-odd years as music director of the Singakademie. Among the works of Bach he performed were several concertos, numerous cantatas, motets, and parts of the B minor Mass. It was his enthusiasm for Bach that led his pupils Mendelssohn and Eduard Devrient (1801–77) to perform the *St Matthew Passion* in Leipzig. Zelter was also an important collector of Bach manuscripts. PW

G. Schünemann, 'Die Bachpflege der Berliner Singakademie', *BJb* 25 (1928), 138–71; H.-J. Schulze, 'Karl Friedrich Zelter und der Nachlaß des Bach-Biographen Johann Nikolaus Forkel', in *Jahrbuch des Staatlichen Instituts für Musikforschung Preußischer Kulturbesitz 1993* (Stuttgart, 1993), 141–50.

***Zerreißet, zersprenget, zertrümmert die Gruft*** ('Tear apart, burst open, shatter the vault') [*Der zufriedengestellte Aeolus* ('Aeolus placated')]. Secular cantata, BWV205, first performed in Leipzig on 3 August 1725. This is in effect a serenata, to words by Picander, composed expressly to mark the nameday of a loved and respected member of the academic community in Leipzig, August Friedrich Müller (1684–1761). After taking a doctorate in law at Erfurt in 1714, Müller took up a post at Leipzig University, where he was made a professor in 1731 and later dean of the faculty of philosophy. Cantata 205 was probably performed by torchlight in front of his house in the Catherinenstraße.

As often in *drammi per musica* of this type, the libretto brings together characters from classical mythology, but the 'plot' is a simple one. In an opening da capo chorus the winds complain of having been confined during the summer months. Aeolus (bass), god of the winds, agrees to release them, and in an impassioned recitative and aria looks forward to the havoc they will cause. In a series of recitatives and arias Zephyrus (tenor), god of evening breezes, Pomona (alto), goddess of fruit trees, and Pallas (soprano), goddess of wisdom call in turn on Aeolus to delay. He is at first unresponsive, but when he learns of the reason for their requests—so that they might join in Müller's nameday celebrations—he relents and commands the winds to be calm. All then join in a rondo chorus to greet Müller with the wish that his teaching may 'raise plants that will one day adorn the country'.

With its two choruses, seven recitatives, five arias, and one duet—15 'movements' in all—*Zerreißet, zersprenget* is one of the most substantial works of its kind, and to accompany his four vocal soloists Bach employed the largest orchestra he was ever to assemble: three trumpets, timpani, two horns, two flutes, two oboes (one doubling on oboe d'amore), strings (including viola d'amore and viola da gamba), and continuo. The opening chorus provides much for them to do in

Gottfried Zimmermann's coffee-house in Leipzig, where Bach directed meetings of his collegium musicum

suggesting the fettered turbulence of the impatient winds, with rushing scales in the woodwind and strings, impetuous blasts from the brass, and rumblings from the timpani, and the wilder forces of nature are no less colourfully evoked in the bass recitative that follows, accompanied (most unusually) by the whole orchestra. But the entire cantata is notable for its inventive instrumentation: the duet for viola d'amore and viola da gamba that accompanies Zephyrus's attempt to quell Aeolus's temper (no. 5); the graceful virtuoso (and unusually high-lying) violin obbligato for Pallas's 'Angenehmer Zephyrus' (no. 9); the entry of two flutes at the point in the recitative (no. 10) when Pallas's entreaties towards Aeolus finally have their effect; and the accompaniment to Aeolus's second aria (no. 11) for brass, timpani, and continuo only—unique in Bach's music and without obvious parallels elsewhere. Only in such a context would the delightful obbligatos for oboe d'amore in no. 7 and for flutes in no. 13 go unremarked.

Some eight and a half years later Bach was able to revive the music with a new text (author unknown) to celebrate the coronation of Augustus III as King of Poland on 19 February 1734. In this version, *Blast Lärmen, ihr Feinde! verstärket die Macht* bwv205a, Pallas Athene retains her identity, while the other three dramatis personae are Tapferkeit ('Courage', bass), Gerechtigkeit ('Justice', tenor), and Gnade ('Mercy', alto). Before then, in 1728, Bach had parodied the duet between Pomona and Zephyrus (no. 13) in a wedding cantata, *Vergnügte Pleißenstadt* (bwv216), but the only number that found its way into a sacred work was Pallas's aria (no. 9), which, transposed a tone lower, was used for the aria 'Jesus soll mein erstes Wort' in Cantata 171. If Bach had been able to transform *Zerreißet, zersprenget* into a whole church cantata or part of an oratorio, one of his most fascinating and rewarding scores would undoubtedly have become better known than it is.

For bibliography, *see* CANTATA, §2.

**Ziegler** (née Romanus), **Christiane Mariane von** (bap. 30 June 1695; d. 1 May 1760). Poet, born in Leipzig. In 1722 the writer and literary reformer Johann Christoph Gottsched began to support her, and in 1728 she published her anthology *Versuch in gebundener Schreib-Art*; this contains the texts of the nine cantatas that Bach composed between 22 April and 27 May 1725, thus succeeding, after a gap of three weeks, the series of the chorale cantatas which was inaugurated in June 1724 and came to an end (for no known reason) around Easter 1725. Perhaps the collaboration between Bach and Ziegler ended because Bach came into contact with Picander, who was not in sympathy with Gottsched's circle.

Bach's Ziegler cantatas are nos. 68, 74, 87, 103, 108, 128, 175, 176, and 183. They share a common structure: each one begins with a biblical text; after a series of recitatives and arias (normally two of each), the cantata is concluded by a chorale.

KK

S. Ehrmann, 'Johann Sebastian Bachs Textdichterin Christiane Mariane von Ziegler', *Beiträge zur Bach-Forschung*, 9–10 (1991), 261–8; H.-J. Schulze, 'Neuerkenntnisse zu einigen Kantatentexten Bachs auf Grund neuer biographischer Daten', in M. Geck, ed., *Bach-Interpretationen* (Göttingen, 1969), 22–8.

**Ziegler, Johann Gotthilf** (b. 25 March 1688; d. 15 Sept. 1747). Organist and composer, born in Leubnitz, near Dresden in Saxony. His teachers included F. W. Zachow (1663–1712, Handel's teacher) in Halle and J. S. Bach, with whom he studied in Weimar before reading law and theology at Halle University in 1712–15. In 1718 he was appointed organist and *director musices* at the Ulrichskirche, Halle, where he remained for the rest of his life. In 1746 he competed unsuccessfully for the post of organist at the Liebfrauenkirche, which went to Wilhelm Friedemann Bach. Ziegler composed four cycles of church cantatas as well as other music, but little of it has survived. *See also* SOURCES, §2.

G. G. Butler, 'Johann Gotthilf Ziegler: der Notenstecher der Partiten III bis VI von Johann Sebastian Bach?', W. Hoffmann and A. Schneiderheinze, eds., *Bericht über die Wissenschaftliche Konferenz zum V. Internationalen Bachfest der DDR in Verbindung mit dem 60. Bachfest der Neuen Bachgesellschaft* (Leipzig, 1988), 277–81.

**Zimmermann, Gottfried** (d. May 1741). Coffee-house owner, resident in Leipzig. It was at his coffee-house in the Catherinenstraße that the COLLEGIUM MUSICUM which Bach directed used to meet during the winter months. In the summer they performed in Zimmermann's garden outside the Grimmische Tor.

**Zink.** *See* CORNETT.

**Zugtrompete.** A slide TRUMPET.

# LIST OF BACH'S WORKS

This list is divided into the following categories:

1. Church cantatas
2. Secular cantatas
3. Latin church music
4. Motets
5. Oratorios and Passions
6. Chorale harmonizations and sacred Lieder
7. Secular Lieder
8. Organ works
9. Keyboard works
10. Solo instrumental music (other than keyboard)
11. Ensemble and orchestral music
12. Canons
13. Doubtful and spurious works

## Numbering
The numbers in the left-hand column (BWV) are those of *Schmieder 2*; for the vocal works the *BC* catalogue numbers are also given.

## Titles
These are shown in the form in which they appear in the main A–Z section of the volume; major keys are indicated by upper-case letters, minor keys by lower-case letters.

## Dates
Precise dates (e.g. 25 March 1725) are those of the first known performance; other dates are either of publication (in the case of works printed during Bach's lifetime) or of composition.

## Scoring
The following abbreviations and contractions are used:

| | | | | | |
|---|---|---|---|---|---|
| A | alto | insts | instruments | tle | taille |
| B | bass | ob | oboe(s) | tr | trumpet(s) |
| bc | basso continuo | obda | oboe(s) d'amore | trdt | tromba da tirarsi |
| bn | bassoon | obdc | oboe(s) da caccia | va | viola(s) |
| cdc | corno da caccia | org | organ | vada | viola d'amore |
| cdt | corno da tirarsi | rec | recorder(s) | vadg | viola(s) da gamba |
| cnt | cornett | S | soprano | vc | violoncello |
| fl | flute(s) | str | violins 1 and 2, viola | vcp | violoncello piccolo |
| flp | flauto piccolo | T | tenor | vn | violin(s) |
| hn | horn(s) | tbn | trombone(s) | vnp | violino piccolo |
| hpcd | harpsichord | timp | timpani | | |

Instruments added for later performances are enclosed in square brackets, [ ]; no distinction is made between solo and choral voices.

## Editions
The volume numbers of the two collected editions are shown; those of the *NBA* that have not yet been published are placed in square brackets, [ ].

# Appendix 1

## 1. Church cantatas

| BWV | BC | Title (librettist) | Date | Scoring | First published | BG vol. | NBA vol. | Autograph score (facsimile) |
|---|---|---|---|---|---|---|---|---|
| 1 | A 173 | Wie schön leuchtet der Morgenstern | 25 March 1725 | SATB, 2 hn, 2 obdc, str, bc | BG, 1851 | i | I/28.2 | |
| 2 | A 98 | Ach Gott, vom Himmel sieh darein | 18 June 1724 | SATB, 4 tbn, 2 ob, str, bc | BG, 1851 | i | I/16 | Private collection, London |
| 3 | A 33 | Ach Gott, wie manches Herzeleid | 14 Jan. 1725 | SATB, hn, tbn, 2 obda, str, bc | BG, 1851 | i | I/5 | Private collection, Switzerland |
| 4 | A 54 | Christ lag in Todes Banden | ?1707/8 | SATB, cnt, str, bc [3 tbn] | BG, 1851 | i | I/9 | |
| 5 | A 145 | Wo soll ich fliehen hin | 15 Oct. 1724 | SATB, trdt, 2 ob, str, bc | BG, 1851 | i | I/24 | Private collection, London |
| 6 | A 57 | Bleib bei uns, denn es will Abend werden | 2 April 1725 | SATB, 2 ob, obdc, vcp, str, bc | BG, 1851 | i | I/10 | Berlin, Staatsbibliothek |
| 7 | A 177 | Christ unser Herr zum Jordan kam | 24 June 1724 | SATB, 2 obda, str, bc | BG, 1851 | i | I/29 | |
| 8 | A 137 | Liebster Gott, wenn werd ich sterben | 24 Sept. 1724 | SATB, hn, fl, 2 obda, str, bc | BG, 1851 | i | I/23 | |
| 9 | A 107 | Es ist das Heil uns kommen her | ? 20 July 1732 | SATB, fl, obda, str, bc | BG, 1851 | i | I/17.2 | Library of Congress, Washington (New York, 1985) |
| 10 | A 175 | Meine Seel erhebt den Herren | 2 July 1724 | SATB, tr, 2 ob, str, bc | BG, 1851 | i | I/28.s | Library of Congress, Washington (New York, 1985) |
| 12 | A 68 | Weinen, Klagen, Sorgen, Zagen (? S. Franck) | 22 April 1714 | SATB, tr, ob, bn, str, bc | BG, 1852 | ii | I/11.2 | Berlin, Staatsbibliothek |
| 13 | A 34 | Meine Seufzer, meine Tränen (G. C. Lehms) | 20 Jan. 1726 | SATB, 2 rec, obdc, str, bc | BG, 1852 | ii | I/5 | Berlin, Staatsbibliothek |
| 14 | A 40 | Wär Gott nicht mit uns dieser Zeit | 30 Jan. 1735 | SATB, hn, 2 ob, str, bc | BG, 1852 | ii | I/6 | Berlin, Staatsbibliothek (Leipzig, 1955) |
| 16 | A 23 | Herr Gott, dich loben wir (G. C. Lehms) | 1 Jan. 1726 | SATB, cdc, 2 ob(dc), str, bc | BG, 1852 | ii | I/4 | Berlin, Staatsbibliothek |
| 17 | A 131 | Wer Dank opfert, der preiset mich | 22 Sept. 1726 | SATB, 2 ob, str, bc | BG, 1852 | ii | I/21 | Berlin, Staatsbibliothek |
| 18 | A 44 | Gleichwie der Regen und Schnee (E. Neumeister) | 1713–15 | SATB, 4 va, bc [2 fl] | BG, 1852 | ii | I/7 | |
| 19 | A 180 | Es erhub sich ein Streit (after Picander) | 29 Sept. 1726 | SATB, 3 tr, timp, 2 ob(da), tle, str, bc | BG, 1852 | ii | I/30 | Berlin, Staatsbibliothek |
| 20 | A 95 | O Ewigkeit, du Donnerwort | 11 June 1724 | SATB, trdt, 3 ob, str, bc | BG, 1852 | ii | I/15 | Basle, Paul-Sacher-Stiftung |

| BWV | BC | Title (librettist) | Date | Scoring | First published | BG vol. | NBA vol. | Autograph score (facsimile) |
|---|---|---|---|---|---|---|---|---|
| 21 | A 99 | Ich hatte viel Bekümmernis (? S. Franck) | 17 June 1714 | SATB, 3 tr, ob, str, bc [4 tbn] | BG, 1855 | v/1 | I/16 | |
| 22 | A 48 | Jesus nahm zu sich die Zwölfe | 7 Feb. 1723 | SATB, ob, str, bc | BG, 1855 | v/1 | I/8.1 | Berlin, Staatsbibliothek |
| 23 | A 47 | Du wahrer Gott und Davids Sohn | 7 Feb. 1723 | SATB, 2 ob, str, bc [cnt, 3 tbn] | BG, 1855 | v/1 | I/8.1 | Berlin, Staatsbibliothek |
| 24 | A 102 | Ein ungefärbt Gemüte (E. Neumeister) | 20 June 1723 | SATB, tr, 2 ob(da), str, bc | BG, 1855 | v/1 | I/17.1 | Berlin, Staatsbibliothek |
| 25 | A 129 | Es ist nichts Gesundes an meinem Leibe | 29 Aug. 1723 | SATB, cnt, 3 tbn, 3 rec, 2 ob, str, bc | BG, 1855 | v/1 | I/21 | Berlin, Staatsbibliothek |
| 26 | A 162 | Ach wie flüchtig, ach wie nichtig | 19 Nov. 1724 | SATB, hn, fl, 3 ob, str, bc | BG, 1855 | v/1 | I/27 | Berlin, Staatsbibliothek |
| 27 | A 138 | Wer weiß, wie nahe mir mein Ende | 6 Oct. 1726 | SATB, hn, 2 ob(dc), org, str, bc | BG, 1855 | v/1 | I/23 | Berlin, Staatsbibliothek |
| 28 | A 20 | Gottlob! nun geht das Jahr zu Ende (E. Neumeister) | 30 Dec. 1725 | SATB, cnt, 3 tbn 2 ob, tle, str, bc | BG, 1855 | v/1 | [I/3] | Berlin, Staatsbibliothek |
| 29 | B 8 | Wir danken dir, Gott | 27 Aug. 1731 | SATB, 3 tr, timp, tbn, 2 ob, org, str, bc | BG, 1855 | v/1 | I/32.2 | Berlin, Staatsbibliothek |
| 30 | A 178 | Freue dich, erlöste Schar (? Picander) | ? 1738–42 | SATB, 2 fl, 2 ob(da), str, bc | BG, 1855 | v/1 | I/29 | Berlin, Staatsbibliothek |
| 31 | A 55 | Der Himmel lacht! die Erde jubilieret (S. Franck) | 21 April 1715 | SSATB, 3 tr, timp, 2 ob(da), str, bc [ob, tle, bn] | BG, 1857 | vii | I/9 | |
| 32 | A 31 | Liebster Jesu, mein Verlangen (G. C. Lehms) | 13 Jan. 1726 | SATB, ob, str, bc | BG, 1857 | vii | I/5 | Berlin, Staatsbibliothek |
| 33 | A 127 | Allein zu dir, Herr Jesu Christ | 3 Sept. 1724 | SATB, 2 ob, str, bc | BG, 1857 | vii | I/21 | Private collection, Princeton, NJ (New York, 1985) |
| 34 | A 84 | O ewiges Feuer, o Ursprung der Liebe | c.1746–7 | SATB, 3 tr, timp, 2 fl, 2 ob, str, bc | BG, 1857 | vii | I/13 | Berlin, Staatsbibliothek |
| 34a | B 13 | O ewiges Feuer, o Ursprung der Liebe [inc.] | ? 1726 | SATB, 3 tr, timp, 2 fl, 2 ob, str, bc | BG, 1894 | xli | I/33 | |
| 35 | A 125 | Geist und Seele wird verwirret (G. C. Lehms) | 8 Sept. 1726 | A, 2 ob, tle, org, str, bc | BG, 1857 | vii | I/20 | Berlin, Staatsbibliothek |
| 36 | A 3 | Schwingt freudig euch empor | c.1725–30 | SATB, 2 obda, str, bc | BG, 1857 | vii | I/1 | Berlin, Staatsbibliothek |
| 37 | A 75 | Wer da gläubet und getauft wird | 18 May 1724 | SATB, 2 ob(da), str, bc | BG, 1857 | vii | I/12 | Berlin, Staatsbibliothek |
| 38 | A 152 | Aus tiefer Not schrei ich zu dir | 29 Oct. 1724 | SATB, 4 tbn, 2 ob, str, bc | BG, 1857 | vii | [I/25] | Berlin, Staatsbibliothek |
| 39 | A 96 | Brich dem Hungrigen dein Brot | 23 June 1726 | SATB, 2 rec, 2 ob, str, bc | BG, 1857 | vii | I/15 | Berlin, Staatsbibliothek |
| 40 | A 12 | Darzu ist erschienen der Sohn Gottes | 26 Dec. 1723 | SATB, 2 hn, 2 ob, str, bc | BG, 1857 | vii | [I/3] | Berlin, Staatsbibliothek |

# Appendix 1

| BWV | BC | Title (librettist) | Date | Scoring | First published | BG vol. | NBA vol. | Autograph score (facsimile) |
|---|---|---|---|---|---|---|---|---|
| 41 | A 22 | Jesu, nun sei gepreiset | 1 Jan. 1725 | SATB, 3 tr, timp, 3 ob, vcp, str, bc | BG, 1860 | x | I/4 | dispersed (Leipzig, n.d.) |
| 42 | A 63 | Am Abend aber desselbigen Sabbaths | 8 April 1725 | SATB, 2 ob, bn, str, bc | BG, 1860 | x | I/11.1 | Berlin, Staatsbibliothek |
| 43 | A 77 | Gott fähret auf mit Jauchzen | 30 May 1726 | SATB, 3 tr, timp, 2 ob, str, bc | BG, 1860 | x | I/12 | Berlin, Staatsbibliothek |
| 44 | A 78 | Sie werden euch in den Bann tun | 21 May 1724 | SATB, 2 ob, str, bc | BG, 1860 | x | I/12 | Berlin, Staatsbibliothek |
| 45 | A 113 | Es ist dir gesagt, Mensch, was gut ist | 11 Aug. 1726 | SATB, 2 fl, 2 ob, str, bc | BG, 1860 | x | I/18 | Berlin, Staatsbibliothek |
| 46 | A 117 | Schauet doch und sehet, ob irgend ein Schmerz sei | 1 Aug. 1723 | SATB, 2 rec, 2 obdc, trdt, str, bc | BG, 1860 | x | I/19 | |
| 47 | A 141 | Wer sich selbst erhöhet, der soll erniedriget werden (J. F. Helbig) | 13 Oct. 1726 | SATB, 2 ob, org, str, bc | BG, 1860 | x | I/23 | Berlin, Staatsbibliothek |
| 48 | A 144 | Ich elender Mensch, wer wird mich erlösen | 3 Oct. 1723 | SATB, tr, 2 ob, str, bc | BG, 1860 | x | I/24 | Berlin, Staatsbibliothek |
| 49 | A 150 | Ich geh und suche mit Verlangen | 3 Nov. 1726 | SB, obda, org, vcp, str, bc | BG, 1860 | x | [I/25] | Berlin, Staatsbibliothek |
| 50 | A 194 | Nun ist das Heil und die Kraft [frag.] | ? 29 Sept. 1723 | SATB, SATB, 3 tr, timp, 3 ob, str, bc | BG, 1860 | x | I/30 | |
| 51 | A 134 | Jauchzet Gott in allen Landen | 17 Sept. 1730 | S, tr, str, bc | BG, 1863 | xii/2 | I/22 | Berlin, Staatsbibliothek (Leipzig, 1985; Stuttgart, 1985) |
| 52 | A 160 | Falsche Welt, dir trau ich nicht | 24 Nov. 1726 | SATB, 2 hn, 3 ob, bn, str, bc | BG, 1863 | xii/2 | I/26 | Berlin, Staatsbibliothek |
| 54 | A 51 | Widerstehe doch der Sünde (G. C. Lehms) | 24 March 1715 | A, str, bc | BG, 1863 | xii/2 | I/18 | |
| 55 | A 157 | Ich armer Mensch, ich Sündenknecht | 17 Nov. 1726 | SATB, fl, obda, str, bc | BG, 1863 | xii/2 | I/26 | Berlin, Staatsbibliothek |
| 56 | A 146 | Ich will den Kreuzstab gerne tragen | 27 Oct. 1726 | SATB, 2 ob, tle, str, bc | BG, 1863 | xii/2 | I/24 | Berlin, Staatsbibliothek (Munich, 1921) |
| 57 | A 14 | Selig ist der Mann (G. C. Lehms) | 26 Dec. 1725 | SATB, 3 ob, str, bc | BG, 1863 | xii/2 | [I/3] | Berlin, Staatsbibliothek |
| 58 | A 26 | Ach Gott, wie manches Herzeleid | 5 Jan. 1727 | SB, str, bc [2 ob, tle] | BG, 1863 | xii/2 | I/13 | Berlin, Staatsbibliothek |
| 59 | A 82 | Wer mich liebet, der wird mein Wort halten (E. Neumeister) | 28 May 1724 | SATB, 2 tr, timp, str, bc | BG, 1863 | xii/2 | I/13 | Berlin, Staatsbibliothek |
| 60 | A 161 | O Ewigkeit, du Donnerwort | 7 Nov. 1723 | SATB, hn, 2 obda, str, bc | BG, 1863 | xii/2 | I/27 | |
| 61 | A 1 | Nun komm, der Heiden Heiland (E. Neumeister) | 2 Dec. 1714 | SATB, str, bc | BG, 1868 | xvi | I/1 | Berlin, Staatsbibliothek |

| BWV | BC | Title (librettist) | Date | Scoring | First published | BG vol. | NBA vol. | Autograph score (facsimile) |
|---|---|---|---|---|---|---|---|---|
| 62 | A 2 | Nun komm, der Heiden Heiland | 3 Dec. 1724 | SATB, hn, 2 ob, str, bc | BG, 1868 | xvi | I/1 | Berlin, Staatsbibliothek |
| 63 | A 8 | Christen, ätzet diesen Tag (? J. M. Heineccius) | c.1714–15 | SATB, 4 tr, timp, 3 ob, str, bc [org] | BG, 1868 | xvi | I/2 | |
| 64 | A 15 | Sehet, welch eine Liebe hat uns der Vater erzeiget (Knauer) | 27 Dec. 1723 | SATB, cnt, 3 tbn, obda, str, bc | BG, 1868 | xvi | [I/3] | |
| 65 | A 27 | Sie werden aus Saba alle kommen | 6 Jan. 1724 | SATB, 2 hn, 2 rec, 2 obdc, str, bc | BG, 1868 | xvi | I/5 | Berlin, Staatsbibliothek |
| 66 | A 56 | Erfreut euch, ihr Herzen | 10 April 1724 | SATB, tr (ad lib), 2 ob, str, bc | BG, 1868 | xvi | I/10 | Berlin, Staatsbibliothek |
| 67 | A 62 | Halt im Gedächtnis Jesum Christ | 16 April 1724 | SATB, cdt, fl, 2 obda, str, bc | BG, 1868 | xvi | I/11.1 | Berlin, Staatsbibliothek |
| 68 | A 86 | Also hat Gott die Welt geliebt | 21 May 1725 | SATB, hn (cnt), 3 tbn, 2 ob, tle, vcp, str, bc | BG, 1868 | xvi | I/14 | |
| 69 | B 10 | Lobe den Herrn, meine Seele (Knauer) | ? 26 Aug. 1748 | SATB, 3 tr, timp, 3 ob, str, bc | BG, 1868 | xvi | I/32.2 | |
| 69a | A 123 | Lobe den Herrn, meine Seele (Knauer) | 15 Aug. 1723 | SATB, 3 tr, timp, rec, 3 ob, str, bc | BG, 1868 | xvi [inc.] | I/20 | |
| 70 | A 165 | Wachet! betet! betet! wachet! (S. Franck, adapted) | 21 Nov. 1723 | SATB, tr, ob, str, bc | BG, 1868 | xvi | I/27 | |
| 70a | A 4 | Wachet! betet! betet! wachet! (S. Franck) [lost] | 6 Dec. 1716 | — | — | — | — | |
| 71 | B 1 | Gott ist mein König | 4 Feb. 1708 | SATB, 3 tr, timp, 2 rec, vc, 2 ob, org, str, bc | Mühlhausen, 1708 | xviii | I/32.1 | Berlin, Staatsbibliothek (Leipzig, 1970) |
| 72 | A 37 | Alles nur nach Gottes Willen | 27 Jan. 1726 | SATB, 2 ob, str, bc | BG, 1870 | xviii | I/6 | Berlin, Staatsbibliothek |
| 73 | A 35 | Herr, wie du willt, so schicks mit mir | 23 Jan. 1724 | SATB, hn/org, 2 ob, str, bc | BG, 1870 | xviii | I/6 | |
| 74 | A 83 | Wer mich liebet, der wird mein Wort halten (C. M. von Ziegler) | 20 May 1725 | SATB, 3 tr, timp, 2 ob, obdc, str, bc | BG, 1870 | xviii | I/38 | |
| 75 | A 94 | Die Elenden sollen essen | 30 May 1723 | SATB, tr, 2 ob(da), str, bc | BG, 1870 | xviii | I/15 | Berlin, Staatsbibliothek |
| 76 | A 97 / A 185 | Die Himmel erzählen die Ehre Gottes | 6 June 1723 | SATB, tr, 2 ob, obda, vadg, str, bc | BG, 1870 | xviii | I/16 | Berlin, Staatsbibliothek |
| 77 | A 126 | Du sollt Gott, deinen Herren, lieben (Knauer) | 22 Aug. 1723 | SATB, trdt, 2 ob, str, bc | BG, 1870 | xviii | I/21 | Berlin, Staatsbibliothek |
| 78 | A 130 | Jesu, der du meine Seele | 10 Sept. 1724 | SATB, hn, fl, 2 ob, str, bc | BG, 1870 | xviii | I/21 | Berlin, Staatsbibliothek |
| 79 | A 184 | Gott der Herr ist Sonn und Schild | 31 Oct. 1725 | SATB, 2 hn, timp, 2 fl (ad lib), 2 ob, str, bc | BG, 1870 | xviii | I/31 | Berlin, Staatsbibliothek |

# Appendix 1

| BWV | BC | Title (librettist) | Date | Scoring | First published | BG vol. | NBA vol. | Autograph score (facsimile) |
|---|---|---|---|---|---|---|---|---|
| 80 | A 183 | Ein feste Burg ist unser Gott (S. Franck) | 1727–31 | SATB, ob, str, bc [2 ob(da, dc)] | Leipzig, 1821 | xviii | I/31 | — |
| 80a | A 52 | Alles, was von Gott geboren (S. Franck) [lost] | 15 March 1716 | — | — | — | — | — |
| 81 | A 39 | Jesus schläft, was soll ich hoffen? | 30 Jan. 1724 | SATB, 2 rec, 2 obda, str, bc | BG, 1872 | xx/1 | I/6 | Berlin, Staatsbibliothek |
| 82 | A 169 | Ich habe genung | 2 Feb. 1727 | B, ob, str, bc | BG, 1872 | xx/1 | I/28.1 | Berlin, Staatsbibliothek |
| 83 | A 167 | Erfreute Zeit im neuen Bunde | 2 Feb. 1724 | SATB, 2 hn, 2 ob, str, bc | BG, 1872 | xx/1 | I/28.1 | Berlin, Staatsbibliothek |
| 84 | A 43 | Ich bin vergnügt mit meinem Glücke (Picander) | 9 Feb. 1727 | SATB, ob, str, bc | BG, 1872 | xx/1 | I/7 | Berlin, Staatsbibliothek |
| 85 | A 66 | Ich bin ein guter Hirt | 15 April 1725 | SATB, 2 ob, vcp, str, bc | BG, 1872 | xx/1 | I/11.1 | Berlin, Staatsbibliothek |
| 86 | A 73 | Wahrlich, wahrlich, ich sage euch | 14 May 1724 | SATB, 2 obda, str, bc | BG, 1872 | xx/1 | I/12 | Berlin, Staatsbibliothek |
| 87 | A 74 | Bisher habt ihr nichts gebeten in meinem Namen (C. M. von Ziegler) | 6 May 1725 | SATB, 2 ob, obdc, str, bc | BG, 1872 | xx/1 | I/12 | Berlin, Staatsbibliothek |
| 88 | A 105 | Siehe, ich will viel Fischer aussenden | 21 July 1726 | SATB, 2 hn, 2 obda, obdc, str, bc | BG, 1872 | xx/1 | I/17.2 | Berlin, Staatsbibliothek |
| 89 | A 155 | Was soll ich aus dir machen, Ephraim? | 24 Oct. 1723 | SATB, hn, 2 ob, str, bc | BG, 1872 | xx/1 | I/26 | Berlin, Staatsbibliothek |
| 90 | A 163 | Es reißet euch ein schrecklich Ende | 14 Nov. 1723 | SATB, tr, str, bc | BG, 1872 | xx/1 | I/27 | Berlin, Staatsbibliothek |
| 91 | A 9 | Gelobet seist du, Jesu Christ | 25 Dec. 1724 | SATB, 2 hn, timp, 3 ob, str, bc | BG, 1875 | xxii | I/2 | Berlin, Staatsbibliothek |
| 92 | A 42 | Ich hab in Gottes Herz und Sinn | 28 Jan. 1725 | SATB, 2 obda, str, bc | BG, 1875 | xxii | I/7 | Berlin, Staatsbibliothek |
| 93 | A 104 | Wer nur den lieben Gott läßt walten | 9 July 1724 | SATB, 2 ob, str, bc | BG, 1875 | xxii | I/17.2 | Berlin, Staatsbibliothek |
| 94 | A 115 | Was frag ich nach der Welt | 6 Aug. 1724 | SATB, fl, 2 ob(da), str, bc | BG, 1875 | xxii | I/19 | Berlin, Staatsbibliothek |
| 95 | A 136 | Christus, der ist mein Leben | 12 Sept. 1723 | SATB, hn, 2 ob(da), str, bc | BG, 1875 | xxii | I/23 | Berlin, Staatsbibliothek |
| 96 | A 142 | Herr Christ, der einge Gottessohn | 8 Oct. 1724 | SATB, hn, tbn, flp, 2 ob, vcp, str, bc | BG, 1875 | xxii | I/24 | Berlin, Staatsbibliothek |
| 97 | A 189 | In allen meinen Taten | 1734 | SATB, 2 ob, str, bc | BG, 1875 | xxii | I/34 | New York Public Library (New York, 1985) |
| 98 | A 153 | Was Gott tut, das ist wohlgetan | 10 Nov. 1726 | SATB, 3 ob, str, bc | BG, 1875 | xxii | [I/25] | Berlin, Staatsbibliothek |
| 99 | A 133 | Was Gott tut, das ist wohlgetan | 17 Sept. 1724 | SATB, hn, fl, obda, str, bc | BG, 1875 | xxii | I/22 | Berlin, Staatsbibliothek (inc.) |

| BWV | BC | Title (librettist) | Date | Scoring | First published | BG vol. | NBA vol. | Autograph score (facsimile) |
|---|---|---|---|---|---|---|---|---|
| 100 | A 191 | Was Gott tut, das ist wohlgetan | c.1732–5 | SATB, 2 hn, timp, fl, obda, str, bc | BG, 1875 | xxii | I/34 | Berlin, Staatsbibliothek |
| 101 | A 118 | Nimm von uns, Herr, du treuer Gott | 13 Aug. 1724 | SATB, cnt, 3 tbn, fl, 2 ob, obdc, str, bc | BG, 1876 | xxiii | I/19 | Berlin, Staatsbibliothek |
| 102 | A 119 | Herr, deine Augen sehen nach dem Glauben | 25 Aug. 1726 | SATB, fl, 2 ob, vcp, str, bc | Bonn, 1830 | xxiii | I/19 | Berlin, Staatsbibliothek |
| 103 | A 69 | Ihr werdet weinen und heulen (C. M. von Ziegler) | 22 April 1725 | SATB, tr, flp, 2 obda, str, bc | Bonn, 1830 | xxiii | I/11.2 | Berlin, Staatsbibliothek |
| 104 | A 65 | Du Hirte Israel, höre | 23 April 1724 | SATB, 2 ob(da), tle, str, bc | Bonn, 1830 | xxiii | I/11.1 | Berlin, Staatsbibliothek |
| 105 | A 114 | Herr, gehe nicht ins Gericht | 25 July 1723 | SATB, hn, 2 ob, str, bc | Bonn, 1830 | xxiii | I/19 | Berlin, Staatsbibliothek (Leipzig, 1983) |
| 106 | B 18 | Gottes Zeit ist die allerbeste Zeit; 'Actus tragicus' | ? 1707–8 | SATB, 2 rec, 2 vadg, bc | Bonn, 1830 | xxiii | I/34 | Berlin, Staatsbibliothek |
| 107 | A 109 | Was willst du dich betrüben | 23 July 1724 | SATB, hn, 2 fl, 2 obda, str, bc | BG, 1876 | xxiii | I/18 | Berlin, Staatsbibliothek |
| 108 | A 72 | Es ist euch gut, daß ich hingehe (C. M. von Ziegler) | 29 April 1725 | SATB, 2 obda, str, bc | BG, 1876 | xxiii | I/12 | Berlin, Staatsbibliothek |
| 109 | A 151 | Ich glaube, lieber Herr, hilf meinem Unglauben | 17 Oct. 1723 | SATB, hn, 2 ob, str, bc | BG, 1876 | xxiii | [I/25] | Berlin, Staatsbibliothek |
| 110 | A 10 | Unser Mund sei voll Lachens (G. C. Lehms) | 25 Dec. 1725 | SATB, 3 tr, timp, 2 fl, 3 ob, str, bc | BG, 1876 | xxiii | I/2 | Berlin, Staatsbibliothek (Leipzig, 1990) |
| 111 | A 36 | Was mein Gott will, das g'scheh allzeit | 21 Jan. 1725 | SATB, 2 ob, str, bc | BG, 1876 | xxiv | I/6 | Kraków, Biblioteka Jagiellońska |
| 112 | A 67 | Der Herr ist mein getreuer Hirt | 8 April 1731 | SATB, 2 hn, 2 obda, str, bc | BG, 1876 | xxiv | I/11.1 | New York, Pierpont Morgan Library (New York, 1985) |
| 113 | A 122 | Herr Jesu Christ, du höchstes Gut | 20 Aug. 1724 | SATB, fl, 2 ob(da), str, bc | BG, 1876 | xxiv | I/20 | Stuttgart, Internationale Bachakademie |
| 114 | A 139 | Ach, lieben Christen, seid getrost | 1 Oct. 1724 | SATB, hn, fl, 2 ob, str, bc | BG, 1876 | xxiv | I/23 | ?USA, private collection |
| 115 | A 156 | Mache dich, mein Geist, bereit | 5 Nov. 1724 | SATB, hn, fl, obda, vcp, str, bc | BG, 1876 | xxiv | I/26 | Cambridge, Fitzwilliam Museum |
| 116 | A 164 | Du Friedefürst, Herr Jesu Christ | 26 Nov. 1724 | SATB, hn, 2 obda, str, bc | BG, 1876 | xxiv | I/27 | Paris, Bibliothèque Nationale |
| 117 | A 187 | Sei Lob und Ehr dem höchsten Gut | 1728–31 | SATB, 2 fl, 2 ob(da), str, bc | BG, 1876 | xxiv | I/34 | Berlin, Staatsbibliothek |
| 119 | B 3 | Preise, Jerusalem, den Herrn | 30 Aug. 1723 | SATB, 4 tr, timp, 2 rec, 3 ob, str, bc | BG, 1876 | xxiv | I/32.1 | Berlin, Staatsbibliothek |

# Appendix 1

| BWV | BC | Title (librettist) | Date | Scoring | First published | BG vol. | NBA vol. | Autograph score (facsimile) |
|---|---|---|---|---|---|---|---|---|
| 120 | B 6 | Gott, man lobet dich in der Stille | ? 27 Aug. 1742 | SATB, 3 tr, timp, 2 obda, str, bc | BG, 1876 | xxiv | I/32.2 | Kraków, Biblioteka Jagiellońska |
| 120a | B 15 | Herr Gott, Beherrscher aller Dinge [inc.] | ? 1729 | SATB, 3 tr, timp, 2 ob(da), org, str, bc | BG, 1894 | xli | I/33 | Berlin, Staatsbibliothek |
| 120b | B 28 | Gott, man lobet dich in der Stille (Picander) [lost] | 26 June 1730 | — | — | — | — | — |
| 121 | A 13 | Christum wir sollen loben schon | 26 Dec. 1724 | SATB, cnt, 3 tbn, obda, str, bc [obdc] | BG, 1878 | xxvi | [I/3] | Kraków, Biblioteka Jagiellońska |
| 122 | A 19 | Das neugeborne Kindelein | 31 Dec. 1724 | SATB, 3 rec, 2 ob, tle, str, bc | BG, 1878 | xxvi | [I/3] | Berlin, Staatsbibliothek |
| 123 | A 28 | Liebster Immanuel, Herzog der Frommen | 6 Jan. 1725 | SATB, 2 fl, 2 obda, str, bc | BG, 1878 | xxvi | I/5 | Kraków, Biblioteka Jagiellońska |
| 124 | A 30 | Meinen Jesum laß ich nicht | 7 Jan. 1725 | SATB, hn, obda, str, bc | BG, 1878 | xxvi | I/5 | Berlin, Staatsbibliothek |
| 125 | A 168 | Mit Fried und Freud ich fahr dahin | 2 Feb. 1725 | SATB, hn, fl, ob(da), str, bc | BG, 1878 | xxvi | I/28.1 | Berlin, Staatsbibliothek |
| 126 | A 46 | Erhalt uns, Herr, bei deinem Wort | 4 Feb. 1725 | SATB, tr, 2 ob, str, bc | BG, 1878 | xxvi | I/7 | |
| 127 | A 49 | Herr Jesu Christ, wahr' Mensch und Gott | 11 Feb. 1725 | SATB, tr, 2 rec, 2 ob, str, bc | BG, 1878 | xxvi | I/8.1 | Berlin, Staatsbibliothek |
| 128 | A 76 | Auf Christi Himmelfahrt allein (C. M. von Ziegler) | 10 May 1725 | SATB, tr, 2 hn, 3 ob, str, bc | BG, 1878 | xxvi | I/12 | Winterthur, Switzerland, private collection |
| 129 | A 93 | Gelobet sei der Herr, mein Gott | ? 31 Oct. 1726 | SATB, 3 tr, timp, fl, 2 ob(da), str, bc | BG, 1878 | xxvi | I/15 | Berlin, Staatsbibliothek |
| 130 | A 179 | Herr Gott, dich loben alle wir | 29 Sept. 1724 | SATB, 3 tr, timp, fl, 3 ob, str, bc | BG, 1878 | xxvi | I/30 | Berlin, Staatsbibliothek, permanent loan |
| 131 | B 25 | Aus der Tiefen rufe ich, Herr, zu dir (? G. C. Eilmar) | 1707/8 | SATB, ob, bn, vn, 2 va, bc | BG, 1881 | xxviii | I/34 | New York, private collection (New York, 1985) |
| 132 | A 6 | Bereitet die Wege, bereitet die Bahn (S. Franck) | 22 Dec. 1715 | SATB, ob, str, bc | BG, 1881 | xxviii | I/1 | Berlin, Staatsbibliothek |
| 133 | A 16 | Ich freue mich in dir | 27 Dec. 1724 | SATB, cnt, 2 obda, str, bc | BG, 1881 | xxviii | [I/3] | Berlin, Staatsbibliothek |
| 134 | A 59 | Ein Herz, das seinen Jesum lebend weiß | 11 April 1724 | SATB, 2 ob, str, bc | BG, 1881 | xxviii | I/10 | Berlin, Staatsbibliothek |
| 135 | A 100 | Ach Herr, mich armen Sünder | 25 June 1724 | SATB, cnt, tbn, 2 ob, str, bc | BG, 1881 | xxviii | I/16 | Leipzig, Bach-Archiv (Leipzig, 1926) |
| 136 | A 111 | Erforsche mich, Gott, und erfahre mein Herz | 18 July 1723 | SATB, hn, 2 ob(da), str, bc | BG, 1881 | xxviii | I/18 | Berlin, Staatsbibliothek |
| 137 | A 124 | Lobe den Herren, den mächtigen König der Ehren | 19 Aug. 1725 | SATB, 3 tr, timp, 2 ob, str, bc | BG, 1881 | xxviii | I/20 | Berlin, Staatsbibliothek [inc.] |

| BWV | BC | Title (librettist) | Date | Scoring | First published | BG vol. | NBA vol. | Autograph score (facsimile) |
|---|---|---|---|---|---|---|---|---|
| 138 | A 132 | Warum betrübst du dich, mein Herz? | 5 Sept. 1723 | SATB, 2 obda, str, bc | Leipzig, 1847 | xxviii | I/22 | Berlin, Staatsbibliothek |
| 139 | A 159 | Wohl dem, der sich auf seinen Gott | 12 Nov. 1724 | SATB, 2 obda, str, bc | BG, 1881 | xxviii | I/26 | |
| 140 | A 166 | Wachet auf, ruft uns die Stimme | 25 Nov. 1731 | SATB, hn, 2 ob, tle, vnp, str, bc | Leipzig, 1847 | xxviii | I/27 | |
| 144 | A 41 | Nimm, was dein ist, und gehe hin | 6 Feb. 1724 | SATB, 2 ob(da), str, bc | Berlin, 1843 | xxx | I/7 | Berlin, Staatsbibliothek |
| 145 | A 60 | Ich lebe, mein Herze, zu deinem Ergötzen (Picander) | ? 19 April 1729 | SATB, tr, fl, 2 obda, str, bc | BG, 1884 | xxx | I/10 | |
| 146 | A 70 | Wir müssen durch viel Trübsal in das Reich Gottes eingehen | ? 12 May 1726/ ? 18 April 1728 | SATB, fl, 2 ob(da), tle, org, str, bc | BG, 1884 | xxx | I/11.2 | |
| 147 | A 174 | Herz und Mund und Tat und Leben (S. Franck, adapted) | 2 July 1723 | SATB, tr, 2 ob(da, dc), str, bc | BG, 1884 | xxx | I/28.2 | Berlin, Staatsbibliothek |
| 147a | A 7 | Herz und Mund und Tat und Leben (S. Franck) | 20 Dec. 1716 | — | — | — | — | |
| 148 | A 140 | Bringet dem Herrn Ehre seines Namens (after Picander) [lost] | ? 19 Sept. 1723 | SATB, tr, 3 ob, str, bc | BG, 1884 | xxx | I/23 | |
| 149 | A 181 | Man singet mit Freuden vom Sieg (Picander) | 29 Sept. ? 1728/9 | SATB, 3 tr, timp, 3 ob, bn, str, bc | BG, 1884 | xxx | I/30 | |
| 150 | B 24 | Nach dir, Herr, verlanget mich | ?1704–7 | SATB, bn, 2 vn, bc | BG, 1884 | xxx | [I/41] | |
| 151 | A 17 | Süßer Trost, mein Jesus kömmt (G. C. Lehms) | 27 Dec. 1725 | SATB, fl, str, bc [obda] | BG, 1886 | xxxii | [I/3] | Coburg, Kunstsammlungen der Veste |
| 152 | A 18 | Tritt auf die Glaubensbahn (S. Franck) | 30 Dec. 1714 | SB, rec, ob, vada, vadg, bc | BG, 1886 | xxxii | [I/3] | Berlin, Staatsbibliothek |
| 153 | A 25 | Schau, lieber Gott, wie meine Feind | 2 Jan. 1724 | SATB, str, bc | BG, 1886 | xxxii | I/4 | |
| 154 | A 29 | Mein liebster Jesus ist verloren | 9 Jan. 1724 | SATB, 2 obda, str, bc | BG, 1886 | xxxii | I/5 | |
| 155 | A 32 | Mein Gott, wie lang, ach lange (S. Franck) | 19 Jan. 1716 | SATB, bn, str, bc | BG, 1886 | xxxii | I/5 | Berlin, Staatsbibliothek |
| 156 | A 38 | Ich steh mit einem Fuß im Grabe (Picander) | ? 23 Jan. 1729 | SATB, ob, str, bc | BG, 1886 | xxxii | I/6 | |
| 157 | A 170 B 20 | Ich lasse dich nicht, du segnest mich denn (Picander) | ? 6 Feb. 1728, or later | SATB, fl, ob(da), str, bc | BG, 1886 | xxxii | I/34 | |
| 158 | A 61 A 171 | Der Friede sei mit dir | ? 1723–35 | SATB, ob, vn, bc | BG, 1886 | xxxii | I/10 | |
| 159 | A 50 | Sehet, wir gehn hinauf gen Jerusalem | ? 27 Feb. 1729 | SATB, ob, str, bc | BG, 1886 | xxxii | I/8.1 | |

# Appendix 1

| BWV | BC | Title (librettist) | Date | Scoring | First published | BG vol. | NBA vol. | Autograph score (facsimile) |
|---|---|---|---|---|---|---|---|---|
| 161 | A 135 | Komm, du süße Todesstunde (S. Franck) | 27 Sept. 1716 | SATB, 2 rec, org, str, bc | BG, 1887 | xxxiii | I/23 | |
| 162 | A 148 | Ach, ich sehe, itzt da ich zur Hochzeit gehe (S. Franck) [inc.] | 25 Oct. 1716 | SATB, cdt, str, bc | BG, 1887 | xxxiii | [I/25] | |
| 163 | A 158 | Nur jedem das Seine (S. Franck) | 24 Nov. 1715 | SATB, str, bc | BG, 1887 | xxxiii | I/26 | Berlin, Staatsbibliothek |
| 164 | A 128 | Ihr, die ihr euch von Christo nennet (S. Franck) | 26 Aug. 1725 | SATB, 2 fl, 2 ob, str, bc | BG, 1887 | xxxiii | I/21 | Berlin, Staatsbibliothek |
| 165 | A 90 | O heiliges Geist- und Wasserbad (S. Franck) | 16 June 1715 | SATB, str, bc | BG, 1887 | xxxiii | I/15 | |
| 166 | A 71 | Wo gehest du hin? [inc.] | 7 May 1724 | SATB, ob, str, bc | BG, 1887 | xxxiii | I/12 | |
| 167 | A 176 | Ihr Menschen, rühmet Gottes Liebe | 24 June 1723 | SATB, tr(dt), ob(dc), str, bc | BG, 1887 | xxxiii | I/29 | |
| 168 | A 116 | Tue Rechnung! Donnerwort (S. Franck) | 29 July 1725 | SATB, 2 obda, str, bc | BG, 1887 | xxxiii | I/19 | Berlin, Staatsbibliothek |
| 169 | A 143 | Gott soll allein mein Herze haben | 20 Oct. 1726 | SATB, 2 ob(da), tle, org, str, bc | BG, 1887 | xxxiii | I/24 | Berlin, Staatsbibliothek |
| 170 | A 106 | Vergnügte Ruh, beliebte Seelenlust (G. C. Lehms) | 28 July 1726 | A, obda, org, str, bc | BG, 1887 | xxxiii | I/17.2 | Berlin, Staatsbibliothek |
| 171 | A 24 | Gott, wie dein Name, so ist auch dein Ruhm (Picander) | 1 Jan. ?1729 | SATB, 3 tr, timp, 2 ob, str, bc | BG, 1888 | xxxv | I/4 | New York, Pierpont Morgan Library (New York, 1985) |
| 172 | A 81 | Erschallet, ihr Lieder (? S. Franck) | 20 May 1714 | SATB, 3 tr, timp, fl, ob(da), str, bc | BG, 1888 | xxxv | I/13 | Berlin, Staatsbibliothek |
| 173 | A 85 | Erhöhtes Fleisch und Blut | ? 29 May 1724 | SATB, 2 fl, str, bc | BG, 1888 | xxxv | I/14 | Berlin, Staatsbibliothek |
| 174 | A 87 | Ich liebe den Höchsten von ganzem Gemüte (Picander) | 6 June 1729 | SATB, 2 cdc, 2 ob, tle, str, bc | BG, 1888 | xxxv | I/14 | Berlin, Staatsbibliothek [inc.] (Berea, Ohio, 1985) |
| 175 | A 89 | Er rufet seinen Schafen mit Namen | 22 May 1725 | SATB, 2 tr, 3 rec, vcp, str, bc | BG, 1888 | xxxv | I/14 | Berlin, Staatsbibliothek |
| 176 | A 92 | Es ist ein trotzig und verzagt Ding (C. M. von Ziegler) | 27 May 1725 | SATB, 3 ob, str, bc | BG, 1888 | xxxv | I/15 | Berlin, Staatsbibliothek |
| 177 | A 103 | Ich ruf zu dir, Herr Jesu Christ | 6 July 1732 | SATB, 2 ob(dc), bn, str, bc | BG, 1888 | xxxv | I/17.1 | Berlin, Staatsbibliothek |
| 178 | A 112 | Wo Gott der Herr nicht bei uns hält | 30 July 1724 | SATB, hn, 2 ob(da), str, bc | BG, 1888 | xxxv, xii | I/18 | |
| 179 | A 121 | Siehe zu, daß deine Gottesfurcht nicht Heuchelei sei | 8 Aug. 1723 | SATB, 2 ob(dc), str, bc | Berlin, 1843 | xxxv | I/20 | Berlin, Staatsbibliothek |
| 180 | A 149 | Schmücke dich, o liebe Seele | 22 Oct. 1724 | SATB, 2 rec, fl, ob, obdc, vcp, str, bc | BG, 1888 | xxxv | [I/25] | Stuttgart, Internationale Bachakademie |

| BWV | BC | Title (librettist) | Date | Scoring | First published | BG vol. | NBA vol. | Autograph score (facsimile) |
|---|---|---|---|---|---|---|---|---|
| 181 | A 45 | Leichtgesinnte Flattergeister [inc.] | 13 Feb. 1724 | SATB, tr, bc [fl, ob] | BG, 1891 | xxxvii | I/7 | Berlin, Staatsbibliothek |
| 182 | A 53 A 172 | Himmelskönig, sei willkommen (? S. Franck) | 25 March 1714 | SATB, rec, str, bc | Berlin, 1843 | xxxvii | [I/8.2] | |
| 183 | A 79 | Sie werden euch in den Bann tun (C. M. von Ziegler) | 13 May 1725 | SATB, 2 obda, 2 obdc, vcp, str, bc | BG, 1891 | xxxvii | I/12 | Berlin, Staatsbibliothek |
| 184 | A 88 | Erwünschtes Freudenlicht | 30 May 1724 | SATB, 2 fl, str, bc | BG, 1891 | xxxvii | I/14 | |
| 185 | A 101 | Barmherziges Herze der ewigen Liebe (S. Franck) | 14 July 1715 | SATB, ob, str, bc | Berlin, 1843 | xxxvii | I/17.1 | |
| 186 | A 108 | Ärgre dich, o Seele, nicht (S. Franck, adapted) | 11 July 1723 | SATB, 2 ob, tle, str, bc | BG, 1891 | xxxvii | I/18 | |
| 186a | A 5 | Ärgre dich, o Seele, nicht (S. Franck) [lost] | 13 Dec. 1716 | — | — | — | — | |
| 187 | A 110 | Es wartet alles auf dich | 4 Aug. 1726 | SATB, 2 ob, str, bc | BG, 1891 | xxxvii | I/18 | |
| 188 | A 154 | Ich habe meine Zuversicht (Picander) [inc.] | ? 17 Oct. 1728 | SATB, 3 ob, org, str, bc | BG, 1891 | xxxvii | [I/25] | dispersed [inc.] |
| 190 | A 21 | Singet dem Herrn ein neues Lied [inc.] | 1 Jan. 1724 | SATB, 3 tr, timp, 3 ob, str, bc | BG, 1891 | xxxvii | I/4 | Berlin, Staatsbibliothek [inc.] |
| 190a | B 27 | Singet dem Herrn ein neues Lied (Picander) [lost] | 25 June 1730 | — | — | — | — | |
| 192 | A 188 | Nun danket alle Gott [inc.] | ? autumn 1730 | SATB, 2 fl, 2 ob, str, bc | BG, 1894 | xli | I/34 | |
| 193 | B 5 | Ihr Tore zu Zion [inc.] | 25 Aug. 1727 | SATB, 2 ob, str, bc | BG, 1894 | xli | I/32.1 | |
| 194 | A 91 B 31 | Höchsterwünschtes Freudenfest | ? 2 Nov. 1723 | SATB, 3 ob, str, bc | BG, 1881 | xxix | I/31 | Berlin, Staatsbibliothek |
| 195 | B 14 | Dem Gerechten muß das Licht immer wieder aufgehen | 1727–31 | SATB, 3 tr, timp, 2 hn, 2 fl, 2 ob(da), str, bc | BG, 1864 | xiii/1 | I/33 | |
| 196 | B 11 | Der Herr denket an uns | ? 1707/8 | SATB, str, bc | BG, 1864 | xiii/1 | I/33 | |
| 197 | B 16 | Gott ist unsre Zuversicht | 1736/7 | SATB, 3 tr, timp, 2 ob(da), str, bc | BG, 1864 | xiii/1 | I/33 | Berlin, Staatsbibliothek |
| 197a | A 11 | Ehre sei Gott in der Höhe (Picander) [inc.] | ? 25 Dec. 1728 | SATB, 2 fl, obda, vc/bn, str, bc | BG, 1894 | xli | I/2 | New York, Pierpont Morgan Library [frag.] |
| 199 | A 120 | Mein Herze Schwimmt im Blut (G. C. Lehms) | 12 Aug. 1714 | S, ob, str, bc | BG, 1912 | xli [inc.] | I/20 | Copenhagen, Kongelige Bibliotek |
| 200 | A 192 | Bekennen will ich seinen Namen [inc.] | c.1742 | A, ? 2vn, bc | Leipzig, 1935 | — | I/28.1 | Berlin, Staatsbibliothek [frag.] |
| 223 | A 186 | (Meine seele soll Gott loben) [frag.] | ? c.1707–8 | ? | — | — | — | |

| BWV | BC | Title (librettist) | Date | Scoring | First published | BG vol. | NBA vol. | Autograph score (facsimile) |
|---|---|---|---|---|---|---|---|---|
| 244a | B 22 | Klagt, Kinder, klagt es aller Welt (Picander) [lost] | 24 March 1729 | — | — | — | — | — |
| 1045 | A 193 | (Sinfonia) [frag.] | c.1743–6 | vn, 3 tr, timp, 2 ob, str, bc | BG, 1874 | xxi/1 | I/34 | Berlin, Staatsbibliothek |
| 1083 | | Tilge, Höchster, meine Sünden [arr. of Pergolesi, *Stabat mater*] | c.1745–7 | SA, str, bc | Stuttgart, 1963 | — | — | |
| Anh. I 2 | A 147 | ? [frag.] | ? Oct. 1729 | SATB, str, bc | — | — | — | |
| Anh. I 3 | B 7 | Gott, gib dein Gerichte dem Könige (Picander) [lost] | 28 Aug. 1730 | — | — | — | — | |
| Ang. I 4 | B 4, 29 | Wünschet Jerusalem Glück (Picander) [lost] | 26 Aug. 1726/30 Aug. 1728 | — | — | — | — | |
| Anh. I 14 | B 12 | Sein Segen fließt daher wie ein Strom [lost] | 12 Feb. 1725 | — | — | — | — | |
| Anh. I 15 | B 32 | Siehe, der Hüter Israel [lost] | ? 27 April 1724 | SATB, 3 tr, timp, 2 ob, str, bc | — | — | — | |
| Anh. 190 | | Ich bin ein Pilgrim auf der Welt (Picander) [frag.] | 18 April 1729 | SATB, insts, bc | — | — | — | |
| Anh. 192 | | ? [lost] | Feb. 1709 | — | — | — | — | |
| Anh. 193 | | Herrscher des Himmels, König der Ehren [lost] | 29 Aug. 1740 | — | — | — | — | |
| Anh. 197 | | Ihr wallenden Wolken | ? 1718–23 | — | — | — | — | |

## 2. Secular cantatas

| BWV | BC | Title (librettist) | Date | Scoring | First published | BG vol. | NBA vol. | Autograph score (facsimile) |
|---|---|---|---|---|---|---|---|---|
| 30a | G 31 | Angenehmes Wiederau, freue dich in deinen Auen (? Picander) | 28 Sept. 1737 | SATB, 3 tr, timp, 2 fl, 2 ob(da), str, bc | BG, 1856 | v/1 | I/39 | Berlin, Staatsbibliothek (Leipzig, 1980) |
| 36a | G 12 | Steigt freudig in die Luft (Picander) [lost] | 30 Nov. 1726 | — | BG, 1887 | xxxiv | — | — |
| 36b | G 38 | Die Freude regt sich [inc.] | 1735 | SATB, fl, obda, str, bc | BG, 1887 | xxxiv | I/38 | Berlin, Staatsbibliothek |
| 36c | G 35 | Schwingt freudig euch empor | April–July 1725 | SATB, obda, vada, str, bc | BG, 1887 | xxxiv | I/39 | Berlin, Staatsbibliothek |
| 66a | G 4 | Der Himmel dacht auf Anhalts Ruhm und Glück (C. F. Hunold) [lost] | 10 Dec. 1718 | — | — | — | — | — |

| BWV | BC | Title (librettist) | Date | Scoring | First published | BG vol. | NBA vol. | Autograph score (facsimile) |
|---|---|---|---|---|---|---|---|---|
| 134a | G 5 | Die Zeit, die Tag und Jahre macht (C. F. Hunold) | 1 Jan. 1719 | SATB, 2 ob, str, bc | BG, 1881 [inc.] | xxxiv [inc.] | I/35 | Paris, Bibliothèque Nationale [inc.] |
| 173a | G 9 | Durchlauchtster Leopold | 10 Dec. ?1720/2 | SB, 2 fl, bn, str, bc | BG, 1887 | xxxiv | I/35 | Berlin, Staatsbibliothek |
| 184a | G 8 | ? [lost] | 10 Dec. 1720 or 21 Jan. 1721 | — | — | — | — | — |
| 193a | G 15 | Ihr Häuser des Himmels, ihr scheinenden Lichter (Picander) [lost] | 3 Aug. 1727 | — | — | — | — | — |
| 194a | G 11 | ? [lost] | before Nov. 1723 | — | — | — | — | — |
| 198 | G 34 | Laß, Fürstin, laß noch einen Strahl: Trauer Ode (J. C. Gottsched) | 17 Oct. 1727 | SATB, 2 fl, 2 obda, 2 vadg, 2 lt, str, bc | BG, 1865 | xiii/3 | I/38 | Berlin, Staatsbibliothek |
| 201 | G 46 | Geschwinde, ihr wirbelnden Winde: Der Streit zwischen Phoebus und Pan (Picander) | ? autumn 1729 | SATTBB, 3 tr, timp, 2 fl, 2 ob(da), str, bc | BG, 1862 | xi/2 | I/40 | Berlin, Staatsbibliothek |
| 202 | G 41 | Weichet nur, betrübte Schatten | before 1730 | S, ob, str | BG, 1862 | xi/2 | I/40 | — |
| 203 | G 51 | Amore traditore | ? before 1723 | B, hpcd | BG, 1862 | xi/2 | [I/41] | — |
| 204 | G 45 | Ich bin in mir vergnügt | 1726/7 | S, fl, 2 ob, str, bc | BG, 1862 | xi/2 | I/40 | Berlin, Staatsbibliothek |
| 205 | G 36 | Zerreißet, zersprenget, zertrümmert die Gruft: Der zufriedengestellte Äolus (Picander) | 3 Aug. 1725 | SATB, 3 tr, timp, 2 fl, 2 ob(da), vada, vadg, str, bc | BG, 1862 | xi/2 | I/38 | Berlin, Staatsbibliothek (Leipzig, 1978; New York, n.d.) |
| 205a | G 20 | Blast Lärmen, ihr Feinde! Verstärket die Macht [lost] | ? 19 Feb. 1734 | — | BG, 1887 | — | — | — |
| 206 | G 23, 26 | Schleicht, spielende Wellen, und murmelt gelinde | 7 Oct. 1736 | SATB, 3 tr, timp, 3 fl, 2 ob(da), str, bc | BG, 1873 | xx/2 | I/36 | Berlin, Staatsbibliothek |
| 207 | G 37 | Vereinigte Zwietracht der wechselnden Saiten | 11 Dec. 1726 | SATB, 3 tr, timp, 2 fl, 2 ob(da), tle, str, bc | BG, 1873 | xx/2 | I/38 | Berlin, Staatsbibliothek |
| 207a | G 22 | Auf, schmetternde Töne der muntern Trompeten | ? 3 Aug. 1735 | SATB, 3 tr, timp, 2 fl, 2 ob(da), tle, str, bc | BG, 1873 | xx/2, xxxiv | I/37 | Berlin, Staatsbibliothek |
| 208 | G1, 3 | Was mir behagt, ist nur die muntre Jagd (S. Franck) | 23 Feb. ?1713/16 | SSTB, 2 cdc, 2 rec, 2 ob, tle, bn, str, bc | BG, 1881 | xxix | I/35 | Berlin, Staatsbibliothek |
| 209 | G 50 | Non sa che sia dolore | after 1729 | S, fl, str, bc | BG, 1881 | xxix | [I/41] | — |
| 210 | G 44 | O holder Tag, erwünschte Zeit | ? 1738–46 | S, fl, obda, str, bc | BG, 1881 | xxix | I/40 | (Leipzig, 1967) |
| 210a | G 29 | O angenehme Melodei [frag.] | 12 Jan. 1729 | — | BG, 1881 | xxix | I/39 | — |
| 211 | G 48 | Schweigt stille, plaudert nicht: Coffee Cantata (Picander) | c.1734 | STB, fl, str, bc | Berlin, Vienna, and Leipzig, 1837 | xxix | I/40 | Berlin, Staatsbibliothek (Vienna, 1923; Leipzig, 1971) |

# Appendix 1

| BWV | BC | Title (librettist) | Date | Scoring | First published | BG vol. | NBA vol. | Autograph score (facsimile) |
|---|---|---|---|---|---|---|---|---|
| 212 | G 32 | Man han en neue Oberkeet: Peasant Cantata (Picander) | ? 30 Aug. 1742 | S, B, hn, fl, str, bc | BG, 1881 | xxix | I/39 | Berlin, Staatsbibliothek (Munich, 1965) |
| 213 | G 18 | Laßt uns sorgen, laßt uns wachen: Herkules at the Crossroads (Picander) | 5 Sept. 1733 | SATB, 2 cdc, 2 ob(da), str, bc | BG, 1887 | xxxiv | I/36 | Berlin, Staatsbibliothek |
| 214 | G 19 | Tönet, ihr Pauken! Erschallet, Trompeten! | 8 Dec. 1733 | SATB, 3 tr, timp, 2 fl, 2 ob(da), str, bc | BG, 1887 | xxxiv | I/36 | Berlin, Staatsbibliothek |
| 215 | G 21 | Preise dein Glücke, gesegnetes Sachsen (J. C. Clauder) | 5 Oct. 1734 | SATB, SATB, 3 tr, timp, 2 fl, 2 ob(da), str, bc | BG, 1887 | xxxiv | I/37 | Berlin, Staatsbibliothek |
| 216 | G 43 | Vergnügte Pleißen-Stadt (Picander) [inc.] | 5 Feb. 1728 | SA, insts | Berlin, 1924 | — | I/40 | |
| 216a | G 47 | Erwählte Pleißenstadt: Apollo et Mercurius [lost] | after 1728 | — | BG, 1887 | — | — | |
| 249a | G 2 | Entfliehet, verschwindet, entweichet, ihr Sorgen (Picander) [lost] | 23 Feb. 1725 | SATB, 3 tr, timp, 2 rec, fl, 2 ob, str, bc | Kassel, 1943 | — | — | |
| 249b | G 28 | Verjaget, zerstreuet, zerrüttet ihr Sterne: Die Feier des Genius (Picander) [lost] | 25 Aug. 1726 | — | — | — | — | |
| Anh. I 5 | B 30 | Lobet den Herrn, alle seine Heerscharen (C. F. Hunold) [lost] | 10 Dec. 1718 | — | — | — | — | |
| Anh. I 6 | G 6 | Dich loben die lieblichen Strahlen (C. F. Hunold) [lost] | 1 Jan. 1720 | — | — | — | — | |
| Anh. I 7 | G 7 | Heut ist gewiß ein guter Tag [lost] | 10 Dec. ?1720 | — | — | — | — | |
| Anh. I 8 | G 10 | ? [lost] | 1 Jan. 1723 | — | — | — | — | |
| Anh. I 9 | G 14 | Entfernet euch, ihr heitern Sterne (C. F. Haupt) [lost] | 12 May 1727 | — | — | — | — | |
| Anh. I 10 | G 30 | So kämpfet nur, ihr mintern Töne (Picander) [lost] | 25 Aug. 1731 | — | — | — | — | |
| Anh. I 11 | G 16 | Es lebe der König, der Vater im Lande (Picander) [lost] | 3 Aug. 1732 | — | — | — | — | |
| Anh. I 12 | G 17 | Frohes Volk, vergnügte Sachsen (Picander) [lost] | 3 Aug. 1733 | — | — | — | — | |
| Anh. I 13 | G 24 | Willkommen! Ihr herrschenden Götter der Erden! (J. C. Gottsched) [lost] | 28 April 1738 | — | — | — | — | |

| BWV | BC | Title (librettist) | Date | Scoring | First published | BG vol. | NBA vol. | Autograph score (facsimile) |
| --- | --- | --- | --- | --- | --- | --- | --- | --- |
| Anh. I 18 G 39 | | Froher Tag, verlangte Stunden (J. H. Winckler) [lost] | 5 June 1732 | — | — | — | — | |
| Anh. I 19 G 40 | | Thomana saß annoch betrübt (J. A. Landvoigt) [lost] | 21 Nov. 1734 | — | — | — | — | |
| Anh. I 20 G 33 | | ? [lost] | 9 Aug. 1723 | | — | — | — | |
| Anh. 194 | | ? [lost] | 9 Aug. 1722 | | — | — | — | |
| Anh. 196 | | Auf! süß-entzückende Gewalt (J. C. Gottsched) [lost] | 27 Nov. 1725 | | — | — | — | |

## 3. Latin church music

| BWV | BC | Title | Date | Scoring | First published | BG vol. | NBA vol. | Autograph score (facsimile) |
| --- | --- | --- | --- | --- | --- | --- | --- | --- |
| 191 | E 16 | Gloria in excelsis Deo | Christmas 1745 | SSTB, 3 tr, timp, 2 fl, 2 ob, str, bc | BG, 1894 | xli | I/2 | Berlin, Staatsbibliothek |
| 232 | E 1 | Mass in B minor, comprising: | 1748–9 | | Bonn, 1845 | vi | II/1 | Berlin, Staatsbibliothek (Leipzig, 1924; Kassel, 1965; Leipzig, 1983; Stuttgart, 1983 [missa only]) |
| 232^I | | Missa | 1733 | SSATB, 3 tr, timp, cdc, 2 fl, 2 ob(da), str, bc | Bonn, 1833 | | | |
| 232^II | | Symbolum Nicenum | | SSATB, 3 tr, timp, 2 fl, 2 ob(da), str, bc | | | | |
| 232^III | | Sanctus | 25 Dec. 1724 | SSAATB, 3 tr, timp, 3 ob, str, bc | | | | |
| 232^IV | | Osanna, Benedictus, Agnus Dei | | SATB, SATB, 3 tr, timp, 2 fl, 2 ob, str, bc | | | | |
| 233 | E 6 | Missa in F | ? 1738/9 | SATB, 2 hn, 2 ob, bn, str, bc | BG, 1858 | viii | II/2 | |
| 233a | E 7 | Kyrie 'Christe du Lamm Gottes' | ? 1708–17 | SSATB, bc | BG, 1894 | xli | II/2 | |
| 234 | E 3 | Missa in A | c.1738 | SATB, 2 fl, str, bc | BG, 1858 | viii | II/2 | Darmstadt, Hessische Landes- und Hochschulbibliothek (Wiesbaden, 1985) |
| 235 | E 5 | Missa in g | ? 1738–9 | SATB, 2 ob, str, bc | BG, 1858 | viii | II/2 | |

# Appendix 1

| BWV | BC | Title | Date | Scoring | First published | BG vol. | NBA vol. | Autograph score (facsimile) |
|---|---|---|---|---|---|---|---|---|
| 236 | E 4 | Missa in G | c.1738–9 | SATB, 2 ob, str, bc | Bonn, 1828 | viii | II/2 | Darmstadt, Hessische Landes- und Hochschulbibliothek |
| 237 | E 10 | Sanctus in C | ? 24 June 1723 | SATB, 3 tr, timp, 2 ob, str, bc | BG, 1862 | xi/1 | II/2 | Berlin, Staatsbibliothek |
| 238 | | Sanctus in D | ? Christmas 1723 | SATB, cnt, str, bc | BG, 1862 | xi/1 | II/2 | Berlin, Staatsbibliothek |
| 239 | | Sanctus in d | c.1735–46 | SATB, str, bc | BG, 1862 | xi/1 | [II/9] | Berlin, Staatsbibliothek |
| 240 | | Sanctus in G | c.1735–46 | SATB, 2 ob, str, bc | BG, 1862 | xi/1 | [II/9] | Berlin, Staatsbibliothek |
| 241 | E 17 | Sanctus in D | 1747–8 | SATB, SATB, 2 obda, bn, str, bc | BG, 1894 | xli | [II/9] | Coburg, Kunstsammlungen der Veste |
| 242 | E 8 | Christe eleison [for Mass in c by Durante] | 1727–31 | SA, bc | BG, 1894 | xli | II/2 | Leipzig, Bach-Archiv |
| 243 | E 14 | Magnificat (2 versions: E♭, D) | 25 Dec. 1723 | SSATB, 3 tr, timp, 2 rec/fl, 2 ob/obda, str, bc | BG, 1862 | xi/3 | II/3 | Berlin, Staatsbibliothek (Leipzig, 1985) |
| 1081 | E 9 | Credo in unum Deum [for Mass in F by Bassani] | c.1747–8 | SATB, bc | Wiesbaden, 1968 | — | II/2 | Berlin, Staatsbibliothek |
| 1082 | E 15 | Suscepit Israel [after Magnificat by Caldara] | c.1740–2 | SATB, ? 2 vn, bc | Wiesbaden, 1968 | — | — | Berlin, Staatsbibliothek |

## 4. Motets

| BWV | BC | Title | Date | Scoring | First published | BG vol. | NBA vol. | Autograph score (facsimile) |
|---|---|---|---|---|---|---|---|---|
| 118 | B 23 | O Jesu Christ, meins Lebens Licht 1st version 2nd version | c.1736–7 c.1746–7 | SATB, 2 litui, cnt, 3 tbn SATB, 2 litui, str, bc [3 ob, bn ad lib] | BG, 1876 | xxiv | III/1 | Princeton University Library, loan (New York, 1985) |
| 225 | C 1 | Singet dem Herrn ein neues Lied | 1726/7 | SATB, SATB | Leipzig, 1802 | xxxix | III/1 | Berlin, Staatsbibliothek (Kassel, 1958) |
| 226 | C 2 | Der Geist hilft unser Schwachheit auf | 20 Oct. 1729 | SATB, SATB, 2 ob, tle, bn, str, bc | Leipzig, 1803 | xxxix | III/1 | Berlin, Staatsbibliothek |
| 227 | C 5 | Jesu, meine Freude | before 1735 | SSATB | Leipzig, 1803 | xxxix | III/1 | |
| 228 | C 4 | Fürchte dich nicht, ich bin bei dir | ? 1708–17 | SATB, SATB | Leipzig, 1802 | xxxix | III/1 | |
| 229 | C 3 | Komm, Jesu, komm | before 1733 | SATB, SATB | BG, 1892 | xxxix | III/1 | |
| 230 | C 6 | Lobet den Herrn alle Heiden | ? | SATB, bc | Leipzig, 1821 | xxxix | III/1 | |

| BWV | BC | Title | Date | Scoring | First published | BG vol. | NBA vol. | Autograph score (facsimile) |
|---|---|---|---|---|---|---|---|---|
| 231 | | Sei Lob und Preis mit Ehren [from BWV28 and Telemann] | after 1724 | SATB, SATB | Berlin, n.d. [1818–28] | xxix | — | Berlin, Staatsbibliothek |
| Anh. III 159 | C 9 | Ich lasse dich nicht, du segnest mich denn | before 1714 | SATB, SATB | Leipzig, 1802 | — | [inc.] | — |

## 5. Oratorios and Passions

| BWV | BC | Title (Librettist) | Date | Scoring | First published | BG vol. | NBA vol. | Autograph score (facsimile) |
|---|---|---|---|---|---|---|---|---|
| 11 | D 9 | Ascension Oratorio | 19 May 1735 | SATB, 3 tr, timp, 2 fl, 2 ob(da), str, bc | BG, 1853 | ii/1 | II/8 | Berlin, Staatsbibliothek |
| 244 | D 3 | St Matthew Passion (Picander) | 11 April 1727 | S, SATB, 2 rec, 2 fl, 2 ob(da, dc), str, bc [vadg]; SATB, 2 fl, 2 ob(da), vadg, str, bc | Berlin, 1830 | iv/1 | II/5 | Berlin, Staatsbibliothek (Leipzig, 1922; Leipzig, 1966) |
| 245 | D 2 | St John Passion | 7 April 1724 | SATB, 2 fl/?rec, 2 ob, 2 vada, vadg, lt, str, bc | Berlin, 1831 | xii/1 | II/4 | Berlin, Staatsbibliothek [inc.] (NBA II/4, 1973) |
| 247 | D 4 | St Mark Passion (Picander) [lost] | 23 March 1731 | — | | — | XX/2 | |
| 248 | D 7 | Christmas Oratorio: | | | BG, 1856 | v/2 | II/6 | Berlin, Staatsbibliothek (Kassel, 1960; Leipzig, 1984) |
| 248$^I$ | | Jauchzet, frohlocket, auf, preiset die Tage | 25 Dec. 1734 | SATB, 3 tr, timp, 2 fl, 2 ob(da), str, bc | | | | |
| 248$^{II}$ | | Und es waren Hirten in derselben Gegend | 26 Dec. 1734 | SATB, 2 fl, 2 obda, 2 obdc, str, bc | | | | |
| 248$^{III}$ | | Herrscher des Himmels, erhöre das Lallen | 27 Dec. 1734 | SATB, 3 tr, timp, 2 fl, 2 ob(da), str, bc | | | | |
| 248$^{IV}$ | | Fallt mit Danken, fallt mit Loben | 1 Jan. 1735 | SSATB, 2 cdc, 2 ob, str, bc | | | | |
| 248$^V$ | | Ehre sei dir, Gott, gesungen | 2 Jan. 1735 | SATB, 2 obda, str, bc | | | | |
| 248$^{VI}$ | | Herr wenn die stolzen Feinde schnauben | 6 Jan. 1735 | SATB, 3 tr, timp, 2 ob(da), str, bc | | | | |
| 249 | D 8 | Easter Oratorio | 1 April 1725 | SATB, 3 tr, timp, 2 rec, fl, 2 ob(da), str, bc | BG, 1874 | xxi/3 | II/7 | Berlin, Staatsbibliothek |
| 1088 | C 10 | So heb ich denn mein Auge sehnlich auf [arioso for pasticcio Passion] | ? | B, insts, bc | BJb 51 (1965), pp. 27–30 | — | — | |

## 6. Chorale harmonizations and sacred Lieder

THREE WEDDING CHORALES FOR SATB, 2 HN, 2 OB(DA), STR, BC; *BG* XXX/1, *NBA* III/2.1

| BWV | BC | Breitkopf | Title |
| --- | --- | --- | --- |
| 250 | F 193.3 | — | Was Gott tut, das ist wohlgetan |
| 251 | F 59.4 | — | Sei Lob und Ehr dem höchsten Gut |
| 252 | F 148.2 | — | Nun danket alle Gott |

FOUR-PART CHORALES IN *JOH. SEB. BACHS VIERSTIMMIGE CHORALGESÄNGE, ED. J. P. KIRNBERGER AND J. C. BACH* (LEIPZIG, 1784–7) [BREITKOPF]; *BG* XXXIX [INC.], *NBA* III/2.1 AND III/2.2

| BWV | BC | Breitkopf | Title |
| --- | --- | --- | --- |
| 253 | F 35.1 | 177 | Ach bleib bei uns, Herr Jesu Christ |
| 254 | F 1.1 | 186 | Ach Gott, erhör mein Seufzen und Wehklagen |
| 255 | F 2.1 | 40 | Ach Gott und Herr |
| 483 | A 144.3 | 279 | Ach Gott und Herr |
| 77.6 | A 126.6 | 253 | Ach Gott, vom Himmel sieh darein |
| 153.1 | F 3 | 3 | Ach Gott, vom Himmel sieh darein |
| 2.6 | A 98.6 | 262 | Ach Gott, vom Himmel sieh darein |
| 3.6 | A 33.6 | 156, 307 | Ach Gott, wie manches Herzeleid |
| 153.9 | A 25.9 | 217 | Ach Gott, wie manches Herzeleid |
| 114.7 | A 139.7 | 300 | Ach, lieben Christen, seid getrost |
| 256 | F 212.1 | 31 | Ach, lieben Christen, seid getrost |
| 259 | F 5.1 | 39 | Ach, was soll ich Sünder machen |
| 26.6 | A 162.6 | 48 | Ach wie flüchtig, ach wie nichtig |
| 104.6 | A 65.6 | 125, 325 | Allein Gott in der Höh sei Ehr |
| 112.5 | A 62.5 | 312, 352 | Allein Gott in der Höh sei Ehr |
| 260 | F 10.1 | 249 | Allein Gott in der Höh sei Ehr |
| 33.6 | A 127.6 | 13 | Allein zu dir, Herr Jesu Christ |

| BWV | BC | Breitkopf | Title |
| --- | --- | --- | --- |
| 261 | F 11.1 | 358 | Allein zu dir, Herr Jesu Christ |
| 262 | F 8.1 | 153 | Alle Menschen müssen sterben |
| 263 | F 12.1 | 128 | Alles ist an Gottes Segen |
| 264 | F 13.1 | 159 | Als der gütige Gott |
| 265 | F 14.1 | 180 | Als Jesus Christus in der Nacht |
| 266 | F 15.1 | 208 | Als vierzig Tag nach Ostern warn |
| 267 | F 17.1 | 5, 308 | An Wasserflüssen Babylon |
| 268 | F 19.1 | 124 | Auf, auf, mein Herz, und du, mein ganzer Sinn |
| 5:7 | F 20.1 | 303 | Auf meinen lieben Gott |
| 269 | F 21.1 | 1 | Aus meines Herzens Grunde |
| 38:6 | F 22 | 10 | Aus tiefer Not schrei ich zu dir |
| 270 | F 92.1 | 285 | Befiehl du deine Wege |
| 271 | F 92.2 | 366 | Befiehl du deine Wege |
| 272 | F 136.2 | 339 | Befiehl du deine Wege |
| 161:6 | A 135:6 | 270 | Christ, der du bist der helle Tag |
| 273 | F 24.1 | 230 | Christ, der du bist der helle Tag |
| 274 | F 27.1 | 245 | Christe, der du bist Tag und Licht |
| 275 | F 28.1 | 210 | Christe, du Beistand deiner Kreuzgemeinde |
| 276 | F 25.1 | 197 | Christ ist erstanden |
| 277 | F 26.1 | 15 | Christ lag in Todes Banden |
| 278 | F 26.2 | 370 | Christ lag in Todes Banden |
| 279 | A 61:4 | 261 | Christ lag in Todes Banden |
| 4:8 | A 54:8 | 184 | Christ lag in Todes Banden |
| 121:6 | F 29 | 55 | Christum wir sollen loben schon |
| 280 | F 65.1 | 65 | Christ, unser Herr, zum Jordan kam |
| 176:6 | A 92:6 | 119 | Christ, unser Herr, zum Jordan kam |
| 281 | F 30.1 | 7 | Christus, der ist mein Leben |
| 282 | F 30.2 | 315 | Christus, der ist mein Leben |
| 283 | F 31.1 | 198, 306 | Christus, der uns selig macht |
| 245:15 | D 2:15 | 80 | Christus, der uns selig macht |
| 245:37 | D 2:37 | 113 | Christus, der uns selig macht |

| Title | Breitkopf | BC | BWV |
|---|---|---|---|
| Erschienen ist der heilig Tag | 17 | A 60:5 | 145:5 |
| Erstanden ist der heil'ge Christ | 176 | F 58.1 | 306 |
| Es ist das Heil uns kommen her | 4 | F 59.3 | 86:6 |
| Es ist das Heil uns kommen her | 289 | A 107:7 | 9:7 |
| Es ist das Heil uns kommen her | 334 | A 32:5 | 155:5 |
| Es ist genung | 216 | F 60 | 60:5 |
| Es ist gewißlich an der Zeit | 260 | F 150.1 | 307 |
| Es ist gewißlich an der Zeit | 361 | D 7:59 | 248:59 |
| Es spricht der Unweisen Mund wohl | 27 | F 62.1 | 308 |
| Es stehn vor Gottes Throne | 166 | F 63.1 | 309 |
| Es wird schier der letzte Tag herkommen | 238 | F 64.1 | 310 |
| Es woll uns Gott genädig sein | 16 | F 66.1 | 311 |
| Es woll uns Gott genädig sein | 351 | F 66.2 | 312 |
| Es woll uns Gott genädig sein | 332 | B 10:6 | 69:6 |
| Freue dich sehr, o meine Seele | 29 | A 31:6 | 32:6 |
| Freue dich sehr, o meine Seele | 63, 256 | A 91:6 | 194:6 |
| Freue dich sehr, o meine Seele | 67 | A 96:7 | 39:7 |
| Freue dich sehr, o meine Seele | 76 | A 178:6 | 30:6 |
| Freue dich sehr, o meine Seele | 254, 282 | A 129:6 | 25:6 |
| Freuet euch, ihr Christen alle | 8 | F 67 | 40:8 |
| Für deinen Thron tret ich hiermit | 333 | F 105:2 | 327 |
| Für Freuden laßt uns springen | 163 | F 68.1 | 313 |
| Gelobet seist du, Jesu Christ | 287 | F 69.1 | 314 |
| Gelobet seist du, Jesu Christ | 53 | A 9:6 | 91:6 |
| Gelobet seist du, Jesu Christ | 160 | A 15:2 | 64:2 |
| Gib dich zufrieden und sei stille | 271 | F 70.1 | 315 |
| Gott, der du selber bist das Licht | 225 | F 71.1 | 316 |
| Gott der Vater wohn uns bei | 134 | F 72.1 | 317 |
| Gott des Himmels und der Erden | 34 | F 73 | 248:53 |
| Gottes Sohn ist kommen | 18 | F 143.1 | 318 |
| Gott hat das Evangelium | 181 | F 74.1 | 319 |
| Gott lebet noch, Seele, was verzagt du doch | 234 | F 75.1 | 320 |
| Gottlob, es geht nunmehr zu Ende | 192 | F 77.1 | 321 |

| BWV | BC | Breitkopf | Title |
|---|---|---|---|
| 284 | F 32.1 | 200 | Christus ist erstanden |
| 285 | F 34.1 | 196 | Da der Herr Christ zu Tische saß |
| 1089 | F 109.1 | | Da Jesus an dem Kreuze stand |
| 286 | F 183.1 | 228 | Danket dem Herren, denn er ist sehr freundlich |
| 287 | F 119.1 | 310 | Dank sei Gott in der Höhe |
| 288 | F 36.1 | 162 | Das alte Jahr vergangen ist |
| 289 | F 36.2 | 313 | Das alte Jahr vergangen ist |
| 122:6 | F 37 | 52, 178 | Das neugeborne Kinderlein |
| 290 | F 38.1 | 224 | Das walt Gott Vater und Gott Sohn |
| 291 | F 39.1 | 75 | Das walt mein Gott, Vater, Sohn, und heiliger Geist |
| 292 | F 40.1 | 239 | Den Vater dort oben |
| 293 | F 42.1 | 154 | Der du bist drei in Einigkeit |
| 294 | F 43.1 | 158 | Der Tag der ist so freudenreich |
| 295 | F 178.1 | 207 | Des heiligen Geistes reiche Gnad |
| 296 | F 44.1 | 231 | Die Nacht ist kommen |
| 297 | F 161.1 | 232 | Die Sonn hat sich mit ihrem Glanz gewendet |
| 298 | F 46.1 | 127 | Dies sind die heilgen zehn Gebot |
| 299 | F 47.1 | 209 | Dir, dir, Jehova, will ich singen |
| 67:7 | A 62:7 | 42 | Du Friedefürst, Herr Jesu Christ |
| 300 | F 51.1 | 164 | Du großer Schmerzensmann |
| 301 | F 50.1 | 137 | Du, o schönes Weltgebäude |
| 56:5 | A 146:5 | 86 | Du, o schönes Weltgebäude |
| 18:5 | F 52.1 | 100, 126 | Durch Adams Fall ist ganz verderbt |
| 302 | F 53.1 | 20 | Ein feste Burg ist unser Gott |
| 303 | F 53.2 | 250 | Ein feste Burg ist unser Gott |
| 80:8 | A 183:8 | 273 | Ein feste Burg ist unser Gott |
| 304 | F 54.1 | 280 | Eins ist Not, ach Herr, dies eine |
| 305 | F 55.1 | 33 | Erbarm dich mein, o Herre Gott |
| 6:6 | F 56 | 72 | Erhalt uns, Herr, bei deinem Wort |
| 248:12 | F 57 | 9, 360 | Ermuntre dich, mein schwacher Geist |
| 43:11 | A 77:11 | 102 | Ermuntre dich, mein schwacher Geist |

# Appendix 1

| BWV | BC | Breitkopf | Title |
|---|---|---|---|
| 322 | F 76:1 | 70 | Gott sei gelobet und gebenedeit |
| 323 | F 140:1 | 319 | Gott sei uns gnädig und barmherzig |
| 57:8 | F 78 | 90 | Hast du denn, Liebster, dein Angesicht gänzlich verborgen |
| 325 | F 79:1 | 235, 318 | Heilig, heilig |
| 28:6 | F 80 | 23, 88 | Helft mir Gotts Güte preisen |
| 16:6 | A 23:6 | 99 | Helft mir Gotts Güte preisen |
| 183:5 | A 79:5 | 123 | Helft mir Gotts Güte preisen |
| 164:6 | F 81 | 101 | Herr Christ, der einge Gottessohn |
| 96:6 | A 142:6 | 302 | Herr Christ, der einge Gottessohn |
| 326 | F 105:1 | 167 | Herr Gott, dich loben alle wir |
| 328 | F 83:1 | 205 | Herr Gott, dich loben wir |
| 329 | F 134:1 | 212 | Herr, ich denk an jene Zeit |
| 330 | F 84:1 | 35 | Herr, ich habe mißgehandelt |
| 331 | F 84:2 | 286 | Herr, ich habe mißgehandelt |
| 332 | F 85:1 | 136 | Herr Jesu Christ, dich zu uns wend |
| 333 | F 86:1 | 226 | Herr Jesu Christ, du hast bereit't |
| 334 | F 202:1 | 73 | Herr Jesu Christ, du höchstes Gut |
| 168:6 | A 116:6 | 92 | Herr Jesu Christ, du höchstes Gut |
| 48:7 | A 144:7 | 266 | Herr Jesu Christ, du höchstes Gut |
| 113:8 | A 122:8 | 293 | Herr Jesu Christ, du höchstes Gut |
| 335 | F 170:1 | 236, 294 | Herr Jesu Christ, meins Lebens Licht |
| 336 | F 88:1 | 189 | Herr Jesu Christ, wahr' Mensch und Gott |
| 127:5 | A 49:5 | 283b | Herr Jesu Christ, wahr' Mensch und Gott |
| 337 | F 89:1 | 190 | Herr, nun laß in Friede |
| 338 | F 90:1 | 221 | Herr, straf mich nicht in deinem Zorn |
| 339 | F 23:1 | 144, 317 | Herr, wie du willst, so schicks mit mir |
| 156:6 | A 38:6 | 316 | Herr, wie du willst, so schick's mit mir |
| 340 | F 91:1 | 277 | Herzlich lieb hab ich dich, o Herr |
| 174:5 | A 87:5 | 56 | Herzlich lieb hab ich dich, o Herr |

| BWV | BC | Breitkopf | Title |
|---|---|---|---|
| 245:40 | D 2:40 | 107 | Herzlich lieb hab ich dich, o Herr |
| 153:5 | F 92:5 | 21 | Herzlich tut mich verlangen |
| 57:3 | F 93 | 58 | Herzliebster Jesu, was hast du verbrochen |
| 244:3 | D 3:3 | 78 | Herzliebster Jesu, was hast du verbrochen |
| 245:17 | D 2:17 | 111 | Herzliebster Jesu, was hast du verbrochen |
| 244:46 | D 3:46 | 105 | Herzliebster Jesu, was hast du verbrochen |
| 341 | F 94:1A | 168 | Heut ist, o Mensch, ein großer Trauertag |
| 342 | F 95:1 | 79 | Heut triumphiret Gottes Sohn |
| 343 | F 96:1 | 199, 301 | Hilf, Gott, laß mirs gelingen |
| 344 | F 97:1 | 155 | Hilf, Herr Jesu, laß gelingen |
| 248:42 | F 98:1 | 367 | Hilf, Herr Jesu, laß gelingen |
| 345 | F 99:1 | 251 | Ich bin ja, Herr, in deiner Macht |
| 346 | F 100:1 | 223 | Ich dank dir, Gott |
| 347 | F 101:1 | 2 | Ich dank dir, lieber Herre |
| 348 | F 101:2 | 272 | Ich dank dir, lieber Herre |
| 37:6 | A 75:6 | 340 | Ich dank dir, lieber Herre |
| 349 | F 4:1 | 188 | Ich dank dir schon durch deinen Sohn |
| 350 | F 139:1 | 229 | Ich dank dir, o Gott, in deinem Throne |
| 133:6 | A 16:6 | 61 | Ich freue mich in dir |
| 103:6 | A 69:6 | 120, 348 | Ich hab, in Gottes Herz und Sinn |
| 351 | F 102:1 | 19 | Ich hab mein Sach Gott heimgestellt |
| 177:5 | F 103 | 71 | Ich ruf zu dir, Herr Jesu Christ |
| 366 | F 104:1 | 161 | Ihr Gestirn, ihr hohlen Lüfte |
| 367 | F 107:1 | 140 | In allen meinen Taten |
| 244:37 | D 337 | 50 | In allen meinen Taten |
| 248:46 | F 108 | 77 | In dich hab ich gehoffet, Herr |
| 248:32 | D 7:32 | 118 | In dich hab ich gehoffet, Herr |
| 368 | D 110:1 | 143 | In dulci jubilo |

| BWV | BC | Breitkopf | Title |
|---|---|---|---|
| 85:6 | A 66:6 | 122 | Ist Gott mein Schild und Helfersmann |
| 352 | F 187.1 | 37 | Jesu, der du meine Seele |
| 353 | F 187.2 | 269 | Jesu, der du meine Seele |
| 354 | F 187.3 | 368 | Jesu, der du meine Seele |
| 78:7 | A 130:7 | 296 | Jesu, der du selbsten wohl |
| 355 | F 112.1 | 169 | Jesu, du mein liebstes Leben |
| 356 | F 113.1 | 243 | Jesu, Jesu, du bist mien |
| 357 | F 114.1 | 244 | Jesu Leiden, Pein und Tod |
| 159:5 | F 115 | 59 | Jesu Leiden, Pein und Tod |
| 245:14 | D 2:14 | 82 | Jesu Leiden, Pein und Tod |
| 245:28 | D 2:28 | 106 | Jesu, meine Freude |
| 358 | F 116.1 | 355 | Jesu, meine Freude |
| 87:7 | A 74:7 | 96 | Jesu, meine Freude |
| 64:8 | A 15:8 | 138 | Jesu, meine Freude |
| 227:1, 11 | C 51, 11 | 263 | Jesu, meine Freude |
| 227:7 | C 57 | 283a | Jesu, meiner Seelen Wonne |
| 81:7 | A 39:7 | 323 | Jesu, meiner Seelen Wonne |
| 359 | F 206.1 | 364 | Jesu, meines Herzens Freud |
| 360 | F 206.2 | 349 | Jesu, nun sei gepreiset |
| 361 | F 117.1 | 264 | Jesu, nun sei gepreiset |
| 362 | F 118.1 | 252 | Jesu, nun sei gepreiset |
| 41:6, 171:6 | A 22:6, A 24:6 | 11 | Jesus Christus, unser Heiland, der den Tod |
| 190:7 | A 21:7 | 326 | Jesus Christus, unser Heiland der von uns |
| 363 | F 121.1 | 30 | Jesus, meine Zuversicht |
| 364 | F 120.1 | 174 | Jesus, meine Zuversicht |
| 365 | F 123.1 | 175 | Jesus, meine Zuversicht |
| 145:8 | A 60:8 | 337 | Keinen, Gott hat Gott verlassen |
| 369 | F 124.1 | 129 | Komm, Gott Schöpfer, heiliger Geist |
| 370 | F 125.1 | 187 | Komm, heiliger Geist, Herre Gott |
| 226 | F 126.2 | 69 | Kommt her zu mir, spricht Gottes Sohn |
| 108:6 | F 128 | 46 | Kommt her zu mir, spricht Gottes Sohn |

| BWV | BC | Breitkopf | Title |
|---|---|---|---|
| 74:8 | A 83:8 | 369 | Kommt her zu mir, spricht Gottes Sohn |
| 371 | F 129.1 | 132 | Kyrie, Gott Vater in Ewigkeit |
| 372 | F 82.1 | 218 | Laß, o Herr, dein Ohr sich neigen |
| 8:6 | F 131.1 | 43 | Liebster Gott, wenn werd ich sterben |
| 123:6 | A 28:6 | 194 | Liebster Immanuel, Herzog der Frommen |
| 373 | F 133.1 | 131, 327 | Liebster Jesu, wir sind hier |
| 374 | F 135.1 | 227 | Lobet den Herren, denn er ist freundlich |
| 375 | F 127.1 | 276 | Lobt Gott, ihr Christen, allzugleich |
| 376 | F 128.1 | 341 | Lobt Gott, ihr Christen, allzugleich |
| 151:5 | A 17:5 | 54 | Lobt Gott, ihr Christen, allzugleich |
| 377 | F 137.1 | 44 | Machs mit mir, Gott, nach deiner Güte |
| 245:22 | D 2:22 | 309 | Machs mit mir, Gott, nach deiner Güte |
| 378 | F 138.1 | 258 | Mein Augen schließ ich jetzt in Gottes Namen zu |
| 379 | F 122.1 | 151 | Meinen Jesum laß ich nicht, Jesus |
| 380 | F 141.1 | 298 | Meinen Jesum laß ich nicht, weil |
| 154:8 | A 29:8 | 152 | Meinen Jesum laß ich nicht, weil |
| 70:11 | A 165:11 | 347 | Meinen Jesum laß ich nicht, weil |
| 324 | F 140.1 | 130 | Meine Seele erhebet den Herrn |
| 10:7 | A 175:7 | 357 | Meine Seele erhebet den Herrn |
| 381 | F 142.1 | 345 | Meines Lebens letzte Zeit |
| 382 | F 144.1 | 49 | Mit Fried und Freud ich fahr dahin |
| 83:5 | A 167:5 | 324 | Mit Fried und Freud ich fahr dahin |
| 383 | F 145.1 | 214 | Mitten wir im Leben sind |
| 384 | F 146.1 | 149 | Nicht so traurig, nicht so sehr |
| 101:7 | A 118:7 | 291 | Nimm von uns, Herr, du treuer Gott |
| 385 | F 147.1 | 36 | Nun bitten wir den heilgen Geist |
| 197:5 | B 16:5 | 83 | Nun bitten wir den heilgen Geist |
| 169:7 | A 143:7 | 97 | Nun bitten wir den heilgen Geist |
| 252 | F 148.2 | 329 | Nun danket alle Gott |

| BWV | BC | Breitkopf | Title |
| --- | --- | --- | --- |
| 386 | F 148.1 | 32 | Nun danket alle Gott |
| 387 | F 106.1 | 185 | Nun freut euch, Gottes Kinder all |
| 388 | F 149.1 | 183 | Nun freut euch, lieben Christen, gmein |
| 36:8 | F 151.1 | 28 | Nun komm, der Heiden Heiland |
| 62:6 | A 2:6 | 170 | Nun komm, der Heiden Heiland |
| 194:12 | F 152 | 93, 257 | Nun laßt uns Gott dem Herren |
| 11:6 | D 9:6 | 342 | Nun lieget alles unter dir |
| 389 | F 153.1 | 268 | Nun lob, mein Seel, den Herren |
| 390 | F 153.2 | 295 | Nun lob, mein Seel, den Herren |
| 17:7 | A 131:7 | 6 | Nun lob, mein Seel, den Herren |
| 29:8 | B 8:8 | 116 | Nun lob, mein Seel, den Herren |
| 391 | F 154.1 | 222 | Nun preiset alle Gottes Barmherzigkeit |
| 392 | F 166.1 | 288 | Nun ruhen alle Wälder |
| 245:11 | D 2:11 | 62 | Nun ruhen alle Wälder |
| 13:6 | A 34:6 | 103 | Nun ruhen alle Wälder |
| 244:10 | D 3:10 | 117 | Nun ruhen alle Wälder |
| 44:7 | A 78:7 | 354 | Nun sich der Tag geendet hat |
| 396 | F 155.1 | 240 | O Ewigkeit, du Donnerwort |
| 397 | F 156.1 | 274 | O Ewigkeit, du Donnerwort |
| 207:7 | A 95:7 | 26 | O Gott, du frommer Gott |
| 398 | F 45.2b | 311 | O Gott, du frommer Gott |
| 399 | F 157.1 | 314 | O Gott, du frommer Gott |
| 45:7 | A 113:7 | 84 | O Gott, du frommer Gott |
| 24:6 | A 102:6 | 336 | O großer Gott von Macht |
| 46:6 | F 158 | 81 | O Haupt voll Blut und Wunden |
| 244:54 | D 3:54 | 74 | O Haupt voll Blut und Wunden |
| 244:44 | D 3:44 | 87 | O Haupt voll Blut und Wunden |
| 244:62 | D 3:62 | 89 | O Haupt voll Blut und Wunden |
| 244:15, 17 | D 3:15, 17 | 98 | O Haupt voll Blut und Wunden |
| 248:5 | D 7:5 | 344 | O Haupt voll Blut und Wunden |
| 184:5 | F 159 | 14 | O Herre Gott, dein göttlich Wort |
| 400 | F 160.1 | 173 | O Herzensangst, o Bangigkeit und Zagen |
| 401 | F 162.1 | 165 | O Lamm Gottes, unschuldig |

| BWV | BC | Breitkopf | Title |
| --- | --- | --- | --- |
| 402 | F 61.1 | 201, 305 | O Mensch, bewein dein Sünde groß |
| 403 | F 163.1 | 203 | O Mensch, schau Jesum Christum an |
| 404 | F 165.1 | 60 | O Traurigkeit, o Herzeleid |
| 393 | F 166.2 | 275 | O Welt, sieh hier dein Leben |
| 394 | F 166.5 | 365 | O Welt, sieh hier dein Leben |
| 395 | F 166.9 | 362 | O Welt, sieh hier dein Leben |
| 405 | F 167.1 | 213 | O wie selig seid ihr doch, ihr Frommen |
| 406 | F 7.1 | 219 | O wie selig seid ihr doch, ihr Frommen |
| 407 | F 168.1 | 202 | O wir armen Sünder |
| 65:2 | F 169 | 12 | Puer natus in Bethlehem |
| 408 | F 94.1B | 171 | Schaut, ihr Sünder! Ihr macht mir große Pein |
| 180:7 | F 171.1 | 22 | Schmücke dich, o liebe Seele |
| 40:6 | F 172 | 142 | Schwing dich auf zu deinem Gott |
| 409 | F 173.1 | 141 | Seelenbräutigam, Jesu, Gottes Lamm |
| 410 | F 174.1 | 172 | Sei gegrüßet, Jesu gütig |
| 117:4 | A 187:4 | 248, 353 | Sei Lob und Ehr dem höchsten Gut |
| 251 | F 59.4 | 328 | Sei Lob und Ehr dem höchsten Gut |
| 187:7 | A 110:7 | 109 | Singen wir aus Herzensgrund |
| 411 | F 175.1 | 246 | Singet dem Herrn ein neues Lied |
| 412 | F 177.1 | 206 | So gibst du nun, mein Jesu, gute Nacht |
| 413 | F 130.1 | 220 | Sollt ich meinem Gott nicht singen |
| 115:6 | F 179 | 38 | Straf mich nicht in deinem Zorn |
| 414 | F 35.2 | 148 | Uns ist ein Kindlein heut geboren |
| 415 | F 18.1 | 24 | Valet will ich dir geben |
| 245:26 | D 2:26 | 108 | Valet will ich dir geben |
| 416 | F 181.4a | 47 | Vater unser im Himmelreich |
| 102:7 | A 119:7 | 110 | Vater unser im Himmelreich |
| 90:5 | A 163:5 | 267 | Vater unser im Himmelreich |
| 427 | F 182.1 | 91, 259 | Verleih uns Frieden gnädiglich |
| 126:6 | A 46:6 | 215 | Verleih uns Frieden gnädiglich |
| 248:9 | F 184 | 45 | Vom Himmel hoch da komm ich her |
| 248:23 | D 7:23 | 343 | Vom Himmel hoch da komm ich her |

| BWV | BC | Breitkopf | Title |
| --- | --- | --- | --- |
| 417 | F 185.1 | 363 | Von Gott will ich nicht lassen |
| 418 | F 185.2 | 331 | Von Gott will ich nicht lassen |
| 419 | F 185.3 | 114 | Von Gott will ich nicht lassen |
| 735 | A 35.5 | 191 | Von Gott will ich nicht lassen |
| 140:7 | A 166:7 | 179 | Wachet auf, ruft uns die Stimme |
| 145 | F 188 | 182 | Wär Gott nicht mit uns diese Zeit |
| 257 | F 212.2 | 284 | Wär Gott nicht mit uns diese Zeit |
| 420 | F 189.1 | 145 | Warum betrübst du dich, mein Herz |
| 421 | F 189.2 | 299 | Warum betrübst du dich, mein Herz |
| 475 | A 141:5 | 94 | Warum betrübst du dich, mein Herz |
| 422 | F 190.1 | 356 | Warum sollt ich mich denn grämen |
| 248:33 | D 7:33 | 139 | Warum sollt ich mich denn grämen |
| 423 | F 191.1 | 237 | Was betrübst du dich, mein Herz |
| 424 | F 192.1 | 193 | Was bist du doch, o Seele, so betrübt |
| 64:4 | A 15:4 | 255 | Was frag ich nach der Welt |
| 94:8 | A 155:8 | 290 | Was frag ich nach der Welt |
| 144:3 | F 193 | 64 | Was Gott tut, das ist wohlgetan |
| 127:7, 69a:6 | A 68:7, A 123:6 | 292 | Was Gott tut, das ist wohlgetan |
| 250 | F 193.3 | 346 | Was Gott tut, das ist wohlgetan |
| 65:7 | A 27:7 | 41 | Was mein Gott will, das g'scheh allzeit |
| 144:6 | A 41:6 | 265 | Was mein Gott will, das g'scheh allzeit |
| 244:25 | D 3:25 | 115 | Was mein Gott will, das g'scheh allzeit |
| 425 | F 195.1 | 241 | Was willst du dich, o meine Seele |
| 19:7 | A 180:7 | 297 | Weg, mein Herz, mit den Gedanken |
| 27:6 | A 138:6 | 150 | Welt, ade! ich bin dein müde |
| 426 | F 197.1 | 211 | Weltlich Ehr und zeitlich Gut |
| 427 | F 200.1 | 147 | Wenn ich in Angst und Not |
| 428 | F 201.1 | 321 | Wenn mein Stündlein vorhanden ist |
| 429 | F 201.2 | 51 | Wenn mein Stündlein vorhanden ist |
| 430 | F 201.3 | 350 | Wenn mein Stündlein vorhanden ist |
| 431 | F 203.1 | 68 | Wenn wir in höchsten Nöten sein |

| BWV | BC | Breitkopf | Title |
| --- | --- | --- | --- |
| 432 | F 203.2 | 247 | Wenn wir in höchsten Nöten sein |
| 555.5 | A 157.5 | 95 | Werde munter, mein Gemüte |
| 1543 | A 29.3 | 233 | Werde munter, mein Gemüte |
| 244:40 | D 3:40 | 121 | Werde munter, mein Gemüte |
| 433 | F 204.1 | 135 | Wer Gott vertraut, hat wohl gebaut |
| 434 | F 205.1 | 146 | Wer nur den lieben Gott läßt walten |
| 845 | A 43.5 | 112 | Wer nur den lieben Gott läßt walten |
| 88:7 | A 105:7 | 104 | Wer nur den lieben Gott läßt walten |
| 179:6 | A 121:6 | 338 | Wer nur den lieben Gott läßt walten |
| 197:10 | B 16:10 | 66 | Wer nur den lieben Gott läßt walten |
| 166:6 | A 71:6 | 204 | Wer weiß, wie nahe mir mein Ende |
| 435 | F 207.1 | 242 | Wie bist du, Seele, in mir so gar betrübt |
| 436 | F 109.1 | 278 | Wie schön leuchtet der Morgenstern |
| 36:4 | A 3:4 | 85, 195, 304 | Wie schön leuchtet der Morgenstern |
| 172:6 | A 81:6 | 322 | Wie schön leuchtet der Morgenstern |
| 40:3 | F 210 | 320 | Wir Christenleut |
| 110:7 | A 10:7 | 57 | Wir Christenleut |
| 248:35 | D 7:35 | 359 | Wir Christenleut |
| 437 | F 211.1 | 133 | Wir glauben all an einen Gott |
| 258 | F 212.3 | 335 | Wo Gott, der Herr, nicht bei uns hält |
| 438 | F 213.1 | 157 | Wo Gott zum Haus nicht gibt sein Gunst |
| 89:6 | A 155:6 | 281 | Wo soll ich fliehen hin |
| 136:6 | A 111:6 | 330 | Wo soll ich fliehen hin |
| 148:6 | A 140:6 | 25 | Wo soll ich fliehen hin |

SACRED LIEDER IN G. C. SCHEMELLI, *MUSICALISCHES GESANG-BUCH* (LEIPZIG, 1736), S, BC; *BG* XXXIX, *NBA* III.2.** = MELODY BY BACH; * = MELODY POSSIBLY BY BACH

| BWV | BC | Schemelli | Title |
| --- | --- | --- | --- |
| 439 | F 274 | 831 | Ach, daß nicht die letzte Stunde |
| 440 | F 229 | 171 | Auf, auf die rechte Zeit is hier* |

| BWV | BC | Schemelli | Title |
| --- | --- | --- | --- |
| 441 | F 245 | 320 | Auf, auf, mein Herz, mit Freuden |
| 442 | F 257 | 570 | Beglückter Stand getreuer Seelen |
| 443 | F 265 | 689 | Beschränkt, ihr Weisen dieser Welt* |
| 444 | F 242 | 303 | Brich entzwei, mein armes Herze |
| 445 | F 247 | 355 | Brunnquell aller Güter |
| 446 | F 220 | 39 | Der lieben Sonnen Licht und Pracht |
| 447 | F 221 | 40 | Der Tag ist hin, die Sonne gehet nieder |
| 448 | F 222 | 43 | Der Tag mit seinem Lichte |
| 449 | F 249 | 396 | Dich bet ich an, mein höchster Gott* |
| 450 | F 235 | 258 | Die bittre Leidenzeit beginnet abermal |
| 451 | F 219 | 13 | Die güldne Sonne, voll Freud und Wonne |
| 452 | F 250 | 397 | Dir, dir, Jehovah, will ich singen** |
| 453 | F 225 | 112 | Eins ist not! ach Herr, dies eine?* |
| 454 | F 230 | 187 | Ermuntre dich, mein schwacher Geist |
| 455 | F 261 | 580 | Erwürgtes Lamm, das die verwahrten Siegel |
| 456 | F 258 | 572 | Es glänzet der Christen inwendiges Leben |
| 457 | F 275 | 847 | Es ist nun aus mit meinem Leben |
| 458 | F 243 | 306 | Est ist vollbracht! Vergiß ja nicht |
| 459 | F 256 | 522 | Es kostet viel, ein Christ zu sein |
| 460 | F 263 | 647 | Gib dich zufrieden und sei stille |
| 461 | F 255 | 488 | Gott lebet noch; Selle, was verzagst du doch? |
| 462 | F 248 | 360 | Gott, wie groß ist deine Güte* |
| 463 | F 223 | 78 | Herr, nicht schicke deine Rache |
| 464 | F 276 | 861 | Ich bin ja, Herr, in deiner Macht |
| 465 | F 231 | 194 | Ich freue mich in dir |
| 466 | F 264 | 657 | Ich halte treulich still* |
| 467 | F 269 | 734 | Ich laß dich nicht, du mußt mein Jesu bleiben |

| BWV | BC | Schemelli | Title |
| --- | --- | --- | --- |
| 468 | F 270 | 737 | Ich liebe Jesum alle Stund* |
| 469 | F 232 | 195 | Ich steh an deiner Krippen hier* |
| 470 | F 271 | 741 | Jesu, Jesu, du bist mein* |
| 471 | F 228 | 139 | Jesu, deine Liebeswunden* |
| 472 | F 226 | 119 | Jesu, meines Glaubens Zier |
| 473 | F 266 | 696 | Jesu, meines Herzens Freud |
| 474 | F 251 | 463 | Jesus ist das schönste Licht |
| 475 | F 246 | 333 | Jesus, unser Trost und Leben |
| 476 | F 233 | 197 | Ihr Gestirn, ihr hohlen Lüfte |
| 477 | F 278 | 869 | Kein Stündlein geht dahin |
| 478 | F 277 | 868 | Komm, süßer Tod, komm, selge Ruh* |
| 479 | F 285 | 936 | Kommt, Seelen, dieser Tag* |
| 480 | F 286 | 938 | Kommt wieder aus der finstern Gruft* |
| 481 | F 236 | 281 | Lasset uns mit Jesu ziehen |
| 482 | F 252 | 467 | Liebes Herz, bedenke doch |
| 483 | F 279 | 873 | Liebster Gott, wenn werd ich sterben |
| 484 | F 280 | 874 | Liebster Herr Jesu! wo bleibst du so lange?* |
| 485 | F 272 | 761 | Liebster Immanuel, Herzog der Frommen |
| 486 | F 227 | 121 | Mein Jesu! dem die Seraphinen |
| 487 | F 237 | 283 | Mein Jesu, was für Seelenweh* |
| 488 | F 281 | 881 | Meines Lebens letzte Zeit |
| 489 | F 259 | 574 | Nicht so traurig, nicht so sehr |
| 490 | F 267 | 700 | Nur mein Jesus ist mein Leben |
| 491 | F 238 | 284 | O du Liebe meiner Liebe |
| 492 | F 282 | 891 | O finstre Nacht, wenn wirst du doch vergehen |
| 493 | F 234 | 203 | O Jesulein süß, o Jesulein mild |
| 494 | F 260 | 575 | O liebe Seele, zieh die Sinnen* |
| 495 | F 283 | 894 | O wie selig seid ihr doch, ihr Frommen |
| 496 | F 253 | 472 | Seelen bräutigam Jesu, Gottes Lamm |

| BWV | BC | Schemelli | Title |
|---|---|---|---|
| 497 | F 268 | 710 | Seelenweide, meine Freude |
| 498 | F 239 | 292 | Selig, wer an Jesum denkt* |
| 499 | F 240 | 293 | Sei gegrüßet, Jesu gütig |
| 500 | F 241 | 296 | So gehst du nun, mein Jesu, hin** |
| 501 | F 244 | 315 | So gibst du nun, mein Jesu, gute Nacht |
| 502 | F 284 | 901 | So wünsch ich mir zu guter Letzt |
| 503 | F 287 | 945 | Steh ich bei meinem Gott |
| 504 | F 254 | 475 | Vergiß mein nicht, daß ich dein nicht vergesse |
| 505 | F 262 | 627 | Vergiß mein nicht, vergiß mein nicht* |
| 506 | F 273 | 779 | Was bist du doch, o Seele, so betrübet |

| BWV | BC | Schemelli | Title |
|---|---|---|---|
| 507 | F 224 | 108 | Wo ist mein Schäflein, das ich liebe |

LIEDER FROM THE *CLAVIERBÜCHLEIN* FOR ANNA MAGDALENA BACH (1725), S, BC; BG XXXIX AND XLIII/2, NBA V/4

| BWV | BC | Title |
|---|---|---|
| 452 | F 217, 250 | Dir, dir, Jehova, will ich singen |
| 511 | F 214a | Gib dich zufrieden und sei stille (g) |
| 512 | F 214b | Gib dich zufrieden und sei stille (e) |
| 513 | F 218 | O Ewigkeit, du Donnerwort |
| 514 | F 216 | Schaffs mit mir, Gott, nach deinem Willen |
| 516 | F 215 | Warum betrübst du dich |

## 7. Secular Lieder

| BWV | BC | Title (facsimile) | Scoring | BG | NBA |
|---|---|---|---|---|---|
| 515 | H 2 | So oft ich meine Tobackspfeife | S, bc | xxix | V/4 |
| 524 | H 1 | Was seind das für große Schlösser [quodlibet; frag.] (Leipzig, 1973) | SATB, bc | — | — |

## 8. Organ works

(A) NOT CHORALE-BASED

| BWV | Title (nickname) | Date | First published | BG vol. | NBA vol. | Autograph (facsimile) |
|---|---|---|---|---|---|---|
| 525–30 | Six sonatas, in E♭, c, d, e, C, G | c.1730 | Zurich, 1815/27 | xv | IV/5 | Berlin, Staatsbibliothek |
| 531 | Prelude and Fugue in C | ? before 1705 | Leipzig, 1846 | xv | IV/5 | |
| 532 | Prelude and Fugue in D | ? before 1710 | Leipzig, 1833 | xv | IV/5 | |
| 533 | Prelude and Fugue in e | ? before 1705 | Mannheim, 1831/2 | xv | IV/5 | |
| 534 | Prelude and Fugue in f | ?1710 | Leipzig, 1846 | xv | IV/5 | |
| 535 | Prelude and Fugue in g | ?1705–17 | Leipzig, 1832 | xv | IV/5, 6 | |
| 536 | Prelude and Fugue in A | ?1708–17 | Leipzig, 1844 | xv | IV/5 | |
| 537 | Fantasia and Fugue in c | ? after 1723 | Erfurt, c.1841–7 | xv | IV/5 | |
| 538 | Toccata and Fugue in d (Dorian) | ?1712–17 | Leipzig, 1832–4 | xv | IV/5 | |
| 539 | Prelude and Fugue in d (Fiddle) | ? after 1720 | Leipzig, 1833 | xv | IV/5 | |
| 540 | Toccata and Fugue in F | ? after 1712 | Leipzig, 1832–4 | xv | IV/5 | |
| 541 | Prelude and Fugue in G | ? after 1712; rev. c.1724 | Leipzig, 1832 | xv | IV/5 | Berlin, Staatsbibliothek |
| 542 | Fantasia and Fugue in g (Great) | ?1710–25 | Leipzig, 1833 | xv | IV/5 | |
| 543 | Prelude and Fugue in a | ? after 1715 | Vienna, 1812 | xv | IV/5 | |
| 544 | Prelude and Fugue in b | 1727–31 | Vienna, 1812 | xv | IV/5 | Zurich, private collection (Vienna, 1923; London, 1942; New York, 1955) |
| 545 | Prelude and Fugue in C | ? before 1708; rev. ?1712–17 | Vienna, 1812 | xv | IV/5 | |
| 546 | Prelude and Fugue in c | ?1723–9 | Vienna, 1812 | xv | IV/5 | |
| 547 | Prelude and Fugue in C | ? c.1719–25 | Vienna, 1812 | xv | IV/5 | |
| 548 | Prelude and Fugue in e (Wedge) | ?; rev. 1727–31 | Vienna, 1812 | xv | IV/5 | |
| 549 | Prelude and Fugue in c/d | before 1705; rev. ? after 1723 | Brussels, 1825 | xxxviii | IV/5, IV/6 | |

| BWV | Title (nickname) | Date | First published | BG vol. | NBA vol. | Autograph (facsimile) |
|---|---|---|---|---|---|---|
| 550 | Prelude and Fugue in G | ? before 1710 | Leipzig, 1833 | xxxviii | IV/5 | |
| 551 | Prelude and Fugue in a | ? before 1707 | Leipzig, 1832 | xxxviii | IV/6 | |
| 552 | Prelude and Fugue in E♭ (St Anne) | in Clavier-Übung III, 1739 | Nuremberg, 1739 | iii | IV/6 | |
| 562 | Fantasia and Fugue in c | ? 1730–45 | Leipzig, 1841 (Fantasia only) | xxxviii | IV/6 | Berlin, Staatsbibliothek [inc.] |
| 563 | Fantasia con imitazione in b | ? before 1708 | Leipzig, 1867 | xxxviii | IV/6 | |
| 564 | Toccata, Adagio and Fugue in C | ? c.1712 | Erfurt, 1846 | xv | IV/6 | |
| 566 | Prelude and Fugue in E/C | ? before 1708 | Leipzig, 1833 [inc.]; Leipzig, 1845 | xv | IV/6 | |
| 568 | Prelude in G | ? before 1705 | Leipzig, 1852 | xxxviii | IV/6 | |
| 569 | Prelude in a | ? before 1705 | Leipzig, 1833 | xxxviii | IV/6 | |
| 570 | Fantasia in C | ? before 1705 | Leipzig, 1852 | xxxviii | IV/6 | |
| 571 | Fantasia in G | ? | Leipzig, 1881 | xxxviii | — | |
| 572 | Pièce d'orgue in G | ? before 1712 | London, c.1818 | xxxviii | IV/7 | |
| 573 | Fantasia in C [frag.] | c.1722 | BG, 1891 | xxxviii | IV/6 | Berlin, Staatsbibliothek [frag.] |
| 574 | Fugue in C, after Legrenzi | ? before 1707 | Mannheim, c.1833 | xxxviii | IV/6 | |
| 575 | Fugue in c | ? 1708–17 | London, 1881 | xxxviii | IV/6 | |
| 577 | Fugue in G (Jig) | ? | Leipzig, 1881 | xxxviii | — | |
| 578 | Fugue in g (Little) | ? before 1707 | Leipzig, 1821 | xxxviii | IV/6 | |
| 579 | Fugue in b, after Corelli | ? before 1710 | Erfurt, c.1841–7 | xxxviii | IV/6 | |
| 582 | Passacaglia in c | ? 1708–12 | Frankfurt, c.1830 | xv | IV/7 | |
| 583 | Trio in d | ? 1723–9 | Leipzig, 1845 | xxxviii | IV/7 | |
| 588 | Canzona in d | ? before 1705 | Erfurt, 1846 | xxxviii | IV/7 | |
| 589 | Alla breve in D | ? | Leipzig, 1852 | xxxviii | IV/7 | |

| BWV | Title (nickname) | Date | First published | BG vol. | NBA vol. | Autograph (facsimile) |
|---|---|---|---|---|---|---|
| 590 | Pastorella in F | ? after 1720 | Berlin, 1825 [inc.] Erfurt, c.1841–7 Erfurt, c.1841–7 | xxxviii | IV/7 | |
| 592–6 | Concerto arrangements: Concerto in G, after Johann Ernst Concerto in a, after Vivaldi, RV522 Concerto in C, after Vivaldi, RV208 Concerto in C, after Johann Ernst Concerto in d, after Vivaldi, RV565 | ? 1713–14 | Leipzig, 1845 (BWV596); Leipzig, 1852 (BWV592–5); BG, 1891 | xxxviii | IV/8 | Berlin, Staatsbibliothek [BWV596 only] |
| 802–5 | Four duets, in e, F, G, a | in Clavier-Übung III, 1739 | Nuremberg, 1739 | iii | IV/4 | |
| 921 | Prelude (Fantasia) in c | before 1705 | BG, 1890 | xxxvi | [V/12] | |
| 1027a | Trio in G, after BWV1027 | ? | — | — | — | |
| Anh. 205 | Fantasia in c | before 1705 | — | — | — | |

(B) CHORALE-BASED

| BWV | Title | Date | First published | BG vol. | NBA vol. | Autograph (facsimile) |
|---|---|---|---|---|---|---|
| 599–644 | Orgel-Büchlein: | mainly 1713–15 | Erfurt, ?; 2nd edn. c.1847 | xxv/1 | IV/1 | Berlin, Staatsbibliothek (Kassel, 1981; Leipzig, 1981) |
| 599 | Nun komm, der Heiden Heiland | | | | | |
| 600 | Gott, durch deine Güte | | | | | |
| 601 | Herr Christ, der einge Gottes Sohn | | | | | |
| 602 | Lob sei dem allmächtigen Gott | | | | | |
| 603 | Puer natus in Bethlehem | | | | | |
| 604 | Gelobet seist du, Jesu Christ | | | | | |
| 605 | Der Tag, der ist so freudenreich | | | | | |

| BWV | Title | Date | First published | BG vol. | NBA vol. | Autograph (facsimile) |
|---|---|---|---|---|---|---|
| 606 | Vom Himmel hoch da komm ich her | | | | | |
| 607 | Vom Himmel kam der Engel Schar | | | | | |
| 608 | In dulci jubilo | | | | | |
| 609 | Lobt Gott, ihr Christen, allzugleich | | | | | |
| 610 | Jesu, meine Freude | | | | | |
| 611 | Christum wir sollen dich loben schon | | | | | |
| 612 | Wir Christenleut | | | | | |
| 613 | Helft mir Gottes Güte preisen | | | | | |
| 614 | Das alte Jahr vergangen ist | | | | | |
| 615 | In dir ist Freude | | | | | |
| 616 | Mit Fried und Freud ich fahr dahin | | | | | |
| 617 | Herr Gott, nun schleuß den Himmel auf | | | | | |
| 618 | O Lamm Gottes unschuldig | | | | | |
| 619 | Christe, du Lamm Gottes | | | | | |
| 620 | Christus, der uns selig macht | | | | | |
| 621 | Da Jesus an dem Kreuze stund | | | | | |
| 622 | O Mensch, bewein dein Sünde groß | | | | | |
| 623 | Wir danken dir, Herr Jesu Christ | | | | | |
| 624 | Hilf Gott, daß mirs gelinge | | | | | |
| Anh. 200 | O Traurigkeit, o Herzeleid [frag.] | | | | | |
| 625 | Christ lag in Todes Banden | | | | | |
| 626 | Jesus Christus, unser Heiland | | | | | |
| 627 | Christ ist erstanden | | | | | |
| 628 | Erstanden ist der heilge Christ | | | | | |
| 629 | Erschienen ist der herrliche Tag | | | | | |
| 630 | Heut triumphieret Gottes Sohn | | | | | |
| 631 | Komm, Gott Schöpfer, heiliger Geist | | | | | |

| BWV | Title | Date | First published | BG vol. | NBA vol. | Autograph (facsimile) |
|---|---|---|---|---|---|---|
| 632 | Herr Jesu Christ, dich zu uns wend | | | | | |
| 633 | Liebster Jesu, wir sind hier | | | | | |
| 634 | Liebster Jesu, wir sind hier | | | | | |
| 635 | Dies sind die heilgen zehn Gebot | | | | | |
| 636 | Vater unser im Himmelreich | | | | | |
| 637 | Durch Adams Fall ist ganz verderbt | | | | | |
| 638 | Est ist das Heil uns kommen her | | | | | |
| 639 | Ich ruf zu dir, Herr Jesu Christ | | | | | |
| 640 | In dich hab ich gehoffet, Herr | | | | | |
| 641 | Wenn wir in höchsten Nöten sein | | | | | |
| 642 | Wer nur den lieben Gott läßt walten | | | | | |
| 643 | Alle Menschen müssen sterben | | | | | |
| 644 | Ach wie nichtig, ach wie flüchtig | | | | | |
| 645–50 | Schübler Chorales: | — | Zella, 1748/9 | xxv/2 | IV/1 | |
| 645 | Wachet auf, ruft uns die Stimme | | | | | |
| 646 | Wo soll ich fliehen hin | | | | | |
| 647 | Wer nur den lieben Gott läßt walten | | | | | |
| 648 | Meine Seele erhebet den Herrn | | | | | |
| 649 | Ach bleib bei uns, Herr Jesu Christ | | | | | |
| 650 | Kommst du nun, Jesu, vom Himmel | | | | | |
| 651–68 | Eighteen Chorales: | ?; rev. after 1740 | | xxv/2 | IV/2 | Berlin, Staatsbibliothek [BWV651–65 only] (Merseburg, 1949; Berlin, 1950) |
| 651 | Komm, heiliger Geist, Herre Gott | | Leipzig, 1846 | | | |
| 652 | Komm, heiliger Geist, Herre Gott | | Leipzig, 1847 | | | |

| BWV | Title | Date | First published | BG vol. | NBA vol. | Autograph (facsimile) |
|---|---|---|---|---|---|---|
| 653 | An Wasserflüssen Babylon | | Leipzig, 1846 | | | |
| 654 | Schmücke dich, o liebe Seele | | Mainz, 1843 | | | |
| 655 | Herr Jesu Christ, dich zu uns wend | | Leipzig, 1846 | | | |
| 656 | O Lamm Gottes, unschuldig | | Leipzig, 1846 | | | |
| 657 | Nun danket alle Gott | | Leipzig, 1846 | | | |
| 658 | Von Gott will ich nicht lassen | | Leipzig, 1846 | | | |
| 659 | Nun komm, der Heiden Heiland | | Mainz, 1843 | | | |
| 660 | Nun komm, der Heiden Heiland | | Leipzig, 1846 | | | |
| 661 | Nun komm, der Heiden Heiland | | Leipzig, 1846 | | | |
| 662 | Allein Gott in der Höh sei Ehr | | Leipzig, 1846 | | | |
| 663 | Allein Gott in der Höh sei Ehr | | Leipzig, 1846 | | | |
| 664 | Allein Gott in der Höh sei Ehr | | Leipzig, 1847 | | | |
| 665 | Jesus Christus, unser Heiland | | Leipzig, 1847 | | | |
| 666 | Jesus Christus, unser Heiland | | Leipzig, 1847 | | | |
| 667 | Komm, Gott Schöpfer, Heiliger Geist | | Leipzig, 1846 | | | |
| 668 | Vor deinen Thron tret ich hiermit | | Leipzig, 1847 | | | |
| 669–89 | Clavier-Übung III: | — | Leipzig, 1739 | iii | IV/4 | |
| 669 | Kyrie, Gott Vater in Ewigkeit | | | | | |
| 670 | Christe, aller Welt Trost | | | | | |
| 671 | Kyrie, Gott heiliger Geist | | | | | |
| 672 | Kyrie, Gott Vater in Ewigkeit (manualiter) | | | | | |
| 673 | Christe, aller Welt Trost (manualiter) | | | | | |
| 674 | Kyrie, Gott heiliger Geist (manualiter) | | | | | |
| 675 | Allein Gott in der Höh sei Ehr | | | | | |
| 676 | Allein Gott in der Höh sei Ehr | | | | | |
| 677 | Allein Gott in der Höh sei Ehr (manualiter) | | | | | |

# Appendix 1

| BWV | Title | Date | First published | BG vol. | NBA vol. | Autograph (facsimile) |
|---|---|---|---|---|---|---|
| 678 | Dies sind die heilgen zehn Gebot | | | | | |
| 679 | Dies sind die heilgen zehn Gebot (manualiter) | | | | | |
| 680 | Wir glauben all an einen Gott | | | | | |
| 681 | Wir glauben all an einen Gott (manualiter) | | | | | |
| 682 | Vater unser im Himmelreich | | | | | |
| 683 | Vater unser im Himmelreich (manualiter) | | | | | |
| 684 | Christ unser Herr zum Jordan kam | | | | | |
| 685 | Christ unser Herr zum Jordan kam (manualiter) | | | | | |
| 686 | Aus tiefer Not schrei ich zu dir | | | | | |
| 687 | Aus tiefer Not schrei ich zu dir (manualiter) | | | | | |
| 688 | Jesus Christus unser Heiland | | | | | |
| 689 | Jesus Christus unser Heiland (manualiter) | | | | | |
| 690 | Wer nur den lieben Gott läßt walten | before 1705 | Leipzig, 1847 | xl | IV/3 | |
| 691 | Wer nur den lieben Gott läßt walten | c.1720–3 | Leipzig, 1803 | xl | IV/3 | New Haven, Conn., Yale University Library |
| 694 | Wo soll ich fliehen hin | before 1708 | Leipzig, 1881 | xl | IV/3 | |
| 695 | Christ lag in Todes Banden | ? before 1708 | Leipzig, 1847 | xl | IV/3 | |
| 696 | Christum wir sollen loben schon | ? | Leipzig, 1846 | xl | IV/3 | |
| 697 | Gelobet seist du, Jesu Christ | ? | Leipzig, 1805 | xl | IV/3 | |
| 698 | Herr Christ, der einge Gottes Sohn | ? | Leipzig, 1806 | xl | IV/3 | |
| 699 | Nun komm, der Heiden Heiland | ? | Leipzig, 1806 | xl | IV/3 | |
| 700 | Vom Himmel hoch, da komm ich her | before 1708; rev. after 1740 | Leipzig, 1806 | xl | IV/3 | |
| 701 | Vom Himmel hoch, da komm ich her | ? | Leipzig, 1806 | xl | IV/3 | |

| BWV | Title | Date | First published | BG vol. | NBA vol. | Autograph (facsimile) |
|---|---|---|---|---|---|---|
| 702 | Das Jesulein soll doch mein Trost | ? | | xl | [IV/9] | |
| 703 | Gottes Sohn ist kommen | ? | Leipzig, 1846 | xl | IV/3 | |
| 704 | Lob sei dem allmächtigen Gott | ? | Leipzig, 1803 | xl | IV/3 | |
| 705 | Durch Adams Fall ist ganz verderbt | ? | | xl | [IV/9] | |
| 706 | Liebster Jesu, wir sind hier | ? 1708–14 | Leipzig, 1806 | xl | IV/3 | |
| 707 | Ich hab mein Sach Gott heimgestellt | ? | | xl | [IV/9] | |
| 708 | Ich hab mein Sach Gott heimgestellt | ? | | xl | [IV/9] | |
| 709 | Herr Jesu Christ, dich zu uns wend | ? | Leipzig, 1846 | xl | IV/3 | |
| 711 | Allein Gott in der Höh sei Ehr | ? 1708–17; rev. after 1740 | Leipzig, 1805 | xl | IV/3 | |
| 712 | In dich hab ich gehoffet, Herr | ? | Leipzig, 1847 | xl | IV/3 | |
| 713 | Jesu, meine Freude | ? | Leipzig, 1847 | xl | IV/3 | |
| 714 | Ach Gott und Herr | ? | Leipzig, 1881 | xl | IV/3 | |
| 715 | Allein Gott in der Höh sei Ehr | ? | BG, 1893 | xl | IV/3 | |
| 716 | Allein Gott in der Höh sei Ehr | ? | | xl | [IV/9] | |
| 717 | Allein Gott in der Höh sei Ehr | ? | Leipzig, 1847 | xl | IV/3 | |
| 718 | Christ lag in Todes Banden | ? | Leipzig, 1847 | xl | IV/3 | |
| 719 | Der Tag, der ist so freudenreich | ? | | xl | [IV/9] | |
| 720 | Ein feste Burg ist unser Gott | ? | Leipzig, 1847 | xl | IV/3 | |
| 721 | Erbarm dich mein, o Herre Gott | ? | BG, 1893 | xl | IV/3 | |
| 722 | Gelobet seist du, Jesu Christ | ? | Leipzig, 1846 | xl | IV/3 | |
| 724 | Gott, durch deine Güte | before 1705 | Leipzig, 1847 | xl | IV/3 | |
| 725 | Herr Gott, dich loben wir | ? | Leipzig, 1847 | xl | IV/3 | |
| 726 | Herr Jesu Christ, dich zu uns wend | ? | BG, 1893 | xl | IV/3 | |
| 727 | Herzlich tut mich verlangen | ? | Leipzig, 1846 | xl | IV/3 | |
| 728 | Jesus, meine Zuversicht | ? | Leipzig, 1846 | xl | IV/3 | |
| 729 | In dulci jubilo | ? | Leipzig, 1846 | xl | IV/3 | |
| 730 | Liebster Jesu, wir sind hier | ? | Leipzig, 1846 | xl | IV/3 | Berlin, Staatsbibliothek |

# Appendix 1

| BWV | Title | Date | First published | BG vol. | NBA vol. | Autograph (facsimile) |
|---|---|---|---|---|---|---|
| 731 | Liebster Jesu, wir sind hier | ? | Leipzig, 1846 | xl | IV/3 | |
| 732 | Lobt Gott, ihr Christen, allzugleich | ? | Leipzig, 1846 | xl | IV/3 | |
| 733 | Meine Seele erhebet den Herren | ? | BG, 1893 | xl | IV/3 | |
| 734 | Nun freut euch, lieben Christen gmein | ? | Leipzig, 1847 | xl | IV/3 | |
| 735 | Valet will ich dir geben | ? 1708–17; rev. after ?1723 | Leipzig, 1847 | xl | IV/3 | |
| 736 | Valet will ich dir geben | ? | Leipzig, 1847 | xl | IV/3 | |
| 737 | Vater unser im Himmelreich | ? | Leipzig, 1847 | xl | IV/3 | |
| 738 | Vom Himmel hoch da komm ich her | ? | Leipzig, 1846 | xl | IV/3 | |
| 739 | Wie schön leuchtet der Morgenstern | ? before 1700 | BG, 1893 | xl | [IV/9] | Berlin, Staatsbibliothek |
| 741 | Ach Gott, vom Himmel sieh darein | ? 1705 | Leipzig, 1881 | xl | IV/3 | |
| 743 | Ach, was ist doch unser Leben | ? | BG, 1893 | — | — | |
| 744 | Auf meinen lieben Gott | ? | Leipzig, 1881 | xl | — | |
| 747 | Christus, der uns selig macht | ? | BG, 1893 | — | — | |
| 749 | Herr Jesu Christ, dich zu uns wend | ? before 1700 | Berlin, 1839 | — | — | |
| 750 | Herr Jesu Christ, meins Lebens Licht | ? before 1700 | Berlin, 1839 | — | — | |
| 753 | Jesu, meine Freude [frag.] | ? before 1723 | Leipzig, 1846 | xl | V/5 | New Haven, Conn., Yale University Library |
| 754 | Liebster Jesu, wir sind hier | ? | BG, 1893 | — | — | |
| 756 | Nun ruhen alle Wälder | ? before 1700 | Berlin, 1839 | — | — | |
| 757 | O Herre Gott, dein göttlichs Wort | ? | BG, 1893 | — | — | |
| 758 | O Vater, allmächtiger Gott | ? | BG, 1893 | xl | — | |
| 762 | Vater unser im Himmelreich | ? | BG, 1893 | — | — | |
| 764 | Wie schön leuchtet der Morgenstern [frag.] | ? before 1705 | BG, 1893 | xl | [IV/9] | Berlin, Staatsbibliothek |
| 765 | Wir glauben all an einen Gott | ? | Leipzig, 1881 | — | — | |
| 1085 | O Lamm Gottes unschuldig | ? | | — | IV/3 | |
| Anh. II 49 | Ein feste Burg ist unser Gott | ? | | — | — | |

| BWV | Title | Date | First published | BG vol. | NBA vol. | Autograph (facsimile) |
|---|---|---|---|---|---|---|
| Anh. II 50 | Erhalt uns, Herr, bei deinem Wort | ? | | — | — | |
| Anh. II 58 | Jesu, meine Freude | ? | | — | — | |
| Anh. II 75 | Herr Christ, der einig Gottes Sohn | ? | | — | — | |
| Anh. II 76 | Jesu, meine Freude | ? | | — | — | |
| 766 | Christ, der du bist der helle Tag (partita) | c.1700 | London, 1846 | xl | IV/1 | |
| 767 | O Gott, du frommer Gott (partita) | ? | Leipzig, 1846 | xl | IV/1 | |
| 768 | Sei gegrüßet, Jesu gütig | ? before 1710; rev.? | London, 1846 | xl | IV/1 | |
| 769 | Canonic Variation on *Vom Himmel hoch* | 1747 | Nuremberg, 1748 | xl | IV/2 | Berlin, Staatsbibliothek (Nuremberg, 1973; Leipzig, 1986) |
| 770 | Ach, was soll ich Sünder machen (variations) | | BG, 1893 | xl | — | |
| 1090–1120 | Neumeister Chorales: | before 1705 | New Haven, Conn., 1985 | — | IV/9 | |
| 1090 | Wir Christenleut | | | | | |
| 1091 | Das alte Jahr vergangen ist | | | | | |
| 1092 | Herr Gott, nun schleuß den Himmel auf | | | | | |
| 1093 | Herzliebster Jesu, was hast du verbrochen | | | | | |
| 1094 | O Jesu, wie ist dein Gestalt | | | | | |
| 1095 | O Lamm Gottes unschuldig | | | | | |
| 1097 | Ehre sei dir, Christe | | | | | |
| 1098 | Wir glauben all an einen Gott | | | | | |
| 1099 | Aus tiefer Not schrei ich zu dir | | | | | |
| 1100 | Allein zu dir, Herr Jesu Christ | | | | | |
| 1101 | Durch Adams Fall ist ganz verderbt | | | | | |
| 1102 | Du Friedefürst, Herr Jesu Christ | | | | | |
| 1103 | Erhalt uns, Herr, bei deinem Wort | | | | | |
| 1104 | Wenn dich Unglück tut greifen an | | | | | |

| BWV | Title | Date | First published | BG vol. | NBA vol. | Autograph (facsimile) |
|---|---|---|---|---|---|---|
| 1105 | Jesu, meine Freude | | | | | |
| 1106 | Gott ist mein Heil, mein Hilf und Trost | | | | | |
| 1107 | Jesu, meines Lebens Leben | | | | | |
| 1108 | Als Jesus Christus in der Nacht | | | | | |
| 1109 | Ach Gott, tu dich erbarmen | | | | | |
| 1110 | O Herre Gott, dein göttlich Wort | | | | | |
| 1111 | Nun laßt uns den Leib begraben | | | | | |
| 1112 | Christus, der ist mein Leben | | | | | |
| 1113 | Ich hab mein Sach Gott heimgestellt | | | | | |
| 1114 | Herr Jesu Christ, du höchstes Gut | | | | | |
| 1115 | Herzlieblich lieb hab ich dich, o Herr | | | | | |
| 1116 | Was Gott tut, das ist wohlgetan | | | | | |
| 1117 | Alle Menschen müssen sterben | | | | | |
| 1118 | Werde munter, mein Gemüte | | | | | |
| 1119 | Wie nach einer Wasserquelle | | | | | |
| 1120 | Christ, der du bist der helle Tag | | | | | |

## 9. Keyboard works

| BWV | Title | Date | First published | BG | NBA | Autograph (facsimile) |
|---|---|---|---|---|---|---|
| 772–86 | Two-part Inventions, C, c, D, d, E♭, E, e, F, f, G, g, A, a, B♭, b | completed 1723 | Vienna, 1801 | iii, xlv | V/3, V/5 | Berlin, Staatsbibliothek (Leipzig, 1942; New York, 1950) |
| 787–801 | Three-part Inventions, C, c, D, d, E♭, E, e, F, f, G, g, A, a, B♭, b | completed 1723 | Leipzig, 1801 | iii | V/3, V/5 | Berlin, Staatsbibliothek (Leipzig, 1942; New York, 1950) |

| BWV | Title | Date | First published | BG | NBA | Autograph (facsimile) |
|---|---|---|---|---|---|---|
| 806–11 | English Suites, A, a, g, F, e, d | ? before 1720 | Leipzig, 1881 | xlv/1 | V/7 | Berlin, Staatsbibliothek [BWV812–16 only, inc.] |
| 812–17 | French Suites, d, c, b, E♭, G, E | c.1722–5 | Leipzig, 1881 | xlv/1 | V/8 | |
| 818 | Suite in a | c.1705 | Leipzig, 1866 | xxxvi | V/8 | |
| 819 | Suite in E♭ | c.1725 | Leipzig, 1866 | xxxvi | V/8 | |
| 820 | Ouverture in F | c.1705 | Leipzig, 1876 | xxxvi | V/10 | |
| 821 | Suite in B♭ | ? | BG, 1894 | xlii | | |
| 822 | Suite in g | before 1707 | Leipzig, 1904 | — | V/10 | |
| 823 | Suite in f | before 1715 | Leipzig, 1843 | xxxvi | V/10 | |
| 825–30 | Partitas, B♭, c, a, D, G, e (Clavier-Übung I) | — | Leipzig, 1726–31 | iii | V/1 | |
| 831 | Ouverture in the French Style (in Clavier-Übung II) | — | Leipzig, 1735 | iii | V/2 | |
| 832 | Partita in A | ? before 1707 | BG, 1894 | xlii | V/10 | |
| 833 | Prelude and Partita in F | before 1708 | BJb, 1912 | — | V/10 | |
| 841–3 | Minuets in G, g, G | c.1720 | Leipzig, 1867 | xxxvi | V/5 | |
| 846–69 | The Well-tempered Clavier, Part 1 | 1722; rev. ? | Bonn, 1801 | xiv | V/6.1 | Berlin, Staatsbibliothek [inc.] (Leipzig, 1962) |
| 870–93 | The Well-tempered Clavier, Part 2 | c.1740 | Bonn, 1801 | xiv | V/6.2 | Berlin, Staatsbibliothek [inc.] (London, 1980) |
| 894 | Prelude and Fugue in a | c.1715–25 | Leipzig, 1843 | xxxvi | [V/9] | |
| 895 | Prelude and Fugue in a | before 1725 | Leipzig, 1843 | xxxvi | [V/12] | |
| 896 | Prelude and Fugue in A | before 1710 | Leipzig, 1866 | xxxvi | [V/9] | |
| 900 | Prelude and Fughetta in e | before 1726 | Leipzig, 1843 | xxxvi | [V/9] | |
| 901 | Prelude and Fughetta in F | before 1730 | Leipzig, 1866 | xxxvi | [V/9] | |
| 902 | Prelude and Fughetta in G | ? before 1730 | Leipzig, 1866 | xxxvi | [V/9] | |
| 903 | Chromatic Fantasia and Fugue in d | before 1723 | Leipzig, 1802 | xxxvi | [V/9] | |
| 904 | Fantasia and Fugue in a [inc.] | ? | Leipzig, 1839 | xxxvi | [V/9] | |
| 906 | Fantasia and Fugue in c [inc.] | c.1726–31 | Leipzig, 1802/3 | xxxvi | [V/9] | Dresden, Sächsische Landesbibliothek (Leipzig, 1976; Leipzig, 1984) |
| 910 | Toccata in f♯ | c.1712 | Berlin, 1837 | iii | [V/9] | |
| 911 | Toccata in c | before 1714 | Leipzig, 1839 | iii | [V/9] | |

# Appendix 1

| BWV | Title | Date | First published | BG | NBA | Autograph (facsimile) |
|---|---|---|---|---|---|---|
| 912 | Toccata in D | before 1710 | Leipzig, 1843 | xxxvi | [V/9] | |
| 913 | Toccata in d | ? before 1708 | Vienna, 1801 | iii | [V/9] | |
| 914 | Toccata in e | c.1710 | Leipzig, 1843/4 | iii | [V/9] | |
| 915 | Toccata in g | ? c.1710 | Leipzig, 1839 | xxxvi | [V/9] | |
| 916 | Toccata in G | before 1714 | Leipzig, 1866/7 | xxxvi | [V/9] | |
| 917 | Fantasia in g | ? before 1710 | Leipzig, 1866/7 | xxxvi | [V/12] | |
| 918 | Fantasia in c | ? after 1740 | BG, 1890 | xxxvi | [V/12] | |
| 922 | Fantasia in a | before 1714 | Leipzig, 1866/7 | xxxvi | [V/12] | |
| 923 | Prelude in b | before 1725 | Berlin, 1826 | xlii | [V/12] | |
| 924 | Prelude in C (in Clavierbüchlein for W. F. Bach) | after 1719 | Leipzig, 1843 | xxxvi | V/5 | New Haven, Conn., Yale University Library |
| 926 | Prelude in d (in Clavierbüchlein for W. F. Bach) | after 1719 | Leipzig, 1843 | xxxvi | V/5 | New Haven, Conn., Yale University Library |
| 927 | Prelude in F (in Clavierbüchlein for W. F. Bach) | after 1719 | Leipzig, 1843 | xxxvi | V/5 | |
| 928 | Prelude in F (in Clavierbüchlein for W. F. Bach) | after 1719 | Leipzig, 1843 | xxxvi | V/5 | New Haven, Conn., Yale University Library |
| 929 | Trio in g (after Stölzel; in Clavierbüchlein for W. F. Bach) | after 1719 | Leipzig, 1843 | xxxvi | V/5 | New Haven, Conn., Yale University Library |
| 930 | Prelude in g (in Clavierbüchlein for W. F. Bach) | after 1719 | Leipzig, 1843 | xxxvi | V/5 | New Haven, Conn., Yale University Library |
| 933–8 | Six Little Preludes, C, c, d, D, E, e | ? 1717–23 | Vienna, 1802 | xxxvi | [V/9] | |
| 939–43 | Five Preludes, C, d, e, a, C | ? 1717–23 | Leipzig, 1843 | xxxvi | [V/9] | |
| 944 | Fantasia and Fugue in a (after Torelli) | ? | Vienna, 1820–4 | iii | [V/9] | |
| 946 | Fugue in C (after Albinoni) | ? before 1708 | Leipzig, 1852 | xxxvi | [V/9] | |
| 947 | Fugue in a | ? | Leipzig, 1843 | xxxvi | [V/12] | |
| 948 | Fugue in d | before 1727 | Leipzig, 1843 | xxxvi | [V/12] | |
| 949 | Fugue in A | ? | Leipzig, 1867 | xxxvi | [V/12] | |
| 950 | Fugue in A (after Albinoni) | c.1710 | Leipzig, 1867 | xxxvi | [V/9] | |
| 951 | Fugue in b | ? | Leipzig, 1866 | xxxvi | [V/9] | |
| 952 | Fugue in C | ? | Leipzig, 1843 | xxxvi | [V/12] | |
| 953 | Fugue in C | after 1723 | London, 1822–31 | xxxvi | V/5 | New Haven, Conn., Yale University Library |

| BWV | Title | Date | First published | BG | NBA | Autograph (facsimile) |
|---|---|---|---|---|---|---|
| 954 | Fugue in B♭ (after Reincken) | ? before 1705 | Leipzig, 1880 | xlii | [V/11] | |
| 956 | Fugue in e | ? | Leipzig, 1880 | xlii | [V/12] | |
| 958 | Fugue in a | ? | BG, 1894 | xlii | [V/9] | |
| 959 | Fugue in a | ? | BG, 1894 | xlii | [V/9] | |
| 961 | Fughetta in c | ? | Leipzig, 1840 | xxxvi | [V/12] | |
| 963 | Sonata in D | ? c.1704 | Leipzig, 1867 | xxxvi | V/10 | |
| 964 | Sonata in d | ? | Leipzig, 1866 | xlii | — | |
| 965 | Sonata in a (after Reincken) | ? before 1705 | Leipzig, 1866 | xlii | [V/11] | |
| 966 | Sonata in C (after Reincken) | ? before 1705 | Leipzig, 1866 | xlii | [V/11] | |
| 967 | Sonata in a | c.1705 | BG, 1897 | xlv/1 | [V/11] | |
| 968 | Adagio in G | ? | Leipzig, 1880 | xlii | — | |
| 971 | Italian Concerto in F (in Clavier-Übung II) | — | Leipzig, 1735 | iii | V/2 | |
| 972–87 | Concerto arrangements: | | | | | |
| 972 | Concerto in D (after Vivaldi, RV230) | 1713–14 | Leipzig, 1850 | xlii | [V/11] | |
| 973 | Concerto in G (after Vivaldi, RV299) | | | | | |
| 974 | Concerto in d (after A. Marcello) | | | | | |
| 975 | Concerto in g (after Vivaldi, RV316) | | | | | |
| 976 | Concerto in C (after Vivaldi, RV265) | | | | | |
| 977 | Concerto in C (? after Vivaldi) | | | | | |
| 978 | Concerto in F (after Vivaldi, RV310) | | | | | |
| 979 | Concerto in b (after Torelli) | | | | | |
| 980 | Concerto in G (after Vivaldi, RV381) | | | | | |
| 981 | Concerto in c (after Marcello, op. 1 no. 2) | | | | | |
| 982 | Concerto in B♭ (after Johann Ernst) | | | | | |

| BWV | Title | Date | First published | BG | NBA | Autograph (facsimile) |
|---|---|---|---|---|---|---|
| 983 | Concerto in g | | | | | |
| 984 | Concerto in C (after Johann Ernst) | | | | | |
| 985 | Concerto in g (after Telemann) | | | | | |
| 986 | Concerto in G | | | | | |
| 987 | Concerto in d (after Johann Ernst) | | | | | |
| 988 | Goldberg Variations | | Nuremberg, 1741/2 | iii | V/2 | |
| 989 | Aria variata in a | ? before 1710 | Leipzig, 1867 | xxxvi | V/10 | |
| 990 | Sarabande and Partita in C | ? | BG, 1894 | xlii | [V/12] | |
| 991 | Air and Variations in c [frag.] (in Clavierbüchlein for A. M. Bach, 1722) | after 1721 | BG, 1894 | xliii | V/4 | Berlin, Staatsbibliothek [frag.] |
| 992 | Capriccio in B♭ 'sopra la lontananza del fratello dilettissimo' | ? | Leipzig, 1839 | xxxvi | V/10 | |
| 994 | Applicatio in C (in Clavierbüchlein 1720 for W. F. Bach) | 1720 | Leipzig, 1873 | xxxvi | V/5 | New Haven, Conn., Yale University Library (NBA, V/5, 1962) |
| 1080 | The Art of Fugue | c.1742–9 | Leipzig, 1751 | xxv/1 | VIII/2 | Berlin, Staatsbibliothek (Leipzig, 1979) |

## 10. Solo instrumental music (other than keyboard)

| BWV | Title; scoring | Date | First published | BG | NBA | Autograph (facsimile) |
|---|---|---|---|---|---|---|
| 995 | Suite in g; lute | c.1730 | Wolfenbüttel, 1925 | — | V/10 | Brussels, Bibliothèque Royale (Brussels, 1936; Leipzig, 1975; Leipzig, 1977; NBA V/10, 1982) |
| 996 | Suite in e; lute | ? after 1712 | Leipzig, 1866 | xlv/1 | V/10 | |

| BWV | Title; scoring | Date | First published | BG | NBA | Autograph (facsimile) |
|---|---|---|---|---|---|---|
| 997 | Partita in c; lute | c.1740 | Leipzig, 1881 | xlv/1 | V/10 | (Leipzig, 1975) |
| 998 | Prelude, Fugue, and Allegro in E♭; lute | c.1740–5 | Leipzig, 1866 | xlv/1 | V/10 | Tokyo, Ueno-Gakuen Music Academy (Tokyo, 1974; Rovereto, 1977) |
| 999 | Prelude in c; lute | c.1720 | Leipzig, 1843 | xxxvi | V/10 | (Leipzig, 1975) |
| 1000 | Fugue in g; lute | after 1720 | Wolfenbüttel, 1925 | — | V/10 | Tokyo, Musashino Music Academy (Rovereto, 1977) |
| 1006a | Suite in E; lute | c.1736–7 | BG, 1894 | xlii | V/10 | |
| 1001–6 | Six Sonatas and Partitas; vn | by 1720 | Bonn, 1802 | xxxvii/1 | VI/1 | Berlin, Staatsbibliothek (Kassel, 1950; Leipzig, 1958; Frankfurt, 1962; Leipzig, 1988) |
| 1001 | Sonata in g | | | | | |
| 1002 | Partita in b | | | | | |
| 1003 | Sonata in a | | | | | |
| 1004 | Partita in d | | | | | |
| 1005 | Sonata in C | | | | | |
| 1006 | Partita in E | | | | | |
| 1007–12 | Six Suites, in G, d, C, E♭, c, D; vc | c.1720 | Leipzig, 1825 | xxvii/1 | VI/2 | (Paris, 1922; Vienna, 1944; Munich and Basle, 1951) |
| 1013 | Partita, a; fl | by c.1723 | Leipzig, 1917 | | | |

11. Chamber, ensemble, and orchestral music

| BWV | Title; scoring | Date | First published | BG | NBA | Autograph (facsimile) |
|---|---|---|---|---|---|---|
| 1014–19 | Six Sonatas, in b, A, E, c, f, G; vn, hpcd | before 1725 | Zurich, 1802 | ix | VI/1 | |
| 1021 | Sonata in G; vn, bc | 1733–5 | Leipzig, 1929 | — | VI/1 | |
| 1023 | Sonata in e; vn, bc | after 1723 | Leipzig, 1867 | xliii/1 | VI/1 | |
| 1025 | Suite in A (after S. L. Weiß); vn, hpcd | c.1740 | Leipzig, 1866/7 | ix | | |
| 1026 | Fugue in g; vn, hpcd | before 1712 | Leipzig, 1866/7 | xliii/1 | | |

# Appendix 1

| BWV | Title; scoring | Date | First published | BG | NBA | Autograph (facsimile) |
|---|---|---|---|---|---|---|
| 1027 | Sonata in G; vadg, hpcd | before 1741 | Leipzig, 1866/7 | ix | VI/4 | Berlin, Staatsbibliothek |
| 1028 | Sonata in D; vadg, hpcd | before 1741 | Leipzig, 1866/7 | ix | VI/4 | |
| 1029 | Sonata in g; vadg, hpcd | before 1741 | Leipzig, 1866/7 | ix | VI/4 | Berlin, Staatsbibliothek |
| 1030 | Sonata in b; fl, hpcd | c.1736 | Erfurt, 1855 | ix | VI/3 | (Leipzig, 1961; Bern, 1980) |
| 1031 | Sonata in Eb; fl, hpcd | 1730–4 | Leipzig, 1867 | ix | VI/3 | Berlin, Staatsbibliothek [inc.] |
| 1032 | Sonata in A [inc.]; fl, hpcd | c.1736 | Leipzig, 1866 | ix | VI/3 | (Leipzig, 1979; Kassel, 1980) |
| 1033 | Sonata in C; fl, bc | c.1736 | Leipzig, 1867 | xliii/1 | | |
| 1034 | Sonata in e; fl, bc | c.1724 | Leipzig, 1867 | xliii/1 | VI/3 | |
| 1035 | Sonata in E; fl, bc | c.1741 | Leipzig, 1867 | xliii/1 | VI/3 | |
| 1038 | Sonata in G; fl, vn, bc | 1732–5 | BG, 1860 | ix | | |
| 1039 | Sonata in G; 2 fl, bc | c.1736–41 | BG, 1860 | ix | VI/3 | |
| 1040 | Trio in F (in bwv208); vn, ob, bc | — | BG, 1881 | xxix | I/35 | Berlin, Staatsbibliothek |
| 1041 | Concerto in a; vn, str, bc | ? | Leipzig, 1852 | xxi/1 | VII/3 | |
| 1042 | Concerto in E; vn, str, bc | ? | Leipzig, 1857 | xxi/1 | VII/3 | |
| 1043 | Concerto in d; 2 vn, str, bc | ? | Leipzig, 1852 | xxi/1 | VII/3 | |
| 1044 | Concerto in a; fl, vn, str, bc | 1729–41 | Mainz, c.1844 | xvii | VII/3 | |
| 1046–51 | Brandenburg Concertos: | before 1722 | Leipzig, 1850–2 | xix | VII/2 | Berlin, Staatsbibliothek (Leipzig, ?1950) |
| 1046 | no. 1 in F; 2 cdc, ob, vnp, 2 ob, bn, str, bc | | | | | |
| 1047 | no. 2 in F; tr, rec, ob, vn, str, bc | | | | | |
| 1048 | no. 3 in G; 3 vn, 3 va, 3 vc, bc | | | | | |
| 1049 | no. 4 in G; vn, 2 rec, str, bc | | | | | |
| 1050 | no. 5 in D; fl, vn, hpcd, str, bc | | | | | Berlin, Staatsbibliothek [parts, early version] (Leipzig, 1975) |
| 1051 | no. 6 in Bb; 2 va, 2 vadg, vc, bc | | | | | |
| 1052 | Concerto in d; hpcd, str, bc | c.1738 | Leipzig, 1838 | xvii | [VII/4] | Berlin, Staatsbibliothek |
| 1053 | Concerto in E; hpcd, str, bc | c.1738 | Leipzig, 1851 | xvii | [VII/4] | Berlin, Staatsbibliothek |

| BWV | Title; scoring | Date | First published | BG | NBA | Autograph (facsimile) |
|---|---|---|---|---|---|---|
| 1054 | Concerto in D (arr. of bwv1042); hpcd, str, bc | c.1738 | Leipzig, 1851 | xvii | [VII/4] | Berlin, Staatsbibliothek |
| 1055 | Concerto in A; hpcd, str, bc | c.1738 | Leipzig, 1851 | xvii | [VII/4] | Berlin, Staatsbibliothek |
| 1056 | Concerto in f; hpcd, str, bc | c.1738 | Leipzig, 1851 | xvii | [VII/4] | Berlin, Staatsbibliothek |
| 1057 | Concerto in F (arr. of bwv1049); hpcd, 2 rec, str, bc | c.1738 | Leipzig, 1851 | xvii | [VII/4] | Berlin, Staatsbibliothek |
| 1058 | Concerto in g (arr. of bwv1041); hpcd, str, bc | c.1738 | Leipzig, 1851 | xvii | [VII/4] | Berlin, Staatsbibliothek |
| 1059 | Concerto in d [frag.]; hpcd, ob, str, bc | c.1738 | BG, 1869 | xvii | [VII/4] | Berlin, Staatsbibliothek [frag.] |
| 1060 | Concerto in c; 2 hpcd, str, bc | c.1738 | Leipzig, 1848 | xxi/2 | VII/5 | |
| 1061 | Concerto in C; 2 hpcd, str, bc | 1732–5 | Leipzig, 1847 | xxi/2 | VII/5 | |
| 1062 | Concerto in c (arr. of bwv1043); 2 hpcd, str, bc | c.1736 | BG, 1874 | xxi/2 | VII/5 | Berlin, Staatsbibliothek (Leipzig, 1979; Kassel, 1980) |
| 1063 | Concerto in d; 3 hpcd, str, bc | c.1730 | Leipzig, 1845 | xxxi/3 | VII/6 | |
| 1064 | Concerto in C; 3 hpcd, str, bc | c.1730 | Leipzig, 1850 | xxxi/3 | VII/6 | |
| 1065 | Concerto in a (arr. of Vivaldi, rv580); 4 hpcd, str, bc | c.1730 | Leipzig, 1865 | xliii/1 | VII/6 | |
| 1066 | Ouverture in C; 2 ob, bn, str, bc | before 1725 | Leipzig, 1853 | xxxi/1 | VII/1 | |
| 1067 | Ouverture in b; fl, str, bc | 1738/9 | Leipzig, 1853 | xxxi/1 | VII/1 | |
| 1068 | Ouverture in D; 3 tr, timp, 2 ob, str, bc | c.1731 | Leipzig, 1853 | xxxi/1 | VII/1 | |
| 1069 | Ouverture in D; 3 tr, timp, 3 ob, bn, str, bc | 1729–41 | Paris, c.1816 | xxxi/1 | VII/1 | |
| 1079 | Musical Offering; fl, vn, bc | 1747 | Leipzig, 1747 | xxxi/2 | VIII/1 | |

## 12. Canons

| BWV | Title | Date | First published | BG | NBA | Autograph (facsimile) |
|---|---|---|---|---|---|---|
| 1072 | Trias harmonica | ? | Berlin, 1754 | xlv | VIII/1 | |
| 1073 | Canon à 4 . . . perpetuus | 1713 | BG, 1897 | xlv | VIII/1 | Cambridge, Mass., Harvard University, Houghton Library (NBA, 1974) |

| BWV | Title | Date | First published | BG | NBA | Autograph (facsimile) |
|---|---|---|---|---|---|---|
| 1074 | Canon a 4 | 1727 | Hamburg, 1728 | xlv | VIII/1 | (Berlin, 1929; NBA, 1974) |
| 1075 | Canon a 2 perpetuus | 1734 | Berlin, 1881 | — | VIII/1 | Wildegg, Switzerland, private collection |
| 1076 | Canon triplex à 6 | before 1747 | Leipzig, 1747 | xlv | VIII/1 | Private collection (NBA, 1974) |
| 1077 | Canone doppio sopr'il soggetto | 1747 | Berlin, 1929 | — | VIII/1 | |
| 1078 | Canon super Fa Mi, a 7 | 1749 | Berlin, 1754 | xlv | VIII/1 | (NBA, 1974) |
| 1086 | Canon, Concordia discors | ? | Die Musikforschung 13 (1960), p. 449 | — | VIII/1 | (NBA, 1974) |
| 1087 | 14 canons (MS addition to bwv988) | after 1745 | Kassel, 1976 | — | V/2 | Paris, Bibliothèque Nationale (NBA, 1977) |

## 13. Doubtful and spurious works

| BWV | Title (librettist) | First published | BG | NBA | Remarks |
|---|---|---|---|---|---|
| **CHURCH CANTATAS AND PASSIONS** | | | | | |
| 15 | Denn du wirst meine Seele nicht in der Hölle lassen | ii | — | | by Johann Ludwig Bach |
| 53 | Schlage doch, gewünschte Stunde (? S. Franck) | xii/2 | — | | by ? M. Hoffmann |
| 141 | Das ist je gewißlich wahr (J. F. Helbig) | xxx | — | | by G. P. Telemann |
| 142 | Uns ist ein Kind geboren (E. Neumeister) | xxx | — | | spurious |
| 143 | Lobe den Herrn, meine seele | xxx | I/4 | | doubtful |
| 160 | Ich weiß, daß mein Erlöser lebt (E. Neumeister) | xxxii | — | | by G. P. Telemann |
| 189 | Meine Seele rühmt und preist | xxxvii | — | | by ? M. Hoffmann |
| 217 | Gedenke, Herr, wie es uns gehet | xli | — | | doubtful |
| 218 | Gott der Hoffnung erfülle euch (E. Neumeister) | xli | — | | by G. P. Telemann |
| 219 | Siehe, es hat überwunden der Löwe | xli | — | | by G. P. Telemann |
| 220 | Lobt ihn mit Herz und Münde | xli | — | | doubtful |
| 221 | Wer sucht die Pracht, wer wünscht den Glanz | — | — | | doubtful |
| 222 | Mein Odem ist schwach | — | — | | by Johann Ernst Bach |
| 224 | Reißt euch los, bekränkte Sinne [frag.] | — | — | | by ? C. P. E. Bach |

| BWV | Title (librettist) | BG | NBA | Remarks |
| --- | --- | --- | --- | --- |
| 246 | St Luke Passion | xlv/2 | — | spurious |
| **ORGAN WORKS** | | | | |
| 536a | Prelude and Fugue in A | — | IV/6 | spurious |
| 561 | Fantasia and Fugue in a | xxxviii | — | doubtful |
| 565 | Toccata in d | xv | — | doubtful |
| 567 | Prelude in C | xxxviii | — | by J. L. Krebs |
| 576 | Fugue in G | xxxviii | — | doubtful |
| 580 | Fugue in D | xxxviii | — | doubtful |
| 581 | Fugue in G | — | — | doubtful |
| 584 | Trio in g | — | — | arr. of BWV166:2 |
| 585 | Trio in c, after J. F. Fasch | xxxviii | IV/5 | doubtful |
| 586 | Trio in G, after Telemann | — | IV/8 | doubtful |
| 587 | Aria in F, after F. Couperin | xxxviii | IV/8 | doubtful |
| 597 | Concerto in E♭ | — | — | arr. by ? C. P. E. Bach |
| 691a | Wer nur den lieben Gott läßt walten | xl | [IV/9] | doubtful |
| 692 | Ach Gott und Herr | xl | — | by J. G. Walther |
| 693 | Ach Gott und Herr | xl | — | by J. G. Walther |
| 695a | Christ lag in Todes Banden | xl | — | doubtful |
| 710 | Wir Christenleut | xl | IV/3 | doubtful |
| 713a | Jesu, meine Freude | — | — | doubtful |
| 723 | Gelobet seist du, Jesu Christ | xl | [IV/9] | doubtful |
| 740 | Wir glauben all an einen Gott, Vater | xl | [IV/9] | by ? J. L. Krebs |
| 742 | Ach Herr, mich armen Sünder | — | — | doubtful |
| 745 | Aus der Tiefe rufe ich | xl | — | by C. P. E. Bach |
| 746 | Christ ist erstanden | xl | — | by J. C. F. Fischer |
| 748 | Gott der Vater wohn bei uns | xl | — | by J. G. Walther |
| 751 | In dulci jubilo | — | — | by Johann Michael Bach |
| 752 | Jesu, der du meine seele | — | — | doubtful |
| 755 | Nun freut euch, lieben Christen | — | — | doubtful |
| 759 | Schmücke dich, o liebe Seele | xl | — | by G. A. Homilius |
| 760 | Vater unser im Himmelreich | xl | — | by G. Böhm |
| 761 | Vater unser im Himmelreich | xl | — | by G. Böhm |

| BWV | Title | BG | NBA | Remarks |
|---|---|---|---|---|
| 763 | Wie schön leuchtet der Morgenstern | — | — | doubtful |
| 771 | Allein Gott in der Höh sei Ehr | xl | — | by ? A. N. Vetter |
| 1096 | Christe, der du bist Tag und Licht | — | IV/9 | by J. Pachelbel |
| | **KEYBOARD WORKS** | | | |
| 824 | Suite in A | xxxvi | — | by G. P. Telemann |
| 834 | Allemande in c | xlii | [V/12] | doubtful |
| 835 | Allemande in a | xlii | — | by J. P. Kirnberger |
| 836 | Allemande in g | xlv/1 | V/5 | ? by W. F. and J. S. Bach |
| 837 | Allemande in g | xlv/1 | V/5 | ? by W. F. and J. S. Bach |
| 838 | Allemande and Courante in A | xlii | [V/12] | by J. C. Graupner |
| 839 | Sarabande in g | — | — | doubtful |
| 840 | Courante in G | — | — | by G. P. Telemann |
| 844 | Scherzo in d/e | xlii | — | by ? W. F. Bach |
| 845 | Gigue in f | xlii | — | doubtful |
| 897 | Prelude and Fugue in a | xlii | [V/12] | Prelude by C. H. Dretzel |
| 898 | Prelude and Fugue in B♭ on the name Bach | — | [V/12] | doubtful |
| 899 | Prelude and Fugue in d | — | [V/12] | doubtful |
| 905 | Fantasia and Fugue in d | xlii | [V/12] | doubtful |
| 907 | Fantasia and Fughetta in B♭ | xlii | [V/12] | by ? G. Kirchhoff |
| 908 | Fantasia and Fughetta in D | xlii | [V/12] | by ? G. Kirchhoff |
| 909 | Concerto and Fugue in c | xlii | [V/12] | doubtful |
| 919 | Fantasia in c | xxxvi | [V/12] | by ? Johann Bernhard Bach |
| 920 | Fantasia in g | xlii | [V/12] | doubtful |
| 924a | Prelude in C | xxxvi | V/5 | by ? W. F. Bach |
| 925 | Prelude in D | xxxvi | V/5 | by ? W. F. Bach |
| 931 | Prelude in a | xxxvi | V/5 | by ? W. F. Bach |
| 932 | Prelude in e [frag.] | xxxvi | V/5 | by ? W. F. Bach |
| 945 | Fugue in e | xlii | [V/12] | doubtful |
| 957 | Fugue in B♭ | xlii | [V/9] | doubtful |
| 960 | Fugue in e | xlii | [V/12] | doubtful |
| 962 | Fugue in e | xlii | — | by J. G. Albrechtsberger |
| 969 | Andante in g | xlii | [V/12] | doubtful |
| 970 | Presto in d | — | [V/12] | by W. F. Bach |

| BWV | Title | BG | NBA | Remarks |
|---|---|---|---|---|
| CHAMBER, ENSEMBLE, AND ORCHESTRAL MUSIC | | | | |
| 1020 | Sonata in g; vn/?fl, hpcd | ix | | by ? C. P. E. Bach |
| 1022 | Sonata in F; vn, hpcd | — | | by ? a Bach pupil |
| 1024 | Sonata in c; vn, bc | — | | by ? J. G. Pisendel |
| 1036 | Sonata in d; 2 vn, hpcd | — | | by C. P. E. Bach |
| 1037 | Sonata in C; 2 vn, hpcd | ix | | by J. G. Goldberg |
| 1070 | Ouverture in g; str, bc | xlv/1 | — | spurious |

# TEXT INCIPITS

The following alphabetical list includes arias, ensembles, and choruses in the vocal works; ariosos, recitatives, and isolated chorales are not included.

## Scoring
The following abbreviations and contractions are used:

| | | | |
|---|---|---|---|
| A | alto | org | organ |
| B | bass | rec | recorder(s) |
| bc | basso continuo | S | soprano |
| bn | bassoon | str | violins 1 and 2, viola |
| cdc | corno da caccia | T | tenor |
| cdt | corno da tirarsi | timp | timpani |
| cnt | cornett | tle | taille |
| fl | flute(s) | tr | trumpet(s) |
| flp | flauto piccolo | trdt | tromba da tirarsi |
| hn | horn(s) | va | viola(s) |
| hpcd | harpsichord | vada | viola d'amore |
| insts | instruments | vadg | viola(s) da gamba |
| ob | oboe(s) | vc | violoncello |
| obda | oboe(s) d'amore | vcp | violoncello piccolo |
| obdc | oboe(s) da caccia | vn | violin(s) |
| orch | orchestra (normally the full complement of instruments in the work concerned) | vnp | violino piccolo |

'chorale' indicates a harmonization for SATB (unless otherwise indicated), with instruments doubling the vocal parts.

| Incipit | Scoring | BWV | BC |
|---|---|---|---|
| Ach bleib bei uns, Herr Jesu Christ | S, vcp, bc | 6:3 | A 57:3 |
| Ach, bleibe doch, mein liebstes Leben | A, vns, bc | 11:4 | D 9:4 |
| Ach, es bleibt in meiner Liebe | A, tr, bc | 77:5 | A 126:5 |
| Ach, es schmeckt doch gar zu gut | S, vn, va, bc | 212:4 | G 32:4 |
| Ach Gott, vom Himmel sieh darein | SATB, orch | 2:1 | A 98:1 |
| Ach Gott, wie manches Herzeleid | SATB, orch | 3:1 | A 33:1 |
| Ach Gott, wie manches Herzeleid | T, bn, bc | 44:4 | A 78:4 |
| Ach großer König, groß zu allen Zeiten | chorale | 245:17 | D 2:17 |
| Ach! Herr Gott, durch die Treue dein | S, bc | 101:3 | A 118:3 |
| Ach Herr, laß dein lieb Engelein | chorale | 149:7 | A 181:7 |
| Ach Herr, laß dein lieb Engelein | chorale | 245:40 | D 2:40 |
| Ach Herr, mein Gott, vergib mir's doch | SA, bc | 113:7 | A 122:7 |
| Ach Herr, mich armen Sünder | SATB, orch | 135:1 | A 100:1 |
| Ach, Herr Schösser, geht nicht gar zu schlimm | B, vn, va, bc | 212:6 | G 32:6 |
| Ach Herr, vergib all unsre Schuld | chorale | 127:5 | A 49:5 |
| Ach Herr, was ist ein Menschenkind | A, ob(da), bc | 110:4 | A 10:4 |
| Ach, ich habe schon erblicket | chorale | 162:6 | A 148:6 |
| Ach, ich sehe, itzt, da ich zur Hochzeit gehe | B, cdt, bn, str, bc | 162:1 | A 148:1 |
| Ach, lege das Sodom der sündlichen Glieder | A, ob, bc | 48:4 | A 144:4 |

584

| Incipit | Scoring | BWV | BC |
|---|---|---|---|
| Ach, lieben Christen, seid getrost | SATB, orch | 114:1 | A 139:1 |
| Ach mein herzliebes Jesulein | SATB, orch | 248:9 | D 7:9 |
| Ach, mein Sinn, wo willt du endlich hin | T, str, bc | 245:13 | D 2:13 |
| Ach, nun ist mein Jesus hin | SATB, orch | 244:30 | D 3:30 |
| Ach schläfrige Seele, wie? | A, obda, str, bc | 115:2 | A 156:2 |
| Ach, schlage doch bald | T, 2 obda, str, bc | 95:5 | A 136:5 |
| Ach senke doch den Geist der Freuden | T, ob, bc | 73:2 | A 35:2 |
| Ach, unaussprechlich ist die Not | A, obda, bc | 116:2 | A 164:2 |
| Ach, wenn wird die Zeit erscheinen | SAT, vn, org, bc | 248:51 | D 7:51 |
| Ach wie flüchtig, ach wie nichtig | SATB, orch | 26:1 | A 162:1 |
| Ach wie flüchtig, ach wie nichtig | chorale | 26:6 | A 162:6 |
| Ach windet euch nicht so, geplagte Seelen | T, 2 ob, org, bc | 245c | D 2b:19 |
| Ach, wir bekennen unsre Schuld | STB, bc | 116:4 | A 164:4 |
| Ach, wo hol ich Armer Rat | B, bc | 25:3 | A 129:3 |
| Ächzen und erbärmlich Weinen | B, 2 rec, vn, bc | 13:5 | A 34:5 |
| Ach, ziehe die Seele mit Seilen der Liebe | T, fl, bc | 96:3 | A 142:3 |
| Adam muß in uns verwesen | T, 2 vn, 2 va, 2 vc, bc | 31:6 | A 55:6 |
| Agnus Dei, qui tollis peccata mundi | A, 2 vn, bc | 232:26 | E 1:25 |
| Allein zu dir, Herr Jesu Christ | SATB, orch | 33:1 | A 127:1 |
| Alleluja | S, tr, str, bc | 51:5 | A 134:5 |
| Alleluja, Alleluja, Alleluja | chorale | 66:6 | A 56:6 |
| Alleluja, gelobet sei Gott | chorale | 110:7 | A 10:7 |
| Aller Augen warten, Herr | SATB, orch | 23:3 | A 47:3 |
| Alles nun, das ihr wollet | SATB, orch | 24:3 | A 102:3 |
| Alles nur nach Gottes Willen | SATB, orch | 72:1 | A 37:1 |
| Alles, was von Gott geboren | SB, ob, str, bc | 80:2 | A 183:2 |
| All solch dein Güt wir preisen | chorale | 16:6 | A 23:6 |
| All solch dein Güt wir preisen | chorale | 28:6 | A 20:6 |
| Alsdann so wirst du mich | chorale | 128:5 | A 76:5 |
| Also hat Gott die Welt geliebt | SATB, orch | 68:1 | A 86:1 |
| Amen, amen, komm, du schöne Freudenkrone | SATB, orch | 61:6 | A 1:6 |
| Amore traditore | B, bc | 203:1 | G 51:1 |
| Andern hat er geholfen | SATB, orch | 244:58d | D 3:58d |
| An dir, du Vorbild großer Frauen | SATB, orch | 198:7 | G 34:7 |
| Angenehme Hempelin | — | 216:3 | G 43:3 |
| Angenehmer Zephyrus | S, vn, bc | 205:9 | G 36:9 |
| Angenehmes Wiederau, freue dich | SATB, orch | 30a:1 | G 31:1 |
| Angenehmes Wiederau, prange nun | SATB, orch | 30a:13 | G 31:13 |
| An irdische Schätze das Herze zu hängen | B, 3 ob, bc | 26:4 | A 162:4 |
| Ärgre dich, o Seele, nicht | SATB, orch | 186:1 | A 108:1 |
| Ätzet dieses Angedenken | A, 2 fl, str, bc | 207:7 | G 37:7 |
| Auch die harte Kreuzesreise | T, 2 obda, bc | 123:3 | A 28:3 |
| Auch mit gedämpften, schwachen Stimmen | S, vn, bc | 36(1):4 | A 3:4 |
| Auf, auf, mit hellem Schall | B, tr, str, bc | 128:3 | A 76:3 |
| Auf Christi Himmelfahrt allein | SATB, orch | 128:1 | A 76:1 |
| Auf daß wir also allzugleich | chorale | 176:6 | A 92:6 |
| Aufgeblasne Hitze | A, 2 fl, bc | 201:13 | G 46:13 |
| Auf, Gläubige! singet die lieblichen Lieder | T, 2 ob, str, bc | 134:2 | A 59:2 |
| Auf Gott steht meine Zuversicht | B, str, bc | 138:4 | A 132:4 |
| Auf ihn magst du es wagen | B, str, bc | 107:3 | A 109:3 |
| Auf meinen Flügeln sollst du schweben | T, ob, vn, bc | 213:7 | G 18:7 |
| Auf meinen lieben Gott | chorale | 188:6 | A 154:6 |
| Auf, schmetternde Töne der muntern Trompeten | SATB, orch | 207a:1 | G 22:1 |

| Incipit | Scoring | BWV | BC |
|---|---|---|---|
| Auf sperren sie den Rachen weit | SATB, bc | 178:5 | A 112:5 |
| Auf, und rühmt des höchsten Güte | — | 195 | [B 14b:6] |
| August lebe, lebe, König | SATB, orch | 207a:9 | G 22:9 |
| Augustus Namenstages Schimmer | T, obda, str, bc | 207a:3 | G 22:3 |
| Aus der Tiefen rufe ich, Herr, zu dir | SATB, orch | 131:1 | B 25:1 |
| Aus Gottes milden Vaterhänden | T, obda, bc | 36b:3 | G 38:3 |
| Aus Liebe will mein Heiland sterben | S, fl, 2 obdc | 244:49 | D 3:49 |
| Aus tiefer Not schrei ich zu dir | SATB, orch | 38:1 | A 152:1 |
| Bäche von gesalznen Zähren | T, str, bc | 21:5 | A 99a:5 |
| Bald zur Rechten, bald zur Linken | B, 2 ob, str, bc | 96:5 | A 142:5 |
| Barmherziges Herze der ewigen Liebe | ST, ob/tr, bc | 185:1 | A 101:1 |
| Beglückte Herde, Jesu Schafe | B, obda, str, bc | 104:5 | A 65:5 |
| Beglückte Neißenstadt [frag.] | SA, ? | 216:1 | G 43:1 |
| Bekennen will ich seinen Namen | A, 2 vn, bc | 200 | A 192 |
| Benedictus qui venit | T, fl/vn, bc | 232:25 | E 1:24 |
| Bereite dich, Zion, mit zärtlichen Trieben | A, obda, vn, bc | 248:4 | D 7:4 |
| Bereite dir, Jesu, noch itzo die Bahn | S, vn, bc | 147:5 | A 174:5 |
| Bereitet die Wege, bereitet die Bahn | S, ob, str, bc | 132:1 | A 6:1 |
| Beruft Gott selbst, so muß der Segen | SA, 2 obda, 2 vn, bc | 88:5 | A 105:5 |
| Bete aber auch dabei | S, fl, vcp, bc | 115:4 | A 156:4 |
| Betorte Welt, betorte Welt | A, fl, bc | 94:4 | A 115:4 |
| Beweis dein Macht, Herr Jesu Christ | chorale | 6:6 | A 57:6 |
| Bewundert, o Menschen, dies große Geheimnis | T, 2 ob, str, bc | 62:2 | A 2:2 |
| Bin ich gleich von dir gewichen | chorale | 55:5 | A 157:5 |
| Bisher habt ihr nichts gebeten | B, 2 ob, obdc, str, bc | 87:1 | A 74:1 |
| Bist du, der mir helfen soll | B, bc | 186:3 | A 108:3 |
| Bist du nicht seiner Junger einer | SATB, 2 ob, str, bc | 245:12b | D 2:12b |
| Blast die wohlgegriffnen Flöten | S, 2 fl, bc | 214:3 | G 19:3 |
| Blast Lärmen, ihr Feinde! Verstarket die Macht | — | 205a:1 | [G 20:1] |
| Bleib bei uns, denn es will Abend werden | SATB, orch | 6:1 | A 57:1 |
| Bleibet nun in eurer Ruh | — | 244a:20 | [B 22:20] |
| Bleibt, ihr Engel, bleibt bei mir | T, tr, str, bc | 19:5 | A 180:5 |
| Blühet, ihr Linden in Sachsen | SATB, orch | 214:9 | G 19:9 |
| Blute nur, du liebes Herz | S, 2 fl, str, bc | 244:8 | D 3:8 |
| Brich an, o schönes Morgenlicht | chorale | 248:12 | D 7:12 |
| Brich dem Hungrigen dein Brot | SATB, orch | 39:1 | A 96:1 |
| Bringet dem Herrn Ehre seines Namens | SATB, tr, str, bc | 148:1 | A 140:1 |
| Buß und Reu knirscht das Sündenherz entzwei | A, 2 fl, bc | 244:6 | D 3:6 |
| Capital und Interessen | T, 2 obda, bc | 168:3 | A 116:3 |
| Cedern müssen von den Winden | ATB, bn, bc | 150:5 | B 24:5 |
| Chi in amore ha nemica la sorte | B, hpcd | 203:3 | G 51:3 |
| Christe, du Lamm Gottes | SATB, orch | 23:4 | A 47:4 |
| Christe eleison | SS, 2 vn, bc | 232:2 | E 1:2 |
| Christe eleison | SA, bc | 242 | E 8 |
| Christen, ätzet diesen Tag | SATB, orch | 63:1 | A 8:1 |
| Christenkinder, freuet euch | T, 2 hn, 2 ob, bc | 40:7 | A 12:7 |
| Christen müssen auf der Erden | A, ob, bc | 44:3 | A 78:3 |
| Christi Glieder, ach bedenket | A, vn, bc | 132:5 | A 6:5 |
| Christ lag in Todes Banden | SATB, orch | 4:2 | A 54:2 |
| Christum wir sollen loben schon | SATB, orch | 121:1 | A 13:1 |
| Christ unser Herr zum Jordan kam | SATB, orch | 7:1 | A 177:1 |
| Christus, der ist mein Leben | SATB, orch | 95:1 | A 136:1 |
| Christus, der uns selig macht | chorale | 245:15 | D 2:15 |

| Incipit | Scoring | BWV | BC |
|---|---|---|---|
| Confiteor unum baptisma | SSATB, bc | 232:20 | E 1:20 |
| Credo in unum Deum | SSATB, 2 vn, bc | 232:13 | E 1:13 |
| Credo in unum Deum | SSATB, orch | 232:14 | E 1:14 |
| Crucifixus | SATB, 2 fl, str, bc | 232:17 | E 1:17 |
| Cum Sancto Spiritu | SSATB, orch | 232:12 | E1 1:12 |
| Cum Sancto Spiritu | SATB, orch | 233:6 | E6:6 |
| Cum Sancto Spiritu | SATB, 2 fl, str, bc | 234:6 | E3:6 |
| Cum Sancto Spiritu | SATB, 2 fl, str, bc | 235:6 | E5:6 |
| Cum Sancto Spiritu | SATB, 2 ob, str, bc | 236:6 | E4:6 |
| Dahero Trotz der Höllen Heer | chorale | 139:6 | A 159:6 |
| Darum ob ich schon dulde | — | 186a | [A 5:6] |
| Darum sollt ihr nicht sorgen | B, 2 vn, bc | 187:4 | A 110:4 |
| Darum wir billig loben dich | chorale | 130:6 | A 179:6 |
| Darzu ist erschienen der Sohn Gottes | SATB, orch | 40:1 | A 12:1 |
| Das Aug allein das Wasser sieht | chorale | 7:7 | A 177:7 |
| Das Blut, so meine Schuld durchstreicht | T, fl, bc | 78:4 | A 130:4 |
| Das Brausen von den rauhen Winden | B, bc | 92:6 | A 42:6 |
| Das Gute, das dein Gott beschert | A, fl, str, bc | 36b:5 | G 38:5 |
| Das hat er alles uns getan | chorale | 64:2 | A 15:2 |
| Das ist der Christen Kunst | B, bc | 185:5 | A 101:5 |
| Das ist des Vaters Wille | chorale | 73:5 | A 35:5 |
| Das ist galant | S, vn, va, bc | 212:10 | G 32:10 |
| Das Lamm, das erwürget ist | SATB, orch | 21:11 | A 99:11 |
| Das neue Regiment | SATB, orch | 71:7 | B 1:7 |
| Das neugeborne Kindelein | SATB, orch | 122:1 | A 19:1 |
| Das Unglück schlägt auf allen Seiten | B, 2 obda, vn, bc | 139:4 | A 159:4 |
| Das wollst du, Gott, bewahren rein | chorale | 2:6 | A 98:6 |
| Das Wort sie sollen lassen stahn | chorale | 80:8 | A 183:8 |
| Dein Alter sei wie deine Jugend | SATB, bc | 71:3 | B 1:3 |
| Dein Blut, der edle Saft | SATB, orch | 136:6 | A 111:6 |
| Das Blut, so meine Schuld durchstreicht | T, fl, bc | 78:4 | A 130:4 |
| Deine Hilfe zu mir sende | chorale | 194:6 | A 91a:6, B 31:6 |
| Dein Geist, den Gott vom Himmel gibt | chorale | 108:6 | A 72:6 |
| Dein Glanz all Finsternis verzehrt | chorale | 248:46 | D 7:46 |
| Dein ist allein die Ehre | chorale | 41:6 | A 22:6 |
| Dein Name gleich der Sonnen geh | B, vc, bn, hpcd, violone | 173a:7 | G 9:7 |
| Dein sonst hell beliebter Schein | S, str, bc | 176:3 | A 92:3 |
| Dein Wachstum sei feste und lache vor Lust | B, vn, bc | 212:20 | G 32:20 |
| Dein Wetter zog sich auf von weiten | B, trdt/cdt, str, bc | 46:3 | A 117:3 |
| Dein Will gescheh, Herr Gott, zugleich | chorale | 245:5 | D 2:5 |
| Dein Wort laß mich bekennen | — | 147a | [A 7:6] |
| Dem Gerechten muß das Licht | SATB, orch | 195:1 | B 14:1 |
| Dem wir das Heilig itzt | SATB, orch | 129:5 | A 93:5 |
| Den Glauben mir verleihe | chorale | 37:6 | A 75:6 |
| Den Himmel und auch die Erden | chorale | 178:7 | A 112:7 |
| Denn das Gesetz des Geistes | SSA | 227:4 | C 5:4 |
| Denn du willst kein Opfer haben | SA, str, bc | 1083:12 | B 26:12 |
| Den soll mein Lorbeer schützend decken | SB, bc | 207:5 | G 37:5 |
| Den Tod niemand zwingen kunnt | SA, cnt, tr, bc | 4:3 | A 54:3 |
| Deposuit potentes | T, vns, bc | 243:8 | E 14:8 |
| Der alte Drache brennt vor Neid | B, 3 tr, timp, bc | 130:3 | A 179:3 |
| Der du bist dem Vater gleich | T, 2 obda, bc | 36(2):6 | A 3:6 |
| Der du den Tempel Gottes zerbrichst | SATB, SATB, 2 orch | 244:58b | D 3:58b |
| Der Ewigkeit saphirnes Haus | T, insts, bc | 198:8 | G 34:8 |
| Der ewig reiche Gott | SB, fl, ob, str, bc | 192:2 | A 188:2 |

# Appendix 2

| Incipit | Scoring | BWV | BC |
|---|---|---|---|
| Der Geist hilft unser Schwachheit auf | SATB, SATB | 226:1 | C 2:1 |
| Der Glaube ist das Pfand der Liebe | T, bc | 37:2 | A 75:2 |
| Der Glaube schafft der Seele Flügel | B, obda, str, bc | 37:5 | A 75:5 |
| Der Gott, der mir hat versprochen | A, rec, obdc, str, bc | 13:3 | A 34:3 |
| Der Heiland kennet ja die Seinen | A, 2 ob, bc | 109:5 | A 151:5 |
| Der Herr denket an uns | SATB, orch | 196:2 | B 11:2 |
| Der Herr hat Guts an uns getan | SATB, orch | 119:7 | B 3:7 |
| Der Herr ist mein getreuer Hirt | SATB, orch | 112:1 | A 67:1 |
| Der Herr ist mein getreuer Hirt | S, 2 ob, bc | 85:3 | A 66:3 |
| Der Herr ist mein getreuer Hirt | chorale | 104:6 | A 65:6 |
| Der Herr segne euch je mehr und mehr | TB, str, bc | 196:4 | B 11:4 |
| Der Himmel lacht! die Erde jubilieret | SATB, orch | 31:2 | A 55:2 |
| Der Leib zwar in der Erden | SATB, bc | 161:6 | A 135:6 |
| Der rufet dem Elias! | SATB, bc | 244:61b | D 3:61b |
| Der schädlichen Dornen unendliche Zahl | T, bc | 181:3 | A 45:3 |
| Der Tag, der dich vordem gebar | B, str, bc | 36c:5 | G 35:5 |
| Der Zeiten Herr hat viel vergnügte Stunden | A, bc | 134a:6 | G 5:6 |
| Der zeitlichen Ehrn will ich gern entbehrn | chorale | 47:5 | A 141:5 |
| Des Höchsten Gegenwart allein | T, bc | 194:8 | A 91a:8, B 31:8 |
| Des Vaters Stimme ließ sich hören | T, 2 vn, bc | 7:4 | A 177:4 |
| Dich erzürnt mein Tun und Lassen | A, str, bc | 1083:4 | B 26:4 |
| Dich hab ich je und je geliebet | SB, obda, str, org, bc | 49:6 | A 150:6 |
| Die Anmut umfange, das Glück bediene | SSTB, orch | 208:15 | G 1:15 |
| Die Armen will der Herr umarmen | S, 2 vn, bc | 186:8 | A 108:8 |
| Die Armut, so Gott auf sich nimmt | SA, 2 vn, bc | 91:5 | A 9b:5 |
| Die Augen sehn nach deiner Leiche | — | 244a:24 | [B 22:24] |
| Die Dankbarkeit, so Tag und Nacht | — | 36a | [G 12:4] |
| Die Elenden sollen essen | SATB, orch | 75:1 | A 94:1 |
| Die Feind sind all in deiner Hand | chorale | 178:7 | A 112:7 |
| Die Freude reget sich | SATB, bc | 36b:1 | G 38:1 |
| Die Himmel erzählen die Ehre Gottes | SATB, orch | 76:1 | A 97:1 |
| Die himmlische Vorsicht der ewigen Gute | SATB, orch | 206:11 | G 23, 26:11 |
| Die Hoffnung wart' der rechten Zeit | chorale | 86:6 | A 73:6 |
| Die Hoffnung wart' der rechten Zeit | SATB, orch | 186:11 | A 108:11 |
| Die Katze läßt das Mausen nicht | STB, fl, str, bc | 211:10 | G 48:10 |
| Die Kön'ge aus Saba kamen dar | chorale | 65:2 | A 27:2 |
| Die Liebe führt mit sanften Schritten | T, obda, bc | 36c:3 | G 35:3 |
| Die Liebe zieht mit sanften Schritten | T, obda, bc | 36(2):3 | A 3a:3 |
| Die Obrigkeit ist Gottes Gabe | A, 2 rec, bc | 119:5 | B 3:5 |
| Die Schätzbarkeit der weiten Erden | S, vn, bc | 204:4 | G 45:4 |
| Die schäumenden Wellen von Belials Bächen | T, str, bc | 81:3 | A 39:3 |
| Die Seele ruht in Jesu Händen | S, 2 rec, ob, str, bc | 127:3 | A 49:3 |
| Dies hat er alles uns getan | chorale | 248:28 | D 7:28 |
| Die Sonne zieht mit sanftem Triebe | — | 36a:3 | [G 12:3] |
| Die Sund macht Leid | chorale | 40:3 | A 12:3 |
| Die Welt ist wie ein Rauch und Schatten | B, bc | 94:2 | A 115:2 |
| Die Welt kann ihre Lust und Freud | T, str, bc | 94:6 | A 115:6 |
| Die Welt mit allen Königreichen | B, vn, bc | 59:4 | A 82:4 |
| Doch bin und bleibe ich vergnügt | S, vns, bc | 150:3 | B 24:3 |
| Doch Jesus will auch bei der Strafe | A, 2 rec, 2 obdc | 46:5 | A 117:5 |
| Doch, Königin! du stirbest nicht | SATB, orch | 198:10 | G 34:10 |
| Doch weichet, ihr tollen, vergeblichen Sorgen | B, fl, str, bc | 8:4 | A 137:4 |
| Domine Deus, Agnus Dei | SA, 2 vn, bc | 236:4 | E 4:4 |

| Incipit | Scoring | BWV | BC |
|---|---|---|---|
| Domine Deus, rex coelestis | ST, fl, str, bc | 232:8 | E 1:8 |
| Domine Deus, rex coelestis | B, str, bc | 233:3 | E 6:3 |
| Domine Deus, rex coelestis | B, vn, bc | 234:3 | E 3:3 |
| Domine Fili unigenite | ST, fl, str, bc | 232:8 | E 1:8 |
| Domine Fili unigenite | A, ob, str, bc | 235:4 | E 5:4 |
| Dona nobis pacem | SATB, orch | 232:27 | E 1:26 |
| Drum fahrt nur immer hin, ihr Eitelkeiten | chorale | 123:6 | A 28:6 |
| Drum ich mich ihm ergebe | T, 2 fl, bc | 107:6 | A 109:6 |
| Drum so laßt uns immerdar | chorale | 115:6 | A 156:6 |
| Drum will ich, weil ich lebe noch | chorale | 153:9 | A 25:9 |
| Drum wir auch billig fröhlich sein | chorale | 145:5 | A 60:5 |
| Du bereitest für mir einen Tisch | ST, str, bc | 112:4 | A 67:4 |
| Du bist ein Geist, der lehret | chorale | 183:5 | A 79:5 |
| Du bist geboren mir zugute | B, 2 ob, tle, bc | 68:4 | A 86:4 |
| Du Friedefürst, Herr Jesu Christ | SATB, orch | 116:1 | A 164:1 |
| Du Friedefürst, Herr Jesu Christ | chorale | 67:7 | A 62:7 |
| Du heilige Brunst, süßer Trost | — | 120*b*:6 | B 28:6 |
| Du heilige Brunst, süßer Trost | chorale | 226:2 | C 2:2 |
| Du Herr, du krönst allein das Jahr | A, ob, str, bc | 187:3 | A 110:3 |
| Du Hirte Israel, höre | SATB, orch | 104:1 | A 65:1 |
| Du Lebensfürst, Herr Jesu Christ | chorale | 43:11 | A 77:11 |
| Du machst, o Tod, mir nun nicht ferner bange | A, ob, str, bc | 114:5 | A 139:5 |
| Du mußt glauben, du mußt hoffen | AT, bn, bc | 155:2 | A 32:2 |
| Durch die von Eifer entflammeten Waffen | S, 2 fl, vn, va | 215:7 | G 21:7 |
| Durch mächtige Kraft | A, 3 tr, timp, bc | 71:5 | B 1:5 |
| Durchs Feuer wird das Silber rein | T, 2 ob, str, bc | 2:5 | A 98:5 |
| Du sollt Gott, deinen Herren, lieben | SATB, orch | 77:1 | A 126:1 |
| Du süße Lieb(e), schenk uns deine Gunst | chorale | 197:5 | B 16:5 |
| Du wahrer Gott und Davids Sohn | SA, 2 ob, bc | 23:1 | A 47:1 |
| Du wollest dem Feinde nicht geben | SATB, orch | 71:6 | B 1:6 |
| Ehre sei dir, Gott, gesungen | SATB, orch | 248:43 | D 7:43 |
| Ehre sei Gott in der Höhe | — | 197*a*:1 | A 11:1 |
| Ehre sei Gott in der Höhe | SATB, orch | 248:21 | D 7:21 |
| Ehr sei Gott in dem höchsten Thron | chorale | 33:6 | A 127:6 |
| Ehr sei ins Himmels Throne | chorale | 135:6 | A 100:6 |
| Eile, Herz, voll Freudigkeit | T, str, bc | 83:3 | A 167:3 |
| Eilt, ihr angefochtnen Seelen | SATB, str, bc | 245:24 | D 2:24 |
| Eilt, ihr Stunden, kommt herbei | S, vns, bc | 30:10 | A 178:10 |
| Eine Stimme läßt sich hören | chorale | 30:6 | A 178:6 |
| Ein feste Burg ist unser Gott | SATB, orch | 80:1 | A 183:1 |
| Ein Fürst ist seines Landes Pan | B, 2 ob, tle, bc | 208:7 | G 1, 3:7 |
| Ein geheiligtes Gemüte | T, 2 fl, str, bc | 173:2 | A 85:2 |
| Ein unbarmherziges Gerichte | A, bc | 89:3 | A 155:3 |
| Ein unbegreiflich Licht erfüllt | TB, 2 vn, bc | 125:4 | A 168:4 |
| Ein ungefärbt Gemüte | A, str, bc | 24:1 | A 102:1 |
| Ei nun, mein Gott, so fall ich dir | chorale | 65:7 | A 27:7 |
| Ei nun, mein Gott, so fall ich dir | chorale | 92:7 | A 42:7 |
| Ei! wie schmeckt der Coffee süße | S, fl, bc | 211:4 | G 48:4 |
| Empfind ich Höllenangst und Pein | B, bc | 3:3 | A 33:3 |
| Endlich, endlich wird mein Joch | B, ob, bc | 56:3 | A 146:3 |
| Entfliehet, verschwindet, entweichet, ihr Sorgen | — | 249*a*:3 | [G 2:3] |
| Entsetze dich, mein Herze, nicht | B, bc | 111:2 | A 36:2 |
| Entziehe dich eilends, mein Herze, der Welt | SA, bc | 124:5 | A 30:5 |

| Incipit | Scoring | BWV | BC |
|---|---|---|---|
| Entzücket uns beide, ihr Strahlen der Freude | ST, vn, bc | 208:12 | G 1, 3:12 |
| Erbarm dich mein in solcher Last | A, vns, bc | 113:2 | A 122:2 |
| Erbarme dich! Laß die Tränen | T, fl, bc | 55:3 | A 157:3 |
| Erbarme dich, mein Gott | A, str, bc | 244:39 | D 3:39 |
| Er denket der Barmherzigkeit | AT, tr, 2 ob, bc | 10:5 | A 175:5 |
| Erforsche mich, Gott, und erfahre mein Herz | SATB, orch | 136:1 | A 111:1 |
| Erfreue dich, Seele | T, bc | 21:10 | A 99:10 |
| Erfreut euch, ihr Herzen | SATB, orch | 66:1 | A 56:1 |
| Erfreute Zeit im neuen Bunde | A, 2 ob, 2 hn, str, bc | 83:1 | A 167:1 |
| Erfüllet, ihr himmlischen göttlichen Flammen | A, obdc, bc | 1:3 | A 173:3 |
| Ergieße dich reichlich, du göttliche Quelle | T, va, bc | 5:3 | A 145:3 |
| Ergötzet auf Erden | SATB, 2 ob, str, bc | 134a:8 | G 5:8 |
| Erhalt mein Herz im Glauben rein | chorale | 3:6 | A 33:6 |
| Erhalt mein Herz im Glauben rein | chorale | 153:9 | A 25:9 |
| Erhalt uns, Herr, bei deinem Wort | SATB, orch | 126:1 | A 46:1 |
| Erholet euch, betrübte Sinnen | T, tr, str, bc | 103:5 | A 69:5 |
| Er ist auf Erden kommen arm | SB, ob, obda, bc | 248:7 | D 71:7 |
| Er ist das Heil und selig Licht | chorale | 83:5 | A 167:5 |
| Er ist das Heil und selig Licht | chorale | 125:6 | A 168:6 |
| Er kann und will dich lassen nicht | SATB, 2 obda, str, bc | 138:3 | A 132:3 |
| Erkenne mich, mein Hüter | chorale | 244:15 | D 3:15 |
| Er kennt die rechten Freudenstunden | SA, str, bc | 93:4 | A 104:4 |
| Erleucht auch meine finstre Sinnen | B, obda, bc | 248:47 | D 7:47 |
| Erleucht auch unser Sinn und Herz | chorale | 116:6 | A 164:6 |
| Ermuntert euch, furchtsam | A, 2 ob, obda, bc | 176:5 | A 92:5 |
| Ermuntre dich, mein Heiland klopft | T, fl, bc | 180:2 | A 149:2 |
| Er nahm alles wohl in acht | chorale | 245:28 | D 2:28 |
| Er richts zu seinen Ehren | S, 2 obda, bc | 107:5 | A 109:5 |
| Erschallet, ihr Himmel, erfreue dich, Erde | SATB, 2 ob, str, bc | 134:6 | A 59:6 |
| Erschallet, ihr Lieder | SATB, orch | 172:1, 7 | A 81:1, 7 |
| Erschienen ist der herrlich Tag | chorale | 67:4 | A 62:4 |
| Erschrecke doch, du allzu sichre Seele | T, fl/vnp, bc | 102:5 | A 119:5 |
| Erschüttre dich nur nicht, verzagte Seele | T, fl, bc | 99:3 | A 133:3 |
| Er segnet, die den Herrn fürchten | S, vns, bc | 196:3 | B 11:3 |
| Ertöt uns durch dein Güte | SATB, ob, str, bc | 22:5 | A 48:5 |
| Ertöt uns durch dein Güte | chorale | 96:6 | A 142:6 |
| Ertöt uns durch dein Güte | — | 132:6 | A 6:6 |
| Ertöt uns durch dein Güte | chorale | 164:6 | A 128:6 |
| Erwäge, wie sein blutgefärbter Rücken | T, 2 vada, bc | 245:20 | D 2:20 |
| Erwahlte Pleißen-Stadt | — | 216a:1 | [G 47:1] |
| Erzählet, ihr Himmel die Ehre Gottes | — | 197a:2 | [A 11:2] |
| Es bringt das rechte Jubeljahr | chorale | 122:6 | A 19:6 |
| Es danke, Gott, und lobe dich | chorale | 69:6 | B 10:6 |
| Es danke, Gott, und lobe dich | SATB, orch | 76:14 | A 97:14 |
| Es danke, Gott, und lobe dich | — | 190a:7 | B 27:7 |
| Es dünket mich, ich seh dich kommen | T, vcp, bc | 175:4 | A 89:4 |
| Es erhub sich ein Streit | SATB, orch | 19:1 | A 180:1 |
| Es halt es mit der blinden Welt | S, obda, bc | 94:7 | A 115:7 |
| Es ist das Heil uns kommen her | SATB, orch | 9:1 | A 107:1 |
| Es ist dir gesagt, Mensch, was gut ist | SATB, orch | 45:1 | A 113:1 |
| Es ist ein trotzig und verzagt Ding | SATB, orch | 176:1 | A 92:1 |
| Es ist genung | chorale | 60:5 | A 161:5 |
| Es ist euch gut, daß ich hingehe | B, obda, str, bc | 108:1 | A 72:1 |
| Es ist nichts Gesundes an meinem Leibe | SATB, orch | 25:1 | A 129:1 |

| Incipit | Scoring | BWV | BC |
|---|---|---|---|
| Es ist und bleibt der Christen Trost | S, 2 ob, bn, str, bc | 44:6 | A 78:6 |
| Es ist vollbracht, das Leid ist alle | B, ob, str, bc | 159:4 | A 50:4 |
| Es ist vollbracht! O Trost | A, vadg, bc | 245:30 | D 2:30 |
| Es kommt aber die Zeit | SATB, orch | 44:2 | A 78:2 |
| Es kommt ein Tag | A, obda, bc | 136:3 | A 111:3 |
| Es nehme zehntausend Dukaten | B, hn, vn, va, bc | 212:16 | G 32:16 |
| Es reißet euch ein schrecklich Ende | T, str, bc | 90:1 | A 163:1 |
| Es strahle die Sonne, es lache die Wonne | — | 66a:8 | [G 4:8] |
| Es streiten, es siegen/prangen | AT, str, bc | 134a:4 | G 5:4 |
| Esurientes implevit bonis | A, 2 fl, bc | 243:9 | E 13:9, E 14:9 |
| Es war ein wunderlicher Krieg | SATB, bc | 4:5 | A 54:5 |
| Es wartet alles auf dich | SATB, orch | 187:1 | A 110:1 |
| Es woll uns Gott genädig sein | SATB, orch | 76:7 | A 97:7, A 185:7 |
| Et expecto resurrectionem | SSATB, orch | 232:21 | E 1:21 |
| Et exsultavit | S, str, bc | 243:2 | E 13:2, E 14:2 |
| Et incarnatus est | SSATB, 2 vn, bc | 232:16 | E 1:16 |
| Et in Spiritum Sanctum | SSATB, orch | 232:19 | E 1:19 |
| Et in terra pax | SSATB, orch | 191:1 | E 16:1 |
| Et in terra pax | SSATB, orch | 232:5 | E 1:5 |
| Et in terra pax | SATB, orch | 234:2 | E 3:2 |
| Et in unum Dominum | SA, 2 obda, str, bc | 232:15 | E 1:15 |
| Et misericordia | AT, 2 fl, str, bc | 243:6 | E 13:6, E 14:6 |
| Et resurrexit | SSATB, orch | 232:18 | E 1:18 |
| Ewigkeit, du machst mir bange | T, str, bc | 20:3 | A 95:3 |
| Fahr hin, abgöttische Zunft | B, tr, str, bc | 76:5 | A 97:5, A 185:5 |
| Fallt mit Danken, fallt mit Loben | SATB, orch | 248:36 | D 7:36 |
| Falscher Heuchler Ebenbild | T, 2 ob, str, bc | 179:3 | A 121:3 |
| Fecit potentiam | SSATB, orch | 243:7 | E 13:7, E 14:7 |
| Flößt, mein Heiland, flößt dein Namen | SS, ob, bc | 248:39 | D 7:39 |
| Freilich trotzt Augustus Name | T, 2 obda, str, bc | 215:3 | G 21:3 |
| Freu dich sehr, o meine Seele | chorale | 70:7 | A 165:7 |
| Freue dich, erlöste Schar | SATB, orch | 30:1 | A 178:1 |
| Freue dich, geheiligte Schar | SATB, orch | 30:12 | A 178:12 |
| Freut euch und jubiliert | SSATB, bc | 243a:B | E 13:B |
| Friede sei mit euch | SATB, orch | 67:6 | A 62:6 |
| Friede über Israel! Dankt | SATB, orch | 34:5 | A 84:5 |
| Friede über Israell Eilt | SATB, orch | 34a:4 | B 13:4 |
| Frische Schatten, meine Freude | T, vada, vadg, bc | 205:5 | G 36:5 |
| Frohe Hirten, eilt, ach eilet | T, fl, bc | 248:15 | D 7:15 |
| Fromme Musen! meine Glieder | A, 2 ob, bc | 214:5 | G 19:5 |
| Führ auch mein Herz und Sinn | chorale | 5:7 | A 145:7 |
| Führ auch mein Herz und Sinn | chorale (SB) | 163:6 | A 158:6 |
| Fünfzig Taler bares Geld | B, vn, va, bc | 212:12 | G 32:12 |
| Fürchte dich nicht, ich bin bei dir | SATB, SATB | 228:1 | C 4:1 |
| Fürchte dich nicht, ich bin mit dir | B, bc | 153:3 | A 25:3 |
| Fürst des Lebens, starker Streiter | B, vc, bc | 31:4 | A 55:4 |
| Fürwahr, wenn mir das kömmet ein | B, 2 ob(da), bc | 113:3 | A 122:3 |
| Gebt mir meinen Jesum wieder | B, str, bc | 244:42 | D 3:42 |
| Gedenk an Jesu bittern Tod | SA, fl, obdc, bc | 101:6 | A 118:6 |
| Gedenk an uns mit deiner Liebe | S, ob, str, bc | 29:5 | B 8:5 |
| Geduld, wenn mich falsche Zungen stechen | T, vadg, bc | 244:35 | D 3:35 |
| Gegrüßet seist du, Judenkönig | SATB, SATB, 2 orch | 244:53b | D 3:53b |
| Geht, ihr Wünsche, geht behende | — | 249b:9 | [G 28:9] |
| Geh, Leopold, zu deiner Ruh | — | 244a:19 | [B 22:19] |
| Geist und Seele wird verwirret | A, 2 ob, tle, str, bc | 35:2 | A 125:2 |
| Geliebter Jesu, du allein | T, obdc/va, bc | 16:5 | A 23:5 |

## Appendix 2

| Incipit | Scoring | BWV | BC |
|---|---|---|---|
| Gelobet sei der Herr, mein Gott | SATB, orch | 129:1 | A 93:1 |
| Gelobet sei der Herr, mein Gott | B, bc | 129:2 | A 93:2 |
| Gelobet sei der Herr, mein Gott | S, fl, vn, bc | 129:3 | A 93:3 |
| Gelobet sei der Herr, mein Gott | A, obda, bc | 129:4 | A 93:4 |
| Gelobet sei Gott, gelobet sein Name | B, str, bc | 30:3 | A 178:3 |
| Gelobet seist du, Jesu Christ | SATB, orch | 91:1 | A 9:1 |
| Genügsamkeit ist ein Schatz in diesem Leben | S, obda, bc | 144:5 | A 41:5 |
| Gerechter Gott, ach, rechnest du | S, ob, bc | 89:5 | A 155:5 |
| Gerne will ich mich bequemen | B, 2 vn, bc | 244:23 | D 3:23 |
| Geschwinde, ihr wirbelnden Winde | SSAATTBB, orch | 201:1 | G 46:1 |
| Gesegnete Christen, glückselige Herde | SA, 2 fl, str, bc | 184:2 | A 88:2 |
| Getrost! es faßt ein heilger Leib | A, 2 obda, bc | 133:2 | A 16:2 |
| Gewaltige stößt Gott vom Stuhl | B, bc | 10:4 | A 175:4 |
| Gib, daß ich tu mit Fleiß | chorale | 45:7 | A 113:7 |
| Gib, höchster Gott, auch hier dem Worte Kraft | SATB, str, bc | 34a:7 | B 13:7 |
| Gib, Schöne, viel Söhne | S, hn, vn, va, bc | 212:18 | G 32:18 |
| Gleichwie die wilden Meereswellen | B, str, bc | 178:3 | A 112:3 |
| Gloria in excelsis Deo | SSATB, orch | 191:1 | E 16:1 |
| Gloria in excelsis Deo | SSATB, orch | 232:4 | E 1:4 |
| Gloria in excelsis Deo | SATB, orch | 233:2 | E 6:2 |
| Gloria in excelsis Deo | SATB, 2 fl, str, bc | 234:2 | E 3:2 |
| Gloria in excelsis Deo | SATB, 2 ob, str, bc | 235:2 | E 5:2 |
| Gloria in excelsis Deo | SATB, 2 ob, str, bc | 236:2 | E 4:2 |
| Gloria in excelsis Deo | SSATB, orch | 243a:C | E 13:C |
| Gloria Patri et Filio | ST, 2 fl, str, bc | 191:2 | E 16:2 |
| Gloria Patri, gloria Filio | SSATB, orch | 243:12 | E 13:12, E 14:12 |
| Gloria sei dir gesungen | chorale | 140:7 | A 166:7 |
| Glorie, Lob, Ehr und Herrlichkeit | SATB, 2 fl, vadg, bc | 106:4 | B 18:4 |
| Glück und Heil bleibe dein beständig Teil | — | 249a:11 | [G 2:11] |
| Glück und Segen sind bereit | T, vn, bc | 184:4 | A 88:4 |
| Gold aus Ophir ist zu schlecht | B, 2 obdc, bc | 65:4 | A 27:4 |
| Gott, ach Gott, verlaß die Deinen nimmermehr | SB, 2 vn, bc | 79:5 | A 184:5 |
| Gott, bei deinem starken Schützen | B, 2 ob, bc | 14:4 | A 40:4 |
| Gott, dem der Erden Kreis zu klein | T, 3 ob, bc | 91:3 | A 9:3 |
| Gott, der du die Liebe heißt | TB, 2 ob, bc | 33:5 | A 127:5 |
| Gott der Herr ist Sonn und Schild | SATB, orch | 79:1 | A 184:1 |
| Gott, du hast es wohl gefüget | SB, ob, bc | 63:3 | A 8:3 |
| Gottes Engel weichen nie | S, str, bc | 149:4 | A 181:4 |
| Gottes Wort, das trüget nicht | SA, obdc, bc | 167:3 | A 176:3 |
| Gottes Zeit ist die allerbeste Zeit | SATB, 2 fl, 2 vadg, bc | 106:2 | B 18:2a |
| Gott fähret auf mit Jauchzen | SATB, orch | 43:1 | A 77:1 |
| Gott hat alles wohlgemacht | A, org, bc | 35:4 | A 125:4 |
| Gott hat die Erde zugericht | chorale | 187:7 | A 110:7 |
| Gott hat uns im heurigen Jahre gesegnet | AT, bc | 28:5 | A 20:5 |
| Gott hilft gewiß | T, str, bc | 86:5 | A 73:5 |
| Gott ist gerecht in seinen Werken | B, 3 ob, bc | 20:5 | A 95:5 |
| Gott ist mein Freund; was hilft das Toben | T, vn, bc | 139:2 | A 159:2 |
| Gott ist mein König | SATB, orch | 71:1 | B 1:1 |
| Gott ist unsre Sonn und Schild | A, ob/fl, bc | 79:2 | A 184:2 |
| Gott ist unsre Zuversicht | SATB, orch | 197:1 | B 16:1 |
| Gottlob! nun geht das Jahr zu Ende | S, 2 ob, tle, str, bc | 28:1 | A 20:1 |
| Gott Lob und Dank, der nicht zugab | chorale | 14:5 | A 40:5 |
| Gott, man lobet dich in der Stille | A, 2 obda, str, bc | 120:1 | B 6:1 |
| Gott, nimm dich ferner unser an | SATB, SATB | 225:2 | C 1:2 |

| Incipit | Scoring | BWV | BC |
|---|---|---|---|
| Gott schickt uns Mahanaim zu | S, 2 obda, bc | 19:3 | A 180:3 |
| Gott soll allein mein Herze haben | A, org, bc | 169:3 | A 143:3 |
| Gott versorget alles Leben | S, ob, bc | 187:5 | A 110:5 |
| Gott, wie dein Name, so ist auch deim Ruhm | SATB, orch | 171:1 | A 24:1 |
| Gott will, o ihr Menschenkinder | A, str, bc | 173:3 | A 85:3 |
| Gott, wir danken deiner Güte [inc.] | S, ob, str | 193:3 | B 5:3 |
| Gratias agimus tibi | SATB, orch | 232:7 | E 1:7 |
| Gratias agimus tibi | B, 2 vn, bc | 235:3 | E 5:3 |
| Gratias agimus tibi | B, str, bc | 236:3 | E 4:3 |
| Greifet zu, faßt das Heil | B, str, bc | 174:4 | A 87:4 |
| Großer Flemming, alles Wissen [inc.] | S, [fl, obda, str, bc] | 210a:8 | G 29:8 |
| Großer Gönner, dein Vergnügen | S, obda, str, bc | 210:8 | G 44:8 |
| Großer Herr, o starker König | B, tr, fl, str, bc | 248:8 | D 7:8 |
| Großer König unsrer Zeit | — | 205a:9 | [G 20:9] |
| Grüne, blühe, lebe lange | — | 36a:9 | [G 12:9] |
| Güldner Sonnen frohe Stunden | S, 2 fl, str, bc | 173a:2 | G 9:2 |
| Gute Nacht, du Weltgetümmel | B, str, bc | 27:5 | A 138:5 |
| Gute Nacht, o Wesen | chorale | 64:8 | A 15:8 |
| Gute Nacht, o Wesen | SSAT | 227:9 | C 5:9 |
| Guter Hirte, Trost der Deinen | SATB, 2 fl, str, bc | 184:6 | A 88:6 |
| Gutes und die Barmherzigkeit | chorale | 112:5 | A 67:5 |
| Halleluja, Stärk und Macht | T, vn, bc | 29:3 | B 8:3 |
| Halleluja, Stärk und Macht | A, org, bc | 29:7 | B 8:7 |
| Halt im Gedächtnis Jesum Christ | SATB, orch | 67:1 | A 62:1 |
| Händen, die sich nicht verschließen | SB, 2 fl, 2 ob, 2 vn, bc | 164:5 | A 128:5 |
| Handle nicht nach deinen Rechten | T, vn, bc | 101:2 | A 118:2 |
| Hasse nur, hasse mich recht | T, vadg, bc | 76:10 | A 97:10 |
| Hat er es denn beschlossen | SB, bc | 97:7 | A 189:7 |
| Hat man nicht mit seinen Kindern | B, str, bc | 211:2 | G 48:2 |
| Hebt euer Haupt empor | T, ob, str, bc | 70:8 | A 165:8 |
| Heilger Geist ins Himmels Throne | chorale | 194:6 | A 91a:6 |
| Heiligste Dreieinigkeit | B, 3 tr, timp, bc | 172:3 | A 81:3 |
| Heil und Lust kron unendlich deine Brust | — | 249b:11 | [G 28:11] |
| Heil und Segen [frag.] | SA, ? | 216:7 | G 43:7 |
| Heil und Segen | — | 216a:7 | G 47:7 |
| Hemme dein gequältes Kränken | — | 244a:22 | [B 22:22] |
| Herr, bin ichs | SATB, str, bc | 244:9e | D 3:9e |
| Herr Christ, der einge Gottessohn | SATB, orch | 96:1 | A 142:1 |
| Herr, deine Augen sehen nach dem Glauben | SATB, 2 ob, str, bc | 102:1 | A 119:1 |
| Herr, deine Güte reicht, so weit der Himmel ist | S, 2 vn, bc | 17:3 | A 131:3 |
| Herr! Dein Eifer vor die Rechte | — | 205a:5 | [G 20:5] |
| Herr, dein Mitleid, dein Erbarmen | SB, 2 obda, bc | 248:29 | D 7:29 |
| Herr, der du stark und mächtig bist | S, 2 ob, str, bc | 10:2 | A 175:2 |
| Herr, du siehst statt guter Werke | SA, fl, obda, bc | 9:5 | A 107:5 |
| Herr, fange an und sprich den Segen | T, 2 obda, str, bc | 120a:6 | B 15:6 |
| Herr, gehe nicht ins Gericht mit deinem Knecht | SATB, orch | 105:1 | A 114:1 |
| Herr, gib, daß ich dein Ehre | SATB, orch | 107:7 | A 109:7 |
| Herr Gott, Beherrscher aller Dinge | SATB, orch | 120a:1 | B 15:1 |
| Herr Gott, dich loben alle wir | SATB, orch | 130:1 | A 179:1 |
| Herr Gott, dich loben wir | SATB, orch | 16:1 | A 23:1 |
| Herr Gott, dich loben wir | SATB, orch | 190:2 | A 21:2 |
| Herr Gott Vater, mein starker Held | SA, bc | 37:3 | A 75:3 |
| Herr, ich glaube, hilf mir Schwachen | chorale | 78:7 | A 130:7 |

## Appendix 2

| Incipit | Scoring | BWV | BC |
|---|---|---|---|
| Herr, ich hoff je, du werdest die | chorale | 184:5 | A 88:5 |
| Herr Jesu Christ, du höchstes Gut | SATB, orch | 113:1 | A 122:1 |
| Herr Jesu Christ, einiger Trost | chorale | 48:7 | A 144:7 |
| Herr Jesu Christ, wahr' Mensch und Gott | SATB, orch | 127:1 | A 49:1 |
| Herrscher des Himmels, erhöre das Lallen | SATB, orch | 248:24 | D 7:24 |
| Herrscher über Tod und Leben | chorale | 8:6 | A 137a:6 |
| Herr, so du willt | B, str, bc | 73:4 | A 35:4 |
| Herr, so groß als dein Erhöhen | — | 193a:7 | [G 15:7] |
| Herr, so weit die Wolken gehen | T, 2 vn, bc | 171:2 | A 24:2 |
| Herr, unser Herrscher | SATB, orch | 245:1 | D 2:1 |
| Herr, was du willt, soll mir gefallen | A, ob, vn, bc | 156:4 | A 38:4 |
| Herr, wenn die stolzen Feinde schnauben | SATB, orch | 248:54 | D 7:54 |
| Herr, wie du willt, so schicks mit mir | SATB, orch | 73:1 | A 35:1 |
| Herr, wie du willt, so schicks mit mir | chorale | 156:6 | A 38:6 |
| Herr, wir haben gedacht | SATB, SATB, 2 orch | 244:66b | D 3:66b |
| Herzlich lieb hab ich dich, o Herr | chorale | 174:5 | A 87:5 |
| Herzliebster Jesu, was hast du verbrochen | chorale | 244:3 | D 3:3 |
| Herz und Mund und Tat und Leben | SATB, orch | 147:1 | A 174:1 |
| Herz, zerreiß des Mammons Kette | SA, bc | 168:5 | A 116:5 |
| Heute noch, lieber Vater, tut es doch | S, str, bc | 211:8 | G 48:8 |
| Heute wirst du mit mir im Paradies sein | B, 2 vadg, bc | 106:3b | B 18:3b |
| Heut lebst du, heut bekehre dich | chorale | 102:7 | A 119:7 |
| Heut schleußt er wieder auf die Tür | chorale | 151:5 | A 17:5 |
| Hier, in meines Vaters Stätte | B, vn, bc | 32:3 | A 31:3 |
| Hier ist das rechte Osterlamm | B, 2 vn, 2 va, bc | 4:6 | A 54:6 |
| Hier ist das rechte Osterlamm | chorale | 158:4 | A 61:4, A 171:1 |
| Hilf deinem Volk, Herr Jesu Christ | chorale | 119:9 | B 3:9 |
| Hilf, Gott, daß es uns gelingt | S, str, bc | 194:5 | A 91:5 |
| Hilf, Jesu, hilf, daß ich auch dich bekenne | T, bc | 147:7 | A 174:7 |
| Hilf mir mein Sach recht greifen an | chorale | 153:9 | A 25:9 |
| Himmel, erhöre das betende Land | — | 193a:11 | [G 15:11] |
| Himmel, reiße, Welt, erbebe | SB, 2 fl, bc | 245a | D 2b:11+ |
| Himmelskönig, sei willkommen | SATB, orch | 182:2 | A 53, 172:2 |
| Himmlische Vergnügsamkeit | S, fl, 2 ob, str, bc | 204:8 | G 45:8 |
| Hochgelobter Gottessohn | A, obdc, bc | 6:2 | A 57:2 |
| Höchster, mache deine Güte | S, bc | 51:3 | A 134:3 |
| Höchster, schau in Gnaden an | SATB, orch | 63:7 | A 8:7 |
| Höchster, schenke diesem Paar | — | 195:8 | [B 14b:8] |
| Höchster Tröster, heilger Geist | S, 2 obdc, str, bc | 183:4 | A 79:4 |
| Höchster, was ich habe | S, 2 fl, bc | 39:5 | A 96:5 |
| Höchsterwünschtes Freudenfest | SATB, orch | 194:1 | A 91:1 |
| Höllische Schlange, wird dir nicht bange | B, 2 ob, str, bc | 40:4 | A 12:4 |
| Hört doch! der sanften Flöten Chor | S, 3 fl, bc | 206:9 | G 23, 26:9 |
| Hört, ihr Augen, auf zu weinen | S, ob, bc | 98:3 | A 153:3 |
| Hört, ihr Völker, Gottes Stimme | S, vn, bc | 76:3 | A 97, 185:3 |
| Hunderttausend Schmeicheleien | — | 249a:5 | [G 2:5] |
| Ich armer Mensch, ich armer Sünder | chorale | 179:6 | A 121:6 |
| Ich armer Mensch, ich Sündenknecht | T, fl, obda, 2 vn, bc | 55:1 | A 157:1 |
| Ich bin deine, du bist meine | AT, 2 va, bc | 213:11 | G 18:11 |
| Ich bin ein guter Hirt | B, ob, str, bc | 85:1 | A 66:1 |
| Ich bin herrlich, ich bin schön | S, obda, vcp, bc | 49:4 | A 150:4 |
| Ich bin nun achtzig Jahr | ST, org | 71:2 | B 1:2 |
| Ich bins, ich sollte büßen | chorale | 244:10 | D 3:10 |
| Ich bin vergnügt in meinem Leiden | S, vn, bc | 58:3 | A 26:3 |
| Ich bin vergnügt mit meinem Glücke | S, ob, str, bc | 84:1 | A 43:1 |
| Ich bitte dich, Herr Jesu Christ | S, str, bc | 166:3 | A 71:3 |
| Ich bitt noch mehr, o Herre Gott | A, bc | 177:2 | A 103:2 |

| Incipit | Scoring | BWV | BC |
|---|---|---|---|
| Ich bitt, o Herr, aus Herzens Grund | chorale | 18:5 | A 44:5 |
| Ich, dein betrübtes Kind | S, va, bc | 199:6 | A 120:6 |
| Ich elender Mensch, wer wird mich erlösen | SATB, orch | 48:1 | A 144:1 |
| Ich ende behende mein irdisches Leben | S, vn, bc | 57:7 | A 14:7 |
| Ich esse mit Freuden mein weniges Brot | S, ob, vn, bc | 84:3 | A 43:3 |
| Ich folge Christo nach | B, 2 vn, bc | 12:5 | A 68:5 |
| Ich folge dir gleichfalls mit freudigen Schritten | S, 2 fl, bc | 245:9 | D 2:9 |
| Ich folge dir nach | SA, ob, bn, bc | 159:2 | A 50:2 |
| Ich freue mich auf meinen Tod | B, ob, str, bc | 82:5 | A 169:5 |
| Ich freue mich in dir | SATB, orch | 133:1 | A 16:1 |
| Ich fürchte nicht des Todes Schrecken | T, vcp, bc | 183:2 | A 79:2 |
| Ich fürchte zwar nicht des Grabes Finsternissen | AT, vn, bc | 66:5 | A 56:5 |
| Ich gehe hin und komme wieder | B, bc | 74:4 | A 83:4 |
| Ich geh und suche mit Verlangen | B, org, bc | 49:2 | A 150:2 |
| Ich glaube, lieber Herr, hilf meinem Unglauben | SATB, orch | 109:1 | A 151:1 |
| Ich hab dich einen Augenblick | chorale | 103:6 | A 69:6 |
| Ich habe genung | B, ob, str, bc | 82:1 | A 169:1 |
| Ich habe meine Zuversicht | T, ob, str, bc | 188:2 | A 154:2 |
| Ich hab für mir ein schwere Reis | SB, 2 ob, tle, str, bc | 58:5 | A 26:5 |
| Ich hab in Gottes Herz und Sinn | SATB, orch | 92:1 | A 42:1 |
| Ich halte meinen Jesum feste | T, obda, bc | 157:2 | A 170:2, B 20:2 |
| Ich halt es mit dem lieben Gott | S, 3 ob, bn, bc | 52:5 | A 160:5 |
| Ich harre des Herrn | SATB, insts | 131:3 | B 25:3 |
| Ich hatte viel Bekümmernis | SATB, orch | 21:2 | A 99:2 |
| Ich höre mitten in dem Leiden | T, 2 ob, bc | 38:3 | A 152:3 |
| Ich lasse dich nicht, du segnest mich denn | SATB, SATB | Anh. III 159 | C 9 |
| Ich lasse dich nicht, du segnest mich denn | TB, fl, ob, vn, bc | 157:1 | A 170:1, B 20:1 |
| Ich lasse dich nicht, ich schließe dich ein | B, obda, bc | 197a:6 | A 11:6 |
| Ich lebe, mein Herze, zu deinem Ergötzen | ST, vn, bc | 145:1 | A 60:1 |
| Ich leb indes in dir vergnüget | chorale | 84:5 | A 43:5 |
| Ich liebe den Höchsten von ganzem Gemüte | A, 2 ob, bc | 174:2 | A 87:2 |
| Ich lieg im Streit und widerstreb | chorale | 177:5 | A 103:5 |
| Ich nehme mein Leiden mit Freuden auf mich | S, obda, bc | 75:5 | A 94:5 |
| Ich rief dem Herrn in meiner Not | chorale | 117:4 | A 187:4 |
| Ich ruf zu dir, Herr Jesu Christ | SATB, orch | 177:1 | A 103:1 |
| Ich ruf zu dir, Herr Jesu Christ | SATB, orch | 185:6 | A 101:6 |
| Ich säe meine Zähren | S, fl, 2 obda, bc | 146:5 | A 70:5 |
| Ich sehe schon im Geist | A, 2 ob, bc | 43:9 | A 77:9 |
| Ich steh an deiner Krippen hier | chorale | 248:59 | D 7:59 |
| Ich steh mit einem Fuß im Grabe | ST, str, bc | 156:2 | A 38:2 |
| Ich traue seiner Gnaden | T, vn, bc | 97:4 | A 189:4 |
| Ich weiche nun/nicht, ich will/du sollst | — | 66a:4 | [G 4:4] |
| Ich will alle meine Tage | chorale | 25:6 | A 129:6 |
| Ich will an den Himmel denken | T, ob, bc | 166:2 | A 71:2 |
| Ich will auch mit gebrochnen Augen | A, fl, obda, bc | 125:2 | A 168:2 |
| Ich will auf den Herren schaun | S, ob, bc | 93:6 | A 104:6 |
| Ich will bei meinem Jesu wachen | T, SATB, 2 fl, str, bc | 244:20 | D 3:20 |
| Ich will den Kreuzstab gerne tragen | B, 2 ob, tle, str, bc | 56:1 | A 146:1 |
| Ich will dich all mein Leben lang | A, fl, str, bc | 117:7 | A 187:7 |
| Ich will dich halten | B, ob, str, bc | 30a:7 | G 31:7 |
| Ich will dich mit Fleiß bewahren | chorale | 248:33 | D 7:33 |

# Appendix 2

| Incipit | Scoring | BWV | BC |
|---|---|---|---|
| Ich will dich nicht hören | A, vn, bc | 213:9 | G 18:9 |
| Ich will dir mein Herze schenken | S, 2 obda, bc | 244:13 | D 3:13 |
| Ich will doch wohl Rosen brechen | A, vn, bc | 86:2 | A 73:2 |
| Ich will/Du sollt rühmen, ich will/du sollt sagen | — | 193a:5 | [G 15:5] |
| Ich will hier bei dir stehen | SA, ob, bn, bc | 159:2 | A 50:2 |
| Ich will leiden, ich will schweigen | T, str, bc | 87:6 | A 74:6 |
| Ich will nach dem Himmel zu | A, vn, bc | 146:3 | A 70:3 |
| Ich will nun hassen und alles lassen | B, obda, str, bc | 30:8 | A 178:8 |
| Ich will nur dir zu Ehren leben | T, 2 vn, bc | 248:41 | D 7:41 |
| Ich will von Jesu Wundern singen | B, tr, 2 ob, str, bc | 147:9 | A 174:9 |
| Ich wünsche nur, bei Gott zu leben | A, 2 ob, tle, str, org, bc | 35:7 | A 125:7 |
| Ich wünschte mir den Tod | S, str, bc | 57:3 | A 14:3 |
| Ihm hab ich mich ergeben | S, 2 ob, bc | 97:8 | A 189:8 |
| Ihr aber seid nicht fleischlich | SSATB | 227:6 | C 5:6 |
| Ihr, die ihr euch von Christo nennet | T, str, bc | 164:1 | A 128:1 |
| Ihr Felder und Auen, laßt grunend euch schauen | B, bc | 208:14 | G 1, 3:14 |
| Ihr Gedanken und ihr Sinnen | T, s fl, bn, bc | 110:2 | A 10:2 |
| Ihr Häuser des Himmels, ihr scheinenden Lichter | — | 193a:1 | [G 15:1] |
| Ihr lieblichste Blicke!, ihr freudige Stunden | SSTB, orch | 208:15 | G 1, 3:15 |
| Ihr Menschen, rühmet Gottes Liebe | T, str, bc | 167:1 | A 176:1 |
| Ihr Pforten (Tore) zu Zion [inc.] | SA, insts | 193:1 | B 5:1 |
| Ihr seid die Gesegneten des Herrn | SATB, str, bc | 196:5 | B 11:5 |
| Ihr Söhne, laßt doch künftig lesen | — | 205a:12 | [G 20:12] |
| Ihr Tore zu Zion [inc.] | SA, insts | 193:1 | B 5:1 |
| Ihr werdet weinen und heulen | SATB, orch | 103:1 | A 69:1 |
| Immerhin, immerhin | S, 2 vn, bn, bc | 52:3 | A 160:3 |
| In allen meinen Taten | SATB, orch | 97:1 | A 189:1 |
| In deine Hände befehl ich meinen Geist | AB, 2 vadg, bc | 106:3 | B 18:3 |
| In der Welt habt ihr Angst | B, bc | 87:5 | A 74:5 |
| In dich hab ich gehoffet, Herr | chorale | 52:6 | A 160:6 |
| In Jesu Demut kann ich Trost | A, obda, str, bc | 151:3 | A 17:3 |
| In meinem Gott bin ich erfreut | AT, bc | 162:5 | A 148:5 |
| In meines Herzens Grunde | chorale | 245:26 | D 2:26 |
| Israel hoffe auf den Herrn | SATB, insts | 131:5 | B 25:5 |
| Ist Gott mein Schutz und treuer Hirt | chorale | 85:6 | A 66:6 |
| Ist Gott versöhnt und unser Freund | SAT, str, bc | 122:4 | A 19:4 |
| Ist mein herz in Missetaten | SS, str, bc | 1083:2 | B 26:2 |
| Jagen ist die Lust der Götter | S, 2 cdc, bc | 208:2 | G 1, 3:2 |
| Ja, ja, ich halte Jesum feste | B, fl, vn, bc | 157:4 | A 170:4, B 20:4 |
| Ja, ja, ich kann die Feinde schlagen | B, str, bc | 57:5 | A 14:5 |
| Ja nicht auf das Fest | SATB, SATB, 2 orch | 244:4b | D 3:4b |
| Ja tausendmal tausend begleiten den Wagen | T, str, bc | 43:3 | A 77:3 |
| Jauchzet, frohlocket, auf, preiset die Tage | SATB, orch | 248:1 | D 7:1 |
| Jauchzet Gott in allen Landen | S, tr, str, bc | 51:1 | A 134:1 |
| Jauchzet, ihr erfreuten Stimmen | SATB, orch | 120:2 | B 6:2 |
| Jede Woge meiner Wellen | T, vn, bc | 206:5 | G 23, 26:5 |
| Jesu, beuge doch mein Herze | B, ob, vn, bc | 47:4 | A 141:4 |
| Jesu, Brunnquell aller Gnaden | S, bc | 162:3 | A 148:3 |
| Jesu, deine Gnadenblicke | S, 2 fl, ob, vn, va | 11:8 | D 9:8 |
| Jesu, deine Passion | chorale | 159:5 | A 50:5 |
| Jesu, deine Passion | SATB, rec, vn, vc, bc | 182:7 | A 53:7 |
| Jesu, deine Passion | SB, 2 fl, bc | 245a | D 1:2a |

| Incipit | Scoring | BWV | BC |
|---|---|---|---|
| Jesu, der aus großer Liebe | A, bc | 165:3 | A 90:3 |
| Jesu, der du meine Seele | SATB, orch | 78:1 | A 130:1 |
| Jesu, der du warest tot | SATB, bc | 245:32 | D 2:32 |
| Jesu, laß dich finden | A, 2 obda, str | 154:4 | A 29:4 |
| Jesu, laß durch Wohl und Weh | T, bc | 182:6 | A 53:6, A 172:6 |
| Jesu, laß uns auf dich sehen | T, str, bc | 6:5 | A 57:5 |
| Jesu, meine Freude | chorale | 227:1 | C 5:1 |
| Jesu, meines Todes Tod | T, str, bc | 165:5 | A 90:5 |
| Jesu, mein Hort und Erletter | chorale | 154:3 | A 29:3 |
| Jesum laß ich nicht von mir | chorale | 124:6 | A 30:6 |
| Jesum laß ich nicht von mir | chorale | 244b:29 | D 3a:29 |
| Jesum von Nazareth | SATB, orch | 245:2b, d | D 2:2b, d |
| Jesu, nimm dich deiner Glieder | chorale | 40:8 | A 12:8 |
| Jesu, nun sei gepreiset | SATB, orch | 41:1 | A 22:1 |
| Jesus bleibet meine Freude | SATB, orch | 147:10 | A 174:10 |
| Jesus Christus, Gottes Sohn | T, 2 vn, bc | 4:4 | A 54:4 |
| Jesus ist ein guter Hirt | A, vcp, bc | 85:2 | A 66:2 |
| Jesus ist ein Schild der Seinen | B, vns, bn, bc | 42:6 | A 63:6 |
| Jesus macht mich geistlich reich | A, vns, bc | 75:10 | A 94:10 |
| Jesus nimmt die Sünder an | T, fl, bc | 113:5 | A 122:5 |
| Jesus, richte mein Beginnen | SATB, orch | 248:42 | D 7:42 |
| Jesus schläft, was soll ich hoffen? | A, 2 rec, str, bc | 81:1 | A 39:1 |
| Jesus soll mein alles sein | TB, bc | 190:5 | A 21:5 |
| Jesus soll mein erstes Wort | S, vn, bc | 171:4 | A 24:4 |
| Jesu, wahres Brot des Lebens | chorale | 180:7 | A 149:7 |
| Johannis freudenvolles Springen | B, str, bc | 121:4 | A 13:4 |
| Kann ich nur Jesum mir zum Freunde machen | T, hn, str, bc | 105:5 | A 114:5 |
| Kann wohl ein Mensch zu Gott im Himmel | SB, bc | 194:9 | A 91a:9, B 31:9 |
| Kapital und Interessen | T, 2 obda, bc | 168:3 | A 116:3 |
| Kein Arzt ist außer dir zu finden | A, vn/fl, bc | 103:3 | A 69:3 |
| Kein Frucht das Weizenkörnlein bringt | S, bc | 114:4 | A 139:4 |
| Kein Menschenkind hier auf der Erd | chorale | 74:8 | A 83:8 |
| Klagt, Kinder, klagt es aller Welt | — | 244a:1 | [B 22:1] |
| Klein-Zschocher müsse so zart und süße | S, fl, str, bc | 212:14 | G 32:14 |
| Komm doch, Flora, komm geschwinde | — | 249a:9 | [G 2:9] |
| Komm, du süße Todesstunde | A, 2 rec, org, bc | 161:1 | A 135:1 |
| Komm, heiliger Geist, Herre Gott | chorale | 59:3 | A 82:3 |
| Komm in mein Herzenshaus | S, bc | 80:4 | A 183:4 |
| Komm, Jesu, komm | SATB, SATB | 229:1 | C 3:1 |
| Komm, Jesu, komm zu deiner Kirche | T, 2 vn, va, bc | 61:3 | A 1:3 |
| Komm, komm, mein Herze steht dir offen | S, obdc, bc | 74:2 | A 83:2 |
| Komm, laß mich nicht langer warten | SA, ob, vc | 172:5 | A 815 |
| Komm, leite mich | A, 3 rec, bc | 175:2 | A 89:2 |
| Komm, mein Jesu, und erquicke | SB, bc | 21:8 | A 99:8 |
| Komm, o Tod, du Schlafes Bruder | chorale | 56:5 | A 146:5 |
| Komm, süßes Kreuz | B, vadg, bc | 244:57 | D 3:57 |
| Kommt, eilet, stimmet Sait und Lieder | T, str, bc | 74:5 | A 83:5 |
| Kommt, eilet und laufet | TB/SATB, orvh | 249:3 | D 8:3 |
| Kommt, ihr angefochtnen Sünder | A, fl, str, bc | 30:5 | A 178:5 |
| Kommt, ihr Töchter, helft mir klagen | S, SATB, SATB, 2 orch | 244:1 | D 3:1 |
| Komm wieder, teurer Fürstengeist | — | 244a:7 | [B 22:7] |
| Können nicht die roten Wangen | A, obda, bc | 205:7 | G 36:7 |
| Können Tränen meiner Wangen | A, vns, bc | 244:52 | D 3:52 |
| Kortte lebe, Kortte blühe | SATB, orch | 207:9 | G 37:9 |

# Appendix 2

| Incipit | Scoring | BWV | BC |
|---|---|---|---|
| Kraft und Stärke sei gesungen | B, violone, bc | 149:2 | A 181:2 |
| Kreuzige, kreuzige | SATB, orch | 245:21*d* | D 2:21*d* |
| Kreuz und Krone sind verbunden | A, ob, bc | 12:4 | A 68:4 |
| Kron und Preis gekrönter Damen | B, tr, str, bc | 214:7 | G 19:7 |
| Kyrie eleison | SSATB, orch | 232:1 | E 1:1 |
| Kyrie eleison | SATB, orch | 232:3 | E 1:3 |
| Kyrie eleison | SATB, orch | 233:1 | E 6:1 |
| Kyrie eleison | SATB, orch | 234:1 | E 3:1 |
| Kyrie eleison | SATB, orch | 235:1 | E 5:1 |
| Kyrie eleison | SATB, orch | 236:1 | E 4:1 |
| Labt das Herz, ihr holden Saiten | SSATB, orch | 201:15 | G 46:15 |
| Laß dein Engel mit mir fahren | chorale | 19:7 | A 180:7 |
| Laß dein Zion blühend dauern | SA, str, bc | 1083:13 | B 26:13 |
| Lässest du diesen los | SATB, orch | 245:23*b* | D 2:23*b* |
| Lasset dem Höchsten ein Danklied erschallen | B, 2 ob, bn, str, bc | 66:3 | A 56:3 |
| Lasset uns den nicht zerteilen | SATB, orch | 245:27*b* | D 2:27*b* |
| Lasset uns nun gehen gen Bethlehem | SATB, orch | 248:26 | D 7:26 |
| Laß, Fürstin, laß noch einen Strahl | SATB, orch | 198:1 | G 34:1 |
| Laß, Höchster, uns zu allen Zeiten | SATB, orch | 181:5 | A 45:5 |
| Laß ihn kreuzigen | SATB, SATB, 2 orch | 244:45*b* | D 3:45*b* |
| Laß ihn kreuzigen | SATB, SATB, 2 orch | 244:50*b* | D 3:50*b* |
| Laß, Leopold, dich nicht begraben | — | 244*a*:15 | [B 22:15] |
| Laß mein Herz die Münze sein | B, 2 vc, bc | 163:3 | A 158:3 |
| Laß mich der Rufer Stimmen hören | — | 147*a*:5 | [A 7:5] |
| Laß mich kein Lust noch Furcht von dir | T, vn, bn, bc | 177:4 | A 103:4 |
| Laß, o Fürst der Cherubinen | T, fl, bc | 130:5 | A 179:5 |
| Laß, o Welt, mich aus Verachtung | B, fl, bc | 123:5 | A 28:5 |
| Laß, Seele, kein Leiden von Jesu dich scheiden | SA, 2 ob, tle, str, bc | 186:10 | A 108:10 |
| Laßt uns jauchzen, laßt uns freuen | SATB, orch | 16:3 | A 23:3 |
| Laßt uns sorgen, laßt uns wachen | SATB, orch | 213:1 | G 18:1 |
| Laßt uns zum Augusto fliehen | — | 205*a*:7 | [G 20:7] |
| Laß uns das Jahr vollbringen | SATB, orch | 171:6 | A 24:6 |
| Laß uns das Jahr vollbringen | chorale | 190:7 | A 21:7 |
| Laß uns, o Höchster Gott, das Jahr vollbringen | S, 3 ob, bc | 41:2 | A 22:2 |
| Laudamus te | S, vn, str, bc | 232:6 | E 1:6 |
| Lebens Sonne, Licht der Sinnen | S, 2 rec, 2 ob, str, bc | 180:5 | A 149:5 |
| Lebe, Sonne dieser Erden | SSTB, orch | 208:11 | G 1, 3:11 |
| Leget euch dem Heiland unter | A, rec, bc | 182:5 | A 53, 172:5 |
| Leg ich mich späte nieder | A, str, bc | 97:6 | A 189:6 |
| Leichtgesinnte Flattergeister | B, fl, ob, str, bc | 181:1 | A 45:1 |
| Leit uns mit deiner rechten Hand | chorale | 90:5 | A 163:5 |
| Leit uns mit deiner rechten Hand | chorale | 101:7 | A 118:7 |
| Leopolds Vortrefflichkeiten | B, str, bc | 173*a*:3 | G 9:3 |
| Letzte Stunde, brich herein | S, ob, 2 vn, 2 va, vc, bc | 31:8 | A 55:8 |
| Liebster Gott, erbarme dich | S, 2 obdc, bc | 179:5 | A 121:5 |
| Liebster Gott, wenn werd ich sterben | SATB, orch | 8:1 | A 137:1 |
| Liebster Immanuel, Herzog der Frommen | SATB, orch | 123:1 | A 28:1 |
| Liebster Jesu, mein Verlangen | S, ob, str, bc | 32:1 | A 31:1 |
| Liebt, ihr Christen, in der Tat | A, obda, vadg, bc | 76:12 | A 97:12 |
| Lobe den Herren, den mächtigen König | SATB, orch | 137:1 | A 124:1 |
| Lobe den Herren, der alles so herrlich regieret | A, vn, bc | 137:2 | A 124:2 |
| Lobe den Herren, der deinen Stand | SATB, orch | 120*a*:8 | B 15:8 |
| Lobe den Herren, der deinen Stand | T, tr, bc | 137:4 | A 124:4 |

| Incipit | Scoring | BWV | BC |
|---|---|---|---|
| Lobe den Herren, der künstlich und fein | SB, 2 ob, bc | 137:3 | A 124:3 |
| Lobe den Herren, was in mir ist, lobe den Namen | SATB, orch | 137:5 | A 134:5 |
| Lobe den Herrn, meine Seele | SATB, orch | 69:1 | B 10:1 |
| Lobe den Herrn, meine Seele | SATB, orch | 69a:1 | A 123:1 |
| Lob, Ehr und Dank sei dir gesagt | chorale | 121:6 | A 13:6 |
| Lob, Ehr und Preis sei Gott [inc.] | SAB, orch | 192:3 | A 188:3 |
| Lobet den Herrn, alle Heiden | SATB, bc | 230 | C 6 |
| Lobet den Herrn in seinen Taten | SATB, SATB | 225:3 | C 1:3 |
| Lobet Gott in seinen Reichen | SATB, orch | 11:1 | D 9:1 |
| Lobe, Zion, deinen Gott | A, str, bc | 190:3 | A 21:3 |
| Lob sei Gott, dem Vater, g'ton | chorale | 36(2):8 | A 3b:8 |
| Lob sei Gott, dem Vater, g'ton | chorale | 62:6 | A 2:6 |
| Lob und Preis sei Gott dem Vater und dem Sohn | chorale | 10:7 | A 175:7 |
| Lust der Völker, Lust der Deinen | SATB, orch | 213:13 | G 18:13 |
| Mache dich, mein Geist, bereit | SATB, orch | 115:1 | A 156:1 |
| Mache dich, mein Herze, rein | B, 2 obdc, str, bc | 244:65 | D 3:65 |
| Machs mit mir, Gott, nach deiner Gut | ST, str, bc | 156:2 | A 38:2 |
| Mädchen, die von harten Sinnen | B, bc | 211:6 | G 48:6 |
| Magnificat anima mea | SSATB, orch | 243:1 | E 13:1, E 14:1 |
| Man halte nur ein wenig stille | T, str, bc | 93:3 | A 104:3 |
| Man nehme sich in acht | A, ob, str, bc | 166:5 | A 71:5 |
| Man singet mit Freuden vom Sieg | SATB, orch | 149:1 | A 181:1 |
| Mein alles in allem, mein ewiges Gut | T, str, bc | 22:4 | A 48:4 |
| Meine Augen sehen stets zu dem Herrn | SATB, bn, 2 vn, bc | 150:6 | B 24:6 |
| Meinem Hirten bleib ich treu | S, obda, str, bc | 92:8 | A 42:8 |
| Meinen Jesum laß ich nicht | B, 2 vn, bc | 98:5 | A 153:5 |
| Meinen Jesum laß ich nicht | SATB, orch | 124:1 | A 30:1 |
| Meinen Jesum laß ich nicht | chorale | 154:8 | A 29:8 |
| Meinen Jesum laß ich nicht | chorale | 157:5 | A 170:5, B 20:5 |
| Mein Erlöser und Erhalter | B, obda, str, bc | 69:5 | A 123:5, B 10:5 |
| Meine Seel erhebt den Herren | SATB, orch | 10:1 | A 175:1 |
| Meine Seele, auf, erzähle | A, ob, vn, bc | 69:3 | B 10:3 |
| Meine Seele sei vergnügt | S, fl, bc | 204:6 | G 45:6 |
| Meine Seele soll Gott loben | — | 223:1 | A 186:1 |
| Meine Seele wartet auf den Herrn | AT, bc | 131:4 | B 25:4 |
| Meine Seufzer, meine Tränen | T, 2 rec, obdc, bc | 13:1 | A 34:1 |
| Meine Tage in dem Leide | SATB, bn, 2 va, bc | 150:7 | B 24:7 |
| Mein Freund ist mein | SB, ob, bc | 140:6 | A 166:6 |
| Mein gläubiges Herze | S, ob, vn, vcp, bc | 68:2 | A 86:2 |
| Mein Gott, ich liebe dich von Herzen | S, 2 ob, bc | 77:3 | A 126:3 |
| Mein Gott, öffne mir die Pforten | chorale | 32:6 | A 31:6 |
| Mein Heiland läßt sich merken | T, obdc, bc | 186:5 | A 108:5 |
| Mein Herze glaubt und liebt | B, tr, str, bc | 75:12 | A 94:12 |
| Mein Jesus hat nunmehr das Heilandwerk | S, 2 ob, str, bc | 43:5 | A 77:5 |
| Mein Jesus ist erstanden | T, obda, str, bc | 67:2 | A 62:2 |
| Mein Jesus soll mein alles sein | B, str, bc | 75:3 | A 94:3 |
| Mein Jesus will es tun | S, ob, str, bc | 72:5 | A 37:5 |
| Mein Jesu, ziehe mich nach dir | A, ob, bc | 22:2 | A 48:2 |
| Mein letztes Lager will mich schrecken | AT, obda, vn, bc | 60:3 | A 161:3 |
| Mein liebster Jesus ist verloren | T, str, bc | 154:1 | A 29:1 |
| Mein Seelenschatz ist Gottes Wort | S, 2 fl, 4 va, bc | 18:4 | A 44:4 |
| Mein teurer Heiland, laß dich fragen | SATB, bc | 245:32 | D 2:32 |
| Mein Verlangen ist, den Heiland zu umfangen | T, str, bc | 161:3 | A 135a–b:3 |
| Menschen, glaubt doch dieser Gnade | A, 2 obda, str, bc | 7:6 | A 177:6 |

| Incipit | Scoring | BWV | BC |
|---|---|---|---|
| Mer hahn en neue Oberkeet | SB, vn, va, bc | 212:2 | G 32:2 |
| Merke, mein Herze, beständig nur dies | B, tr, fl, 2 obda, 2 vn, bc | 145:3 | A 60:3 |
| Merkt und hört, ihr Menschenkinder | B, bc | 7:2 | A 177:2 |
| Messias läßt sich merken | — | 186a:2 | [A 5:3] |
| Mich kann die süße Ruhe laben | SB, bc | 207a:5 | G 22:5 |
| Mich kann kein Zweifel stören | T, vn, bc | 108:2 | A 72:2 |
| Mir ekelt mehr zu leben | A, obda, org, str, bc | 170:5 | A 106:5 |
| Mir hat die Welt trüglich gericht' | chorale | 244:32 | D 3:32 |
| Mir mangelt zwar sehr viel | chorale | 89:6 | A 155:6 |
| Missetaten, die mich drücken | SA, str, bc | 1083:3 | B 26:3 |
| Mit allem, was ich hab und bin | A, 2 vn, bc | 72:2 | A 37:3 |
| Mit Freuden sei die Welt verlassen | — | 244a:12 | [B 22:12] |
| Mit Fried und Freud ich fahr dahin | SATB, orch | 125:1 | A 168:1 |
| Mit Lachen und Scherzen, mit freudigen Hersen | — | 216a:5 | [G 47:5] |
| Mit Segen mich beschütte | chorale | 194:12 | A 91:12, B 31:12 |
| Mit unsrer Macht ist nichts getan | SB, ob, str, bc | 80:2 | A 183:2 |
| Mit Verlangen drück ich deine zarten Wangen | B, fl, obda, str, bc | 201:5 | G 46:5 |
| Mit zarten und vergnügten Trieben | S, fl, vn, bc | 36b:7 | G 38:7 |
| Mund und Herze steht dir offen | A, 3 ob, bc | 148:4 | A 140:4 |
| Murre nicht, lieber Christ | A, str, bc | 144:2 | A 41:2 |
| Muß ich sein betrübet | chorale | 87:7 | A 74:7 |
| Nach dir, Herr, verlanget mich | SATB, bn, 2 vn, bc | 150:2 | B 24:2 |
| Nein, Gott ist allezeit geflißen | T, 2 obda, str, bc | 88:3 | A 105:3 |
| Nenne deinen August: Gott | — | 193a:3 | [G 15:3] |
| Nicht diesen, sondern Barrabam | SATB, orch | 245:18b | D 2:18b |
| Nicht nach Welt, nach Himmel nicht | chorale | 70:11 | A 165:11 |
| Nichts ist es spat und frühe | B, bc | 97:2 | A 189:2 |
| Nichts kann mich erretten von höllischen Ketten | A, 2 ob, obdc, vn, str, bc | 74:7 | A 83:7 |
| Nimm auch, großer Fürst, uns auf | SATB, orch | 173a:8 | G 9:8 |
| Nimm mich dir zu eigen hin | T, orch | 65:6 | A 27:6 |
| Nimm mich mir und gib mich dir | SA, vn, va, bc | 163:5 | A 158:5 |
| Nimm von uns, Herr, du treuer Gott | SATB, orch | 101:1 | A 118:1 |
| Nimm, was dein ist, und gehe him | SATB, bc | 144:1 | A 41:1 |
| Noch eins, Herr, will ich bitten dich | chorale | 111:6 | A 36:6 |
| Nun blühet das Vergnügen | — | 205a:3 | [G 20:3] |
| Nun danket alle Gott [inc.] | SAB, orch | 192:1 | A 188:1 |
| Nun danket alle Gott | SATB, orch | 79:3 | A 184:3, B 17:3 |
| Nun danket all und bringet Ehr | chorale | 195:6 | B 14c:6 |
| Nun du wirst mein Gewissen stillen | B, ob, str, bc | 78:6 | A 130:6 |
| Nun hilf uns, Herr, den Dienern dein | chorale | 120:6 | B 6:6 |
| Nun, ich weiß, du wirst mir stillen | chorale | 105:6 | A 114:6 |
| Nun ist das Heil und die Kraft [frag.] | SATB, SATB, orch | 50 | A 194 |
| Nun komm, der Heiden Heiland | SA, 2 obda, bc | 36(2):2 | A 3b:2 |
| Nun komm, der Heiden Heiland | SATB, orch | 61:1 | A 1:1 |
| Nun komm, der Heiden Heiland | SATB, orch | 62:1 | A 2:1 |
| Nun lieget alles unter dir | chorale | 11:6 | D 9:6 |
| Nun lob, mein Seel, den Herren | SATB, orch | 28:2 | A 20:2 |
| Nun mögt ihr stolzen Feinde schrecken | T, 2 obda, bc | 248:62 | D 7:62 |
| Nun seid ihr wohl gerochen | SATB, orch | 248:64 | D 7:64 |
| Nun verschwinden alle Plagen | SB, ob, str, bc | 32:5 | A 31:5 |
| Nun, werter Geist, ich folg dir | chorale | 175:7 | A 89:7 |
| Nur durch Lieb und durch Erbarmen | A, 2 fl, bc | 164:3 | A 128:3 |
| Nur ein Wink von seinen Händen | S, obda, str, bc | 248:57 | D 7:57 |
| Nur jedem das Seine | T, str, bc | 163:1 | A 158:1 |

| Incipit | Scoring | BWV | BC |
|---|---|---|---|
| Ob bei uns ist der Sünden viel | chorale | 38:6 | A 152:6 |
| Ob sichs anließ, als wollt er nicht | chorale | 9:7 | A 107:7 |
| Ob sichs anließ, als wollt er nicht | chorale | 155:5 | A 32:5 |
| Ob sichs anließ, als wollt er nicht | SATB, 2 ob, str, bc | 186:6 | A 108:6 |
| O du angenehmer Schatz [inc.] | A, 2 fl, bc | 197a:4 | A 11:4 |
| O du angenehmes Paar | B, ob, 2 vn, bn, bc | 197:6 | B 16:6 |
| O du von Gott erhöhte Creatur | T, obda, bc | 121:2 | A 13:2 |
| O ewiges Feuer, o Ursprung der Liebe | SATB, orch | 34:1 | A 84:1, B 13:1 |
| O Ewigkeit, du Donnerwort | SATB, orch | 20:1 | A 95:1 |
| O Ewigkeit, du Donnerwort | chorale | 20:11 | A 95:11 |
| O Ewigkeit, du Donnerwort | AT, orch | 60:1 | A 161:1 |
| Öffne dich, mein ganzes Herze | S, bc | 61:5 | A 1:5 |
| Öffne Lippen, Mund und Seele | A, str, bc | 1083:11 | B 26:11 |
| Öffne meinen schlechten Liedern | S, 3 fl, 2 ob, str, bc | 25:5 | A 129:5 |
| Öffnet euch, ihr beiden Ohren | B, 2 tr, bc | 175:6 | A 89:6 |
| O Gott, du frommer Gott | SATB, orch | 24:6 | A 102:6 |
| O große Lieb, o Lieb ohn' alle Maße | chorale | 245:3 | D 2:3 |
| O großer Gott von Treu | SATB, orch | 46:6 | A 117:6 |
| O Haupt voll Blut und Wunden | chorale | 244:54 | D 3:54 |
| O heilges Geist- und Wasserbad | S, str, bc | 165:1 | A 90:1 |
| O hilf, Christe, Gottes Sohn | chorale | 245:37 | D 2:37 |
| O Jesu Christ, meins Lebens Licht | SATB, insts | 118 | B 23 |
| O Mensch, bewein dein Sünde groß | SATB, orch | 244:29 | D 3:29 |
| O Menschen, die ihr täglich sündigt | B, bc | 122:2 | A 19:2 |
| O Menschenkind, hör auf geschwind | AT, bc | 20:10 | A 95:10 |
| O Mensch, errette deine Seele | A, str, bc | 20:6 | A 95:6 |
| Omnes generationes | SSATB, orch | 243:4 | E 13:4, E 14:4 |
| Osanna in excelsis | SATB, SATB, orch | 232:24 | E 1:23 |
| O Seelenparadies | T, 2 vn, 2 va, bc | 172:4 | A 81:4 |
| O wie wohl ist uns geschehn | SB, 2 ob, bc | 194:10 | A 91:10, B 31:10 |
| O wohl uns, die wir an ihn glauben | SAT, str, bc | 122:4 | A 19:4 |
| Pan ist Meister, laßt ihn gehn | T, 2 vn, bc | 201:11 | G 46:11 |
| Parti pur e con dolore | S, fl, str, bc | 209:3 | G 50:3 |
| Patrem omnipotentem | SATB, orch | 232:14 | E 1:14 |
| Patron, das macht der Wind | S, bc | 201:3 | G 46:3 |
| Petrus, der nicht denkt zurück | chorale | 245:14 | D 2:14 |
| Phoebus, deine Melodei | T, obda, bc | 201:9 | G 46:9 |
| Phoebus eilt mit schnellen Pferden | S, bc | 202:3 | G 41:3 |
| Preise dein Glücke, gesegnetes Sachsen | SATB, SATB, orch | 215:1 | G 21:1 |
| Preise, Jerusalem, den Herrn | SATB, orch | 119:1 | B 3:1 |
| Preiset, späte Folgezeiten | A, 2 fl, str, bc | 207a:7 | G 22:7 |
| Preis und Dank | SATB, orch | 249:11 | D 8:11 |
| Quia fecit mihi magna | B, bc | 243:5 | E 13:5, E 14:5 |
| Quia respexit humilitatem | S, obda, bc | 243:3 | E 13:3, E 14:3 |
| Qui sedes ad dextram Patris | A, obda, str, bc | 232:12 | E 1:10 |
| Qui tollis peccata mundi | S, ob, bc | 233:4 | E 6:4 |
| Qui tollis peccata mundi | S, 2 fl, str | 234:4 | E 3:4 |
| Qui tollis peccata mundi | T, ob, bc | 235:5 | E 5:5 |
| Quoniam tu solus sanctus | B, cdc, 2 bn, bc | 232:11 | E 1:11 |
| Quoniam tu solus sanctus | A, vn, bc | 233:5 | E 6:5 |
| Quoniam tu solus sanctus | A, vn, va, bc | 234:5 | E 3:5 |
| Quoniam tu solus sanctus | T, ob, bc | 236:5 | E 4:5 |
| Rase nur, verwegner Schwarm | B, ob, str, bc | 215:5 | G 21:5 |
| Reis von Habsburgs hohem Stamme | A, 2 obda, bc | 206:7 | G 23:7, G 26:7 |
| Ricetti gramezza e pavento | S, fl, str, bc | 209:5 | G 50:5 |
| Richte dich, Liebste, nach meinem Gefallen | chorale | 57:8 | A 14:8 |

# Appendix 2

| Incipit | Scoring | BWV | BC |
|---|---|---|---|
| Ruft und fleht den Himmel an | AT, str, bc | 63:5 | A 8:5 |
| Ruhet hie, matte Sinnen (Töne) | S, [obda, vn, bc] | 210a:4 | G 29:4, G 44:4 |
| Ruhig und in sich zufrieden | S, 2 ob, bc | 204:2 | G 45:2 |
| Rühmet Gottes Güt und Treu | B, 2 ob(da), str, bc | 195:3 | B 14:3 |
| Rühre, Höchster, unsern Geist | SATB, orch | 173:6 | A 85:6 |
| Ruht wohl, ihr heiligen Gebeine | chorale | 245:39 | D 2:39 |
| Sachsen, komm zum Opferherd | — | 193a:9 | [G 15:9] |
| Saget, saget mir geschwinde | A, obda, str, bc | 249:9 | D 8:9 |
| Sanctus, sanctus, sanctus Dominus Deus Sabaoth | SSAATB, orch | 232:22 | E 1:22 |
| Sanctus, sanctus, sanctus Dominus Deus Sabaoth | SATB, orch | 237 | E 10 |
| Sanctus, sanctus, sanctus Dominus Deus Sabaoth | SATB, str, bc | 238 | E 11 |
| Sanctus, sanctus, sanctus Dominus Deus Sabaoth | SATB, str, bc | 239 | E 12 |
| Sanctus, sanctus, sanctus Dominus Deus Sabaoth | SATB, 2 ob, str, bc | 240 | E 13 |
| Sanctus, sanctus, sanctus Dominus Deus Sabaoth | SATB, SATB, orch | 241 | E 14 |
| Sanfte soll mein Todeskummer | T, 2 rec, 2 vn, bc | 249:7 | D 8:7 |
| Schafe können sicher weiden | S, 2 fl, bc | 208:9 | G 1:9, G 3:9 |
| Schäme dich, o Seele, nicht | A, obda, bc | 147:3 | A 174:3 |
| Schäme dich, o Seele, nicht | — | 147a:2 | A 7:2 |
| Schaue nicht auf meine Sünden | SA, str, bc | 1083:10 | B 26:10 |
| Schauet doch und sehet, ob irgend ein Schmerz | SATB, orch | 46:1 | A 117:1 |
| Schau, lieber Gott, wie meine Feind | chorale | 153:1 | A 25:1 |
| Schaut hin, dort liegt im finstern Stall | chorale | 248:17 | D 71:17 |
| Schlafe, mein Liebster, genieße der Ruh | A, fl, 2 obda, 2 obdc, str, bc | 248:19 | D 7:19 |
| Schlafe, mein Liebster, und pflege der Ruh | S, str, bc | 213:3 | G 18:3 |
| Schleicht, spielende Wellen, und murmelt | SATB, orch | 206:1 | G 23:1, G 26:1 |
| Schleuß des Janustempels Türen | B, str, bc | 206:3 | G 23:3, G 26:3 |
| Schließe, mein Herze, dies selige Wunder | A, vn, bc | 248:31 | D 7:31 |
| Schlummert ein, ihr matten Augen | B, str, bc | 82:3 | A 169:3 |
| Schmücke dich, o liebe Seele | SATB, orch | 180:1 | A 149:1 |
| Schreibe nicht: der Juden König | SATB, orch | 245:25b | D 2:25b |
| Schüttle deinen Kopf und sprich | chorale | 40:6 | A 12:6 |
| Schweig, aufgetürmtes Meer | B, 2 obda, str, bc | 81:5 | A 39:5 |
| Schweig, schweig nur, taumelnde Vernunft | T, str, bc | 178:6 | A 112:6 |
| Schweigt, ihr Flöten, schweigt, ihr Töne | S, fl, bc | 210:6 | G 29:6, G 44:6 |
| Schwingt freudig euch empor | SATB, 2 obda, str, bc | 36:1 | A 3:1 |
| Seele, deine Spezereien | S, fl/vn, bc | 249:5 | D 8:5 |
| Sehet in Zufriedenheit | S, ob, str, bc | 202:9 | G 41:9 |
| Sehet, Jesus hat die Hand | A, SATB, 2 ob, 2 obdc, str, bc | 244:60 | D 3:60 |
| Sehet, welch eine Liebe | SATB, orch | 64:1 | A 15:1 |
| Seht, seht! wie reißt, wie bricht, wie fällt | T, str, bc | 92:3 | A 42:3 |
| Seht, was die Liebe tut | T, str, bc | 85:5 | A 66:5 |
| Sei bemüht in dieser Zeit | A, ob, str, bc | 185:3 | A 101:3 |
| Seid beglückt, edle beide | S, fl, obda, str, bc | 210:10 | G 44:10 |
| Seid froh dieweil | chorale | 248:35 | D 7:35 |
| Seid vergnügt, werte Gönner | S, [fl, obda, str, bc] | 210a:10 | G 29:10 |
| Seid wachsam, ihr heiligen Wächter | AT, bn, bc | 149:6 | A 181:6 |

| Incipit | Scoring | BWV | BC |
|---|---|---|---|
| Sei gegrüßet, lieber Judenkönig | SATB, orch | 245:21*b* | D 2:21*b* |
| Sei getreu, alle Pein | T, tr, bc | 12:6 | A 68:6 |
| Sei Lob und Ehr dem höchsten Gut | SATB, orch | 117:1 | A 187:1 |
| Sei Lob und Preis mit Ehren | chorale | 29:8 | B 8:8 |
| Sei Lob und Preis mit Ehren | S, 2 vn, bc | 51:4 | A 134:4 |
| Sei Lob und Preis mit Ehren | SATB, orch | 167:5 | A 176:5 |
| Sei Lob und Preis mit Ehren | SATB, orch | 28:2 | C 7:2 |
| Sei mir willkommen, werter Schatz | B, str, bc | 36(1):3 | A 3*a*:3 |
| Sein Allmacht zu ergründen | AT, ob(da), bc | 128:4 | A 76:4 |
| Sein Blut komme über uns | SATB, SATB, 2 orch | 244:50*d* | D 3:50*d* |
| Seinem Schöpfer noch auf Erden | A, ob, vn, bc | 39:3 | A 96:3 |
| Sei nun wieder zufrieden, meine Seele | SATB, org | 21:9 | A 99:9 |
| Sei uns willkommen, schönster Tag | — | 36*a*:5 | [G 12:5] |
| Sei vergnügt, großer Flemming [inc.] | S, [fl, obda, str, bc] | 210*a*:10 | G 29:10 |
| Selig ist der Mann | B, orch | 57:1 | A 14:1 |
| Selig sind, die aus Erbarmen | chorale | 39:7 | A 96:7 |
| Selig sind wir durch das Wort | — | 190*a*:5 | [B 27:5] |
| Seligster Erquickungs-Tag | B, tr, str, bc | 70:10 | A 165:10 |
| Sende deine Macht von oben | T, 2 ob, bc | 126:2 | A 46:2 |
| Sende, Herr, den Segen ein [inc.] | A, [insts] | 193:5 | B 5:5 |
| Senket euch nur ohne Kummer | — | 249*b*:7 | [G 28:7] |
| Seufzer, Tränen, Kummer, Not | S, ob, bc | 21:3 | A 99:3 |
| Sich üben im Lieben | S, ob, bc | 202:7 | G 41:7 |
| Sicut erat in principio | SSATB, orch | 191:3 | E 16:3 |
| Sicut locutus est | SSATB, bc | 243:11 | E 13:11, E 14:11 |
| Sieh, du willst die Wahrheit haben | S, str, bc | 1083:7 | B 26:7 |
| Siehe, also wird gesegnet der Mann | AT, str, bc | 34*a*:3 | B 13:3 |
| Siehe, ich will viel Fischer aussenden | B, orch | 88:1 | A 105:1 |
| Siehe zu, daß deine Gottesfurcht | SATB, orch | 179:1 | A 121:1 |
| Sieh, ich bin in Sünd empfangen | SA, str, bc | 1083:6 | B 26:6 |
| Sie stellen uns wie Ketzern nach | T, 2 obda, bc | 178:4 | A 112:4 |
| Sie werden aus Saba alle kommen | SATB, orch | 65:1 | A 27:1 |
| Sie werden euch in den Bann tun | TB, 2 ob, bc | 44:1 | A 78:1 |
| Sind Blitze, sind Donner in Wolken | SATB, SATB, 2 orch | 244:27*b* | D 3:27*b* |
| Sing, bet und geh auf Gottes Wegen | chorale | 88:7 | A 105:7 |
| Sing, bet und geh auf Gottes Wegen | chorale | 93:7 | A 104:7 |
| Singet dem Herrn ein neues Lied | SATB, orch | 190:1 | A 21:1 |
| Singet dem Herrn ein neues Lied | SATB, SATB | 225:1 | C 1:1 |
| So aber Christus in euch ist | ATB | 227:8 | C 5:8 |
| So du willst, Herr, Sünde zurechnen | SB, ob, bc | 131:2 | B 25:2 |
| So fahr ich hin zu Jesu Christ | chorale | 31:9 | A 55*a*:9 |
| So feiern wir das hohe Fest | ST, bc | 4:7 | A 54:7 |
| So hat Gott die Welt geliebt | SB, 2 fl, str, bc | 173:4 | A 85:4 |
| So ist mein Jesus nun gefangen | SA, SATB, orch | 244:27*a* | D 3:27*a* |
| Solang ein Gott im Himmel lebt | chorale | 20:7 | A 95:7 |
| So lasset uns gehen in Salem der Freuden | SATB, orch | 182:8 | A 53:8 |
| So lebet, ihr Musen! auf Helikons-Höhen | — | 205*a*:11 | [G 20:11] |
| Soll ich auf dieser Welt | ST, org | 71:2 | B 1:2 |
| Soll ich denn auch des Todes Weg | chorale | 92:9 | A 42:9 |
| Soll ich meinen Lebenslauf | A, str, bc | 153:8 | A 25:8 |
| Solls ja so sein | chorale | 48:3 | A 144:3 |
| So löschet im Eifer der rächende Richter | B, tr, str, bc | 90:3 | A 163:3 |
| So nun der Geist | SSATB | 227:10 | C 5:10 |
| Sooft ich meine Tobacks-Pfeife | voice, bc | 515 | H 2 |
| So schau dies holden Tages Licht | S, 2 fl, str, bc | 173*a*:6 | G 9:6 |
| So schnell ein rauschend Wasser schießt | T, fl, vn, bc | 26:2 | A 162:2 |
| So sei nun, Seele, deine | chorale | 13:6 | A 34:6 |

# Appendix 2

| Incipit | Scoring | BWV | BC |
|---|---|---|---|
| So sei nun, Seele, deine | chorale | 44:7 | A 78:7 |
| So sei nun, Seele, deine | chorale | 97:9 | A 189:9 |
| So wandelt froh auf Gottes Wegen | chorale | 197:10 | B 16:10 |
| So wie ich die Tropfen zolle | T, fl, obda, str, bc | 30a:11 | G 31:11 |
| Spielet, ihr beseelten Lieder | S, obda, str, bc | 210:2 | G 44:2 |
| Spielet, ihr beseelten Lieder [inc.] | S, [obda, str, bc] | 210a:2 | G 29:2 |
| Sprich Ja zu meinen Taten | chorale | 194:12 | A 91:12, B 31:12 |
| Starkes Lieben, das dich, großer Gottessohn | B, str, bc | 182:4 | A 53:4, A 172:4 |
| Stärk mich mit deinem Freudengeist | chorale | 113:8 | A 122:8 |
| Stärk mich mit deinem Freudengeist | chorale | 168:6 | A 116:6 |
| Steigt freudig in die Luft | — | 36a:1 | [G 12:1] |
| Stein, der über alle Schätze | S, rec, vada, bc | 152:4 | A 18:4 |
| Stifter der Reiche, Beherrscher der Kronen | SATB, orch | 215:9 | G 21:9 |
| Stirb in mir, Welt | A, str, org, bc | 169:5 | A 143:5 |
| Streite, siege, starker Held | B, str, bc | 62:4 | A 2:4 |
| Stumme Seufzer, stille Klagen | S, ob, bc | 199:2 | A 120:2 |
| Stürmt nur, stürmt, ihr Trübsalswetter | T, str, bc | 153:6 | A 25:6 |
| Stürze zu Boden schwülstige Stolze | B, bc | 126:4 | A 46:4 |
| Suscepit Israel | SSA, 2 ob, vc, org | 243:10 | E 13:10, E 14:10 |
| Suscepit Israel | SATB, 2 vn, bc | 1082 | E 15 |
| Süßer Trost, mein Jesus kommt | S, fl, obda, str, bc | 151:1 | A 17:1 |
| Süße, wundersüße Triebe | — | 249b:5 | [G 28:5] |
| Tief gebückt und voller Reue | S, str, bc | 199:4 | A 120:4 |
| Tilge, Höchster, meine Sünden | SA, str, bc | 1083:1 | B 26:1 |
| Tilg, o Gott, die Lehren | A, vn, bc | 2:3 | A 98:3 |
| Tönet, ihr Pauken! Erschallet, Trompeten! | SATB, orch | 214:1 | G 19:1 |
| Traget, ihr Lüfte, den Jubel von hinnen | — | 66a:2 | [G 4:2] |
| Treues Echo dieser Orten | AA, obda, bc | 213:5 | G 18:5 |
| Treu im Glauben, unbeweglich in der Not | — | 120b:4 | [B 28:4] |
| Treu und Wahrheit sei der Grund | T, 2 obda, bc | 24:5 | A 102:5 |
| Tritt auf die Glaubensbahn | B, ob, bc | 152:2 | A 18:2 |
| Tröste mir, Jesu, mein Gemüte | T, 2 ob, bc | 135:3 | A 100:3 |
| Trotz dem alten Drachen | SSATB | 227:5 | C 5:5 |
| Tue Rechnung! Donnerwort | B, str, bc | 168:1 | A 116:1 |
| Und bitten dich, wollst allezeit | chorale | 130:6 | A 179:6 |
| Und daß ihrs alle wißt | S, vn, va, bc | 212:22 | G 32:22 |
| Und ob gleich alle Teufel | chorale | 153:5 | A 25:5 |
| Und was der ewig gütig Gott | S, 2 ob(da), bc | 86:3 | A 73:3 |
| Und weil ich denn in meinem Sinn | AT, bc | 131:4 | B 25:4 |
| Und wenn der harte Todesschlag | T, obda, str, bc | 124:3 | A 30:3 |
| Und wenn die Welt voll Teufel war | SATB, orch | 80:5 | A 183:5 |
| Unerforschlich ist die Weise | A, vc, org | 188:4 | A 154:4 |
| Unser Mund sei voll Lachens | SATB, orch | 110:1 | A10:1 |
| Unser Mund und Ton der Saiten | T, str, bc | 1:5 | A 173:5 |
| Unser trefflicher, lieber Kammerherr | S, vn, va, bc | 212:8 | G 32:8 |
| Unsre Stärke heißt zu schwach | S, cdc, str, bc | 14:2 | A 40:2 |
| Uns treffen zwar der Sünden Flecken | TB, 2 vn, bc | 136:5 | A 111:5 |
| Unter deinem Schirmen | chorale | 81:7 | A 39:7 |
| Unter deinem Schirmen | SSATB | 227:3 | C 5:3 |
| Unter seinem Purpursaum | SB, 2 fl, str, bc | 173a:4 | G 9:4 |
| Valet will ich dir geben | S, 2 obda, bc | 95:3 | A 136:3 |
| Verbirgt mein Hirte sich zu lange | T, 2 obda, bc | 104:3 | A 65:3 |
| Vereinigte Zwietracht der wechselnden Saiten | SATB, orch | 207:1 | G 37:1 |
| Vergib, o Vater, unsre Schuld | A, 2 obdc, bc | 87:3 | A 74:3 |

604

| Incipit | Scoring | BWV | BC |
|---|---|---|---|
| Vergibt mir Jesus meine Sünden | T, ob, str, bc | 48:6 | A 144:6 |
| Vergnügen und Lust | S, 2 ob(da), vn, bc | 197:8 | B 16:8 |
| Vergnügte Pleißen-Stadt [inc.] | SA[TB, orch] | 216:1 | G 43:1 |
| Vergnügte Ruh, beliebte Seelenlust | A, obda, str, bc | 170:1 | A 106:1 |
| Verjaget, zerstreuet, zerrüttet, ihr Sterne | — | 249b:3 | [G 28:3] |
| Verleih, daß ich aus Herzens Grund | S, obdc, bc | 177:3 | A 103:3 |
| Verleih uns Frieden gnädiglich | chorale | 42:7 | A 63:7 |
| Verleih uns Frieden gnädiglich | chorale | 126:6 | A 46:6 |
| Verstumme, Höllenheer | B, tr, 2 ob, str, bc | 5:5 | A 145:5 |
| Verstummt, verstummt, ihr holden Saiten | S, str, bc | 198:3 | G 34:3 |
| Verzage nicht, o Häuflein klein | ST, bn, vc, bc | 42:4 | A 63:4 |
| Virga Jesse floruit | SB, bc | 243a:D | E 13:D |
| Vivat! August, August, vivat | SATB, orch | 205a:15 | [G 36:15] |
| Vom Himmel hoch da komm ich her | SSATB | 243a:A | E 13:A |
| Von den Stricken meiner Sünden | A, 2 ob, bc | 245:7 | D 2:7 |
| Von der Welt verlang ich nichts | A, obda, bc | 64:7 | A 15:7 |
| Von Gott kommt mir ein Freudenschein | SATB, orch | 172:6 | A 81:6 |
| Wachet auf, ruft uns die Stimme | SATB, orch | 140:1 | A 166:1 |
| Wachet! betet! betet! wachet! | SATB, orch | 70:1 | A 165:1 |
| Wachet! betet! betet! wachet! | — | 70a:1 | A 4:1 |
| Wacht auf, ihr Adern und ihr Glieder | B, tr, 2 ob, obdc, str, bc | 110:6 | A 10:6 |
| Wacht auf, wacht auf, verlornen Schafe | B, tr, 3 ob, str, bc | 20:8 | A 95:8 |
| Wann kommst du, mein Heil | SB, vnp, bc | 140:3 | A 166:3 |
| Wann soll es doch geschehen | SATB, orch | 11:9 | D 9:9 |
| Wäre dieser nicht ein Übeltäter | SATB, orch | 245:16b | D 2:16b |
| Wär Gott nicht mit uns diese Zeit | SATB, orch | 14:1 | A 40:1 |
| Wahrlich, dieser ist Gottes Sohn gewesen | SATB, SATB, 2 orch | 244:63b | D 3:63b |
| Wahrlich, du bist auch einer von denen | SATB, orch | 244:38b | D 3:38b |
| Wahrlich, wahrlich, ich sage euch | B, str, bc | 86:1 | A 73:1 |
| Warum betrübst du dich, mein Herz? | SATB, orch | 138:1 | A 132:1 |
| Warum willst du so zornig sein | B, 2 ob, tle, bc | 101:4 | A 118:4 |
| Was betrübst du dich, meine Seele | SATB, orch | 21:6 | A 99:6 |
| Wasche mich doch rein von Sünden | A, str, bc | 1083:8 | B 26:8 |
| Was des Höchsten Glanz erfüllt | B, ob, str, bc | 194:3 | A 91:3, B 31:3 |
| Was die Seele kann ergötzen | A, fl, str, bc | 30a:5 | G 31:5 |
| Was die Welt in sich hält | S, str, bc | 64:5 | A 15:5 |
| Was frag ich nach der Welt | chorale | 64:4 | A 15:4 |
| Was frag ich nach der Welt | SATB, orch | 94:1 | A 115:1 |
| Was frag ich nach der Welt | chorale | 94:8 | A 115:8 |
| Was gehet uns das an | SATB, SATB, 2 orch | 244:41b | D 3:41b |
| Was Gott tut, das ist wohlgetan | chorale | 12:7 | A 68:7 |
| Was Gott tut, das ist wohlgetan | chorale | 69a:6 | A 123:6 |
| Was Gott tut, das ist wohlgetan | SATB, orch | 75:7 | A 94:7 |
| Was Gott tut, das ist wohlgetan | SATB, orch | 98:1 | A 153:1 |
| Was Gott tut, das ist wohlgetan | SATB, orch | 99:1 | A 133:1 |
| Was Gott tut, das ist wohlgetan | SATB, orch | 100:1 | A 191:1 |
| Was Gott tut, das ist wohlgetan | AT, bc | 100:2 | A 191:2 |
| Was Gott tut, das ist wohlgetan | S, fl, bc | 100:3 | A 191:3 |
| Was Gott tut, das ist wohlgetan | B, str, bc | 100:4 | A 191:4 |
| Was Gott tut, das ist wohlgetan | A, obda, bc | 100:5 | A 191:5 |
| Was Gott tut, das ist wohlgetan | SATB, orch | 100:6 | A 191:6 |
| Was ist die Ursach aller solcher Plagen | T, SATB, orch | 244:19 | D 3:19 |
| Was mein Gott will, das g'scheh allzeit | chorale | 72:6 | A 37:6 |
| Was mein Gott will, das g'scheh allzeit | SATB, 2 ob, str, bc | 111:1 | A 36:1 |
| Was mein Gott will, das g'scheh allzeit | chorale | 144:6 | A 41:6 |
| Was mein Gott will, das g'scheh allzeit | chorale | 244:25 | D 3:25 |
| Was seind das für große Schlosser [inc.] | SATB, bc | 524 | H 1 |

# Appendix 2

| Incipit | Scoring | BWV | BC |
|---------|---------|-----|-----|
| Was soll ich aus dir machen, Ephraim? | B, 2 ob, hn, str, bc | 89:1 | A 155:1 |
| Was unser Gott geschaffen hat | T, 2 obda, bc | 117:3 | A 187:3 |
| Was willst du dich betrüben | SATB, orch | 107:1 | A109:1 |
| Was willst du dich, mein Geist, entsetzen | T, obda, bc | 8:2 | A 137:2 |
| Was wir dir vor Glücke gönnen | SATB, orch | 36b:8 | G 38:8 |
| Weg mit allen Schatzen | SATB | 227:7 | C 5:7 |
| Weg, weg mit dem | SATB, orch | 245:23d | D 2:23d |
| Weh! der Seele, die den Schaden | A, ob, bc | 102:3 | A 119:3 |
| Weh und Ach krankt die Seelen tausendfach | — | 244a:3 | [B 22:3] |
| Weichet nur, betrübte Schatten | S, ob, str, bc | 202:1 | G 41:1 |
| Weicht, all ihr Übeltäter | B, str, bc | 135:5 | A 100:5 |
| Weicht, ihr Trauergeister | SATB | 227:11 | C 5:11 |
| Weil die wollenreichen Herden | S, bc | 208:13 | G 1:13, G 3:13 |
| Weil du mein Gott und Vater bist | SATB, orch | 138:6 | A 132:6 |
| Weinen, Klagen, Sorgen, Zagen | SATB, 2 vn, 2 va, bc | 12:2 | A 68:2 |
| Weissage uns | SATB, SATB, 2 orch | 244:36d | D 3:36d |
| Weiß ich Gottes Rechte | T, str, bc | 45:3 | A 113:3 |
| Welch Übermaß der Güte | T, str, bc | 17:5 | A 131:5 |
| Welt, ade! ich bin dein müde, ich will | chorale (SSATB) | 27:6 | A 138:6 |
| Welt, ade, ich bin dein müde, Salems Hütten | SB, ob, vn, bc | 158:2 | A 61:2, A 171:1 |
| Wenn aber jener, der Geist der Wahrheit | SATB, orch | 108:4 | A 72:4 |
| Wenn des Kreuzes Bitterkeiten | SA, fl, obda, vc | 99:5 | A 133:5 |
| Wenn die Frühlingslüfte streichen | S, vn, bc | 202:5 | G 41:5 |
| Wenn es meines Gottes Wille | SATB, 2 rec, str, bc | 161:5 | A 135:5 |
| Wenn ich einmal soll scheiden | chorale | 244:62 | D 3:62 |
| Wenn kommst du, mein Heil | SB, vnp, bc | 140:3 | A 166:3 |
| Wenn kömmt der Tag, an dem wir ziehen | — | 70a:3 | A 165:3 |
| Wenn meine Trübsal als mit Ketten | SAB, bc | 38:5 | A 152:5 |
| Wenn soll es doch geschehen | SATB, orch | 11:9 | D 9:9 |
| Wenn Sorgen auf mich dringen | SA, 2 obda, vn, bc | 3:5 | A 33:5 |
| Wenn Trost und Hülf ermangeln muß | B, vn, bc | 117:6 | A 187:6 |
| Wer an ihn glaubet, der wird nicht gerichtet | SATB, orch | 68:5 | A 86:5 |
| Wer bist du? Frage dein Gewissen | B, bc | 132:3 | A 6:3 |
| Wer da glaubet und getauft wird | SATB, 2 obda, str, bc | 37:1 | A 75:1 |
| Wer Dank opfert, der preiset mich | SATB, orch | 17:1 | A 131:1 |
| Wer ein wahrer Christ will heißen | S, org, bc | 47:2 | A 141:2 |
| Wer Gott bekennt aus wahrem Herzensgrund | A, fl, bc | 45:5 | A 113:5 |
| Wer hat dich so geschlagen | chorale | 244:37 | D 3:37 |
| Wer hat dich so geschlagen | chorale | 245:11 | D 2:11 |
| Wer hofft in Gott und dem vertraut | SATB, orch | 109:6 | A 151:6 |
| Wer mich liebet, der wird mein Wort halten | SB, orch | 59:1 | A 82:1 |
| Wer mich liebet, der wird mein Wort halten | SATB, orch | 74:1 | A 83:1 |
| Wer nur den lieben Gott läßt walten | SATB, orch | 21:9 | A 99:9 |
| Wer sich selbst erhöhet | SATB, orch | 47:1 | A 141:1 |
| Wer Sünde tut, der ist vom Teufel | A, 2 vn, 2 va, bc | 54:3 | A 51:3 |
| Werte Gönner, alles Wissen | S, [obda, 2 vn, bc] | 210a:8 | G 29:8 |
| Wer weiß, wie nahe mir mein Ende | SATB, orch | 27:1 | A 138:1 |
| Wer wird seine Schuld verneinen | SA, str, bc | 1083:5 | B 26:5 |
| Widerstehe doch der Sünde | A, str, bc | 54:1 | A 51:1 |
| Wie bin ich doch so herzlich froh | chorale | 1:6 | A 173:6 |
| Wie die Jahre sich verneuen | SATB, orch | 36c:9 | G 35:9 |

| Incipit | Scoring | BWV | BC |
|---|---|---|---|
| Wie freudig ist mein Herz | S, ob, str, bc | 199:8 | A 120:8 |
| Wie furchtsam wankten meine Schritte | A, str, bc | 33:3 | A 127:3 |
| Wieget euch, ihr satten Schafe | — | 249a:6 | [G 2:6] |
| Wie jammern mich doch | A, vn, va, org, bc | 170:3 | A 106:3 |
| Wie lieblich klingt es in den Ohren | S, str, bc | 133:4 | A 16:4 |
| Wie schön leuchtet der Morgenstern | SATB, orch | 1:1 | A 173:1 |
| Wie selig sind doch die | AT, obdc, vn, bc | 80:7 | A 183:7 |
| Wie soll ich dich empfangen | chorale | 248:5 | D 7:5 |
| Wie starb die Heldin so vergnügt | A, 2 vadg, 2 lutes, bc | 198:5 | G 34:5 |
| Wie will ich lustig lachen | B, str, bc | 205:3 | G 36:3 |
| Wie will ich mich freuen | TB, 2 ob, str, bc | 146:7 | A 70:7 |
| Wie wunderbarlich ist doch diese Strafe | chorale | 244:46 | D 3:46 |
| Wie zittern und wanken | S, ob, str | 105:3 | A 114:3 |
| Wie zweifelhaftig ist mein Hoffen | T, str, bc | 109:3 | A 151:3 |
| Willkommen in Heil | B, str, bc | 30a:3 | G 31:3 |
| Willkommen, werte Schatz | B, str, bc | 36(2):5 | A 3:5 |
| Willkommen! will ich sagen | A, obdc, org, bc | 27:3 | A 138:3 |
| Willst du dich nicht mehr ergetzen | T, bc | 208:4 | G 1:4, G 3:4 |
| Wir danken dir, Gott | SATB, orch | 29:2 | B 8:2 |
| Wir danken sehr und bitten ihn | chorale | 187:7 | A 110:7 |
| Wir danken, wir preisen | AT, str, bc | 134:4 | A 59:4 |
| Wird auch gleich nach tausend Zahren | — | 244a:17 | [B 22:17] |
| Wir dürfen niemand töten | SATB, orch | 245:16d | D 2:16d |
| Wir eilen mit schwachen | SA, bc | 78:2 | A 130:2 |
| Wir essen und leben wohl | chorale | 4:8 | A 54:8 |
| Wirf, mein Herze, wirf dich noch | S, str, bc | 155:4 | A 32:4 |
| Wir gehn nun wo der Tudelsack | SB, vn, va, bc | 212:24 | G 32:24 |
| Wir haben einen Gott, da der hilft | — | 244a:8 | [B 22:8] |
| Wir haben ein Gesetz | SATB, orch | 245:21f | D 2:21f |
| Wir haben keinen König | SATB, orch | 245:23f | D 2:23f |
| Wir kommen, deine Heilgkeit | SATB, orch | 195:5 | B 14:5 |
| Wir müssen durch viel Trübsal in das Reich | SATB, orch | 146:2 | A 70:2 |
| Wir setzen uns mit Tränen | SATB, SATB, 2 orch | 244:68 | D 3:68 |
| Wir singen dir in deinem Heer | SATB, orch | 248:23 | D 7:23 |
| Wir wachen oder schlafen ein | chorale | 114:7 | A 139:7 |
| Wir waren schon zu tief gesunken | T, vn, bc | 9:3 | A 107:3 |
| Woferne du den edlen Frieden | T, vcp, bc | 41:4 | A 22:4 |
| Wo gehest du hin? | B, ob, str, bc | 166:1 | A 71:1 |
| Wo Gott der Herr nicht bei uns halt | SATB, orch | 178:1 | A 112:1 |
| Wohlan! so will ich mich an dich | chorale | 133:6 | A 16:6 |
| Wohlan! so will ich mich an dich | chorale | 197a:7 | A 11:7 |
| Wohl dem, der sich auf seinen Gott | SATB, orch | 139:1 | A 159:1 |
| Wohl dir, du Volk der Linden | T, 2 obdc, bc | 119:3 | B 3:3 |
| Wohl euch, ihr auserwählten Schafe | A, 2 fl, str, bc | 34a:5 | B 13:5 |
| Wohl euch, ihr auserwählten Seelen | A, 2 fl, str, bc | 34:3 | A 84:3 |
| Wohl mir, daß ich Jesum habe | SATB, orch | 147:6 | A 174:6 |
| Wohl mir, Jesus ist gefunden | AT, 2 obda, str, bc | 154:7 | A 29:7 |
| Wohlzutun und mitzuteilen vergesset nicht | B, bc | 39:4 | A 96:4 |
| Wo ist der neugeborne König der Juden | SATB, orch | 248:45 | D 7:45 |
| Wo soll ich fliehen hin | SATB, orch | 5:1 | A 145:1 |
| Wo willst du, daß wir dir bereiten | SATB, orch | 244:9b | D 3:9b |
| Wo wird in diesem Jammertale | T, fl, bc | 114:2 | A 139:2 |
| Wozu dienet dieser Unrat | SATB, orch | 244:4d | D 3:4d |
| Wo zwei und drei versammlet sind | A, 2 ob, bn, str, bc | 42:3 | A 63:3 |
| Zage nur, du treues Land | — | 244a:5 | [B 22:5] |

# Appendix 2

| Incipit | Scoring | BWV | BC |
|---|---|---|---|
| Zahle, Zion, die Gelübde | — | 120*b*:2 | [B 28:2] |
| Zedern mussen von den Winden | ATB, bn, bc | 150:5 | B 24:5 |
| Zerfließe, mein Herze, in Fluten der Zähren | S, 2 fl, 2 obdc, bc | 245:35 | D 2:35 |
| Zerreißet, zersprenget, zertrümmert die Gruft | SATB, orch | 205:1 | G 36:1 |
| Zerschmettert mich, ihr Felsen und ihr Hügel | T, str, bc | 245*b* | D 2*b*:13 |
| Zieht euren Fuß nur nicht zurücke | T, str, bc | 207:3 | G 37:3 |
| Zion hört die Wächter singen | T, str, bc | 140:4 | A 166:4 |
| Zudem ist Weisheit und Verstand | A, 2 obda, bc | 92:4 | A 42:4 |
| Zum reinen Wasser er mich weist | A, obda, bc | 112:2 | A 67:2 |
| Zurücke, zurücke, geflügelten Winde | B, 3 tr, timp, 2 hn, bc | 205:11 | G 36:11 |
| Zu Tanze, zu Sprunge, so wackelt das Herz | B, 2 vn, bc | 201:7 | G 46:7 |
| Zwar ist solche Herzensstube | chorale | 248:53 | D 7:53 |
| Zweig und Äste | AT, 2 fl, bc | 205:13 | G 36:13 |
| Zwingt die Saiten in Cythara | chorale | 36(2):4 | A 3*b*:4 |

# APPENDIX 3

# CHRONOLOGIES

(*a*) **General**

For performance dates of sacred cantatas, see separate chronology below.

| Year | Domestic events | Bach's music (*except sacred cantatas*) | Other musicians | Contemporary events |
|---|---|---|---|---|
| 1685 | Birth in Eisenach, 21 March; baptism in Georgenkirche, 23 March; burial of brother Johann Jonas, 22 May | | Birth of G. F. Handel, 23 Feb; birth of S. L. Weiß, 12 Oct; birth of D. Scarlatti, 26 Oct. | Edict of Potsdam, offering Huguenots refuge in Brandenburg |
| 1686 | Burial of sister Johanna Juditha, 3 May | | Birth of B. Marcello, 24 June | |
| 1687 | | | death of Jean-Baptiste Lully, 22 March; birth of Francesco Geminiani, 5 Dec.; birth of J. G. Pisendel, 26 Dec. | Publication of Newton's *Principia mathematica* |
| 1688 | | | Birth of J. F. Fasch, 15 April | Death of Frederick William, the Great Elector, 9 May; accession of Frederick III as Elector of Brandenburg; birth of Frederick William I of Prussia, 15 Aug. |
| 1689 | | | Death of G. Legrenzi, 2 May | Coronation of William III and Mary II as British sovereigns, 21 April |
| 1690 | | | | |
| 1691 | | | | |
| 1692 | Enrolment in Lateinschule, Eisenach | | | |
| 1693 | | | | |
| 1694 | Death of mother, 1 May; remarriage of father Johann Ambrosius, 27 Nov. | | Birth of Giuseppe Tartini, 8 April | |
| 1695 | Death of father, 20 Feb.; transfer to Ohrdruf and enrolment in lyceum there | | Birth of P. A. Locatelli, 3 Sept.; death of Henry Purcell, 21 Nov. | |
| 1696 | | | | Death of Jan Sobieski, King of Poland, 17 June |

# Appendix 3

| Year | Domestic events | Bach's music (except sacred cantatas) | Other musicians | Contemporary events |
|---|---|---|---|---|
| 1697 | | | Birth of J. J. Quantz, 30 Jan. | Frederick Augustus, Elector of Saxony, elected King of Poland; death of Charles XI of Sweden, 5 April; accession of Charles XII |
| 1698 | | | | |
| 1699 | | | Bap. of J. A. Hasse, 25 March | |
| 1700 | Enrolment in Michaelisschule, Lüneburg | | | Birth of J. C. Gottsched, 2 Feb.; change from Julian to Gregorian calendar in Protestant Germany, 18/28 Feb.; attack on Livenia by Augustus II, Elector of Saxony; outbreak of Great Northern War |
| 1701 | | | | Frederick III of Brandenburg made King of Prussia |
| 1702 | Application for organist post at Sangerhausen unsuccessful, July | | | Outbreak of War of the Spanish Succession |
| 1703 | Appointment as court musician (Laquey) at Weimar, March–Sept.; appointment as organist at Neue Kirche, Arnstadt, 9 Aug. | | Death of N. de Grigny, 30 Nov. | Defeat of Saxons by Charles XII at Pultusk |
| 1704 | | | Death of H. I. F. von Biber, 3 May | Deposition of Augustus II as King of Poland; election of Stanislaus Lesczinski in his place |
| 1705 | Altercation with J. H. Geyersbach, 4 Aug.; prolonged visit to Lübeck, ?Nov. | | | Death of Emperor Leopold I, 5 May; accession of Joseph I |
| 1706 | Return to Arnstadt, Feb.; reprimand by church consistory for long absence, 21 Feb.; testing of organ at Langewiesen, 28 Nov. | | Bur. of Johann Pachelbel, 9 March | Swedish invasion of Saxony |
| 1707 | Appointment at Blasiuskirche, Mühlhausen, 15 June; marriage to Maria Barbara Bach at Dornheim, 17 Oct. | | Death of D. Buxtehude, 9 May | Alliance formed between Sweden and Prussia |
| 1708 | Appointment as organist and chamber musician at Weimar, June; bap. of daughter Catharina Dorothea, 29 Dec. | | | |

| Year | Domestic events | Bach's music (except sacred cantatas) | Other musicians | Contemporary events |
| --- | --- | --- | --- | --- |
| 1709 | | | Death of Giuseppe Torelli, 8 Feb.; bap. of Franz Benda, 22 Nov. | Coalition formed between Denmark, Saxony, and Russia, against Sweden |
| 1710 | Testing of organ at Taubach, 26 Oct.; son Wilhelm Friedemann born, 22 Nov. | | birth of G. Pergolesi, 4 Jan. | Augustus II reinstated as King of Poland |
| 1711 | Godfather to Magdalena Dorothea Backer, 17 Jan. | | | Death of Emperor Joseph I, 17 April; accession of Archduke Charles |
| 1712 | Godfather to son of J. G. Walther, 27 Sept. | | Publication of A. Vivaldi, *L'estro armonico*, op. 3 | Birth of future King Frederick the Great, 24 Jan. |
| 1713 | Visit to Weißenfels, Feb.; birth of twins Johann Christoph (d. 23 Feb.) and Maria Sophia (bur. 13 March), 23 Feb.; godfather to J. G. Trebs, 27 Nov.; competition for organist post at Halle, Dec. | ?Cantata 208 perf., 23 Feb.; *Orgel-Büchlein* (part) comp. | Death of A. Corelli, 8 Jan. | Signing of Treaty of Utrecht by France and other European countries, 11 April; death of Frederick I of Prussia; accession of Frederick William I |
| 1714 | Offer of Halle post declined, Feb./March; promoted to *Konzertmeister* at Weimar, 2 March; birth of son Carl Philipp Emanuel, 8 March | *Orgel-Büchlein* (part) comp. | Publication of A. Corelli, Concerti grossi, op. 6; birth of C. W. Gluck, 2 July | Conclusion of Utrecht treaties, bringing to an end the War of the Spanish Succession |
| 1715 | Birth of son Johann Gottfried Bernhard, 11 May | *Orgel-Büchlein* (part) comp. | Birth of J. F. Doles, 23 April | Death of Prince Johann Ernst, 1 Aug.; death of Louis XIV, 1 Sept. |
| 1716 | Testing of organs in Liebfrauenkirche, Halle, 29 April–2 May and Augustinerkirche, Erfurt, 31 July | Cantata 208 perf., 23 Feb. | | Death of Gottfried Wilhelm Leibnitz, 14 Nov. |
| 1717 | Appointment as *Kapellmeister* at Cöthen, 5 Aug.; competition with Louis Marchand at Dresden, autumn; imprisonment at Weimar, 6 Nov.–2 Dec.; transfer to Cöthen; testing of organ in Paulinerkirche, Leipzig, 16 Dec. | | | |
| 1718 | Visit to Carlsbad, May–June; bap. of son Leopold Augustus, 17 Nov. | Cantatas 66a and Anh. 15 perf., 10 Dec. | | Treaty of Passarowitz, concluding Turkish war with Austria and Venice, 21 July; death of Charles XII of Sweden, 30 Nov. |

| Year | Domestic events | Bach's music (except sacred cantatas) | Other musicians | Contemporary events |
|---|---|---|---|---|
| 1719 | Visit to Berlin for purchase of harpsichord, ?Feb.: attempted meeting with Handel, May–July; death of son Leopold Augustus, 26 Sept. | Cantata 134a perf., 1 Jan. | Birth of Leopold Mozart, 14 Nov. | |
| 1720 | Godfather to S. C. Abel, 10 Jan.; visit to Carlsbad, May–July; death of wife Maria Barbara, bur. 7 July; visit to Hamburg, Nov.; offer of organist post at Jakobikirche declined | Cantata 134a perf., 1 Jan.; fair copy of Sonatas and Partitas BWV1001–6; ?Cantata Anh. 17 perf., 10 Dec. | Bap. of J. C. Altnickol, 1 Jan.; birth of J. F. Agricola, 4 Jan. | |
| 1721 | Death of brother Johann Christoph, 22 Feb.; godfather to J. C. H. Bähr, 28 June, and J. C. Hahn, 25 Sept.; marriage to Anna Magdalena Wülcken at Cöthen, 3 Dec. | Brandenburg Concertos, dedicated 24 March | Bap. of J. P. Kirnberger, 24 April | Marriage of Prince Leopold of Anhalt-Cöthen, 11 Dec. |
| 1722 | Death of brother Johann Jacob, 16 April; godfather to S. D. Schulze, 26 Oct.; candidature entered for post of Thomaskantor, Leipzig, 21 Dec. | Cantata Anh. 194 perf., 9 Aug.; ?Cantata 173a perf., 10 Dec.; The Well-tempered Clavier Part 1 completed | Death of Johann Kuhnau, 5 June; death of J. A. Reincken, 24 Nov. | |
| 1723 | Birth of daughter Christiana Sophia Henrietta; godfather to J. F. Bähr, 4 March; appointment as Thomaskantor, 5 May; transfer to Leipzig, 22 May; testing of organ at Störmthal, Nov. | Cantata Anh. 1 8 perf., 1 Jan.; fair copy of Inventions; Cantata Anh. 1 20 perf. 9 Aug.; Magnificat perf., 25 Dec. | | |
| 1724 | Birth of son Gottfried Heinrich, 26 Feb.; testing of organ in Johanniskirche, Gera, 25 June; visit to Cöthen with wife, July; godfather to J. C. Kunadt, 15 Oct. | St John Passion perf., 7 April | | |
| 1725 | Bap. of son Christian Gottlieb, 14 April; recitals in Sophienkirche, Dresden, 19–20 Sept; visit to Cöthen with wife, Dec. | Cantata 249a perf., 23 Feb; St John Passion perf., 30 March; Easter Oratorio perf. 1 April; Cantata 205 perf., 3 Aug.; Cantata Anh. 196 perf. 27 Nov. | Death of A. Scarlatti, 22 Oct.; publication of J. J. Fux, Gradus ad Parnassum | Death of Peter the Great of Russia, 28 Jan./8 Feb. |
| 1726 | Bap. of daughter Elisabeth Juliana Friederica, 5 April; death of daughter Christiana Sophia Henrietta, 29 June | Keyboard Partita no. 1 pubd.; Cantata 249b perf. 25 Aug.; Cantata 36a perf, 30 Nov.; Cantata 207 perf., Dec. | | |

| Year | Domestic events | Bach's music (except sacred cantatas) | Other musicians | Contemporary events |
|---|---|---|---|---|
| 1727 | Bap. of son Ernestus Andreas, 30 Oct. (d. 1 Nov.) | Keyboard Partitas nos. 2 and 3 pubd.; *St Matthew Passion* perf., 11 April; Cantata Anh. 1 9 perf., 12 May; Cantata 193*a* perf., 3 Aug.; Cantata 198 perf., 17 Oct. | | Death of Isaac Newton, 20/31 March |
| 1728 | Godfather to L. Spieß, 11 Aug.; death of son Christian Gottlieb, 21 Sept.; bap. of daughter Regina Johanna, 10 Oct.; bur. of sister Maria Salome, 27 Dec. | Keyboard Partita no. 4 pubd.; Cantata 216 perf., 5 Feb. | | Death of Prince Leopold of Anhalt-Cöthen, 19 Nov. |
| 1729 | Visits to Weißenfels, Feb., and Cöthen, 23–4 March; directorship of collegium musicum, March; second attempt to meet Handel, June; death of sister-in-law Friedelena Margaretha Bach, 28 July | Cantata 210*a* perf., 12 Jan.; *St Matthew Passion* perf., 15 April | Death of J. A. Heinichen, 16 July | Death of Thomasschule Rector J. H. Ernesti, 16 Oct. |
| 1730 | Bap. of daughter Christiana Benedicta Louisa, 1 Jan. (d. 4 Jan.); godfather to M. R. Schramm, 13 March; *Entwurff* addressed to town council, 23 Aug.; letter to G. Erdmann inquiring about opportunities at Danzig, 28 Oct.; godfather to J. M. Wilde, 30 Oct. | Keyboard Partitas nos. 5 ? and 6 pubd. | | Appointment of J. M. Gesner as Rector of Thomasschule; bicentenary of the Augsburg Confession |
| 1731 | Bap. of daughter Christiana Dorothea, 18 March; organ recitals in Dresden, 14–21 Sept.; testing of organ at Stöntzsch, 12 Nov. | *Clavier-Übung I* pubd.; *St Mark Passion* perf., 23 March; Cantata Anh. 1 10 perf. 25 Aug. | Première of J. A. Hasse, *Cleofide*, 13 Sept. | |
| 1732 | Birth of son Johann Christoph Friedrich, 21 June; death of daughter Christiana Dorothea, 31 Aug; opening of rebuilt Thomasschule, Sept.; testing of organ in Martinskirche, Kassel, 7–8 Sept. | ?*St John Passion* perf., 11 April; Cantata Anh. 1 18 perf. 5 June; Cantata Anh. 1 11 perf. 3 Aug. | Birth of Joseph Haydn, 31 March; death of L. Marchand, 17 Feb.; publication of J. G. Walther's *Lexicon* | |
| 1733 | Death of daughter Regina Johanna, 25 April; appointment of son Wilhelm Friedemann as organist at Sophien kirche, Dresden, 23 June; visit to Dresden, July; bap. of son Johann August Abraham, 5 Nov. (d. 6 Nov.) | *Missa* bwv 232[1] comp; Cantata Anh. 1 12 perf. 3 Aug.; Cantata 213 perf., 5 Sept.; Cantata 214 perf., 8 Dec. | Death of G. Böhm, 18 May; death of F. Couperin, 11 Sept. | Death of Elector of Saxony, Friedrich August I, 2 Feb; War of the Polish Succession |

# Appendix 3

| Year | Domestic events | Bach's music (except sacred cantatas) | Other musicians | Contemporary events |
|---|---|---|---|---|
| 1734 | | ?Cantata 205a perf., 19 Feb.; Cantata 215 perf., 5 Oct.; Cantata Anh. I 19 perf. 21 Nov.; Christmas Oratorio, Parts 1–3 perf., 25–7 Dec. | | Coronation of Elector Friedrich August II as King of Poland, 17 Jan.; appointment of J. A. Ernesti as Rector of Thomasschule, Nov. |
| 1735 | Testing of organ in Marienkirche, Mühlhausen, June; appointment of son Gottfried Bernhard as organist there, 16 June; bap. of son Johann Christian, 7 Sept. | Christmas Oratorio, Parts 4–6 perf., 1–6 Jan.; Clavier-Übung II pubd.; Ascension Oratorio perf., 19 May; ?Cantata 207a perf., 3 Aug. | | |
| 1736 | Conflict with Rector J. A. Ernesti over choice of school prefects, July onwards; appointment as Hofcomponisteur to Dresden court, 19 Nov.; recital in Frauenkirche, Dresden, 1 Dec. | St Matthew Passion perf., 30 March; Schemelli Songbook pubd.; Cantata 206 perf., 7 Oct. | Death of G. Pergolesi, 16 March | |
| 1737 | Appointment of son Johann Gottfried Bernhard as organist of Jakobikirche, Sangerhausen, 14 Jan.; temporary break in directorship of collegium musicum, spring; adverse criticism of music by J. A. Scheibe, May; arrival of Johann Elias Bach as tutor and secretary, Oct.; bap. of daughter Johanna Carolina, 30 Oct. | Cantata 30a perf., 28 Sept. | Birth of Michael Haydn, 14 Sept. | |
| 1738 | Appointment of son Carl Philipp Emanuel as harpsichordist to Crown Prince Frederick of Prussia; visit to Dresden, May | Cantata Anh. I 13 perf. 28 April | | |
| 1739 | Death of son Johann Gottfried Bernhard, 27 May; testing of organ and recital in Schloßkirche, Altenburg; resumption of directorship of collegium musicum, 2 Oct.; visit to Weißenfels with wife, 7–14 Nov. | Clavier-Übung III pubd. | Publication of D. Scarlatti, Essercizi, ?Jan.; death of B. Marcello, 24 July; death of Reinhard Keiser, 12 Sept. | |
| 1740 | Visit to Halle, April | | Publication of G. F. Handel, Grand Concertos, op. 6 | Accession of Frederick II (the Great) of Prussia, 31 May; death of Emperor Charles VI, 20 Oct.; War of the Austrian Succession; Invasion of Silesia by Frederick the Great |

| Year | Domestic events | Bach's music (except sacred cantatas) | Other musicians | Contemporary events |
|---|---|---|---|---|
| 1741 | Visit to son Carl Philipp Emanuel in Berlin, Aug.; illness of wife Anna Magdalena; visit to Dresden, Nov. | | Death of J. J. Fux, 13 Feb.; death of A. Vivaldi, 27/8 July | |
| 1742 | Bap. of daughter Regina Susanna, 22 Feb.; departure of Johann Elias Bach, 31 Oct. | ?St Matthew Passion perf., 23 March; ?Cantata 212 perf., 30 Aug.; Goldberg Variations pubd. | Handel's Messiah perf. Dublin, 13 April | Treaty of Berlin between Austria and Prussia, ending First Silesian War |
| 1743 | Godfather to J. S. Weyrauch, 18 April; testing of organ in Johanniskirche, Leipzig, Dec. | | | |
| 1744 | Marriage of son Carl Philipp Emanuel to Johanna Maria Dannemann in Berlin | | | Invasion of Bohemia by Frederick the Great; Second Silesian War |
| 1745 | Birth of grandson Johann August, 30 Nov. | Gloria BWV191 perf., Christmas | Death of Jan D. Zelenka, 23 Dec. | Occupation of Leipzig by Prussian troops; end of Second Silesian War, 25 Dec. |
| 1746 | Appointment of son Wilhelm Friedemann as organist of the Liebfrauenkirche, Halle, 16 April; testing of organs in Zschortau, 7 Aug., and Wenzelskirche, Naumburg, 27 Sept. | | | Departure of Prussian troops from Leipzig, 1 Jan. |
| 1747 | Visit to Frederick the Great at Potsdam, 7–8 May; enrolment in Lorenz Mizler's Society of Musical Sciences, June; birth of granddaughter Anna Carolina Philippina, 4 Sept. | Musical Offering pubd. | Death of A. Marcello, 19 June | |
| 1748 | Birth of grandson Johann Sebastian, 24 Sept. | Canonic Variations pubd.; Schübler Chorales pubd. (?, or 1749) | Death of J. G. Walther, 23 March | Treaty of Aix-la-Chapelle, ending War of the Austrian Succession, 24 April |
| 1749 | Marriage of daughter Elisabeth Juliana Friederica to J. C. Altnickol in Leipzig, 20 Jan.; Probe of J. G. Harrer with a view to his succeeding Bach as Thomaskantor, 8 June; birth of grandson Johann Sebastian Altnickol, 4 Oct. (bur. 21 Dec.) | Mass in B minor completed; St John Passion perf., 4 April | | |

| Year | Domestic events | Bach's music (except sacred cantatas) | Other musicians | Contemporary events |
|---|---|---|---|---|
| 1750 | Appointment of son Johann Christoph Friedrich as court musician at Bückeburg, Jan.; operations by oculist John Taylor, March–April; final communion, 22 July; death of J. S. Bach, 28 July; burial at Johanniskirche, 31 July | Work on *The Art of Fugue* (since c.1742; pubd. 1751) | Death of S. L. Weiß, 16 Oct. | |

(b) Performance dates of sacred cantatas

*revival or new version

Trinity/Epiphany/Easter 1 (etc.): 1st (etc.) Sunday after Trinity/Epiphany/Easter

1 (etc.) Advent/Lent/Easter/Christmas/Whitsun: 1st (etc.) day of Advent/Lent/Easter/Christmas/Whitsun

| Date | Occasion | BWV | Short title |
|---|---|---|---|
| PRE-WEIMAR CANTATAS | | | |
| ? 1704–7 | Unspecified, ?Arnstadt | 150 | Nach dir, Herr, verlanget mich |
| 1707–8 | Unspecified, Mühlhausen | 131 | Aus der Tiefen rufe ich, Herr |
| ? 1707–8 | ?Funeral, Mühlhausen | 106 | Gottes Zeit ist die allerbeste Zeit |
| ? 1707–8 | 1 Easter, ?Mühlhausen | 4 | Christ lag in Todes Banden |
| ? 1707–8 | ? Wedding, Mühlhausen | 196 | Der Herr denket an uns |
| 4 Feb. 1708 | Council election, Mühlhausen | 71 | Gott ist mein König |
| WEIMAR CANTATAS | | | |
| 25 March 1714 | Palm Sunday/Annunciation | 182 | Himmelskönig, sei willkommen |
| 22 April 1714 | Easter 3 | 12 | Weinen, Klagen, Sorgen, Zagen |
| 20 May 1714 | 1 Whitsun | 172 | Erschallet, ihr Lieder |
| 17 June 1714 | Trinity 3 | 21 | Ich hatte viel Bekümmernis |
| 12 Aug. 1714 | Trinity 11 | 199 | Mein Herze schwimmt im Blut |
| 2 Dec. 1714 | 1 Advent | 61 | Nun komm, der Heiden Heiland |
| 30 Dec. 1714 | Sunday after Christmas | 152 | Tritt auf die Glaubensbahn |
| 24 Feb. 1715 | Sexagesima | ?18 | ?Gleichwie der Regen und Schnee |
| 24 March 1715 | 3 Lent | 54 | Widerstehe doch der Sünde |
| 21 April 1715 | 1 Easter | 31 | Der Himmel lacht! die Erde jubilieret |
| 16 June 1715 | Trinity Sunday | 165 | O heilges Geist- und Wasserbad |

| Date | Occasion | BWV | Short title |
|---|---|---|---|
| 14 July 1715 | Trinity 4 | 185 | Barmherziges Herze der ewigen Liebe |
| 24 Nov. 1715 | Trinity 23 | 163 | Nur jedem das Seine |
| 22 Dec. 1715 | 4 Advent | 132 | Bereitet die Wege, bereitet die Bahn |
| 19 Jan. 1716 | Epiphany 2 | 155 | Mein Gott, wie lang, ach lange |
| 15 March 1716 | 3 Lent | 80a | Alles, was von Gott geboren |
| 12 April 1716 | 1 Easter | 31 | *Der Himmel lacht! die Erde jubilieret |
| 7 June 1716 | Trinity Sunday | 165 | *O heilges Geist- und Wasserbad |
| 5 July 1716 | Trinity 4 | 185 | *Barmherziges Herze der ewigen Liebe |
| 27 Sept. 1716 | Trinity 16 | 161 | Komm, du süße Todesstunde |
| 25 Oct. 1716 | Trinity 20 | 162 | Ach, ich sehe, itzt, da ich zur Hochzeit gehe |
| 6 Dec. 1716 | 2 Advent | 70a | Wachet! betet! betet! wachet! |
| 13 Dec. 1716 | 3 Advent | 186a | Ärgre dich, o Seele, nicht |
| 20 Dec. 1716 | 4 Advent | 147a | Herz und Mund und Tat und Leben |

CANTATAS FOR LEIPZIG *Probe*

| | | | |
|---|---|---|---|
| 7 Feb. 1723 | Estomihi | 22 | Jesus nahm zu sich die Zwölfe |
| | | 23 | Du wahrer Gott und Davids Sohn |

FIRST LEIPZIG JAHRGANG, 1723–4

| | | | |
|---|---|---|---|
| 30 May 1723 | Trinity 1 | 75 | Die Elenden sollen essen |
| 6 June 1723 | Trinity 2 | 76 | Die Himmel erzählen die Ehre Gottes |
| 13 June 1723 | Trinity 3 | 21 | *Ich hatte viel Bekümmernis |
| 20 June 1723 | Trinity 4 | 24 | Ein ungefärbt Gemüte |
| | | 185 | *Barmherziges Herze der ewigen Liebe |
| 24 June 1723 | Feast of St John the Baptist | 167 | Ihr Menschen, rühmet Gottes Liebe |
| 2 July 1723 | Feast of the Visitation | 147 | *Herz und Mund und Tat und Leben |
| 11 July 1723 | Trinity 7 | 186 | *Ärgre dich, o Seele, nicht |
| 18 July 1723 | Trinity 8 | 136 | Erforsche mich, Gott, und erfahre mein Herz |
| 25 July 1723 | Trinity 9 | 105 | Herr, gehe nicht ins Gericht |
| 1 Aug. 1723 | Trinity 10 | 46 | Schauet doch und sehet |
| 8 Aug. 1723 | Trinity 11 | 179 | Siehe zu, daß deine Gottesfurcht |
| | | 199 | *Mein Herze schwimmt im Blut |
| 15 Aug. 1723 | Trinity 12 | 69a | Lobe den Herrn, meine Seele |
| 22 Aug. 1723 | Trinity 13 | 77 | Du sollt Gott, deinen Herren, lieben |
| 29 Aug. 1723 | Trinity 14 | 25 | Es ist nichts Gesundes an meinem Leibe |

# Appendix 3

| Date | Occasion | BWV | Short title |
|---|---|---|---|
| 5 Sept. 1723 | Trinity 15 | 138 | Warum betrübst du dich, mein Herz? |
| 12 Sept. 1723 | Trinity 16 | 95 | Christus, der ist mein Leben |
| 19 Sept. 1723 | Trinity 17 | 148 | ? Bringet dem Herrn Ehre seines Namens |
| 29 Sept. 1723 | Feast of St Michael | ?50 | ? Nun ist das Heil und die Kraft |
| 3 Oct. 1723 | Trinity 19 | 48 | Ich elender Mensch, wer wird mich erlösen |
| 10 Oct. 1723 | Trinity 20 | 162 | *Ach, ich sehe, itzt, da ich zur Hochzeit gehe |
| 17 Oct. 1723 | Trinity 21 | 109 | Ich glaube, lieber Herr, hilf meinem Unglauben |
| 24 Oct. 1723 | Trinity 22 | 89 | Was soll ich aus dir machen, Ephraim? |
| 31 Oct. 1723 | Trinity 23/Reformation festival | 80b | Ein feste Burg ist unser Gott |
| 2 Nov. 1723 | Organ dedication, Störmthal | 194 | Höchsterwünschtes Freudenfest |
| 7 Nov. 1723 | Trinity 24 | 60 | O Ewigkeit, du Donnerwort |
| 14 Nov. 1723 | Trinity 25 | 90 | Es reißet euch ein schrecklich Ende |
| 21 Nov. 1723 | Trinity 26 | 70 | *Wachet! betet! betet! wachet! |
| 28 Nov. 1723 | 1 Advent | 61 | *Nun komm, der Heiden Heiland |
| 25 Dec. 1723 | 1 Christmas | 63 | *Christen, ätzet diesen Tag |
| 26 Dec. 1723 | 2 Christmas | 40 | Darzu ist erschienen der Sohn Gottes |
| 27 Dec. 1723 | 3 Christmas | 64 | Sehet, welch eine Liebe |
| 1 Jan. 1724 | New Year | 190 | Singet dem Herrn ein neues Lied |
| 2 Jan. 1724 | Sunday after New Year | 153 | Schau, lieber Gott, wie meine Feind |
| 6 Jan. 1724 | Epiphany | 65 | Sie werden aus Saba alle kommen |
| 9 Jan. 1724 | Epiphany 1 | 154 | Mein liebster Jesus ist verloren |
| 16 Jan. 1724 | Epiphany 2 | 155 | *Mein Gott, wie lang, ach lange |
| 23 Jan. 1724 | Epiphany 3 | 73 | Herr, wie du willt, so schicks mit mir |
| 30 Jan. 1724 | Epiphany 4 | 81 | Jesus schläft, was soll ich hoffen? |
| 2 Feb. 1724 | Feast of the Purification | 83 | Erfreute Zeit im neuen Bunde |
| 6 Feb. 1724 | Septuagesima | 144 | Nimm, was dein ist, und gehe hin |
| 13 Feb. 1724 | Sexagesima | 181 | Leichtgesinnte Flattergeister |
| 20 Feb. 1724 | Estomihi | 18 | *Gleichwie der Regen und Schnee |
| | | 22 | *Jesus nahm zu sich die Zwölfe |
| | | 23 | *Du wahrer Gott und Davids Sohn |
| 25 March 1724 | Feast of the Annunciation | 182 | *Himmelskönig, sei willkommen |
| 9 April 1724 | 1 Easter | 31 | *Der Himmel lacht! die Erde jubilieret |
| 10 April 1724 | 2 Easter | 66 | Erfreut euch, ihr Herzen |
| 11 April 1724 | 3 Easter | 134 | Ein Herz, das seinen Jesum lebend weiß |
| 16 April 1724 | Easter 1 | 67 | Halt im Gedächtnis Jesum Christ |

618

| Date | Occasion | BWV | Short title |
|---|---|---|---|
| 23 April 1724 | Easter 2 | 104 | Du Hirte Israel, höre |
| 30 April 1724 | Easter 3 | 12 | *Weinen, Klagen, Sorgen, Zagen |
| 7 May 1724 | Easter 4 | 166 | Wo gehest du hin? |
| 14 May 1724 | Easter 5 | 86 | Wahrlich, wahrlich, ich sage euch |
| 18 May 1724 | Ascension | 37 | Wer da gläubet und getauft wird |
| 21 May 1724 | Sunday after Ascension | 44 | Sie werden euch in den Bann tun |
| 28 May 1724 | 1 Whitsun | 172 | *Erschallet, ihr Lieder |
| | | 59 | *Wer mich liebet, der wird mein Wort halten (at Paulinerkirche) |
| 29 May 1724 | 2 Whitsun | ?173 | ?Erhöhtes Fleisch und Blut |
| 30 May 1724 | 3 Whitsun | 184 | Erwünschtes Freudenlicht |
| 4 June 1724 | Trinity Sunday | 194 | *Höchsterwünschtes Freudenfest |

SECOND LEIPZIG JAHRGANG, 1724–5

| Date | Occasion | BWV | Short title |
|---|---|---|---|
| 11 June 1724 | Trinity 1 | 20 | O Ewigkeit, du Donnerwort |
| 18 June 1724 | Trinity 2 | 2 | Ach Gott, vom Himmel sieh darein |
| 24 June 1724 | Feast of St John the Baptist | 7 | Christ unser Herr zum Jordan kam |
| 25 June 1724 | Trinity 3 | 135 | Ach Herr, mich armen Sünder |
| 2 July 1724 | Trinity 4 | 10 | Meine Seel erhebt den Herren |
| 9 July 1724 | Trinity 5 | 93 | Wer nur den lieben Gott läßt walten |
| 23 July 1724 | Trinity 7 | 107 | Was willst du dich betrüben |
| 30 July 1724 | Trinity 8 | 178 | Wo Gott der Herr nicht bei uns hält |
| 6 Aug. 1724 | Trinity 9 | 94 | Was frag ich nach der Welt |
| 13 Aug. 1724 | Trinity 10 | 101 | Nimm von uns, Herr, du treuer Gott |
| 20 Aug. 1724 | Trinity 11 | 113 | Herr Jesu Christ, du höchstes Gut |
| 3 Sept. 1724 | Trinity 13 | 33 | Allein zu dir, Herr Jesu Christ |
| 10 Sept. 1724 | Trinity 14 | 78 | Jesu, der du meine Seele |
| 17 Sept. 1724 | Trinity 15 | 99 | Was Gott tut, das ist wohlgetan |
| 24 Sept. 1724 | Trinity 16 | 8 | Liebster Gott, wenn werd ich sterben |
| 29 Sept. 1724 | Feast of St Michael | 130 | Herr Gott, dich loben alle wir |
| 1 Oct. 1724 | Trinity 17 | 114 | Ach, lieben Christen, seid getrost |
| 8 Oct. 1724 | Trinity 18 | 96 | Herr Christ, der einge Gottessohn |
| 15 Oct. 1724 | Trinity 19 | 5 | Wo soll ich fliehen hin |
| 22 Oct. 1724 | Trinity 20 | 180 | Schmücke dich, o liebe Seele |
| 29 Oct. 1724 | Trinity 21 | 38 | Aus tiefer Not schrei ich zu dir |
| 5 Nov. 1724 | Trinity 22 | 115 | Mache dich, mein Geist, bereit |

| Date | Occasion | BWV | Short title |
|---|---|---|---|
| 12 Nov. 1724 | Trinity 23 | 139 | Wohl dem, der sich auf seinen Gott |
| 19 Nov. 1724 | Trinity 24 | 26 | Ach wie flüchtig, ach wie nichtig |
| 26 Nov. 1724 | Trinity 25 | 116 | Du Friedefürst, Herr Jesu Christ |
| 3 Dec. 1724 | 1 Advent | 62 | Nun komm, der Heiden Heiland |
| 25 Dec. 1724 | 1 Christmas | 91 | Gelobet seist du, Jesu Christ |
| 26 Dec. 1724 | 2 Christmas | 121 | Christum wir sollen loben schon |
| 27 Dec. 1724 | 3 Christmas | 133 | Ich freue mich in dir |
| 1 Jan. 1725 | New Year | 41 | Jesu, nun sei gepreiset |
| 6 Jan. 1725 | Epiphany | 123 | Liebster Immanuel, Herzog der Frommen |
| 7 Jan. 1725 | Epiphany 1 | 124 | Meinen Jesum laß ich nicht |
| 14 Jan. 1725 | Epiphany 2 | 3 | Ach Gott, wie manches Herzeleid |
| 21 Jan. 1725 | Epiphany 3 | 111 | Was mein Gott will, das g'scheh allzeit |
| 28 Jan. 1725 | Septuagesima | 92 | Ich hab in Gottes Herz und Sinn |
| 2 Feb. 1725 | Feast of the Purification | 125 | Mit Fried und Freud ich fahr dahin |
| 4 Feb. 1725 | Sexagesima | 126 | Erhalt uns, Herr, bei deinem Wort |
| 11 Feb. 1725 | Estomihi | 127 | Herr Jesu Christ, wahr' Mensch und Gott |
| 25 March 1725 | Feast of the Annunciation | 1 | Wie schön leuchtet der Morgenstern |
| 1 April 1725 | 1 Easter | 249 | Kommt eilet und laufet (*Easter Oratorio*) |
| 2 April 1725 | 2 Easter | 6 | Bleib bei uns, denn es will Abend werden |
| 3 April 1725 | 3 Easter | ?4 | ?*Christ lag in Todes Banden |
| 8 April 1725 | Easter 1 | 42 | Am Abend aber desselbigen Sabbaths |
| 15 April 1725 | Easter 2 | 85 | Ich bin ein guter Hirt |
| 22 April 1725 | Easter 3 | 103 | Ihr werdet weinen und heulen |
| 29 April 1725 | Easter 4 | 108 | Es ist euch gut, daß ich hingehe |
| 6 May 1725 | Easter 5 | 87 | Bisher habt ihr nichts gebeten |
| 10 May 1725 | Ascension | 128 | Auf Christi Himmelfahrt allein |
| 13 May 1725 | Sunday after Ascension | 183 | Sie werden euch in den Bann tun |
| 20 May 1725 | 1 Whitsun | 74 | Wer mich liebet, der wird mein Wort halten |
| 21 May 1725 | 2 Whitsun | 68 | Also hat Gott die Welt geliebt |
| 22 May 1725 | 3 Whitsun | 175 | Er rufet seinen Schafen mit Namen |
| 27 May 1725 | Trinity Sunday | 176 | Es ist ein trotzig und verzagt Ding |
| **JUNE–OCTOBER 1725** | | | |
| [17 June 1725 | Trinity 3 | — | Ich ruf zur dir, Herr Jesu Christ, by ?] |
| [24 June 1725 | Trinity 4, feast of St John | — | Gelobet sei der Herr, by ?Telemann] |
| [1 July 1725 | Trinity 5 | — | Der Segen des Herrn, by ?Telemann] |

| Date | Occasion | BWV | Short title |
|---|---|---|---|
| [2 July 1725] | Feast of the Visitation | — | Meine seele erhebt den Herrn, by ?] |
| [8 July 1725] | Trinity 6 | — | Wer such rächet, by ?Telemann] |
| 29 July 1725 | Trinity 9 | 168 | Tue Rechnung! Donnerwort |
| 19 Aug. 1725 | Trinity 12 | 137 | Lobe den Herren, den mächtigen König |
| 26 Aug. 1725 | Trinity 13 | 164 | Ihr, die ihr euch von Christo nennet |
| 31 Oct. 1725 | Reformation festival | 79 | Gott der Herr ist Sonn und Schild |
| **THIRD LEIPZIG JAHRGANG, 1725–6** | | | |
| 25 Dec. 1725 | 1 Christmas | 110 | Unser Mund sei voll Lachens |
| 26 Dec. 1725 | 2 Christmas | 57 | Selig ist der Mann |
| 27 Dec. 1725 | 3 Christmas | 151 | Süßer Trost, mein Jesus kömmt |
| 1 Jan. 1726 | New Year | 16 | Herr Gott, dich loben wir |
| 13 Jan. 1726 | Epiphany 1 | 32 | Liebster Jesu, mein Verlangen |
| 20 Jan. 1726 | Epiphany 2 | 13 | Meine Seufzer, meine Tränen |
| 27 Jan. 1726 | Epiphany 3 | 72 | Alles nur nach Gottes Willen |
| 2 Feb. 1726 | Feast of the Purification | — | Mache dich auf, werde licht, by L. Bach] |
| 3 Feb. 1726 | Epiphany 4 | — | Gott ist unsre Zuversicht, by J. L. Bach] |
| 10 Feb. 1726 | Epiphany 5 | — | Der Gottlosen Arbeit wird fehlen, by J. L. Bach] |
| [17 Feb. 1726] | Septuagesima | — | Darum will ich auch erwählen, by J. L. Bach] |
| [24 Feb. 1726] | Sexagesima | — | Darum säet euch Gerechtigkeit, by J. L. Bach] |
| [3 March 1726] | Estomihi | — | Ja, mir hast du Arbeit gemacht, by J. L. Bach] |
| [25 March 1726] | Feast of the Annunciation | — | ? Ich habe meinen König eingesetzt, by J. L. Bach] |
| [21 April 1726] | 1 Easter | — | Den du wirst meine seele, by J. L. Bach] |
| [22 April 1726] | 2 Easter | — | Er ist aus der Angst und Gericht, by J. L. Bach] |
| [23 April 1726] | 3 Easter | — | Er machet uns lebendig, by J. L. Bach] |
| [28 April 1726] | Easter 1 | — | Wie lieblich sind au den Bergen, by J. L. Bach] |
| [5 May 1726] | Easter 2 | — | Und ich will ihnen einen einigen Hirten, by J. L. Bach] |
| 12 May 1726 | Easter 3 | ?146 | ?Wir müssen durch viel Trübsal |
| [19 May 1726] | Easter 4 | — | Die Weisheit kömmt nicht, by J. L. Bach] |

# Appendix 3

| Date | Occasion | BWV | Short title |
| --- | --- | --- | --- |
| [26 May 1726 | Easter 5 | — | ? Der Herr ist nahe allen, by J. L. Bach] |
| 30 May 1726 | Ascension | 43 | Gott fähret auf mit Jauchzen |
| 16 June 1726 | Trinity Sunday | 194 | *Höchsterwünschtes Freudenfest (shortened) |
| 23 June 1726 | Trinity 1 | 39 | Brich dem Hungrigen dein Brot |
| [24 June 1726 | Feast of St John the Baptist | — | Siehe, ich will meinen Engel senden, by J. L. Bach] |
| 30 June 1726 | Trinity 2 | ? | ? Und der Herr Zebaoth wird allen Völkern, by ? J. S. Bach |
| [2 July 1726 | Feast of the Visitation | — | Der Herr wird ein Neues im Lande, by J. L. Bach] |
| 7 July 1726 | Trinity 3 | ? | ? Wo sich aber der Gottlose bekehret, by ? J. S. Bach |
| [14 July 1726 | Trinity 4 | — | ? Ich tue Barmherzigkeit, by J. L. Bach] |
| 21 July 1726 | Trinity 5 | 88 | Siehe, ich will viel Fischer aussenden |
| 28 July 1726 | Trinity 6 | [— | Ich will meinen Geist in euch geben, by J. L. Bach] |
| 4 Aug. 1726 | Trinity 7 | 170 | Vergnügte Ruh, beliebte Seelenlust |
| 11 Aug. 1726 | Trinity 8 | 187 | Es wartet alles auf dich |
| 18 Aug. 1726 | Trinity 9 | 45 | Es ist dir gesagt, Mensch, was gut ist |
|  |  | ? | ? Wer sich des Armen erbarmet, by J. L. Bach] |
| 25 Aug. 1726 | Trinity 10 | 102 | Herr, deine Augen sehen nach dem Glauben |
| 26 Aug. 1726 | Council election | ?Anh. I.4 | ? Wünschet Jerusalem Glück |
| [1 Sept. 1726 | Trinity 11 | — | Durch sein Erkenntnis, wird er, by J. L. Bach] |
| 8 Sept. 1726 | Trinity 12 | 35 | Geist und Seele wird verwirret |
| 15 Sept. 1726 | Trinity 13 | — | Ich aber ging für dir über, by J. L. Bach] |
| 22 Sept. 1726 | Trinity 14 | 17 | Wer Dank opfert, der preiset mich |
| 29 Sept. 1726 | Trinity 15 | 19 | Es erhub sich ein Streit |
| 6 Oct. 1726 | Trinity 16 | 27 | Wer weiß, wie nahe mir mein Ende |
| 13 Oct. 1726 | Trinity 17 | 47 | Wer sich selbst erhöhet, der soll erniedriget werden |
| 20 Oct. 1726 | Trinity 18 | 169 | Gott soll allein mein Herze haben |
| 27 Oct. 1726 | Trinity 19 | 56 | Ich will den Kreuzstab gerne tragen |
| 3 Nov. 1726 | Trinity 20 | 49 | Ich geh und suche mit Verlangen |
| 10 Nov. 1726 | Trinity 21 | 98 | Was Gott tut, das ist wohlgetan |

| Date | Occasion | BWV | Short title |
|---|---|---|---|
| 17 Nov. 1726 | Trinity 22 | 55 | Ich armer Mensch, ich Sündenknecht |
| 24 Nov. 1726 | Trinity 23 | 52 | Falsche Welt, dir trau ich nicht |

LATER LEIPZIG PERFORMANCES

| Date | Occasion | BWV | Short title |
|---|---|---|---|
| 5 Jan. 1727 | Sunday after New Year | 58 | Ach Gott, wie manches Herzeleid |
| 2 Feb. 1727 | Feast of the Purification | 82 | Ich habe genung |
| 9 Feb. 1727 | Septuagesima | 84 | Ich bin vergnügt mit meinem Glücke |
| 31 Aug. 1727 | Trinity 12 | 69a | *Lobe den Herrn, meine Seele |
| 30 Aug. 1728 | Council election | ?Anh. I.4 | ? Wünschet Jerusalem Glück |
| 29 Sept. 1728 | Feast of St Michael | ?149 | ? Man singet mit Freuden vom Sieg |
| 17 Oct. 1728 | Trinity 21 | ?188 | ? Ich habe meine Zuversicht |
| 25 Dec. 1728 | 1 Christmas | ?197a | ? Ehre sei Gott in der Höhe |
| 1 Jan. 1729 | New Year | ?171 | ? Gott, wie dein Name, so ist auch dein Ruhm |
| 23 Jan. 1729 | Epiphany 3 | ?156 | ? Ich steh mit einem Fuß im Grabe |
| 27 Feb. 1729 | Estomihi | ?159 | ? Sehet, wir gehn hinauf gen Jerusalem |
| 18 April 1729 | 2 Easter | Anh. 190 | Ich bin ein Pilgrim auf der Welt |
| 19 April 1729 | 3 Easter | ?145 | ? Ich lebe, mein Herze, zu deinem Ergötzen |
| 6 June 1729 | 2 Whitsun | 174 | Ich liebe den Höchsten von ganzem Gemüte |
| 17 Sept. 1730 | Trinity 15 | 51 | Jauchzet Gott in allen Landen |
| 31 Oct. 1730 | Reformation festival | 79 | *Gott der Herr ist Sonn und Schild |
| 2 Feb. 1731 | Feast of the Purification | ?82 | ?*Ich habe genung |
| 25 March 1731 | 1 Easter | 31 | *Der Himmel lacht! die Erde jubilieret |
| 26 March 1731 | 2 Easter | 66 | *Erfreut euch, ihr Herzen |
| 27 March 1731 | 3 Easter | 134 | *Ein Herz, das seinen Jesum lebend weiß |
| 8 April 1731 | Easter 2 | 112 | Der Herr ist mein getreuer Hirt |
| 15 April 1731 | Easter 3 | 103 | *Ihr werdet weinen und heulen |
| 3 May 1731 | Ascension | 37 | *Wer da gläubet und getauft wird |
| 13 May 1731 | 1 Whitsun | 172 | *Erschallet, ihr Lieder |
| 14 May 1731 | 2 Whitsun | 173 | *Erhöhtes Fleisch und Blut |
| 15 May 1731 | 3 Whitsun | 184 | *Erwünschtes Freudenlicht |
| 20 May 1731 | Trinity Sunday | 194 | *Höchsterwünschtes Freudenfest (shortened) |
| 27 Aug. 1731 | Council election | 29 | Wir danken dir, Gott |
| 18 Nov. 1731 | Trinity 26 | 70 | *Wachet! betet! betet! wachet! |
| 25 Nov. 1731 | Trinity 27 | 140 | Wachet auf, ruft uns die Stimme |
| 2 Dec. 1731 | 1 Advent | 36(2) | Schwingt freudig euch empor (revised) |

| Date | Occasion | BWV | Short title |
| --- | --- | --- | --- |
| 6 July 1732 | Trinity 4 | 177 | Ich ruf zu dir, Herr Jesu Christ |
| 24 Oct. 1734 | Trinity 18 | ?96 | ?*Herr Christ, der einge Gottessohn |
| 30 Jan. 1735 | Epiphany 4 | 14 | Wär Gott nicht mit uns dieser Zeit |
| 11 April 1735 | 2 Easter | ?66 | ?*Erfreut euch, ihr Herzen |
| 12 April 1735 | 3 Easter | ?134 | ?*Ein Herz, das seinen Jesum lebend weiß |
| 19 May 1735 | Ascension | 11 | Lobet Gott in seinen Reichen (*Ascension Oratorio*) |
| 31 Aug. 1739 | Council election | 29 | *Wir danken dir, Gott |
| 29 Aug. 1740 | Council election | Anh. 193 | Herrscher des Himmels, König der Ehren |
| 1 Oct. 1747 | Trinity 18 | ?96 | ?*Herr Christ der einge Gottessohn |
| 1 Jan. 1749 | New Year | 16 | *Herr Gott, dich loben wir |
| 25 Aug. 1749 | Council election | 29 | *Wir danken dir, Gott |

*Schmieder* 2, pp. 917–25; S. Daw, *The Music of Johann Sebastian Bach: The Choral Works* (East Brunswick, NJ, 1981), 219–36; K. Hofmann, 'Neue Überlegungen zu Bachs Weimarer Kantaten-Kalender', *Blb* 79 (1993), 9–29; H.-J. Schulze, ed. *Kalendarium zur Lebensgeschichte Johann Sebastian Bachs* (2nd edn., Leipzig, 1979); G. Stauffer and E. May, eds., *J. S. Bach as Organist* (London, 1986), 295–300.

# GLOSSARY

**alternatim** The practice of performing sections of the liturgy (including the Mass) by alternating soloist and choir, choir and organ, chant and polyphony etc.

**arpeggio** The notes of a chord sounded in succession rather than together. The practice of writing or playing arpeggios is known as 'arpeggiation'.

**bariolage** In string music, the rapid alternation of a stopped string and a neighbouring open string.

**bassetto, Bassetgen, Bassettchen** The lowest instrumental part in a movement or passage from which the normal bass instruments (and usually the accompanying harmony instruments) are excluded. Among several examples in Bach's music is the alto aria 'Doch Jesus will auch bei der Strafe' in Cantata 46.

**cadence** A phrase and/or chord sequence that brings a piece, a movement, or a passage to a close, or (in the case of the interrupted cadence) anticipates a close.

**cantional** A simple harmonic texture in four parts, with the melody in the highest voice; 'hymn-tune style'.

**circle of 5ths** The 12 major or minor keys arranged in sequence with a perfect 5th between each pair, so that extension by a further 5th would bring the sequence 'full circle', e.g.: C–F–D–A–E–B–F♯(=G♭)–D♭–A♭–E♭–B♭–F–[C]; *see* TEMPERAMENTS. Modulations in Bach's music frequently move through a 'segment' of the circle.

*colla parte* ('with the part') An indication to accompanying instruments to follow the tempo of the solo part. By '*colla parte* accompaniment' is meant the instrumental doubling of the vocal lines, for example in a Bach chorale.

**comma** A small interval—about a ninth of a whole tone in equal temperament—of importance in determining methods of tempered, unequal tuning. *See* 'meantone', below.

**concertino** A group of soloists, for example in a concerto or in a body of singers.

**concitato** ('agitated') A compositional style characterized above all by rapid reiteration, usually of a single note or chord.

*divisi* An indication to two or more performers that they should cease to sing or play in unison and instead take different notes or parts (often notated on the same staff). *Divisi* passages in a four-part chorus could result in textures of eight or more parts.

**Dorian, Mixolydian** Modal ancestors of the modern minor and major keys respectively. The octave species extended from *d* to *d'* (Dorian) and *g* to *g'* (Mixolydian), without 'accidentals' (i.e. as if on the white notes of the modern piano). Modal inflections—including some derived from the Phrygian (*e* to *e'*) and Lydian (*f* to *f'*) modes—are evident in Bach's music, particularly in pieces based on older chorale melodies. The modality of such pieces is often indicated by reference to a tonic in the modern sense: G-Dorian (with B♭), G-Mixolydian (with F♮) etc.

**figured bass** A bass line, above or below which figures are placed to indicate to an accompanying player the chords that are to be 'realized'. *See* CONTINUO.

*fioritura* ('flourish') Embellishment, usually of a melodic line by means of rapid, decorative passages.

**ground bass** A bass melody or phrase which is repeated throughout a piece or section while other parts change and develop above it. 'Crucifixus etiam pro nobis' in Bach's B minor Mass provides a well-known example.

**harmonic series** The sequence of natural harmonics (overtones) produced when a string or column of air is made to vibrate. *See* HORN and TRUMPET.

**hemiola** The displacing of natural accents so that two bars of triple time are made to sound like three bars of duple, e.g.: ♩ ♩ | ♩ ♩ ♩ . Hemiola is a feature of cadences in the courante, but is frequently found elsewhere as well.

**Lombardic rhythm** A strongly characterized rhythm produced by an accented short note followed by an unaccented longer one, e.g.: ♫. Also known as the 'Scotch snap'.

**Lydian** See Dorian.

**meantone** A tuning system used in the Renaissance and Baroque periods, in which the tones (i.e. major 2nds) were rendered equal by making the 5ths smaller and the 4ths larger than they are in the natural harmonic series. The system lent itself to various refinements, expressed in terms of the fractions of a comma (e.g. $\frac{1}{6}$-comma meantone) by which the tempered 5th deviated from a pure 5th. See also 'comma' and 'harmonic series', above.

# GLOSSARY

**mediant** The third note in a major or minor scale.

**melisma** A phrase of several notes fitted to a single syllable of text. In Bach's music the word 'Freude' ('joy') and its derivatives are often expressed in long melismas.

**Mixolydian** See Dorian.

**modality** A term used to define the harmonic resource and characteristics of Medieval and Renaissance music; the counterpart to 'tonality' in the later major-minor system. See Dorian.

**modulation** Movement from one key centre to another in the course of a piece.

**motto** (*Devise*). The vocal opening of an aria which is cut short and then taken up again after a brief instrumental ritornello.

**murky** A type of bass line, typically for keyboard, consisting of broken octaves.

**ostinato** A rhythmic or melodic phrase repeated many times while other elements of the composition change.

**obbligato** An instrumental part, essential (*obbligato*) to the performance of an aria, duet, etc., and of more or less equal importance to the vocal part(s). Obbligato parts are usually for solo instruments.

**pasticcio** A musical composition (especially an opera or oratorio) made up of items originally belonging elsewhere and usually by a number of different composers.

**pedal** (1) A key on the pedal-board of an organ or other instrument. (2) A long-held note, usually (but not necessarily) in the bass, above, below, or around which the harmonies change; also known as a 'pedal point'.

**pedal piano** A piano fitted with an organ-type pedal-board. Such pedal-boards were also fitted to harpsichords.

**Phrygian** See Dorian.

**ripieno** A body of instrumentalists or singers from which a solo group (concertino) may be drawn.

**supertonic** The second note in a major or minor scale.

**syncopation** The displacing of the regular accents in a particular rhythmic scheme, usually by removing them from the beginning of a bar. The many examples in Bach's music include the main theme of the last movement of Brandenburg Concerto no. 6 and the tenor aria 'Schweig nur' from Cantata 178.

**thorough-bass** English term for *basso continuo*, practically synonymous with 'figured bass'. *See* CONTINUO.

**tonic** The first note of a major or minor scale, defining the key of the music.

**tonus peregrinus** ('wandering tone') One of the medieval psalm tones. Its name probably derives from the fact that its recitation note (tenor), unlike that of other psalm tones, changes after the central mediation. It is associated particularly with Psalm 114, *In exitu Israel*. Bach introduced it into the trio 'Suscepit Israel' in the *Magnificat*.